Dictionary of Literary Biography

1 *The American Renaissance in New England,* edited by Joel Myerson (1978)

2 *American Novelists Since World War II,* edited by Jeffrey Helterman and Richard Layman (1978)

3 *Antebellum Writers in New York and the South,* edited by Joel Myerson (1979)

4 *American Writers in Paris, 1920–1939,* edited by Karen Lane Rood (1980)

5 *American Poets Since World War II,* 2 parts, edited by Donald J. Greiner (1980)

6 *American Novelists Since World War II, Second Series,* edited by James E. Kibler Jr. (1980)

7 *Twentieth-Century American Dramatists,* 2 parts, edited by John MacNicholas (1981)

8 *Twentieth-Century American Science-Fiction Writers,* 2 parts, edited by David Cowart and Thomas L. Wymer (1981)

9 *American Novelists, 1910–1945,* 3 parts, edited by James J. Martine (1981)

10 *Modern British Dramatists, 1900–1945,* 2 parts, edited by Stanley Weintraub (1982)

11 *American Humorists, 1800–1950,* 2 parts, edited by Stanley Trachtenberg (1982)

12 *American Realists and Naturalists,* edited by Donald Pizer and Earl N. Harbert (1982)

13 *British Dramatists Since World War II,* 2 parts, edited by Stanley Weintraub (1982)

14 *British Novelists Since 1960,* 2 parts, edited by Jay L. Halio (1983)

15 *British Novelists, 1930–1959,* 2 parts, edited by Bernard Oldsey (1983)

16 *The Beats: Literary Bohemians in Postwar America,* 2 parts, edited by Ann Charters (1983)

17 *Twentieth-Century American Historians,* edited by Clyde N. Wilson (1983)

18 *Victorian Novelists After 1885,* edited by Ira B. Nadel and William E. Fredeman (1983)

19 *British Poets, 1880–1914,* edited by Donald E. Stanford (1983)

20 *British Poets, 1914–1945,* edited by Donald E. Stanford (1983)

21 *Victorian Novelists Before 1885,* edited by Ira B. Nadel and William E. Fredeman (1983)

22 *American Writers for Children, 1900–1960,* edited by John Cech (1983)

23 *American Newspaper Journalists, 1873–1900,* edited by Perry J. Ashley (1983)

24 *American Colonial Writers, 1606–1734,* edited by Emory Elliott (1984)

25 *American Newspaper Journalists, 1901–1925,* edited by Perry J. Ashley (1984)

26 *American Screenwriters,* edited by Robert E. Morsberger, Stephen O. Lesser, and Randall Clark (1984)

27 *Poets of Great Britain and Ireland, 1945–1960,* edited by Vincent B. Sherry Jr. (1984)

28 *Twentieth-Century American-Jewish Fiction Writers,* edited by Daniel Walden (1984)

29 *American Newspaper Journalists, 1926–1950,* edited by Perry J. Ashley (1984)

30 *American Historians, 1607–1865,* edited by Clyde N. Wilson (1984)

31 *American Colonial Writers, 1735–1781,* edited by Emory Elliott (1984)

32 *Victorian Poets Before 1850,* edited by William E. Fredeman and Ira B. Nadel (1984)

33 *Afro-American Fiction Writers After 1955,* edited by Thadious M. Davis and Trudier Harris (1984)

34 *British Novelists, 1890–1929: Traditionalists,* edited by Thomas F. Staley (1985)

35 *Victorian Poets After 1850,* edited by William E. Fredeman and Ira B. Nadel (1985)

36 *British Novelists, 1890–1929: Modernists,* edited by Thomas F. Staley (1985)

37 *American Writers of the Early Republic,* edited by Emory Elliott (1985)

38 *Afro-American Writers After 1955: Dramatists and Prose Writers,* edited by Thadious M. Davis and Trudier Harris (1985)

39 *British Novelists, 1660–1800,* 2 parts, edited by Martin C. Battestin (1985)

40 *Poets of Great Britain and Ireland Since 1960,* 2 parts, edited by Vincent B. Sherry Jr. (1985)

41 *Afro-American Poets Since 1955,* edited by Trudier Harris and Thadious M. Davis (1985)

42 *American Writers for Children Before 1900,* edited by Glenn E. Estes (1985)

43 *American Newspaper Journalists, 1690–1872,* edited by Perry J. Ashley (1986)

44 *American Screenwriters, Second Series,* edited by Randall Clark, Robert E. Morsberger, and Stephen O. Lesser (1986)

45 *American Poets, 1880–1945, First Series,* edited by Peter Quartermain (1986)

46 *American Literary Publishing Houses, 1900–1980: Trade and Paperback,* edited by Peter Dzwonkoski (1986)

47 *American Historians, 1866–1912,* edited by Clyde N. Wilson (1986)

48 *American Poets, 1880–1945, Second Series,* edited by Peter Quartermain (1986)

49 *American Literary Publishing Houses, 1638–1899,* 2 parts, edited by Peter Dzwonkoski (1986)

50 *Afro-American Writers Before the Harlem Renaissance,* edited by Trudier Harris (1986)

51 *Afro-American Writers from the Harlem Renaissance to 1940,* edited by Trudier Harris (1987)

52 *American Writers for Children Since 1960: Fiction,* edited by Glenn E. Estes (1986)

53 *Canadian Writers Since 1960, First Series,* edited by W. H. New (1986)

54 *American Poets, 1880–1945, Third Series,* 2 parts, edited by Peter Quartermain (1987)

55 *Victorian Prose Writers Before 1867,* edited by William B. Thesing (1987)

56 *German Fiction Writers, 1914–1945,* edited by James Hardin (1987)

57 *Victorian Prose Writers After 1867,* edited by William B. Thesing (1987)

58 *Jacobean and Caroline Dramatists,* edited by Fredson Bowers (1987)

59 *American Literary Critics and Scholars, 1800–1850,* edited by John W. Rathbun and Monica M. Grecu (1987)

60 *Canadian Writers Since 1960, Second Series,* edited by W. H. New (1987)

61 *American Writers for Children Since 1960: Poets, Illustrators, and Nonfiction Authors,* edited by Glenn E. Estes (1987)

62 *Elizabethan Dramatists,* edited by Fredson Bowers (1987)

63 *Modern American Critics, 1920–1955,* edited by Gregory S. Jay (1988)

64 *American Literary Critics and Scholars, 1850–1880,* edited by John W. Rathbun and Monica M. Grecu (1988)

65 *French Novelists, 1900–1930,* edited by Catharine Savage Brosman (1988)

66 *German Fiction Writers, 1885–1913,* 2 parts, edited by James Hardin (1988)

67 *Modern American Critics Since 1955,* edited by Gregory S. Jay (1988)

68 *Canadian Writers, 1920–1959, First Series,* edited by W. H. New (1988)

69 *Contemporary German Fiction Writers, First Series,* edited by Wolfgang D. Elfe and James Hardin (1988)

70 *British Mystery Writers, 1860–1919,* edited by Bernard Benstock and Thomas F. Staley (1988)

71 *American Literary Critics and Scholars, 1880–1900,* edited by John W. Rathbun and Monica M. Grecu (1988)

72 *French Novelists, 1930–1960,* edited by Catharine Savage Brosman (1988)

73 *American Magazine Journalists, 1741–1850,* edited by Sam G. Riley (1988)

74 *American Short-Story Writers Before 1880,* edited by Bobby Ellen Kimbel, with the assistance of William E. Grant (1988)

75 *Contemporary German Fiction Writers, Second Series,* edited by Wolfgang D. Elfe and James Hardin (1988)

76 *Afro-American Writers, 1940–1955,* edited by Trudier Harris (1988)

77 *British Mystery Writers, 1920–1939,* edited by Bernard Benstock and Thomas F. Staley (1988)

78 *American Short-Story Writers, 1880–1910,* edited by Bobby Ellen Kimbel, with the assistance of William E. Grant (1988)

79 *American Magazine Journalists, 1850–1900,* edited by Sam G. Riley (1988)

80 *Restoration and Eighteenth-Century Dramatists, First Series,* edited by Paula R. Backscheider (1989)

81 *Austrian Fiction Writers, 1875–1913,* edited by James Hardin and Donald G. Daviau (1989)

82 *Chicano Writers, First Series,* edited by Francisco A. Lomelí and Carl R. Shirley (1989)

83 *French Novelists Since 1960,* edited by Catharine Savage Brosman (1989)

84 *Restoration and Eighteenth-Century Dramatists, Second Series,* edited by Paula R. Backscheider (1989)

85 *Austrian Fiction Writers After 1914,* edited by James Hardin and Donald G. Daviau (1989)

86 *American Short-Story Writers, 1910–1945, First Series,* edited by Bobby Ellen Kimbel (1989)

87 *British Mystery and Thriller Writers Since 1940, First Series,* edited by Bernard Benstock and Thomas F. Staley (1989)

88 *Canadian Writers, 1920–1959, Second Series,* edited by W. H. New (1989)

89 *Restoration and Eighteenth-Century Dramatists, Third Series,* edited by Paula R. Backscheider (1989)

90 *German Writers in the Age of Goethe, 1789–1832,* edited by James Hardin and Christoph E. Schweitzer (1989)

91 *American Magazine Journalists, 1900–1960, First Series,* edited by Sam G. Riley (1990)

92 *Canadian Writers, 1890–1920,* edited by W. H. New (1990)

93 *British Romantic Poets, 1789–1832, First Series,* edited by John R. Greenfield (1990)

94 *German Writers in the Age of Goethe: Sturm und Drang to Classicism,* edited by James Hardin and Christoph E. Schweitzer (1990)

95 *Eighteenth-Century British Poets, First Series,* edited by John Sitter (1990)

96 *British Romantic Poets, 1789–1832, Second Series,* edited by John R. Greenfield (1990)

97 *German Writers from the Enlightenment to Sturm und Drang, 1720–1764,* edited by James Hardin and Christoph E. Schweitzer (1990)

98 *Modern British Essayists, First Series,* edited by Robert Beum (1990)

99 *Canadian Writers Before 1890,* edited by W. H. New (1990)

100 *Modern British Essayists, Second Series,* edited by Robert Beum (1990)

101 *British Prose Writers, 1660–1800, First Series,* edited by Donald T. Siebert (1991)

102 *American Short-Story Writers, 1910–1945, Second Series,* edited by Bobby Ellen Kimbel (1991)

103 *American Literary Biographers, First Series,* edited by Steven Serafin (1991)

104 *British Prose Writers, 1660–1800, Second Series,* edited by Donald T. Siebert (1991)

105 *American Poets Since World War II, Second Series,* edited by R. S. Gwynn (1991)

106 *British Literary Publishing Houses, 1820–1880,* edited by Patricia J. Anderson and Jonathan Rose (1991)

107 *British Romantic Prose Writers, 1789–1832, First Series,* edited by John R. Greenfield (1991)

108 *Twentieth-Century Spanish Poets, First Series,* edited by Michael L. Perna (1991)

109 *Eighteenth-Century British Poets, Second Series,* edited by John Sitter (1991)

110 *British Romantic Prose Writers, 1789–1832, Second Series,* edited by John R. Greenfield (1991)

111 *American Literary Biographers, Second Series,* edited by Steven Serafin (1991)

112 *British Literary Publishing Houses, 1881–1965,* edited by Jonathan Rose and Patricia J. Anderson (1991)

113 *Modern Latin-American Fiction Writers, First Series,* edited by William Luis (1992)

114 *Twentieth-Century Italian Poets, First Series,* edited by Giovanna Wedel De Stasio, Glauco Cambon, and Antonio Illiano (1992)

115 *Medieval Philosophers,* edited by Jeremiah Hackett (1992)

116 *British Romantic Novelists, 1789–1832,* edited by Bradford K. Mudge (1992)

117 *Twentieth-Century Caribbean and Black African Writers, First Series,* edited by Bernth Lindfors and Reinhard Sander (1992)

118 *Twentieth-Century German Dramatists, 1889–1918,* edited by Wolfgang D. Elfe and James Hardin (1992)

119 *Nineteenth-Century French Fiction Writers: Romanticism and Realism, 1800–1860,* edited by Catharine Savage Brosman (1992)

120 *American Poets Since World War II, Third Series,* edited by R. S. Gwynn (1992)

121 *Seventeenth-Century British Nondramatic Poets, First Series,* edited by M. Thomas Hester (1992)

122 *Chicano Writers, Second Series,* edited by Francisco A. Lomelí and Carl R. Shirley (1992)

123 *Nineteenth-Century French Fiction Writers: Naturalism and Beyond, 1860–1900,* edited by Catharine Savage Brosman (1992)

124 *Twentieth-Century German Dramatists, 1919–1992,* edited by Wolfgang D. Elfe and James Hardin (1992)

125 *Twentieth-Century Caribbean and Black African Writers, Second Series,* edited by Bernth Lindfors and Reinhard Sander (1993)

126 *Seventeenth-Century British Nondramatic Poets, Second Series,* edited by M. Thomas Hester (1993)

127 *American Newspaper Publishers, 1950–1990,* edited by Perry J. Ashley (1993)

128 *Twentieth-Century Italian Poets, Second Series,* edited by Giovanna Wedel De Stasio, Glauco Cambon, and Antonio Illiano (1993)

129 *Nineteenth-Century German Writers, 1841–1900,* edited by James Hardin and Siegfried Mews (1993)

130 *American Short-Story Writers Since World War II,* edited by Patrick Meanor (1993)

131 *Seventeenth-Century British Nondramatic Poets, Third Series,* edited by M. Thomas Hester (1993)

132 *Sixteenth-Century British Nondramatic Writers, First Series,* edited by David A. Richardson (1993)

133 *Nineteenth-Century German Writers to 1840,* edited by James Hardin and Siegfried Mews (1993)

134 *Twentieth-Century Spanish Poets, Second Series,* edited by Jerry Phillips Winfield (1994)

135 *British Short-Fiction Writers, 1880–1914: The Realist Tradition,* edited by William B. Thesing (1994)

136 *Sixteenth-Century British Nondramatic Writers, Second Series,* edited by David A. Richardson (1994)

137 *American Magazine Journalists, 1900–1960, Second Series,* edited by Sam G. Riley (1994)

138 *German Writers and Works of the High Middle Ages: 1170–1280,* edited by James Hardin and Will Hasty (1994)

139 *British Short-Fiction Writers, 1945–1980,* edited by Dean Baldwin (1994)

140 *American Book-Collectors and Bibliographers, First Series,* edited by Joseph Rosenblum (1994)

141 *British Children's Writers, 1880–1914,* edited by Laura M. Zaidman (1994)

142 *Eighteenth-Century British Literary Biographers,* edited by Steven Serafin (1994)

143 *American Novelists Since World War II, Third Series,* edited by James R. Giles and Wanda H. Giles (1994)

144 *Nineteenth-Century British Literary Biographers,* edited by Steven Serafin (1994)

145 *Modern Latin-American Fiction Writers, Second Series,* edited by William Luis and Ann González (1994)

146 *Old and Middle English Literature,* edited by Jeffrey Helterman and Jerome Mitchell (1994)

147 *South Slavic Writers Before World War II,* edited by Vasa D. Mihailovich (1994)

148 *German Writers and Works of the Early Middle Ages: 800–1170,* edited by Will Hasty and James Hardin (1994)

149 *Late Nineteenth- and Early Twentieth-Century British Literary Biographers,* edited by Steven Serafin (1995)

150 *Early Modern Russian Writers, Late Seventeenth and Eighteenth Centuries,* edited by Marcus C. Levitt (1995)

151 *British Prose Writers of the Early Seventeenth Century*, edited by Clayton D. Lein (1995)

152 *American Novelists Since World War II, Fourth Series*, edited by James R. Giles and Wanda H. Giles (1995)

153 *Late-Victorian and Edwardian British Novelists, First Series*, edited by George M. Johnson (1995)

154 *The British Literary Book Trade, 1700–1820*, edited by James K. Bracken and Joel Silver (1995)

155 *Twentieth-Century British Literary Biographers*, edited by Steven Serafin (1995)

156 *British Short-Fiction Writers, 1880–1914: The Romantic Tradition*, edited by William F. Naufftus (1995)

157 *Twentieth-Century Caribbean and Black African Writers, Third Series*, edited by Bernth Lindfors and Reinhard Sander (1995)

158 *British Reform Writers, 1789–1832*, edited by Gary Kelly and Edd Applegate (1995)

159 *British Short-Fiction Writers, 1800–1880*, edited by John R. Greenfield (1996)

160 *British Children's Writers, 1914–1960*, edited by Donald R. Hettinga and Gary D. Schmidt (1996)

161 *British Children's Writers Since 1960, First Series*, edited by Caroline Hunt (1996)

162 *British Short-Fiction Writers, 1915–1945*, edited by John H. Rogers (1996)

163 *British Children's Writers, 1800–1880*, edited by Meena Khorana (1996)

164 *German Baroque Writers, 1580–1660*, edited by James Hardin (1996)

165 *American Poets Since World War II, Fourth Series*, edited by Joseph Conte (1996)

166 *British Travel Writers, 1837–1875*, edited by Barbara Brothers and Julia Gergits (1996)

167 *Sixteenth-Century British Nondramatic Writers, Third Series*, edited by David A. Richardson (1996)

168 *German Baroque Writers, 1661–1730*, edited by James Hardin (1996)

169 *American Poets Since World War II, Fifth Series*, edited by Joseph Conte (1996)

170 *The British Literary Book Trade, 1475–1700*, edited by James K. Bracken and Joel Silver (1996)

171 *Twentieth-Century American Sportswriters*, edited by Richard Orodenker (1996)

172 *Sixteenth-Century British Nondramatic Writers, Fourth Series*, edited by David A. Richardson (1996)

173 *American Novelists Since World War II, Fifth Series*, edited by James R. Giles and Wanda H. Giles (1996)

174 *British Travel Writers, 1876–1909*, edited by Barbara Brothers and Julia Gergits (1997)

175 *Native American Writers of the United States*, edited by Kenneth M. Roemer (1997)

176 *Ancient Greek Authors*, edited by Ward W. Briggs (1997)

177 *Italian Novelists Since World War II, 1945–1965*, edited by Augustus Pallotta (1997)

178 *British Fantasy and Science-Fiction Writers Before World War I*, edited by Darren Harris-Fain (1997)

179 *German Writers of the Renaissance and Reformation, 1280–1580*, edited by James Hardin and Max Reinhart (1997)

180 *Japanese Fiction Writers, 1868–1945*, edited by Van C. Gessel (1997)

181 *South Slavic Writers Since World War II*, edited by Vasa D. Mihailovich (1997)

182 *Japanese Fiction Writers Since World War II*, edited by Van C. Gessel (1997)

183 *American Travel Writers, 1776–1864*, edited by James J. Schramer and Donald Ross (1997)

184 *Nineteenth-Century British Book-Collectors and Bibliographers*, edited by William Baker and Kenneth Womack (1997)

185 *American Literary Journalists, 1945–1995, First Series*, edited by Arthur J. Kaul (1998)

186 *Nineteenth-Century American Western Writers*, edited by Robert L. Gale (1998)

187 *American Book Collectors and Bibliographers, Second Series*, edited by Joseph Rosenblum (1998)

188 *American Book and Magazine Illustrators to 1920*, edited by Steven E. Smith, Catherine A. Hastedt, and Donald H. Dyal (1998)

189 *American Travel Writers, 1850–1915*, edited by Donald Ross and James J. Schramer (1998)

190 *British Reform Writers, 1832–1914*, edited by Gary Kelly and Edd Applegate (1998)

191 *British Novelists Between the Wars*, edited by George M. Johnson (1998)

192 *French Dramatists, 1789–1914*, edited by Barbara T. Cooper (1998)

193 *American Poets Since World War II, Sixth Series*, edited by Joseph Conte (1998)

194 *British Novelists Since 1960, Second Series*, edited by Merritt Moseley (1998)

195 *British Travel Writers, 1910–1939*, edited by Barbara Brothers and Julia Gergits (1998)

196 *Italian Novelists Since World War II, 1965–1995*, edited by Augustus Pallotta (1999)

197 *Late-Victorian and Edwardian British Novelists, Second Series*, edited by George M. Johnson (1999)

198 *Russian Literature in the Age of Pushkin and Gogol: Prose*, edited by Christine A. Rydel (1999)

199 *Victorian Women Poets*, edited by William B. Thesing (1999)

200 *American Women Prose Writers to 1820*, edited by Carla J. Mulford, with Angela Vietto and Amy E. Winans (1999)

201 *Twentieth-Century British Book Collectors and Bibliographers*, edited by William Baker and Kenneth Womack (1999)

202 *Nineteenth-Century American Fiction Writers*, edited by Kent P. Ljungquist (1999)

203 *Medieval Japanese Writers*, edited by Steven D. Carter (1999)

204 *British Travel Writers, 1940–1997*, edited by Barbara Brothers and Julia M. Gergits (1999)

205 *Russian Literature in the Age of Pushkin and Gogol: Poetry and Drama*, edited by Christine A. Rydel (1999)

206 *Twentieth-Century American Western Writers, First Series*, edited by Richard H. Cracroft (1999)

207 *British Novelists Since 1960, Third Series*, edited by Merritt Moseley (1999)

208 *Literature of the French and Occitan Middle Ages: Eleventh to Fifteenth Centuries*, edited by Deborah Sinnreich-Levi and Ian S. Laurie (1999)

209 *Chicano Writers, Third Series*, edited by Francisco A. Lomelí and Carl R. Shirley (1999)

210 *Ernest Hemingway: A Documentary Volume*, edited by Robert W. Trogdon (1999)

211 *Ancient Roman Writers*, edited by Ward W. Briggs (1999)

212 *Twentieth-Century American Western Writers, Second Series*, edited by Richard H. Cracroft (1999)

213 *Pre-Nineteenth-Century British Book Collectors and Bibliographers*, edited by William Baker and Kenneth Womack (1999)

214 *Twentieth-Century Danish Writers*, edited by Marianne Stecher-Hansen (1999)

215 *Twentieth-Century Eastern European Writers, First Series*, edited by Steven Serafin (1999)

216 *British Poets of the Great War: Brooke, Rosenberg, Thomas. A Documentary Volume*, edited by Patrick Quinn (2000)

217 *Nineteenth-Century French Poets*, edited by Robert Beum (2000)

218 *American Short-Story Writers Since World War II, Second Series*, edited by Patrick Meanor and Gwen Crane (2000)

219 *F. Scott Fitzgerald's* The Great Gatsby: *A Documentary Volume*, edited by Matthew J. Bruccoli (2000)

220 *Twentieth-Century Eastern European Writers, Second Series*, edited by Steven Serafin (2000)

221 *American Women Prose Writers, 1870–1920*, edited by Sharon M. Harris, with the assistance of Heidi L. M. Jacobs and Jennifer Putzi (2000)

222 *H. L. Mencken: A Documentary Volume*, edited by Richard J. Schrader (2000)

223 *The American Renaissance in New England, Second Series*, edited by Wesley T. Mott (2000)

224 *Walt Whitman: A Documentary Volume*, edited by Joel Myerson (2000)

225 *South African Writers*, edited by Paul A. Scanlon (2000)

226 *American Hard-Boiled Crime Writers*, edited by George Parker Anderson and Julie B. Anderson (2000)

227 *American Novelists Since World War II, Sixth Series*, edited by James R. Giles and Wanda H. Giles (2000)

228 *Twentieth-Century American Dramatists, Second Series*, edited by Christopher J. Wheatley (2000)

229 *Thomas Wolfe: A Documentary Volume*, edited by Ted Mitchell (2001)

230 *Australian Literature, 1788–1914,* edited by Selina Samuels (2001)

231 *British Novelists Since 1960, Fourth Series,* edited by Merritt Moseley (2001)

232 *Twentieth-Century Eastern European Writers, Third Series,* edited by Steven Serafin (2001)

233 *British and Irish Dramatists Since World War II, Second Series,* edited by John Bull (2001)

234 *American Short-Story Writers Since World War II, Third Series,* edited by Patrick Meanor and Richard E. Lee (2001)

235 *The American Renaissance in New England, Third Series,* edited by Wesley T. Mott (2001)

236 *British Rhetoricians and Logicians, 1500–1660,* edited by Edward A. Malone (2001)

237 *The Beats: A Documentary Volume,* edited by Matt Theado (2001)

238 *Russian Novelists in the Age of Tolstoy and Dostoevsky,* edited by J. Alexander Ogden and Judith E. Kalb (2001)

239 *American Women Prose Writers: 1820–1870,* edited by Amy E. Hudock and Katharine Rodier (2001)

240 *Late Nineteenth- and Early Twentieth-Century British Women Poets,* edited by William B. Thesing (2001)

241 *American Sportswriters and Writers on Sport,* edited by Richard Orodenker (2001)

242 *Twentieth-Century European Cultural Theorists, First Series,* edited by Paul Hansom (2001)

243 *The American Renaissance in New England, Fourth Series,* edited by Wesley T. Mott (2001)

244 *American Short-Story Writers Since World War II, Fourth Series,* edited by Patrick Meanor and Joseph McNicholas (2001)

245 *British and Irish Dramatists Since World War II, Third Series,* edited by John Bull (2001)

246 *Twentieth-Century American Cultural Theorists,* edited by Paul Hansom (2001)

247 *James Joyce: A Documentary Volume,* edited by A. Nicholas Fargnoli (2001)

248 *Antebellum Writers in the South, Second Series,* edited by Kent Ljungquist (2001)

249 *Twentieth-Century American Dramatists, Third Series,* edited by Christopher Wheatley (2002)

250 *Antebellum Writers in New York, Second Series,* edited by Kent Ljungquist (2002)

251 *Canadian Fantasy and Science-Fiction Writers,* edited by Douglas Ivison (2002)

252 *British Philosophers, 1500–1799,* edited by Philip B. Dematteis and Peter S. Fosl (2002)

253 *Raymond Chandler: A Documentary Volume,* edited by Robert Moss (2002)

254 *The House of Putnam, 1837–1872: A Documentary Volume,* edited by Ezra Greenspan (2002)

255 *British Fantasy and Science-Fiction Writers, 1918–1960,* edited by Darren Harris-Fain (2002)

256 *Twentieth-Century American Western Writers, Third Series,* edited by Richard H. Cracroft (2002)

257 *Twentieth-Century Swedish Writers After World War II,* edited by Ann-Charlotte Gavel Adams (2002)

258 *Modern French Poets,* edited by Jean-François Leroux (2002)

259 *Twentieth-Century Swedish Writers Before World War II,* edited by Ann-Charlotte Gavel Adams (2002)

260 *Australian Writers, 1915–1950,* edited by Selina Samuels (2002)

261 *British Fantasy and Science-Fiction Writers Since 1960,* edited by Darren Harris-Fain (2002)

262 *British Philosophers, 1800–2000,* edited by Peter S. Fosl and Leemon B. McHenry (2002)

263 *William Shakespeare: A Documentary Volume,* edited by Catherine Loomis (2002)

Dictionary of Literary Biography Documentary Series

1 *Sherwood Anderson, Willa Cather, John Dos Passos, Theodore Dreiser, F. Scott Fitzgerald, Ernest Hemingway, Sinclair Lewis,* edited by Margaret A. Van Antwerp (1982)

2 *James Gould Cozzens, James T. Farrell, William Faulkner, John O'Hara, John Steinbeck, Thomas Wolfe, Richard Wright,* edited by Margaret A. Van Antwerp (1982)

3 *Saul Bellow, Jack Kerouac, Norman Mailer, Vladimir Nabokov, John Updike, Kurt Vonnegut,* edited by Mary Bruccoli (1983)

4 *Tennessee Williams,* edited by Margaret A. Van Antwerp and Sally Johns (1984)

5 *American Transcendentalists,* edited by Joel Myerson (1988)

6 *Hardboiled Mystery Writers: Raymond Chandler, Dashiell Hammett, Ross Macdonald,* edited by Matthew J. Bruccoli and Richard Layman (1989)

7 *Modern American Poets: James Dickey, Robert Frost, Marianne Moore,* edited by Karen L. Rood (1989)

8 *The Black Aesthetic Movement,* edited by Jeffrey Louis Decker (1991)

9 *American Writers of the Vietnam War: W. D. Ehrhart, Larry Heinemann, Tim O'Brien, Walter McDonald, John M. Del Vecchio,* edited by Ronald Baughman (1991)

10 *The Bloomsbury Group,* edited by Edward L. Bishop (1992)

11 *American Proletarian Culture: The Twenties and The Thirties,* edited by Jon Christian Suggs (1993)

12 *Southern Women Writers: Flannery O'Connor, Katherine Anne Porter, Eudora Welty,* edited by Mary Ann Wimsatt and Karen L. Rood (1994)

13 *The House of Scribner, 1846–1904,* edited by John Delaney (1996)

14 *Four Women Writers for Children, 1868–1918,* edited by Caroline C. Hunt (1996)

15 *American Expatriate Writers: Paris in the Twenties,* edited by Matthew J. Bruccoli and Robert W. Trogdon (1997)

16 *The House of Scribner, 1905–1930,* edited by John Delaney (1997)

17 *The House of Scribner, 1931–1984,* edited by John Delaney (1998)

18 *British Poets of The Great War: Sassoon, Graves, Owen,* edited by Patrick Quinn (1999)

19 *James Dickey,* edited by Judith S. Baughman (1999)

See also DLB 210, 216, 219, 222, 224, 229, 237, 247, 253, 254, 263

Dictionary of Literary Biography Yearbooks

1980 edited by Karen L. Rood, Jean W. Ross, and Richard Ziegfeld (1981)

1981 edited by Karen L. Rood, Jean W. Ross, and Richard Ziegfeld (1982)

1982 edited by Richard Ziegfeld; associate editors: Jean W. Ross and Lynne C. Zeigler (1983)

1983 edited by Mary Bruccoli and Jean W. Ross; associate editor Richard Ziegfeld (1984)

1984 edited by Jean W. Ross (1985)

1985 edited by Jean W. Ross (1986)

1986 edited by J. M. Brook (1987)

1987 edited by J. M. Brook (1988)

1988 edited by J. M. Brook (1989)

1989 edited by J. M. Brook (1990)

1990 edited by James W. Hipp (1991)

1991 edited by James W. Hipp (1992)

1992 edited by James W. Hipp (1993)

1993 edited by James W. Hipp, contributing editor George Garrett (1994)

1994 edited by James W. Hipp, contributing editor George Garrett (1995)

1995 edited by James W. Hipp, contributing editor George Garrett (1996)

1996 edited by Samuel W. Bruce and L. Kay Webster, contributing editor George Garrett (1997)

1997 edited by Matthew J. Bruccoli and George Garrett, with the assistance of L. Kay Webster (1998)

1998 edited by Matthew J. Bruccoli, contributing editor George Garrett, with the assistance of D. W. Thomas (1999)

1999 edited by Matthew J. Bruccoli, contributing editor George Garrett, with the assistance of D. W. Thomas (2000)

2000 edited by Matthew J. Bruccoli, contributing editor George Garrett, with the assistance of George Parker Anderson (2001)

2001 edited by Matthew J. Bruccoli, contributing editor George Garrett, with the assistance of George Parker Anderson (2002)

Concise Series

Concise Dictionary of American Literary Biography, 7 volumes (1988–1999): *The New Consciousness, 1941–1968; Colonization to the American Renaissance, 1640–1865; Realism, Naturalism, and Local Color, 1865–1917; The Twenties, 1917–1929; The Age of Maturity, 1929–1941; Broadening Views, 1968–1988; Supplement: Modern Writers, 1900–1998.*

Concise Dictionary of British Literary Biography, 8 volumes (1991–1992): *Writers of the Middle Ages and Renaissance Before 1660; Writers of the Restoration and Eighteenth Century, 1660–1789; Writers of the Romantic Period, 1789–1832; Victorian Writers, 1832–1890; Late-Victorian and Edwardian Writers, 1890–1914; Modern Writers, 1914–1945; Writers After World War II, 1945–1960; Contemporary Writers, 1960 to Present.*

Concise Dictionary of World Literary Biography, 10 volumes projected (1999–   ): *Ancient Greek and Roman Writers; German Writers; African, Caribbean, and Latin American Writers; South Slavic and Eastern European Writers.*

Dictionary of Literary Biography® • Volume Two Hundred Sixty-Three

William Shakespeare
A Documentary Volume

Dictionary of Literary Biography® • Volume Two Hundred Sixty-Three

William Shakespeare
A Documentary Volume

Edited by
Catherine Loomis
University of New Orleans

A Bruccoli Clark Layman Book

GALE®

THOMSON
GALE

Detroit • New York • San Diego • San Francisco • Cleveland • New Haven, Conn. • Waterville, Maine • London • Munich

© 2002 by Gale. Gale is an imprint of The Gale Group, Inc., a division of Thomson Learning, Inc.

Gale and Design™ and Thomson Learning™ are trademarks used herein under license.

For more information, contact
The Gale Group, Inc.
27500 Drake Rd.
Farmington Hills, MI 48331-3535
Or you can visit our Internet site at
http://www.gale.com

LIBRARY OF CONGRESS CATALOGING-IN-PUBLICATION DATA

William Shakespeare: A Documentary Volume / edited by Catherine Loomis.
    p. cm.—(Dictionary of literary biography; v. 263)
"A Bruccoli Clark Layman book."
    Includes bibliographical references and index.
    ISBN 0-7876-6007-8 (alk. paper)
    1. Shakespeare, William, 1564–1616—Biography—Sources.
    2. Dramatists, English—Early modern, 1500–1700—Biography—
Sources. I. Loomis, Catherine. II. Series.

PR2893 .W55 2002
822.3'3—dc21
           2002007920

Printed in the United States of America
10 9 8 7 6 5 4 3 2 1

Contents

Plan of the Series xxvii

Introduction xxix

A Note on the Text xxxv

Acknowledgments xxxvi

Short Titles of Works Cited in this Volume 3

Baptism through the "Lost Years": 1564–1591 5

1564
William Shakespeare's Birth and Name 5

> *Box:* A Note on Dates during Shakespeare's Life
> *Facsimile:* Shakespeare's Baptismal Record

1566
Gilbert Shakespeare's Baptismal Record 9

1569
Joan Shakespeare's Baptismal Record 10

The Queen's Players and the Earl of Worcester's Players
> Visit Stratford-upon-Avon 10

1571
Anne Shakespeare's Baptismal Record 10

1573
Visit of the Earl of Leicester's Players 10

1574
Richard Shakespeare's Baptismal Record 10

> *Box:* Money in the Elizabethan and Jacobean Eras

1576
Visit of the Earl of Worcester's Players 12

1578
Visit of the Earl of Worcester's Players 12

1579
Anne Shakespeare's Burial Record 12

Visits of the Lord Strange's Players and the Countess
> of Essex's Players 12

1580

Inquest on the Body of Katherine Hamlett 13

Edmund Shakespeare's Baptismal Record 13

Visit of the Earl of Derby's Players 13

     Box: An Age of Exploration and Colonization

     Box: A Touring Company Performance

1581

The Will of Alexander Hoghton of Lea, Esquire .16

Visits of the Earl of Worcester's Players and Lord Berkley's Players 17

1582

Visit of the Earl of Worcester's Players 17

Records of Shakespeare's Marriage 17

     Entry in Bishop Whitgift's *Register* naming Anne Whatley

     Facsimile and transcription: Shakespeare and Anne Hathaway's
        Marriage License Bond

     Box: Acting as a Profession

1583

Susanna Shakespeare 19

     Fascimile: Susanna Shakespeare's Baptismal Record

     Epitaph

1584

Visits of the Lord Berkley's Players and the Lord Chandos's Players 20

1585

Visits of the Earl of Oxford's Players, the Earl of Worcester's Players,
   and the Earl of Essex's Players 21

Hamnet and Judith Shakespeare's Baptismal Record 21

     Facsimile: Hamnet and Judith Shakespeare's Baptismal Record

1587

Visit of Unidentified Players 21

1588

Visits of the Queen's Players, the Earl of Essex's Players, the Earl
   of Leicester's Players, and an Unidentified Company 21

     Box: On the Charms of Plays

Record of John Shakespeare's Lawsuit against John Lambert
   in which William Shakespeare Is Named. 23

1589

Allusion to an ur-*Hamlet* in Nashe's Preface to Greene's *Menaphon* 25

The Elizabethan Years: 1592–March 1603 27

1592

Henslowe Records Performances of a Play about King Henry VI 28

John Shakespeare Cited for Failing to Attend Church 30

Allusion to Shakespeare in *Greene's Groats-worth of Witte* 30

    Box: Signature Designations

Possible Allusion to *1 Henry VI* in Nashe's *Pierce Penilesse* 32

    Box: Shakespeare's Work on *Sir Thomas More*

1593

Possible Allusion to Shakespeare in Chettle's *Kind-Harts Dreame* 35

Henslowe Records Performances of a Play about Henry VI 38

Shakespeare's First Publication. 38

    Stationers' Entry for *Venus and Adonis*

    Fascimile: Title page for *Venus and Adonis*

    Box: Quartos and Folios

    Box: The Stationers' Company

The Dedication of *Venus and Adonis* to the Earl of Southampton 39

Stonley Buys a Copy of *Venus and Adonis* 40

Reynolds Interprets *Venus and Adonis* 40

1594

Henslowe Records Performances of *Titus Andronicus* and Other Plays. 40

Stationers' Register Entries. 41

    Entries for *Titus Andronicus, The First Part of the Contention*
        betwixt the two famous Houses of Yorke and Lancaster,
        The Taming of a Shrew, The Rape of Lucrece, and *Venus and Adonis*

Publications 41

    Transcribed title page for *Venus and Adonis*

    Facsimile: Title page for *The Rape of Lucrece*

    Facsimile: Title page for *Titus Andronicus*

    Facsimile: Title page for *The First Part of the Contention betwixt*
        the two famous Houses of Yorke and Lancaster

The Dedication of *The Rape of Lucrece* to the Earl of Southampton. 42

Shakespeare's Company Paid for a Court Performance 42

Probable Allusion to *Titus Andronicus* in *A Knacke to know a Knave* 43

Possible Allusion to *The Rape of Lucrece* in Drayton's *Matilda* 44

Allusion to *The Rape of Lucrece* in Har.'s *Epicedium* 44

Allusion to W. S. and *The Rape of Lucrece* in *Willobie His Avisa*. 45

    Box: On Printing Plays

    Box: The Reliability of Shakespeare's Texts

Account of an Attempted Performance of *The Comedy of Errors*
   in *Gesta Grayorum* 50

1595

Stationers' Register Entry 52

    Entry for *Edward III*

Possible Allusion to Richard III in Hoby's Letter to Cecil 53

Publications 53

    Facsimile: Title page for *The True Tragedy of Richard Duke of York*
    Facsimile: Title page for *The Lamentable Tragedy of Locrine*

Allusion to Shakespeare in Covell's *Polimanteia* 54

1596

A New Year's Performance of *Titus Andronicus* .55

Stationers' Register Entry 55

    Entry for *Venus and Adonis*

Publications 55

    Transcribed title pages for *Venus and Adonis* and *Edward III*
    Facsimile: Hamnet Shakespeare's burial record
    Box: The Price of a Play

John Shakespeare's Request for a Grant of Arms 56

    Box: The Hierarchy of the Gentry

Writ of Attachment Requested against Shakespeare and Others 58

Possible Allusion to *The Taming of the Shrew* in
    Harington's *The Metamorphosis of Ajax* 58

Allusion to *Hamlet* in Lodge's *Wits Miserie* 59

Shakespeare's Company Paid for Court Performance 60

1597

Shakespeare's Purchase of New Place 61

Shakespeare Confirms Ownership of New Place .63

    Box: London's Mayor Requests a Ban on Plays

Stationers' Register Entries 65

    Entries for *Richard II* and *Richard III*

Publications 66

    Transcribed title page for *Richard II*
    Facsimile: Title page for *Richard III*
    Facsimile: Title page for *Romeo and Juliet*

Record Showing Shakespeare as a Tax Defaulter 66

    Box: The Table of Contents of the Northumberland Manuscript

Lord Chamberlain's Men Paid for Court Performances 67

1598

Letter from Sturley to Quiney Mentioning Shakespeare 67

Shakespeare Listed as Hoarding Grain 71

Stationers' Register Entries. 72

      Entries for *1 Henry IV* and *The Merchant of Venice*

Publications 72

      Transcribed title pages for *The Rape of Lucrece, Richard II,*
        and *Richard III*
      Facsimile: Title page for *1 Henry IV*
      Facsimile: Title page for *Love's Labor's Lost*

London Tax Indenture Listing Shakespeare 72

Letter from Richard Quiney to Shakespeare 73

Letter from Adrian to Richard Quiney Mentioning Shakespeare. 75

Letter from Sturley to Richard Quiney Mentioning Shakespeare 75

      Box: Blood Sports and Executions

Shakespeare Is Paid for a Load of Stone 78

Allen's Bill of Complaint Regarding The Theatre 78

      Facsimile: Page from *The Workes of Benjamin Jonson*
        listing Shakespeare

Allusion to Shakespeare in Barnfield's *The Encomion of Lady Pecunia* 82

Allusion to *Romeo and Juliet* in Marston's *The Scourge of Villanie*. 82

Allusions to Shakespeare and His Plays in Meres's *Palladis Tamia*. 82

Allusion to *Love's Labor's Lost* in Tofte's *Alba* 86

Shakespeare Listed as a Tax Defaulter. 86

The Lord Chamberlain's Men Paid for Performances. 86

Harvey's Comments on Shakespeare. 86

Shakespeare's Poetry Mocked in *The First Part of the Return
  from Parnassus* 87

      Box: The Globe in Southwark

1599
Shakespeare Identified as a Sharer in the Globe. 90

Further Details of Shakespeare's Share of the Globe 95

Possible Allusion to *1 Henry IV* in Whyte's Letter to Sidney 96

      Box: A Royal Edict on the Production of Plays

Brend's Property Inventory Listing Shakespeare 99

Platter Sees *Julius Caesar* 99

Shakespeare Listed on Exchequer Pipe Roll. 100

Publications 100

    Transcribed title pages for *Venus and Adonis, Romeo and Juliet,*
      1 Henry IV, and *The Passionate Pilgrime*

Weever's Poem About Shakespeare in *Epigrammes* 100

    Box: Shakespeare Cited on the Title Page of
      Pinner of Wakefield

John Shakespeare's Grant of Arms 101

Shakespeare's Company Paid for Court Performances 102

1600
A Contract to Build the Fortune Theater 102

Stationers' Register Entries 104

    Entries for *As You Like It, Henry V, Much Ado about Nothing,*
      2 Henry IV, A Midsummer Night's Dream, and *The Merchant of Venice*

Publications 104

    Transcribed title pages for *The Rape of Lucrece, Titus Andronicus,*
      The True Tragedy of Richard Duke of York, and *The First Part*
      of the Contention betwixt the two famous houses of York and Lancaster
    Facsimile: Title page for *The Merchant of Venice*
    Facsimile: Title page for *A Midsummer Night's Dream*
    Facsimile: Title page for *Much Ado about Nothing*
    Facsimile: Title page for *2 Henry IV*
    Facsimile: Title page for *Henry V*

Allusion to *1 Henry IV* in the *Life of Sir John Oldcastle* 105

The Publication of *Englands Helicon* 106

Shakespeare Listed on Exchequer Pipe Roll .107

Allusion to Justices Silence and Shallow in Percy's Letter 107

Allusion to Shakespeare in Bodenham's *Bel-vedere* 107

Allusion to Falstaff in Jonson's *Every Man Out of His Humor* 110

Possible Allusions to Shakespeare and an Early Version of *Macbeth*
    in *Kemp's Nine Daies Wonder* 110

Allusions to *Venus and Adonis* and *Lucrece* in Lane's
    Tom Tel-Troths Message 112

Allusion to the Globe in Rowlands's *The Letting Of Humours Blood* 112

Allusion to Falstaff in a Letter from the Countess of Southampton
    to the Earl of Southampton 112

Shakespeare's Company Paid for Court Performances 113

1601
A Performance of *Richard II* and the Essex Rebellion 113

Shakespeare and His Wife Named in Whittington's Will 116

John Shakespeare's Burial Record 116

The Publication of Chester's *Love's Martyr* 117

Allusions to *Richard III* and *1 Henry IV* in *The Whipping of the Satyre* 117

Allusion to *1 Henry IV* in Weever's *The Mirror of Martyrs* 117

Allusions to Shakespeare in *The Returne From Pernassus* 118

Allusion to *Richard III* in Marston's *What You Will* 122

Shakespeare's Company Paid for Court Performances 122

1602
Stationers' Register Entries 122

> Entries for *The Merry Wives of Windsor, 1 and 2 Henry VI,
> Titus Andronicus,* and *Hamlet*

Publications 123

> Transcriptions of the title pages for *Venus and Adonis, Henry V,*
> and *Richard III*
> *Facsimile:* Title page for *The Merry Wives of Windsor*

Manningham Sees *Twelfth Night* and Reports a Story
about Shakespeare and Richard Burbage 124

The Shakespeare Coat of Arms Questioned 126

John Shakespeare Defended in the College of Arms 126

Deed of Conveyance for Land in Stratford 126

Hercules Underhill Acknowledges Shakespeare's Ownership
of New Place 129

> *Box:* The Swan and the Other Theaters of London

Shakespeare Buys a Cottage in Chapel Lane 131

Richard Vennar Causes a Scandal at the Swan .132

> *Box:* John Chamberlain's Account of the Vennar Incident

Allusions to *The Comedy of Errors* and Justice Shallow in
Dekker's *Satiro-mastix* 133

Shakespeare's Company Paid for Court Performances 134

1603
Stationers' Register Entries 134

> Entries for *Troilus and Cressida, Richard II, Richard III,*
> and *1 Henry IV*
> *Facsimile:* Title page for *Hamlet*
> *Box:* The First Quarto of *Hamlet*

Allusion to Shakespeare in Chettle's *Englandes Mourning Garment* 134

Allusion to Shakespeare in "A mournefull Dittie" 136

The Jacobean Years: April 1603–1616 137

1603
Shakespeare's Company Becomes the King's Men 138

    Box: A Stationer's Record of Shakespeare's Plays

The King's Men Paid for Court Performances .139

Possible Allusions to *The Rape of Lucrece* and Two Plays in
    Saint Marie Magdalens Conversion 141

Shakespeare Named in Camden's "Certaine Poemes" 141

Possible Allusion to Shakespeare in Davies's *Microcosmos* 142

The King's Men Paid for Court Performances .142

1604
Possible Allusion to *A Midsummer Night's Dream* in Carleton's
    Letter to Chamberlain 143

    Box: Satan at the Globe

The King's Men Paid for Being Unable to Perform 145

The King's Men Paid for Court Performances .145

The King's Men Congratulated in Dugdale's *The Time Triumphant* 146

Allusion to *Love's Labor's Lost* in Cope's Letter to Cecil 146

    Box and Facsimile: The King's Men in the Coronation Procession

The King's Men Paid for Attendance on the Spanish Ambassador 146

Shakespeare Listed in Survey of Rowington Manor 146

Shakespeare's Involvement in Belott's Suit against Mountjoy 146

Shakespeare's Suit against Rogers 151

Publications 152

    Transcription of the title page for *1 Henry IV*
    Facsimile: Title page for *Hamlet*

Allusion to Shakespeare in Cooke's *Epigrames* .153

Allusion to *The Comedy of Errors* in Dekker's *The Honest Whore* 153

Allusions to Falstaff and *The Comedy of Errors* in *The Meeting of Gallants* 153

Allusion to *Titus Andronicus* in Middleton's *Father Hubburds Tales* 154

Allusion to Falstaff in Persons's *Of Three Conversions of England* 155

Allusions to Shakespeare and *Hamlet* in Scoloker's *Daiphantus* 155

The King's Men Paid for Court Performances .157

1605
Publications 158

    Transcription of the title page for *Richard III*
    Facsimile: Title page for *The London Prodigall*

Shakespeare Named in Phillips's Will 158

Shakespeare Leases the Stratford Tithes 158

Hubaud's Bond to Shakespeare 165

Allusion to Shakespeare in Poulet's Letter to Vincent 165

Allusion to *Hamlet* in *Ratseis Ghost* 166

Allusion to *2 Henry IV* in Breton's *A Poste with a Packet
       of madde Letters* 168

Allusion to *Hamlet* in *Eastward Hoe* 168

Possible Allusion to *The Rape of Lucrece* in *The Strange Fortune of Alerane* 169

Allusion to *Hamlet* in Smith's *Voiage and Entertainment in Rushia* 169

Allusion to Justice Shallow in Woodhouse's *The Flea* 171

The King's Men Paid for Court Performances 171

1606
Shakespeare Listed in Hubaud's Inventory 173

The Globe Ordered to Repair Its Sewers 173

       Box: A Statute on Blasphemy

Shakespeare Listed in Survey of Rowington Manor 173

Allusion to *Richard III* in Barnes's *Foure Bookes of Offices* 173

The King's Men Paid for Court Performances 174

1607
Stationers' Register Entries 174

       Entries for *Romeo and Juliet, Love's Labor's Lost, The
       Taming of a Shrew, Hamlet,* and *King Lear*

Publications 174

       Transcriptions of title pages for *The Taming of a
       Shrew, The Rape of Lucrece,* and *Venus and Adonis*

Raworth Sanctioned for Printing *Venus and Adonis* 174

Susanna Shakespeare's Marriage to John Hall 175

Edward Shakespeare's Burial Record 175

Edmund Shakespeare's Burial Record 175

Allusion to *Venus and Adonis* in *The Fayre Mayde of the Exchange* 175

Allusion to Shakespeare in Barksted's *Mirrha The Mother of Adonis* 176

Possible Allusions to *Richard III* and *Twelfth Night* in Dekker's
       A Knights Conjuring 177

Allusion to *Hamlet* in Dekker and Webster's *West-ward Hoe* 179

Allusion to *Venus and Adonis* in *Merrie Conceited Jests of George Peele* 179

Allusion to *A Midsummer Night's Dream* in Sharpham's *The Fleire* 179

The King's Men Paid for Court Performances 180

Shipboard Performances of *Richard II* and *Hamlet*. 180

    Box: Playwrights as Directors

1608
Elizabeth Hall's Baptismal Record 180

Stationers' Register Entries. 181

    Entries for *A Yorkshire Tragedy, Pericles,* and *Antony and Cleopatra*

Publications 181

    Transcribed title pages for *1 Henry IV, Richard II,*
        and *Venus and Adonis*
    Facsimile: Title page for *King Lear*
    Facsimile: Title page for *A Yorkshire Tragedy*

Allusion to Performances of Shakespeare's Play in
    Wilkins's *The Painfull Adventures of Pericles Prince of Tyre*. 182

Shakespeare's Lease for the Blackfriar's Theater 182

Mary Shakespeare's Burial Record. 186

Allusion to *Hamlet* in Armin's *A Nest of Ninnies* 186

Allusion to *Hamlet* in Dekker's *The Dead Tearme*. 187

Allusion to *Hamlet* in Dekker's *Lanthorne and Candle-light*. 188

Allusion to *Venus and Adonis* in Machin and Markham's
    The Dumbe Knight 190

Allusion to *Venus and Adonis* in Middleton's *A Mad World,*
    My Masters 190

The Venetian Ambassador Attends a Performance of *Pericles* 190

Possible Allusion to Anne Hathaway 190

The King's Men Paid for Court Performances .191

Shakespeare's Suit against Addenbrooke 191

1609
Stationers' Register Entries. 195

    Entries for *Troilus and Cressida* and *Sonnets*

Publications 195

    Transcribed title page for *Romeo and Juliet*
    Facsimile: Title page and dedication page for *Shakespeare's Sonnets*
    Facsimile: Title page for *Troilus and Cressida*
    Facsimile: Title page for *Pericles*

Preface to *The Famous Historie of Troylus and Cresseid*. 195

Alleyn Buys a Copy of Shakespeare's *Sonnets*. .196

Greene Stays at New Place. 196

Pericles and *King Lear* Performed at Gowthwaite Hall 196

Possible Allusion to Shakespeare in Davies's *Humours
Heav'n on Earth* 197

Possible Allusion to *Julius Caesar* in *Everie Woman in her Humor* 198

Possible Allusion to *Pericles* in *Pimlyco* 198

Possible Allusion to *The Taming of the Shrew* in *A whole crew
of kind Gossips* 199

The King's Men Paid for Being Unable to Perform. 200

1610
Publication 200

Transcribed title page for *Venus and Adonis*

The Prince of Wirtemberg Sees *Othello* at the Globe. 200

Jackson sees *Othello* in Oxford. 201

Allusion to the Globe in Heath's *Two Centuries Of Epigrammes* 201

Allusion to Falstaff in Sharpe's *More Fooles Yet* 202

Forman Sees *Macbeth*, *Cymbeline*, and *The Winter's Tale*. 202

The King's Men Paid for Court Performances .206

1611
Publications 206

Transcribed title pages for *Hamlet*, *Pericles*, and *Titus Andronicus*
Facsimile: Title page for *King John*

Shakespeare's Land Purchase Confirmed 206

Shakespeare Named in Stratford Highway Bill .207

Shakespeare Listed in Johnson's Inventory 207

Bill of Complaint Regarding the Stratford Tithes. 208

Allusion to the Globe in Cooke's *Greene's Tu quoque*. 208

Poem about Shakespeare and an Allusion to *Venus and Adonis*
in Davies's *The Scourge of Folly*. 209

Allusion to Falstaff in Field's *Amends for Ladies* 209

Allusion to Falstaff in Speed's *The History of Great Britaine*. 210

The Master of the Revels' Account of Plays Performed. 210

The King's Men Paid for Court Performances .211

Harington's List of Shakespeare's Plays 211

1612
Gilbert Shakespeare's Burial Record 213

Vaux's Complaint about an Incident at the Globe. 213

Publications 215

> Transcribed title pages for *Richard III and The Passionate Pilgrim*
> *Facsimile:* Title page for *A Funerall Elegy*

Allusions to Shakespeare and *Henry V* in Heywood's
    An Apology For Actors 215

Allusion to Shakespeare in Webster's Preface to *The White Divel* 216

1613
Richard Shakespeare's Burial Record. 217

Publications 217

> Transcribed title pages for *1 Henry IV* and *Thomas Cromwell*

Shakespeare's Purchase of the Blackfriar's Gatehouse 217

Shakespeare Mortgages the Blackfriar's Gatehouse 219

Shakespeare and Burbage Paid for Impresa 221

The King's Men Paid for Court Performances .221

Allusion to Shakespeare in Digges's Inscription in
    de Vega's *Rimas* 222

Account of the Burning of the Globe in Lorkin's Letter
    to Puckering. 222

Account of the Burning of the Globe in Wotton's Letter
    to Bacon. 222

Account of the Burning of the Globe in Bluett's Letter
    to Weeks 223

Account of the Burning of the Globe in Chamberlain's
    Letter to Winwood 223

Account of the Burning and Rebuilding of the Globe in
    The Annales 223

Report of the Burning of the Globe in *The Abridgement of the*
    English Chronicle 224

Allusion to the Burning of the Globe in Taylor's
    A nest of Epigrams 224

Allusion to the Globe in Taylor's *The Water Mens Suit* 224

The King's Men Paid for Court Performances 227

Shakespeare Named in the Will of John Combe 227

1614
Rights to Publish *The Rape of Lucrece* Transferred. 227

Allusion to the Rebuilt Globe in Chamberlain's Letter
    to Carleton. 227

A Preacher Is Entertained at New Place. 228

Publication 228

      Transcribed title page for *Englands Helicon*

Possible Allusion to *Richard III* in Brooke's *The Ghost Of*
Richard The Third 228

Allusion to Shakespeare in Camden's *Remaines*. 229

Allusions to Plays in Johnson's Preface to *Bartholomew Fayre*. 230

Allusion to *Hamlet* in Scott's *The Philosopher's Banquet* 232

Allusion to *Pericles* in Tailor's *The Hogge Hath Lost His Pearle*. 232

Porter's Epigram on Shakespeare. 233

Epigram on Shakespeare in Freeman's *Rubbe, And a great Cast* 233

Shakespeare's Possible Involvement in an Enclosure Effort. 233

The King's Men Paid for Court Performances 235

1615
Publication 236

      Transcribed title page for *Richard II*

The King's Men Paid for Court Performances 236

Allusion to Shakespeare in F.B.'s Poem 236

Possible Allusion to Shakespeare in *The New Metamorphosis* 236

Shakespeare Named in Howes and Stow's *The Annales*. 238

Shakespeare's Suit against Bacon 238

1616
Shakespeare Named in Bolton's Draft for *Hypercritica*. 239

Judith Shakespeare's Marriage to Thomas Quiney 239

The King's Men Paid for Court Performances 240

      Fascimile: William Shakespeare's Burial Record

Shakespeare's Epitaphs. 240

Shakespeare's Will 240

      Transcriptions and facsimile

Publication 249

      Transcribed title page for *The Rape of Lucrece*

Possible Allusions to *Antony and Cleopatra* and *The Comedy of Errors*
in Anton's *The Philosophers Satyrs*. 249

Allusion to *Richard III* in Breton's *The Good And The Badde*. 251

Allusions to *Hamlet* and *The Rape of Lucrece* in Beaumont
and Fletcher's *The Scornful Ladie* 251

Basse's Poem about Shakespeare 251

Shakespeare's Posthumous Reputation and the First Folio 253

1617
Publication 253

    Transcribed title page for *Venus and Adonis*

1619
Stationers' Register Entry 253

    Entry for *The Merchant of Venice*

Publications 253

    Transcribed title pages for *Henry V, King Lear, The Merry Wives
    of Windsor, The Whole Contention between the Two Famous Houses,
    Lancaster and York,* and *A Yorkshire Tragedy*

Allusions to Shakespeare in Jonson's "Conversations with Drummond" 254

1620
Publication 255

    Title page of *Venus and Adonis*

1621
Stationers' Register Entry 255

    Entry for *Othello*

1622
Publications 255

    Transcribed title pages for *Richard III, Romeo and Juliet,*
    and *1 Henry IV*
    Facsimile: Title page for *Othello*

Epistle to the Reader from *Othello* 256

1623
Anne Hathaway's Burial 256

Stationers' Register Entries 256

    Entries for plays to be included in the First Folio

Preliminary Material in the First Folio 257

    Facsimile: Title page for the First Folio
    Facsimile: Jonson's note "To the Reader"
    Facsimile and transcription: "To the great Variety of Readers"

    Dedication
    Commendatory Verses by Jonson, Hugh Holland,
        L. Digges, and I.M.
    Facsimile: List of actors
    Facsimile: Table of Contents
    Facsimile: First page of *The Tempest*
    Facsimile: Last page of *Othello*
    Facsimile: Last page of *Henry VIII*
    Facsimile: Page from Hamlet

Jonson's *Timber, or Discoveries*. 265

Epistle to the Reader and Commendatory Verse from *Poems:
Written By Wil. Shakespeare. Gent*. 265

Entries from Ward's Diary. 268

Facsimile: Title page for *The Taming of the Shrew*

Aubrey's *Lives*. 269

Appendix

Eyewitnesses and Historians. 275
Platter's Observations (1599)
Baron Waldstein's Diary (1600)
Letter of Ottaviano Lotti (1605)
Letter of John Chamberlain (1608)
Letter of Antimo Galli (1613)

Politics and the Theater 278
Letter of Dudley Carleton (1605)
Letter of John Harington (1606)

Regulations for the Theater 281
The Book of Common Prayer (1559)
An Act of the Privy Council (1600)
An Act of the Privy Council (1601)
A Privy Council Warrant (1604)
A Letter Attributed to George Chapman (1608)
George Buc's License to Perform *The Second Maiden's Tragedy* (1611)

Prologues, Epilogues, Epistles to Readers, and Excerpts from Plays. 285

Marston's Letter to the Reader of *The Malcontent* (1604)
Commendatory Poem for Jonson's *Sejanus* (1605)
Prologue and Epilogue for Marston's *Parasitaster* (1606)
Note to the Reader of Marston's *The Wonder of women* (1606)
Heywood's Preface to *The Rape of Lucrece* (1608)
Jonson's Prefatory Poem for *Epicoene* (1609)
Jonson on the Audience in *The Masque of Queenes* (1609)
Address to the Reader and Prologue for *The Roaring Girle* (1611)

Epigrams and Satires 289

Greene's *Francescos Fortunes* (1590)
Greenes, Groats-worth of witte (1592)
Nashe's *Christs Teares Over Jerusalem* (1593)
Rankins's *Seaven Satyres Applyed to the Weeke* (1598)
Davies and Marlowe's *Epigrammes and Elegies* (1599)
Weever's *Epigrammes in the oldest cut, and newest fashion* (1599)
Rowlands's *The Letting Of Humours Blood In The Head-Vaine* (1600)

A Translation of Dedekind's *Grobianus et Grobiana* (1605)

Merrie Conceited Jests of George Peele Gentleman (1607)

Dekker's *The Guls Horne-booke* (1609)

Parrot's *Laquei ridiculosi* (1613)

Wither's *Abuses Stript, And Whipt* (1613)

Breton's *I would, And would not* (1614)

Overbury's *New And Choice Characters* (1615)

Stephens's *Satyrical Essayes Characters And Others* (1615)

Jonson's *Epigrammes* (1616)

Anti-Theatrical Tracts 304

Stubbes's "Of Stage-playes and Enterluds, with their wickednes" (1583)

Rainolds's *Th'overthrow of Stage-Playes* (1599)

Vaughan's *The Golden grove* (1600)

A Defense of Actors 306

Heywood's *An Apology for Actors* (1612)

Practical Matters 310

Inventories of Theatrical Costumes and Properties (1598)

Serlio's *The Second Booke of Architecture* (1611)

Rid's *The Art of Jugling or Legerdemaine* (1612)

Education 312

Letter of Gager (1592)

Checklist of Further Reading 313

Cumulative Index 319

Plan of the Series

The advisory board, the editors, and the publisher of the *Dictionary of Literary Biography* are joined in endorsing Mark Twain's declaration. The literature of a nation provides an inexhaustible resource of permanent worth. Our purpose is to make literature and its creators better understood and more accessible to students and the reading public, while satisfying the needs of teachers and researchers.

To meet these requirements, *literary biography* has been construed in terms of the author's achievement. The most important thing about a writer is his writing. Accordingly, the entries in *DLB* are career biographies, tracing the development of the author's canon and the evolution of his reputation.

The purpose of *DLB* is not only to provide reliable information in a usable format but also to place the figures in the larger perspective of literary history and to offer appraisals of their accomplishments by qualified scholars.

The publication plan for *DLB* resulted from two years of preparation. The project was proposed to Bruccoli Clark by Frederick G. Ruffner, president of the Gale Research Company, in November 1975. After specimen entries were prepared and typeset, an advisory board was formed to refine the entry format and develop the series rationale. In meetings held during 1976, the publisher, series editors, and advisory board approved the scheme for a comprehensive biographical dictionary of persons who contributed to literature. Editorial work on the first volume began in January 1977, and it was published in 1978. In order to make *DLB* more than a dictionary and to compile volumes that individually have claim to status as literary history, it was decided to organize volumes by topic, period, or

From an unpublished section of Mark Twain's autobiography, copyright by the Mark Twain Company

genre. Each of these freestanding volumes provides a biographical-bibliographical guide and overview for a particular area of literature. We are convinced that this organization—as opposed to a single alphabet method—constitutes a valuable innovation in the presentation of reference material. The volume plan necessarily requires many decisions for the placement and treatment of authors. Certain figures will be included in separate volumes, but with different entries emphasizing the aspect of his career appropriate to each volume. Ernest Hemingway, for example, is represented in *American Writers in Paris, 1920–1939* by an entry focusing on his expatriate apprenticeship; he is also in *American Novelists, 1910–1945* with an entry surveying his entire career, as well as in *American Short-Story Writers, 1910–1945, Second Series* with an entry concentrating on his short fiction. Each volume includes a cumulative index of the subject authors and articles.

Since 1981 the series has been further augmented by the *DLB Yearbooks,* which update published entries, add new entries to keep the *DLB* current with contemporary activity, and provide articles on literary history. There have also been nineteen *DLB Documentary Series* volumes which provide illustrations, facsimiles, and biographical and critical source materials for figures, works, or groups judged to have particular interest for students. In 1999 the *Documentary Series* was incorporated into the *DLB* volume numbering system beginning with *DLB 210: Ernest Hemingway.*

We define literature as the *intellectual commerce of a nation:* not merely as belles lettres but as that ample and complex process by which ideas are generated, shaped, and transmitted. *DLB* entries are not limited to "creative writers" but extend to other figures who in their time and in their way influenced the mind of a people. Thus the series encompasses historians, journalists, publishers, book collectors, and screenwriters. By this means readers of *DLB* may be aided to perceive literature not as cult scripture in the keeping of intellectual high priests but firmly positioned at the center of a nation's life.

DLB includes the major writers appropriate to each volume and those standing in the ranks behind them. Scholarly and critical counsel has been sought in deciding which minor figures to include and how full their entries should be. Wherever possible, useful references are made to figures who do not warrant separate entries.

Each *DLB* volume has an expert volume editor responsible for planning the volume, selecting the figures for inclusion, and assigning the entries. Volume editors are also responsible for preparing, where appropriate, appendices surveying the major periodicals and literary and intellectual movements for their volumes, as well as lists of further readings. Work on the series as a whole is coordinated at the Bruccoli Clark Layman editorial center in Columbia, South Carolina, where the editorial staff is responsible for accuracy and utility of the published volumes.

One feature that distinguishes *DLB* is the illustration policy—its concern with the iconography of literature. Just as an author is influenced by his surroundings, so is the reader's understanding of the author enhanced by a knowledge of his environment. Therefore *DLB* volumes include not only drawings, paintings, and photographs of authors, often depicting them at various stages in their careers, but also illustrations of their families and places where they lived. Title pages are regularly reproduced in facsimile along with dust jackets for modern authors. The dust jackets are a special feature of *DLB* because they often document better than anything else the way in which an author's work was perceived in its own time. Specimens of the writers' manuscripts and letters are included when feasible.

Samuel Johnson rightly decreed that "The chief glory of every people arises from its authors." The purpose of the *Dictionary of Literary Biography* is to compile literary history in the surest way available to us—by accurate and comprehensive treatment of the lives and work of those who contributed to it.

The *DLB* Advisory Board

Introduction

We no longer use the Nine Muses to explain artistic inspiration; instead, we turn to biography. When reading about an artist's life, even in its most mundane details, we look for material that has been transformed or translated into the finished works we admire and study: the lover whose face is recognizable even when cubed, the parent who metamorphoses into a villain, the letter to a cousin that evolves into a chapter. We try to determine how a painter was trained or a writer educated, what she read, what he wore, where they went; we look at parents, friends, lovers, spouses, and rivals to try to place the artist in a social context; we study historical events that took place during the artist's life to try to determine what might have influenced her or worried him, or how they formed or were formed by the culture around them. Most of us assume there is a link between life and art, and that knowing more about the artist's life will help us better understand his or her work.

Artists do not always agree. Some take careful steps to ensure that biographers will have little to work with: papers, sketches, and early drafts are burned or even buried at sea, and family and friends sworn to silence. Others leave an abundance of material, giving the biographer the impossible task of determining what mattered. Whether there is too little material or too much, the passage of time makes constructing a biography more and more difficult. Documents decay or are destroyed; family and acquaintances die, forget, or exaggerate; the artist's reputation shifts; works disappear or are recovered.

In the case of William Shakespeare, the problems a biographer faces are compounded by several factors: Shakespeare's fame and reputation are extensive–in the year 2000, he was voted England's Man of the Millennium, and scholars and students all over the world study his works with care; any account of his life is bound to emphasize some details and exclude others in ways likely to offend some workers in the Shakespeare Industry. In the nearly 400 years that have passed since his death in 1616, many documents have been lost, or their use or relevance is no longer clear to us. Shakespeare's plays are still frequently performed, and his extraordinary artistic reputation is often at odds with the ordinary realities a biographer must cope with: many of the surviving documents naming Shakespeare have to do with taxes and real estate purchases, not with poetry. Shakespeare's life story contains several intriguing mysteries: What did he do from 1585 to 1592, the "lost years" during which he disappears from the public records? Who is the Dark Lady of the sonnets? Why, in his will, does he leave his wife Anne Hathaway his second best bed? Any responsible account of his life is bound to tell you the answer to each of these questions is we do not know.

The temptation to assume Shakespeare's plays and poems, and his sonnets in particular, reveal biographical information is a strong one, made all the stronger by the absence of any personal papers. Whether they were destroyed consciously or accidentally, or whether they still await discovery, any letters, notes, journals, drafts, or other private writings by Shakespeare are not available to us. What is available from his lifetime are records that were public: legal documents, authorizations for payments, references in printed texts to Shakespeare or his poems and plays. *Dictionary of Literary Biography 263: William Shakespeare, A Documentary Volume* presents the available documents in chronological order.

The biographical documents are of mixed origin. There are long and dull conveyances and feet of fine, showing Shakespeare's title to a large house and a substantial piece of land in Stratford. There are regular payments from King James's accounts to Shakespeare and his fellow actors. There are poems praising him, plays mocking him, pamphlets excoriating him. There are records of lawsuits to collect debts and regain possession of legal documents. Putting these records in chronological order rather than sorting them by type provides a sense of the complexity of Shakespeare's life–he was not working in an ivory tower of London when he wrote the sonnets, *Venus and Adonis,* and *Hamlet*; he was helping to manage a large and busy theater, investing the profits, suing and being sued, dodging the tax collectors. Not everything that happened to him was equally important, and hardly any of it was poetic, but even seemingly trivial events may help us interpret the plays or poems, or understand more about the man who created them.

The story the documents tell begins in an ordinary way. William Shakespeare was baptized on 26 April 1564 in Holy Trinity Church, Stratford. He was the son of Mary Arden, a farmer's daughter, and John Shakespeare, a farmer's son who had become a glover and wool dealer and who held a series of increasingly important public offices in Stratford. The Shakespeares had eight children who were baptized in Holy Trinity Church: Joan in 1558, Margaret in 1562; William in 1564; Gilbert in 1566; another Joan in 1569; Anne in 1571; Richard in 1574; and Edmund in 1580.

The Shakespeares lived in a house in Henley Street; when John Shakespeare's fortunes were rising, he also bought the house next door. The two houses, joined and remodeled, still stand. After many years of success as a town official, John Shakespeare's fortunes shifted: he mortgaged some of the land that had been his wife's dowry; he stopped attending meetings of the Stratford council; and he stopped attending church, claiming he feared being arrested for debt. The records that document this decline provide no clue as to what caused it; reasonable explanations include illness, bad luck, or recusancy. The early modern period—the late sixteenth and early seventeenth centuries—was a tumultuous time for England's Christians who in one lifetime might have had to metamorphose from Catholic to Anglican to Catholic to Anglican until the matter was settled by Queen Elizabeth's accession to the throne in 1558; non-Christians and atheists, when not subjected to persecution or expulsion, were forced to conform outwardly with the official religion of the state. John Shakespeare may have chosen to remain Catholic, a decision whose consequences grew more serious as the penalties against Catholics increased in severity in the sixteenth century, or he may have been another kind of nonconformist, such as a Puritan.

John Shakespeare's services as ale taster, alderman, and bailiff entitled him to send his sons to the town grammar school; unfortunately, the school's records for the years Shakespeare might have attended it do not survive. From his use of Latin and of classical sources in his play, he seems to have had the sort of education Stratford's grammar school would have provided. Such an education featured careful study of Latin grammar and translation of classical texts, including poetry and drama. The Shakespeares may have attended theatrical performances by troupes of players whose regular visits to Stratford are reported in the town's financial accounts.

William Shakespeare next appears in the public records in 1582 when he was granted a license to marry Anne Whatley of Temple Grafton. The entry of this name in the bishop of Worcester's registry book has caused a great deal of consternation, because Shakespeare eventually married Anne Hathaway of Shottery. The simplest explanation is that the clerk who recorded the license made a mistake; he was prone to them. The need to make Shakespeare's life as complicated as the plot of one of his early comedies, though, has provoked romantic speculations in which Shakespeare is in love with one Anne but forced to marry another. Proof is lacking for any account of a runaway bride or reluctant groom, but we do know that six months after the wedding, Susanna Shakespeare was born to Anne Hathaway and Shakespeare, who went on to produce twins, Hamnet and Judith, in 1585. The twins were probably named after Hamnet and Judith Sadler, who lived in Stratford near John Shakespeare's Henley Street houses.

From 1585 until 1592, Shakespeare appears in surviving records only once: he is named along with his parents in a lawsuit his father initiated in 1589 to attempt to recover land mortgaged and lost through nonpayment of the debt. Unfortunately, the bill of complaint does not give William Shakespeare's occupation or address. Scholars continue to search for any evidence of Shakespeare's activities in this period, known as the "lost years." A variety of intriguing explanations have been offered for how a young man from Stratford, a country market town, came to be a London playwright, one of the few without credentials from Oxford or Cambridge. Shakespeare may have joined a company of actors who were on tour in the countryside; such companies visited Stratford frequently in the 1580s. Shakespeare may, as antiquarian John Aubrey reports in *Lives of Eminent Men* (1813), have worked as a schoolmaster in the country. Shakespeare may have assumed an alias, William Shakeshafte, a variant on the family name that his grandfather Richard Shakespeare had sometimes used, and gone to work in a Catholic household in Lancashire from which he entered the service of the earl of Derby's players. He may have run away to London because, as an enduring but unproven story has it, he was caught poaching deer on a nearby estate, or because he wanted to be an actor: another story from well after his death tells of Shakespeare holding horses at the theater door in order to break into the business. Until further documentation is found, however, any account of the lost years remains speculative.

Although scholars have been unable to determine which of the London acting companies could claim him, by 1592 Shakespeare was in London and was known as a playwright. In that year two prose writers, Robert Greene and Thomas Nashe, allude to him. Greene is not particularly flattering: he calls him "Shake-scene" and describes him as "an upstart crow."

Nashe alludes to an especially valiant character from Shakespeare's *1 Henry VI*, John Talbot, the earl of Shrewsbury, as a prologue to a defense of actors against the intense and lengthy criticism of London's conservative religious community. Shakespeare was a notable enough playwright to have drawn Greene's sniping and Nashe's compliment, but any success he experienced with his early comedies and history plays was interrupted in 1593 by an epidemic of bubonic plague in London that forced the theaters to close. Shakespeare's response was to write two long poems, *Venus and Adonis*, published in 1593, and *The Rape of Lucrece*, published in 1594, both of which were successful, remaining in print throughout Shakespeare's lifetime and referred to often, nearly always in complimentary ways. Both poems are dedicated to Henry Wriothesley, Earl of Southampton, a courtier whose relationship to Shakespeare is otherwise undocumented. Southampton is one of several English aristocrats whose life accords in some ways with the story told in Shakespeare's sonnets, the first 126 of which are addressed to a young man whose social position is much higher than the poet's and whose beauty and inconstancy are a source of immense frustration. Aside from the clues some readers find in the sonnets themselves, and some inexact references in Henry Willobie's poem *Avisa* (1594), there is no evidence to identify the sonnets' young man or the Dark Lady by whom he is eventually seduced. It is perhaps helpful to remember that, technically, they are both fictional characters.

When the theaters reopened after the plague subsided, the professional acting companies in London reorganized. The acting companies were patronized by various aristocrats; Shakespeare became a member of the Lord Chamberlain's Men, who drew their players from various other companies and who eventually became London's premier theatrical troupe. The Lord Chamberlain was the title of the member of the queen's household who planned her entertainment; in 1594 the position was held by Henry Carey, Lord Hundson. Royal performances were given at court, and the Chamberlain's Men appeared there in December 1594 and regularly thereafter. They were allowed to play at the public theaters in order to be ever at the ready should the queen desire to see a play. Although by 1595–1596 the Chamberlain's Men were performing at an outdoor theater called The Theater, they appeared elsewhere in 1594: Shakespeare's *Titus Andronicus* and one of his *Henry VI* plays are probably the plays by those names recorded in Philip Henslowe's 1594 financial accounts for his theater, the Rose; the play *Taming of a Shrew*, whose revenue Henslowe reports, may also be Shakespeare's. His *Comedy of Errors* was supposed to be part of the elaborate 1594–

1595 Christmas entertainments at Gray's Inn, a sort of guildhall for lawyers, but, as the official account of the events explains, the evening ended in confusion. There are few other records from 1594 to 1596, but Shakespeare continued to write plays: *Richard II, Richard III*, and a textually corrupt version of *Romeo and Juliet* were published in 1597. He was also probably working as an actor; he is identified as such in the first edition of his collected works, published in 1623, and is among the cast list in Ben Jonson's *Every Man in His Humor* (1598) and *Sejanus* (1603).

The surviving documents for 1596 exemplify the frustrations such evidence presents: they tell us what happened but not why or how. In August 1596 Shakespeare's son Hamnet died. The only surviving record is the entry in the Holy Trinity church burial register, which does not list a cause of death. In October, Shakespeare's father John requested a grant of arms, a way of marking himself and his heirs as gentlemen, but the formal words of the request do not explain John Shakespeare's motive. In November an arrest warrant was issued for William Shakespeare, Francis Langley, Dorothy Soer, and Anne Lee for disturbing the peace of William Wayte, who was perhaps retaliating for a similar warrant Langley earlier requested against Wayte; the warrant does not tell us who Soer and Lee were or what Shakespeare did that Wayte found so disturbing.

In 1597 Shakespeare began a series of cautious legal transactions to purchase New Place, one of the largest houses in Stratford. He also defaulted on his London taxes, a habit that continued for several years. By 1598 he was perceived as wealthy enough for some of Stratford's governors to approach him for a loan. It is not clear whether he profited from the publication of several of his plays in 1597 and 1598—when a playwright sold his work to an acting company, he sold the publication rights along with it—but by 1598 Shakespeare's name began appearing on the title pages of his plays, meaning the publishers thought it would improve sales. In 1598 Francis Meres published a collection of maxims and comparisons; included in it is a chapter of literary criticism in which Shakespeare is one of dozens of contemporary writers named. Meres's list of plays by Shakespeare is extremely helpful in dating Shakespeare's early work, but it is also the source of another mystery: one of the plays he claims Shakespeare wrote is *Love's Labor's Won*, a play that is either lost or that survived under another title.

In December 1598, after a dispute with the ground landlord of The Theater, Shakespeare's company decided to move to a new location. Richard Burbage, the leading actor in Shakespeare's company, whose father had built The Theater, hired carpenter Peter Street to dismantle the playhouse, ferry its materials across the Thames, and reconstruct it on more reasonably priced land in Southwark. The new theater was called the Globe; it opened in 1599 and was noted for its splendor. The Burbages and several other members of the company, including Shakespeare, formed a syndicate by which they shared both the costs and the profits of the Globe; these shares were later the subject of several lawsuits that provide details of the original agreement. The Burbages owned half the shares and the others an equal share of the remaining half. Perhaps in response to the financial demands of the new theater, several of Shakespeare's plays were published or republished in 1600.

As his fame increased, Shakespeare, and his plays and poems, continued to be mentioned or commented on by other writers. In the Parnassus plays, a series of satirical dramas by Cambridge University students, Shakespeare is mocked, but he is more often admired. His contemporaries praise him in highest terms, from John Weever's 1599 epigram to "Honie-tong'd *Shakespeare*" to Leonard Digges's 1640 assertion that, to do him justice, "Some second *Shakespeare* must of *Shakespeare* write." These allusions, of which there is a goodly number, help to date the plays and poems and also serve as convincing evidence that Shakespeare is indeed their author. The assertion that only a man of aristocratic birth could have produced plays with such an intimate knowledge of court politics is based on a misunderstanding of what dramatic poets do best: they hold a mirror up to nature.

At the turn of the century Shakespeare and his fellow actors continued to appear in the court's financial accounts, which unfortunately do not record the names of the plays the Lord Chamberlain's Men were paid to perform. In 1601 the company was commissioned to perform Shakespeare's *Richard II* for the earl of Essex and his supporters, a performance that took place the night before Essex launched a rebellion against Elizabeth I. The testimony of one member of Shakespeare's company, Augustine Phillips, survives; the actors do not appear to have been charged with crimes or sanctioned. Essex and several of his followers were executed; other participants in the rebellion, including Shakespeare's patron the earl of Southampton, were imprisoned until released by King James. The incident is one of many showing the close link between the drama the court watched and the dramas it enacted.

In September of 1601 Shakespeare's father died. Again, the Holy Trinity parish register offers no information except the date of burial, and no will has been found. In 1602 Shakespeare purchased 107 acres of land in Stratford and a cottage near New Place; several of his plays were published or republished; and the Lord Chamberlain's Men were paid for performances

at court. This pattern continues through the years in which Shakespeare was producing his great tragedies: *Hamlet* was probably completed by 1601 and was followed in relatively short order by *Othello, King Lear, Macbeth,* and *Antony and Cleopatra.* Although the dates these plays were composed are still in dispute, they were performed, printed, or registered with the Stationers' Company between 1604 and 1608. The documents tell us little about what inspired this shift from comedies and histories to tragedies; they instead record careful business transactions, regular court performances, and occasional publications. They also show Shakespeare dividing his attention between London and Stratford: in 1603, upon the death of Queen Elizabeth and the accession of King James, the Lord Chamberlain's Men became the King's Men, the court's official players; in the early financial accounts of the new bureaucracy, the plays performed for the king are named, helping us to date their composition. In 1604 Shakespeare sued a Stratford apothecary, Phillip Rogers, to collect a debt; that same year he was living in London in the home of Christopher Mountjoy, a maker of women's headdresses who made promises to his daughter's fiancé that Shakespeare was later asked to recall. In 1605 he made additional investments in Stratford; in 1606 the Globe's sewers needed attention; in 1607 his daughter Susanna married the physician John Hall, and his brother Edmund, and Edmund's illegitimate child, died and were buried in London. In 1608 his granddaughter Elizabeth Hall was born, and his mother Mary Arden died; later that year he sued John Addenbrooke of Stratford to recover a debt; that same year the King's Men began performing in an indoor theater, the Blackfriars.

In 1609 Shakespeare's sonnets were published, perhaps without Shakespeare's knowledge or consent. The sonnets had been mentioned by Francis Meres in 1598 in his survey of England's poets, but Meres described them as circulating among Shakespeare's friends, not appearing in print. The 1609 edition of the sonnets is prefaced by an address to the reader that has caused additional disputes about the young man to whom they are addressed, and the order of the sonnets may have more to do with the manuscript the printer used than with the order of composition or Shakespeare's own arrangement of them. The sonnets joined *Venus and Adonis* and *The Rape of Lucrece* as objects of admiration for other poets. Edward Alleyn, the leading actor of the Lord Admiral's Men, rivals of the King's Men, bought a copy.

From 1609 to Shakespeare's death in 1616, the records continue in the familiar pattern: the King's Men are paid for court performances; Shakespeare's plays and long poems are published or republished;

other writers allude to Shakespeare or his works; and Shakespeare conducts business in London and Stratford. The best-documented event of this period is the burning of the Globe theater in 1613; the fire started during a performance of Shakespeare's *All Is True,* a play also known as *Henry VIII.* The theater was quickly rebuilt. Also in 1613 Shakespeare purchased a house in London and took steps that seemed designed to ensure that his daughter Susanna, rather than his wife, would inherit it. The Stratford records for 1614 and 1615 include some transactions concerned with one of the most contentious issues of the early modern period: efforts to enclose some of the town's common pasture. Shakespeare's role in the enclosure controversy, as recorded in the surviving documents, is ambiguous. His late plays are equally mysterious. *The Winter's Tale, Cymbeline,* and *The Tempest* belong to a genre called romance when the play is written by Shakespeare and tragicomedy when the play is written by someone else. Characters experience terrible trials; spouses and children die, or seem to; miraculous interventions, both theatrical and divine, occur regularly; the final scenes involve extraordinary acts of forgiveness and a troubling redefinition of what constitutes a happy ending. These plays make full use of Shakespeare's poetic and intellectual skills, but they also make use of every resource the theater had to offer. Their project is to please, and they do so in ways that make many of us sorry there are not more of them.

The Tempest delivers two farewells to the stage and its rough magic, but it is not the last play Shakespeare wrote. *All Is True* and *Two Noble Kinsmen* followed, as well as the lost play *Cardenio.* Shakespeare wrote his late plays in collaboration with John Fletcher, who succeeded Shakespeare as the playwright of the King's Men. Shakespeare probably spent his final years in Stratford, although there are few records from this period. In February 1616 his daughter Judith married a man who had been convicted of fornication with another woman; Shakespeare rewrote his will on 25 March 1616 and was careful to ensure that Judith's new husband had no access to her inheritance; his brother-in-law William Hart was buried on 17 April; Shakespeare himself was buried on 25 April 1616, having died, according to the inscription on his monument in Holy Trinity Church, on 23 April.

One reason Shakespeare's plays are set apart from those of his contemporaries is that his characters leave us with the sense that they are more than airy nothings, that they have that within which passes show, that more is felt than they have power to tell. Unfortunately, this sense of a complex inner life is exactly what is missing from Shakespeare's own biography. Using the poems and plays, we can construct a dashing poet who understood erotic passion, battle strategy, the burdens of kingship, the habits of fairies, and the minds of madmen. Using the documents in which Shakespeare's name appears, we can construct a practical businessman who understood marriage contracts, real estate transactions, the politics of courtly entertainment, investment strategies, and tax laws.

—*Catherine Loomis*

A Note on the Text

When possible, manuscript documents were transcribed from facsimiles; the transcripts done by other scholars are noted in the headnote. In manuscripts and printed texts, spelling has been slightly modified: *i* has been transformed to *j* as appropriate, and *u* and *v* have been made to conform to their modern forms. The turned *u* and *n* have been silently corrected, and double *v* has become *w*. Transcriptions of the title pages of Shakespeare's works have been kept in their original spelling. Italics have been preserved as in the original except in the cases of documents primarily in italics; there, roman and italic fonts have been reversed. Words that are entirely in uppercase letters in the original text are generally given in upper- and lowercase letters. The expansion of contractions and abbreviations is noted in the headnote. The position of marginal notes is approximated or, in many cases, such notes are bracketed and embedded in the text. All quotations from Shakespeare's plays and poems follow *The Riverside Shakespeare,* edited by G. Blakemore Evans and others, second edition (1997).

Acknowledgments

Any collector of early modern documents depends heavily on the work of generations of scholars who found, gathered, transcribed, transliterated, collated, and preserved manuscripts and early printed editions of these texts. I have benefited greatly from their careful work.

Russ McDonald is responsible for what is best about this project; I have had the great good fortune to study with him as well as with Cyrus Hoy, Stanley Wells, and Carolyn Asp, each of whom provided a model of scholarly excellence and generosity. The University of New Orleans provided photocopying support and a summer research grant, for which I am grateful. Drs. Susan Krantz, Miriam Miller, Robert Sturges, and Edward Johnson provided advice and support on numerous occasions, for which this is small but sincere thanks. Dr. Gary Richards provided encouragement during all phases of this book's production, and tolerated the associated clutter. I had very helpful research assistance from Sharon Guerino and Christopher Loomis as well as from librarians at the University of Rochester, the University of New Orleans, the Louisiana State University Law School, and Tulane University, where Connie Cannon often went out of her way to be helpful. I am grateful to my family and friends for their confidence and support during this project. This work is dedicated to my mother, Pat Loomis.

––––––––––

This book was produced by Bruccoli Clark Layman, Inc. Karen L. Rood is senior editor. George Anderson was the in-house editor.

Production manager is Philip B. Dematteis.

Administrative support was provided by Ann M. Cheschi, Carol A. Cheschi, and Amber L. Coker.

Accountant is Ann-Marie Holland.

Copyediting supervisor is Sally R. Evans. The copyediting staff includes Phyllis A. Avant, Brenda Carol Blanton, Caryl Brown, Melissa D. Hinton, Philip I. Jones, Rebecca Mayo, Nancy E. Smith, and Elizabeth Jo Ann Sumner. Freelance copyeditor is Brenda Cabra.

Editorial associates are Michael S. Allen, Michael S. Martin, and Catherine M. Polit.

Database manager is José A. Juarez.

Layout and graphics supervisor is Janet E. Hill. The graphics staff includes Zoe R. Cook and Sydney E. Hammock.

Office manager is Kathy Lawler Merlette.

Photography supervisor is Paul Talbot. Photography editor is Scott Nemzek.

Digital photographic copy work was performed by Joseph M. Bruccoli.

Systems manager is Marie L. Parker.

Typesetting supervisor is Kathleen M. Flanagan. The typesetting staff includes Patricia Marie Flanagan, Mark J. McEwan, and Pamela D. Norton. Freelance typesetter is Wanda Adams.

Walter W. Ross did library research. He was assisted by Jo Cottingham and the following librarians at the Thomas Cooper Library of the University of South Carolina: circulation department head Tucker Taylor; reference department head Virginia W. Weathers; reference department staff Brette Barron, Marilee Birchfield, Paul Cammarata, Gary Geer, Michael Macan, Tom Marcil, Rose Marshall, and Sharon Verba; interlibrary loan department head John Brunswick; and interlibrary loan staff Robert Arndt, Hayden Battle, Alex Byrne, Jo Cottingham, Bill Fetty, Marna Hostetler, and Nelson Rivera.

Dictionary of Literary Biography® • Volume Two Hundred Sixty-Three

William Shakespeare
A Documentary Volume

Dictionary of Literary Biography

Short Titles of Works Cited in this Volume

Baptismal Register
> *Baptismal register of Holy Trinity Church, Stratford-on-Avon* (Shakespeare Birthplace Trust Records Office, DR 243/1).

Bibliography of the English Printed Drama
> W. W. Greg, *A Bibliography of the English Printed Drama to the Restoration,* 4 volumes (London: Printed for the Bibliographical Society at the University Press, Oxford, 1939–1959).

Burial Register
> *Burial register of Holy Trinity Church, Stratford-on-Avon* (Shakespeare Birthplace Trust Records Office, DR 243/1).

Calendar of State Papers
> *Calendar of State Papers, Domestic Series, of the Reign of Elizabeth, 1598–1601,* edited by Mary Anne Everett Green (London: Her Majesty's Stationery Office, 1869; reprinted, Nendeln, Liechtenstein: Kraus Reprint, 1967).

Dramatic Records
> David Cook and F. P. Wilson, eds., *Malone Society Collections Vol. VI: Dramatic Records in the Declared Accounts of the Treasurer of the Chamber 1558–1642* (Oxford: Printed by Vivian Ridler at the University of Oxford Press, 1961).

Facts and Problems
> E. K. Chambers, *William Shakespeare: A Study of Facts and Problems,* 2 volumes (Oxford: Clarendon Press, 1930).

Henslowe's Diary
> R. A. Foakes and R. T. Rickert, eds., *Henslowe's Diary: Edited with Supplementary Material, Introduction and Notes* (Cambridge: Cambridge University Press, 1961).

Minutes and Accounts
> Richard Savage and Edgar I. Fripp, eds., *Minutes and Accounts of the Corporation of Stratford-Upon-Avon and Other Records 1553–1620,* volume 3 (London: Oxford University Press, 1926).

Lewis, *Shakespeare Documents*
> B. Roland Lewis, ed., *The Shakespeare Documents: Facsimiles, Transliterations, Translations & Commentary,* 2 volumes (Stanford, Cal. & London: Stanford University Press & Oxford University Press, 1940).

Stationers' Registers
> Edward Arber, *A Transcript of the Registers of the Company of Stationers of London 1554–1640 A.D.,* 5 volumes (London: Privately printed, 1875–1894).

John Taylor's portrait of William Shakespeare (courtesy of The National Portrait Gallery, London)

Baptism through the "Lost Years": 1564–1591

The first surviving document naming William Shakespeare is his baptismal record. Shakespeare was baptized at Holy Trinity Church in Stratford-upon-Avon, a small market town in Warwickshire in the English midlands. Shakespeare's mother, Mary Arden, was the youngest daughter of a prosperous farmer. His father, John Shakespeare, was a glover and maker of small leather goods who may also have dealt in cattle; he owned a house, which is still standing, on Henley Street.

John Shakespeare held increasingly important positions in the Stratford-upon-Avon government until 1576, when for reasons unknown he stopped attending council meetings and began suffering from financial difficulties; one of the lawsuits John Shakespeare filed in this period identifies William as his son. Shakespeare probably attended grammar school in Stratford; unfortunately, the records of The King's New School for this period have not survived. As the son of a town official Shakespeare may have attended performances by troupes of traveling players who visited Stratford on their provincial tours.

The documents for the years 1564 to 1591 record the births of Shakespeare's brothers Gilbert (1566), Richard (1574), and Edmund (1580) and his sisters Joan (1569) and Anne (1571) as well as the burial of Anne in 1579. Other surviving documents show Shakespeare marrying Anne Hathaway in November 1582 and record the baptisms of their daughter Susanna (1583) and their twin son and daughter Hamnet and Judith (1585). The account of Katherine Hamlett's inquest and the reference to a play called Hamlet in a London writer's preface may be related to Shakespeare's tragedy.

The years between the birth of Hamnet and Judith (1585) and the first published reference to Shakespeare as a playwright (1592) are called the "lost years." E. A. J. Honigmann and others see a connection between Shakespeare and the William Shakeshaft named in the 1581 will included here. Shakespeare may have spent part of the lost years as a "schoolmaster in the country" as John Aubrey reports in his seventeenth-century biographical notes, included at the end of this volume. Shakespeare may also have joined a touring company of actors, or worked as a sailor, soldier, or member of one of the professions he refers to with detailed knowledge in his plays. He may also have remained in Stratford, leading a life that kept his name out of the surviving public records. In his first 28 years Shakespeare's name appears in just a handful of documents: his baptismal record, the record of his marriage, and a lawsuit brought by his father against John Lambert.

1564

William Shakespeare's Birth and Name

The Holy Trinity parish registers record baptisms, marriages, and burials in the parish and begin in the year 1558. The entries recording the years from 1558 to 1600 are in the same hand, having been made in accordance with an October 1597 provisional constitution in which parishes were ordered to make copies of their records. Richard Bifield was vicar of Holy Trinity in 1597; he and four churchwardens signed each page of the copied records.

A Note on Dates during Shakespeare's Life

There was wide variation in dating practices in England until the calendar was reformed in 1752. The calendar in general use during Shakespeare's time was the Julian, or Old Style, calendar. Because of an original miscalculation in the length of the solar year, the Julian calendar fell slowly behind the seasons over the centuries. In 1582 Pope Gregory decreed a change in the calendar, moving time forward 10 days to compensate for the accruing error. However, the Gregorian, or New Style, calendar was not adopted in England and its colonies for another 170 years. After 1582 many English writers cited a double-year date for the days from 1 January to 24 March because, though 1 January was recognized as the beginning of the year by many on the Continent, the 25th of March—the feast of the Annunciation, or "Lady Day"—was widely regarded as the beginning of the year in England.

Since Shakespeare was born after 25 March, even those who celebrated the feast of the Annunciation as New Year's Day would have agreed that his birth year was 1564. Reckoning by a modern calendar, though, his birth would have occurred not in the last third of April but in the first week of May. Dates in DLB 263 have not been modernized, but the first of January has been regarded as the beginning of the year.

5

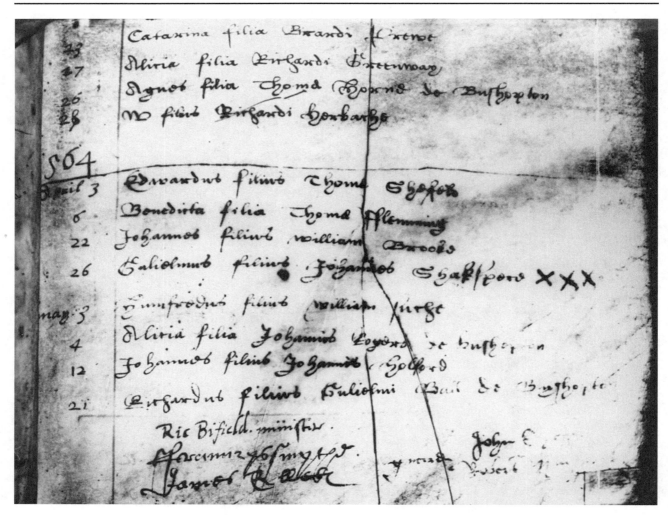

*William Shakespeare's baptismal record from Holy Trinity Church,
Stratford-upon-Avon (shelfmark DR 243/1, folio 5; courtesy of
the Shakespeare Birthplace Trust Records Office)*

Although the date of Shakespeare's baptism is recorded, the date of his birth is not. His birthday is traditionally celebrated on 23 April, which is convenient for two reasons: it is the feast day of St. George, England's patron saint, and it is the day on which Shakespeare died in 1616. The Book of Common Prayer *enjoins the faithful to have infants baptized on the Sunday or holy day following the birth; this ensures a crowd will be present to witness the ceremony. Shakespeare was baptized on a Wednesday, and the 26th of April is not a holy day.*

Shakespeare's name may have been chosen in honor of a family member or his godfather or because of something else the name represented to his family. William Camden, in Remaines of a Greater Worke, Concerning Britaine, the inhabitants thereof, their Languages, Names, *Surnames, Empreses, Wise speeches, Poesies, and Epitaphes (London, 1605) provides an early-seventeenth-century interpretation of Shakespeare's first and last names.*

WILLIAM, *ge:* For sweeter sound drawne from *Wilhelm,* which is interpreted by *Luther,* Much Defence, or, Defence to many, as *Wilwald,* Ruling many. *Wildred,* Much reverent feare, or Awfull. *Wilfred,* Much peace. *Willibert,* Much brightnessse, or Very bright. *Willibrod* Much increase. So the French that cannot pronounce *W* have turnd it into *Philli,* as *Phillibert,* for *Willibert,* Much brightnes. Many names wherein wee have *Will,* seeme translated from the Greeke names composed of Πολὺς, as *Polydamas, Polybius, Polyxenus, &c. Helm* yet remaineth with us, and *Villi, Willi,* and *Billi* yet with the Germans for *Many.* Other turne *William,* a Willing Defender, and so it answereth the Roman *Titus,* if it

*The Henley Street houses of John and Mary Arden Shakespeare, now joined as a single house
and known as The Birthplace (photograph ©2001 by Gary Vernon)*

Holy Trinity Church, Stratford-upon-Avon, site of Shakespeare's baptism and burial (photograph ©2001 by Gary Vernon)

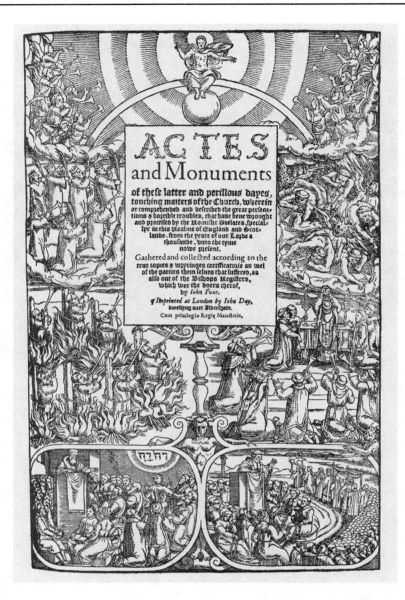

Title page for John Foxe's collection of accounts of Protestant martyrs persecuted during the reign of Mary Tudor (1553–1558). The Church of England required that a copy of the book be placed in each church (by permission of the Folger Shakespeare Library).

come from *Tuendo*, as some will have it. The Italians that liked the name, but could not pronounce the *W* if wee may beleeve *Gesner*, turned it into *Galeazo*, retaining the sence in part for *Helme*. But the Italians report, that *Galeazo* the first Viscount of *Müllaine* was so called, for that many Cockes crew lustily at his birth. This name hath beene most common in *England* since king *William* the Conqueror, insomuch that upon a festivall day in the Court of king *Henry* the second, when Sir *William Saint-John*, and Sir *William Fitz-Hamon* especiall Officers had commaunded that none but of the name of *William* should dine in the great Chamber with them, they were accompanied with an hundred and twentie *Williams*, all Knights, as *Robert Montensis* recordeth *Anno* 1173. (pp. 73–74)

Camden's lengthy survey of English surnames includes this entry:

Some [surnames derive] from that which they commonly carried, as *Palmer*, that is, Pilgrime, for that they carried *Palme* when they returned from *Hierusalem*. *Long-sword*, *Broad-speare*, *Fortescu*, that is, Strong-shield, and in some such respect, *Breake-speare*, *Shake-Speare*, *Shotbolts*, *Wagstaffe*, *Bagot*, in the old Norman, the same with *Scipio*, that is, a stay or walking staffe with the Latines, which became a surname, for that *Cornelius* served as a stay to his Blinde father. Likewise *Billman*, *Hookeman*, *Talevas*, of a shield so called, whereof *William* sonne of *Robert de Belisme* Earle of *Shrewsbury* had his name. (p. 111)

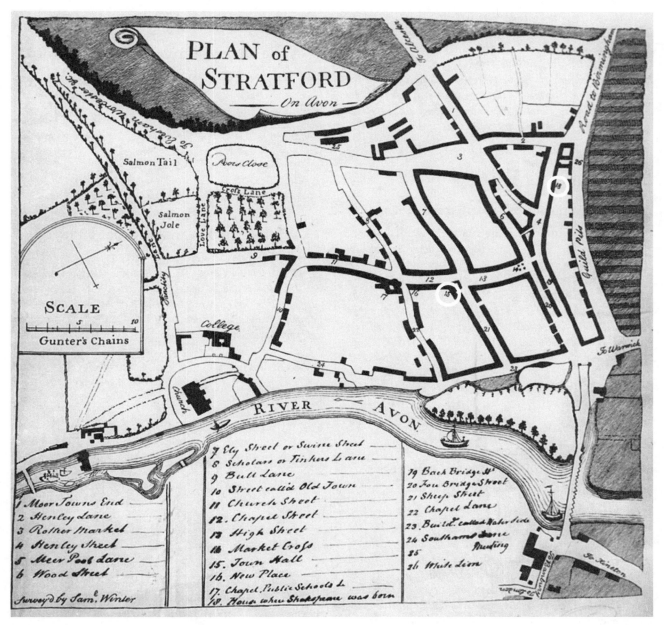

Map of Stratford-upon-Avon showing the location of the house where Shakespeare was born and also New Place, the home he bought in 1597 (shelfmark ER 1/48 fol. 22; courtesy of the Shakespeare Birthplace Trust Records Office)

Before William Shakespeare's birth, two other children born to John and Mary Shakespeare had been baptized at Holy Trinity, daughters Joan ("Jone Shakspere daughter to John Shakespere," on 15 September 1558) and Margaret ("Margareta filia Johannis Shakspere," on 2 December 1562). The parish register records that Margaret was buried within a few months of her birth ("Margareta filia Johannis Shakspere," on 30 April 1563). In 1569 the Shakespeares christened another daughter named Joan, so presumably the first Joan died, although her burial is not recorded. The parish burial records for 1564 record the fact that Stratford suffered an outbreak of the bubonic plague in which approximately one-sixth of the town's population died.

1566

Gilbert Shakespeare's Baptismal Record

[13 October 1566] Gilbertus filius Johannis Shakspere

                —*Baptismal Register*, folio 7

Shakespeare's brother Gilbert appears in several legal records. In 1597, at the Queen's Bench in London, he paid a substantial sum of money, £19, as bail for William Sampson of Stratford; the documents describe Gilbert as a haberdasher. In 1602, in Stratford, the indenture recording William Shakespeare's purchase of land from William Combe was "Sealed and delivered to Gilbert Shakespere." In 1609, in London, the Court of Requests summoned Gilbert Shakespeare to appear; details of the case have not survived. In 1610, in Stratford, Gilbert was witness to a lease. In 1612 the Holy Trinity burial register records his death.

1569

Joan Shakespeare's Baptismal Record

[15 April 1569] Jone the daughter of John Shakspere
—Baptismal Register, folio 9

Shakespeare's sister Joan survived him and is mentioned in his will. She married William Hart, a hatter; the marriage is not recorded in the Holy Trinity register and it may have taken place in another parish. Joan Hart bore four children: William (1600–1639), Mary (1603–1607), Thomas (1605–after 1670), and Michael (1608–1618). Her husband was buried on 17 April 1616, six days before Shakespeare's death. Joan Hart was buried on 4 November 1646.

The Queen's Players and the Earl of Worcester's Players Visit Stratford-upon-Avon

Early modern acting companies went on tour for a variety of reasons, including to escape outbreaks of the bubonic plague in London. Stratford was visited regularly. Because Shakespeare's father served the corporation of Stratford in various official capacities, including alderman and bailiff, he probably attended at least some of the performances listed here and below. Some scholars speculate that Shakespeare may have joined one of the traveling troupes that visited Stratford in the 1580s, because from 1585 to 1592 he disappears from the surviving public records in Stratford, reappearing in 1592 in London, where he is associated with the theater. The payments, recorded on 27 February 1570, were charged to the account of Robert Salisbury and John Sadler. Unfortunately, the Stratford financial records do not provide the titles of the plays the touring companies performed.

Item payd to the Quenes Pleyers   ix^s

. . . .

Item to the Erle of Worcesters Pleers   xii^d
—Minutes and Accounts, vol. II, p. 35

1571

Anne Shakespeare's Baptismal Record

[28 September 1571] Anna filia magistri Shakspere
—Baptismal Register, folio 10

Born in 1571, Anne Shakespeare died in 1579 and was buried on 4 April. That John Shakespeare's social status had improved by 1571 is indicated by the designation "magistri."

1573

Visit of the Earl of Leicester's Players

In Minutes and Accounts Richard Savage and Edgar I. Fripp note that the Earl of Leicester's players "were in Nottingham on 1 September and in Bristol in the week 20–27 October 1573. Between these dates they may have paid their visit to Stratford." The payment, recorded on 17 February 1574, was charged to the account of John Tayler and William Smith.

pd to m^r bayly for the earle of lecesters players   v^s viii^d
—Minutes and Accounts, vol. II, p. 77

1574

Richard Shakespeare's Baptismal Record

[11 March 1574] Richard sonne to Mr John Shakspeer
—Baptismal Register, folio 11

After Richard Shakespeare's baptism, no further records naming him have been found until his burial on 4 February 1613.

Money in the Elizabethan and Jacobean Eras

English money in this period is recorded as pounds, shillings, and pence; abbreviations for these units come from their Latin names. A pound is represented by an £ or l for libra; a shilling by an s for solidus; a pence by a d for denarius. There are twenty shillings to the pound and twelve pence to the shilling. In financial records such as Philip Henslowe's and the court accounts, Roman numerals are used to designate the numbers of pounds, shillings, and pence.

Unskilled men could earn five or six pence for a day's labor; unskilled women earned less than that. A loaf of bread cost a penny, as did admission to a play; a printed version of the play cost sixpence. In 1597 Shakespeare purchased New Place, a large house in Stratford, for £60. The legal documents recording the sale probably understate the amount paid, but £60 was a substantial sum of money, representing nearly two and a half years' wages for an actor.

The Guildhall Chapel and The King's New School in Stratford-upon-Avon (photograph ©2001 by Gary Vernon)

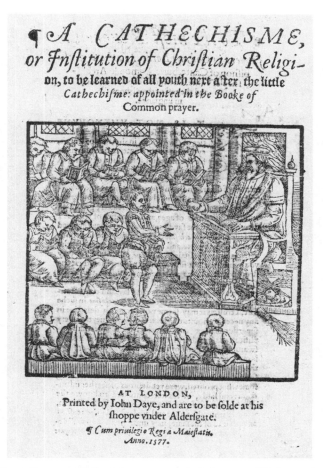

Title page for a textbook showing a grammar-school classroom of Shakespeare's time
(shelfmark C.132.i.15.[3]); courtesy of The British Library, London)

1576

Visit of the Earl of Worcester's Players

Savage and Fripp note of this entry that the Earl of Worcester's players "were in Stratford about Christmas time, probably early in January 1576, having come on tour from Leicester and Coventry." The payment, recorded on 24 March 1576, was charged to the account of John Tayler and William Smith.

p^d the earle of worcester players   v^s viii^d
                                      —*Minutes and Accounts*, vol. II, p. 106

1578

Visit of the Earl of Worcester's Players

Savage and Fripp note of this entry, "About Christmas time. They proceeded to Coventry, and were at Nottingham on the 19 January." The payment, recorded on 29 January 1578, was charged to the account of John Tayler and Antony Tanner.

Paid to my lord of Wosters players   iii^s iiii^d
                                      —*Minutes and Accounts*, vol. III, p. 14

1579

Anne Shakespeare's Burial Record

[4 April 1579]   Anne daughter to Mr John Shakspere
                                      —*Burial Register*, folio 15

Shakespeare's sister Anne, age seven years, died in the month before he turned fifteen.

Visits of the Lord Strange's Players and the Countess of Essex's Players

Savage and Fripp note that the Countess of Essex's players "were in Stratford on the 26 July or soon after, on a tour, apparently, from Coventry to Oxford or vice versa." The payments, recorded on 20 January 1580, were charged to the account of Peter Smart and William Wilson.

Paid to my lord Straunge men the xith day of february
at the commaundment of Mr Baliffe   v^s
                                      —*Minutes and Accounts*, Vol. III, p. 43

Paid at the commaundement of M^r baliffe to the countys of Essex plears   xiiii^s vi^d
                                      —*Minutes and Accounts*, Vol. III, p. 46

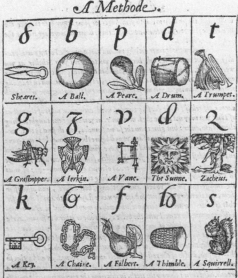
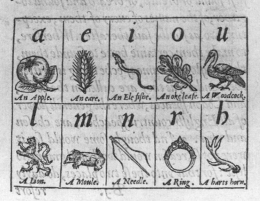

A table from John Hart's A Methode or comfortable beginning for all unlearned, whereby they may bee taught to read English, in a very short time, with pleasure. *Shakespeare, seven when this work was published, may have used such a book (1570; by permission of the Folger Shakespeare Library).*

1580

Inquest on the Body of Katherine Hamlett

Some scholars see a link between the drowning of Katherine Hamlett and the death of Ophelia (and the gravediggers' discussion of it) in Shakespeare's Hamlet *(4.7.163 ff; 5.1.1-29). A dissenting view is offered in* William Shakespeare: A Study of Facts and Problems *(Oxford, 1930) by E. K. Chambers, who argues "The resemblance of the name to that of the hero of Shakespeare's tragedy, which has a different Scandinavian origin, can hardly be more than a coincidence" (vol. II, p. 4). The inquest at Tiddington into the death of the young woman, whose body was found in the Avon, took place on 11 February 1580.*

Warwicensis

Inquisicio indentata capta apud Tidington in comitatu predicto undecimo die Februarii Anno Regni domine nostre Elizabethe dei gracia Anglie francie et Hibernie Regine fidei defensoris etcetera vicesimo secundo coram Henrico Rogers uno coronatorum dicte domine Regine comitatus predicti super visum corporis Katherine Hamlett nuper de Tidington predicta in comitatu predicto spinster ibidem mortua et submersa inventa per sacramentum Johannis pearse, Thome Tounsend, Egidii Walker, Edmundi Baker, Thome Baker, Ricardi Godwine, Willelmi Fawkener, Johannis lord, Thome Gibbes, Thome Hickes, Thome Warde, Roberti Simcocks et Roberti Griffine Qui dicunt super sacramentum suum Quod predicta Katherina Hamlett decimo septimo die Decembris Anno Regni predicte domine Regine vicesimo secundo iens cum quodam mulctrale Anglice a Paile ad afferendam aquam ad Rivum vocatum Havon in Tidington predicta Ita accidit quod predicta Katherina stans super ripam eiusdem Rivi subito ac per infortunium lapsit et cecidit in Rivum predictum et ibidem in aqua eiusdem Rivi dicto decimo septimo Die Decembris Anno predicto apud Tidington predictam in comitatu predicto per infortunium submersa fuit, et non aliter nec alio modo ad mortem suam devenit. In cuius rei testimonium tam prefatus coronator quam Juratores predicti huic inquisicioni indentato sigillam suam apposuerunt die anno et loco primo supradictis

per infortunium

[Warwick.

Inquisition indented taken at Tiddington in the County aforesaid on the eleventh day of February in the twenty-second year of the reign of our Lady Elizabeth, by the grace of God Queen of England, France and Ireland, defender of the Faith &c. before Henry Rogers, a coroner of the said lady the Queen in the County aforesaid, on a view of the body of Katherine Hamlett, late of Tiddington aforesaid in the County aforesaid, spinster, found there dead and drowned, on the oath of John Pearse, Thomas Townsend, Giles Walker, Edmund Baker, Thomas Baker, Richard Godwine, William Fawkener, John Lord, Thomas Gibbes, Thomas Hickes, Thomas Warde, Robert Simcocks and Robert Griffine: Who say on their oath that the aforesaid Katherine Hamlett, on the seventeenth day of December in the twenty-second year of the reign of the aforesaid lady the Queen, going with a certain vessel, in English *a pail*, to draw water at the river called Avon in Tiddington aforesaid, it so happened that the aforesaid Katherine, standing on the bank of the same river, suddenly and by accident slipped and fell into the river aforesaid, and there, in the water of the same river on the said seventeenth day of December in the year aforesaid at Tiddington aforesaid in the County aforesaid by accident was drowned, and not otherwise nor in other fashion came by her death. In testimony whereof both the coroner aforesaid and the jury aforesaid have set their seal to this inquisition indented on the day, in the year, and in the place abovesaid.

By accident.]

–*Minutes and Accounts,* vol. III, pp. 50–51

Edmund Shakespeare's Baptismal Record

[3 May 1580] Edmund sonne to M[r] John Shakspere

–*Baptismal Register,* folio 17

In 1607 Edmund Shakespeare appears in the parish register of a London church, St. Giles without Cripplegate, where he is identified as a "Player" and as the father of an illegitimate child. Edmund was buried on 31 December 1607.

Visit of the Earl of Derby's Players

The payment, recorded on 26 January 1581, was charged to the account of William Wilson and Peter Smart.

Paid to the Earle of Darbyes players at the commaundement of M[r] Baliffe   viii[s] iiii[d]

–*Minutes and Accounts,* vol. III, p. 83

An *A*ge of *E*xploration and *C*olonization

Early modern English explorers, like their continental counterparts, were "discovering" the Americas, often to the dismay of the native inhabitants. While the rhetoric describing these explorations often emphasizes that the Europeans were bringing Christianity, and hence salvation, to the native populations, the money to be made in the trade of spices, gold, and slaves was also a powerful motivation. In his late romance The Tempest, *Shakespeare gives a native inhabitant of Prospero's island, Caliban, a chance to explain colonialism from his perspective:*

This island's mine by Sycorax my mother,
Which thou tak'st from me. When thou cam'st first,
Thou strok'st me and made much of me, wouldst give me
Water with berries in't, and teach me how
To name the bigger light, and how the less,
That burn by day and night; and then I lov'd thee
And show'd thee all the qualities o' th' isle,

The fresh springs, brine-pits, barren place and fertile.
Curs'd be I that did so! All the charms
Of Sycorax, toads, beetles, bats, light on you!
For I am all the subjects that you have,
Which first was mine own king. . .

—The Tempest, 1.2.331-342

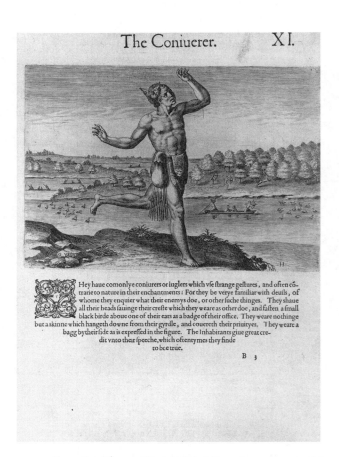

Pages from Thomas Harriot's A briefe and true report of the new found land of Virginia *(1590). Illustrations accompanying accounts of the new English colonies often make the native inhabitants appear primitive or ridiculous—and hence conquerable (by permission of the Folger Shakespeare Library).*

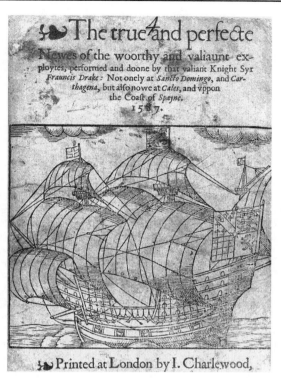

Illustration from Nicholas Monardes's 1580 book Joyfull newes out of the newe founde worlde. *Tobacco, imported from the Americas, was praised for its medicinal value and denounced by King James and others for its addictive qualities (by permission of the Folger Shakespeare Library).*

Title page for one of many works that heralded the accomplishments of England's explorers and privateers (by permission of the Folger Shakespeare Library)

Pages from Nicholas Nicholay's The Navigations, peregrinations and voyages, made into Turkie (1585). *The author claimed that his illustrations show "the diversitie of nations, their port, intreatie, apparrell, lawes, religion, and manner of living, aswel in time of warre as peace" (by permission of the Folger Shakespeare Library).*

A Touring Company Performance

The following account of attending a play performed by a touring company is from Robert Willis's Mount Tabor. Or Private Exercises Of A Penitent Sinner . . . *(London, 1639). According to the title page, Willis was seventy-five when this book was published in 1639, meaning that he was born in 1563 or 1564.*

Upon a Stage-play which I saw when I was a child.

In the City of *Gloucester* the manner is (as I think it is in other like corporations) that when Players of Enterludes come to towne, they first attend the Mayor to enforme him what noble-mans servants they are, and so to get licence for their publike playing; and if the Mayor like the Actors, or would shew respect to their Lord and Master, he appoints them to play their first play before himselfe and the Aldermen and common Counsell of the City; and that is called the Mayors play, where every one that will comes in without money, the Mayor giving the players a reward as hee thinks fit to shew respect unto them. At such a play, my father tooke me with him and made mee stand betweene his leggs, as he sate upon one of the benches where wee saw and heard very well. The play was called (the Cradle of security,) wherin was personated a King or some great Prince with his Courtiers of severall kinds, amongst which three Ladies were in speciall grace with him; and they keeping him in delights and pleasures, drew him from his graver Counsellors, hearing of Sermons, and listning to good counsell, and admonitions, that in the end they got him to lye downe in a cradle upon the stage, where these three Ladies joyning in a sweet song rocked him asleepe, that he snorted againe, and in the meane time closely conveyed under the cloaths where withall he was covered, a vizard like a swines snout upon his face, with three wire chaines fastned thereunto, the other end whereof being holden severally by those three Ladies, who fall to singing againe, and then discovered his face, that the spectators might see how they had transformed him, going on with their singing, whilst all this was acting, there came forth at another doore at the farthest end of the stage, two old men, the one in blew with a Serjeant at Armes, his mace on his shoulder, the other in red with a drawn sword in his hand, and leaning with the other hand upon the others shoulder, and so they two went along in a soft pace round about by the skirt of the Stage, till at last they came to the Cradle, when all the Court was in greatest jollity, and then the foremost old man with his Mace stroke a fearfull blow upon the Cradle; whereat all the Courtiers with the three Ladies and the vizard all vanished; and the desolate Prince starting up bare faced, and finding himselfe thus sent for to judgement, made a lamentable complaint of his miserable case, and so was carried away by wicked spirits. This Prince did personate in the morall, the wicked of the world; the three Ladies, Pride, Covetousnesse, and Luxury, the two old men, the end of the world, and the last judgement. This sight tooke such impression in me, that when I came towards mans estate, it was as fresh in my memory, as if I had seen it newly acted. From whence I observe out of mine owne experience, what a great care should bee had in the education of children, to keepe them from seeing of spectacles of ill examples, and hearing of lascivious or scurrilous words: for that their young memories are like faire writing tables, wherein if the faire sentences or lessons of grace bee written, they may (by Gods blessing) keepe them from many vicious blots of life, wherewithall they may otherwise bee tainted; especially considering the generall corruption of our nature, whose very memories are apter to receive evill then good, and that the well seasoning of the new Caske at the first, keepes it the better and sweeter ever after, and withall wee may observe, how farre unlike the Plaies and harmelesse morals of former times, are to those which have succeeded, many of which, (by report of others,) may bee termed schoolmasters of vice, and provocations to corruptions: which our deprived nature is too prone unto: nature and grace being contraries.

—pp. 110–114

1581

The Will of Alexander Hoghton of Lea, Esquire

Between the death of his brother Thomas in 1580 and his own death in 1581, Alexander Hoghton was head of a prominent Catholic family in Lancashire. In his will, dated 3 August 1581 and proved 12 September that same year, Hoghton asks that either his stepbrother Thomas or his brother-in-law Sir Thomas Hesketh take special care of two of his servants, Fulke Gillom and William Shakeshafte. Shakeshafte, a surname sometimes used by John Shakespeare's father, but one also found in other Lancashire records of the period, may have been an alias used by Shakespeare to prevent his being identified as a Catholic recusant. *There is a link between Hoghton and John Cottam, master of Stratford's grammar school from 1579 until 1581 or 1582: Cottam, whose brother Thomas was a priest, was from Tarnacre, about ten miles from Hoghton's estate in Lea. Cottam may have recommended Shakespeare for employment with Hoghton. Hesketh, into whose care Shakeshafte is trusted, had close links to the Earl of Derby (Ferdinando Stanley, Lord Strange) who was patron of a company of players. There is not yet enough evidence to prove that Shakespeare left Stratford for the Hoghton household, and from there joined Lord Strange's Men, and it is possible he became a playwright by some other means, such as joining a company of traveling players.*

The following excerpt is quoted from E. A. J. Honigmann's Shakespeare: The "Lost Years" *(Totowa, New Jersey, 1985):*

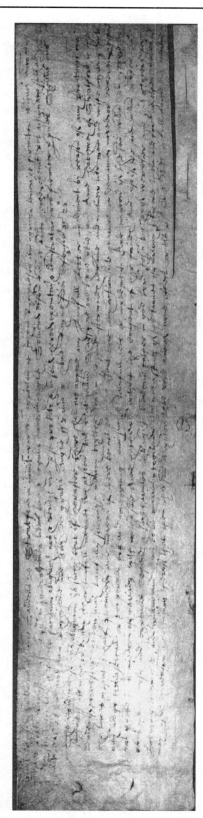

Shakespeare and Anne Hathaway's marriage-license bond (courtesy of the Bishop of Worcester and the Worcester Diocesan Registrar; Worcestershire Record Office, X797 BA 2783)

Item, it is my mind & will that the said Thomas Hoghton of 'brynescoules' my brother shall have all my instruments belonging to musics, & all manner of play clothes if he be minded to keep & do keep players. And if he will not keep & maintain players, then it is my mind & will that Sir Thomas Hesketh knight shall have the same instruments & play clothes. And I most heartily require the said Sir Thomas to be friendly unto Fulk Gillom & William Shakeshafte now dwelling with me & either to take them unto his service or else to help them to some good master, as my trust is he will. (pp. 136–137)

Later in the document Shakeshafte is named as part of a syndicate of servants who are to share the rents generated by one of Hoghton's properties; as members of the syndicate died, the remaining heirs were to receive larger portions.

Visits of the Earl of Worcester's Players and Lord Berkley's Players

The payment, recorded on 31 January 1582, was charged to the account of Philip Green and Thomas Godwin.

Paid to the Earle of Worcester his players　　　iii^s iiii^d
Paid to the L: Bartlett his players　　　　　　iii^s ii^d
　　　　　　　　　　　—Minutes and Accounts, vol. III, p. 98

1582

Visit of the Earl of Worcester's Players

The payment, recorded on 11 January 1583, was charged to the account of Thomas Godwin and Philip Green.

Payed to Henry Russell for the Earle of Worcesters players　　　　　　　　　　　　　　　v^s
　　　　　　　　　　　—Minutes and Accounts, vol. III, p. 119

Records of Shakespeare's Marriage

The following documents have caused a great deal of speculation about William Shakespeare's personal life. The first document shows that the bishop of Worcester granted a special marriage license to Shakespeare and Anne Whatley of Temple Grafton, one of ninety-eight such licenses the bishop granted in 1582. The second document is one of three on which the grant of this license was based: a bond exempting the bishop from legal action and guaranteeing money to help care for the bride and any children should an impediment arise to nullify the marriage.

The usual process for legal marriages in the early modern period was that banns were announced in the parish church on three Sundays or holy days. If there were no objections—i.e. that the bride or groom were unfit, close relatives, or already married to someone else—a wedding ceremony took place. Less formally, a couple could hold hands and, in front of witnesses, make a promise to marry; this sort of marriage, called a "handfast," was legal, but its existence was more difficult to prove than a marriage that had been recorded in a church register.

The church prohibited marriage ceremonies during certain times of the ecclesiastical year, including the Advent and Christmas seasons. If for some compelling reason, such as the bride's pregnancy, a couple needed to be married during this prohibited time, they could request a special license from a consistory court. They would have to identify themselves and their parents, prove they had their parents' consent, particularly if one or both were minors, and promise there were no known impediments to the marriage. The couple was also obligated to provide the bond that indemnified the Bishop against later suits related to the marriage.

In November 1582, during Advent, William Shakespeare and Anne Hathaway were granted a special license to marry. Anne, who was from Shottery, a village near Stratford, was three months pregnant. Two records have survived from the request for the license: an entry in the Bishop of Worcester's consistory court register indicating the license was granted and the bond that the couple had to provide. The bond was guaranteed by Fulke Sandells and John Richardson, whose names appear in the 1581 last will and testament of Richard Hathaway, Anne's father; presumably the two men represented the bride's interests. The bond is dated 28 November 1582 and is written in conventional early modern legalese.

The problem is the entry in the Bishop's register. On 27 November the notary, Robert Warmstry, wrote that the bride was Anne Whatley of Temple Grafton, rather than Anne Hathaway of Shottery. The least troubling explanation for this is also the most reasonable one: Warmstry made a mistake. In several other entries in the register he miswrites names, and on the same day that he wrote "Whatley" where one expects to see "Hathaway," he had recorded a suit brought by William Whatley. Anne Hathaway may have attended church in Temple Grafton or may have wanted to be married there for reasons of sentiment or privacy. Until and unless additional documents emerge, however, the discrepancy between the Anne of the Bishop's register and the Anne of the bond will continue to cause speculation.

Shakespeare's license to marry "Anne Whatley" is dated 27 November 1582 in John Whitgift Bishop of Worcester's Register (Worcester Record Office, vol. XXXII, folio 43v):

Item eodem die similis emanavit licencia inter Willelmum Shaxpere et Annam Whateley de Temple Grafton.

[Item: the same day a similar license was issued between William Shakespeare and Anne Whateley of Temple Grafton.]

—*Minutes and Accounts*, vol. III, pp. 111–112

In this Latin and English transcript (followed by an English translation of the Latin portion) of Shakespeare's marriage license bond, legal abbreviations have been silently expanded.

Noverint universi per presentes nos ffulconem Sandells de Stratford in Comitatu Warwicensi agricolam et Johannem Rychardson ibidem agricolam teneri et firmiter obligari Ricardo Cosin generoso et Roberto Warmstry notario publico in quadraginta libris bone et legalis monete Anglie solvendis eisdem Ricardo et Roberto heredibus executoribus vel assignatis suis ad quam quidem solucionem bene et fideliter faciendam obligamus nos et utrumque nostrum per se pro toto et in solidum heredes executores et administratores nostros firmiter per presentes sigillis nostris sigillatas datas 28 die novembris Anno Regni domine nostre Elizabethe Dei gratia Anglie ffrancie et Hibernie Regine fidei defensoris &c. 25°.

The condicion of this obligacion ys suche that if herafter there shall not appere any lawfull lett or impediment by reason of any precontract consanguinitie affinitie or by any other lawfull meanes whatsoever but that William Shagspere one thone partie, and Anne Hathwey of Stratford in the Dioces of worcester maiden may lawfully solemnize matrimony together and in the same afterwards remaine and continew like man and wiffe according unto the lawes in that behalf provided and moreover if there be not at this present time any action sute quarrell [or] demaund moved or depending before any judge ecclesiasticall or temporall for and concerning any suche lawfull lett or impediment. And moreover if the said William Shagspere do not proceed to solennizacion of mariadg with the said Anne Hathwey without the consent of hir frindes. And also if the said William do upon his owne proper costes and expenses defend & save harmles the right Reverend father in god lord John bushop of worcester and his offycers for licencing them the said William and Anne to be maried together with once asking of the bannes of matrimony betwene them and for all other causes which may ensue by reason or occasion thereof that then the said obligacion to be voyd and of none effect or els to stand & abide in full force and vertue.

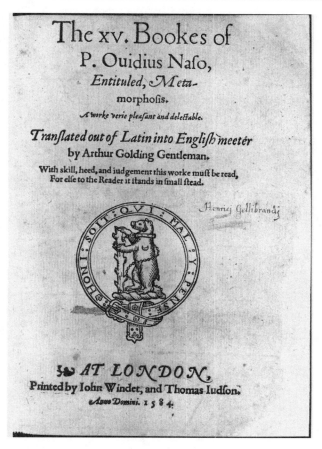

Title page for a book that Shakespeare used as a source, both in its original Latin and in Golding's translation (by permission of the Folger Shakespeare Library)

Acting as a Profession

Actors who did not belong to an acting company were classified as vagabonds and masterless men, making them subject to arrest and harassment. By 1583, according to The Annales, Or Generall Chronicle of England *(1615) for that year, Queen Elizabeth decided to maintain a company of actors among the royal household's servants, and assembled her company by choosing the best actors from the existing companies:*

[*Marginal note:* Players.] Comedians and stage-players, of former times were very poore and ignorant, in respect of these of this time, but being nowe growne very skillfull and exquisite Actors for all matters, they were entertained into the service of divers great Lords, out of which companies, there were xii. of the best chosen, and at the request of Sir *Francis Walsingham,* they were sworne the Queenes servants, & were allowed wages, and liveries, as groomes of the chamber: and untill this yeere 1583, the Queene hadde no players, amongst these xii. players were two rare men, viz. *Thomas Wilson* for a quicke delicate refined extermporall witte, and *Richard Tarleton* for a wondrous plentifull pleasant extemporall wit, hee was the wonder of his time: hee lyeth buried in *Shore-ditch* Church. [*Marginal note:* Tarleton so beloved that men use his picture for their signes.]

–p. 697

1583

Susanna Shakespeare

Susanna Shakespeare was born six months after her parents' marriage. This circumstance may indicate she was conceived out of wedlock, although it is also possible that William Shakespeare and Anne Hathaway had, before consummating their relationship, performed a handfast marriage, a secular ceremony that, under certain conditions, was recognized as a legal marriage.

Susanna appears in the public records several times. On 6 May 1606 a church court in Stratford cited her for failing to take communion on the previous Easter Sunday, perhaps indicating Susanna was a Catholic recusant or a Puritan; her case was later dismissed. On 5 June 1607 she married the Puritan physician John Hall. Her daughter Elizabeth was baptized on 21 February 1608. On 15 July 1613 Susanna sued John Lane for slander after Lane announced Susanna "had the Runninge of the raynes & had bin naught with Ralph Smith at John Palmer['s]" (British Library, Harleian Manuscript 4064). She was buried on 16 July 1649; her epitaph credits Shakespeare with responsibility for her wit as well, perhaps, for her faith:

[Let all men know by these presents that we Fulke Sandells of Stratford in the County of Warwick, husbandman, and John Rychardson there husbandman, are held and firmly bound by Richard Cosin gentleman and Robert Warmstry public notary to pay forty pounds of good and lawful money of England to the same Richard and Robert, their heirs executors or assigns: to make which payment well and faithfully we bind ourselves and each of us severally for the whole and total amount, our heirs executors and administrators firmly by these presents sealed with our seals. Given on the 28th day of November in the 25th year of the reign of our Lady Elizabeth, by the grace of God Queen of England, France and Ireland, Defender of the Faith, &c.]

–*Minutes and Accounts,* vol. III, pp. 112–113

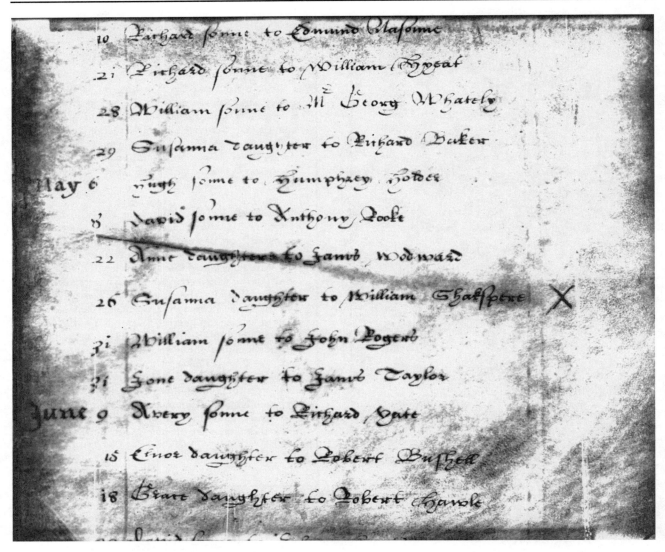

Susanna Shakespeare's baptismal record (shelfmark DR 243/1, fol. 20; courtesy of the Shakespeare Birthplace Trust Records Office)

Heere lyeth the body of Susanna
wife to John Hall, Gent: the daugh
ter of William Shakespeare, Gent:
shee deceased the . 11th of July. Aº.
1649, aged 66.

Witty above her sexe, but that's not all,
Wise to salvation was good Mistris Hall,
Something of Shakespeare was in that, but this
Wholy of him with whom she's now in blisse.
Then, Passenger, hast nere a teare,
To weepe with her that wept with all;
That wept, yet set her self to chere
Them up with comforts cordiall.
Her love shall live, her mercy spread,
When thou has't ner'e a teare to shed.

1584

Visits of the Lord Berkley's Players and the Lord Chandos's Players

These payments, recorded on 11 January 1584, were charged to the account of Richard Court and John Smith.

Payd to Mr Alderman that he layd downe to ye lord Bartlite his players & to a preacher   vs

payd to the lord {saunders} (shandowes) players   iiis iiiid
—*Minutes and Accounts,* vol. III, pp. 136–137

1585

Visits of the Earl of Oxford's Players, the Earl of Worcester's Players, and the Earl of Essex's Players

These payments, recorded on 20 January 1585, were charged to the account of Richard Court and John Smith.

geven to my lord of oxfordes pleers	iii^s iiii^d
geven to the earle of worceter pleers	iii^s iiii^d

. . . .

geven to the earle of essex pleers   iii^s viii^d
             —*Minutes and Accounts,* vol. III, pp. 148, 149

Hamnet and Judith Shakespeare's Baptismal Record

Baptized on 2 February 1585, Shakespeare's twin son and daughter, Hamnet and Judith, were probably named after the Shakespeares' neighbors Hamnet Sadler and Judith Staunton Sadler. Hamnet Sadler, a baker, was a witness to Shakespeare's will in 1616.

Hamnet died in 1596; aside from the burial record, no information survives about his life or death. Judith witnessed a deed of sale on 4 December 1611, and on 10 February 1616 she married Thomas Quiney. She bore three sons: Shaksper (baptized 23 November 1616; buried 8 May 1617), Richard (1618–1639), and Thomas (1620–1639). Judith lived until 1662.

1587

Visit of Unidentified Players

This payment, recorded on 13 January 1587, was charged to the account of William Parsons and George Bardwell.

paide to Mr Tiler for the pleyers   v^s
             —*Minutes and Accounts,* vol. IV, p. 16

1588

Visits of the Queen's Players, the Earl of Essex's Players, the Earl of Leicester's Players, and an Unidentified Company

These payments, recorded on 12 January 1588, were charged to the account of John Gybbes and Richard Quyney.

It. p^d for mendinge of a forme that was broken by the quenes players   xvi^d

. . . .

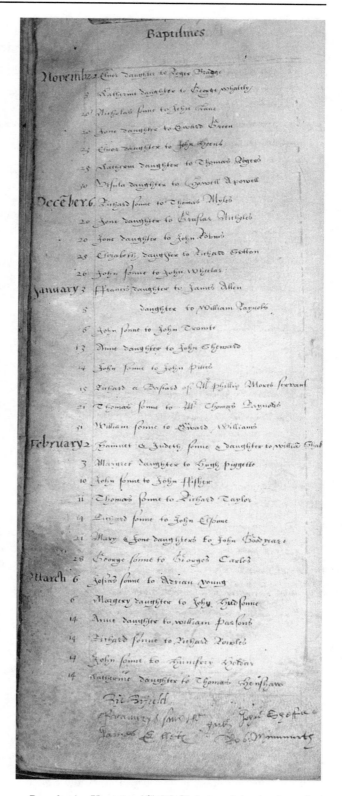

Page showing Hamnet and Judith Shakespeare's baptismal record (shelfmark DR 243/1; courtesy of the Shakespeare Birthplace Trust Records Office)

On the Charms of Plays

Richard Norwood ultimately became the pious surveyor of Bermuda, but in the following entries from his journal, concerning events that took place circa 1605–1610, he describes the temptations playgoing and acting presented for him when he was a young man. Norwood's struggle to reconcile his theatrical desires and his religion's anti-theatrical beliefs is a compelling reminder of the difficulty of choosing to become an actor or playwright. These excerpts are from The Journal of Richard Norwood Surveyor of Bermuda *(1945), edited by Wesley Frank Craven and Walter B. Hayward.*

I was born of Christian parents and under them educated till about fifteen years of age; in whom there was a severe disposition and carriage towards me suitable to that mass of sin and folly which was bound up in my heart, whereby it was moderated in some good measure.

–p. 4

. . . .

Norwood recalls the difficulty he had in leaving a favorite schoolmaster and the temptations he soon experienced.

Then my heart was ready to break and my eyes to gush out abundantly with tears. And not without cause, for from that time forwards I went no more to school to any purpose, not meeting with an able schoolmaster and my father much decaying in his estate, but passed my time in a more fruitless and dissolute manner. At Stratford when I was near fifteen years of age, being drawn in by other young men of the town, I acted a woman's part in a stage play. I was so much affected with that practice that had not the Lord prevented it I should have chosen it before any other course of life.

–pp. 5–6

. . . .

In this three years, especially whilst I was at London by the fishmonger, the corruption of my heart showed itself abundantly *in lust, as touching the maid at my Aunt Edwards, the maid at Billing . . . wantonness with my master's daughter . . . also in the . . . sin, in appareling, etc., also* [deleted] in vanity of mind and self-conceitedness. Which notwithstanding, the Lord was pleased somewhat to moderate by sending usually some sharp chastisement or affliction upon me when that sin did much prevail, insomuch as I took notice of it and did expect and fear it, which did something repress that vice. Also as a fruit and fomenter of the former I had a great delight in reading in vain and corrupt books as *Palmerin de Oliva, The Seven Champions,* and others like. Also as soon as I was recovered of the plague, and before I was quite recovered, I fell to reading of Virgil's *Aeneid* with much affection, but had no love nor delight nor faith in the word of God, never spent any time (that I remember) in those three years and much less in many years after in reading of that. I think that acting a part in a play, the reading of playbooks and other such books as aforementioned, and the vain conceits which they begat in me was the principal thing that alienated my heart from the word of God which afterwards grew to that height that scarce any book seemed more contemptible to me than the word of God.

–pp. 16–17

. . . .

And now lying at home in the ship, having means allowed me and leisure enough for half a year together, (for about so long it was as I remember before she was sold) a man would have thought I should have made a very good progress in my studies, but it fell out clean contrary, for though I might seem now to be my own man, being gotten free from a good master (who I think respected me well and intended his daughter to me for wife as I have heard) yet I was under an evil master, Satan, who in this time finding me idle and unsettled, employed me in his drudgery, tyrannizing over me, and I became more his vassal than ever before.

–pp. 41–42

. . . .

For at this time (as I say) I did not prosecute my laudable exercise but went often to stage plays wherewith I was as it were bewitched in affection and never satiated, which was a great means to withdraw and take off my mind from anything that was serious, true, or good, and to set it upon frivolous, false, and feigned things. Yea, so far was I affected with these lying vanities that I began to make a play and had written a good part of it. It happened after some time that I fell out with the players at the Fortune (which was the house I frequented) about a seat which they would not admit me to have, whereupon out of anger, and as it were to do them a despite, I came there no more that I remember. It was God's mercy to give me this rub that I had not run myself over head and ears in these vanities.

–p. 42

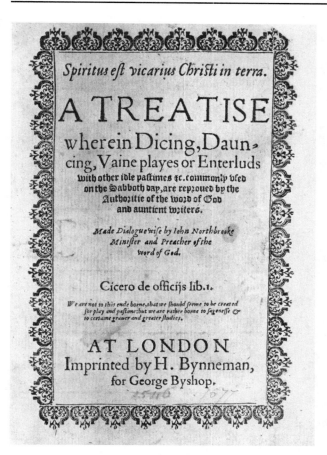

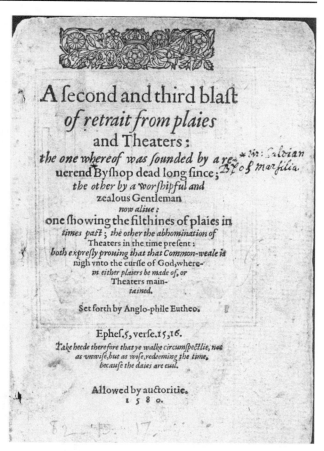

Title pages for two of the anti-theatrical tracts linking play attendance to various vices
(by permission of the Folger Shakespeare Library)

It. gyven to the Quenes players	xx^s
It. gyven to my Lo: of Essex players	v^s
It. gyven to therle of leycester his players	x^s
It. gyven to another Companye	iii^s iiii^d

—*Minutes and Accounts*, vol. IV, pp. 31, 32

Record of John Shakespeare's Lawsuit against John Lambert in which William Shakespeare Is Named

In 1578, apparently in response to financial difficulties, John Shakespeare mortgaged land in Wilmcote to Edmund Lambert, husband of one of Mary Arden's sisters. John Shakespeare was unable to repay the debt as promised; he made later efforts to clear the debt and reclaim the land, initiating lawsuits when these efforts were rejected. The following excerpt from the 1588 complaint (PRO KB27/1311 rot. 516), transcribed in Tucker Brooke's Shakespeare of Stratford: A Handbook for Students *(1926), is from a suit to recover this land and includes William Shakespeare's name, probably to establish or protect his ability to inherit the land. When the*

suit was eventually settled, however, the land was awarded to Lambert's heirs.

Et quod dictus Johannes Shackespere et Maria uxor ejus, simulcum Willielmo Shackespere filio suo, cum inde requisiti essent, assurarent mesuagium predictum et cetera premissa, cum pertinentiis, prefato Johanni Lamberte, et deliberarent omnia scripta et evidencias premissa predicta concernentia; predictus Johannes Lamberte vicesimo sexto die Septembris anno regni dicte domine regine vicesimo nono, apud Stratford-super-Avon in comitatu predicto, in consideracione inde super se assumpsit et prefato Johanni Shackespere, adtunc et ibidem fideliter promisit, quod ipse, idem Johannes Lambert, viginti libras legalis monete Anglie prefato Johanni Shackespere [. . .] bene et fideliter solvere et contentare vellet; et predictus Johannes Shackespere in facto dicit quod ipse hucusque non implacitavit dictum Johannem Lambert pro premissis, nec aliqua inde parcella, et insuper quod ipse, idem Johannes Shackespere et Maria uxor ejus, simulcum Willielmo Shackespere filio suo, sem-

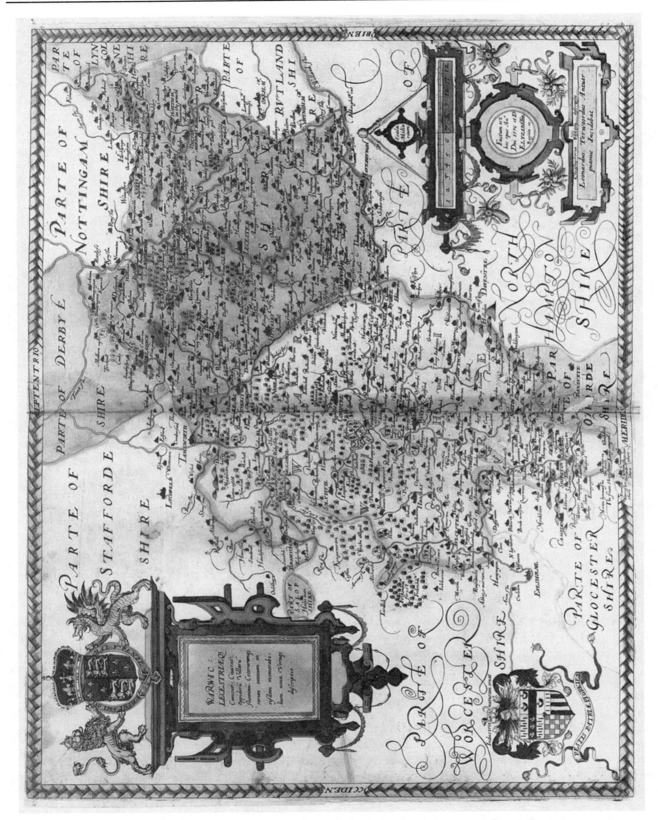

Map of Warwickshire from Christopher Saxton's Atlas, London *(circa 1590), showing Stratford-upon-Avon (Stretford) and the surrounding towns and villages (by permission of the Folger Shakespeare Library)*

per hactenus parati fuerunt tam ad assurandum premissa predicta quam ad deliberandum eidem Johanni
Lamberte omnia scripta et evidencias eadem premissa
concernentia; predictus tamen Johannes Lamberte,
promissionem et assumpcionem suas predictas min-
ime curans, set machinans et fraudulenter intendens
ipsum Johannem Shackspere de predictis viginti libris
callide et subdole decipere et defraudare, easdem viginti libras prefato Johanni Shackespere juxta promissionem et assumpcionem, suas hucusque non
solvit . . .

[And that the said John Shakespeare and Mary his
wife, together with William Shakespeare their son,
when they should be asked to do so, would confirm
the aforesaid messuage and other premises with their
appurtenances to the said John Lambert, and would
deliver all writings and evidences concerning the
aforesaid premises. The aforesaid John Lambert, on
the twenty-sixth day of September in the
twenty-ninth year of the reign of our said lady the
Queen (1587), at Stratford-on-Avon in the aforesaid
county, in consideration of this took upon himself
and then and there faithfully promised the said John
Shakespeare that he, the same John Lambert, would
well and faithfully pay and satisfy to the said John
Shakespeare twenty pounds of legal money of
England; and the said John Shakespeare says in fact
that he has not hitherto sued the said John Lambert
for the premises nor any part of them, and moreover
that he the said John Shakespeare and Mary his wife,
together with William Shakespeare their son, have
always been ready both to confirm [John Lambert's
possession of] the aforesaid premises and to deliver
to the same John Lambert all writings and evidences
concerning the said premises. Nevertheless the said
John Lambert, very little regarding his promise and
undertaking aforesaid, but scheming and fraudulently intending to deceive and defraud John Shakespeare of the said twenty pounds, has not hitherto
paid the twenty pounds to the said John Shakespeare
according to his promise and undertaking.]

　　　　　　　　　　　　　－*Shakespeare of Stratford*, pp. 8–9

1589

Allusion to an ur-*Hamlet*
in Nashe's Preface to Greene's *Menaphon*

*Thomas Nashe was a satirist who, like Shakespeare,
dedicated some of his work to the Earl of Southampton. In
this excerpt from "To the Gentlemen Students of both Universities," Nashe's preface to Robert Greene's* Menaphon

*Camillas alarum to slumbering Euphues, in his mel-
ancholie Cell at Silexedra (London: Printed by T. O. for
Sampson Clarke, 1589), the* Hamlet *referred to is probably
a play by Thomas Kyd. The allusion is sometimes cited as
proof that Shakespeare was known in London by 1589.*

Curteous and wise, whose judgements (not
entangled with envie) enlarge the deserts of the
Learned by your liberall censures; vouchsafe to welcome your scholler-like Shepheard with such Universitie entertainement, as either the nature of your
bountie, or the custome of your common civilitie
may afford. To you he appeales that knew him *ab
extrema pueritia*, whose *placet* he accounts the *plaudite*
of his paines; thinking his daie labour was not altogether lavisht *sine linea*, if there be anie thing of all in
it, that doth *olere atticum* in your estimate. I am not
ignorant how eloquent our gowned age is growen of
late; so that everie mœchanicall mate abhorres the
english he was borne too, and plucks with a
solemne periphrasis, his *ut vales* from the inkhorne:
which I impute not so much to the perfection of
arts, as to the servile imitation of vainglorious
tragœdians, who contend not so seriouslie to excell
in action, as to embowell the clowdes in a speach of
comparison; thinking themselves more than initiated in poets immortalitie, if they but once get
Boreas by the beard, and the heavenlie bull by the
deaw-lap. But herein I cannot so fully bequeath
them to follie, as their idiote art-masters, that
intrude themselves to our eares as the alcumists of
eloquence; who (mounted on the stage of arro-
gance) think to outbrave better pens with the swell-
ing bumbast of a bragging blanke verse. Indeed it
may be the ingrafted overflow of some kilcow conceipt, that overcloieth their imagination with a more
than drunken resolution, beeing not extemporall in
the invention of anie other meanes to vent their
manhood, commits the disgestion of their cholerick
incumbrances, to the spacious volubilitie of a drum-
ming decasillabon. Mongst this kinde of men that
repose eternitie in the mouth of a player, I can but
ingrosse some deepe read Grammarians, who having no more learning in their scull, than will serve
to take up a commoditie; nor Art in their brain,
than was nourished in a serving mans idlenesse, will
take upon them to be the ironicall censors of all,
when God and Poetrie doth know, they are the simplest of all.

　　　　　　　　　　　　　　　　　　　　　　－pp. I–verso

. . . .

It is a common practise now a daies amongst a
sort of shifting companions, that runne through every

arte and thrive by none, to leave the trade of *Nouerint* whereto they were borne, and busie themselves with the indevors of Art, that could scarcelie latinize their necke-verse if they should have neede; yet Engish *Seneca* read by candlelight yeeldes manie good sentences, as *Bloud is a begger*, and so foorth: and if you intreate him faire in a frostie morning, he will affoord you whole *Hamlets*, I should say handfulls of tragical speaches. But ô griefe*! tempus edax rerum*, what's that will last alwaies? The sea exhaled by droppes will in continuance be drie, and *Seneca* let bloud line by line and page by page, at length must needes die to our stage: which makes his famisht followers to imitate the Kidde in *Æsop*, who enamored with the Foxes newfangles, forsooke all hopes of life to leape into a new occupation; and these men renowncing all possibilities of credit or estimation, to intermeddle with Italian translations: wherein how poorelie they have plodded,

(as those that are neither provenzall men, nor are able to distinguish of Articles,) let all indifferent Gentlemen that have travailed in that tongue, discerne by their twopenie pamphlets: & no mervaile though their home-born mediocritie be such in this matter; for what can be hoped of those, that thrust *Elisium* into hell, and have not learned so long as they have lived in the spheares, the just measure of the Horizon without an hexameter. Sufficeth them to bodge up a blanke verse with ifs and ands, & other while for recreation after their candle stuffe, having starched their beardes most curiouslie, to make a peripateticall path into the inner parts of the Citie, & spend two or three howers in turning over French *Doudie*, where they attract more infection in one minute, than they can do eloquence all dayes of their life, by conversing with anie Authors of like argument.

–pp. 3–verso

Illustration from Georgette de Montenay's Emblemes ou Devises Chrestiennes *(1571). Emblem books, in which readers are encouraged to scrutinize illustrations for their philosophical or theological significance, may have prepared Shakespeare's audiences to interpret dramas symbolically (shelfmark 89.k.7; courtesy of The British Library, London).*

The Elizabethan Years: 1592–March 1603

Shakespeare's professional career opened with a complaint: in 1592 a fellow dramatist, Robert Greene, protests that an "upstart crow," nicknamed "Shake-scene," is elbowing his way into the group of Oxford- and Cambridge-trained playwrights currently dominating London. Shakespeare's professional career closed with collaborations: he and playwright John Fletcher wrote the history play All Is True, the tragicomedy Two Noble Kinsmen, and the lost play Cardenio. In between are the brilliant comedies, tragedies, romances, and poems for which he is best known. There is no convenient breaking point to use when presenting a history of Shakespeare's literary career; the usual practice is to divide events by the reigns of the two English monarchs for whom Shakespeare and his acting company often performed: Queen Elizabeth (1533–1603) and King James (1566–1625).

Shakespeare arrived in London at a time when, following the construction of purpose-built theaters such as the Curtain and the Theatre, there was a growing demand for new plays. Between 1592 and 1603, Shakespeare wrote popular historical dramas about the War of the Roses, the fourteenth- and fifteenth-century English civil war being much on the minds of the aging and heirless Queen Elizabeth's subjects; comedies ranging from the farcical Comedy of Errors to the romantic Twelfth Night; and tragedies, beginning with the gruesome stage effects of Titus Andronicus and evolving into the sophisticated psychological portraits in Hamlet. Establishing a precise chronology of when Shakespeare wrote what is impossible because many of his early plays were not published until 1623, when his fellow actors John Heminges and Henry Condell collected them in a volume now called the First Folio. Fewer than half of Shakespeare's early plays were published in his lifetime, probably because publication reduced their value to the acting company. One sign of Shakespeare's growing success as a playwright is that unscrupulous publishers sometimes put his name or initials on plays written by others.

Shakespeare also worked as an actor early in his career, but the documents provide few details about how often he acted or in what parts. The first acting company of which he is known to have been a member is the Lord Chamberlain's Men, the company that performed for Queen Elizabeth and her court during the Christmas and winter holidays. The Lord Chamberlain's Men performed in other venues, such as the London Inns of Court and the Theatre, and they eventu-

Portrait of Queen Elizabeth I, daughter of Henry VIII and Anne Boleyn, who ruled England from 1558 to 1603 (artist unknown; courtesy of The National Portrait Gallery, London)

ally became successful enough to be able to build their own theater, the Globe, on the south bank of the Thames in Southwark, near where a modern reproduction of the theater now stands. Shakespeare was a householder—a part owner—of the Globe.

Shortly after Shakespeare began being noticed as a playwright, there was an outbreak of bubonic plague. One response by London officials was to close the theaters, throwing the actors and playwrights out of work. During the 1592–1594 plague closings, Shakespeare wrote or completed two long poems, Venus and Adonis and The Rape of Lucrece. *The first is an erotic account of Venus's pursuit of the beautiful but reluctant young man Adonis; the second is a complaint by the chaste but violated Lucrece. Both were reprinted several times during Shakespeare's lifetime and are frequently alluded to by readers and writers. There are many other allusions to characters from Shakespeare's plays, particularly the comic hero of the* Henry IV *plays, Sir John Falstaff. Despite the low esteem in which playwrights were generally held by early modern critics, Shakespeare himself is the subject of praise in poems and prose by several of his contemporaries.*

Although his theatrical career was centered in London, Shakespeare bought property in Stratford: a large house, New Place, and 107 acres of land. Some of his fellow Stratfordians made plans to approach him for loans, and Shakespeare or his father took steps to have the Shakespeares' social status raised to the level of the gentry by applying for a coat of arms. Some of the surviving documents show Shakespeare engaged in mundane activities: he fails to pay his taxes, may have hoarded grain, and was involved in minor legal skirmishes. Some documents record but do not provide many details about personal losses: Shakespeare's son, Hamnet, died in 1596 and his father, John, in 1601. What emerges from the documents is the portrait of an artist developing his skills and receiving increasing recognition, most but not all of it flattering.

1592

Henslowe Records Performances of a Play about King Henry VI

Much of what is known about the day-to-day operations of an early modern theater is derived from the diary of theatrical producer Philip Henslowe. Henslowe's records are jumbled: his money-lending activities, the receipts from his theater, records of purchases, medical recipes, descriptions of card tricks, and personal and business notes are all intermixed. The diary shows the range of theatrical companies' repertories, gives some sense of how the plays were financed, and helps scholars to date, and sometimes assign authors to, early modern plays; it also provides the only information we have about some plays of which no copy survives. Sometimes these "lost" plays provide tantalizing links to the work of other playwrights: in May 1592 Henslowe's top-earning play was The Tanner of Denmark, *a play whose existence may add to the complexity of Hamlet's gravedigger's remark that "A tanner will last you nine year" (5.1.144-5).*

The plays named by Henslowe in 1592 as well as in 1593 and 1594 may or may not be those Shakespeare wrote. As Neil Carson notes in A Companion to Henslowe's Diary *(1988), Henslowe's entries for seven "Shakespearian" titles–King Lear, Hamlet, Henry V, Troilus and*

Cressida, Henry VI, Titus Andronicus, *and* Taming of a Shrew–*provide no definitive answers about Shakespeare's career:*

> only the last three conform to the orthodox notions concerning Shakespearian chronology. Consequently, it is probable (although not, by the nature of the evidence, absolutely certain) that *Hamlet* and *Troilus* are lost plays which Shakespeare may have known, and that *Henry V* and *King Lear* refer to the old Queen's Men's plays preserved as *The Famous Victories of Henry V*, and *King Leir*. Until the complicated relationship between *a Shrew* and *the Shrew* is fully understood, it is impossible to know if Henslowe's title refers to a source play or to Shakespeare's version of the story. Similar uncertainties surround both *Henry VI* and *Titus Andronicus*, described as "ne" (new?) plays on 3 March 1592 (f. 7), and 23 January 1594 (f. 8v) respectively. Commentators who feel that *Titus* must have been written earlier suggest that perhaps the performance by Sussex's Men was a revision. Of course, all such speculation is completely unverifiable. (p. 68)

Regardless of who wrote it, the play about Henry VI was popular and a steady earner.

Henslowe's abbreviation "ne" is still in dispute; it may mean "new"–newly written or new to Henslowe's company, or "newly entered"–that is, recently approved for public performance by the Master of the Revels. It may also mean something known only to Henslowe. "Rd" means "received," but it is not clear if the amounts reflect the play's total takings or only Henslowe's share. The diary entries follow the English calendar, in which the new year begins on 25 March, although Henslowe does not always remember to write the new date.

ne–Rd at harey the vi the 3 of marche 1591 . . . . . . iiiˡⁱ xviˢ 8d

. . . .

Rd at harey the vi the 7 of marche 1591. . . . . iii li

. . . .

Rd at harey the vi the 11 of marche 1591. . . . xxxxviiˡⁱ viᵈ

. . . .

Rd at harey the vi the 16 of marche 1591. . . . . xxxi s vi d

. . . .

Rd at harey the vi the 28 of marche 1591. . . . . . . iiiˡⁱ viii s

. . . .

Rd at harey the vi the 5 of apˡell 1591 . . . . xxxxi s

. . . .

Rd at harey the vi the 13 of apˡell 1591. . . . . xxvi s

. . . .

Images of Queen Elizabeth I: (top) illustration from Edmund Spenser's The Shepheardes Calender *(1586) showing Elizabeth being entertained by shepherds and musicians; (bottom) title page for Christopher Saxton's* Atlas *(circa 1590), in which Elizabeth is surrounded by iconographic figures that assert her ability to explore and conquer the world (by permission of the Folger Shakespeare Library)*

Rd at harey the vi the 21 of ap^rell 1591 . . . . xxxiii s

. . . .

Rd at harey the vi the 4 of maye 1592 . . . . lvi s

. . . .

Rd at harey the vi the 7 of maye 1592 . . . . xxii s

. . . .

Rd at harey the 6 the 14 of maye 1592 . . . . ls

. . . .

——Rd at harey the vi the 19 of maye 1592 . . . . xxx^s

. . . .

——Rd at harey the vi the 25 of maye 1592 . . . . .xxiiii s

. . . .

——Rd at harey the vi the 12 of June 1592 . . . . xxxii s

. . . .

Rd at harey the vi the 19 of June 1592 . . . . xxxi s

–Henslowe's Diary, pp. 16–19

John Shakespeare Cited for Failing to Attend Church

John Shakespeare's appearance on a list citing those who "have bene hearetofore presented for not comminge monethlie to the churche according to hir Majestys lawes" (a 25 September report of the royal commissioners, Public Record Office, State Papers Domestic, Elizabeth I SP 12/243, number 76) is an official version of a list made earlier in the year in which he was also identified as one who refused to attend church for fear of being arrested for debt. This document has caused a great deal of speculation, most of it centered on John Shakespeare's religious beliefs. Does his failure to attend services indicate he was a Catholic recusant, or perhaps a Puritan, who avoided church for ideological reasons? Although he may, as the document states, have stayed away from church to avoid arrest for debt, it is also possible that his colleagues on the town council listed him as fearing process for debt in order to protect him from prosecution as a recusant or nonconformist. John Shakespeare's religious beliefs, orthodox or not, may have had no effect on his son, but the possibility that members of William Shakespeare's family were Catholic has raised questions about the playwright's own faith.

Additional support for John Shakespeare's Catholicism includes a pamphlet discovered on 29 April 1757 by a workman retiling the roof of John Shakespeare's house on Henley Street. The pamphlet, which has since disappeared, was printed by Edmund Malone in The Plays and Poems of William Shakespeare *(1790); Malone at first supported, then doubted, its authenticity. The text Malone printed is similar to a 1638*

edition of The Contract and Testament of the Soule *by Carlo Borromeo; the person who signs the text pledges his or her support of Catholic doctrine. Such a document would need to be carefully hidden in order for the person signing it to avoid prosecution. For further details of the history of John Shakespeare's "last spiritual will, testament, confession, protestation, and confession of faith" (Malone, Vol. I, Part 2, p. 166), see Samuel Schoenbaum's* William Shakespeare: A Documentary Life *(1975), pp. 41–46. For accounts of John Shakespeare's possible recusancy, see Peter Milward's* Shakespeare's Religious Background *(1973) and Richard Wilson's "Shakespeare and the Jesuits" in* TLS: Times Literary Supplement *(19 December 1997), pp. 11–13.*

In the parrishe of Stratford upon Avon./

Mr. John Wheeler.
John Wheeler his Soon.
Mr John Shackespere.
Mr Nicholas Barneshurste
Thomas James, alias Gyles.
William Bainton.
Richard Harrington,
William ffluellen,
George Bardolfe.

A large bracket was drawn to the right of the list of names and the following note is written:

It is sayd that these laste nine, coom
not to Churrrche for feare of
processe for Debtte./

–William Shakespeare: A Documentary Life, p. 39

Allusion to Shakespeare in *Greene's Groats-worth of Witte*

In this excerpt from Greene's Groats-worth of Witte *(1592), playwright and pamphlet writer Robert Greene (circa 1560–1592) derides Shakespeare as "an upstart Crow," a designation usually interpreted as an insult to Shakespeare's lack of a university education. Greene's description of Shakespeare as "beautified with our feathers" may be an accusation that Shakespeare, in adapting or revising old plays, was adhering too closely to the original or borrowing too heavily from his fellow playwrights. Greene then deliberately misquotes a line from Shakespeare's history play* Henry VI, Part III. *Shakespeare's line, spoken by Richard, Duke of York as an insult to Queen Margaret, is: "O tiger's heart wrapp'd in a woman's hide!" (1.4.137); Greene renders it "Tygers hart wrapt in a Players hyde," and he perhaps hoped Shakespeare would remember*

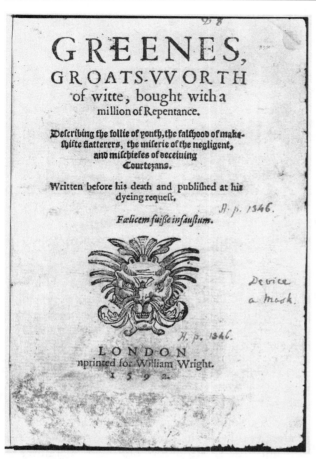

Title page for the pamphlet in which Robert Greene derides Shakespeare as "an upstart crow" (by permission of the Folger Shakespeare Library)

the preceding lines: *"Thou art as opposite to every good / As the antipodes are unto us"* (3 Henry VI, *1.4.134–5*).

To those Gentlemen his Quondam acquaintance,
that spend their wits in making plaies, R. G.
wisheth a better exercise, and wisdome
to prevent his extremities.

If wofull experience may move you (Gentlemen) to beware, or unheard of wretchednes intreate you to take heed: I doubt not but you wil looke backe with sorrow on your time past, and indevour with repentance to spend that which is to come. Wonder not, (for with thee wil I first begin) thou famous gracer of Tragedians, that *Greene*, who hath said with thee (like the foole in his heart) There is no God, shoulde now give glorie unto his greatnes: for penetrating is his power, his hand lyes heavie upon me, hee hath spoken unto mee with a voice of thunder, and I have felt he is a God that can punish enemies. Why should thy excellent wit, his gift, bee so blinded, that thou shouldst give no glorie to the

giver? Is it pestilent Machivilian pollicy that thou hast studied? O peevish follie! What are his rules but meere confused mockeries, able to extirpate in small time the generation of mankind. For if *Sic volo, sic jubeo*, hold in those that are able to commaund: and if it be lawfull *Fas & nefas* to do any thing that is beneficiall; onely Tyrants should possesse the earth, and they striving to exceed in tyrannie, should each to other be a slaughter man; till the mightiest outliving all, one stroke were lefte for Death, that in one age mans life should end. The brocher of this Diabolicall Atheisme is dead, and in his life had never the felicitie hee aymed at: but as he began in craft; lived in feare, and ended in despaire. *Quam inscrutabilia sunt Dei judicia?* This murderer of many brethren, had his conscience seared like *Caine*: this betrayer of him that gave his life for him, inherited the portion of *Judas*: this Apostata perished as ill as *Julian*: and wilt thou my friend be his disciple? Looke but to me, by him perswaded to that libertie, and thou shalt find it an infernall bondage. I knowe the least of my demerits merit this miserable death, but wilfull striving against knowne truth, exceedeth all the terrors of my soule. Defer not (with me) till this last point of extremitie; for litle knowst thou how in the end thou shalt be visited.

With thee I joyne yong *Juvenall*, that byting Satyrist, that lastly with mee together writ a Comedie. Sweet boy, might I advise thee, be advisde, and get not many enemies by bitter wordes: inveigh against vaine men, for thou canst do it, no man better, no man so well: thou hast a libertie to reproove all, and name none; for one being spoken to, all are offended; none being blamed no man is injured. Stop shallow water still running, it will rage, or tread on a worme and it will turne: then blame not Schollers vexed with sharpe lines, if they reprove thy too much liberty of reproofe.

And thou no lesse deserving than the other two, in some things rarer, in nothing inferiour; driven (as my selfe) to extreme shifts, a litle have I to say to thee: and were it not an idolatrous oth, I would sweare by sweet S. George, thou art unworthy better hap, sith thou dependest on so meane a stay. Base minded men all three of you, if by my miserie you be not warnd: for unto none of you (like mee) sought those burres to cleave: those Puppets (I meane) that spake from our mouths, those Anticks garnisht in our colours. Is it not strange, that I, to whom they all have beene beholding: is it not like that you, to whome they all have beene beholding, shall (were yee in that case as I am now) bee both at once of them forsaken? Yes trust them not: for there is an upstart Crow, beautified with our feathers, that with his *Tygers hart wrapt in a Players hyde*, supposes he is as well able to bombast out a blanke verse as the best of you: and beeing an absolute *Johannes fac totum*, is in his owne conceit the onely Shake-scene in a countrey. O that I might intreat your rare wits to be imploied in more profitable courses: & let those Apes imitate your past excellence, and never more acquaint them with your admired inventions. I knowe the best husband of you all will never prove an Usurer, and the kindest of them all will never prove a kind nurse: yet whilest you may, seeke you better Maisters; for it is pittie men of such rare wits, should be subject to the pleasure of such rude groomes.

In this I might insert two more, that both have writ against these buckram Gentlemen: but lette their owne workes serve to witnesse against their owne wickednesse, if they persevere to maintaine any more such peasants. For other new-commers, I leave them to the mercie of these painted monsters who (I doubt not) will drive the best minded to despise them: for the rest, it skils not though they make a jeast at them.

But now returne I againe to you three, knowing my miserie is to you no newes: and let mee hartily intreat you to be warned by my harms. Delight not (as I have done) in irreligious oathes; for from the blasphemers house, a curse shall not depart. Despise drunkennes, which wasteth the wit, and maketh men all equall unto beasts. Flie lust, as the deathsman of the soule; and defile not the Temple of the holy Ghost. Abhore those Epicures, whose loose life hath made religion lothsome to your eares: and when they sooth you with tearms of Mastership, remember *Robert Greene*, whome they have often so flattered, perishes now for want of comfort. Remember Gentlemen, your lives are like to many lighted Tapers, that are with care delivered to all of you to maintaine: these with wind-puft wrath may be extinguisht, which drunkennes put out, which negligence let fall: for mans time is not of it selfe so short but it is more shortned by sinne. The fire of my light is now at the last snuffe, and for want of wherewith to sustaine it, there is no substance lefte for life to feede on. Trust not then (I beseech ye) to such weake staies: for they are as changeable in minde, as in many attyres. Wel, my hand is tyrde, and I am forst to leave where I would begin: for a whole booke cannot containe their wrongs, which I am forst to knit up in some few lines of words.

> *Desirous that you should live,*
> *though himselfe be dying:*
> *Robert Greene.*

—sigs. E4v–F2v

Possible Allusion to *1 Henry VI* in Nashe's *Pierce Penilesse*

In the course of defending actors in Pierce Penilesse his Supplication to the Divell. Describing the over-spreading of Vice, and suppression of Vertue. Pleasantly interlac't with variable delights: and pathetically intermixt with conceipted reproofes. (1592), *Thomas Nashe alludes to popular stage figures such as "brave Talbot"; the reference may be to Lord Talbot, a prominent figure in the first part of Shakespeare's* Henry VI.

That State or Kingdome that is in league with all the World, and hath no forreyne sword to vexe it, is not halfe so strong or confirmed to endure, as that which lives everie houre in feare of invasion. There is a certaine wast of the people for whom there is no use, but warre: and these men must have some employment still to cut them off: *Nam si foras hostens non habent domi invenient*, If they have no service abroad, they will make mutinies at home. Or if the affaires of the State be such, as cannot exhale all these corrupt excrements, it is verie expedient they have some lyght toyes to busie their heads withall, to cast before them as bones to gnaw uppon, which may keepe them from having leasure to intermeddle with higher matters.

[*Marginal note*: The defence of Playes.] To this effect, the policie of Playes is verie necessarie, however some shallow-braynd censurers (not the deepest serchers into the secrets of government) mightily oppugne them. For whereas the after-noone being the eldest time of the day; wherein men that are their owne masters, (as Gentlemen of the Court, the Innes of the Court, and the number of Captaines and Souldiours about *London*) doo wholly bestow themselves upon pleasure, and that pleasure they devide (how vertuously it skills not) either into gameing, following of harlots, drinking, or seeing a Play: is it not then better (since of foure extreames

Shakespeare's Work on *Sir Thomas More*

"The Booke of Sir Thomas More*" (British Library, Harleian manuscript 7368) is an extensively revised play manuscript, written in at least six different hands; one of these, known as Hand D, is thought to be Shakespeare's. The play was probably written in 1592–1593, but the revisions are more difficult to date; conjecture has ranged from 1592 to 1604. The manuscript also contains comments by the Master of the Revels, Edmund Tilney, suggesting revisions. No printed copy of the play or record of its performance survives. The document is useful for studying the process by which playwrights wrote and collaborated on their work.*

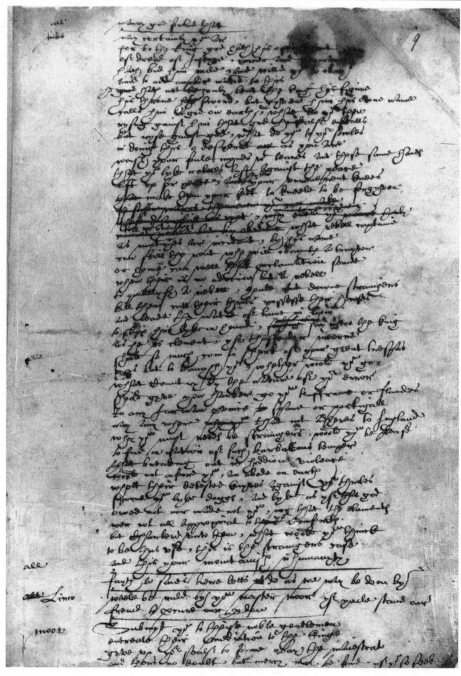

A page from the manuscript of a censored play about Sir Thomas More; some scholars believe this page is in Shakespeare's handwriting
(MS Harley 7368, folio 9; courtesy of The British Library, London)

all the world cannot keepe them but they will choose one) that they should betake them to the least, which is Playes? Nay, what if I proove Playes to be no extreame, but a rare exercise of vertue? First, for the subject of them (for the most part) it is borrowed out of our English Chronicles, wherein our forefathers valiant actes (that have lyne long buried in rustie brasse and worme-eaten bookes) are revived, and they themselves raysed from the Grave of Oblivion, and brought to pleade their aged Honours in open presence: than which, what can bee a sharper reproofe, to these degenerate effeminate dayes of ours?

How would it have joyd brave *Talbot* (the terror of the French) to thinke that after he had lyne two hundred yeare in his Tomb, he should triumph againe on the Stage, and have his bones new embalmed with the teares of ten thousand spectators at least, (at severall times) who in the Tragedian that represents his person, imagine they behold him fresh bleeding.

I will defend it against anie Collian, or club-fisted Usurer of them all, there is no immortalitie can be given a man on earth like unto Playes. What talke I to them of immortalitie, that are the onely underminers of Honour, and doo envie anie man that is not sprung up by base Brokerys like themselves. They care not if all the auncient Houses were rooted out, so that like the Burgomasters of the Low-countries they might share the government amongst them as States, & be quarter- masters of our Monarchy. Al Arts to them are vanitie: and if you tell them what a glorious thing it is to have *Henry* the fifth represented on the Stage leading the French King prisoner, and forcing both him and the Dolphin sweare fealtie, I, but (will they say) what doo we get by it? Respecting neither the right of Fame that is due to true Nobilitie deceased, nor what hopes of eternitie are to be proposed to adventrous minds, to encourage them forward, but onely their execrable lucre, and filthie unquenchable avarice.

They know when they are dead they shall not bee brought upon the Stage for any goodnes, but in a merriment of the Usurer and the Divel, or buying Armes of the Herald, who gives them the Lyon without tongue, tayle, or tallents, because his master whom he must serve is a Townsman, and a man of peace, and must not keepe anie quarrelling beasts to annoy his honest neighbours.

[*Marginal note:* The use of Playes.] In Playes, all coosonages, all cunning drifts overguylded with outward holinesse, all stratagems of warre, all the canker-wormes that breede on the rust of peace, are most lively anotomizd: they shew the ill successe of treason, the fall of hastie climbers, the wretched ende of usurpers, the miserie of civill dissention, & howe just God is evermore in punishing of murther. And to proove everie one of these allegations, could I propound the circumstaunces of this play and that play, if I meant to handle this Theame otherwise than *obiter*. What should I say more? they are sower pills of reprehension wrapt up in sweete words. [*Marginal note:* The confutation of Cittizens objections against Playes.] Whereas some Petitioners to the Counsaile against them object, they corrupt the youth of the Citie, and withdrawe Prentises from their worke; they heartely wish they might bee troubled with none of their youth nor their prentises; for some of them (I meane the ruder handicraftes servaunts) never come abroad, but they are in danger of undooing: and as for corrupting them when they come, thats false; for no Playe they have, encourageth anie man to tumults or rebellion, but layes before such the halter and the gallowes; or prayseth or approoveth pride, lust, whoredome, prodigalitie, or drunkennes, but beates them downe utterly. As for the hindrance of Trades and Traders of the Citie by them, that is an Article foysted in by the vintners, alewives, and victuallers, who surmise if there were no Playes, they should have all the companie that resort to them, lye bowzing and beere-bathing in their houses everie after-noone Nor so, nor so, good brother bottle-ale, for there are other places besides where money can bestow it selfe: the signe of the smocke will wype your mouth clean; and yet I have heard ye have made her a tenaunt to your tap-houses. But what shall he doo that hath spent himselfe? where shall he haunt? Faith, when dice, lust, and drunkennes, and all have dealt uppon him, if there bee never a Playe for him to goe too for his peny, he sits melancholy in his chamber, devising upon felonie or treason, and how hee may best exalt himselfe by mischiefe.

In *Augustus* time (who was the Patrone of all wittye sports) there hapned a great Fray in *Rome* about a Player, insomuch as all the Citie was in an uproare: whereupon, the Emperour (after the broyle was somwhat over-blown) cald the Player before him, and askt what was the reason that a man of his qualitie durst presume to make such a brawle about nothing. He smilingly replide, *It is good for thee O Cæsar, that the peoples heads are troubled with brawles and quarrels about us and our lights matters: for otherwise they would looke into thee and thy matters.* [*Marginal note:* A Players witty answere to Augustus.] Read *Lipsius* or anie prophane or Christian Politician, and you shall finde him of this opinion. [*Marginal note:* A comparison twixt our Players and the Players beyond the

Sea.] Our Players are not as the players beyond sea, a sort of squirting baudie Comedians, that have whores and common Curtizans to play womens parts, and forbeare no immodest speach or unchast action that may procure laughter, but our Sceane is more stately furnisht than ever it was in the time of *Roscius*, our representations honorable, and full of gallaunt resolution, not consisting like theirs of a Pantaloun, a Whore, and a Zanie but of Emperours, Kings and Princes: whose true Tragedies (*Sophocleo cothurno*) they doo vaunt.

Not *Roscius* nor *Æsope* those Tragedians admyred before Christ was borne, could ever performe more in action, than famous *Ned Allen*. [*Marginal note:* The due commendation of Ned Allen.] I must accuse our Poets of sloth and partialitie that they will not boast in large impressions what worthie men (above all Nations) *England* affoords. Other Countreyes cannot have a Fidler breake a string, but they will put it in Print, and the olde *Romanes* in the writings they published, thought scorne to use anie but domestical examples of their owne home-bred Actors, Schollers and Champions. and them they woulde extoll to the third and fourth Generation: Coblers, Tinkers, Fencers, none escapt them, but they mingled them all in one Gallimafry of glory.

Heere I have used a like Methode, not of tying my selfe to mine owne Countrey, but by insisting in the experience of our time; and if I ever write any thing in Latine, (as I hope one day I shall) not a man of any desert heere amongst us, but I will have up. *Tarlton, Ned Allen, Knell, Bentley,* shall be made knowen to *Fraunce, Spayne* and *Italie:* and not a part that they surmounted in, more than other, but I will there note and set downe, with the manner of their habites and attyre.

–pp. 25–27

1593

Possible Allusion to Shakespeare in Chettle's *Kind-Harts Dreame*

Henry Chettle's Kind-Harts Deame. Conteining five Apparitions, with their Invectives against abuses raigning, *a work entered in the Stationers' Register on 8 December 1592, consists of descriptions of, and letters from, five ghosts, all of whom offer critiques of contemporary London morals. One of the ghosts is the playwright and pamphlet writer Robert Greene. In* Kind-Hart's *prefatory epistle, Chettle, a playwright and printer, apologizes for his part in the publication of Greene's 1592* Greenes Groats-worth of witte, *bought with a million of Repentance, in which Shakespeare is derided as "an*

upstart Crow." The first author Chettle refers to in the epistle is probably Christopher Marlowe; the second, the one Chettle describes as civil, upright, and honest, is almost certainly Shakespeare.

To the Gentlemen Readers.

It hath beene a custome Gentlemen (in my mind commendable) among former Authors (whose workes are no lesse beautified with eloquente phrase, than garnished with excellent example) to begin an exordium to the Readers of their time, much more convenient I take it, should the writers in these daies (wherein that gravitie of enditing by the elder excercised, is not observ'd, nor that modest decorum kept, which they continued) submit their labours to the favourable censures of their learned overseers. For seeing nothing can be said, that hath not been before said, the singularitie of some mens conceits, (otherwayes exellent well deserving) are no more to be soothed, than the peremptorie posies of two very sufficient Translators commended. To come in print is not to seeke praise, but to crave pardon: I am urgd to the one; and bold to begge the other, he that offendes being forst, is more excusable than the wilfull faultie, though both be guilty, there is difference in the guilt. To observe custome, and avoid as I may cavill, opposing your favors against my feare, Ile shew reason for my present writing, and after proceed to sue for pardon. About three moneths since died M. *Robert Greene,* leaving many papers in sundry Booke sellers hands, among other his Groats-worth of wit, in which a letter written to divers play-makers, is offensively by one or two of them taken, and because on the dead they cannot be avenged, they wilfully forge in their conceites a living Author: and after tossing it two and fro, no remedy, but it must light on me. How I have all the time of my conversing in printing hindred the bitter inveying against schollers, it hath been very well knowne, and how in that I dealt I can sufficiently proove. With neither of them that take offence was I acquainted, and with one of them I care not if I never be: The other, whome at that time I did not so much spare, as since I wish I had, for that as I have moderated the heate of living writers, and might have usde my owne discretion (especially in such a case) the Author beeing dead, that I did not, I am as sorry, as if the originall fault had beene my fault, because my selfe have seene his demeanor no lesse civill than he exelent in the qualitie he professes: Besides, divers of worship have reported, his uprightnes of dealing, which argues his honesty, and his facetious grace in writting, that aprooves his Art. For the first, whose learning I reverence, and at the perusing of *Greenes* Booke, stroke out what then in conscience I thought he in some displeasure writ: or had it beene true, yet to publish it, was intollerable: him I would wish to use me no worse than I deserve. I had only in the copy this share, it was ilwritten, as sometime

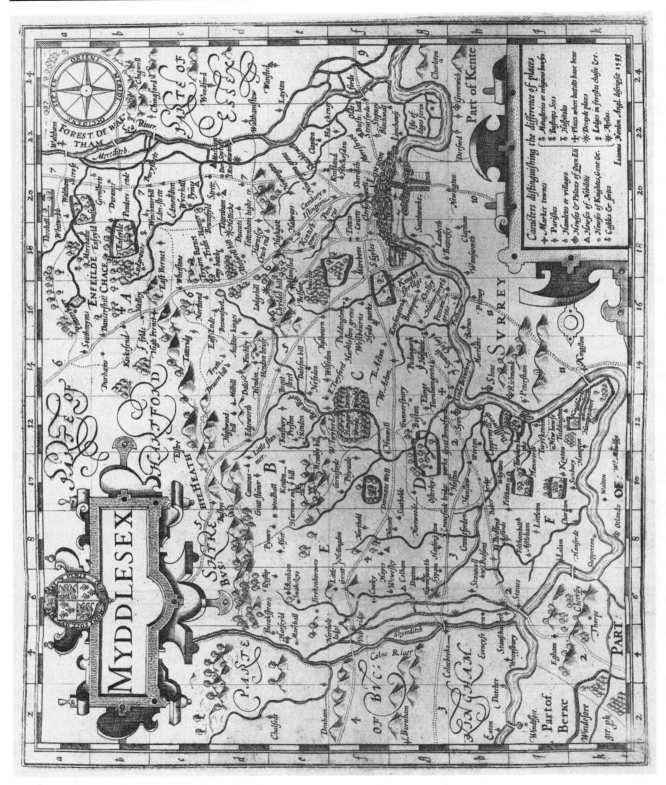

John Norden's map of Middlesex, showing London and Southwark from Speculum Britanniae, *London, 1593*
(by permission of the Folger Shakespeare Library)

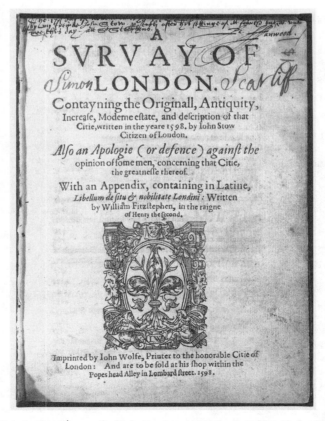

Illustration from Bidpai's The Morall Philosophie of Doni *(1570). Beggars, often with disabling injuries, were a common sight in Shakespeare's London (courtesy of the Library of Congress, Prints and Photographs Division, Rosenwald Collection).*

Title page for John Stowe's guide to London. The year for Shakespeare's arrival in the city is debatable, but it is certain that the playwright was established in the city in the early 1590s (by permission of the Folger Shakespeare Library).

Greenes hand was none of the best, licensd it must be, ere it could bee printed which could never be if it might not be read. To be breife I writ it over, and as neare as I could, followed the copy, only in that letter I put something out, but in the whole booke not a worde in, for I protest it was all *Greenes*, not mine nor Maister *Nashes*, as some unjustly have affirmed. Neither was he the writer of an Epistle to the second part of Gerileon, though by the workemans error T. N. were set to the end: that I confesse to be mine, and repent it not.

Thus Gentlemen, having noted the private causes, that made me nominate my selfe in print; being aswell to purge Master *Nashe* of that he did not, as to justifie what I did, and withall to confirme what M. *Greene* did: I beseech yee accept the publike cause, which is both the desire of your delight, and common benefite: for though the toye bee shadowed under the Title of *Kind-hearts Dreame*, it discovers the false hearts of divers that wake to commit mischiefe. Had not the former reasons been, it had come forth without a father: and then shuld I have had no cause to feare offending, or reason to sue for favour. Now am I in doubt of the one, though I hope of the other; which if I obtaine, you shall bind me hereafter to bee silent, till I can present yee with some thing more acceptable.

Henrie Chettle.
—sigs. A3r–A4v

Henslowe Records Performances of a Play about Henry VI

These entries show the continuing popularity of Henslowe's company's Henry VI *play, which may be by Shakespeare.*

Rd at harey the 6 of 16 of Jeneway 1593 . . . . . . xxxxvi s

. . . .

Rd at harey the vi the 31 of Jenewarye 1593 . . . . . . xxvî
—*Henslowe's Diary, pp.* 19, 20

Quartos and Folios

Elizabethan printers worked with large sheets of paper, all of it handmade. Once these sheets had been imprinted, they were folded. When the sheet was folded once, the two leaves, making up four pages, were formed; these leaves are called "folios." When the sheet was folded twice, making four leaves (eight pages), the result is called a "quarto." When the sheet was folded four times, making eight leaves or sixteen pages, the result is an "octavo." To assemble a book, small groups of pages were sewn together using the signature, a sequential letter and number at the bottom of the page, to keep them in order. Most plays—and all of Shakespeare's plays prior to the First Folio of 1623—were published in quarto, which measured about 9 x 7 inches.

Shakespeare's First Publication

A precise chronology of Shakespeare's plays and poems is impossible to determine. No manuscripts of the plays or poems have been discovered, and the surviving records show when a play was performed, and when the plays and poems were published, not when they were written.

Printer Richard Field, who registered Venus and Adonis *as well as* The Rape of Lucrece *the next year with the Stationers' Company, produced texts that are remarkably free from errors. Shakespeare is supposed to have fully participated in the publication of these poems, presumably not only furnishing fair copies for the printer but also proofreading the texts. Like Shakespeare, Field was from Stratford-upon-Avon.*

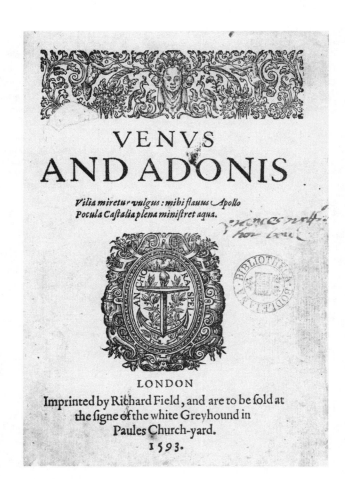

Title page for the first of Shakespeare's poems to be published; the printer, Richard Field, was also from Stratford. The Latin epigraph is from Book 15 of Ovid's Amores; *Christopher Marlowe translated the lines as "Let base conceipted witts admire vile things / Fair Phoebus lead me to the Muses springs" (courtesy of the Bodleian Library, Oxford).*

The Stationers' Company

The Stationers' Company, a trade guild for printers, publishers, booksellers, book binders, and others involved in the business of publishing, was formed by royal charter in 1557. Like most guilds, it regulated, promoted, and protected the business of its members, supervised apprentices, and settled disputes. Publication and printing was a particularly lucrative trade in the early modern period when the demand for books, pamphlets, and broadsides increased steadily, but the potential danger of using printed materials to spread seditious or treasonous ideas meant printing needed careful regulation.

A publisher who agreed to produce and distribute an author's work usually paid the author—the going rate for a play was about 40 shillings—then took the manuscript to the Stationers' Hall, where it would be inspected by an official called a warden to make sure that another member of the company had not been licensed to publish it. The publisher paid a fee—sixpence to register the work and another four pence to have the registration recorded—and was then licensed to publish the text; subsequent editions of a work did not need to be relicensed. The Stationers' Registers, the books in which the entries and fees were recorded, have survived, and it is through their entries that we know when some of Shakespeare's plays were written. Many works were printed without being registered, but Stationers' Company members who did so and were caught faced substantial fines. Some works were entered by one publisher to prevent them from being produced by another; these "blocking entries" were of particular use to acting companies who wanted to protect their plays.

Not all members of the Stationers' Company were scrupulous businesspeople. In his chapter "The Publication of Shakespeare's Plays" in Shakespeare, In Fact *(1994), Irvin Matus notes "How a stationer came by the work he was entering, whether or not his copy was corrupt, whether or not the author wished it to be published, had been compensated for it, or could in any way be damaged by its publication, were not questions asked by the wardens of the company when licensing a work" (85). This carelessness helps explain why the texts of Shakespeare's plays published during his lifetime are so full of errors; the friends who later published Shakespeare's collected works, John Heminges and Henry Condell, describe these early texts as "stolne, and surreptitious copies, maimed, and deformed by the frauds and stealthes of injurious impostors, that expos'd them." Some of the texts, such as the first quarto of* The Merry Wives of Windsor *(1602), seem to have been reported from memory by actors who played minor parts in them. Even the plays for which a legitimate manuscript was provided, such as the second quarto of* Hamlet *(1604/1605), do not seem to have been proofread by Shakespeare. The only texts with which he seems to have taken some care are the poems* Venus and Adonis *(1593) and* The Rape of Lucrece *(1594), both printed by Richard Field, formerly of Stratford-upon-Avon.*

Portrait of Shakespeare's patron Henry Wriothesley, the Earl of Southampton, by John de Critz (by kind permission of his Grace the Duke of Buccleuch and Queensberry, K. T., from his collection at Boughton House)

                   xviii° Aprilis [1593]
Richard ffield Entred for his copie under th[e h]and o
the Archbisshop of Canterbury and master warden Stirrop, a booke intituled / Venus and Adonis   vi^s

This entry has a note written in the margin: "Assigned over to master Harrison senior 25 Junii1594/"
          —*Stationers' Registers,* vol. II, folio 297b

The Dedication of *Venus and Adonis* to the Earl of Southampton

Shakespeare dedicated Venus and Adonis *and* The Rape of Lucrece *to Henry Wriothesley, the third Earl of Southampton (1573–1624), a patron of writers including Barnabe Barnes, Thomas Nashe, and Gervase Markham. Southampton is sometimes proposed as the young man to whom most of Shakespeare's sonnets are addressed. Poets dedicated their works to patrons in the hope of receiving a gratuity and new commissions. Shakespeare's address to Southampton is suitably formal, humble, and complimentary; its success may be gauged by the much warmer dedication to Southampton in Shakespeare's next published poem,* The Rape of Lucrece.

TO THE RIGHT HONORABLE
Henrie Wriothesley, Earle of Southampton,
and Baron of Titchfield.

Right Honourable, I know not how I shall offend in dedicating my unpolisht lines to your Lordship, nor how the worlde will censure mee for choosing so strong a proppe to support so weake a burthen, onelye if your Honour seeme but pleased, I account my selfe highly praised, and vowe to take advantage of all idle houres, till I have honoured you with some graver labour. But if the first heire of my invention prove deformed, I shall be sorie it had so noble a god-father: and never after eare so barren a land, for feare it yeeld me still so bad a harvest, I leave it to your Honourable survey, and your Honor to your hearts content, which I wish may alwaies answere your owne wish, and the worlds hopefull expectation.

Your Honors in all dutie,
William Shakespeare.

Stonley Buys a Copy of *Venus and Adonis*

Richard Stonley recorded his purchase of Venus and Adonis *in the 12 June 1593 entry in his Diary Account Book (Folger Shakespeare Library MS V.a.460, fol. 9). In* William Shakespeare: A Documentary Life, *Samuel Schoenbaum notes that "Stonley has the minor distinction of being the first recorded purchaser of Shakespeare's first publication" (p. 130).*

Books　for the Survey of ffraunce wᵗʰ
　　　the Venus & Adhonay pʳ } xiiᵈ
　　　Shakspere

Reynolds Interprets *Venus and Adonis*

William Reynolds, a skilled soldier who displayed signs of severe mental illness, wrote long, rambling letters to Queen Elizabeth and the Privy Council. In the following excerpt from his 21 September 1593 letter to "wellbeloved cuntrymen, and people of this honourable Cittie [London]" (British Library, Lansdowne Manuscript 99), he comments on Shakespeare's poem. This excerpt was transcribed by Katherine Duncan-Jones in her 1993 article "Much Ado with Red and White: The Earliest Readers of Shakespeare's Venus and Adonis *(1593)."*

Also within thees few dayes ther is another boke made of Venus and Adonis wherin the queene represents the person of Venus, which queene is in great loue (forsoth) with adonis, and greatly desiares to kise him, and she woes him most intierly, teling him allthough she be oulde, yet she is lustie freshe & moyst, full of love & life (I beleve a goodell more then a bushell full) and she can trip it as lightly as a phery nimphe upon the sandes and her foote stepes not seene, and much ado with redde & whyte, But adonis regardid her not, wherfore she condemnes him for unkindnesse...
—*Review of English Studies*, 44 (November 1993): 479–501

1594

Henslowe Records Performances of *Titus Andronicus* and Other Plays

Henslowe recorded entries for a play called Titus Andronicus, *which may be Shakespeare's play, in early 1594.*

ne—Rd at titus & ondronicus the 23 of Jeneway. . . . iiiˡⁱ viii s

. . . .

Rd at titus & ondronicous the 28 of Jenewary. . . . . . xxxxˢ
—*Henslowe's Diary*, p. 21

Henslowe noted the monies—or his share of the monies—collected in June of 1594. As the following list of plays Henslowe's company performed in that month shows, the actors needed good memories as well as a steady supply of new plays. The Hamlet *performed on 9 June is unlikely to be Shakespeare's;* Andronicus *and* Taming of a Shrew *may be Shakespeare's plays or may be plays that shared a common source with, or were a source for, Shakespeare's plays.*

In the name of god Amen begininge at newing ton my Lord Admeralle men & my Lorde chamberlen men As ffolowethe 1594

¶ 3 of June 1594　Rd at heaster & asheweros . . . . viii s
¶ 4 of June 1594　Rd at the Jewe of malta . . . . x s
¶ 5 of June 1594　Rd at andronicous . . . . xii s
¶ 6 of June 1594　Rd at cutlacke . . . . xi s
¶ 8 of June 1594　ne—Rd at bellendon. . x. . . . . . xvii s
¶ 9 of June 1594　Rd at hamlet . . . . viii s
¶ 10 of June 1594　Rd at heaster . . . . v s
¶ 11 of June 1594　Rd at the tamynge of A shrowe . ix s
¶ 12 of June 1594　Rd at andronicous . . . . vii s
¶ 13 of June 1594　Rd at the Jewe . . . . .iiii s
¶ 15 of June 1594　Rd at bellendon . . . . iiiˡⁱ iiii s
¶ 17 of June 1594　Rd at cutlacke. . . . . xxxv s
¶ 18 of June 1594　Rd at the Rangers comodey. . . xxii s
¶ 19 of June 1594　Rd at the Gwies . . . . liiii s
¶ 20 of June 1594　Rd at bellendon . . . . xxxˢ
¶ 22 of June 1594　––Rd at the Rangers comodey . . lviiii s
¶ 23 of June 1594　Rd at the Jewe . . . . xxiii s
¶ 24 of June 1594　Rd at cutlacke . . . . xxvˢ
¶ 25 of June 1594　Rd at the masacer. . . . . xxxvi s
¶ 26 of June 1594　ne—Rd at galiaso. . . . . iiiˡⁱ iiii s
¶ 27 of June 1594　Rd at cuttlacke . . . . xxxvi s
¶ 30 of June 1594––Rd at the Jewe of malta. . . . . . xxxxis
—*Henslowe's Diary*, pp. 21–22

Stationers' Register Entries

Titus Andronicus is the first of Shakespeare's plays known to have appeared in print. The First Part of the Contention is generally accepted as a memorial reconstruction of Shakespeare's 2 Henry VI, meaning that the text, published by the notorious pirate John Dantler, was re-created by actors or auditors and is unlikely to have been authorized for publication by the author or his acting company. The entry for Taming of a Shrew refers to a play about which scholars are divided: it has been identified as a memorial reconstruction of Shakespeare's play, a play Shakespeare wrote and then later revised, Shakespeare's source for his play, and a play by another author who used the same source Shakespeare did. In these transcribed entries from the Stationers' Register (Stationer's Hall, Register B, folios 304v, 305v, 306v), abbreviated words have been silently expanded.

vi° die ffebruarii./.

John Danter./. Entred for his Copye under thandes of bothe the wardens a booke intituled a*n* . . . Rom [deleted] Noble Roman Historye of Tytus *&* [deleted] Andronicus   vi^d

John Danter./. Entred alsoe unto him by warraunt from Mr Woodcock the ballad thereof   vi^d

. . . .

xii° marcii

Thomas Myllington/ Entred for his copie under the handes of bothe the wardens / a booke intituled, the firste parte of the Contention of the twoo famous houses of york and Lancaster with the deathe of the good Duke Humfrey and the banishement and deathe of the duke of Suffolk and the tragicall ende of the prowd Cardinall of winchester / with the notable rebellion of Jack Cade and the duke of yorkes firste clayme unto the Crowne   vi^d

Secundo die maii

Peter Shorte/ Entred unto him for his copie under m^r warden Cawoodes hande/ a booke intituled A plesant Conceyted historie called the Tayminge of a Shrowe   vi^d
— *Bibliography of the English Printed Drama*, p. 10

9 maii [1594]

Master Harrison   Entred for his copie uner th[e h]and
                        of master
Senior   Cawood Warden, a booke intituled
                        the Ravyshement of
                        Lucrece   vi^d C
                  —*Stationers' Registers*, folio 306b

25 Junii [1594]

Master Harrison Assigned over to him from Richard ffield in open Court holden this Day
Senior   a book called Venus and Adonis   vi^d
The which was before entred to Richard ffield. 18. aprilis /1593/

                  —*Stationers' Registers*, folio 310a

Publications

Editions of four Shakespearean works published in 1954 survive. His two poems The Rape of Lucrece *and* Venus and Adonis *were published by Richard Field, the former for the first time and the latter for the second. As the title pages show, Shakespeare was not named as the author of these works.*

VENVS / AND ADONIS / *Vilia miretur vulgus: mihi flavus Apollo / Pocula Castalia plena ministret aqua.* / [*Publisher's device*] / LONDON. / Imprinted by Richard Field, and are to be ſold / at the ſigne of the white Greyhound / in Paules Church-yard. / 1594.

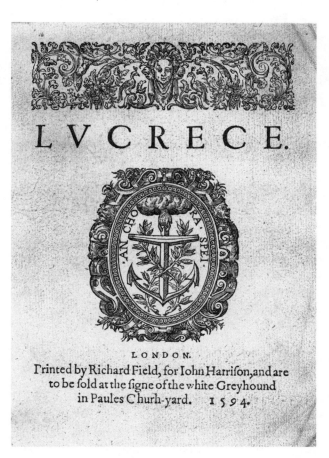

Title page for the first quarto of Shakespeare's poem recounting the rape and suicide of the Roman matron Lucrece; the work is better known as The Rape of Lucrece *(by permission of the Folger Shakespeare Library)*

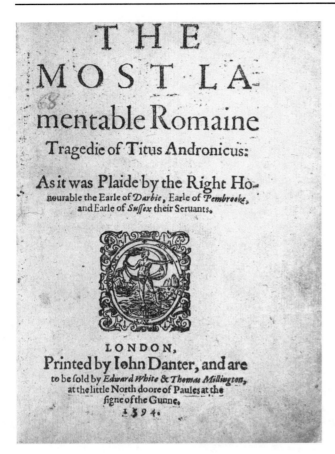

Title page for the quarto of Titus Andronicus, *the first known edition of any of Shakespeare's plays (by permission of the Folger Shakespeare Library)*

Title page for the play that is probably a memorial reconstruction of Shakespeare's 2 Henry VI, *though scholars also have argued that it is a first draft, a source text, or a touring version of the play (by permission of the Folger Shakespeare Library)*

The Dedication of *The Rape of Lucrece* to the Earl of Southampton

Shakespeare's second long poem, Lucrece, *or, as it is more widely known,* The Rape of Lucrece, *is probably the "graver labour" Shakespeare promised to Southampton in his dedication to* Venus *and* Adonis. *The tone of the dedication to Southampton here is warmer and more personal than that of* Venus and Adonis; *this implies Southampton was pleased with the first poem and rewarded the poet accordingly.*

TO THE RIGHT
HONOURABLE, HENRY
Wriothesley, Earle of Southhampton,
and Baron of Titchfield.

The love I dedicate to your Lordship is without end: wherof this Pamphlet without beginning is but a superfluous Moity. The warrant I have of your Honourable disposition, not the worth of my untutord Lines makes it assured of acceptance. What I have done is yours, what I have to doe is yours, being part in all I have, devoted yours. Were my worth greater, my duety would shew greater, meane time, as it is, it is bound to your Lordship; To whom I wish long life still lengthned with all happinesse.

Your Lordships in all duety.
William Shakespeare.

–sig. A2r

Shakespeare's Company Paid for a Court Performance

Shakespeare and his fellow actors, identified as the Lord Chamberlain's Men, are paid for performances at court during the 1594 Christmas season. "March 1594" is in Old Style dating in which the new year began on the feast of the Annunciation, 25 March. At the time the Lord Chamberlain was Henry Carey, Baron Hunsden. As Lord Chamberlain, his responsibilities included arranging for the Queen's entertainment.

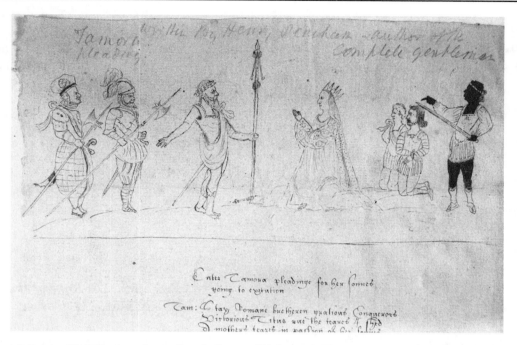

Drawing attributed to Henry Peacham of events from the first act of Shakespeare's Titus Andronicus *(Longleat Portland Papers I fol. 159v; courtesy of the Marquess of Bath, Longleat House, Warminster, Wiltshire, Great Britain)*

To Will^am Kempe Will^am Shakespeare & Richarde Burbage servauntes to the Lord Chamberleyne upon the Conncells warr^t dated at Whitehall xv^to Martii 1594 for twoe severall Comedies or Enterludes shewed by them before her ma^tie in xpmas tyme laste paste vizt upon St Stephens daye & Innocents daye xiii^l vi^s viii^d and by waye of her ma^tes Rewarde vi^l xiii^s iiii^d in all xx^li
—Exchequer records, Public Record Office Pipe Office, Declared Accounts, E. 351/542, fol. 107v.

Probable Allusion to *Titus Andronicus* in *A Knacke to know a Knave*

The anonymous play A most pleasant and merie new Comedie, Intituled, A Knacke to knowe a Knave *(1594) includes a probable reference to act 1 scene 1 of Shakespeare's* Titus Andronicus, *perhaps more as an advertisement than an allusion.*

Enter the King, Dunston, and Perin to Ethenwald.
[*King:*] Earle *Osricke*, you must needs hold us excused,
Though boldly thus unbid we visite you:
But knowe the cause that mooved us leave our Court,
Was to doe honour to Earle *Ethenwald*:
And see his lovelie Bride, faire *Alfrida*.

[*Osrick:*] My gratious Lord, as welcome shall you be,
To me, my Daughter, and my sonne in Law,
As *Titus* was unto the Roman Senators,

Title page for a pamphlet inspired by extreme weather. Because many plays were performed in open-air theaters, weather was of particular concern to Elizabethan playwrights (by permission of the Folger Shakespeare Library).

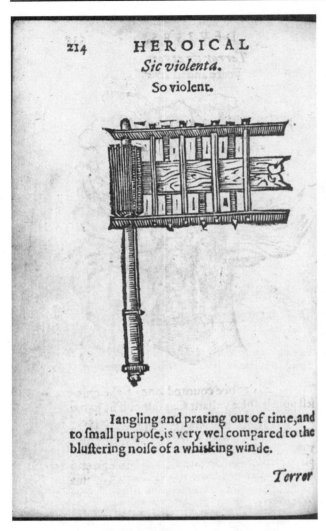

Page from Claude Paradin's Herociall Devises *(1591) showing a wind machine. A similar device may have been used to provide sound effects for stage storms (by permission of the Folger Shakespeare Library).*

When he had made a conquest on the Goths:
That in requitall of his service done,
Did offer him the imperiall Diademe:
As they in *Titus*, we in your Grace still fynd,
The perfect figure of a Princelie mind.

—sig. F2v

Possible Allusion to *The Rape of Lucrece* in Drayton's *Matilda*

In this stanza from Michael Drayton's Matilda. The faire and chaste Daughter of the Lord Robert Fitzwater *(London: Printed by James Roberts, for N. L. and John Busby, 1594), Matilda is complaining that, although the stories of other notable women can be seen and read in London, her story has been ignored. In* William Shakespeare *E. K. Chambers says of this stanza "It does not seem to me clear that the reference is to* Lucrece. *The wording suggests a play" (vol. II, p. 192).*

Lucrece, of whom proude Rome hath boasted long,
Lately reviv'd to live another age,
And here ariv'd to tell of *Tarquins* wrong.
Her chast deniall, and the Tyrants rage,
Acting her passions on our stately stage.
She is remembred, all forgetting me,
Yet I as fayre and chast, as ere was she.

—sig. B2r

Allusion to *The Rape of Lucrece* in Har.'s *Epicedium*

In Epicedium. A Funerall Song, upon the vertuous life, and godly death, of the right worshipfull the Lady Helen Branch *(London: Printed by Thomas Creede, 1594), the author, identified only as W. Har., enjoins his fellow poets to turn their attention to contemporary, rather than classical, models of female virtue; his reference to* Lucretia *is probably an allusion to Shakespeare's* The Rape of Lucrece.

You that to shew your wits have taken toyle,
In registring the deeds of noble men:
And sought for matter in a forraine soyle,
(As worthie subjects of your silver pen)
Whom you have rais'd from darke oblivions den.
You that have writ of chaste *Lucretia,*
Whose death was witnesse of her spotlesse life:
Or pend the praise of sad *Cornelia,*
Whose blamelesse name hath made her fame so rife:
As noble *Pompeys* most renoumed wife.
Hither unto your home direct your eies:
Whereas unthought on, much more matter lies.

Matter that well deserves your golden stile,
And substance that will fit your shadowes right,
Whereon his wits a Scholler well may file:
Whereof a Poet needs not blush to write,
When strangers causes should be banisht quite.
And this bright Comet, of whose splendant raies,
My too-unworthie pen shall give a sight,
A Ladie was of whose deserved praise
A farre more learned Artist ought to write:
Lesse wits should speake of starres of lesser light.
Yet since their waies, by her light many finde,
I (mongst the rest) may shew my thankfull minde.

—sig. A2r

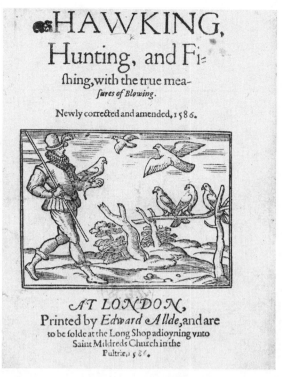

Title page for a book on popular pastimes. In The Rape of Lucrece, *Lucretia is likened to a fowl hearing "falcon's bells" in the voice of her attacker (shelfmark C.31.b.4; courtesy of The British Library, London).*

Allusion to W. S. and *The Rape of Lucrece* in *Willobie His Avisa*

Willobie His Avisa. The true Picture of a modest Maid, and of a chast and constant wife *(1594) is a series of poems, with prose bridges, describing efforts to court a much-desired lady, Avisa. In a prefatory epistle, a man named Hadrian Dorrell, otherwise unidentified, tells the reader he found the manuscript among the papers of his friend Henry Willobie, probably the Henry Willobie who took a degree from Oxford in 1595. Dorrell claims Willobie is the author of the poems that follow and assures the readers that, although Willobie has disguised the names of the persons, he is writing about actual events: "me thinks it a matter almost impossible that any man could invent all this without some ground or foundation to build on . . . though the matter be handled poetically, yet there is some thing under these fained names and showes that hath bene done truely. Now judge you, for I can give no sentence in that I know not."*

Willobie's own courtship of Avisa is the subject of Canto 44; in its prose preface, Willobie describes his "familiar" friend W. S., an "old player" who is himself recovering from a failed courtship. Willobie and W. S. then trade laments and advice about courtship. If Willobie's friend is William Shakespeare, the unsuccessful courtship ascribed to W. S. may be the one described in Shakespeare's sonnets. An additional reason to suspect Willobie's W. S. is Shakespeare is the anonymous prefatory poem comparing Willobie's poetic efforts to The Rape of Lucrece, *and naming Shakespeare.*

> But she hath lost a dearer thing than life,
> And he hath won what he would lose again;
> This forced league doth force a further strife,
> This momentary joy breeds months of pain,
> This hot desire converts to cold disdain;
>   Pure Chastity is rifled of her store,
>   And Lust, the thief, far poorer than before.
>
> —*The Rape of Lucrece, 687–693*

In praise of Willobie *his* Avisa, *Hex-ameton to the Author.*

In Lavine Land though Livie bost,
There hath beene seene a Constant *dame:*
Though Rome *lament that she have lost*
The Gareland *of her rarest fame,*
    Yet now we see, that here is found,
    As great a Faith *in* English *ground.*

Though Collatine *have deerely bought,*
To high renowne, a lasting life,
And found, that most in vaine have sought,
To have a Faire, *and* Constant *wife,*
    Yet Tarquyne *pluckt his glistering grape,*
    And Shake-speare, *paints poore* Lucrece *rape.*

Though Susan *shine in faithfull praise,*
As twinckling Starres in Christall skie,
Penelop's *fame though* Greekes *do raise,*
Of faithfull wives to make up three,
    To thinke the Truth, *and say no lesse,*
    Our Avisa *shall make a messe.*

This number knits so sure a knot,
Time *doubtes, that she shall adde no more,*
Unconstant Nature, *hath begot,*
Of Fleting Feemes, *such fickle store,*
    Two thousand yeares, have scarcely seene,
    Such as the worst of these have beene.

Then Avi-Susan *joyne in one,*
Let Lucres-Avis *be thy name,*
This English Eagle *sores alone,*
    And farre surmounts all others fame,
    Where high or low, where great or small,
    This Brytan Bird *out-flies them all.*

Were these three happie, that have found,
Brave Poets *to depaint their praise?*
Of Rurall Pipe, *with sweetest sound,*
That have beene heard these many daies,
Sweete wylloby his AVIS blest,
That makes her mount above the rest.

Contraria Contrariis:
    Vigilantius: Dormitanus.

—sigs.A4r-v

. . . .

On Printing Plays

In his epistle to the readers of Christopher Marlowe's tragedy Tamburlaine the Great *(1590), the play's publisher, Richard Jones, points out that stage directions are considered inelegant and obtrusive, and so he has omitted many of them. An alternative explanation is that detailed stage directions would allow touring companies of actors (or imaginative readers) to replicate a London performance, thus hurting business. Whether the reason is aesthetic or commercial, stage directions for most printed plays from this period are minimal at best.*

To the Gentlemen Readers:
and others that take pleasure
in reading Histories.

Gentlemen, and curteous Readers whosoever: I have here published in print for your sakes, the two tragical Discourses of the Scythian Shepheard, *Tamburlaine*, that became so great a Conquerour, and so mightie a Monarque: My hope is, that they wil be now no lesse acceptable unto you to read after your serious affaires and studies, then they have bene (lately) delightfull for many of you to see, when the same were shewed in London upon stages: I have (purposely) omitted and left out some fond and frivolous Jestures, digressing (and in my poore opinion) far unmeet for the matter, which I thought, might seeme more tedious unto the wise, than any way els to be regarded, though (happly) they have bene of some vaine conceited fondlings greatly gaped at, what times they were shewed upon the stage in their graced deformities: nevertheles now, to be mixtured in print with such matter of worth, it wuld proove a great disgrace to so honorable & stately a historie: Great folly were it in me, to commend unto your wisedomes, either the eloquence of the Authour that writ them, or the worthinesse of the matter it selfe; I therefore leave unto your learned censures, both the one and the other, and my selfe the poore printer of them unto your most curteous and favourable protection; which if you vouchsafe to accept, you shall ever more binde mee to imploy what travell and service I can, to the advauncing and pleasuring of your excellent degree.

Yours, most humble at commaundement,
R. I. Printer
–Sigs. A2r–A3r

Images of *W*riting and *P*rinting

Frontispiece for John Partridge's The Treasurie of Commodius Conceits *(1573; by permission of The Huntington Library, San Marino, California)*

Illustration from Janos Zsamboki's Emblemata, et aliquot
nummi antiqui operis *(1599; courtesy of Special
Collections, Howard-Tilton Library, Tulane
University, New Orleans, Louisiana)*

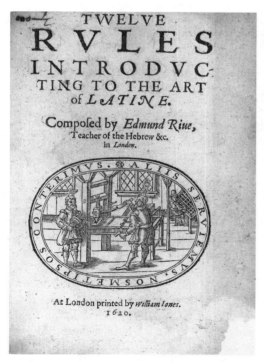

*Title page showing early printers at work (by permission
of the Folger Shakespeare Library)*

Page from Stephen Bateman's The Doome warning all men to the
Judgement *(1581; by permission of the Folger Shakespeare Library)*

The Reliability of Shakespeare's Texts

No manuscripts survive for Shakespeare's published plays; in their absence, Shakespeare's editors depend on printed texts. Just under half of Shakespeare's plays, both of his long poems, and his sonnets were published in his lifetime; the remainder of his plays were published seven years after his death in the 1623 First Folio. The first editions of these plays were printed from one or a combination of sources: foul papers—the author's handwritten copy of a play; a fair copy—a legible copy prepared by the author or a professional scrivener; or a theatrical prompt-book—manuscripts prepared for use in the playhouse, and thus marked with cues for entrances, props, and sound effects. Later editions were sometimes printed from earlier ones, with or without corrections. Some of the quarto editions of Shakespeare's plays came from a less legitimate source: they appear to be memorial reconstructions by actors who played minor roles in the plays; other contemporary authors complained that their plays were recorded by stenographers in the audience, who then sold the stolen copy to a publisher.

No matter how a printer acquired a manuscript, he or she transformed it into type one letter at a time. This work was not often appreciated by authors: prefaces to many Elizabethan and Jacobean works are filled with complaints about careless printing, including Thomas Nashe's declaration in The Unfortunate Traveler *(1594) that "Printers are mad whoresons." Errors abound in early modern printed texts, just as they do in modern ones. The compositor, in picking up each piece of type to form words, might choose a wrong letter, misread or misspell a word, skip a line, or run out of space. Sometimes the type was improperly inked or the paper was of poor quality; sometimes the press continued running while the proofreader worked, with the result that some copies of an edition have corrections that others lack; sometimes the author made a mistake or wrote illegibly. Without Shakespeare's manuscripts, editors cannot always determine who is responsible for errors in the text or what the correct word or phrase might be.*

The work habits of early modern printers have been studied carefully, as have handwriting, spelling, and grammatical conventions of the period. Such examination helps editors of Shakespeare in their efforts to produce as accurate a text as possible. But it is impossible to determine exactly what Shakespeare wrote. The problem of editing Shakespeare is particularly difficult when there are great differences between the quarto text or texts and the First Folio. Hamlet, *for example, exists in three versions: the First Quarto, published in 1603, which may be a memorial reconstruction, a touring version, an early draft, or some combination of the three; the Second Quarto, published in 1604 and 1605, whose title page promises the play has been "enlargd to almost as much againe as it was, according to the true and perfect copie"; and the First Folio version, shorter than the Second Quarto, but with new material and many variant readings, a possible indication that the text was revised, although not necessarily by Shakespeare. Editors must make difficult choices when preparing an edition of* Hamlet, *and standards of what makes a text accurate change over time. Most modern editors explain their decisions in a note on the text.*

The problem of the reliability of the text of Shakespeare's plays is compounded by the low regard in which plays were held in the contemporary period. Plays, like other works whose primary purpose was entertainment, were thought of as cheap, disposable, lightweight reading and were printed with far less care than was devoted to printing Bibles or royal proclamations. Shakespeare seems to have taken little interest in the publication of his plays. Thomas Nashe, in The Unfortunate Traveler, *recommends using the pages of that comic narrative as "a privy token"—toilet paper. Thomas Bodley, in a 1612 letter to his friend Thomas James, insisted that plays be left out of the collection that would evolve into Oxford's Bodleian Library: "Were it so againe, that some litle profit might be reaped (which God knowes is very litle) out of some of our playbookes, the benefit therof will nothing neere contervaile, the harme that the scandal will bring unto the Librarie, when it shalbe given out, that we stuffe it full of baggage bookes. And though they should be but a fewe, as they would be very many, if your course should take place, yet the having of those fewe (suche is the nature of malicious reporters) would be mightily multiplied by suche as purpose to speake in disgrace of the Librarie" (Letters of Sir Thomas Bodley to Thomas James First Keeper of the Bodleian Library [1926], edited by G. W. Wheeler, pp. 221–222).*

CANT. XLIIII.
Henrico Willobego. Italo-Hispalensis.

H. W. being sodenly infected with the contagion of a fantasticall fit, at the first sight of *A,* pyneth a while in secret griefe, at length not able any longer to indure the burning heate of so fervent a humour, bewrayeth the secresy of his disease unto his familiar frend W. S. who not long before had tryed the curtesy of the like passion, and was now newly recovered of the like infection; yet finding his frend let bloud in the same vaine, he took pleasure for a tyme to see him bleed, & in steed of stopping the issue, he inlargeth the wound, with the sharpe rasor of a willing conceit, perswading him that he thought it a matter very easy to be compassed, & no doubt with payne, diligence & some cost in time to be obtayned. Thus this miserable comforter comforting his frend with an impossibilitie, eyther for that he now would secretly laugh at his frends folly, that had given occasion not long before unto others to laugh at his owne, or because he would see whether an other could play his part better then himselfe, & in vewing a far off the course of this loving Comedy, he determined to see whether it would sort to a happier end for this new actor, then it did for the old player. But at length this Comedy was like to have growen to a Tragedy, by the weake & feeble estate that H. W. was brought unto, by a desperate vewe of an impossibility of obtaining his purpose, til Time & Necessity, being his best Phisitions brought him a plaster, if not to heale, yet in part to ease his maladye. In all which discourse is lively represented the unrewly rage of unbrydeled fancy, having the raines to rove at liberty, with the dyvers & sundry changes of affections & temptations, which Will, set loose from Reason, can devise. &c.

H. W.

What sodaine chance or change is this,
That doth bereave my quyet rest?
What surly cloud eclipst my blisse,
What sprite doth rage within my brest?
 Such fainty qualmes I never found,
 Till first I saw this westerne ground.

Can change of ayre complexions change,
And strike the sences out of frame?
Though this be true, yet this is strange,
Sith I so lately hither came:
 And yet in body cannot find
 So great a change as in my mynd.

My lustlesse limmes do pyne away,
Because my hart is dead within,
All lively heat I feele decay,
And deadly cold his roome doth win,
 My humors all are out of frame,
 I frize amid'st the burning flame.

I have the feaver Ethicke right,
I burne within, consume without,
And having melted all my might,
Then followes death, without all doubt:
 O fearefull foole, that know my greefe,
 Yet sew and seeke for no releefe.

I know the tyme, I know the place,
Both when and where my eye did vew
That novell shape, that frendly face,
That so doth make my hart to rew,
 O happy tyme if she inclyne,
 If not, O wourth theese lucklesse eyne.

I love the seat where she did sit,
I kisse the grasse, where she did tread,
Me thinkes I see that face as yet,
And eye, that all these turmoyles breed,
 I envie that this seat, this ground,
 Such frendly grace and favour found.

I dream't of late, God grant that dreame
Protend my good, that she did meete
Me in this greene by yonder streame,
And smyling did me frendly greete:
 Where wandring dreames be just or wrong,
 I mind to try ere it be long.

But yonder comes my faythfull frend,
That like assaultes hath often tryde,
On his advise I will depend,
Where I shall winne, or be denyde,
 And looke what counsell he shall give,
 That will I do, where dye or live.

CANT. XLV.
W. S.

Well met, frend Harry, what's the cause
You looke so pale with Lented cheeks?
Your wanny face & sharpened nose
Shew plaine, your mind some thing mislikes,
 If you will tell me what it is,
 Ile help to mend what is amisse.

What is she, man, that workes thy woe,
And thus thy tickling fancy move?
Thy drousie eyes, & sighes do shoe,
This new disease proceedes of love,
 Tell what she is that witch't thee so,
 I sweare it shall no farder go.

A heavy burden wearieth one,
Which being parted then in twaine,
Seemes very light, or rather none,
And boren well with little paine:
 The smothered flame, too closely pent,
 Burnes more extreame for want of vent.

So sorrowes shrynde in secret brest,
Attainte the hart with hotter rage,
Then griefes that are to frendes exprest,
Whose comfort may some part asswage:
 If I a frend, whose faith is tryde,
 Let this request not be denyde.

Excessive griefes good counsells want,
And cloud the sence from sharpe conceits;
No reason rules, where sorrowes plant,
And folly feedes, where fury fretes,
 Tell what she is, and you shall see,
 What hope and help shall come from mee.

CANT. XLVI.
H. W.

Seest yonder howse, where hanges the badge
Of Englands Saint, when captaines cry
Victorious land, to conquering rage,
Loe, there my hopelesse helpe doth ly:
 And there that frendly foe doth dwell,
 That makes my hart thus rage and swell.

CANT. XLVII.
W. S.

Well, say no more: I know thy griefe,
And face from whence these flames aryse,
It is not hard to fynd reliefe,
If thou wilt follow good advyse:
    She is no Saynt, She is no Nonne,
    I thinke in tyme she may be wonne.

At first repulse you must not faint,
Nor flye the field though she deny
You twise or thrise, yet manly bent,
Againe you must, and still reply:
    When tyme permits you not to talke,
    Then let your pen and fingers walke.
[*Marginal note to lines 1–2: "Ars veteratoia"*]

Apply her still with dyvers thinges,
(For giftes the wysest will deceave)
Sometymes with gold, sometymes with ringes,
No tyme nor fit occasion leave,
    Though coy at first she seeme and wielde,
    These toyes in tyme will make her yielde.
[*Marginal note to lines 2–4: "Muneris (crede mihi) pl.tant homi-nesq; Deosq"*]

Looke what she likes; that you must love,
And what she hates, you must detest,
Where good or bad, you must approve,
The wordes and workes that please her best:
    If she be godly, you must sweare,
    That to offend you stand in feare.

You must commend her loving face,
For women joy in beauties praise,
You must admire her sober grace,
Her wisdome and her vertuous wayes,
    Say, t'was her wit & modest shoe,
    That made you like and love her so.
[*Marginal note to lines 1–4: "Wicked wiles to deceave witles women."*]

You must be secret, constant, free,
Your silent sighes & trickling teares,
Let her in secret often see,
Then wring her hand, as one that feares
    To speake, then wish she were your wife,
    And last desire her save your life.

When she doth laugh, you must be glad,
And watch occasions, tyme and place,
When she doth frowne, you must be sad,
Let sighes & sobbes request her grace:
    Sweare that your love is truly ment,
    So she in tyme must needes relent.

CANT. XLVIII.
H. W.

The whole to sicke good counsell give,
Which they themselves cannot performe,
Your wordes do promise sweet reliefe,
To save my ship from drowning storme:
    But hope is past, and health is spent,
    For why my mynd is *Mal-content*.

                –pp. 40–44

Account of an Attempted Performance of *The Comedy of Errors* in *Gesta Grayorum*

Gesta Grayorum: Or The HISTORY Of the High and mighty PRINCE, HENRY *(1688) is an anonymous account of the holiday revels at Gray's Inn, one of the London Inns of Court, where lawyers and law students lived, worked, and studied. The account includes a reference to Shakespeare's* The Comedy of Errors. *A company of actors attempted to perform it but were thwarted by their unruly audience. The account provides details about the misrule that prevailed during the twelve days of Christmas, a period during which plays were often performed for the royal court. The injunction from the Lord of Misrule that follows the description of the revels shows the close link between the Inns of Court and the public theaters.*

Henry *Prince of* Purpoole, *Arch-Duke of* Stapulia *and* Bernardia, *Duke of* High *and* Nether Holborn, *Marquis of* St. *Giles's and* Tottenham, *Count Palatine of* Bloomsbury *and* Clerkenwell, *Great Lord of the Canton of* Islington, Kentish-Town, Paddington *and* Knightsbridge, *Knight of the most Heroical Order of the* Helmet, *and Sovereign of the same, To all, and all manner of Persons to whom these Presents shall appertain;* Greeting.

                –p. 14

. . . .

The next grand Night was intended to be upon *Innocents-Day* at Night; at which time there was a great Presence of Lords, Ladies, and worshipful Personages, that did expect some notable Performance at that time; which, indeed, had been effected, if the multitude of Beholders had not been so exceeding great, that thereby there was no convenient room for those that were Actors; by reason whereof, very good Inventions and Conceipts could not have opportunity to be applauded, which otherwise would have been great Contentation to the Beholders. Against which time, our Friend, the *Inner Temple*, determined to send their Ambassador to our Prince of State, as sent from *Frederick Templarius*, their Emperor, who was then busied in his Wars against the

Turk. The Ambassador came very gallantly appointed, and attended by a great number of brave Gentlemen, which arrived at our Court about Nine of the Clock at Night. Upon their coming thither, the King at Arms gave notice to the Prince, then sitting in his Chair of State in the Hall, that there was come to his Court an Ambassador from his ancient Friend the State of *Templaria*, which desired to have present Access unto His Highness; and shewed his Honour further, that he seemed to be of very good sort, because he was so well attended; and therefore desired that it would please His Honour that some of his Nobles and Lords might conduct him to His Highness's Presence; which was done. So he was brought in very solemnly, with Sound of Trumpets, the King at Arms and Lords of *Purpoole* making to his Company, which marched before him in order. He was received very kindly of the Prince, and placed in a Chair besides His Highness, to the end that he might be Partaker of the Sports intended. But first, he made a Speech to the Prince, wherein he declared how his excellent Renown and Fame was known throughout all the whole World; and that the Report of his Greatness was not contained within the Bounds of the Ocean, but had come to the Ears of his noble Sovereign, *Frederick Templarius*, where he is now warring against the *Turks*, the known Enemies to all *Christendom*; who having heard that His Excellency kept his Court at *Graya* this *Christmas*, thought it to stand with his ancient League of Amity and near Kindness, that so long hath been continued and increased by their noble Ancestors of famous Memory and Desert, to gratulate his Happiness, and flourishing Estate; and in that regard, had sent him his Ambassador, to be residing at His Excellency's Court, in honour of his Greatness, and token of his tender Love and Good Will he beareth to His Highness; the Confirmation whereof he especially required, and by all means possible, would study to increase and eternize: Which Function he was the more willing to accomplish, because our State of *Graya* did grace *Templaria* with the Presence of an Ambassador about thirty Years since, upon like occasion.

Our Prince made him this Answer, That he did acknowledge that the great Kindness of his Lord, whereby he doth invite to further degrees in firm and Loyal Friendship, did deserve all honourable Commendations, and effectual Accomplishment, that by any means might be devised; and that he accounted himself happy, by having the sincere and stedfast Love of so gracious and renowned a Prince, as his Lord and Master deserved to be esteemed; and that nothing in the World should hinder the due Observation of so inviolable a Band as he esteemed his Favour and Good Will. Withal, he entred into Commendations of his noble and courageous Enterprizes, in that he chuseth out an Adversary fit for his Greatness to encounter with, his Honour to be

illustrated by, and such an Enemy to all *Christendom*, as that the Glory of his Actions tend to the Safety and Liberty of all Civility and Humanity; yet, notwithstanding that he was thus employed, in this Action of honouring us, he shewed both his honourable Mindfulness of our Love and Friendship, and also his own Puissance, that can afford so great a number of brave Gentlemen, and so gallantly furnished and accomplished: And so concluded, with a Welcome both to the Ambassador himself, and his Favourites, for their Lord and Master's sake, and so for their own good Deserts and Condition.

When the Ambassador was placed, as aforesaid, and that there was something to be performed for the Delight of the Beholders, there arose such a disordered Tumult and Crowd upon the Stage, that there was no Opportunity to effect that which was intended: There came so great a number of worshipful Personages upon the Stage, that might not be displaced; and Gentlewomen, whose Sex did privilege them from Violence, that when the Prince and his Officers had in vain, a good while, expected and endeavoured a Reformation, at length there was no hope of Redress for that present. The Lord Ambassador and his Train thought that they were not so kindly entertained, as was before expected, and thereupon would not stay any longer at that time, but, in a sort, discontented and displeased. After their Departure the Throngs and Tumults did somewhat cease, although so much of them continued, as was able to disorder and confound any good Inventions whatsoever. In regard whereof, as also for that the Sports intended were especially for the gracing of the *Templarians*, it was thought good not to offer any thing of Account, saving Dancing and Revelling with Gentlewomen; and after such Sports, a Comedy of Errors (like to *Plautus* his *Menechmus*) was played by the Players. So that Night was begun, and continued to the end, in nothing but Confusion and Errors; whereupon, it was ever afterwards called, *The Night of Errors*.

This mischanceful Accident sorting so ill, to the great prejudice of the rest of our Proceedings, was a great Discouragement and Disparagement to our whole State; yet it gave occasion to the Lawyers of the Prince's Council, the next Night, after Revels, to read a Commission of *Oyer* and *Terminer*, directed to certain Noble-men and Lords of His Highness's Council, and others, that they should enquire, or cause Enquiry to be made of some great Disorders and Abuses lately done and committed within His Highness's Dominions of *Purpoole*, especially by Sorceries and Inchantments; and namely, of a great Witchcraft used the Night before, whereby there were great Disorders and Misdemeanours, by Hurly-burlies, Crowds, Errors, Confusions, vain Representations and Shews, to the utter Discredit of our State and Policy.

The next Night upon this Occasion, we preferred Judgments thick and threefold, which were read publickly by the Clerk of the Crown, being all against a Sorcerer or Conjurer that was supposed to be the Cause of that confused Inconvenience. Therein was contained, How he had caused the Stage to be built, and Scaffolds to be reared to the top of the House, to increase Expectation. Also how he had caused divers Ladies and Gentlewomen, and others of good Condition, to be invited to our Sports; also our dearest Friend, the State of *Templaria*, to be disgraced, and disappointed of their kind Entertainment, deserved and intended. Also that he caused Throngs and Tumults, Crowds and Outrages, to disturb our whole Proceedings. And Lastly, that he had foisted a Company of base and common Fellows, to make up our Disorders with a Play of Errors and Confusions; and that that Night had gained to us Discredit, and it self a Nickname of Errors. All which were against the Crown and Dignity of our Sovereign Lord, the Prince of *Purpoole*.

Under Colour of these Proceedings, were laid open to the View, all the Causes of note that were committed by our chiefest States-men in the Government of our Principality; and every Officer in any great Place, that had not performed his Duty in that Service, was taxed hereby, from the highest to the lowest, not sparing the Guard and Porters, that suffered so many disordered Persons to enter in at the Court-Gates: Upon whose aforesaid Indictments, the Prisoner was arraigned at the Bar, being brought thither by the Lieutenant of the Tower (for at that time the Stocks were graced with that Name;) and the Sheriff impannelled a Jury of Twenty four Gentlemen, that were to give their Verdict upon the Evidence given. The Prisoner appealed to the Prince his Excellency for Justice, and humbly desired, that it would please His Highness to understand the Truth of the Matter by his Supplication, which he had ready to be offered to the Master of the Requests. The Prince gave leave to the Master of the Requests, that he should read the Petition; wherein was a Disclosure of all the Knavery and Juggling of the Attorney and Sollicitor, which had brought all this Law-stuff on purpose to blind the Eyes of his Excellency, and all the honourable Court there, going about to make them think, that those things which they all saw and perceived sensibly to be in very deed done, and actually performed, were nothing else but vain Illusions, Fancies, Dreams and Enchantments, and to be wrought and compassed by the Means of a poor harmless Wretch, that never had heard of such great Matters in all his Life: Whereas the very Fault was in the Negligence of the Prince's Council, Lords and Officers of his State, that had the Rule of the Roast, and by whose Advice the Commonwealth was so soundly mis-governed. To prove these things to be true, he brought divers Instances of great Absurdities committed by the greatest; and made such Allegations, as could not be denied. These were done by some that were touched by the Attorney and Sollicitor, in their former Proceedings, and they used the Prisoners Names for means of Quittance with them in that behalf. But the Prince and States-men (being pinched on both sides, by both the Parties) were not a little offended at the great Liberty that they had taken, in censuring so far of His Highness's Government; and thereupon the Prisoner was freed and pardoned, the Attorney, Sollicitor, Master of the Requests, and those that were acquainted with the Draught of the Petition, were all of them commanded to the Tower; so the Lieutenant took charge of them. And this was the End of our Law-sports, concerning the Night of Errors.

–pp. 20–24

The following excerpt is from The Articles of the Orders.

Item, Every Knight of this Order shall endeavour to add Conference and Experience by Reading; and therefore shall not only read and peruse *Guizo*, the *French Academy*, *Galiatto* the Courtier, *Plutarch*, the *Arcadia*, and the Neoterical Writers, from time to time; but also frequent the Theatre, and such like places of Experience; and resort to the better sort of Ord'naries for Conference, whereby they may not only become accomplished with Civil Conversations, and able to govern a Table with Discourse; but also sufficient, if need be, to make Epigrams, Emblems, and other Devices appertaining to His Honour's learned Revels.

–pp. 29–30

1595

Stationers' Register Entry

Although the authorship of Edward III *is still vigorously disputed, many scholars, including Eric Sams, Richard Proudfoot, and Eliot Slater, now accept that Shakespeare is responsible for all or part of it. Abbreviated words have been silently expanded in this transcription.*

Primo die decembr'
Cuthbert Burby   Entred for his copie under the handes of the wardens A book Intitled Edward the Third and the blacke prince their warres wth kinge John of Fraunce.
vi[d]
–*Bibliography of the English Printed Drama*, p. 12

An edition of Shakespeare's Venus and Adonis *whose title page has not survived was probably published in 1595. See* Short Title Catalog, *entry 22356 for details.*

Possible Allusion to Richard III in Hoby's Letter to Cecil

In a 1925 essay "Elizabethan Stage Gleanings," E. K. Chambers quoted this 7 December 1595 letter from scholar and diplomat Edward Hoby to his cousin Robert Cecil, a privy councillor and later secretary of state (Cecil Manuscript 36, 60). Chambers notes that the letter "seems to suggest a performance of Richard II., *and, if so, confirms the date of 1595 for Shakespeare's play," an observation still disputed.*

Sir, findinge that you wer not convenientlie to be at London to morrow night I am bold to send to knowe whether Teusdaie may be anie more in your grace to visit poore Channon rowe where as late as it shal please you a gate for your supper shal be open: & K. Richard present him self to your vewe. Pardon my boldnes that ever love to be honored with your presence nether do I importune more then your occasions may willingly assent unto, in the meanetime & ever restinge

At your command
Edw. Hoby.
—*RES,* 1 (1925): 75–76

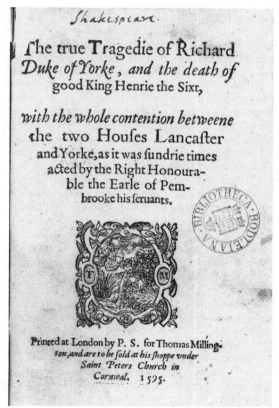

Title page for a quarto of a play that is closely related to Shakespeare's 3 Henry VI. *The many variations between this edition and its publication in the First Folio have relegated it to a place among the "bad" quartos (courtesy of the Bodleian Library, Oxford).*

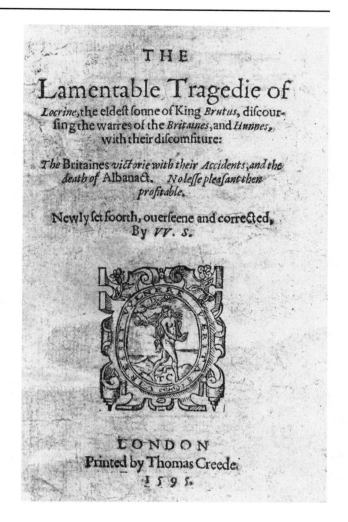

Title page for a play sometimes attributed to Shakespeare. The practice of identifying an author only by his or her initials was common in the Elizabethan period (by permission of the Folger Shakespeare Library).

Publications

The True Tragedy of Richard Duke of York, *a play that is clearly related to Shakespeare's* 3 Henry VI, *is the only surviving work credited to Shakespeare published in 1595. This text is probably a memorial reconstruction of Shakespeare's* 3 Henry VI, *but some scholars have argued that it is a first draft, a source text, or a touring version of the play.*

Few scholars accept that Shakespeare wrote another play published in 1595, The Lamentable Tragedy of Locrine, *despite its title page claim that the play is "Newly set forth, overseene and corrected, by W. S." Another play,* Locrine, *is published, with the author identified as "W. S." Efforts to attribute the play to Shakespeare have not been successful.*

Title page for Stephen Gosson's 1595 pamphlet that is also known by its subtitle, A Glasse, to view the Pride of vainglorioius Women. Sumptuary laws, designed to keep both men and women from dressing above their social station, were passed more often than they were enforced, but violators were sometimes lampooned in works such as this one (by permission of the Folger Shakespeare Library).

Allusion to Shakespeare in Covell's *Polimanteia*

Protestant divine William Covell alludes to Shakespeare in "England To Her Three Daughters, Cambridge, Oxford, Innes of Court, and to all her Inhabitants," a letter appended to Polimanteia, Or, The meanes lawfull and unlawfull, to Judge Of The Fall Of A Common-Wealth, Against the frivolous and foolish conjectures of this age *(1595).* Polimanteia *mixes social and literary criticism.*

Let your children (daughters) content themselves: leave to repine at baser fortunes: let them be perswaded of this, [*In margin: "Schollers must learne patience."*] that Fame shall be their servant, Honour

> **Lord Say**
>
> Tell me: wherein have I offended most?
> Have I affected wealth or honour? Speak.
> Are my chest fill'd up with extorted gold?
> Is my apparel sumptuous to behold?
>
> – *2 Henry VI*,
> 4.7.97–100

shall bee their subject, Glory shalbe their crown, Eternitie their inheritance: (then indeard wit decking admired daughters) write and let the worlde know that heavens harmonie is no musicke, in respect of your sweete, and well arte tuned strings: that *Italian Ariosto* did but shadowe the meanest part of thy muse, that *Tassos Godfrey* is not worthie to make compare with your truelie eternizing *Elizas* stile: [*In margin: "M. Alablaster. Spenser and others."*] let France-admired *Bellaw* and courtlike amarous *Rousard* confesse that there be of your children, that in these latter times have farre surpassed them. [*In margin: "Lylia clouded, whose teares are making."*] Let divine *Bartasse* eternally praise worthie for his weeks worke, say the best thinges were made first: Let other countries (sweet *Cambridge*) envie, (yet admire) my *Virgil*, thy petrarch, divine *Spenser*. And unlesse I erre, (a thing easie in such simplicitie) deluded by dearlie beloved *Delia*, and fortunatelie fortunate *Cleopatra*; *Oxford* thou maist extoll thy courte-deare-verse happie *Daniell*, whose sweete refined muse, in contracted shape, were sufficient amongst men, to gaine pardon of the sinne to *Rosemond*, pittie to distressed *Cleopatra*, and everliving praise to her loving *Delia*. Register your childrens petegree in Fames forehead, so may you fill volumes with *Chaucers* praise, with *Lydgate*, the Scottish Knight, and such like, whose unrefined tongues farre shorte of the excellencie of this age, wrote simplie and purelie as the times weare. [*In margin: "All praise worthy. Lucrecia Sweet Shakspeare. Eloquent Gaveston. Wanton Adonis. Watsons heyre. So well graced Anthonie deserveth immortall praise from the hand of that divine Lady who like Corinna contending with Pindarus was oft victorious. Sir David Lynsay. Matilda honorably honored by so sweet a Poem. Diana."*] And when base and injurious trades, the sworne enemies to Learnings eternitie (a thing usuall) shall have devoured them, either with the fretting cancker worme of mouldie time: with *Arabian* spicerie: with english honnie: with outlandish butter (matters of imployment for the aged dayes of our late authors) yet that then such (if you thinke them worthie) in despite of base Grosers, [*In margin: "Procul hinc, proculite profani."*] (whome I charge upon paine of learnings curse, not to handle a leafe of mine) may live by your meanes, canonized in learnings catalogue.

– sigs. R2r–R3v

1596

A New Year's Performance of *Titus Andronicus*

Jacques Petit was a tutor in the household of Sir John Harington and a servant to Anthony Bacon, secretary to the Earl of Essex. His letter to Anthony Bacon, "Letter Referring to the Performance of 'Titus Andronicus' at Burley-on-the-Hill" (Lambeth Palace MS. 654, no. 167), describes a production of Titus Andronicus *that was part of the Christmas entertainment for the nine hundred or so holiday visitors and guests at Burley-on-the-Hill, Rutland, one of Harington's manors. In the essay in which this letter is transcribed and edited, "An Unrecorded Elizabethan Performance of* Titus Andronicus," *Gustaz Ungerer offers a careful account of the "commediens de Londres" who were available to perform the play and concludes that it is impossible to determine which of the professional troupes Petit saw.*

Le Jour de lan fut monstree la liberalité de ces bon[s gens] & principalem^t de Mad: la Contesse [Russell] car depuis le plus [grand] jusques au plus petit elle en donna bon tesmoignage, mesm[e] j'en puis dire quelque chose. Les commediens de Londres son[t] venus icy po^r en avoir leur pt. on les feit jouer le soir [de] leur venue & le lendemain on les despecha

On a fait icy une mascarade de linvention de Sr Edw: wingfild on a aussi joué la tragedie de Titus Andronicus mais la monstre a plus valeu que le suject.

—*Shakespeare Survey,* 14 (1961): 102–109

[On New Year's Day was demonstrated the liberality of these good people and principally of Madame the Countess, for to the greatest unto the least (of the guests) she gave good proof of it; I myself can say something to this account. The London actors came here to have their share in it. They were bid to perform the evening of their arrival and the next day they were sent on their way.

A masque of Sir Edward Wingfield's invention was performed here, and also the tragedy *Titus Andronicus,* but the show was worth more than the play (itself).]

—translated by Julia Reagin

Stationers' Register Entry

Venus and Adonis was entered into the Stationers' Register for a third time in 1596, showing its continued popularity.

25 Junii [1596]

William leeke Assigned over unto him for his copie from master harrison th[e] elder, in full Court holden this day. by the said master harrisons consent. A booke called.   Venus and Adonis   vi^d

—*Stationers' Register,* folio 11

Publications

Venus and Adonis and Edward III, *which had been entered in the Stationers' Register in December 1595, were published in 1596; the consensus among scholars is that Shakespeare wrote part or all of the play. The title pages for these works follow.*

VENVS / AND ADONIS. / *Vilia miretur vulgus: mihi fla-uus Apollo / Pocula Caſtalia plena miniſtret aqua.* / [*Publisher's device*] / Imprinted at London by R. F. for / Iohn Hariſon. / 1596.

THE / RAIGNE OF / KING EDVVARD / the third: / *As it hath bin ſundrie times plaied about / the Citie of London.* / [*Publisher's device*] / LONDON, / *Printed for Cuthbert Burby.* / 1 5 9 6.

The Price of a Play

The pricing system at a London theater–a penny to enter, and additional pennies for a better seat–is described in an aside by William Lambarde in his travelogue A Perambulation of Kent: Conteining the Description, Hystorie, and Customes of that Shyre *(1596). At Boxley abbey, penitent pilgrims had to complete several purifying steps, each of which might involve a fee; the clerics collecting the offerings often tricked the pilgrims into giving up more money.*

But marke heere (I beseech you) their policie in picking plaine mens purses. It was in vaine (as they persuaded) to presume to the Roode without shrifte: yea, and money lost there also, if you offered before you were in cleane life: And therefore, the matter was so handled, that without treble oblation (that is to say) first to the *Confessour,* then to *Sainct Rumwald,* and lastly to the *Gracious Roode,* the poore Pilgrimes could not assure themselves of any good, gained by all their labour. No more than such as goe to *Paris-gardein,* the *Bell Savage,* or *Theatre,* to beholde Beare baiting, Enterludes, or Fence play, can account of any pleasant spectacle, unlesse they first pay one pennie at the gate, another at the entrie of the Scaffolde, and the thirde for a quiet standing.

—p. 233

Burial record for Shakespeare's only son, Hamnet, who died at age eleven. Nothing is known about the cause of his death (shelfmark DR 234/1; courtesy of the Shakespeare Birthplace Trust Records Office).

John Shakespeare's Request for a Grant of Arms

The 20 October 1596 document in which Shakespeare's father applies for a grant of arms presents particular difficulty. Two drafts of the request are in the records of the College of Arms (Vincent Manuscript 157, articles 23 and 24); no final or fair copy has been discovered. Neither draft is in perfect condition; the preliminary draft has been heavily revised, and the second, also revised, is written on paper that has decayed and crumbled in a particularly crucial spot: the section of the document that lists the reasons John Shakespeare is qualified for the grant of arms.

A transcript that takes account of the many additions, deletions, and absences is extremely difficult to read. The usual practice—and the one followed here—is to transcribe the second draft, using the first draft to supply the missing words and phrases. Unfortunately, the second text does not follow the first closely enough to allow this reconstruction to be done without conjecture and rearrangement, resulting in a set of typographical impediments. Words supplied from similar sentences in the first draft are in angled brackets; words from the first draft that have had to be rearranged in order to make sense in the second draft are in square brackets. Missing words and phrases not found in the first draft are noted as [. . .]. Shorthand characters have been silently expanded. Diplomatic transcripts of both drafts can be found in B. Roland Lewis's The Shakespeare Documents: Facsimiles, Transliterations, Translations & Commentary (1940) and clear facsimiles of the manuscripts are in S. Schoenbaum's William Shakespeare: A Documentary Life (1975). For an alternative reconstruction of the text, see E. K. Chambers's William Shakespeare: A Study of Facts and Problems.

There are many differences between the two drafts, beginning with their first words. The upper left corner of the preliminary draft contains the motto "Non, Sanz Droict." These same words, with the comma after "Non," are written *immediately below the motto, then crossed out. To the right of both mottos is written: "NON SANZ DROICT." It is now sans comma; the comma is also absent in the second draft. An insoluble problem is presented by the differences between the two drafts' accounts of the service provided by John Shakespeare's "antecessors." In the second draft, "antecessors" appears with the word "Grandfather" written above it. This split-level subject is followed by the phrase "were for theyr faithfull & va. . . ." in which "were" is deleted, "theyr" is deleted and replaced by "his," and "va" is all that remains of the rest of the sentence. In the first draft, the service of the "parentes & late antecessors" is lauded; the grandfather's contributions are not mentioned.*

The Shakespeare arms, as sketched in the upper left corner of both drafts, appear on the monument to Shakespeare in Holy Trinity Church, and on Susanna Hall's seal.

To all singuler Noble, and Gentilmen: of what Estate, degree, bearing Arms to whom these presentes shall come. William Dethick Garter princip<all> king of Arms sendethe greetinges. Knowe yee. that whereas by the authoriti<e> and auncyent pryveleges perteyning to my office from the Queenes most excellent Majestie and by her highnesse most noble & victorious progenitors. I am to take generall notice & record and to make declaration & testemonie for all causes of Arms and matters of Gentrie thorough all her majesties kingdoms, dominions, principalites, Isles and provinces. To the'nd that as manie gentillmen by theyr auncyent names of families, kyndredes, & descentes have & enjoye certeyne enseignes & cottes of Arms So it is v[. . .] expedient in all Ages that some men for theyr valeant factes, magnanimite, vertu, dignites & des<ertes> maye use & beare suche tokens of honor and worthinesse. whereby theyr Name & good fame may be the better knowen & divulged. and theyr Children & posterite (in all vertue to the service of theyr prynce & Contrie) encouraged: Wherefore being solicited and by credible report <info>rmed. That John Shakespeare of Stratford uppon Avon <in> the count<e of> Warwike <whose> parentes <& late> antecessors. Grandfather for his faithfull & va<leant> [service was] <advanced & rewar>ded <by the most pruden[. . .]> prince King Henry the seventh of <famous memorie sythence which tyme they have> continewed in those partes being of good reputacion <& credit and that the s>aid John hath maryed the daughter <& one of the heyres of Robert Arden of Wilm^cote in the said> Counte esquire, and for the encouragement of his posterite to whom [these achivmentes by the a]uncyent Custome of the Lawes of Arms maye descend. I the said G[arter king] of Arms have assigned, graunted, and by these presentes confirmed: This sh<ield> or <Cote of> Arms. viz. Gould. on A Bend Sables. a Speare of the first steeled argent. And for his Creast or Cognizaunce a falcon. his winges displayed Argent. standing on a

---

The Hierarchy of the Gentry

By applying for a coat of arms, John Shakespeare sought to improve his social status. One version of the complex gentry hierarchy is found in Thomas Milles's The Catalogue of Honor or tresury of true nobility perculiar to Great Britaine *(London, 1610).*

These are the Orders and Degrees, of both our sortes of *Nobility, Named and Unnamed. Now into what rankes they are among themselves divided, and what honour they owe one of them unto another (by a certaine right of precedence) receive here in briefe.*

1 The Kings Majesty.
2 The Prince of Wales.
3 Dukes discended of the Royall bloud.
4 Dukes not discended of Royall bloud.
5 Dukes eldest Sonnes discended of the Royall bloud.
6 Marquesses.
7 Dukes eldest Sonnes.
8 Earles.
9 Marquesses eldest Sonnes.
10 Dukes younger Sonnes of the bloud Royall.
11 Dukes second Sonnes.
12 Vicounts.
13 Earles eldest Sonnes.
14 Marquesses second Sonnes.
15 Barons.

16 Vicounts eldest Sonnes.
17 Earles second Sonnes.
18 Barons eldest Sonnes.
19 Knights Bannarets.
20 Vicounts second Sonnes.
21 Barons second Sonnes.
22 Knights Batchellers.
23 Esquires for the body.
24 Knights Bannarets eldest Sonnes.
25 Knights Batchellers eldest Sonnes.
26 Esquires.
27 Gentlemen.

–p. 87

wrethe of his Coullors. suppo<rting> a Speare Gould. steeled as aforesaid sett uppon a helmett with mantelles & tasselles as hath ben accustomed and doth more playnely appeare depicted on this margent: Signefieing hereby & by the authorite of my office aforesaid Ratefieing that it shalbe lawfull for the said John Shakespeare. gent. and for his cheldren yssue & posterite (at all tymes & places convenient) to beare and make demonstracion of the same Blazon or Atchevment uppon theyre Shieldes, Targetes, escucheons, Cotes of Arms, pennons, Guydons, Seales, Ringes, Edefices, Buyldinges, utensiles, Lyveries, Tombes, or monumentes. or otherwise for all lawfull warrlyke factes or Civile use or exercises: according to the Lawes of Arms, and Customes that to gentillmen belongethe: without let or interruption of any other person or persons for use or bearing the same. In wittnesse & perpetuall remembrance hereof I have hereunto subscribed my name & fastened the Seale of my office endorzed with the signett of my Arms. At the office of Arms London the xx. daye of October the xxxviii^th yeare of the reigne of our Soveraigne Lady Elizabeth by the grace of God Quene of England, ffrance and Ireland defender of the ffayth etc. 1596.

This John sheweth A patierne therof under Clarent Cookes hand.
—paper. xx years past.
A Justice of peace And was Baylyf [illegible] officer & cheffe of the towne of Stratford uppon Avon xv or xvi years past.
That he hath Landes & tenementes of good wealth & Substance 500^li.
That he mar [. . . .]

Writ of Attachment Requested Against Shakespeare and Others

The 29 November 1596 writ of attachment requested by William Wayte against William Shakespeare, Francis Langley, Dorothy Soer, and Anna Lee (PRO Controllment Rolls KB 29/234) was an order issued by the Court of the Queen's Bench to the sheriff for the arrest of the persons named. Those arrested as the result of such a writ were required to post bond to guarantee their peaceful behavior. The phrase "ob metum mortis" ("for fear of death") was conventional. No further documents have survived to indicate what, if any, further action took place. The women have not been identified. Samuel Schoenbaum in William Shakespeare: A Documentary Life *notes, "it is a minor solace that nobody has yet cast either for the part of Dark Lady" (p. 146).*

While it is possible the writ refers to another William Shakespeare, it is unlikely, since the other man named, Francis Langley, built and owned the Swan Theatre. On 3 November 1596, Langley requested a writ of attachment against William Wayte and Wayte's step-father, William Gardiner, a Surrey justice of the peace. The writ naming Langley and Shakespeare may have been issued in retaliation. Both writs may be connected with efforts by Gardiner and the Puritans to suppress the theaters in Southwark. See the discussion in B. Roland Lewis's The Shakespeare Documents: Facsimiles, Transliterations, Translations & Commentary, *Vol. I (Stanford, 1940). The following transcript and translation are from Lewis's book.*

Anglia scire scilicet Willielmus Wayte petit securitates pacis versus Willielmum Shakspere Franciscum Langley Dorotheam Soer uxorem Johannis Soer & Annam Lee ob metum mortis &c Attachiamentum Vicecomiti Surreie retornabile xviii Martini

[England. Be it known that William Wayte craves sureties of the peace against William Shakspere, Francis Langley, Dorothy Soer wife of John Soer, and Anne Lee, for fear of death and so forth. Writ of Attachment issued and directed to the Sheriff of Surrey, returnable on the eighteenth of St. Martin.]
—p. 218

Possible Allusion to *The Taming of the Shrew* in Harington's *The Metamorphosis of Ajax*

After a pun-filled account of his main topic—indoor plumbing—John Harington in A New Discourse Of A Stale Subject, Called The Metamorphosis of Ajax *(1596) turns to other sorts of household advice, including a brief account of how to cope with the "three things that make a man weary of his house, a smoking chimney, a dropping eves, and a brauling woman" (p. 84). The "booke" Harington recommends may be Shakespeare's play* The Taming of the Shrew, *or may be another, older play,* The Taming of a Shrew.

For the shrewd wife, read the booke of taming a shrew, which hath made a number of us so perfect, that now every one can rule a shrew in our countrey, save he that hath her. But indeed there are but two good rules. One is, let them never have their willes; the other differs but a letter, let them ever have their willes, the first is the wiser, but the second is more in request, and therefore I make choice of it.
—p. 86

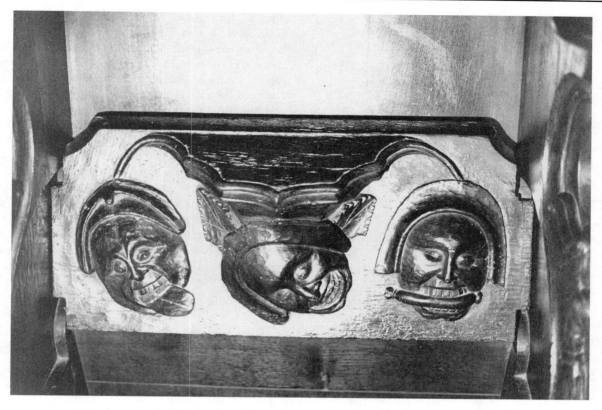

A fifteenth-century misericord from Holy Trinity Church, Stratford-upon-Avon, perhaps illustrating the taming of a shrewish woman (photograph ©2001 by Gary Vernon)

Allusion to *Hamlet* in Lodge's *Wits Miserie*

In Wits Miserie, and the Worlds Madnesse: Discovering the Devils Incarnat of this Age *(1596) Thomas Lodge satirizes and chastises the evils of his day by describing the devils who embody each of the deadly sins; their demonic offspring represent the lesser vices. In this excerpt from "Of the great Devill Belzebub, and what monstrous and strange Devils he hath bred in our age," Belzebub embodies the sin of envy. He marries Jealousie, who avoids contact with him. Their three sons are conceived when Jealousie drinks some of Belzebub's blood and steals a kiss from him. Lodge compares the first of these sons, Hate-Vertue, to the ghost in* Hamlet, *though the reference is probably to the ur-Hamlet, not to Shakespeare's play.*

The first by Sathan (his grandsire) was called *Hate-Vertue,* or (in words of more circumstance) *Sorrow for another mans good successe)* who after he had learnt to lie of *Lucian,* to flatter with *Aristippus,* & conjure of *Zoroastes,* wandred a while in France, Germanie, & Italy, to learn languages & fashions, & now of late daies is stoln into England to deprave all good deserving. And though this fiend be begotten of his fathers own blood, yet is he different from his nature, & were he not sure that *Jealousie* could not make him a cuckold, he had long since published him for a bastard: you shall know him by this, he is a foule lubber, his tongue tipt with lying, his heart steeld against charity, he walks for the most part in black under colour of gravity, & looks as pale as the Visard of the ghost which cried so miserally at the Theator like an oister wife, *Hamlet, revenge:* he is full of infamy & slander, insomuch as if he ease not his stomack in detracting somwhat or some man before noontide, he fals into a fever that holds him while supper time: he is alwaies devising of Epigrams or scoffes, and grumbles, murmures continually, although nothing crosse him, he never laughes but at other mens harmes, briefly in being a tyrant over mens fames, he is a very Titius (as *Virgil* saith) to his owne thoughts.

Titiique vultur intus
Qui semper lacerat comest que mentem.

THE
Brideling, Sadling and Ryding, of
a rich Churle in Hampſhire, by the ſubtill practiſe of one
Iudeth Philips, a profeſſed cunning woman, or
Fortune teller.

VVith a true diſcourſe of her vnwomanly vſing of a Trype wife, a widow,
lately dwelling on the back ſide of S. Nicholas ſhambles in London, whom ſhe with her conferates, likewiſe coſoned:

For which fact, ſhee was at the Seſſions houſe without New-gate arraigned,
where ſhe confeſſed the ſame, and had iudgement for her offence,
to be whipped through the Citie, the 14. of February, 1594.

Printed at London by T. C. and are to be ſolde by
William Barley, at his ſhop in New-gate
Market, neare Chriſt-Church. 1595.

Title page for a pamphlet that indicates apprehension about the changing
roles of women in Shakespeare's era (reproduced by permission of
The Huntington Library, San Marino, California)

The mischiefe is that by grave demeanure, and newes bearing, hee hath got some credite with the greater sort, and manie fooles there bee that because hee can pen prettilie, hold it Gospell what ever hee writes or speakes: his custome is to preferre a foole to credite, to despight a wise man, and no Poet lives by him that hath not a flout of him. Let him spie a man of wit in a Taverne, he is an arrant dronckard; or but heare that he parted a fray, he is a harebraind quarreller: Let a scholler write, Tush (saith he) I like not these common fellowes: let him write well, he hath stollen it out of some note booke: let him translate, Tut, it is not of his owne: let him be named for preferment, he is insufficient, because poore: no man shall rise in his world, except to feed his envy: no man can continue in his friendship, who hateth all men. Divine wits, for many things as sufficient as all antiquity (I speake it not on slight surmise, but con-

siderate judgement) to you belongs the death that doth nourish this poison: to you the paine, that endure the reproofe. *Lilly*, the famous for facility in discourse: *Spencer*, best read in ancient Poetry: *Daniel*, choise in word, and invention: *Draiton*, diligent and formall: *Th. Nash*, true English Aretine. All you unnamed professours, or friends of Poetry, (but by me inwardly honoured) knit your industries in private, to unite your fames in publike: let the strong stay up the weake, & the weake march under conduct of the strong; and all so imbattell your selves, that hate of vertue may not imbase you. But if besotted with foolish vain-glory, emulation, and contempt, you fall to neglect one another, *Quod Deus omen auertat*, Doubtles it will be as infamous a thing shortly, to present any book whatsoever learned to any *Mæcenas* in England, as it is to be headsman in any free citie in Germanie:

Clauditie iam rivos pueri sat prata viverunt.

The meane hath discoursed, let the mighty prevent the mischiefe. But to our Devill, by his leave, we can not yet shake him off: hearke what *Martial* saith to thee, thou depraver:

Omnibus invideas, invide nemo tibi.
Envy thou all men, let none envy thee.
—pp. 56–57

Shakespeare's Company
Paid for Court Performance

The Lord Hunsdon's men, formerly the Lord Chamberlain's men, are paid for their Christmas holiday performances before the queen. Unfortunately, the queen's bookkeeper did not record the titles of the plays Shakespeare's company performed. "Lord Hunsden" is George Carey, son of the former Lord Chamberlain, Henry Carey, who died in 1596.

To John Hemynge and George Bryan servauntes to the late Lorde Chamberlayne and now servauntes to the Lorde Hunsdon upon the Councelles warraunte Dated at whitehall xxi^{mo} die Decembris 1596 for five Enterludes or playes shewed by them before her majestie on St Stephans daye at nighte, the Sondaye nighte followeing Twelfe nighte, one St Johns daye and on Shrovesunday at nighte laste the Some of xxxiii^{li} vi^s viii^d and by waye of her majesties rewarde   xvi^{li} xiii^s iiii^d.
In all the Some of

—*Dramatic Records*, p. 29

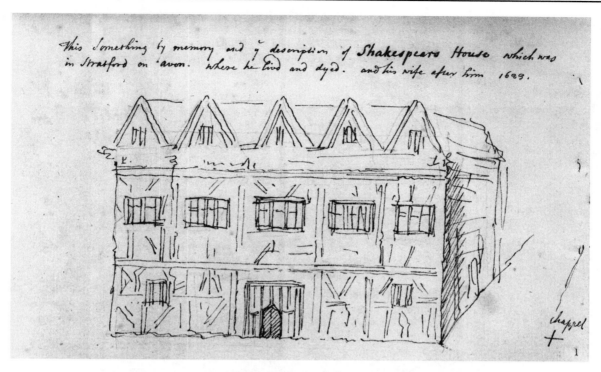

George Vertue's sketch of New Place as it appeared in 1737 (Portland Loan 29/246, page 18; courtesy of The British Library, London)

1597

Shakespeare's Purchase of New Place

This document (PRO CP 25(2)/237, Easter 39 Eliz. I) records Shakespeare's purchase of New Place, the second-largest house in Stratford-upon-Avon. The amount Shakespeare paid for the house, granaries, and gardens, £60, is probably understated, as was conventional in a foot of fine. The purchase price represents a substantial sum of money, particularly for an actor and playwright, to have accumulated. It is impossible to determine how much time Shakespeare spent in Stratford during his active theatrical career, but he continued to buy property in Stratford and returned there at the end of his life. Shakespeare left New Place to his daughter Susanna and her husband, John Hall; its eighteenth-century owner, Francis Gastrell, tore the house down in 1759.

Haec est finalis concordia facta in curia domine Regine apud Westmonasterium a die pasche in quinque Septimanca anno regnorum Elizabeth dei gratia Anglie ffrancie & hibernie regine fidei defensor &c a conquestu tricesimo Nono coram Edmundo Anderson Thoma Walmsley ffrancisco Seammons & Thoma Owen Justiciariis & aliis domine Regine fidelibus tunc ibi presentibus Inter Willielmum Shakespeare querentem et Willielmum Underhill generosum deforciantem de uno messuagio duobus horreis & duobus gardinis cum pertinenciis in Stratford super Avon unde placitum convencionis summonitum fuit inter eos in eadem curia Scilicet quod predictus Willielmus Underhill recognovit predicta tenementa cum pertinenciis esse ius ipsius Willielmi Shakespeare ut illa que idem Willielmus habet de dono predicti Willielmi Underhill et illa remisit & quietumclamavit de se & heredibus suis predicto Willielmo Shakespeare & heredibus suis Imperpetuum et pretera idem Willielmus Underhill concessit pro se & heredibus suis quod ipsi Warantizabunt predicto Willielmo Shakespeare & heredibus suis predicta tenementa cum pertinenciis Imperpetuum et pro hac recognicione remissione quietaclamancia Warantia fine & concordia idem Willielmus Shakespeare dedit predicto Willielmo Underhill Sexaginta libras sterlingorum.

Warr

–Lewis, *Shakespeare Documents,* Vol. 1, p. 237

[This is the final agreement made in the court of her majesty the Queen at Westminster from Easter Day five weeks in the year of the reign of Elizabeth by the grace of God Queen of England, France, and Ireland and defender of the faith, etc., and from the conquest thirty

The King's Gardener's Assistant

Why should we in the compass of a pale
Keep law and form and due proportion,
Showing as in a model our firm estate,
When our sea-walled garden, the whole land,
Is full of weeds, her fairest flowers chok'd up,
Her fruit trees all unprun'd, her hedges ruin'd,
Her knots disordered, and her wholesome herbs
Swarming with caterpillars?

—Richard II, 3.4.40–47

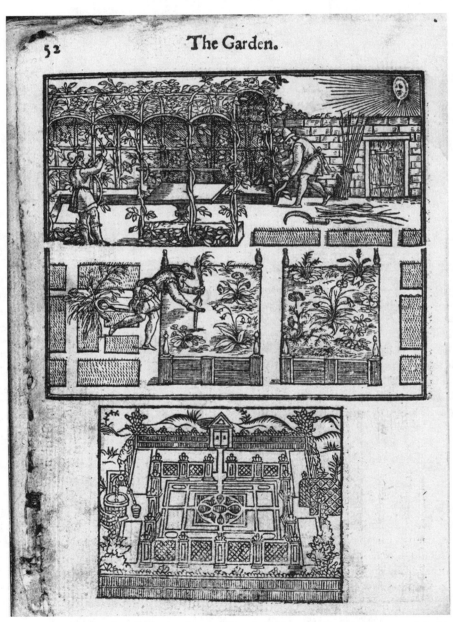

Page from The Orchard, and the Garden *(1594) showing the type of formal, highly patterned garden that was admired in the Elizabethan period (shelfmark C.27.f.16; courtesy of The British Library, London)*

THE
Silkewormes, and
their Flies:

Liuely defcribed in verfe, by T. M.
a *Countrie Farmar*, and an apprentice in Phyficke.

For the great benefit and enriching of England.

Printed at London by V. S. for Nicholas Ling, and
are to be fold at his fhop at the Weft ende of
Paules. 1599.

*Title page for a book on silkworms. The presence of mulberry
trees in Shakespeare's garden at New Place may indicate that he
was raising silkworms (by permission of the Folger
Shakespeare Library).*

nine years in the presence of Edmond Anderson, Thomas Walmsley, Francis Seammons, and Thomas Owen,
justices and other loyal to her majesty the Queen then
present there between William Shakespeare, plaintiff, and
William Underhill, gentleman, defendant concerning one
messuage, two granaries, and two gardens with appurtenances in Stratford upon Avon from which place a plea of
agreement had been summoned between them in the
same court, to wit that the aforesaid William Underhill
recognized the aforesaid tenement with appurtenances to
be the right of William Shakespeare himself and those
which the same William holds by gift of the aforesaid
William Underhill and he has remised and quitclaimed
for himself and his heirs to the aforesaid William Shakespeare and his heirs forever and besides the same William
Underhill has conceded for himself and his heirs that they
themselves warranted to the aforesaid William Shakespeare and his heirs the aforesaid tenement with appurtenances forever and for this recognition, remission,
quitclaim, warranty, fine and agreement the same William Shakespeare has given to the aforesaid William
Underhill sixty pounds sterling.]

Shakespeare Confirms Ownership of New Place

*This 4 May 1597 document conveying New Place from
William Underhill to Shakespeare (Shakespeare Birthplace
Trust MS item 1, case 8) records an additional legal step
Shakespeare took to confirm his ownership of New Place. Legal
abbreviations have been silently expanded.*

Elizabeth dei gratia Anglie ffrancie & hibernie Regina
fidei Defensor &c Omnibus ad quos presentes hae
nostrae pervenerint Salutem sciatis quod inter recor-
datur ac pedes finium tunc pro clamavit inde factis
Secundum formam Statuti in huiusmodi casu nuper
edito & primis Coram justicus nostris de Banco apud
Wesminsterium & primo pasche Anno regni nostri
tricesimo nono continetur ac warrwick scire scilicet
haec est finalis concordia facta in curia Dominae
Regnae apud Wesminsterium A die Pasche in
quinque septimanca anno regnorum Elizabeth dei
gratia Anglie ffrancie & hibernie reginae fidei Defensor &c A Conquestu tricesimo nono coram Edmundo
Anderson Thoma Walmysley ffrancisco Seammons
& Thoma Owen justiciariis & aliis Dominae Reginae
fidelibus tunc ibi presentibus Inter Willielmum
Shakespeare querentem et Willielmum Underhill
generosum deforciantem de uno mesuagio duobus
horreis & duobus gardinis cum pertinenciis in Stratford super Avon unde placitum convencionis summonitum fuit inter eos in eadem curia Scilicet quod
predictus Willielmus Underhill recognovit predicta
tenementa cum pertinenciis esse jus ipsius Willielmi
Shakespeare ut illa que idem Willielmus habet de
dono predicti Willielmi Underhill et illa remiset &
quietumclamavit de se & heredibus suis predicto
Willielmo Shakespeare & heredibus suis Imperpetuum Et pretetea idem Willielmus Underhill concessit
pro se & heredibus suis quod ipsi Warantizabunt predicto Willielmo Shakespeare & heredibus suis predicta tenementa cum pertinenciis Imperpetuum & pro
hac recognicione remissione quietaclamancia Warantia fine & concordia idem Willielmus Shakespeare
dedit predicto Willielmo Unverhill Sexaginta libras
Sterlingorum In cuius rei testimonium Sigillum nostrum ad Scribat in Banco praedicto Sigillatis deputa-
tis presentibus apponi feam &c Edmundo Anderson
apud Westminsterum iiii° die maii Annoque reginae
supradicto.

Crompton

[Elizabeth by the grace of God Queen of England,
France, & Ireland, Defender of the Faith &c to all to
whom these our presents shall come, greetings. Be it

known to you that it is recorded & that a foot of fine then is proclaimed made there according to the form of the statute in a case of this kind lately published in particular in the presence of our justices of the Bench at Westminster on the first Easter in the thirty-ninth year [1597] of her reign in the County of Warwick. That is to say: This is the final agreement made in the Court of Her Majesty the Queen at Westminster from Easter Day in five weeks in the thirty-ninth year of the reign of Elizabeth by the grace of God Queen of England, France, & Ireland, Defender of the Faith, &c. and in the thirty-ninth year from the Conquest, in the presence of Edmund Anderson, Thomas Walmsley, Francis Seamons, & Thomas Owen, Justices & others faithful to the Queen's Majesty then there present in Court. Between William Shakespeare complainant and William Underhill gentleman defendant in regard to one messuage, two granaries, & two gardens with appurtenances in Stratford-upon-Avon, whence a plea of meeting between them has been summoned in the same Court To wit that the aforesaid William Underhill has recognized the aforesaid tenement with appurtenances to be the right of William Shakespeare himself that those which the same William holds by gift of the aforesaid William Underhill, he remised & quitclaimed them for himself & his heirs to the aforesaid William Shakespeare & his heirs forever and, besides, the same William Underhill has granted for himself & his heirs that they themselves will warrant to the aforesaid William Shakespeare & his heirs the aforesaid tenements with appurtenances forever, & for this recognition, remission, quitclaim, warrant, fine, & agreement, the same William Shakespeare has given the aforementioned William Underhill sixty pounds sterling. In witness whereof our hands are written and seals are appended in the aforesaid Court in the presence of Edmund Anderson at Westminster the fourth day of May in the year and reign above written.

Crompton]
—Lewis, *Shakespeare Documents,* Vol. I, pp. 238–239

Site of New Place, the Stratford house Shakespeare purchased in 1597. The house was torn down in 1759 by its then-owner Francis Gastrell (photograph ©2001 by Gary Vernon).

London's Mayor Requests a Ban on Plays

The social position of actors improved little in Shakespeare's time, and London's mayor and council frequently requested royal support for bans on plays and players. The following excerpt from a 28 July 1597 letter from the Lord Mayor and Aldermen of London to the Privy Council lists the reasons for the City's opposition to theater.

[*Marginal note:* The inconveniences that grow by Stage playes abowt the Citie of London.]

1. They are a speaciall cause of corrupting their Youth conteninge nothinge but unchast matters, lascivious devices, shiftes of Coozenage, & other lewd & ungodly practizes, being so as that they impresse the very qualitie & corruption of manners which they represent Contrary to the rules & art prescribed for the makinge of Comedies eaven amonge the Heathen, who used them seldom & at certen sett tymes, and not all the year longe as our manner is. Whearby such as frequent them beinge of the base & refuze sort of people or such young gentlemen as have small regard of credit or conscience, drawe the same into imitacion and not to the avoidinge the like vices which they represent.

2. They are they ordinary places for vagrant persons, Maisterles men, thieves, horse stealers, whoremongers, Coozeners, Conycatchers, contrivers of treason and other idele and daungerous persons to meet together & to make theire matches to the great displeasure of Almightie God & the hurt & annoyance of her Majesties people, which cannot be prevented nor discovered by the Governors of the Citie for that they are owt of the Citiees jurisdiction.

3. They maintaine idlenes in such persons as have no vocation & draw apprentices and other servantes from theire ordinary workes and all sortes of people from the resort unto sermons and other Christian exercies to the great hinderance of traides & prophanation of religion established by her highnes within this Realm.

4. In the time of sicknes it is fownd by experience, that many having sores and yet not hart sicke take occasion hearby to walk abroad & to recreat themselves by heareinge a play. Whearby others are infected, and them selves also many things miscarry.

—Malone Society *Collections, Vol. I, Part I,* pp. 79–80

Stationers' Register Entries

Richard II and Richard III are entered in the Stationers' Register (Stationer's Hall, Register C, folios 23r, 25r). Abbreviated words have been silently expanded.

29º Augusti./.
Andrew Wise./.Entred for his Copie by appoyntment from m[r] Warden man / The Tragedye of Richard the Second   vi[d]

20 Octobr'
Andrewe wise / Entred for his copie under thandes of m[r] Barlowe, and m[r] warden man. / The tragedie of kinge Richard the Third with the death of the duke of Clarence   vi[d]

—*Bibliography of the English Printed Drama,* p. 13

King Richard

Thoughts tending to content flatter themselves
That they are not the first of fortune's slaves,
Nor shall not be the last–like seely beggars
Who sitting in the stocks refuge their shame
That many have and others must [sit] there;
And in this thought they find a kind of ease,
Bearing their own misfortunes on the back
Of such as have before endur'd the like.

– *Richard II,* 5.5.23–30

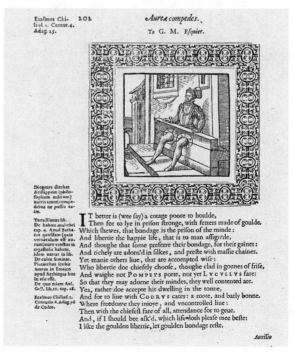

Page from Geoffrey Whitney's A Choice of Emblemes and Other Devices *(1586) showing the humiliating punishment of the stocks (by permission of the Folger Shakespeare Library)*

Publications

Richard II *and* Richard III *are published without attribution in 1597;* Romeo and Juliet *was also published without attribution.* Richard II *appears without the scene in which King Richard is deposed (4.1.154–318), perhaps because it was considered too controversial or too dangerous to Queen Elizabeth.* Richard III *may be a memorial reconstruction, meaning the play was written down or dictated to a scribe, usually by some or all of the actors who performed it.* Romeo and Juliet *also seems to be a memorially reconstructed text, but of much poorer quality than* Richard III. Richard III *and* Romeo and Juliet *are frequently quoted by Shakespeare's contemporaries, indicating the plays were popular and well known. This makes their publication something of a mystery: more profit might be made if a theater company had exclusive access to an unpublished play. It may be that Shakespeare or his company had an urgent need for cash, or it may be that the publication of* Romeo and Juliet, *and perhaps* Richard III, *was unauthorized.* Romeo and Juliet *was published in 1599 in an edition the title page describes as "Newly corrected, augmented, and amended."*

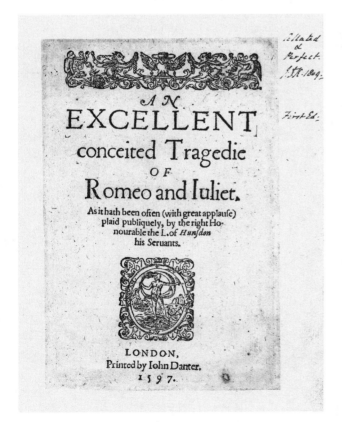

The first quarto of Romeo and Juliet, *published without credit (reproduced by permission of The Huntington Library, San Marino, California)*

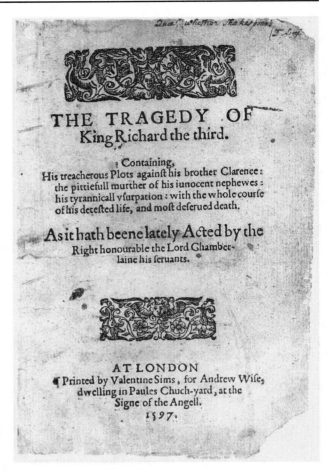

The first quarto of Richard III, *probably a memorial reconstruction (by permission of the Folger Shakespeare Library)*

THE / Tragedie of King Ri- / chard the ſe- / cond. / *As it hath beene publikely acted* / *by the right Honourable the* / *Lorde Chamberlaine his Ser-* / *uants.* / [Publisher's device] / L O N D O N / Printed by Valentine Simmes for Androw Wiſe, and / are to be ſold at his ſhop in Paules church yard at / the ſigne of the Angel. / 1 5 9 7.

Record Showing Shakespeare as a Tax Defaulter

Shakespeare was certainly not alone in avoiding the London tax collectors, but he was persistent in doing so. Surviving records list Shakespeare as a tax defaulter in 1598 and 1599. "The tax records are valuable for the Shakespearean biographer," David Thomas notes in Shakespeare in the Public Records *(1985), "as they provide the only evidence as to where [Shakespeare] was living between 1596 and 1600. In 1596 or at the latest February 1597, he was a parishioner of St Helen's Bishopsgate, conveniently close to Shoreditch where the Lord*

Chamberlain's company performed. By the time the commissioners came to look for him in 1597 he had moved away. In 1598–9 he was found by the authorities living somewhere in Surrey; in the next year he was certainly in the liberty of the Clink in Southwark" (p. 8). This excerpt is from the tax commissioners' report dated 15 November 1597 (PRO Exchequer, King's Remembrancer, Subsidy Roll E 179/146/354). Legal abbreviations have been silently expanded.

. . . We whose names are subscribed Commissioners of our soveraigne Ladye the Quenes ma^tye amongst others assigned within the sayde Cytye for the taxacõn leveying and gathering of the second payment of the last Subsydye of the three entire subsydyes latelye graunted unto her majestye by her highnes laye subjectes by acte of parliament holden at westminster in ye xxxvth year [1593] of her majesties reigne Do signifye and declare unto the right honorable the Lorde highe Treasorer of England the Barons of her ma^ties Cort of Exchequer and to all others her ma^to officers ministers and loving subjectes to whom in this behalf yt maye apperteyne and by everie of them. That on the daye of the date hereof there did appeare and come personallie before us the sayde Commissioners John Robinson the younger merchantailo^ur and Benjamin Firwyn Grocer petty collect^ours of the sayde second payment of the sayde last subsydye within the warde of Byshopsgate London who upon their corporall othes upon the holye Evangeliste of Allmightye God then and there solempmlye taken & made dyd saye and affirme that the persons hereunder named are all ether dead departed and gone out of the sayde warde or their goodes soe eloigned or conveyed out of the same or in such pryvate or Coverte manner kepte whereby the severall Somes of money on them severally taxed and assessed towarde the sayde second payment of the sayde laste subsydye neither might nor could by anye meanes by them the sayde petty collecto^urs or either of them be leveyed of them or anye of them to her ma^ties use.

The list of defaulters, organized by parish, follows. The amount in the first column is the assessed value of goods; the amount in the second column is the tax owed.

St Ellens parishe

Peter Dallila	1^li	1^s
William Shackspere	v^li	v^s
Thomas Stythe	xxx^li	xxx^s
William Boyese	xxx^li	xxx^s

—Lewis, *Shakespeare Documents*, Vol. I, pp. 264–265

Lord Chamberlain's Men Paid for Court Performances

Shakespeare's acting acompany continued to be chosen to entertain Queen Elizabeth during her holiday revels. The court's financial records do not list the names of the six plays the actors performed.

To Thomas Pope & John Hemynges servauntes to the Lorde Chamberleyne upon the Councelles warrant dated at the Courte at whitehall xxvii^mo die Novembr 1597 for six interludes or playes played before her majestie on St Stephens night St Johns night, newyeares nighte, Twelfe nighte Shrovesondaie at night and Shrovetuesday at night last past xl^li and by waie of her majesties Rewarde xx^li in all   lx^li

—*Dramatic Records*, pp. 29–30

1598

Letter from Sturley to Quiney Mentioning Shakespeare

In this 24 January 1598 letter (Shakespeare Birthplace Trust Records Office, Miscellaneous Documents I, 135) Abraham Sturley, a Stratford businessman and town official, tells his brother-in-law Richard Quiney, also of Stratford, that William Shakespeare might have money to lend. Richard Quiney was the son of Adrian Quiney, a mercer who, like John Shakespeare's family, lived in Henley Street; Richard's son Thomas later married William Shakespeare's daughter Judith. In the letter Sturley speculates about ways to target Shakespeare's money but does not fully explain the purpose of the loan.

Most loving and belovedd in the Lord, in plaine Englishe we remember u in the Lord, and ourselves unto u. I would write nothinge unto u nowe, but come home. I prai God send u comfortabli home. This is one speciall remembrance from ur fathers motion. Itt semeth bi him that our countriman, M^r. Shaksper, is willinge to disburse some monei upon some od yarde land or other att Shotterie or neare about us; he thinketh it a veri fitt patterne to move him to deale in the matter of our tithes. Bi the instruccions u can geve him theareof, and bi the frendes he can make therefore, we thinke it a faire marke for him to shoote att, and not unpossible to hitt. It obtained would advance him in deede, and would do us muche good. Hoc movere, et quantum in te est permovere, ne necligas, hoc enim et sibi et nobis maximi erit momenti. Hic labor, hic opus esset eximie et gloriæ et laudis sibi. U shall understande, brother, that our neighbours are growne with the wantes they feele throughe the dearnes of corne, which heare is beionde all other countries that I can heare of

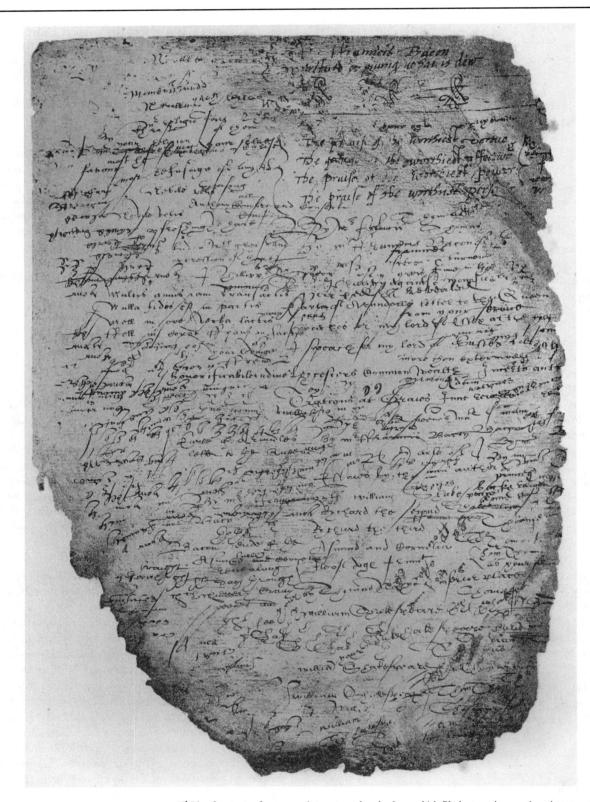

Table of contents of a manuscript commonplace book on which Shakespeare's name is written several times and Frank Burgoyne's "modern script rendering" (Northumberland manuscript 525; courtesy of His Grace the Duke of Northumberland, Alnwick Castle)

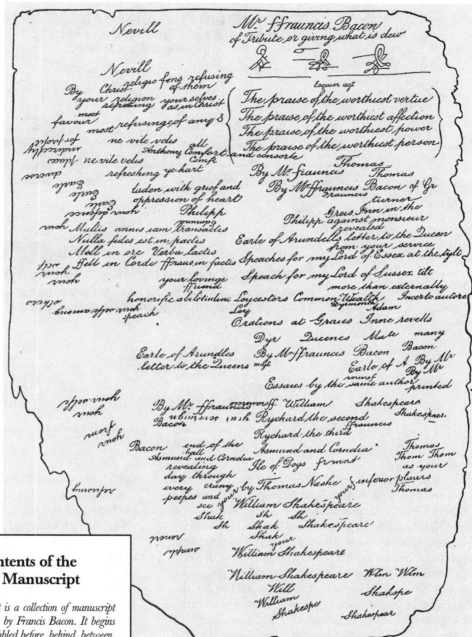

The Table of Contents of the Northumberland Manuscript

The Northumberland Manuscript is a collection of manuscript copies of various works, most of them by Francis Bacon. It begins with a table of contents (folio 1). Scribbled before, behind, between, above, and below the titles of Bacon's works is Shakespeare's name; the names of two of his plays, Richard II *and* Richard III; *a near-quotation from* The Rape of Lucrece, *"Revealing day through every cranny spies, / And seems to point her out where she sits weeping" (1086–1087); and a variant of the longest word in Shakespeare, "honorificabilitudinitatibus," from* Love's Labor's Lost *(5.1.41). Although the proximity of Shakespeare's name to that of Francis Bacon pleases conspiracy theorists who believe that Bacon was the true author of the plays attributed to Shakespeare, a close examination of the manuscript page shows a partial table of contents that has become a doodle-pad. Some scholars think it is the work of Adam Dyrmouth, whose name appears near the end of the list of the manuscript's contents.*

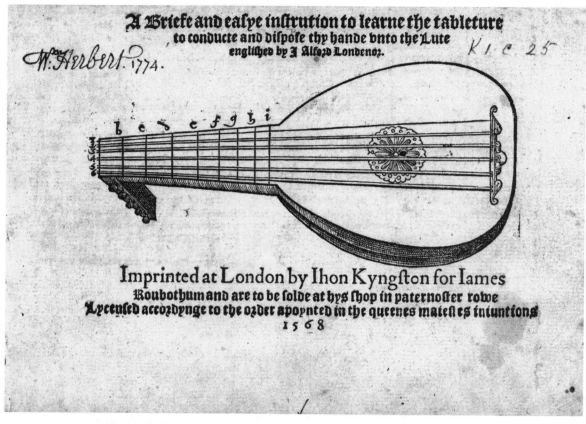

Title page for a 1568 music primer showing a lute, an instrument that was played in Richard III as well as other plays (shelfmark K.1.c.25; courtesy of The British Library, London)

deare and over deare, malecontent. Thei have assembled togeather in a great nomber, and travelld to Sir Tho. Luci on Fridai last to complaine of our malsters; on Sundai to Sir Foulke Gre. and Sir Joh. Conwai. I should have said on Wensdai to Sir Ed. Grevll first. Theare is a metinge heare expected tomorrowe. The Lord knoweth to what end it will sorte. Tho. West, returninge from the ii. knightes of the woodland, came home so full that he said to M^r. Baili that night, he hoped within a weeke to leade some of them in a halter, meaninge the malsters; and I hope, saith Jho. Grannams, if God send mi Lord of Essex downe shortli, to se them hanged on gibbettes att their owne dores. To this

---

Richard III

Grim-visag'd War hath smooth'd his wrinkled front;
And now, in stead of mounting barbed steeds
To fright the souls of fearful adversaries,
He capers nimbly in a lady's chamber
To the lascivious pleasing of a lute.

—*Richard III,* 1.1.9–13

---

end I write this chiefli, that, as ur occasion shall suffer u to stai theare, theare might bi Sir Ed. Grev. some meanes made to the Knightes of the Parliament for an ease and discharge of such taxes and subsedies wherewith our towne is like to be charged, and I assure u I am in great feare and doubte bi no meanes hable to paie. Sir Ed. Gre. is gonne to Brestowe, and from thence to Lond., as I heare, who verie well knoweth our estates, and wil be willinge to do us ani good. Our great bell is broken, and W^m. Wiatt is mendinge the pavemente of the bridge. Mi sister is chearefull, and the Lord hath bin mercifull and comfortable unto hir in hir labours, and, so that u be well imploied, geveth u leave to followe ur occasions for i. weeke or fortnight longer. I would u weare furnisht to pai W^m. Pattrike for me xi.^li. and bring his quittance, for I thinke his specialtie is in Jho. Knight hand, due on Candlls. daie. Yestrdai I spake to M^r. Sheldon att Sir. Tho. Lucies for the staie of M^r. Burtons suite, and that the cause might be referred to M^r. Walkrs of Ellyngton; he answered me that M^r. Bur. was nowe att Lond., and, with all his harte and good will, the suite should be staied, and the matter so referred. I have here inclosed a breife of the reckoninge betwene him and me, as I would have it passe, and as in æqitie it should passe, if he wil be but as good as his faith and promise. Good brother, speake to Mr. Goodale that there be no more proceading in tharches bi Mr. Clopton, whom I am content and most willinge to compounde withall, and have bin ever since the beginninge of the laste terme, and thearefore much injured bi somebodie, that I have bin put to an unnecessarie charge of xx.s and upwardes that terme; whereas I had satisfied Mr. Clopton, as I was credibli made beleve by some of his servantes. I was allso assured of the staie of suit bi Mr. Barnes in the harvest, and bi Mr. Pendleburi the latter end of the terme. Mi brothr Woodwarde commeth up att the latter end of this weeke, who will speake with Mr. Clopton himselfe to that purpose. U understand bi mi letter I sent bi our countriman Burnell that masse Brentt dispatchd 50l. for u. Jh. Sdlr bounde alone as yeat. Because Mr. Brbr might not have it for 12. moneths, he would none att all, wherebi I lost mi expectation, and leafte, I assure u, in the greatest neede of 30l. that possibli maie be. In truth, brother, to u be it spoken and to nonne els, for want thereof knowe skarce wc. waie to turne me. Det Deus misericordiæ dominus exitum secundum bene placitum suum. Ur fathr with his blessinge and comendation, mi sister with her lovinge remembrance, comendes hir; in health both, with all ur children and houshold: ur fathr, extraordinari hartie, chearefull and lustie, hath sent u this remembrance innclosed. It maie be u knowe him his executr and brother, I meane of whom our brother Whte borowed for me the 80li. paihable att Mai next; his name I have not att hand. He dwelleth in Watlinge Streate. If 40li. thereof might be procured for 6. monethes more, it would make me whole. I knowe it doeth u good to be doinge good, and that u will do all the good u can. I would Hanlett weare at home, satisfied for his paines taken before his cominge, and so freed from further travell. Nunc Deus omnipotens, opt. max., pater omnimodæ consolationis, benedicat tibi in viis tuis, et secundet te in omnibus tuis, per Jhesum Christum, Dominum nostrum. Amen. Dum ullus sum tuis tum. Stretfordiæ, Januarii 24.

Abrah. Strl.

Comend me to Mr. Tom Bur'll, and prai him for me and mi bro. Da. Bakr. to looke that J. Tub maie be well hooped, that he leake not out lawe to our hurte for his cause; quod partim avidio non nihill suspicor et timeo.

Receved of Mr. Buttes:

In beanes 23 qrs., att 3s. 4d. the strike . . . . . . 30l. 13s. 4d.
Barlei 8 qrs., and 4 str., att 4s. the str . . . . . 13l. 12s. 0d.
Wheate 4 qrs. 4 str., att 6s. 8d. the str . . . . . 12l. 0s. 0d.
                                                          56l. 5s. 4d.

I have paid and sowed theareof, 52l. 11s. 8d. Mi Lad. Gre. is run in arreages with mi sister for malt, as it semeth, which hindreth and troubleth hir not a littell.
—*Shakespeare Documents,* vol. I, pp. 227–228

Shakespeare Listed as Hoarding Grain

By order of the Privy Council in 1594 and 1595, Stratford's Justices of the Peace prepared a list of the amount of grain held by Stratford's "townesmen" and "straingers" (Shakespeare Birthplace Trust Records Office, Misc. Doc. I, 106). In the mid 1590s poor weather, the practice of enclosing arable land for grazing, and two severe fires in Stratford caused shortages of grain. To try to prevent the practices of engrossing (hoarding grain) and forestalling (buying grain directly from the farmer rather than through the market) the justices ordered this inventory and were empowered to confiscate and resell the grain if necessary. The beginning of the list sets its scope and date:

Stratforde Burrowhe, Warrwicke. } The noate of corne & malte Taken the iiiith of ffebruarii, 1597, in the xlth yeare of the raigne of or moste gracious Soveragine Ladie Queen Elizabethe, &c.

—*Shakespeare Documents,* vol. I, pp. 281

The holdings of the residents of the Wood Street, Henley Street, Bridge Street, and Sheep Street wards are listed, followed by the holdings of the Chapel Street ward, where Shakespeare lived. Shakespeare's ten quarters of grain are among the largest holdings, but not out of keeping with those of his neighbors. The document does not say whether the grain was confiscated or what other citizens of Stratford thought about the grain hoarders, although the assemblies by citizens angry at the grain hoarders and "malsters" that Abraham Sturley describes in his 24 January 1598 letter indicate that many people were angry about the shortages and high prices of wheat and malt.

Chapple Street Warde. Townsmens corne.

ffrauncys Smythe jun. iii. quarters.
Jhon Coxe v. quarters.
Mr. Thomas Dyxon xvii. quarters.
Mr. Thomas Barber iii. quarters.
Mychaell Hare v. quarters.
Mr. Bifielde vi. quarters.
Hughe Aynger vi. quarters.
Thomas Badsey vi. quarters, bareley i. quarter.
Jhon Rogers x. str[ikes].
wm. Emmets viii. quarters.
Mr. Aspinall about xi. quarters.
wm Shackespere x. quarters.
Julii Shawe vii. quarters.
—*Shakespeare Documents,* vol. I, pp. 283

The holdings of the Chapel Street ward's strangers and the High Street ward follow. The document ends with a summary of the town's grain holdings.

Somme iiii. c.xxxviii. quarters vi. str. of malte of townes mens.
Wheate and mylecorne xliiii. quarters halfe.
Pease, beanes, and fetches, xv. quarters.
Barley ix. quarters vi. stricke.
Somme of straingers malte ii. c. li. quarters halfe.
—*Shakespeare Documents*, vol. I, pp. 284

Stationers' Register Entries

1 Henry IV *and* The Merchant of Venice *are entered in the Stationers' Register (Stationer's Hall, Register C, folios 31r, 39v). Abbreviated words have been silently expanded.*

xxvᵗᵒ die ffebruarii
Andrew Wyse./. Entred for his Copie under thandes of Mʳ Dix: and mʳ Warden man a booke intituled The historye of Henry the iiiiᵗʰ with his battaile of Shrewsburye against Henry Hottspurre of the Northe with the conceipted mirthe of Sir John ffalstoff'   viᵈ./.

xxiiᵒ Julii
James Robertes./ Entred for his copie under the handes of bothe the wardens, a booke of the Marchaunt of Venyce or otherwise called the Jewe of Venyce./ Provided that yt bee not prynted by the said James Robertes; or anye other whatsoever without lycence first had from the Right honorable the lord Chamberlen.   viᵈ
—*Bibliography of the English Printed Drama*, p. 13

Publications

Shakespeare's Lucrece *is published again.* 1 Henry IV *is published without attribution; a second edition was also published, but the title page has not survived; see the* Short Title Catalog, *entry 22279a.* Love's Labour's Lost *and* Richard III *are published with attribution. Two editions of Shakespeare's* Richard II *are published with attribution; in one imprint the book is "to be sold," and in the other the book is "to be solde."*

LVCRECE. / [*Printer's device*] / AT LONDON. / Printed by P.S. for Iohn / Harriſon. 1598.

THE / TRAGEDIE / of King Richard / the third. / Conteining his treacherous Plots againſt his / brother *Clarence*: the pitiful murther of his innocent / Nephewes: his tyrannicall vſurpation: with / the whole courſe of his deteſted life, and moſt / deſerued death. / As it hath beene lately Acted by the Right honourable / the Lord Chamberlaine his ſeruants. / By

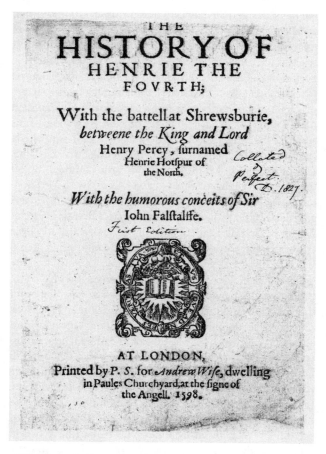

THE
HISTORY OF
HENRIE THE
FOVRTH;
With the battell at Shrewsburie,
betweene the King and Lord
Henry Percy, ſurnamed
Henrie Hotſpur of
the North.
With the humorous conceits of Sir
Iohn Falſtalffe.
AT LONDON,
Printed by P. S. for *Andrew Wiſe*, dwelling
in Paules Churchyard, at the ſigne of
the Angell. 1598.

Title page for the first quarto of Henry IV, *published without credit. The printer clearly believed that Falstaff was a selling point for the play (reproduced by permission of The Huntington Library, San Marino, California).*

William Shake-ſpeare. / [*Publisher's device*] / LONDON / Printed by Thomas Creede, for Andrew Wiſe, / dwelling in Paules Church-yard, at the ſigne / of the Angell. 1 5 9 8.

THE / Tragedie of King Ri- / chard the ſecond. / As it hath beene publikely acted by the Right Ho- / nourable the Lord Chamberlaine his / ſeruants. / By William Shake-ſpeare. / [*Publisher's device*] / L O N D O N / Printed by Valentine Simmes, for Andrew Wiſe, and / are to be ſold at his ſhop in Paules churchyard, at / the ſigne of the Angel. / 1 5 9 8.

London Tax Indenture Listing Shakespeare

This 1 October 1598 indenture between the London Commissioners for the 1597–1598 parliamentary subsidy and the petty collectors of Bishopsgate (PRO Exchequer, King's Remembrancer,

Subsidy Roll E 179/146/369) authorizes Ferdinando Clutterbrooke and Thomas Symons to collect taxes in Bishopgate Ward where Shakespeare was a resident.

Busshopsgate

This Indenture made yᵉ first day of October in yᵉ fortyth yeare of yᵉ reigne of our sovereigne Lady Elizabeth by yᵉ grace of God Queene of England ffraunce and Ireland Defendeʳ of yᵉ Faithe &c Between yᵉ right honorable Sʳ Richard Salltonstall knight Lord Maioʳ of yᵉ cyttie of London Sʳ John Hart and Sʳ Henry Billingsley knightes yᵉ Queenes Maᵗᵉˢ Commissioners amongest otheʳˢ authorized by hir highnes Commission under yᵉ greate seale of England for yᵉ taxation levyeing and gatheringe of yᵉ first subsydie of yᵉ three entire subsidies latelie graunted to hir Maᵗⁱᵉ by yᵉ highnes lay subjectes by Act of Parliamᵗ holden at Westmᵉʳ in yᵉ xxxixᵗʰ yeare of hir Maᵗᵉˢ reigne wᵗʰin yᵉ said Cytie of London on *thone* [deleted] thone partie and fferdynando clutterbooke Draper & Thomas Symons Skynner Cittizens of yᵉ said Cytie whome yᵉ said Commissioneʳˢ have named deputed and chosen and by theise presentes doe name depute & choose to bee Pettye collectoᵘʳˢ of yᵉ said first subsydie in yᵉ ward of Bushoppsgate wᵗʰin yᵉ sayd Cytie on thothᵉʳ partie Witnesseth yᵗ yᵉ sayd fferdinando Clutterbooke and Thomᵃˢ Symons soe named deputed appointed and chosen to bee pettie collectoᵘʳˢ in yᵉ sayd warde and authorized thereunto by theise presentes shall receive levye collect and gathᵉʳ of all and everye the sevᵉʳall persons hereafter named to yᵉ queenes Maᵗᵉˢ use all such sevᵉʳall sommes of monye as in this presente extract beene taxed and assessed upon them and every of them for their several values and substances rated specified and conteyned as hereafter followeth yᵗ is to saye of . . .

A list of delinquent taxpayers follows. Included in the list for "S.ᵗ Hellens parishe" is the following entry. The petty collectors placed the abbreviation for "Affidavit" to the left of Shakespeare's name as their legal assurance that the tax was not collected.

Affid   William Shakespeare   vˡⁱ   xiiiˢ   iiiiᵈ
            —*Shakespeare Documents*, vol. I, pp. 266–268

Letter from Richard Quiney to Shakespeare

The 25 October 1598 letter from Richard Quiney to Shakespeare (Shakespeare Birthplace Trust, MS. ER 27/4) was found among Quiney's papers and was apparently not sent, perhaps because Quiney met with Shakespeare in person. The letter is addressed "H [possibly "In haste"] / To my Loveinge good ffrend / & counterman mʳ Wᵐ / Shackespere del[iver] thees." This letter is probably part of the borrowing campaign Abraham Sturley suggested in his letter of 24

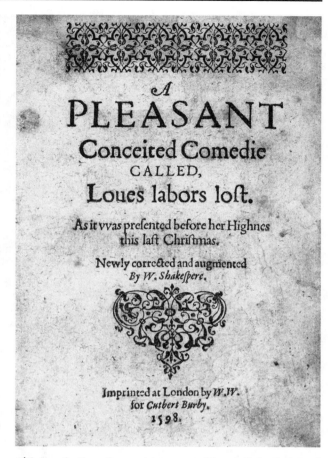

Title page for the earliest surviving quarto of Love's Labor's Lost. *It is the first of Shakespeare's comedies to be credited to him on the title page (by permission of the Folger Shakespeare Library).*

January. No additional surviving records explain why Quiney needed the money.

Loveinge Countreyman I am bolde of yoᵂ as of a ffrende, cravinge yoᵂʳ helpe wᵗʰ xxxˡˡ upon mʳ Bushells & my securytee or mʳ Myttons wᵗʰ me mʳ Rosswell is nott come to London. as yeate & I have especiall cause yoᵂ shall ffrende me much in helping me out of all the debettes I owe in London I thancke god & muche quiet my mynde wᶜʰ wolde nott be indebeted I am nowe towards the Cowrte in hope of answer for the dispatche of my Buysenes yoᵂ shall neither loase creddytt nor monney by me the Lorde wyllinge & nowe butt perswade yoᵂʳ selfe soe as I hope & yoᵂ shall nott need to feare butt wᵗʰ all hartie thanckefullnes I wyll holde my tyme & content yoᵂʳ ffrende & yf we bargaine farther yoᵂ shalbe the paiemʳ yoᵂʳ selfe. my tyme biddes me hasten to an ende & soe I committ this yoᵂʳ care & hope of yoᵂʳ helpe I feare I shall nott be backe thys night ffrom the Cowrte. haste the Lorde be wᵗʰ yoᵂ & wᵗʰ us all amen / ffrom the Bell in Carter Lane the 25 October 1598 /
            Yoᵂʳˢ in all kyndenes
            (signed) Ryc. Quyney

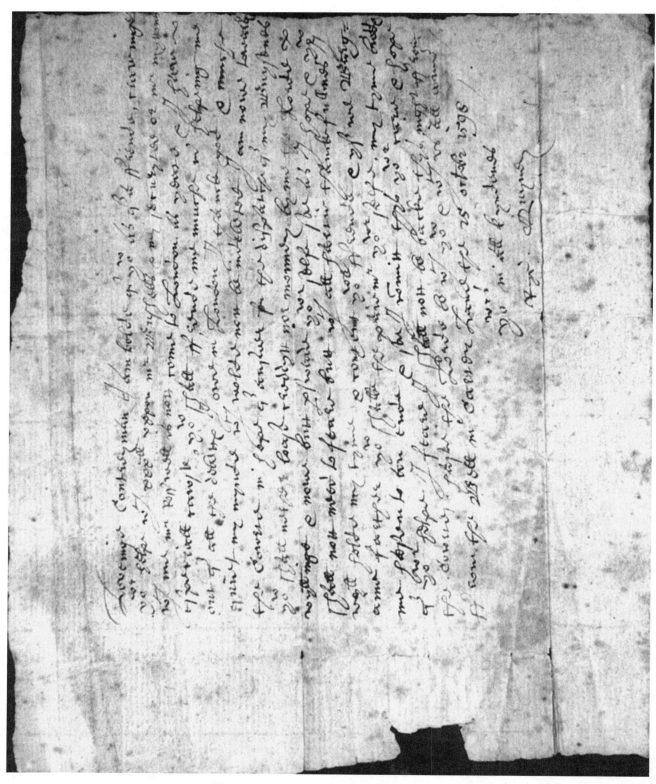

Richard Quiney's 25 October 1598 letter to Shakespeare (shelfmark ER 27/4; courtesy of the Shakespeare Birthplace Trust Records Office)

Letter from Adrian to Richard Quiney Mentioning Shakespeare

In this letter from father to son written in October or November 1598 (Shakespeare Birthplace Trust Records Office, Miscellaneous Documents I, 131) Adrian Quiney assumes his son Richard Quiney will approach Shakespeare for a loan.

Yow shalle, God wyllyng, receve from youre wyfe by M[r.] Baylye, thys b[ea]r[e]r, asowrance of x.[s.], and she wold have yow to bye some grocerye, yff hyt be resonable; yow maye have carryage by a woman who I wyllyd to com to you. M[r.] Layne by reporte hath receved a great summ of money of M[r.] Smyth of Wotten, but wylle not be knowyn of hyt, and denyd to lende your wyff any, but hys wyff sayd that he had receved v.[li.] which was gevyn hyr, and wysshd hym to lent that to your wyff, which he dyde; she hopyth to mayk provyssyon to paye M[r.] Combes and alle the rest. I wrot to yow concerning Jhon Rogers; the howsse goythe greatlye to dekaye; ask secretli therin, and doo somewhat therin, as he ys in doubt that M[r.] Parsonss wylle not paye the 3[li.] 13[s.] 4[d.] Wherfor wryte to hym, yff yow maye have carryage, to bye some such warys as yow may selle presentlye with profet. Yff yow bargen with W[m.] Sha . . or receve money therfor, brynge youre money homme that yow maye; and see howe knite stockynges be sold; ther ys gret byinge of them at Aysshome. Edward Wheat and Harrye, youre brother man, were both at Evyshome thys daye senet, and, as I harde, bestow 20[li.] ther in knyt hosse; wherefore I thynke yow maye doo good, yff yow can have money.

—Lewis, *Shakespeare Documents,* vol. I, p. 230

Letter from Sturley to Richard Quiney Mentioning Shakespeare

Shakespeare is again seen as a potential source of a substantial loan in a second letter from Stratford businessman Abraham Sturley to Richard Quiney, dated 4 November 1598 (Shakespeare Birthplace Trust Records Office, Miscellaneous Documents I, 136).

To his most lovinge brother, Mr. Richard Quinei, att the Bell in Carterlane att London, geve there.   Paid 2[d.]

All health, happines of suites and wellfare, be multiplied unto u and ur labours in God our Father bi Christ our Lord. Ur letter of the 25. of Octobr came to mi handes the laste of the same att night per Grenwai, which imported a stai of suites bi S[r.] Ed. Gr. advise, untill &c., and that onli u should followe on for tax and sub. presentli, and allso ur travell and hinderance of answere therein bi ur longe travell and thaffaires of the Courte; and that our countriman M[r.] W[m.] Shak. would procure us monei, which I will like of as I shall heare when, and wheare, and howe; and I prai let not go that occasion if it mai sorte to ani indifferent condicions. Allso that if monei might be had for 30 or 40[L.], a lease, &c., might be procured. Oh howe can u make dowbt of monei, who will not beare xxx. tie or xl.[s.] towards sutch a match. The latter end of ur letter which concerned ur houshold affaires I delivered presentli. Nowe to ur other letter of the 1[o] of Novmbr received the 3d. of the same. I would I weare with u; nai, if u continue with hope of those suietes u wrighte of, I thinke I shall wt. concent; and I will most willingli come unto u, as had u but advise and compani, and more monei presente, much might be done to obtaine our charter enlargd, ii. faires more, with tole of corne, bestes and sheepe, and a matter of more valewe then all that; for (sai u) all this is nothinge that is in hand, seeinge it will not rise to 80[L.], and the charges wil be greate. What this matter of more valewe meaneth I cannot undrstand; but me thinketh whatsoever the good would be, u are afraid of want of monei. Good thinges in hand or neare hand can not choose but be worth monei to bringe to hand, and, beinge assured, will, if neede be, bringe monei in their mouthes, there is no feare nor dowbte. If it be the rest of the tithes and the College houses and landes in our towne u speake of, the one halfe weare aboundantli ritch for us; and the other halfe to increase S[r.] Ed. riallties would both beare the charge and sett him sure on; the which I take to be your meaninge bi the latter parte of ur letter, where u write for a copie of the particulars, which allso u shall have accordingli. Oh howe I feare when I se what S[r.] Ed. can do, and howe neare it sitteth to himselfe, leaste he shall thinke it to good for us, and procure it for himselfe, as he served us the last time; for it semeth bi ur owne wordes theare is some of hit in ur owne conceite, when u write if S[r.] Ed. be as forward to do as to speake, it will be done; a dowbt I assure u not without dowbt to be made; whereto allso u ad, notwithstandinge that dowbt, no want but monei. Somewhat must be to S[r.] Ed. and to each one that dealeth somewhat and great reason. And me thinketh u need not be affraid to promise that as fitt for him, for all them, and for urselfe. The thinge obtained no dowbte will pai all. For present advise and encouragmente u have bi this time M[r.] Baili, and for monei, when u certifie what u have done and what u have spent, what u will do, and what u wante; somewhat u knowe we have in hand, and God will provide that wc. shall be sufficient. Be of good cowrage. Make fast S[r.] Ed. bi all meanes, or els all our hope and ur travelles be utterli disgraced. Consider and advise if S[r.] Ed. will be faste for us, so that bi his goodwill to us and his meanes for us these things be brought about. What weare it for the fee-farme of his

*B*lood *S*ports and *E*xecutions

London's theaters often competed for audiences with promoters of blood sports, including cock fighting and bearbaiting. The Bear Gardens, where bears, bulls, and dogs fought vicious battles, was next door to Shakespeare's Globe. Public executions were held frequently and had the additional advantage of being free.

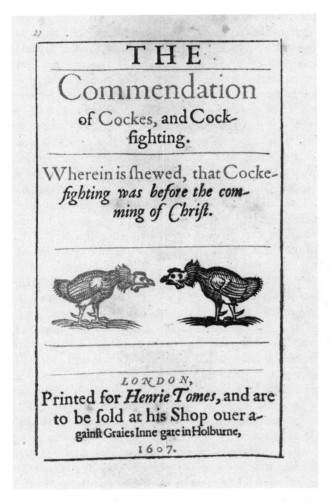

*Title page for a book about one of the popular entertainments of the day
(by permission of the Folger Shakespeare Library)*

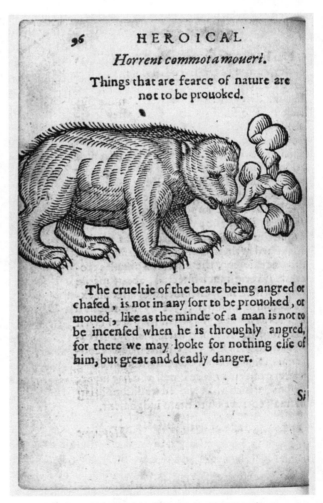

Page from Paradin's Heroicall Devises (1591). *The bear that pursues Antigonus as he makes his final exit from* The Winter's Tale *may have been borrowed from the bear garden near the Globe or may have been a costumed actor (by permission of the Folger Shakespeare Library).*

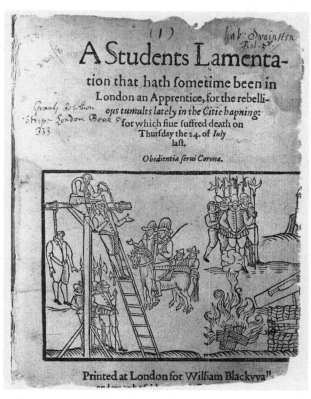

Title page for a pamphlet that describes noteworthy executions. Such illustrations may provide clues about how executions in plays were staged (by permission of the Folger Shakespeare Library).

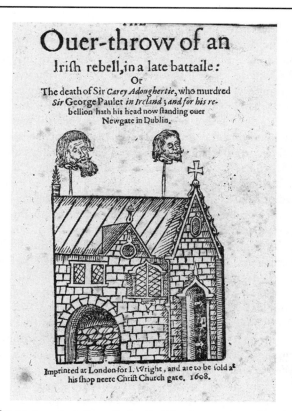

This title page, part of a continuing English print campaign to demonize Irish rebels, shows the heads of traitors being posted as a warning. Visitors to London frequently remarked about the heads of criminals posted on the city's gates (shelfmark G. 5543; courtesy of The British Library, London).

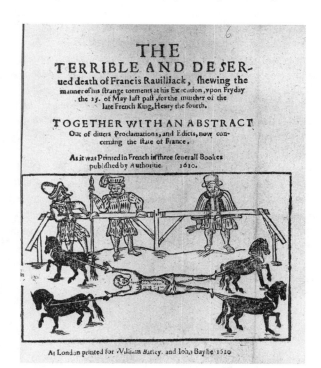

Title page showing the punishment for traitors (by permission of the Folger Shakespeare Library)

Philip the Bastard

Drawn in the flattering table of her eye!
Hang'd in the frowning wrinkle of her brow!
And quarter'd in her heart! he doth espy
Himself love's traitor. This is pity now,
That hang'd and drawn and quarter'd there should be
In such a love so vile a lout as he.

—*King John*, 2.1.504–509

rialties, nowe not above xii. or xiiii.^{l}, he weare assured of the dowble, when these thinges come to hande, or more, as the goodnes of the thinge procured proveth. But whi do i travell in these thinges, when I knowe not certainli what u intende, neither what ur meanes are, nor what are ur difficulties preciseli and bi name, all which must be knowen bi name, and specialli with an estimate of the charge before ani thinge can be added either for advise or supplie. I leave these matters therefore unto the Allmighties mercifull disposition in ur hand, untill a more neare possibilitie or more leisure will encourage u or suffer u to write more plainli and particularli. But withall the Chancell must not be forgotten, which allso obtained would yeald some pretti gub of monei for ur present busines, as I thinke. The particulars u write for shalle this morninge be dispatched and sent as soone as mai be. All is well att home; all ur paimentes made and dispatchd; mi sister saith if it be so that u can not be provided for M$^{rs.}$ Pendllbur, she will, if u will, send u up x.^{l} towardes that bi the next after, or if u take it up, pai it to whom u appointe. W$^m.$ Wallford sendeth order and monei per W$^m.$ Court nowe cominge, who hathe some cause to feare, for he was neweli served with proces on Twsdai last att Alcr. per Roger S. M$^r.$ Parsons supposeth that Wenlock came the same dai with M$^r.$ Baili that u writt ur letter. He saith he supposeth u mai use that x.^{l} for our brwinge matters. W$^m.$ Wiatt answered M$^r.$ Ba., and us all, that he would neither brwe himselfe, nor submitt himselfe to the order, but bi those veri wordes make against it with all the strength he could possibli make, yeat we do this dai begin M$^r.$ Bar. and miselfe a littell for assai. My bro. D. B. att Shrewsburi or homeward from thence. But nowe the bell hath runge mi time spent. The Lord of all power, glori, merci, and grace and goodnes, make his great power and mercie knowen towardes us in ur weakenes. Take heed of tabacco whereof we heare per. W$^m.$ Perri; against ani longe journei u mai undertake on foote of necessiti, or wherein the exercise of ur bodi must be imploied, drinke some good burned wine, or aqavitæ and ale strongli mingled without bread for a toste, and, above all, kepe u warme. Farewell, mi dare harte, and the Lord increase our loves and comfortes one to another, that once it mai be sutch as becometh Christianiti, puritie, and sinceriti, without staine or blemishe. Fare ye well; all ur and ours well. From Stretford, Novem. 4th, 1598. Urs in all love in the best bond,

Abrah. Sturlei.

M$^{rs.}$ Coomb, when Gilbert Charnocke paid them their monei, as he told me, said that if ani but he had brought it, she would not receve it, because she had not hir gowne; and that she would arrest u for hit as soone as u

come home, and much twattell; but att the end, so that youe would pai 4^l toward hit, she would allowe u xx.$^s.$, and we shall heare att some leasure howe fruictes are, and hoppes, and sutch knakkes. Att this point came W$^m.$ Sheldon, the silke man, with a warrant to serve W$^m.$ Walford againe upon a trespasse of 500^l.

—*Shakespeare Documents*, vol. I, pp. 230

Shakespeare Is Paid for a Load of Stone

Shakespeare's payment for a load of stone was recorded in the Stratford-upon-Avon Chamberlain's accounts, 1598 (Shakespeare Birthplace Trust Corporation Records, Chamberlain's Accounts 1585–1619, page 44). The stone was used to repair Clopton Bridge, which crosses the river Avon, linking Stratford to the Oxford road.

pd to m^r Shaxspere for on lod of ston x^d

Allen's Bill of Complaint Regarding The Theatre

Giles Allen was the ground landlord of the property on which James Burbage built The Theatre. When Burbage's sons Cuthbert and Richard were unable to negotiate a new lease with Allen, the Burbages, along with their carpenter Peter Street and "divers other persons to the number of twelve," dismantled the Theatre building, transported the timber and ironwork across the Thames, and used the pieces to construct the Globe theater. The dismantling took place on 28 December 1598; on 21 February 1599 the Burbages and five of their fellow actors, including Shakespeare, signed a lease for the land on which the Globe was built.

The following bill of complaint, dated November 1601, documents one of many lawsuits Allen filed against the Burbages; it and other depositions and interrogatories were transcribed by Charles William Wallace in his essay "The First London Theatre: Materials for a History" in University Studies (1913). Legal abbreviations have been silently expanded. Wallace notes that the words and letters in brackets at the end of the document are conjectures from the context, made necessary because "rats or mice gnawed through one side of the roll" of parchment on which the bill is written (p. 283).

Lune vicesino Tercio
Novembris Anno xliiii^{to}
Elizabethe Regine
    William Mill
  To the Queenes most excellent Majestie: . /
In most humble wyse complayninge sheweth unto your most Excellent Majestie: your highnes obedient and faythfull Subject Gyles Allein of Haseleigh in your highnes Countye of Essex gentleman That whereas your sayd

subject together with Sara his wyfe did heretofore by their Indenture bearinge date the thirteenth daye of Aprill in the eighteenth yeere of your highnes Raigne demise unto one James Burbage late of London Joyner certen howseing and voyde Groundes lyeing and being in Hollywell in the Countye of Middlesex for the Terme of one and twentye yeeres then next following for the yeerelye Rente of foureteene powndes, wherin it was covenanted on the parte of your sayd subject and the sayd Sara to make a newe Lease of the premisses to the sayde James Burbage or his assignes att any tyme within the firste Tenne yeers upon his or their Request for the terme of one and twenty yeeres from the making hereof. And it was by the same Indenture covenaunted on the parte of the sayd James Burbage That he or his assignes should within the sayd first Tenne yeeres bestowe the somme of two hundred powndes in alteringe and amendinge of the buyldings there (The value of the olde stuffe therof to be accompted parcell) In Consideracion of which somme of two hundred powndes soe to be bestowed It was covenanted on the parte of your Subject that it should be lawfull for the sayd James Burbage and his Assignes att anie tyme within the first one and twentye yeeres graunted, or within the one and twentye yeeres by vertue of the Covenante aforesayd to be graunted to take downe such Buylding as should within the sayd Tenne yeeres be erected on the sayd voyde grownedes for a Theater or playinge place, And afterwardes the sayd James Burbage did within the sayde Tenne yeeres (A Theater being then there erected att the Costes and Charges of one Braynes and not of the sayd James Burbage to the value of one Thowsand Markes) tender unto your subject a Draught of a newe lease of the premisses requiring your Subjecte to seale the same which your subject refused to doe, by reason that the sayd Draught soe tendred varyed much from the Covenantes in the former lease, And also for that the sayd James Burbage had before that tyme assigned all his Interest and terme in the sayd premisses unto one John Hide and had also bene a verye badd and troblesome tenante unto your sayd Subject. So that your Subject was in noe wyse bounde either in lawe or conscience to seale the same, And afterwardes the sayd Hide conveyed all his Interest and terme in the premisses unto one Cuthbert Burbage the sonne of the sayd James Burbage, whoe being desirous still to make gayne of the sayd Theater suffered the same there to contynue till the expiracion of the sayd Terme, Wherby the right and Interest of the sayd Theater was both in lawe and Conscience absolutely vested in your sayd Subject, Wheruppon your Subject seeing the greate and greevous abuses that grewe by the sayd Theater intended to pull downe the same, and to convert the wood and timber therof to some better use for the benefitt of your Subject which

your Subject had just Cause to doe, the rather for that your Subject had noe other meanes to be releived for thirtye powndes Arrerages of Rentes which the sayd James Burbage in his lyefe tyme did owe unto your Subject for the premisses, and for the breach of divers Covenantes in not repayring the howses and otherwise for that the sayd James Burbage had in his lyefe tyme made A deede of guift of all his goodes to the sayd Cuthbert Burbage and Richard Burbage his sonnes, whoe after the death of the sayd James Burbage procured Ellen Burbage his widdowe being a verye poore woman to take the Administracion uppon her which was done to defraude your Subject and other Creditors of the sayd James Burbage. But so it is yf it maye please your excellent Majestie: that the sayd Cuthbert Burbage having intelligence of your Subjectes purpose herein, and unlawfullye combyninge and confederating himselfe with the sayd Richard Burbage and one Peeter Streat, William Smyth and divers other persons to the number of twelve to your Subject unknowne did aboute the eight and twentyth daye of December in the one and fortyth yeere of your highnes Raygne, and sythence your highnes last and generall pardon by the Confederacye aforesayd ryotouslye assemble themselves together and then and there armed themselves with divers and manye unlawfull and offensive weapons, as namely, swordes daggers billes axes and such like And soe armed did then repayre unto the sayd Theater And then and there armed as aforesayd in verye ryotous outragious and forcyble manner and contrarye to the lawes of your hignes Realme attempted to pull downe the sayd Theater wheruppon divers of your Subjectes servauntes and farmers then goinge aboute in peacable manner to procure them to desist from that their unlawfull enterpryse, They the sayd ryotous persons aforesayd notwithstanding procured then therein with greate vyolence not onlye then and there forcyblye and ryotouslye resisting your subjectes servauntes and farmers but allso then and there pulling breaking and throwing downe the sayd Theater in verye outragious violent and riotous sort to the great disturbance and terrefyeing not onlye of your subjectes sayd servauntes and farmers but of divers others of your majesties loving subjectes there neere inhabitinge. And having so done did then also in most forrcible and ryotous manner take and carrye away from thence all the wood and timber therof unto the Banckside in the parishe of Sᵗ Marye Overyes and there erected a newe playe howse with the sayd Timber and wood, Wheruppon your Subjecte in Hillarye Terme following did commence an Accion of Trespas agaynst the sayd Peeter Streate in your highnes Courte at Westminster commonlye called the kinges Benche for the sayde wrongfull entringe into your subjectes groundes and pullinge downe and taking away of the

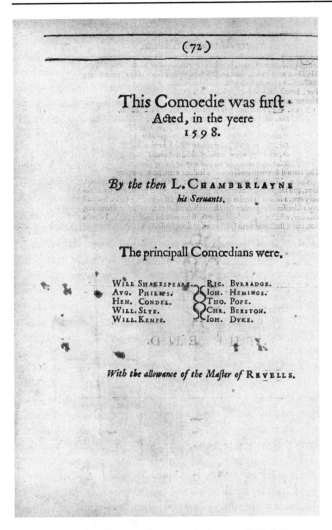

Page from The Workes of Benjamin Jonson *(1616) listing Shakespeare among the cast in* Every Man In His Humor *(by permission of the Folger Shakespeare Library)*

sayd Theater, Howbeit the sayd Cuthbert Burbage maliciouslye intending to vexe and molest your subjecte in Easter Terme followinge exhibited a Bill unto your highnes agaynst your subject in your hignes Courte of Requestes pretending matter of Equitye for the staye of your subjectes sayd sute att the Common lawe wherunto your subjecte appeared and made Aunswere, And afterwardes in Trinytye terme in the xlii[th] yeare of your highnes raigne an order was conceived and then published and pronounced by your highnes Councell of the sayd Courte by the Consent of your subjecte that your subjects sayd sute att the Common Lawe should staye till the cause in Equitye were heard in the sayd Courte of Requestes which was appoynted to be in Michellmas Terme following yett soe that the Demurrer which was formerlye joyned in the sayd sute betweene your subjecte and the sayd Peeter Streate might be made

upp which was expreslye graunted and allowed by the sayd order uppon the speciall mocion and desire of your subjectes Councell, wheruppon your subjecte gave order to his Attorney to cause the Demurrer to be made uppe accordinglye. / But maye it please your excellent Majestie the sayd Cuthbert Burbage myndinge further to intrappe your subjecte and to circumvent him to his great Daunger as the sequell sheweth did verye malycouslye and fraudulentlye after the sayd Order pronounced as aforesayd combyne and practise with one John Maddoxe then his Attorney in that sute with one Richard Lane the Register of the sayd Courte and by confederacye as aforesayd procured the sayd John Maddox to drawe an order (which appertayned not to him to doe but unto the Regyster of the sayd Courte of Requestes and likewyse procured the same to be entred and sett downe directly contrarye to that which was delivered and pronounced as aforesayd by your highnes Counsell of the sayd Courte, namelye that your subject should not proceed to the making upp of the Demurrer aforesayd. Therein verye highlye abusing your highnes sayd honorable Courte and greatlye injuringe your subjecte, Howbeit your subject having formerlye given Order to his Attorney for the making upp of the Demurrer nothing doubtinge but that safelye he might so doe being altogether ignorant of the fraudulent and sinister practise and confederacye aforesayd, And your subjectes Attorney havinge made upp the sayd Demurrer your subject made repayre home into the Countrye thinking all matters should rest in peace till the tyme appoynted for the hearing of the sayd Cause. But the sayd Cuthbert Burbage pursuing his former wicked and ungodlye purpose and seeking to plunge your subjecte in very greivous and inevitable mischeifs did the last daye of the sayd Trynitye Terme by the practise and confederacye of the sayd John Maddoxe make oath in your highnes sayd Courte of Requestes that your subjecte had broken the order of that Courte by making upp of the Demurrer aforesayd, Wheruppon your subject for that supposed Contempt was in the vacacion tyme then next followinge by the procurement of the sayd Cuthbert Burbage and by the confederacye aforesayd fetched upp to London by a Pursevant to his great vexacion and troble (beinge a man verye aged and unfitt to travell) and to his excessive charges in his Journey and otherwise to his great discreditt and disgrace in the Countrye, And your subject then by the sayd Pursevant brought before one of the masters of your highnes sayd Courte did (by the sayd masters order then made) become bounde unto the sayd Cuthbert Burbage in a bonde of two hundred powndes to appeare in the sayd Court of Requestes in the begining of the Terme of S[t] Michell then next following to aunswere the sayd supposed contempt and to stand to the Order of the sayd

Courte upon the hearinge of the Cause. And afterwardes your sayd subject at the sayd Terme appeared in the sayd Court accordingly, And the matter aforesayd being opened to your highnes Counsell there your subject was therupon by order of that Courte discharged of the supposed Contempt And afterwardes in the sayd Terme of St Michaell at the day appoynted for the hearing of the sayd Cause your subject appearing in your highnes sayd Courte and having divers witnesses there presente to testifie viva voce on the behaulfe of your subjecte, The sayd Cuthbert Burbage and the sayd Richard Burbage still persisting in their unlawfull and malicious Courses agaynst your subject did by the Confederacye aforesayd then and there very shamefully and unlawfullye revile with manye reproachfull termes your subjectes sayd witnesses and affirmed that they had formerly testified in the sayd Cause divers untruthes, and threatned to stabb some of your subjectes sayd witnesses because they had testified of the fraudulent deede of Guift made by James Burbage to the sayd Cuthbert Burbage and Richard Burbage as aforesayd, By which their furyous and unlawfull threates your subjectes witnesses were then soe terrefyed that they durst not testifie the truth on the behalfe of your subjecte in the sayd Cause. And further so it is yf it maye please your excellent Majestie That the sayd Cuthbert Burbage did verye maliciouslye and corruptlye and contrarye to the Lawes and statutes of your highnes Realme suborne and procure one Richard Hudson of the parishe of St Albons in London Carpenter and Thomas Osborne of the parishe of ffanchurche in London Carpenter to commit verye greivous and wilfull perjurye in the sayd sute in your highnes Court of Requestes in divers materyall poyntes concerninge the sayd sute The sayd Richard Hudson testifieing and deposing in the sayd sute on the behalfe of the sayd Cuthbert Burbage That he was present at a veiwe and estimate made of the Costes bestowed by the aforesayd James Burbage in his lyefe tyme upon the howses and Tenementes demised unto him by your subject which veiwe was taken the eighteenth daye of Julye in the yeere of our Lord god one thowsand five hundred eightye six by himselfe and others And that then it did appeare unto them That before that tyme The sayd James Burbage had bestowed uppon the sayd Howses and Tenementes the somme of two hundred and fortye poundes. And the sayd Thomas Osborne in like manner testyfieing and deposing in the sayd sute on the behalfe of the sayd Cuthbert Burbage That he likewise was present at the same veiwe and that it did then appeare that within foure or five yeeres before that veiwe taken there had bene bestowed uppon the sayd howses and Tenementes by the sayd James Burbage the somme of two hundred and fortye powndes. Wheras in truth the sayd Richard Hudson was not present at

any veiwe taken in the yeere aforesayd, but onlye at veiwe taken in the three and thirtyth yeere of your highnes Raigne as by the Deposicion of the sayd Richard Hudson himselfe heretofore made in your highnes Court of Chauncery and there remaynyng of record it doth evidentlye appeare neither had the sayd James Burbage at the tyme of the sayd veiwe supposed to be made the eighteenth daye of Julye in the sayd yeere of our Lord God 1586 bestowed anye thinge neere the somme of two hundred and fortye powndes wherof your Subject hopeth he shall be able to make verye sufficient proofe. By which unlawfull practices of the sayd Cuthbert Burbage your Subject did then lose his sayd Cause. And further so it is maye it please your excellent majestye, That aswell the sayd sute betweene your Subject and the sayd Streate As also the sayd sute betweene your subject and the sayd Cuthbert Burbage were prosecuted agaynst your subjecte by the maliciouse procurement and the unlawfull mayntenance of the aforesayd William Smyth (he t[he sayd] William unlawfullye [bringing]e the sayd sutes for th[e sayd] Cuthbert Burbage a[nd th]en unlawfullye expen[din]g and layeing out divers sommes of money in the same for and in the behalfe of the sayde Cuthbert Burbage [contrarye] to the Lawes and [statutes] of this your highnes R[ealme an]d to the great [prejud]ice of your subjecte In Consideracion wherof and for that the Ryott routes forcible Entries confederacies abuse of Justice maynten[ance and] other the misdem[eanors a]foresayd are contrar[ye to y]our highnes lawes [statutes] and ordinances [made] and established for [the] quiet and happye governement of this your highnes Realme and are not onlye ve[rye grei]vous unto your say[d subjec]t but also verye de[leteri]ous in example to [others] yf such and so fow[le m]isdemeanors should [esc]ape their due and condigne punishment Maye it therefore please your excellen[t Majestie] the premisses conside[red to g]raunt unto your su[bjecte] your highnes most [graci]ous writtes of Su[bpoen]a to be directed u[nto] the sayd Cuthbert Burbage, Richard Burbage, Peeter Streate William Smyth, [Richar]d Lane Richard H[udson] and Thomas Osbo[rne c]ommaunding them and [everye] of them therbye [on a] certen daye and u[nder] a certen payne therein to be lymitted personallye to be and appeare before yo[ur highnes] most honorable p[rivie] Counsell in your high[nes most] honorable Court [of Sta]rr-chamber to an[swer]e the misdemean[ors a]foresayd. And yo[ur] sayd subject shall according to his bounden dutye daylye praye t[o Almig]htye god for your ro[yall] majesties long lyfe [and pro]sperous Raigne./

J. Jeffreys [attorney]

—*University Studies*, 12 (1913): 276–283

Allusion to Shakespeare in Barnfield's *The Encomion of Lady Pecunia*

Like Shakespeare, poet Richard Barnfield had poems included in the collection The Passionate Pilgrim. *Barnfield, an Oxford graduate, also wrote the satiric* The Encomion of Lady Pecunia: or The praise of Money *(1598). In a prefatory poem Barnfield praises Shakespeare as a poet, not a playwright, and places him in the company of his contemporaries Edmund Spenser, Samuel Daniel, and Michael Drayton.*

A Remembrance of some English Poets.

Live *Spenser* ever, in thy *Fairy Queene*:
Whose like (for deepe Conceit) was never seene.
Crownd mayst thou bee, unto thy more renowne,
(As King of Poets) with a Lawrell Crowne.

And *Daniell*, praised for thy sweet-chast Verse:
Whose Fame is grav'd on *Rosamonds* blacke Herse.
Still mayst thou live: and still be honored,
For that rare Worke, *The White Rose and the Red*.

And *Drayton*, whose wel-written Tragedies,
And sweete Epistles, soare thy fame to skies.
Thy learned Name, is æquall with the rest;
Whose stately Numbers are so well addrest.

And *Shakespeare* thou, whose hony-flowing Vaine,
(Pleasing the World) thy Praises doth containe.
Whose *Venus* and whose *Lucrece* (sweete and chaste)
Thy Name in fames immortall Booke have plac't.
Live ever you, at least in Fame live ever:
Well may the Bodye dye, but Fame die never.

– sig. E2v

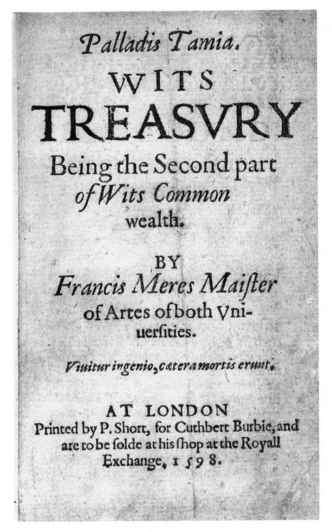

Allusion to *Romeo and Juliet* in Marston's *The Scourge of Villanie*

John Marston (circa 1575–1634), playwright and satirist, had a particularly vicious tongue. His The Scourge of Villanie. Three Bookes of Satyres *(1598) relentlessly mocks what Marston sees as the great abuses of the age: hypocrisy, idleness, pride, and other deadly sins. The excerpt below is from "Satyre X. Humours" and derides young men for their habit of quoting from popular plays, in this case Shakespeare's* Romeo and Juliet.

Luscus what's playd to day? faith now I know
I set thy lips abroach, from whence doth flow
Naught but pure *Juliat* and *Romio*.
Say, who acts best? *Drusus*, or *Roscio*?
Now I have him, that nere of ought did speake
But when of playes or Plaiers he did treate.
H'ath made a common-place booke out of plaies,
And speakes in print, at least what ere he sayes
Is warranted by Curtaine *plaudeties*,

If ere you heard him courting *Lesbias* eyes;
Say (Curteous Sir) speakes he not movingly
From out some new pathetique Tragedie?
He writes, he railes, he jests, he courts, what not,
And all from out his huge long scraped stock
Of well penn'd playes.

–sig. H4r

Allusions to Shakespeare and His Plays in Meres's *Palladis Tamia*

Francis Meres's Palladis Tamia *(1598) is a collection of analogies, most of them translated from classical sources. As in the selection here, Meres sometimes draws comparisons between classical and contemporary figures. In addition to Shakespeare's published works, Meres also speaks of the author's "sugred Sonnets" (which were not published until 1609) and several plays that had not then been published–"Gentlemen of Verona," "Errors," "Love labours wonne," "Midsummers night dreame," and "Merchant of Venice." Meres's inclusion of a play called* Love labours wonne *continues to draw critical attention. He may refer here to a lost play, a sequel to* Love's Labor's Lost, *or an alternative title for an extant play.*

Poets.

As the Greeke and Latine Poets have wonne immortall credit to their native speech, beeing encouraged and graced by liberall patrones and bountifull Benefactors: so our famous and learned Lawreat masters of England would entitle our English to far greater admired excellency, if either the Emperor *Augustus*, or *Octavia* his sister, or noble *Mecænas* were alive to rewarde and countenaunce them; or if our witty Comedians and stately Tragedians (the glorious and goodlie representers of all fine witte, glorified phrase and queint action) bee still supported and uphelde, by which meanes for lacke of Patrones (ô ingratefull and damned age) our Poets are soly or chiefly maintained, countenanced and patronized.

–pp. 277–278

A comparative discourse of our English Poets, with the *Greeke, Latine, and Italian Poets.*

As Greece had three Poets of great antiquity, *Orpheus, Linus* and *Musæus*; and *Italy,* other three auncient Poets, *Livius Andronicus, Ennius* & *Plautus*: so hath England three auncient Poets, *Chaucer, Gower* and *Lydgate*.

As *Homer* is reputed the Prince of Greek Poets; and *Petrarch* of Italian Poets: so *Chaucer* is accounted the God of English Poets.

As *Homer* was the first that adorned the Greek tongue with true quantity: so *Piers Plowman* was the first that observed the true quantitie of our verse without the curiositie of Rime.

Ovid writ a Chronicle from the beginning of the world to his own time, that is, to the raign of *Augustus* the Emperour: so hath *Harding* the Chronicler (after his maner of old harsh riming) from *Adam* to his time; that is, to the raigne of King Edward the fourth.

As *Sotades Maronites* the Iambicke Poet gave himselfe wholy to write impure and lascivious things: so *Skelton* (I know not for what great worthines, surnamed the Poet Laureat) applied his wit to scurrilities and ridiculous matters, such among the Greeks were called *Pantomimi*, with us Buffons.

As *Consaluo Periz* that excellent learned man, and Secretary to King *Philip* of Spayne, in translating the *Ulysses* of *Homer* out of Greeke into Spanish, hath by good judgement avoided the faulte of Ryming, although not fully hit perfect and true versifying: so hath *Henrie Howarde* that true and noble Earle of *Surrey* in translating the fourth book of *Virgils Æneas*, whom *Michael Drayton* in his *Englands heroycall Epistles* hath eternized for an Epistle to his faire *Geraldine*.

As these Neoterickes *Jovianus Pontanus, Politianus, Marullus Tarchaniota,* the two *Strozæ* the father and the son, *Palingenius, Mantuanus, Philelphus, Quintianus Stoæ* and *Germanus Brixius* have obtained renown and good place among the auncient Latine Poets: so also these English men being Latine Poets, *Gualter Haddon, Nicholas Car, Gabriel Harvey, Christopher Ocland, Thomas Newton* with his *Leyland, Thomas Watson, Thomas Campion, Brunswerd* & *Willey*, have attained good report and honorable advancement in the Latin Empyre.

As the Greeke tongue is made famous and eloquent by *Homer, Hesiod, Euripedes, Aeschilus, Sophocles, Pindarus, Phocylides* and *Aristophanes*; and the Latine tongue by *Virgill, Ovid, Horace, Silius Italicus, Lucanus, Lucretius, Ausonius,* and *Claudianus*: so the English tongue is mightily enriched, and gorgeouslie invested in rare ornaments and resplendent abiliments by sir *Philip Sidney, Spencer, Daniel, Drayton, Warner, Shakespeare, Marlow* and *Chapman*.

As *Xenophon*, who did imitate so excellently, as to give us *effigiem justi impery*, the portraiture of a just Empyre under the name of *Cyrus* (as *Cicero* saieth of him) made therein an absolute heroicall Poem; and as *Heliodorus* writ in prose his sugred invention of that picture of Love in *Theagines* and *Cariclea*, and yet both excellent admired Poets: so sir *Philip Sidney* writ his immortal Poem, *The Countesse of Pembrookes Arcadia*, in Prose, and yet our rarest Poet.

As *Sextus Propertius* saide; *Nescio quid magis nascitur Iliade*: so I say of *Spencers Fairy Queene*, I knowe not what more excellent or exquisite Poem may be written.

As *Achilles* had the advantage of *Hector*, because it was his fortune to bee extolled and renowned by the heavenly verse of *Homer*: so *Spensers Elisa* the *Færy Queen* hath the advantage of all the Queenes in the worlde, to bee eternized by so divine a Poet.

As *Theocritus* is famoused for his *Idyllia* in Greeke, and *Virgill* for his *Eclogs* in Latine: so *Spencer* their imitatour in his *Shepheardes Calender*, is renowned for the like argument, and honoured for fine Poeticall invention, and most exquisit wit.

As *Parthenius Nicæus* excellently sung the praises of his *Arete*: so *Daniel* hath divinely sonetted the matchlesse beauty of his *Delia*.

The Rapier and Dagger.

greater time, becaufe the point of the fworde is farther off from the enimie. The firft (being more neere)
with the onely encreafe of the foote forwardes, ftriketh more readily, yet not more forcible than the fe-
cond, which, when it ftriketh with the encreafe of a
ftraight pace, ioyneth to the force of the arme & hand,
the ftrength of the whole bodie.

Beginning then with the firft, as with that which
each man doth moft eafelie find: I faie, he ought if he
will keepe himfelfe within the boundes of true Arte,
to thruft onely with the increafe of the foote forwards,
fetling himfelfe in the lowe warde.

In

The firft Booke.   8

handes, therefore begin I pray you.
V. That which I haue promifed you I will now performe, therfore I fay, that when a teacher will begin to
make a Scholler, (as for me I wil begin with the fingle

Rapier, and at this weapon will firfte enter you, to
the ende you maye frame your hand, your foote, and
your body, all which partes muft goe together, and vn-
leffe you can ftirre and moue all thefe together, you
fhall neuer be able to performe any great matter, but
with great danger) I come therefore to the point and
fay, that when the teacher wil enter his fcholler, he fhal
D 3   caufe

Pages showing the proper use of the rapier and dagger and sword: (left) from the 1594 book Giacomo di Grassi his True arte of defence *(1594) and (right) from the 1595 book* Vincentio Saviolo his Practise *(by permission of the Folger Shakespeare Library). These books may indicate how weapon play was staged in plays such as* Hamlet.

As every one mourneth, when hee heareth of the lamentable plangors of *Thracian Orpheus* for his dearest *Euridice*: so every one passionateth, when he readeth the afflicted death of *Daniels* distressed *Rosamund*.

As *Lucan* hath mournefully depainted the civil wars of *Pompey* & *Caesar*: so hath *Daniel* the civill wars of Yorke and Lancaster: and *Drayton* the civill wars of *Edward* the second, and the Barons.

As *Virgil* doth imitate *Catullus* in the like matter of *Ariadne* for his story of Queene *Dido*: so *Michael Drayton* doth imitate *Ovid* in his *Englands Heroical Epistles*.

Hamlet and Osric

Hamlet: What's his weapon?

Osric: Rapier and dagger.

Hamlet: That's two of his weapons—but well.

—*Hamlet*, 5.2.144–146

As *Sophocles* was called a Bee for the sweetnes of his tongue: so in *Charles Fitz-Jefferies Drake*, *Drayton* is termed *Golden-mouth'd*, for the purity and pretiousnesse of his stile and phrase.

As *Accius, M. Attilius* and *Milithus* were called *Tragœdiographi*, because they writ Tragedies: so may wee truly terme *Michael Drayton Tragœdiographus*, for his passionate penning the downfals of valiant *Robert of Normandy*, chast *Matilda*, and great *Gaveston*.

As *Joan. Honterus* in Latine verse writ 3. Bookes of Cosmography with Geographicall tables: so *Michael Drayton* is now in penning English verse a Poem called *Polu-olbion* Geographical and Hydrographicall of all the forests, woods, mountaines, fountaines, rivers, lakes, flouds, bathes and springs that be in England.

As *Aulus Persius Flaccus* is reported among al writers to be of an honest life and upright conversation: so *Michael Drayton (quem toties honoris & amoris causa nomino)* among schollers, souldiours, Poets, and all sorts of people, is helde for a man of vertous disposition, honest conversation, and wel governed cariage, which is almost miraculous among good wits in these declining and corrupt times, when there is nothing but rogery in villanous man, & when cheating and craftines is counted the cleanest wit, and soundest wisdome.

As *Decius Ausonius Gallus in libris Fastorum*, penned the occurrences of the world from the first creation of it to his time, that is, to the raigne of the Emperor *Gratian*: so *Warner* in his absolute *Albions Englande* hath most admirably penned the historie of his own country from *Noah* to his time, that is, to the raigne of Queene *Elizabeth*; I have heard him termd of the best wits of both our Universities, our English *Homer*.

As *Euripedes* is the most sententious among the Greek Poets: so is *Warner* among our English Poets.

As the soule of *Euphorbus* was thought to live in *Pythagoras*: so the sweete wittie soule of *Ovid* lives in mellifluous & hony-tongued *Shakespeare*, witnes his *Venus and Adonis*, his *Lucrece*, his sugred Sonnets among his private friends, &c.

As *Plautus* and *Seneca* are accounted the best for Comedy and Tragedy among the Latines: so *Shakespeare* among the English is the most excellent in both kinds for the stage; for Comedy, witnes his *Gentlemen of Verona*, his *Errors*, his *Love labors lost*, his *Love labours wonne*, his *Midsummers night dreame*, & his *Merchant of Venice*: for Tragedy his *Richard the 2. Richard the 3. Henry the 4. King John, Titus Andronicus* and his *Romeo and Juliet*.

As *Epius Stolo* said, that the Muses would speake with *Plautus* tongue, if they would speak Latin: so I say that the Muses would speake with *Shakespeares* fine filed phrase, if they would speake English.

As *Musæus*, who wrote the love of *Hero* and *Leander*, had two excellent schollers, *Thamaras* & *Hercules*: so hath he in England two excellent Poets, imitators of him in the same argument and subject, *Christopher Marlow*, and *George Chapman*.

As *Ovid* saith of his worke;
Iamq[ue] opus exegi, quod nec Jovis ira, nec ignis,
Nec poterit ferrum, nec edax abolere vetustas.

And as *Horace* saith of his; *Exegi monumentum ære perennius; Regaliq; situ pyramidum altius; Quod non imber edax; Non Aquilo impotens possit diruere; aut innumerabilis annorum series & fuga temporum*: so say severally of sir *Philip Sidneys, Spencers Daniels, Draytons, Shakespeares*, and *Warners* workes;
Non Jovis ira: imbres: Mars: ferrum: flamma, senectus,
Hoc opus unda: lues: turbo: venena ruent.
Et quanquam ad plucherrimum hoc opus evertendum tres illi Diü conspirabunt, Cronus, Vulcanus, & pater ipse gentis;
Non tamen annorum series, non flamma, nec ensis,
Æternum potuit hoc abolere Decus.

As Italy had *Dante, Boccace, Petrarch, Tasso, Celiano* and *Ariosto*: so England had *Mathew Roydon, Thomas Atchelow, Thomas Watson, Thomas Kid, Robert Greene* & *George Peele*.

As there are eight famous and chiefe languages, *Hebrew, Greek, Latine, Syriack, Arabicke, Italian, Spanish* and *French*: so there are eight notable severall kindes of Poets, *Heroick, Lyricke, Tragicke, Comicke, Satiricke, Iambicke, Elegiacke* & *Pastoral*.

As *Homer* and *Virgil* among the Greeks and Latines are the chiefe Heroick Poets: so *Spencer* and *Warner* be our chiefe heroicall Makers.

As *Pindarus, Anacreon* and *Callimachus* among the Greekes; and *Horace* and *Catullus* among the Latines are the best Lyrick Poets: so in this faculty the best among our Poets are *Spencer* (who excelleth in all kinds) *Daniel, Drayton, Shakespeare, Bretton*.

As these Tragicke Poets flourished in Greece, *Aeschylus, Euripedes, Sophocles, Alexander Aetolus, Achæus Erithriæus, Astydamas Atheniensis, Apollodorus Tarsensis, Nicomachus Phrygius, Thespis Atticus*, and *Timon Apolloniates*; and these among the Latines, *Accius, M. Attilius, Pomponius Secundus* and *Seneca*: so these are our best for Tragedie, the Lorde *Buckhurst*, Doctor *Leg* of Cambridge, Doctor *Edes* of Oxforde, maister *Edward Ferris*, the Authour of the *Mirrour for Magistrates, Marlow, Peele, Watson, Kid, Shakespeare, Drayton, Chapman, Decker*, and *Benjamin Johnson*.

As *M. Anneus Lucanus* writ two excellent Tragedies, one called *Medea*, the other *de Incendio Troiæ cum Priami calamitate*: so Doctor *Leg* hath penned two famous tragedies, the one of *Richard the 3*. the other of the destruction of *Jerusalem*.

The best Poets for Comedy among the Greeks are these, *Menander, Aristophanes, Eupolis Atheniensis, Alexis Terius, Nicostratus, Amipsias Atheniensis, Anaxandrides Rhodius, Aristonymus, Archippus Atheniensis* and *Callias Atheniensis*; and among the Latines, *Plautus, Terence, Nævius, Sext. Turpilius, Licinius Imbrex*, and *Virgilius Romanus*: so the best for Comedy amongst us bee, *Edward* Earle of Oxforde, Doctor *Gager* of Oxforde, Maister *Rowley* once a rare Scholler of learned Pembrooke Hall in Cambridge, Maister *Edwardes* one of her Majesties Chappell, eloquent and wittie *John Lilly, Lodge, Gascoyne, Greene, Shakespeare, Thoms Nash, Thomas Heywood, Anthony Mundye* our best plotter, *Chapman, Porter, Wilson, Hathway*, and *Henry Chettle*.

As *Horace, Lucilius, Juvenall, Persius* & *Lucullus* are the best for Satyre among the Latines: so with us in the same faculty these are chiefe, *Piers Plowman, Lodge, Hall* of Imanuel Colledge in Cambridge; the Author of *Pigmalions Image, and certaine Satyrs*; the Author of *Skialetheia*.

Among the Greekes I wil name but two for *Iambicks, Archilochus Parius*, and *Hipponax Ephesius*: so amongst us I name but two Iambical Poets, *Gabriel Harvey*, and *Richard Stanyhurst*, bicause I have seene no mo in this kind.

As these are famous among the Greeks for Elegie, *Melanthus, Mymnerus Colophonius, Olympius Mysius, Parthenius Nicæus, Philetas Cous, Theogenes Megarensis,* and *Pigres Halicarnassæus*; and these among the Latines, *Mecænas, Ovid, Tibullus, Propertius, T. Valgius, Cassius Severus & Clodius Sabinus*: so these are the most passionate among us to bewaile and bemoane the perplexities of Love, *Henrie Howard* Earle of Surrey, sir *Thomas Wyat* the elder, sir *Francis Brian*, sir *Philip Sidney*, sir *Walter Rawley*, sir *Edward Dyer, Spencer, Daniel, Drayton, Shakespeare, Whetstone, Gascoyne, Samuell Page* sometimes fellowe of *Corpus Christi* Colledge in Oxford, *Churchyard, Bretton.*

–pp. 279–284

Allusion to *Love's Labor's Lost* in Tofte's *Alba*

Poet and translator Robert Tofte cites Shakespeare's comedy in his poem Alba. The Months Minde of a Melancholy Lover *(1598) as a further example of the narrator's romantic difficulties.*

Loves Labor Lost, I once did see a Play,
Ycleped so, so called to my paine,
Which I to heare to my small Joy did stay,
Giving attendance on my froward Dame,
   My misgiving minde presaging to me Ill,
   Yet was I drawne to see it gainst my Will.

This *Play* no *Play*, but Plague was unto me,
For there I lost the Love I liked most:
And what to others seemde a jest to be,
I, that (in earnest) found unto my cost.
   To every one (save me) twas *Comicall,*
   Whilst *Tragick* like to me it did befall.

Each Actor plaid in cunning wise his part,
But chiefly Those entrapt in *Cupids* snare:
Yet All was fained, twas not from the hart,
They seemde to grieve, but yet they felt no care:
   Twas I that Griefe (indeed) did beare in brest,
   The others did but make a show in Jest.

Yet neither faining theirs, nor my meere Truth,
Could make her once so much as for to smile:
Whilst she (despite of pitie milde and ruth)
Did sit as skorning of my Woes the while.
   Thus did she sit to see Love lose his Love,
   Like hardned Rock that force nor power can move.

–sig. G5r

Shakespeare Listed as a Tax Defaulter

*This document (PRO Exchequer, Lord Treasurer's Remembrancer, Accounts of Subsidies, E 359/56) shows Shake-*speare in default on his taxes. Legal abbreviations have been silently expanded.*

. . . . In Warda de Bishopsgate. . . . in parochia sancta helene Robertus Honiewoode generosus viii. li. Willielmus Shakespeare ibidem xiii. s. iiii. d. . . .
–Lewis, *Shakespeare Documents,* vol. I, p. 269

[In Bishopsgate ward in the parish of St. Helen: Robert Honiewoode, gentleman, 8 pounds; likewise William Shakespeare, 13 shillings 4 pence. . . .]

The Lord Chamberlain's Men Paid for Performances

Although Queen Elizabeth's accountants kept careful track of the payments made to Shakespeare's acting company, they did not note the titles of the plays performed during the 1598–1599 winter holidays.

To John Heminges and Thomas Pope servauntes to the Lorde Chamberleyne upon the Councelles warrant dated at Whitehall tercio Decembris 1598 for fower Interludes or playes played before her Majestie on S[t] Stephens nighte Newyeares nighte, Twelfe nighte, and Shrovesundaye at nighte laste paste togeather with theire Chardges and paynes the somme of xxvi[li] xiii[s] iiii[d] and by waye of her Majesties rewarde xiii[li] vi[s] viii[d] in all   xl[li]
–Dramatic Records, p. 30

Harvey's Comments on Shakespeare

Like many readers, scholar Gabriel Harvey (1550–1631) made marginal notes in his books. These notes, found in Harvey's copy of Thomas Speght's edition of The Workes of our Antient and lerned English Poet, Geffrey Chaucer *(1598), were transcribed by G. C. Moore Smith in* Gabriel Harvey's Marginalia *(1913). In* William Shakespeare: A Study of Facts and Problems *(1930), E. K. Chambers notes that it is impossible to date the marginalia, concluding "any date from 1598 to the opening weeks of 1601 seems . . . possible" (p. 197).*

Like Gascoigns flowers, herbs, and weeds. Heywoods proverbs, with His, & Sir Thomas Mores Epigrams, may serve for sufficient supplies of manie of theis devises. And now translated Petrarch, Ariosto, Tasso, & Bartas himself deserve curious comparison with Chaucer, Lidgate, & owre best Inglish, auncient & moderne. Amongst which, the Countesse of Pembrokes Arcadia, & the Faerie Queene ar now freshest in request: & Astrophil, & Amyntas ar none of the idlest pastimes of sum fine humanists. The Earle of Essex much commendes Albions England: and not unworthily for diverse notable pageants, before, & in the Chronicle. Sum Inglish, & other Histories nowhere more sensibly described, or more inwardly discovered. The Lord Mountjoy makes the like account of Daniels peece of the Chronicle, touching the Usurpation of Henrie of Bullingbrooke. which in deede is a fine, sententious, & politique peece of Poetrie: as proffitable, as pleasurable. The younger sort takes much delight in Shakespeares Venus, & Adonis: but his Lucrece, & his tragedie of Hamlet, Prince of Denmarke, have it in them, to please the wiser sort. Or such poets: or better: or none.

    Vilia miretur vulgus: mihi flavus Apollo
    Pocula Castaliæ plena ministret aquæ:
quoth Sir Edward Dier, betwene jest, & earnest. Whose written devises farr excell most of the sonets, and cantos in print. His Amaryllis, & Sir Walter Raleighs Cynthia, how fine & sweet inventions? Excellent matter of emulation for Spencer, Constable, France, Watson, Daniel, Warner, Chapman, Silvester, Shakespeare, & the rest of owr florishing metricians. I looke for much, aswell in verse, as in prose, from mie two Oxford frends, Doctor Gager, & M. Hackluit: both rarely furnished for the purpose: & I have a phansie to Owens new Epigrams, as pithie as elegant, as plesant as sharp, & sumtime as weightie as breife: & amongst so manie gentle, noble, & royall spirits meethinkes I see sum heroical thing in the clowdes: mie soveraine hope. Axiophilus shall forgett himself, or will remember to leave sum memorials behinde him: & to make an use of so manie rhapsodies, cantos, hymnes, odes, epigrams, sonets, & discourses, as at idle howers, or at flowing fitts he hath compiled. God knowes what is good for the world, & fitting for this age.

        –Gabriel Harvey's Marginalia, pp. 232–233

Harvey's marginal comments on Shakespeare in Francesco Guicciardini's Detti, et Fatti *(Venice, 1571) are reprinted in* Gabriel Harvey: His Life, Marginalia and Library *(1979), edited by Virginia F. Stern. The first part of his remark may be translated, "Above all, and for myself, before all, are the most penetrating disputes and round sentences in Seneca's tragedies."*

Now Domenichi, & the 4. Of Guazzo. Super omnes: & for miself, ante omnes, Argutissimae altercationes, et rotundus Logismus in Senecae Tragaed. Eliots dialogs: Gascoignes steel-glasse: Greenes quip for an upstart Courtier; & his art of Conniecatching: Diets drie dinner; a fresh supplie of Mensa philosophica; the Tragedie of Hamlet: Richard 3.

                    –p. 128

Shakespeare's Poetry Mocked in *The First Part of the Return from Parnassus*

*The students at St. John's College, Cambridge, wrote and produced the three Parnassus plays as part of their Christmas celebrations. The plots of each play concern the misfortunes of two students, Studioso and Philomusus, as they travel to Cambridge (*The Pilgrimage to Parnassus*), find their first jobs (*The First Part of the Returne from Parnassus*), and wind up as con men (*The Second Part of the Returne from Parnassus*). Some of the characters are satirical "types," such as the studious and poetical students, and others seem to be based on real persons. Very little is safe from the student mockery, including Shakespeare's poetry.*

In the following excerpts a wily poet, Ingenioso, who may be based on satirist Thomas Nashe, attempts to extract more money from his patron, Gullio, who may represent Henry Wriothesley, the Earl of Southampton and Shakespeare's patron. In the first excerpt Gullio quotes from and praises Shakespeare, but Gullio's stupidity does little to enhance the poet and playwright's reputation. In the second excerpt Ingenioso steals and rewrites lines from several poets, including Shakespeare, in his effort to help Gullio court a scornful mistress.

Ingenioso Amonge other of youre vertues I doe observe youre stile to be most pure, youre English tonge comes as neere Tullies as anie mans livinge.

Gullio Oh Sʳ, that was my care, to prove a complet gentleman, to be *tam Marti quàm Mercurio*; insomuche that I am pointed at for a poet in Pauls church yarde, and in the tilte yarde for a champion,—nay every man enquires after my abode: Gnats are unnoted where soe ere they flie, But Eagles waited on with every eye. I had in my dayes not unfitly bene likned to Sʳ Phillip Sidney, only with this diference, that I had the better legg, and more amiable face. His *Arcadia* was prittie, soe are my sonnetes; he had bene at Paris, I at Padua; he fought, and so dare I; he dyed in the lowe cuntries, and soe I thinke shall I; he loved a scholler, I mantaine them, witness thy selfe, nowe, because I sawe thee have the wit to acknowledge those vertus to be mine, which indeede are, I have restored thy dylaniated back & ruinous estate to those prettie clothes wherin thou now walkest.

Ingenioso Oh it is a moste lousie caste sute of his, that he before bought of an Irish souldier.—Durste envie otherwise reporte of your excellencie than I have done, I would bob him on the pate, & make forlorne malice recante. If I live, I will lime out your vertues in such rude colours as I have, that youre late nephwes may knowe what good witts were youre worshipps most bounden.

Gullio Nay I have not onlie recreated thy could state with the warmth of my bountie, but also mantaine other poetical spirites, that live upon my trenchers; in so muche that I cannot come to my Inn in Oxforde without a dozen congratulorie orations, made by Genus and Species and his ragged companions. I reward the poore ergoes moste bountifullie, and send them away. I am verie latelie registered in the roules of fame, in an Epigram made by a Cambridge man, one Weaver-fellow, I warrant him, els coulde he never have had such a quick sight into my vertues, howsoever I merit his praise: if I meet with him I will vouchsafe to give him condigne thankes.

Ingenioso Great reason the Muses shoulde flutter about youre immortal heade, since youre bodye is nothinge but a faire Inne of fairer guestes, that dwell ther in. But you have digrest from your M^{ris}, for whose sake you & I began this parley.

Gullio Marrie well remembred, Ile repeat unto you an enthusiasticall oration, wherwith my new M^{ris} ears were made happie. The carriage of my body, by the reporte of my mistriss, was excellent: I stood stroking up my haire, which became me very admirably, gave a low congey at the beginninge of each period, made every sentence end sweetly with an othe. It is the part of an Oratoure to perswade, & I know not how better, than to conclude with such earnest protestations. Suppose also that thou wert my M^{ris}, as somtime woodden statues represent the goddesses, thus I woulde looke amorously, thus I would pace, thus I woulde salute thee.

Ingenioso It will be my lucke to dye noe other death than by hearinge of his follies, I feare this speach thats a comminge will breede a deadly disease in my ears.

Gullio Pardon faire lady, thoughe sicke thoughted Gullio maks a maine unto thee, & like a bould faced sutore gins to woo thee.

Ingenioso We shall have nothinge but pure Shakspeare, and shreds of poetrie that he hath gathered at the theators.

Gullio Pardon mee moy mittressa, ast am a gentleman the moone in comparison of thy bright hue a meere

slutt, Anthonies Cleopatra a blacke browde milkmaide, Hellen a dowdie.

Ingenioso Marke Romeo and Juliet: o monstrous theft, I thinke he will runn throughe a whole booke of Samuell Daniells.

Gullio Thrise fairer than my selfe, thus I began,
The gods faire riches, sweete above compare,
Staine to all Nimphes, [m]ore lovely the[n] a man,
More white and red than doves and roses are:
Nature that made thee, with herselfe at strife,
Saith that the worlde hath ending with thy life.

Ingenioso Sweete Mr Shakspeare.

Gullio As I am a scholler, these arms of mine are long and strong withall:
Thus elms by vines are compast ere they falle.

Ingenioso Faith gentleman, youre reading is wonderfull in our English poetts.

Gullio Sweet M^{ris}, I vouchsafe to take some of there wordes and applie them to mine owne matters by a scholasticall imitation. Report thou upon thy credit, is not my vayne in courtinge gallant & honorable?

Ingenioso Admirable sanes compare, never was soe mellifluous a witt joynet to so pure a phrase, such comly gesture, suche gentleman like behaviour.

Gullio But stay, its verie true, good wittes have badd memories: I had almoste forgotten the cheife pointe I cald thee out for: new years day approcheth, and wheras other gallants bestowe Jewells upon there Mistrisses (as I have done whilome), I now count it base to do as the common people doe; I will bestow upon them the precious stons of my witt, a diamonde of Invention, that shall be above all value & esteeme; therfore, sithens I am employed in some weightie affayrs of the courte, I will have thee, Ingenioso, to make them, and when thou hast done, I will peruse, pollish, and correcte them.

Ingenioso My pen is youre bounden vassall to commande, but what vayne woulde it please you to have them in?

Gullio Not in a vaine veine (prettie y faith): make mee them in two or three divers vayns, in Chaucers, Gowers and Spencers, and Mr Shakspeares. Marry I thinke I shall entertaine those verses which run like these:

The Globe in Southwark

John Stowe's detailed description of London streets and neighborhoods, A Survay Of London. Contayning the Originall, Antiquity, Increase, Moderne estate, and description of that Citie, written in the year 1598 *(1598), includes the following description of Southwark, the area where Shakespeare's Globe was built.*

Now to returne to the West banke, there be the two Beare-gardens, the old and new places wherein be kept Beares, Bulles, and other beastes, to be bayted. As also Mastives in severall kenels are there nourished to bait them. These Beares and other beastes are there bayted in plottes of grounde, scaffolded about for the beholders to stand safe.

Next on this banke was sometime the *Bordello* (or Stewes) a place so called, of certaine stew houses priviledged there, for the repaire of incontinent men to the like women . . . .

– p. 331

Even as the sunn with purple coloured face
Had tane his laste leave on the weeping morne,
etc. O sweet Mr Shakspeare, Ile have his picture in my study at the courte.

Ingenioso Take heede my maisters, hele kill you with tediousness ere I can ridd him of the stage.

Gullio Come, let us in. Ile eate a bit of phesante, & drincke a cupp of wine in my cellar, & straight to the courte Ile goe: a countess and twoo lordes expect mee to day at dinner, they are my very honorable frendes, I muste not disapointe them.

Exeunt. . . .
—lines 925–1040

Gullio . . . But have you finished those verses in an Ambrosiall veyne, that must kiss my M^{ris} daintie hande? Ile nowe steale some time from my weightie affayres to peruse them.

Ingenioso Yes S^r, I have made them in there severall vayns; lett them be judged by youre elegante eares, and soe acquitted or condemned.

Gullio Lett mee heare Chaucers vaine firste, I love antiquitie, if it be not harshe.

Ingenioso Even as the flowers in the coulde of night
Yclosed slepen in there stalkes lowe,
Redressen them [against] the sunne brighte
And spreaden in theire kinde course by rowe,
Right soe mine eyne when I up to thee throwe,
They bene y cleard; therfore o Venus deare,

Thy might, thy grace y heried be it here.
Nor scrivenly nor craftilie I write;
Blott I a litell the paper with my teares,
Nought might mee gladden while I [did] endite
But this poore scroule, that thy name y bears.
Go blessed scroule, a blisfull destinie
Is shapen thee, my lady shalt thou see.
Nought fitteth mee in this sad thing I feare
To usen jolly tearmes of meriment;
Solemne tearmes better fitten this mattere
Then to usen tearmes of good content:
For if a painter a pike woulde painte
With asses feet, and headed like an ape,
It cordeth not, soe were it but a jape.

Gullio Noe more, nowe in my discreet judgment this I judge of them, that they are dull, harshe, and spiritless; my M^{ris} will soone finde them not to savoure of my sweet vayne. Besides, thers a worde in the laste canto, which my chaste Ladye will never endure the readinge of: thou shouldest have insinuated soe much, and not toulde it plainlye. What is becomne of arte? Well, dye when I will, I shall leave but litell learninge behinde mee upon the earthe. Well, those verses have purchast my implacable anger; lett mee heare youre other vayns.

Ingenioso S^r, the worde as Chaucer useth it, hath no unhonest meaninge in it, for it signifieth a jeste.

Gullio Tush, Chaucer is a foole, and you are another for defendinge of him.

Ingenioso Then you shall heare Spe[n]cers veyne.
A gentle pen rides prickinge on the plaine,
This paper plaine, to resalute my love.

Gullio Stay man, why thou haste a very lecherous witt, what wordes are these? Though thou comes somwhat neare my meaninge, yet it doth not become my gentle witt to sett it downe so plainlye. Youe schollers are simple felowes, men that never came where Ladies growe; I that have spente my life amonge them knowes best what becometh my pen, and theire Ladishipps ears. Let mee heare Mr Shakspears veyne.

Ingenioso Faire Venus, queene of beutie and of love,
Thy red doth stayne the blushinge of the morne,
Thy snowie neck shameth the milke white dove,
Thy presence doth this naked worlde adorne;
Gazinge on thee all other nymphes I scorne.
When ere thou dyest slowe shine that Satterday,
Beutie and grace muste sleepe with thee for aye.

Gullio Noe more, I am one that can judge according to the proverb *bovem ex unguibus.* Ey marry S^r, these have some life in them: let this duncified worlde esteeme of Spencer and Chaucer, Ile worshipp sweet Mr Shakspeare, and to honoure him will lay his *Venus and Adonis* under my pillowe, as wee reade of one (I do not well remember his name, but I am sure he was a kinge) slept with Homer under his beds heade. Well, Ile bestowe a Frenche crowne in the faire writinge of them out, and then Ile instructe thee about the delivery of them. Meane while, Ile have thee make an elegant description of my M^ris; liken the worste part of her to Cynthia, make also a familiar Dialogue be twixt her and my selfe. Ile now in, and correct these verses.   *Exit*

Ingenioso Why, who coulde endure this post put into a sattin sute, this haberdasher of lyes, this Bracchi-dochio, this Ladye munger, this meere rapier and dagger, this cringer, this foretopp, but a man thats ordayned to miserie? Well madame Pecunia, onc more for thy sake will I waite on this truncke, and with soothinge him upp in time will leave him a greater foole than I founde him.   *Exit*

–lines 1137–1217
–translated by Virginia F. Stern

1599

Shakespeare Identified as a Sharer in the Globe

In Witter vs. Hemings and Condell *(Court of Proceedings, James I), John Hemings and William Condell's answer to the complaint John Witter lodged against them reveals many details of the financial arrangements of the actors who owned the Globe theater, Shakespeare among them. Witter had married the widow of Augustine Phillips, one of the Globe sharers. The lawsuit was filed in 1619, but the events described occurred in 1599 and 1613. The text is from Charles William Wallace's "Shakespeare and his London Associates as Revealed in Recently Discovered Documents,"* which was published in University Studies *in 1910. Legal abbreviations have been silently expanded.*

The joynt and severall answers of John Hemings and Henry Condell gentlemen defendantes to the bill of Complaint of John Witter gentleman Complaynant.

The said Defendantes and either of them saveing to themselves and either of them nowe and at all times hereafter all advantages of excepcion to the incertentie & insufficiencie of the said bill of complaint for answer to so many of the matters therein conteyned as any way concerne them the said defendantes or is materiall for them or either of them to answer unto Do say & either of them for himself saith That he thincketh it to be true that the said Augustine Phillipps in the said bill of Complaint named was in his life time lawfully possessed of such terme of yeeres of & in a fiveth parte of the moitie of the said galleryes of the said Playhowse Called the globe in the said bill mencioned and of divers gardens thereunto belonging & adjoyning And that the said Nicholas Brend in the said bill named was thereof seised in his demesne as of fee as in the said bill is alledged But the said defendantes say that they do not thincke that the said Augustine Phillips was so possessed of the said terme of yeeres by force of a demise or lease to him the said Augustine Phillipps made of all the same by the said Nicholas Brend ymediatly/ ffor the said gardens and groundes whereupon the said Playhowse & galleryes were afterwardes builded were demised & letten by the said Nicholas Brend by his Indenture of lease tripartite bearing date in or about the xxi^th day of ffebruary in the xli^th yeere of the raigne of the late Queene Elizabeth unto Cuthbert Burbadge Richard Burbadge William Shakespeare the said Augustine Phillipps Thomas Pope the said John Heminges one of the said defendantes and William Kempe To have and to hould the one moitie of the said garden plottes and ground to the said Cuthbert Burbadge and Richard Burbadge their executors administrators & assignes from the ffeast or the birth of our Lord god Last past before the date of the said Indenture unto thend & terme of xxxi yeeres from thence next ensuing for the yeerely rent of seaven poundes & five shillinges And to have & to hould thother moitie of the said garden plottes & groundes unto the said William Shakespeare Augustine Phillipps Thomas Pope the said John Heminges one of the said defendantes & William Kempe their executors administrators & assignes from the said ffeast of the Birth of our Lord god then last past before the date of the said Indenture unto the said full end & terme of xxxi yeeres from thence next ensuing for the like yeerely rent of seaven poundes & five shillinges. Which said William Shakespeare Augustine Phillips Thomas Pope John Heminges & William Kempe did shortlie after graunte & assigne all the said Moitie of & in the said gardens & groundes unto William Levinson and Thomas Savage who regraunted & reassigned to everye of them severally a fift parte of the said Moitie of the said gardens & groundes, Upon which premisses or some parte thereof there was shortly after built the said then Playhowse. So as the said Augustine Phillipps had a fiveth parte of the moitie of the said gardens & groundes & after the said Play-

The Globe theater, circa 1600, from Claes Janzoon de Visscher's 1616 "View of London." Visscher worked from sketches or descriptions by other artists (Map L85c, number 7; courtesy of the Folger Shakespeare Library).

howse was built he had a fiveth parte of the said galleryes of the said Playhowse in joynt tenancie with the said William Shakespeare Thomas Pope the said John Heminges & William Kempe & as tenant in Common during the said terme of yeeres demised by the said Nicholas Brend as aforesaid as the said defendantes do take it But the said defendantes do say that about the time of the building of the said Playhowse & galleryes or shortlie after a third parte of the fiveth parte of the said Moitie of the said Playhowse galleryes gardens & ground which was the fiveth parte of the said William Kempe did come unto the said Augustine Phillipps by a graunt or assignement of the said fiveth parte made by the said William Kempe to the said William Shakespeare the said John Heminges one of the said defendantes and the said Augustine Phillips./ Which said Last mencioned fiveth parte did shortlie after come to Thomas Cressey by the graunte & assignement of the said William Shakespeare the said John Heminges and Augustine Phillipps which said Cressey did shortlie after regraunte and reassigne the said fiveth parte to the said William Shakespeare John Heminges Augustine Phillipps & Thomas Pope as the said defendantes do take it. So as the said Augustine Phillipps then had a fiveth parte and the fourth parte of another fiveth parte of the said moitie of the said playhowse galleryes gar-

dens and groundes as the said defendantes do verily beleeve for & during the same terme of yeeres/ And the said defendant John Heminges doth also say that he thincketh it to be true that the said Augustine Phillipps being so of one fiveth parte and of the fourth parte of another fiveth parte of the said moitie so possessed in or about the time in the said bill mencioned made his Last will & testament in writing & thereby made his then wife Anne his executrix of his said Last will & testament & shortlie after died so possessed of the said terme of & in the said parte of the said moitie as is aforesaid And that shortly after his decease his said will was proved in the Prerogative Court of Canterbury as in the said bill is alledged. And the said defendant John Heminges doth say that he likewise thincketh it to be true that by vertue of her the said Annes being Executrix of the said will shee into the said partes of the moitie of the said galleryes ground & playhowse late of the said Augustine Phillipps as aforesaid did enter & was thereof possessed accordingly and did receive & take the yssues proffittes and commodities thereof But whether her said entrie into the said parte or into any parte thereof was by virtue of a divise or guift in & by the said will & testament to her geven & devised or not this defendant saith he knoweth not And yet he thincketh it to be true that the said testator Augustine Phillipps in & by his said Last will & testament did geve & bequeath one third parte of all his goodes & chattells to the said Anne But this defendant saith that he doth not thinck that the said Anne made her eleccion to have a third parte of the partes Late of the said Augustine her said husband of the said moitie of the said galleryes gardens & ground as a legacie geven unto her by the said will And this defendant John Heminges doth also say that although the said testator Augustine Phillipps in & by his said Last will and testament did ordeyne & make the said Anne his wife Executrix of his said Last will & testament yet the same was not absolutely but onley with proviso or upon condicion in the said will expressed that if the said Anne his wife should at any time marrie after his decease That then & from thenceforth shee should cease to be any more or longer Executrix of his said Last will or any wayes intermedle with the same And that then and from thenceforth this defendant John Heminges the said Richard Burbadge William Slye & Tymothie Whitehorn should be fully & wholie his executors of his said Last will and testament as though the same Anne had never byn named As by the same last will and testament ready to be shewed to this honorable courte (to which the said will this said defendant for the more certentie thereof doth referre himself) more playnely appeareth. And this defendant John Heminges further saith that the said Complainant in or about the Moneth of November in the fourth Yeere of the Kinges Majesties raigne of England Did come to this defendant, and making shewe and affirming that the said Anne and himself then stood in greate nede of money did make offer to procure the said Anne to mortgage her said terme of and in the said fiveth parte of the said Playhowse galleryes gardens and groundes which was so regraunted to the said Augustine Phillipps by the said Levison and Savage as is aforesaid unto this defendant for the somme of fiftie poundes or thereaboutes wherewith to relieve their wantes and would have had the said Anne by herself to have made the said Mortgage to this defendant. But this defendant then suspecting that the said Complainant and Anne having then by a good space byne in treatie of a mariage betwene them might then be secretlie marryed and so her assuraunce alone nothing worth and nothing at all then doubting that the said Anne had assigned over the said terme of yeeres of & in the said fiveth parte of the said moitie to the said Complainant this defendant required the said Complainant to joyne in the said assuraunce of the said terme of yeeres of the said fiveth parte of the said moitie in Mortgage for his said money which he the said complainant yeelded unto And thereupon both the said complainant & the said Anne then confessing themselves to be maried joyned in the said Mortgage to this defendant and he paid unto them the said some of 50li which together with 50s for consideracion for the forbearaunce thereof this defendant Confesseth was repaid unto him on the day lymmitted in & by the said dede of assuraunce in mortgage for the repayment thereof. But this defendant did not knowe or thincke that the said Anne had assigned or settover the said terme of yeeres & the said interest of & in the said fiveth parte of the said moitie unto the said complainant which if shee had donne this defendant thincketh he had byne meerely deceived & defrauded of his said 50li if he would have lent the same without the said Complainantes joyning with the said Anne in the said Mortgage But if any such assignement of the said terme of yeeres was made by the said Anne unto the said Complainant before the said complainant & the said Anne intermaried the same was done contrary to the said testators meaning in & by his said Last will and to the trust by him reposed in the said Anne thereby & with purpose to take away & avoid theffect of the said condicion made by the said testator in his said will which was intended for the good & preferment of his children Which Course of dealing this defendant thincketh deserveth no favor or relief in any Court of equitie And this defendant hopeth to prove that the said Anne did not make the said supposed assignement of the said terme of yeeres & interest of & in the said fiveth parte of the said moitie to the said Complainant before their intermariage for that after their said intermariage the said complainant claymed the same parte only in the right of the said Anne his wife as Executrix of the said Augustine Phillipps as will appeare by divers writinges & otherwise And this defendant verely thincketh that if the said supposed assignement be produced & brought to light that it will not abide the touch in the triall thereof Or if the said Anne did make the said assignement unto the said Complainant before their intermariage this defendant hopeth to prove that it was and is meerely void in Lawe And this defendant saith that after the said intermariage of the said Complainant with the said Anne he the said complainant did joyne in the graunting of two sixth partes of the said Moitie of & in the said Playhowse galleryes gardens and groundes with this defendant & the rest then interessed therein unto William Slye and the said other defendant Henry Condell / And this defendant doth deny that he or to his knowledge the said other defendant Henry Condell hath the said assignement or graunt so supposed to be made by the said Anne to the said Complainant. But Confesseth that he hath the said last will and testament of the said Augustine Phillips and the said dede whereby the said Augustine Phillipps had onely a fiveth parte of the said Moitie of the said Playhowse galleryes gardens & ground during the said terme yeeres and that at & upon the earnest solicitacion & intreatie of the said Anne before the said repayment of the said fiftie poundes unto this defendant shee then in urgent manner affirming unto him that the deliverye thereof unto the said Complainant would be her utter undoing he this defendant did forbeare to deliver the same unto the said Complainant but kept the same And this defendant hath also in his handes and Custody the said originall lease so made by the said Nicholas Brend to him & others as is aforesaid and keepeth the same to the use of himself & the rest which have any interest thereunto by & with their Consentes And this defendant further saith that by meanes that the said Complainant & the said Anne were intermaryed whereby the said Condicion in the said will of the said Augustine Phillipps was broken and especially to keepe the Complainant from receaving or recovering of the some of 300^{li} which did then remaine in the handes of Sir Eusebius Isam Knight least he should spend the same as he had before lavishly and riotously spent wasted & consumed almost all the rest of the said goodes & chattells which were of the said Augustine Phillipps and as he after spent 80^{li} of the said 300^{li} which he gott out of this defendantes handes after that he had received the same 300^{li} of the said Sir Eusebius and with the consent and intreatie of the said Anne the administracion of the goodes and chattells of the said Augustine Phillipps in or about the Moneth of May in the fiveth yeere of his Majeties said raigne was Committed to this defendant in the prerogative Court of Canterbury as Executor of the said Last will & testament of the said Augustine Phillipps By virtue whereof he this defendant did enter into the said fiveth parte of the said moitie of the said Playhowse galleryes gardens and groundes and did take the rentes yssues and proffittes thereof as well & lawfull it was as he hopeth for him to doe After which said administracion so taken by this defendant he paid a legacie of five poundes to or for the poore of Mortlack in the County of Surrey which the said Anne & the said Complainant had left unpaid by all the time wherein shee was executrix as aforesaid and he this defendant is to pay more legacyes to others when the same shalbe due & payable by the same last will and this defendant in Charitie also to relieve the said Complainant & the said Anne his wife & her children did from time to time divers & many times deliver sometimes unto the said Complainant & sometimes to the said Anne divers sommes of money amounting in the whole to a greate some untill about the Moneth of ffebruary in the Eight yeere of his Majesties said raigne about which time the said complainant & Anne his wife by their dede pole bearing date

the tenth day of ffebruary in the said Eight yeere of his Majesties said raigne (this defendant then being in possession of the said fiveth parte of the said moitie of the said playhowse galleryes groundes & gardens) did remise & release unto this defendant all & al manner of accions debtes bills bondes accomptes matters & demaundes whatsoever as by the said dede pole ready to be shewed to this honorable Courte may appeare By which said release this defendant hopeth that the said Complainant is barred both in lawe & equitie to sue for or demaund the said fiveth parte of the said moitie of the said playhowse galleryes ground or gardens & Contrary or against which said Complainantes owne dede of release this defendant hopeth that this honorable Courte will not permitt the said Complainant to sue this defendant for the said fiveth parte or any parte of the said moitie of the said playhowse in this honorable Courte And this defendant further saith that shortlie after the makeing of the said release by the said Complainant & his wife to this defendant the said Complainant & his said wife did take a lease of this defendant by Indenture bearing the date the xiiiith day of the said Moneth of february which was but foure dayes after the date of the said release, of a sixth parte of the said moitie of the said playhowse garden plottes and premisses for the terme of Eighteene yeeres from the birth of our Lord god then last past yelding & paying therefore yeerely during the said terme unto this defendant his executors administrators & assignes xxiiii^{s} ii^{d} of Lawfull money of England at the ffeastes of thanunciacion of the blessed virgin Mary the Nativity of St John Baptist St Michael Tharchangell & the birth of our Lord god or within tenne dayes after everye of the same ffeast dayes by even porcions Provided alwayes that if it should happen the said yeerely rent of xxiiii^{s} ii^{d} to be behinde unpaid in parte or in all by the said space of tenne dayes next over or after any of the ffeast dayes of payment thereof aforesaid in which the same ought to be paid being lawfully demaunded Or if the said Complainant his executors administrators or assignes should not within one yeere then next Comeing pay and discharge the said legacie of five poundes geven & bequeathed by the last will & testament aforesaid unto the poore of the parish of Mortlack or should not within the space of one whole yeere then next Comeing Cause & procure a sufficient acquittaunce or dischardge under the handes & seales of the parson or Curat and Churchwardens of the said parish to be geven & delivered to this defendant his executors administrators or assignes for his & their dischardge of & for the said legacie of five poundes with divers others partes of the said Condicion hereafter to be performed by the said Complainant his executors

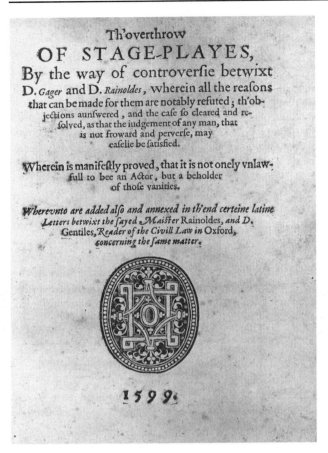

Th'overthrow

OF STAGE-PLAYES,

By the way of controverſie betwixt
D. *Gager* and D. *Rainoldes*, wherein all the reaſons
that can be made for them are notably refuted; th'objections aunſwered, and the caſe ſo cleared and reſolved, as that the iudgement of any man, that
is not froward and perverſe, may
eaſelie be ſatisfied.

Wherein is manifeſtly proved, that it is not onely vnlaw-
full to bee an Actor, but a beholder
of thoſe vanities.

Whereunto are added alſo and annexed in th'end certeine latine
Letters betwixt the ſayed *Maiſter* Rainoldes, *and* D.
Gentiles, *Reader of the Civill Law in* Oxford,
concerning the ſame matter.

1599.

*Title page for John Rainolds's anti-theatrical tract that indicts both
players and audience members (by permission of the
Folger Shakespeare Library)*

administrators & aſſignes That then the demiſe &
graunte aforeſaid of the premiſes ſhould be void &
of none effect. In which ſaid Indenture of leaſe it is
recited and expreſſed that the ſaid ſixth parte of the
ſaid Moitie of the ſaid Playhowſe garden plottes &
premiſſes was then Lawfully Come to the handes &
poſſeſſion of this defendant by his being adminiſtrator of the goodes chattells rightes & debtes aforeſaid
of the ſaid Auguſtine Phillipps, And that this defendant in conſideracion that the ſaid Complainant
ſhould pay & diſchardge the ſaid Legacie of five
poundes and two other legacies of tenne poundes a
peece mencioned in the ſaid Condicion did make the
ſaid demiſe & leaſe As by the Counterparte of the
ſaid Indenture of leaſe ready to be ſhewed to this
honorable Courte (whereto this defendant referreth
himſelf) more playnely appeareth /. whereby this
defendant thinccketh that it manifeſtly appeareth that
the ſaid Complainant then claymed not the ſaid ſixth
parte of the ſaid Moitie by the ſaid ſuppoſed aſſigne-
ment by him pretended to be thereof made unto him

by the ſaid Anne & that this defendant was Lawfully
intereſſed in the ſaid ſixth parte as adminiſtrator
when the ſaid releaſe was ſo made unto him or by the
ſaid releaſe when the ſaid defendant made the ſaid
Leaſe unto the ſaid Complainant & his ſaid wife of
the ſaid ſixth parte of the ſaid moitie of the ſaid playhowſe gardens & ground And this defendant further
ſaith that about the ſaid terme of five yeeres Laſt paſt
mencioned in the ſaid bill of Complaint or about Six
Monethes before the ſaid Playhowſe and galleryes
were caſually burnt downe & conſumed with fier/.
Shortlie after which this defendant and his partners in
the ſaid Playhowſe reſolved to reedifie the ſame &
the rather becauſe they were by Covenante on their
parte in the ſaid originall leaſe conteyned to main-
teyne & repaire all ſuch buildinges as ſhould be built
or erected upon the ſaid gardens or ground during
the ſaid terme as by the ſaid originall leaſe may
appeare And thereupon this defendant did write his
Lettre to the ſaid Complainant ſignifieing the ſame
unto him & therein required him to come & bring or
ſend 50^{li} or 60^{li} by a day therein mencioned for &
towardes the reedifieing of a howſe in regard of his
the ſaid Complainantes parte of the ſaid ground
which this defendant had ſo demiſed unto him & his
ſaid wife by the ſaid leaſe if he would adventure ſo
much (he the ſaid Complainant having latly before
joyned with the ſaid defendantes & the reſt then intereſſed in the ſaid moitie of the ſaid playhowſe gardens
& ground to William Oſtler of a ſeaventh parte of the
ſaid moitie) But the ſaid Complainant neither
brought or ſent any money towardes the reedifieing
of the ſaid Playhowſe Nor did this defendant ever
receive any anſwer by or from him the ſaid Complainant of his this defendantes ſaid Lettre which
when this defendant perceived although the ſaid
Complainant had broken the ſaid Condicion of the
ſaid leaſe by not paying the ſaid legacie of five
poundes & by not procuring of the ſaid acquittaunce
or diſchardge from the ſaid parſon or Curatt &
Churchwardens of Mortlack aforeſaid yet he this
defendant demaunded the two next quarters rentes
reſerved upon the ſaid leaſe on the ſeverall tenth
dayes after the ſaid two next ffeaſtes of payment &
there Continuing his ſaid demaundes untill the ſunne
was ſett on either of the ſaid dayes But neither the
ſaid Complainant nor any for him paid or came to
pay either of the ſaid quarters rentes on either of the
ſaid dayes And thereupon this defendant did enter
into the ſaid parte ſo demiſed as aforeſaid for the ſaid
Condicion broken & becauſe he found that the reedifieing of the ſaid playhowſe would be a verie great
charge & doubted what benefitt would ariſe thereby &
for that the ſaid originall Leaſe had then but a fewe

yeeres to come he this defendant did geve away his said terme of yeeres & interest of & in the one Moitie of the said parte of the said Moitie of the said garden plottes & ground to the said other defendant Henry Condell gratis The reedifieing of which parte hath sithence Cost the said defendantes about the somme of Cxx^{li}, and yet one other sixth parte of the said moitie of the said playhowse galleryes gardens & ground before the said playhowse was burned & Consumed with fier was absolutely sould for lesse money then the half of the said charges of the said defendantes in the newe building thereof when there were more yeeres to come therein then there were at the time of the said burning thereof & yet the said Complainant was in Lawe chardgeable with the reedifieing of the said parte of the said moitie by the said lease, And this defendant further saith that sithence the said release & lease made as is aforesaid he hath also from time to time divers & manie times in Charitie & to relieve the said Complainant his said wife & her children delivered sometimes unto the said Complainant himself, sometimes to his said wife & sometimes to others for them divers other sommes of money amounting to a further greate some of money untill about the said time of the burning of the said playhowse & the said Complainant divers yeeres before the said Anne dyed did suffer her to make shift for herself to live & at her death this defendant out of charitie was at the charges of the buryeing of her. / Without that that the said Nicholas Brend made a demise or lease of the said sixth parte of the said moitie to the said Augustine Phillipps or of any parte otherwise then as is aforesaid or that the said Anne to this defendantes knowledge did or could graunte or assigne the said supposed originall lease to the said Complainant or that the said Augustine Phillipps died possessed of a sixth parte onely of the said playhowse gardens & groundes as in the said bill of Complaint is pretended/ And the said other defendant Henry Condell for himself saith that the said other defendant John Heminges a litle before the reedifieing of the said newe playhowse did freely geve & assure unto him one moitie of the said parte of the said garden plottes & groundes but denyeth that he or to his knowledge the said other defendant John Heminges hath the said assignement or graunt so supposed to be made by the said Anne to the said Complainant or that he this defendant hath the said Last will & testament of the said Augustine Phillipps or the said dede whereby the said Augustine had onely a sixth parte of the said moitie of the said playhowse galleryes gardens & ground during the said terme of yeeres or the said originall lease made by the said Brend but he thincketh that the said other defendant hath the same

will dede & originall lease. And both the said defendantes Do say & confesse that a litle space before the reedifieing of the said playhowse they the said defendantes did enter into the said moitie of the said parte of the said moity of the said Garden plotts and grounds which was of the said Augustine Phillipps and doe yet keepe the same and from and after the reedifying of the said playhowse did and yet doe receive and take the rents and proffitts thereof and doe keepe the same from the said Complainant as well & Lawfull it was & is for them as they hope to doe, Without that that the said defendantes have made or contrived to themselves or to any other person or persons any estate or estates of the said parte other then is above mencioned & one Eight parte of the said moitie of the said playhowse galleryes gardens & groundes graunted by the said defendantes & other their partners in the said moitie to Nathan ffield & one other estate made to John Atkins gent in trust for the said defendant John Heminges of two litle parcells of the said ground by the said defendant John Heminges & the rest of the partners in the said Playhowse & premisses upon parte whereof the said John Heminges hath built a howse And without that that the said defendantes have made or contrived to themselves or to any other person or persons any secrett subtill or fraudulent estates of purpose to defraud or defeate the said Complainant or otherwise as in & by the said bill of Complaint is very falsely & slaunderously suggested And without that that any other matter or thing in the said bill of Complaint conteyned materiall or effectuall for the said defendantes or either of them to answer unto & herein & hereby not sufficiently answered unto confessed & avoided denyed or traversed to these defendantes knowledges is true All which matters the said defendantes & either of them are ready to averre & prove as this Court shall award & do pray to be dismissed forth of the same with either of their reasonable costes & charges in this behalf most wrongfully susteyned/

Seb: Kele:
—University Studies, 10 (1910): 312–323

Further Details of Shakespeare's Share of the Globe

The Burbages provided details about the theaters their family built and owned and about their financial arrangements with the "sharers" in the theaters in the answer of Cuthbert Burbage and others to the 1635 petition by Robert Benfield and others (PRO LC 5/133 pages 50–51). The events described in this document occurred circa 1599; the lawsuit was filed in 1635.

To ye Right Honble Philip Earle of Pembroke & Montgomery Lord Chamberlaine of his Mates Houshold.

Right Honble & our singular good Lord. Wee your humble suppl[ian]tes Cutbert Burbage & Winifrid his Brothers wife & Wm his sonne doe tender to your honble consideration for what respectes & good reasons wee ought not in all charity to bee disabled of or lively-hoodes by men soe soone shott up, since it hath beene the custome that they should come to it by farre more antiquity and desert, then those can justly attribute to them selves.

And first humbly shewing to your honor the infinite Charges, the manifolde law suites, the leases expiration by the restraintes in sicknes times & other accidentes that did cutt from them the best part of the gaines that yr honor is informed they have received. /

The father of us Cuthbert & Richd Burbage was the first builder of Playhowses & was himselfe in his younger yeeres a Player. The Theater hee built wth many Hundred poundes taken up at interest. The Players that lived in those first times had onely the profitts arising from the dores, but now the players receave all the commings in at the dores to them selves & halfe the Galleries from the Houskeepers. Hee built this house upon leased ground, by wch meanes the Landlord & Hee had a great suite in law & by his death, the like troubles fell on us, his sonnes; wee then bethought us of altering from thence, & at like expence built the Globe wth more summes of money taken up at interest, which lay heavy on us many yeeres, & to or selves wee joyned those deserving men, Shakspere Hemings, Condall, Philips and others partners in ye profittes of that they call the House, but making the Leases for 21 yeares hath beene the destruction of or selves & others, for they dyeing at the expiration of 3 or 4 yeeres of their lease, the subsequent yeeres became dissolved to strangers as by marrying wth their widdowes & the like by their Children.

Thus Right Honble, as concerning the Globe, where wee or selves are but Lessees. Now for the Blackfriers that is or inheritance, or father purchased it at extreame rates & made it into a play house wth great charge and trouble, which after was leased out to one Evans that first sett up the Boyes commonly called the Queenes Mates Children of the Chappell. In process of time the boyes growing up to bee men which were Underwood, Field, Ostler, & were taken to strengthen the Kings service, & the more to strengthen the service, the boyes dayly wearing out, it was considered that house would bee as fitt for or selves, & soe purchased the lease remaining from Evans wth or money & placed men Players, which were Hemings, Condall Shakspeare &c'. And Richard Burbage, who for 35

yeeres paines, cost, and Labour made meanes to leave his wife and Children, some estate (& out of whose estates, soe many of other Players and their families have beene mayntained) these new men that were never bred from Children in the kings service, would take away wth Oathes & menaces that wee shall bee forced, & that they will not thanke us for it, soe that it seemes they would not pay us for what they would have or wee can spare which, more to satisfie your honor then their threatning pride, wee are for or selves willing to part wth a part betweene us, they paying according as ever hath beene ye custome and ye number of yeeres the lease is made for. /

Then, to shew yr Honor against these sayinges that wee eat the fruit of their Labours. Wee referre it to yr honors judgemt to consider their profittes, which wee may safely maintaine, for it appeareth by their owne Accomptes for one whole yeere last past beginning from Whitson-Munday 1634 to Whitson Munday 1635 each of these compl[ainan]tes gained severally as hee was a Player and noe Howskeeper 180li, Besides Mr Swanston hath received from the Blackfriers this yeere as hee is there a Houskeeper above 30li, all which beeing accompted together may very well keepe him from starving.

Wherfore yor honors most humble suppl[ian]tes intreates [sic] they may not further bee trampled upon then their estates can beare seeing, how deerly it hath beene purchased by the infinite cost & paynes of the family of the Burbages, & the great desert of Richd Burbage for his quality of playing that his wife should not sterve in hir old age, submitting or selves to part wth one part to them for valuable consideration & let them seeke further satisfaccion else where (that is) of the Heires or assignes of Mr Hemings & Mr Condall who had theirs of the blackfriers of us for nothing, it is onely wee that suffer continually. /

Therefore humbly relyeing upon yr honble Charity in discussing their clamor against us / wee shall, as wee are in duty bound, still pray for the dayly increase of yr honors health & happines. /

–The Malone Society, *Collections, Vol. II, Part III,*
pp. 370–372

Possible Allusion to *1 Henry IV* in Whyte's Letter to Sidney

In his 8 March 1599 letter to his employer, Sir Robert Sidney, steward Rowland Whyte reports on the negotiations between the English government and Lodowick Verreyken, a diplomat from Brussels who represented the interests of the Archduke Albert of Austria and his wife, Isabella, Infanta of Spain, monarchs of the Spanish Netherlands. Whyte's letter includes a reference to Sir John Old-

castle, *a play presented for Verreyken. Whyte may mean Shake-speare's* 1 Henry IV, *a play that, despite its questionable treatment of honor, emphasizes English military superiority, particularly in the face of internal political rebellion. Shakespeare appears to have changed the name of* 1 Henry IV's *comic hero from Oldcastle to Fal-staff. That a professional production of the play was performed in the Lord Chamberlain's house demonstrates the flexibility of early modern staging and acting. The text of this letter is from* Letters and Memorials of State, in the Reigns of Queen Mary, Queen Elizabeth, King James, King Charles the First, Part of the Reign of King Charles the Second, and Oliver's Usurpa-tion, *Vol. II (1746), edited by Arthur Collins.*

My Duty very humbly remembred,

Your Lordship, I know is desirous to understand what these Conferences of Peace doth bring forth, and you have Reason to take yt unkyndly at sume of your Frends Hands here, if they doe not acquaint you with the Pro-ceedings, seing by there Place and Imploiments, they must needs know more Particulars than is possible for me to send you. But out of my Care, I wryte what I heare of, especially of the Town of *Flushing*; whereof I am (by your Lordships Favor towards me) a Member.

And this is conceaved here, that a Peace is greatly desired; that both Parties have made great Demands and Difficulties, which have bene gravely discussed of by the Lords and *Vereiken.* That *Vereiken* hath no Authority to conclude, or agree unto any Thing, only to propownd, and heare what wilbe propownded by us; and so referre yt to the *Archduke* and *Infantas* Consideration, to what by hym hath bene demanded; Mr. *Edmonds* is sent over instructed, as yt shuld seeme with her Majesties Pleasure, to what hath bene by the Lords propownded. *Vereiken,* who goes over within 3 or 4 Daies, with Mr. *Edmonds,* will procure Resolution from the *Archduke,* which Mr. *Edmonds,* shall bring over, or rather yt is thought *Vereiken* will hymself, come hither again, and untill then, theire wilbe no Comis-sioners named, or Place, or Tyme apointed, or agreed upon. The *Hollanders* and *Zelanders* Resolution to Warr, are a great Lett unto yt, for her Majestie hath a very gracious Care of them, as I heare; besides the King of *France* is an Intercessor for them to her Majestie, that they may not be wholy abandoned.

Of *Flushing*, this I heare, that her Majestie hath assured *Vereiken* she will keape yt, till the States give her Satisfaction, and then is she in Honor, and by her Word, ingaged to deliver yt safe to their Hands again; he then desired (as in my last I signified) to know how farre the Limitts of *Flushing* might stretch unto; that if his Master had an Intention to invade that Island, how neare he might aproach without Offence to her Majes-ties Government, and this is the Point in Deliberacion, not yet resolved upon.

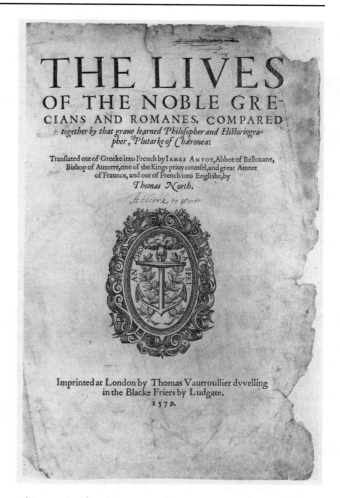

Title page for Thomas North's translation of Plutarch's Lives *that was one of Shakespeare's most frequently used sources (by permission of the Folger Shakespeare Library)*

28 (who in the Ciphre between your Lordship and me, is put in *Wilkes* Place) the other Day told me, that he wold speake with me; the next Morning I attended hym at his Lodging; he then demanded of me, how neare *Flushing* the Chanell went, that led to *Midelboro*; I answered, that yt went neare the Head of *Flushing,* and under the Comand of the Shott of the Town; then he asked, yf there were not another Channell neare the Land towards *Flanders,* by which a Fleet might goe towards *Midelboro*; I answered, that I thought there was none for Ships of any Burthen to pass thorough. He demanded how farre the Limitts of *Flushing* extended; I answered, that I cold not well tell, but as I thought one Way, which was towards the *Ramakins,* both Sea and Land within Daunger of the great Ordinance was comprehended; then he asked if a Fleet might cast Anker between *Flushing* and

Ramakins, and be free from the Danger of Shott. I told hym, I cold not tell, but of these Matters of such Moment, there was no Body cold better inform theire Lordships, both what was fitt to be yelded unto, or demanded, for the Safety of *Flushing*, then your self, who was Governor of the Place, and that it wold be a kynd of Wrong, not to acquaint you withall; I besought hym to make a Motion how needfull yt is to have you here for a While, to be talked withall, both in these Things, and many others, that the Lords, peradventure, did not thincke upon; which he promised to doe. He likewise told me, that the Lords did begin to consider of the leaving of the *Brill*, and soe to strengthen *Flushing*, and keape yt as a Cawtion for all; only one Doubt was made by 200 [Sir *Robert Cecil*] that if *Brill* were left, whither the States of *Holland*, might not choose to contribute towards her Majesties Satisfaction. He promises to wryte within 3 or 4 Daies hymself; I told hym how unkyndly you tooke yt at his Hands, and 15, that they did not wryte all this While.

All this Weeke the Lords have bene in *London*, and past away the Tyme in Feasting and Plaies; for *Vereiken* dined upon *Wednesday*, with my Lord Treasurer, who made hym a Roiall Dinner; upon *Thursday* my Lord Chamberlain feasted hym, and made hym very great, and a delicate Dinner, and there in the After Noone his Plaiers acted, before *Vereiken*, Sir *John Old Castell*, to his great Contentment. This Day the Lords are going to Court. My Lord *Harbert* wil be here upon *Wednesday*, he must be the honorable Instrument of much good to your Lordship, and I find your Lordship wilbe thoroughly delt withall upon your Return, by 600 [Earl of *Nottingham*] in the Matter I soe often mentioned unto you; if yt bring you Honor, and Contentment to all Parties, I shall thinke myself happy to have bene the first Motioner of yt.

Here was an Expectation all this Weeke, that my Lord of *Essex*, shuld have come to his own Howse, but why, or how yt was staied is not spoken of. This is conjectured, that the great Ladies, *Lester, Southhampton, Northumberland,* and *Rich*, assembled themselves, at *Essex* House, to receve hym, which hyndred yt at that Tyme. He hath his Health well again, and is much troubled at the Indiscretion of his Frends and Servants, which makes hym, by their Tatle, to suffer the more; I heare it now reported, that old Mrs. *Ratcliffe* is Deade, which may welbe, for I lefte her very sicke at my being at Courte. *Baynards* Castell, this *Saturday*, 8 of *March*, 1599.

Your Honors, &c.

Row. Whyte.

That 200 and 24 shuld be fallen out was but a Tale, for I know and see the contrary.

—*Letters and Memorials of State*, pp. 174–176

A Royal Edict on the Production of Plays

On 16 May 1599 Queen Elizabeth I issued the following proclamation forbidding the production of plays (Interludes) except as permitted by local or royal officials and urging her "nobilitie and gentlemen" to keep their players as liveried servants. Among those who complied with her request were the earls of Leicester, Worcester, and Derby, whose acting companies were among those stopping in Stratford on their provincial tours. The proclamation was first printed by Richard Jugge and John Cawood, "Printers to the Quenes Majestie."

By the Quene

Forasmuche as the tyme wherein common Interludes in the Englishe tongue ar wont usually to be played, is now past untyll AllHallontyde, and that also some that have ben of late used, are not convenient in any good ordred Christian Common weale to be suffred. The Quenes Majestie doth straightly forbyd al maner Interludes to be playde eyther openly or privately, except the same be notified before hande, and licenced within any Citie or towne corporate, by the Maior or other chiefe officers of the same, and within any shyre, by such as shalbe Lieuetenauntes for the Quenes Majestie in the same shyre, or by two of the Justices of peac[e] inhabyting within that part of the shire where any shalbe played.

And for instruction to every of the sayde officers, her majestie doth likewise charge every of them as they will aunswere: that they permyt none to be played wherin either matters of religion or of the governaunce of the estate of the common weale shalbe handled or treated, beyng no meete matters to be wrytten or treated upon, but my menne of aucthoritie, learning and wisedome, nor to be handled before any audience, but of grave and discrete persons: All which partes of this proclamation, her majestie chargeth to be inviolably kepte. And if anye shal attempte to the contrary: her majestie giveth all maner of officers that have authoritie to see common peac kepte in commaundement, to arrest and enprison the parties so offendinge for the space of fourtene dayes or more, as cause shall nede: And furder also untill good assuraunce may be founde and gyven, that they shalbe of good behaviour, and no more to offende in the like.

And further her majestie gyveth speciall charge to her nobilitie and gentilmen, as they professe to obey and regarde her majestie, to take good order in thys behalfe wyth their servauntes being players, that this her majesties commaundement may be dulye kepte and obeyed.

Yeven at our Palayce of Westminster the .xvi. daye of Maye, the first yeare of oure Raygne.

Brend's Property Inventory Listing Shakespeare

Thomas Brend owned the land on which the Globe theater was built. This excerpt, from a 16 May 1599 document listing Brend's property and the tenants living on that property after his death, has been used to support two assertions: that the Globe theater (the "Domo de nova edificata" or new-built house) was completed by 16 May 1599, and that Shakespeare, the only one of the Globe sharers named, was the most prominent among the theater's owners. The Times (London) published the passage in an article on the work of Charles William Wallace.

Ac de et in una Domo de novo edificata cum gardino eidem pertinenti in parochia S^{ci} Salvatoris praedicta in Comitatu Surria praedicta in occupacione Willielmi Shakespeare et aliorum.

[And of and in a newly built house and garden belonging to the same in the parish of St. Savior's aforesaid in the county of Surrey aforesaid in the possession of William Shakespeare and others.]
–"New Light on Shakespeare," *Times* (London), 1 May 1914, p. 4

Platter Sees *Julius Caesar*

Thomas Platter's visit to what may have been the Globe theater provides evidence for reconstructing some of the theater's architectural details. The translation from the German of Platter's comments remains in dispute. This first translation is from Thomas Platter's Travels in England 1599 *(1937), edited and translated by Clare Williams.*

On September 21st after lunch, about two o'clock, I and my party crossed the water, and there in the house with the thatched roof witnessed an excellent performance of the tragedy of the first Emperor Julius Caesar with a cast of some fifteen people; when the play was over, they danced very marvellously and gracefully together as is their wont, two dressed as men and two as women.

On another occasion not far from our inn, in the suburb at Bishopsgate, if I remember, also after lunch, I beheld a play in which they presented diverse nations and an Englishman struggling together for a maiden; he overcame them all except the German who won the girl in a tussle, and then sat down by her side, when he and his servant drank themselves tipsy, so that they were both fuddled and the servant proceeded to hurl his shoe at his master's head, whereupon they both fell asleep; meanwhile the Englishman stole into the tent and absconded with the German's prize, thus in his turn outwitting the German; in conclusion they danced very charmingly in English and Irish fashion. Thus daily at two in the after-

noon, London has two, sometimes three plays running in different places, competing with each other, and those which play best obtain most spectators. The playhouses are so constructed that they play on a raised platform, so that everyone has a good view. There are different galleries and places, however, where the seating is better and more comfortable and therefore more expensive. For whoever cares to stand below only pays one English penny, but if he wishes to sit he enters by another door, and pays another penny, while if he desires to sit in the most comfortable seats which are cushioned, where he not only sees everything well, but can also be seen, then he pays yet another English penny at another door. And during the performance food and drink are carried round the audience, so that for what one cares to pay one may also have refreshment. The actors are most expensively and elaborately costumed; for it is the English usage for eminent lords or Knights at their decease to bequeath and leave almost the best of their clothes to their serving men, which it is unseemly for the latter to wear, so that they offer them then for sale for a small sum to the actors.

How much time then they may merrily spend daily at the play everyone knows who has seen them play or act.
–*Thomas Platter's Travels in England 1599,* pp. 166–167

In "Thomas Platter's Observations on the Elizabethan Stage" Ernest Schanzer notes that Platter's comments were "written in a slovenly form of sixteenth century Alemannic, which renders some of their content obscure even to German scholars." He offers what he calls a "very literal and therefore inelegant translation":

On the 21st of September, after dinner, at about two o'clock, I went with my party across the water; in the straw-thatched house we saw the tragedy of the first Emperor Julius Caesar, very pleasingly performed, with approximately fifteen characters; at the end of the play they danced together admirably and exceedingly gracefully, according to their custom, two in each group dressed in men's and two in women's apparel.

On another occasion, also after dinner, I saw a play not far from our inn, in the suburb, at Bishopsgate, as far as I remember. There they presented various nations with whom each time an Englishman fought for a maiden, and overcame them all, except the German, who won the maiden in fights, sits down beside her, and hence got himself and his servant very fuddled, so that they both became drunk, and the servant threw his shoe at his master's head, and they both fell asleep. Meanwhile the Englishman went [or, possibly, 'climbed'] into the tents and carries off the German's prize, and so he outwits the German too. At the end they danced, too, very gracefully, in the English and the Irish mode. Thus every day around two o'clock in the afternoon in the city of London two and sometimes even three plays are performed at different places, in order to make people merry [literally 'so that one make the other merry']; then those who acquit themselves best have also the largest audience. The places are built in such a way that they act on a raised scaffold, and everyone can well see everything. However, there are separate galleries and places, where one sits more pleasantly and better, therefore also pays more. For he who remains standing below pays only one English penny, but if he wants to sit he is let in at another door, where he gives a further penny; but if he desires to sit on cushions in the pleasantest place, where he not only sees everything well but can also be seen, then he pays at a further door another English penny. And during the play food and drink is carried around among the people, so that one can also refresh oneself for one's money.

—*Notes and Queries* (November 1956): 466

Shakespeare Listed on Exchequer Pipe Roll

The Exchequer Pipe Roll of 6 October 1599 (PRO Exchequer, Lord Treasurer's Remembrancer, E 372/444, m. Residuum London) shows Shakespeare in default on his taxes. Legal abbreviations have been silently expanded.

Surr R   . . . Robertus honiewood generosus in parochia sancta helen in Ward ibidem viii. li. de eodem subsidio ibidem Willielmus Shakspeare in parochia sancta helene in Warda prædicta debet xiii. s. iiii. d. de eodem subsidio ibidem [*Added in a different hand:*] Respondebit in rotulo sequente in residuum Sussex.

[Robert Honiewood gentleman in the parish of St. Helen in the same ward viii. li. of the same subsidy; likewise William Shakspeare in the parish of St. Helen in the ward aforesaid owes 13*s.* 4*d.* of the same subsidy there. He answers in the following [year's] roll in "residuum Sussex."]

—Lewis, *Shakespeare Documents,* p. 269

Publications

Three of Shakespeare's previously published works were published again in 1599: two editions of Venus and Adonis, *which had been published previously in 1593, 1594, and 1596;* Romeo and Juliet, *published previously in 1597 and 1598; and* 1 Henry IV, *first published in 1598. Among the regulations early modern printers faced were restrictions on the number of copies of a work they could print; the number varied but was limited. The existence of two separate editions of* Venus and Adonis *is probably a sign of continuing demand for the*

poem. *Although the title page of* 1 Henry IV *describes the play as "Newly corrected by* W. Shake-speare," *the text appears to have been set from a copy of the 1598 quarto. The transcribed title pages of these works follow.*

VENVS / AND ADONIS. / *Vilia miretur vulgus: mihi flavus Apollo / Pocula Castalia plena ministret aqua.* / [*Printer's device*] / Imprinted at London for William Leake, dwel- / ling in Paules Churchyard at the ſigne of / the Greyhound. 1599.

VENVS. / AND ADONIS. *Vilia miretur vulgus: mihi flavus Apollo / Pocula Castalia plena ministret aqua.* / [*Printer's device*] / Imprinted at London for William Leake, dwel- / ling in Paules Churchyard, at the ſigne of / the Greyhound. 1599.

THE / MOST EX- / cellent and lamentable / Tragedie, of Romeo / and *Iuliet.* / *Newly corrected, augmented, and / amended:* / As it hath bene ſundry times publiquely acted, by the / right Honourable the Lord Chamberlaine / his Seruants. / [*Printer's device*] / LONDON / Printed by Thomas Creede, for Cuthbert Burby, and are to / be ſold at his ſhop neare the Exchange. / 1 5 9 9.

THE / HISTORY OF / HENRIE THE / FOVRTH; / With the battell at Shrewsburie, / *betweene the King and Lord* Henry / Percy, ſurnamed Henry Hot- / ſpur of the North. / *With the humorous conceits of Sir* / Iohn Falſtaffe. / Newly corrected by *W. Shake-ſpeare.* / [*Printer's device*] / AT LONDON, / Printed by *S. S.* for *Andrew Wiſe,* dwelling / in Paules Churchyard, at the ſigne of / the Angell. 1599.

Also published in 1599 was the anthology The Passionate Pilgrime, *which included two of Shakespeare's sonnets (138 and 144) and three poems from* Love's Labour's Lost, *published in 1598. As the transcription of the title page shows, Shakespeare was identified as the author of this miscellaneous collection of the work of several poets.*

THE / PASSIONATE / PILGRIME. / *By* W. Shake-ſpeare. / [*Printer's device*] / *AT LONDON* / Printed for W. Iaggard, and are / to be ſold by W. Leake, at the Grey- / hound in Paules Churchyard. / 1 5 9 9.

Weever's Poem About Shakespeare in *Epigrammes*

Poet and satirist John Weever (1576–1632) writes about Shakespeare in Epigrammes of the oldest cut, and newest fashion *(1599). Epigrams, short and often nasty topical poems, were a popular turn-of-the-century genre; here,*

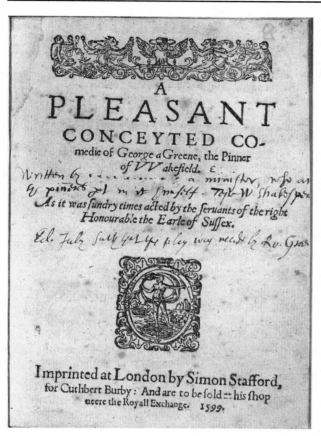

The handwritten notation below the play's title (see box below) identifies Shakespeare as the source of information about its still-unidentified author (by permission of the Folger Shakespeare Library)

Shakespeare Cited on the Title Page of *Pinner of Wakefield*

The following comments were almost certainly written by George Buc (1560–1622), who served King James as Master of the Revels beginning in 1610. For a detailed analysis of the handwriting, and of the implications of Buc's comments for theatrical and literary historians, see Alan H. Nelson's "George Buc, William Shakespeare, and the Folger George a Greene" *in* Shakespeare Quarterly, *49 (1998): 74–83. Nelson notes that* George a Greene *was performed at the Rose in 1593/ 1594, where it was followed by* Titus Andronicus, *a circumstance that may explain why Buc consulted Shakespeare about the identity of the author. The title page has been cropped, truncating the words at the end of each line.*

Written by .... a minister, who a[cted]
the piners part in it himself. Test W. Shakespe[are]
Ed. Juby saith that this play was made by Ro. Gre[ene]

Weever uses the form to praise Shakespeare's skill as a poet and playwright. In Shakespeare: The "Lost Years" (1985), E. A. J. Honigman discusses possible links between Weever and Shakespeare.

The fourth weeke.

Epig. 22. Ad Gulielmum Shakespear

Honie-tong'd *Shakespeare* when I saw thine issue
I swore *Apollo* got them and none other,
Their rosie-tainted features cloth'd in tissue;
Some heaven born goddesse said to be their mother:
Rose-checkt *Adonis* with his amber tresses,
Faire fire-hot *Venus* charming him to love her,
Chaste *Lucretia* virgine-like her dresses,
Prowd lust-stung *Tarquine* seeking still to prove her:
Romea Richard; more whose names I know not,
Their sugred tongues, and power attractive beuty
Say they are Saints althogh that Sts they shew not
For thousands vowes to them subjective dutie:
They burn in love thy children *Shakespear* het them,
Go, wo thy Muse more Nymphish brood beget them.
—sig. E6r.

John Shakespeare's Grant of Arms

This document, circa 1599 (College of Arms Manuscript R. 21, page 347), grants John Shakespeare permission to combine the coats of arms of the Shakespeare and Arden families. The combined crest, featured in a drawing in the upper left corner of the manuscript, was not used on Shakespeare's monument.

To all and Singuller Noble and Gentilmen of all estates & degrees bearing Arms. To whom the presentes shall come William Dethick Garter. principall king of Arms of England and William Camden alias Clarentieulx king of Arms. for the Sowthe, East and weste partes of this Realme Sendethe greetinges. Knowe yee. That in all nations and kingdoms the Record & remembrances of the valeant factes & verteous dispositions of worthie men have ben made knowen and divulged by certeyne Shieldes of Arms & tokens of Chevalrie The grant & testemonie wheof apperteynethe unto us by vertu of our offices from the Quenes most excellent majestie, & her highenes most noble & victorious Progenitors. Wherfore being solicited and by credible report informed. That John . Shakespere. nowe of Stratford uppon Avon in the Counte of Warwik Gent. whose parent great Grandfather and late Antecessor, for his faithefull & approved service to the late most prudent prince king H. 7 of famous memorie. was advanced & rewarded with Landes & Tementes geven to him in those partes of Warwikeshere where they have continewed bie some descentes in good reputacion & credit And for that the said John .Shakespere. having maryed the daughter & one of the heyrs of Robert Arden of Welling Cote in the said Countie. And also produced this his Auncient Cote of Arms heretofore Assigned to him whilest he was her majesties officer & Baylife of that Towne. In Consideration of the premisses And for the encouragement of his posterite unto whom suche Blazon of Arms & Atchevementes of inheritance from theyre said mother. by the auncyent Custome & Lawes of Arms maye Lawfullie descend. We the said Garter and Clarentieulx have Assigned, graunted, & confirmed & by these presentes exemplefied. Unto the said John Shakespere. and to his posterite that Shield & Cote of Arms viz. in A field of Gould. upon A Bend Sables. A Speare. of the first the poynt upward hedded Argent And for his Creast or Cognizance A ffalcon. with his wynges displayed. standing on A wrethe of his Coullors. Supporting a Speare Armed hedded or & steeled Sylver fixed upon A helmet with mantelles & tasselles as more playnely maye appeare depicted on this Margent. And we have lykewise upon on other escucheone impaled the same with the Auncyent Arms of the said Arden of Wellingcote. Signefeing thereby That it maye & shalbe Lawefull for the said John Shakespere gent. to beare & use the same Shieldes of Arms Single or impaled as aforesaid during his natural Lyffe: And that it shalbe Lawfull for his children yssue & posterite (Lawfully begotten) to beare use & quarter & shewe forthe the same with theyre dewe differences in all Lawfull warlyke factes, and Civile use or exercises. according to the Lawes of Arms & Custome that to Gent. belongethe. without let or Interruption of any person or persons for use or persons bearing the same. In wyttnesse & testemonye wherof we hav[e] subscribed our Names & fastened the Seales of our offices. yeven at the office of Arms London the [. . .] in the xlii^te yeare of the reigne of our Most gratious Soveraigne Elizabeth by the grace of God [. . .] ffrance & Ireland defender of the fayth etc. 1599.

—p. 301

Shakespeare's Company Paid for Court Performances

Shakespeare's acting company, the Lord Chamberlain's Men, are paid for court performances during the 1599–1600 winter holidays. The financial records do not provide the titles of the plays the company performed.

To John Heminges and Thomas Pope servantes unto the Lorde Chamberleyne uppon the Councells warraunt dated at the Courte at Nonesuche secundo die Octobris 1599 for three Enterludes or playes played before her Majestie uppon St Stephens daye at nighte, Newyeares daye at nighte and shrove-tuesdaye at nighte laste paste xx^li and to them more by waye of her Majesties rewarde x^li In all amounting to   xxx^li

. . . .

To John Hemynge servaunt to the Lorde Chamberlaine uppon the Councells Warraunt dated at the Courte at Richmond xvii^mo die Februarii 1599 for three Enterludes or playes playde before her Majestie on St Stephens daye at nighte, Twelfth daye at night and Shrove sondaye at night laste paste   xxx^li

—*Dramatic Records,* pp. 30–31

1600

A Contract to Build the Fortune Theater

On the site of the original Globe theater there currently stands a building with its own claim to historical significance, thus limiting any efforts to excavate the site of the Globe. Efforts to determine the size and orientation of the Globe's stage and seating areas, however, continue. One document that helps with these efforts is Philip Henslowe and Edward Alleyn's contract (18 January 1600) with Peter Street for the construction of the Fortune theater. The contract describes the dimensions and some of the structural details of a theater meant to be built, with a few noteworthy exceptions, "according to the manner and fashion of the saide howse Called the Globe." The carpenter named in the contract, Peter Street, helped dismantle the Burbadges' Theatre in December 1599 and used its timbers to build the Globe. His work was impressive enough to convince Henslowe to hire him to build a new theater, the Fortune. The following text is from Henslowe's Diary: Edited with Supplementary Material, Introduction and Notes *(1961). Abbreviations have been silently expanded.*

This Indenture made the Eighte daie of Januarye 1599 And in the Twoe and ffortyth yeare of the Reigne of our sovereigne Ladie Elizabeth by the grace of God Queene of England ffraunce and Irelande defender of the ffaythe &ces Betwene Phillipp Henslowe and Edwarde Allen of the parishe of Ste Saviours in Southwark in the Countie of Surrey gentlemen on thone parte And Peeter Streete Cittizen and Carpenter of London on thother parte witnesseth That whereas the saide Phillipp Henslowe & Edward Allen the daie of the date hereof Have bargayned Compounded & agreed with the saide Peter Streete ffor the erectinge buildinge & setinge upp of a newe howse and Stadge, for a Plaiehowse in and uppon a certeine plott or parcell of grounde appoynted oute for that purpose Scytuate and beinge nere Goldinge lane in the parishe of Ste Giles withoute Cripplegate of London To be by him the saide Peeter Streete or somme other sufficyent woorkmen of his provideinge and appoyntemente and att his propper Costes & Chardges for the consideracion hereafter in theis presentes expressed / Made erected, builded and sett upp In manner & forme followeinge (that is to saie) The frame of the saide howse to be sett square and to conteine ffowerscore foote of lawfull assize everye waie square withoute and fiftie five foote of like assize square everye waie within, with a good suer and stronge foundacion of pyles brick lyme and sand, both withoute & within, to be wroughte one foote of assize att the leiste above the grounde And the saide fframe to conteine Three Stories in heighth The first or lower Storie to Conteine Twelve foote of lawfull assize in heighth The first or lower Storie to Conteine Twelve foote of lawfull assize in heighth The second Storie Eleaven foote of lawfull assize in heighth And the Third or upper Storie to conteine Nyne foote of lawfull assize in height / All which Stories shall conteine Twelve foote and a half of lawfull assize in breadth througheoute besides a Juttey forwardes in eyther of the saide Two upper Stories of Tenne ynches of lawfull assize, with ffower convenient divisions for gentlemens roomes and other sufficient and convenient divisions for Twoe pennie roomes with necessarie Seates to be placed and sett Aswell in those roomes as througheoute all the rest of the galleries of the saide howse and with suche like steares Conveyances & divisions withoute & within as are made & Contryved in and to the late erected Plaiehowse On the Banck in the saide parishe of Ste Saviours Called the Globe With a Stadge and Tyreinge howse to be made erected & settupp within the saide fframe, with a shadowe or cover over the saide Stadge, which Stadge shalbe placed & sett As alsoe the stearecases of the saide fframe in suche sorte as is prefigured in a Plott thereof drawen And which Stadge shall conteine in length ffortie and Three foote of lawfull assize and in breadth to extende to the middle of the yarde of the saide howse, The same Stadge to be paled in belowe with good stronge and sufficyent newe oken bourdes And likewise the lower Storie of the saide fframe withinside, and the same lower storie to be alsoe laide over and fenced with stronge yron pykes And the saide Stadge to be in all other proporcions Contryved and fashioned like unto the Stadge of the saide Plaiehowse Called the Globe, With convenient windowes and lightes glazed to the saide Tyreinge howse And the saide fframe Stadge and Stearecases to be covered with Tyle, and to have a sufficient gutter of lead to Carrie & convey the water frome the Coveringe of the saide Stadge to fall backwardes And alsoe all the saide fframe and the Stairecases thereof

to be sufficyently enclosed withoute with lathe lyme & haire and the gentlemens roomes and Twoe pennie roomes to be seeled with lath lyme & haire and all the fflowers of the saide Galleries Stories and Stadge to be bourded with good & sufficyent newe deale bourdes of the whole thicknes wheare neede shalbe And the saide howse and other thinges beforemencioned to be made & doen To be in all other Contrivitions Conveyances fashions thinge and thinges effected finished and doen accordinge to the manner and fashion of the saide howse Called the Globe Saveinge only that all the princypall and maine postes of the saide fframe and Stadge forwarde shalbe square and wroughte palasterwise with carved proporcions Called Satiers to be placed & sett on the Topp of every of the same postes And saveinge alsoe that the said Peeter Streete shall not be chardged with anie manner of pay<ntin>ge in or aboute the saide fframe howse or Stadge or anie parte thereof nor Rendringe the walls within Nor seelinge anie more or other roomes then the gentlemens roomes Twoe pennie roomes and Stadge before remembred / nowe theiruppon the saide Peeter Streete dothe covenante promise and graunte ffor himself his executors and administrators to and with the saide Phillipp Henslowe and Edward Allen and either of them and thexecutors and administrators of them and either of them by theis presentes In manner & forme followeinge (that is to saie) That he the saide Peeter Streete his executors or assignes shall & will att his or their owne propper costes & Chardges well woorkmanlike & substancyallie make erect, sett upp and fully finishe In and by all thinges accordinge to the true meaninge of theis presentes with good stronge and substancyall newe Tymber and other necessarie stuff All the saide fframe and other woorkes whatsoever In and uppon the saide plott or parcell of grounde (beinge not by anie aucthoretie Restrayned, and haveinge ingres egres & regres to doe the same) before the ffyve & Twentith daie of Julie next Commeinge after the date hereof And shall alsoe at his or theire like costes and Chardges Provide and finde All manner of woorkemen Tymber Joystes Rafters boordes dores boltes hinges brick Tyle lathe lyme haire sande nailes leede Iron Glasse woorkmanshipp and other thinges whatsoever which shalbe needefull Convenyent & necessarie for the saide fframe & woorkes & everie parte thereof And shall alsoe make all the saide fframe in every poynte for Scantlinges lardger and bigger in assize Then the Scantlinges of the Timber of the saide newe erected howse, Called the Globe And alsoe that he the saide Peeter Streete shall furtherwith aswell by himself As by suche other and soemanie woorkmen as shalbe Convenient & necessarie enter into and uppon the saide buildinges and woorkes And shall in reasonable manner proceede therein withoute anie wilfull detraccion untill the same shalbe fully effected and finished / In consideracion of all which buildinges and of all stuff & woorkemanshipp thereto belonginge The saide Phillipp Henslowe & Edwarde Allen and either of them ffor themselves theire and either of theire executors & administrators doe Joynctlie & severallie Covenante & graunte to & with the saide Peeter Streete his executors & administrators by theis presentes That they the saide Phillipp Henslowe & Edward Allen or one of them Or the executors administrators or assignes of them or one of them Shall & will well & truelie paie or Cawse to be paide unto the saide Peeter Streete his executors or assignes Att the place aforesaid appoynted for the erectinge of the saide fframe The full somme of ffower hundred & ffortie Poundes of lawfull money of Englande in manner & forme followeinge (that is to saie) Att suche tyme And when as the Tymberwoork of the saide fframe shalbe rayzed & sett upp by the saide Peeter Streete his executors or assignes, Or within Seaven daies then next followeinge Twoe hundred & Twentie poundes And att suche time and when as the saide fframe & woorkes shalbe fullie effected & ffynished as is aforesaide Or within Seaven daies then next followeinge, thother Twoe hundred and Twentie poundes withoute fraude or Coven Provided allwaies and it is agreed betwene the saide parties That whatsoever somme or sommes of money the saide Phillipp Henslowe and Edward Allen or either of them or thexecutors or assignes of them or either of them shall lend or deliver unto the saide Peter Streete his executors or assignes or anie other by his appoyntemente or consent ffor or concerninge the saide Woorkes or anie parte thereof or anie stuff thereto belonginge before the raizeinge & settinge upp of the saide fframe, shalbe reputed accepted taken & accoumpted in parte of the firste paymente aforesaid of the saide some of ffower hundred & ffortie poundes And all suche somme & sommes of money as they or anie of them shall as aforesaid lend or deliver betwene the razeinge of the saide fframe & finishinge thereof and of all the rest of the saide woorkes Shalbe reputed accepted taken & accoumpted in parte of the laste paymente aforesaid of the same somme of ffower hundred & ffortie poundes Anie thinge abovesaid to the contrary notwithstandinge / In witnes whereof the parties abovesaid to theis presente Indentures Interchaungeably have sett theire handes and Seales / Yeoven the daie and yeare ffirste abovewritten

P S

Sealed and delivered by the saide Peter Streete in the presence of me william Harris Pub Scr And me frauncis Smyth appr to the said Scr /

[endorsed:]
Peater Streat ffor The Building of the ffortune

　　　　　　　　　　　　　　　　　　　　　—pp. 307–310

Stationers' Register Entries

In 1600, six previously unpublished plays were registered with the Stationers (Stationer's Hall, Register C, fly leaf and folios C 63r–v, 65v, 66r.): As You Like It, Henry V, Much Ado about Nothing, 2 Henry IV, A Midsummer Night's Dream, *and* The Merchant of Venice.

In W. W. Gregg's transcription of these entries abbreviated words have been silently expanded.

4. Augusti

as yo^w like yt: / a booke Henry the ffift: / a booke Every man in his humo^r. / a booke
The commedie of muche A doo about nothinge. / a booke /　　　　　　　　　　to be staied

. . . .

14. Augusti

Thomas Pavyer Entred for his Copyes by direction of m^r white warden under his hand wrytinge: These [12] Copyes followinge beinge thinges formerlye printed & sett over to the sayd Thomas Pavyer: viz.
. . . [2] The historye of Henrye the vth with the battell of Agencourt　　　　　　　　　　　　　　vi^d

. . . .

23 Augusti

Andrewe Wyse William Aspley Entred for their copies under the handes of the wardens. Twoo bookes. the one called: Muche a Doo about nothinge. Thother the second parte of the history of kinge henry the iiii^th with the humo^rs of Sr John ffallstaff': Wrytten by m^r Shakespere　　　　　　　　　　　　　　　　xii^d

. . . .

8. octobr'

Thomas ffyssher Entred for his copie under the handes of m^r Rodes / and the Wardens. A booke called A mydsommer nightes dreame　　　　　　　　　　vi^d

. . . .

28 octobr'

Thomas haies Entred for his copie under the handes of the Wardens & by Consent of m^r Robertes. A booke called the booke of the m'chant of Venyce　　vi^d
　　　—*Bibliography of the English Printed Drama*, pp. 15–16

Publications

During 1600 five of the six plays registered with the Stationers—all save As You Like It—*were published for the first time (see facsimiles). Also published that year were four previously published works:* The Rape of Lucrece *(1594, 1598),* Titus Andronicus *(1594),* The First Part of the Conten-

A Booke of fishing
with Hooke & Line, and
of all other inſtruments thereunto belonging.

Another of ſundrie Engines and
Trappes to take Polcats, Buzards, Rattes,
Mice and all other kindes of *Vermine & Beaſt*
whatſoeuer, moſt profitable for all Warri-
ners, and ſuch as delight in this kinde
of ſport and paſtime.

Made by L. M.

DONDON.
Printed by Iohn Wolfe, and are to be ſolde
by Edwarde White dwelling at the little North
doꝛe of Paules at the ſigne of the Gunne.
1 5 9 9.

Title page for a fishing guide. Shakespeare often evoked common activities in his writing, as in his use of fishing in Much Ado about Nothing, *3.1.26–239 (by permission of the Folger Shakespeare Library)*

---

tion betwixt the two famous houses of York and Lan-caster *(1594), and* The True Tragedy of Richard Duke of York *(1595). The transcribed title pages for the previously published works follow.*

LVCRECE. / [*Printer's device*] / LONDON, / Printed by I.H. for Iohn Hariſon. / 1 6 0 0.

A second edition of Lucrece was also published in 1600; its title page lacked a period after the title.

The moſt lamenta- / ble Romaine Tragedie of *Titus* / *Andronicus.* / As it hath ſundry times beene playde by the / Right Honourable the Earle of Pembrooke, the / Earle of Darbie, the Earle of Suſſex, and the / Lorde Chamberlaine theyr / Seruants. / [*Printer's device*] / AT LONDON, / Printed by I.R. for Edward White / and are to bee ſolde at his ſhoppe; at the little / North doore of Paules, at the ſigne of / the Gun. 1 6 0 0.

Ursula

The pleasant'st angling is to see the fish
Cut with her golden oars the silver stream,
And greedily devour the treacherous bait;
So angle we for Beatrice . . .

—*Much Ado about Nothing,* 3.1.26-29

THE / True Tragedie of / Richarde Duke of / Yorke, and the death of good / King Henrie the ſixt: / With the whole contention betweene the two / Houſes, Lan-caſter and Yorke; as it was / ſundry times acted by the Right / Honourable the Earle / of Pembrooke his / ſeru-antes. / [*Printer's device*] / Printed at London by *W. W.* for *Thomas Millington,* / and are to be ſold at his ſhoppe vnder Saint / Peters Church in Cornewall. / 1 6 0 0.

THE / Firſt part of the Con- / tention betwixt the two famous hou- / ſes of Yorke and Lancaſter, with the / death of the good Duke / Humphrey: / And the baniſhment and death of the Duke of / Suffolke, and the Tragical end of the prowd Cardinall / of Wincheſter, with the notable Rebel-lion of / Iacke Cade: / And the Duke of Yorkes first clayme to the / Crowne. / [*Printer's device*] / LONDON / Printed by Valen-tine Simmes for Thomas Millington, and / are to be ſold at his ſhop under S. Peters church / in Cornewall. / 1600.

Allusion to *1 Henry IV*
in the *Life of Sir John Oldcastle*

As the following transcribed title page shows, Shakespeare was credited as the author of the Life of Sir John Oldcastle *in one published edition.*

The firſt part / Of the true & hono- / rable hiſtory, of the Life of / *Sir Iohn Old-caſtle, the good* / Lord Cobham. / *As it hath bene lately acted by the Right* / honorable the Earle of Noting-ham / Lord High Admirall of England, / his Seruants. / Written by William Shakeſpeare. / [*Printer's device*] / London printed for T.P. / 1600.

Despite its similarities to Shakespeare's 1 Henry IV, *the history play* Life of Sir John Oldcastle *was written by Antony Munday, Michael Drayton, Richard Hathway, and Robert Wil-son. The 1619 edition of the play, however, names Shakespeare as its author, which may have been done to improve sales. In the pro-logue to the play, Munday criticizes Shakespeare's characterization of the historical John Oldcastle, a Protestant martyr. Shakespeare's corrupt and corpulent Sir John Falstaff appears to have been called John Oldcastle at an early stage in the composition of the two* Henry IV *plays, but in an epilogue to the second part of* Henry

IV, *Shakespeare assures the audience that "Oldcastle died [a] martyr, and this [Falstaff] is not the man" (Epil, 32).*

The Prologue.

The doubtful Title (Gentlemen) prefixt
Upon the Argument we have in hand,
May breede suspence, and wrongfully disturbe
The peacefull quiet of your setled thoughts:
To stop which scruple, let this briefe suffise.
It is no pamperd glutton we present,
Nor aged Councellor to youthfull sinne,
But one, whose vertue shone above the rest,
A valiant Martyr, and a vertuous peere,
In whose true faith and loyaltie exprest
Unto his soveraigne, and his countries weale:
We strive to pay that tribute of our Love,
Your favours merite, let faire Truth be grac'te,
Since forg'de invention former time defac'te.

—A2r

. . . .

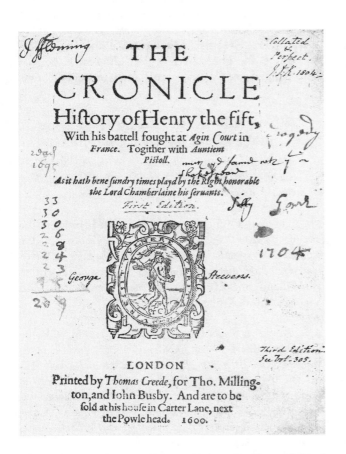

Title page for the first quarto of Henry V *(reproduced by permission of The Huntington Library, San Marino, California)*

The excerpt from the scene that follows shows Munday's audience still expected Oldcastle to be accompanied by the same questionable associates he had with him in Shakespeare's plays.

Enter Sir John.

Sir John Stand true-man saies a thiefe.
King Stand thiefe, saies a true man, how if a thiefe?
Sir John Stand thiefe too.
King Then thiefe or true-man I see I must stand, I see how soever the world wagges, the trade of theeving yet will never downe, what art thou?
Sir John A good fellow.
King So am I too; I see thou dost know me.
Sir John. If thou be a good fellow, play the good fellowes part, deliver thy purse without more adoe.
King I have no mony.
Sir John I must make you find some before we part, if you have no mony you shal have ware, as many sound drie blows as your skin can carrie.
King Is that the plaine truth?
Sir John Sirra no more adoe, come, come, give me the mony you have, dispatch, I cannot stand all day.
King Wel, if thou wilt needs have it, there tis: just the proverb, one thiefe robs another, where the divel are all my old theeves, that were wont to keepe this walke? Falstaffe the villaine is so fat, he cannot get on's horse, but me thinkes Poines and Peto should be stirring here abouts.

—F2r

The Publication of *Englands Helicon*

ENGLANDS / HELICON. / Caſta placent ſuperis, / pura cum veſte venite, / Et manibus puris / ſumite ſontis aquam. / [Printer's device] / AT LONDON / Printed for I.R. by Iohn Flasket, and are / to be ſold in Paules Church-yard, at the ſigne / of the Beare. 1600.

One sign of Shakespeare's growing fame and popularity as a poet is the inclusion of his poetry in anthologies. These miscellaneous collections of short poems, or excerpts from longer works, sometimes print bits of Shakespeare's plays as if they were poems. The 1600 anthology England's Helicon *includes Dumaine's sonnet from* Love's Labor's Lost *(4.3.99–118).*

Francis Davison, the compiler of another anthology of poetry, A Poetical Rhapsody *(1602), made a list of the poems in* England's Helicon. *This list, now in the British Library (Harleian Manuscript 280, folios 99–101), includes Shake-speare's name on folio 99 next to the title "On a day alack the day," the first line of Dumaine's sonnet. The sonnet also appears in the 1599 anthology* The Passionate Pilgrim.

Shakespeare Listed on Exchequer Pipe Roll

This listing from the Exchequer pipe roll, 6 October 1600 (PRO Exchequer, Lord Treasurer's Remembrancer, E 372/ 445, m. Residuum Sussex), shows Shakespeare in default on his taxes. The marginal note indicates the case was transferred to the jurisdiction of the Bishop of Winchester. No documents survive to indicate whether Shakespeare eventually paid his taxes. Legal abbreviations in this transcript have been silently expanded.

London R:

On[i] Episcopo wintonensi T Willielmus Shakspeare in parochia sancta helene xiii. s. iiii. d. de primo integro subsidio prædicto Anno XXXIX[no] concesso Qui requiritur super eundem ibidem

[William Shakspeare, in the parish of St. Helen, 13s. 4d. of the first entire subsidy aforesaid granted in the said 39th year which is required upon the same there.]

—Lewis, *Shakespeare Documents*, p. 270

Allusion to Justices Silence and Shallow in Percy's Letter

In his 27 December 1600 letter written from Dumbleton, Gloucestershire, to Mr. Carlington (possibly English diplomat Dudley Carleton), Sir Charles Percy, third son of the Earl of Northumberland and a participant in the Earl of Essex's brief and unsuccessful 1601 rebellion against Queen Elizabeth, alludes to the foolish country justices Silence and Shallow from Shakespeare's 2 Henry IV.

I am so pestered with country business, that I cannot come to London. If I stay here long, you will find me so dull that I shall be taken for Justice Silence or Justice Shallow; therefore take pity of me and send me news from time to time, the knowledge of which, though perhaps it will not exempt me from the opinion of a Justice Shallow at London, yet will make me pass for a very sufficient gentleman in Gloucestershire. If I do not always answer, pray do not desist from your charitable office, that place being so fruitful and here so barren that it will make my head ache for invention. Direct your letters to the Three Cups in Bread Street, where I have taken order for the sending of them down.

P.S.—You need not forbear sending news hither in respect of their staleness, for I assure you they will be very new here.

—*Calendar of State Papers*, p. 502

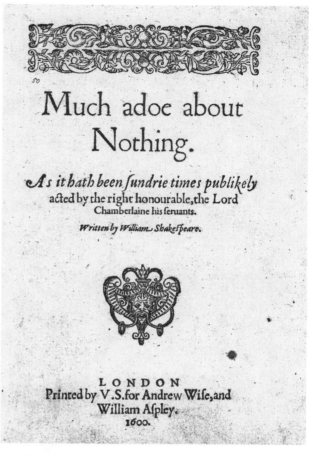

Title page for the first quarto of Much Ado about Nothing *(by permission of the Folger Shakespeare Library)*

Allusion to Shakespeare in Bodenham's *Bel-vedere*

In this address to the readers of the anthology Bel-vedere *or* The Garden of the Muses, *editor John Bodenham, who is described in a prefatory sonnet as "Art's lover, [and] Learning's friend," explains the standards he used to select works for inclusion in his collection of "excellent flowres"—short extracts from poems and prose works by a wide variety of English writers. Bodenham then lists the authors whose works make up the collection and includes Shakespeare among the "Moderne and extant Poets."*

To the Reader.

It shall be needlesse (gentle Reader) to make any Apologie for the defence of this labour, because the same being collected from so many singular mens workes; and the worth of them all having been so especially approved, and past with no meane applause the censure of all in generall; doth both disburden me of that paines, and sets the better approbation on this excellent booke. It

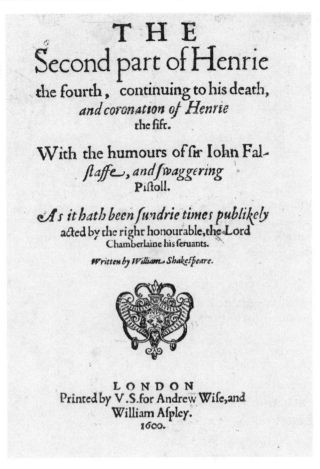

Title page for the first quarto of 2 Henry IV *(by permission of the Folger Shakespeare Library)*

shall be sufficient for me then to tell thee, that here thou art brought into the Muses Garden, (a place that may beseeme the presence of the greatest Prince in the world.) Imagine then thy height of happinesse, in being admitted to so celestiall a Paradise. Let thy behaviour then (while thou art here) answere thy great fortune, and make use of thy time as so rich a treasure requireth.

The walkes, alleys, and passages in this Garden, are almost infinite; every where a turning, on all sides such windings in and out: yet all extending both to pleasure and profit, as very rare or seldome shalt thou see the like. Marke then, what varietie of flowres grow all along as thou goest, and trample on none rudely, for all are right precious. If thy conscience be wounded, here are store of hearbs to heale it: If thy doubts be fearefull, here are flowres of comfort. Are thy hopes frustrated? here's immediate helpes for them. In briefe, what infirmitie canst thou have, but here it may bee cured? What delight or pleasure wouldst thou have, but here it is affoorded?

Concerning the nature and qualitie of these excellent flowres, thou seest that they are most learned, grave, and wittie sentences; each line being a severall sentence, and none exceeding two lines at the uttermost. All which, being subjected under apt and proper heads, as arguments what is then dilated and spoken of: even so each head hath first his definition in a couplet sentence; then the single and double sentences by variation of letter do follow: and lastly, Similes and Examples in the same nature likewise, to conclude every Head or Argument handled. So let this serve to shew thee the whole intent of this worke.

Now that every one may be fully satisfied concerning this Garden, that no one man doth assume to him-selfe the praise thereof, or can arrogate to his owne deserving those things which have been derived from so many rare and ingenious spirits; I have set down both how, whence, and where these flowres had their first springing, till thus they were drawne together into the *Muses Garden*, that every ground may challenge his owne, each plant his particular, and no one be injuried in the justice of his merit.

First, out of many excellent speeches spoken to her Majestie, at Tiltings, Triumphes, Maskes, Shewes, and devises perfourmed in prograce: as also out of divers

Title page for the first quarto of A Midsummer Night's Dream. *The image on the title page is a printer's device, not an illustration for the play (by permission of the Folger Shakespeare Library).*

choise Ditties sung to her; and some especially, proceeding from her owne most sacred selfe: Here are great store of them digested into their meete places, according as the method of the worke plainly deliuereth. Likewise out of priuat Poems, Sonnets, Ditties, and other wittie conceits, given to her Honorable Ladies, and vertuous Maids of Honour; according as they could be obtained by sight, or favour of copying, a number of most wittie and singular Sentences.

Secondly, looke what workes of Poetrie have been put to the worlds eye, by that learned and right royall king and Poet, JAMES king of Scotland, no one Sentence of worth hath escaped, but are likewise here reduced into their right roome and place.

Next, out of sundry things extant, and many in privat, done by these right Honourable persons following:

Thomas, Earle of Surrey.
The Lord Marquesse of Winchester.
Mary, Countesse of Pembrooke.
Sir Philip Sidney.

From Poems and workes of these noble personages, extant.

Edward, Earle of Oxenford.
Ferdinando, Earle of Derby.
Sir Walter Raleigh.
Sir Edward Dyer.
Fulke Grevile, Esquier.
Sir John Harrington.

From divers essayes of their Poetrie, some extant among other Honourabe personages writings; some from private labours and translations.

Edmund Spencer.
Henry Constable Esquier.
Samuell Daniell.
Thomas Lodge, Doctor of Physicke.
Thomas Watson.
Michaell Drayton.
John Davies.
Thomas Hudson.
Henrie Locke Esquier.
John Marstone.
Christopher Marlow.
Benjamin Johnson.
William Shakspeare.
Thomas Churchyard Esquier.
Thomas Nash.
Thomas Kidde.
George Peele.
Robert Greene.
Joshua Sylvester.
Nicholas Breton.
Gervase Markham.
Thomas Storer.
Robert Wilmot.
Christopher Middleton.
Richard Barnefield.

These being Moderne and extant Poets, that have liv'd togither; from many of their extant workes, and some kept in privat.

Thomas Norton Esquier.
George Gascoigne Esquier.
Frauncis Kindlemarsh Esquier.
Thomas Atchlow.
George Whetstones.

These being deceased, have left divers extant labours, and many more held back from publishing, which for the most part have been perused, and their due right here given them in the Muses Garden.

Besides, what excellent Sentences have been in any presented Tragedie, Historie, Pastorall, or Comedie, they have been likewise gathered, and are here inserted in their proper places.

—sigs. A3r–A6r

Allusion to Falstaff
in Jonson's *Every Man Out of His Humor*

In the epilogue to The comicall Satyre of Every Man Out Of His Humor *(1600) Ben Jonson refers to Falstaff as he has the malcontent Macilente beg for applause.*

[Macilente:] . . . Well, Gentlemen, I should have gone in, and return'd to you as I was *Asper* at the first: but (by reason the shift would have bene somewhat long, and we are loth to draw your patience any farder) wee'le intreat you to imagine it. And now (that you may see I will be out of my Humor for company) I stand wholly to your kind Approbation; and (indeed) am nothing so peremptorie as I was in the beginning: Marie I will not do as *Plautus* in his *Amphitryo* for all this (*Summi Jovis causa, Plaudite*:) begge a *Plaudite* for Gods sake; but if you (out of the bountie of your good liking) will bestow it; why, you may (in time) make leane *Macilente* as fat as *Sir John Fall-staffe.*

–Sig.Qiv^v

Possible Allusions to Shakespeare
and an Early Version of *Macbeth*
in *Kemp's Nine Daies Wonder*

In his "humble request" appended to Kemps nine daies wonder *(1600) William Kemp, a noted comedian and, until 1599, a member of the Lord Chamberlain's Men, addresses unnamed ballad makers, asking them to refrain from writing about his nine-day morris dance. "Shakerags," and the "penny Poet" who wrote the "stolne story of Macdoel, or Macdobeth, or Macsomewhat," are sometimes understood as references to Shakespeare and to a conjectured earlier version of* Macbeth, *but in 1599 Shakespeare was 35, not quite in keeping with Kemp's description of the penny poet as "a proper upright youth." Kemp also describes finding another "fat filthy ballet-maker" at the theater, and expresses his horror that a playwright has abused his father by portraying him on stage as a merry innkeeper.*

Kemps humble request to the impudent generation of Ballad-makers and their coherents; that it would please their rascalities to pitty his paines in the great journey he pretends, and not fill the country with lyes of his never done actes, as they did in his late Morrice to Norwich.

To the tune of Thomas Delonies Epitaph.

My notable Shakerags, the effect of my sute is discovered in the Title of my supplication. But for your better understandings: for that I know you to be a

Title page for the first quarto of The Merchant of Venice *(by permission of the Folger Shakespeare Library)*

sort of witles beetle-heads, that can understand nothing, but what is knockt into your scalpes; These are by these presentes to certifie unto your block-headships, that I William Kemp, whom you had neer hand rent in sunder with your unreasonable rimes, am shortly God willing to set forward as merily as I may; whether I my selfe know not. Wherefore by the way I would wish ye, imploy not your little wits in certifying the world that I am gone to Rome, Jerusalem, Venice, or any other place at your idle appoint. I knowe the best of ye by the lyes ye writ of me, got not the price of a good hat to cover your brainles heads: If any of ye had come to me, my bounty should have exceeded the best of your good masters the Ballad-buiers, I wold have apparrelled your dry pates in party coloured bonnets, & bestowd a leash of my cast belles to have crown'd ye with cox-combs. I have made a privie search, what private Jigmonger of your jolly number, hath been the Author of these abhominable ballets written of me: I was told it was the great ballet-maker *T. D.,* alias

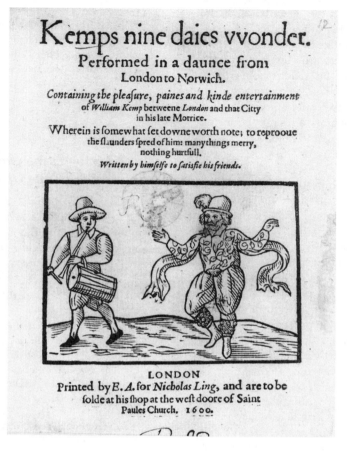

Title page for a pamphlet by comedian William Kempe, a member
of Shakespeare's acting company, the Lord Chamberlain's Men,
and shareholder in the Globe (courtesy of the
Bodleian Library, Oxford)

Tho. Deloney, Chronicler of the memorable lives of the 6. yeomen of the west, Jack of Newbery, the Gentle-craft, & such like honest men: omitted by Stow, Hollinshead, Grafton, Hal, froysart, & the rest of those wel desrving writers: but I was given since to understand your late generall Tho. dyed poorely, as ye all must do, and was honestly buried: which is much to bee doubted of some of you. The quest of inquiry finding him by death acquited of the Inditement, I was let to wit, that another Lord of litle wit, one whose imployment for the Pageant, was utterly spent, he being knowne to be Eldertons immediate heyre, was vehemently suspected: but after due inquisition was made, he was at that time knowne to live like a man in a mist, having quite given over the mistery. Still the search continuing, I met a proper upright youth, onely for a little stooping in the shoulders: all hart to the heele, a penny Poet whose first making was the miserable stolne story of Macdoel, or Macdobeth, or Macsomewhat: for I am sure a Mac it was, though I never had the maw to see it: & hee tolde me there was a fat filthy ballet-maker, that should have once been his Journeyman to the trade: who liv'd about the towne; and ten to one, but he had thus terribly abused me & my Taberer: for that he was able to do such a thing in print. A shrewd presumption: I found him about the bank-side, sitting at a play, I desired to speake with him, had him to a Taverne, charg'd a pipe with Tobacco, and then laid this terrible accusation to his charge. He swels presently like one of the foure windes, the violence of his breath, blew the Tobacco out of the pipe, & the heate of his wrath drunke dry two bowlefuls of Rhenish wine. At length having power to speake, Name my accuser saith he, or I defye thee Kemp at the quart staffe. I told him, & all his anger turned to laughter: swearing it did him good to have ill words of a hoddy doddy, a habber de hoy, a chicken, a squib, a squall: One that hath not wit enough to make a ballet, that by *Pol* and *Aedipol* would Pol his father, Derick his dad: doe anie thing how ill soever, to please his apish humor. I hardly beleeved, this youth that I tooke to be gracious, had bin so graceles: but I heard afterwards his mother in law was eye and eare witnes of his fathers abuse by this blessed childe on a publique stage, in a merry Hoast of an Innes part. Yet all this while could not I finde out the true ballet-maker. Till by chaunce a friend of mine puld out of his pocket a booke in Latine called *Mundus Furiosus*: printed at *Cullen*, written by one of the vildest and arrantest lying Cullians that ever writ booke, his name Jansonius, who taking upon him to write an abstract of all the turbulent actions that had beene lately attempted or performed in Christendome, like an unchristian wretch, writes only by report, partially, and scoffingly, of such whose pages shooes hee was unworthy to wipe, for indeed he is now dead: farewell he, every dog must have a day. But see the luck on't: this beggerly lying busie-bodies name, brought out the Ballad-maker: and it was generally confirmd, it was his kinsman: he confesses himselfe guilty, let any man looke on his face: if there be not so redde a colour that all the sope in the towne will not washe white, let me be turned to a Whiting as I passe betweene Dover and Callis. Well, God forgive thee honest fellow, I see thou hast grace in thee: I prethee do so no more, leave writing these beastly ballets, make not good wenches Prophetesses, for litle or no profit, nor for a sixe-penny matter, revive not a poore fellowes fault thats hanged for his offence: it may be thy owne destiny one day, prethee be good to them. Call up thy olde Melpomene, whose straubery quill may write the blood lines of the blew Lady, and the Prince of the burning crowne: a better subject I can tell ye: than your Knight of the Red Crosse. So farewel, and crosse me no more I prethee with thy rabble of bald rimes, least at my returne I set a crosse on thy forehead, that all men may know thee for a foole.

Allusions to *Venus and Adonis* and *Lucrece* in Lane's *Tom Tel-Troths Message*

Poet John Lane's satire of contemporary vices, Tom Tel-Troths Message, And His Pens Complaint. A worke not unpleasant to read, nor unprofitable to be followed *(1600) contains an allusion to Shakespeare's* Venus and Adonis *and* The Rape of Lucrece *to support Lane's censure of lechery.*

Now last of all though perhaps chiefe of all,
My pen hath hunted out lewde Lecherie,
Which many sinnes and many faults doth call,
To bee pertakers to her trecherie:
　　Her love is lust, her lust is sugred sower,
　　Her paine is long, her pleasure but a flower.

When chast *Adonis* came to mans estate,
Venus straight courted him with many a wile;
Lucrece once seene, straight *Tarquine* laid a baite,
With foule incest her bodie to defile:
　　Thus men by women, women wrongde by men,
　　Give matter still unto my plaintife pen.

　　　　　　　　　　　　　　　　　　　　　　–sig. F2r.

Allusion to the Globe in Rowlands's *The Letting Of Humours Blood*

The allusion to visiting the Globe theater to see a play in poet Samuel Rowland's collection of epigrams and satires The Letting of Humours Blood In The Head-Vaine *(1600) shows that a trip to the theater was one of many options for young men in search of entertainment.*

EPIG. 7.

Speake Gentlemen, what shall we do to day?
Drinke some brave health upon the Dutch carouse?
Or shall we to the *Globe* and see a Play?
Or visit *Shorditch* for a bawdie house?
Lets call for Cardes or Dice, and have a Game,
To sit thus idle, is both sinne and shame.

This speakes *Sir Revell*, furnisht out with fashion,
From dish-crowned Hat, unto the Shoo's square toe
That haunts a Whore-house but for recreation,
Playes but at Dice to connycatch or so.
Drinkes drunke in kindnes, for good fellowship.
Or to Play goes but some Purse to nip.

　　　　　　　　　　　　　　　　　　　　　　–sig. A7r.

Allusion to Falstaff in a Letter from the Countess of Southampton to the Earl of Southampton

In a postscript to a letter from Elizabeth Vernon, the Countess of Southampton, to her husband, Shakespeare's patron Henry Wriothesley, Earl of Southampton, endorsed "Chartly the 8th of July" but otherwise undated, the countess refers to Shakespeare's popular character. The identities of "Falstaff" and his mistress have not been discovered. The text of the postscript is from the appendix of the Third Report of The Royal Commission on Historical Manuscripts *(1872).*

All the nues I can send you that I thinke wil make you mery is that I reade in a letter from London that Sir John Falstaf is by his Mrs Dame Pintpot made father of a godly milers thum, a boye thats all heade and veri litel body; but this is a secrit.

　　　　　　　　　　　　　　　　　　　　　　–p. 148

A theater in Shoreditch from "A View of the Cittye of London from the North towards the Sowth" circa 1597–1600 (courtesy of the University Library, University of Utrecht)

Shakespeare's Company Paid for Court Performances

The Lord Chamberlain's Men are paid for performances.

To John Hemynges and Richarde Cowley servuntes to the Lord Chambrleine uppon the Councelles warraunte dated at Whitehall ultimo Marcii 1601 for three playes showed before her highnes on St Stephens day at nighte Twelfth day at nighte and Shrovetwesday at nighte xxx^li
  —*Dramatic Records*, p. 31

1601

A Performance of *Richard II* and the Essex Rebellion

The following documents record one aspect of the attempted coup against Queen Elizabeth led by Robert Devereux, the second Earl of Essex (1566–1601). In an apparent effort to generate support or enthusiasm among his followers Essex commissioned Shakespeare's acting company, the Lord Chamberlain's Men, to perform Shakespeare's Richard II, *a play about a monarch to whom Elizabeth was sometimes unfavorably compared. The play includes a scene in which King Richard is deposed by Henry Bullingbrook, who thereby becomes King Henry IV. Essex himself knew theatrical representations had the power to influence public perceptions: in a 1600 letter to Queen Elizabeth, he complained, "The prating tavern haunter speaks of me what he lists; they print me and make me speak to the world, and shortly they*

will play me upon the stage" (Calendar of State Papers Domestic, p. 435).

Essex's coup was a spectacular failure: the conspirators were quickly arrested and tried, and many of them were executed. Among Essex's supporters was Shakespeare's patron, Henry Wriothesley, Earl of Southampton, who was imprisoned by Queen Elizabeth, then pardoned by King James shortly after he acceded to the English throne in 1603. Although Augustine Phillips, a member of the Lord Chamberlain's Men and a sharer (part owner) of the Globe theater, was brought in for questioning, no records survive documenting the questioning or arrest of other actors or of Shakespeare. Essex, once a court favorite, was executed on 25 February 1601.

The following excerpt, from the "Analytical abstract of the evidence in support of the charge of treason against the Earl of Essex" (circa June, 1600), a legal document describing earlier charges against Essex, shows that the earl had a previous association with printed and dramatic representations of the life of Henry IV. Although the specific reference here is to John Hayward's The First Part of the Life and Raigne of King Henrie IIII, *a prose history dedicated to Essex, the accusation that Essex attended "the playing" of Henry IV's story means he saw a theatrical representation such as Shakespeare's* Richard II *or* 1 Henry IV.

Essex's own actions confirm the intent of this treason. His permitting underhand that treasonable book of Henry IV. to be printed and published; it being plainly deciphered, not only by the matter, and by the epistle itself, for what end and for whose behalf it was made, but also the Earl himself being so often present at the playing thereof, and with great applause giving countenance to it. His idle and fruitless journeys into Munster, Lex, and Ophaly, on purpose to harass and waste the Queen's army and treasure, and let the fit time for the northern journey pass away; all which he effected contrary to Her Majesty's directions, and to the manifest peril and loss of the whole realm of Ireland. His giving pardon to his father-in-law and Capt. Lea, secretly sent by his said father-in-law to Tyrone, notwithstanding that neither the Earl himself, as he says, nor any of the Council, as they affirm, were made privy thereto by either of them. His private speech and meeting with Tyrone, none but they two being present, while the Earl of Southampton sought to keep all men from standing near, and hearing what was said between them. His sudden return into England, contrary to the express command of Her Majesty, leaving that kingdom in so apparent danger, and wholly to the will and power of that proud and pernicious traitor, Tyrone.
  —*Calendar of State Papers*, p. 455

The following excerpt is from "Examination of Sir William Constable and two others, in answer to interrogatories," dated 16 February 1601 (New Style). The interrogation of Constable, one of Essex's coconspirators in the February 1601 rebellion, describes the conspirators' visit to the Globe theater to see Richard II. *The document's internal date, "Saturday the 7th inst." is Old Style; "inst." is an abbreviation for "instar," a Latin term here meaning "or its equivalent."*

On Saturday the 7th inst., he with Lord Monteagle, Sir Christ. Blount, Sir Gelly Merrick, Sir Chas. Percy, Hen. Cuffe, Edw. Bushell, Ellis Jones, and Sir Jo. Davies met, for all he knows by chance, at one Gunter's house, over against Temple gate, where they dined, after which Thos. Lea came to the play, where they were all assembled, at the Globe on the Bankside, saving Cuffe. After the play, examinate and Edw. Bushell went to Essex House, where they supped and lay all night, which he had never done before; the reason was that after supper, the Earl signified to those assembled in the withdrawing chamber, where Lord Monteagle, Sir Gelly Merrick, Sir Robt. Vernon, and others were, that there was a plot laid by his enemies to draw him to the Lord Treasurer's, and to take his life, as he was then called to the Council, which he had not been before since his disgrace. The Earl moved examinate to lie there all night, which he did with Sir Robt. Vernon.

–*Calendar of State Papers*, p. 573

The examination of Sir Gelly Merrick, another of the Essex conspirators, is dated 17 February 1601 (New Style) and provides further details about the conspirators' trip to the Globe theater.

Examination of Sir Gelly Merrick before Lord Chief Justice Popham and Edw. Fenner. On Saturday last was sevennight, dined at Gunter's in company with Lord Monteagle, Sir Christ. Blount, Sir Chas. Percy, Ellis Jones, Edw. Bushell, and others. On the motion of Sir Chas. Percy, they went all together to the Globe over the water, where the Lord Chamberlain's men used to play, and were there somewhat before the play began, Sir Charles telling them that the play would be of Harry the Fourth. Cannot say whether Sir John Danvers was there or not, but he said he would be if he could; thinks it was Sir Chas. Percy who procured that play to be played at that time. The play was of King Henry the Fourth, and of the killing of Richard the Second, and played by the Lord Chamberlain's players.

–*Calendar of State Papers*, p. 575

The examination of actor Augustine Phillips (PRO SP 12/278/85) is dated 18 February 1601 (New Style). Phillips was a member of Shakespeare's acting company, the Lord Chamberlain's Men, and a sharer (part owner) of the Globe theater. His arrest and interrogation illustrates the dangers actors and

playwrights faced when their work was linked to contemporary political events. Phillips's defense—that the play was an old one— is strategically sound because it implies the actors were ignorant of the political relevance of their production and concerned only with their potential financial profit.

The ex[aminati]on of Augustyn Phillypps
servant unto the L. Chamberlyne
and one of hys players taken
the xviii[th] of Februarij 1600
vpon hys oth.

He sayeth that on Fryday last was senyght or Thursday S[r] Charles Percy S[r] Jostlyne Percy and the L Montegle w[th] some thre more spak to some of the players in the presens of this exa to have the play of the deposying and kyllyng of Kyng Rychard the Second to be played the *next day* [deleted] *Satedy next* [interlined] promysyng to gete them xls more then their ordynary to play yt. Wher thys exa and hys freindes were determyned to have playd some other play holdyng that play of Kyng Rychard to be so old & so long out of use as that they shold have small or no company at yt. But at their request this exa and hys freindes were content to play yt the Saterday and hadd their xls. more then their ordynary for yt and so played y[t] accordyngly.

Augustine Phillips (signed)

ex per
Jo Popham
Edmund Anderson
Edward Fenner

Francis Bacon, once Essex's friend and promoter, made the politically adept choice to support the earl's prosecutors in Essex's final trial. The excerpt from Bacon's account of the Essex conspiracy provides a published, and publically available, description of the conspirators' commissioning of the performance of Shakespeare's Richard II; *it is from* A Declaration of the Practices & Treasons attempted and committed by Robert late Earle of Essex and his Complices, against her Majestie and her Kingdoms *(1601).*

THE EFFECT OF THAT
which passed at the Arraignements of
Sir *Christopher Blunt*, Sir *Charles Davers*,
Sir *John Davies*, Sir *Gillie Mericke*,
and *Henry Cuffe*.

The 5. of March by a very honorable Commission of *Oier* and *Determiner*, directed to the Lord high Admiral, the Lord Chamberlaine, Master Secretary, the Lord chiefe Justice of *England*, Master Chancellour of the Exchequer, Master Secretary *Herbert*, with divers of the Judges, the Commissioners sitting in the Court of the Queenes Bench, there were arraigned and tried by a Jury both of Aldermen of London, and other Gentlemen of good credit and sort, Sir *Christopher Blunt*, Sir *Charles Davers*, Sir *John Davies*, Sir *Gillie Mericke* & *Henry Cuffe*.

–sig. I3v

. . . .

Against Sir *Gilly Merrick*, the Evidence that was given, charged him chiefly with the matter of the open Rebellion, that hee was as Captaine or commander over the house, and tooke upon him charge to keepe it, and make it good as a place of Retraict for those which issued into the Citie, and fortifying and barriccadoing the same house, and making provision of Muskets, Powder, Pellets and other munition and weapons for the holding and defending of it, and as a busie, forward, and noted Actor in that defence and resistance, which was made against the Queenes forces brought against it, by her Majesties Lieutenant.

And further to proove him privie to the plot, it was given in Evidence, that some fewe dayes before the Rebellion, with great heat and violence hee had displaced certaine Gentlemen lodged in an house fast by *Essex house*, and there planted divers of my Lords followers and Complices, all such as went foorth with him in the Action of Rebellion.

That the afternoone before the Rebellion, *Merricke*, with a great company of others, that afterwards were all in the Action, had procured to bee played before them, the Play of deposing King *Richard* the second.

Neither was it casuall, but a Play bespoken by *Merrick*.

And not so onely, but when it was told him by one of the Players, that the Play was olde, and they should have losse in playing it, because fewe would come to it: there was fourty shillings extraordinarie given to play it, and so thereupon playd it was.

So earnest hee was to satisfie his eyes with the sight of that Tragedie, which hee thought soone after his Lord should bring from the Stage to the State, but that GOD turned it upon their owne heads.

–K2r–K3r.

In The Progresses and Public Processions of Queen Elizabeth *(1823), editor John Nichols notes that this document–"That which passed from the Excellent Majestie of Queen ELIZABETH, in her Privie Chamber at East Greenwich, 4° Augusti 1601, 43° Reg. sui, towards WILLIAM LAMBARDE"–was "Communicated, from the original, by Thomas Lambard, of Sevenoaks, Esq." William Lambarde, an historian and antiquary, had been given the responsibility of organizing the*

royal records stored in the Tower of London. The following excerpt reports a conversation he had with the queen when he delivered his report on those records to her. Lambarde notes that Queen Elizabeth compared herself to King Richard II and was aware of theatrical representations of that king's story. This provides further evidence that the Essex conspirators hoped the audience assembled to watch their specially commissioned production of Shakespeare's Richard II *would link Elizabeth and Richard and would see the queen as someone who deserved to be deposed.*

He presented her Majestie with his Pandecta of all her rolls, bundells, membranes, and parcells that be reposed in her Majestie's Tower at London; whereof she had given to him the charge 21st January last past.

Her Majestie chearfullie received the same into her hands, saying, "You intended to present this book unto me by the Countess of Warwicke: but I will none of that; for if any subject of mine do me a service, I will thankfully accept it from his own hands;" then, opening the book, said, "You shall see that I can read;" and so, with an audible voice, read over the epistle, and the title, so readily, and distinctly pointed, that it might perfectly appear, that she well understood, and conceived the same. Then she descended from the beginning of King John, till the end of Richard III. that is 64 pages, serving eleven kings, containing 286 years: in the 1st page she demanded the meaning of *oblata, cartæ, literæ clausæ,* and *literæ patentes.*

W. L. He severally expounded the meaning, and laid out the true differences of every of them; her Majestie seeming well satisfied, and said, "that she would be a scholar in her age, and thought it no scorn to learn during her life, being of the mind of that philosopher, who in his last years began with the Greek alphabet." Then she proceeded to further pages, and asked where she found cause of stay, as what *ordinationes, parliamenta, rotulus cambii, rediseisnes.*

W. L. He likewise expounded these all according to their original diversities, which she took in gratious and full satisfaction; so her Majestie fell upon the reign of King Richard II. saying "I am Richard II. know ye not that?"

W. L. "Such a wicked imagination was determined and attempted by a most unkind Gent. the most adorned creature that ever your Majestie made."

Her Majestie. "He that will forget God, will also forget his benefactors; this tragedy was played 40^tie times in open streets and houses."

Her Majestie demanded "what was *præstita?*"

W. L. He expounded it to be "monies lent by her Progenitors to her subjects for their good, but with assurance of good bond for repayment."

Her Majestie. "So did my good Grandfather King Henry VII. sparing to dissipate his treasure or lands." Then returning to Richard II. she demanded, "Whether I

Portrait of William Sly by an unknown painter. Sly, an actor with the King's Men, was a shareholder in the Globe and Blackfriars theaters (by permission of the Trustees of Dulwich Picture Gallery).

W. L. "Yea, and therefore these be the rolls of fines assessed and levied upon such wrong-doers, as well for the great and wilful contempt of the crown and royal dignity, as disturbance of common justice."

Her Majestie. "In those days force and arms did prevail; but now the wit of the fox is every where on foot, so as hardly a faithful or vertuouse man may be found." Then came she to the whole total of all the membranes and parcels aforesaid, amounting to . . . ; commending the work; "not only for the pains there in taken, but also for that she had not received since her first coming to the crown any one thing that brought therewith so great delectation unto her;" and so being called away to prayer, she put the book in her bosom, having forbidden me from the first to the last to fall upon my knee before her; concluding, "Farewell, good and honest Lambarade."
—*The Progresses and Public Processions of Queen Elizabeth,*
volume III, pp. 552–553

Shakespeare and His Wife Named in Whittington's Will

In this extract from Thomas Whittington's will, dated 25 March 1601 (Worcestershire Record Office, 008.7, 16/1601), one of the questions raised by Shakespeare's marriage documents is settled: it is Anne Hathaway, rather than Anne Whatley, who is identified here as Shakespeare's wife. Whittington, a shepherd employed by Hathaway's father, was owed 40 shillings by Anne Hathaway, and Whittington asked that the debt be settled by having Hathaway pay his bequest to the poor people of Stratford.

Item I geve & bequeth unto the poore people of Stratford xl^s that is in the hand of Anne Shaxspere Wyf unto Mr Wyllyam Shaxspere & is due dett unto me beyng payd to myne executor by the sayd Wyllyam Shaxspere or his assigns accordyng to the true meanyng of this my wyll./

John Shakespeare's Burial Record

[8 September 1601] Mr Johannes Shakspeare
—*Burial Register,* folio 34v

The cause of John Shakespeare's death is not known, nor, in the absence of a record of his birth, is his age. William Shakespeare, as the eldest son, would have inherited his father's property, and Shakespeare's own will (1616) shows he owned the family home in Henley Street and made provisions for his sister Joan to continue to live there.

had seen any true picture, or lively representation of his countenance and person?"

W. L. "None but such as be in common hands."

Her Majestie. "The Lord Lumley, a lover of antiquities, discovered it fastened on the backside of a door of a base room; which he presented unto me, praying, with my good leave, that I might put it in order with the Ancestors and Successors; I will command Tho. Kneavet, Keeper of my House and Gallery at Westminster, to shew it unto thee." Then she proceeded to the Rolls,

Romæ, Vascon, Aquitaniæ, Franciæ, Scotiæ, Walliæ, et Hiberniæ.

W. L. He expounded these to be records of estate, and negotiations with foreign Princes or Counteries.

Her Majestie demanded again, "if *rediseisnes* were unlawful and forcible throwing of men out of their lawfull possessions?"

The Publication of Chester's *Love's Martyr*

LOVES MARTYR: / OR, / ROSALINS COM-PLAINT. / *Allegorically ſhadowing the truth of Loue,* / in the Conſtant Fate of the Phoenix / *and Turtle.* / A Poeme enterlaced with much varietie and raritie; / *now firſt tranſlated out of the venerable Italian* Torquato / Cæliano, *by* ROBERT CHESTER. / With the true legend of famous King *Arthur,* the laſt of the nine / Worthies, being the firſt *Eſſay* of a new *Brytiſh* Poet, collected / out of diuerſe anthenticall Records. / *To theſe are added ſome new compoſitions, of ſeuerall moderne Writers* / *whoſe names are ſubſcribed to their ſeuerall workes, upon the* / *firſt Subject: viz. the* Phoenix *and* Tur-tle. / *Mar:—Mutare dominum non poteſt liber notus.* / [*Printer's device*] / LONDON / Imprinted for F.B.

Poet Robert Chester, in the anthology containing Shakespeare's allegorical poem "The Phoenix and the Tur-tle," lists Shakespeare among the "best and chiefest of our modern writers" who contributed "divers poetical essays" to his collection.

Allusions to *Richard III* and *1 Henry IV* in *The Whipping of the Satyre*

The author of The Whipping of the Satyre (*Imprinted for John Flasket, 1601*) is identified only by the ini-tials "W. I." The excerpt's first stanza deliberately misquotes Shakespeare's history play Richard III's "A horse, a horse! my kingdom for a horse!" (5.4.7) in its excoriation of contemporary vices. The fourth stanza provides further evidence that Shake-speare's Falstaff is, as he himself admits, "A goodly portly man, i' faith, and a corpulent" (1 Henry IV, 2.4.421).

But harke, I heare the *Cynicke Satyre* crie,
A man, a man, a kingdome for a man.
Why, was there not a man to serve his eye?
No, all were turn'd to beasts that headlong ran.
Who cried a man, (c) a man then was he none,
No, but a beast by his confession.
    (c) *Nec vox hominis sonat: O fera certe.*

Fayth, Satyre, thou art overmuch severe:
For say, that we had brutish bene indeede;
I shall make proofe, & proofe shal make it cleare,
That brutishnesse to us small shame can breede.
An Englishman may better brutish be,
Then any nation in the world save he.

For doth it us become a shame to stand,
Of our most noble Ancestours this day,
The valiant Brute, first father of our land?
Shall not we shewe of whom we come, I pray?
If we be brutish, you must it impute,
That we be so in memory of Brute.

I dare here speake it, and my speach mayntayne,
That Sir John Falstaffe was not any way
More grosse in body, then you are in brayne.
But whether should I (helpe me nowe, I pray)
For your grosse brayne, you like I, Falstaffe, graunt,
Or for small wit, suppose you John of Gaunt?

                     –sigs. D2r–D3r.

Allusion to *1 Henry IV* in Weever's *The Mirror of Martyrs*

Shakespeare's Sir John Falstaff was originally called Sir John Oldcastle. Early modern accounts of the historical Oldcas-tle–such as John Weever's The Mirror of Martyrs, Or The life and death of that thrice valiant Capitaine, and most godly Martyre Sir John Old-castle knight, Lord Cob-ham (*Printed by V.S. for William Wood, 1601*)–often stress the ways in which this Protestant hero differed from Shake-speare's "old fat man" (1 Henry IV, 2.4.448). Here, Oldcas-tle himself is the narrator of his life's history, and in the third and fourth stanzas of this excerpt he comments on the large audiences drawn to the London theaters and compares this to an incident staged in act 3 scene 2 of Shakespeare's tragedy Julius Cæsar.

The Life and death of Sir
Jo: Oldcastle knight,
Lord Cobham.

Faire *Lucifer,* the messenger of light,
Upon the bosome of the star-deckt skie,
Begins to chase the raven-fethered night:
That stops the passage of his percing eie:
    And heaving up the brim of his bright bever,
    Would make that day, which day was counted never.

But *Mercurie,* be thou the morning Star,
Beare my embassage from *Elysium,*
Shew to my countrie hence removed far,
From these pavilions I can never come:
    Staind vice ascends from out th'infernall deepes,
    But in the heavens unspotted vertue keepes.

Deliver but in swasive eloquence,
Both of my life and death the veritie,
Set up a *Si quis,* give intelligence,
That such a day shall be my Tregedie:
    If thousands flocke to heare a Poets pen,
    To heare a god, how many millions then?

The many-headed multitude were drawne
By *Brutus* speach, that *Cæsar* was ambitious,
When eloquent *Mark Antonie* had showne
His vertues, who but *Brutus* then was vicious:
    Mans memorie with new forgets the old,
    One tale is good untill another's told.

Sing thou my dirgies like a dying Swan,
Whose painfull death requires a playning dittie:
That my complaint may pierce the hart of man,
Plaine be thy song, sweete, pleasing, full of pittie:
   And more, to move the multitude to ruth,
   Let my apparell be the naked truth.

. . . .

   Weever returns to his criticism of the theater in the poem's
final stanza.

Wit, spend thy vigour, Poets, wits quintessence,
Hermes make great the worlds eies with teares;
Actors make sighes a burden for each sentence:
That he may sob which reades, he swound which heares.
Mean time, till life in death you doe renew,
Wit, Poets, Hermes, Actors, all adew.

               –sigs. A3r-v, F3v.

Allusions to Shakespeare
in *The Returne From Pernassus*

   The third Parnassus play, The Returne From Pernassus: Or The Scourge of Simony *(1606), the only*
one to be printed, was performed by the students of St. John's
College, Cambridge, probably in 1601. The play continues
the tradition of the first two (circa 1598-1601) by both eval-
uating and mocking contemporary poets, including Shake-
speare. In this excerpt, two characters, Ingenioso, who may be
based on satirist Thomas Nashe, and Judicio, who edits pam-
phlets, discuss the poets whose works are featured in John
Bodenham's anthology Bel-vedere *(1600), a collection of*
poetical extracts considered unworthy of scholars such as the
heroes of the Parnassus plays Studioso and Philomusus.

[*Judicio*] . . . [H]ere is a booke *Ing[enioso]*: why to condemne it to cleare the usuall Tiburne of all misliving
papers, weare too faire a death for so foule an
offender.

[*Ingenioso*] What's the name of it, I pray thee
Jud [icio]?

Jud. Looke its here *Belvedere.*

Ing. what a belwether in Paules Churchyeard, so cald
because it keeps a bleating, or because it hath the tinck-
ling bel of so many Poets about the neck of it, what is
the rest of the title.

Jud. The garden of the Muses.

Ing. What have we here, the Poet garish gayly bedeket
like fore horses of the parish? what follows.

Jud. Quem referent musæ, viuet dum robora tellus,
    Dum celum stellas, dum vehit amnis aquas.
Who blurres fayer paper, with foule bastard rimes,
Shall live full many an age in latter times:
Who makes a ballet for an alehouse doore,
Shall live in future times for ever more.
Then [Bodenham] thy muse shall live so long,
As drafty ballats to thy praise are song.

   But what's his devise, Parnassus with the sunne
and the lawrel: I wonder this owle dares looke on the
sunne and I marvaill this go[o]se flies not the lawrell:
his devise might have bene better a foole going in to the
market place to be seene, with this motto, *scribimus*
indocti, or a poore beggar gleaning of eares in the end of
harvest, with this word, *sua cuiq[ue] gloria.*

Jud. Turne over the leafe, *Ing[enioso]*: and thou shalt see
the paynes of this worthy gentleman, Sentences gathered out of all kind of Poetts, referred to certaine
methodicall heades, profitable for the use of these times,
to rime upon any occasion at a little warning: Read the
names.

Ing. So I will, if thou wilt helpe me to censure them.
   Edmund Spencer.   *Michaell Drayton.*
   Henry Constable.   *John Davis.*
   Thomas Lodge.   *John Marston.*
   Samuel Daniell.   *Kit: Marlowe.*
   Thomas Watson.
Good men and true; stand togither: heare your cen-
sure, what's thy judgement of *Spencer*?

Jud. A sweeter swan then ever song in Poe,
A shriller Nightingale then ever blest
The prouder groves of selfe admiring Rome.
Blith was each vally, and each sheapeard proud,
While he did chaunt his rurall minstralsye.
Attentive was full many a dainty eare.
Nay hearers hong upon his melting tong,
While sweetly of his Faiery Queene he song.
While to the waters fall he tun'd for fame,
And in each banke engrav'd Elizaes name.
And yet for all this, unregarding soile
Unlac't the line of his desired life,
Denying mayntenance for his deare releife.
Carelesse care to prevent his exequy,
Scarce deigning to shut up his dying eye.

Ing. Pitty it is that gentler witts should breed,
Where thickskin chuffes laugh at a schollers neede.

But softly may our honors ashes rest,
That lie by mery *Chaucers* noble chest.
 But I pray thee proceede breefly in thy censure, that I may be proud of my selfe, as in the first, so in the last, my censure may jumpe with thine. *Henry Constable, Samuel Daniel, Thomas Lodg, Thomas Watson.*

Jud. Sweete *Constable* doth take the wondring eare,
And layes it up in willing prisonment:
Sweete hony dropping *Daniell* doth wage
Warre with the proudest big Italian,
That melts his heart in sugred sonetting.
Onely let him more sparingly make use,
Of others wit, and use his owne the more:
That well may scorne base imitation.
For *Lodge* and *Watson,* men of some desert,
Yet subject to a Critticks marginall.
Lodge for his oare in every paper boate,
He that turnes over Galen every day,
To sit and simper *Euphues* legacy.

Ing. Michael Drayton.

[*Judicio*] *Draytons* sweete muse is like a sanguine dy,
Able to ravish the rash gazers eye.

Ing. How ever he wants one true note of a Poet of our times, and that is this, hee cannot swagger it well in a Taverne, nor dominere in a hothouse.

Jud. Acute *John Davis,* I affect thy rymes,
That ierck in hidden charmes these looser times:
Thy playner verse, thy unaffected vaine,
Is grac't with a fayre and a sooping trayne.

Ing. Locke and *Hudson.*

Jud. Locke and *Hudson,* sleepe you quiet shavers, among the shavings of the presse, and let your bookes lie in some old nookes amongst old bootes and shooes, so you may avoyde my censure.

Ing. Why then clap a locke on their feete, and turne them to commons.
 John Marstox.

Jud. What, *Monsier Kinsayder,* lifting up your legge and pissing against the world, put up man, put up for shame.
Me thinks he is a Ruffian in his stile,
Withouten bands or garters ornament,
He quaffes a cup of frenchmans Helicon.
Then royster doyster in his oylie tearmes,
Cutts, thrusts, and foines at whomesoever he meets.

And strewes about Ram-ally meditations,
Tut what cares he for modest close coucht termes,
Cleanly to gird our looser libertines.
Give him plaine naked words stript from their shirts
That might beseeme plaine dealing *Aretine:*
I there is one that backes a paper steed
And manageth a pen-knife gallantly,
Strikes his poinado at a buttons breadth,
Brings the great battering ram of tearms to towns
And at first volly of his Cannon shot,
Batters the walles of the old fustie world.

Ing. Christopher Marlowe.

Jud. Marlowe was happy in his buskind muse,
Alas unhappy in his life and end,
Pitty it is that wit so ill should dwell,
Wit lent from heaven, but vices sent from hell.

Ing. Our *Theater* hath lost, *Pluto* hath got,
A Tragick penman for a driery plot.
Benjamin Johnson.

Jud. The wittiest fellow of a Bricklayer in England.

Ing. A meere Empyrick, one that getts what he hath by observation, and makes onely nature privy to what he endites, so slow an Inventor, that he were better betake himselfe to his old trade of Bricklaying, a bould whorson, as confident now in making of a booke, as he was in times past in laying of a brick.
William Shakespeare.

Jud. Who loves *Adonis* love, or *Lucre's* rape,
His sweeter verse contaynes hart robbing life,
Could but a graver subject him content,
Without loves foolish lazy languishment.

Ing. Churchyard.
Hath not *Shor's* wife although a light skirts she,
Given him a chast long lasting memory?

Jud. No all light pamphlets once I finden shall,
A Churchyard and a grave to bury all.

Ing. Thomas Nashdo.
I heare is a fellowe *Judicio* that carryed the deadly stocke in his pen, whose muse was armed with a gag-tooth, and his pen possest with *Hercules* furies.

Jud. Let all his faultes sleepe with his mournfull chest,
And then for ever with his ashes rest.
His stile was wittie, though he had some gal,
Something he might have mended, so may all.

Yet this I say, that for a mother witt,
Fewe men have ever seene the like of it.

Ing. Reades the rest.

Jud. As for these, they have some of them beene the old hedgstakes of the presse, and some of them are at this instant the botts and glanders of the printing house. Fellowes that stand onely upon tearmes to serve the tearme, with their blotted papers, write as men goe to stoole, for needes, and when they write, they write as a Beare pisses, now and then drop a pamphlet.

Ing. Durum telum necessitas. Good fayth they do as I do, exchange words for mony, I have some traffique this day with *Danter*, about a little booke which I have made, the name of it is a Catalogue of *Cambrige* Cuckolds, but this Belvedere, this methodicall asse, hath made me almost forget my time: Ile now to Paules Churchyard meete me an houre hence, at the signe of the Pegasus in Cheap-side, and Ile moyst thy temples with a cuppe of Claret, as hard as the world goes. *Ex[it] Judicio.*

—lines 169–335

. . . .

In a later scene, actors impersonating the actors Richard Burbage and William Kempe provide a comic look at early modern celebrity. Parnassus graduates Studioso and Philomusus, unable to find gainful employment, are searching for ways to make money. Having tried making a living as con men, they decide, with Burbage and Kemp's encouragement, to take up the "basest trade" and become actors. Burbage hopes the Cambridge graduates will also be able to write plays, but Kemp insists their dramas will be too intellectual for the audience, unlike the plays written by "our fellow Shakespeare." *This observation prompts the actors to exchange professional gossip; the "purge" that Kemp claims Shakespeare gave Ben Jonson is usually understood as a reference to Shakespeare's bitter comedy* Troilus and Cressida. *The two professional actors then audition the former students; Studioso quotes from Thomas Kyd's* The Spanish Tragedy, *and Philomusus quotes the opening lines of Shakespeare's* Richard III. *In a later scene, the students reappear as musicians, having decided "Better it is mongst fidlers to be chiefe / Then at plaiers trencher beg reliefe" (lines 1916–1917); they ultimately decide to become shepherds.*

Bur. Now *Will Kempe* if we can intertaine these schollers at a low rate, it wil be well, they have oftentimes a good conceite in a part.

Kempe Its true indeede, honest *Dick*, but the slaves are somewhat proud, and besides, it is a good sport in a part to see them never speake in their walke, but at the end of the stage, just as though in walking with a fellow we should never speake but at a stile, a gate, or a ditch, where a man can go no further. I was once at a Comedie in Cambridge, and there I saw a parasite make faces and mouths of all sorts on this fashion.

Bur. A little teaching will mend these faults, and it may bee besides they will be able to pen a part.

Kemp. Few of the university pen plaies well, they smell too much of that writer *Ovid*, and that writer *Metamorphosis*, and talke too much of *Proserpina* & *Juppiter*. Why heres our fellow *Shakespeare* puts them all downe, I and *Ben Jonson* too. O that *Ben Jonson* is a pestilent fellow, he brought up *Horace* giving the Poets a pill, but our fellow *Shakespeare* hath given him a purge that made him beray his credit.

Bur. Its a shrewd fellow indeed: I wonder these schollers stay so long, they appointed to be here presently that we might try them: oh here they come.

[*Enter Philomusus and Studioso.*]

Stud. Take heart these lets our clouded thoughts refine,
The sun shines brightest when it gins decline.

Burb. M. *Phil[omusus]* and M. *Stud[ioso]*. God save you.

Kemp. M. *Phil.* and M. *Otioso*, well met.

Phil. The same to you good M. *Burbage.* What M. *Kempe* how doth the Emperour of Germany?

Stud. God save you M. *Kempe*: welcome M. *Kempe* from dancing the morrice over the Alpes.

Kemp. Well you merry knaves you may come to the honor of it one day, is it not better to make a foole of the world as I have done, then to be fooled of the world, as you schollers are? But be merry my lads, you have happened upon the most excellent vocation in the world for money: they come North and South to bring it to our playhouse, and for honours, who of more report, then *Dick Burbage* & *Will Kempe,* he is not counted a Gentleman, that knowes not *Dick Burbage* & *Will Kemp,* there's not a country wench that can dance Sellengers Round but can talke of *Dick Burbage* and *Will Kempe.*

Phil. Indeed M. *Kempe* you are very famous, but that is as well for workes in print as your part in kne.

Kempe. You are at Cambridge still with sice kne, and be lusty humorous poets, you must untrusse, I road this

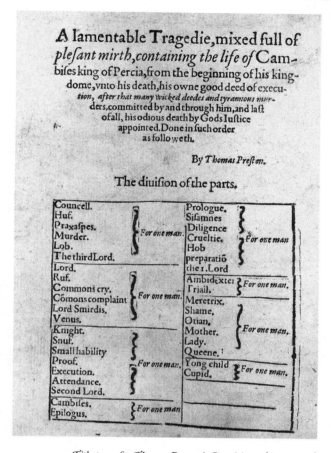
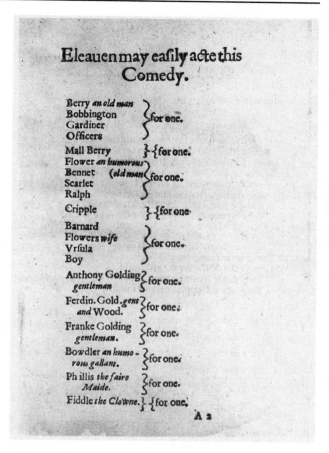

Title page for Thomas Preston's Cambises (circa 1595) *and page from* The Fayre Mayde of the Exchange *(1607),*
showing the common practice of doubling in which one actor plays two or more parts
(by permission of the Folger Shakespeare Library)

my last circuit, purposely because I would be judge of your actions.

Burb. M. *Stud* I pray you take some part in this booke and act it, that I may see what will fit you best, I thinke your voice would serve for *Hieronimo,* observe how I act it and then imitate mee.

Stud. Who call *Hieronimo* from his naked bed?
    And &c.

Bur. You will do well after a while.

Kemp. Now for you, me thinkes you should belong to my tuition, and your face me thinkes would be good for a foolish Mayre or a foolish justice of peace: marke me.——
Forasmuch as there be two states of a common wealth, the one of peace, the other of tranquility: two states of warre, the one of discord, the other of dissention: two states of an incorporation, the one of the Aldermen, the

other of the Brethren: two states of magistrates the one of governing, the other of bearing rule, now, as I said even now for a good thing thing cannot be said too often: Vertue is the shooinghorne of justice, that is, vertue is the shooinghorne of doing well, that is, vertue is the shooinghorne of doing justly, it behooveth mee and is my part to commend this shooinghorne unto you. I hope this word shooinghorne doth not offend any of you my worshipfull brethren, for you beeing the worshipfull headsmen of the towne, know well what the horne meaneth. Now therefore I am determined not onely to teach but also to instruct, not onely the ignorant, but also the simple, not onely what is their duty towards their betters but also what is their dutye towards their superiours: come let mee see how you can doe, sit downe in the chaire.

Phil. Forasmuch as there be &c.

Kemp. Thou wilt do well in time, if thou wilt be ruled by thy betters, that is by my selfe, and such grave Aldermen of the playhouse as I am.

Bur. I like your face, and the proportion of your body for *Richard* the 3. I pray M. *Phil.* let me see you act a little of it.

Phil. Now is the winter of our discontent,
Made glorious summer by the sonne of Yorke,

Bur. Very well I assure you, well M. *Phil.* and M. *Stud.* wee see what ability you are of: I pray walke with us to our fellows, and weele agree presently.

Phil. We will follow you straight M. *Burbage.*

Kempe. Its good manners to follow us, Maister *Phil.* and Maister *Otioso.*
[*Exuent Burbage & Kempe.*]

Phil. And must the basest trade yeeld us reliefe?
Must we be practis'd to those leaden spouts,
That nought downe vent but what they do receive?
Some fatall fire hath scorcht our fortunes wing,
And still we fall, as we do upward spring:
As we strive upward to the vaulted skie,
We fall and feele our hatefull destiny.
　　　　　　　　　　　　　　　　　　–lines 1753–1852

After further complaint, Studioso and Philomusus end the scene with this exchange.

Stud. Lets learne to act that Tragick part we have.

Phil. Would I were silent actor in my grave.
　　　　　　　　　　　　　　　　　　–lines 1911–1912

Allusion to *Richard III* in Marston's *What You Will*

Satirist and playwright John Marston's comedy What You Will *(1607) was performed circa 1601 as part of the War of the Theaters, a literary conflict in which rival playwrights depicted each other in often-vicious stage caricatures. In the following exchange of insults the two speakers, Lampatho and Quadratus, probably represent Marston and Ben Jonson, although critical consensus is divided over which character represents which playwright. Quadratus quotes Shakespeare's* Richard III *(5.4.7), then calls attention to his fashionable habit of quoting from plays.*

[*Lampatho*] So *Phœbus* warme my braine, Ile rime thee dead,
Looke for the Satyre, if all the sower juice
Of a tart braine, can sowse thy estimate,
Ile pickle thee.

[*Quadratus*] Ha he mount *Chirall* on the wings of fame.
A horse, a horse, my kingdom for a horse,
Looke the I speake play scrappes. *Bydet* Ile downe
Sing, sing, or stay weele quaffe or any thing
Rivo, Saint *Marke*, lets talke as losse as ayre
Un-wind youthes coullors, display our selves
So that yon envy-starved Curre may yealpe
And spend his chappes at our Phantastickenesse.

Shakespeare's Company Paid for Court Performances

The Lord Chamberlain's men are paid for performances before the Queen during the winter holidays. The titles of the plays were not recorded.

To John Hemyng Servaunte to the Lorde Chamberleyne upon the Counselles warraunt dated at the Courte at Richmond ultimo die Februar' 1601 for iii-i^{or} Playes or Enterludes by him and the rest of his Company presented before her majestie at Christyanmas and Shrovetyde laste paste after the rate of vi^{li} xiii^s iiii^d for every playe viz' one on St Stevens day at night \ Sundaie at night / following Newyeares day at night and Shrovesonday at night xxvi^{li} xiii^s iiii^d and to them more by way of her majesties rewarde for each Play after the rate of lxvi^s viii^d xiii^{li} vi^s viii^d In all the some of xl^{li}
　　　　　　　　　　　　　　　　–*Dramatic Records*, pp. 32–33re,

1602

Stationers' Register Entries

The Merry Wives of Windsor, 1 *and* 2 Henry VI, Titus Andronicus, *and* Hamlet *are registered with the Stationers' Company (Stationer's Hall, Register C, folios 78r, 80v, 84v). In the following transcriptions W. W. Greg has silently expanded abbreviated words. He notes that the second entry is in a different hand than the first and suggests it was written by Arthur Johnson.*

18 Januarii
John Busby. Entred for his copie under the hand of m^r Seton / A booke called. An excellent & pleasant conceited commedie of S^r Jo ffaulstof and the merry wyves of windesor　　　　　　　　　　　　　　vi^d
[*Marginal note:* Conceited Commedie]

Arthure Johnson Entred for his Copye *under the handes of* [deleted] *by assignement from* John Busbye / A booke

Called an excellent and pleasant conceyted Comedie of Sir John ffaulstafe and the merye wyves of windsor vi^d

19 April'

Thomas Pavier Entred for his copies by assignement from Thomas millington these [3] bookes folowinge, Salvo Jure cuiuscunque viz.

. . . [2] The first and Second parte of henry the vi^t ii bookes   xii^d

[3] A booke called Titus and Andronicus vi^d Entred *for* [deleted] by warrant under m^r Setons hand /

. . . .

xxvi^{to} Julii

James Roberte Entred for his Copie under the hande of m^r Pasfeild & m^r waterson warden A booke called the Revenge of Hamlett Prince Denmarke as yt was latelie Acted by the Lo: Chamberleyn his servante vi^d
—*Bibliography of the English Printed Drama*, p. 18

Publications

Three of Shakespeare's previously published works were published again in 1602: Venus and Adonis *(1593, 1594, 1595, 1596, and 1599),* Richard III *(1597 and 1598), and* Henry V *(1600). Published for the first time in 1602 was* The Merry Wives of Windsor, *but this quarto edition seems to be a memorial reconstruction of the play. There are three editions of* Venus and Adonis *bearing the date 1602 and a fourth edition (Short Title Catalogue [STC] 22359) thought to be from this year but missing its title page. A careful study of the type used to print the three editions whose title pages have survived indicates that all three of them may have been published later, circa 1607 (STC 22360), circa 1608 (STC 22360a), and circa 1610 (STC 22360b). It is not clear why the later editions of the poem bear an incorrect date. Only the first "1602" edition is transcribed.*

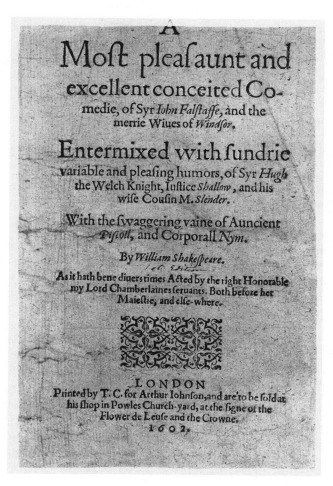

Title page for the first quarto of The Merry Wives of Windsor, *an abridged and textually corrupt version (by permission of the Folger Shakespeare Library)*

VENVS / AND ADONIS. / *Vilia miretur vulgus : mihi / flauus Apollo / Pocula Caſtalia plena miniſtret aqua.* / [*Printer's device*] / Imprinted at London for *VVilliam Leake,* / dwelling at the ſigne of the Holy Ghoſt, in / Pauls Church-yard. 1602.

THE / CHRONICLE / Hiſtory of Henry the fift, / VVith his battell fought at *Agin Court* / in *France.* Together with *Auntient* / *Piſtoll.* / *As it hath bene ſundry times playd by the Right honorable* / *the Lord Chamberlaine his ſeruants.* / [*Printer's device*] / LONDON / Printed by Thomas Creede, for Thomas / Pauier,and are to be ſold at his ſhop in Cornhill, / at the ſigne of the Cat and Parrets neare / the Exchange. 1602.

THE / TRAGEDIE / of King Richard / the third. / *Conteining his treacherous Plots againſt his brother* / *Clarence*: *the pittifull murther of his innocent Ne-* /*phewes: his tyrannicall vſur-*pation: *with the* / *whole courſe of his deteſted life, and* / *moſt deſerued death.* / *As it hath bene lately Acted by the Right Honourable* / *the Lord Chamberlaine his ſervants.* / Newly aug-mented, / By *William Shakeſpeare.* / [*Printer's device*] / LON-DON / Printed by Thomas Creede, for Andrew Wiſe, dwelling / in Paules Church-yard, at the ſigne of the / Angell. 1 6 0 2.

Manningham Sees *Twelfth Night* and Reports a Story about Shakespeare and Richard Burbage

From January 1602 until April 1603 John Manningham, who was studying law at the Middle Temple, kept a diary. In it he recorded his daily activities, political gossip, jests, and witty sayings and stories. The first excerpt describes an Inns of Court performance of Shakespeare's Twelfth Night. *Olivia is here described as a widow as she is in Shakespeare's source, Barnabe Rich's prose account of Apollonius and Silla in* Rich his Farewell to the Military Pro-fession *(1581); in Shakespeare's play she is unmarried. In the sec-ond excerpt Manningham reports a piece of theatrical gossip in which Shakespeare outwits the leading actor of Lord Chamberlain's Men, Richard Burbage, the first actor to play Hamlet and Othello.*

FEBR. 1601. [1602 New Style]

2. At our feast wee had a play called "Twelve night, or what you will"; much like the commedy of errores, or Menechmi in Plautus, but most like and neere to that in Italian called Inganni.

A good practise in it to make the steward beleeve his Lady widdowe was in Love with him, by counterfayting a letter, as from his Lady, in generall termes, telling him what shee liked best in him, and prescribing his gesture in smiling, his apparraile, &c., and then when he came to practise, making him beleeve they tooke him to be mad.

Portrait of Richard Burbage by an unknown painter. As the leading actor in the Lord Chamberlain's and King's Men companies, Burbage's roles included Richard III, Hamlet, Lear, and Othello (by permission of the Trustees of Dulwich Picture Gallery).

–p. 48

Marche. 1601. [1602 New Style]

13. Mr. Watts and Mr. Danvers had fiery wordes.

Commonly those which speake most against Tullie are like a dog, which comming into a roome where he espies a shoulder of mutton lying upon some high place, falls to barking at it, because he cannot reache it. (Watts.)

Upon a tyme when Burbidge played Rich[ard] 3. there was a Citizen grewe soe farr in liking with him, that before shee went from the play shee appointed him to come that night unto hir by the name of Ri[chard] the 3. Shakespeare, overhearing their conclusion, went before, was intertained, and at his game ere Burbidge came. Then message being brought that Richard the 3^d. was at the dore, Shakespeare caused returne to be made that William the Conquerour was before Rich[ard] the 3. Shakespeare's name William. (Mr. [Curle])
(Folio 29b)

–pp. 74–75

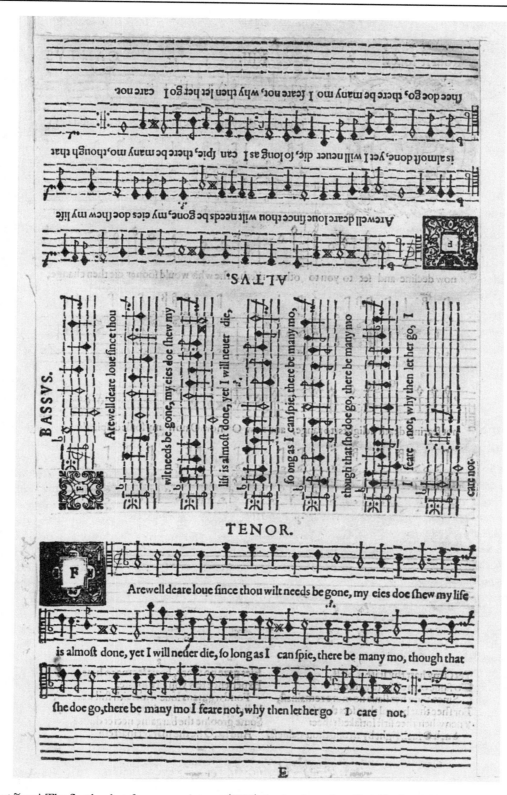

Page from Robert Jones's The first booke of songes and ayres *(1600) showing the music and lyrics for the madrigal "Farewell, Dear Love." The parts are laid out to allow three singers to share a single page. During a late-night songfest in* Twelfth Night *(2.3.102–112) Sir Toby Belch and Feste exchange lines from this song (by permission of the Folger Shakespeare Library).*

The Shakespeare Coat of Arms Questioned

Ralph Brooke, the York Herald of Arms, prepared this list of the names of men who were suspected of having been granted coats of arms without sufficient reason (Folger Manuscript V.a.156). Among Brooke's objections was that some of the men on the list were of too low a social status. The list includes a goldsmith, a haberdasher, an innkeeper, a ropemaker, a fishmonger, a vintner, a seller of stockings, a stationer, and, of course, an actor/playwright.

1 Norton	12 Cowley
2 Lound	13 Macatret
3 Hall	14 Laurence
4 Shakespeare	15 Wythens
5 Clarke	16 whitmore
6 Sanderson	17 Gibson
7 Smyth	18 Elkyn
8 Parre	19 Hickman
9 Pettous	20 Thwate
10 yonge	21 Lee
11 Peake	22 Molesworth
	23 Heyward

John Shakespeare Defended in the College of Arms

Dissension among members of the College of Arms appears to have prompted complaints regarding some of the college's activities, including Brooke's questioning the awarding of coats of arms to those who did not deserve them. Among those defended from this charge was John Shakespeare. In "The answeres of Garter and Clarencieux Kings of Arms to the Scrowle of Arms exhibited by Raffe Brokesmouth caled York Herauld" (Bodleian Library, Ashmolean Manuscript 846, f. 50), dated 21 March 1602, the reference of the trick of coat described as "the Speare on the Bend" is to that of John Shakespeare.

It maye as well be said That Harley who bearethe Gould a bend 2 Cotizes Sable. or ferrers .&c. or any other that beare Silver. or Gould a bend charged in like manner. Usurpe the Coate of the Lo: Mauley. As for the Speare on the Bend. is a patible difference. And the man was A magestrat in Stratford upon Avon. A Justice of peace he maryed A daughter and heyre of Ardern. and was of good substance and habelite / .

Deed of Conveyance for Land in Stratford

In this transcription of the 1 May 1602 deed of conveyance for Shakespeare's purchase of 107 acres of land from William and John Combe (Shakespeare Birthplace Trust Records Office manuscript ER 27/1), abbreviations and contractions have been silently expanded. The £320 Shakespeare paid for the land is nearly two and a half times what he paid for New Place in 1597, indicating he had managed to make his work as a player and dramatist, and his share in the Globe, quite profitable.

This Indenture made the ffirste daie of Maye in the ffowre and ffortieth yeare of the Raigne of our Soveraigne Ladie Elizabeth by the grace of god of England ffraunce and Ireland Queene Defendresse of the faithe &c Betweene william Combe of warrwicke in the Countie of warrwick Esquier and John Combe of Olde Stretford in the Countie aforesaide gentleman on the one partie And william Shakespere of Stretford uppon Avon in the Countie aforesaide gentleman on thother partye Witnesseth that the saide William Combe and John Combe for and in Consideracion of the somme of Three hundred and Twentie Poundes of Currant Englishe money to them in hande at and before the ensealinge and Deliverie of theis presentes well and trulie satisfied Contented and paide wherof and wherwith they acknowledge themselves fullie satisfied Contented and paide and therof and of everie parte and parcell therof doe clearlie exonerate acquite and discharge the said william Shakespere his heires Executors Administrators and Assignes forever by theis presentes have aliened bargayned solde geven graunted and Confirmed and by theis presentes doe fullye Clearlie and absolutelie alien bargayne sell give graunte and Confirme unto the said william Shakespere All and singuler those errable landes with thappurtenaunces Conteyninge by estymacion ffowre yarde lande of errable land scytuate lyinge and beinge within the parrishe feildes or towne of Olde Stretford aforesaide in the saide Countie of Warrwick Conteyninge by estimacion One hundred and Seaven acres be they more or lesse And also all the Common of pasture for Sheepe horse kyne or other Cattle in the feildes of Olde Stretford aforesaide to the saide ffowre yarde lande belonginge or in any wise apperteyninge A[nd] also all hades leys tyinges proffites advantages and Commodities whatsoever with their and everie of their Appurtenaunces to the saide bargayned premisses belonginge or apperteyninge or hertofore reputed taken knowne or occupied as parte parcell or member of the same And the revercion and reverciones of all and singuler the same bargayned premisses and of everie parte and parcell therof nowe or late in the severall tenures or occupacions of Thomas Hiccoxe and Lewes Hiccoxe or of either of them or of their Assignes or any of them Together also with all Charters deedes writinges escriptes and mynumentes whatsoever touchinge or concerninge the same premisses onlie or only any parte or parcell therof And

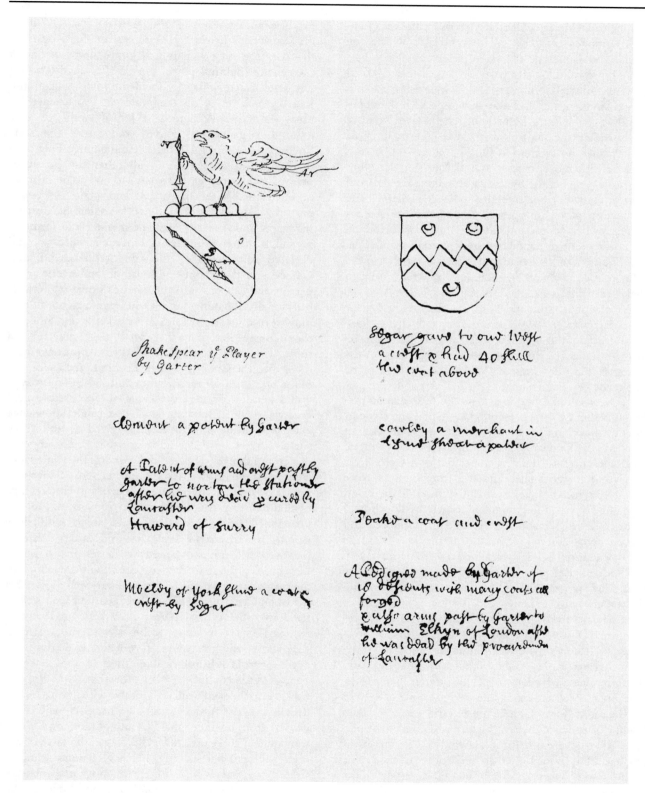

Page 28 of the York Herald's complaint about men granted coats of arms undeservedly. Beneath the design for Shakespeare's coat of arms, Ralph Brooke, the York Herald of Arms, has noted Shakespeare's occupation as an actor (Folger manuscript V.a.350; by permission of the Folger Shakespeare Library).

also the true Copies of all other deedes Evidences Charteres writinges escriptes and mynumentes which doe touche and Concerne the saide premisses before bargayned and solde or any parte or parcell therof which the saide william Combe or John Combe nowe have in their custodie or herafter may have or which they may lawfullye gett or come by without suite in lawe To have and to holde the saide ffower yarde of errable lande Conteyninge by estimacion One Hundred and seaven acres be they more or lesse and all and singuler other the premisses before by theis presentes aliened and solde or mencioned or entended to be aliened and solde and everie parte and parcell therof And all deedes Charters writinges escriptes and mynumentes before by theis presentes bargayned and solde unto the saide William Shakespere his heires and Assignes forever to the onlie proper use and behoofe of the saide William Shakespere his heires and Assignes forever And the saide william Combe and John Combe for them their heires Executors & Administrators doe Covenant promise and graunte to and with the saide William Shakespere his heires Executors and Assignes by theis presentes that they the saide William and John Combe are seazde or one of them is seazde of a good sure perfect and absolute estate in fee simple of the same premisses before by theis presentes bargayned and solde or ment or mencioned to be bargayned and solde without any further Condicion or lymyttacion of use or estate uses or estates and that he the saide John Combe his heires and Assignes shall and will from tyme to tyme and at all tymes herafter well and sufficientlie save and keepe harmles and indempnified aswell the said ffowre yardes of errable lande Conteyninge One hundred and Seaven acres and all other the premisses with their Appurtenaunces before bargayned and solde or mencioned or entended to be bargayned and solde and everie parte and parcell therof as also the saide william Shakespere and his heires and Assignes and everie of them of and from all former bargaynes sales Leases Joyntures Dowers wills Statutes Recognizances writinges obligatorie fynes feoffamentes entayles Judgmentes Execucions Charges titles forfeytures and encombrances whatsoever at any tyme before the ensealinge herof had made knowledged done or suffred by the saide John Combe or by the saide William Combe or either of them or by any other person or persons whatsoever any thinge lawfullye Clayminge or havinge from by or under them or either of them The Rentes and services herafter to be due in respect of the premisses before mencioned or entended to be bargayned and solde to the Cheife Lord or Lordes of the fee or fees onlie excepted and foreprized. And the saide william Combe and John Combe for them their heires Executors Adminstrators and Assignes doe Covenant promise and graunte to and with the saide William Shakespere his heires and Assignes for theis presentes that they the saide william and John Combe or one of them hathe rightfull power and lawfull aucthortie for any acte or actes done by them the saide william and John Combe or by the sufferance or procurement of them the saide William and John Combe to geve graunte bargayne sell convey and assure the saide ffowre yardes of errable lande Conteyninge One hundred and Seaven acres and all other the premisses before by theis presentes bargayned and solde or ment or mencioned to be bargayned and solde and everie parte and parcell therof to the saide william Shakespere his heires and Assignes in suche manner and forme as in and by theis presentes is lymytted expressed and declared And that they the saide William and John Combe and their heires and also all and everie other person and persons and their heires nowe or herafter havinge or Clayminge any lawfull estate righte title or interest of in or to the saide errable lande and all other the premisses before by theis presentes bargayned and solde with their and everie of their Appurtenaunces other then the Cheife Lorde or Lordes of the fee or fees of the premisses for their Rentes and services only at all tymes herafter duringe the space of ffyve yeares next ensewinge the date herof shall doe cause knowledge and suffer to be done and knowledged all and every suche further lawfull and reasonable acte and actes thinge and thinges devise and devises Conveyances and assurances whatsoever for the further more better and perfect assurance suretie sure makinge and Conveyinge of all the saide premisses before bargayned and solde or mencioned to be bargayned and solde with their Appurtenaunces and everie parte and parcell therof to the saide william Shakespere his heires and Assignes forever accordinge to the true entent and meaninge of theis presentes by the saide william Shakespere his heires and assignes or his or their Learned Counsell in the Lawe shalbe reasonablye devized or advized and required Be yt by fyne or fynes with proclamacion Recoverye [with] voucher or vouchers over deede or deedes enrolled Enrollment of theis presentes feoffament Releaze confirmacion or otherwise with Warrantie against the said william Combe with John Combe their heires and Assignes and all other persons Clayminge by from or under them or any of them or without warrantie at the Costes and Charges in the lawe of the saide william Shakespere his heires Executors Administrators or Assignes so as for the makinge of any suche estate or assurance this saide William and John Combe be not Compeld to travell above Sixe myles And the saide William Combe and John Combe for them their heires Executors Administrators and Assignes doe Covenant promise and graunte to and with the saide William Shakespere his heires Executors Administrators and Assignes by theis presentes that the saide william Shakespere his heires and Assignes shall or may from tyme to tyme from henceforth forever peaceably and quietlye have holde occupie possesse and enjoye the saide ffowre yardes of errable lande and all other the bargayned premisses with their Appurtenaun[ces] and everie parte and parcell therof without any manner of lett trouble or eviccion of them the saide william Combe and John Combe their heires or Assignes and without the lawfull lett trouble or eviccion of any other person or persons whatsoever lawfullie havinge or clayming any thinge in of or out of the saide premisses or any parte therof by from or under them the said william Combe and John Combe or either of them or the heires or Assignes of them or either of them or their or any of their estate title or interest In wytnes wherof the parties to theis presentes have enterchangeably sette their handes and seales the daie and yeare first above Written 1602.

    [Signed] W. Combe   Jo. Combe

[*Endorsed verso:*] Sealed and delivered to Gilbert Shakespere to the use of the within named William Shakespere in the presence of

[*Signed*]
Anthony Nasshe   Jhon Nashe
William Sheldon
Humfrey Maynwaringe
Rychard Mason

Hercules Underhill Acknowledges Shakespeare's Ownership of New Place

Following the death of William Underhill, former owner of New Place, Shakespeare took the precaution of having the sale of the house recognized by Underhill's son Hercules. The following document (PRO Court of Common Pleas, Feet of Fines, C. P. 25(2)/237, Michaelmas 44 & 45 Eliz. I, no. 15) reconveys New Place to Shakespeare and offers additional legal protection for his claim to the property. In this edited version of Lewis's transcription and translation, legal abbreviations have been silently expanded.

Haec est finalis concordia facta in curia dominæ Reginæ apud Wesminsterem A die sancti michaelis in unum mensem Anno regnorum Elizabethae dei gratia Angliæ ffranciæ & Hiberniæ Reginae fidei defensor &c A conquestu quadragesimo quarto coram Edouarduo Anderson Thomas Walmysley Georgio Kingermyll & petro Warburton Justiciis &

aliis dominæ Reginæ fidelibus tunc ibi praesentibus Inter Willielmum Shakespeare generosum quaerentum et herculem Underhill generosum deforciantem de uno mesuagio duobus horreis duobus gardinis & duobus pomariis cum pertinenciis in Stretford super Avon unde placitum convencionis summonitum fuit inter eos in eadem Curia Scilicet quod praedictus hercules recognovit praedictum tenementum cum pertinenciis esse jus ipsius Willielmi et illa que idem Willielmus habet de dono praedicti herculis et illa remisit & quietclamavit de se & heredibus suis praedicto Willielmo & heredibus suis Imperpetuum et praeterea idem hercules concessit pro se & heredibus suis quod ipsi Warantizabant praedicto Willielmo & heredibus suis praedicta tenementa cum pertinenciis contra praedictum herculem & heredes suos Imperpetuum et pro hac recognicione remissione quietaclamancia Warantia fine & concordia idem Willielmus dedit praedicto herculi sexaginta libras sterlingorum

[This is the final agreement made in the court of her majesty the Queen at Westminster On the day of Saint Michael in one month in the [forty-fourth] Year of the reign of Elizabeth by the grace of God Queen of England France & Ireland defender of the faith & From the Conquest forty-four in the presence of Edward Anderson Thomas Walmysley George Kingermyll & Peter Warburton Justices & others loyal to her majesty the Queen then present there Between William Shakespeare gentleman complaining [plaintiff] and Hercules Underhill gentleman deforcing [defendant] concerning one messuage two barns two gardens & two orchards with appurtenances in Stratford-upon-Avon from which place [whence] a plea of agreement had been summoned between them in the same Court To wit that the aforesaid Hercules recognized the aforesaid tenement with appurtenances to be the right [owned] of William himself and those which the same William holds by gift of aforesaid Hercules and he [the latter] hath remised & quitclaimed for himself & his heirs to the aforesaid William & his heirs forever and besides the same Hercules has conceded for himself & his heirs that they themselves Warranted to the aforesaid William & his heirs the aforesaid tenements with appurtenances against the aforesaid Hercules & his heirs forever and for this recognition remission quitclaim Warranty fine & agreement the same William has given to the aforesaid Hercules sixty pounds sterling.]

—Lewis, *Shakespeare Documents,* volume II, pp. 355–356

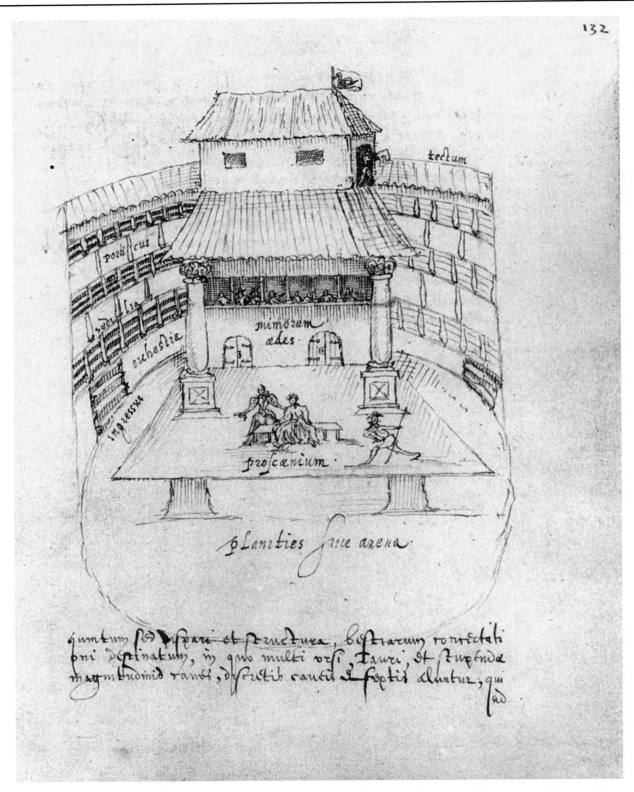

Arend van Buchell's copy of Johannes de Witt's drawing of the Swan Theatre (courtesy of the University Library, University of Utrecht)

The Swan and the Other Theaters of London

Appended to the drawing of the Swan theater is a record of Johannes de Witt's comments, "Ex Observationibus Londinensibus," transcribed by Arend van Buchel. The following Latin transcript is from an unsigned note in the Shakespeare Survey.

Amphiteatra Londinii sunt IV visendæ pulcritudinis quæ a diversis intersigniis diversa nomina sortiuntur; in iis varia quotidie scæna populo exhibetur. Horum duo excellentio:ra ultra Tamisim ad meridiem sita sunt, a suspensis sig:nis Rosa et Cygnus nominata. Alia duo extra urbem ad septentrionem sunt, viâ quâ itur per Episcopalem portam vulgariter Biscopgat nuncupatam. Est et quintum sed dispari et structura, bestiarum concertationi destinatum, in quo multi ursi, Tauri, et stupendæ magnitudinis canes, discretis caveis et septis aluntur, qui ad pugnam adservantur, jucundissim_m hominibus spectaculum præbentes. Theatrorum autem omnium prestantissimum est et amplissimum id cuius intersignium est cygnus (vulgo te theater off te ciin) quippe quod tres mille homines in sedilibus admittat, constructum ex coaceruato lapide pyrritide (quorum ingens in Brittannia copia est) ligneis suffultum columnis quæ ob illitum marmoreum colorem, nasutissimos quoque fallere posse[n]t. Cuius quidem forma[m] quod Romani operis umbram videatur exprimere supra adpinxi.

—"A Note on the Swan Theatre Drawing,"
Shakespeare Survey, 1 (1948): 23–24

The translation is from Joseph Quincy Adams's Shakespearean Playhouses: A History of English Theatres from the Beginnings to the Restoration *(1917).*

[There are four amphitheatres in London [the Theatre, Curtain, Rose, and Swan] of notable beauty, which from their diverse signs bear diverse names. In each of them a different play is daily exhibited to the populace. The two more magnificent of these are situated to the southward beyond the Thames, and from the signs suspended before them are called the Rose and the Swan. The two others are outside the city towards the north on the highway which issues through the Episcopal Gate, called in the vernacular Bishopgate. There is also a fifth [the Bear Garden], but of dissimilar structure, devoted to the baiting of beasts, where are maintained in separate cages and enclosures many bears and dogs of stupendous size, which are kept for fighting, furnishing thereby a most delightful spectacle to men. Of all the theatres, however, the largest and the most magnificent is that one of which the sign is a swan, called in the vernacular the Swan Theatre; for it accommodates in its seats three thousand persons, and is built of a mass of flint stones (of which there is a prodigious supply in Britain), and supported by wooden columns painted in such excellent imitation of marble that it is able to deceive even the most cunning. Since its form resembles that of a Roman work, I have made a sketch of it above.]

—pp. 167–168

Shakespeare Buys a Cottage in Chapel Lane

This document transfers the ownership of a cottage in Chapel Lane, across the street from New Place, to Shakespeare. The copyhold (Shakespeare Birthplace Trust Records Office, MS. ER 28/1) is dated 28 September 1602.

In this edited version of Lewis's transcription and translation, abbreviated names and legal terms have been silently expanded. The left margin contains the notation "28 Sep^r / 1602. / C. M." in another hand.

Rowington ss Visus ffranci plegii cum curia baronis prenobilis domine Anne Comitesse Warwici ibidem tentus xxviii° die Septembris Anno regni domine nostre Elizabethe dei gracia Anglie ffranci & Hibernie Regine fidei defensoris &c quadragesimo quarto coram Henrico Michell Generoso deputato Scenescallo Johannis Huggeford Armigeri Capitlis Scenescalli ibidem Ad hanc Curian venit Walterus Getley per Thomas Tibbottes juniorem Attornatum suum unum Customari-

orum Tenencium mannerii predicta (predicto Thomam Tibbottes jurato pro veritate inde) & sursumreddidit in manus domine manerii predicti unum cotagium cum perinenciis scituatum iacens & existens in Stratford super Avon in quodam vico ibidem vocato walkers streete alias dead lane ad opus & usum Willielmi Shackespere & heredum suorum im perpetuum secundum Consuetudinem manerii predicti & sic remanet in manibus domine manerii predicti quousque predictus Willielmus Shakespere venit ad capiendum premissa predicta In cujus rei testimonium predicta Henricus Michell huic presenti copie sigillum suum apposuit die & anno supradictis.

Per me Henricum Michell

[Rowington Manor / scire scilicet / 28 September / 1602. / Court of the Manor   A View of Frank Pledge with the court baron of the noble Lady Anne Countess of Warwick held in the same place on the xxviii day of September in the forty-fourth year of the reign of our Lady Elizabeth by the Grace of God

Queen of England, France, & Ireland, Defender of the Faith, &c., in the Court before Henry Michell, gentleman, deputy seneschal for John Huggeford, esquire, chief seneschal in the same Court. To this Court came Walter Getley, through his attorney Thomas Tibbotts junior, one of the customary tenants of the manor aforesaid (the aforesaid Thomas Tibbotts being sworn for the truth), and restored into the hands of the Lady of the aforesaid Manor a cottage with its appurtenances situated, lying, and being in Stratford upon Avon in a certain street there called Walker's Street, otherwise Dead Lane, to the behoof and use of William Shakespeare and his heirs forever according to the custom of the manor aforesaid. And so it remains in the hands of the Lady of the Manor aforesaid until such time as the aforesaid William Shakespeare shall come to receive the premises aforesaid. In testimony of which the aforesaid Henry Michell has affixed his seal to the present copy on the day and year aforesaid.

By me Henry Michell]

–Lewis, *Shakespeare Documents,*
volume II, pp. 348–349

Richard Vennar Causes a Scandal at the Swan

In November 1602 Richard Vennar advertised a spectacular theatrical event, Englands Joy, *to be performed at the Swan theater. In a bill titled "The Plot of the Play Called Englands Joy" (1602) he announced that a cast of men and women would, in a series of plays, re-create the history of England on stage. The plays would open, "by shew and in Action," with "the civill warres of England from* Edward *the third, to the end of* Queene Maries *raigne" and would end with the stage occupied by the Nine Worthies and the souls of the blessed while "beneath under the Stage set forth with strange fireworkes, divers blacke and damned Soules, wonderfully discribed in their severall torments." Unfortunately, the audience assembled at the Swan saw nothing of the sort.*

In the following excerpt from An Apology: Written, By Richard Vennar of Lincolnes Inne, abusively called Englands Joy *(Printed by Nicholas Okes, 1614) Vennar offers a defense of his actions; the story begins with Vennar in prison, in need of cash, and inspired by the money being made at the Globe theater. Every day, Shakespeare and his fellow sharers produced plays that were a feast for their audience's eyes, and, at least when Vennar attended, the profits were large. The "burning pestle" to which Vennar compares his play is Francis Beaumont's* Knight of the Burning Pestle, *a comedy written circa 1607 and not particularly well received when first produced. Vennar concludes by arguing that, by being a source of gossip and scandal, he had given people their money's worth despite failing to provide the show he promised.*

Thus lived I a long time as a Bird in a cage, not fed like Birds at their keepers cost, but as a hurt Deere in an enclosed ground, hunted with the continuall cries of the fastidious and pittilesse hel-hounds of a Jayle: Howbeit I never held my selfe so fatally unfortunate as to expire my last breath in a prison, for at last I got my freedome, and casting up my reckoning with Counters, wanting money both for that use and others, my minde became diversly distracted with plurallity of purposes, some times carried one way, some times another; the last, that I stood not least upon in resolution, was a second intendment for *Scotland,* but to this purpose there wanted Armes, or rather the sinewes of Armes, money; I saw a daily offring to the God of pleasure, resident at the Globe on the Banke-side, of much more then would have supplyed my then want; I noted every mans hand ready to feed the luxury of his eye, that puld downe his hat to stop the sight of his charity, wherefore I concluded to make a friend of Mammon, and to give them sound for words, both being but aire, for which they should give double payment, to the intent onely, men of ability might make the purchase without repentance, and my selfe observe that wise rule of Phylosophy; *Non fiat per plura quod potest fieri per pauciora:* My devise was all sorts of Musique, beginning with Chambers, the Harpe of war, and ending with Hounds, the cry of peace, of which I was doubly provided, for Fox and Hare.

The report of Gentlemen and Gentlewomens actions, being indeed the flagge to our Theater, was not meerely falcification, for I had divers Chorus to bee spoken by men of good birth, Schollers by profession; protesting that the businesse was meerely abused, by the comming of some Beagles upon mee, that were none of the intended Kennell, I meane Baylifes, who seizing mee before the first entrance, spoke an Epilogue instead of a Prologue, this changed the play into the hunting of the Fox; which, that the world may know for a verity, I heere promise the next Tearme, with a true history of my life, to bee publiquely presented, to insert in place of Musicke, for the actes, all those intendments prepared for that daies entertainment: Which, seeing it must rest in your beliefes till then, I will bee content so long to weare your Apellation, preferring onely in this Imputation, so farre the part of an Apologist, that drawing the accident it selfe, without defence, into judicious question, this Scoggins Crow, that hath filled so many mouths will prove but a Rooke. For suppose that the play was hist, was I the first Poet made my Clients penitents, let the burning pestle bee heard in my cause, which rang so dismally in your eares, and yet the Writer in state of Grace.

The difference was, I presented you with a Dumbe Show, and the Players say, that is alwaies as good as a bad act, neither could the cost bee great, that for one twelve pence, afforded mirth for a Twelve-month after: At the highest rate, you lent mee but an after-noones hearing, the expectation being worth the money; since Phylosophers say, that the sweetnesse of hope is beyond the enjoying, and in this sense, I bettered that daies travell, the errour being your owne, that being ignorant of a Logitian, stile mee an Impostor, from which I am so farre, that the Law shall speake for mee, which presupposeth every man good, till hee bee convicted bad; And I presume it came not within the compasse of an inditement: The conclusion is this, I had too many Patrons for so slender a worke, and for that fault, this Apologie is my sufficient answere. Neither is it strange to have so much mony for six verses, since *Bonum quo communius eo melius.* And Poetry in a more legitimate age, hath beene held cosin-germane to goodnesse, but were there no more holes in this vessell, you might soone stop the leake.

–pp. 21–27

Allusions to *The Comedy of Errors* and Justice Shallow in Dekker's *Satiro-mastix*

A weapon in the War of the Theaters, a literary battle among rival playwrights, Thomas Dekker's play Satiro-mastix. Or The untrussing of the Humorous Poet *(1602) mocks, among others, Ben Jonson, here represented by the character Horace. In the first excerpt, from the address to the play's readers, Dekker borrows the title of Shakespeare's early play* The Comedy of Errors *as an ironic description of his own satirical project; in a later excerpt, Horace alludes to Justice Shallow, the butt of many of Falstaff's jokes in* 2 Henry IV.

Ad Lectorem.

In steed of the Trumpets sounding thrice, before the Play begin: it shall not be amisse (for him that will read) first to beholde this short Comedy of Errors, and where the greatest enter, to give them in stead of a hisse, a gentle correction.

–sig. A4v

John Chamberlain's Account of the Vennar Incident

Scholar and letter writer John Chamberlain wrote to diplomat Dudley Carleton on 19 November 1602 and included descriptions of two sorts of public theater: the celebration held in honor of Elizabeth's accession day (November 17) and Richard Vennar's "famous play" at the Swan theater. Chamberlain's account of the damage inflicted by the outraged Swan audience shows the danger actors faced when they failed to please their audience. This excerpt is from the second volume of The Letters of John Chamberlain *(1939), edited by Norman Edgar McClure.*

The Quene came to Whitehall on Monday by water, though the Lord Mayor with his troupes of 500 velvet coates and chaines of gold was alredy mounted and marching to receve her at Charing Crosse. The sodain alteration grew upon inckling or suspicion of some daungerous attempt. Her day passed with the ordinarie solemnitie of preaching, singing, shooting, ringing and running: the bishop of Limmericke Dr. Thornborough made a dull sermon at Paules Crosse. At the tilt were many younge runners as you may perceve by the paper of theyre names: your foole Garret made as fayre a shew as the prowdest of them, and was as well disguised, mary not altogether so well mounted, for his horse was no bigger than a good bandogge, but he delivered his scutchion with his *impresa* himself and had goode audience of her Majestie and made her very merry. And now we are in mirth I must not forget to tell you of a cousening prancke of one Venner of Lincolns Ynne that gave out bills of a famous play on Satterday was sevenight on the Banckeside, to be acted only by certain gentlemen and gentlewomen of account. The price at comming in was two shillings or eighteen pence at least and when he had gotten most part of the mony into his hands, he wold have shewed them a fayre payre of heeles, but he was not so nimble to get up on horsebacke, but that he was faine to forsake that course, and betake himselfe to the water, where he was pursued and taken and brought before the Lord Cheife Justice, who wold make nothing of yt but a jest and a merriment, and bounde him over in five pound to appeare at the sessions: in the meane time the common people when they saw themselves deluded, revenged themselves upon the hangings, curtaines, chaires, stooles, walles and whatsoever came in theyre way very outragiously and made great spoyle: there was great store of good companie and many noble men. . . .

–pp. 171–172

Enter Horace *in his true attyre,* Asinius *bearing his Cloake.*

Asi. If you flye out Ningle, heer's your Cloake; I thinke it raines too.

Ho. Hide my shoulders in't.

Asi. Troth so th'adst neede, for now thou art in thy Pee and Kue; thou hast such a villanous broad backe, that I warrant th'art able to beare away any mans jestes in England.

Hor. It's well Sir, I ha strength to beare yours mee thinkes; fore God you are growne a piece of a Critist, since you fell into my hands: ah little roague, your wit has pickt up her crums prettie and well.

Asi. Yes faith, I finde my wit a the mending hand Ningle; troth I doe not thinke but to proceede Poetaster next Commencement, if I have my grace perfectlie: everie one that confer with me now, stop their nose in merriment and sweare I smell somewhat of Horace; one calles me Horaces Ape, another Horaces Beagle, and such Poeticall names it passes. I was but at Barbers last day, and when he was rencing my face, did but crie out, fellow thou makst me *Connive* too long, & sayes he sayes hyee, Master *Asinius Bubo,* you have eene Horaces wordes as right as if he had spit them into your mouth.

Hor. Well, away deare Asinius, deliver this letter to the young Gallant *Druso,* he that fell so strongly in love with mee yesternight.

Asi. It's a sweete Muske-cod, a pure spic'd-gull; by this feather I pittie his *Ingenuities*; but hast writ all this since Ningle? I know thou hast a good running head and thou listest.

Hor. Foh come, your great belly'd wit must long for every thing too; why you *Rooke,* I have a set of letters readie starcht to my hands, which to any fresh suited gallant that but newlie enters his name into my rowle, I send the next morning, ere his ten a clocke dreame has rize from him, onelie with claping my hand to't, that my Novice shall start, ho and his haire stand an end, when hee sees the sodaine flash of my writing; what you prettie Diminitive roague, we must have false fiers to amaze these spangle babies, these true heires of Ma. Justice Shallow.

Ais. I wod alwaies have thee sawce a foole thus.

Hor. Away, and, stay: heere be Epigrams upon Tucca, divulge these among the gallants; as for Crispinus, that Crispin-asse and Fannius his Play-dresser; who (to make the Muses beleeve, their subjects eares were starv'd, and that there was a dearth of Poesie) cut an Innocent Moore i'th middle, to serve him in twice; & when he had done, made Poules-worke of it, as for these Twynnes these *Poet-apes*:

Their Mimicke trickes shall serve
With mirth to feast our Muse, whilst their owne starve.

—sigs. E2v–E3r

Shakespeare's Company Paid for Court Performances

The Lord Chamberlain's Men are paid for performances.

To John Hemynges and the rest of his companie servauntes to the Lorde Chamberleyne uppon the Councelles warrant dated at Whitehall the xx[th] day of Aprill 1603 for their paynes and expences in presentinge before the late Quenes Majestie twoe playes the one uppon S[t] Stephens day at nighte and thother uppon Candlemas nighte for eche of which they were allowed by way of her Majesties rewarde tenne poundes amountinge in all to the some of   xx[li]

—*Dramatic Records,* p. 35

1603

Stationers' Register Entries

Troilus and Cressida is registered with the Stationers' Company. Richard II, Richard III, and 1 Henry IV are transferred to another publisher. There are no surviving editions of any of these plays from 1603. In the following transcription W. W. Greg has silently expanded abbreviated words.

7 Febr'

m[r] Robertes. Ent[r]ed for his copie in Full Court holden this day. to print when he hath gotten sufficient aucthority for yt. The booke of Troilus and Cresseda as yt is acted by my lo: Chamblens Men   vi[d]

. . . .

25 Junii

Matthew Lawe. Entred for his copies in full courte Holden this Day. These ffyve copies folowinge   ij[s] vj[d]
       viz [1-3] iii enterludes or playes. The ffirst is of Richard the .3.
       The second of Richard the .2. The Third of Henry the .4 the first parte. all kinges . . .
All whiche by consent of the Company are sett ou' to him from Andrew Wise.

—*Bibliography of the English Printed Drama,* p. 18

Allusion to Shakespeare in Chettle's *Englandes Mourning Garment*

Henry Chettle's memorial to Elizabeth, Englandes Mourning Garment: Worne heere by plaine Shepheardes, in memorie of their sacred Mistresse, ELIZABETH; Queene of Vertue while she lived, and Theame of Sorrow, being dead (Printed by V.S. for Thomas Millington, 1603), *is in part a diatribe against "the negligence of many better able" writers*

The First Quarter of *Hamlet*

The first edition of Shakespeare's Hamlet, *known as the First, or Bad, Quarto, differs substantially from the Second Quarto (1604/05) and Folio (1623) editions of the play. The First Quarto has been described as a memorial reconstruction (by actors or stenographic pirates), as an early draft, or as a touring version of the play. Although the text of the quarto is corrupt, its stage directions are often incorporated into editions based on the later texts.*

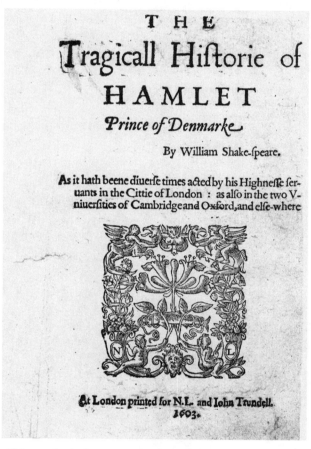

THE

Tragicall Historie of

HAMLET

Prince of Denmarke.

By William Shake-speare.

As it hath beene diuerse times acted by his Highnesse seruants in the Cittie of London : as also in the two V-niuersities of Cambridge and Oxford, and else-where

At London printed for N.L. and Iohn Trundell.
1603.

Title page for the first quarto of Hamlet *(reproduced by permission of The Huntington Library, San Marino, California)*

(A2), and Chettle castigates his fellow poets for their failure to produce appropriate elegies for the Queen. The "Acadian Shepheard" is probably Philip Sidney; "Collin" is Edmund Spenser; the thinly disguised poets described in the second through eighth stanzas are usually identified as Samuel Daniel ("He that so well could sing the fatall strife . . ."); John Lyly ("He that sung fotie yeares her life and birth"); George Chapman (Coryn); Ben Jonson (Horace); Shakespeare (Melicert); and Michael Drayton (Coridon). The identification of Shakespeare with Melicert is based in part on Chettle's reference to Tarquin, the villain in Shakespeare's poem The Rape of Lucrece.

I want but the Arcadian Shepheards inchaunting phrase of speaking, that was many times witnesse to her just mercies, and mercifull justice: yet rude as I am, I have presumed to handle this excellent Theame, in regard the Funerall hastens on, of that sometime most Serene Lady, and yet I see none, or at least past one or two that have sung any thing since her departure worth the hearing; and of them they that are best able, scarce remember her Majestie. I cannot now forget the excellent and cunning *Collin* indeed; (for alas, I confesse my selfe too too rude,) complaining that a liberal *Mecænas* long since dying, was immediately forgotten, even by those that living most laboured to advance his fame; and these as I thinke close part of his songs:

> Being dead no Poet seekes him to revive,
> Though many Poets flattred him alive.

Somewhat like him, or at least to that purpose, of a person more excellent, though in ruder verse I speake.

> Death now hath ceaz'd her in his ycie armes,
> That sometime was the Sun of our delight:
> And pittilesse of any after-harmes,
> Hath veyld her glory in the cloude of night.
> Nor doth one Poet seeke her name to raise,
> That living hourely striv'd to sing her praise.
> He that so well could sing the fatall strife
> Betweene the royall Roses White and Red,
> That prais'd so oft *Eliza* in her life,
> His Muse seemes now to dye, as shee is dead:
> Thou sweetest song-man of all English swaines,
> Awake for shame, honour ensues thy paines.
> But thou alone deserv'dst not to be blamde,
> He that sung fortie yeares her life and birth,
> And is by English Albions so much famde,
> For sweete mixt layes of majestie with mirth,
> Doth of her losse take now but little keepe;
> Or else I gesse, he cannot sing, but weepe.
> Neither doth *Coryn* full of worth and wit,
> That finisht dead *Musæus* gracious song,
> With grace as great, and words, and verse as fit;
> Chide meager death for dooing vertue wrong:
> He doth not seeke with songs to deck her herse,
> Nor make her name live in his lively verse.
> Nor does our English *Horace*, whose steele pen
> Can drawe Characters which will never die,
> Tell her bright glories unto listning men,
> Of her he seemes to have no memorie.
> His Muse an other path desires to tread,
> True Satyres scourge the living leave the dead.
> Nor doth the silver tongued *Melicert*,
> Drop from his honied Muse one sable teare
> To mourne her death that graced his desert,
> And to his laies opend her Royall eare.
> Shepheard remember our *Elizabeth*,
> And sing her Rape, done by that *Tarquin*, Death.
> No lesse doe thou (sweet singer *Coridon*)
> The Theame exceedeth *Edwards Isabell*.
> Forget her not in *Poly-Albion*;

Make some amends, I know thou lovdst her well.
 Thinke twas a fault to have thy Verses seene
 Praising the King, ere they had mournd the Queen.
And thou delicious sportive *Musidore*,
 Although thou have resignd thy wreath of Bay
With Cypresse bind thy temples and deplore
 Elizas winter in a mournfull Lay:
 I know thou canst and none can better sing
 Herse songs for her, and *Pæans* to our King.
Quicke *Antihorace* though I place thee heere,
 Together with yong *Mælibee* thy frend:
And *Hero's* last *Musæus*, all three deere,
 All such whose vertues highly I commend:
 Prove not ingrate to her that many a time
 Hath stoopt her Majestie, to grace your rime.
And thou that scarce hast fligd thy infant muse,
 (I use thine owne word) and commend thee best,
In thy proclaiming *James*: the rest misuse
 The name of Poetry, with lines unblest;
 Holding the Muses to be masculine.
 I quote no such absurditie in thine.
Thee doe I thanke for will; thy worke let passe:
But wish some of the former had first writ
That from their Poems like reflecting glasse
 Steeld with the puritie of Art and wit,
 Eliza might have livde in every eye,
 Alwaies beheld till Time and Poems dye.
But cease you Goblins, and you under Elves;
That with rude rimes and meeters reasonlesse;
Fit to be sung for such as your base selves,
Presume to name the Muses Patronesse:
 Keepe your low Spheres, she hath an Angell spirit:
 The learnedst Swaine can hardly sing her merit.
Onely her brother King, the Muses trust
(Blood of her Grandsires blood, plac'd in her Throne)
Can raise her glory from the bed of dust
To praise her worth belongs to Kings alone.
 In him shall we behold her Majestie,
 In him her vertue lives and cannot die.

—sigs. D2r–D3v

Allusion to Shakespeare in "A mournefull Dittie"

In this anonymous ballad elegy for Queen Elizabeth, "A mournefull Dittie, entituled Elizabeths *losse, together with a welcome for King* James. *To a pleasant new tune" (circa 1603), the author enjoins various figures—nymphs and musicians among them—to mourn the loss of the queen. Three poets who have yet to memorialize the late queen are named.*

Farewell, farewell, farewell,
 brave Englands joy:
Gone is thy friend
 that kept thee from annoy.
Lament, lament, lament
 you English Peeres,

Lament your losse
 possest so many yeeres.

Gone is thy Quéene, the
 paragon of time,
On whom grim Death
 hath spred his fatall line.
Lament, lament, &c.

. . . .

You Poets all brave *Shakspeare*,
 Johnson, *Greene*,
Bestow your time to write
 for Englands Queene.
Lament, lament, &c.

Returne your songs and Sonnets
 and your sayes:
To set foorth swéete
 Elizabeths praise.
Lament, lament, &c.

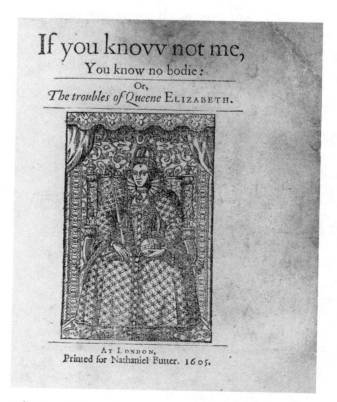

Title page for Thomas Heywood's play that features Queen Elizabeth. Although actors were forbidden to impersonate living royalty, dead kings and queens were fair game; shortly after the queen's death, Heywood, along with other London playwrights, began using her as a stage character (by permission of the Folger Shakespeare Library).

The Jacobean Years: April 1603–1616

Queen Elizabeth I died on 24 March 1603 and was succeeded by her distant cousin King James VI of Scotland, who became James I of England. The new king's reign, called the Jacobean period after the Latin translation of his name, marked the beginning of several changes in England: James negotiated an end to the decades-old conflict with Spain; the Americas were colonized; court favorites exerted undue influence and reaped enormous financial benefits. James held and exercised his royal power quite differently than Elizabeth had, and his absolutist approach to governing, intensified by his son Charles, ultimately culminated in the English Civil War. His reign is not considered a great political success, but it did mark a fruitful period in English literary history.

For Shakespeare and his fellow actors, the change in monarchs meant a change in their repertory. During Queen Elizabeth's reign, most of the plays Shakespeare wrote were histories that warned of the dire consequences of civil war and tyrannical misrule or romantic comedies with powerful female characters; the many court appearances by Shakespeare's company, the Lord Chamberlain's Men, indicate that these plays pleased or flattered the queen. In 1603 the Lord Chamberlain's Men became the King's Men, and financial accounts show them performing for the king and the court. Perhaps in response to the new king's taste, or perhaps because he had exhausted the possibilities of comedy, Shakespeare shifted to tragedy—his Jacobean plays include Othello, King Lear, Macbeth, Antony and Cleopatra, and Coriolanus—and to romance, a genre that maintains a careful balance between comic and tragic events. Shakespeare's Jacobean comedies—Measure for Measure and All's Well that Ends Well—do more to disturb than amuse but are less bitter than the satiric city comedies his fellow playwrights were producing.

Shakespeare's Jacobean romances—Pericles, The Winter's Tale, Cymbeline, and The Tempest—are full of magical stage effects that mark another change for Shakespeare and his acting company: in 1608 they acquired an indoor theater, giving them access to elements such as artificial lighting and stage machinery that permitted more elaborate effects than could be achieved at the outdoor Globe. The Globe continued to be a popular destination for Londoners looking for entertainment, though, as several allusions to it attest. In 1613, during a performance of Shakespeare's his-

Portrait of James I by Nicholas Hilliard, circa 1605. Formerly James VI of Scotland, he became the first Stuart king of England upon Elizabeth I's death on 24 March 1603. He ruled until his death in 1625 (courtesy of the New Orleans Museum of Art, New Orleans, Louisiana).

tory of Henry VIII, All is True, the Globe caught fire and burned to the ground, but the theater was quickly rebuilt.

Shakespeare's growing fame, illustrated by the publication and republication of his plays and long poems as well as by allusions, quotes, and acts of outright theft by his fellow playwrights and poets, may be responsible for the publication of his sonnets in 1609. The sonnets were first mentioned in 1598 by Francis Meres, who stated they were circulating among Shakespeare's friends. The story they tell—the narrator *has two tumultuous love affairs, both with unhappy endings—has prompted much speculation about the identity of the young man and the Dark Lady to whom the sonnets are addressed, but no documents survive to show they are anything other than fictional creations.*

Legal and business documents place Shakespeare in Stratford and in London between 1603 and his death in 1616. A lawsuit concerning an unpaid dowry includes testimony from Shakespeare and others showing he lived with the Mountjoy family in London in 1604; the exceptionally detailed stage directions in The Tempest, *first performed in 1611, are sometimes used to argue that Shakespeare had retired to Stratford by then. Shakespeare made further investments in Stratford and was involved, perhaps only peripherally, in an enclosure controversy in the town. He and his fellow Globe owners bought the Blackfriars theater, and Shakespeare himself bought a house in the Blackfriars in 1613. Both of his daughters married, and in 1608 the elder, Susanna, produced Shakespeare's first grandchild, Elizabeth Hall.*

On 23 April 1616 Shakespeare died and was buried two days later in Holy Trinity Church, where he had been baptized in 1564. The cause of his death is unknown. Shakespeare's will, written shortly before his death, leaves the bulk of his property to his daughter Susanna and her husband, John Hall. Their daughter Elizabeth died childless, and if she kept any of her grandfather's papers or manuscripts, their whereabouts are unknown.

1603

Shakespeare's Company Becomes the King's Men

After Queen Elizabeth's death on 24 March 1603, the royal household continued its ordinary functions until the arrival of King James. The king reorganized the household, replacing some officials and servants and keeping or promoting others. Shakespeare and his fellow actors were, as the following documents show, transformed from the Lord Chamberlain's Men into the King's Men.

On 17 May 1603, ten days after his arrival in London, King James directed the Keeper of the Privy Seal to execute a warrant for a royal patent, a legal document that authorized Shakespeare's company to perform for the king's own "Solace and pleasure" as well as for the benefit of the king's subjects. The royal patent, which ensured James's patronage and protection for the King's Men, was issued two days later. In the transcriptions of the warrant (PRO, Privy Seal Office, Warrants for the Privy Seal, PSO 2/22) and the patent (PRO C66/1608 m. 4), abbreviations have been silently expanded.

By the king

Right trusty and welbeloved Counsellour we greete you well and will and Commaund you that under our privie Seale in your Custody for the time being you Cause our letteres to be directed to the keep[er] of our greate seale of England, Comaunding him that under our said great Seale he cause our letteres to be made patentes in forme following: James by the grace of God king of England Scotland ffraunce Ireland defendour of the faith &c. To all Justices Maiours Sheriffs Constables hedboroughes and other our officers and loving subjectes greeting. Know ye that we of our speciall grace certaine knowledge & meere motion, have licenced and authorized & by these presentes doo licence & authorize these our servantes Lawrence ffletcher William Shakespeare Richard Burbage Augustine Phillippes John Heminges Henry Condell William Sly Robt Armyn Richard Cowlye and the rest of their associates freely to use and exercise the Arte and facultie of playing Comedies Tragedies Histories Enterludes Moralles Pastoralles Stage plaies & such other like as they have already studie or hereafter shall use or studied aswell for the recreation of our loving subjectes as for our solace and pleasure when we shall thinke good to see them during our pleasure And the said Comedies Tragedies Histories Enterludes Moralles Pastoralles Stage plaies & such like To shew and exercise publiquely to their best Commoditie, when the infection of the plague shall decrease as well within their now usuall howse called the Globe within our Countie of Surrey as also within any towne Halles or Mouthalls or other convenient places within the liberties and freedome of any other Cittie Universitie Towne or Borough whatsoever within our said Realmes and dominions. Willing and Comaunding you and every of you as you tender our pleasure not only to permitt and suffer them herein without any your letts hinderances or molestacions during our said pleasure, but also to be ayding and assisting to them yf any wrong be to them offered And to allowe them such former Courtesies as hath bene given to men of their place and qualitie. And also what further favour you shall shew to these our servantes for our sake we shall take kindely at your handes. In witnes wherof &c And these our letteres shall be your sufficient warrant and discharge in this behalf. Given under our Signet at our Mannour of Greenwiche the seavententh day of May in the first yeere of our raigne of England ffraunce and Irland, and of Scotland the six and thirtieth.

EX per Lake

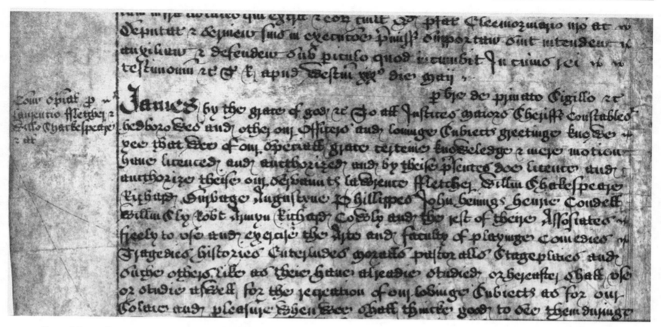

Part of the 19 May 1603 patent licensing Shakespeare and his fellow actors as the King's Men (PRO C66/1608 m. 4; courtesy of the Public Records Office, London)

The royal patent was issued on 19 May 1603.

Commissio specialis
pro Laurencio Fletcher
& Willo Shackespeare
& aliis

James by the grace of god &c. To all Justices Mayors Sheriffes Constables Hedborowes and other our Officers and lovinge Subjects greetinge Knowe yee that Wee of our speciall grac certeine knowledge & mere motion have licenced and aucthorized and by theise presentes doe licence and aucthorize theise our Servaunts Lawrence ffletcher Willm Shakespeare Richard Burbage Augustyne Phillippes John Hemings Henrie Condell Willm Sly Robt Armyn Richard Cowly and the rest of theire Assosiates freely to use and exercise the Arte and faculty of playinge Comedies Tragedies Histories Enterludes Moralls pastoralls Stageplaies and suche others like as theie have alreadie studied or hereafter shall use or studie aswell for the recreation of our lovinge Subjects as for our Solace and pleasure when Wee shall thincke good to see them duringe our pleasure And the said Comedies tragedies Histories Enterludes Morralls Pastoralls Stageplayes and suche like to shewe and exercise publiquely to theire best Comoditie when the infection of the plague shall decrease aswell within theire nowe usuall house called the Globe within our County of Surrey as alsoe within anie towne halls or Moute halls or other conveniente places within the lib[er]ties and freedome of anie other Cittie universitie towne or Boroughe whatsoever within our said Realmes and domynions Willinge and Commaunding you and everie of you as you tender our pleasure not onelie to permitt and suffer them herein without anie your lettes hindrances or molestacions during our said pleasure but alsoe to be aiding and assistinge to them yf anie wronge be to them offered And to allowe them such former Courtesies as hath bene given to men of theire place and quallitie and alsoe what further favour you shall shewe to theise our Servauntes for our sake wee shall take kindlie at your handes In Wytnesse Whereof &c

Witnesse our selfe at Westmi[nster] the nyntenth day of May

per breve de privato sigillo &c.

The King's Men Paid for Court Performances

To John Hemyngs one of his majesties players uppon the Councelle warraunte dated at the Courte at Wilton iii° die december 1603 for the paynes and expences of himselfe and the rest of the Company in coming from mortelacke in the Countie of Surrie unto the Courte aforesaid and there presenting before his majestie one playe on the second of december laste by way of his majesties rewarde xxx[li]
            —*Dramatic Records,* p. 38

A Stationer's Record of Shakespeare's Plays

Before being used as binding, the manuscript leaf used to bind Thomas Gataker's Certaine Sermon *(1637) was used by an unidentified stationer to record sales (from 9 August 1603 to 17 August 1603 on the recto, and on 19 August on the verso) and to keep a list, or perhaps an inventory, of books. Among the plays are three by Shakespeare:* The Merchant of Venice, The Taming of the Shrew, *and* Love's Labor's Lost; *paired with* Love's Labor's Lost *is a play Francis Meres attributes to Shakespeare,* Love's Labor's Won. *The manuscript is analyzed by T. W. Baldwin in* Shakspere's Love's Labor's Won: New Evidence from the Account Books of an Elizabethan Bookseller *(1957), which is the source of the transcription below.*

[inte]rludes & tragedyes
mother bombye
like will to like quoth yᵉ divell to yᵉ colliar
Jack Jugler
nise wanton
2 sir Jhon oldcastell
2 of yᵉ lord cromwell
2 of Jane shore
2 appius & Virginia
4 enuf as good as afeaste
3 friar bacon
marchant of vennis
taming of a shrew
knak to know an honest man
loves labor won
ovid metamorfosis 16
ovids epistels 16
ovid de tristibus fastor_ & ponto 16
senecas sentences 16
ciceros sentences 16
textoris epitheton 16
manutius epistels 16J
glas of vaine glory in 12
orders set forth lately by yᵉ Kings majesty & yᵉ counsell
to be used in tyme of siknes
gouryes conspiracye
Jewell on yᵉ thesalonians
napier on yᵉ revelation
kings lectures on Jonas
babington on genesis

---

gouryes conspiracye yᵉ last 1 for mᵣ archar
4 dod on yᵉ comandments in qᵗᵒ
bushop of winchester sermon at yᵉ coronation4
bushop ruds sermon
a kenning glas for a christian ki[n]ge by doctor thorne
doctor doves perswasion to recusants
muriels answer to yᵉ recusants petition

To valentyne at bremor
was mr doringtons cooke
19 of august 1603 for b
bindinge a servis booke 16–8d

T[o] mᵣ gwin 1 boke of
knak to know a knaveprayer 4ᵈ

T[o] mr gwin 1 boke
of prayer 4d

To mᵣ paynter 1 boke of
loves labor lostof prayer 4ᵈ

gentil crafte
first & 2nd part
bevis of hampton
dreame of divel & dives
dainty devises
Jack of nubery both
                    Parts

to mr gouldesborow
1 farest 8 d pener

8 terences 8ᵗᵒ
tullis officis 8ᵗᵒ_

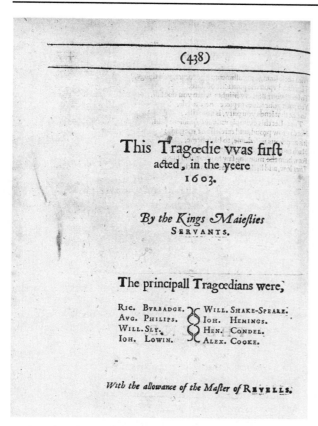

(438)

This Tragœdie vvas firſt
acted, in the yeere
1603.

By the Kings Maieſties
SERVANTS.

The principall Tragœdians were,

RIC. BVRBADGE.   WILL. SHAKE-SPEARE.
AVG. PHILIPS.   IOH. HEMINGS.
WILL. SLY.   HEN. CONDEL.
IOH. LOWIN.   ALEX. COOKE.

With the allowance of the Maſter of REVELLS.

Page from The Workes of Beniamin Jonson *(1616) listing Shakespeare among the cast in* Sejanus *(by permission of the Folger Shakespeare Library)*

Possible Allusions to *The Rape of Lucrece* and Two Plays in *Saint Marie Magdalens Conversion*

Playwrights of Shakespeare's era often retold stories from classical Greece and Rome as well as from England's medieval past. The author of the pro-Catholic Saint Mary Magdalens Conversion *(1603), identified only by the initials I.C., would like contemporary writers to consider New Testament sources as well as classical and historical ones. In the second stanza the poet may be alluding to Shakespeare's* Troilus and Cressida, Richard III, *and* The Rape of Lucrece.

Of Romes great conquest in the elder age,
When she the worlde made subject to her thrall,
Of lovers giddy fancies, and the rage,
Wherwith that passion is possest withall,
When jelousie with love doth share apart,
And breedes a civill warre within the harte.

Of *Helens* rape, and *Troyes* beseiged *Towne*,
Of *Troylus* faith, and *Cressids* falsitie,
Of *Rychards* stratagems for the english crowne,
Of *Tarquins* lust, and lucrece chastitie,
Of these, of none of these my muse nowe treates,
Of greater conquests, warres, and loves she speakes,

A womans conquest of her one affects,
A womans warre with her selfe-appetite,
A womans love, breeding such effects,
As th'age before nor since nere brought to light,
Of these; and such as these, my muse is prest,
To spend the idle houres of her rest.

Shakespeare Named in Camden's "Certaine Poemes"

In "Certaine Poemes, or Poesies, Epigrammes, Rythmes, and Epitaphs of the English Nation in former Times," the dedicatory epistle (dated 12 June 1603) to his Remaines of a Greater Worke, Concerning Britaine, the inhabitants thereof, their Languages, Names, Surnames, Empreses, Wise speeches, Poesies, and Epitaphes *(Printed by G.E. for Simon Waterson, 1605) historian William Camden names Shakespeare as one of the poets whom future generations "may justly admire."*

Of the dignity of Poetry much hath beene said by the worthy Sir *Philipp Sidney*, and by the Gentleman which proved that Poets were the first *Politicians*, the first *Philosophers*, the first *Historiographers*. I will onely adde out of *Philo*, that they were Gods owne creatures, who in his Booke *de Plantatione Noe*, reporteth, that when he had made the whole worlds masse; he created Poets to celebrate and set out the Creator himselfe, and all the creatures: you Poets read the place and you will like it. Howsoever it pleaseth the *Italian* to censure us, yet neither doth the Sunne so farre retire his chariot from our Climate, neither are there lesse favourable aspects betweene *Mercurie*, *Jupiter*, and the Moone, in our inclination of heaven, if Poets are *Fato*, as it pleased *Socrates*, neither are our Poets destitute of Arte prescribed by reason, and grounded upon experience, but they are as pregnant both in witty conceits and devises, and also in imitation, as any of them. Yea and according to the argument excell in granditie and gravity, in smoothnesse and proprietie, in quicknesse and briefnesse. So that for skill, varietie, efficacie, and sweetnesse, the foure materiall points required in a Poet, they can both teach and delight perfectly.

. . . .

These may suffice for some Poeticall descriptions of our auncient Poets, if I would come to our time, what a world could I present to you out of Sir *Philipp Sidney, Ed. Spencer, Samuel Daniel, Hugh Holland, Ben: Johnson, Th. Campion, Mich. Drayton, George Chapman, John Marston, William Shakespeare,* & other most pregnant witts of these our times, whom succeeding ages may justly admire.

–pp. 1, 8

Possible Allusion to Shakespeare in Davies's *Microcosmos*

In this excerpt from John Davies of Hereford's Microcos-mos. The Discovery of the Little World, with the govern-ment thereof *(Oxford: Printed by Joseph Barnes, 1603), the "W.S." referred to in footnote c is thought to be Shakespeare; "R.B." probably refers to Richard Burbage, one of the chief actors in Shake-speare's company. Davies, a poet and epigram writer, was also noted for his penmanship, and worked as a writing master.* Microcosmos *is one of several long poems Davies wrote in an attempt to survey all human knowledge. In this excerpt he examines an instance of the sin of pride: bad acting. Burbage and Shakespeare appear to be exceptions to the general condemnation of theatrical types.*

But that which grates my *Galle*, and mads my *Muse*,
Is (ah that ever such just cause should *Bee*)
To see a *Player* at the put-downe *stewes*
Put up his *Peacockes* Taile for al to see,
And for his hellish voice, as prowde as *hee*;
What *Peacocke* art thou prowd? Wherefore? because
Thou *Parrat*-like canst speake what is taught thee:
A *Poet* must teach thee from clause to clause,
Or thou wilt breake *Pronunciations* Lawes.

[*Marginal note:*
"The stewes once stoode where now Play-houses stand. The Peacock."]

Lies al thy *vertue* in thy *Tongue* stil taught,
And yet art prowd? alas poore *skum* of *pride*!
Peacocke, looke to thy *legs* and be not haught,
No *patience* can least *pride* in thee abide;
Looke not upon thy *Legs* from side to side
To make thee prowder, though in *Buskine* fine,
Or *silke* in graine the same be beautifide;
For *Painters* though they have no skil divine,
Can make as faire a *legge*, or *limbe* as thine.

[*Marginal note:*
"Neither delighteth he in any mans legs. Psal. 147.10."]

Good *God*! that ever *pride* should stoope so low,
That is by nature so exceeding hie:
Base *pride*, didst thou thy selfe, or others know,
Wouldst thou in *harts* of Apish *Actors* lie,
That for a ᵃ *Cue* wil sel their *Qualitie*?
Yet they through thy perswasion (being strong)
Doe weene they merit *immortality*,
Onely because (forsooth) they use their ᵇ *Tongue*,
To speake as they are taught, or right or *wronge*.

[*Marginal note:*
ᵃ Reproofes wher they are wel deserved, must bee well paied.
ᵇ Meant of those that have nothing to commende them but affected acting, & offensive mouthing.]

If *pride* ascende the *stage* (ô base ascent)
Al men may see her, for nought comes thereon
But to be seene, and where *Vice* should be shent,

Yea, made most odious to ev'ry one,
In blazing her by demonstration
Then *pride* that is more then most vicious,
Should there endure open damnation,
And so shee doth, for shee's most odious
In *Men* most base, that are ambitious.

Players, I love yee, and your *Qualitie*,
As ye are Men, *that* pass time not abus'd:
And ᶜsome I love for ᵈ*painting, poesie*,
And say fell *Fortune* cannot be excus'd,
That hath for better *uses* you refus'd:
Wit, Courage, good shape, good partes, and all *good*,
As long as al these *goods* are no *worse* us'd,
And though the *stage* doth staine pure gentle *bloud*,
Yet ᵉ*generous* yee are in *minde* and *moode*.

[*Marginal note:*
ᶜ W.S. R. B.
ᵈ Simonides saith, that painting is a dumb Poesy, & Poesy a speaking painting.
ᵉ Roscius was said for his excéllency in his quality, to be only worthie to come on the stage, and for his honesty to be more worthy then to come thereon.]

Your *Qualitie*, as farre as it reproves
The *World* of *Vice*, and grosse *incongruence*
Is good; and *good*, the *good* by nature loves,
As ᶠ recreating in and outward *sense*;
And so deserving *praise* and *recompence*:
But if *pride* (otherwise then morally)
Be *acted* by you, you doe *all* incense
To mortal hate; if *all* hate mortally,
Princes, much more *Players* they vilifie.

[*Marginal note:*
ᶠTher is good use of plaies & pastimes in a Commó-weale for thereby those that are most uncivill, prone to move war and dissention, are by these recreations accus-tomed to love peace & ease. Tac 14. An. Ca 6.]

–pp. 214–215

The King's Men Paid for Court Performances

To John Hemynges one of his majesties players upon the Councelles warrant dated at Hamptoncoute xviiiᵘᵒ die Jan-uary 1603 for his paynes and expences of himselfe and the rest of his Company in presenting of six interludes or playes before the kinges majesty and the prince viz one one Sᵗ Stephins Day at night St Johnes Day at night Innocentes Day and Newyers day at night before the kinges majestie for each of the saide playes twentie nobles a peece and to them by way of his majesties rewarde fyve markes and for two playes before the prince on the xxxᵗʰ of December and the firste of January 1603 twentie nobles a peece in all amounting to the some of   liiiˡⁱ

–*Dramatic Records*, p. 38

1604

Possible Allusion to *A Midsummer Night's Dream* in Carleton's Letter to Chamberlain

Dudley Carleton, diplomat and secretary to Sir Thomas Parry, maintained a long correspondence with John Chamberlain, a Londoner who kept Carleton informed of court news and gossip during the latter's trips to the Continent. In this 15 January 1604 letter, Carleton describes his experiences as an audience member at the court's 1604 masques and provides a detailed account of the social and political complexities of this form of courtly entertainment. He also comments on the king's failure to take "extraordinary pleasure" in plays, which may have had worrying implications for Shakespeare's acting company, now the King's Men. The "play of Robin Goodfellow" probably refers to Shakespeare's A Midsummer Night's Dream; *unfortunately, Carleton is less forthcoming about that play than about the masques. This excerpt is from* Dudley Carleton to John Chamberlain 1603–1624: Jacobean Letters *(1972), edited by Maurice Lee Jr.*

Sir, I perceived by Sir Rowland Lytton that in this time of your good leisure a small matter will serve for good entertainment, and therefore I send you such idle stuff as I received last out of France: but you must take the copies no otherwise than as lent, though you may keep them as long as you please; and for interest if they be worth it, I would gladly hear how you do in the country and with what contentment you pass your time; we have had here a merry Christmas and nothing to disquiet us save brabbles amongst our ambassadors, and one or two poor companions that died of the plague. The first holy days we had every night a public play in the great hall, at which the king was ever present and liked or disliked as he saw cause, but it seems he takes no extraordinary pleasure in them. The queen and prince were more the players' friends, for on other nights they had them privately and have since taken them to their protection. On New Year's night we had a play of Robin Goodfellow and a mask brought in by a magician of China. There was a heaven built at the lower end of the hall out of which our magician came down, and after he had made a long sleepy speech to the king of the nature of the country from whence he came, comparing it with ours for strength and plenty, he said he had brought in clouds certain Indian and China knights to see the magnificency of this court; and thereupon a traverse was drawn and the maskers seen sitting in a vaulty place with their torchbearers and other lights, which was no unpleasing spectacle. The maskers were brought in by two boys and two musicians, who began with a song, and whilst that went forward they presented themselves to the king. The first gave the king an impresa in a shield with a sonnet in a

paper to express his device and presented a jewel of £40,000 value which the king is to buy of Peter van Lore. But that is more than every man knew, and it made a fair show to the French ambassador's eye, whose master would have been well pleased with such a maskers' present, but not at that price. The rest in their order delivered their escutcheons with letters, and there was no great stay at any of them save only at one who was put to the interpretation of his device. It was a fair horse-colt in a fair green field, which he meant to be a colt of Bucephalus' race and had this virtue of his sire that none could mount him but one as great at least as Alexander. The king made himself merry with threatening to send this colt to the stable, and he could not break loose till he promised to dance as well as Banks his horse. The first measure was full of changes and seemed confused but was well gone through withal, and for the ordinary measures they took out the queen, the ladies of Derby, Harford, Suffolk, Bedford, Susan Vere, Southwell the elder, and Rich. In the corantoes they ran over some other of the young ladies and so ended as they began, with a song; and, that done, the magician dissolved his enchantment and made the maskers appear in their likeness to be the earl of Pembroke, the duke [of Lennox], Monsieur d'Aubigny, young Somerset, Philip Herbert the young Bucephal, James Hay, Richard Preston, and Sir Henry Goodier. Their attire was rich but somewhat too heavy and cumbersome for dancers, which put them beside their galliards. They had loose robes of crimson satin embroidered with gold and bordered with broad silver laces, doublets and bases of cloth of silver, buskins, swords, and hats alike, and in their hats each of them an Indian bird for a feather, with some jewels. The twelfth day the French ambassador was feasted publicly, and at night there was a play in the queen's presence, with a masquerade of certain Scotchmen who came in with a sword dance, not unlike a matachin, and performed it cleanly; from thence the king went to dice into his own presence and lost £500, which marred a gamester, for since, he appeared not there, but once before was at it in the same place and parted a winner. The Sunday following was the great day of queen's mask, at which was present the Spanish and Polack ambassadors with their whole trains and the most part of the Florentines and Savoyards but not the ambassadors themselves, who were in so strong competition for place and precedence that to displease neither it was thought best to let both alone. The like dispute was betwixt the French and the Spanish ambassadors and hard hold for the greatest honor, which the Spaniard thinks he hath carried away by being first feasted (as he was the first holiday and the Polack the next) and invited to the greatest mask; and the French seems to be greatly discontented that he was flatly refused to be admitted to the last, about which he

HISTORIE OF PLANTS.

455

✱ The place.

It ioyeth in barren and fandie grounds, and is likewife founde in dankifh places that lie wide open to the funne, it doth growe and profper in my garden exceedingly.

✱ The time.

It flowreth and flourifheth in Maie, Iune, Iulie, and Auguft.

✱ The names.

It is called of the latter Herbariftes *Herniaria*, and *Herniola* : taken from the effect in curing the difeafe *Hernia* : of diuers *Herba Turca*, and *Empetron* : in French *Boutonet* : in Englifh Rupture woort, and Burftwoort.

✱ The temperature.

Rupture woort doth notably drie, and throughly clofeth vp togither and faftneth.

✱ The vertues.

It is reported, that being drunke it is fingular good for ruptures, and that very many that haue A beene burften, were reftored to health by the vfe of this herbe : alfo the powder heereof taken with wine, doth make a man to piffe that hath his water ftopt, and that it wafteth awaie the ftones in the kidneies, and expelleth them.

Of wilde Time.   Chap. 164.

1 *Serpillum vulgare.*
Wilde Time.

2 *Serpillum vulgare flore albo.*
White wilde Time.

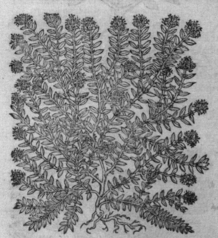 

✱ The defcription.

1   BOth *Diofcorides* and *Plinie* make two kindes of *Serpillum*, that is, of creeping or wilde Time, whereof the firft is our common creeping Time, which is fo well knowen, that it needeth no defcription; yet this ye fhall vnderftand, that it beareth flowers of a purple colour, as euerie bodie knoweth. Of which kinde I found another fort, with flowers as white as fnowe, and haue planted it in my garden, where it becommeth an herbe of great beautie.

2   This wilde Time that bringeth foorth white flowers, differeth not from the other, but onely in the colour of the flowers.

There is another kinde of *Serpillum*, which groweth in gardens, in fmell and fauour refembling Marierom. It hath leaues like Organie, or wilde Marierome, but fomewhat whiter, putting foorth many fmall ftalkes, fet full of leaues like Rue, but longer, narrower, and harder. The flowers are of a biting tafte, and pleafant fmell. The whole plant groweth vpright, whereas the other creepeth along vpon the earth, catching hold where it groweth, and fpreading it felfe far abroad.

Ff 4   3 *Serpillum*

Page from John Gerard's The Herball or Generall Historie of Plantes *(1597). In act 2, scene 1, of* A Midsummer Night's Dream, *Oberon tells Puck, "I know a bank where the wild thyme blows . . ." (courtesy of Special Collections, Howard-Tilton Library, Tulane University, New Orleans, Louisiana).*

used unmannerly expostulations with the king and for a few days troubled all the court; but the queen was fain to take the matter upon her, who as a masker had invited the Spaniard as the duke before had done the French, and to have them both there could not well be without bloodshed. The hall was much lessened by the works that were in it, so as none could be admitted but men of appearance; the one end was made into a rock and, in several places, the waits placed, in attire like savages; through the midst from the top came a winding stair, of breadth for three to march, and so descended the maskers by three and three, which being all seen on the stairs at once was the best presentation I have at any time seen. Their attire was alike, loose mantles and petticoats, but of different colors, the stuffs embroidered satins and cloth of gold and silver, for which they were beholden to Queen Elizabeth's wardrobe. Their heads by their dressing did only distinguish the difference of the goddesses they did represent. Only Pallas had a trick by herself; for her clothes were not so much below the knee but that we might see a woman had both feet and legs, which I never knew before. She had a pair of buskins set with rich stones, a helmet full of jewels, and her whole attire embossed with jewels of several fashions. Their torch-bearers were pages in white satin loose gowns, set with stars of gold, and their torches of white virgin wax gilded. Their *démarche* was slow and orderly; and first they made their offerings at an altar in a temple which was built on the left side of the hall towards the upper end; the songs and speeches that were there used I send you here enclosed. Then after the walking of two rounds fell into their measure, which for variety was nothing inferior but had not the life as the former. For the common measures they took out the earl of Pembroke, the duke, the lord chamberlain, Lord Henry Howard, Southampton, Devonshire, Sidney, Nottingham, Monteagle, Northumberland, Knollys, and Worcester. For galliards and corantoes they went by discretion, and the young prince was tossed from hand to hand like a tennis ball. The Lady Bedford and Lady Susan took out the two ambassadors and they bestirred themselves very lively, especially the Spaniard, for his Spanish galliard shewed himself a lusty old reveller. The goddesses they danced with did their parts, and the rest were nothing behindhand when it came to their turns; but of all for good grace and good footmanship Pallas bore the bell away. They retired themselves toward midnight in order as they came and quickly returned unmasked but in their masking attire. From thence they went with the king and the ambassadors to a banquet provided in the presence, which was dispatched with the accustomed confusion; and so ended that night's sport with the end of our Christmas gambols.

−pp. 53–56

Satan at the Globe

In this excerpt from Thomas Middleton's satire of London life, The Blacke Booke *(1604), the narrator, Satan, compares the world to a theater. His reference to the "Stage-rayles" of the "earthen Globe" is sometimes thought to be a literal description of a feature of the Globe theater: railings to prevent the actors from tumbling off the raised stage. Among those Satan expects to find in his audience are "Strumpets that follow Theators and Faires" (sig. B2).*

And now that I have vaulted up so hye
Above the Stage-rayles of this earthen Globe,
I must turne Actor, and joyne Companies
To share my Comick sleek-eyde villanies
For I must weave a thousand Ills in one,
To please my blacke and burnt affection: . . .

– sig. Bv

The King's Men Paid for Being Unable to Perform

One official response to outbreaks of bubonic plague was to close the theaters. The actors could either go on provincial tours, find other employment, or, as in the following document, be paid enough by the company's patron to tide them over until they could begin playing again.

To Richard Burbadg one of his majesties Comedians uppon the Councelles warraunte dated at Hampton-courte viiiᵒ die Februarii 1603 for the mayntenaunce and releife of himselfe and the rest of his Company being prohibited to presente any playes publiquelie in or neere London by reason of great perill that might growe throughe the extraordinary Concourse and assemblie of people to a newe increase of the plague till it shall please god to settle the Cittie in a more perfecte health by way of his Majesties free gifte   xxxˡⁱ

−*Dramatic Records,* p. 39

The King's Men Paid for Court Performances

To John Hemynges one of his majesties players uppon the Councelles warraunte dated at the Courte at White-hall ultimo die February 1603 for himselfe and the rest of his Company for two playes presented before his majestie viz the one on Candelmas Day at night and the other on Shrovesonday at night the some of thirtene poundes six shilling and eight pence and way of his majesties rewarde for the same twoe playes six poundes thirteene shilling and iiiiᵒʳ pence in all the some of   xxˡⁱ

−*Dramatic Records,* p. 39

The King's Men Congratulated in Dugdale's *The Time Triumphant*

In his account of the ceremonies and festivities celebrating King James's coronation, The Time Triumphant, Declaring in briefe, the arival of our Soveraigne liedge Lord, King James into England, His Coronation at Westminster: Together with his late royal progresse, from the Towre of London through the Cittie, to his Highnes mannor of WhiteHall *(1604), Gilbert Dugdale interprets the king's elevation of Shakespeare's acting company to royal service as a sign of royal magnanimity.*

In the meane time, his grace together with his *Queene* and children, progrest in the country, and dealt honours as freely to our Nation as their harts would wish, as creating Knights of gentlemen, Lordes of Knights and Earles of Lords & no doubt hereafter Dukes of Earles, I, and raised up an honor to *England,* that to this day have bin long in oblivion, which as now it is honorably living, so it will never die, I meane our noble knights of the Bath, young and gallant, worthy and valiant, nay see the beauty of our all kinde Soveraigne, not onely to the indifferent of worth, and the worthy of honor, did he freely deale about thiese causes: but to the meane gave grace, as taking to him the late Lord chamberlaines servants now the *Kings* acters: the *Queene* taking to her the Earle of *Worsters* servants that are now her acters, the Prince their sonne *Henry* Prince of Wales full of hope, tooke to him the Earle of *Nottingham* his servants who are now his acters, so that of Lords servants they are now the servants of the *King Queene* and *Prince.*

–sig. Bv

Allusion to *Love's Labor's Lost* in Cope's Letter to Cecil

In an undated letter endorsed 1604, Sir Walter Cope, an antiquarian and Member of Parliament who later became Master of the Court of Wards, writes to Secretary of State Robert Cecil to suggest a performance of Love's Labor's Lost *for Queen Anne. The text of the letter is from the Historical Manuscripts Commission's* Third Report *(1872).*

Sir,– I have sent and bene all thys morning huntyng for players Juglers & Such kinde of Creaturs, but fynde them harde to finde; wherefore leaving notes for them to seek me. Burbage ys come, and sayes there is no new playe that the quene hath not seene, but they have revyved an olde one, cawled *Loves Labore Lost,* which for wytt & mirthe he sayes will please her excedingly. And thys ys appointed to be playd to morowe

night at my Lord of Sowthampton's, unless yow send a wrytt to remove the Corpus Cum Causa to your howse in Strande. Burbage ys my messenger ready attending your pleasure.

yours most humbly,
Walter Cope.

Dated From your library.

[*Addressed:*] To the right honorable the Lorde Viscount Cranborne at the Courte.

[*Endorsed:*] 1604, Sir Walter Cope to my Lord.

–p. 148

The King's Men Paid for Attendance on the Spanish Ambassador

In August 1604 the King's Men were paid for their attendance on the Spanish ambassador, Juan Fernandez de Velasco, who was staying in Somerset House while in London to negotiate a peace treaty to end the longstanding hostilities between England and Spain (PRO Declared Accounts, Treasurer of the Chamber, A.O. 1/388/41).

To Augustine Phillippes and John Hemynges for the allowaunce of themselves and tenne of theire ffellowes his Ma^tes groomes of the chamber, and Players for waytinge and attendinge on his Ma^tes service by commandemente uppon the Spanishe Ambassador at Somersette House the space of xviii dayes viz from the xv^th day of Auguste 1604 untill the xxvii^th day of the same as appeareth by a bill therof signed by the Lord chamberlayne [for] xxi^li xii^s.

Shakespeare Listed in Survey of Rowington Manor

The survey of Rowington Manor (PRO Exchequer, Special Commission, E. 178/4661), dated 24 October 1604, lists Shakespeare's Chapel Lane cottage among the property it documents; the survey was conducted when Anne, Countess of Warwick, the lady of Rowington Manor, died and the property reverted to the Crown.

Willm Shakespere lykewise holdeth there one cottage & one garden by estimation a quarter of one acre and payeth Rent yeerely   ii^s vi^d

Shakespeare's Involvement in Belott's Suit against Mountjoy

The documents in this section record a lawsuit filed in 1612 by Stephen Belott against Christopher Mountjoy, his father-in-law. Mountjoy was a tire-maker—a maker of

The King's Men in the Coronation Procession

As the King's Men, Shakespeare and his fellow actors were entitled to take part in James's coronation procession, which took place on 15 March 1604, nearly a year after the death of Queen Elizabeth. The public celebration of the coronation was delayed because of an outbreak of the bubonic plague. Members of the household were granted scarlet cloth, to be used as their identifying livery. Entries in the royal account books for King James's "royall proceeding through the Citie of London" list the names of those receiving cloth. The listing of nine players—William Shakespeare, Augustine Phillips, Lawrence Fletcher, John Hemminges, Richard Burbidge, William Slye, Robert Armyn, Henry Cundell, and Richard Cowley—is included under the entries for "Chamber," a division of the royal household. Each player received four and a half yards of "Skarlet Red cloth," the abbreviation "di" standing for "dimidium," or "half."

Page from the royal account book kept by Sir George Hume, Master of the Great Wardrobe, showing that the King's Men were allotted scarlet cloth for the coronation procession of James I. As servants of the king, the actors were to take part in the procession, which, because of an outbreak of bubonic plague, was postponed until March 1604 (PRO LC 2/4 [5]; courtesy of the Public Records Office, London).

women's headdresses—whose house and business were located at the corner of Monkswell and Silver Streets in London. Belott had been Mountjoy's apprentice, but by the time of the events described in the documents he was a tire-maker in his own right.

Court records establish that Shakespeare was living in the Mountjoy house in 1604. On 19 November 1604 Mountjoy's daughter, Mary, married Stephen Belott. According to the depositions Shakespeare assisted in the courtship, and Mountjoy promised the couple money and goods upon the marriage. The lawsuit began when Mountjoy failed to keep his end of the bargain. After examining the testimony the court transferred the case to the jurisdiction of "the Reverend & grave overseers and Elders of the french Church in London," who on 6 May 1613 fined Mountjoy twenty nobles. A noble was equal to ten shillings, sixpence; the fine is about 1/6 of the amount Shakespeare paid for New Place in 1597.

Many documents from the case survive; those presented here name Shakespeare. He is listed in a court summons and among the witnesses for the case; he is asked questions during the interrogatory stage; and his deposition is taken. Also included here are excerpts from the depositions of other witnesses in which they testify about Shakespeare's actions. "What we learn of Shakespeare," E. K. Chambers concludes in William Shakespeare: A Study of Facts and Problems, "is that he had known the Mountjoy household since 1602, had been a lodger in it, but perhaps only temporarily in 1604, was described as of Stratford-upon-Avon in 1612 and therefore presumably had no London residence, was present at Westminster on 11 May 1612, and, perhaps, was then of failing memory" (vol. II, p. 95).

The records presented here from the Belott-Mountjoy lawsuit were transcribed from various sources by Charles William Wallace in his October 1910 essay in University Studies, "Shakespeare and his London Associates as Revealed in Recently Discovered Documents." Abbreviated names and legal terms have been silently expanded.

In this summons (Process Book 6-11 James I, Miscellaneous Books, Vol. 183, f. 269), Wallace notes that "Nil pauper" refers to the defendant and "r Imed" means "returnable immediately."

Septimo die Maii/

Nil pauper

| A compulsory to William Shakespeare gent and others ad testificandum inter Stephanum Bellott querentem et Xpoferum Mountjoy defendentem | r Imed |

– University Studies, 10 (October 1910): 277

Wallace transcribed this witness list from the Witness Book, 44 Elizabeth I to 16 James I, Miscellaneous Books, vol. 199.

| Stephen Belott plaintiff Xpofer Mountjoy def | danyell Nicholas Johan Johnson uxor Tho: Johnson William Shakespeare gent |

The first set of interrogatories (PRO Court of Requests, Documents of Shakespearian Interest, Req. 4/1) are dated 11 May 1612.

Interrogatories to bee mynistred to Wittnesses to bee produced on the parte and behalf of Stephen Belott Complainant against Christopher Mountjoye Defendant.

1 Imprimis whether doe you knowe the parties plainant and defendant and howe long have you knowne them and either of them.

2 Item whether did you knowe the Complainant when he was servant wth the said defendant howe and in what sort did he behave himselfe in the service of the said defendant and whether did not the said defendant Confesse that hee had got great profitt and Comodytie by the service of the said Complainant.

3 Item whether did not the said defendant seeme to beare great good will and affeccione towardes the said Complainant during the time of his said service and what report did he then give of the said Complainant touching his said service and whether did not the said defendant make a mocion unto the said Complainant of marriage wth the said Mary in the Bill mencioned being the said defendantes sole Child and daughter and willingly offer to performe the same yf the said Complainant should seeme to be content and well lyke thereof. and whether did not hee lykewise send anie person or noe to perswade the said Complainant to the same. declare the truthe of yor knowledge herin.

4 Item what some or somes of moneye did the said defendant promise to give the said Complainant for a porcion in marriage wth the said Marye his daughter whether the some of threscore powndes or what other somme as you knowe or have hard and when was the same to be paied whether at the daie of Marriage of the said Complainant and the said Marye or whath other tyme and what further porcion did the said defendant promise to give unto the said Complainant wth the said Marye at the tyme of his decease whether the some twoe hundred poundes or what

other somes and whether uppon the said per-swaciones and promises of the said defendant did not the said Complainant shortly after marrye wth her the said Marye declare the truthe herein as you knowe verylie believe or have Credybly hard.

5/ Item what parcells of goodes or houshold stuffe did the defendant promise to geve unto the com-plainant in Marriadge wth his said wiefe And what parcelles of goodes did he geve him in Marriage wth his said wyffe. did he not geve them these parcels (vizt.) One ould ffetherbed, one oulde ffether boul-ster, A flocke boulster, a thine greene Rugg, two ordanarie blanckettes woven, two paire sheetes, A dozine of napkines of Course Dyaper, twoe short table Clothes, six short Towelles & one longe one, An ould drawinge table, two ould Joyned stooles, one Wainscott Cubberd, one Twistinge wheele of woode, twoe paire of litle Scyssers, one ould Truncke and a like old Truncke. / One Bobbine box: And what doe youe thincke in yor Conscyence all these said parcelles might be woorthe at the tyme when they weare delivered by the defendauntes appoyntm^t, unto the plaintiffes declare the truthe hearein at lardge./

—*University Studies,* 10 (October 1910): 278–279

Shakespeare's deposition was included in "Depositiones Captae apud Westmonasterium undecimo die maii Ann° Regni Jacobi Regis Angliae &c decimo et Scotiae xlv^to ex parte Stepha-nei Bellott quaerentis versus Christopherum Mountjoye defen-dentem."

William Shakespeare of Stratford upon Aven in the Countye of Warwicke gentleman of the Age of xlviii yeres or thereaboutes sworne and examined the daye and yere abovesaid deposethe & sayethe

1 To the first Interrogatory this deponent sayethe he knowethe the partyes plaintiff and deffendant and hathe know[ne] them bothe as he now remembrethe for the space of tenne yeres or thereaboutes./

2 To the second Interrogatory this deponent sayeth he did know the complainant when he was servant wth the deffendant, and that duringe the tyme of his the complainantes service wth the said deffendant he the said Complainant to this deponentes knowledge did well and honestly behave himselfe, but to this deponentes remembrance he hath not heard the def-fendant confesse that he had gott any great proffitt and comodytye by the *said* [deleted] service of the said complainant, but this deponent saith he verely thinckethe that the said complainant was a very good and industrious servant in the said service And more he canott depose to the said Interrogatory:/

3/ To the third Interrogatory this deponent sayethe that it did evydentlye appeare that the said deffen-dant did all the tyme of the said complainantes ser-vice wth him beare and shew great good will and affeccion towardes the said complainant, and that he hath hard the deffendant and his wyefe diverse and sundry tymes saye and reporte that the said com-plainant was a very honest fellowe: And this depo-nent sayethe that the said deffendant did make a mocion unto the complainant of marriadge wth the said Mary in the bill mencioned beinge the said def-fendantes sole chyld and daughter and willinglye offered to performe the same yf the said Complain-ant shold seeme to be content and well like thereof: And further this deponent sayethe that the said def-fendantes wyeffe did sollicitt and entreat this depo-nent to move and perswade the said Complainant to effect the said Marriadge and accordingly this depo-nent did move and perswade the complainant therunto: And more to this Interrogatorye he cannott depose:/

4/ To the ffourth Interrogatory this deponent sayth that the defendant promissed to geve the said Com-plainant a porcion *of monie and goodes* [deleted] in Mar-riadg[e] wth Marye his daughter./ but what certayne porcion he Rememberithe not./ nor when to be payed *yf any some weare promissed,* [deleted] nor knoweth that the defendant promissed the *defendant* [deleted] plaintiff twoe hundered poundes wth his daughter Marye at the tyme of his decease./ But sayth that the plaintiff was dwellinge wth the defen-dant in his house And they had Amongeste them-selves manye Conferences about there Marriadge w^ch [afterwardes] was Consumated and Solempnized. And more he cann[ott depose./]

5/ To the vth Interrogatory this deponent sayth he can saye noth[inge] touchinge any parte or poynte of the same Interrogatory for he knoweth not what Implementes and necessaries of househould stuffe the defendant gave the plaintiff in Marriadge wth his daughter Marye./

[*Signed*] Willm Shak[sper]
—*University Studies,* 10 (October 1910): 282–283

Joan Johnson, described as "the wyffe of Thomas Johnsone of the parishe of Elinge in the Countye of Middlesex Baskettmaker of the Age of ffortye yeres or th'aboutes," mentioned Shakespeare in one of her answers in her deposition.

3/ To the thirde Interrogatory this deponent sayth that the defendant seemed to beare greate good will and affection towardes the plaintiff when he served him, gevinge him reporte to be A verry good servaunte for pl[ ] his service./ But that the defendant moved the plaintiff to Marrye wth his daughter Marye she knoweth not./ But sayth that there was a shewe of goodwill betweene the plaintiff and defendantes daughter Marye wch the defendantes wyffe did geve Countenaunce unto and thinke well of./ And as shee Remembereth the defendant did send and perswade one Mr Shakespeare that laye in the house to perswade the plaintiff to the same Marriadge./ And more shee cannott depose.

—*University Studies*, 10 (October 1910): 280

Daniel Nichols, described as "of the parishe of S^d Olphadge w^thin Criplegate London gent of the Age of ffyftye twoe yeres or th^raboutes," referred to Shakespeare in two of his answers.

3 To the thirde Interrogatory this deponent sayth he herd one W^m: Shakespeare saye that the defendant did beare A good opinnion of the plaintiff and affected him well when he served him, And did move the plaintiff by him the said Shakespeare to have [a] marriadge betweene his daughter Marye Mountjoye [and] the plaintiff And for that purpose sent him the said Sh[akespeare] to the plaintiff to perswade the plaintiff to the same, as Shakespere tould him this deponent wch was effected and Solempnized uppon promise of a porcion wth her./ And more he cannott depose./

4 To the iiii^th Interrogatory this deponent sayth that the plaintiff did Requeste him this deponent to goe wth his wyffe to Shakespe[are] to und^rstande the truthe howe muche and what the defendant did promise [to] bestowe on his daughter in marriadge wth him the plaintiff, who did soe./ And askinge Shakespeare th^rof, he Answered that he promissed yf the plaintiff would marrye wth Marye his the defandantes onlye daughter, he the defendant would by his promise as he Remembered geve the plaintiff wth her in marriadge about the some of ffyftye poundes in money and Certayne Houshould stuffe./ And more he cannott depose touchinge the said Interrogatory to his Rememberaunce for he remembereth not any daye sett downe for paym^t of the porcion or deliverye of the houshould Stuffe. but only that he would geve her soe much at the tyme of her marriadge./

—*University Studies*, 10 (October 1910): 281

In the second set of interrogatories, dated 19 June 1612, Shakespeare's name is noted in the margin beside question 4, perhaps to remind the interrogator either to ask Shakespeare this question or to use Shakespeare's name when questioning other witnesses. Several witnesses report what they remember from discussions with Shakespeare; if Shakespeare gave a second deposi-

tion, it does not survive. The absence of this second deposition is sometimes taken as evidence that, by 1612, Shakespeare's memory was failing.

4. Item whether did not the said defendant or some other by his appointment send you or any other person to yor knowledge unto the said Complainant to make a mocion of marriadge betwixt the said Complainant and the said Mary Mountjoy beinge the defendantes sole Childe and daughter, and what wordes did the said defendant use unto you or to any other to yor knowledge touchinge the marryage of the said Complainant wth the said Mary? whether did not the defendant then say that yf shee the said Mary did not marry the said Complainant, that [*Marginal note:* William Shakespeare 4.] shee the said Mary should not Coste him nor have a groate from him, and whether did not the said defendant likewise promise that yf the Complainant and the said Mary did marry together then hee would give a porcion wth the said Mary unto the said Complainant? howe muche was the said porcion that hee then promised, whether not the somme of threescore pounds or what other somme as you thinke in yor Conscience to bee true? and before whome did the said defendant soe promise the same, whether before you or any other to yor knowledge, and whether upon the said promisses and perswacions did not the said Complainant Contracte himselfe wth the said Mary?

—*University Studies*, 10 (October 1910): 285–286

Daniel Nichols again refers to Shakespeare in his second deposition, dated 19 June 1612.

4 To the iiii^th Interrogatory this deponent sayth that the defendant did never send him this deponent unto the Complainant to make mocion of Marriadge betwixte the Complainant and the said Marye Mountjoye beinge the defendantes sole daughter and Childe but Mr William Shakespeare tould him this deponent that the defendant sent him the said Mr Shakespeare to the plaintiff about suche a marriage to be hadd betweene them. And Shakespeare tould this deponent that the defendant tould him that yf the plaintiff would Marrye the said Marye his daughter he would geve hime the plaintiff A some of money wth her for A porcion in Marriadge wth her./ And that yf he the plaintiff did not marry wth her the said Marye and shee wth the plaintiff shee should never coste him the defendant her ffather A groat, whereuppon And in Regard Mr Shakespeare hadd tould them that they should have A some of money for a porcion from the fath^r they weare made suer by Mr Shakespeare by gevinge there Consent, and

agreed to Marrye, *gevinge eache others hand to the hande* [deleted] And did marrye./ But what some yt was that Mr *Shake* [deleted] Mountjoye promissed to geve them he the said Mr Shakespeare could not remember, but said yt was ffyftye poundes or th^raboutes to his beste Rememberaunce. / And as he Rememberith Mr Shakespeare said he promissed to geve them A porcion of his goodes: but what, or to what valewe he Rememberithe not/ And more he Cannott depose./

　　　　　　　　　　　　—*University Studies*, 10 (October 1910): 287–288

William Eaton, described as "apprentice wth the Complainant of the Age of nynteene yeres or th^raboutes," refers to Shakespeare in his 19 June 1612 deposition.

4 To the iiii^th Interrogatory this deponent sayth he hath herd one Mr Shakspeare saye that he was sent by the defendant to the plaintiff to move the plaintiff to have A marriadge betweene them the plaintiff and the defendantes daughter Marye Mountjoye, And herd Mr Shakespeare saye that he was wished by the defendant to make proffer of A certayne some that the defendant said he would geve the plaintiff wth his daughter Marye Mountjoye in Marriadge, but he had forgott the some./ And *m^r Shakespeare tould the plaintiff* [deleted] more he cannott depose touchinge the same Interrogatory./

　　　　　　　　　　　　—*University Studies*, 10 (October 1910): 289

Nowell Mountjoy, described as "of the parishe of S.^d Olaves in Sylver Streete Londone Tyremaker of the Age of thirtye yeares or th^raboutes," refers to Shakespeare in his 19 June 1612 deposition.

4 To the iiii^th Interrogatory this deponent sayth he was never sent by the defendant unto the Complainant to make A mocon to him of A marriadge to be hadd betwixte the Complainant and Marye Mountjoy the defendantes sole Child and daughter, nor knoweth of any other that was by the defendant sent unto the plaintiff uppon that messaiege: but the plaintiff tould this deponent that one Mr Shakespeare was Imployed by the defendant about that buysnes: in what mann^r: or to what effecte he knoweth not: And sayth he never herd the defendant saye that yf his daughter Mary married not wth the plaintiff shee should neve^r have groate from him./ nor knoweth that the defendant promissed to geve the plaintiff Any porcion of monney wth his daughter Mary in marriadge nor howe much he promissed yf he promissed any, nor knoweth uppon what promise the Complainant contracted him selfe wth the said Marye/. And more he Cannott depose.

　　　　　　　　　　　　—*University Studies*, 10 (October 1910): 292–293

Shakespeare's Suit against Rogers

This document (Shakespeare Birthplace Trust Records Office, manuscript ER 27/5) records the beginning of a suit Shakespeare filed against Stratford apothecary Philip Rogers to collect a debt of 35 shillings, 10 pence, plus 10 pence damages. Shakespeare sold Rogers 20 bushels of malt, apparently on credit, and loaned him 2 shillings. The outcome of the suit, brought in Stratford's Court of Record, is unknown.

Stretford
Burgus
R.

Philipus Rogers sommonitus fuit per servientem ad clavam ibidem ad respondendum Willielmo Shexpere de placito quod reddat ei triginta et quinque solidos decem denarios quos ei debet et injuste detinet, et sunt plegii de prosequendo Johannes Doe et Ricardus Roe, &c., et unde idem Willielmus, per Willielmum Tetherton attornatum suum, dicit quod cum predictus Phillipus Rogers, vicesimo septimo die Marcii, anno regni domini nostri Jacobi regis, nunc Anglie, Francie et Hibernie, primo [*sic*] et Scocie tricesimo septimo [1604], hic apud Stretford predictam, ac infra jurisdiccionem huius curie, emisset de eodem Willielmo tres modios brasii pro sex solidis de predictis triginta et quinque solidis decem denariis; ac etiam quod cum predictus Phillipus Rogers, decimo die Aprillis, anno regni dicti domini regis nunc Anglie, &c., secundo, hic apud Stretford predictam ac infra jurisdiccionem huius curie, emisset de eodem Willielmo quatuor modios brasii pro octo solidis de predictis triginta et quinque solidis decem denariis; ac etiam quod cum predictus Phillipus, vicesimo quarto die dicti Aprillis, anno regni dicti domini regis nunc Anglie, &c., secundo, hic apud Stretford predictam, infra jurisdiccionem huius curie, emisset de eodem Willielmo alios tres modios brasii pro sex solidis de predictis triginta et quinque solidis decem denariis; ac etiam quod cum predictus Phillipus, tercio die Maii anno regni dicti domini regis nunc Anglie, &c., secundo, hic apud Stretford predictam, ac infra jurisdiccionem huius curie, emisset de eodem Willielmo alios quatuor modios brasii pro octo solidis de predictis triginta et quinque solidis decem denariis; ac etiam quod cum predictus Phillipus, decimo sexto die Maii, anno regni dicti domini regis nunc Anglie, &c., secundo, hic apud Stretford predictam, infra jurisdiccionem huius curie, emisset de eodem Willielmo alios quatuor modios brasii pro octo solidis de predictis triginta et quinque solidis decem denariis; ac etiam quod cum predictus Phillipus, tricesimo die Maii, anno regni dicti domini regis nunc Anglie, &c., secundo, hic apud Stretford predictam, ac infra jurisdiccionem huius curie, emisset de eodem Willielmo duas modios brasii pro tres solidis decem denariis de predictis triginta et quinque solidis decem denariis; ac etiam quod cum predictus Phillipus, vicesimo quinto die Junii, anno dicti domini regis nunc Anglie, &c., hic apud Stretford predictam, ac infra jurisdiccionem huius curie, mutuatus fuisset duos solidos legalis monete, &c., de predictis triginta et quinque solidis decem denariis residuos, solvendos eidem Willielmo cum inde requisitus fuisset. Que omnia separales somme attingunt se in toto ad quadraginta et unum solidos decem denarios. Et predictus Phillipus Rogers de sex solidis inde eidem Willielmo postea satisfecisset. Predictus tamen Phillipus, licet sepius requisitus, predictos triginta et quinque solidos decem denarios residuos eidem Willielmo nondum reddidit, sed illos ei huc usque reddere contradixit et adhuc contradicit, unde dicit quod deterioratus est et dampnum habet ad valencian decem solidorum. Et inde producit sectam, &c.

| Stratford Borough. | Phillip Rogers was summoned by the sergeant at mace in the same place to reply to William Shakespeare concerning the |

judgment that he return to him thirty-five shillings ten pence which he owes him and unjustly retains, and there are pledges, John Doe and Richard Roe, to prosecute, etc.; and therefore the same William, by William Tetherton, his attorney, says that when aforesaid Phillip Rogers, on the twenty-seventh day of March, in the year of the reign of our master James, King, now in England, France, and Ireland, the first, and in Scotland the thirty-seventh, here at aforesaid Stratford and within the jurisdiction of this court, had bought from the same William three measures [bushels] of malt for six shillings of the aforesaid thirty-five shillings and ten pence; and also that when aforesaid Phillip Rogers on the tenth day of April in the year of the reign of our said master, King, now in England, etc., the second, here at aforesaid Stratford and within the jurisdiction of the court had bought from the same William four measures of malt for eight shillings of the aforesaid thirty-five shillings ten pence; and also that when aforesaid Phillip on the twenty-fourth day of said April, in the year of the reign of said master, King, now in England, etc., the second, here at aforesaid Stratford within the jurisdiction of this court, had bought from the same William another three measures of malt for six shillings of the aforesaid thirty-five shillings ten pence; and also that when the aforesaid Phillip on the third day of May, in the year of the reign of the master, King, now in England, etc., the second, here at aforesaid Stratford and within the jurisdiction of this court, had bought from the same William

another four measures of malt for eight shillings of the aforesaid thirty-five shillings ten pence; and also that when aforesaid Phillip on the sixteenth day of May, in the year of the reign of said master, King, now in England, etc., the second, here at the aforesaid Stratford within the jurisdiction of this court, had bought from the same William another four measures of malt for eight shillings of the aforesaid thirty-five shillings ten pence; and also that when aforesaid Phillip, on the thirtieth day of May, in the year of the reign of the said master, King, now in England, etc., the second, here at aforesaid Stratford and within the jurisdiction of this court, had bought from the same William two measures of malt for three shillings ten pence of the aforesaid thirty-five shillings ten pence; and also that when the aforesaid Phillip on the twenty-fifth day of June, in the year of said master, King of England, etc., here at aforesaid Stratford and within the jurisdiction of this court, had borrowed two shillings of legal money, etc., when therefore he had demanded that the residue of the aforesaid thirty-five shillings ten pence be paid to the said William. That all the separate sums added themselves in toto to forty-one shillings ten pence. And the aforesaid Phillip Rogers would afterwards have satisfied the same William with six shillings; nevertheless, the aforesaid Phillip, although often having been demanded, has not yet paid the residue of the aforesaid thirty-five shillings ten pence; but has even to this time refused to repay it and still refuses, therefore he says that he has been injured and has damage to the value of ten shillings, and therefore he brings this suit, etc.

–Lewis, *Shakespeare Documents,* pp. 369–371

Publications

Two of Shakespeare's plays were published again in 1604: 1 Henry IV *(1598, 1599) and* Hamlet *(1603). The description of this edition of* Hamlet, *known as the Second Quarto, as "enlarged to almost as much againe, as it was, according to the true and perfect Coppie," implies a manuscript or theatrical promptbook was used to set the text into type.*

The / *HISTORY OF* / HENRIE the fourth, / With the battell at Shrewsburie, / *betweene the King, and Lord* / Henry Percy, surnamed Henry Hot-*spur* / *of the North.* / *With the humorous conceits of Sir* / Iohn Falstalffe. / Newly corrected by *W. Shakspeare.* / [*Printer's device*] / LONDON / Valentine Simmes, for *Mathew Law,* / and are to be ſolde at his ſhop in / Paules Churchyard, at the signe of the Fox. 1604. [*Copy is damaged; publication information is conjectural.*]

Allusion to Shakespeare in Cooke's *Epigrames*

In Epigrames. Served out in 52. severall Dishes for every man to tast without surfeting *(1604?) dramatist and poet John Cooke answers the anonymous ballad "A mournefull Dittie" (circa 1603) that called on "Shakspeare, Johnson, Grene" to memorialize Queen Elizabeth; Cooke assumes the "Greene" referred to in the ballad is Robert Greene, dead since 1592.*

12

Who er'e will go unto the presse may see,
The hated Fathers of vilde balladrie,
One sings in his base note the River Thames,
Shal sound the famous memory of noble king *James*
Another sayes that he will to his death,
Sing the renowned worthinesse of sweet *Elizabeth,*
So runnes their verse in such disordered straine,
And with them dare great majesty prophane,
Some dare do this, some other humbly craves,
For helpe of spirits in their sleeping graves,
As he that calde to *Shakespeare, Johnson, Greene,*
To write of their dead noble Queene,
But he that made the Ballads of oh hone,
Did wondrous well to whet the buyer on,
These fellowes are the slaunderers of the time,
Make ryming hatefull through their bastard rime.
But were I made a judge in poetry,
They all should burne for their vilde heresie.

                            —sigs. B1r–v

Allusion to *The Comedy of Errors* in Dekker's *The Honest Whore*

In Thomas Dekker's play The Honest Whore, With, The Humours of the Patient Man, and the Longing Wife *(1604) Candido, the patient man of the play's subplot, is being tested by his wife, who is trying to arouse his jealousy. In this excerpt a servant, George, is putting on Candido's clothes while the wife encourages the other servants to take part in the masquerade by treating George as if he were the master of the house. This device prompts the reference to one of Shakespeare's earliest plays,* The Comedy of Errors.

Enter George.
Wife. Be redy with your legs then let me see,
How curtzy would become him: gallantly!
Beshrew my bloud a proper seemely man,
Of a choice carriage walkes with a good port,
Geo. I thanke you mistris, my back's broad enough,
now my Maister's gown's on.
Wif. Sure I should thinke it were the least of sin,
To mistake the maister, and to let him in.
Geo. Twere a good Comedy of errors that yfaith.
2. Pre. whist, whist, my maister.

                            —sig. G4r

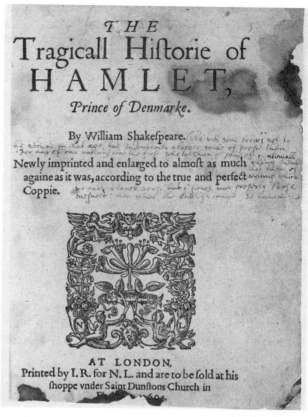

Title page of the corrected and expanded second quarto edition of Hamlet, *which serves as the basis for most modern editions of the play. In some copies, the title page is dated 1605 (by permission of the Folger Shakespeare Library).*

Allusions to Falstaff and *The Comedy of Errors* in *The Meeting of Gallants*

In this first excerpt from The Meeting of Gallants at an Ordinarie: Or The Walkes in Powles *(1604), a work attributed to dramatist and satirist Thomas Dekker, the gallants have gathered at an ordinary, or tavern, and compare their host to Sir John Oldcastle; the emphasis on the host's fat belly indicates the allusion is to the earlier name of Shakespeare's Sir John Falstaff, who was probably first called Sir John Oldcastle, rather than to the historical Oldcastle, a Protestant martyr. In the second excerpt a gruesome story of mistaken identity is called a "Comedy of Errors."*

Entring into the Ordinarie.
Host.

What Gallants are you come, are you come? welcome Gentlemen; I have newes enough for you all, welcome againe, and againe: I am so fatte and pursie, I cannot speake loude enough, but I am sure you heare mee, or you shall heare me: Welcome, welcome Gentlemen, I have Tales, and Quailes for you: seate your selves Gallantes, enter Boyes & Beardes with dishes and Platters; I will be with you againe in a trice ere you looke for me.

Sig. Shuttlecocke.

Now *Signiors* howe like you mine Host? did I not tell you he was a madde round knave, and a merrie one too: and if you chaunce to talke of fatte Sir *John Old-castle*, he wil tell you, he was his great Grand-father, & not much unlike him in Paunch, if you marke him well by all descriptions: and see where hee appeares againe. Hee told you he would not be longe from you, let his humor have scope enough I pray, and there is no doubt but his Tales will make us laugh ere we be out of our Porridge. . . .

—sig. B4v

Host.

And now I returne to more pleasant Arguments, Gentlemen Gallants, to make you laugh ere you be quite out of your Capen: this that I discourse of now is a prettie merrie accident that happened about *Shoreditch*, although the intent was sad and Tragicall, yet the event was mirthfull and pleasant: The goodman (or rather as I may fitlier tearme him, the bad-man of a House) being sorely pesterd with the death of servants, and to avoyde all suspition of the Pestilence from his house above all others, did very craftily and subtilly compound with the Maisters of the Pest-cart, to fetch away by night as they past by, all that should chance to die in his house, having three or foure servants downe at once, and told them that he knew one of them would be readie for them by that time the Cart came by, and to cleare his house of all suspition, the dead body should bee laide upon a stall, some five or six houses of: where, there they should entertaine him and take him in amongst his dead companions: To conclude, night drewe on-ward, and the servant concluded his life, and according to their appointment was enstalde to be made knight of the Pest-cart. But here comes in the excellent Jest, Gentlemen Gallants of five and twentie, about the darke and pittifull season of the night: a shipwracke drunkard, (or one drunke at the signe of the Ship,) new cast from the shore of an Ale-house, and his braines sore beaten with the cruell tempests of Ale and Beere, fell Flounce upon a lowe stall hard by the house, there being little difference in the Carecasse, for the other was dead, and he was dead drunke, (the worse death of the twaine) there taking up his drunken Lodging, and the Pest-cart comming by, they made no more adoe, but taking

him for the dead Bodie, placed him amongst his companions, and away they hurred with him to the Pest-house: but there is an oulde Proverbe, and now confirmed true, a Druncken man never takes harme: to the Approbation of which, for all his lying with infectious Bedfellowes, the next morning a little before he should be buried, he strecht and yawnde as wholesomely, as the best Tinker in ill *Banburie*, and returned to his olde Vomit againe, and was druncke in *Shoreditch* before Evening.

Gingle-spur.

This was a prettie Commedie of Errors, my round Host.

Host.

O my Bullies, there was many such a part plaide uppon the Stage both of the Cittie and the Suburbs. . . .

—sigs. Dr–D2r

Allusion to *Titus Andronicus* in Middleton's *Father Hubburds Tales*

The allusion to Shakespeare's play occurs in the chapter titled "The Ants Tale when he was a Souldier" in playwright Thomas Middleton's prose satire Father Hubburds Tales: Or The Ant, And the Nightingale *(1604). In this excerpt the Ant describes the travails of a soldier's life; like many early modern soldiers, the Ant has lost limbs, thus prompting the comparison to* Titus Andronicus, *who severs his own hand in a desperate effort to save the lives of two of his sons.*

To conclude, they usde me very curteously and gentleman-like awhile, like an old cunning Bowler to fetch in a yong [betling?] Gamester, who will suffer him to win one Six-penny game at the first, and then lurch him in Six pounds afterward: and so they plaide with me, still training me (with their faire promises) in to farre deeper and deadlier Battayles, where like villainous cheating Bowlers, they lurcht me of two of my best Limbes, *viz.* My right Arme, and right Legge, that so of a man of war, I became in shew a monster of warre: yet comforted in this, because I knew warre begot many such Monsters as my selfe in lesse then a Twlve-month. Now I could discharge no more, having paide the shot deare enough I thinke, but rather desirde to be dischargde, to have Pay, and be gone: whereupon I appeared to my Captaine and other Commanders, kissing my left hand which then stood for both; (like one Actor that plaies two Parts) who seemd to pittie my unjoynted fortunes, and playster my wounds up with words, tolde me I had done valiant service in their knowledge, marry as for Pay, they must goe on the score with me, for all their money was thumpt out in Powder: And this was no pleasing salve for a greene sore Madame: twas too much for me, Lady, to trust Calivers with my Limbes, and then Cavaleeres with my mony. Neverlesse (for all my lamentable Action of one Arme like old *Titus Andronicus*) I could purchase no more then one months Pay, for a ten-months paine and perill, nor that neither; but to convey away my miserable clamours that lay roaring against the Arches of their Eares, marry their bountiful favours were extended thus farre: I had a Passport to beg in all Countries.

—sigs. E2v–E3r

Allusion to Falstaff in Persons's *Of Three Conversions of England*

Robert Persons, a Jesuit priest, was an active opponent of the Church of England and the monarch who was head of that church. Although his desire to see a Catholic monarch succeed Queen Elizabeth went unfulfilled, Persons continued to write for and visit England's Catholic community. Had he been captured in England, Persons would have faced execution. The Third Part Of A Treatise Intituled Of Three Conversions of England *(1604), which Persons wrote as N.D. (Nicholas Dolman), was subtitled* Conteyninge an examen of the Calendar or Catalogue of Protestant Saintes, Martyrs and Confessors, devised by *Fox, and prefixed before his huge Volume of Actes and Monuments: With a Paralel or Comparison therof to the Catholike Roman Calendar, and Saintes therin conteyned. *In the following excerpt the popular association of Shakespeare's Falstaff with the historical Sir John Oldcastle affords Persons an easy opportunity to criticize a Protestant hero; the passage shows Persons's familiarity with popular culture, which is perhaps also intended to imply the ineffectiveness of anti-Jesuit statutes.*

FEBRUARY.

The second Moneth of *February* is more fertile of rubricate Martyrs, then *January*, for that yt hath 8. in number, two Wickliffians, *Syr John Oldcastle* a Ruffian- knight as all England knoweth, & commonly brought in by comediants on their stages: he was put to death for robberyes and rebellion under the foresaid *K. Henry* the fifth and *Syr Roger Onely* Priest-martyr, condemned for conjuringe and wichcraft under *K. Henry* the sixt.

Allusions to Shakespeare and *Hamlet* in Scoloker's *Daiphantus*

Anthony Scoloker alludes to Shakespeare and Hamlet in his parodic epistle to Daiphantus, or The Passions of Love. Comicall to Reade, But Tragicall to Act: As full of Wit, as Experience *(1604), a mixture of prose and poetry that recounts an unfortunate love affair.*

TO THE MIGHTIE, LEARNED,
and Ancient Potentate *Quisquis*; Emperour of ✠
King of Great and Little *A.* Prince of *B. C.* And *D.* &c.
Aliquis, wisheth the much increase of true Subjects,
free from *Passion Spleene,* and *Melancholy:* and
indued with Vertue, Wisedome, and Magnanimitie.
Or, to the Reader.

An epistle to the *Reader*; why? that must have his Forehead, or first Entrance like a Courtier, *Faire-spoken,* and full of *Expectation.* His middle or Center like your Citizens ware-house, beautified with inticing vanities, though the true Riches consist of Bald Commodities. His Randevow or conclusion like The Lawyers Case, able to pocket up any matter: But let good word be your best *Evidence.* In the Generall, or Foundation he must be like *Paules-Church,* resolved to let every *Knight* and *Gull* travell upon him, yet his Particulars, or Lyneaments may be Royall at the *Exchange,* with attending steps, promising Newe but costly devices & fashions: It must have Teeth like a *Satyre,* Eyes like a *Cryticke,* and yet may your Tongue speake false *Latine,* like your Panders and Bawdes of *Poetrie.* Your *Genius* and *Species* should march in battle aray with our Politicians: yet your *Genius* ought to live with an honest soule indeed. It should be like the *Never-too-well read Arcadia,* where the *Prose* and *Verce,* (*Matter* and *Words*) are like his *Mistresses* eyes one still excelling another and without Corivall: or to come home to the vulgars *Element,* like *Friendly Shake-speares Tragedies,* where the *Commedian* rides, when the *Tragedian* stands on Tip-toe: Faith it should please all, like Prince *Hamlet.* But in sadnesse, then it were to be feared he would runne mad: Insooth I will not be moone-sicke to please: nor out of my wits though I displeased all. What? *Poet,* are you in Passion, or out of Love? This is as *Strange as True*: Well, well if I seeme misticall, or tyrannicall, whether I be a *Foole* or a *Lords- Ingle,* alls one: If you be angry, you are not well advised. I will tell you, tis an Indian *Humour,* I have snuft up from divine *Tabacco*: and tis most Gentleman-like to puffe it out at any place or person. Ile no *Epistle,* (it were worse then one of *Hercules* Labours) But will conclude, honesty is a mans best vertue. And but for the *Lord Mayor,* and the two *Sheriffes,* the Innes of

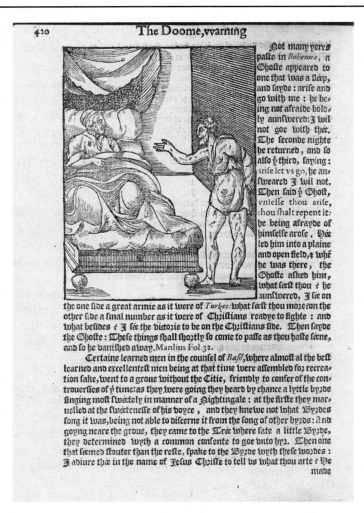

Page from Stephen Bateman's The Doome warning all men to the Judgement *(1581)*. Belief in ghosts was widespread in Shakespeare's era, and the playwright used apparitions in Hamlet *and other plays (by permission of the Folger Shakespeare Library).*

Court, and many Gallants elsewhere this last yeare might have bene burned. As for *Momus,* Carpe and Barke who will: of the *Noble Asse* bray not, I am as good a Knight Poet, as *Etatis suæ,* Maister *An. Dom.* Sonne in Law. Let your *Cryticke* looke to the Rowels of his spurs, the pad of his Saddle, and the Jerke of his Wand: then let him ride me and my Rimes as hotely as he would ride his Mistresse, I care not: We shall meete and be friends againe, with the breaking of a Speare or two: And who would do lesse, for a faire Lady. There I leave you, where you shall ever finde me.

Passionate *Daiphantus*: Your loving *Subject,*

Gives you to understand, *He is A man in Print,* and tis enough he hath under-gone a *Pressing* (yet not like a *Ladie*) though for your sakes and for *Ladyes,* protesting for this poore Infant of his Brayne, as it was the price of his *Virginitie* borne into the world in teares; So (but for a many his deare friends that tooke much paines for it) it had dyed and never bene laught at: And that if *Truth* have wrote lesse than *Fixion,* yet tis better to erre in Knowlege then in Judgment. Also if he have caught up half a Line of any others, It was out of his *Memorie* not of any ignorance. Why, he Dedicates it to all, and not to any Particular, as his *Mistresse,* or So. His answere is, he is better Borne, than to creepe into *Womens Favours,* and aske their leave afterwards. Also he desireth you to helpe Correct such errors of the Printer; which because the *Authour* is dead (or was out of the Citie) hath beene committed. And twas his folly, or the *Stationers,* You had not an *Epistle* to the purpose.

Thus like a Lover, wooes he for your Favor,
Which if You grant then *Omnia vincit Amor.* . . .

—sigs. A2r–v

Daiphantus's love-induced madness seems modeled on the behavior of Shakespeare's Hamlet, *particularly as Orphelia describes him in act 2, scene 1.*

At length he grew, as in an extasie
Twixt love and love, whose beautie was the truer,
His thoughts thus divers as in a Lunacie,
He starts and stares, to see whose was the purer:
    Oft treads a Maze, runs, suddenly then stayes,
    Thus with himselfe himself makes many frayes.

Now with his fingers, like a Barber snaps,
Playes with the fire-pan, as it were a Lute,
Unties his shoe-strings, then his lips he laps,
Whistles awhile, and thinkes it is a Flute:
    At length, a glasse presents it to his sight,
    Where well he acts, fond love in passions right.

His chin he strokes, sweares beardles men kisse best,
His lips anoynts, sayes Ladyes use such fashions,
Spets on his Napkin; termes that the Bathing Jest,
Then on the dust, describes the Courtiers passion.
    Then humble cal's: though they do still aspire,
    Ladies then fall, when Lords rise by Desire.

Then stradling goes, saies Frenchmen feare no Beares
Vowes he will travaile, to the Siege of *Brest*,
Swears Captaines, they doe all against the heare:
Protests Tabacco, is A smoke-dride Jest,
    Takes up his pen, for a Tabacco-pipe;
    Thus all besmeard, each lip the other wipe.

His breath, he thinkes the smoke, his tongue a cole,
Then calls for bottell ale; to quench his thirst:
Runs to his Inke-pot, drinkes, then stops the hole,
And thus growes madder, then he was at first.
    Tasso, he finds, by that of *Hamlet*, thinkes
    Tearmes him a mad-man; than of his Inkhorne drinks.

Calls Players fooles, the foole he judgeth wisest,
Will learne them Action, out of *Chaucers* Pander:
Proves of their Poets bawdes even in the highest,
The drinkes a health; and sweares it is no slander.
    Puts off his cloathes; his shirt he onely weares,
    Much like mad-*Hamlet*; thus as Passion teares.

Who calls me forth from my distracted thought?
Oh *Serberus*, if thou, I prethy speake?
Revenge if thou? I was thy Rivall ought,
In purple gores Ile make the ghosts to reake:
    Vitullia, oh *Vitullia*, be thou still,
    Ile have revenge, or harrow up my will.

                      –sigs. E4r–v

Ophelia

He took me by the wrist, and held me hard.
Then, goes he to the length of all his arm,
And with his other hand thus o'er his brow,
He falls to such perusal of my face
As 'a would draw it. Long stay'd he so.
At last, a little shaking of mine arm,
And thrice his head thus waving up and down,
He rais'd a sigh so piteous and profound
As it did seem to shatter all his bulk
And end his being. That done, he lets me go,
And with his head over his shoulder turn'd,
He seem'd to find his way without his eyes,
For out a'doore he went without their helps,
And to the last bended their light on me.

                      –Hamlet, 2.1.84–97

The King's Men
Paid for Court Performances

To John Hemynges one of his Majesties players uppon the Counselles warraunte dated at the Courte at Whitehalle xxi^mo die Januarii 1604 for the paines and expences of himselfe and his companie in playinge and presentinge of sixe Enterludes or plaies before his Majestie viz on all Saintes daie at nighte the Sonday at nighte followinge beinge the iiii^th of November 1604 St Stephens daie at nighte Innocentes day at nighte and on the vii^th and viii^th daies of Januarie for everie of the saide plaies accordinge to the usualle allowaunce of vi^li xiii^s iiii^d the peece xl^li and lxvi^s viii^d for everie plaie by waie of his Majesties rewarde xx^li in all the some of   lx^li

. . . .

To John Heminges one of his Majesties plaiers uppon the Counselles warraunte dated at the Courte at Whitehalle xxiiii^to die Februarii 1604 for himselfe and the reste of his companie for iiii^or Interludes or plaies presented by them before his Majestie at the Courte viz on Candlemas daie at nighte on Shrovesundaye at nighte Shrovemundaye at nighte and Shrovetuesdaie at nighte 1604 at vi^li xiii^s iiii^d for everie plaie and lxvi^s viii^d by waye of his Majesties rewarde for each playe in all the some of   xl^li

To the same John Heminges upon the Counselles Warraunte dated at the Courte at Grenewich xxviii^uo

die Aprilis 1605 for the paines and expences of himselfe and the reste of his companie for one enterlude
or plaie presented by them before his Majestie at the
Courte the third daye of Februarie 1604 vi^li xiii^s iiii^d
and to them more by waie of his Majesties rewarde
lxvi^s viii^d in all x^li

—*Dramatic Records, pp. 41–42*

1605

Publications

Richard III, *previously published in 1597, 1598,
and 1602, was published again. One other play,* The London Prodigall, *was published with Shakespeare named as
the author. The play is not thought to be by Shakespeare;
scholars assume an unscrupulous publisher used Shakespeare's name in order to improve sales.*

THE / TRAGEDIE / of King Richard / the third. /
Conteining his treacherous Plots again∫t his brother / Clarence: *the pittifull murther of his innocent Ne-* /
phewes: *his tyrannicall v∫urpation: with the* / *whole
cour∫e of his dete∫ted life, and* / mo∫t de∫erued
death. / *As it hath bin lately Acted by the Right Honourable*
/ *the Lord Chamberlaine his ∫eruants.* / Newly augmented, / By *William Shake-∫peare.* / [*Printer's device*] /
LONDON, / Printed by Thomas Creede, and are to
be ∫old by *Mathew* / *Lawe,* dwelling in Paules
Church-yard, at the Signe / of the Foxe, neare S.
Au∫tins gate, 1605.

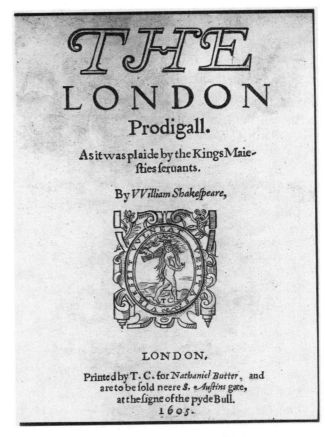

*Title page for a play that is only rarely credited to Shakespeare
(by permission of the Folger Shakespeare Library)*

Shakespeare Named in Phillips's Will

*In this excerpt from his will dated 4 May 1605
(PROB 11/105 s. 31) Shakespeare's fellow actor and
Globe sharer Augustine Phillips makes a bequest to Shake-
speare and other members of the King's Men.*

Item I give and bequeath unto and amongest the
hired men of the company wch I am of wch shall be at
the tyme of my decease the somme of five poundes
of lawfull money of England to be equally dystrib-
uted amongeste them Item I give and bequeath to
my fellowe William Shakespeare a xxx^s peece in
gould, To my fellow Henry Condell one other xxx^s
peece in gould To my servaunte [Christ]ofer Besone
xxx^s in gould, To my fellow Lawrence ffletcher xx^s
in gould, To my fellow Robte Armyne xx^s in gould
To my fellow Richard Cowley xx^s in gould To my
fellow Allexander Cooke xx^s in golde, To my fellow
Nicholas Tooley xx^s in gould.

Shakespeare Leases the Stratford Tithes

*The transcribed indenture here (Shakespeare Birthplace
Trust Records Office, ER 27/2) records Shakespeare's purchase
of a moiety, or share, in the Stratford tithes. Robert Bearman
explains the nature of this investment in* Shakespeare in the
Stratford Records *(1994):*

Tithes originated as a payment to the rector of a
parish of a tenth part of agricultural produce. Over the
years the right to the tithes of some parishes passed into
the hands of monasteries and other religious houses
who appointed a vicar and paid him out of the pro-
ceeds. When these foundations were suppressed during
the reigns of Henry VIII and Edward VI the rights to
such tithes passed, with their other possessions, into the
Crown's hands and were then liable to be sold off in
the same way as any other piece of property. In the
case of Stratford, the tithes had been appropriated in
the Middle Ages by the college of priests attached to
Holy Trinity Church. When, at the Reformation, this
college was suppressed, the ownership part of the tithes
(those of Old Stratford, Bishopton and Welcombe, and

the lesser tithes of the whole parish) was granted to the newly incorporated borough.

The owners of the tithes at this period rarely collected them themselves. Instead, for a fixed sum, they let the right to collect them to a tenant who was free to make what profit he could. At Stratford the college had in 1544 leased its tithes and other property for ninety-two years to William Barker, whose relative John sub-let them in 1580 to Sir John Hubaud. The situation then becomes extraordinarily confused; suffice it to say for our purposes that the lease of one half of the tithes of Old Stratford, Bishopton and Welcombe ended up in the hands of John's brother, Ralph Hubaud. This is what Shakespeare bought in 1605, subject to annual payments of £17 to the Corporation (as the owners) and a further £5 to John Barker, the principal sub-tenant. A few years later these tithes were actually valued at £60 a year, which would have left Shakespeare with an annual surplus in the region of £40. In ten years or so he would therefore have made good the £440 he had had to pay Hubaud; and for the remaining twenty-one years of the 1544 lease the £40 surplus would have been clear profit. (pp. 41–42)

In this transcription, names and legal abbreviations have been silently expanded; closing parentheses have been added. When the text proved illegible in the facsimiles, Lewis's transcription in The Shakespeare Documents *has been substituted and is shown in brackets.*

This Indenture made the ffowre & twentythe daye of Julye in the yeares of the Raigne of our Soveraigne Lorde James by the grace of god of Englande Scotlande ffraunce & Irelande Kinge Defender of the ffayeth &tc That is to saye of Englande ffraunce & Irelande the Thirde & of Scotlande the Eighte & Thirtythe Betweene Raphe Hubaude of Ippesley in the Countye of warrick Esquier on thone parte And William Shakespear of Stratforde upon Avon in the sayed Countye of warrick gentleman on thother parte Whereas Anthonye Barker Clarke late warden of the Colledge or Collegiate Churche of Stratforde upon Avon aforesayed in the sayed countye of warrick And Gyles Coventrie subwarden there And the whole Chapiter of the same Late Colledge by their Deade Indented Sealed with their Chapiter seale Dated the Seaventh daye of September in the Six & Thirtyth yeare of the Raigne of the late kinge of famous memorie kinge Henrye the Eighte Demysed graunted & to farme Lett amongste Diverse other thinges unto one William Barker of Sonnynge in the countye of Barkshire gentleman All & All manner of Tythes of Corne Grayne Blade & Heye yearelye & from tyme to tyme Comynge encreasinge Reneweinge Arrysinge groweinge yssueinge or Happeninge or to bee had recyved perceyved or taken out upon of or in the townes villages Hamlettes groundes & ffyeldes of Stratforde upon Avon Oldestratforde Welcombe &

Bushopton in the sayed Countye of warrick And Alsoe All & All manner of Tythes of wooll Lambe & other small & pryvie Tythes oblacions obvencions Alterages mynumentes & offeringes whatsoever yearelye & from tyme to tyme cominge encreasinge reneweinge or happeninge or to bee had recevyed perceyved or taken within the parishe of Stratforde upon Avon aforesayed in the sayed Countye of warrick by the name or names of All & singuler their Mannors Landes Tenementes meadowes pastures feedinges woodes underwoodes rentes revercions services Courtes leetes Releeves wardes marriages harriottes perquisites of Courtes liberties Jurisdiccions and all other hereditamentes withall & singuler other rightes commodities & their Appurtenaunces togeather with all manner of Parsonages Gleebe Landes Tythes Alterages oblacions obvencions mynumentes offeringes & All other issues proffittes Emolumentes & Advantages in the Countye of warrick or worcester or elce where whatsoever they bee unto the sayed then Colledge Apperteyninge (The mancion house & the Scite of the sayed Colledge with their Appurtenaunces within the precinctes of the walles of the sayed Colledge unto the sayed warden & subwarden onelye excepted) To have and to holde All the sayed Mannors Landes Tenementes & all other the premisses with all & singuler their Appurtenaunces (excepte before excepted) unto the sayed Colledge belonginge or in Anie wyse Apperteyninge unto the sayed William Barker his Executors & Assignes from the feast of St Michaell tharchangell then Laste paste before the Date of the sayed Indenture unto thend & terme of ffourescore & Twelve yeares then nexte ensueinge Yeldinge & payeinge therefore yearelye unto the sayed warden & subwarden & their Successors att the sayed Colledge Cxxii¹ xviiiˢ ix^d of lawfull money of Englande as more playnely appeareth by the sayed Indenture And Whereas Alsoe the revercion of All & singuler the sayed premisses (Amonge other thinges by vertue of the Acte of Parliament made in the ffyrst yeare of Raigne of the late soveraigne Lorde kinge Edwarde the Sixte for the Dissolucion of Chauntries Colledges & ffree Chappels or by some other meanes) Came to the handes & possession of the sayed Late kinge Edwarde And Whereas the sayed Late kinge Edwarde the Sixte beinge seised as in right of his Crowne of Englande of & in the revercion of All & singler the premisses by his Lettres Patentes bearinge Date the Eight & twentyth Daye of June in the Seaventh yeare of his raigne for the Consideracion therein expressed Did gyve & graunte unto the Baylief & Burgesses of Stratforde aforesayed & to their Successors Amonge other thinges All & All manner of the sayed Tythes of Corne graine & Heye Comynge encreasinge or Arrysinge in the Villages & ffyeldes of Oldestratforde

Pages from financial accounts in which are recorded performances of several of Shakespeare's plays before James I and the court. Between 1 November 1604 and the beginning of Lent in 1605, the King's Men performed seven plays by Shakespeare: Othello *(The Moor of Venis),* The Merry Wives of Windsor *(Merry wives of winsor),* Measure for Measure *(Mesur for Mesur),* The Comedy of Errors *(The plaie of: Errors),* Love's Labor's Lost *(A play of Loves Labours Lost),* Henry V *(Henry the fift), and* The Merchant of Venice *(A play of the Marchant of Venis) (PRO Audit Office 3/908/13, folio 2r–v; courtesy of the Public Records Office, London).*

The plaiers	On Twelfe Night	The poete
	A Maske & moures with tth steven layticit of th omis to Attu payneo for ma no ht camy in great showes off debiste with th pay sett In with ep etlent musike	
By his Ma^tis plaiers:	On the: 7: off January was played the play off Henry the fift:	
By his Ma^tis plaiers:	The: 8: off January: A play Cauled Euery on out of his Tmor	
By his Ma^tis plaiers:	On Candelmas night A play Euery one In his Tmor	
	The Sunday following A playe probied And disspreged	
By his Ma^tis plaiers:	On Shrousunday A play off the Marthant of Vems	Shaxberd
By his Ma^tis plaiers:	On Shroumonday A Tragidy of the Spamshe Maz:	
By his Ma^tis plaiers:	On Shroutusday A play Cauled The Martchant of Venis Againe Comanded By the Kings Matie	Shaxberd:

welcombe & Bushopton aforesayed in the sayed Countye of warrick then or Late in the tenure of John Barker & to the late Colledge of Stratforde upon Avon in the sayed countye of warrick of late belonginge & Apperteyninge & parcell of the possessions thereof beinge And alsoe All & All manner of the sayed Tythes of wooll Lambe & other smalle & pryvie tythes oblacions & Alterages whatsoever within the parishe of Stratford upon Avon aforesayed & to the sayed late Colledge of Oldstratforde upon Avon belonginge or apperteyninge & then or Late in the tenure of William Barker or of his Assignes And the Revercion & Revercions whatsoever of All & singler the sayed Tythes & everye parte & parcell thereof And the Rentes revenues & other yearelye proffittes whatsoever Reserved upon anye Demise or graunte of the sayed Tythes or anie parte or parcell thereof And Whereas Alsoe the interest of the sayed premisses in the sayed originall lease mencioned and the interest of Certein Copieholdes in Shotterie in the parishe of Stratford aforesayed beinge by good & lawfull Conveyans & Assurance in the Lawe before that tyme conveyed & Assured to John Barker of Hurste in the sayed countye of Berkshire Hee the sayed John Barker by his Indenture bearinge Date the ffoure & twentyth Daye of June in the twoe & twentythe yeare of the Raigne of the late Queene Elizabeth for the Consideracions therein specifyed Did gyve graunte Assigne & sett over unto Sir John Hubaude Knighte brother of the sayed Raphe Hubaude All & singuler the sayed laste mencioned premisses And all his estate right title & interest that hee then had to come of in & to all & singuler the sayed premisses and of all other mannors Messuages landes Tenementes gleebe landes tythes oblacions Commodities & proffittes in the sayed originall lease mencioned for & duringe All the yeares & terme then to come unexpired in the sayed originall lease (exceptinge as in & by the sayed laste mencioned Indenture is excepted as by the same Indenture more att large maye Appeare) To Have & To holde All & singuler the sayed recyted premisses (excepte before excepted) to the sayed Sir John Hubaude his Executors and Assignes for & duringe the yeares then to come of & in the same yeldinge & payeinge therefore yearelye after the ffeast of St Michaell tharchangell nexte ensueinge the Date of the sayed laste mencioned Indenture for & duringe all the yeares mencioned in the sayed first mencioned Indenture then to come & not expired unto the sayed John Barker his executors Administrators and Assignes one Annuall or yearelye Rente of Twentye Seaven Poundes Thirteene shillinges ffoure Pence by the yeare to be yssueinge & goeinge out of All the Mannors Landes Tenementes Tythes & hereditamentes in the sayed Indenture specyfied To bee payed yearlye to the sayed John Barker his executors Admin-

istrators & Assignes by the sayed Sir John Hubaude his executors Administrators & Assignes Att the ffeastes of the Anunciacion of our Ladye & St Michaell tharchangell or within ffortye dayes after the sayed ffeastes in the Porche of the parishe Churche of Stratford aforesayed by even porcions And further payeinge doeinge and performinge All suche other Rentes Dutyes & servyces as att anie tyme from thencefourth & from tyme to tyme for & duringe the terme aforesayed shoulde become due to anie personne or personns for the same premisses or anie parte thereof and thereof to discharge the sayed John Barker his executors & Administrators And yf yt shoulde happen the sayed Twentye Seaven Poundes thirteene shillinges ffoure pence to bee behinde & unpayed in parte or in All by the space of ffortye Dayes nexte after anie of the sayed ffeastes or Daies of payement in which as is aforesayed it ought to bee payed beinge lawfullie asked That then yt shoulde bee lawfull to & for the sayed John Barker his executors Administrators & Assignes into All & singuler the premisses with their Appurtenaunces & everye parte & parcell thereof to reenter & the same to have againe as in his or their former righte And that then & from thenceforthe the sayed recyted Indenture of Assignement and everye Article Covenaunte Clause provisoe & Agreement therein conteyned on the parte & behalfe of the sayed John Barker his executors Administrators & Assignes to bee performed should Ceasse & bee utterlie voyde & of none effect with Diverse other Covenauntes grauntes Articles & Agreementes in the sayed Indenture of Assignementes specified to bee observed & performed by the sayed Sir John Hubaude his executors & Assignes As in & by the sayed recyted Indenture it Doth & maye Appeare And Whereas the sayed Sir John Hubaude Did by his Deade Obligatorie bynd himself and his heires to the sayed John Barker in A greate some of money for the performance of All & singuler the Covenauntes grauntes Articles & Agreementes which on the parte of the sayed Sir John Hubaud were to bee observed & performed conteyned & specyfied as well in the sayed recyted Indenture of Assignment as alsoe in one other Indenture bearinge the date of the sayed recyted Indenture of Assignement made betweene the sayed John Barker on theone partie and the sayed Sir John Hubaude on thother partie As by the sayed Deade obligatorie more att large it doth & maye Appeare And Whereas Alsoe the sayed Sir John Hubaude by his laste will & testament in writinge Did gyve & bequeath unto his Executors amongst other thinges the Moytie or one half of All & singuler the sayed Tythes aswell greate as smalle before mencioned to bee graunted to the sayed Baylyffe & Burgesses of Stratford for & duringe soe Longe tyme & untill of the yssues & proffittes thereof soe much as with other thinges in his sayed will to that purposse willed Lymitted or Appointed shoulde bee sufficient to Discharge beare & paye his funeralls Debtes & Legacies And alsoe by his sayed laste will & testament did gyve & bequeath the other moytie or one half of the sayed Tythes unto the sayed Raphe Hubaude & his assignes duringe All the yeares to come in the sayed ffirst mencioned Indenture & not expired payeinge the one half of the rentes & other Charges Dewe or goeinge out of or for the same That is to saye the one half of Tenne poundes by yeare to bee payed to the sayed John Barker over & above the rentes thereof reserved upon the sayed originall lease for the same As by the sayed will & testament more playnelye Appeareth This Indenture nowe witnesseth that the sayed Raphe Hubaude for & in consideracion of the somme of ffoure Hundred & ffourtye Poundes of lawfull Englishe money to him by the sayed William Shakespeare before thensealinge & Deliverye of thees presentes well & truelye contented & payed whereof & of everye parte & parcell whereof hee the sayed Raphe Hubaude dothe by thees presentes acknowledge the Receipt And thereof & of everye parte & parcell thereof dothe clerely acquite exonerate & discharge the sayed the sayed William Shakespear his Executors and Administrators forever by thees presentes Hathe Demised graunted Assigned & sett over & by thees presentes Dothe Demise graunte Assigne & sett over unto the sayed William Shakespear his executors & Assignes the xxxx Moytie or one half of All & singuler the sayed Tythes of Corne grayne blade & heye yearelye & from tyme to tyme cominge encreasinge Reneweinge Arrysinge groweinge issueinge or happenynge or to bee had receyved perceyved or taken out of upon or in the Townes villages hamlettes groundes & ffyeldes of Stratforde Oldestratforde welcombe & Bushopton aforesayed in the sayed Countye of warrick And Alsoe the xxxx Moytie or one half of All & singuler the sayed Tythes of wooll Lambe & other smalle & Pryvie Tythes Herbage oblacions obvencions Alterages mynumentes & offeringes whatsoever yearelye & from tyme to tyme cominge encreasinge reneweinge or happeninge or to bee had receyved perceyved or taken within the parishe of Stratforde upon Avon aforesayed And Alsoe the Moytie or one half of All & All manner of Tythes as well great as smalle whatsoever which were by the laste will & testament of the sayed Sir John Hubaude Gyven & bequeathed to the sayed Raphe Hubaude Arrysing encreasinge reneweinge or groweinge within the sayed Parishe of Stratforde upon Avon And whereof the sayed Raphe Hubaude hath att anie tyme heretofore been or of right ought to have been possessed or whereunto hee nowe hath or att anie tyme hereafter should have Anie

estate right or interest in possession or Revercion And All thestate right tytle interest terme claime & Demaunde whatsoever of the sayed Raphe Hubaude of in & to all & singuler the premisses hereby lastelye mencioned to bee graunted & assigned & everie or anie parte or parcell thereof And the Revercion & Revercions of all & singuler the sayed premisses And All & singuler Rentes & yearely proffyttes Reserved upon Anie Demise graunte or Assignement thereof or of anie parte or partes thereof heretofore made (The Pryvie Tythes of Luddington And suche parte of the Tythe Heye & pryvie Tythes of Bushopton as of Right Doe belonge to the vicar Curate or minister there for the tyme beinge Always excepted & foreprised) To have and to holde All & everye the sayed Moyties or one halfe of All & singuler the sayed Tythes before in & by thees presentes lastelye mencioned to bee graunted & Assigned & everye parte & parcell of them & everye of them And All thestate righte tytle & intereste of the sayed Raphe Hubaud of in & to the same And All other thafore Demised premisses & everye parte & parcell thereof (except before excepted) unto the sayed William Shakespear his Executors & Assignes from the Daye of the Date hereof for & duringe the Residewe of the sayed terme of ffourescore & twelve yeares in the sayed first recyted Indenture mencioned & for suche & soe Longe terme & tyme & in as large ample & benefyciall manner as the sayed Raphe Hubaude shoulde or oughte enjoye the same Yeldinge & payeinge therefore yearely duringe the Residewe of the sayed terme of ffourescore & twelve yeares which bee yet to come & unexpired the rentes hereafter mencioned in manner and forme followeinge That is to saye unto the Baylyffe & Burgesses of Stratford aforesaied & their Successors the yearelye rent of Seaventeene poundes Att the ffeastes of S Michaell tharchangell & the Anunciacion of blessed Marye the virgin by equall porcions And unto the sayed John Barker his Executors Administrators or Assignes the Annuall or yearelye rente of ffyve Poundes Att the ffeaste Dayes & place lymitted appointed & mencioned in the sayed recyted Indenture of Assignement made by the sayed John Barker or within ffortye Dayes after the sayed feaste Dayes by even porcions As parcell of the sayed Annuall Rent of twentye Seaven Poundes Thirteene shillinges foure pence in the sayed Assignement mencioned And the sayed Raphe Hubaude Dothe by thees presentes for him his heires executors & Administrators Covenaunte & graunte to & with the sayed William Shakespear his executors administrators & Assignes That Hee the sayed Raphe Hubaude Att the tyme of thensealinge & Delyverie of thees presentes hath & att the tyme of the first Execucion or intencion of anie execucion of Anie estate by force of thees presentes shall Have full power & lawfull & sufficient Aucthoritie certeinlie suerlye & absolutelie to graunte Demise Assigne & sett over All & everye the sayed Moyties or one Halfe of All & singuler the sayed Tythes & other the premisses before in thees presentes lastelye Mencioned to bee Assigned & sett over & everye parte & parcell thereof unto the sayed William Shakespear his executors & assignes accordinge to the true meaninge of thees presentes And Alsoe that the sayed William Shakespear his executors Administrators or assignes shall & maye from tyme to tyme & att all tymes duringe the Residewe of the sayed terme of ffoure score & Twelve yeares yet to come & unexpired for the yearelye severall Rentes above by thees presentes reserved peaceablie lawfullye & quietlie have holde occupie, possesse & enjoye All & everye the sayed Moyties or one halfe of All & singuler the sayed Tythes of Corne graine blade Heye woolle lambe & other small & pryvie Tythes Herbage oblacions obvencions offeringes & other the premisses before by thees presentes graunted & assigned & everye parte & parcell thereof (excepte before excepted) without anie lett trouble entire distresse claime Deniall interrupcion or molestacion whatsoever of the sayed Raphe Hubaude his executors Administrators or Assignes or of anie other personne or personnes havinge or clayminge to have or which att anie tyme or tymes hereafter shall or maye have or claime to have anie thinge of in or to the afore graunted premisses or anie parte thereof by from or under the sayed Raphe Hubaud his executors Administrators or Assignes or anie of them or by from or under the sayed Sir John Hubaude or by their or anie of their meanes consent forfeiture act or procurement And without anie Lawfull lett trouble distresse claime Denyall entrie or demaunde whatsoever other then for the sayed yearely rent of Twentye seaven poundes thirteene shillinges ffoure pence by the sayed recyted assignement reserved of the sayed John Barker his executors Administrators or Assignes or anie of them or of anie personne or personnes clayeming by from or under them or anie of them Thestate & interest of the Lorde Carewe of in & to the Tythes of Bridgtowne & Ryen Clyfforde & the interest of Sir Edwarde Grevill knight of & in the Moytie of the Tythe Heye woolle lambe & other smalle & pryvie Tythes oblacions obvencions offeringes & proffittes before by thees presentes graunted & assigned unto the sayed William Shakespear which is to endure untill the feast of St Michaell tharchangell next ensueinge the Date hereof & noe longer onelye excepted & foreprised And the sayed Raphe Hubaude doth by thees presentes for him his heires executors & administrators Covenaunte & graunte to & with the

sayed William Shakespear his executors Administrators & Assignes That All & everye the sayed Moyties of the sayed Tythes before mencioned to be graunted to the sayed William Shakespear & other the premisses (except before excepted) nowe are & soe from tyme to tyme & att All tymes hereafter during the Residewe of the saied terme of ffourescore & Twelve yeares yet to come & unexpired according to the true meaninge hereof shalbe remaine & Contynewe unto the sayed William his executors or Assignes ffree & Clere & freelye & clerelye acquyted exonerated & discharged or well & sufficientlie saved & kept harmelesses of & from All & All manner of bargaines sales guiftes Assignementes leases Recognizances statutes mercheant & of the Staple outlaries Judgementes execucions titles troubles Charges encumbraunces & Demaundes whatsoever heretofore had made done committed omitted or suffered or hereafter to bee had made Done committed omitted or suffered by the sayed Raphe Hubaude Sir John Hubaude & John Barker or anie of them their or anie of their executors administrators or Assignes or anie of them or anie personne or personnes whatsoever Clayminge by from or under them or anie of them or by their or anie of their meanes Act title graunte forfeiture [consent or procurement (except before excepted) and alsoe that Hee the sayed] Raphe Hubaude his executors administrators & assignes shall & will from tyme to tyme & att all tymes duringe the space of Three yeares next ensueing upon reasonable Requeste & att the Costes & charges in the lawe of the sayed William Shakespear his executors or assignes Doe performe & execute & cause permitt and suffer to bee Done performed & executed All & everye suche further & reasonable Acte & Actes thinge & thinges devyse and devyses in the Lawe whatsoever bee yt or they by anie meane course Acte Devise or Assurans in the lawe whatsoever As by the sayed William Shakespear his executors or assignes or his or their learned Councell shalbe reasonablie Devised advised or Required for the Confirmacion of thees presentes or for the further or more better or firmer Assurans suertye suermakinge & Conveyeinge of All & singler the premisses before by thees presentes Demised & assigned or ment or intended to bee Demised & assigned & everye parte & parcell thereof unto the sayed William Shakespear his executors & assignes for & duringe all the residewe of the sayed terme of ffourescore & twelve yeare which bee yet to come & unexpired According to the tenor & true meaninge of thees presentes Soe as the sayed the sayed Raphe Hubaude his executors or Assignes bee not hereby compelled to travell from Ippesley aforesayed for the Doeinge thereof and the sayed William Shakespear doth by thees presentes for him his heires executors & administrators Covenaunte & graunte to & with the sayed Raphe Hubaude his executors administrators & assignes That hee the sayed William Shakespeare his executors administrators or assignes shall & will Duringe the Residewe of the sayed terme of ffourescore & twelve yeares which bee yet to comme & unexpired yearelie content & paye the severall rentes above mencioned vidlt Seaventene poundes to the Baylief & burgesses of Stratford aforesayed & fyve poundes to the sayed John Barker his executors or assignes att the Dayes & places aforesayed in which it ought to bee payed accordinge to the purporte & true meaninge of thees presentes And thereof shall & will Discharge the saied Raphe Hubaude his executors Administrators & assignes In witnes whereof the partyes abovesayed to thees presentes interchangeablie have sett their seales the Daie & yeare ffyrst above written.

Raffe Hubaud.
Sealed and delivered in the presence of

William Hubaud
Antony Nasshe
Fra: Collyns

Hubaud's Bond to Shakespeare

Lewis notes that Ralph Hubaud's bond to Shakespeare for the lease of the Stratford Tithes, dated 24 July 1605, is a "thoroughly conventional procedure" that Shakespeare used to guarantee that Hubaud would keep his end of the bargain.

Nouerint universi per presentes me Radulphum Huband de Ippesley in comitatu Warwici, armigerum, teneri et firmiter obligari Willielmo Shakespear de Stratforde super Avon in dicto comitatu Warwici, generoso, in octingentis libris bone et legalis monete Anglie solvendis eidem Willielmo, aut suo certo attornato, executoribus vel assignatis suis, ad quam quidem solucionem bene et fideliter faciendam obligo me, heredes, executores et administratores meos, firmiter per presentes sigillo meo sigillatas. Datum vicesimo quarto die Julii, annis regni domini nostri Jacobi, Dei gracia Anglie, Scocie, Francie et Hibernie regis, fidei defensoris, &c. scilicet, Anglie, Francie et Hibernie tercio & Scocie tricesimo octavo.

The condicion of this obligacion is suche that if thabove bounden Raphe Hubande, his heires, executors, administrators and assignes, and everye of them, shall and doe, from tyme to tyme and att all tymes, well and truelye observe, performe, fulfill and keepe all and everye covenaunte, graunte, article, clause, sentence and thinge mencioned, expressed and declared, in a certein writinge indented, bearinge date with thees presentes, made betweene the sayed Raphe Hubande on thone parte and the abovenamed William Shakespear on thother parte, and which, on the parte and behalf of the saied Raphe, his heires, executors, administrators and assignes, or anie of them, are to bee observed, performed, fulfilled or kept, according to the purporte and true meaninge of the saied writinge, that then this present obligacion to bee voyde and of none effect, or els to stand and abide in full force, power and vertue.

Raffe Huband
Sealed and delivered in the presens of

William Huband
Antony Nasshe
Fra Collyns

[Know all men by these presents that I Ralph Huband, armiger, of Ipsley, in the county of Warwick am held and firmly bound to William Shakespeare, gentleman, of Stratford-on-Avon in the said county of Warwick in the sum of eighty pounds of good and legal English money to be paid to the same William or his certain attorney, executors, or assigns, to the certain payment of which I firmly bind myself, my heirs, executors, and administrators by these presents, sealed with my seal. Given the twenty-fourth day of July in the year of the reign of our master James, by the grace of God, King of England, Scotland, Ireland, and France, and Defender of the Faith, etc., to-wit: the third year of his reign over England, France, and Ireland and the thirty-eighth year of his reign over Scotland.]

–Lewis, *Shakespeare Documents,* pp. 384–385

Allusion to Shakespeare in Poulett's Letter to Vincent

The casual reference to Shakespeare in this 10 October 1605 letter from John Poulett, a twenty-year-old who was touring the Continent as the culmination of his education, to his uncle Sir Francis Vincent (British Library Additional Manuscript 11757, fols. 105–106b) is a good indication of Shakespeare's contemporary reputation. The text of this letter is an edited version of Hilton Kelliher's transcription in "A Shakespeare Allusion of 1605 and Its Author."

Sir I receaved your letter the 8th of October, which by the date you gave him, seemed to be long a comming, yet was it never the lesse wellcomme, comming from your selfe, and bringing so good news. I would I knewe how to expresse sufficientlye to my

Aunt, the joye I hadde to heare her desyre accomplished, for I remembre, to have heard her often wish for an other daughter. I have beene so wearyed with traveling this sommer, that synce my comming to this towne I have beene sicke, but (I thanke god) am now well agayne, and my Lo: Norreys hath taken the reversion of my sicknesse, which (I feare me) will not Leave him so soone; wee came out of Spayne together with an intention to have gone into the Lowe Countryes but these accidents of sicknesse, have hyndred us so long that the tyme of the yeare is now past, and the armyes gone into Garison: There are verye lyke to be warres in this countrye forthwith, for the King is in the field with a verye galant Armye, and hath marched above a 100 - and 60 miles, so that we daylye looke for somme exploite; I thanke you, for putting me in mynd to write to my Lo: Cheefe Justice, I have written to him twice allreadye, once from this place, agayne out of Spayne, but I perceave he hath not receaved any, I have written to him now agayne, which I hope he will receave. I am gladde to heare you are so well hawked, I shall manye tymes this winter, in a delicious morning wish my selfe with you one the top of Burtrig, and to eate a coke and bacon. I praye yf you hawk at Sydberye this winter to remember me to Sir Thomas Prediox, and Mistress More; Thus leaving you in the myddest of your Sportes, (which in respect of those which this countrye allowes, seeme rather fitt for Ladyes then, for Cavalliers: wee for to passe the winters bitter cold, doe with a Javelin chasse the brisseled bore, and sometymes, mounted one a fowming Curtol, doe rend the woods to hounde the furious bulle, and sometymes for to have more gentle sport doe hunt the fearfull Roe, these did I offten see the Last winter, and now the season commeth in agayne; the danger in these sports makes them seeme good, men seeme in them as actors in a Tragedye, and my thinkes I could play Shackesbeare in relating; Sir I hadde leaft you in your sports a greate whyle agone, but this desyre to relate you our tragicke sports made me forgett when to take my Leave; yf I knew how to gossope, I should use a greate manye gossoping Phrases, (you may thanke god I cannot) that you be not troubled with delivering them.) I will onlye commend my best love to your selfe and my Aunt, and without any more ceremonie[s], take my leave allwayes resting

> Your Most assured loving
> Nephew.
> Jo: Poulett:

> Paris the 10th of
> October. 1605.
> —*The British Library Journal*, 3, no. 1 (1977): 7–12

Allusion to *Hamlet* in *Ratseis Ghost*

In the anonymous prose narrative Ratseis Ghost. or The second Part of his madde Prankes and Robberies *(1605), Gamaliell Ratsey has a variety of adventures, including one in which he finds an actor worthy of playing the part of Hamlet. The following excerpt describes some of the difficulties early modern actors faced on provincial tours, illustrates the risks of misbehaving while under the protection of an aristocratic patron, and offers advice for actors who want to join a London company.*

A pretty prancke passed by *Ratsey*, upon certaine
Players that he met by chance in an Inne; who
denied their owne Lord and Maister,
and used another Noble-
mans name.

Gamaliell Ratsey and his company, travailing up and downe the Countrey, (as they had often times done before) *per varios casus, & tot discrimina rerum*; still hazarding their severall happes as they had severall hopes; came by chance into an Inne, where that night there harbored a company of Players: and *Ratsey* framing himselfe to an humor of merriment, caused one or two of the chiefest of them to be sent for up into his chamber, where hee demanded whose men they were, and they answered they served such an honorable Personage. I pray you (quoth *Ratsey*) let me heare your musicke, for I have often gone to plaies more for musicke sake, then for action. For some of you not content to do well, but striving to over-doe and go beyond your selves, oftentimes (by S. *George*) mar all; yet your Poets take great paines to make your parts fit for your mouthes, though you gape never so wide. Othersome I must needs confesse, are very wel deserving both for true action and faire deliverie of speech, and yet I warrant you the very best have sometimes beene content to goe home at night with fifteene pence share apeece.

Others there are whom Fortune hath so wel favored, that what by penny-sparing and long practise of playing, are growne so wealthy, that they have expected to be knighted, or at least to be conjunct in authority, and to sit with men of great worship, on the Bench of Justice. But if there were none wiser then I am, there should more Cats build Colledges, and more whoores turne honest women then one, before the world should be filled with such a wonder.

Well, musicke was plaide, and that night passed over with such singing, dauncing, and revelling, as if my Lord Prodigall hadde beene there in his ruines of excesse and superfluitie. In the morning

Ratsey made the Players taste of his bountie, and so departed.

But everie day hee had new inventions to obtaine his purposes: and as often as fashions alter, so often did he alter his Stratagems, studying as much how to compasse a poore mans purse, as Players doe, to win a full audience.

About a weeke after hee met with the same Players, although hee had so disguised himselfe with a false head of hayre and beard, that they could take no notice of him, and lying as they did before in one Inne together, hee was desirous they should play a private play before him, which they did not in the name of the former Noblemans servants. For like Camelions they had changed that colour; but in the name of another, (whose indeede they were) although afterwardes when he heard of their abuse, hee discharged them, and tooke away his warrant. For being far off, (for their more countenance) they would pretend to be protected by such an honourable man, denying their Lord and Maister; and comming within ten or twenty miles of him againe, they would shrowd themselves under their owne Lords favour.

Ratsey heard their Play, and seemed to like that, though he disliked the rest, and verie liberally out with his purse, and gave them fortie shillings, with which they held themselves very richly satisfied, for they scarce had twentie shillings audience at any time for a Play in the Countrey. But *Ratsey* thought they should not enjoy it long, although he let them beare it about them till the next day in their purses. For the morning being come, and they having packt away their luggage, and some part of their companie before in a Waggon, discharged the house, and followed them presently.

Ratsey intended not to bee long after: but having learned which way they travailed, hee being verie wel horsed, and mounted upon his blacke gelding soone overtooke them. And when they saw it was the Gentleman that had beene so liberall with them the night before, they beganne to doe him much courtesie, and to greete his late kindesse with many thankes. But that was not the matter which he aymed at: therefore he roundly tolde them, they were deceived in him, hee was not the man they tooke him for. I am a Souldier (sayth he) and one that for meanes hath ventured my fortunes abroade, and now for money am driven to hazard them at home. I am not to bee played upon by Players: therefore, be short, deliver mee your money, I will turne Usurer now, my fortie shillings againe will not serve without interest they beganne to make many faces, and to cappe and [kneel?], but all would not serve their turne. Hee bade them leave off their cringing, and complements, and their apish trickes, and dispatch: Which they did, for feare of the worst, seeing to begge

was bootelesse. And having made a desperate tender of their stocke into *Ratseyes* handes, he had them play for more, for (sayes hee) it is an idle profession that brings in much profite, & every night where you come, your playing beares your charges, and somewhat into purses besides you have Fidlers fare, meat, drink & mony. If the worst be, it is but pawning your apparell, for as good actors and stalkers as you are have done it, though now they scorne it: but in any case heereafter be not counterfaites, abuse not honorable Personages, in using their names and countenance without their consent and privitie. And because you are now destitute of a Maister, I will give you leave to play under my protection for a senights space, and I charge you doe it, lest when I meet you again, I cut you shorter by the hams, and share with you in a sharper manner, then I have done at this time. And for you (sirra saies hee to the chiefest of them) thou hast a good presence upon a stage, me thinks thou darkenst thy merite by playing in the country: Get thee to London, for if one man were dead, they will have much neede of such a one as thou art. There would be none in my opinion, fitter then thy selfe to play his parts: my conceipt is such of thee, that I durst venture all the mony in my purse on thy head, to play Hamlet with him for a wager, There thou shalt learne to be frugall (for Players were never so thriftie as they are now about London) & to feed upon all men, to let none feede upon thee; to make thy hand a stranger to thy pocket, thy hart slow to performe thy tongues promise: and when thou feelest thy purse well lined, buy thou some place or Lordship in the Country, that growing weary of playing, thy mony may there bring thee to dignitie and reputation: then thou needest care for no man, nor not for them that before made thee prowd, with speaking their words upon the Stage. Sir, I thanke you (quoth the Player) for this good counsell, I promise you I will make use of it; for I have heard indeede, of some that have gone to London very meanly, and have come in time to be exceeding wealthy. And in this presage and propheticall humor of mine, (sayes *Ratsey*) kneele downe, Rise up Sir *Simon* two shares and a halfe: Thou art now one of my Knights, and the first Knight that ever was Player in England. The next time I meete thee, I must share with thee againe for playing under my warrant, and so for this time adiew.

How ill hee brooked this new knighthood, which hee durst not but accept of, or liked his late counsell, which he lost his coine for, is easie to be imagined. But whether he met with them againe after the senights space, that he charged them to play in his name, I have not heard it reported.

—sigs. A3v–Bv

Allusion to *2 Henry IV* in Breton's *A Poste with a Packet of madde Letters*

Among the mocking exchanges in poet Nicholas Breton's A Poste with a Packet of madde Letters. *The first part (1605), a collection of fictional letters, is the following reply to the insulting "A Letter of scorne to a coy Dame."*

Maister *Swash*, it is not your hufty rufty, can make me afraid of your bigge lookes: for I saw the plaie of Ancient *Pistoll*, where a craking coward was well cudgeled for his knavery: your railing is so neere the Rascal, that I am almost ashamed to bestow so good a name as the rogue upon you: but for modesties sake, I will a little forbeare you, & onely tell you, that a hanging looke, and a hollow heart, a cunning wit, & a corrupted conscience, will make you so fit a mate for the divel, that there is no christian wil desire your company: now for your state, it is much upon fortune, which brings many of your fellows to a deadly fal, when the paine of their heads is only healed with a halter: & for your linage, when the bearewards Ape, and the hangmans monky met together on a hay mowe, what a whelp came of such a litter, let the world judge, I say nothing: now for your stump feet, & your lame hand, suting kindly with your wry neck, who would not make of their eyes, that could indure the sight of such a picture? now, your wealth being but a fewe words, which you have almost all spent in idle humors, hoping that the Tortus will not quarell with the Crabbe, and that when you have slept upon your Ale, you wil get a medicine for your madnesse, till the Woodcocke do tell you how the Dawcocke hath caught you leaving further to think on you, more then utterly to loath you, glad that your entertainment was so much to your discontentment: In full measure with your malice, I rest

Yours as you see. A. W.

Allusion to *Hamlet* in *Eastward Hoe*

This excerpt from the satiric city comedy Eastward Hoe *(1605) by George Chapman, Ben Jonson, and John Marston, shows that Shakespeare's* Hamlet *was popular enough to be parodied. In this scene Gertrude, the vain daughter of a rich merchant, has married a titled but impoverished lord. On her way to visit what she thinks is her lavish new home, Gertrude stops at an inn. The scene includes several references to Shakespeare's tragedy: in the excerpt below, Hamlet, the inn's footman, behaves like a madman. Later in the scene, Gertrude sings a variation on one of Ophelia's mad songs, and Gertrude's sister Mildred's thriftiness is mocked when Gertrude is told "the cold meat left at [Gertrude's] wedding, might serve to furnish [Mildred's] Nuptiall table," a parody of Shakespeare's Hamlet's bitter observation that, when his recently widowed mother remarried, "the funeral baked meats / Did coldly furnish forth the marriage tables" (1.2.180–181).*

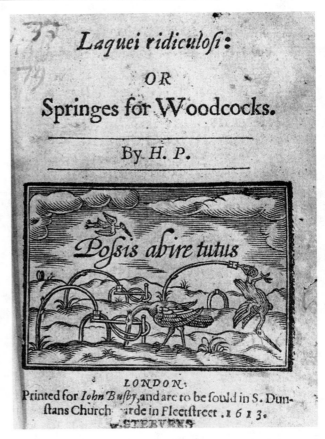

Title page for Henry Parrot's book in which he satirizes social pretentions. Polonius, disgusted by his daughter's gullibility, compares Hamlet's words and promises to Ophelia to "springes to catch woodcocks" (Hamlet, 1.3.115; by permission of the Folger Shakespeare Library).

Actus tertii. Scena Secunda.

Enter a Coachman in hast in's frock feeding.

Coach. Heer's a stirre when Cittizens ride out of Towne indeed, as if all the house were afire; Slight they will not give a man leave, to eat's breakfast afore he rises.

Enter Hamlet a footeman in haste.

Ham. What Coachman? my Ladyes Coach for shame; her ladiships ready to come downe;

Enter Potkinn, *a Tankerd bearer.*

Pot. Sfoote *Hamlet*; are you madde? whether run you now you should brushe up my olde Mistresse?
—sigs. D2v–D3r

Possible Allusion to *The Rape of Lucrece* in *The Strange Fortune of Alerane*

The Strange Fortune of Alerane: Or, My Ladies Toy (London, 1605), a poem by H.M., tells the story of King Othoe's daughter Radigund and her son William, who becomes a warrior despite being raised as a collier. In this excerpt the author refers to Henry Willobie's 1594 poem Avisa, *which mentions Shakespeare by name, and, possibly, to Shakespeare's* Rape of Lucrece. *The allusion was first identified by R. C. Horne in "Two Unrecorded Contemporary References to Shakespeare" in the June 1984 issue of* Notes and Queries.

Faire Ladies, since your pleasure is to passe
Away the time with Stories grave and fit,
I am not grave nor wise, my Silver's brasse,
My with is willing, but my will wants wit:
　Virgils verse, and one of *Tullies* imps,
　Agreeth better with *Dianaes* Nimphs.

To speake divinely, t'is above my reach,
To speake of dutie, you know more then I,
To speake of dainties, heere you stay my speach,
To speake of doting, I ne're knew it, I:
　But for to speake of things now most in fashion,
　Are lovely Ladies of most milde condition.

Pan counts her lovely which doth make men love;
I say, She is lovely which doth love againe;
For if no plaints nor prayers her can moove,
She is not lovely, but a lowring Swaine:
　Needes must I thinke she springs of savage kinde,
　Whom no desires, love, or deserts, can binde.

We read (*Avisa*) as reports the Writer,
We reade that *Lucrece* was pursude after;
T'is read in prose, but never yet in miter,
The *Saxon* storie of King *Othoes* daughter:
　Daine with patience, if you please to reede,
　T'is very strange, but yet t'is true indeede.

　　　　　　　　　　　　　　　　　—sig. B2v

Allusion to *Hamlet* in Smith's *Voiage and Entertainment in Rushia*

In Sir Thomas Smithes Voiage and Entertainment in Rushia *(1605), Smith (circa 1558–1625) compares the acts of vengeance committed by members of the Russian royal family with those found in a "horrid and wofull" stage tragedy, Shakespeare's* Hamlet. *Smith, a London merchant, became the first governor of the East India Company, sponsor of voyages for trade and exploration. An experienced traveler, Smith was named special ambassador to the Russian czar by King James in June 1604.*

Now I shall tell you of a 18. yeare esteemed dead Princes reviving of an other Princes (that twise 18. yeares might have lyved) poysoning, like (and indeed not unfit for the same) Stage crowners, within one day dying and reviving; as it were to make *Time* a lyer, who is the Sonne and Heire of *Trueth*.

Of the Almighties providence, by the benefite of Patience, Innocencie of past-yeares, Right of Inheritaunce, and his just Judgement upon the contrarie; and to the eternall happines of this never yet civill Nation, in effecting his exceeding mercie (that Ages wonderment) this last yeere: But it will be a Laborinth to mee, as it were to ravish my selfe with, if not a Dylemma wherein I may (not having the Art of Logicke or Rhetoricke) needlesse, if at any time (to my tyme and discourse, though incident to the general) rather confound my selfe, then satisfie the Readers expectation, or every particuler proprietie, it not onely beeing very tragicall and comicall in the event: But as all such State pollicies are beyond ordinary intelligence, or a writers honest patience; but what Trueth hath been servant, and my Eares subject unto, I will without either flatterie to the living, or envie to the dead, compendiously diliver.

After the suspitious death of the old Emperour *Boris Pheodoricke, &c.* by the appoyntment of the *Prince* (then their expected Emperour) and the Counsell, *Peter Basman* (that noble Sparke) was speedely dispatched and sent a Generall unto their ill succeeding Warres, as their last hope, (indeed hee prooved so in a contrary sence) and the onely refuge to the Commons: Whither being come, (bemeeting as you may imagine) he insenced the Counsell, A loving and beloved *Prince*, of such heroyicall spirit, so worthy selfe-acting and politique a Souldier, so generally good a Scholler, as being reported to be both well Letterd, well traveld; as great a Linguest as he was Statist; feared, as being aleyed; hee for speciall grace and favour, whose bountie & curtesie, sent Defiance to *Pride* and *Extortion*; in whom *Industrie* & *Labour* were twins, *Innocensie* and *Freedome* brothers; that held *Wisedome* as his rest, *True Valour* as his Servant, *Flatterie* as his Enemie, and *Envie* as his Slave; not being himselfe subject to any greater Potentate, but *Princely povertie*; Hee (I say) reviewing the Majestie of his person, and comparing the age of his Youth with the gray heades of his Honour: not in all, but in every particuler hereof, not lesse to this Nation then a *Phenix*; was resolved, hee could not lesse be than (beeing a Prince of so many Vertues) the Heire of the Kingdome, his Emperour, Lord and Maister: whereupon hee speeded with the winges of *Hope*, *Honour*, and *Confidence*, to deliver himselfe in such an

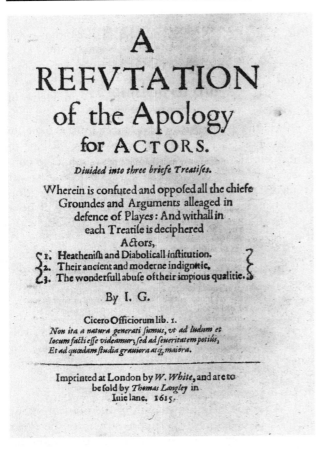

Title page for a pamphlet in which the author, thought to be John Greene, refutes a defense of players (by permission of the Folger Shakespeare Library)

infected and pestiferous a time, to the handes of him either whose Enemie beeing, he was without beeing; or whose Subject and Patient received, hee might well fall away; but neither from his right Soveragine, nor Loyaltie: Also he prostrated, or presented most of his Commaund, as many as freely would offer themselves: Under which, were all the *English*, *Scots*, *French*, *Dutch*, and *Flemings*, whatsoever: and with him, or rather before him (as least suspected) *Ries Vasili Evanch Goleeche*, the other Generall a man of great birth, and in the prioritie of place, to be received before *P. Basman*.

All which, the now well knowne newly opinionated Emperour very gratiously received, happely not without some jealowsie of many particulers; as of the Generals, the world surmizing a former correspondence to be held ever since a Parle had, at what time he was besiedged, and is aforesaid to performe very honorable service; and for the same had so applausable a receiving by the olde Emperours appoyntment into the *Moskoe*.

After this Generall, from the *Prince* amd Counsell was foorthwith sent many thousand [Rolles?] or Markes, they ever having the discretion of wise and politique States to account it as the Nerves and Sinewes; but now were perswaded it would proove the Soule and Hart of the Warres: but the generall received, he could not accept it and his Generall, being offered it by the faythfull treasorers, would not, but gave them this answere.

Hee would, they that sent that (though in-directly to him) should know, Hee who had the Patience to forbeare a Tyrant usurper, sitting upon his Throne so long; And hitherto of himselfe (by his stranger Friends) had thus happely and farre, entered into his Right, could not now want that should incourage those noble Spirites, fought with him in so just a quarrell: neither did he hold it Princelike, to receive, from his Enemie in that kinde, especially by their hands could not shew their face without blushing to their commaunding Lord: Yet when hee came to receive the Crowne and Kingdome, (which he assured himselfe and them, would be very shortly) hee doubted not this monegs would be then infinitely increased, as should be his honour, and their affection. So hee let them have safe conduct to depart.

This falling away of them, the State so greatly blinded upon (especially *Peter Basman*, whom I neither dare commend, nor will condemne, because I am not studious in his arguments: and the answere from the Emperour) with the many continually doubts of the issue, hastied the last breath of the once hoped-for *Prince*, as from him that (though an Emperour, was much hoodwinckt by his politique kinsmen great counsellours) now might easilie discerne those times to outrun his, and must notoriously know (though happely his youth and innocencie shadowed the reflection) that his Sonne was setting or beclouded at noone-dayes, and that the right heire was (and would be when he was not) apparant: that his fathers Empire and Government, was but as the *Poeticall Furie in a Stage-action*, compleat yet with horrid and wofull Tragedies: a first, but no second to any *Hamlet*; and that now *Revenge*, just *Revenge* was comming with his Sworde drawne against him, his royall Mother, and dearest Sister, to fill up those Murdering Sceanes; the *Embryon* whereof was long since Modeld, yea digested (but unlawfully and too-too vive-ly) by his dead selfe-murdering Father: such and so many being their feares and terrours; the Divell advising, Despaire counselling, Hell it selfe instructing; yea, wide-hart-opening to receive a King now, rather than a Kingdome; as *L. Bartas* divenely sayth: *They who expect not Heaven, finde a hell every where.*

These wicked instruments, the whole familie of the *Godonoves*, their adherents and factors, making a second (but no devine) damned Jurie; these dejected and abjected, as not knowing how to trust any, they so distrusted themselves, like men betweene murdering others, and being massacred them selves; holding this their onely happinesse, that they were then onely myserable (Noblenesse yet esteeming any preferment felicitie, but Honorable imployment): As those whose unmercifull greatnes gayned a pittifull commiseration, accounting Securitie neither safetie, nor reward; Indeed they were like Beastes, that have strength, but not power.

Oh for some excellent pen-man to deplore their state: but he which would lively, naturally, or indeed poetically delyneate or enumerate these occurrents, shall either lead you thereunto by *a poeticall spirit*, as could well, if well he might the dead living, life-giving *Sydney* Prince of *Poesie*; or deifie you with the Lord *Salustius* devinity, or in an Earth-deploring, Sententious, high rapt Tragedie with the noble *Foulk-Grevill*, not onely give you the *Idea*, but the soule of the acting *Idea*; as well could, if so we would, the elaborate English *Horace* that gives number, waight, and measure to every word, to teach the reader by his industries, even our Lawreat worthy *Benjamen*, whose Muze approves him with (our mother) the *Ebrew* signification to bee, *The elder Sonne*, and happely to have been the Childe of *Sorrow*: It were worthy so excellent rare witt: for my selfe I am neither *Apollo* nor *Appelles*, no nor any heire to the *Muses*: yet happely a younger brother, though I have as little bequeathed me, as many elder Brothers, and right borne Heires gaine by them: but *Hic labor, Hoc opus est*.

I am with the late *English* quick-spirited, cleare-sighted *Ovid*: It is to be feared Dreaming, and thinke I see many strange and cruell actions, but say my selfe nothing all this while: Bee it so that I am very drowsie, (the heate of the Clymate, and of the State) will excuse mee; for great happinesse to this mightie Empire is it, or would it have been, if the more part of their State affayres had been but Dreames, as they proove phatasmaes for our yeares.

—sigs. I3r–K2r

Allusion to Justice Shallow in Woodhouse's *The Flea*

In his dedicatory epistle to The Flea: Sic parva componere magnis *(1605), a satiric account of a dispute between an elephant and a flea, poet Peter Woodhouse alludes to one of the inept justices from* 2 Henry IV *to highlight the shallow judgment of the "giddie multitude" he addresses.*

The Epistle Dedicatorie.
To the giddie multitude.

Custome (that imperious King, or rather cruell Tyrant) hath so farre prevayled in these our dayes, that every Pamphlet must have his Patron, or els all the fatte is in the fire: Now I not knowing anye one whose name I might be so bolde with, as to make a shelter for this substance-wanting shadow, dedicate it to you al, so shal I be sure to offend none. And as he that speaketh in the defence of women, having a flock of femals for his Auditors (how-soever his cause be) is sure to want no wordes on his side: So let him that shall speake against this Toy, looke for more fists then his owne about his eares, & take heed of Club lawe, since the brainlesse multitude hath vouchsafed to take it into their protection. Now therefore, thou many-headed beast, censure me at thy pleasure: like or dislike what thou listest; but have an especial care of this, that thou beest not over constant in thine opinions: But what even now thou praysest to the heavens, by and by dispraise againe, as the vildest stuffe thou ever heardest of. Extoll that with admiration, which but a little before thou didst rayle at, as most carterly: And when thou sittest to consult about any weighty matter, let either justice *Shallowe*, or his Cousen Mr. *Weathercocke* be foreman of the Jurie. Thus relying on thy Moonlike constancie, I will shrowde this shadowe under thy alwaies-unstedfast favour.

P. W.

—sigs. A2r–v

The King's Men Paid for Court Performances

The "marks" and "nobles" in this entry are measures of money: a mark equals 13 shillings and 4 pence; a noble equals 10 shillings and sixpence.

To John Hemynges one of his Majesties players upon the Councells warrant dated at the Courte at whitehall xxiiii° Die Marcii 1605 for himselfe and the rest of his Companie for presenting tenn severall playes or enterludes before his Majestie in the tyme of Christmas laste and since upon the nightes mencioned in a Schedule annexed unto the said warrant after the rate of twentie nobles for everie play and by way of his Majesties rewarde fyve markes in all the some of   C^{li}

—*Dramatic Records*, pp. 43–44

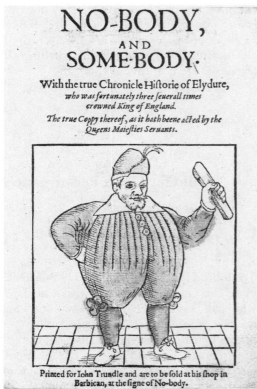

Illustrations depicting actors in comic roles: (top) a title-page illustration showing two stock characters, the pantaloon and the zany, from Italian commedia dell'arte (courtesy of the Bodleian Library, Oxford) and (bottom) pages from the anonymous comedy No-body, and Some-body *(1605; reproduced by permission of The Huntington Library, San Marino, California)*

1606

Shakespeare Listed in Hubaud's Inventory

In an inventory dated 31 January 1606 (Birmingham Probate Registry), Ralph Hubaud lists Shakespeare among those in his debt. B. Roland Lewis writes that it "is not known why Shakespeare owed Hubaud money; there is no evidence that a mortgage was used as partial payment for the Stratford Tithes."

There was Owinge by Mr. Shakespre . . . . xx*li*.
—Lewis, *Shakespeare Documents*, p. 385

The Globe Ordered to Repair Its Sewers

Charles William Wallace transcribed these orders of the Sewer Commission, issued 14 February 1606, in his article "Shakespeare and the Globe" for The Times *(London). Wallace notes that the second order was repeated on 25 April with a deadline of 1 June and that this second entry was labeled "done." Shakespeare was a sharer in the King's Men, meaning he was part owner of the company's resources (playbooks, costumes, props) and shared its profits, but he was also a householder, a part owner of the Globe theater. Householders were responsible for arranging and paying for repairs such as the ones the following documents describe.*

A Statute on Blasphemy

The following 1606 statute prohibits the use of God's name in stage plays; playwrights usually substituted the name of a classical god, particularly Jove or Jupiter. Abbreviations are silently expanded. The following transcript of "An Acte to restraine Abuses of Players" (3 Jac. I c. 21) is from The Statutes of the Realm *(1819), vol. IV, part II, p. 1097.*

For the preventing and avoyding of the greate Abuse of the Holy Name of God in Stageplayes Interludes Maygames Shewes and such like; Be it enacted by our Soveraigne Lorde the Kinges Majesty, and by the Lordes Spirituall and Temporall, and Commons in this present Parliament assembled, and by the authoritie of the same, That if at any tyme or tymes after the end of this present Session of Parliament, any person or persons doe or shall in any Stage play Interlude Shewe Maygame or Pageant jestingly or prophanely speake or use the holy Name of God or of Christ Jesus, or of the Holy Ghoste or of the Trinitie, which are not to be spoken but with feare and reverence, shall forfeit for everie such Offence by hym or them committed Tenne Pounde, the one Moytie thereof to the Kinges Majestie his Heires and Successors, the other Moytie thereof to hym or them that will sue for the same in any Courte of Recorde at Westminster, wherein no Essoigne Protection or Wager of Lawe shalbe allowed.

It is Ordered that Burbidge and Heminges and others, the owners of the Playhouse called the Globe in Maid-lane shall before the xxth day of Aprill next pull up and take cleane out of the Sewar the props or postes w[hi]ch stand under theire bridge on the North side of Mayd-lane upon paine to forf[eit]   xxs.
[Labelled "done."]

It is ordered that the said Burbidge and Heminges and others as aforesaid shall before the xxth day of Aprill next well and sufficiently pyle boorde and fill up viii poles more or lesse of theire wharfe against theire said Playhouse upon payne to forfeict for every pole then undone   xxs.
[Labelled "not done decret non levand."]
—*The Times* (London), 30 April 1914, p. 10

Shakespeare Listed in Survey of Rowington Manor

Shakespeare was listed as a Stratford copyhold tenant in a 1 August 1606 survey of Rowington Manor in the Accounts of the Auditors of the Land Revenue.

Tenentes Custumarii

Stratfor super Avon	Willielmus Shakespere tenet per copiam datam—anno —vidilicet	
	Domum mansionalem	ii.s
	Reddendo per annum	finis
	Habendum	heriettum
		annualis valor
		dimmittenda

—Public Records Office Exchequer, LR 2/228, fol. 199

Allusion to *Richard III* in Barnes's *Foure Bookes of Offices*

Port Barnabe Barnes alludes to Shakespeare's Richard III *in* Foure Bookes of Offices: Enabling Privat persons for the speciall service of all good Princes and Policies *(1606), an advice manual for would-be courtiers. Barnes's scorn for the theater was shared by many of his contemporaries.*

I will not omit that which is yet fresh in our late Chronicles; and hath been many times represented unto the vulgar upon our English Theaters, of *Richard Plantaginet*, third sonne to *Richard* Duke of *Yorke*, who (being eldest brother next surviving to King *Edward* the fourth, after hee had unnaturally made away his elder brother, *George* Duke of *Clarence* (whom he thought a grievous eye-sore betwixt him and the marke at which he levelled) did upon death of the King his brother, take upon him protection of this Realme, under his two Nephewes left in his butcherly tuition: both which he caused at once to be smothered together, within a keepe of his Majesties Tower, at *London*: which ominous bad lodging in memoriall thereof, is to this day knowne, and called by name of *the bloody Tower.*

                                        –sig. Qr

The King's Men
Paid for Court Performances

To John Heminges one of his majesties Players uppon the Councelles warrant dated xiiii^{to} Octobris 1606 for iii^{re} plaies before his majestie and the kinge of Denmarke twoe of them at Grenewich and one at Hamptoncourte   xxx^{li}

To John Heminges one of his majesties Players uppon the Councelles warrant dated xxx^{mo} marcii 1607 for ix^{en} playes presented before his hignes viz the xxvi^{th} and xxix^{th} of December 1606 the iiii^{th} the vi^{th} and viii^{th} of Januarye and the seconde the fifthe the xv^{th} and the xxvii^{th} of Februarye   iiii x^{li}

                        –*Dramatic Records,* pp. 44–45

1607

Stationers' Register Entries

Romeo and Juliet, Love's Labor's Lost, The Taming of a Shrew, Hamlet, *and* King Lear *were registered with the Stationers (Stationer's Hall, Register C, folios 147r, 161r-v). In the following transcription W. W. Greg has silently expanded abbreviated words.*

.22. Januar'.

Mr Linge. Entred for his copies by direccion of A Court, and with consent of M^r. Burby under his hand-wrytinge These. iii copies. viz.

Romeo & Juliett. Loves Labour Loste. The taminge of A Shrewe   xviiid R

. . . .

19. Novembr'

Jo. Smythick. Entred for his copies under thandes of the wardens. these [16] bookes followinge Whiche dyd belonge to Nicholas Lynge .viz.
. . . 6 a booke called Hamlett   vi^d
. . . 9 The taminge of A Shrewe   vi^d
      10 Romeo and Julett   vi^d
      11 Loves labour Lost   vi^d

26 Nov
Nathaniel Butter John Busby Entred for their copie under thandes of Sr George Buck knight & Thwardens A booke called. Mr William Shakespeare his historye of Kynge Lear as yt was played before the kinges majestie at Whitehall uppon St Stephans [deleted] night at Christmas Last by his majesties servantes playinge usually at the globe on the Banksyde   vi^d
–*Bibliography of the English Printed Drama,* pp. 22, 24

Publications

The relationship between the text of The Taming of a Shrew *published in 1607 and the version published in the First Folio has not been established. The 1607 version of the play may be a memorial reconstruction of, an early draft of, or a play that shares a source with Shakespeare's play.*

A / Pleaſaunt Conceited / Historie, called / *The Taming of a Shrew.* / As it hath beene ſundry times acted by the right / Honourable the Earle of *Pembrooke* / his Seruants. / [*Printer's device*] / G. STEEVENS. / Printed at London by *V. S* for *Nicholas Ling,* / and are to be ſold at his ſhop in Saint / Dunſtons Church yard in / Fleetſtreet. 1607.

Two previously published works by Shakespeare were published in 1607: Lucrece *(1594, 1598, 1600) and* Venus and Adonis *(1593, 1594, 1596, 1599). Despite its title-page listing of 1602, this edition of* Venus and Adonis *is believed to have been published in 1607 (see the* Short Title Catalog *entry 22360).*

LVCRECE. / [*Printer's device*] / AT LONDON, / Printed by N. O. for Iohn Ha- /rison. 1607.

VENVS / AND ADONIS. / *Vilia miretur vulgus: mihi flauus Apollo / Pocula Caſtalia plena miniſtret aqua.* / [*Printer's device*] / Imprinted at London for *VVilliam Leake,* / dwelling at the ſigne of the Holy Ghoſt, in / Pauls Churchyard. 1602.

Raworth Sanctioned for Printing
Venus and Adonis

The Stationers' Company regulated the behavior of its members, the printers and publishers of London. Once a work had been entered on the Stationers' Register, the person who paid for the entry usually held the copyright. Unscrupulous publishers and printers sometimes ignored this, however, and produced copies of works for which they did not hold copyright as Robert Raworth did in 1607 when he published Shakespeare's Venus and Adonis. *He was sanctioned for doing so; Raworth's case is discussed by Edward Arber*

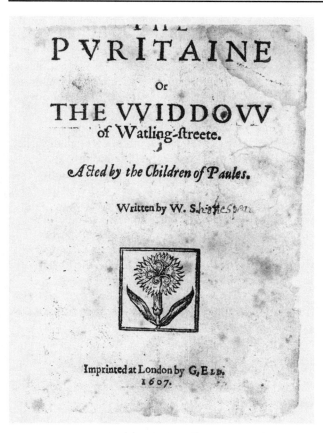

THE
PVRITAINE
Or
THE VVIDDOVV
of Watling-ftreete.

Acted by the Children of Paules.

Written by W. Shakespeare.

Imprinted at London by G, E L D.
1607.

Title page for a work sometimes attributed to Shakespeare. The publishers may have printed "W.S." on the title page to increase sales, as readers were free to assume, as some continue to do, that Shakespeare wrote the play (by permission of the Folger Shakespeare Library).

In Shakespeare: The Poet in His World *(1978), M. C. Bradbrook briefly describes the life of John Hall:*

John Hall, the son of a well-known physician, William Hall of Acton, Middlesex, had graduated at Queens' College, Cambridge, in 1594; he was thirty-two when he married Susannah and been in Stratford practising physic since 1600. His degree was not in medicine but he probably learned, as many learned their profession, from his father's skill; at all events, John Hall made a conscientious and skilful physician, who treated rich and poor, rode forty miles to visit a patient (admittedly a nobleman) and kept a case-book (in Latin). The first volume is missing or we might know more than we do of Shakespeare's later years and the cause of his death, for John Hall treated his family and recorded giving his daughter a purge (for fever) and his wife an enema (for colic).

–p. 222

Edward Shakespeare's Burial Record

The burial of Shakespeare's nephew Edward Shakespeare, the son of his brother Edmund, is noted in the parish records of St. Giles's Church without Cripplegate.

[12 August 1607]
Edward sonne of Edward Shackspeere
Player base-borne.
    –Guildhall Library, MS 6419/2

Edmund Shakespeare's Burial Record

The burial of Shakespeare's brother Edmund is noted in the parish register and a fee book of St. Saviour's, Southwark. Nothing more than the brief mentions in his son's and his own burial records is known about Edmund Shakespeare's life and profession; he is not named in the surviving records of the London acting companies. The register entry for 31 December 1607 reads:

Edmond Shakespeare a player in the Church
    –Greater London Record Office, P92/SAV/2001

The fee book entry for 31 December 1607 reads:

wth a fore noone knell of ye great bell ––––––––––– xx^s
    –Greater London Record Office, P92/SAV/370/10

Allusion to *Venus and Adonis* in *The Fayre Mayde of the Exchange*

In this scene from the comedy The Fayre Mayde of the Exchange: With The pleasaunt Humours of the Crip-

in an addendum to A Transcript of the Registers of the Company of Stationers of London 1554–1640 A.D. *(1876).*

1607 Robert Raworth supprest for printing anothers Copy [of *Venus and Adonis*]
    –*Stationers' Register,* vol. III, folio 703

Susanna Shakespeare's Marriage to John Hall

The marriage of Shakespeare's daughter Susanna to John Hall (circa 1575–1635) was recorded in the marriage register of Holy Trinity Church, Stratford-upon-Avon.

Junii 5. [1607] John Hall gentleman & Susanna Shaxspere
    –Shakespeare Birthplace Trust Records Office
    DR 243/1, folio 11

ple of Fanchurch *(1607) possibly written by Thomas Heywood, the playwright notes and mocks the use of Shakespeare's erotic poem* Venus and Adonis *(1593) as a means of seduction. Mall, the Fair Maid of the play's title, is pursued by an ardent lover, Bowdler, whose overwrought language owes much to the poetry he reads.*

[*Cripple*] What say you to your sweet heart, *Mall Berry.*

[*Bowdler*] Peace Cripple, silence, name her not, I could not indure the carrire of her wit, for a million, shee is the onely shee *Mercury* under the heavens; her wit is all spirit; that spirit fire, that fire flies from her tongue, able to burne the radix of the best invention; in this Element shee is the abstract and breefe of all the eloquence since the incarnation of *Tullie*: I tell thee Cripple, I had rather incounter *Hercules* with blowes, than *Mall Berry* with words: And yet by this light I am horribly in love with her.

Enter Mall Berry.

Crip. See where she comes, O excellent!
Bowd. Now have I no more blood than a bull-rush.
　[*Barnard*] How now; what aile you sir?
Crip. Whats the matter man?
Bowd. See, see that glorious angell doth approach, What shall I doe?
Crip. Shee is a saint indeed; Zounds to her, court her, win her, weare her, wed her, and bed her too.
Bowd. I would it were come to that, I win her! by heaven, I am not furnish'd of a courting phrase, to throw at a dogge.
Crip. Why no, but at a woman you have; O sir, seeme not so doultish now, can you make no fustian, aske her if sheele take a pipe of Tobacco.
Bow. It wil offend her judgement, pardon me.
Crip. But heare you sir? reading so much as you have done,
　Doe you not remember one pretty phrase,
　To scale the walles of a faire wenches love?
Bow. I never read any thing but *Venus* and *Adonis*.
Crip. Why thats the very quintessence of love,
　If you remember but a verse or two,
　Ile pawne my head, goods, lands and all twill doe.
Bow. Why then have at her.
　Fondling I say, since I have hemd thee heere,
　Within the circle of this ivory pale,
　Ile be a parke.
Mal. Hands off fond sir.
Bow. And thou shalt be my deere;
　Feede thou on me, and I will feede on thee,
　And Love shall feede us both.
Ma. Feede you on woodcockes, I can fast awhile.

Bow. Vouchsafe thou wonder to alight thy steede.
Crip. Take heede, shees not on horsebacke.
Bow. Why then she is alighted,
　Come sit thee downe where never serpent hisses,
　And being set, ile smother thee with kisses.
Ma. Why is your breath so hot? now God forbid
　I should buy kisses to be smotherd.
Bow. Meane you me? you gull me not?
Ma. No, no, poore *Bowdler*, thou dost gull thy selfe:
　Thus must I do to shadow the hid fire,
　That in my heart doth burne with hot desire:
　O I doe love him well what ere I say,
　Yet will I not my selfe selfe love bewray.
　If he be wise hee'l sue with good take heede:
　Bowdler, doe so, and thou art sure to speede:
　I will flie hence to make his love the stronger,
　Though my affection must lie hid the longer.
　What maister *Bowdler*, not a word to say?
Bowd. No by my troth, if you stay heere all day.
Ma. Why then ile beare the bucklers hence away.
Exit.

The faire Maide

Crip. What maister *Bowdler*, have you let her passe unconquerd?
Bow. Why what could I doe more? I lookt upon her with judgement, the strings of my tongue were well in tune, my embraces were in good measure, my palme of a good constitution, onely the phrase was not mooving; as for example, *Venus* her selfe with all her skill could not winne *Adonis*, with the same wordes: O heavens! was I so fond then to thinke that I could conquer *Mall Berry*? O the naturall fluence of my owne wit had beene farre better!
　　　　　　　　　　　　　　　　　　–sigs. G2v–G3v

Allusion to Shakespeare in Barksted's *Mirrha The Mother of Adonis*

Actor and poet William Barksted praises Shakespeare's superior poetic skills in Mirra The Mother of Adonis: Or, Lustes Prodegies *(1607). The poem's content is borrowed from the tenth book of Ovid's* Metamorphoses *and its style from Shakespeare's* Venus and Adonis.

But stay my Muse in thine owne confines keepe,
　& wage not warre with so deere lov'd a neighbor
But having sung thy day song, rest & sleepe
　preserve thy small fame and his greater favor:
His song was worthie merrit (*Shakspeare* hee)
　sung the faire blossome, thou the withered tree
Laurell is due to him, his art and wit
　hath purchast it, *Cypres* thy brow will fit.
　　　　　　　　　　　　　　　　　　–sig. Er

Possible Allusions to *Richard III* and *Twelfth Night* in Dekker's *A Knights Conjuring*

In this first excerpt from his rant against London's corruption, A Knights Conjuring. Done in earnest: Discovered in Jest (1607), playwright and pamphlet writer Thomas Dekker probably refers to Shakespeare's Richard III; *the passage also suggests the popularity of new plays.*

Will Sommers gives not *Richard* the third the cushions, the Duke of *Guyze* & the Duke of *Shoreditche* have not the bradth of a benche betweene them, *Jane Shore* and a Gold-smiths wife are no better then one another.

Kings and Clownes, Souldiers and Cowards, Church-men and Sextons, Aldermen and Coblers, are all one to *Charon*: For his *Navlum, Lucke* (the old Recorders foole) shall have as much mat, as *Syr Launcelot* of the Lake: He knowes, though they had an oar in every mans Boat in the World, yet in his they cannot challenge so much as a stretcher: And therefore (though hee sayles continually with wind and Tyde) he makes the prowdest of them all to stay his leasure. It was a Comedy, to see what a crowding (as if it had bene at a newe Play,) there was upon the *Acheronticque Strond*, (so that the Poste was faine to tarry his turne, because he could not get neere enough the shore: He purpos'd therefore patiently to walke up and downe, til the Coast was cleare, and to note the condition of all the passengers.

—sigs. F1v–F2r

Dekker satirizes London's vices by imagining a Knight of the Post has been sent to find the Devil; the Knight's journey takes him through London. Once he reaches hell, the Knight attends a mock Court of Sessions; the following excerpt describes what happens after court is adjourned. The name of the petition reader, Malvolio, may be borrowed from Shakespeare's Twelfth Night; the passage concludes with a reference to Shakespeare's early play The Comedy of Errors.

Let us therfore sithence the *Infernall Sessions* are rejourned, & the Court breaking up, seeke out his knightship, who having wayted all this while for the *Divell*, hath by this time deliverd to his *paws* the *Supplication*, about *Golde*, & to *Malvolio* his *Secretary* is reading it to him, but before he was up to the middle of it, the work-maister of *Witches*, snatched away the Paper, & thrust it into his bosome in great choller, rayling at his Letter-carryer, and threatning to have him la'sht by the *Furies*, for his loytring so long, or Cauteriz'de with hotte Irons for a Fugitive. But *Mephostophiles* discoursing from point to point; what paines hee had taken in the Survey of every Countrey, and how hee had spent his time there, Serjeant Sathan gave him his blessing, and told him that dur-

ing his absence, the *Wryter* that penn'd the *Supplication* had ben landed by *Charon*, of whom he willed to enquire within what part of their dominion hee had taken up his lodging, his purpose is to answere every worde by word of mouth yet because he knowes, that at the returne of his *Post-ship*, and walking upon the *Exchange* of the *Worlde*, (which he charges him to hasten, for the good of the *Stygian* kingdome, that altogether stands upon quicke tafficque) they will flutter about him, crying, What newes? what newes? what squibs, or rather what peeces of ordinance doth the *McGunner of Gehenna* discharge against so sawcie a suitor, that by the Artillarie of his Secretaries penne, hath shaken the walles of his Kingdome, and made so wide a breache, that anie *Syr Giles* may looke into his, and his Officers dooings: to stop their mouthes with some thing, stop them with this: That touching the enlargement of *Gold* (which is the first branch of the *Petition*:) So it is, that *Plutus* his kinsman (being the onely setter up of tempting Idolles,) was borne a Cripple, but had his eye sight as faire as the daye, for hee could see the faces & fashions of all men in the world in a twinkling. At which time, for all he went upon Crutches, hee made shifte to walke abroad with many of his friends, Marrie they were none but good men. A Poet, or Philosopher, might then have sooner had his company, than a Justice of Peace: Vertue at that time, went in good cloaths, & vice fed upon beggery. Almes baskets, honestie, and plaine dealing, had all the Trades in their owne handes, So that Unthrifts, Cheaters, and the rest of their Faction, (though it were the greater) were borne downe, for not an Angell durst bee seene to drink in a Taverne with them: whereupon they were all in danger to be famisht: Which enormity *Jupiter* wisely looking into, and seeing *Plutus* dispersing his giftes amongst none but his honest brethren, strucke him (either in anger or envie) starke blinde, so that ever since hee hath play'de the good fellowe, for now every gull may leade him up and downe like *Guy*, to make sports in any drunken assemblie, now hee regards not who thrusts his handes into his pockets, nor how it is spent; a foole shall have his heart nowe, assoone as a Physition: And an Asse that cannot spell, goe laden away with double Duckets from his *Indian* store-house, when *Ibis Homere*, that hath layne sick seventeene yeeres together of the Universitie plague, (watching and want) only in hope at the last to finde some cure, shall not for an hundred waight of good Latine, receive a two penny waight in Silver, his ignorance (arising from his blindenes) is the onely cause of this Comedie of errors: so that untill some Quack-salver or other (either by help of Tower hill water, or any other, either Physicall or Chirurgicall meanes) can picke out that pin and webbe which is stucke into both his eyes, (and that will very hardly be.)

—sigs. G3v–G4r

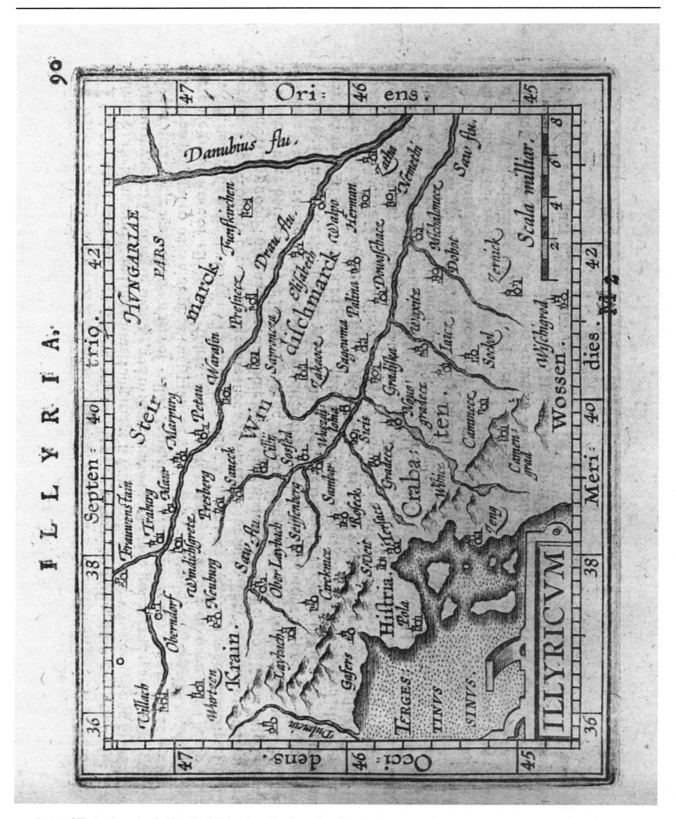

A map of Illyria, the setting for Twelfth Night, *from* Abraham Ortelius his Epitome of the Theater of the World *(1603). Although Shakespeare errs in giving Bohemia a coast in* The Winter's Tale, *his geographic knowledge is generally accurate (by permission of the Folger Shakespeare Library).*

Allusion to *Hamlet* in Dekker and Webster's *West-ward Hoe*

In Thomas Dekker and John Webster's city comedy West-ward Hoe (1607), three jealous husbands plot to uncover and avenge their wives' supposed infidelities.

Enter Tenter-hooke, Hony-suckle, Wafer, Parenthesis, *and his wife with* Ambush *and* Chamberlayn.

[*Hony-suckle*] Serjeant *Ambush*, as th'art an honest fellow, scowte in some back roome, till the watch-word be given for sallying forth. [*Ambush*] Duns the Mouse. *Exit.*

[*Tenter-hooke*] —A little low-woman saist thou, —in a Velvet-cappe—and one of 'him in a Beaver? brother *Honny-suckle*, and brother *Wafer*, hearke—they are they.

[*Wafer*] But art sure theyr husbands are a bed with 'hem?

[*Chamberlayne*] I thinke so Sir, I know not, I left 'hem together in one roome: and what division fell amongst 'hem, the fates can descover not I.

Tent. Leave us good Chamberlaine, wee are some of their friends: leave us good Chamberlaine: be merry a little: leave us honest Chamberlaine—*Exit.* Wee are abuzd, wee are bought and sold in *Brainford* Market; never did the sicknesse of one belyed nurse-child, sticke so cold to the heartes of three Fathers: never were three innocent Cittizens so horribly, so abhominably wrung under the withers.

Both. What shall wee do? how shall we helpe our selves?

Hony. How shall we pull this thorne out off our foote before it rancle?

Tent. Yes, yes, yes, well enough; one of us stay here to watch: doe you see: to watch: have an eye, have an eare. I and my brother *Wafer,* and Maist. *Justiniano,* will set the towne in an insurrection, bring hither the Constable, and his Billmen, breake open upon 'hem, take 'hem in their wickednesse, and put 'hem to their purgation.

Both. Agreed. [*Parenthesis*] Ha, ha purgation.

Tent. Wee'le have 'hem before some Countrey Justice of *Corans* (for we scorne to be bound to the Peace) and this Justice shall draw his Sword in our defence, if we finde 'hem to be Malefactors wee'le tickle 'hem.

Hony. Agreed: doe not say, but doo: come.

Par. Are you mad? do you know what you doe? whether will you runne?

All 3. To set the Towne in an uprore.

Par. An uprore! will you make the Townesmen think, that *Londoners* never come hither but upon Saint *Thomases* night? Say you should rattle up the Constable: thrash all the Countrey together, hedge in the house with Flayles, Pike-staves, and Pitch-forkes, take your wives napping, these Western Smelts nibling, and that like so many *Vul-*cans, every Smith should discover his *Venus* dancing with *Mars*, in a net? wud this plaster cure the head-ake.

Tent. I, it wood. *All 3.* Nay it shud.

Par. Nego, Nego, no no, it shall bee prov'd unto you, your heads would ake worse: when women are proclaymed to bee light, they strive to be more light, for who dare disprove a Proclamation.

Tent. I but when light Wives make heavy husbands, let these husbands play mad *Hamlet*, and crie revenge, come, and weele do so.

—sigs. H4v–H5r

Allusion to *Venus and Adonis* in *Merrie Conceited Jests of George Peele*

George Peele refers to Venus and Adonis *in the beginning of a story in* Merrie Conceited Jests of George Peele Gentleman, sometimes a student in Oxford. Wherein is shewed the course of his life how he lived: a man very well knowne in the Citie of London and elsewhere *(1607). Putting Shakespeare's poem into the hands of a bartender is not meant to be a compliment to the poet.*

How he served a Tapster

George was making merry with three or four of his frindes in picorner, where the Tapster of the house was much given to Poetrie: for hee had ingrosed into his hands the Knight of the sunne: *Venus*, and *Adonis*, and other phamphlets which the stripling had collected together, and knowing *George* to be a Poet, tooke great delight in his companie, and out of his bountie would needes bestow a brace of cans of him.

—p. 29

Allusion to *A Midsummer Night's Dream* in Sharpham's *The Fleire*

In The Fleir *(1607), a bitter comedy featuring a father who disguises himself and watches his daughters sell themselves into prostitution, Edward Sharpham parodies many lines from Shakespeare. This excerpt may provide details about a piece of stage business for the comic suicide of Thisbe in* A Midsummer Night's Dream, *act 5, scene 1. Thisbe's lines "Come, trusty sword, / Come blade, my breast imbrue!" (343–344) imply that she stabs herself with her lover Pyramus's sword, but Sharpham claims that Thisbe uses the scabbard instead; Sharpham himself is punning on the Latin word for "scabbard," "vagina."*

[*Knight*]: *Fleir*, is the gentleman usher that I preferd to your Ladies in any favour with them?

[*Fleir*]: Great, great: a kisses his hand with an excellent grace, and a will leire and fleire upon am,

hee's partly their Phisitian, a makes am Supposito-
ries, and gives am Glisters.

Kni. And how lives he with am.

Fle. Faith like *Thisbe* in the play, a has almost
kil'd himselfe with the scabberd. . . .

—sig. E1v

The King's Men
Paid for Court Performances

to John Hemynges one of his Majesties Players upon the
Councelles warraunt dat viii^{uo} die Februarii 1608 for himself and the rest of his fellowes for xiii plaies presented by
them before his Majestie at the Court at Whitehall viz on
St Stephens night St Johns night Childermas night the seconde of January Twelfenight two plaies the seaventh of
January the ninth of January the xviith of January two
plaies the xxvith of January, Candlemas night and Shrove
sunday at night iiii vi^{li} xiii^s iiii^d and by waies of his Majesties
reward xliiii^{li} vi^s viii^d In all Cxxx^{li}

—*Dramatic Records,* p. 46

Shipboard Performances
of *Richard II* and *Hamlet*

In his journal William Keeling, captain of the Dragon, *a ship
sailing to the East Indies, mentions shipboard performances of* Richard II *and* Hamlet. *Thomas Rundall, the editor of* Narratives of
Voyages towards the North-West in search of a Passage to
Cathay and India 1496–1631 *(1849), notes that "the drama
appears to have been considered a beneficial source of recreation."*

1607.

September 4. [At Serra Leona.] Towards night, the
kinges interpter came, and brought me
a letter from the Portingall, wher in (like
the faction) he offered me all kindly services. The bearer is a man of marvail-
ous redie witt, and speakes in eloquent
Portugues. He layt abord me.

5. I sent the interpreter, according to his
desier, abord the Hector, whear he
brooke fast, and after came abord mee,
wher *we gave the tragedie of Hamlett.*

30. Captain Hawkins dined with me,
wher *my companions acted Kinge Richard
the Second.*

[1608]

[March] 31. I envited Captain Hawkins to a ffishe dinner, and *had Hamlet acted* abord me: wch I
p'mitt to keepe my people from idlenes and unlawfull games, or sleepe.

—*Narratives of Voyages,* p. 231

Playwrights as Directors

As the surviving cast lists from Ben Jonson's Every
Man in his Humor *and* Sejanus *show, Shakespeare acted
in plays in addition to writing them. But did he direct the
actors who performed at the Globe? The following preface to
a German translation of Thomas Tomkis's 1607 academic
comedy* Lingua, or the Combat of the Tongue and
five Senses for Superiority *suggests that playwrights did
some directing. The excerpt is from Johannes Rhenanus,
preface to Speculum Aistheticum (1613), translated by
David Klein in his article "Did Shakespeare Produce His
Own Plays?"*

Was aber die *actores* antrifft, werden solche (wie
ich in England in acht genommen) gleichsam in
einer schule täglich *instituiret,* dass auch die
vornembsten *actores* deren orter sich von den Poëten
müssen underwayssen lassen, welches dann einer
wolgeschriebenen *Comoedien* das leben und zierde
gibt und bringet; Dass also kein wunder ist, warumb
die Engländische *Comoedianten* (Ich rede von
geübten) andern vorgehen und den Vorzug haben.

[So far as the actors are concerned they, as I have
noticed in England, are daily instructed, as it were in
a school, so that even the most eminent actors have
to allow themselves to be taught their places by the
dramatists, and this gives life and ornament to a
well-written play, so that it is no wonder that the
English players (I speak of skilled ones) surpass others and have the advantage over them.]

—*Modern Language Review,* 57 (1962): 556

1608

Elizabeth Hall's Baptismal Record

*The baptism of Shakespeare's granddaughter Elizabeth
Hall was recorded in the baptismal register of Holy Trinity
Church, Stratford-upon-Avon.*

[21 February 1608] Elizabeth dawghter to John Hall geñ

—*Baptismal Register,* 42r

*Elizabeth Hall married Thomas Nash on 22 April 1626;
the date is sometimes thought to have been chosen in honor of her
grandfather, leading to speculation that it was Shakespeare's
birthday. Thomas Nash died in 1647, and Hall married John
Bernard in 1649. There is no record of children from either marriage, although Bernard had eight children from his first marriage. When Bernard became a baronet, Elizabeth Hall became
Lady Bernard. She died in 1670.*

Stationers' Register Entries

A Yorkshire Tragedy, *which is attributed to Shakespeare in the entry,* Pericles, *and* Antony and Cleopatra *(Stationer's Hall, Register C, folios 167r-v.) were registered with the Stationers's Company. In both of the 20 May entries the sum is followed by an "R," which has been deleted. Abbreviated words have been silently expanded in these entries.*

2do. die maii

m^r Pavyer　Entered for his Copie under the handes of m^r Wilson & m^r Warden Seton A booke Called A yorkshire Tragedy written by Wylliam Shakespere　　　vi^d

20 maii

Edward Blount. Entred for his copie under thandes of Sr George Buck knight & m^r warden Seton a booke called. The booke of Pericles Prynce of Tyre.　　vi^d
Edward Blunt　Entred also for his copie by the lyke Aucthoritie. A booke Called. Anthony. & Cleopatra　　vi^d
　　　—*Bibliography of the English Printed Drama*, p. 24

Publications

King Lear *was published for the first time in 1608; three other works by Shakespeare were published again:* Venus and Adonis *(1593, 1594, 1596, 1599),* Richard II *(1597, 1598), and* 1 Henry IV *(1598, 1599, 1604).*

The title page for the edition of Venus and Adonis *published in 1608 was printed with the year 1602. Some copies of this edition have a colon rather than a comma between "vulgus" and "mihi." For further information, see the* Short Title Catalog *entry 22360a.*

Venus and Adonis. *Vilia miretur vulgus, mihi flavus Apollo / Pocula Castalia plena ministret aqua.* Imprinted at London for *William Leake,* dwelling at the signe of the Holy Ghost, in Paules Church-yard. 1602.

Richard II *was published with the deposition scene that had not been included in earlier editions; one of the title pages printed with this edition noted the addition of the scene.*

THE / Tragedie of King / Richard the ſecond. / As it hath been publikely acted by the Right / Honourable the Lord Chamberlaine / his ſeruantes. / By *William Shake- ſpeare.* / [*Printer's device*] / LONDON, / Printed by W. W. for *Mathew Law,* and are to be / ſold at his ſhop in Paules Church-yard, at / the ſigne of the Foxe. / 1608.

Page from Edward Topsell's The Historie of Serpents *(1608). "What manner o' thing is your crocodile?" Lepidus asks in* Antony and Cleopatra *(2.7.41; by permission of the Folger Shakespeare Library)*

The Tragedie of King Richard the Second: With new additions to the Parliament Sceane, and the deposing of King Richard. As it hath been lately acted by the Kinges Majesties servantes, at the Globe. By *William Shake-speare.* At London, Printed by W. W. for *Mathew Law,* and are to be sold at his shop in Paules Church-yard, at the signe of the Foxe. 1608.

THE / HISTORY OF / Henry the fourth, / VVith the battell at Shrewſeburie, / *betweene the King, and* Lord / Henry Percy, ſurnamed Henry / *Hotſpur of the North.* / *With the humorous conceites of Sir* / John Falstalffe. / *Newly corrected by W. Shake-ſpeare.* / [*Printer's device*] / LONDON, / Printed for *Mathew Law,* and are to be ſold at / his ſhop in Paules Church-yard, neere unto S. / *Augustines* gate, at the ſigne of / the Foxe. 1608.

Allusion to Performances of Shakespeare's Play in Wilkins's *The Painfull Adventures of Pericles Prince of Tyre*

George Wilkins's prose account of the adventures of Pericles in The Painfull Adventures of Pericles Prince of Tyre. Being The true History of the Play of Pericles, as it was lately presented by the Worthy and ancient Poet John Gower *(1608) follows Shakespeare's play closely; his book is used to argue that* Pericles *in its present form is missing at least one scene. The excerpt here is the conclusion of Wilkins's "Argument," a summary of the story with which he begins his narrative.*

Onely intreating the Reader to receive this Historie in the same maner as it was under the habite of ancient *Gower* the famous English Poet, by the Kings Majesties Players excellently presented.

—sig. A3r

Shakespeare's Lease for the Blackfriar's Theater

Thomasina Hemings Ostler, a widow at age 19, had inherited shares in the Globe and Blackfriars theaters from her husband, the actor William Ostler. In 1615, after a series of disputes with her father, John Hemings, Thomasina Ostler initiated a lawsuit to recover income from the shares and damages for being denied that income. The outcome of the case is not recorded; it may have been settled out of court. The section of Ostler's plea transcribed below provides details of the legal means by which Shakespeare became a householder of the Globe and Blackfriars theaters. Ostler's plea establishes that Shakespeare and others leased the Blackfriars on 9 August 1608, giving the company access to an indoor theater with artificial lighting and a more elaborate set of stage machinery than was available at the Globe. The plea has also been used to attempt to establish the value of shares in the theater, but Ostler does not provide enough information about the financial arrangements to prove her claim that a seventh part of the Blackfriars and a fourteenth part of the Globe were each worth £300.

For further details from Thomasina Ostler's 1615 plea in William Ostler v. John Heminges *(PRO Coram Rege Roll 1454, 12 Jac. Hilary Term, membrane 692), see Charles William Wallace's two-part ariticle, "Shakespeare in London," in* The Times *(London) on 2 and 4 October 1909. For a transcript of the Latin original, see volume two of B. Roland Lewis's* The Shakespeare Documents: Facsimiles, Transliterations, Translations & Commentary.

That whereas by a certain indenture between Richard Burbadge of London, gentleman on the one party and the forementioned William Osteler of London, gentleman, in his life late the husband of the fore-said Thomasina Osteler, on the other party, at London aforesaid, in the parish of the blessed Mary-le-Bow, in the ward of Cheap, London, made, bearing date the twentieth day of May in the year of the reign of the Lord James now King of England the ninth [1611], it being necessarily recited by the same indenture;

That, whereas the foresaid Richard Burbadge, by a certain other indenture of lease bearing date the ninth day of August in the year of the Lord one thousand six hundred and eight and in the year of the reign of the said Lord King now of England the sixth, for considerations in this same last recited indenture of lease specified, did lease and to farm let to one William Slye, of London, gentleman, deceased, one full seventh part of all that playhouse and divers other possessions of the said Richard Burbadge particularly specified both in the foresaid recited indenture of lease and in five other separate indentures of lease of the same date separately granted of parts of the foresaid playhouse and premises (except just as by the foresaid separate indentures is excepted) by and from the foresaid Richard Burbadge to the forementioned John Hemyngs and to these certain others, William Shakespeare, Cuthbert Burbadge, Henry Condell, Thomas Evans, of London aforesaid, gentlemen, situate in the precinct of the Blackfryers, London, for the term of twenty-one years and for and under an annual rental of five pounds, fourteen shillings, and four pence;

Which particular first recited indenture of lease, just as is set forth, to the forementioned William Slye made and granted as has been abovesaid, one Cecilia Brown, executrix of the last will and testament of the same William Slye, for good considerations her thereunto moving, by virtue of her executorship aforesaid, surrendered and to him the forementioned Richard Burbadge delivered up to be cancelled and made void, together with all her right and interest of and in the foresaid seventh part of the same playhouse and premises, just as by the foresaid indenture of lease and of surrender thereupon endorsed more fully may appear;

And which particular seventh part of the same playhouse and premises so to the foresaid William Slye demised, and surrendered as has been said above, afterwards was divided, demised, and reserved by the foresaid Richard Burbadge to the forementioned John Hemyngs, Henry Condell, the forementioned Richard Burbadge and others by separate indentures of lease, all which particular indentures of lease were surrendered and delivered up to the forementioned Richard Burbadge to be cancelled and made void;

The foresaid Richard Burbadge, for divers good and reasonable considerations him the forementioned

Richard thereunto moving, did demise and to farm let to the forementioned William Osteler all the foresaid seventh part of the foresaid playhouse and premises, just as is set forth to the forementioned William Slye and others demised, having been surrendered as is abovesaid (except just as in the foresaid first recited indenture of lease and in the foresaid five other indentures of lease first beforementioned is excepted)

To have and to hold the foresaid seventh part of the foresaid playhouse and premises, in the manner formerly by the foresaid indenture to the forementioned William Osteler [apparently an error for William Slye] demised (except excepted), to the forementioned William Osteler, his executors, administrators, and assigns, from the feast of the Annunciation of the blessed Virgin Mary [25 March 1611], last past before the date of the said indentures unto the end and term of eighteen years and one quarter of a year then next ensuing, fully to be completed and finished;

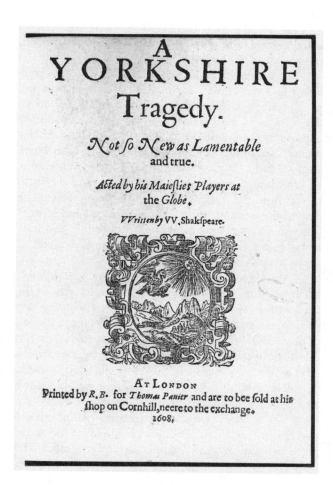

Title page for a quarto play that was not included in the First Folio. The authorship of the work is still vigorously disputed (by permission of the Folger Shakespeare Library).

Title page for the first quarto of King Lear. *Substantial differences between the quarto and Folio texts have led some editors to include both editions in Shakespeare's complete works in lieu of a conflated edition (by permission of the Folger Shakespeare Library).*

Yielding and paying therefore annually during the said term to the forementioned Richard Burbadge, his heirs and assigns, five pounds, fourteen shillings, and fourpence of lawful money of England at the four chief usual feasts or terms in the year—namely, at the feasts of the Nativity of St. John Baptist [24 June], St. Michael the Archangel [29 Sept.], the Birth of the Lord [25 Dec.] and the Annunciation of the blessed Virgin Mary [25 March], or within twenty-one days next after any one of the same feast days by equal portions.

And whereas by a certain other indenture between Basil Nicholl, William Shakespeare, John Witter, John Hemyngs, Henry Condall, and John Edmonds and Mary, his wife, of the one party and the forementioned William Osteler of the other party at London aforesaid in the foresaid parish of the blessed Mary-le-Bow in the ward of Cheap, London, made bearing date the twentieth day of February in the year of the reign of the said Lord King now of England the ninth [1611] abovementioned, it being necessarily recited;

That whereas one Nicholas Brend of West Moulsey in the county of Surrey, esquire, by his indenture tripartite, bearing date the twenty-first day of February in the year of the reign of the Lady Elizabeth, recently Queen of England, the forty-first [1599], for considerations in the same indenture tripartite mentioned and expressed, did demise, grant, and to farm let to these certain ones, Cuthbert Burbadge and Richard Burbadge, of London, gentlemen, to the forementioned William Shakespeare, and to Augustine Phillips and Thomas Pope, of London, gentlemen, deceased, to the foresaid John Hemyngs and to William Kempe, recently of London, gentleman, deceased, all that parcel of ground just recently before enclosed and made into four separate garden plots recently in the tenure and occupation of Thomas Burt and Isbrand Morris, diers, and of Lactantius Roper, salter, citizen of London, containing in length from east to west two hundred and twenty feet of assize or thereabouts, lying and adjoining upon a way or lane there on one [*i.e.*. south] side and abutting upon a piece of land called The Park upon the north, and upon a garden then or recently in the tenure or occupation of one John Cornishe toward the west and upon another garden plot then or recently in the tenure or occupation of one John Knowles toward the east, with all the houses, buildings, structures, ways, easements, commodities, and appurtenances thereunto belonging or in any manner pertaining;

Which said premises are situate, lying, and being within the parish of Saint Savior in Southwark in the county of Surry;

And also all that parcel of land just recently before enclosed and made into three separate garden plots whereof two of the same [were] recently in the tenure or occupation of John Roberts, carpenter, and another recently in the occupation of one Thomas Ditcher, citizen and merchant tailor, of London, situate, lying, and being in the parish aforesaid in the foresaid county of Surry, containing in length from east to west by estimation one hundred fifty and six feet of assize or thereabouts and in breadth from the north to the south one hundred feet of assize by estimation or thereabouts; lying and adjoining upon the other side of the way or lane aforesaid, and abutting upon a garden plot there then or recently just before in the occupation of William Sellers toward the east, and upon one other garden plot there then or recently just before in the tenure of John Burgram, sadler, toward the west, and upon a lane there, called Maiden Lane, toward the south; with all the houses, buildings, structures, ways, easements, commodities, and appurtenances to the last recited premises or to any part or parcel thereof belonging or in any

manner pertaining, together with free ingress, egress, and regress, and passage to and for the foresaid Cuthbert Burbadge and Richard Burbadge and to the forementioned William Shakespeare, Augustine Phillips, Thomas Pope, John Hemyngs, and William Kempe, their executors, administrators, and assigns, and to all and every other person or persons having occasion to come to them by and through the foresaid way or lane, lying and being between the premises aforesaid, mentioned to be demised as is abovesaid, to and from the foresaid premises mentioned to be demised as is aforesaid, and at all and every time and times during the said term below written;

To have and to hold one moiety or half part of the said separate garden plots and all and singular other the forementioned and demised premises, with all and singular the appurtenances to the forementioned Cuthbert Burbadge and Richard Burbadge, their executors, administrators, and assigns, from the Feast of the Birth of the Lord [25 December 1598] last past before the date of the said indenture unto the full end and term of thirty-one years immediately next ensuing and fully to be complete and finished, for an annual rental of seven pounds and five shillings.

And to have and to hold the foresaid other moiety or half part of the foresaid separate garden plots and all and singular other the premises mentioned to be demised as is abovesaid, with all and singular their appurtenances to the forementioned William Shakespeare, Augustine Phillips, Thomas Pope, John Hemyngs, and William Kempe, their executors, administrators, and assigns, from the feast of the Birth of the Lord [25 December 1598] last past before the date of the said indenture until the full end and term of thirty-one years immediately next succeeding and fully to be complete and finished, for an annual rental of seven pounds and five shillings;

Which particular separate amounts were payable upon the four feasts or terms in the year, namely, at the feast of the Annunciation of the blessed Virgin Mary [25 March], of the Nativity of St. John Baptist [24 June], of Saint Michael the Archangel [29 September], and of the Birth of the Lord [25 December], or within sixteen days next after any feast of the feasts aforesaid by equal portions, just as by the foresaid recited indenture among other things may and doth appear.

Upon which particular premises, or upon some part thereof, a certain playhouse, suitable for the showing forth and acting of comedies and tragedies, did exist.

Of which particular playhouse, garden plots, and premises one moiety or half part, into six equal parts and portions divided, the foresaid Basil Nicholl, William Shakespeare, John Witter, John Hemyngs, Henry

Condell, John Edmonds, and Mary his wife, at the time of the making of the foresaid indenture, to the foresaid William Osteler made, did have and enjoy;

Namely, the foresaid Basil Nicholl, John Edmonds, and Mary his wife had one equal sixth part thereof, the foresaid William Shakespeare had one other equal sixth part thereof, the foresaid John Witter had one other equal sixth part thereof, and the foresaid John Hemyngs and Henry Condell had three equal sixth parts thereof, just as by the separate conveyances thereof made more fully may appear;

The foresaid Basil Nicoll, William Shakespeare, John Witter, John Hemyngs, Henry Condell, John Edmonds, and Mary his wife, in consideration of a certain competent sum of money to the same Basil, William, John, John, Henry, John, and Mary by the foresaid William Osteler before the sealing of the said indenture in hand paid, whereof the same Basil, William, John, John, Henry, John, and Mary acknowledged the receipt at London aforesaid, in the foresaid parish of the blessed Mary-le-Bow in the ward of Cheap, London, aforesaid, did demise, bargain, sell, assign, and set over to the foresaid William Osteler, one equal seventh part and portion of the foresaid moiety and half part and portion of the foresaid garden plots, playhouse, and premises in and by the foresaid recited indenture of lease demised (the same moiety and half part of the foresaid garden plots, playhouse, and premises into seven parts and portions being divided)

To have and to hold the foresaid seventh part and portion of the foresaid moiety or half part of the foresaid garden plots, playhouse, and premises, by the foresaid indenture to the forementioned William Osteler mentioned to be granted, bargained, sold, assigned, and set over, to the forementioned William Osteler, his executors, administrators, and assigns from the time of the making of that indenture for and during the residue then still to come of the foresaid term of thirty-one years by the foresaid indenture of lease granted, in such ample manner and form as the foresaid Basil Nicoll, William Shakespeare, John Witter, John Hemyngs, Henry Condell, John Edmonds, and Mary his wife or any one of them the premises aforesaid had or enjoyed.

By virtue of which particular separate leases, the same William Osteler was possessed both of the foresaid seventh part of all the foresaid playhouse and other premises aforesaid situate in the precinct of the Blackfriars, London, in the foresaid indenture of lease before specified, and also of the foresaid other seventh part and portion of the moiety of the foresaid garden plots, playhouse, and other premises aforesaid, in the foresaid second indenture of lease before similarly specified, situate in the foresaid parish of Saint Savior in Southwark, in the foresaid county of Surry.

And so thereof being possessed, the same William Osteler afterwards—namely, on the 16th day of December in the year of the reign of the Lord James, now King of England, the 12th [1614], at London aforesaid, namely, in the parish of the blessed Mary-le-Bow, in the ward of Cheap, London, died intestate;

After whose death the administration of all and singular the goods, chattels, rights, and credits which were belonging to the foresaid William Osteler at the time of his death, by the right reverend father in Christ, the Lord George, by divine favor Archbishop of Canterbury, Primate, and Metropolitane of all England, to the forementioned Thomasina on the twenty-second day of December, in the year of the Lord one thousand six hundred and fourteen, at London aforesaid, in the foresaid parish of the blessed Mary-le-Bow in the ward of Cheap, London aforesaid, was granted;

By force of which, both the foresaid seventh part of all the foresaid playhouse and other the premises aforesaid situate in the precinct of the Blackfriars, London, aforesaid, and the foresaid other seventh part and portion of the foresaid moiety or half part of the garden plots aforesaid, of the playhouse, and of other the premises aforesaid, situate in the foresaid parish of Saint Savior in Southwark in the foresaid county of Surry, specified in the foresaid separate indentures of lease aforesaid to the foresaid William Osteler as set forth granted, and all the profit theron arising and accruing, to the same Thomasina, by virtue of the administration aforesaid, of right did belong and pertain.

Which particular separate indentures of lease, both of the foresaid seventh part of the whole foresaid playhouse and other the premises aforesaid situate in the precinct of the Blackfriars, London aforesaid, and of the foresaid seventh part and portion of the foresaid moiety of the foresaid garden plots, playhouse, and other the premises aforesaid situate in the foresaid parish of Saint Savior in Southwark, in the foresaid county of Surry, after the death of the foresaid William Osteler, namely, on the foresaid twenty-second day of December, in the year of the reign of the said Lord King now of England the twelfth [1614] abovesaid, at London aforesaid, in the foresaid parish of the blessed Mary-le-Bow, in the ward of Cheap, London aforesaid, to the hands and possession of the foresaid John Hemyngs merely to be safe kept did come and then still in the hands of the same John Hemyngs did remain and continue, and yet still do remain and be.

And the same John Hemyngs the gains, profits, and commodities both of and for the foresaid seventh part of all the foresaid playhouse and other the premises aforesaid situate in the foresaid precinct of the

Blackfriars, London aforesaid, and of the foresaid seventh part and portion of the moiety of the foresaid garden plots, playhouse, and other the premises aforesaid situate in the foresaid parish of Saint Savior in Southwark in the foresaid county of Surry, specified in the foresaid indentures of lease, as is set forth, from day to day increasing and growing and to the foresaid Thomasina, after the death of the foresaid William Osteler as is set forth, belonging and pertaining, being all the estate which she the same Thomasina had to herself, by the death of the foresaid William Osteler her husband, left remaining both for her relief and maintenance and for paying the debts of the same William Osteler, amounting to a very great value from the time of the death of the same William Osteler unto the present, by color of a certain pretended grant and assignment (to the same Thomasina totally unknown) to him the forementioned John Hemyngs by the foresaid William Osteler of trust made, as the same John Hemyngs to the forementioned Thomasina has declared and affirmed, has received and had and them to his own private use has converted without giving any compensation therefore to the same Thomasina for the same, and those indentures of lease aforesaid from the forementioned Thomasina has detained and yet still doth detain and them to her the forementioned Thomasina to render and deliver up has utterly refused, although the same John has very frequently been required to do this by the foresaid Thomasina both after the death of the foresaid William Osteler, and after the administration aforesaid granted to her the forementioned Thomasina, as is set forth. . . .

And the same Thomasina further in fact says that the true value of the foresaid seventh part of all the foresaid playhouse and other the premises situate in the foresaid precinct of the Blackfriars, London aforesaid, from the time of the death of the foresaid William Osteler unto the present and for the residue of the term of years in the foresaid indenture of lease thereof, to the forementioned William Osteler made as is set forth, amounts to three hundred pounds of legal money of England; and that the true value of the foresaid seventh part of the moiety of the foresaid garden plots, playhouse, and other the premises aforesaid situate in the parish of Saint Savior in Southwark in the foresaid county of Surry, from the time of the death of the foresaid William Osteler unto the present and for the residue of the term of years in the foresaid indenture of lease thereof, to the same William Osteler made as is set forth, amounts to three hundred pounds of legal money of England; and that the true value of the foresaid garden plots, playhouse, and other the premises aforesaid situate in the foresaid parish of Saint Savior in Southwark, in the foresaid county of Surry, from the time of the death of the foresaid William Osteler unto

the present and for the residue of the term of years in the foresaid indenture of lease thereof, to the same William Osteler made as is set forth, amounts to three hundred pounds of legal money of England.

Yet nevertheless the foresaid John, very little regarding his promise and undertaking aforesaid but plotting and basely intending the same Thomasina in this part cunningly and craftily to deceive and defraud, the foresaid six hundred pounds for the true value of the same two seventh parts of the playhouses aforesaid to the forementioned Thomasina not yet has paid nor in any way for the same satisfied, although, thereunto by the same Thomasina afterwards, namely on the fifth day of October in the year of the reign of the said Lord King now of England the thirteenth [1615] abovesaid, at London aforesaid, in the parish and ward aforesaid very often demand has been made of him.

By which means the same Thomasina the whole gain, commodity, and profit which she with the foresaid six hundred pounds would have and enjoy, to buy, sell, and lawfully bargain, if the foresaid John his promise and undertaking aforesaid in the form aforesaid had performed, is utterly deprived of and has wholly lost, whereby she says that she has received harm and has sustained damage to the value of six hundred pounds, and therefore has brought suit, &c.

–*The Times* (London), 4 October 1909, p. 9

Mary Shakespeare's Burial Record

The burial of Shakespeare's mother, Mary, was recorded in the register of Holy Trinity Church, Stratford-upon-Avon.

[9 September 1608]   Mayry Shaxspere, wydowe
                    –Shakespeare Birthplace Trust Records Office,
                                        DR 243/1, folio 39v

Allusion to *Hamlet* in Armin's *A Nest of Ninnies*

A Nest of Ninnies Simply of themselves without Compound, *Robert Armin's collection of jests first published in 1600 as* Foole upon Foole, *was subsequently published in 1605 and 1608. The third edition includes a reference to Hamlet in the jest of John, an "innocent Ideot" (G1r), who is involved in a variety of misadventures. The excerpt follows the second jest, in which John tolls the church bell, forcing parish officials to place the rope out of his reach; when asked for whom the bell tolls, John replies that it tolls for his chicken. While Hamlet complains about "the whips and scorns of time" (3.1.69), he does not speak the line Armin assigns him here. Armin was an actor in Shakespeare's company, and a playwright. In the dedicatory epistle to his translation of* The Italian Taylor, *and his Boy (1609), Armin humbly describes himself as a "Begger, who hath been writ downe for an Asse in his time, & pleades under* forma pauperis *in it still, notwithstanding his Constableship and Office" (sig. A3r); this statement implies Armin played the role of Dogberry in Shakespeare's comedy* Much Ado About Nothing *in which the misspeaking constable several times wishes that he "had been writ down an ass" (4.2.86–87).*

A number of things more *John* did, which I omit, fearing to be tedious: not long after he dyed, and was old, for his beard was full of white haires, as his picture in christs Hospitall (now to be seene) can witnesse: buryed he is, but with no Epitaph. Mee thinks, those that in his life time could afford him his picture, might with his grave yeeld so much as foure lynes, that people may see where he lyes, whom they so well knew, and if I might perswade, his Motto should bee to this effect:

Here sleepes blew John, *that gives*
Food to feed wormes, and yet not lives:
You that passe by looke on his grave,
And say, your selves the like must have.
Wise men and fooles all one end makes:
Gods will be done who gives and takes.

Surely sayes mistris Nicetie this pleases well to see one so naturally silly to be simply subtill, it is strange, but I heare it and like a tale out of a poore mans mouth hardly credit it. This foole sayes *Sotto* signifies many who come to Church to meete acquaintance, more then for piety, & will sooner sell the Church for mony, then pawne ought to underprop it. At these the boyes and children of this world wonder, while manly ages sees and will not see. For these as the second tale saies, Folly towles the bell, and a number longs to heare it ring out, when the losse of *Johns* Chickin is of more want then theirs, but a rope ont it, it will one day be better. Ther are as *Hamlet* sayes things cald whips in store.

—sig. G3v

Allusion to *Hamlet* in Dekker's *The Dead Tearme*

In Thomas Dekker's The Dead Tearme. Or Westminsters Complaint for long Vacations and short Termes. *Written in manner of a Dialogue betweene the two Cityes London and Westminster (1608), a young man dies of the plague, and two unscrupulous porters are hired to bury him. In order to be able to return to the room where the plague victim died and steal the rest of his property, one of the two porters pretends to be mad, a trick that prompts a comparison to* Hamlet. *The first-person narrator in this excerpt is the city of London.*

[*In margin:* The death of a young man a linnen Draper dwelling in Friday-street.] A token had hee sent from heaven, by which hee was bidden to make hast thither: hee obeyed the bringer of it, and in pawne of his soule that was gone of the journey, left hee his cold body behind.

[*In margin:* The two Porters of London.] To keepe which safe, Two fellowes were hyred to hide it in the earth: they did so, using the body, as Souldiers do Townes which are taken; they rifled it, of all that belonged unto it, and what al men else were affraid to touch or come neere, did they (being armed with the desire of money) nimbly, and Jocundly packe uppe, intending at theyre comming home to share it.

No sooner had they dispatched their deadly busines, but those that had Authorities of the place, and who made much of these two *Sharkers* before, when they stoode in neede of their helpe, make now as much hast as they can, to ridde them out of theyre company: Away therefore like Pedlers from the end of a Fayre, so doe they send them away trudging.

The Town looked even sick so long as they were in it. It was a killing to any Countrey fellowe to have looked uppon them, if hee had but heard what parts in this black Tragedy of death they had played. And both of them being Porters, were taken by reason of their white Frocks, for two Ghosts walking in white Shirts: to have drunk with these Pot-tossers hadde beene no way but one, to have solde any drinke to them, had beene for a Tapster to have drunke his last: nay, whosoever did but spy them 12. score off, or were but told that two such *Ravens* (who preied uppon a dead body) flew that way, cryed presently out, *Lord have mercy uppon us*, clapping their hard handes on their Country-breastes, and looking more pale then the sheete in which the man was buryed.

But the best was these *Partners* (that dealt in such a dead commodity) were borne to beare, & tooke all things patiently.

But ambling on their way towards their owne home, (which is under my wing) where they knewe they should finde better entertainement, their mindes were troubled, and their teeth watered, at the remembraunce of not onely Money, but also of apparell, and other luggage which was left in the Bed-chamber where the sicke man dyed; neere which they perswaded themselves no man (upon payne of life) unlesse it were *They two* durst or would once venture.

They shrugged as they went, and on a sudden starting backe, would they stand stone-still, for their braines were buzzing about severall plottes how to purchase this booty. But the powder of their wit being wet, and not so apt to take fire, they shooke their addle heads like a couple of rattles, and bit their lips

187

for anger, that their tongues would speak nothing to helpe them in this peck of troubles. Faine would they have returned backe, but durst not: their fingers itched to lay hold upon the prize, but all the craft was in the catching.

At length one of them having a more plaugy pate than his fellow, swore he would counterfet himselfe to be struck with sicknes, and with the poyson of infection, to run mad if he got not the bayt that he nibled at, (without choaking himselfe with the hooke) onely by this tricke, he would dye for it: but if he went away with it cleare, all the fresh men in Cambridge should throw their cappes at him, and not mend the devise.

The other scratched at this, and grind, insteed of gyving a plaudit, which proved that he had a liking to this parte of the Comedy. Their faces therefore do they turne upon *Barnwell* (neere *Cambridge*) for ther was it to be acted: thither comes this counterfet mad-man running: his fellow Jugler following a loose, crying stoppe the mad-man, take heed of the man, hees mad with the plague. Sometimes would he over take him, and lay hands upon him (like a Catch-pole) as if he had arrested him, but furious *Hamlet* would presently eyther breake loose like a Beare from the stake, or else so set his pawes on this dog that thus bayted him; that with tugging and tearing one anothers frockes off, they both looked like mad Tom of Bedlam. Wheresoever they cam, there needed no Fencers, nor Whifflers to flourish before them to make way, for (as if a Bul had run up and downe) the streetes were cleared, and none sought to stop him.

At length he came to the house where the deade man had bin lodged: from the dore would not this olde *Jeronimo* be driven, that was his Inne, there he would lie, that was his Bedlam, and there or nowhere must his mad tricks be plaid.

In the end, the feare of further daunger to flowe from him (as being thought to have the plague) and the authority of those that could command, made this unruly guest be let into the same house, where entring, none durst keep him company, but the Byrd of his own feather, and that was the sport which hee looked for: In no other chamber must he be lodged, but onely that where al the dead mans goods lay; and that was the feast to which they longed to be bidden: where lying, and none comming neare them, they plaied the merchants and packed up such commodities as they liked, and about the houre of the night when spyrits use to walk, did these *Quicke Ghosts* silently steale forth, and before they were missed, were laughing on their way, how they had cozend them that deal in nothing but *Learning*.

—sigs. G2r–G3v

Page from Edward Topsell's The Historie of Serpents *(1608). Hamlet describes himself to King Claudius as "of the chameleon's dish: I eat the air, promise-cramm'd" (3.2.93–94; by permission of the Folger Shakespeare Library).*

Allusion to *Hamlet* in Dekker's *Lanthorne and Candle-light*

Thomas Dekker alludes to Hamlet *in* Lanthorne and Candle-light *(1608), a sequel to Dekker's lively account of London rogues, crimes, con men, and scams,* Belman of London *(1608). In the following description of "moon-men," Dekker compares one of their deceptive practices to a stage play, and labels an unwitting victim of the scam a "mad Hamlet."*

Moone-men,

A discovery of a strange wild people, very dangerous to townes and country villages.

A Moone-man signifies in English, a mad-man, because the Moone hath greatest domination (above any other Planet) over the bodies of Franticke persons. But these Moone-men (whose Images are now to be carved) are neither absolute mad, nor yet perfectly in their wits. Their name they borrow from the Moone, because as the Moone is never in one shape two nights together, but wanders up and downe Heaven like an Anticke, so these changeable-stuff-companions never tary one day in a place, but are the onely, and the onely base Ronnagats upon earth. And as in the Moone there is a man, that never stirres without a bush of thornes at his backe, so these Moone-men lie under bushes, and are indeed no better then Hedge-creepers.

They are a people more scattred then Jewes, and more hated: beggerly in apparell, barbarous in condition, beastly in behavior: and bloudy if they meete advantage. A man that sees them would sweare they had all the yellow jawndis, or that they were Tawny Moores bastardes, for no Red-oaker man caries a face of a more filthy complexion, yet are they not borne so, neither has the Sunne burnt them so, but they are painted so, yet they are not good painters neither; for they do not make faces, but marre faces. By a by name they are called Gipsies, they call themselves Egiptians, others in mockery call them Moone-men.

If they be Egiptians, sure I am they never discended from the tribes of any of those people that came out of the Land of Eigpt: *Ptolomy* (King of the Egiptians) I warrant never called them his Subjects; no nor *Pharao* before him. Looke what difference there is betweene a civill cittizen of Dublin and a wild Irish Kerne, so much difference there is betweene one of these counterfeit Egiptians and a true English Begger. An English Roague is just of the same livery.

. . . .

Their apparell is od, and phantasticke, tho it be never so full of rents: the men weare scarfes of Callico, or any other base stuffe having their bodies like Morris dancers, with bells, and other toyes, to intice the countrey people to flocke about them, and to wounder at their fooleries or rather rancke knaveryes. The women as ridiculously attrire them-selves, and (like one that plaies, the Roague on a Stage) weare rags, and patched filthy mantles uppermost, when the under garments are handsome and in fashion.

The battailes these Out-lawes make, are many and very bloudy. Whosoever falles into theyr hands never escapes alive, and so cruell they are in these murders, that nothing can satisfie them but the very heart-bloud of those whom they kill. And who are they (thinke you) that thus go to the pot? Alasse! Innocent Lambs, Sheep, Calves, Pigges &c. Poultrie- ware are more churlishly handled by them, then poore prisoners are by keepers in the counter it'h Poultry. A goose comming amongst them learnes to be so wise, that hee never will be Goose any more. The bloudy tragedies of al these, are only acted by the Women, who carrying long knives or Skeanes under theyr mantles, do thus play theyr parts: The Stage is some large Heath, or a Firre-bush Common, far from any houses; Upon which casting them-selves into a Ring, they inclose the Murderers, till the Massacre be finished. If any passenger come by, and wondring to see such a conjuring circle kept by Hel-houndes, demaund what spirits they raise there? one of the Murderers steps to him poysons him with sweete wordes and shifts him off, with this lye, that one of the women is falne in labour. But if any mad *Hamlet* hearing this, smell villanie, and rush in by violence to see what the tawny Divels are dooing; then they excuse the fact, lay the blame on those that are the Actors, and perhaps (if they see no remedie) deliver them to an officer, to be had to punishment: But by the way a rescue is surely laid & very valiantly (tho very villanously) do they fetch them off, and guard them.

—sigs. G4v–G5v

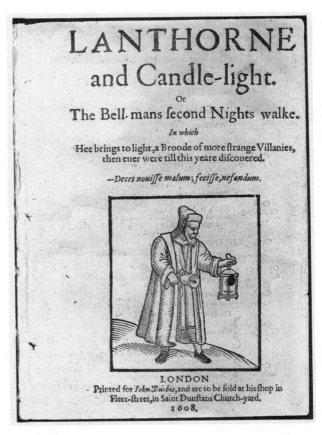

Title page for a work that includes an allusion to the madness of Hamlet (by permission of the Folger Shakespeare Library)

Allusion to *Venus and Adonis* in Machin and Markham's *The Dumbe Knight*

In Lewis Machin and Gervase Markham's The dumbe Knight. A historicall Comedy *(1608), President, a master of the double entendre and clerk to the orator, Prate, is interrupted by Drap, a country gentleman, and Veloups, a citizen; the book with which President busies himself is not work related.*

Enter Veloups and Drap, President sitting at his deske.

[*Veloups*] This is his chamber, lets enter, heeres his clarke.

[*President*] Fondling, said he, since I have hem'd thee heere,

　　　Within the circuit of this Ivory pale.

[*Drap*] I pray you sir help us to the speech of your master.

[*President*] Ile be a parke, and thou shalt be my Deere:

He is very busie in his study.

Feed where thou wilt, in mountaine or on dale.

Stay a while he will come out anon.

Graze on my lips, and when those mounts are drie,

Stray lower where the pleasant fountaines lie.

Go thy way thou best booke in the world.

[*Veloups*] I pray you sir, what booke doe you read?

[*President*] A book that never an Orators clarke in this kingdome but is be-

holden unto; it is called maides philosophie, or *Venus and Adonis*:

Looke you gentlemen, I have divers other pretty bookes. . . .

　　　　　　　　　　　　　　　　　　　　　–sig. Fr

Allusion to *Venus and Adonis* in Middleton's *A Mad World, My Masters*

Among the steps that Harebraine takes to make his wife behave more chastely in playwright Thomas Middleton's comedy A Mad World, My Masters *(1608) is to hide her copy of* Venus and Adonis.

[*Harebraine*] . . . Oh Lady *Gulman*, my wifes onely company! welcome; and how do's the vertuous Matron, that good old Gentlewoman thy mother? I perswade my selfe, if modesty be in the world she has part on't: a woman of an excellent carriage all her life time, in Court, Citie, and Countrey.

[*Curtizan*] Sha's alwaies carried it well in those places sir; witnesse three bastards a peece: how do's your sweete bedfellow sir? you see Ime her boldest visitant.

Hareb. And welcome sweete Virgin, the onely companion, my soule wishes for her; I left her within at her Lute, prethee give her good counsell.

Curtiz. Alas, she needes none sir.

Hareb. Yet, yet, yet, a little of thy instructions will not come amisse to her.

Curtiz. Ile bestow my labour sir.

Hareb. Doe, labour her prethee; I have convay'd away all her wanton Pamphlets, as Hero and Leander, Venus and Adonis, oh two lushious mary-bone pies for a yong married wife, here, here, prethie take the resolution, and reade to her a little.

Curt. Sha's set up her resolution alreadie sir.

Hareb. True, true, and this will confirme it the more, ther's a chapter of Hell, tis good to reade this cold weather, terrifie her, terrifie her; goe, reade to her the horrible punishments for itching wantonnes, the paines alotted for adulterie; tell her her thoughts, her very dreames are answerable, say so; rip up the life of a Curtizan, & show how loathsom tis.

Curt. The gentleman would perswade mee in time to disgrace my selfe, and speake ill of mine owne function.

　　　　　　　　　　　　　　　　　　　　Exit.

　　　　　　　　　　　　　　　　　　–sigs. B1r–v

The Venetian Ambassador Attends a Performance of *Pericles*

Zorzi Giustinian served as the Venetian ambassador from 5 January 1606 to 23 November 1608. This report of his attending Pericles *was made by Odoardo Guatz, his interpreter, and included in* Calendar of State Papers and Manuscripts Relating to English Affairs, Existing in the Archives and Collections of Venice, and in the Other Libraries of Northern Italy *(1908).*

Believes that all the ambassadors who have come to England have gone to the play more or less.

The Ambassador Giustinian went with the French ambassador and his wife to a play called "Pericles," which cost Giustinian more than 20 crowns. He also took the Secretary of Florence.

　　　　　　　　–*Calendar of State Papers*, vol. XIV, p. 600

Possible Allusion to Anne Hathaway

*F. C. Morgan in "Honorificabilitudinitatibus" (*Notes & Queries, *October, 1978, p. 445) reports finding a letter beginning "Good Mrs. Shakespeare" in the binding of* Analysis Logica Omnium Epistolarum Pauli *(1608) by J. Piscator. The letter is not signed or dated, but it does mention the name "Bott" and the street "Trinity Lane"; William Bott once owned New Place, and Trinity Lane is a street in Stratford-upon-Avon. The printer of the book, Richard Field, was from Stratford and printed Shakespeare's* Venus and Adonis *and* The Rape of Lucrece.

The King's Men
Paid for Court Performances

The King's Men are also compensated for being unable to perform due to an outbreak of the plague.

To John Hemynges one of his majesties plaiers uppon the Councelles warraunte dated v^{to} Aprilis 1609 for twelve playes by him and the rest of his Companye presented before the Kinge Queene Prince and Duke of Yorke at severall times in xpmas 1608   Cxx^{li}

. . . .

To John Hemynges one of his majesties plaiers uppon the Councelles warraunte dated xxvi^{to} Aprilis 1609 in the behalfe of himselfe and the rest of his Company by way of his majesties rewarde for their private practise in the time of infeccion that thereby they mighte be inhabled to performe their service before his majestie in Christmas hollidaies 1609   xl^{li}

—*Dramatic Records*, p. 47

Shakespeare's Suit against Addenbrooke

These documents record Shakespeare's lawsuit against John Addenbrooke who owed the playwright £6 plus court costs of £1, 4 s. (Shakespeare Birthplace Trust Records Office, Miscellaneous Documents V, 115; 116; 127a; 127b; 139; Manuscripts ER 27/6; 27/7). The first document is dated 17 August 1608 and the last 7 June 1609. The documents include orders for Addenbrooke's arrest, for the empanelling and appearance of a jury, and for the court appearance of the defendant, along with a record of the names of and the verdict reached by the jurors. Addenbrooke lost the case and apparently disappeared because the final document is an order for his surety, Thomas Hornby, to pay the debt and court costs. For a detailed discussion of the case see B. Roland Lewis's The Shakespeare Documents: Facsimiles, Transliterations, Translations & Commentary (pp. 393–400).

This first court document recording the arrest of John Addenbrooke is dated 17 June 1608.

Stratford Burgus. Preceptum est servientibus ad clavam ibidem quod capiant, seu etc., Johannem Addenbrooke, generosum, si etc., et eum salvo etc., ita quod habeant corpus ejus coram ballivo burgi prediti, ad proximam curiam de recordo ibidem tenendam, ad respondendum Willielmo Shackspeare, generoso, de placito debiti, et habeant ibi tunc hoc preceptum. Teste Henrico Walker, generoso, ballivo ibidem, xvii. die Augusti, annis regni domini nostri Jacobi, Dei gratia regis Anglie, Francie et Hibernie, sexto, et Scotie quadragesimo.

[Signed]: Greene.

[Endorsed]: Virtute istius precepti cepi infranominatum Johannem, cujus corpus paratum habeo prout interius mihi precipitur. Manucaptor pro defendente, Thomas Hornebye.

[Signed]: Gilbertus Charnock, serviens.

[Borough of Stratford.] John Addenbrooke, gentleman, was ordered by the sergeants at mace, the same which they executed, etc., etc., greetings, etc., thus that they have his body in the presence of the bailiff of the borough aforesaid, at the next Court of Record to be held at that place, to answer to William Shakespeare, gentleman, concerning the payment of a debt, and they have there and then this order. Henry Walker, gentleman, being witness for the same bailiff on the seventeenth day of August, in the sixth year of the reign of our good James, by the Grace of God King of England, France and Ireland, and the fortieth year of Scotland.

[Signed]: Greene

[Endorsed]: By virtue of this order I have taken the within-named John, whose body I have presented as I was ordered so to do. Mainpernor for the defendant, Thomas Hornby.

[Signed]: Gilbert Charnock, sergeant.

—Lewis, *Shakespeare Documents*, vol. II, pp. 393–394

The jury was summoned on 21 December 1608.

Stratford Burgus. Preceptum est servientibus ad clavam ibidem quod habeant, seu etc., corpora Philippi Greene, Jacobi Elliottes, Edwardi Hunt, Roberti Wilson, Thome Kerby, Thome Bridges, Ricardi Collyns, Johannis Ingraham, Danielis Smyth, Willilmi Walker, Thome Mylls, Johannis Tubb, Ricardi Pincke, Johannis Smyth pannarii, Laurencii Holmes, Johannis Boyce, Hugonis Piggen, Johannis Samvell, Roberti Cawdry, Johannis Castle, Pauli Bartlett, Johannis Yeate, Thome Bradshowe, Johannis Gunne, juratorum summonitorum in curia domini regis hic tenta coram ballivo ibidem, ad faciendum quandam juratam patrie inter Willielmum Shackspeare, generosum, querentem, et Johannem Addenbrooke, defendentem, in placito debiti, et habeant ibi tunc hoc preceptum. Teste Francisco Smyth juniore, generoso, ballivo ibidem, xxi. die Decembris, annis regni domini nostri Jacobi, Dei gratia regis Anglie, Fraucie et Hibernie, sexto, et Scotie quadragesimo secundo.

[Signed]: Greene.

[Endorsed]: Executio istius precepti patet in quodam panello huic precepto annexo.

[Signed]: Gilbertus Charnock, serviens.

[Borough of Stratford. There is an order from the sergeants at mace, the same which they executed, etc. The bodies of Philip Greene, James Elliott, Edward Hunt, Robert Wilson, Thomas Kerby, Thomas Bridges, Richard Collins, John Ingraham, Daniel Smyth, William Walker, Thomas Mills, John Tubb, Richard Pink, John Smyth, panniers, Lawrence Holmes, John Boyce, Hugo Piggen, John Samwell, Robert Cawdry, John Castle, Paul Bartlett, John Yeate, Thomas Bradshaw, John Gunn, the jurors summoned in the King's Court here held in the presence of the same bailiff, for the certain selection of a jury between William Shakespeare, gentleman, plaintiff, and John Addenbrooke, defendant, in the payment of a debt, and they have there and then this order. Francis Smyth, Jr., gentleman, being a witness before the same bailiff at that place, on the twenty-first day of December, the sixth year of the reign of our Master James, by the Grace of God King of England, France and Ireland, and the forty-second year of Scotland.

[Signed]: Greene.
[Endorsed]: The execution of this order appears in a certain panel attached to this order.
[Signed]: Gilbert Charnock, sergeant.
—Lewis, *Shakespeare Documents,* vol. II, pp. 394–395

The jurors were then selected.

Nomina juratorum inter Willielmum Shakespere, generosum, versus Johannem Addenbroke de placito debiti. Philippus Greene; Jacobus Elliott; Edwardus Hunte; Robertus Wilson; Thomas Kerbye; Thomas Bridges; Ricardus Collins; Johannes Ingraham; Daniell Smyth; Willielmus Walker; Thomas Mills; Johannes Tubb; Ricardus Pincke; Johannes Smyth, draper; Laurencius Holmes; Johannes Boyce; Hugo Piggon; Johannes Samwell; Robertus Cawdry; Johannes Castle; Paulus Bartlett; Johannes Yeate; Thomas Bradshowe; Johannes Gunne. Quilibet jurator predictus, pro se separatim, manucaptus est per plegios, Johannem Doo et Ricardum Roo.

[The names of the jurors between William Shakespeare, gentleman, versus John Addenbrooke concerning the payment of a debt. Philip Greene; James Elliott; Edward Hunt; Robert Wilson; Thomas Kerby; Thomas Bridges; Richard Collins; John Ingraham; Daniel Smyth; William Walker; Thomas Mills; John Tubb; Richard Pink; John Smyth, draper; Lawrence Holmes; John Boyce; Hugo Piggen; John Samwell; Robert Cawdry; John Castle; Paul Bartlett; John Yeate; Thomas Bradshaw; John Gunn. Each of the aforesaid jurors, for himself separately, has been made bondsman by pledge by John Doe and Richard Roe.]
—Lewis, *Shakespeare Documents,* vol. II, p. 395

The jury was ordered to appear on 15 February 1609.

Stratford Burgus. Preceptum est servientibus ad clavam ibidem quod distringant, seu etc., Philippum Greene, Jacobum Elliottes, Edwardum Hunt, Robertum Wilson, Thomam Kerbey, Thomam Bridges, Ricardum Collins, Johannem Ingraham, Danielem Smyth, William Walker, Thomam Mylls, Johanem Tubb, Ricardum Pincke, Johannem Smyth, pannarium, Laurencium Holmes, Johannem Boyce, Hugonem Piggin, Johannem Samwell, Robertum Cawdry, Johannem Castle, Paulum Bartlett, Johannem Yate, Thomam Bradshawe, et Johannem Gunne, juratores summonitos in curia domini regis de recordo hic tenta inter Willielmum Shackspeare, querentem, et Johannem Addenbroke, defendentem, in placito debiti, per omnes terras et cattalla sua in balliva sua, ita quod nec ipsi nec aliquis per ipsos ad ea manum apponant, donec aliud inde a curia predicta habuerint preceptum, et quod de exitibus eorundem de curia predicta respondeant. Et quod habeant corpora corum coram ballivo burgi predicti, ad proximam curaim de recordo ibidem tenendam, ad faciendum juratam illam et ad audiendum judicium suum de pluribus defaltis; et habeant ibi tunc hoc preceptum. Teste Francisco Smyth juniore, generoso, ballivo ibidem, xvº. die Februarii, annis regni domini nostri Jacobi Dei gratia regis Anglie, Francie et Hibernie, sexto, et Scotie quadragesimo-secundo.

[Signed]: Greene.
[Endorsed]: Executio istius precepti patet in quodam panello huic precepto annexo.
[Signed]: Franciscus Boyce, serviens.

[Borough of Stratford. There is an order to the sergeants of the mace in the same place that they distrain, etc. Philip Greene, James Elliott, Edward Hunt, Robert Wilson, Thomas Kerby, Thomas Bridges, Richard Collins, John Ingraham, Daniel Smyth, William Walker, Thomas Mills, John Tubb, Richard Pink, John Smyth, panniers, Lawrence Holmes, John Boyce, Hugo Piggen, John Samwell, Robert Cawdry, John Castle, Paul Bartlett, John Yeate, Thomas Bradshaw, and John Gunn, jurors summoned in the King's Court of Record held here between William Shakespeare, plaintiff, and John Addenbrooke, defendant, for the payment of a debt for all lands and chattels in his bailiwick; so that neither they nor any of them, in any way, interfere with them until further order of the said court and that they shall make answer after the withdrawal of the same from said court. And that they appear before the bailiff of the aforesaid borough at the next court of record held at that place to empanel a jury to render its judgment concerning the many defaults; and that they have there this order. Witnessed by Francis Smyth, Jr., gentleman, before the same bailiff on the fifteenth day of February, the sixth year of our Master James, by Grace of God King of England, France and Ireland, and in the forty-second of Scotland.

[Signed]: Greene.

[Endorsed]: The execution of this order is shown in a certain panel attached to this order.

[Signed]: Francis Boyce, sergeant.

—Lewis, *Shakespeare Documents*, vol. II, pp. 395–396

The list of the jurors who served and the record of their verdict were recorded.

Nomina juratorum inter Willielmum Shackspere, querentem, et Johannem Addenbrooke, de placito debiti. Philippus Greene; Jacobus Elliottes egrotat; Edwardus Hunt; Robertus Wilson, juratus; Thomas Kerby; Thomas Bridges; Ricardus Collyns, juratus; Johannes Ingraham, juratus; Daniel Smyth, juratus; Willielmus Walker, juratus; Thomas Mills, juratus; Johannes Tubb, juratus; Ricardus Pincke, juratus; Johannes Smyth, pannarius, juratus; Laurencius Holmes; Johannes Boyce; Hugo Piggin, juratus; Johannes Samvell; Robertus Cawdrey, juratus; Johannes Castle; Paulus Bartlett; Johannes Yate, juratus; Thomas Bradshawe et Johannes Gunne. Quilibet juratorum predictorum, per se separatim, attachiatus est per plegios, Johannem Doo et Ricardum Roo. Exitus cujuslibet eorum per se, vi.*s.* viii.*d.* Juratores dicunt pro querente; misas iiii.*d.*; dampna ii.*d.*

[The names of the jurors between William Shakespeare, plaintiff, and John Addenbrooke, concerning the payment of a debt. Philip Greene and James Elliott were ill; Edward Hunt; Robert Wilson, juror; Thomas Kerby; Thomas Bridges; Richard Collins, juror; John Ingraham, juror; Daniel Smyth, juror; William Walker, juror; Thomas Mills, juror; John Tubb, juror; Richard Pink, juror; John Smyth, pannier, juror; Lawrence Holmes; John Boyce; Hugo Piggen, juror; John Samwell; Robert Cawdry, juror; John Castle; Paul Bartlett; John Yeate, juror; Thomas Bradshaw; and John Gunn. Each of the aforesaid jurors, for himself separately, was made mainpernor by pledges of John Doe and Richard Roe. And all and each of them having retired, the jurors return verdict for plaintiff. Costs 6*s.* 8*d.* [for the jurors]; [other court] cost, 4*d.*; damages [to the complainant] 2*d.*]

—Lewis, *Shakespeare Documents*, vol. II, p. 397

John Addenbrooke was ordered to pay the debt, costs, and damages on 15 March 1609.

Stratford Burgus. Preceptum est servientibus ad clavam ibidem quod capiant, seu etc., Johannem Addenbrooke, si etc., et eum salvo etc., ita quod habeant corpus ejus coram ballivo burgi predicti, ad proximam curiam de recordo ibidem tenendam, ad satisfaciendum Willielmo Shackspeare, generoso, tam de sex libris debiti quas predictus Willielmus in eadem curia versus eum recuperavit quam de viginti et quatuor solidis qui ei adjudicati fuerunt pro dampnis et custagiis suis quos sustinuit occacione detencionis debiti predicti, et habeant ibi tunc hoc preceptum. Teste Francisco Smyth juniore, generoso, ballivo ibidem, xv die Marcii, annis regni domini nostri Jacobi, Dei gracia regis Anglie, Francie et Hibernie sexto, et Scotie xliiº.

[Signed]: Greene.

[Endorsed]: Infranominatus Johannes non est inventus infra libertatem hujus burgi.

[Signed]: Franciscus Boyce, serviens.

[Borough of Stratford. John Addenbrooke was summoned by the sergeants at mace the same which they executed, whether etc., greetings, etc., thus they have his body in the presence of the bailiff of the aforesaid borough, at the next Court of Record held there, to satisfy William Shakespeare, gentleman, concerning not only a debt of six pounds which said William recovered in said court against him but also twenty-four shillings which were adjudged to him for damages and costs which he sustained on the occasion of withholding said debt, and that they have here then this order. Witnessed by Francis Smyth, Jr., gentleman, for the same bailiff, this fifteenth day of March, the sixth year of the reign of our Master James, by the Grace of God King of England, France and Ireland, and the forty-second of Scotland.

[Signed]: Greene.

[Endorsed]: The within-named John has not been found within the jurisdiction of this borough.

[Signed]: Francis Boyce, sergeant.

—Lewis, *Shakespeare Documents*, vol. II, pp. 397–398

Addenbrooke's surety, Thomas Hornby, was ordered to pay the debt, costs, and damages on 7 June 1609.

Stratford Burgus. Preceptum est servientibus ad clavam ibidem quod cum quidam Willielmus Shackspeare, generosus, nuper in curia domini Jacobi, nunc regis Anglie, burgi predicti, ibidem tenta virtute literarum patentium domini Edwardi, nuper regis Anglie, sexti, levavit quandam querelam suam versus quendam Johannem. Addenbrooke de placito debiti, cumque eciam quidam Thomas Horneby de burgo predicto in eadem querela devenit plegius et manucaptor predicti Johanne, scilicet, quod si predictus Johannes in querela illa legitimo modo convincaretur quod idem Johannes satisfaceret prefato Willielmo Shackspeare tam debitum in querela illa per prefatum Willielmum versus predictum Johannem in curia predicta recuperandum quam misas et custagia que eidem Willielmo in querelailla per eandem curiam adjudicata forent versus eundem Johannem, vel idem se redderet prisone dicti domini regis Jacobi nunc, burgi predicti, ad satisfaciendum eidem Willielmo eadem debitum misas et custagia; et ulterius quod si idem Johannes non satisfaceret eidem Willielmo debitum et misas et custagia, nec se redderet predicte prisone dicti domini regis nunc ad satisfaciendum eidem Willielmo in forma predicta, quod tunc ipse idem Thomas Horneby debitum sic recuperandum et misas et custagia sic adjudicata eidem Willielmo satisfacere vellet. Cumque eciam in querela illa taliter processum fuit in eadem curia quod predictus Willielmus in loquela illa, per judicium eiusdem curie, recuperabat versus predictum Johannem tam sex libras de debito quam viginti et quatuor solidos pro decremento misarum et custagiorum ipsius Willielmi in secta querela illius appositos. Super quo preceptum fuit servientibus ad clavam ibidem quod capiant, seu etc., predictum Johannem, si etc., et eum salvo etc., ita quod habeant corpus eius coram ballivo burgi predicti, ad proximam curiam de recordo ibidem tenendam, ad satisfaciendum predicto Willielmo [tam] de debito predicto sic recuperato, quam de viginti et quatuor solidis pro predictis dampnis et custagiis adjudicatis; unde Franciscus Boyce, tunc et nunc serviens ad clavam, ad diem retorni inde mandavit quod predictus Johannes non est inventus in balliva sua, unde idem Willielmus, ad predictam curiam dicti domini regis, supplicaverit sibi de remedio congruo versus predictum manucaptorem in hac parte provideri, super quod preceptum est servientibus ad clavam ibidem quod per probos et legales homines de burgo predicto scire faciant, seu etc., prefatum Thomam quod sit coram ballivo burgi predicti, ad proximam curiam de recordo in burgo predicto tenendam, ostensurus si quid de se habeat vel dicere sciat quare predictus Willielmus execucionem suam versus eundem Thomam de debito et misis et custagiis illis habere non debeat, juxta vim, formam et effectum manucapcionis predicti, si sibi viderit expedire, et ulterius facturus et recepturus quod predicta curia dicti domini regis consideret in ea parte, et habeant ibi tunc hoc preceptum. Teste Francisco Smyth juniore, generoso, ballivo ibidem, septimo die Junii, annis regni domini nostri Jacobi, Dei gracia regis Anglie, Francie et Hibernie, septimo, et Scotie xiii°.

[Signed]: Greene.

[Endorsed]: Virtute istius precepti mihi directi per Johannem Hemynges et Gilbertum Chadwell, probos et legales homines burgi infrascripti, scire feci infranominatum Thomam Hornbye, prout interius mihi precipitur.

[Signed]: Franciscus Boyce, serviens.

[Borough of Stratford. There is an order to the sergeants at mace that when a certain William Shakespeare, gentleman, recently in the court of James, now King of England, of the aforesaid borough, same held by virtue of letters patent from King Edward VI, recently king of England, carried his own certain complaint against a certain John Addenbrooke concerning the payment of a debt; and when a certain Thomas Hornby of said borough in the same complaint became a pledge and mainpernor for the said John, to wit; that if the said John in said suit were convicted in a legal manner that the same John would satisfy said William Shakespeare not only for the debt in said complaint by said William against said John to be recovered in the aforesaid court but also for the loss and cost to the same William in that complaint by said court that would be adjudged against said John; or that he would go to prison in the said year of the reign of James, now King in said borough, to satisfy to William Shakespeare the said debt, loss and costs; and furthermore, that if the same John does not satisfy for same William the debt, loss, and costs, and does not go to the aforesaid prison in the said year of our king to satisfy the said William in form aforesaid, then the same Thomas Hornby wishes to satisfy for the recovery of the debt, losses, and costs thus adjudged to the same William. And since also in that complaint such proceeding were had in the same court that the said William in said case by the judgment of said court recovered against the said John not only six pounds for debt but also twenty-four shillings for the payment of losses and costs of the same William, appropriate to his suit and complaint. For which there was the order to the sergeant at mace the same which they executed, etc., etc., said John, if etc., greetings, that they have his body in the presence of the bailiff of said borough at the next Court of Record there held to satisfy said William concerning said debt so recovered; namely, to the extent of twenty-four shillings for said damages and costs adjudged. Wherefore Francis Boyle, then and now sergeant at mace on the day for returning the writ, announced that said John was not found within his bailiwick. Wherefore the said William prays to said court of said Lord King that there be provided to him said suitable remedy against aforesaid mainpernor in the suit concerning which it was ordered to the sergeants at mace which they make known through upright and legal men of said borough, whether etc., that the aforesaid Thomas be in the presence of the bailiff of the said borough at the next court of record held in said district to show either if he has anything to say or whether or not he knows why the aforesaid William ought not have his execution against the said Thomas, concerning the debt, the losses, and the costs, according to the force, form, and effect of said mainpernor, whether or not he should see how to extricate himself and furthermore, whether or not he would do and would accept what said court of said King decrees in this matter, and therefore they have this order. Witnessed by Francis Smyth, Jr., gentleman, before the same bailiff on the seventh day of June in the seventh year of the reign of James, by Grace of God King of England, France and Ireland and forty-second year of his reign of Scotland.

[Signed]: Greene.

[Endorsed]: By virtue of this order they have directed me through John Heminges and Gilbert Chadwell, good and legal men of the borough named within, to execute the within-named writ upon Thomas Hornby, that he shall be seized and brought before me.

        [Signed]: Francis Boyce, sergeant.

    —Lewis, *Shakespeare Documents*, vol. II, pp. 398–400

1609

Stationers' Register Entries

In 1609 Troilus and Cressida *and Shakespeare's* Sonnets *were registered with the Stationers. Abbreviated words have been silently expanded in the first entry.*

28^{uo} Januarii/.

Richard Bonion   Henry Walleys   Entred for their Copy under thandes of m^r Segar deputy to Sr George Bucke and m^r war^d. Lownes a booke called.   The history of Troylus and Cressida   vi^d/

    —*Bibliography of the English Printed Drama*, p. 25

20 Maii

Thomas Thorpe Entred for his copie under th[e h]andes of master Wilson and master Lownes Warden a Booke called Shakespeares Sonnettes   vi^d

    —*Stationers' Register*, volume III, folio 183b

Publications

Four works by Shakespeare were published in 1609, including Romeo and Juliet, *which had been previously published in 1597 and 1599.*

THE / MOST EX- / CELLENT AND / Lamentable Tragedie, of / *Romeo and Juliet.* / As it hath beene ſundrie times publiquely Acted, / by the KINGS Maieſties Seruants / at the Globe. / Newly corrected, augmented, and / amended: / [*Printer's device*] / LONDON / Printed for IOHN SMETHVVICK, and are to be ſold / at his Shop in Saint Dunſtanes Church-yard, / in Fleeteſtreete vnder the Dyall. / 1609.

Three works by Shakespeare were published for the first time: Troilus and Cressida, Shakespeare's Sonnets, *and* Pericles. *There are two issues of the 1609 edition of* Troilus and Cressida, *each with a different title page; the second issue also includes a letter from the printer. A variant title page for the edition of Shakespeare's* Sonnets *substituted "to be ſolde by Iohn Wright, dwelling / at Chriſt Church gate" for "to be ſolde by William Aſpley." Two editions of* Pericles *were published with identical title pages but variations in the texts.*

Preface to *The Famous Historie of Troylus and Cresseid*

James Roberts registered Troilus and Cressida *with the Stationers' Company in February 1603 but did not publish it, perhaps because he was unable to get the "sufficient aucthority" that he claimed to be awaiting. Roberts said the play had been performed by Shakespeare's company, the Lord Chamberlain's Men. In 1609, the play was re-registered by Richard Bonian and Henry Walley, who then published it. The first 1609 title page claimed the play had been performed at the Globe, although it calls the Lord Chamberlain's Men by their new name, the King's Men. As the play was being printed, however, this title page was replaced with one that makes no mention of a performance, and the following epistle to the reader, probably written by Bonian and/or Walley, insists that the play was never performed. The epistle also offers lavish praise for Shakespeare's skill as a playwright.*

A never writer, to an ever
reader. Newes.

Eternall reader, you have heere a new play, never stal'd with the Stage, never clapper-clawd with the palmes of the vulger, and yet passing full of the palme comicall; for it is a birth of your braine, that never under-tooke any thing commicall, vainely: And were but the vaine names of commedies changde for the titles of Commodities, or of Playes for Pleas; you should see all those grand censors, that now stile them such vanities, flock to them for the maine grace of their gravities: especially this authors Commedies, that are so fram'd to the life, that they serve for the most common Commentaries, of all the actions of our lives, shewing such a dexteritie, and power of witte, that the most displeased with Playes, are pleasd with his Commedies. And all such dull and heavy-witted worldlings, as were never capable of the witte of a Commedie, comming by report of them to his representations, have found that witte there, that they never found in them-selves, and have parted better wittied then they came: feeling an edge of witte set upon them, more then ever they dreamd they had braine to grinde it on. So much and such savored salt of witte is in his Commedies, that they seeme (for their height of pleasure) to be borne in that sea that brought forth Venus. *Amongst all there is none more witty then this: And had I time I would comment upon it, though I know it needs not, (for so much as will make you thinke your testerne well bestowd) but for so much worth, as even poore I know to be stuft in it. It deserves such a labour, as well as the best Commedy in* Terence *or* Plautus. *And beleeve this, that when hee is gone, and his Commedies out of sale, you will scramble for them, and set up a new English Inquisition. Take this for a warning, and at the perrill of your pleasures losse, and Judgements, refuse not, nor like this the lesse, for not being sullied, with the smoaky breath of the multitude; but thanke fortune for the scape it hath made amongst you. Since by the grand possessors wills I beleeve you should have prayd for them rather then beene prayd. And so I leave all such to bee prayd for (for the states of their wits healths) that will not praise it.*

Vale.

    —sigs. 2r–v

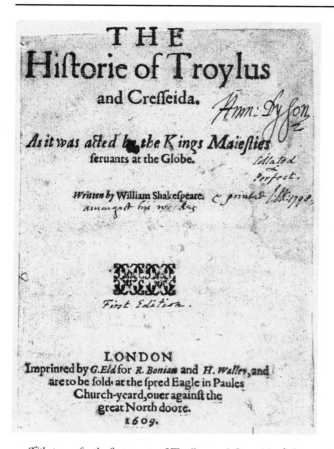

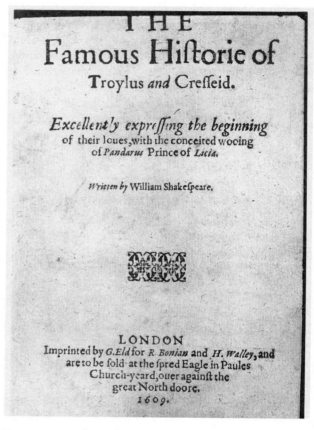

Title pages for the first quarto of Troilus and Cressida (left; reproduced by permission of The Huntington Library, San Marino, California)
and the second issue of that edition, to which was added an anonymous address to the reader
(by permission of the Folger Shakespeare Library)

Alleyn Buys a Copy of Shakespeare's *Sonnets*

Edward Alleyn, the leading actor in the Admiral's Men, used the back of a 19 June letter from Thomas Bowker to record what he spent on "purchase," "rent," "lawe," "aparell," and "Howshowld stuff"; his copy of Shakespeare's sonnets is recorded under the last category. The letter, from Bowker, is dated 19 June. The text is from George F. Warner's Catalogue of the Manuscripts and Muniments of Alleyn's College of God's Gift at Dulwich *(1881).*

a book. Shaksper sonetts 5ᵈ.

—p. 72

Greene Stays at New Place

Thomas Greene's notes concern his negotiations with George Browne regarding a house. His memorandum was dated 9 September 1609 (Shakespeare Birthplace Trust, Stratford Corporation Records, Miscellaneous Documents XII, 103).

He doubted whether he might sowe his garden, untill about my goinge to the Terme. (seeing I could gett noe carryages to help me here with tymber) I was content to permytt yt without contradiccion & the rather because I perceyved I mighte stay another yere at newe place.

—*Facts and Problems,* vol. II, p. 96

Pericles and *King Lear* Performed at Gowthwaite Hall

The performances at Gowthwaite Hall during the Christmas season drew official attention because at least one of the plays, Saint Christopher, *was perceived to be pro-Catholic. In his April 1942 essay "Shakespeare Quartos as Prompt-Copies with Some Account of Cholmeley's Players and a New Shakespeare Allusion," C. J. Sisson notes that one of the players, Richard Simpson, defended himself during the Star Chamber proceedings by arguing "that booke by which he and the other persons did act the said play . . . was a printed booke, And they onelie acted the same according to the contents therein printed, and not otherwise" (138). Public*

196

Hunc capient alio mediante
colorem.

Non quemvis subito probè colorem
Panni concipiunt, diúve servant:
Quin perfusi alia tenace quadam
Tinctura fuerint paratiores.
Haud secus humanas non quæque scientia mentes
Imbuit extemplò: Physicasq̃, addiscere primum
Res decet: ante sacros quam progrediaris ad arces.

Page from Nicolaas Taurellus's Emblemata physico-ethica *(1599) showing a dyer at work. In Sonnet 111 Shakespeare writes,
"[My] nature is subdu'd / To what it works in, like the dyer's hand" (courtesy of Special Collections,
Howard-Tilton Library, Tulane University, New Orleans, Louisiana).*

*performance of a play and its appearance in print were both
signs that it had been seen and allowed by government censors. Sisson then quotes William Harrison, an English Catholic priest who had fled to the Continent but who visited
England from 1608 to 1609. Harrison lists* King Lear *and*
Pericles *as among the plays performed.*

. . . one of the playes acted and played was Perocles
prince of Tire, And the other was Kinge Lere . . . these
plaies which they so plaied were usuall playes And such
as were acted in Common and publicke places and
Staiges . . . and such as were played publicly and prynted
in the bookes.

                    —*The Review of English Studies,* 18 (April 1942): 138

Possible Allusion to Shakespeare in Davies's *Humours Heav'n on Earth*

In Humours Heav'n on Earth; With The Civile
Warres of Death and Fortune. As also The Triumph of
Death: Or, The Picture of the Plague, according to the Life;
as it was in Anno Domini. 1603 *(1609), John Davies of Hereford describes various followers of Fortune—the "her" referred to in the
quoted stanza's first line. Leading up to the description of stage players
are stanzas describing orators, astronomers, musicians, linguists,
"Penne-men or faire writers" (207), and fencers.*

*This stanza from "The Second Tale: Containing, The
Civile Warres of Death and Fortune" was printed with three
notes in the left margin: "* Stage plaiers." (lines 1–2); "*Shewing the vices of the time." (lines 4–5); and "*W.S.R.B." (line 6).*

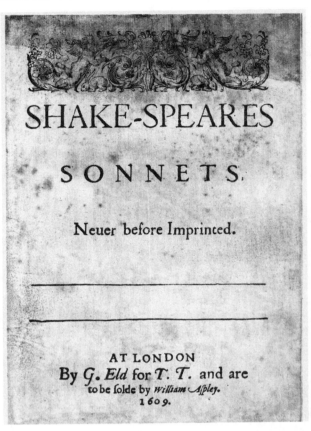

Title page and dedication page for the only known edition of the sonnets published in Shakespeare's lifetime. The identity of "Mr. W. H." is one of the many mysteries surrounding Shakespeare's sonnets; the dedication is usually attributed to the publisher Thomas Thorpe (by permission of the Folger Shakespeare Library).

The "W.S." in the margin is probably William Shakespeare, and "R.B." is probably Richard Burbage, a leading member of Shakespeare's acting company.

76

Some followed her by * acting all mens parts,
These on a Stage she rais'd (in scorne) to fall:
And made them Mirrors, by their acting Arts,
Wherein men saw their * faults, thogh ne'r so small:
Yet some she guerdond not, to their* desarts;
But, othersome, were but ill-Action all:
Who while they acted ill, ill staid behinde,
(By custome of their maners) in their minde.

       –p. 208

Possible Allusion to *Julius Caesar* in *Everie Woman in her Humor*

The play these characters from satiric comedy Everie Woman in her Humor *(1609) have been to see may be Shakespeare's* Julius Caesar, *although they have seen a production by one of the children's companies or by puppeteers.*

[Gettica:] I pray yee what showe will be heere to night? I have seen the Babones already, the Cittie of new Ninivie, and *Julius Cæsar* acted by the Mammets.

[Graccus:] Oh gentlewoman, those are showes for those places they are used in, marry here you must expect some rare device as *Diana* bathing her selfe, being discovered or occulated, by *Acteon*, he was transfigured to a hart, & werried to death with his own dogs.

[Citizen's Wife:] Thats prettie in good truth, & must *Diana* be naked?

[Graccus:] Oh of necessitie, if it be that show.

[Hostess:] And *Acteon* too? thats prettie ifaith.

       –sig. Hr

Possible Allusion to *Pericles* in *Pimlyco*

Pimlyco. Or, Runne Red-Cap. *Tis a mad world at Hogsdon (1609) reprints and expands "The Tunning of Elinour Rumming," a mock encomium to an alewife by John Skelton (circa 1460–1529). The anonymous author of* Pimlyco *satirizes London's drinkers, and compares the crowd gathered to eat and drink in Pimlyco to the*

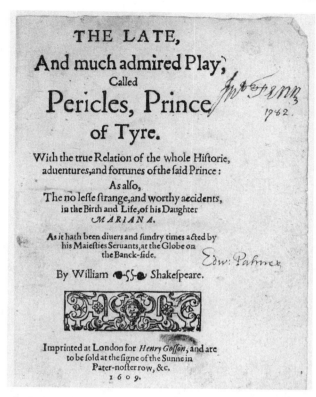

THE LATE,
And much admired Play,
Called
Pericles, Prince
of Tyre.

With the true Relation of the whole Historie,
aduentures, and fortunes of the said Prince:
As also,
The no lesse strange, and worthy accidents,
in the Birth and Life, of his Daughter
MARIANA.

As it hath been diuers and sundry times acted by
his Maiesties Seruants, at the Globe on
the Banck-side.

By William Shakespeare.

Imprinted at London for *Henry Gosson*, and are
to be sold at the signe of the Sunne in
Pater-noster row, &c.
1 6 0 9.

Title page for the first quarto of Pericles. *Although four quarto editions were published before 1619, the play was not included in the First Folio (by permission of the Folger Shakespeare Library).*

crowd that might gather to see two plays: Jane Shore, *otherwise unknown but in telling the tale of Shore, mistress to Edward IV, sure to be full of sensational detail, and Shakespeare's* Pericles, *a play whose features include incest, a wicked stepmother, pirates, a shipwreck, and a brothel.*

Into their *Parke* I forthwith went,
Being entred, all the ayre was rent
With a most strange confused noyse,
That sounded nothing but meere voyce.
Amazde I stood to see a Crowd
Of *Ciuill Throats* stretch'd out so lowd:
(As at a *New-play*) all the Roomes
Did swarme with *Gentiles* mir'd with Groomes.
So that I truly thought, all These
Came to see *Shore*, or *Pericles*,
And that (to have themselves well plac'd)
Thus brought they victualls (they fed so fast)
But then (agen mee thought) This shoale
Swom thither for *Bakers* doale
Or *Brewers*, and that for their soules sakes,
They thus were serv'd with Ale and cakes:
For *Iugs* of Ale came reeling in,
As if the *Pots* had drunkards bin.

—sig. Cr

Possible Allusion to *The Taming of the Shrew* in *A whole crew of kind Gossips*

In the satiric poem A whole crew of kind Gossips, all met to be merry *(1609), a group of drinkers takes turns complaining about their lives. In this excerpt, one of the narrators explores ways of dealing with his unruly wife. He claims to be seeking guidance from "a worke cald taming of the Shrow," which may be Shakespeare's early comedy.*

The fift, complained on by his wife to be a common Drunkard.

My Maisters heer's good stuffe, if this geare hold,
When honest men by sluts are thus contrould:
In absence, to have credit overthrowne,
And we made Guls for them to play upon,
Shall we endure it, and be made fooles still:
No, Ile curbe mine, upon my life I will,
And keepe her somewhat shorter in a doore,
A Taverne tell-tale she shall be no more.
Neighbours, I thinke you know me, all are heere,
Although I love a Cup of Wine or Beere:
And as good-fellow, sometime trade therewith,
Yet did you never see me *Smug the Smith*?
Did any of you ever know me reele?
Or in a storme of Ale turneup the Keele?
In all your lives did any see me so,
That with these paire of legs I could not go?
pray speake my Maisters, for I may mistake,
A man will venter much for good wines sake.
But if I have bin sometimes over-shot,
In calling for too much by t'other pot;
Shall my wife chatter till her tongue be weary,
And terme me Drunkard, when I am but merry;
Wil any loving wife be so unkinde?
Or doth not duty and good manners binde
A woman to forbeare, to winke, and hide,
And not to raile, to slaunder, and to chide,
She might have saide in private certainly,
Husband, last night you sung a pot to hye,
Or my deere love, pray thee where hast thou bin?
In truth (Sweet-hart) you are a little in.
All this were well indifferent to be borne:
But shall she lay me open (as in scorne)
To her companions scoffing at me so,
As if I daily could not stand nor go.
She tearmes me *Sound card for a womans stay,*
Drunke once a weeke, and that is every day,
The filthiest Drunkard (thus she doth protest)
That ever was of giddy braine possest.
And further, to the world she doth disclose,
That I come into bed in shooes and hose:
And horrible Tobacco do so drinke,
That she is almost poyson'd with the stinke.

Well, this is good, but marke the end at last,
In a new mould this woman I will cast,
Her tongue in other order I will keepe,
Better she had bin in her bed asleepe,
Then in a Taverne, when those words she spake;
A little paines with her I meane to take:
For she shall find me in another tune,
Betweene this February and next June:
In sober sadnesse I do speake it now,
And to you all I make a solemne vow,
The chiefest Art I have I will bestow,
About a worke cald taming of the Shrow.
It makes my heart to fret, my lookes to frowne,
That we should let our wives thus put us downe.
But for mine owne part I have now decreed,
To do a good and charitable deed.
If she begin her former course a fresh,
I have a tricke to mortifie her flesh:
Unto you all example I will give,
Perhaps youle thanke me for it while you live.
But for your selves, to nothing Ile perswade,
Because the blame on me shall not be laid:
Other mens wives I meane to let alone,
I shall have worke enough to tame mine owne.

—sigs. D4r–Er

Title page for a play that, like The Taming of the Shrew, addresses
the role of women in society. Although boy actors were expected to
dress as women while performing, women who appeared in
public dressed as men faced scorn and censure
(by permission of the Folger
Shakespeare Library).

The King's Men
Paid for Being Unable to Perform

*The King's Men are compensated during an outbreak of the
plague and for the performances they did render.*

To John Heminges uppon the Counsells warrant dated at
the Courte at Whitehall x^mo die Marcii 1609 for himselfe
and the reste of his companie beinge restrayned from publique playinge within the Citie of London in the tyme of
infeccion duringe the space of six weekes in which tyme
they practised pryvately for his Majesties service
xxx^li

. . . .

To John Heminges one of the kinges Majesties players
uppon the Counsells Warraunt dated at the Courte at
Whitehall secundo die Marcii 1609 in the behalfe of himselfe and the reste of his felowes for presenting thirteene
playes before his Majestie the Queenes Majestie the Prince
the Duke and the Ladie Elizabeth before xpmas Anno
prēd 1609 and in the tyme of the holidayes and afterwardes on severall nightes expressed in the saide warraunte iiii vi^li xiii^s iiii^d and by waye of his Majesties
rewarde xliii^li vi^s viii^d in al
Cxxx^li

—Dramatic Records, pp. 48–49

1610

Publication

Despite its title-page imprint of 1602, this edition of
Venus and Adonis *is believed to have been published in 1610
(see the* Short Title Catalog *entry 22360b).*

VENVS / AND ADONIS. / *Vilia miretur vulgus: mihi flauus
Apollo* / *Pocula Castalia plena ministret aqua* / [*Printer's device*]
/ Imprinted at London for *William Leake* / dwelling at the
signe of the Holy Ghost in / Paules Church-yard. 1602.

The Prince of Wirtemberg Sees *Othello*
at the Globe

*Lewis Frederick, Prince of Wirtemberg, saw a performance
of* Othello *on 30 April 1610; the prince's travel diary was kept by
his secretary Hans Jacob Wurmsser von Vendenheym. The excerpt*

and its translation are taken from William Brenchley Rye,
England as Seen by Foreigners in the Days of Elizabeth
and James the First *(1865; reprinted 1967).*

Lundi, 30. S. E. Alla au Globe lieu ordinaire ou l'on
joue les Commedies, y fut representé l'histoire du More
de Venise.

[Monday, 30th. His Excellency went to the *Globe*, the
usual place for acting Plays; the history of the Moor of
Venice was represented there.]

–p. 61

Jackson sees *Othello* in Oxford

*Henry Jackson, a member of Corpus Christi College at
Oxford, recorded seeing* Othello *at Oxford in his Latin correspondence. William Fulman, a later member of the college, transcribed excerpts from Jackson's letters, which were subsequently
published by Geoffrey Tillotson in his article* "Othello *and* The
Alchemist *at Oxford in 1610" for* The Times Literary
Supplement (TLS). *Fulman's excerpt identifies the date of the
letter as September 1610.*

Habuerunt et Tragœdias, quas decorè, et aptè agebant.
In quibus non solùm dicendo, sed etiam facièndo
quædam lachrymas movebant.
–At verò Desdemona illa apud nos a marito occisa,
quanquam optimè semper causam egit, interfecta tamen
magis movebat; cum in lecto decumbens spectantium
misericordiam ipso vultu imploraret.

–*TLS,* 20 July 1933, p. 494

[They also had tragedies which were acted out both
beautifully and appropriately and in which certain ones
moved tears not only by the speaking but also by the
doing (acting).
–But indeed that (famous) Desdemona when cut down
by her husband in our midst, although she always
pleaded her case in the best possible way, nevertheless
when slain moved (us) more; when lying down on her
bed she implored the pity of those watching with her
very countenance.]

–translated by Rayford Shaw

Allusion to the Globe in Heath's *Two Centuries Of Epigrammes*

In the satirical Two Centuries Of Epigrammes *(1610),
John Heath describes the efforts of his protagonist, who, hoping to
improve his acting skills, visits three of London's public playhouses,
beginning with the Globe. Heath, like many of his contemporaries, did
not have much regard for the Globe audience, the customers Shakespeare strove to please.*

Title page for Timothy Kendall's Flowers of Epigrams *(1577) with an
emblematic illustration of a swan's death song. "I will play the swan /
And die in music"* (Othello, *5.2.247–248; by permission of the
Folger Shakespeare Library).*

Epigram. 39.
In Momum.

Momus would act the fooles part in a play,
And cause he would be exquisite that way,
Hies me to London, where no day can passe,
But that some play-house still his presence has.
Now at the *Globe* with a judicious eye,
Into the Vice's action doth he prie.
Next to the *Fortune*, where it is a chaunce,
But he mark's something worth his cognisance.
Then to the *Curtaine*, where as at the rest,
He notes that action downe that likes him best.
Being full fraught, at length he gets him home,
And *Momus* now, know's how to play the Mome.
There want's nought but a fooles cap on his head,
As for the action tut, hee'le strike it dead.
When the time came, he comes me on the stage,
Rap't as it were with an unwieldy rage,
Of a fantastique braine, and gables out
Some senselesse wordes, well fitting such a lout:

Then his unsavory speech he enterlaces,
With wreathed mouths, and filthy antike faces.
Fie on this Mimick skill, it marres his part:
Nature would doe farre better without art.

—sigs. E3r–v

Allusion to Falstaff in Sharpe's *More Fooles Yet*

In an epigram in More Fooles Yet *(1610), Roger Sharpe satirizes his subject's girth by comparing it to Falstaff's.*

In Virosum.

How *Falstafe* like, doth sweld *Virosus* looke,
As though his paunch did foster every sinne:
And sweares he is injured by this booke,
His worth is taxt he hath abused byn:
Swell still *Virosus*, burst with emulation,
I neither taxe thy vice nor reputation.

—sig. E3r

Forman Sees *Macbeth*, *Cymbeline*, and *The Winter's Tale*

*Astrologer and physician Simon Forman describes three of Shakespeare's plays—*Macbeth, Cymbeline, *and* The Winter's Tale—*he saw at the Globe in his manuscript collection* The Book of Plaies and Notes thereof per Forman, for common Pollicie. *The* Richard II *Forman saw is not Shakespeare's play. The date of the first entry contains an error: either the year is 1610, or the day of the week is not Saturday. The following document was transcribed from the facsimilies in S. Schoenbaum,* William Shakespeare: Records and Images *(1981), pp. 9–19.*

IN Mackbeth at the glod 1610 the 20 of Aprill [astrological sign representing "Saturday"]. ther was to be observed firste how Mackbeth and Bancko 2 noble men of Scotland Ridinge thorowe a wod ther stode before them 3 women feiries or Nimphes And saluted Mackbeth sayinge .t. 3 tyms unto him haille Mackbeth. king of Codon for thou shalt be a kinge but shalt beget No kinges &c. Then said Bancko What all to Mackbeth And nothing to me. Yes said the nimphes haille to thee Bancko thou shalt beget kinges. yet be no kinge And so they departed & cam to the Courte of Scotland to Dunkin king of Scotes and yt was in the dais of Edward the Confessor. And Dunkin bad them both kindly wellcome. And made Mackbeth forth with Prince of Northumberland and sent him hom to his own castell and appointed Mackbeth to provid for him for he wold

Sup wth him the next dai at night. & did soe. And Mackbeth contrived to kill Dunkin & thorowe the persuasion of his wife did that night Murder the kinge in his own Castell beinge his guest And ther were many prodigies seen that night & the dai before. And when Mack Beth had murdred the kinge the blod on his handes could not be washed of by Any meanes. nor from his wives handes wch handled the bloddi daggers in hiding them By wch means they became both moch amazed & Affronted. The murder being knowen Dunkins 2 sonns fled the on to England the [other to] Walles to save them selves. they beinge fled they were supposed guilty of the murder of their father which was nothinge so Then was Mackbeth crowned kinge and then he for feare of Banko his old companion that he should beget kinges but be no kinge him selfe. he contrived the death of Banko and caused him to be Murdred on the way as he Rode The next night beinge at supper wth his noble men whom he had bid to a feaste to the wch also Banco should have com. he began to speake of Noble Banco and to wish that he wer ther And as he thus did standing up to drincke a Carouse to him. the ghoste of Banco came and sate down in his cheier behind him. And he turninge About to sit down Again sawe the goste of banco which fronted him so. that he fell into a great passion of fear and fury. Utterynge many wordes about his murder by wch when they hard that Banco was Murdred they Suspected Mackbet.

Then Mack dove fled to England to the kinges sonn. And soe they Raised an Army And cam into scotland and at dunston Anyse overthrue Mackbet. In the meantyme whille Mackdove was in England Mackbet slewe Mackdoves wife & children. and after in the battelle Mackdove slewe Mackbet.

Observe Also howe Mackbetes quen did Rise in the night in her slepe & walke and talked and confessed all & the docter noted her wordes.

Of Cimbalin king of England.

Remember also the storri of Cymbalin King of England in Lucius tyme. howe Lucius cam from Octavus Cesar for Tribut and being denied. after sent Lucius wth a greate Armi of Souldiars who landed at milford haven. and After wer Vanquished by Cimbalin and Lucius taken prisoner and all by means of 3 outlawes of the wch 2 of them were the sonns of Cimbalin stolen from him when they were but 2 yers old. by an old man whom Cymbalin banished. and he kept them as his own sonns 20 yers wth him in A cave. And howe of of them slewe Clotan that was the quens sonn goinge to milford haven to seke the love of Innogen the kinges daughter whom he had banished also for lovinge his daughter. and howe the Italian that cam from her love. conveied him selfe into A Cheste. and said yt was a chest of plate sent from her love & others to be presented to the kinge. And in the depest of the night she being aslepe. he opened the cheste & cam forth of yt. And vewed her in her bed and the markes of her body. & toke awai her braslet & after Accused her of adultery to her love &c And in thend howe he came wth the Romains into England & was taken prisoner and after Reveled to Innogen. Who had turned her self into mans apparrell & fled to mete her love at milford haven. & chanchsed to fall on the Cave in the wodes wher her 2 brothers were & howe by eating a sleping Dram they thought she had bin deed & laid her in the wodes & the body of cloten by her. in her loves apparrell that he left behind him & howe she was found by Lucius &c.

IN Richard the 2 At the glob
1611 the 30 of Aprill / [astrological sign representing
Tuesday]

Remember therin howe Jack Straw. by his overmoch boldnes. not beinge pollitick nor suspecting Anye thinge: was Soddenly at Smithfeld Bars – stabbed by Walworth the major of London & soe he and his wholle Army was overthrowen Therfore in such a case or the like, never admit any party w^thout a bar betwen for A man cannot be to wise, nor kepe him selfe to safe.

Also remember howe the duke of Gloster. The Erell of Arundell Oxford and oth[ers] crossing the kinge in his humor. about the duke of Erland and Bushy wer glad to fly and Raise an hoste of men and beinge in his Castell. howe the d of Erland cam by nighte to betray him wth 300 men. but having pryvie warninge thereof kept his gates faste And wold not suffer the Enimie to Enter wch went back Again wth a flie in his eare. and after was slainte by the Errell of Arundell in the battell

Remember also: when the duke and Arundell cam to London wth their Army. king Richard came forth to them and met them and gave them fair wordes and promised them pardon and that all should be well yf they wold discharge their Army. upon. whose promises and faier Speaches they did yt and After the king byd them all to A banket and soe betraid them And Cut of their heades &c because they had not his pardon under his hand & sealle before but his worde

Remember therin Also howe the ducke of Lankaster pryvily contryved all villany. to set them all together by the ears and to make the nobilyty to Envy the kinge and mislyke of him and his governmentes by which means. he made his own sonn king which was henry Bullinbrocke

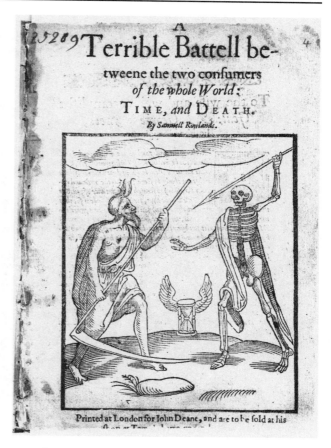

The title-page illustration for Rowland's pamphlet shows that for Shakespeare's audience Time had a recognizable costume and props. Act 4 of The Winter's Tale *opens with the stage direction "Enter* Time, the Chorus*" (courtesy of the Bodleian Library, Oxford).*

Remember also howe the duke of Lankaster asked A wise man, wher him self should ever be kinge And he told him no, but his sonn should be a kinge. And when he had told him he hanged him up for his labor. because he should not brute yt abrod or speke therof to others. This was a pollicie in the common wealthes opinion But I sai yt was a villaines p[ar]te and a Judas kisse to hange the man. for telling him the truth Beware by this Example of noble men / and of their fair wordes & sai lytell to them, lest they doe the like by thee for thy good will/

IN the Winters Talle at the glob
1611 the 15 of maye [astrological sign representing
Wednesday].

Observe ther howe Lyontes the kinge of Cicillia was overcom wth Jelosy of his wife with the kinge of Bohemia his frind that came to see him. and howe he Contrived his death and wold have had his cup berer to have poisoned.

THE
WITCHES
OF NORTHAMPTON-
SHIRE.

Agnes Browne. Arthur Bill.
Ioane Vaughan. Hellen Ienkenson } Witches.
Mary Barber.

Who were all executed at *Northampton* the 22. of
Iuly laſt. 1612.

LONDON,
Printed by *Tho: Purfoot*, for *Arthur*
Iohnſon. 1612.

Title page showing witches and their animal familiar
(shelfmark G.2394; courtesy of The
British Library, London)

Macbeth's
Witches

Illustration from Raphael Holinshed's Chronicles *(1577) showing Macbeth and Banquo meeting*
the three witches (by permission of the Folger Shakespeare Library)

Banquo

What are these
So wither'd and so wild in their attire,
That look not like th' inhabitants o' th' earth,
And yet are on't? Live you? or are you aught
That man may question? You seem to understand me,
By each at once her choppy finger laying
Upon her skinny lips. You should be women,
And yet your beards forbid me to interpret
That you are so.

—*Macbeth*, 1.3.39–47

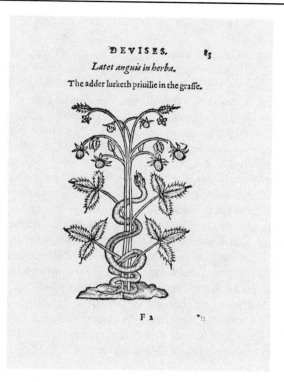

Page from Paradin's Heroicall Devises *(1591). Lady Macbeth's advice to "look like th' innocent flower, / But be the serpent under 't" (*Macbeth *1.5.65–66) is illustrated in this emblem (by permission of the Folger Shakespeare Library).*

Witches being subjected to trial by water, from the anonymous 1613 pamphlet Witches Apprehended, Examined and Executed, for notable villanies by them committed both by Land and Water *(by permission of The Huntington Library, San Marino, California)*

who gave the king of bohemia warning therof & fled with him to bohemia

Remember also howe he sent to the Orakell of appollo & the Annswer of apollo. that she was giltles. and that the king was jelouse &c and howe Except the Child was found Again that was loste the kinge should die wth out yssue for the Child was caried into bohemia & ther laid in a forrest & brought up by a sheppard And the kinge of bohemia his sonn maried that wentch & howe they fled into Cicillia to Leontes. and the sheppard having showed the letter of the nobleman by whom Leontes sent a way that child and the jewells found about her. she was knowen to be Leontes daughter and was then 16 yers old

Remember also the Rog that cam in all tottered like coll pixci /. and howe he feyned him sicke & to have bin Robbed of all that he had and howe he cosoned the por man of all his money. and after cam to the shep sher with a pedlers packe & ther cosoned them Again of all their money And howe he changed apparrell wth the kinge of bomia his sonn. and then howe he turned Courtiar &c / beware of trustinge feined beggars or fawninge fellouse.

—Bodleian Ashmolean Manuscript 208, ff. 200–213

The King's Men
Paid for Court Performances

Item paid to Jhon Heminges one of the Kinges Majesties players uppon the Cowncells warrant dated at whitehall xii⁰ Die februarii 1610 for him self and the rest of his company for presentinge unto His Majestie the Queene the Prince xv playes uppon severall nightes mentioned in the warrant C^li and by waye of his Majesties reward l^li in all the some of　　　　　　　　　　　　　　　　　Cl^li

—*Dramatic Records*, p. 50

1611

Publications

Three previously published plays were published again: Titus Andronicus *(1594, 1600),* Hamlet *(1603, 1604/1605), and* Pericles *(1609). Also published was* The Troublesome Reign of King John, *a play that may or may not be related to Shakespeare's* King John.

THE / MOST LAMEN- / TABLE TRAGEDIE / *of Titus Andronicus.* / *AS IT HATH SVNDRY* / *times beene plaide by the Kings* / Maiesties Seruants. / [*Printer's device*] / LONDON, / Printed for Eedward White, and are to be solde / at his shoppe, nere the little North dore of / Pauls, at the signe of the / Gun. 1 6 1 1.

THE / TRAGEDY / OF / HAMLET / Prince of Denmarke. / BY / WILLIAM SHAKESPEARE. / Newly imprinted and enlarged to almost as much / againe as it was, according to the true / and perfect Coppy. / [*Printer's device*] / AT LONDON, / Printed for *Iohn Smethwicke*, and are to be sold at his shoppe / in Saint *Dunstons* Church yeard in Fleetstreet. / Vnder the Diall. 1611.

THE LATE, / And much admired Play, / Called / Pericles, Prince / of Tyre. / With the true Relation of the whole History, / aduentures, and fortunes of the sayd Prince: / *As also,* / The no lesse strange, and worthy accidents, / in the Birth and Life, of his Daughter / *MARIANA.* / As it hath beene diuers and sundry times acted by / his Maiestyes Seruants, at the Globe on / the Banck-side. / By *VVilliam Shakspeare.* / [*Printer's device*] / Printed at London by *S. S.* / 1611.

Shakespeare's Land Purchase Confirmed

The foot of fine confirms Shakespeare's title to the 107 acres of arable land he purchased in 1602 from John and William Combe and also gives a more precise account of 20 acres of pastureland than was provided in the original deed of conveyance.

Inter Willielmum Shakespere generosum querentem et Willielmum Combe armigerum et Johannem Combe generosum deforciantes de centum et septem acris terre et viginti acris pasture cum pertinenciis in Old Stratford et super Avon Unde placitum convencionis summonitum fuit inter eos in eadem curia [&c] scilicet quod predicti Willielmus Combe et Johannes recognoverunt predicta tenementa cum pertinenciis esse ius ipsius Willielmi Shakespere ut illa que idem Willielmus habet de dono predictorum Willielmi Combe et Johannis et illa remiserunt et quietumclamaverunt de ipsis Willielmo Combe et Johanne et heredibus suis predicto Willielmo Shakespere et heredibus suis imperpetuum Et preterea idem Willielmus Combe concessit pro se et heredibus suis quod ipsi warantizabunt predicto Willielmo Shakespere et heredibus suis predicta tenementa cum pertinenciis contra predictum Willielmum Combe et heredes suos imperpetuum Et ulterius idem Johannes Concessit pro se et heredibus suis quod ipsi warantizabunt predicto Willielmo Shakespere et heredibus suis predicta tenementa cum pertinenciis contra predictum Johannem et heredes suos imperpetuum Et pro hac recognicione . . . idem Willielmus Shake-

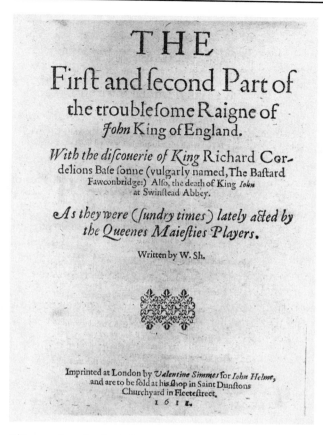

Title page for a play that has an uncertain relationship to Shakespeare's King John *(courtesy of the Folger Shakespeare Library)*

spere dedit predictis Willielmo Combe et Johanni centum libras sterlingorum.

[Between William Shakespeare, gentleman, plaintiff, and William Combe, Esquire, and John Combe, gentleman, defendants, concerning one hundred and seven acres of land and twenty acres in pasture with their appurtenances in Old Stratford and Stratford-upon-Avon; to which place a summons to meeting in the said Court was agreed upon between them; to-wit: that the aforementioned William Combe and John Combe recognize the aforesaid tenements with their appurtenances to be the right of William Shakespeare himself and that the same mentioned William has them from the gift of the aforesaid William and John Combe and [that] those things they remise and quitclaim from the said William and John Combe and their heirs to the aforementioned William Shakespeare and his heirs in perpetuity. And furthermore the same William Combe concedes on behalf of himself and his heirs that they warrant the said tenements with appurtenances to the said William Shakespeare and his heirs against the aforesaid William Combe and his heirs in perpetuity. And furthermore the said John concedes on behalf of himself and his

heirs that they warrant the said tenements with appurtenances to the said William Shakespeare and his heirs against the said John and his heirs in perpetuity. And for this recognition . . . the same William Shakespeare gave to the aforementioned William and John Combe one hundred pounds sterling.]

—Lewis, *Shakespeare Documents,* p. 413

Shakespeare Named in Stratford Highway Bill

Shakespeare's name is probably a late addition to the following list of the names of Stratford residents providing financial support for a Highway Bill to be presented to Parliament. The bill is dated 11 September 1611; Parliament did not take action on the bill. Abbreviations have been silently expanded in the transcription.

Wednesdaye the xi[th] of September /1611/
Colected towards the Charge of prosecutyng the Bill in parliament for the better Repayre of the highe waies and amendinge divers defectes in the Statutes alredy made

Imprimis of m[r]
Item of m[r] ffraunces Smythe gent
    of m[r] Thomas Greene esquire   ii[s] vi[d]
    of m[r] Thomas Barbar
    of m[r] John Gibbes
    of m[r] William Parsons
    of m[r] Henry Willson
    of m[r] Danyell Baker
    of m[r] John Sadler
    of m[r] ffraunces Smith senior
    of m[r] Abraham Sturley
    of m[r] John Smithe
    of m[r] William Wyatt   m[r] William shackspere
    of m[r] Henry Walker
    of m[r] Robert Butler
    of m[r] Julius Shawe
    of m[r] John Lawe
    —Shakespeare Birthplace Trust Records Office,
        Miscellaneous Documents I, 4

Shakespeare Listed in Johnson's Inventory

From the postmortem inventory of goods of Robert Johnson of Henley Street, Stratford-upon-Avon, dated 5 October 1611. For a detailed account of Johnson's relationship to Shakespeare, see E. K. Chambers, William Shakespeare: A Study in Facts and Problems, *vol. II (Oxford, 1930), pp. 32–34.*

A lease of a barne that he holdeth of M[r] Shaxper, xx[li]
    —*Facts and Problems,* vol. II, p. 32

Bill of Complaint
Regarding the Stratford Tithes

This draft copy of a bill of complaint regarding the Stratford Tithes held by William Shakespeare and others (Shakespeare Birthplace Trust Records Office Miscellaneous Documents ii, II) marks the beginning of legal action taken by the holders to ensure that the rents paid for the Stratford Tithes were equitable. Records documenting the outcome of the case have not been discovered. Abbreviations have been silently expanded.

Richard Lane et alii querentes et Dominus Carewe et alii defendentes in Cancellaria billa.

To the Right Honorable Thomas Lord Ellesmere Lord Chauncellour of England. In humble wise complayninge, shewen unto your honorable good Lordshipp, your dayly oratours Richard Lane of Awston in the county of Warwiche esquire, Thomas Greene of Stratford uppon Avon in the said county of Warwicke esquire, and William Shackspeare of Stratford uppon Avon aforesaid in the said county of Warwicke gentleman, that whereas Anthonie Barker, clarke, late warden of the late dissolved Colledge of Stratford uppon Avon aforesaid in the said county of Warwicke and Gyles Coventrey late subwarden of the same colledge, and the chapter of the said colledge, were heretofore seised in their demesne as of fee in the right of the said colledge, of and in divers messuages landes tenementes and glebe landes, scituate, lyeinge and beinge within the parishe of Stratford uppon Avon aforesaid, and of and in the tythes of corne grayne and haye, and of and in all and all manner of tythes of wooll lambe and all other small and pryvye tythes and oblacions and alterages whatsoever, cominge groweinge aryseinge reneweinge or happeninge within the whole parishe of Stratford uppon Avon aforesaid; and beinge soe thereof seised, by their indenture bearinge date in or aboute the seaventh day of September in the six and thirtyth yeare of the raigne of our late soveraigne lord of famous memory Kinge Henry the Eight, sealed with their chapter seale, they did demise graunte and to ferme lett, amongst divers mannors and other messuages landes tenementes and hereditamentes, unto one William Barker gentleman nowe deceassed, the aforesaid messuages landes tenementes and glebe landes, scituate lyeinge and beinge within the said parishe of Stratford uppon Avon aforesaid, and the aforesaid tythes of corne grayne and hay, and all and all manner other the said tythes of wooll lambe and smale and pryvie tythes, oblacions and alterages whatsoever; To have and to hould from the feast of Ste.

Michaell tharchangell then last past, for and duringe the terme of fourescore and twelve yeares thence next and imediately followeinge and fully to be compleate and ended. . . .

—Lewis, *Shakespeare Documents*, pp. 417–418

The bill then lists those who have owned the tithes since Barker's death, including Shakespeare.

and your oratour William Shackspeare hath an estate and interest of and in the moyty or one half of all tythes of corne and grayne aryseinge within the townes villages and fieldes of Old Stratford, Byshopton and Welcombe, being of and in the said parishe of Stratford, and of and in the moity or half of all tythes of wooll and lambe, and of all small and pryvy tythes oblaciones and alterages arisynge or increasyng in or within the wholl parishe of Stratford upon Avon aforesayd, for and duringe all the residue of the said terme, beinge of the yearely value of threescore powndes. . . .

—Lewis, *Shakespeare Documents*, p. 419

Other tithe holders are then listed, and the plaintiffs ask that "every of them, and every of their executors and assignes, ought in all right, equity, reason and good conscience . . . to pay unto the executors, administrators or assignes of the said John Barker a ratable and proporcionable parte and porcion of the said annuell or yearely rente. . ." (p. 422). The plaintiffs then turn to the "negligence or willfullnes of divers or anie other of the said partyes, which manie tymes will pay nothinge, whenas your oratours Richard Lane and William Shackspeare, and some fewe others of the said parties, are wholly, and against all equity and good conscience, usually dryven to pay the same for preservacion of their estates of and in the partes of the premisses belonginge unto them. . ." (pp. 423–424). The plaintiffs express concern about the effect the inequitable division has on poor tenants of the land who are "daylye in doubte to be turned out of doores, with their wives and families, thorough the practice or wilfullnes of such others" (p. 424). They conclude by asking the court to order and establish an equitable solution.

Allusion to the Globe
in Cooke's *Greenes Tu quoque*

In J. Cooke's satire of would-be gentlemen Greenes Tu quoque, Or, The Cittie Gallant *(1614), the characters mock Thomas Greene, the company clown of the Queen's Men; he played the part of Bubble in early productions of the play but died in August 1612. In the following excerpt, Bubble continues his attempt to learn how to be a gentleman, and the question of where to see a play is one social marker. The plays and audience at the Globe were considered more sophisticated than those at the Red Bull, a London theater built in 1605 where the Queen's Men often performed.*

[*Will Rash:*] . . . But what shall's doe when wee have dinde, shall's goe see a Play?

[*Scattergood:*] Yes fayth Brother: if it please you, let's goe see a Play at the Gloabe.

[*Bubble:*] I care not; any whither, so the Clowne have a part: For Ifayth I am no body without a Foole.

[*Geraldine:*] Why then wee'le goe to the Red Bull; they saye *Green's* a good Clowne.

[*Bubble:*] *Greene? Greene's* an Asse.

[*Scattergood:*] Wherefore doe you say so?

[*Bubble:*] Indeed I ha no reason: for they say, hee is as like mee as ever hee can looke.

[*Rash:*] Well then, to the Bull.

—sig. G2v

Poem about Shakespeare and an Allusion to *Venus and Adonis* in Davies's *The Scourge of Folly*

John Davies of Hereford's The Scourge of Folly *(1611) is a collection of often-vicious epigrams. His poem addressed to Shakespeare is an exception: Davies describes Shakespeare as the English equivalent of the Roman comedian Terence and comments on Shakespeare's gentle behavior. In the second excerpt, from "Paper's Complaint," a poem appended to* The Scourge of Folly, *Davies is less kind when he alludes to* Venus and Adonis.

To our English Terence Mʳ. Will:
    Shake-speare.

Epig. 159.

Some say (good *Will*) which I, in sport, do sing,
Had'st thou not plaid some Kingly parts in sport,
Thou hadst bin a companion for a *King*;
And, beene a King among the meaner sort.
Some others raile; but, raile as they thinke fit,
Thou hast no rayling, but, a raigning Wit:
    And honesty *thou sow'st, which they do reape;*
    So, to increase their Stocke *which they do keepe.*

—pp. 76–77

From "Papers Complaint, compild in ruthfull Rimes / Against the Paper-spoylers of these Times."

Another (ah Lord helpe) mee vilifies
With Art of Love, and how to subtilize,
Making lewd *Venus*, with eternall Lines,
To tye *Adonis* to her loves designes:
Fine wit is shew'n therein: but finer twere
If not attired in such bawdy Geare.
But be it as it will: the coyest Dames,
In private read it for their Closet-games:
For, sooth to say, the Lines so draw them on,
To the venerian speculation,
That will they, nill they (if of flesh they bee)
They will thinke of it, sith *loose* Thought is free.

—pp. 231–232

Allusion to Falstaff in Field's *Amends for Ladies*

In Amends for Ladies. A Comedie *(1618), performed in 1611, actor and playwright Nathan Field alludes to Falstaff's mock catechism in* 1 Henry IV, *5.1.127–141.*

Enter Lord Proudly *with a riding rod.*
[*Proudly*]: My Horse there, Z'oones I would not
    for the world
He should alight before me in the field,
My name and honor were for ever lost.
[*Seldome*]: Good morrow to your Honor, I doe
    heare
Your Lordship this faire morning is to fight,
And for your honor: Did you never see
The Play, where the fat Knight hight *Old-castle*,
Did tell you truly what this honor was?

—sig. Gr

Falstaff

'Tis not due yet, I would be loath to pay him before his day. What need I be so forward with him that calls not on me? Well, 'tis no matter, honor pricks me on. Yea, but how if honor prick me off when I come on? how then? Can honor set to a leg? No. Or an arm? No. Or take away the grief of a wound? No. Honor hath no skill in surgery then? No. What is honor? A word. What is in that word honor? What is that honor? Air. A trim reckoning! Who hath it? He that died a' Wednesday. Doth he feel it? No. Doth he hear it? No. 'Tis insensible then? Yea, to the dead. But will['t] not live with the living? No. Why? Detraction will not suffer it. Therefore I'll none of it, honor is a mere scutcheon. And so ends my catechism.

—*1 Henry IV,* 5.1.127–141

Allusion to Falstaff
in Speed's *The History of Great Britaine*

Historian John Speed, in his account of the martyrdom of the Protestant hero John Oldcastle in The History of Great Britaine Under the Conquests of Romans, Saxons, Danes, and Normans *(1611), responds to the Jesuit Robert Persons's* The Third Part Of A Treatise Intituled Of Three Conversions of England *(1604). Speed's scathing reference to Persons's use of a stage play to support his argument concludes with a swipe at "this Papist and his Poet." The poet who created the most famous stage version of Sir John Oldcastle is Shakespeare, who brings the knight, renamed Sir John Falstaff, onstage in the two parts of* Henry IV *and* The Merry Wives of Windsor. *Speed's reference is too vague to be linked definitively to Shakespeare, however.*

(46) [*Marginal note: The story of Sir John Ouldcastle.*] The Kings affaires thus effected in the *North*, the Clergies eye-sore was also somewhat eased by the apprehension of Sir *John Ouldcastle* their disturber in the *South*, who not contented to set the *God of Rome* at nought, but likewise defaced the faces of his Saints, trimly limmed in their Letanyes and other like masse bookes; a matter indeed of such moment, that the Abbot of *Saint Albans* (in whose precinct they were taken) sent these poore misused and scratched faced pictures, to complaine of their injuries unto the King, but his peace not broken, [*Marginal note:* Scratched faced pictures shewed at *Paules Crosse.*] for no blood was drawne, he remitted the offence and punishment thereof unto *Chichley* Archbishop of *Canterbury*, who sent them to *Paules* Crosse to shew their Countenances unto the people, the Preacher that day being their mouth, insinuating the offence to be done unto the triumphant Saints in heaven.

(47) [*Marginal note: Ex. Record. Parla. 5. H. 5.*] A Parliament assembled by the Regents authority for the supply of mony to maintaine the warres in *France*, a matter of as great importance was therein to be paid, and that was the apprehension and judgement of the Lord *Cobham*, with a consideration of reward for his taker the Lord *Powesse* in *Wales*, from whence sore wounded he was brought to *Westminster* before the Lords, and having heard his convictions would not thereunto answere in his excuse, upon which record and processe, it was adjudged that he should be taken as a traitour to the King and the Realme, that hee should bee carried to the Tower of *London*, [*Marginal note: Fox. Acts* and *Monuments.*] & from thence drawn through the streetes unto Saint *Giles* fields, and there to bee hanged, and burned hanging, which accordingly was done. [*Marginal note:* The review by *N. D.* pag. 31.] That *N. D.* author of the three conversions hath made *Ouldcastle* a Ruffian, a Robber, and a Rebell, and his authority taken from the *Stage-plaiers*, is more befitting the pen of his slanderous report, then the Credit of the judicious, being only grounded from this Papist and his Poet, of like conscience for lies, the one ever faining, and the other ever falsifying the truth [*Marginal note:* Papists and Poets of like conscience for fictions.].

–p. 637

The Master of the Revels' Account
of Plays Performed

Sir George Buc, Master of the Revels, kept the following account of the plays performed for the court in 1611 and 1612.

The names, of all the playes And by what Cumpaney played them hearafter ffollowethe: As All so what maskes, and Triumphes att the Tilte were presented before the kinges ma^tie in this year./1611

By the Kings players:	Hallomas; nyght was presented att Whithall before ye kinges ma^tie A play Called the Tempest:
The Kings players:	The 5th of november: A play Called ye winters nightes Tayle/
The Kings players:	On St Stivenes night A play called A Kinge & no king & Running at the Ring
The Queens players:	St John: night A play Called the City Gallant.
The princes players:	The Sunday ffollowinge A play called the Almanak
The kings players:	On neweres, night A play Called the Twinnes Tragedie And Running att the Ring.
The Childern of whitfriers	The Sunday ffollowing A play Called Cupids Reveng
This day the King & prince, with diver of his Nobelmen	Twelfe, night The princes Maske performed by Gentelmen of his did run att the Ring for a prize.

By the Queens players and the Kings men	The Sunday ffollowinge att Grenwidg before the Queen and the prince was played the Silver Aiedg: and ye next night following Lucre[ce]
By the Queens players	Candelmas: night A play Called The coque
By the kings players	Shrove Sunday: A play Called the Noblman
By the Duke of Yorks	Shrove Munday: A play Called Himens Holiday players/
By the Ladye Elizabeths	Shrove Teusday A play Called the proud Mayds Tragedie players

On the :24th: day of Marche Being the Kings Ma^{tis} day
Of his Entrie to the Croune of England was performed
at the
Tilt A Triumphe
—PRO, AO 3/908/14

The King's Men
Paid for Court Performances

To John Heminges for himselfe and his fellowes the kinges Majesties servauntes and Players upon the Counselles warraunt dated at whithall primo die Junii 1612 for presenting vi^x severall playes before his Majesty viz on upone the last of October one upon the first of November one upon the vth of November one upon the xxvith of December one upon the vth of January and one other upon Shrovesunday at night being the xxiiith of Febraary viz at twenty nobles for every play and five Markes for a reward for every play   lx^{li}

To the sayd John Heminges upon the lyke warraunt dated at whithall primo die Junii 1612 for himselfe and his fellowes for presenting xii severall playes before the Princes hignes and the Duke of yorke on severall nightes viz one upon the ninth of November last one upon the xixth of the same one other upon the xvith of December one other upon the last of the same one other upon the viith of January one other upon the xvth of the same one other upon the xixth of February one upon the xxth of the same one upon the xxviiith of February one upon the third of Aprill and an other upon the xvith of the same at twenty Nobles a Play   iiii^{li}

To the say John Heminges upon the Counselles warraunt dated at whithall primo die Junii 1612 for himselfe and his fellowes for presenting fowre playes before the Princes highnes the Lady Elizabeth and the Duke of yorke viz one the ixth of February last one other before the Prynce the xxth of the same one other the xxviiith of the Moneth of March before the Lady Elizabeth and one upon the xxvith of Aprill after the said rate

xxvi^{li} xiii^s iiii^d
—*Dramatic Records*, pp. 52–53

Harington's List of Shakespeare's Plays

The courtier and writer John Harington, who died in 1613, included "a list of eleven bound volumes of plays, besides several single comedies and other dramas" (British Museum Additional Manuscript 27, 632 lf. 43) in a family miscellany. As F. J. Furnivall observes in "Sir John Harington's Shakspeare Quartos" (Notes and Queries, 1890), "Among these are eighteen quartos of fifteen of Shakespeare's plays, three being duplicates of 'Pericles,' 'Lear,' and 'The Merry Wives.'" Also on the list are The Yorkshire Tragedy *and* The Puritan Widow. *Many of the numbers on this list probably refer to the volumes in Harington's collection. Furnival suggests that "the 13 at the side refers to the plays intended to form a vol. 13, or in a shelf 13." The meaning for some of the annotations is unknown.*

Leaf 43

Names of Comedyes.

13 A mad world my M^{rs}.
13 What yow will.
12 The dumb Knight [*struck through*]
12 Northward hoe [*struck through*] Stet.
12 Perocles, pr. of Tyre. [*struck through*]
12 Humor out of Breth. [*struck through*]
12 Law tricks, or who wold.
13 The case is Altred. [*struck through*] Stet.
12 Thre english Brothers. [*struck through*]
12 Lingua. [*struck through*]
12 Family of love. [*struck through*]
12 Yo^r fyve gallants. [*struck through*]
12 Mustaffa tragedy.
12 Byroun tragedy.
   Faythful Sheppard.   5
   Mery wyves of winsor.
   Looke about you.   2
   Ed. the 3.
   More foole.
   K. Leir of Shakspear.
13 Evry wom. in her humour.

Cupids whirlegigg.
The weakest to wall.   2
Cornelia Tragedy.
13 Alex. vi. papa. trag.   2
13 Revengers tragedy.   2
13 Bussy D'Amboys.
Ferrex & Porrex quære.
Belynus. Brennus.
Rape of Lucres.   13
Puritan widdow.   13
Muliasees the turk.   13
Poetaster. Ben Johnson.
Satiromastix. Jo. Decker   2
Alexander Campaspe.
Erl of Hungtington.
Sᵣ Tho. Wyat.   13
Glasse of government.
Grisild.
Yorkshyre tragedy.

.
1 Tom. 13 pl[ays].
1 The Marchant of Venice.
The London prodigall.
Tryall of Chyvalrie.
Everie man in his humoᵣ.
Eastward hoe.
Monsieur D'Olyve.
Henry the fourth.   1.
Henry the fourth.   2.
Richard yᵉ 3ᵈ tragedie.
King Leire. old.
Locryne.
Hamlet.
Sejanus. Ben. Johnson.
2 tome. xi. pl.

2 All Fooles.
Gentleman Usher.
The Queens Arcadia.
Sᵣ Giles Goose capp.
Liberalitie & Prodigal.
Good wife and bad.
The Malcontent.
Lord Cromwell.
Larum for London.
Pasquill & Katherin.
Alphonso of Arragon.

3 Tom. 9 pl.
Scourge of Symony re-
tire from.
Blurt mᵣ Constable.
Henry the viiiᵗ.

Everie man out of his
humour.
Fleyre.
The fawn.
The Isle of gulls.
Romeo and Julyet.
Sophonisba.

4 Tome. 12 [plays].
The taming of a shrow.
Orlando foolioso.
Moch adoe about nothing.
Queen Elis.
Queen Elis. hobs tawny coat
Wil somers will.
Loves labor lost.
Pastor fido.
Midsomer night dream.
Volpone the fox.
Spanish tragedy. Romeo.
Richard the 2.
Note yᵗ Guiana ys sorted
wᵗʰ Virginia and Maundey.

5 Tome. 13.
Thre Ladyes of London.
Warning for fayr wimen.
Looking glasse for London.
Fayr mayd of Bristow.
The Lords of London.
Stukly.
Fortunatus.
Tamberlane.
Tamberlane.
Edward 4.
Edward 4.
Arden of Feversham.
Doctor Faustus.

6 Tome. 13.
Nobody.
Loves metamorph.
Pedlers prophecy.
Doctor Dodypol.
Musidorus.
Antonio & Melida.
Woman in the moon.
Jeronimo. i. part.
David and Bersabe.
Arraignment of paris.
Blynde begger of Alexandria.
Antonius (?).
Solimon and Perseda.

Leaf 43 bk.:–

7 Tome. 13.
Lusty Juventus.
Cambyses.
Henry the fift. Pistol.
Supposes.
Marius and Scilla.
Two tragedyes in one.
Jack Straw. wat tiler.
Mayds metamorpd.
Edward the first.
Menechmus.
Selimus. i. part.
Cinthias revels.

8 Tome.
Downfal of Rob. E. Hunt.   1
Alexander Campaspe.   F
Merry wyves winsor. W. S.   G
King Leyr. W. Sh.   L
Glas of government. gaskin.   n
Ed. the third.   J
Cornelia. tra.   L
Dutch cortesan. marston.   H
Yorksh. Traged. W. S.   D
Pacient Grisild.   L
Faythful shepardes. Jo.
fle. [Fletcher].   L

12. 9 Tome.
The dumb Knight.
Northward hoe.
Pericles.
Humor out of breth.
Law tricks.
Three Engl. brother.
Lingua.
Famyly of love.
Yo^r fyve gallants.
Mustaffa. i.
Biron i.
Biroun 2.

12. 10 Tome.
Sr. Tho. wyat. Decker.   g
Cupids whirligig. E. S.   L
Puritan wyddow. W. S.   H
Revengers tragedy.   I
Devils charter. Bar. Barns.   H
Bussy d Amboys.   I
What you wil. Marston.   H
Mad world. T. M.   I
Y^e Rape of Lucress. Tho.
        heywood   K

Y^e case ys altered. I
Evry woman in humour.   H
Mulliassis. John Mason.   K

11 Tome. 11.
Mother Bombee.   h
Whore of Babylon. J. d.   K
Cæsar and Pompey.   I
Coblers prophesy.   g
Westward hoe. J. De. Web.
[Decker, Webster].   I
Taming of a shrow.   g
Pinner of wakfeeld.   g
Return from pernass.   h
Phœnix.   K
Michelmas term.   I
Willy beguild.   K
        —*Notes and Queries*, 7th series, 9 (1890): 382–383

1612

Gilbert Shakespeare's Burial Record

The burial of Shakespeare's brother Gilbert Shakespeare is noted in the parish records of Holy Trinity Church in Stratford. The term "adolescens" is perhaps used here, as it seems to be elsewhere in the register, to mean "unmarried."

[3 February 1612]   Gilbert Shakspere, adolescens
        —*Burial Register*, folio 41v

Vaux's Complaint about an Incident at the Globe

Ambrose Vaux courted and married Elizabeth Wyborne, a widow "possessed of divers goodes and Chattells as well reall as personall and then haveing greate store of money in hir handes or in the handes of some of hir freindes" (p. 568). According to Vaux's complaint against Sir Richard Blunt, Edward Wyborne, Dudley Norton, and Joseph Mules (PRO STAC 8/289/3), before the marriage took place, Blunt, Wyborne, and Norton persuaded Elizabeth Wyborne "to make over hir money goodes plate leases landes Joynture and dowre" (p. 568) in order to keep this property out of his control. Vaux alleges the deeds transferring the property were "fraudulently and deceitfuly made framed and contrived" (p. 569), and that once the men had the property, they attempted to persuade Elizabeth to leave Vaux. Shortly after that, the following incident took place in the Globe theater.

The excerpts in this section are from Mary A. Blackstone and Cameron Louis's "Towards 'A Full and Understanding Auditory': New Evidence of Playgoers at the First

Globe Theatre." Italics in the text indicate expanded abbreviations.

". . . about the moneth of August last past and after the said entermarriage betweene your subject and the said Elizabeth your said subject about the same tyme havinge some intelligence that the said Elizabeth your said subjectes wife was gon to a playe in the Companye of the said Dudley Norton to the Globe in Southwarke in your highnes County of Surrey Therupponn your said subject then and there resorted [to the said] and then went to the said playe house Called the Globe in Southwarke aforesaid And your said subject then perseavinge the said Elizabeth your said subjectes wife to be there in ye Company of the said Elizabeth and lovingly desired hir to go with him and to live with him And the said Dudley Norton seeinge your subject earnest to have his said wife home with him he the said Dudley Norton then began to be much distempered and with greate violences and blasphemous oathes the said Dudley Norton Joseph Mules servant to the said Dudley Norton and divers others to the number of twelve persons whose names are unknowen to your subject but humbly desireth they maye be incerted in this bill when they shalbe knowen unto your said subject beinge all of them then and there armed arraied and weaponed with Rapiars daggers Pystalls and other weapons as well defensive as offencive they the said Dudley Norton Joseph Mules and the said other riotous persons then and there assaulted your said subject and there held your said subject the said Dudley Norton then and there swearinge Godes woondes thether hee brought hir your said subjectes wife and from thence hee wold carry hir againe aweae in dispite of your said subjecte And accordingli theye the said Dudley Norton Joseph Mules and the said other persons to the number of xii persons beinge then and there armed and arraied as aforesaid did then and there in a Riotus forceable and outragiouse manner take from your said subject the said Elizabeth and with force and in a ryotous manner did then and there take and Carry aweae the said Elizabeth in dispite of your said subject and the said Dudley Norton ever since hath and still doth Carry and keepe aweae your said Subjectes wife from him in his house against your highnes lawes and the lawes of god and against all Christian Charitie and to the evill example of your highnes lovinge and obedient subjectes by reason whereof your subject is bereft of his wife and of all hir estate . . .

The defendants' answer describes the events in Vaux's complaint as "slaunderously and untrewlie alleaged" (p. 570), and they claim they took control of the widow's property to pay her late husband's debts and to execute his will. The answer concludes with their version of what happened at the Globe.

. . . and touchinge to the pretended misdemenure and riott supposed to bee committed by the said Dudley Norton And Joseph Mulis his servant at the globe in Southwarke the said defendant Dudley Norton for the manifestacion of the truth thereof saith that for his recreation hee together with the said Elizabeth ^ 'and' her late husbandes neece and one gentleman more onely attended by the said Joseph Mulis the other defendant went to the Globe in Southwarke where hee this defendant Dudley Norton never was above foure or five times in his whole life and sitting there togither the said Complaynant came in and tould the said Elizabeth shee must goe away with him whereuppon this defendant Dudley Norton perceivinge the great feare and perplexitie shee was in tooke pitty on her and advised him to forbeare at that time and the said gentleman did the like desieringe him with many faire wordes that hee the said Complaynant would bee contented to meete her and to conferre orderly and peaceablie with her at an other time but the Complaynant would harken to noe tearmes of peace but in a verie outragious manner offered to draw his dagger which the said defendant Dudley Norton perceivinge where it was half out Laid one of his handes onely uppon the said Complaynantes wristes for the preservacion of his Majesties peace and thereby to prevent the mischief hee the said Complaynant intended to have done and in the meane season the said Elizabeth went away in the Companie of her said neece and the said other defendant Joseph Mulis and lastlie this defendant Dudley Norton saith that whereas the said Complaynant chargeth him this defendant with keepinge the said Elizabeth away from him in his house That the said Elizabeth hath her setled place of abode at one Billyes house in ffleetstreet where for the most part shee remayneth but hee this defendant acknowledgeth that out of the good will of a kinswoman shee doth now and then as shee and her late husband Wybarne were wont to doe in his life time repayre to the defendan house sometimes uppon busines and sometimes in curtesie to visitt the defendantes parentes and his wif when shee is in the towne the said Elizabeth and her late husband beinge the kinsfolke and auncient acquaintance of the said defendant Dudley Norton of five and twentie yeares continuance All which matters & thinges the sayd defendantes are redy to aver manetaine & prove as this most honorable Court shall award & therefore most humbly pray to be dismissed from the same with theire costes & chardges in that behalfe wrongfully sustayned.

—MLR, 90 (July 1995): 556–571

Publications

Shakespeare's Richard III, *previously published in 1597, 1598, 1602, and 1606, was published again in 1612.*

THE / TRAGEDIE / of King Richard / the third. / Containing his treacherous Plots againſt his brother / Clarence: the pittifull murther of his innocent Ne- / phewes: his tyrannicall vſurpation: with the / whole courſe of his deteſted life, and / moſt deſerved death. / *As it hath beene lately Acted by the Kings Maieſties / ſervants.* / Newly augmented, / by *William Shake-ſpeare.* / [Printer's device] / LONDON, / Printed by Thomas Creede, and are to be ſold by Mathew / Lawe, dwelling in Pauls Church-yard, at the Signe / of the Foxe, neare S. Auſtins gate, 1 6 1 2.

The Passionate Pilgrim, previously published in 1599, was published again in 1612. It contains several poems by Shakespeare. The first title page below, which lists Shakespeare as the author, was cancelled, and Shakespeare's name does not appear on the replacement title page.

THE / PASSIONATE / PILGRIME. / OR / *Certaine Amorous Sonnets,* / betweene Venus and Adonis, / *newly corrected and aug-* / *mented.* / By *W. Shakeſpere.* / The third Edition. / Where-unto is newly ad- / ded two Loue-Epiſtles, the firſt / [page damaged] to *Hellen,* and / [page damaged] nſwere backe / [page damaged] ne to *Paris.* / [page damaged] by W. Iaggard. 1612. [Cancelled]

THE / PASSIONATE / PILGRIME. / OR / *Certaine Amorous Sonnets,* / betweene *Venus* and *Adonis,* / *newly corrected and* / *aug-* / *mented.* / The third Edition. / Where-unto is newly ad- / ded two Loue-Epiſtles, the firſt / from *Paris* to *Hellen,* and / *Hellens anſwere backe* [?] *againe to Paris.* / Printed by W. Iaggard. / 1612.

Allusions to Shakespeare and *Henry V* in Heywood's *An Apology For Actors*

Shakespeare is probably the offended author Heywood refers to near the end of his epistle to the printer Nicholas Okes that follows An Apology For Actors *(1612). As E. K. Chambers and others have noted, two poems from Heywood's* Troia Britannica *(1609) were printed in William Jaggard's 1612 edition of* The Passionate Pilgrim. Or Certaine Amorous Sonnets, betweene Venus and Adonis, newly corrected and augmented. *The work initially appeared with a title page identifying Shakespeare as the author; this page was cancelled, and Shakespeare's name removed. Both title pages add, "The third Edition. Where-unto is newly added two Love-Epistles, the first from Paris to Hellen, and Hellens answere backe againe to Paris."*

In the body of his work Heywood vigorously defends actors against charges of immorality and argues that a well-governed commonwealth needs drama for a variety of reasons. In this excerpt he describes the role of drama in promoting patriotism and national pride and alludes to plays portraying Edward III and Henry V, possibly Shakespeare's plays about those monarchs.

To turne to our domesticke hystories, what English blood seeing the person of any bold English man presented and doth not hugge his frame, and hunnye at his valor, pursuing him in his enterprise with his best wishes, and as beeing wrapt in contemplation, offers to him in his hart all prosperous performance, as if the Personater were the man Personated, so bewitching a thing is lively and well spirited action, that it hath power to new mold the harts of the spectators and fashion them to the shape of any noble and notable attempt. What coward to see his own countryman valiant would not bee ashamed of his owne cowardise? What English Prince should hee behold the true portrature of that famous King *Edward* the third, foraging France, taking so great a King captive in his owne country, quartering the English Lyons with the French Flower-delyce, and would not bee suddenly Inflam'd with so royall a spectacle, being made apt and fit for the like atchievement. So of *Henry* the fift: but not to be tedious in any thing. . . .

To my approved good Friend, Mr. *Nicholas Okes.*

The infinite faults escaped in my booke of *Britaines Troy,* by the negligence of the Printer, as the misquotations, mistaking of sillables, misplacing halfe lines, coining of strange and never heard of words. These being without number, when I would have taken a particular account of the *Errata,* the Printer answered me, hee would not publish his owne disworkemanship, but rather let his owne fault lye upon the necke of the Author: and being fearefull that others of his quality, had beene of the same nature, and condition, and finding you on the contrary, so carefull, and industrious, so serious and laborious to doe the Author all the rights of the presse, I could not choose but gratulate your honest indeavours with this short remembrance. Here likewise, I must necessarily insert a manifest injury done me in that worke, by taking the two Epistles of *Paris* to *Helen,* and *Helen to Paris,* and printing them in a lesse volume, under the name of another, which may put the world in opinion I might steale them from him; and hee to doe himselfe right, hath since published them in his owne name: but as I must acknowledge my lines not worthy his patronage,

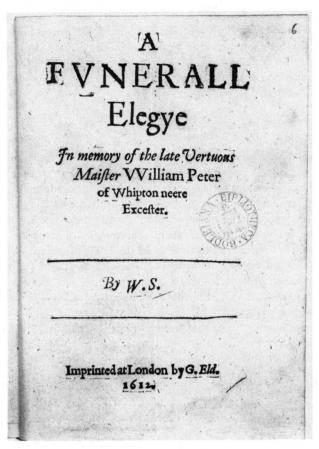

Title page for a work that is often attributed to Shakespeare. Various plausible candidates have been put forth as the author of William Peter's funeral elegy (courtesy of the Bodleian Library, Oxford).

under whom he hath publisht them, so the Author I know much offended with M. *Jaggard* (that altogether unknowne to him) presumed to make so bold with his name. These, and the like dishonesties I know you to bee cleere of; and I could wish but to bee the happy Author of so worthy a worke as I could willingly commit to your care and workmanship.

Yours ever
THOMAS HEYWOOD.
—sigs. G4r–v

Allusion to Shakespeare in Webster's Preface to *The White Divel*

Coachmaker and playwright John Webster (circa 1578–circa 1632) lists Shakespeare among other worthy contemporaries in his address to the readers of his sophisticated revenge tragedy The White Divel, Or, The Tragedy of Paulo Giordano Ursini, Duke of Brachiano, With The Life and Death of Vittoria Corombona the famous Venetian Curtizan *(1612).*

To the Reader.

In publishing this Tragedy, I do but challenge to my selfe that liberty, which other men have tane before mee; not that I affect praise by it, for, *nos hæc novimus esse nihil*, onely since it was acted, in so dull a time of Winter, presented in so open and blacke a Theater, that it wanted (that which is the onley grace and setting out of a Tragedy) a full and understanding Auditory: and that since that time I have noted, most of the people that come to that Play-house, resemble those ignorant asses (who visiting Stationers shoppes their use is not to inquire for good bookes, but new bookes) I present it to the generall veiw with this confidence.

Nec Rhoncos metues, maligniorum,
Nec Scombris tunicas, dabis molestas.

If it be objected this is no true Drammaticke Poem, I shall easily confesse it, *non potes in nugas dicere plura meas: Ipse ego quam dixi*, willingly, and not ignorantly, in this kind have I faulted: for should a man present to such an Auditory, the most sententious Tragedy that ever was written, observing all the criticall lawes, as heighth of stile; and gravety of person: inrich it with the sententious *Chorus*, and as it were life'n Death, in the passionate and waighty *Nuntius*: yet after all this divine rapture, *O dura messorum ilia*, the breath that comes from the uncapable multitude, is able to poison it, and ere it be acted, let the Author resolve to fix to every scæne, this of *Horace*,

Hæc hodie Porcis comedenda a relinques.

To those who report I was a long time in finishing this Tragedy, I confesse I do not write with a goose-quill, winged with two feathers, and if they will needes make it my fault, I must answere them with that of *Eurypides* to *Alcestides*, a Tragicke writer: *Alcestides* objecting that *Eurypides* had onely in three daies composed three verses, whereas himselfe had written three hundreth: Thou telst truth, (quoth he) but heres the difference, thine shall onely bee read for three daies, whereas mine shall continue three ages.

Detraction is the sworne friend to ignorance: For mine owne part I have ever truly cherisht my good opinion of other mens worthy Labours, especially of that full and haightned stile of Maister *Chapman*, The labor'd and understanding workes of Maister *Johnson*: The no lesse worthy composures of the both worthily excellent Maister *Beaumont*, & Maister *Fletcher*: And lastly (without wrong last to be named) the right happy and copious industry of M. *Shake-speare*, M. *Decker*, & M. *Heywood*, wishing what I write may be read by their light: Protesting, that in the strength of mine own judgement, I know them so worthy, that though I rest silent in my owne worke, yet to most of theirs I dare (without flattery) fix that of *Martiall*,

non norunt, Hæc monumenta mori.

—sigs. A2r–v

1613

Richard Shakespeare's Burial Record

The burial of Shakespeare's brother Richard is noted in the parish records of Holy Trinity Church in Stratford.

[4 February 1613]   Rich: Shakspeare
—*Burial Register,* folio 42v

Publications

1 Henry IV *(1598, 1599, 1604, 1608) is published again. Also published is* Thomas Cromwell; *although the author is identified as "W. S.", the play is not thought to be by Shakespeare.*

THE / HISTORY OF / Henrie the fourth, / With the Battell at Shrewſeburie, betweene / the King, and Lord Henrie Percy, ſur- / named *Henrie Hotſpur* of the North. / VVith the humorous conceites of Sir / *Iohn Falſtaffe.* / Newly corrected by *W. Shake-speare.* / [*Printer's device*] / LONDON, / Printed by *W. W.* for *Mathew Law,* and are to be ſold / at his ſhop in Paules Church-yard, neere vnto S. / *Auguſtines* Gate, at the ſigne of the Foxe. / 1 6 1 3.

THE / True Chronicle Hi- / ſtorie of the whole life and death / of *Thomas* Lord *Cromwell.* / As it hath beene ſun-dry times pub- / likely Acted by the Kings Maieſties / Seruants. / *Written by* W. S. / [*Printer's device*] / *LONDON:* / Printed by THOMAS SNODHAM. / 1613.

Shakespeare's Purchase of the Blackfriar's Gatehouse

In this transcription of the vendor's copy of the conveyance for the Blackfriar's Gatehouse, a house near the Blackfriar's the-ater (Guildhall Library manuscript), whereby Shakespeare acquired the property, the legal abbreviations have been silently expanded. The transcription is taken from the facsimile in Lewis, Documents, *volume two, following page 438. The purchaser's copy of the conveyance, which Shakespeare would have kept and which he did not have to sign, is in the Folger Shakespeare Library (Manuscript Z.c.22 [45]).*

This Indenture made the Tenthe day of Marche in the yeare of our Lord god according to the Computacion of the church of England one thousand six hundred and twelve, and in the yeares of the reigne of our Soveraigne Lord James by the grace of god king of England Scotland ffraunce and Ireland defender of the faith &c. that is to saie of England ffraunce and Ireland the tenth and of Scotland the six and fortith: Betweene Henry Walker Citizein and Minstrell of London of th'one partie And William Shakespeare of Stratford Upon Avon in the Countie of Warwick gentleman William Johnson Citizein and Vintener of London John Jackson and John Hemmyng of London gentlemen of th'other partie. Witnesseth that the said Henry Walker for and in consideracion of the somme of one hundred and fortie poundes of lawfull money of England to him in hande before th'ensealing hereof by the said William Shakespeare well & trulie paid whereof and wherewith hee the said Henry Walker doth acknowledge himselfe fullie satisfied and contented and thereof and of every part and parcell therof doth cleerlie acquite and dis-charge the saide William Shakespeare his heires execu-tours administratours and assignes and every of them by theis presentes Hath bargayned and soulde and by theis presentes doth fullie cleerlie and absolutlie bar-gayne and sell unto the said William Shakespeare Wil-liam Johnson John Jackson and John Hemmyng their heires and assignes forever; All that dwelling house or Tenement with th'appurtenaunces situate and being within the Precinct, Circuit and Compasse of the late black ffryers London sometymes in the tenure of James Gardyner Esquiour and since that in the tenure of John ffortescue gentleman, and now or late being in the ten-ure or occupacion of one William Ireland or of his assignee or assignes abutting upon a streete leading downe to Pudle wharffe on the east part, right against the kinges Majesties Wardrobe: part of which said Ten-ement is erected over a great gate leading to a capitall Mesuage which sometyme was in the tenure of William Blackwell Esquiour deceased, and since that in the ten-ure or occupacion of the right Honorable Henry now Earle of Northumberland; And also all that plott of ground on the west side of the same Tenement which was lately inclosed with boordes on two sides therof by Anne Bacon widowe soe farre and in such sorte as the same was inclosed by the said Anne Bacon and not oth-erwise, and being on the thirde side inclosed with an old Brick wall; Which said plott of ground was some-tyme parcell and taken out of a great [*"voyde" in vendee's copy*] peece of ground lately used for a garden and also the soyle whereupon the said Tenement standeth: and also the said Brick wall and boordes which doe inclose the said plott of ground: With free entrie, accesse, ingresse, egresse, and regresse in, by, and through the said greate gate and yarde there unto the usuall dore of the said Tenement; And also all and singuler Cel-lours, sollers, romes, lightes, easiamentes, profittes Commodities, and heriditamentes whatsoever; to the said dwelling house or Tenement belonging, or in any wise apperteyning And the reversion and reversions whatsoever of all and singuler the premisses, and of every parcell thereof; And also all rentes and yearlie profittes whatsoever reserved and from hensforth to growe due and paiable upon whatsoever lease dimise, or graunt, leases demises or graunts made of the premisses, or of any parcell thereof; And also all th'estate, right, title, interest, propertie, use, possession, clayme, and demaund whatsoever which hee the said Henry Walker now hath or of right may, might, should, or ought to have of, in, or to the premisses or any parcell thereof; And also all and every the deedes, evidences, Charters, escriptes, minimentes, & writinges whatsoever which hee the said Henry Walker now hath, or any other person or persons to his use have or hath, or which hee may lawfullie come by without suite in the lawe which touch or concerne the premisses onlie or onlie any part or parcell thereof; Togeither with true Coppies of all such deedes, evidences, and writinges as concerne the premisses (among other thinges to be writ-

ten) and taken out at the onlie costes and charges of the said William Shakespeare his heires, or assignes. Which said dwelling house or Tenement and other the premisses above by theis presentes mencioned to bee bargayned and soulde the said Henry Walker late purchased and had to him his heires and assignes forever of Mathie Bacon of Graies Inne in the Countie of Middlesex gentleman by Indenture bearing date the fifteenth day of October in the yeare of our Lord god one thowsand six hundred and fower, and in the yeares of the reigne of our said Sovereigne Lord King James of his Realmes of England, ffraunce, and Ireland the second and of Scotland the eight & thirtith. To have and to holde the said dwelling house or Tenement, shopps, Cellours, sollers, plott of ground and all and singuler other the premisses above by theis presentes mencioned to bee bargayned and soulde and every part and parcell thereof with th'appurtenances, unto the said William Shakespeare, William Johnson, John Jackson, and John

Mortgage, signed by Shakespeare, for the Blackfriar's gatehouse (MS Egerton 1787; courtesy of The British Library, London)

Hemmyng their heires and assignes forever; To th'onlie & proper use and behoofe of the said William Shakespeare, William Johnson, John Jackson, and John Hemmyng their heires and assignes forever. And the said Henry Walker for himselfe, his heires, executours, administratours and assignes, and for every of them Doth Covenaunt promisse and graunt to and with the said William Shakespeare his heires and assignes by theis presentes in forme following that is to saie That hee the said Henry Walker his heires, executours, administratours, or assignes shall and will cleerlie acquite, exonerate, and discharge, or otherwise from tyme to tyme, and at all tymes hereafter well and sufficientlie save and keepe harmles the said William Shakespeare his heires and assignes and every of them of, for, and concernyng the bargayne and sale of the premisses, and the said bargayned premisses, and every part and parcell thereof with th'appurtenances of and from all and almanner of former bargaynes, sales, guiftes, grauntes, leases, statutes, Recognizaunces, Joyntures, Dowers, intailes, lymittacions and lymittacions of use and uses, extentes, Judgmentes, execucions, Annuities and of and from all and every other charges, titles and incumbraunces whatsoever wittinglie and wilfullie had, made, committed, suffered, or donne by him the said Henry Walker or any other under his aucthoritie or right before th'ensealing and deliverye of theis presentes Except the rentes and services to the Cheefe Lord or Lordes of the fee or fees of the premisses from hensforth for or in respecte of his or their seigniorie or seigniories onlie to bee due and donne; [four lines deleted and illegible] And further the saide Henry Walker for himselfe, his heires, executours, and administratours, and for every of them doth Covenaunte promisse, and graunt to and with the said William Shakespeare his heires and assignes by theis presentes in forme following (that is to saie) That for and notwithstanding any acte or thing donne by him the said Henry Walker to the Contrarye hee the said William Shakespeare his heires and assignes shall or lawfullie maye peaceablie & quietlie have, holde occupie and enjoye the said dwelling house or Tenement, Cellours sollers and all and singuler other the premisses above by theis presentes mencioned to bee bargayned and soulde and every part and parcell therof with th'appurtenaunces, and the rentes, yssues, and profittes thereof and of every part and parcell thereof to his and their owne use receave, perceave, take, and enjoye from hensforth forever without the lett troble evicc[ion or] interrupcion of the said Henry Walker his heires, executours, or administratours, or any of them or of or by any other person or persons which have, or may before the date hereof pretend to have any lawfull estate, right title, use or interest in or to the premisses, or any parcell thereof by,

from, or under him the said Henry Walker. And also that hee the said Henry Walker his heires, and all and every other person and persons and their heires which have or that shall lawfullie and rightfullie have or clayme to have any lawfull and rightfull estate righte title or interest in or to the premisses or any parcell thereof by from, or under the said Henry Walker shall and will from tyme to tyme & at all tymes from hensforth for and during the space of three yeares now next ensuing, at or upon the reasonable request and [word deleted] Costes and charges in the lawe of the said William Shakespeare his heires and assignes Doe make knowledge, and suffer to bee donne, made, and knowledged all and every such further lawfull and reasonable acte and actes, thing and thinges, devise and devises in the lawe whatsoever for the conveying of the premisses bee it by deed or deedes, inrolled or not inrolled, inrolment of theis presentes, fyne feoffament, recoverye release, confirmacon, or otherwise with warrantie of the said Henry Walker and his heires against him the said Henry Walker and his heires onlie or otherwise without warrantie, or by all, any, or as many of the wayes, meanes, and devises aforesaid As by the said William Shakespeare his heires or assignes, or his or their Councell learned in the lawe shalbee reasonablie devised or advised: ffor the further, better, and more perfect assurance, suertie, suermaking, and conveying of all and singuler the premisses and every parcell thereof with th'appurtenaunces unto the saide William Shakespeare his heires and assignes forever to th'use and in forme aforesaid, And that all and every fyne and fynes to bee levyed recoveryes to bee suffered, estates and assurances at any tyme or tymes hereafter to bee had, made, executed or passed by or betweene the said parties of the premisses or of any parcell thereof shalbee and shalbee esteemed adjudged, deemed, and taken to bee to th'onlie and proper use and behoofe of the said William Shakespeare his heires and assignes forever and to none other use, intent, or purpose. In witnesse thereof the said parties to theis Indentures Interchaungablie have sett their seales: Yeoven the day and yeares first above written. [Signed] William Shakespeare, William Johnson, John Jackson

Shakespeare Mortgages the Blackfriar's Gatehouse

This 11 March 1613 document (British Library, Edgerton Manuscript 1787) is the deed by which Shakepeare mortgaged the Blackfriar's gatehouse to Henry Walker. Shakespeare may have purchased the gatehouse as an investment; there is no evidence that he ever lived there, and his will shows he leased it to a man named John Robinson. The financial arrangement established in the mortgage would prevent Shakespeare's widow from inheriting her customary one-third share of the property, but it is not possible to determine if that was Shakespeare's primary purpose here. The house was inherited by Shakespeare's daughter Susanna and her husband John Hall; they sold it in 1618.

This Indenture made the Eleaventh day of March in the yeares of the reigne of our Sovereigne Lord James by the grace of god king of England, Scotland, ffraunce and Ireland defender of the faith &c (that is to saie) of England ffraunce and Ireland the tenth and of Scotland the six and fortith: Betweene William Shakespeare of Stratford upon Avon in the Countie of Warwick gentleman, William Johnson Citizein and Vintener of London, John Jackson and John Hemmyng of London gentlemen of thone partie, And Henry Walker Citizein and Minstrell of London of th'other partie. Witnesseth that the said William Shakespeare William Johnson, John Jackson, and John Hemmyng Have dimised graunted and to ferme letten and by theis presentes doe demise graunt and to ferme lett unto the said Henry Walker All that dwelling house or Tenement with th'appurtennces situate and being within the Precinct Circuit and Compasse of the late black ffryers London sometymes in the tenure of James Gardyner Esquiour and since that in the tenure of John ffortescue gentleman and now or late being in the tenure or occupacion of one William Ireland or of his assignee or assignes; abutting upon a streete leading downe to Puddle wharffe on the east part right against the kinges Majesties Wardrobe part of which said Tenement is erected over a great gate leading to a Capitall Mesuage which sometyme was in the tenure of William Blackwell Esquior deceased and since that in the tenure or occupacion of the Right Honourable Henry now Earle of Northumberland And also all that plott of grounde on the west side of the same Tenement, which was lately inclosed with boordes on two sides thereof by Anne Bacon widow soe farre, and in such sorte as the same was inclosed by the said Anne Bacon and not otherwise and being on the third side inclosed with an olde brick wall. Which said plott of ground was sometyme parcell and taken out of a great voyde peece of ground lately used for a garden; and also the soyle whereuppon the said Tenement standeth; and also the said Brick wall and boordes which doe inclose the said plott of ground. With free entrie accesse ingresse, egresse, and regresse in, by, and through the said great gate and yarde there unto the usuall dore of the said Tenement; And also all and singuler Cellours sollers, romes, lightes, easiamentes, profittes, Commodities, and appurtenaunces whatsoever to the said dwelling house or Tenement belonging, or in any wise apperteyning. To have and to holde the said dwell-

Shakespeare's signature on the vendor's copy of the deed for the Blackfriar's gatehouse, 1613 (courtesy of the Guildhall Library; photograph © 2001 Geremy Butler Photography)

ing house or Tenement, Cellers, sollers, romes, plott of ground and all and singuler other the premisses above by theis presentes mencioned to bee dimised, and every part and parcell thereof with th'appurtenaunces, unto the said Henrye Walker his executours, administratours, and assignes from the feast of th'annunciation of the blessed Virgin Marye next comming after the date hereof, unto th'ende and terme of One hundred yeares from thence next ensuing and fullie to bee Compleat and ended without ympeachment of or for any manner of waste. Yeelding and paying therefore yearlie during the said terme unto the said William Shakespeare, William Johnson, John Jackson, and John Hemmyng their heires and assignes a pepper Corne, at the feast of Easter yearlie, yf the same bee lawfullie demaunded, and noe more. / Provided alwayes that if the said William Shakespeare his heires, executours, administratours or assignes or any of them doe well and trulie paie or cause to bee paid to the said Henry Walker his executours, administratours, or assignes the somme of threescore poundes of lawfull money of England, in and upon the nyne & twentith day of September next comming after the date hereof at or in the nowe dwelling house of the said Henry Walker situate and being in the parish of Saint Martyn neere Ludgate of London, at one entier payment without delaie; That then and from thensforth this presente lease demise and graunt and all and every matter and thing herein conteyned (other then this provisoe) shall Cease, determyne, and bee utterlie voyde, frustrate, and of none effect, As though the same had never beene had ne made; Theis presentes, or any thing therein Conteyned to the Contrary thereof in any wise notwithstanding And the said William Shakespeare for himself his heires, executours and administratours and for every of them doth Covenaunt, promisse, and graunt to and with the said Henry Walker his executours, administratours, and assignes and every of them by theis presentes; That hee the said William Shakespeare his heires, executours, administratours, or assignes shall and will cleerlie acquite, exonerate, and discharge, or from tyme to tyme and at all tymes hereafter well and sufficientlie save and keepe harmles the said Henry Walker his executours, administratours and assignes, and every of them and the said premisses by theis presentes dimised and every parcell thereof with th'appurtenaunces of and from all and almanner of former & other bargaynes sales, guiftes, grauntes, leases, Joyntures, dowers, intailes, statutes, Recognizaunces, Judgmentes, execucions, and of and from all & every other charges, titles, trobles, and incumbraunces whatsoever by the said William Shakes-

peare, William Johnson, John Jackson, and John Hemmyng, or any of them, or by their or any of their meanes had, made, committed, or donne before th'ensealing and delivery of theis presentes, or hereafter before the said nyne & twentith day of September next comming after the date hereof to bee had, made, committed, or done Except the rentes and services to the Cheefe Lord or Lordes of the fee or fees of the premisses for or in respect of his or their seigniorie or seigniories onlie to bee due & donne. In witnesse whereof the said parties to theis Indentures Interchaungablie have sett their seales: Yeoven the day and yeares first above written. 1612

[Signed on the seal tabs:]   Wᵐ Shaksp_
                                     Wᵐ Johnson
                                     Jo: Jackson

The endorsement was transcribed by B. Roland Lewis.

Sealed and delivered by the said William Shakespeare William Johnson and John Jackson in the presence of
Will: Atkinson
Ed: Overy
Robert Andrewe Scr
Henry Lawrence, servant to the same Scr
                        —Lewis, *The Shakespeare Documents,* p. 447

Shakespeare and Burbage
Paid for Impresa

Shakespeare designed an impresa–a paper shield bearing an emblem and usually a motto to identify, often in a clever way, the knight who carries it–for Francis Manners, the sixth Earl of Rutland, to carry at a celebration marking the King's Accession day, 24 March 1613. The following entry is from the earl of Rutland's household accounts.

Item 31 Mᵃʳtii. to Mʳ Shakespeare in gold.
about my Lorde Impreso xliiiiˢ / To Rich   iiiiˡⁱ· viiiˢ·
Burbage for paynting & making yt in
gold xliiiiˢ.
                        —Rutland Manuscript, iv. 494

The King's Men
Paid for Court Performances

The King's Men are paid for the performance of several plays. These entries are unusual because they name the plays being performed; the list includes Shakespeare's Much Ado about Nothing *(spelled similarly in the first entry; called*

Benidicte and Betteris *in the third);* The Tempest; The Winter's Tale; 1 Henry IV *(the third entry's* The Hotspurr *and possibly the first entry's* Sr John Falstafe); *possibly another of the plays featuring Falstaff* (2 Henry IV *or* The Merry Wives of Windsor); Othello; *possibly* Julius Caesar *(the first entry's* Caesars Tragedye); *and* Cardenio, *a lost play.*

Item paid to John Heminges upon the Couwncells warrant dated att Whitehall xx° Die Maii 1613 for presentinge before the Princes Highnes the La: Elizabeth and the Prince Pallatyne Elector fowerteene severall playes viz one playe called Pilaster, One other called the Knott: of Fooles, One other Much adoe abowte nothinge, The Mayeds Tragedy, The merye Dyvell of Edmonton, The Tempest, A Kinge and no Kinge The Twins Tragedie The Winters Tale, Sr John Falstafe, The Moore of Venice, The Nobleman, Caesars Tragedye And one other called Love Lyes a bleedinge, All which Playes weare played within the tyme of this Accompte, viz paid the some of   iiii^xx xiii^li vi^s viii^d

To the sayd John Heminges upon the Councells warrante dated the xx^th of May 1613 for presentinge sixe severall playes before the kinges Majestie xl^li, and by way of his Majesties rewarde xx^li, in all lx^li

Item paid to the said John Heminges upon the lyke warrant: dated att Whitehall xx° die Maii 1613 for presentinge sixe severall playes viz one playe called a badd begininge makes a good endinge, One other called the Capteyne, One other the Alcumist. One other Cardenno. One other The Hotspurr. And one other called Benidicte and Betteris All played within the tyme of this Accompte viz paid Fortie powndes, And by waye of his Majesties rewarde twentie powndes In all   lx^li

—*Dramatic Records,* pp. 55–56

Allusion to Shakespeare in Digges's Inscription in de Vega's *Rimas*

Poet Leonard Digges's (1588–1635) fly-leaf inscription in Lope de Vega's Rimas *(Madrid, 1613) was discovered in the library of Balliol College, Oxford, and transcribed by Paul Morgan in "'Our Will Shakespeare' and Lope de Vega: An Unrecorded Contemporary Document." Digges contributed a commendatory verse to the First Folio as did "I.M.", thought to be translator James Mabbe, the same "Mr Mab" referred to in Digges's inscription.*

Will Baker: Knowinge
that Mr Mab: was to
sende you this Booke

of sonets, wch with Spaniards
here is accounted of their
lope de Vega as in Englande
wee sholde of o^r: Will
Shakespeare. I colde not
but insert thus much to
you, that if you like
him not, you muste never
never reade Spanishe Poet.
            Leo: Digges
—*Shakespeare Survey,* 16 (1963): 118–120

Account of the Burning of the Globe in Lorkin's Letter to Puckering

In a 30 June 1613 letter to Sir Thomas Puckering, Reverend Thomas Lorkin reported on the fire that destroyed the Globe theater. This excerpt is from The Court and Times of James the First; Illustrated by Authentic and Confidential Letters, from Various Public and Private Collections *(1848), edited by Thomas Birch.*

No longer since than yesterday, while Burbage's company were acting at the Globe the play of Henry VIII., and there shooting off certain chambers in way of triumph, the fire catched and fastened upon the thatch of the house, and there burned so furiously, as it consumed the whole house, all in less than two hours, the people having enough to do to save themselves.
            —vol. I, p. 253

Account of the Burning of the Globe in Wotton's Letter to Bacon

Diplomat and poet Sir Henry Wotton gave an account of the Globe fire in a letter to Sir Edmund Bacon. This letter is from Logan Pearsall Smith's The Life and Letters of Sir Henry Wotton *(1907).*

July 2, 1613.

Sir,

Whereas I wrote unto you, that I would be at Cambridge as on Saturday next, I am now cast off again till the King's return to London, which will be about the middle of the week following. The delay grows from a desire of seeing Albertus his business settled before we come unto you, where we mean to forget all the world besides. Of this we shall bring you the account.

Now, to let matters of state sleep, I will entertain you at the present with what hath happened this week at the Bank's side. The King's players had a new play, called *All is true*, representing some principal pieces of the reign of Henry VIII, which was set forth with many extraordinary circumstances of pomp and majesty, even to the matting of the stage; the Knights of the Order with their Georges and garters, the Guards with their embroidered coats, and the like: sufficient in truth within a while to make greatness very familiar, if not ridiculous. Now, King Henry making a masque at the Cardinal Wolsey's house, and certain chambers being shot off at his entry, some of the paper, or other stuff, wherewith one of them was stopped, did light on the thatch, where being thought at first but an idle smoke, and their eyes more attentive to the show, it kindled inwardly, and ran round like a train, consuming within less than an hour the whole house to the very grounds.

This was the fatal period of that virtuous fabric, wherein yet nothing did perish but wood and straw, and a few forsaken cloaks; only one man had his breeches set on fire, that would perhaps have broiled him, if he had not by the benefit of a provident wit put it out with bottle ale. The rest when we meet; till when, I protest every minute is the siege of Troy. God's dear blessings till then and ever be with you.

Your poor uncle and faithful servant,
Henry Wotton.

I have this week received your last of the 27th of June, wherein I see my steps lovingly calculated, and in truth too much expectation of so unworthy a guest.

—vol. II, pp. 32–33

Account of the Burning of the Globe in Bluett's Letter to Weeks

Henry Bluett reported the Globe fire in his 4 July 1613 letter to Richard Weeks; "Tuesday last" refers to 29 June 1613 (Somerset Record Office, DD/SF 3066). This transcription is from Maija Jansson Cole's "A New Account of the Burning of the Globe."

On Tuesday last there was acted at the Globe a new play called *All is Triewe*, which had been acted not passing 2 or 3 times before. There came many people to see it insomuch that the house was very full, and as the play was almost ended the house was fired with shooting off a chamber which was stopped with towe which was blown up into the thatch of the house and so burnt down to the ground. But the people escaped all without hurt except one man who was scalded with the fire by adventuring in to save a child which otherwise had been burnt.

—*Shakespeare Quarterly* (Autumn 1981): 352

Account of the Burning of the Globe in Chamberlain's Letter to Winwood

After a long account of court news and gossip, John Chamberlain in his 8 July 1613 letter to Sir Ralph Winwood, England's ambassador to the Hague, comes to the burning of the Globe theater. This excerpt is from The Letters of John Chamberlain *(1939), edited by Norman Egbert McClure.*

Yt may be you have not heard of the earle of Northumberlands swaggering not long since in the Towre and beating Ruthen (the earle Gowries brother) for crossing him in his walke in the garden: but the burning of the Globe or play-house on the banck-side on St. Peters day cannot scape you, which fell out by a peale of chambers (that I know not upon what occasion were to be used in the play,) the tampin or stoppell of one of them lighting in the thatch that covered the house, burned yt downe to the ground in lesse then two howres with a dwelling house adjoyning: and yt was a great marvayle and fayre grace of God, that the people had so litle harme, having but two narrow doores to get out. I am to morrow to go into the countrie for most part of this sommer, but I shall still hearken after you, and will not geve over my hopes. So with the remembrance of my best service to my goode Lady I commend you and all yours to the protection of the Almighty. From London this 8th of July 1613.

Your Lordships to commaund
John Chamberlain.

—vol. I, pp. 465–467

Account of the Burning and Rebuilding of the Globe in *The Annales*

Edmund Howes and John Stow remarked the Globe fire in The Annales, Or Generall Chronicle of England *(1615) for the year 1613.*

If I shuld here set down the severall terrors & damages done this yeere by fire, in very many and sundry places of this kingdome, it would containe many a sheete of paper, as is evident by the incessant collections throughout all churches of this realme for such as have bin spoyled by fire. Also upon *S. Peters* day last, the play-house or Theater called the *Globe*, upon the Banck-side neere London, by negligent discharging of a peale of ordinance, close to the south side thereof, the Thatch tooke fier, & the wind sodainly disperst the flame round about, & in a very short space the whole building was quite consumed, & no man hurt: the house being filled with people, to behold the play, viz. of *Henry* the *8*. And the next spring it was new builded in far fairer manner then before.

—p. 926

Report of the Burning of the Globe in *The Abridgement of the English Chronicle*

Howes and Stow mention the Globe fire in The Abridgement of the English Chronicle *(1618).*

The 17 of Aprill 1613. at Alington in Lancashire was borne a maiden child, having foure Legges, foure Armes, two Bellies joynde to one backe, one head with two faces, the one before and the other behinde, and this yeare likewise was great Ship-wracke, by violent tempests, there happened also sundrie Inundations, and strange accidents, and much dammage done by fire in divers places, and upon Saint Peters day the Globe on the banckside was burned.

–p. 538

Allusion to the Burning of the Globe in Taylor's *A nest of Epigrams*

Poet and waterman John Taylor (1580–1653) recited his poetry as he rowed customers across the Thames. He refers to the Globe fire in one of his poems in A nest of Epigrams, *collected in* All The Workes Of John Taylor The Water Poet Being 63 in number Collected Into One Volum By the Author *(1630).*

Epigram 33.
Upon the burning of the Globe.

Aspiring *Phaeton* wth pride inspir'd,
Misguiding *Phœbus* Carre, the world he fir'd:
But *Ovid* did with fiction serve his turne,
And I in action sawe the Globe to burne.

–p. 265

Allusion to the Globe in Taylor's *The Water Mens Suit*

The watermen made their living ferrying people across the Thames. In The True Cause of the Water Mens suit concerning Players, *John Taylor points out the effect changes in the location of London's theaters would have on the watermen's livelihood. Taylor's petition provides a brief history of the growth and spread of London's theaters. The Globe, the Rose, and the Swan theaters stood on the south bank of the Thames, freeing them from the jurisdiction of London's government but creating a demand for water-taxi service for audience members, most of whom lived north of the river. Taylor's complaint concerns a proposal to open new theaters in London and Middlesex, an action that would reduce the demand for the watermen's services; he refers several times to the Globe and the King's Men, providing a*

useful reminder that Shakespeare and his fellow sharers and householders had to deal with practical as well as artistic matters. The pamphlet was included in All The Workes Of John Taylor The Water Poet Being 63 in number Collected Into One Volum By the Author.

The occasions that hath moved me to write this Pamphlet are many, and forcible, and the Attempt in writing it adventurous and full of danger, for as on the one side I doubt not but with truth to stop the mouthes of Ignorance and Mallice that have and doe daily scandalize mee, (and withall I know I shall purchase a generall thankes from all honest men of my Company) so I am assured to gaine the hatred of some that love mee well, and I affect them no worse, only for my plaine truth and discharging of my conscience: But fall back, fall edge, come what can come, I am resolved, and without feare or flattery, thus I beginne.

In the month of *January* last 1613. there was a motion made by some of the better sort of the company of Watermen, that it were necessary for the reliefe of such a decayed multitude to petition his Majesty, that the Players might not have a play-house in London or in Middlesex, within foure miles of the City on that side of the Thames. Now this request may seeme harsh and not well to bee digested by the Players and their Apendixes. But the reasons that mov'd us unto it, being charitably considered, makes the suite not only seeme reasonable, but past seeming most necessary to be sued for, and tollerable to bee granted.

Our petition being written to purpose aforesaid, I was selected by my company to deliver it to his Majesty and follow the businesse, which I did with that care and integrity, that I am assured none can justly taxe me with the contrary. I did ride twice to Theobalds, once to Newmarket, and twice to Roystone, before I could get a reference upon my petition. I had to beare my charge, of my company first and last, seven pound two shillings, which horshire, horse meat, and mans meat brought to a consumption; besides I wrote severall petitions to most of the Right Honourable Lords of his Majesties Privy Counsell, and I found them all compassionately affected to the necessity of our cause.

First, I did briefly declare part of the services that Watermen had done in Queene *Elizabeths* raigne, of famous memory, in the voyage to Portingale, with the Right Honorable and never to be forgotten Earle of *Essex*; then after that, how it pleased God (in that great deliverance in the yeere 1588.) to make Watermen good serviceable instruments, with their losse of lives and limbs to defend their Prince and Country. Moreover, many of them served with Sir *Francis Drake*,

Sir *John Hawkins*, Sir *Martin Frobusher*, and others: besides in Cales action, the Iland voyage, in Ireland, in the Lowcuntryes, and in the narrow Seas they have beene, (as in duty they are bound) at continuall command, so that every Summer 1500. or 2000. of them were imployed to the places aforesaid, having but nine shillings foure pence the month a peece for their pay, and yet were they able then to set themselves out like men, with shift of Apparell, linnen and wollen, and forbeare charging of their Prince for their pay sometimes sixe months, nine months, twelve months, sometimes more, for then there were so few Watermen and the one halfe of them being at Sea, those that staid at home had as much worke as they would doe.

Afterwards the Players began to play on the Bank-side and to leave playing in London and Middlesex (for the most part) then there went such great concourse of people by water, that the smal number of watermen remaining at home were not able to carry them, by reason of the Court, the Tearmes, the Players, and other imployments, so that we were inforced and encouraged (hoping that this golden stirring world would have lasted ever) to take and entertaine men and boyes: which boyes are growne men, and keepers of houses, many of them being over-charged with families of Wife and Children, so that the number of Water-men, and those that live and are maintained by them, and by the onely labour of the Oare and the Scull, betwixt the Bridge of Windsor and Gravesend, cannot be fewer then forty thousand; the cause of the greater halfe of which multitude, hath beene the Players playing on the Banke-side, for I have knowne three Companies besides the Beare-bayting, at once there; to wit, the Globe, the Rose, and the Swan. And it is an infallible truth, that had they never played there it had beene better for Water-men by the one halfe of their living, for the Company is encreased more then halfe by their meanes of playing there in former times.

And now it hath pleased God in this peaceful time, that there is no imployment at the sea, as it hath beene accustomed, so that all those great numbers of men remaines at home; and the Players have all (except the Kings men) left their usuall residency on the Banke-side, and doe play in Middlesex farre remote from the Thames, so that every day in the weeke they doe draw unto them three or foure thousand people, that were used to spend their monies by water, (to the reliefe of so many thousands of poore people, which by Players former playing on the Banke-side) are encreased, so that oft-times a poore man that hath five or sixe children, doth give good attendance to his labour all day, and at night (perhaps)

hath not gotten a Groat to relieve himselfe, his wife and family.

This was the effect and scope of our petition, though here I have declared it more at large, to which his Majesty graciously granted me a reference to his commissioners for suites, who then were the Right honourable Sir *Julius Cæsar*, Sir *Thomas Parray*, Knights, the Right Worshipfull Sir *Francis Bacon* then the Kings Atturny generall, Sir *Henry Mountague* his Majesties Sergant at Law, Sir *Walter Cope*, Master *George Calvert*, one of the Clarkes of his Majesties privy Counsell, and Baron *Southerton*, one of the Barons of the Kings Exchequer: these Honorable and Worshipfull persons I did oft solicite, by petitions, by friends, and by mine own industrious importunity, so that in the end when our cause was heard, wee found them generally affected to the suit we prosecuted.

His Majesties Players did exhibit a petition against us, in which they said, that our suit was unreasonable, and that we might as justly remove the Exchange, the walkes in *Pauls*, or Moorefields to the Bank-side for our profits, as to confine them; but our extremities and cause being judiciously pondered by the Honorable and Worshipfull Commissioners, Sir *Francis Bacon* very worthily said that so farre forth as the Publike weale was to be regarded before pastimes, or a serviceable decaying multitude before a handful of particular men, or profit before pleasure, so far was our suite to be preferred before theirs. Whereupon the Players did appeale to the Lord Chamberlaine, which was then the Earle of Sommerset who stood well affected to us, having beene moved before in the businesse by Master *Samuel Goldsmith* an especiall friend of mine, and a Gentleman that my selfe and all the rest of my poore company in generall, are generally beholden, and deeply ingaged unto; for of his owne free will to his cost and charge, wee must with thankfulnesse acknowledge he hath beene and is continually our worthy friend. Who seeing the wants of such numbers of us, hee hath often neglected his owne urgent and profitable affaires, spending his time and coyn in any honest occasion that might profit us. Thus much I thought good to insert in the way of thankfulnesse, because of all vices, ingratitude is most hatefull.

The Commissioners did appoint mee to come on the next day that they sate again, and that then the Players and wee should know their determinations concerning our businesses: but before the day came, Sir *Walter Cope* died, and Sir *Julius Cæsar* being chiefe Commissioner was made master of the Rolls, by which means the Commission was dissol'd, and we never yet had further hearing. Thus farre did I proceed in this thanklesse suite; and because it was not effected, some of my company partly through malice

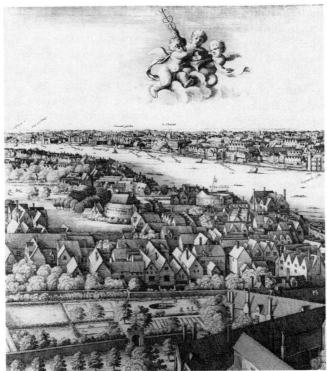

Views of the Globe theater after it was rebuilt, circa 1647. The drawing (top) is from Wenceslaus Hollar's "A View from St. Mary's Southwark, Looking Towards Westminster" (courtesy of the Yale Center for British Art, Paul Mellon Collection). The drawing (bottom) is Hollar's "Long View of London" (courtesy of the Guildhall Library; photograph © 2001 Geremy Butler Photography).

or ignorance, or both, have reported that I tooke bribes of the Players to let the suit fall, and that to that purpose I had a supper with them at the Cardinalls Hat on the Banke-side, and that if I had dealt wel with my Company, and done as I might have done, then all had beene as they would have had it.

These and more the like such pritty aspersions, the out-cast rubbish of my Company hath very liberally, unmannerly and ingratefully bestowed upon mee, whereby my credit hath been blemished, the good opinion which many held of me lost, my name abused, and I a common reproach, a scorne, a bye-word, and bayting-stocke to the poysonous teeth of envy and slander.

But I doubt not but what is before said will satisfie any well disposed or honest mind, and for the rest (if there bee any such) as I found them ignorant knaves, so I leave them unthankfull villanes. And I will regard such Vipers, and their slander so little, that their malice shall not make mee give over to doe service to my Company, by any honest lawfull meanes, my Trade (under God) is my best friend, and though it bee poore, I am sure the calling is honest, therefore I will be an assistant in this suite, or any other that may be availeable unto it; and howsoever we are slightly esteem'd by some Giddy-headed Corkbrains or Mushrom Painted Puckfoysts; yet the estate of this Kingdome knowes, that many of the meanest Scullers that Rowes on the Thames, was, is, or shall be if occasion serve, at command to doe their Prince and Country more service, then any of the Players shall be joyned unto.

−pp. 171–173

The King's Men Paid for Court Performances

To John Heminges and the rest of his fellowes his Majesties servauntes the Players upon the like warrant dated at whithall xxi° Die Junii 1614 for theire Chardges and paines in presenting seaven severall plaies before the Princes highnes viz on the iiii^th of November the xvi^th of November the xth of January the iiii^th of February the viii^th the xth and the xviii^th of the same moneth 1614   xlvi^li xiii^s

To the said John Heminges and the rest of his fellowes upon like warraunte dated at whithall xxi^mo Junii 1614 for theire chardges and paines taken in presenting before his Majesty nine severall plaies viz on the first v^th & xv^th of November 1614 on the xxvii^th of December the first and fourth of January the seconde of February following and the vi^th and viii^th of March following 1614   iiii^x x^li
−*Dramatic Records*, p. 59

Shakespeare Named in the Will of John Combe

John Combe, the richest man in Stratford, bequeathed five pounds to Shakespeare in his 28 January 1613 will (PRO PROB 11.126 s. 118). Combe died in July 1614, and his will was proved in the Prerogative Court of Canterbury in 1615. No documents survive describing a friendship between the two men, but their business dealings are recorded: Shakespeare purchased 107 acres of land from Combe and Combe's uncle William in 1602. In his own will in 1616, Shakespeare left his sword to Thomas Combe, John's nephew. John Combe is rumored to have amassed his fortune through usury—lending money at interest. Many years after Shakespeare's death, anecdotes began appearing claiming Shakespeare had written satiric verses about Combe's money-lending practices, one of which was rumored to have been inscribed on Combe's tomb, but no reliable evidence can be found to support these claims. For one version of the epitaph, see John Aubrey's account of Shakespeare's life at the end of this volume.

/Item/ I give unto William White fortie shillinges wch he oweth me by bond yf he be lyvinge at my decease and the same bonde to be cancelled to m^r William Shackspere five poundes. . .

1614

Rights to Publish *Lucrece* Transferred

John Harrison transfers the rights to The Rape of Lucrece *to another publisher.*

primo Martii .1613. [1614 New Style]
Roger Jackson Entred for his coppies by consent of Master John Harrison the eldest
  and by order of a Court, these 4 bokes followinge ii^s
                  vizt
    Mascalles first booke of Cattell
    Master Dentes sermon of repentance
    Recordes Arithmeticke
    Lucrece
      −*Stationers of London*, vol. III, fol. 248b

Allusion to the Rebuilt Globe in Chamberlain's Letter to Carleton

John Chamberlain mentions the new Globe theater in his 30 June 1614 letter to Alice Carleton. This excerpt is from The Letters of John Chamberlain *(1939), edited by Norman Egbert McClure.*

. . . I have not seen your sister Williams since I came to towne though I have ben there twise. The first time she was at a neighbours house at Cards, and the next she was gon to the new Globe to a play. Indeed I heare much speach of this new play-house, which is saide to be the fayrest that ever was in England, so that yf I live but seven yeares longer I may chaunce make a journy to see yt.

–vol. I, p. 544

A Preacher Is Entertained at New Place

The corporation of Stratford pays part of the expenses for entertaining a visiting preacher at New Place, Shakespeare's home, according to the entry in the Stratford Chamberlain's Accounts for 1614.

Item for one qt of sack and one qt of clarrett winne given to a precher at the newe place _ xx[d]

–Shakespeare Birthplace Trust Records Office, Corporation Records, Chamberlain's Accounts 1585–1619, p. 266

Publication

The second edition of the anthology England's Helicon, *first published in 1600, is published again; it includes "On a day alack the day" from* Love's Labor's Lost.

ENGLANDS / HELICON. / *OR* / THE MVSES / HARMONY. / *The Courts of Kings beare no such straines,* / *As daily lull the Rusticke Swaines.* / [*Printer's device*] / *LONDON:* Printed for RICHARD MORE, and are to / be ſould at his Shop in S. Dunſtanes / Church-yard. 1 6 1 4.

Possible Allusion to *Richard III* in Brooke's *The Ghost Of Richard The Third*

In The Ghost Of Richard The Third. *(1614) Christopher Brooke, in addition to offering a critique of contemporary playwriting, also complains that Richard III has been made common by his appearance in popular plays. In the epistle and excerpts that follow, Brooke probably refers to Shakespeare's history play* Richard III.

The Epistle to the Reader.

An Epistle to the Reader is as ordinary before a new Book, as a *Prologue* to a new Play; but as Plaies are many times exploded, though the Prologue be never so good, and promising; So (*Reader*) if thou findest not

stuffe, in this *Poem,* to fit thy humor: If the wit with the fashion, hold not some tollerable proportion; this Enducement (though nere so formall and obsequious) would little prevaile with thy acceptation, but thou wouldst conjure my *Ghost* downe againe, before his time, or torment him upon earth, with the Hell-fire of thy displeasure. Therefore it matters not whether I humor thee with complement, or insinuate with glozing *Epithites.* I know (in a play or *Poem*) thou liks'st best of *Satyricall* stuffe; though perhaps thou seest therein thine own *Character;* and not without some shew of Reason are things bitter, the better: For the Gluttonous Sences (the Eye and Eare) so cloi'd and surfeited, with variety of effeminate pleasures; the rough Satyre doth sometimes not unfitly enterpose such Courtly delight, which growing a Burthen to it selfe, his entermixt vaine with the others vanity, gives entermission to the humor, and proves no lesse tastfull to the *Gallants* judgement, then tart sauce to whet his dull'd appetite: And of this kind I have enterlaced something, naturally rising out of my subject; where (by way of prevention) if any shall object that I have not amplified the *Legend* to the full scope of the *Story;* I answere; I should then have made the volume too great, to the discouragement of the Buyer, and disadvantage of the Printer; let it suffice I have the substance, if not the circumstance; and when I undertook this I thought with my selfe: That to draw Arguments of Invention from the *Subject,* new, and probable, would be farre more plaucible to the time, then by insisting upon narrations (made so common in *Playes,* and so notorious among all men) have my Labour slighted, and my Pen tax't for triviall. The Generous *Censor* (as hee is Ingenious or Ingenuous) I reverence; likewise the *Crittick* (as he is knowing, and learn'd) but when his censure shall be levell'd with neither of his good parts, but favour more of Spleene, then Braine; of Disease, then Judgement; I doe hartily appeale from him, with all of that faction; And though many did inly wish, that this (not the meanest Issue of my Braine) might have prov'd an Obortive, and seene no comfortable light; Yet they see it is borne, and (without prejudice to Nature) with Teeth too, to oppose theirs, that shall open their lips to deprave mee; but whether to lye upon the Parish, or the Printers hand that rests in clouds; howsoever, I have got sheetes to lye in, (though they be but course) and am sure to be cherish't in good Letters; if I be entertain'd in the world, and prove a companion for the many, I know I shall not be much chargeable; if not, yet this is my comfort, there will be some use made of me in this land of waste; In which Resolution, I set up my Rest.

Thine if thou wilt.

–preliminary page–sig. Av

THE ARAIGNMENT
of *John* Selman, who was executed
neere Charing-Croſſe the 7. of Ianuary, 1611. for
a Fellony by him committed in the Kings Chappell
at White-Hall vpon Chriſtmas day laſt, in preſence
of the King and diuers of the Nobility.

LONDON,
Printed by *W. H.* for *Thomas Archer*, and are to be
ſold at his ſhop in Popes-head Pallace, 1611.

*Title page for a pamphlet on the execution of a thief. Among those who
hoped that a play would hold the audience's attention were pickpockets,
who frequently plied their trade in the theaters (by permission
of the Folger Shakespeare Library).*

*This second excerpt is from the beginning of Part 2, "The
Legend Of Richard The Third."*

To him that Impt my Fame with *Clio's Quill*;
Whose *Magick* rais'd me from *Oblivions* den;
That writ my *Stories* on the *Muses Hill*;
And with my *Actions* Dignifi'd his *Pen*:
He that from *Helicon* sends many a *Rill*;
Whose *Nectared Veines*, are drunke by thirstie *Men*:
Crown'd be his *Stile*, with *Fame*; his *Head*, with *Bayes*;
And none detract, but gratulate his *Praise*.
Yet if his *Scœnes* have not engrost all *Grace*,
The much fam'd Action could extend on *Stage*;
If *Time*, or *Memory*, have left a place
For *Me* to fill; t'enforme this Ignorant Age;
To that intent I shew my horrid *Face*;
Imprest with *Feare*, and *Characters* of *Rage*:
   Nor *Wits*, nor *Chronicles* could ere containe,
   The Hell-deepe Reaches, of my soundlesse Braine.
                                                    —sig. D2r

Allusion to Shakespeare in Camden's *Remaines*

*In these excerpts from "The Excellencie of the English Tongue,"
an essay included in historian William Camden's* Remaines, concerning Britaine: But especially England, and the Inhabitants thereof *(1614), the author, identified by the initials R.C.,
praises the beauties of the English language and lists some contemporary
authors who use it well, Shakespeare among them.*

*The Excellencie of the English
tongue by R. C. Of Anthony
Esquire to W. C.*

It were most fitting (in respect of discretion) that men
should first weigh matters with judgement, and then
encline their affection, where the greatest reason swayeth.
But ordinarily it falleth out to the contrary; for either by
custome, we first settle our affection, & then afterward
draw in those arguments to approve it, which should
have foregone to perswade our selves. This preposterous
course, seeing antiquitie from our elders, and universality
of our neighbours do entitle with a right, I hold my selfe
the more freely warranted *delirare*, not onely *cum vulgo*, but
also *cum sapientibus*, in seeking out with what comendations
I may attire our English language, as *Stephanus* hath done
for the French, and divers others for theirs.

Locutio is defined, *Animi sensus per vocem expressio*. On
which ground I build these consequences, that the first &
principall point sought in every language, is that we may
expresse the meaning of our mindes aptly each to other.
Next that we may do it readily without great adoe. Then
fully, so as others may throughly conceive us. And last of
all handsomly that those to whom we speak may take pleasure in hearing us, so as whatsoever tongue will gaine the
race of perfection, must runne on these foure wheeles, *Significancie*, *Easinesse*, *Copiousnesse*, and *Sweetnesse*, of which the
two foremost import a necessitie, the two latter a delight.
Now if I can proove that our English language, for all, or
the most, is matchable, if not preferrable before any other
in use at this day, I hope the assent of any impartiall
Reader will passe on my side.
                                                    —pp. 36–37

. . . .

I come now to the last and sweetest point of the
sweetnesse of our tongue, which shall appeare the more
plainely, if like two Turkeyses or the London Drapers
wee match it with our neighbours. The Italian is pleasant but without sinewes as a still fleeting water. The
French, delicate, but even nice as a woman, scarce daring to open her lippes for feare of marring her countenance. The Spanish majesticall, but fulsome, running
too much on the O. and terrible like the divell in a play.
The Dutch manlike but withall verie harsh, as one

readie at everie word to picke a quarrell. Now we in borrowing from them, give the strength of consonants to the Italian, the full sound of wordes to the French, the varietie of terminations to the Spanish, and the mollifying of more vowels to the Dutch, and so (like Bees) gather the honey of their good properties and leave the dregges to themselves. And thus when substantialnesse combineth with delightfulnesse, fulnesse with finesse, seemelinesse with portlinesse, and currantnesse with stayednesse, how can the language which consisteth of all these, sound other then most full of sweetnes?

Againe, the long words that we borrow being intermingled with the short of our owne store, make up a perfect harmonie, by culling from out which mixture (with judgement) you may frame your speech according to the matter you must worke on, majesticall, pleasant, delicate, or manly more or lesse, in what sort you please. Adde hereunto, that whatsoever grace any other language carrieth in verse or Prose, in Tropes or Metaphors, in Ecchoes and Agnominations, they may all bee lively and exactly represented in ours: will you have Platoes veine? reade Sir *Thomas Smith*, the *Ionicke?* Sir *Thomas Moore. Ciceroes? Ascham, Varro? Chaucer, Demosthenes?* Sir *John Cheeke* (who in his treatise to the Rebels, hath comprised all the figures of Rhetorick. Will you reade Virgill? take the Earle of Surrey. *Catullus?* Shakespheare and Barlowes fragment, Ovid? Daniell, Lucan? Spencer, Martial? Sir John Davies and others: will you have all in all for Prose and verse? take the miracle of our age Sir Philip Sidney.

And thus if mine owne eyes bee not blinded by affection, I have made yours to see that the most renowned of other nations have layed up, as in treasure, and entrusted the *Divisos orbe Britannos*, with the rarest Jewels of their lips perfections, whether you respect the understanding for significancie, or the memorie of easinesse, or the conceite for plentifulnesse, or the eare for pleasantnesse: wherin if enough be delivered, to adde more then enough were superfluous; if too little, I leave it to be supplyed by better stored capacities; if ought amisse, I submit the same to the discipline of every able and impartiall censurer.

–pp. 43–44

Allusions to Plays in Jonson's Preface to *Bartholomew Fayre*

Some early modern plays, Shakespeare's Taming of the Shrew *among them, feature an induction, a short scene creating a framing device within which the play unfolds. In Ben Jonson's 1614 comedy* Bartholomew Fayre, *the induction is performed by members of the backstage crew: the stage-keeper, who is the theater's maintenance man; the book-holder, who prompts the actors when they forget their lines; and the scrivener, a professional scribe whose work might include producing legible copies of plays as well as legal documents. Jonson uses these characters to mock his audience's tastes as well as the literary skills of some of his fellow playwrights. Shakespeare does not escape censure: the stage-keeper's survey of popular theatrical sights includes a reference to night watchmen who take criminals away "with mistaking words," a reference to Dogberry and Verges in Shakespeare's* Much Ado about Nothing. *Jonson also refers to* The Tempest *and probably* The Winter's Tale *as plays that "make Nature afraid" because of their magical elements. Of particular interest is his dismissal of* Titus Andronicus *as a twenty-five- or thirty-year-old play. Although Jonson is writing here as a poet, not an historian, this would place* Titus Andronicus *in 1589, an earlier date than most scholars accept for Shakespeare's tragedy. The induction is transcribed from* The Workes of Benjamin Jonson (1640).

The Induction.
On the *Stage.*

Stage-Keeper.

Gentlemen, have a little patience, they are e'en upon comming, instantly. He that should beginne the Play, Master *Littlewit,* the *Proctor,* has a stitch new falne in his black silk stocking; 'twill be drawn up ere you can tell twenty. He playes one o'the *Arches,* that dwels about the *Hospitall,* and hee has a very pretty part. But for the whole *Play,* will you ha' the truth on't? (I am looking, lest the *Poet* heare me, or his man, Master *Broome,* behind the Arras) it is like to be a very conceited scurvy one, in plaine English. When't comes to the *Fayre,* once: you were e'en as good goe to *Virginia,* for any thing there is of *Smith-field.* Hee has not hit the humors, he do's not know 'hem; hee has not convers'd with the *Bartholmew*-birds, as they say; he has ne're a Sword, and a Buckler man in his *Fayre,* nor a little *Davy,* to take toll o' the Bawds there, as in my time, nor a *Kind-heart,* if any bodies teeth should chance to ake in his *Play.* Nor a Jugler with a wel-educated Ape to come over the chaine, for the *King* of *England,* and backe againe for the *Prince,* and sit still on his arse for the *Pope,* and the *King* of *Spaine!* None o' these fine sights! Nor has he the Canvas cut i' the night, for a Hobby horse man to creepe into his she-neighbour, and take his leap there! Nothing! No, and some writer (that I know) had had but the penning o' this matter, hee would ha' made you such a *Jig-ajogge* i' the boothes, you should ha' thought an earthquake had beene i'the *Fayre!* But these *Master-Poets,* they will ha' their owne absurd courses; they will be inform'd of nothing! Hee has (sirreverence) kick'd me three, or foure times about the Tyring-house, I thanke him, for but offering to putt in, with my experience. I'le be judg'd by you, *Gentlemen*, now, but for one conceit of mine! would not a fine Pumpe upon the Stage ha' done well, for a property now? and a *Punque* set under upon her head, with her Sterne upward, and ha' beene sous'd by my wity young masters o'the *Innes o' Court?* what thinke you o'this for a shew, now? hee will not heare o' this! I am an Asse! I! and yet I kept the *Stage* in Master *Tarletons* time, I thanke my starres. Ho! and that man had liv'd to have play'd in *Bartholmew Fayre*, you should ha' seene him ha' come in, and ha' beene coozened i'the *Cloath-quarter*, so finely! And *Adams*, the Rogue, ha leap'd and caper'd upon him, and ha' dealt his vermine about, as though they had cost him nothing. And then a substantiall watch to ha' stolne in upon 'hem, and taken 'hem away, with mistaking words, as the fashion is, in the *Stage*-practice.

Booke-holder. Scrivener. To him.

Booke. How now? what rare discourse are you falne upon? ha? ha' you found any familiars here, that you are so free? what's the businesse?

Sta. Nothing, but the understanding Gentlemen o' the ground here, ask'd my judgement.

Booke. Your judgement, Rascall? for what? sweeping the *Stage?* or gathering up the broken Apples for the beares within? Away Rogue, it's come to a fine degree in these *spectacles* when such a youth as you pretend to a judgement. And yet hee may, i'the most o' this matter i'faith: For the *Author* hath writ it just to his *Meridian*, and the *Scale* of the grounded Judgements here, his Play followes in wit. Gentlemen; not for want of a *Prologue*, but by way of a new one, I am sent out to you here, with a *Scrivener*, and certaine Articles drawne out in hast betweene our *Author*, and you; which if you please to heare, and as they appeare reasonable, to approve of; the *Play* will follow presently. Read, *Scribe*, gi' me the Counterpaine.

Scr. Articles of Agreement, indented, between the *Spectators* or *Hearers*, at the *Hope* on the Bankeside, in the County of *Surrey* on the one party; And the *Author* of *Bartholmew Fayre* in the said place, and County on the other party: the one and thirtieth day of *Octob.* 1614. and in the twelfth yeere of the Raigne of our Soveragine Lord, *James* by the grace of God *King of England, France, & Ireland*, Defender of the faith. And of *Scotland* the seaven and fortieth.

Inprimis, It is covenanted and agreed, by and betweene the parties abovesaid, and the said *Spectators*, and *Hearers*, aswell the curious and envious, as the favouring and judicious, as also the grounded Judgements and understandings, doe for themselves severally Covenant, and agree to remaine in the places, their money or friends have put them in, with patience, for the space of two houres and an halfe, and somewhat more. In which time the *Author* promiseth to present them by us, with a new sufficient Play called *Bartholmew Fayre*, merry, and as full of noise, as sport: made to delight all, and to offend none. Provided they have either, the wit or the honesty to thinke well of themselves.

It is further agreed that every person here, have his or their free-will of censure, to like or dislike at their owne charge, the *Author* having now departed with his right: It shall bee lawfull for any man to judge his six pen'orth his twelve pen'orth, so to his eighteene pence, x. shillings, halfe a crowne, to the value of his place: Provided alwaies his place get not above his wit. And if he pay for halfe a dozen, hee may censure for all them too, so that he will undertake that they shall bee silent. Hee shall put in for *Censures* here, as they doe for *lots* at the *lottery*: mary if he drop but six pence at the doore, and will censure a crownes worth, it is thought there is no conscience, or justice in that.

It is also agreed, that every man heere, exercise his owne Judgement, and not censure by *Contagion*, or upon *trust*, from anothers voice, or face, that sits by him, be he never so first, in the *Comission of Wit*: As also, that hee bee fixt and settled in his censure, that what hee approves, or not approves to day, hee will doe the same to morrow, and if to morrow, the next day, and so the next weeke (if neede be:) and not to be brought about by any that sits on the *Bench* with him, though they indite, and arraigne *Playes* daily. Hee that will sweare, *Jeronimo*, or *Andronicus* are the best playes, yet, shall passe unexcepted at, heere, as a man whose Judgement shewes it is constant, and hath stood still, these five and twentie, or thirtie yeeres: Though it be an *Ignorance*, it is a vertuous and stay'd ignorance; and next to *truth*, a confirm'd errour does well; such a one the *Author* knowes where to finde him.

It is further covenanted, concluded and agreed, that how great soever the expectation bee, no person here, is to expect more then hee knowes, or better ware then a *Fayre* will affoord: neyther to looke backe to the sword and buckler-age of *Smithfield*, but content himselfe with the present. In stead of a little *Davy*; to take toll o' the Bawds, the *Author* doth promise a strutting *Horse-courser*, with a *leere*-Drunkard, two or three to attend him, in as good *Equipage* as you would wish. And then for *Kinde-heart*, the Tooth-drawer, a fine oyly *Pig-woman* with her *Tapster*, to bid you welcome, and a consort of *Roarers* for musique. A wise *Justice* of *Peace meditant*, in stead of a *Jugler*, with an *Ape*. A civill *Cutpurse searchant*. A sweete *Singer* of new ballads *allurant*: and as fresh an *Hypocrite*, as ever was broach'd *rampant*. If there bee never a *Servant-monster* i'the *Fayre*, who can helpe it? he sayes; nor a nest of *Antiques*? Hee is loth to make Nature afraid in his *Playes*, like those that beget *Tales*, *Tempests*, and such like *Drolleries*, to mixe his head with other mens heeles; let the concupisence of *Jigges* and *Dances*, raigne as strong as it will amongst you: yet if the *Puppets* will please any body, they shall be entreated to come in.

In *consideration of which*, it is finally agreed, by the foresaid hearers, and *spectators*, that they neyther in themselves conceale, nor suffer by them to be concealed any *State-decipherer*, or politique *Picklocke* of the *Scene*, so solemnly ridiculous, as to search out, who was meant by the *Ginger-bread-woman*, who by the *Hobby-horse-man*, who by the *Costard-monger*, nay, who by their *Wares*. Or that will pretend to affirme (on his owne *inspired ignorance*) what *Mirror of Magistrates* is meant by the *Justice*, what *great Lady* by the *Pigge-woman*, what *conceal'd States-man* by the *Seller* of *Mouse-trappes*, and so of the rest. But that such person, or persons so found, be left discovered to the mercy of the *Author*, as a forfeiture to the *Stage*, and your laughter, aforesaid. As also, such as shall so desperately, or ambitiously, play the foole by his place aforesaid, to challenge the *Author* of scurrilitie, because the language some where savours of *Smithfield*, the Booth, and the Pig-broth, or of prophanenesse, because a *Mad-man* cryes, *God quit you*, or *blesse you*. In *witnesse* whereof, as you have preposterously put to your Seales already (which is your money) you will now adde the other part of suffrage, your hands, The *Play* shall presently begin. And though the *Fayre* be not kept in the same Region, that some here, perhaps, would have it, yet thinke, that therein the *Author* hath observ'd a speciall *Decorum*, the place being as durty as *Smithfield*, and as stinking every whit.

Howsoever, hee prayes you to beleeve, his *Ware* is still the same, else you will make him justly suspect that hee that is so loth to looke on a *Baby*, or an *Hobby-horse*, heere, would bee glad to take up a *Commodity* of them, at any laughter, or losse, in another place.

– The Workes of Benjamin Jonson, vol. II, sigs. A4r–A6v

Allusion to *Hamlet* in Scott's *The Philosopher's Banquet*

In The Philosopher's Banquet *(1614) Sir Michael Scott in his discussion of "good" widows refers to the Player Queen in* Hamlet.

Of good Widdowes.

Macrobius saith, that the word *Vidua*, a Widdowe, comes of *Divisa oras*, one would more properly say, *a Viro divisa*, divided; or divided from a man.

Amongst the ancient Women of elder times, that were contented with single marriages, it was their glorie to be honoured with the crowne of Chastitie: but the experience of manie Mariages hath much increased the suspition of intemperancy, and inconstancie. The daughter of Marcus Cato, when shee had bewayled the death of her Husband a month together, the longest date of our times: shee was asked of some of her Friendes which day should have her last teare, shee answered, the day of her death.

> Truely intending what the Trag. Q. but fainedly spoke,
> In second Husband, let me be accurst:
> None weds the second, but who kills the first.
> A second time, I kill my Husband dead,
> When second Husband kisses me in bed.

And when some of her Kinsfolkes perswaded her to marrie an other Husband, in regard shee was young and beautifull, shee utterly denyed, saying: If I should meete with a good Husband as I had before, I shall ever feare to lose him: if I shall meete with a bad one, what neede I such a sorrow after such a griefe. In like manner, Portia was perswaded, after the death of her Husband, to marrie againe: she answered, a happie and chaste Matrone never marries but once. In like manner Valeria, having lost her husband, would marrie no other: and being asked her reason, answered, that her husband lived alwaies to her. In like manner, of Arthemisia, the wife of Maufoll, king of Corinth, that amongst many of her commendations, this is a principall, that after the death of her Husband, she still remembred him, as if alive: and buylt for his honour and memorie, a Sepulcher of wondrous beautie and cost, the like wherof was not to be found; Of which Women, my Author thus comparatively concludeth;

> Such Wives their living Husbands did not wrong,
> Who after death remembred them so long:
> What our short mourning Widdows usde to doe,
> That so soone marrie, and forget them too:
> I can but gesse, but secret may be tolde,
> That love was nere much hote, that's so soone colde.
>   *– pp. 149–151*

Allusion to *Pericles* in Tailor's *The Hogge Hath Lost His Pearle*

Dramatist Robert Tailor alludes to Pericles *at the end of his preface to his comedy* The Hogge Hath Lost His Pearle *(1614), a satiric attack on John Swinnerton, Lord Mayor of London.*

THE PROLOGUE.

Our long time rumor'd Hogge, so often crost
By unexpected accidents, and tost
From one house to another, still deceiving
Many mens expectations, and bequeathing
To some lost labour, is at length got loose,
Leaving his servile yoake-sticke to the goose,
Hath a Knights licence, and may raunge at pleasure,
Spight of all those that envy our Hogges treasure:
And thus much let me tell you, that our Swyne
Is not as divers Crittickes did define,
Grunting at State affaires, or invecting
Much, at our Citty vices; no, nor detecting
The pride, or fraude, in it, but were it now
He had his first birth, wit should teach him how
To taxe these times abuses, and tell some
How ill they did in running oft from home,
For to prevent (O men more hard then flint)
A matter that shall laugh at them in print:
Once to proceede in this play we were mindlesse,
Thinking we liv'd mongst Jewes that lov'd no swines flesh:
But now that troubles past, if it deserve a hisse,
(As questionlesse it wil through our amisse,)
Let it be favoured by your gentle sufferance,
Wise-men are still indu'd with patience,
Wee are not halfe so skild as strowling Players,
Who could not please heere as at Country faiers,
We may be pelted off for ought we know,
With apples, egges, or stones from thence belowe;
In which weele crave your friendship if we may,
And you shall have a daunce worth all the play,
And if it prove so happy as to please,
Weele say tis fortunate like *Pericles*.

—sigs. A3r–v

Porter's Epigram on Shakespeare

Thomas Porter dedicated a book of Latin poems, dated "12 die Martii mensis 1614," to Sir John Heneningham; included among them is one to the witty poet William Shakespeare.

Gul: Shakespeare Poëtam lepidum.

Quot lepores in Atho tot habet tua musa lepores
Ingenii vena divite metra tua.

—Coke MS. 436, cent. I. 57

[William Shakespeare, the charming poet. Just as many hares are found on Mt. Athos, so many charms does your muse possess. Your verses exist from a rich streak of genius.]

Epigram on Shakespeare in Freeman's *Rubbe, And a great Cast*

Epigram writer Thomas Freeman included a tribute to Shakespeare in his mostly satirical collection Rubbe, And a great Cast. Epigrams *(1614).*

Epigram 92.
To Master W: Shakespeare.

Shakespeare, that nimble *Mercury* thy braine,
Lulls many hundred *Argus* eyes asleepe,
So fit, for all thou fashionest thy vaine,
At th'*horse-foote* fountaine thou hast drunk full deepe,
Vertues or vices theame to thee all one is:
Who loves chaste life, there's *Lucrece* for a Teacher:
Who list read lust there's *Venus* and *Adonis*,
True modell of a most lascivious leatcher.
Besides in plaies thy wit windes like *Meander*:
When needy new-composers borrow more
Thence *Terence* doth from *Plautus* or *Menander*.
But to praise thee aright I want thy store:
 Then let thine owne works thine owne worth upraise,
 And help t'adorne thee with deserved Baies.
—sigs. K2v–K3r

Shakespeare's Possible Involvement in an Enclosure Effort

The process of enclosing land—turning open fields into pasture for grazing sheep or cattle—was controversial during the early modern period. The immediate consequences of enclosure were often grain shortages and unemployment among rural workers; the owners of the land who combined their freeholds to form the enclosure usually profited from the process. Even rumors of enclosure might result in local uprisings; actual efforts to enclose land, such as digging ditches or planting hedges, often prompted those opposed to the enclosure to gather together to, for instance, fill in the ditches.

The following documents form part of a story of an enclosure effort in Stratford. Some of the land in question may be holdings in unenclosed fields north of Stratford that, according to a 1625 survey (Shakespeare Birthplace Trust Records Office DR 37/Box 113/15), belonged to Shakespeare. To enclose the land would have required Shakespeare's permission.

The author of the following memoranda, Thomas Greene, was Stratford's town clerk. He identifies Shakespeare as his cousin, although it is not clear how, exactly, they are related. Greene was also, along with Shakespeare, owner of a moiety, or portion, of the profits from Stratford's tithes. As town clerk, Greene was obliged to oppose enclosure as a cause of social and political disruptions; as a tithe owner, he was probably concerned that he would lose some of his profits were the land to be enclosed. Greene, in January 1615, claims to have joined Shakespeare in an agreement negotiated with William Replingham, an agent for one of the enclosers, that was designed to protect Shakespeare's income from losses caused by the enclosure.

The documents do not reveal Shakespeare's position on enclosure, although it is clear he was careful to protect his assets in the agreement he negotiated with Replingham. Arthur Mainwaring, who employed Replingham, may have been working on behalf of or in collusion with another Stratford encloser, William Combe. Shakespeare had ties to the Combe family: in 1602 Combe's great-uncle William sold Shakespeare the four yardlands referred to in Green's memorandum; Combe's uncle John left Shakespeare £5 in his will; Shakespeare left his sword to Thomas Combe, William's brother.

Some biographers argue that Shakespeare distanced himself from the enclosure conflict, while others believe that Shakespeare favored enclosing the land in question. See, for instance, the discussions in Robert Bearman's Shakespeare in the Stratford Records *(1994) and Samuel Schoenbaum's* William Shakespeare: A Documentary Life *(1975).*

Greene's annotation in the The Particulers of Olde Stratforde *(1603) shows Shakespeare's ownership of land in the area being enclosed.*

5 Septembris .1614.

Auncient ffreeholders in the ffields of Oldstratford and Welcombe.

Wm Shakspeare. 4. yard Land. no common nor ground beyond gospell bushe. nor ground in Sandfield, nor none in slowe hill field beyond Bishopton nor none in that enclosure beyond Bishopton.

—Shakespeare Birthplace Trust Records Office, Miscellaneous Documents I, 94

Greene's "Coppy of the articles with mr Shakspeare" is an extract of the 28 October 1614 Articles between William Shakespeare and William Replingham. Greene's memorandum of 9 January 1615 notes that he was "putt in" to these articles, that is, added or made a party to them. The word "increasing" is usually assumed to be an error for "decreasing."

Vicesimo octavo dio octobris Anno Domini 1614

Articles of agreement indented made betweene william Shackespeare of Stratford in the County of warwicke gent on the one partye & william Replingham of

Greete Harborowe in the Countie of warwicke gent on the other partie. The daye & yeare abovesaid/

Inter alia. Item the said William Replingham for him his heires executo^rs and assignes doth Covenaunate & agree to & with the said William Shackespeare his heires & assignes that he the said William Replingham his heires or assignes shall upon reasonable request satisfie Content & make recompense unto him the said William Shackespeare or his assignes for all such losses detriment & *hinderan* (struck through) hinderance as he the said William Shackespeare his heires & assignes and one Thomas Greene gent shall or maye be thought in the viewe and judgement of foure indifferent persons to be indifferentlie elected by the said william & william and their heires & in default of the said William Replingham by the said william Shackespeare or his heires onely to survey and judge the same to sustayne or incurre for or in respecte of the increasinge of the yearlie value of the Tythes they the said William Shackespeare and Thomas doe joyntlie or severallie hold and enjoy in the said fieldes or anie of them by reason of anie Inclosure or decaye of Tyllage there ment and intended by the said William Replingham And that the said william Replingham and his heires shall procure such sufficient securitie unto the said william Shackespeare and his heires for the performance of theis Covenauntes as shalbee devised by learned Counsell In witnes whereof the parties abovsaid to theis presentes Interchaungeablie their handes and Seales have put the daye & yeare first above wrytten Sealed & delivered in the presence of us

Tho: Lucas   Anthonie Nasshe
Jo: Rogers   Mich: Olney

—Shakespeare Birthplace Trust Records Office
MS. ER 27/3

The following memoranda from 1615 and 1616 (Shakespeare Birthplace Trust Records Office, Corporate Records, Miscellaneous Documents XIII 26a, 27-9) were transcribed by C. M. Ingleby in Shakespeare and the Enclosure of Common Fields at Welcombe, being A Fragment of the Private Diary of Thomas Greene, Town Clerk of Stratford-upon-Avon, 1614–1617 *(1885).*

Jovis 17 No:[vembris] *as* [deleted] my Cosen Shakspeare *has* [deleted] commyng yesterday to towne I went to see him howe he did he told me that they assured him they ment to inclose noe further then to gospell bushe & so upp straight (leavyng out part of the dyngles to the ffield) to the gate in Clopton hedge & take in Salisburyes peece: and that they meane in Aprill to servey the Land & then to gyve satisfaccion & not before & he & Mr. Hall say they think there will be nothyng done at all.

—p. 1

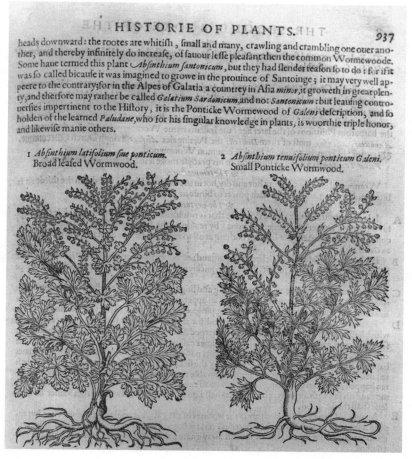

Page from John Gerard's The Herball or Generall Historie of Plantes *(1597) showing wormwood, an herb Hamlet refers to in expressing his bitterness (3.2.181; courtesy of Special Collections, Howard-Tilton Library, Tulane University, New Orleans, Louisiana)*

10 Dec. that the survey there was past, & I *went* [deleted] came from Wilson to look Mr. Replingham at the beare & at new place but missed him & on the narowe sid but he was not to be spoken with:

–p. 3

23. Dec. A Hall. L[ett]res wrytten one to Mr. Manneryng another to Mr Shakspeare with *the* [deleted] almost all the com[panyes] hands to eyther: I alsoe wrytte of myself to my Cosen Shakspeare the Coppyes of all our oathes mde then alsoe a not of the Inconvenyences wold g[row] by the Inclosure.

–p. 4

9 Ja: . . . Mr. Replyngham 28 Oct[o]bris articled w[i]th Mr. Shakspeare & then I was *recommended* [deleted] putt in by T. Lucas.

–p. 6

[11 January] At night Mr. Replingham supped w[i]th me & Mr. W Barnes was to beare him Company where he assured me before Mr. Barnes that I should be well dealt w[i]thall *as n* [deleted] confessyng former promises *& th* [deleted] by himself Mr. Manneryng & his agreement for me w[i]th my Cosen Shakspeare:

–p. 7

1615 14 Aug. Mr. Barker dyed.	Sept W Shakspeares tellyng J Greene that I was not able to *he* [deleted] beare the encloseinge of Welcombe.

–p. 11

The King's Men Paid for Court Performances

To John Hemynges upon the Lorde Chamberleynes warrant dated xix[no] Maii 1615 in the behalfe of himselfe and his fellowes the Kinges majesties players for eighte severall plaies before his majestie   iiii[li]

–Dramatic Records, p. 60

1615

Publication

Richard II, *previously published in 1597, 1598, and 1608, is published again.*

THE / Tragedie of King / Richard the Se- / cond: / *With new additions of the Parliament Sceane, / and the depoſing of King / Richard.* / As it hath been lately acted by the Kinges / Maieſties ſervants, at the Globe. / *By* WIL-LIAM SHAKE-SPEARE. / *[Printer's device]* / At LONDON, / Printed for *Mathew Law,* and are to be ſold / at his ſhop in Paules Church-yard, at the / ſigne of the Foxe. / 1 6 1 5.

The King's Men Paid for Court Performances

Shakespeare's Company performed before Queen Anne on this occasion.

John Heminges one of the Kinges majesties plaiers for so much paid unto him in the behalfe of himselfe and the rest of his fellowes of that companie for one plaie acted before her majestie at Queenes court on St Thomas daye at night being the xxith of December 1615. by warrant signed by the right honorable the Lord Vicount Lisle Lord chamber-laine to her majestie dated at Greenewich the xxiith of Janu-arie 1615. nowe called in seene and examined and remaineing as aforesaid together with an acquittance there-under written for the receipt of   x^li

—Dramatic Records, Appendix B

Allusion to Shakespeare in F.B.'s Poem

The author of this poem, found in the manuscript collection known as the Holgate Miscellany, *is possibly Francis Beau-mont, a witty playwright who collaborated with John Fletcher, Shakespeare's successor as the King's Men's playwright. The poem is dedicated to Ben Jonson. As Jonson will later do in his commendatory poem in Shakespeare's First Folio, Beaumont emphasizes Shakespeare's lack of a formal education: he describes the playwright's works as not marked by signs of learning and as guided by "the dimme light of Nature."*

To Mr B: J:

Neither to follow fashion nor to showe
my witt against the State, nor that I knowe
any thing now, with which I am with childe
till I have tould, nor hopeinge to bee stilde
a good Epist'ler through the towne, with which

I might bee famous, nor with any ytch
like these, wrote I this Letter but to showe
the Love I carrie and mee thinkes do owe
to you above the number, which can best
in something which I use not, be exprest.
to write this I invoake none, but the post
of Dover, or some Carriers pist-ling ghost,
For if this equall but the stile, which men
send Cheese to towne with, and thankes downe agen,
tis all I seeke for: heere I would let slippe
(If I had any in mee) schollershippe,
and from all Learninge keepe these lines as deere
    [In margin: cleere]
as Shakespeares best are, which our heires shall heare
Preachers apte to their auditors to showe
how farr sometimes a mortall man may goe
by the dimme light of Nature, tis to mee
an helpe to write of nothing; and as free,
As hee, whose text was, god made all that is,
I meane to speake: what do you thinke of his
state, who hath now the last that hee could make,
in white and Orrenge tawny on his backe
at Windsor? is not this mans miserie more
then a fallen sharers, that now keepes a doore,
hath not his state almost as wretched beene
as is, that is ordainde to write the grinne
after the fawne, and fleere shall bee? as sure
some one there is allotted to endure
that Cross. there are some, I could wish to knowe
to love, and keepe with, if they woulde not showe
their studdies to me; or I wish to see
their workes to laugh at, if they suffer mee
not to knowe them: And thus I would Commerse
with honest Poets that make scurvie verse.
by this time you perceive you did a misse
to leave your worthier studies to see this,
which is more tedious to you, then to walke
in a Jews Church, or Bretons Common talke.
But know I write not these lines to the end
to please Ben: Johnson but to please my frend: ffinis:
FB:

*—*Pierpont Morgan Library MA 1057, fol. 110

Possible Allusion to Shakespeare in *The New Metamorphosis*

The author of this poem in The New Metamorphosis *(British Library Additional MSS. 14824-26), identified only as J.M., is unknown.*

who hath a lovinge wife & loves her not,
he is no better then a witlesse sotte;

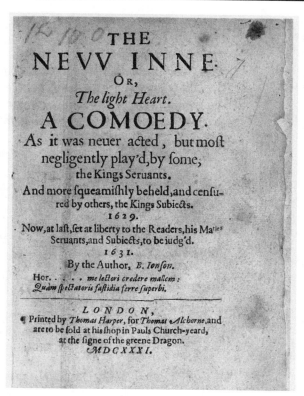

A title page that includes Jonson's complaints about acting and audiences (by permission of the Folger Shakespeare Library)

Two title-page illustrations that may reflect the staging and costuming practices of Jacobean drama (left, by permission of the Folger Shakespeare Library; right, courtesy of Masters and Fellows of Trinity College, Cambridge)

Let such have wives to recompense their merite,
even Menelaus forked face inherite.
Is love in wives good, not in husbands too?
why doe men sweare they love then, when they wooe?
it seemes 't is true that W. S. said,
when once he heard one courting of a Mayde,—
Beleve not thou Mens fayned flatteryes,
Lovers will tell a bushell-full of Lyes!
—Facts and Problems, vol. II, pp. 221–222

Shakespeare Named in Howes and Stow's *The Annales*

Shakespeare was among the "excellent Poets" listed in historian Edmund Howes and John Stow's The Annales, Or Generall Chronicle of England *(1615).*

And as precedent writers, in favour of vertuous merit, in their severall times, have registred such as were most famous, in the high misterie of *Poesey*: by whose singuler paines, and industry, our native language, hath from time to time, beene much refined: and at this time directly by them, brought to great perfection: and the abuse of time, & populer absurdities many wayes disciphered, and amended: the chiefe of our auncient Poets, recommended unto us, by worthy auncient writers, are Frier *Bacon, Thomas Wyclife,* sir *Jeoffry Chaucer* knight, *John Gower,* Esquier, *John Lidgate* monke of Bury, doctor *Skelton,* sir *Thomas More* Lord Chancellor, master *Jasper Heyward* Gentleman, &c.

Our moderne, and present excellent Poets which worthely florish in their owne workes, and all of them in my owne knowledge lived togeather in this Queenes raigne, according to their priorities as neere as I could, I have orderly set downe (viz) *George Gascoigne* Esquire, *Thomas Church-yard* Esquire, sir *Edward Dyer* Knight, *Edmond Spencer* Esquire, sir *Philip Sidney* Knight, Sir *John Harrington* Knight, Sir *Thomas Challoner* Knight, Sir *Frauncis Bacon* Knight, & Sir *John Davie* Knight, Master *John Lillie* gentleman, Maister *George Chapman* gentleman M. *W. Warner* gentleman, M. *Willi. Shake-speare* gentleman, *Samuell Daniell* Esquire, *Michaell Draiton* Esquire, of the bath, M. *Christopher Marlo* gen. M. *Benjamine Johnson* geleman, *John Marston* Esquier, M. *Abraham Frauncis* gen. master *Frauncis Meers* gentle. master *Josua Silvester* gentle. master *Thomas Deckers* gentleman, M. *John Flecher* gentle. M. *John Webster* gentleman, M. *Thomas Heywood* gentlemen, M. *Thomas Middelton* gentleman, M. *George Withers.*

—p. 811

Shakespeare's Suit against Bacon

Shakespeare and other owners of the Blackfriars's properties sue Matthew Bacon for the return of legal documents Bacon inherited from his mother, Ann, the Blackfriars's previous owner. In Shakespeare's case, the documents would be related to the 1608 purchase of the Blackfriars theater (Chancery, Bundle B 11, No. 9, Bills and Answers 1 Jac.). Abbreviations have been silently expanded.

xxvi^{to} die Aprilis 1615
Saunders

To the Right Honorable Sir Thomas Egerton knight Lord Ellesmere and Lord Chancellor of England

Humblie Complayninge sheweth Unto your Honorable Lordship your Daylie Oratores Sir Thomas Bendish Baronet Edward Newport and Willyam Thoresbie Esquire Robert Dormer Esquior and Marie his wife Willyam Shakespere gentleman and Richard Bacon Citezen of London That Wheares Your Orators be and are severally Lawfullie Seised in there Demesne as of ffee of and in One Capitall Messuage or Dwellinge howse with there appurtenances with two Court Yardes and one void plot of grownd sometymes used for a garden on the East parte of the said Dwellinge howse and so Much of one Edifice as now or sometymes served for two Stables and two haye Loftes over the said Stables and one litle Colehowse adjoyninge to the said Stables Lyinge on the South side of the said Dwellinge howse And of another Messuage or Tenemente with thappurtenances now in the occupacion of Anthony Thompson and Thomas Perckes and of there Assignes & of a void peece of grownd wheruppon a Stable is builded to the said meassuage belonginge and of severall othere howses Devided into severall Lodginges or Dwellinge howses Toginther with all and singuler Sellors Sollers Chambers Halls parlors Yardes Back-sides Easementes profites and Comodityes Herunto severallie belonginge And of Certaine Void plots of grownd adjoyninge to the said Messuages and premisses aforesaid or unto some of them And of a Well howse All which messuages Tenementes and premisses aforesaid bye Lyinge within the precinct of Black ffriers in the Cittye of London or Countye of Middlesex late the Messuages Tenementes and enheritances of Willyam Blackwell thelder Henrie Blackwell and Willyam Blackwell the Younger of Ann Bacon or of some of them Unto which foresaid Capitall Messuages Tenementes and premisses aforesaid severall Deedes Chartres Letters patentes Evidences Munimentes and Wrightinges be and are belonginge and apperteyninge and do belonge unto Your Orators and Doe serve for the preservinge of Your Orators Lawfull right title interest and estate in to and unto the foresaid Messuages and premisses All which

foresaid Letters patentes Deedes Evidences Chartres munimentes and Wrightings aforesaid were left in trust with
Ann Bacon deceassed for and unto the use and behoofe of
Your Orators Now so Yt is May Yt please Your Honorable Lordship: that the said Ann Bacon beinge latelie
Dead and Mathy Bacon beinge her sole executor the foresaid Letters patentes Deedes Chartres and Evidences
Muniments and Wrightinges aforesaid be since her Death
come unto and now be in the handes and possession of
the foresaid Mathy Bacon who doth not Clayme any right
estate or interest at all in or unto the foresaid Messuages or
Tenementes Yet nevertheles the said Mathy Bacon Knowinge the Messuages Tenementes Letters patentes Deedes
Evidences Chartres Munimentes and Wrightinges aforesaid to be belonging and onelie to belonge to Your Orators Doth nevertheles Withhould keepe and Deteyne
awaye from Your Orators the foresaid Letters patentes
and other Deedes Evidences Chartres Munimentes and
Wrightinges aforesaid and will not deliver the same unto
your Orators Wherby Your Orators be in great Danger
for to Loose and be Disinherited of the messuages Tenementes and premisses aforesaid In tender Consideracion
Wherof and forasmuch as Your Orators have no
remoudye at and by the Course of the Common Lawes of
this Realme for to have the said Letters patentes Deedes
Charters Munimentes Evidences and Wrightinges Delivered unto Your Orators for that your Orators Doo not
knowe the Certaine Dates nor particuler Contentes of
them nor Whither they be in Box Bag or Chist sealed or
Locked Therfore that the said Mathy Bacon maye make
Direct Answere unto the premisses and maye set Downe
expresslie what Letters patentes Deedes Evidences Chartres munimentes or Wrightinges he hath in his handes or
knoweth where they be which Concerne Your Orators or
the Messuages and premisses aforesaid or any of them
and the same maye bringe into this Honorable Court to
be delivered unto Your Orators Maye Yt please your
Lordship to grant to Your Orators his Majesties most gracious writt of Subpena and also of Ducens tecū unto him
the said Mathew Bacon to be Directed Commandinge
him therby at a Certaine Daye and under a Certaine
payne therein to be Lymited Personalli to be and appeare
before Your Lordship in his Majesties high Court of
Chancerie then and there for to make Answere unto the
premisses and also to bring with him the said Letters patentes Deedes Evidences Chartres and Wrightinges into
this Honorable Court and to stand to and abide such further Order therin as to your Honorable Lordship shalbe
thought fitt And your Lordships Daylie Orators shalbe in
all Dewtye Bownd to pray for your good Lordship in all
health and happines long to Contynue.

Lock

—Lewis, *Shakespeare Documents*, vol. II, pp. 467–468

<hr>

1616

Shakespeare Named in Bolton's Draft for *Hypercritica*

*Scholar and antiquary Edmund Bolton names Shake-
speare in this draft for* Hypercritica *(Bodleian, Rawlinson
manuscript D1, folio 14v); the final version, which remained
unpublished until 1722, did not include the allusion.*

The bookes also out of which wee gather the most
warrantable English are not many to my Remembrance, of which in regard they require a particuler
and curious tract, I forbeare to speake at this
present. But among the cheife, or rather the cheife
are in my opinion these . . . Shakespere, Mʳ Francis
Beamont and innumerable other writers for the
stage and presse tenderly to be used in this Argument.

—*Facts and Problems*, vol. II, p. 225

Judith Shakespeare's Marriage to Thomas Quiney

*The marriage of Shakespeare's daughter Judith to Thomas
Quiney is recorded in the marriage register of Holy Trinity
Church, Stratford-upon-Avon.*

[10 February 1616] Tho Queeny tow Judith Shakspere
—Shakespeare Birthplace Trust Records Office,
DR 243/1, folio 13v

*Thomas Quiney was the son of Richard Quiney, author
of the only surviving letter written to Shakespeare. In 1615
Thomas Quiney got Margaret Wheeler pregnant; Wheeler
and her child were buried on 15 March 1616, a month after
Quiney's marriage to Judith Shakespeare. Quiney confessed
to being the father of the child and was fined five shillings.
His marriage to Judith took place during Lent; this required
a special license that Quiney did not obtain. The couple were
called before the bishop of Worcester's consistory court; when
they failed to answer a second summons, they were excommu-
nicated, a punishment that lasted several months. Shakespeare made special efforts in his will to assure Judith of an
income Quiney could not control.*

*Thomas and Judith Quiney had several children, none
of whom survived their mother. Shakespeare Quiney was
baptized on 23 November 1616 and died on 8 May 1618;
Richard Quiney was born 9 February 1618 and died 26
February 1639; Thomas Quiney was born 23 January
1620 and died 28 January 1639.*

The King's Men
Paid for Court Performances

To John Heminges and the rest of his fellowes the kinges Majesties Players upon a warraunte signed by the Lorde Chamberleyne Dated the xxix^th of Aprill 1616 for presenting before the kinges Majestie and the Queene xiiii^en severall plays from the feaste of all Saintes 1615 to the firste of Aprill 1616   Cxl^li

Item paid to John Heminges and the rest of his Fellowes the Kinges Majesties players for presentinge before his Highnes and the Queenes Majestie Fowerteene severall plays from the Feast of All Sainctes 1615 to the first of April 1616 As appeereth by a Warrant signed by the Lord Chamberleine Dated att Whitehall xxix^o Die April 1616 the some of   Cxl^li

                              —*Dramatic Records*, pp. 65–66

Shakespeare's Epitaphs

Shakespeare was buried in the chancel of Holy Trinity Church in Stratford. In this epitaph from his grave, the word "bleste" in the third line is sometimes read as "blese."

Good frend for Jesus sake forbeare,
To digg the dust encloased heare.
Bleste be the man that spares thes stones,
And curst be he that moves my bones.

In the epitaph on Shakespeare's monument in the church, the word "Sieh" in the penultimate line appears to be an error for "sith."

Judicio Pylium, Genio Socratem, Arte Maronem,
Terra tegit, populus mæret, Olympus habet.

[The earth covers, the people mourn, and Olympus holds (the man who was a) Pylian (Nestor) for his judgement, Socrates for his Genius, and Maro (Vergil) for his art.]

Stay passenger, why goest thou by so fast?
Read if thou canst, whom envious Death hath plast,
With in this monument Shakspeare: with whome,
Quick Nature dide: whose name doth deck [this] tombe,
Far more then cost: sieh all, [that] he hath writt,
Leaves living art, but page, to serve his witt.
                    Obit Año Do^i 1616
                    Ætatis • 53 die 23 Ap^r.

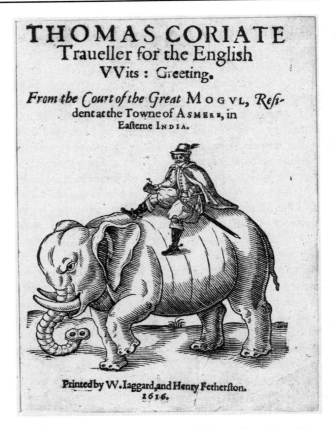

THOMAS CORIATE Traueller for the English VVits : Greeting. From the Court of the Great MOGVL, Resident at the Towne of ASMERE, in Easterne INDIA.

Printed by W. Iaggard and Henry Fetherston. 1616.

The popularity of travel narratives among readers of Shakespeare's time helps explain the exotic locations of many Elizabethan and Jacobean plays, including Shakespeare's (by permission of the Folger Shakespeare Library).

Shakespeare's Will

Although Shakespeare signed his will, he did not write it; the handwriting is that of his lawyer or the lawyer's clerk, who provided the correct legal phrasing, all of which is standard for early modern wills. Shakespeare determined the various legacies, including the infamous "second best bed" he left to his wife, Anne Hathaway. As many scholars have noted, this phrasing is not necessarily a metaphor for an unhappy marriage. The second best bed may have been the marriage bed itself, with the best bed being reserved for guests, so the bed he left his wife may have had sentimental value.

The following is a diplomatic transcription of the will, slightly modified for clarity, prepared by Jane Cox for Shakespeare in the Public Records (1985), a publication of the Public Record Office; it is used by permission of the office.

Vicesimo Quinto die *Januarii* (struck through) M[ar]tii Anno Regni D[omi]ni n[ost]ri Jacobi nunc R[egis] Angliae etc. decimo quarto & Scotie xlix^o Annoque D[omi]ni 1616

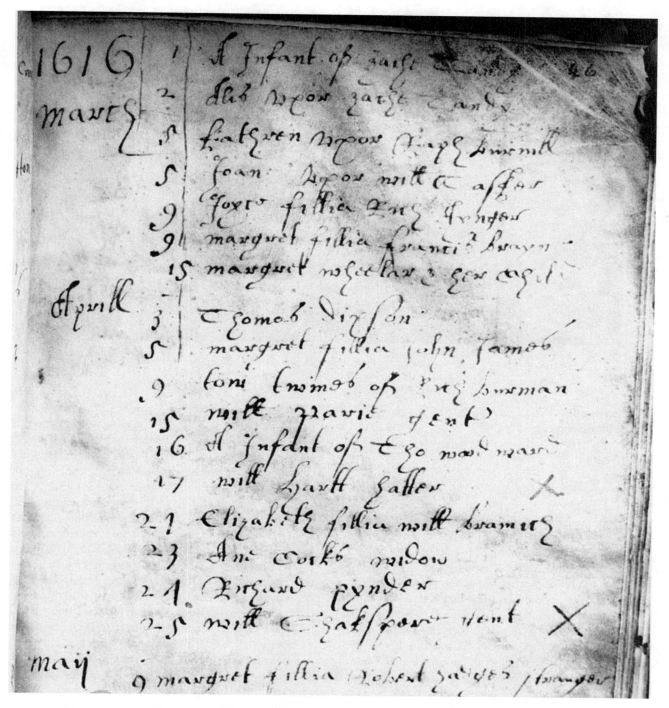

Shakespeare's death is recorded on 25 April 1616 in the burial register of Holy Trinity Church in Stratford. He is identified as a gentleman (shelfmark DR 243/1; courtesy of the Shakespeare Birthplace Trust Records Office).

Shakespeare's gravestone, reinscribed from the original, in Holy Trinity Church, Stratford-upon-Avon
(photograph ©2001 by Gary Vernon)

T[estamentum]
W[ille]mi Shackspeare

R[egistretu]r

In the name of god Amen I Williᵃm Shackspeare of Stratford upon Avon in the countie of Warr[wick] gent[leman] in perfect health & memorie god be praysed doe make & Ordayne this my last will & testam[en]ᵗ in manner & forme followeing That ys to saye first I Comend my Soule into the hands of god my Creator hoping & assuredlie beleeving through thonelie merittes of Jesus Christe my Saviour to be made partaker of lyfe everlastinge And my bodye to the Earth whereof yt ys made. It[e]m I Gyve & bequeath unto my *sonne in L[aw]* (struck through) Daughter Judyth One Hundred & ffyftie pounds of lawfull English money to be paied unto her in manner & forme followeing That ys to saye One Hundred Poundes *in discharge of her marriage porc[i]on* (interlined) within one yeare after my deceas w[i]th considerac[i]on after the Rate of twoe shillinges in the pound for soe long tyme as the same shalbe unpaide unto her after my deceas & the ffyftie pounds Residewe thereof upon her surrendring *of* (interlined) or gyving of such sufficient securitie as the overseers of this my will shall like of to Surrender or graunte All her estate &

Right that shall discend or come unto her after my deceas or *that she* (interlined) nowe hath of in or to one Copiehold ten[emen]te with thappertenances lyeing & being in Stratford upon Avon aforesaied in the saied countie of warr' being parcell or holden of the mannor of Rowington unto my daughter Susanna Hall & her heiries for ever. Item I Gyve & bequeath unto my saied Daughter Judyth One Hundred & ffyftie Poundes more if shee or Anie issue of her bodie be Lyvinge att thend of three Yeares next ensueing the daie of the date of this my will during which tyme my executors to paie her considerac[i]on from my deceas according to the Rate aforesaied. And if she dye within the saied terme without issue of her bodye then my will ys & I doe gyve & bequeath One Hundred Poundes thereof to my Neece Elizabeth Hall & the ffiftie Poundes to be sett fourth by my executors during the lief of my Sister Johane Harte & the use & proffitt thereof Cominge shalbe payed to my saied Sister Jone & after her deceas the saied Lⁱ shall Remaine Amongst the children of my saied Sister Equallie to be devided Amongst them. But if my saied daughter Judith be lyving att thend of the saied three yeares or anie yssue of her bodye then my will ys & soe I devise & bequeath the saied Hundred & ffyftie poundes to be sett out *by my executors & overseers* (interlined) for the best benefitt of her & her issue & *the stock*

The monument to Shakespeare, sculpted by Gheerart Janssen, in Holy Trinity Church, Stratford-upon-Avon (photograph ©2001 by Gary Vernon)

yearelie Rent of xii^d Item I gyve & bequeath (signed bottom left) William Shakespere (end of page 1) unto her three sonnes William Harte (name ommitted) Hart & Michaell Harte ffyve poundes A peece to be payed within one yeare after my decease *to be sett out for her within one yeare after my deceas by my executors with thadvise & direcc[i]ons of my overseers for her best proffitt untill her marriage & then the same with the increase thereof to be paied unto her* (struck through). Item I gyve & bequeath unto *her* (struck through) *the saied Elizabeth Hall* (interlined) All my Plate (*except my brod silver & gilt bole*) (interlined) that I now have att the date of this my will. Item I gyve & bequeath unto the Poore of Stratford aforesaied tenn poundes; to Mr Thomas Combe my Sword; to Thomas Russell Esquier ffyve poundes & to ffrauncis Collins of the Borough of Warr' in the countie of Warr' gent. thirteene poundes Sixe shillinges & Eight pence to be paied within one yeare after my deceas. Item I gyve & bequeath to mr. Richard (struck through) *Hamlett Sadler* (interlined) *Tyler thelder* (struck through) XXVI^s VIII^d to buy him A Ringe; *to William Raynoldes gent. XXVI^s VIII^d to buy him A Ringe* (interlined); to my godson William Walker XX^s in gold; to Anthonye Nashe gent. XXVI^s VIII^d; & to mr. John Nashe XXVI^s VIII^d *in gold* (struck through) *& to my ffellowes John Hemynges, Richard Burbage & Henry Cundell XXVI^s VIII^d A peece to buy them Ringes* (interlined). Item I Gyve Will bequeth & Devise unto my Daughter Susanna Hall *for better enabling of her to performe this my will & towardes the performans thereof* (interlined) All that Capitall Messuage or tenemente with thappurtenances *in Stratford aforesaid* (interlined) called the newe plase wherein I nowe Dwell & two messuages or ten[emen]tes with thappurtenances scituat lyeing & being in Henley Streete within the borough of Stratford aforesaied And all my barnes, stables, Orchardes, gardens, landes, ten[emen]tes & hereditam[en]ts whatsoever scituat lyeing & being or to be had Receyved, perceyved or taken within the townes & Hamletts, villages, ffieldes & groundes of Stratford upon Avon, Oldstratford, Bushopton & Welcombe or in anie of them in the saied countie of warr And alsoe All that Messuage or ten[emen]te with thappurtenances wherein one John Robinson dwelleth, scituat, lyeing & being in the blackfriers in London nere the Wardrobe & all other my landes ten[emen]tes & hereditam[en]tes whatsoever. To Have & to hold All & sing[u]ler the saied premisses with their Appurtenances unto the saied Susanna Hall for & during the terme of her naturall lief & after her deceas to the first sonne of her bodie lawfullie yssueing & to the heiries Males of the bodie of the saied first Sonne lawfullie yssueinge & for defalt of such issue to the second Sonne of her bodie lawfullie issueinge & *of* (struck through) to the heires Males of the bodie of

(interlined) not *to be* (interlined) paied unto her soe long as she shalbe marryed & Covert Baron *by my executors and overseers* (struck through) but my will ys that she shall have the considerac[i]on yearelie paied unto her during her lief & after her deceas the saied stock and considerac[i]on to bee paied to her children if she have Anie & if not to her executors or assignes she lyving the saied terme after my deceas provided that if such husbond as she shall att thend of the saied three yeares be marryed unto or attaine after doe sufficientlie Assure unto her & thissue of her bodie landes answereable to the porc[i]on by this my Will gyven unto her & to be adjudged soe by my executors & overseers then my will ys that the saied CL^li shalbe paied to such husbond as shall make such assurance to his owne use. Item I gyve and bequeath unto my saied sister Jone XX^li & all my wearing Apparrell to be paied & delivered within one yeare after my deceas. And I doe will & devise unto her *the house* (interlined) with thappurtenances in Stratford wherein she dwelleth for her naturall lief under the

the saied Second Sonne lawfullie yssueing & for defalt of such heires to the third Sonne of the bodie of the saied Susanna Lawfullie yssueing & of the heires Males of the bodie of the saied third sonne lawfullie yssueing And for defalt of such issue the same soe to be & Remaine to the ffourth, *sonne* (struck through) ffyfth, sixte & Seaventh sonnes of her bodie lawfullie issueing one after Another & to the heires (signed bottom right) William Shakspere (end of page 2) Males of the bodies of the saied ffourth, fifth, Sixte & Seaventh sonnes lawfullie yssueing in such manner as yt ys before Lymitted to be & Remaine to the first, second & third Sonns of her bodie & to their heires males. And for defalt of such issue the saied premisses to be & Remaine to my sayed Neece Hall & the heires Males of her bodie Lawfull[ie] yssueing for defa[ult of] (page damaged) such iss[u]e to my daughter Judith & the heires Males of her bodie lawfullie issueinge. And for defalt of such issue to the Right heires of me the saied Will[ia]m Shackspere for ever. *Item I gyve unto my wief my second best bed with the furniture* (interlined); Item I gyve & bequeath to my saied daughter Judith my broad silver gilt bole. All the Rest of my goodes Chattel[s], Leases, plate, Jewels & household stuffe whatsoever after my dettes and Legasies paied & my funerall expences discharged, I gyve devise & bequeath to my Sonne in Lawe John Hall gent. & my daughter Susanna his wief whom I ordaine & make executors of this my Last will & testam[en]t. And I doe intreat & Appoint *the saied* (interlined) Thomas Russell Esquier & ffraunci[s] Collins gent. to be overseers hereof And doe Revoke All former wills and publishe this to be my last will & testam[en]t. In Wit[n]es whereof I have hereunto put my *Seale* (struck through) *hand* (interlined) the Daie & Yeare first above Written.

At the end of the text, on the left, the witnesses signed the will.

Witnes to the publishing
hereof (signed) Fra: Collyns
Juliyus Shawe
John Robinson
Hamnet Sadler
Robert Whattcott

Shakespeare signed the will opposite the signatures of his witnesses on the right side of the page.

By me William Shakspeare (signed)

More text appears under Shakespeare's signature.

Probatum coram Mag[ist]ro Willi[a]mo Byrde

legum d[o]c[t]ore Commissar[io] etc. xxii^{do} die mensis Junii Anno d[omi]ni 1616 Juram[en]to Johannis Hall unius ex[ecutorum] etc. Cui etc. de bene etc. Jurat[i] Res[er]vata p[o]t[est]ate etc. Sussanne Hall alt[eri] ex[ecutorum] etc. cum ven[er]it etc. petitur

In[ventariu]m ex[hibi]t[um]

Finally, text appears on the verso of page three at the top.

Juratus vir reservetur
potestas alii ex[ecu]tricii cum
venerit 22 Junii W. Byrde
(signed)

right hand: Mr. Shackspere
his will
left hand: Mr Shackspere
June 16
—*Shakespeare in the Public Records,* pp. 31–32

The following is a modern-spelling version of the will.

In the name of God, Amen. I William Shackspeare of Stratford upon Avon in the county of Warwick, gentleman, in perfect health and memory, God be praised, do make and ordain this my last will and testament in manner and form following. That is to say, first I commend my soul into the hands of God my creator, hoping and assuredly believing through the only merits of Jesus Christ my Savior to be made partaker of life everlasting, and my body to the earth whereof it is made. Item, I give and bequeath unto my daughter Judith one hundred and fifty pounds of lawful English money to be paid unto her in manner and form following: That is to say one hundred pounds in discharge of her marriage portion within one year after my decease with consideration after the rate of two shillings in the pound for so long time as the same shall be unpaid unto her after my decease, and the fifty pounds residue thereof upon her surrendering of, or giving of such sufficient security as the overseers of this my will shall like of, to surrender or grant all her estate and right that shall descend or come unto her after my decease, or that she now hath of in or to one copyhold tenement with the appurtenances lying and being in Stratford upon Avon aforesaid in the said county of Warwick being parcel or holden of the manor of Rowington unto my daughter Susanna Hall and her heirs for ever. Item, I give and bequeath unto my said daughter Judith one hundred and fifty pounds more if she or any issue of her body be living at the end of three years next ensuing the day of the date of this my will during which time my execu-

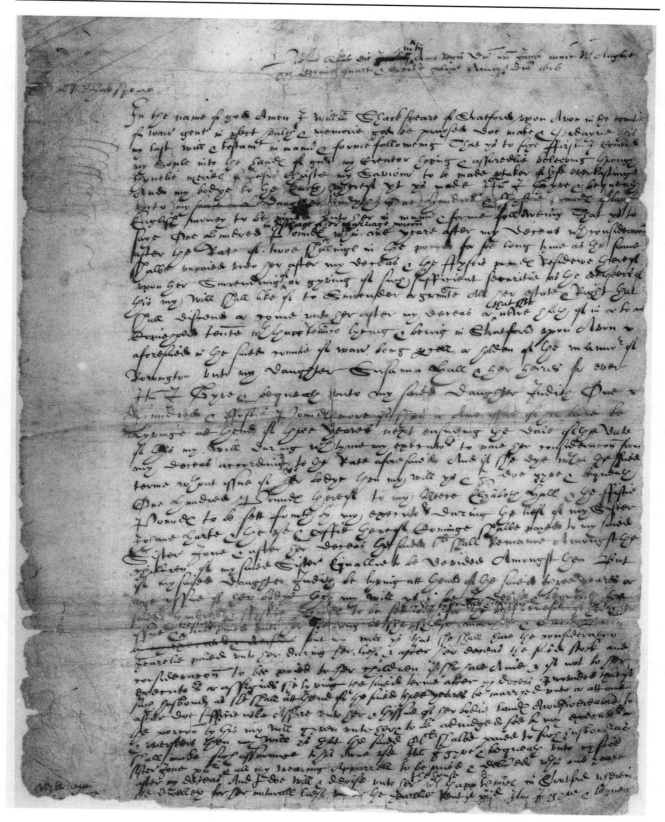

Shakespeare's will, signed by Shakespeare on all three pages (PRO PROB 1/4; courtesy of the Public Records Office, London)

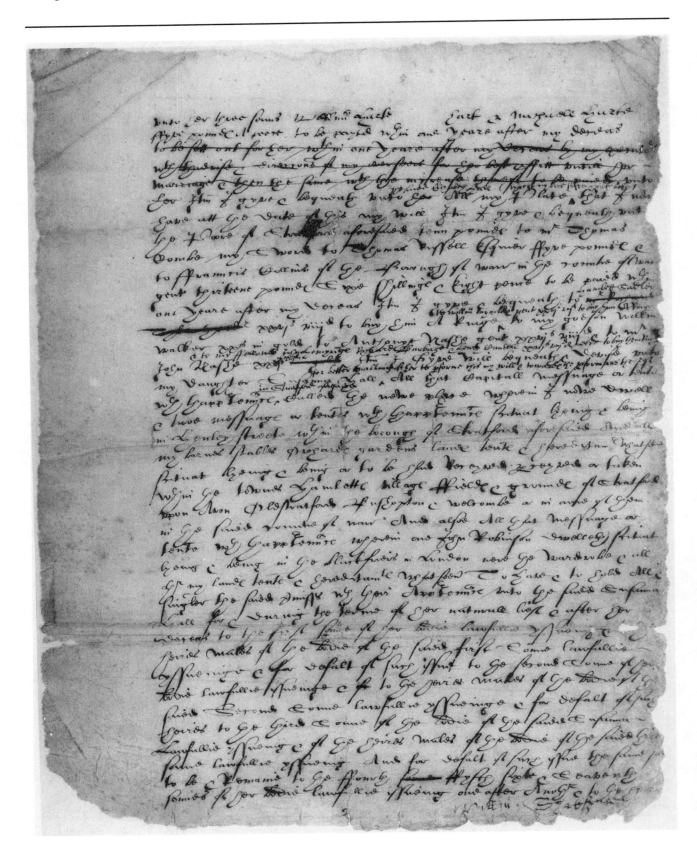

tors to pay her consideration from my decease according to the rate aforesaid. And if she die within the said term without issue of her body then my will is and I do give and bequeath one hundred pounds thereof to my niece Elizabeth Hall and fifty pounds to be set forth by my executors during the life of my sister Johane Harte and the use and profit thereof coming shall be paid to my said sister Jone, and after her decease the said fifty pounds shall remain amongst the children of my said sister equally to be divided amongst them. But if my said daughter Judith be living at the end of the said three years or any issue of her body then my will is and so I devise and bequeath the said hundred and fifty pounds to be set out by my executors and overseers for the best benefit of her and her issue and the stock not to be paid unto her so long as she shall be married and Covert Baron, but my will is that she shall have the consideration yearly paid unto her during her life and after her decease the said stock and consideration to be paid to her children if she have any, and if not, to her executors or assigns she living the said term after my decease provided that if such husband as she shall at the end of the said three years be married unto or attain after do sufficiently assure unto her and the issue of her body lands answerable to the portion by this my will given unto her and to be adjudged so by my executors and overseers then my will is that the said one hundred fifty pounds shall be paid to such husband as shall make such assurance to his own use. Item, I give and bequeath unto my said sister Jone twenty pounds and all my wearing apparel to be paid and delivered within one year after my decease. And I do will and devise unto her the house with the appurtenances in Stratford wherein she dwelleth for her natural life under the yearly rent of twelve pence. Item, I give and bequeath unto her three sons William Harte [blank space] Hart and Michael Harte five pounds a piece to be paid within one year after my decease. Item, I give and bequeath unto the said Elizabeth Hall all my plate (except my broad silver and gilt bowl) that I now have at the date of this my will. Item, I give and bequeath unto the poor of Stratford aforesaid ten pounds; to Mr. Thomas Combe my sword; to Thomas Russell Esquire five pounds and to Frauncis Collins of the borough of Warwick in the county of Warwick gentleman thirteen pounds six shillings and eight pence to be paid within one year after my decease. Item, I give and bequeath to Hamlett Sadler twenty-six shillings eight pence to buy him a ring; to William Raynoldes gentleman twenty-six shillings eight pence to buy him a ring; to my godson William Walker twenty shillings in gold; to Anthony Nashe gentleman twenty-six shillings eight pence; to Mr. John Nashe twenty-six shillings eight pence; and to my fellows John Hemynges, Richard Burbage and Henry Cundell twenty-six shillings eight pence a piece to buy them rings. Item, I give, will, bequeath, and devise unto my daughter Susanna Hall for better enabling of her to perform this my will and towards the performance thereof all that capital messuage or tenement with the appurtenances in Stratford aforesaid called the New Place wherein I now dwell and two messuages or tenements with the appurtenances situate lying and being in Henley Street within the borough of Stratford aforesaid. And all my barns, stables, orchards, gardens, lands, tenements and hereditaments whatsoever situate lying and being or to be had received, perceived or taken within the towns and hamlets, villages, fields and grounds of Stratford upon Avon, Old Stratford, Bishopton and Welcombe or in any of them in the said county of Warwick. And also all that messuage or tenement with the appurtenances wherein one John Robinson dwelleth, situate, lying, and being in the Blackfriars in London near the Wardrobe, and all other my lands tenements and hereditaments whatsoever. To have and to hold all and singular the said premises with their Appurtenances unto the said Susanna Hall for and during the term of her natural life and after her decease to the first son of her body lawfully issuing and to the heirs males of the body of the said first son lawfully issuing, and for default of such issue to the second son of her body lawfully issuing and to the heirs males of the body of the said second son lawfully issuing and for default of such heirs to the third son of the body of the said Susanna lawfully issuing and of the heirs males of the body of the said third son lawfully issuing. And for default of such issue the same so to be and remain to the fourth, fifth, sixth and seventh sons of her body lawfully issuing one after another and to the heirs males of the bodies of the said fourth, fifth, sixth and seventh sons lawfully issuing in such manner as it is before limited to be and remain to the first, second and third sons of her body and to their heirs males. And for default of such issue the said premises to be and remain to my said niece Hall and the heirs males of her body lawfully [issuing for default of] such issue to my daughter Judith and the heirs males of her body lawfully issuing. And for default of such issue to the right heirs of me the said William Shackspere for ever. Item, I give unto my wife my second best bed with the furniture; Item, I give and bequeath to my said daughter Judith my broad silver gilt bowl. All the rest of my goods, chattels, leases, plate, jewels, and household stuff whatsoever after my debts and legacies paid and my funeral expenses discharged, I give devise and bequeath to my son-in-law John Hall, gentleman, and my daughter Susanna his wife, whom I ordain and make executors of this my last will and testament. And I do entreat and appoint the said Thomas Russell, Esquire, and Francis Collins, gentleman, to be overseers hereof, and do revoke all former wills and publish this to be my last will and testament. In witness whereof I have hereunto put my hand the day and year first above written.

By me William Shakspeare

Publication

The Rape of Lucrece, *previously published in 1594, 1598, 1600, and 1607, is published again.*

THE / RAPE / OF / LVCRECE. / By / Mr. *William Shakeſpeare.* / Newly Reuiſed. / [*Printer's device*] / LONDON: / Printed by *T. S.*, for *Roger Iackson*, and are / to be ſolde at his shop neere the Conduit / in Fleet-street. 1616.

Possible Allusions to *Antony and Cleopatra* and *The Comedy of Errors* in Anton's *The Philosophers Satyrs*

In The Philosophers Satyrs *(1616) Robert Anton blames the theater for providing women with models of bad behavior. In addition to using theatrical language to castigate women, Anton also refers to several plays, two of which—one showing Cleopatra's crimes and the other a comedy of errors— may be Shakespeare's. These excerpts are from the "fifth satire, of Venus."*

Why doe our *lustfull Theaters* entice,
And personate in lively action *vice*:
Draw to the *Cities* shame, with *guilded clothes*,
Such *swarmes* of *wives* to breake their *nuptiall othes*:
Or why are *women* rather growne so mad,
That their *immodest feete* like *planets* gad
With such *irregular motion* to base *Playes*,
Where all the *deadly sinnes* keepe *hollidaies*.
There shall they see the *vices* of the *times*,
Orestes incest, *Cleopatres* crimes,
Lucullus surfets, and *Poppeas* pride.
Virgineaes rape, and wanton *Lais* hide
Her *Sirens charmes* in such *eare charming sense*;
As it would turne a modest *audience*,
To *brazen-fac'et profession* of a *whore*.
Their *histories* perswade, but *action* more,
Vices well coucht in pleasing *Sceanes* present,
More *will* to act, then *action* can invent.
And this the reason, unlesse *heaven* prevent,
Why *women* most at *Playes* turne impudent,
And yet not to their *sexe* doe we applie,
A *Stoicall* and stout *necessitie*,
Of shamefull *sinne* to *women* in this *kind*.
But I could wish their *modestie* confin'd,

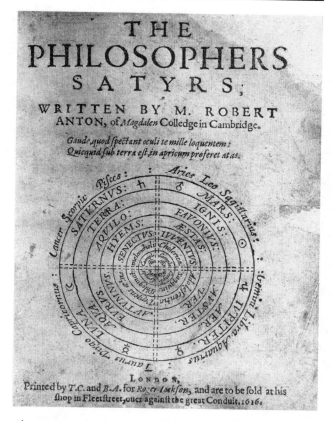

Title page for Robert Anton's book in which he may allude to Shakespeare's works. Anton presents an orderly picture of the universe, linking astrological signs, planets, elements, winds, seasons, and bodily humors (by permission of the Folger Shakespeare Library).

To a more *civill* and *grave libertie*,
Of *will* and *free election*: carefullie
Hating this *hellish confluence* of the *stage*,
That breeds more grosse *infections* to the *age*
Of *separations*, and religious *bonds*,
Then e're *religion* with her *hallowed hands*
Can reunite: rather renew thy *web*,
With chast *Penelope*, then staine thy *bed*
With such base *incantations*: But why in vaine,
Doe I confound the *musicke* of my *straine*
With such unrellisht *Pantomimmicke slaves*,
Whose lives prophane a lashing *Satyr* craves?
Oh yet my grave muse be not to profuse,
Applaud their good, scourge onely their abuse,
No, rather my keene pen with *art* dissect,
The *Anotomie* of *woman*, whose *defect*,
May reade such *Physicke* to their longing *sexe*,
As what most horrid guilt of *lust* detects,
And cast *aspersions* on their *Angels faces*,
May *salve* their *burning feavers* of *disgraces*. . . .

–pp. 46–47

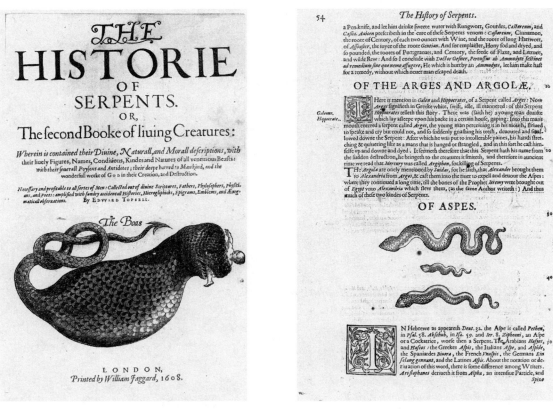

Title page and interior page from Edward Topsell's The Historie of Serpents *(1608). Topsell emphasizes the dangers posed by serpents, including the Asp, Cleopatra's means of suicide in* Antony and Cleopatra *(by permission of the Folger Shakespeare Library).*

Page from Paradin's Heroicall Devises *(1591) showing an emblem that represents Egypt's conquest by Rome (by permission of the Folger Shakespeare Library)*

Sooner may shamelesse wives hate *Braindford feasts*,
Albertus Magnus, or the *pilfred Jests*
Of some spruce *Skipjack Citizen* from *Playes*,
A *Coach*, the secret *Baudihouse* for *waies*,
And *riotous waste* of some new *Freeman* made,
That in one *yeere* to *peices* breakes his *trade*,
Then wash the toadlike speckles of *defame*,
That swell the *world* with *poyson* of their *shame*:
What *Comedies* of *errors* swell the *stage*
With your most *publike vices*, when the *age*
Dares personate in *action*, for, your *eies*
Ranke *Sceanes* of your *lust*-sweating *qualities*. . . .

—p. 51

Allusion to *Richard III* in Breton's *The Good And The Badde*

Nicholas Breton alludes to Richard III *in* The Good And The Badde, Or Descriptions of the Worthies, and Unworthies of this Age *(1616). Breton's book is a collection of "characters," short descriptions of various social types, usually satirical, and, in the early seventeenth century, very popular.*

An Unworthy Lawyer.

An Unlearned and unworthily called a Lawyer, is the figure of a Foot-post, who carries Letters, but knowes not what is in them, only can read the superscriptions, to direct them to their right owners. So trudgeth this simple Clarke, that can scarce read a Case when it is written, with his hand-full of papers, from one Court to another, and from one Counsellors chamber to another, when by his good payment for his paines, hee will bee so sawcy as to call himselfe a Sollicitor: But what a taking are poore Clients in, when this too much trusted cunning companion, better read in *Pierce Plowman*, then in *Ploydon*, and in the Play of *Richard the Third*, then in the Pleas of *Edward* the Fourth; perswades them all is sure, when hee is sure of all? and in what a misery are the poore men, when, upon a *Nihil dicit*, because indeede, this poore fellow, *Nihil potest dicere*, they are in danger of an Execution, before they know wherefore they are condemned: But, I wish all such more wicked then witty, unlearned in the Law and abusers of the same, to looke a little better into their consciences, and to leave their crafty courses, lest when the Law indeede laies them open, insteade of carrying papers in their hands, they weare not papers on their heads, and in stead of giving eare to their Clients causes, or rather eies into their purses, they have nere an Eare left to heare withal, nor good Eie to see withall; or at least honest Face to looke out withall: but as the Grashoppers of Egypt, bee counted the Caterpillers of England, and not the Foxe that stole the Goose, but the great Foxe that stole the Farme, from the Gander.

—pp. 13–14

Allusions to *Hamlet* and *The Rape of Lucrece* in Beaumont and Fletcher's *The Scornful Ladie*

In this excerpt from their comedy The Scornful Ladie *(1616) Francis Beaumont and John Fletcher quote from Hamlet's "to be or not to be" soliloquy (3.1.55 ff.); the "Comick Poet" is probably Shakespeare, with the "loopeholes" reference, from* The Rape of Lucrece, *providing a mocking commentary on Welford: "There might you see the laboring pioner / Begrim'd with sweat, and smeared all with dust, / And from the tow'rs of Troy there would appear / The very eyes of men through loop-holes thrust / Gazing upon the Greeks with little lust" (1380–1384).*

[*Welford*]: But shall wee see these Gentleweomen to night?

[*Sir Roger*]: Have patience Sir, untill our fellowe *Nicholas* bee deceast, that is, asleepe: for so the word is taken; to sleepe to die, to die to sleepe: a very Figure Sir.

Wel. Cannot you cast another for the Gentleweomen?

Ro. Not till the man bee in his bed, his grave; his grave, his bed; the very same againe Sir. Our Comick Poet gives the reason sweetly; *Plenus rimarum est*, he is full of loopeholes, and will discover to our Patronesse.

Wel. Your comment Sir has made me understand you.

Enter Maria the Ladies sister, and Yonglove to them with a posset.

Ro. Sir be addrest, the graces doe salute you with the full bowle of plenty. Is our old enemy entomb'd?

[*Abigail*]: He's fast?

Ro. And does he snore out supinely with the Poet?

[*Maria*] No, he out-snores the Poet.

—sigs. C4r–v

Basse's Poem about Shakespeare

William Basse's poem about Shakespeare (Lansdowne MS. 777. F. 67v.) cannot be dated, but was written after 1616 and appeared in the 1633 edition of Donne's poems as well as in other manuscript and printed verse collections.

On Mr. Wm. Shakespeare
he dyed in Aprill 1616.

Renowned Spencer, lye a thought more nye
To learned Chaucer, and rare Beaumont lye
A little neerer Spenser to make roome
For Shakespeare in your threefold fowerfold Tombe.

Although not as "chop-fallen" as Yorick's skull in Hamlet
(5.1.180 ff.), Geffrey Whitney's emblem from A Choice of
Emblemes and Other Devices *(Leyden, 1586) provides
a similar opportunity for meditation on mortality (by
permission of the Folger Shakespeare Library).*

*Title-page illustration of a corpse ready for burial and some of the tools of
the gravedigger's trade (by permission of the Folger Shakespeare Library)*

To lodge all fowre in one bed make a shift
Untill Doomesdaye, for hardly will a fift
Betwixt this day and that by Fate be slayne
For whom your Curtaines may be drawn againe.
If your precedency in death doth barre
A fourth place in your sacred sepulcher,
Under this carved marble of thine owne
Sleepe rare Tragœdian Shakespeare, sleep alone,
Thy unmolested peace, unshared Cave,
Possesse as Lord not Tenant of thy Grave,
    That unto us and others it may be
    Honore hereafter to be layde by thee.

Wm. Basse.
—Facts and Problems, vol. II, p. 226

First Clown

. . . Here's a skull now hath lien you i' th' earth three
and twenty years.

Hamlet

Whose was it?

First Clown

A whoreson mad fellow's it was. Whose do you think
it was?

Hamlet

Nay, I know not.

First Clown

A pestilence on him for a mad rogue! 'a pour'd a flagon
of Rhenish on my head once. This same skull, sir, was,
sir, Yorick's skull, the King's jester.

Hamlet

This? [*Takes the skull.*]

First Clown

E'en that.

Hamlet

Alas, poor Yorick! I knew him, Horatio, a fellow of infinite jest, of most excellent fancy. He hath bore me on his
back a thousand times, and now how abhorr'd in my
imagination it is! my gorge rises at it. Here hung those lips
that I have kiss'd I know not how oft. Where be your
gibes now, your gambols, your songs, your flashes of merriment, that were wont to set the table on a roar? Not one
now to mock your own grinning–quite chop-fall'n. Now
get you to my lady's [chamber], and tell her, let her paint
an inch thick, to this favor she must come; make her
laugh at that.

—Hamlet, 5.1.173–195

Shakespeare's Posthumous Reputation and the First Folio

Many of the stories about Shakespeare—that he was forced to leave school when his father suffered financial losses, that he was caught poaching Sir Thomas Lucy's deer and had to flee from Stratford, that his first theatrical job in London was providing a sort of valet parking service for audience members' horses, that he played the part of the ghost of Hamlet's father—emerged well after his death in 1616. Although Shakespeare's modern biographers have searched assiduously for documents to corroborate these anecdotes, no evidence has yet emerged to support them. Such stories are appealing because they fill in the gaps of a life story otherwise told by dry legal documents and accompanied by a body of creative work packed with compelling characters about whom we know far more than we do about their author. But these anecdotes do not come from Shakespeare and his contemporaries, and they are told by people who knew Shakespeare only through his published work.

The documents in this section show that the publication of Shakespeare's work continued steadily after his death, culminating in the publication in 1623 of a collection of thirty-six of his plays. (In addition to the thirty-six First Folio plays, most modern complete works now include Pericles, which is credited to Shakespeare on the title pages of its quarto editions, and Two Noble Kinsmen, which Shakespeare wrote in collaboration with John Fletcher; Cardenio, a lost play, brings the total to thirty-nine.) The Folio was a substantial investment for its publishers, and they demanded a substantial price: an unbound copy of the First Folio cost a pound, forty times the price of a single play. The Folio was assembled by Shakespeare's friends and fellow King's Men, John Heminges and Henry Condell, who tell their audience they were motivated to collect the plays in order to preserve and share Shakespeare's "wit," passing on to future readers the obligation to continue to read and praise the works of their friend.

Other documents in this section are memorials written by people who, like Shakespeare's friend and rival playwright Ben Jonson, knew him or who, like vicar John Ward and antiquarian John Aubrey, knew his children or associates. Poet Leonard Digges's 1640 tribute to Shakespeare is also included because it describes performances from Shakespeare's lifetime that Digges witnessed. Anecdotes that cannot be linked to Shakespeare or one of his associates are not included here; they began appearing in the mid seventeenth century in a variety of sources. They can be found in many accounts of Shakespeare's life, beginning with the first scholarly biography, Nicholas Rowe's essay "Some Account of the Life, &c. of Mr. William Shakespear" in the first volume of his 1709 edition of the plays, and continuing in biographies from this century.

1617

Publication

Venus and Adonis, *previously published in 1593, 1594, 1596, 1599, and 1602, is published again.*

VENVS / *AND* / ADONIS / *Vilia miretur vulgus: mihi flavus Apollo* / *Pocula Caſtalia plena miniſtret aqua.* / *LONDON,* / Printed for *W. B.* 1617.

1619

Stationers' Register Entry

The Merchant of Venice *is entered with the Stationers (Stationer's Hall, Register C, folio 303r). Abbreviated words have been silently expanded in the transcription.*

8° Julii 1619
Lau: Hayes Entred for his Copies by Consent of a full Court theis two Copies following which were the Copies of Thomas Haies his fathers   vizt.
    [1] A play Called The Marchant of Venice, . . . xii^d
—Bibliography of the English Printed Drama, vol. I, p. 31

Publications

Several previously published plays by Shakespeare were published again in 1619, including Henry V *(1600 and 1602) and* King Lear *(1608), which were published with a 1608 imprint;* The Merry Wives of Windsor *(1602); and* The First Part of the Contention betwixt the two Famous Houses of York and Lancaster *(1600) and* The True Tragedie of Richard III *(1597, 1598, 1602, 1605, and 1612), which were published together as* The Whole Contention.

THE / Chronicle Hiſtory / of Henry the fift, with his / battell fought at *Agin Court* in / France. Together with an- / *cient Pistoll.* / *As it hath bene ſundry times playd by the Right Honou-* / rable the Lord Chamberlaine his / Seruants. / [*Printer's device*] / Printed for *T. P.* 1608.

M. VVilliam Shake-ſpeare, / *HIS* / True Chronicle Hiſtory of the life / and death of King *Lear*, and his / *three Daughters.* / *With the vnfortunate life of* EDGAR, / ſonne and heire to the Earle of *Gloceſter*, and / *his ſullen and aſſumed humour of* TOM / *of Bedlam.* / *As it was plaid before the Kings Maiesty at White-Hall, vp-* / *pon S. Stephens night, in Christmas Hollidaies.* / *By his Maieſties Seruants, playing vſually at the* / *Globe on the Banck-ſide.* / [*Printer's device*] / Printed for *Nathaniel Butter.* / 1608.

A / Moſt pleaſant and ex- / cellent conceited Comedy, / of *Sir Iohn Falſtaffe, and the* / *merry VViues of VVindſOr.* / VVith the ſwaggering vaine of An- / cient *Pistoll*, and Corporall *Nym.* / Written by W. SHAKESPEARE. / [*Printer's device*] / Printed for *Arthur Johnſon*, 1619.

THE / Whole Contention / betweene the two Famous / Houſes, LANCASTER and / YORKE. / *With the Tragicall ends of the good Duke* / Humfrey, Richard Duke of Yorke, / *and King Henrie the* / *ſixt.* / Divided into two Parts: And newly corrected and / enlarged. Written by *William Shake-* / *ſpeare*, Gent. / [*Printer's device.*] / Printed at LON-DON, for T. P.

Also published was A Yorkshire Tragedy, *a play of disputed authorship that had first been published in 1608, which was again credited to Shakespeare.*

A / YORKSHIRE / TRAGEDIE. / *Not ſo New, as Lamentable* / *and True.* / Written by W. SHAKESPEARE. / [*Printer's device*] / Printed for *T. P.* 1619.

Allusions to Shakespeare in Jonson's "Conversations with Drummond"

William Drummond of Hawthornden, a Scots poet, kept a careful record of his 1619 conversations with playwright Ben Jonson. The "Conversations," first printed in 1711 in The Works of William Drummond, of Hawthornden, *are in* Ben Jonson, *volume one (1925), edited by C. H. Herford and Percy Simpson. Because Drummond's original manuscript has been lost, Herford and Simpson's source for the following excerpt is an early-eighteenth-century transcript by Sir Robert Sibbald. The first comment is from a list of Jonson's brief assessments of his contemporaries; the second comment is from a later list in which Jonson critiques individual works by his contemporaries. Drummond*

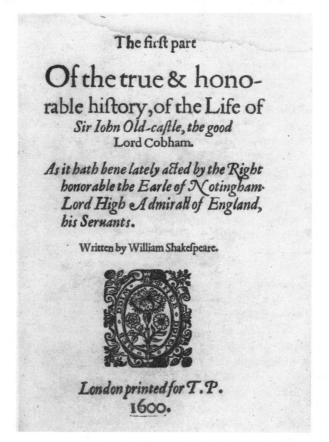

Title page for a quarto that was actually published in 1619. Despite the credit to Shakespeare, the play was written by Anthony Munday, Michael Drayton, Robert Wilson, and Richard Hathway (by permission of the Folger Shakespeare Library).

kept a log of his reading; in 1606, the list includes "Romeo and Julieta Tragedie, loves labors lost comedie, The passionat pilgrime, The rape of lucrece, *and* A midsommers nights Dreame comedie" (*Hawthornden manuscripts 2059, ff. 359–367; transcribed in* The Library of Drummond of Hawthornden, *edited by Robert H. Macdonald [1971]). Drummond's 1611 catalogue of his library includes these entries:* "a midsumers night dreame"; "the tragedies of Romeo & Julieta"; "the rap of Lucrece idem"; *and* "Venus & Adon. by Schaksp" (*Macdonald, p. 200).*

Informations be Ben Johnston
to W. D. When he came to Scotland upon foot
1619

[*Marginal note:*] of Shakspear

That Shaksperr wanted Arte
—*Ben Jonson*, vol. I, pp. 132–133

Sheakspear in a play brought in a number of men saying they had suffered Shipwrack in Bohemia, wher y[r] is no Sea neer by some 100 Miles.
—*Ben Jonson*, vol. I, p. 138

1620

Publication

Venus and Adonis, *published at least six times previously, is published again.*

VENVS / *AND* / ADONIS. / *Vilia miretur vulgus, mihi flauus Apollo, / Pocula Caſtalia plena miniſtret aqua.* / LONDON, / Printed for *I. P.* 1620.

1621

Stationers' Register Entry

Othello *is entered with the Stationers (Stationer's Hall, Register D, page 21). Abbreviated words have been silently expanded in the transcription.*

6°. Octobris. 1621
Thomas Walkley Entred for his copie under the handes of S[r]. George Buck, and M[r] Swinhowe warden, The Tragedie of Othello, the moore of Venice.   vi[d]
—*Bibliography of the English Printed Drama*, vol. I, p. 32

1622

Publications

Three previously published plays by Shakespeare are published again: Richard III *(1597, 1598, 1602, 1605, 1612),* Romeo and Juliet *(1597, 1599, 1609), and* Henry IV *(1598, 1599, 1604, 1608, 1613). Also, the first edition of* Othello *is published.*

THE / TRAGEDIE / *OF* / KING RICHARD / *THE THIRD.* / Contayning his treacherous Plots againſt / *his brother* Clarence: *The pittifull murder of his innocent* / Nephewes: his tyrannicall Vſurpation: with the whole / courſe of his deteſted life, and moſt / *deſerved death.* / As it hath been lately Acted by the Kings Maieſties / Seruants. / Newly augmented. / By *William Shake-ſpeare.* / [*Printer's device*] / LONDON, / Printed by *Thomas Purfoot,* and are to be ſold by *Mathew Law,* dwelling / in *Pauls* Church-yard, at the Signe of the *Foxe,* neere / S. *Auſtines* gate, 1622.

Two editions of Romeo and Juliet *were published, one of which names Shakespeare as author of the play.*

THE MOST / EXCELLENT / And Lamentable Tragedie, / of ROMEO and / IVLIET. / As it hath beene ſundrie times publikely Acted, / by the KINGS Maieſties Seruants / at the GLOBE. / *Newly Corrected, augmented, and amended.* / [*Printer's device*] / *LONDON,* / Printed for *Iohn Smethwicke,* and are to bee ſold at his Shop in / Saint *Dunſtanes* Church-yard, in Fleeteſtreete / vnder the Dyall.

THE MOST / EXCELLENT / And Lamentable Tragedie, / of ROMEO and / IVLIET. / As it hath beene ſundrie times publikely Acted, / by the KINGS Maieſties Seruants / at the GLOBE. / Written by *W. Shake-ſpeare.* / *Newly Corrected, augmented, and amended.* / [*Printer's device*] / *LONDON,* / Printed for *Iohn Smethwicke,* and are to bee ſold at his Shop in / Saint *Dunſtanes* Church-yard, in Fleeteſtreete / vnder the Dyall.

THE / HISTORIE / *OF* / Henry the Fourth. / With the Battell at *Shrewſeburie,* betweene / the King, and Lord *Henry Percy,* ſurnamed / *Henry Hotſpur of the North.* / With the humorous conceits of Sir / *Iohn Falſtaffe.* / Newly corrected. / By *William Shake-ſpeare.* / [*Printer's device*] / LONDON, / Printed by *T. P.* and are to be ſold by *Mathew Law,* dwelling / in *Pauls* Church-yard, at the Signe of the *Foxe,* neere / S. *Auſtines* gate, 1622.

Epistle to the Reader from *Othello*

The printer Thomas Walkley wrote the preface for the 1622 edition of Othello.

The Stationer to the Reader.

To set forth a booke without an Epistle, were like to the old English proverbe, A blew coat without a badge, *& the Author being dead, I thought good to take that piece of worke upon mee: To commend it, I will not, for that which is good, I hope every man will commend, without intreaty: and I am the bolder, because the Authors name is sufficient to vent his worke. Thus leaving every one to the liberty of judgement: I have ventered to print this Play, and leave it to the generall censure.*

Yours,
Thomas Walkley.

—sig. A2r

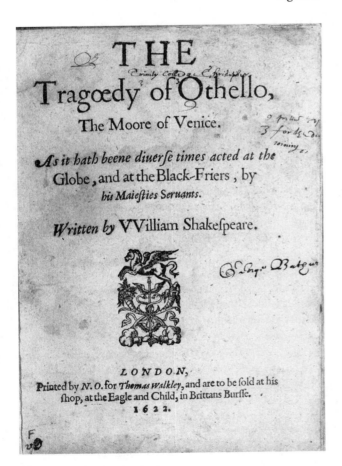

Title page for the first quarto of Othello. *There are hundreds of textual variants between this quarto and the First Folio text, published a year later (by permission of the Folger Shakespeare Library).*

1623

Anne Hathaway's Burial

Anne Hathaway's burial is recorded in the register of Holy Trinity Church in Stratford.

[1623]	Mʳˢ Shakspeare
Aug 8.	Anna uxor Richardi James.

—Lewis, Shakespeare Documents, *vol II., p. 580*

This entry may indicate that Anne Hathaway remarried, but no record of a second marriage survives. It is also possible that two women named Anne were buried on 8 August and that the records were bracketed by the clerk.

It is possible that the epitaph on Anne Hathaway's grave in Holy Trinity Church was composed by her daughter Susanna, who was described in her own epitaph as "Witty above her sexe." The translation of the Latin text is still contended; the translation used here is that of Lewis.

Heere lyeth interred the body of Anne wife
of William Shakespeare who departed this life the
6ᵗʰ day of August: 1623 ß Being of the age of ß 67 ß
yeares

Ubera, tu mater, tu lac, vitamque dedisti.
    Væ mihi: pro tanto munere saxa dabo.
Quam mallem, amoveat lapidem, bonus angelus orem
    Exeatᵘᵗ, christi corpus, imago tua
Sed nil vota valent. venias citò Christe resurget
    Clausa licet tumulo mater et astra petet.

[Thou, mother, gavest [me] breasts, milk, and life. Woe [is] me! for so great a bounty I shall give [thee] stones [a tomb]. How much rather I would entreat the good angel would move the stone, so that thy figure might come forth as did [like] the body of Christ. But my prayers avail nothing. Come quickly, O Christ, so that my mother, [now] lying closed in the tomb, may rise again and seek the stars.]

—Lewis, Shakespeare Documents, *vol. II, pp. 581–582*

Stationers' Register Entries

The plays to be included in the First Folio are entered with the Stationers (Stationer's Hall, Register D, page 69). Greg notes that the "sum 'viî' is added in a different ink. It should normally have been 8s."

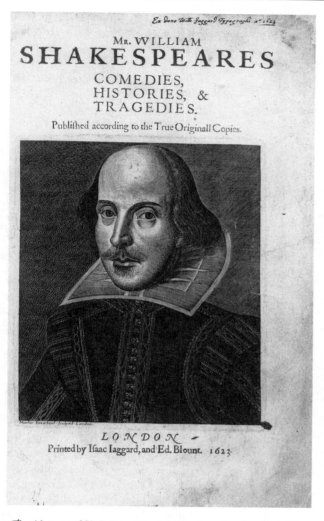

The title page of Shakespeare's collected works, referred to as the First Folio (by permission of the Folger Shakespeare Library)

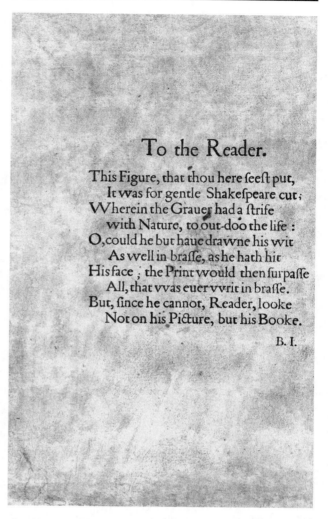

Ben Jonson's prefatory note, referring to the likeness of Shakespeare on the title page of the First Folio (by permission of the Folger Shakespeare Library)

8⁰ Novembris. 1623 . . .

Mʳ. Blounte   Isaak Jaggard. Entred for their Copie under the hands of Mʳ. Doʳ. Worrall and Mʳ. Cole warden Mʳ. William Shakspeers Comedyes Histories, & Tragedyes soe manie of the said Copies as are not formerly entred to other men. vizᵗ.

Comedyes.	Histories
The Tempest	The thirde parte of Henry yᵉ sixt
The two gentlemen of Verona	Henry the eight
Measure for Measure	Tragedies.
The Comedy of Errors	Coriolanus
As you like it	Timon of Athens
All's well that ends well	Julius Cæsar
Twelfe night	Mackbeth
The winters tale	Anthonie & Cleopatra
	Cymbeline

—Bibliography of the English Printed Drama, vol. I, p. 33

Preliminary Material in the First Folio

The preliminary matter for Mʳ William Shakespeares Comedies, Histories, & Tragedies *(1623)* consists of a short poem by Ben Jonson addressed "To the Reader" and commenting on the engraving of Shakespeare on the facing page; a letter from John Heminges and Henry Condell, the two actors from Shakespeare's company who collected the plays for publication in the First Folio, addressed to the Folio's patrons William Herbert Earl of Pembroke, the current Lord Chamberlain, and his brother Philip Herbert, Earl of Montgomery; another letter from Heminges and Condell addressed "To the great Variety of Readers"; commendatory verses by Jonson, poets Hugh Holland and Leonard Digges, and "I. M," who is probably the translator James Mabbe; a table of contents; and a list of the "Principall Actors in all these Playes."

TO THE MOST NOBLE
AND
INCOMPARABLE PAIRE
OF BRETHREN.

WILLIAM
Earle of Pembroke, &c. Lord Chamberlaine to the
Kings most Excellent Majesty.

AND
PHILIP

Earle of Montgomery, &c. Gentleman of his Majesties
Bed-Chamber. Both Knights of the most Noble Order
of the Garter, and our singular good
LORDS.

Right Honourable,

*Whilst we studie to be thankful in our particular, for the
many favors we have received from your L.L we are falne upon
the ill fortune, to mingle two the most diverse things that can bee,
feare, and rashnesse; rashnesse in the enterprize, and feare of the
successe. For, when we valew the places your H. H. sustaine, we
cannot but know their dignity greater, then to descend to the reading of these trifles: and, while we name them trifles, we have
depriv'd our selves of the defence of our Dedication. But since
your L.L. have beene pleas'd to thinke these trifles some-thing,
heeretofore; and have prosequuted both them, and their Authour
living, with so much favour: we hope, that (they out-living him,
and he not having the fate, common with some, to be exequutor to
his owne writings) you will use the like indulgence toward them,
you have done unto their parent. There is a great difference,
whether any Booke choose his Patrones, or finde them: This hath
done both. For, so much were your L L. likings of the severall
parts, when they were acted, as before they were published, the
Volume ask'd to be yours. We have but collected them, and done
an office to the dead, to procure his Orphanes, Guardians; without ambition either of selfe-profit, or fame: onely to keepe the
memory of so worthy a Friend, & Fellow alive, as was our
SHAKESPEARE, by humble offer of his playes, to your most noble
patronage. Wherein, as we have justly observed, no man to come
neere your L.L. but with a kind of religious addresse; it hath bin
the height of our care, who are the Presenters, to make the present
worthy of your H.H. by the perfection. But, there we must also
crave our abilities to be considerd, my Lords. We cannot go
beyond our owne powers. Country hands reach foorth milke,
creame, fruites, or what they have: and many Nations (we have
heard) that had not gummes & incense, obtained their requests
with a leavened Cake. It was no fault to approch their Gods, by
what meanes they could: And the most, though meanest, of things
are made more precious, when they are dedicated to Temples. In
that name therefore, we most humbly consecrate to your H.H.
these remaines of your servant Shakespeare; that what delight*

*is in them, may be ever your L.L. the reputation his, & the faults
ours, if any be committed, by a payre so carefull to shew their
gratitude both to the living, and the dead, as is*

Your Lordshippes most bounden,

JOHN HEMINGE.
HENRY CONDELL.

*Heminges and Condell expected a wide audience for the
First Folio and did their best to teach a range of readers how to
approach Shakespeare's plays. Their first piece of advice—buy the
book—is a good marketing tactic; their explanation of their efforts
to find the best possible texts and their wish that Shakespeare
were still alive to supervise the publication of the Folio marks the
beginning of hundreds of years of editorial efforts to come as close
as possible to Shakespeare's manuscripts; their praise of Shakespeare's artistry and their insistence that he be read and reread
until readers can generate that praise for themselves shows their
confidence in the power of Shakespeare's language to survive the
transition from stage to page.*

To the great Variety of Readers.

From the most able, to him that can but spell:
There you are number'd. We had rather you were
weighd. Especially, when the fate of all Bookes depends
upon your capacities: and not of your heads alone, but
of your purses. Well! It is now publique, & you wil
stand for your priviledges wee know: to read, and censure. Do so, but buy it first. That doth best commend a
Booke, the Stationer saies. Then, how odde soever
your braines be, or your wisedomes, make your licence
the same, and spare not. Judge your sixe-pen'orth, your
shillings worth, your five shillings worth at a time, or
higher, so you rise to the just rates, and welcome. But,
what ever you do, Buy. Censure will not drive a Trade,
or make the Jacke go. And though you be a Magistrate
of wit, and sit on the Stage at *Black-Friers*, or the *Cock-pit*,
to arraigne Playes dailie, know, these Playes have had
their triall alreadie, and stood out all Appeales; and do
now come forth quitted rather by a Decree of Court,
then any purchas'd Letters of commendation.

It had bene a thing, we confesse, worthie to have
bene wished, that the Author himselfe had liv'd to have
set forth, and overseen his owne writings; But since it
hath bin ordain'd otherwise, and he by death departed
from that right, we pray you do not envie his Friends,
the office of their care, and paine, to have collected &
publish'd them; and so to have publish'd them, as
where (before) you were abus'd with diverse stolne,
and surreptitious copies, maimed, and deformed by the
frauds and stealthes of injurious impostors, that expos'd
them: even those, are now offer'd to your view cur'd,

To the great Variety of Readers.

Rom the most able, to him that can but spell: There you are number'd. We had rather you were weighd. Especially, when the fate of all Bookes depends vpon your capacities : and not of your heads alone, but of your purses. Well! It is now publique, & you wil stand for your priuiledges wee know: to read, and censure. Do so, but buy it first. That doth best commend a Booke, the Stationer saies. Then, how odde soeuer your braines be, or your wisedomes, make your licence the same, and spare not. Iudge your sixe-pen'orth, your shillings worth, your fiue shillings worth at a time, or higher, so you rise to the iust rates, and welcome. But, what euer you do, Buy. Censure will not driue a Trade, or make the Iacke go. And though you be a Magistrate of wit, and sit on the Stage at *Black-Friers*, or the *Cock-pit*, to arraigne Playes dailie, know, these Playes haue had their triall alreadie, and stood out all Appeales ; and do now come forth quitted rather by a Decree of Court, then any purchas'd Letters of commendation.

It had bene a thing, we confesse, worthie to haue bene wished, that the Author him selfe had liu'd to haue set forth, and ouerseen his owne writings ; But since it hath bin ordain'd otherwise, and he by death departed from that right, we pray you do not envie his Friends, the office of their care, and paine, to haue collected & publish'd them ; and so to haue publish'd them, as where (before) you were abus'd with diuerse stolne, and surreptitious copies, maimed, and deformed by the frauds and stealthes of iniurious impostors, that expos'd them : euen those, are now offer'd to your view cur'd, and perfect of their limbes ; and all the rest, absolute in their numbers, as he conceiued thē. Who, as he was a happie imitator of Nature, was a most gentle expresser of it. His mind and hand went together: And what he thought, he vttered with that easinesse, that wee haue scarse receiued from him a blot in his papers. But it is not our prouince, who onely gather his works, and giue them you, to praise him. It is yours that reade him. And there we hope, to your diuers capacities, you will finde enough, both to draw, and hold you : for his wit can no more lie hid, then it could be lost. Reade him, therefore ; and againe, and againe : And if then you doe not like him, surely you are in some manifest danger, not to vnderstand him. And so we leaue you to other of his Friends, whom if you need, can bee your guides : if you neede them not, you can leade your selues, and others. And such Readers we wish him.

A 3   *Iohn Heminge.*
                        Henrie Condell.

The address to the readers of the First Folio (by permission of the Folger Shakespeare Library) and perfect of their limbes; and all the rest, absolute in their numbers, as he conceived them. Who, as he was a happie imitator of Nature, was a most gentle expresser of it. His mind and hand went together: And what he thought, he uttered with that easinesse, that wee have scarse received from him a blot in his papers. But it is not our province, who onely gather his works, and give them you, to praise him. It is yours that reade him. And there we hope, to your divers capacities, you will finde enough, both to draw, and hold you: for his wit can no more lie hid, then it could be lost. Reade him, there-fore; and againe, and againe: And if then you doe not like him, surely you are in some manifest danger, not to understand him. And so we leave you to other of his Friends, whom if you need, can bee your guides: if you neede them not, you can leade your selves, and others. And such Readers we wish him.

John Heminge.
Henrie Condell.

Shakespeare's friend and rival Ben Jonson here offers a critical essay in rhyme. He discusses Shakespeare's learning (not enough of it to please the classically inclined Jonson); places him in the context of his contemporary writers; uses the example of Shakespeare to settle the question of whether poets are born or made; and invents several memorable phrases that are still used to describe Shakespeare.

To the memory of my beloved,
The AUTHOR
MR. WILLIAM SHAKESPEARE:
AND
what he hath left us.

To draw no envy (Shakespeare) *on thy name,*
  Am I thus ample to thy Booke, and Fame:
While I confesse thy writings to be such,
  As neither Man, *nor* Muse, *can praise too much.*
Tis true, and all mens suffrage. But these wayes
  Were not the paths I meant unto thy praise:
For seeliest Ignorance on these may light,
  Which, when it sounds at best, but eccho's right;
Or blinde Affection, which doth ne're advance
  The truth, but gropes, and urgeth all by chance;
Or crafty Malice, might pretend this praise,
  And thinke to ruine, where it seem'd to raise.
These are, as some infamous Baud, or Whore,
  Should praise a Matron. What could hurt her more?
But thou art proofe against them, and indeed
  Above th'ill fortune of them, or the need.
I, therefore will begin. Soule of the Age!
  The applause! delight! the wonder of our Stage!
My Shakespeare, *rise; I will not lodge thee by*

Abraham van Blyenberch's portrait of Ben Jonson (courtesy of The National Portrait Gallery, London)

Chaucer, *or* Spenser, *or bid* Beaumont *lye*
A little further, to make thee a roome:
  Thou are a Moniment, without a tombe,
And art alive still, while thy Booke doth live,
  And we have wits to read, and praise to give.
That I not mixe thee so, my braine excuses;
  I meane with great, but disproportion'd Muses:
For, if I thought my judgement were of yeeres,
  I should commit thee surely with thy peeres,
And tell, how farre thou didst our Lily *out-shine,*
  Or sporting Kid, *or* Marlowes *mighty line.*
And though thou hadst small Latine, *and lesse* Greeke,
  From thence to honour thee, I would not seeke
For names; but call forth thund'ring Æschilus,
  Euripides, *and* Sophocles *to us,*
Paccuvius, Accius, *him of* Cordova *dead,*
  To life againe, to heare thy Buskin tread,
And shake a Stage: Or, when thy Sockes were on,
  Leave thee alone, for the comparison
Of all, that insolent Greece, *or haughtie* Rome
  sent forth, or since did from their ashes come.
Triumph, my Britaine, *thou hast one to showe,*
  To whom all Scenes of Europe *homage owe.*
He was not of an age, but for all time!
  And all the Muses *still were in their prime,*
When like Apollo *he came forth to warme*
  Our eares, or like a Mercury *to charme!*
Nature her selfe was proud of his designes,
  And joy'd to weare the dressing of his lines!

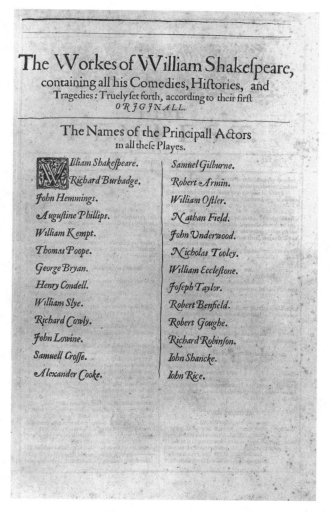

The Workes of William Shakespeare,
containing all his Comedies, Histories, and
Tragedies: Truely set forth, according to their first
ORIGINALL.

The Names of the Principall Actors
in all these Playes.

William Shakespeare.   Samuel Gilburne.
Richard Burbadge.   Robert Armin.
John Hemmings.   William Ostler.
Augustine Phillips.   Nathan Field.
William Kempt.   John Underwood.
Thomas Poope.   Nicholas Tooley.
George Bryan.   William Ecclestone.
Henry Condell.   Joseph Taylor.
William Slye.   Robert Benfield.
Richard Cowly.   Robert Goughe.
John Lowine.   Richard Robinson.
Samuell Crosse.   Iohn Shancke.
Alexander Cooke.   Iohn Rice.

*The list of the actors who performed the plays collected in the Shakespeare First Folio
(by permission of the Folger Shakespeare Library)*

Which were so richly spun, and woven so fit,
  As, since, she will vouchsafe no other Wit.
The merry Greeke, *tart* Aristophanes,
  Neat Terence, *witty* Plautus, *now not please;*
But antiquated, and deserted lye
  As they were not of Natures family.
Yet must I not give Nature all: Thy Art,
  My gentle Shakespeare, *must enjoy a part.*
For though the Poets *matter, Nature be,*
  His Art doth give the fashion. And, that he,
Who casts to write a living line, must sweat,
  (such as thine are) and strike the second heat
Upon the Muses *anvile: turne the same,*
  (And himselfe with it) that he thinkes to frame;
Or for the lawrell, he may gaine a scorne,
  For a good Poet's *made, as well as borne.*
And such wert thou. Looke how the fathers face

Lives in his issue, even so, the race
Of Shakespeares *minde, and manners brightly shines*
  In his well torned, and true-filed lines:
In each of which, he seemes to shake a Lance,
  As brandish't at the eyes of Ignorance.
Sweet Swan of Avon! *what a sight it were*
  To see thee in our waters yet appeare,
And make those flights upon the bankes of Thames,
  That so did take Eliza, *and our* James!
But stay, I see thee in the Hemisphere
  Advanc'd, and made a Constellation there!
Shine forth, thou Starre of Poets, *and with rage,*
  Or influence, chide, or cheere the drooping Stage;
Which, since thy flight from hence, hath mourn'd like night,
  And despaires day, but for thy Volumes light.

BEN: JONSON.

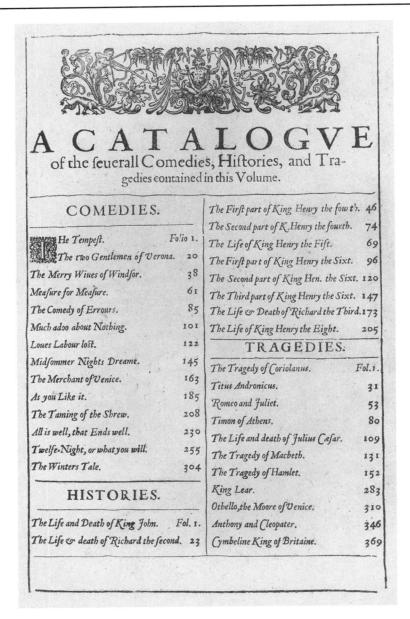

A CATALOGVE
of the feuerall Comedies, Hiftories, and Tragedies contained in this Volume.

COMEDIES.

He Tempeſt.	Folio 1.
The two Gentlemen of Verona.	20
The Merry Wiues of Windsor.	38
Meaſure for Meaſure.	61
The Comedy of Errours.	85
Much adoo about Nothing.	101
Loues Labour loſt.	122
Midſommer Nights Dreame.	145
The Merchant of Venice.	163
As you Like it.	185
The Taming of the Shrew.	208
All is well, that Ends well.	230
Twelfe-Night, or what you will.	255
The Winters Tale.	304

HISTORIES.

The Life and Death of King John.	Fol. 1.
The Life & death of Richard the second.	23

The Firſt part of King Henry the fourth.	46
The Second part of K. Henry the fourth.	74
The Life of King Henry the Fift.	69
The Firſt part of King Henry the Sixt.	96
The Second part of King Hen. the Sixt.	120
The Third part of King Henry the Sixt.	147
The Life & Death of Richard the Third.	173
The Life of King Henry the Eight.	205

TRAGEDIES.

The Tragedy of Coriolanus.	Fol.1.
Titus Andronicus.	31
Romeo and Juliet.	53
Timon of Athens.	80
The Life and death of Julius Cæsar.	109
The Tragedy of Macbeth.	131
The Tragedy of Hamlet.	152
King Lear.	283
Othello, the Moore of Venice.	310
Anthony and Cleopater.	346
Cymbeline King of Britaine.	369

The table of contents for the First Folio. Troilus and Cressida *was included between* The Life of King Henry the Eight *and* The Tragedy of Coriolanus, *although it is not listed (by permission of the Folger Shakespeare Library).*

Poet Hugh Holland provides a conventional encomium.

Upon the Lines and Life of the Famous
Scenicke Poet, Master WILLIAM
SHAKESPEARE.

Those hands, which you so clapt, go now, and wring
You *Britaines* brave; for done are *Shakespeares* dayes:
His dayes are done, that made the dainty Playes,
Which made the Globe of heav'n and earth to ring.
Dry'de is that veine, dry'd is the *Thespian* Spring,

Turn'd all to teares, and *Phoebus* clouds his rayes:
That corp's, that coffin now besticke those bayes,
Which crown'd him *Poet* first, then *Poets* King.
If *Tragedies* might any *Prologue* have,
All those he made, would scarse make one to this:
Where *Fame*, now that he gone is to the grave
(Deaths publique tyring-house) the *Nuncius* is.
 For though his line of life went soone about,
 The life yet of his lines shall never out.

HUGH HOLLAND.

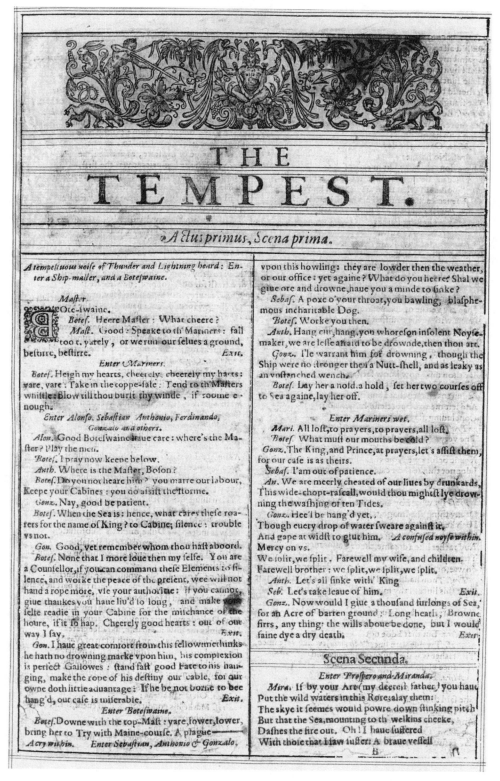

The first page of the first play in the First Folio (by permission of the Folger Shakespeare Library)

the Moore of Venice. 339

*Caf.*This did I feare, but thought he had no weapon:
For he was great of heart.
  Lod. Oh Sparton Dogge:
More fell then Anguish, Hunger, or the Sea:
Looke on the Tragicke Loading of this bed:
This is thy worke:
The Obiect poyfons Sight,

Let it be hid. *Gratiano,* keepe the houfe,
And feize vpon the Fortunes of the Moore,
For they fucceede on you. To you, Lord Gouernor,
Remaines th'eCenfure of this hellifh villaine:
The Time, the Place, the Torture, oh inforce it:
My felfe will ftraight aboord, and to the State,
This heauie Act, with heauie heart relate. *Exeunt.*

FINIS.

The Names of the Actors.
(:*⋆*:)

Thello, *the Moore.*
Brabantio, *Father to Defdemona.*
Caffio, *an Honourable Lieutenant.*
Iago, *a Villaine.*
Rodorigo, *a gull'd Gentleman.*
Duke of Venice.

Senators.
Montano, *Gouernour of Cyprus.*
Gentlemen of Cyprus.
Lodouico, *and* Gratiano, *two Noble Venetians.*
Saylors.
Clowne.

Defdemona, *wife to Othello.*
Æmilia, *wife to Iago.*
Bianca, *a Curtezan.*

The last page of Othello *in the First Folio. Some of the plays in the volume are followed by a list of the characters of the play
(by permission of the Folger Shakespeare Library).*

Poet Leonard Digges had previously expressed his appreciation of Shakespeare in his 1613 inscription to Lope de Vegas Rimas.

TO THE MEMORIE
of the deceased Authour Maister
W. Shakespeare.

Shake-speare, *at length thy pious fellowes give*
The world thy Workes: *thy* Workes, *by which, out-live*
Thy Tombe, *thy name must when that stone is rent,*
And Time dissolves thy Stratford *Moniment,*
Here we alive shall view thee still. This Booke,
When Brasse and Marble fade, shall make thee looke
Fresh to all Ages: when Posteritie
Shall loath what's new, thinke all is prodegie
That is not Shake-speares; *ev'ry Line, each Verse*
Here shall revive, redeeme thee from thy Herse.
Nor Fire, nor cankring Age, as Naso *said,*
Of his, thy wit-fraught Booke shall once invade.
Nor shall I e're beleeve, or thinke thee dead
(Though mist) untill our bankrout Stage be sped
(Impossible) with some new straine t'out-do
Passions of Juliet, *and her* Romeo;
Or till I heare a Scene more nobly take,
Then when thy half-Sword parlying Romans *spake.*
Till these, till any of thy Volumes rest
Shall with more fire, more feeling be exprest,
Be sure, our Shake-speare, *thou canst never dye,*
But crown'd with Lawrell, *live eternally.*

L. Digges.

I. M. is probably the translator James Mabbe.

To the memorie of M. *W. Shake-speare.*

WEE *wondred* (Shake-speare) *that thou went'st so soone*
From the Worlds-Stage, to the Graves-Tyring-roome.
Wee thought thee dead, but this thy printed worth,
Tels thy Spectators, that thou went'st but forth
To enter with applause. An Actors Art,
Can dye, and live, to acte a second part.
That's but an Exit *of Mortalitie;*
This, a Re-entrance to a Plaudite.

I. M.

Jonson's *Timber, or Discoveries*

In this passage from his collection of notes and observations, Timber, or Discoveries, *Ben Jonson complains that Shakespeare did not spend enough time editing or rewriting his work; he also comments on Shakespeare's personality.* Timber

was first printed in the 1640 edition of Jonson's Workes. *On the discrepancy between Jonson's "Caesar did never wrong, but with just cause" and Shakespeare's "Know, Caesar doth not wrong, nor without cause / Will he be satisfied"* (Julius Caesar, *3.1.47–48) see Herford and Simpson's note in* Ben Jonson *(vol. XI, pp. 231–232).*

[Marginal note: *De Shakespeare nostrat.*]

I remember, the Players have often mentioned it as an honour to *Shakespeare,* that in his writing, (whatsoever he penn'd) hee never blotted out line. My answer hath beene, Would he had blotted a thousand. Which they thought a malevolent speech. I had not told posterity this, but for their ignorance, who choose that circumstance to commend their friend by, wherein he most faulted. And to justifie mine owne candor, (for I lov'd the man, and doe honour his memory (on this side Idolatry) as much as any.) Hee was (indeed) honest, and of an open, and free nature: had an excellent *Phantsie*; brave notions, and gentle expressions: wherein hee flow'd with that facility, that sometime it was necessary he should be stop'd: *Sufflaminandus erat*; as *Augustus* said of *Haterius.* [Marginal note: *Augustus in Hat.*] His wit was in his owne power; would the rule of it had beene so too. Many times hee fell into those things, could not escape laughter: As when hee said in the person of *Cæsar,* one speaking to him; *Cæsar thou dost me wrong.* Hee replyed: *Cæsar did never wrong, but with just cause*: and such like; which were ridiculous. But hee redeemed his vices, with his vertues. There was ever more in him to be praysed, then to be pardoned.
                    —Ben Jonson, vol. VIII, pp. 97–98

Epistle to the Reader and Commendatory Verse from *Poems: Written By Wil. Shakespeare. Gent.*

Poems: Written By Wil. Shakespeare. Gent. *(1640) includes words of praise for Shakespeare from publisher John Benson and from poet Leonard Digges, one of the writers who commended him seventeen years before in the First Folio. Benson's praise is fulsome, showing Shakespeare's reputation was far from fading; Digges's poem is a refutation of some of Ben Jonson's less favorable assertions about Shakespeare's artistry in his commendatory poem in the 1623 First Folio.*

To the Reader.

I Here presume (under favour) to present to your view, some excellent and sweetely composed Poems, of Master *William Shakespeare,* Which in themselves appeare of the same purity, the Authour himselfe then living

232   *The Life of King Henry the Eight.*

Holy and Heauenly thoughts still Counsell her:
She shall be lou'd and fear'd. Her owne shall blesse her;
Her Foes shake like a Field of beaten Corne,
And hang their heads with sorrow:
Good growes with her.
In her dayes, Euery Man shall eate in safety,
Vnder his owne Vine what he plants; and sing
The merry Songs of Peace to all his Neighbours.
God shall be truely knowne, and those about her,
From her shall read the perfect way of Honour,
And by those claime their greatnesse;not by Blood.
Nor shall this peace sleepe with her: But as when
The Bird of Wonder dyes, the Mayden Phoenix,
Her Ashes new create another Heyre,
As great in admiration as her selfe.
So shall she leaue her Blessednesse to One,
(When Heauen shal call her from this clowd of darknes)
Who,from the sacred Ashes of her Honour
Shall Star-like rise,as great in fame as she was,
And so stand fix'd. Peace, Plenty,Loue, Truth, Terror,
That were the Seruants to this chosen Infant,
Shall then be his, and like a Vine grow to him;
Where euer the bright Sunne of Heauen shall shine,
His Honour,and the greatnesse of his Name,
Shall be,and make new Nations. He shall flourish,

And like a Mountaine Cedar, reach his branches,
To all the Plaines about him: Our Childrens Children
Shall see this,and blesse Heauen.
  Kin. Thou speakest wonders.
  Cran. She shall be to the happinesse of England,
An aged Princesse; many dayes shall see her,
And yet no day without a deed to Crowne it.
Would I had knowne no more: But she must dye,
She must, the Saints must haue her; yet a Virgin,
A most vnspotted Lilly shall she passe
To th' ground, and all the World shall mourne her.
  Kin. O Lord Archbishop
Thou hast made me now a man, neuer before
This happy Child, did I get any thing.
This Oracle of comfort, ha's so pleas'd me,
That when I am in Heauen, I shall desire
To see what this Child does, and praise my Maker.
I thanke ye all. To you my good Lord Maior,
And you good Brethren, I am much beholding:
I haue receiu'd much Honour by your presence,
And ye shall find me thankfall. Lead the way Lords,
Ye must all see the Queene, and she must thanke ye,
She will be sicke els. This day, no man thinke
'Has businesse at his house; for all shall stay:
This Little-One shall make it Holy-day.   *Exeunt.*

THE EPILOGVE.

'Tis ten to one, this Play can neuer please
  All that are heere: Some come to take their ease,
And sleepe an Act or two; but those we feare
W' haue frighted with our Trumpets: so 'tis cleare,
They'l say tis naught. Others to heare the City
Abus'd extreamly,and to cry that's witty,
Which wee haue not done neither; that I feare

All the expected good w' are like to heare.
For this Play at this time, is onely in
The mercifull construction of good women,
For such a one we shew'd 'em: If they smile,
And say twill doe; I know within a while,
  All the best men are ours; for 'tis ill hap,
  If they hold, when their Ladies bid 'em clap.

FINIS.

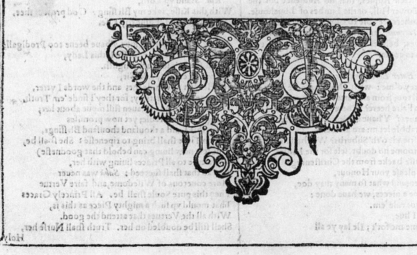

The Epilogue to Shakespeare's Henry VIII *in the First Folio, in which reasons are offered for attending a play
(by permission of the Folger Shakespeare Library)*

The Tragedie of Hamlet.　　265

With turbulent and dangerous Lunacy.

Rosin. He does confesse he feeles himselfe distracted,
But from what cause he will by no meanes speake.

Guil. Nor do we finde him forward to be sounded,
But with a crafty Madnesse keepes aloofe:
When we would bring him on to some Confession
Of his true state.

Qu. Did he receiue you well?

Rosin. Most like a Gentleman.

Guild. But with much forcing of his disposition.

Rosin. Niggard of question, but of our demands
Most free in his reply.

Qu. Did you assay him to any pastime?

Rosin. Madam, it so fell out, that certaine Players
We ore-wrought on the way: of these we told him,
And there did seeme in him a kinde of ioy
To heare of it: They are about the Court,
And (as I thinke) they haue already order
This night to play before him.

Pol. 'Tis most true:
And he beseech'd me to intreate your Maiesties
To heare, and see the matter.

King. With all my heart, and it doth much content me
To heare him so inclin'd. Good Gentlemen,
Giue him a further edge, and driue his purpose on
To these delights.

Rosin. We shall my Lord.　　　　　　　*Exeunt.*

King. Sweet *Gertrude* leaue vs too,
For we haue closely sent for *Hamlet* hither,
That he, as 'twere by accident, may there
Affront *Ophelia.* Her Father, and my selfe (lawful espials)
Will so bestow our selues, that seeing vnseene
We may of their encounter frankely iudge,
And gather by him, as he is behaued,
If t be th'affliction of his loue, or no.
That thus he suffers for.

Qu. I shall obey you,
And for your part *Ophelia*, I do wish
That your good Beauties be the happy cause
Of *Hamlets* wildenesse: so shall I hope your Vertues
Will bring him to his wonted way againe,
To both your Honors.

Ophe. Madam, I wish it may.

Pol. *Ophelia*, walke you heere. Gracious so please ye
We will bestow our selues: Reade on this booke,
That shew of such an exercise may colour
Your lonelinesse. We are oft too blame in this,
'Tis too much prou'd, that with Deuotions visage,
And pious Action, we do surge o're
The diuell himselfe.

King. Oh 'tis true:
How smart a lash that speech doth giue my Conscience?
The Harlots Cheeke beautied with plaist'ring Art
Is not more vgly to the thing that helpes it,
Then is my deede, to my most painted word.
Oh heauie burthen!

Pol. I heare him comming, let's withdraw my Lord.
　　　　　　　　　　　　　　　　Exeunt.

Enter Hamlet.

Ham. To be, or not to be, that is the Question:
Whether 'tis Nobler in the minde to suffer
The Slings and Arrowes of outragious Fortune,
Or to take Armes against a Sea of troubles,
And by opposing end them: to dye, to sleepe
No more; and by a sleepe, to say we end
The Heart-ake, and the thousand Naturall shockes

That Flesh is heyre too? 'Tis a consummation
Deuoutly to be wish'd. To dye to sleepe,
To sleepe, perchance to Dreame; I, there's the rub,
For in that sleepe of death, what dreames may come,
When we haue shuffel'd off this mortall coile,
Must giue vs pawse. There's the respect
That makes Calamity of so long life:
For who would beare the Whips and Scornes of time,
The Oppressors wrong, the poore mans Contumely,
The pangs of dispriz'd Loue, the Lawes delay,
The insolence of Office, and the Spurnes
That patient merit of the vnworthy takes,
When he himselfe might his *Quietus* make
With a bare Bodkin? Who would these Fardles beare
To grunt and sweat vnder a weary life,
But that the dread of something after death,
The vndiscouered Countrey, from whose Borne
No Traueller returnes, Puzels the will,
And makes vs rather beare those illes we haue,
Then flye to others that we know not of.
Thus Conscience does make Cowards of vs all,
And thus the Natiue hew of Resolution
Is sicklied o're, with the pale cast of Thought,
And enterprizes of great pith and moment,
With this regard their Currants turne away,
And loose the name of Action. Soft you now,
The faire *Ophelia?* Nimph, in thy Orizons
Be all my sinnes remembred.

Ophe. Good my Lord,
How does your Honor for this many a day?

Ham. I humbly thanke you: well, well, well.

Ophe. My Lord, I haue Remembrances of yours,
That I haue longed long to re-deliuer.
I pray you now, receiue them.

Ham. No, no, I neuer gaue you ought.

Ophe. My honor'd Lord, I know right well you did,
And with them words of so sweet breath compos'd,
As made the things more rich, then perfume left:
Take these againe, for to the Noble minde
Rich gifts wax poore, when giuers proue vnkinde.
There my Lord.

Ham. Ha, ha: Are you honest?

Ophe. My Lord.

Ham. Are you faire?

Ophe. What meanes your Lordship?

Ham. That if you be honest and faire, your Honesty
should admit no discourse to your Beautie.

Ophe. Could Beautie my Lord, haue better Comerce
then your Honestie?

Ham. I trulie: for the power of Beautie, will sooner
transforme Honestie from what it is, to a Bawd, then the
force of Honestie can translate Beautie into his likenesse.
This was sometime a Paradox, but now the time giues it
proofe. I did loue you once.

Ophe. Indeed my Lord, you made me beleeue so.

Ham. You should not haue beleeued me. For vertue
cannot so innoculate our old stocke, but we shall rellish
of it. I loued you not.

Ophe. I was the more deceiued.

Ham. Get thee to a Nunnerie. Why would'st thou
be a breeder of Sinners? I am my selfe indifferent honest,
but yet I could accuse me of such things, that it were better my Mother had not borne me. I am very prowd, re-
uengefull, Ambitious, with more offences at my becke,
then I haue thoughts to put them in imagination, to giue
them shape, or time to acte them in. What should such
　　　　　　　　　　　　　　　　　　　　　　　　Fel-

*Page from the First Folio that includes Hamlet's "To be or not to be" soliloquy
(by permission of the Folger Shakespeare Library)*

avouched; they had not the fortune by reason of their Infancie in his death, to have the due accomodation of proportionable glory, with the rest of his everliving Workes, yet the lines of themselves will afford you a more authentick approbation than my assurance any way can, to invite your allowance, in your perusall you shall finde them *Seren*, cleere and eligantly plaine, such gentle straines as shall recreate and not perplexe your braine, no intricate or cloudy stuffe to puzzell intellect, but perfect eloquence; such as will raise your admiration to his praise: this assurance I know will not differ from your acknowledgement. And certaine I am, my opinion will be seconded by the sufficiency of these ensuing Lines; I have beene somewhat solicitus to bring this forth to the perfect view of all men; and in so doing, glad to be serviceable for the continuance of glory to the deserved Author in these his Poems.

I. B.
—sigs. *2r–v

Upon Master WILLIAM
SHAKESPEARE, the
Deceased Authour, and his
POEMS.

POets are borne not made, when I would prove
This truth, the glad rememberance I must love
Of never dying *Shakespeare*, who alone,
Is argument enough to make that one.
First, that he was a Poet none would doubt,
That heard th'applause of what he sees set out
Imprinted; where thou hast (I will not say)
Reader his Workes for to contrive a Play:
To him twas none) the patterne of all wit,
Art without Art unparaleld as yet.
Next Nature onely helpt him, for looke thorow
This whole Booke, thou shalt find he doth not borrow,
One phrase from Greekes, nor Latines imitate,
Nor once from vulgar Languages Translate,
Nor Plagiari-like from others gleane,
Nor begges he from each witty friend a Scene
To peece his Acts with, all that he doth write,
Is pure his owne, plot, language exquisite.
But oh! what praise more powerfull can we give
The dead, then that by him the Kings men live,
His Players, which should they but have shar'd the Fate,
All else expir'd within the short Termes date;
How could the Globe have prospered, since through want
Of change, the Plaies and Poems had growne scant.
But happy Verse thou shalt be sung and heard,
When hungry quills shall be such honour bard.
Then vanish upstart Writers to each Stage,
You needy Poetasters of this Age,
Where *Shakespeare* liv'd or spake, Vermine forbeare,

Least with your froth you spot them, come not neere;
But if you needs must write, if poverty
So pinch, that otherwise you starve and die,
On Gods name may the Bull or Cockpit have
Your lame blancke Verse, to keepe you from the grave:
Or let new Fortunes younger brethren see,
What they can picke from your leane industry.
I doe not wonder when you offer at
Blacke-Friers, that you suffer: tis the fate
Of richer veines, prime judgements that have far'd
The worse, with this deceased man compar'd.
So have I seene, when Cesar would appeare,
And on the Stage at halfe-sword parley were,
Brutus and *Cassius*: oh how the Audience,
Were ravish'd, with what wonder they went thence,
When some new day they would not brooke a line,
Of tedious (though well laboured) *Catilines*;
Sejanus too was irkesome, they priz'de more
Honest *Iago*, or the jealous Moore.
And though the Fox and subtill Alchimist,
Long intermitted could not quite be mist,
Though these have sham'd all the Ancients, and might raise,
Their Authours merit with a crowne of Bayes.
Yet these sometimes, even at a friends desire
Acted, have scarce defrai'd the Seacoale fire
And doore-keepers: when let but *Falstaffe* come,
Hall, Poines, the rest you scarce shall have a roome
All is so pestered: let but *Beatrice*
And *Benedicke* be seene, loe in a trice
The Cockpit Galleries, Boxes, all are full
To heare *Malvoglio* that crosse garter'd Gull.
Briefe, there is nothing in his wit fraught Booke,
Whose sound he would not heare, on whose worth looke
Like old coynd gold, whose lines in every page,
Shall passe true currant to succeeding age.
But why doe I dead *Shakespeares* praise recite,
Some second *Shakespeare* must of *Shakespeare* write;
For me tis needlesse, since an host of men,
Will pay to clap his praise, to free my Pen.

Leon. Digges.
—sigs. *3r–*4r

Entries from Ward's Diary

The comments of John Ward (1629–1681), vicar of Stratford from 1662 to 1681, are often dismissed as part of the Shakespeare mythology. Skeptics scorn Ward's claims of extravagant profits for the playwright and his account of the drinking party that led to a fever and Shakespeare's death. As the last of the following passages shows, however, Shakespeare's daughter Judith Quiney—Ward's Mrs. Queeny—was still living, and Ward may have known her. Dying from a fever contracted by excessive drinking was also not unheard of in the period. For instance, in his 16 September 1607 letter to John Chamberlain, Dudley Carleton

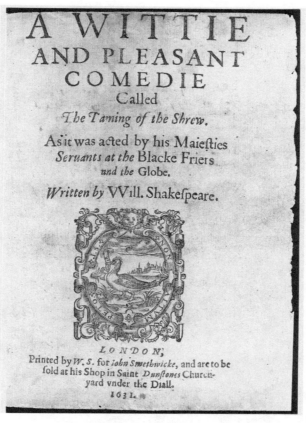

Title page for a quarto published after the 1623 First Folio. Such editions occasionally
provide information about the performance history of a play
(courtesy of the Folger Shakespeare Library).

makes the following report: "Sir William Stone of Cheapside died
on Monday last at his house in Leighton of a fever coming little
short of the plague; he took the infection of a quart of sack which he
drunk of to the king's health the week before" (Dudley Carle-
ton to John Chamberlain 1603–1624: Jacobean Letters
[1972], p. 101). The sixteen volumes of Ward's diary are held in
the Folger Shakespeare Library (MS. V.a.284–299); the follow-
ing excerpts were transcribed by E. K. Chambers.

Shakespear had but 2 daughters, one whereof M. Hall,
yᵉ physitian, married, and by her had one daughter, to
wit yᵉ Lady Bernard of Abbingdon. . . .

   I have heard yᵗ Mʳ. Shakespeare was a natural
wit, without any art at all; hee frequented yᵉ plays all
his younger time, but in his elder days livd at Stratford:
and supplied yᵉ stage with 2 plays every year, and for yᵗ
had an allowance so large, yᵗ hee spent att yᵉ Rate of a
1,000*l.* a year, as I have heard.

   Remem*ber* to peruse Shakespears plays, and bee
versd in *them*, yᵗ I may not bee ignorant in yᵗ matter. . . .

   Shakespear, Drayton, and Ben Jhonson, had a
merry meeting, and itt seems drank too hard, for
Shakespear died of a feavour there contracted. . . .

   A letter to my brother, to see Mrs. Queeny, to
send for Tom Smith for the acknowledgment.
                              —*Facts and Problems,* vol. II, pp. 249–250

Aubrey's *Lives*

   Antiquarian and anecdote collector John Aubrey (1626–
1697) gathered information about many notable sixteenth- and
seventeenth-century figures. Unfortunately, Aubrey never completed
his plan to turn his notes into proper biographies. What follows are
the notes Aubrey collected about Shakespeare. They contain some
intriguing biographical information, and while Aubrey's sources
appear to be generally good, little of what he reports about Shake-
speare can be verified by surviving documents. As he did with his
notes on other poets, Aubrey drew a wreath of bay leaves in the
margin of his notes on Shakespeare. The text is from Oliver Law-
son Dick's edition of Aubrey's Brief Lives (1949).

Mr. William Shakespeare was borne at Stratford upon
Avon in the County of Warwick. His father was a
Butcher, and I have been told heretofore by some of the
neighbours, that when he was a boy he exercised his
father's Trade, but when he kill'd a Calfe he would doe

A performance of Shakespeare's The Tempest *in the reconstructed Globe theater in Southwark, near the site of the original Globe. The new Globe opened for performances in 1997 (copyright 2001 by Donald Cooper, courtesy of Shakespeare's Globe, London).*

it in a high style, and make a Speech. There was at this time another Butcher's son in this Towne that was held not at all inferior to him for a naturall witt, his acquaintance and coetanean, byt dyed young.

This William, being inclined naturally to Poetry and acting, came to London, I guesse about 18: and was an Actor at one of the Play-houses, and did acte exceedingly well: now B. Johnson was never a good Actor, but an excellent Instructor.

He began early to make essayes at Dramatique Poetry, which at that time was very lowe; and his Playes tooke well.

He was a handsome, well-shap't man: very good company, and of a very readie and pleasant smoothe Witt.

The Humour of the Constable in Midsomernight's Dreame, he happened to take at Grendon, in Bucks (I thinke it was Midsomer night that he happened to lye there) which is the roade from London to Stratford, and there was living that Constable about 1642, when I first came to Oxon. Ben Johnson and he did gather Humours of men dayly where ever they came. One time as he was at the Tavern at Stratford super Avon, one Combes, an old rich Usurer, was to be buryed. He makes there this extemporary Epitaph:

Ten in the Hundred the Devill allowes,
But Combes will have twelve he sweares and vowes:
If anyone askes who lies in the Tombe,
Hoh! quoth the Devill, 'Tis my John o' Combe.

He was wont to goe to his native Countrey once a yeare. I thinke I have been told that he left 2 or 300 pounds per annum there and thereabout to a sister.

I have heard Sir William Davenant and Mr. Thomas Shadwell (who is counted the best Comoedian we have now) say that he had a most prodigious Witt, and did admire his naturall parts beyond all other Dramaticall writers.

His Comoedies will remaine witt as long as the English tongue is understood, for that he handles *mores hominum* [the ways of mankind]. Now our present writers reflect so much on particular persons and coxcombeities that twenty yeares hence they will not be understood.

Though, as Ben Johnson sayes of him, that he had little Latine and lesse Greek, He understood Latine pretty well: for he had been in his younger yeares a schoolmaster in the countrey.

He was wont to say that he never blotted out a line in his life. Sayd Ben: Johnson, I wish he had blotted-out a thousand.

—*Aubrey's Brief Lives,* pp. 275–276

Aubrey also writes of Shakespeare in his entry on the dramatist Sir William Davenant.

Sir William Davenant, Knight, Poet Laureate, was borne in the City of Oxford, at the Crowne Taverne. He went to schoole at Oxon to Mr. Sylvester, but I feare he was drawne from schoole before he was ripe enough.

His father was John Davenant, a Vintner there, a very grave and discreet Citizen; his mother was a very beautifull woman and of a very good witt, and of conversation extremely agreable.

Mr. William Shakespeare was wont to goe into Warwickshire once a yeare, and did commonly in his journey lye at this house in Oxon, where he was exceedingly respected. (I have heard Parson Robert say that Mr. William Shakespeare haz given him a hundred kisses.) Now Sir William would sometimes, when he was pleasant over a glasse of wine with his most intimate friends—e.g. Sam Butler, author of *Hudibras,* etc., say, that it seemed to him that he writt with the very spirit that did Shakespeare, and seemed contented enough to be thought his Son. He would tell them the story as above, in which way his mother had a very light report, whereby she was called a Whore.

—*Aubrey's Brief Lives,* p. 85

These notes (Bodleian MSS. Aubrey MS 8, f. 45v) were found in the third part of the manuscript of Aubrey's Brief Lives *and transcribed by Chambers; it is difficult to make sense of them, but Aubrey's source appears to have supplied details about one of Shakespeare's London addresses and to have told Aubrey that Shakespeare preferred a quiet life.*

the more to be admired q[uia] he was not a company
   keeper
lived in Shoreditch, wouldnt be debauched, & if invited to
writ; he was in paine.
     W. Shakespeare.

q[uaere] Mr Beeston who knows most of him fr[om] Mr; *Lacy* (interlined)
he lives in Shore-ditch. *neer Nort* (struck through) at Hoglane
within 6 dores—Norton—folgate.
Q[uaere] etiam B. Jonson.

—*Facts and Problems,* vol. II, p. 252

Appendix

Eyewitnesses and Historians

Politics and the Theater

Regulations for the Theater

Prologues, Epilogues, Epistles to Readers, and Excerpts from Plays

Epigrams and Satires

Anti-Theatrical Tracts

A Defense of Actors

Practical Matters

Education

This appendix records the aesthetic, social, legal, political, and practical aspects of English drama of the period; it is a representative but by no means complete survey of the surviving documents. These documents range from the concise literary criticism many playwrights offered in their prologues to satirical accounts of audience members to detailed arguments from prelates that the theaters must be closed to save London's soul. Church and state regulations on the theater are provided to show the types of regulation and censorship that may have inhibited Shakespeare and his contemporaries. Like the biographical records, these documents tell only part of the story, but they do indicate many of the practical pressures playwrights faced.

Eyewitnesses and Historians

There are dozens of surviving accounts describing visits to professional and amateur theatrical performances in the early modern period. The following selections provide details about the theaters and the audiences for plays by Shakespeare and his contemporaries.

1599

Platter's Observations

Swiss traveler Thomas Platter visited England in 1599 and recorded his observations about many aspects of English life, including popular entertainment. Here he describes two of the theater's main competitors: blood sports, such as cockfighting and bull- and bearbaiting, and public executions. These excerpts are from Thomas Platter's Travels in England 1599 *(1937), edited and translated by Clare Williams.*

There is also in the city of London not far from the horse-market which occupies a large site, a house where cock-fights are held annually throughout three quarters of the year (for in the remaining quarter they told me it was impossible since the feathers are full of blood) and I saw the place which is built like a theatre (theatrum). In the centre on the floor stands a circular table covered with straw and with ledges round it, where the cocks are teased and incited to fly at one another, while those with wagers as to which cock will win, sit closest around the circular disk, but the spectators who are merely present on their entrance penny sit around higher up, watching with eager pleasure the fierce and angry fight between the cocks, as these wound each other to death with spurs and beaks. And the party whose cock surrenders or dies loses the wager; I am told that stakes on a cock often amount to many thousands of crowns, especially if they have reared the cock themselves and brought their own along.* [*Platter's note*: This entertainment usually lasts four or five hours.] For the master who inhabits the house has many cocks besides, which he feeds in separate cages and keeps for this sport, as he showed us. He also had several cocks, none of which he would sell for less than twenty crowns; they are very large but just the same kind as we have in our country. He also told us that if one discovered that the cocks' beaks had been coated with garlic, one was fully entitled to kill them at once. He added

too, that it was nothing to give them brandy before they began to fight, adding what wonderful pleasure there was in watching them.

Every Sunday and Wednesday in London there are bearbaitings on the other side of the water, and I ferried across on Sunday the 18th of September with the Earl of Benthem (?) and my party, and saw the bear and bullbaiting. The theatre is circular, with galleries round the top for the spectators, the ground space down below, beneath the clear sky, is unoccupied. In the middle of this place a large bear on a long rope was bound to a stake, then a number of great English mastiffs were brought in and shown first to the bear, which they afterwards baited one after another: now the excellence and fine temper of such mastiffs was evinced, for although they were much struck and mauled by the bear, they did not give in, but had to be pulled off by sheer force, and their muzzles forced open with long sticks to which a broad ironpiece was attached at the top. The bears' teeth were not sharp so they could not injure the dogs; they have them broken short. When the first mastiffs tired, fresh ones were brought in to bait the bear.

When the first bear was weary, another was supplied and fresh dogs to bait him, first one at a time, then more and more as it lasted, till they had overpowered the bear, then only did they come to its aid. This second bear was very big and old, and kept the dogs at bay so artfully with his paws that they could not score a point off him until there were more of them. When this bear was tired, a large white powerful bull was brought in, and likewise bound in the centre of the theatre, and one dog only was set on him at a time, which he speared with his horns and tossed in such masterly fashion, that they could not get the better of him, and as the dogs fell to the floor again, several men held the sticks under them to break their fall, so that they would not be killed. Afterwards more dogs were set on him, but could not down him. Then another powerful bear was fetched and baited by six or seven dogs at a time, which attacked him bravely on all sides, but could not get the better of him because of his thick pelt.

Lastly they brought in an old blind bear which the boys hit with canes and sticks; but he knew how to untie his leash and he ran back to his stall.

On leaving we descended the steps and went behind the theatre, saw the English mastiffs, of which there were one hundred and twenty together in one enclosure, each chained up to his own separate kennel however. And the place was evil-smelling because of the lights and meat on which the butchers feed the said dogs.

In a stall adjoining were some twelve large bears, and several bulls in another, all of them kept there merely for the sport described above.

With these and many more amusements the English pass their time, learning at the play what is happening abroad; indeed men and womenfolk visit such places without scruple, since the English for the most part do not travel much, but prefer to learn foreign matters and take their pleasures at home.

There are a great many inns, taverns, and beer-gardens scattered about the city, where much amusement may be had with eating, drinking, fiddling and the rest, as for instance in our hostelry, which was visited by players almost daily. And what is particularly curious is that the women as well as the men, in fact more often than they, will frequent the taverns or ale-houses for enjoyment. They count it a great honour to be taken there and given wine with sugar to drink; and if one woman only is invited, then she will bring three or four other women along and they gaily toast each other; the husband afterwards thanks him who has given his wife such pleasure, for they deem it a real kindness.

In the ale-houses tobacco or a species of wound-wort are also obtainable for one's money, and the powder is lit in a small pipe, the smoke sucked into the mouth, and the saliva is allowed to run freely, after which a good draught of Spanish wine follows. This they regard as a curious medicine for defluctions, and as a pleasure, and the habit is so common with them, that they always carry the instrument on them, and light up on all occasions, at the play, in the taverns or elsewhere, drinking as well as smoking together, as we sit over wine, and it makes them riotous and merry, and rather drowsy, just as if they were drunk, though the effect soon passes—and they use it so abundantly because of the pleasure it gives, that their preachers cry out on them for their self-destruction, and I am told the inside of one man's veins after death was found to be covered in soot just like a chimney. The herb is imported from the Indies in great quantities, and some types are much stronger than others, which difference one can immediately taste; they perform queer antics when they take it. And they first learned of this medicine from the Indians, as Mr. Cope a citizen of London who has spent much time in the Indies, informed me.

–pp. 167–171

. . . .

This city of London is not only brimful of curiosities, but so populous also that one simply cannot walk along the streets for the crowd.

Especially every quarter when the law courts sit in London and they throng from all parts of England for the terms (aux termes) to litigate in numerous matters which have occurred in the interim, for everything is saved up till that time; then there is a slaughtering and a hanging, and from all the prisons (of which there are several scattered about the town where they ask alms of the passers by, and sometimes they collect so much by their begging that they can purchase their freedom) people are taken and tried; when the trial is over, those condemned to the rope are placed on a cart, each one with a rope about his neck, and the hangman drives with them out of the town to the gallows, called Tyburn, almost an hour away from the city, there he fastens them up one after another by the rope and drives the cart off under the gallows which is not very high off the ground; then the criminals' friends come and draw them down by their feet, that they may die all the sooner. They are then taken down from the gallows and buried in the neighbouring cemetery, where stands a house haunted by such monsters that no one can live in it, and I myself saw it. Rarely does a law day in London in all the four sessions pass without some twenty to thirty persons—both men and women—being gibbetted.

And since the city is very large, open, and populous, watch is kept every night in all the streets, so that misdemeanour shall be punished. Good order is also kept in the city in the matter of prostitution, for which special commissions are set up, and when they meet with a case, they punish the man with imprisonment and fine. The woman is taken to Bridewell, the King's palace, situated near the river, where the executioner scourges her naked before the populace. And although close watch is kept on them, great swarms of these women haunt the town in the taverns and playhouses.

–pp. 174–175

1600

Baron Waldstein's Diary

Like many young aristocrats, Zdenek Brthnickyz Valdstejna (1581–1623) spent several years traveling through Europe. This excerpt, from The Diary of Baron Waldstein: A Traveller in Elizabethan England *(1981), edited and translated by G. W. Groos, describes his visit to an unnamed London theater.*

Monday, 3 July

Went to see an English play. The theatre follows the ancient Roman plan: it is built of wood and is so designed that the spectators can get a comfortable view of everything that happens in any part of the building.

On the way back we crossed the bridge; it has very fine buildings on it, and fixed to one of them can still be seen the heads of a number of earls and other noblemen who have been executed for treason.

–p. 37

1605

Letter of Ottaviano Lotti

An agent representing Florentine interests in London, Ottaviano Lotti was a careful observer of the English court and its entertainments. Here, he describes the carnival season, the period between the Feast of the Epiphany (6 January or Twelfth Night) and the start of Lent (Ash Wednesday, whose date changes annually). During this holiday season, plays and masques were performed for the court by Shakespeare and the King's Men, among others. This excerpt from a 20 January 1605 letter is from John Orrell's article "The London Stage in the Florentine Correspondence, 1604–1618" in Theatre Research International.

That which in Italy is commonly called '*il Carnovale*' runs its course in these parts from the birthday of Our Lord until Twelfth Night, or in other words, according to our usage, until the day of Epiphany. At this time, even more than at other seasons, all the people turn their minds to festivities and pleasures, but their Majesties' courtiers in particular show themselves all the more ardent in this because of their capacity to spend money, and because it is proper for them to entertain one another. The princes themselves like to mingle with them. This year, therfore, new scenes (*nuovi apparati*) and most lovely theatres have been built. Not an evening has passed without the performance of some lovely play in the royal household in the presence of their Majesties, and then in a different fashion two most superb masques have been staged. . . . The Spanish ambassador prepared a most sumptuous banquet and the word was out that it was a sure thing that the Prince of England and the Duke of York, the second-born, were to have gone, but the Duke of Holstein was there alone, accompanied by a number of ladies and knights, and they were entertained with dances, plays and a most splendid meal at the end.

–New Series, 3 (May 1978): 160–161

1608

Letter of John Chamberlain

When diplomat Dudley Carleton was not in London, he relied on scholar John Chamberlain to provide him with news of the court. Chamberlain's letters offer accounts of political events and also frequently describe the court's entertainment. Here, Chamberlain describes King James's imperious approach to scheduling plays. This excerpt from Chamberlain's 5 January 1608 letter to Carleton is from The Letters of John Chamberlain *(1939), edited by Norman Egbert McClure.*

The maske goes forward at court for Twelfth day, though I doubt the new roome wilbe scant redy. All the holy-dayes there were playes, but with so litle concourse of straungers, that they say they wanted companie. The Kinge was very earnest to have one on Christmas-night, (though as I take yt he and the Prince receved that day) but the Lordes told him yt was not the fashion, which aunswer pleased him not a whit, but said what do you tell me of the fashion? I will make yt a fashion.

–vol. I, p. 250

1613

Letter of Antimo Galli

Antimo Galli, a Florentine visiting London, describes the Venetian ambassador, Antonio Foscarini, attending the theater. Some scholars think the play the crowd is calling for is Robert Greene's The Honorable History of Friar Bacon and Friar Bungay. *The letter provides one of the few accounts we have of the behavior of the "groundlings," the playgoers who stood in the yard directly in front of the stage and who often interacted with the performers. This excerpt from a 22 August 1613 letter was published in John Orrell's article "The London Stage in the Florentine Correspondence, 1604–1618."*

[Foscarini] often goes to the plays in these parts. Among others, he went the other day to a playhouse called the Curtain, which is out beyond his house. It is an infamous place in which no good citizen or gentleman would show his face. And what was worse, in order not to pay a royal, or a scudo, to go in one of the little rooms, nor even to sit in the degrees that are there, he insisted on standing in the middle down below among the gang of porters and carters, giving as his excuse that he was hard of hearing–as if he could have understood the language anyway! But it didn't end there because, at the end of the performance, having received permission from one of the actors, he invited the public to the play for the next day, and named one. But the people, who wanted a different one, began to call out 'Friars, Friars' (that is, 'Frati, frati') because they wanted one that they called 'Friars.' Then, turning to his interpreter, my Tambalone asked what they were saying. The interpreter replied that it was the name of a play about friars. Then he, bursting out of his cloak, began to clap his hands as the people were doing and to yell 'Friars, Friars.' But at this racket the people turned on him, thinking him to be a Spaniard, and began to whistle at him in such a fashion that I don't think he'll ever want to go back there again. But that doesn't stop him frequenting the other theatres, and almost always with just one servant.

–New Series, 3 (May 1978): 171

Politics and the Theater

Court masques grew increasingly elaborate and expensive to produce under King James. There were layers of meaning in the masques, whose plots were taken from classical literature but whose cast of masquers reflected contemporary political realities.

1605

Letter of Dudley Carleton

This letter from Dudley Carleton to John Chamberlain provides a sense of the political complexities of staging a court masque. It also reveals Carleton's repulsion at the sight of the female masquers in blackface, an attitude that complicates efforts to understand how a contemporary audience might have responded to Shakespeare's Othello, *whose title character would have been played by an actor who, like the queen and her ladies, wore black makeup. The text is from* Dudley Carleton to John Chamberlain 1603–1624: Jacobean Letters *(1972), edited by Maurice Lee Jr.*

London, January 7, 1605

Sir, if your little messenger had come a day or two sooner he had come opportunely to have squired Sir William Cecil, now knight of the Bath. How he sped yesterday I know not, for when I saw him on Saturday I gave him the best advice I could and since never set eye on him but once that night, when he was herded with the small game that follows the prince [Henry] and in my opinion could not be better. Our Christmas games are now at an end unless the duke of Holstein come with an after reckoning, who as they say hath somewhat in hand and broges [fishes] about for some others to bear part in the charge, which is not *bien séant à un prince.* We began on Saint John's day with the marriage of Sir Philip and the Lady Susan, which was performed with as much ceremony and grace as could be done a favorite. The prince [Henry] and duke of Holstein led the bride to church, the queen followed her from thence, the king gave her; and she brided and bridled it so handsomely and indeed became herself so well that the king said if he were not married he would not give her but keep her himself. There was none of our accustomed forms omitted, of bride cakes, sops in wine, giving of gloves, laces, and points, which have been ever since the livery of the court; and at night there was sewing into the sheet, casting of the bride's left hose, and twenty other petty sorceries. They were married in the chapel, feasted in the great chamber, and lodged in the council chamber, where the king gave them in the morning before they were up a *reveille-matin* in his shirt and his nightgown and spent a good hour with them in the bed or upon, choose which you will believe best. The plate and presents that were given were valued at £2000, but that which the king gave made it a good marriage, which was a book of 500 land lying in the Isle of Sheppey (whereof Sir Edward Hoby had a lease) passed and delivered that day for the lady's jointure. At night there was a mask performed by my lord of Pembroke, my lord Willoughby, Sir James Hay, Sir Robert Carey, Sir John Lee, Sir Richard Preston, Sir Thomas Germain, and Sir Thomas Bager. Their conceit was a representation of Juno's temple at the lower end of the great hall, which was vaulted, and within it the maskers seated with store of lights about them, and it was no ill show; they were brought in by the four seasons of the year and *Hymeneus,* which for songs and speeches was as good as a play. Their apparel was rather costly than comely, but their dancing full of life and variety; only Sir Thomas Germain had lead in his heels and sometimes forgot what he was doing. The Venetian ambassador was there present and was a wedding guest all the day; but one thing he took ill, and not without cause, that being brought after dinner to the closet to retire himself, he was there forgotten and suffered to walk out his supper, which he took afterwards privately in my lord of Cranborne's chamber; the Spanish ambassador was there likewise, but disguised; the French ambassador by reason of sickness hath been a stranger at court all Christmas. On Thursday last the Spaniard made a solemn dinner to the duke of Holstein and the greatest part of the court. The ladies he presented with fans and gloves and ended his entertainment with a play and a banquet. On New Year's Day there was expectation of new creations both of marquises and earls, but they are put off till the queen's lying down, which will be about three months hence at Greenwich. Yesterday in the morning the little Charles was made great duke of York. The ceremony was performed in the hall, and himself with his ornaments carried by nine earls. There were 11 knights of the Bath besides Sir Charles himself and all of the king's choice, as, namely, the lords Willoughby, Chandos, Compton and Norris; William Cecil, Allen Percy, Francis Manners, Thomas Somerset, Clifford, Howard, and Harrington. They were all lodged and feasted in the court for three days, and yesterday a public dinner was made in the great chamber, where was a table for the little duke and the earls and another apart for these new knights. The mask at night requires much labor to be well described, but there is a pamphlet in press which will save me that pains; meantime you shall only know that the actors were the queen, the ladies Bedford, Suffolk, Derby, Rich, Herbert, Effingham, Susan, Ed. Howard, Bevell, Walsingham, and Wroth. The presentation of the mask at the first drawing of the traverse was very fair and their apparel rich, but too light and courtesanlike. Their black faces and hands, which were painted and bare up the elbows, was a very loathsome sight and I am sorry that strangers should see our court so strangely disguised. The Spanish and Venetian ambassadors were both there and most of the French about the town. The confusion in getting in was so great that some ladies lie by it and complain of the fury of the white staffs. In the passages through the galleries they were shut up in several heaps betwixt doors and there stayed till all was ended; and in the coming out, a banquet which was prepared for the king in the great chamber was overturned, table and all, before it was scarce touched. It were infinite to tell you what losses there were of chains, jewels, purses, and suchlike loose ware, and one woman amongst the rest lost her honesty, for which she was carried to the porter's lodge, being surprised at her business on the top of the terrace. The court comes towards you on Wednesday next, and you will have these accidents more particularly related. Here is no news out of France since the last I showed you, the duke [of Lennox] in his passage being bound for Dieppe was driven up as high as Gravelines and there forced to land and to march with his whole troop on foot as far as Calais, from whence he is gone overland; my lord of Hertford is come up and not knowing how to put off the journey to the archduke hath this day undertaken it. Our lieger into Spain takes state upon him and is proud of the employment to which it was thought he would hardly have been entreated. Here have come of late many dispatches from our ambassador at Venice [Sir Henry Wotton] and his doings not over well liked. Will you not wonder if I shall tell you that Sir Walter Cope is believed not only to aspire but to be in fair forwardness to the secretaryship? I hope you have enough to entertain your thoughts withal and therefore when I have told you that your friends are well here and desired to be remembered where you are I leave further to trouble you and rest,

Yours most assured
—pp. 66–68

1606

Letter of John Harington

A favorite and cousin of Queen Elizabeth, John Harington was one of the courtiers who made a successful transition to life under King James. Harington was not always happy with what he saw, however, as his dry account of a court masque for the king of Denmark shows. The text of this letter from Harington to Secretary Barlow is from The Letters and Epigrams of Sir John Harington Together with The Prayse of Private Life *(1930), edited by Norman Egbert McClure.*

[Theobalds, July, 1606].

My good Friend,

In compliance with your asking, now shall you accept my poor accounte of rich doings. I came here a day or two before the Danish King came, and from the day he did come untill this hour, I have been well nigh overwhelmed with carousal and sports of all kinds. The sports began each day in such manner and such sorte, as well nigh persuaded me of Mahomets paradise. We had women, and indeed wine too, of such plenty, as woud have astonishd each sober beholder. Our feasts were magnificent, and the two royal guests did most lovingly embrace each other at table. I think the Dane hath strangely wrought on our good English nobles; for those, whom I never could get to taste good liquor, now follow the fashion, and wallow in beastly delights. The ladies abandon their sobriety, and are seen to roll about in intoxication. In good sooth, the parliament did kindly to provide his Majestie so seasonably with money, for there hath been no lack of good livinge; shews, sights, and banquetings, from morn to eve.

One day, a great feast was held, and, after dinner, the representation of Solomon his Temple and the coming of the Queen of Sheba was made, or (as I may better say) was meant to have been made, before their Majesties, by device of the Earl of Salisbury and others.—But, alass! as all earthly thinges do fail to poor mortals in enjoyment, so did prove our presentment hereof. The Lady who did play the Queens part, did carry most precious gifts to both their Majesties; but, forgetting the steppes arising to the canopy, overset her caskets into his Danish Majesties lap, and fell at his feet, tho I rather think it was in his face. Much was the hurry and confusion; cloths and napkins were at hand, to make all clean. His Majesty then got up and woud dance with the Queen of Sheba; but he fell down and humbled himself before her, and was carried to an inner chamber and laid on a bed of state; which was not a little defiled with the presents of the Queen which had been bestowed on his garments; such as wine, cream, jelly, beverage, cakes, spices, and other good matters. The entertainment and show went forward, and most of the presenters went backward, or fell down; wine did so occupy their upper chambers. Now did appear, in rich dress, Hope, Faith, and Charity: Hope did assay to speak, but wine renderd her endeavours so feeble that she withdrew, and hope the King would excuse her brevity: Faith was then all alone, for I am certain she was not joyned with good works, and left the court in a staggering condition: Charity came to the King's feet, and seemed to cover the multitude of sins her sisters had committed; in some sorte she made obeysance and brought giftes, but said she would return home again, as there was no gift which heaven had not already given his Majesty. She then returned to Hope and Faith, who were both sick and spewing in the lower hall. Next came Victory, in bright armour, and presented a rich sword to the King, who did not accept it, but put it by with his hand; and, by strange medley of versification, did endeavour to make suit to the King. But Victory did not tryumph long; for, after much lamentable utterance, she was led away like a silly captive, and laid to sleep in the outer steps of the anti-chamber. Now did Peace make entry, and strive to get foremoste to the King; but I grieve to tell how great wrath she did discover unto those of her attendants; and, much contrary to her semblance, most rudely made war with her olive branch, and laid on the pates of those who did oppose her coming.

I have much marvelled at these strange pegeantries, and they do bring to my remembrance what passed of this sort in our Queens days; of which I was sometime an humble presenter and assistant: but I neer did see such lack of good order, discretion, and sobriety, as I have now done! I have passed much time in seeing the royal sports of hunting and hawking, where the manners were such as made me devise the beasts were pursuing the sober creation, and not man in quest of exercise or food. I will now, in good sooth, declare to you, who will not blab, that the gunpowder fright is got out of all our heads, and we are going on, hereabouts, as if the devil was contriving every man shoud blow up himself, by wild riot, excess, and devastation of time and temperance. The great ladies do go well-masked, and indeed it be the only show of their modesty, to conceal their countenance; but, alack, they meet with such countenance to uphold their strange doings, that I marvel not at ought that happens. The Lord of the mansion is overwhelmed in preparations at Theobalds, and doth marvelously please both Kings, with good meat, good drink, and good speeches. I do often say (but not aloud) that the Danes have again conquered the Britains, for I see no man, or woman either, that can now command himself or herself. I wish I was at home:—*O rus, quando te aspiciam?*—And I will; before the Prince Vaudemont cometh.

I hear the uniting the kingdoms is now at hand; when the Parliament is held more will be done in this matter. Bacon is to manage all the affair, as who can better do these state jobs. My cosin, Lord Harington of Exton, doth much fatigue himself with the royal charge of the princess Elizabeth; and, midst all the foolery of these times, hath much labour to preserve his own wisdom and sobriety. If you would wish to see howe folly dothe grow, come up quickly; otherwise, stay where you are, and meditate on the future mischiefs of those our posterity, who shall learn the good lessons and examples helde forthe in these days. I hope to see you at the Bathe, and see the gambols you can perform in the hot waters, very speedily; and shall reste your assured friend in all quiet enjoyments and hearty good affections.

John Harington

–pp. 118–121

Regulations for the Theater

The theaters built within the city of London were under the authority of the London council. Theaters such as Shakespeare's Globe, built in Southwark, were outside the reach of the city's government and were less heavily regulated.

1559

The Book of Common Prayer

The following regulation explains why ceremonies of dramatic interest, such as the marriages in Taming of the Shrew *and* Romeo and Juliet, *must take place offstage. The following excerpt, "An act for the uniformitie of common praier," is from* The Booke of common praier, and administration of the Sacramentes, and other rites and Ceremonies in the Churche of Englande *(1559).*

And it is ordeyned and enacted by the aucthoritie abovesayd, that yf any person or personnes whatsoever, after the sayd feast of the Nativitie of Saynct John Baptiste nexte commynge, shall in any Enterludes, Playes, Songs, Rymes, or by other open wordes, declare or speake any thyng in the derogation, depravying, or despysyng of the same booke, or of any thynge therin conteyned, or any parte therof, or shall by open facte, deede, or by open threatnynges, compell or cause, or otherwyse procure or maintayne any Parson, Vycar, or other Mynister, in any Cathedral or paryshe Churche, or in Chappell, or in any other place to syng or say any common and open prayer, or to minister any Sacramente otherwyse, or in anye other maner and forme then is mencioned in the sayd boke, or that by any of the sayd meanes that unlawfully interrupt or let any parson, vicar, or other minister, in any Cathedral or paryshe Churche, Chappel, or any other place to syng or say comon and open prayer, or to minister the Sacramentes or any of them, in such maner and fourme, as is mencioned in the said boke: That then every suche parson beyng thereof lawefully convicted in fourme above sayde, shal forfeyte to the Quene oure Soveraygne Ladye, her heires and successours, for the fyrste offence a hundreth markes. And yf any parson or parsons, beyng once convict of any suche offence eft-sons offend against any of the last recited offences, and shall in fourme aforesayd be therof lawefully convict: That then the same parson so offendynge and convicte shall for the second offence forfeyte to the Quene our Soveraigne Lady, her heires and successours, foure hundreth markes. And if any parson after he in forme aforesayde, shall have bene twyse convicte of any offence, concernyng any of the last recited offences, shal offend the thyrd time, and be therof in forme abovesayde lawefully convicte: That then every parson so offendyng and convict shal for his thyrd offence, forfeyte to oure Soveraygne Lady the Quene, al his goodes & catelles, and shal suffer imprisonment durynge his lyfe.

—sig. Aiii

1600

An Act of the Privy Council

The Queen's Privy Council often responded to complaints from the London city government about the disorderly behavior associated with playhouses. The 22 June 1600 act, which attempts to restrict the number of theaters as well as the number of performances given at them, names several of the London playhouses, including the Globe. The following excerpt is from Acts of the Privy Council of England, *edited by John Roche Dasent.*

At the Courte at Greenwich, 22 of June.

Order of the Lords for the restrainte of the imoderate use and companye of playhowses and players.

Whereas divers complaintes have bin heretofore made unto the Lords and other of her Majesty's Privye Counsell of the manyfolde abuses and disorders that have growen and do contynue by occasion of many houses erected and employed in and about the cittie of London for common stage-playes, and now verie latelie by reason of some complainte exhibited by sondry persons against the buyldinge of the like house in or next Golding Lane by one Edward Allen, a servant of the right honorable the Lord Admyrall, the matter, aswell in generaltie touchinge all the saide houses for stage-playes and the use of playinge, as in particular concerninge the saide house now in hand to be buylte in or neare Golding Lane, hath bin broughte into question and consultacion ammonge theire Lordships.

Forasmuch as it is manifestly knowen and graunted that the multitude of the saide houses and the mysgover[n]ment of them hath bin and is dayly occasion of the ydle, ryoutous and dissolute living of great nombers of people, that leavinge all such honest and painefull course of life as they should followe, doe meete and assemble here, and of many particular abuses and disorders that doe thereupon ensue, and yet nevertheles it is considered that the use and exercise of such playes (not beinge evill in yt self) may with a good order and moderacion be suffered in a well governed State, and that her Majestie beinge pleased at some tymes to take delight and recreation in the sight and hearinge of them, some order is fitt to be taken for the allowance and mayntenance of such persons as are thought meetest in that kinde to yealde her Majestie recreation and delighte, and consequently of the houses that must serve for publike playinge to keepe them in exercise. To the ende therefore that both the greatest abuses of the playes and playinge-houses may be redressed and yet the aforesaide use and moderation of them retayned, the Lords and the reste of her Majesty's Privie Counsell with one and full consent have ordered in manner and forme as followeth.

Firste, that there shalbe aboute the cittie two houses and no more allowed to serve for the use of the common stage-playes, of the which houses one shalbe in Surrey in that place which is commonly called the Banckeside or thereaboutes, and the other in Middlesex. And forasmuch as their Lordships have bin enformed by Edmund Tylney, esquire, her Majesty's servante and Master of the Revells, that the house nowe in hand to be builte by the saide Edward Allen is not intended to encrease the nomber of the play-houses, but to be insteede of an other (namely the Curtayne) which is ether to be ruyned and plucked downe or to be put to some other good use, as also that the scytuation thereof is meete and convenient for that purpose, it is likewise ordered that the saide house of Allen shalbe allowed to be one of the two houses and namely for the house to be allowed in Middlesex *for the company of players belonging to the Lord Admyrall* [interlined], so as the house called the Curtaine be (as it is pretended) either ruynated or applyed to some other good use, and for the other house allowed to be on Surrey side, whereas *their Lordships are pleased to permitt* [interlined] to the company of players that shall play there to make their owne choice which they will have *of divers houses that are there*

[interlined], choosing one of them and no more, *and the said company of plaiers, beinge the servantes of the Lord Chamberlain and that are to play there, have made choice of the house called the Globe, it is ordered that the said house and none other shalbe there allowed* [interlined]. And especially it is forbidden that any stage-playes shalbe played (as some tymes they have bin) in any common inne for publique assembly in or neare aboute the cittie. [*Marginal note: Memorandum* that the alteracion and interlyning of this order was by reason that the said order after the same was entred in the Booke came againe in question and debate, and the said interlyninge and amendementes were sett downe according to the laste determinacion of their Lordships. (*signed*) Th: Smith.]

Secondly, forasmuch as these stage-plaies by the multitude of houses and company of players have bin to[o] frequent, not servinge for recreation but invitinge and callinge the people dayly from their trade and worke to mispend their tyme, it is likewise ordered that the two severall companies of players assigned unto the two houses allowed may play each of them in their severall house twice a weeke and no oftener, and especially that they shall refrayne to play on the Sabbath day upon paine of imprisonment and further penaltie, and that they shall forbeare altogether in the tyme of Lent, and likewise at such tyme and tymes as any extraordinary sicknes or infection of disease shall appeare to be in or about the cittie.

Thirdly, because the orders wilbe of little force and effecte unlesse they be duely put in execution by those unto whome it appertayneth to see them executed, it is ordered that severall copies of these orders shalbe sent to the Lord Maiour of London and to the Justices of the Peace of the counties of Middlesex and Surrey, and that letters shalbe written unto them from their Lordships straightly charginge them to see to the execucion of the same aswell by comyttinge to prison any owners of play-houses and players as shall disobey and resist these orders, as by any other good and lawfull meanes that in their discretion they shall finde expedient, and to certifie their Lordships from tyme to tyme, as they shall see cause, of their proceedinges therein.

—Acts of the Privy Council, new series, 30
(1905; reprinted, 1974): 395–398

1601

An Act of the Privy Council

The Privy Council, after authorizing London's justices of the peace to close down all but two London theaters, the Fortune and the Globe, shows its impatience with the city's governors' con-

tinuing complaints in the following letters. The text of this 31 December 1601 action is from Acts of the Privy Council of England, *edited by John Roche Dasent.*

Ultimo Decembris.

Lord Keeper.	Earl of Worcester.
Lord Treasurer.	Mr. Comptroler.
Lord Admirall.	Mr. Secretary Cecyll.
Earl of Shrewsbury.	Mr. Secretary Herbert.

Two letters of one tenour to the Justices of Middlesex and Surrey. It is in vaine for us to take knowledg of great abuses and disorders complayned of and to give order for redresse if our directions finde no better execution and observation then it seemeth they do, and wee must needes impute the fault and blame thereof to you or some of you the Justices of the Peace that are put in trust to see them executed and perfourmed, whereof wee may give you a plaine instance in the great abuse contynued or rather encreased in the multitude of plaie howses and stage plaies in and about the cittie of London.

For whereas about a yeare and a half since (upon knowledge taken of the great enormities and disorders by the overmuch frequentinge of plaies) wee did carefullie sett downe and prescribe an order to be observed concerninge the number of playhowses and the use and exercise of stage plaies with lymytacion of tymes and places for the same (namely that there should be but two howses allowed for that use, one in Middlesex called the Fortune and the other in Surrey called the Globe, and the same with observacion of certaine daies and times as in the said order is particularly expressed), in such sorte as a moderate practice of them for honest recreation might be contynued and yet the inordinate concourse of dissolute and idle people be restrayned, wee do now understande that our said order hath bin so farr from takinge dew effect as in steede of restrainte and redresse of the former disorders the multitude of play howses is much encreased, and that no daie passeth over without many stage plaies in one place or other within and about the cittie publiquelie made.

The default of perfourmance of which our said order we must in greate parte the rather impute to the Justices of the Peace, because at the same tyme wee gave earnest direction unto you to see it streightly executed, and to certifie us of the execution, and yet we have neither understoode of any redresse made by you nor received any certificate at all of your proceedinges therein, which default or omission wee do now pray and require you foorthwith to amende and to cause our said former order to be putt duely in execution, and especiallie to call before you the owners of all the other play howses (excepting the two howses in Middlesex and Surrey aforementioned), and to take good and sufficient bondes of them not to exercise, use or practise nor to suffer from henceforth to be exercised, used or practized any stage playinge in their howses, and if they shall refuse to enter into such bondes then to comitt them to prison untill they shall conforme themselves. And so, &c.

Signed and dated as the former.

A letter to the Lord Maiour and Aldermen of London. Wee have received a letter from you renewing a complaint of the great abuse and disorder within and about the cittie of London by reason of the multitude of play howses and the inordinate resort and concourse of dissolute and idle people daielie unto publique stage plaies, for the which information as wee do commende your Lordship because it betokeneth your care and desire to reforme the disorders of the cittie, so wee must lett you know that wee did muche rather expect to understand that our order (sett downe and prescribed about a yeare and a half since for reformation of the said disorders upon the like complaint at that tyme) had bin duelie executed then to finde the same disorders and abuses so muche encreased as they are, the blame whereof as wee cannot but impute in great part to the Justices of the Peace or somme of them in the counties of Middlesex and Surrey, who had speciall direction and charge from us to see our said order executed for the confines of the cittie, wherein the most part of those play howses are scituate, so wee do wishe that it might appeare unto us that any thinge hath bin endeavoured by the predecessours of you, the Lord Maiour, and by you, the Aldermen, for the redresse of the said enormities, and for observation and execution of our said order within the cittie.

Wee do therefore once againe renew heereby our direction unto you (as wee have donne by our letters to the Justices of Middlesex and Surrey) concerninge the observation of our former order, which wee do praie and require you to cause duelie and dilligentlie to be put in execution for all poyntes thereof and especiallie for th'expresse and streight prohibition of any more play howses then those two that are mentioned and allowed in the said order, charging and streightlie comaunding all suche persons as are the owners of any the howses used for stage plaies within the cittie not to permitt any more publique plaies to be used, exercised or shewed from hencefoorth in their said howses, and to take bondes of them (if you shall finde it needefull) for the perfourmaunce thereof, or if they shall refuse to enter into bonde or to observe our said order, then to committ them to prison untill they shall conforme themselves thereunto. And so praying you as your self do make the complaint and finde the ennormitie so to applie your best endeavour to the remedie of the abuse, wee bidd, &c.

—new series, 32 (1907; reprinted, 1974): 466–469

1604

A Privy Council Warrant

The effort to limit the number of theaters continued for several years. Here, the companies that perform at the theaters are named, including Shakespeare's company, the King's Men. The text of this 9 April 1604 privy council warrant to the lord mayor of London and the justices of the peace of Middlesex and Surrey is from Henslowe Papers: Being Documents Supplementary to Henslowe's Diary *(1907), edited by Walter W. Greg.*

After our hart[ie *word(s) missing*]s to your [Lordship] Wheras the kings majesties Plaiers have given ty[*word(s) missing*] hyghnes good service in ther Quallitie of Playinge and for as much Lickwise as they are at all times to be emploied In that Service whensoever they shalbe Comaunded we thinke it therfore fitt the time of Lent being now Passt that your Lordship doe Permitt and suffer the three Companies of Plaiers to the King Queene and Prince publicklie to Exercise ther Plaies in ther severall and usuall howses for that Purpose and noe other vz The Globe scituate in maiden lane on the Banckside in the Countie of Surrey, the fortun in Golding Lane, and the Curtaine In Hollywell in the Cowntie of midlesex without any lett or Interupption In respect of any former Lettres of Prohibition heertofore written by us to your Lordship. Except there shall happen weeklie to die of the Plague Above the Number of thirtie within the Cittie of London and the Liberties therof. Att which time we thinke it fitt they shall Cease and forbeare any further Publicklie to Playe untill the Sicknes be again decreaced to the saide Number. and so we bid your Lordship hartilie farewell ffrom the Court at whitehalle the ix^th of Aprille 1604

Your very Loving ffrends
Nottingham
Suffock
Gill Shrowsberie
Ed Worster
W: Knowles
J: Stanhopp

To our verie good Lord the Lord Maior of the Cittie of London and to the Justices of the Peace of the Counties of Midlesex and Surrey
L. Maiore

—pp. 61–62

1608

A Letter Attributed to George Chapman

George Chapman's play The Conspiracie, and Tragedie of Charles Duke of Byron *(1608) caused offense to the French ambassador to England, Antoine de la Boderie. This letter, written in response to government efforts to censor or suppress the play, was probably addressed to the master of the revels, Edmund Tilney, or his deputy George Buc. It provides details about the process of censorship and helps identify the limits of the playwright's responsibility for the text. The text of the letter, probably written by Chapman in March–June 1608, is from* A Seventeenth-Century Letter-Book: A Facsimile Edition of Folger MS. V.a. 321 *(1983), edited by A. R. Braunmuller. Abbreviations have been silently expanded.*

Sir I have not deserv'd what I suffer by your Austeritie, yf the two or three lynes you crost, were spoken; My uttermost to suppresse them was enough for my discharge; to more then which, no promysse can be rackt by reason; I see not myne owne Plaies; Nor carrie the Actors Tongues in my Mouthe; The action of ye mynde is performance sufficient of any dewtie, before the greatest Authoritie wherein I have quitted all your former favoures, And made them more worthie then any you bestowe on outward observers; Yf the thrice allowance of ye Counsaile for ye Presentment; have not weight–enoughe to drawe youres after for the Presse; My Breath is a hopeles Adition; Yf you say (for your Reason) you know not if more then was spoken be now written no No; Nor can you know that, if you had bothe the Copies; Not seeing the first at all: Or if you had seene it presented, your Memorie could hardly confer with it so strictly in the Revisall, to descerne the Adition; My short Reason therefore can not sounde your Severitie; Whosoever it were yt first plaied the bitter Informer before the frenche Ambassador for a matter so far from offence; And of so muche honor for his Maister, as those two partes containe; performd it with the Gall of a Wulff, and not of a Man; and theise hartie, & secrett vengeances taken for Crost, & Officious humers, are more Politiq then Christian; Which he that hates, will one day discover in ye op[en] Ruyne of their Auctores; And thoughe they be trifles: he yet laie them in Ballance, (as they concerne Justice, and bewray Appetites to the greatest Tyrannye) with the greatest; But how easely soever Illiterate Aucthoritie settes up his Bristles against Pover Me thinkes youres (beinge accompanied with learninge) should rebate ye pointes of them: And soften the fiercenes of those rude Manners; You know Sir, They are sparkes of the lowest Fier in Nature, that flye out uppon weakenes, with everie pufft of Power; I desier not, you should drenche your hand in the least daunger for mee; And therefore (with entreatie of my Papers returne) I cease ever to trooble you./.

By the poore subject of your office for the present./

—pp. 246

1611

George Buc's License to Perform *The Second Maiden's Tragedy*

Before being performed on a public stage, a play had to be "seen and allowed" by the master of the revels to ensure it was free of offensive material. The manuscript of the play Sir Thomas More, *part of which is thought to be by Shakespeare, shows signs of censorship. When plays were approved, they carried an endorsement similar to the one shown below from the manuscript of* The Second Maiden's Tragedy. *The endorsement is by George Buc, who became master of the revels in 1610. For a detailed analysis of Buc's note, see Alan H. Nelson, "George Buc, William Shakespeare, and the Folger* George a Greene" *in* Shakespeare Quarterly, *49 (1998): 74–83.*

This second Maydens tragedy (for it hath no name inscribed) may wth the reformations bee acted publikely. 31. octobe ^r. 1611./. G. Buc.

—British Museum Lansdowne Manuscript 807, folio 56a

Prologues, Epilogues, Epistles to Readers, and Excerpts from Plays

Much theorizing about the purpose and process of playwriting is found in letters to the readers of printed plays and in prologues and epilogues. Playwrights sometimes offer thoughtful or bitter accounts of the difficulties they contend with—bad actors and noisy and unappreciative audiences among them—and of the reasons for writing or publishing their plays. These addresses to readers or audience members sometimes provide details about performances, stage business, or theater architecture but are not always included in modern editions of the plays.

1604

Marston's Letter to the Reader of *The Malcontent*

John Marston first wrote satirical poetry, then switched to comedies and tragedies written for one of London's children's companies, groups of professional boy actors who performed all of the roles in a play. The Malcontent *(1604) is a bitter examination of court corruption. In his epistle Marston is careful to warn his readers not to try to link his characters to the courtly figures living in contemporary London.*

To the Reader.

I Am an ill Oratour; and in truth, use to indite more honestly then eloquently, for it is my custome to speake as I thinke, and write as I speake.

In plainenesse therefore understand, that in some things I have willingly erred, as in supposing a Duke of *Genoa*, and in taking names different from that Cities families: for which some may wittily accuse me; but my defence shall be as honest, as many reproofes unto me have beene most malicious. Since (I hartily protest) it was my care to write so farre from reasonable offence, that even strangers, in whose state I laid my Scene, should not from thence draw any disgrace to any, dead or living. Yet in dispight of my indevors, I understand, some have beene most unadvisedly over-cunning in mis-interpreting me, and with subtilitie (as deepe as hell) have maliciously spread ill rumors, which springing from themselves, might to themselves have heavily returned. Surely I desire to satisfie every firme spirit, who in all his actions, proposeth to himselfe no more ends then God and vertue do, whose intentions are alwaies simple: to such I protest, that with my free understanding, I have not glanced at disgrace of any, but of those, whose unquiet studies labor innovation, contempt of holy policie, reverent comely superioritie, and establisht unity: for the rest of my supposed tartnesse, I feare not, but unto every worthy minde it will be approved so generall and honest, as may modestly passe with the freedome of a Satyre. I would faine leave the paper; onely one thing afflicts me, to thinke that Scænes invented, meerely to be spoken, should be inforcively published to be read, and that the least hurt I can receive, is to do my selfe the wrong. But since others otherwise would doe me more, the least inconvenience is to be accepted. I have my selfe therefore set forth this Comedie; but so, that my inforced absence must much relye upon the Printers discretion: but I shall intreate, slight errors in orthographie may bee as slightly over passed; and that the unhansome shape which this trifle in reading presents, may be pardoned, for the pleasure it once afforded you, when it was presented with the soule of lively action.

Sine aliqua dementia nullus Phœbus.

J. M.

—The Malcontent, sig. A2r

1605

Commendatory Poem for Jonson's *Sejanus*

Ben Jonson's Roman tragedy Sejanus *(1605), for which Shakespeare is listed as a cast member, was not particularly popular on stage. The following commendatory poem, which places the first performance of the play at the Globe theater, is by an author identified only as Ev.B.; it was published with other complimentary verse as a preface to the 1605 edition of the play.*

To the most understanding Poet.

WHē in the GLOBES faire Ring, our Worlds best Stage,
I saw *Sejanus*, set with that rich foyle,
I look't the Author should have borne the spoile
Of conquest, from the Writers of the Age:
But when I veiw'd the Peoples beastly rage,
Bent to confound thy grave, and learned toile,
That cost thee so much sweat, and so much oyle,
My indignation I could hardly asswage.
And many there (in passion) scarce could tell
Whether thy fault, or theirs deserv'd most blame;
Thine, for so showing, theirs, to wrong the same:
But both they left within that doubtfull Hell:
From whence, this Publication setts thee free:
They, for their Ignorance, still damned bee.

—sig. A2v

1606

Prologue and Epilogue for Marston's *Parasitaster*

In his addresses to the readers of his satire of contemporary hypocrisy, Parasitaster, Or The Fawne *(1606), John Marston reminds his readers that plays are meant to be seen, not read.*

Reader, know I have perused this coppy, to make some satisfaction for the first faulty impression: yet so urgent hath been my busines, that some errors have styll passed, which thy discretion may amend: *Comedies* are writ to be spoken, not read: Remember the life of these things consists in action; and for your such courteous survay of my pen, I will present a Tragedy to you which shall boldly abide the most curious perusall. [*Marginal note: Sophonisba.*]

—sig. A2v

Prologus.

Let those once know that here with malice lurke,
Tis base too be to wise, in others worke.
The rest, sit thus saluted:
Spectators know, you may with freest faces
Behould this Sceane, for here no rude disgraces
Shall taint a publique, or a privat name,
This pen at viler rate doth value fame,
Than at the price of others infamy,
To purchase it: Let others dare the rope,
Your modest pleasure is our authors scope.
The hurdle and the racke to them he leaves,
That have naught left to be accompted any,
But by not being: Nor doth he hope to win
Your Laud or hand, with that most common sinne
Of vulgar pennes, ranke baudrie, that smels
Even thorow your maskes, *Usque ad nauseam*:
The venus of this sceane doth loath to weare
So vile, so common, so immodest clothings,
But if the nimble forme of commodie,
Meere spectacle of life, and publique manners
May gracefully arrive to your pleased eares,
We boldly dare the utmost death of feares
For we doe know that this most faire fil'd roome
Is Loaden with most *Atick* judgements, ablest spirits,
Then whome, there are none more exact, full, strong,
Yet none more soft, benigne in sensuring,
I know ther's not one Asse in all this presence,
Not one Callumnious rascall, or base villaine
Of emptiest merit, that would taxe and slaunder
If Innocencie her selfe should write, not one we know't.
O you are all the very breath of *Phebus*
In your pleas'd gracings all the true life bloud
Of our poore author lives, you are his very grace,
  Now if any wonder why he's drawn
  To such base soothings, know his play's the *Fawne*.

—sig. A3r

Epilogus.

And thus in bolde, yet modest phrase we end,
He whose Thalia with swiftest hand hath pend,
This lighter subject, and hath boldly torne,
Fresh bayes from *Daphnes* arme, doth only scorne,
Malitious censures of some envious few,
Who thinke they loose if others have their due.
But let such Addars hisse, know all the sting,
All the vaine fome of all those snakes that ringes
Minervas glassefull shield can never taint,
Poyson or pierce, firme art disdaines to faint,
But yet of you that with impartiall faces,
With no prepared malice, but with graces,
Of sober knowledge, have survaide the frame,
Of his sleight scene, if you shall judge his flame,
Distemperately, weake as faulty much,
In stile, in plot, in spirit, loe if such
He daines in selfe accusing phrase to crave,
For prayse but pardon which he hopes to have.
      Since he protests he ever hath aspirde,
      To be belovde, rather then admirde.

                  −sig. I4v

Note to the Reader of Marston's *The Wonder of women*

John Marston's play The Wonder of women or the tragedie of Sophonisba *tells the tragic story of the death of a noble Roman woman, Sophonisba, and his address to the reader provides a short, sharp reminder of the differences between historical fact and dramatic fiction.*

To the generall Reader.

Know, that I have not labored in this poeme, to tie my selfe to relate any thing as an historian but to inlarge every thing as a Poet, To transcribe Authors, quote authorities, & translate Latin prose orations into English bla[n]ck-verse, hath in this subject beene the least aime of my studies. Then (equall Reader) peruse me with no prepared dislike, and if ought shall displease thee thanke thyselfe, if ought shall please thee thanke not me, for I confesse in this it was not my onely end.

              Jo. Marston.

                  −sig. A2r

1608

Heywood's Preface to *The Rape of Lucrece*

Playwright John Heywood explains his reluctance to publish his work and his decision to publish his play The Rape of Lucrece *(1608) in this preface: he had become embarrassed by the error-filled versions of his works that had found their way to the printers.*

To the Reader.

It hath beene no custome in mee of all other men (curteous Readers) to commit my plaies to the presse: the reason, though some may attribute to my own insufficiencie, I had rather subscribe in that to their seveare censure, then by seeking to avoide the imputation of weakenes, to incurre a greater suspition of honestie: for though some have used a double sale of their labours, first to the Stage, and after to the presse, For my owne part I heere proclaime my selfe ever faithfull in the first, and never guiltie of the last: yet since some of my plaies have (unknown to me, and without any of my direction) accidentally come into the Printers handes, and therfore so corrupt and mangled, (copied onely by the eare) that I have bene as unable to know them, as ashamde to chalenge them. This therefore I was the willinger to furnish out in his native habit: first beeing by consent, next because the rest have beene so wronged in beeing publisht in such savadge and ragged ornaments: accept it Curteous Gentlemen, and proove as favourable Readers as wee have found you gratious Auditors.

              Yours T. H.

                  −sig. A2

1609

Jonson's Prefatory Poem for *Epicoene*

In a second or alternative prologue to Epicoene, or the Silent Woman, *a comedy of a demanding man who finds what he believes is the perfect wife, Ben Jonson, prompted by what he claims in a 1620 marginal note is "some persons impertinent exception" to the play, concisely sets forth the task of a playwright in this prefatory poem.*

Another.

The endes of all, who for the *Scene* doe write,
Are, or should be, to profit, and delight.
And still't hath beene the praise of all best times,
So persons were not touch'd, to taxe the crimes.
Then, in this play, which we present to night,
And make the object of your eare, and sight,
On forfeit of your selves, thinke nothing true:
Least so you make the maker to judge you,
For he knowes, *Poet* never credit gain'd
By writing truths, but things (like truthes) well fayn'd.
If any, yet, will (with particular slight
Of application) wrest what he doth write;
And that he meant or him, or her, will say:
They make a libell, which he made a play.

                  −p. 530

Jonson on the Audience in
The Masque of Queenes

In this excerpt from The Masque of Queenes *(1609) Ben Jonson departs from his description of the masque to offer an assessment of the different classes of audience members a playwright is likely to encounter.*

At this, the *Dame* enter'd to them, naked-arm'd, bare-footed, her frock tuck'd, her haire knotted, and folded with Vipers; In her hand a Torch made of a dead mans arme, lighted; girded with a Snake. To whom they all did reverence, and she spake, uttering, by way of question, the end wherefore they came: which if it had beene done either before, or otherwise, had not beene so naturall. For, to have made themselves, their owne decipherers, and each one to have told, upon their entrance, *what they were, and whether they would*, had bin a most pitious hearing, and utterly unworthy any quality of a *Poeme*: wherein a *Writer* should alwayes trust somewhat to the capacity of the *Spectator*, especially, at these *Spectacles*; where men, beside inquiring eyes, are understood to bring quicke eares, and not those sluggish ones of *Porters*, and *Mechanicks*, that must be bor'd through, at every act, with *narrations*.

—sigs. B2r–v

1611

Address to the Reader and Prologue
to *The Roaring Girle*

Thomas Middleton and Thomas Dekker's play The Roaring Girl. Or Moll Cut-Purse *(1611) features a character, the roaring girl Moll Cut-Purse, based on a real-life Londoner, Marion Firth. Firth appeared in public wearing men's clothes, a daring move given the sumptuary laws—Middleton's "Statute"—which were created and enforced in order to help maintain "proper" social order by attempting to limit how men and women dressed themselves. Both the address to the readers and the prologue demonstrate that women had to overcome some deeply entrenched stereotypes to be taken seriously as readers, as playgoers, and as the subject of plays.*

To the Comicke, Play-readers, Venery, *and Laughter.*

The fashion of play-making, I can properly compare to nothing, so naturally, as the alteration in apparell: For in the time of the Great-crop-doublet, your huge bombasted plaies, quilted with mighty words to leane purpose was onely then in fashion. And as the doublet fell, neater inventions beganne to set up. Now in the time of sprucenes, our plaies followe the nicenes of our Garments, single plots, quaint conceits, letcherous jests, drest up in hanging sleeves, and those are fit for the Times, and the Tearmers:

Such a kind of light-colour Summer stuffe, mingled with diverse coulours, you shall finde this published Comedy, good to keepe you in an afternoone from dice, at home in your chambers; and for venery you shall finde enough, for sixpence, but well couch and you marke it. For *Venus* being a woman passes through the play in doublet and breeches, a brave disguise and a safe one, if the Statute unty not her cod-peece point. The book I make no question, but is fit for many of your companies, as well as the person it selfe, and may bee allowed both Gallery roome at the play-house, and chamber-roome at your lodging: worse things I must needs confesse the world ha's taxt her for, then has beene written of her; but 'tis the excellency of a Writer, to leave things better then he finds 'em; though some obscœne fellow (that cares not what he writes against others, yet keepes a mysticall baudy-house himselfe, and entertaines drunkards, to make use of their pockets, and vent his private bottle- ale at mid-night) though such a one would have ript up the most nasty vice, that ever hell belcht forth, and presented it to a modest Assembly; yet we rather wish in such discoveries, where reputation lies bleeding, a slackenesse of truth, then fulnesse of slander.

THOMAS MIDDLETON.

Prologus.

A Play (expected long) make the Audience looke
For wonders:—that each Scœne should be a booke,
Compos'd to all perfection; each one comes
And brings a play in's head with him: up he summes,
What he would of a Roaring Girle have writ;
If that he findes not here, he mewes at it.
Onely we intreate you thinke our Scœne,
Cannot speake high (the subject being but meane)
A Roaring Girle (whose notes till now never were)
Shall fill with laughter our vast Theater,
That's all which I dare promise: Tragick passion,
And such grave stuffe, is this day out of fashion.
I see attention sets wide ope her gates
Of hearing, and with covetous listning waites,
To know what Girle, this Roaring Girle should be.
(For of that Tribe are many.) One is shee
That roares at midnight in deepe Taverne bowles,
That beates the watch, and Constables controuls;
Another roares i'th day time, sweares, stabbes, gives braves,
Yet sells her soule to the lust of fooles and slaves.
Both these are Suburbe-roarers. Then there's (besides)
A civill Citty Roaring Girle, whose pride,
Feasting, and riding, shakes her husbands state,
And leaves him Roaring through an yron grate.
None of these Roaring Girles is ours: shee flies
With wings more lofty. Thus her character lyes,
Yet what neede characters? when to give a gesse,
Is better then the person to expresse;
But would you know who 'tis? would you heare her name?
Shee is cal'd madde *Moll*; her life, our acts proclaime.

—sigs. A3r–A4r

Epigrams and Satires

Epigrams—short, topical, and frequently nasty poems—and verse and prose satires were popular late-sixteenth-century forms although their availability declined for a time after many collections of them were publicly burned by order of the archbishop of Canterbury and the bishop of London in June 1599. The satirical poems and prose narratives attack London's contemporary vices and the inhabitants who practice them, including people who go to or work at the theater. Satirical works occasionally provide details about theaters, actors, or stage business, although they also reinforce the low reputation of players and playwrights.

1590

Greene's *Francescos Fortunes*

Robert Greene's Francescos Fortunes: Or The second part of Greenes Never too late. Wherein is discoursed the fall of Love, the bitter fruites of Follies pleasure, and the repentant sorowes of a reformed man *(1590) is a loosely autobiographical prose narrative that tells the story of a hapless young man. Betrayed by his lover and deeply in debt, Francesco tries to find work. The profession he chooses prompts the Palmer, who is narrating the tale, to provide a brief history of drama. The following excerpt is from "The Palmers Tale of Francesco."*

Necessitie that stingeth unto the quick, made him set his wits on the tenter, and to stretch his braines as high as *Ela*, to see how he could recover pence to defray his charges by any sinister meanes to salve his sorrowes: the care of his parents and of his owne honor perswaded him from making gaine by labour: he had never been brought up to any mechanicall course of life. Thus every way destitute of meanes to live, he sight out this olde sayd sawe, *Miserrimum est fuisse beatum*: yet at last, as extremities search very farre, he calde to minde that he was a scholler, and that although in these daies Arte wanted honor, and learning lackt his due, yet good letters were not brought to so lowe an ebbe, but that there might some profite arise by them to procure his maintenance. In this humour he fell in amongst a companie of Players, who perswaded him to trie his wit in writing of Comedies, Tragedies, or Pastorals, and if he could performe any thing worth the stage, then they would largelie reward him for his paines. *Francesco* glad of this motion, seeing a meanes to mitigate the extremitie of his want, thought it no dishonor to make gaine of his wit, or to get profite by his pen: and therefore getting him home to his chamber writ a Comedie, which so generally pleased all the audience, that happie were those Actors in short time that could get any of his workes, he grewe so exquisite in that facultie. By this meanes his want was releeved, his credit in his hosts house, recovered his apparell in greater braverie then it was, and his purse well lined with Crownes.

At this discourse of *Francesco*, the Gentleman tooke his guest by the hand and broke off his tale thus. Now gentle Palmer, seeing we are fallen by course of prattle to parlie of Playes, if without offence doo me that favour to shewe me your judgement of Playes, Playmakers and Players. Although (quoth the Palmer) that some for being too lavish against that facultie, have for their satiricall invectives been well canvased, yet seeing here is none but our selves, and that I hope what you heare shall be troden under foote, I will flatlie say what I can both even by reading and experience. The invention of Comedies were first found amongst the *Greekes*, and practised at *Athens*: some thinke by *Menander* whom *Terence* so highlie commends in his *Heautonti morumenon*. The reason was, that under the covert of such pleasant and Comicall events, they aymed at the overthrowe of many vanities that then raigned in the Citie: for therein they painted out in the persons the course of the world, how either it was graced with honor, or discredited with vices: There might you see leveld out the vaine life that boasting *Thrases* use, smoothed up with the selfe conceipt of their owne excellence; the miserable estate of covetous parents, that rather let their sonnes tast of any misfortunes, than to releeve them with the superfluitie of their wealth: the pourtraiture of parasiticall friends and flattering *Gnatos*, that only are time pleasers and trencher friends, which sooth yong Gentlemen subtellie in their follies, as long as they may: *Ex corum susto vivere* was set out in lively colours. In those Comedies the abuse of Bawdes that made sale of honest virgins, and lived by the spoyle of womens honors, was deeply discovered. To be short, Lecherie, Covetousnesse, Pride, selfe-love, disobedience of parents, and such vices predominant both in age and youth were shot at, not onely with examples and instances to feede the eye, but with golden sentences of morall works to please the eare. Thus did *Menander* win honor in *Greece* with his works, & reclaime both old & yong for their vanities by the pleasant effects of his Comedies. After him this facultie grew to be famous in *Rome*, practised by *Plautus*, *Terence*, and other that excelled in this qualitie, all ayming as *Menander* did in all their workes to suppresse vice and advance vertue. Now, so highlie were Comedies esteemed in those daies, that men of great honor and grave account were the Actors, the Senate and the Consuls continuallie present, as auditors at all such sports, rewarding the Author with rich rewards, according to the excellencie of the Comedie. Thus continued this facultie famous, till covetousnesse crept into the qualitie, and that meane men greedie of gaines did fall to practise the acting of such Playes, and in the Theater presented their Comedies but to such onely, as rewarded them well for their paines: when thus Comedians grewe to bee mercinaries, then men of accompt left to practise such pastimes, and disdained to have their honors blemisht with the staine of such base and vile gaines: in so much that both Comedies and Tragedies grew to less accompt in *Rome*, in that the free sight of such sports was taken away by covetous desires: yet the people (who are delighted with such novelties and pastimes) made great resort, paide largely, and highly applauded their doings, in so much that the Actors by continuall use grewe not onely excellent, but rich and insolent. Amongst whome in the daies of *Tully* one *Roscius* grewe to be of such exquisit perfection in his facultie, that he offered to contend with the Orators of that time in gesture, as they did in eloquence; boasting that he could expresse a passion in as many sundrie actions, as *Tully* could discourse it in varietie of phrases: yea so prowde he grewe by the daylie applause of people, that he looked for honour and reverence to bee done him in the streetes: which selfe conceipt when *Tully* entred into with a pearcing insight, he quipt at in this manner.

   It chanced that *Roscius* & he met at a dinner, both guests unto *Archias* the Poet, where the prowd Comedian dared to make comparison with *Tully*: which insolencie made the learned Orator to growe into these termes; why *Roscius*, art thou proud with *Esops* Crow, being pranct with the glorie of others feathers: of thy selfe thou canst say nothing, and if the Cobler hath taught thee to say, *Ave Cæsar*, disdain not thy tutor, because thou pratest in a Kings chamber: what sentence thou utterest on the stage, flowes from the censure of our wittes; and what sentence or conceipte of the invention the people applaud for excellent, that comes from the secrets of our knowledge. I graunt your action, though it be a kind of

mechanical labour; yet wel done tis worthie of praise: but you worthlesse, if for so small a toy you waxe proud. At this *Roscius* waxt red, and bewraied his imperfection with silence: but this check of *Tully* could not keepe others from the blemish of that fault, for it grew to a generall vice amongst the Actors, to excell in pride as they did exceede in excellence, and to brave it in the streetes, as they bragge it on the stage: so that they reveld it in *Rome* in such costly roabes, that they seemed rather men of great patrimonie, than such as lived by the favour of the people. Which *Publius Servilius* very well noted; for hee being the sonne of a Senatour, and a man very valiant, met on a day with a player in the streetes richly apparrelled; who so farre forgat himselfe, that he tooke the wall of the young noble man, which *Servilius* taking in disdaine, countercheckt with this frump: My friend (quoth hee) be not so bragge of thy silken roabes, for I sawe them but yesterday make a great shew in a broakers shop. At this the one was ashamed, and the other smilde, and they which heard the quip, laught at the folly of the one & the wit of the other. Thus sir have you heard my opinion briefly of plaies, that *Menander* devised them for the suppressing of vanities, necessarie in a common wealth, as long as they are used in their right kind; the play makers worthy of honour for their Arte: & players, men deserving both prayse and profite, as long as they wax neither covetous nor insolent. I have caused you sir (quoth the gentleman) to make a large digression, but you have resolved me in a matter that I long doubted of: and therefore I pray you againe to *Francesco*. Why then thus quoth the Palmer: After he grew excellent for making of Comedies, he waxt not onely brave, but full of Crownes: which *Infida* hearing of, and having intelligence what course of life he did take; thought to cast foorth her lure to reclaime him, though by her unkindnesse she was proved haggard; for she thought that *Francesco* was such a tame foole that he would be brought to strike at any stale, decking her selfe therefore as gorgiously as she could, painting her face with the choyce of all her drugges, she walkt abroade where shee thought *Francesco* used to take the ayre; Love and Fortune joyning in league so favoured her, that according to her desire she met him. At which incounter I gesse, more for shame than love she blusht; and fild her countenaunce with such repentant remorse (yet having her lookes full of amorous glaunces) that she seemed like *Venus*, reconciling her selfe to froward *Mars*. The sight of *Infida* was pleasing in the eyes of *Francesco*, and almost as deadly as the basilisk: that had hee not had about him *Moly* as *Ulisses*, he had been inchaunted by the charmes of that wylie *Circes*; but the abuse so stucke in his stomack that she had profered him in his extremitie, that he returned all her glaunces with a frowne, and so parted. . . .

—sigs. B3v–C1v

1592

Greenes, Groats-worth of witte

Robert Greene is reported to have been on his deathbed when he wrote his biography of a debauched young man who lived a life not unlike the author's own: Greenes, Groatsworth of witte, bought with a million of Repentance *(1592). In the following excerpt, an actor's description of his glamorous life convinces Roberto to become a playwright, a decision that contributes to his utter ruin.*

On the other side of the hedge sate one that heard his sorrow: who getting over, came towards him, and brake off his passion. When hee approached, hee saluted *Roberto* in this sort.

Gentleman quoth hee (for so you seeme) I have by chaunce heard you discourse some part of your greefe; which appeareth to be more than you will discover, or I can conceipt. But if you vouchsafe such simple comforte as my abilitie may yeeld, assure your selfe, that I will indevour to doe the best, that either may procure you profite, or bring you pleasure: the rather, for that I suppose you are a scholler, and pittie it is men of learning should live in lacke.

Roberto wondring to heare such good wordes, for that this iron age affoordes few that esteeme of vertue; returnd him thankfull gratulations, and (urgde by necessitie) uttered his present griefe, beseeching his advise how he might be imployed. Why, easily quoth hee, and greatly to your benefite: for men of my profession gette by schollers their whole living. What is your profession, said *Roberto*? Truly sir, saide hee, I am a player. A player, quoth *Roberto*, I tooke you rather for a Gentleman of great living, for if by outward habit men should be censured, I tell you, you would bee taken for a substantiall man. So am I where I dwell (quoth the player) reputed able at my proper cost to build a Windmill. What though the world once went hard with me, when I was faine to carry my playing Fardle a footebacke; *Tempora mutantur*, I know you know the meaning of it better than I, but I thus conster it, its otherwise now; for my very share in playing apparell will not be sold for two hundred pounds. Truly (said *Roberto*) tis straunge, that you should so prosper in that vayne practice, for that it seemes to mee your voice is nothing gratious. Nay then, saide the Player, I mislike your judgement: why, I am as famous for Delphrigus, & the King of Fairies, as ever was any of my time. The twelve labors of Hercules have I terribly thundred on the Stage, and plaid three Scenes of the Devill in the High way to heaven. Have ye so (saide *Roberto*?) then I pray you pardon me. Nay more (quoth the Player) I can serve to make a pretie speech, for I was a countrey

Author, passing at a Morall for twas I that pende the Morall of mans witte, the Dialogue of Dives, and for seven yeers space was absolute Interpreter to the puppets. But now my Almanacke is out of date:

The people make no estimation,
Of Morrals teaching education.

Was not this prettie for a plaine rime extempore? if ye will ye shall have more. Nay its enough, said *Roberto*, but how meane you to use mee? Why sir, in making Playes, said the other, for which you shall be well paid, if you will take the paines.

Roberto perceiving no remedie, thought best in respect of his present necessitie, to try his wit, & went with him willingly: who lodgd him at the Townes end in a house of retayle, where what happened to our Poet, you shall after heare. There by conversing with bad company, he grew *A malo in peius*, falling from one vice to an other: and so having founde a vaine to finger crowns, he grew cranker than *Lucanio*, who by this time began to droope, beeing thus dealt with by *Lami[l]ia*. Shee having bewitched him with hir enticing wiles, caused him to consume in lesse than two yeéres that infinite treasure gathered by his father with so many a poore mans curse. His lands sold, his jewels pawnd, his money wasted, he was casseérd by *Lamilia*, that had coossend him of all. Then walkt he like one of Duke *Humfreys* Squires, in a thread-bare cloake, his hose drawne out with his heeles, his shooes unseamed, least his feete should sweate with heat: now (as witlesse as hee was) he remembred his Fathers words, his unkindnes to his brother, his carelesnes of himselfe. In this sorrow he sate down on pennilesse bench; where when *Opus* and *Usus* told him by the chymes in his stomacke it was time to fall unto meat, he was faine with the Camelion to feed upon the aire, and make patience his best repast.

While he was at this feast, *Lamilia* came flaunting by, garnished with the jewels wherof she beguiled him, which sight served to close his stomacke after his cold cheare. *Roberto* hearing of his brothers beggery, albeit he had little remorse of his miserable state, yet did seeke him out; to use him as a propertie, whereby *Lucanio* was somewhat provided for. But beeing of simple nature, hee served but for a blocke to whet *Robertoes* wit on: which the poore foole perceiving, he forsooke all other hopes of life, and fell to be a notorious Pandar, in which detested course he continued till death. But *Roberto* now famozed for an Arch-plaimaking-poet, his purse like the sea sometime sweld; anon like the same sea fell to a low ebbe; yet seldom he wanted, his labors were so well esteemed. Marry this rule he kept; what ever he fingerd afore hand, was the certaine meanes to unbinde a bargaine, and being askt why hee so slightly dealt with them that did him good? It becoms me, saith hee, to bee contrary to the worlde; for commonly when vulgar men receive earnest, they doo performe, when I am paid any thing afore-hand, I breake my promise.

He had shift of lodgings, where in every place his Hostesse writ up the wofull remembrance of him, his laundresse, and his boy; for they were ever his in houshold, beside retainers in sundry other places. His companie were lightly the lewdest persons in the land, apt for pilferie, perjurie, forgerie, or any villainy. Of these hee knew the casts to cog at cards, coossen at Dice; by these he learnd the legerdemaines of nips, foystes, connycatchers, crosbyters, lifts, high Lawyers, and all the rabble of that uncleane generation of vipers: and pithily could he paint out their whole courses of craft: So cunning he was in all craftes, as nothing rested in him almost but craftines. How often the Gentle-woman his Wife labored vainely to recall him, is lamentable to note: but as one given over to all lewdnes, he communicated her sorrowfull lines among his loose truls, that jested at her bootlesse laments. If he could any way get credite on scores, he would then brag his creditors carried stones, comparing every round circle to a groning O procured by a painfull burden. The shamefull ende of sundry his consorts deservedly punished for their amisse, wrought no compunction in his heart: of which one, brother to a Brothell hee kept, was trust under a tree as round as a Ball.

−sigs. D4r−E2

1593

Nashe's *Christs Teares Over Jerusalem*

In Christs Teares Over Jerusalem. Wherunto is annexed, a comparative admonition to London *(1593) Thomas Nashe laments the excesses to which Londoners are given, comparing their lavish apparel and superficial morality to that seen on the stage.*

Decke our selves how we will, in all our royaltie, wee cannot equalize one of the Lillies of the fielde, as they wither, so shall we wanze and decay, and our place no more be found. Though our span long youthly prime, blossomes foorth eye-banqueting flowers, though our delicious gleaming features, make us seeme the Sonnes and Daughters of the Graces, though we glister it never so in our worme-spunne robes, and golde-florisht garments, yet in the grave shall we rotte: from our redolentest refined compositions, ayre pes-tilenzing stincks, and breath-choking poysnous vapours shall issue.

England, the Players stage of gorgeous attyre, the Ape of all Nations superfluities, the continuall Masquer in out-landish habilements, great plenty-scanting calamities, art thou to await, for wanton disguising thy selfe against kind, and digressing from the plainnesse of thine Auncesters. Scandalous and shamefull is it, that not anie in thee, (Fishermen & Husbandmen set aside) but lyve above their ability and birth; That the outward habite, (which in other Countries is the only distinction of honour,) shoulde yeelde in thee no difference of persons: that all thy auncient Nobilitie, (almost,) with this gorgeous prodigalitie, should be devoured and eaten uppe, and up-starts inhabite their stately Pallaces, who from farre have fetcht in this varietie of pride to entrappe and to spoyle them. Those of thy people that in all other things are miserable, in their apparraile will be prodigal. No Lande can so unfallibly experience this Proverbe, *The hoode makes not the Moncke*, as thou: for Tailers, Serving-men, Make-shifts and Gentlemen, in thee are confounded. For the compasment of bravery, we have them will robbe, steale, cosen, cheate, betray theyr owne Fathers, sweare and for-sweare, or doe any thing. Take away braverie, you kill the hart of lust and incontinencie. Wherefore doe men make themselves brave, but to riot and to revell? Looke after what state theyr apparraile is, that state they take to them and carry, and after a little accustoming to that carriage, perswade themselves they are such indeede.

−folios 73v−74r

Others there are (though not of the same order) that can never heare, but when they are flattered, & they cry continually to their Preachers, *Loquere nobis placentia, Loquere nobis placentia*. Speake to us nothing but pleasing things. And even as *Archabius* the Trumpeter, had more given him to cease then to sound, (the noise that he made was so harsh,) so wil they give them more to cease then to sound, to corrupt them then to make them sound, to feede their sores then to launch them. The noise of judgements which they pronounce, soundeth too harshe in theyr eares. They must have *Orpheus* melodie, whom the *Ciconian* weomen tore in peeces, because with his musique, hee corrupted and effeminated theyr men. *Guido* saith, There are certaine devils that can abide no musick, these are contrary devils, for they delight in nothing but the musique of flattery. Moving words please them, but they heare them but as a passion in a play, which maketh them ravishtly melancholy, and nere renteth the hart.

−folios 81v−82r

1598

Rankins's *Seaven Satyres Applyed to the Weeke*

The following excerpt is from William Rankins's Seaven Satyres Applyed to the Weeke *(1598). Rankins here describes a man whose infatuation with a boy player is exploited by his greedy associates; Ben Jonson uses a similar plot in his city comedy* Epicoene, or The Silent Woman *(circa 1609).*

And once Ile tell you how this gallant sped,
He was inamored of a players boy,
And certaine sharkers that upon him fed,
Did soone instruct the stage boy to be coy,
That but with him, he had no other joy:
In womans queint attyre they drest the lad,
That almost made the foole my maister mad.

They soone perswaded him she was an heyre,
And onely daughter to a knight well knowne,
He saw her young, rich, amorous and faire,
Have her he must, or dye he would with moane,
In sleepy nights his very soule did groane:
Then had not I been stickler in this strife,
The beast had had a male-kinde to his wife.

                     –sigs. C2v–C3r

1599

Davies and Marlowe's *Epigrammes and Elegies*

In Epigrammes and Elegies *(circa 1599) lawyer Sir John Davies and playwright Christopher Marlowe expose the faults of men and women of leisure. The "gallants"—idle young men—they describe spend part of their time at the theater. The epigrams provide a few details about the practices and reputation of the theater: Rufus is rich enough to sit onstage; Cosmus enjoys the song and dance with which plays ended; Fuscus needs to decide whether to spend his money going to see a play or visiting a brothel; and many young gallants spend their time thinking about plays when they should be considering matters of state.*

In Rufum 3

Rufus the Courtier at the theatre,
Leaving the best and most conspicuous place,
Doth either to the stage himselfe transfer,
Or through a grate doth shew his doubtfull face.

For that the clamorous frie of Innes of court,
Filles up the private roomes of greater prise:
And such a place where all may have resort,
He in his singularitie doth despise.

Yet doth not his particular humour shunne,
The common stews and brothels of the towne,
Though all the world in troupes do thither runne,
Cleane and uncleane, the gentle and the clowne:
    Then why should Rufus in his pride abhorre
    A common seate that loves a common whore.

                     –sig. A4r

In Faustum 7

Faustus not lord, nor knight, nor wise, nor old,
To every place about the towne doth ride,
He rides into the fieldes Playes to behold,
He rides to take boate at the water side,
He rides to Poules, he rides to th' ordinarie,
He rides unto the house of bawderie too,
Thither his horse so often doth him carry,
That shortly he will quite forget to go.

                     –sig. Br

In Cosmum 17

Cosmus hath more discoursing in his head,
Then Jove, when Pallas issued from his braine,
And still he strives to be delivered
Of all his thoughts at once, but all in vaine:
For as we see at all the play-house doores,
When ended is the play, the daunce, the song,
A thousand townsmen, gentlemen, and whores
Porters and servingmen togither throng,
So thoughts of drinking, thriving, wenching, warre,
And borrowing money raging in his mind,
To issue all at once so forward are,
As none at all can perfect passage find.

                 –sigs. B2v–B3r

In Fuscum. 39

Fuscus is free, and hath the world at will,
Yet in the course of life that hee doth leade,
Hees like a horse which turning round a mill,
Doth alwaies in the selfe same circle treade:
    First he doth rise at ten, and at eleven
    He goes to Gilles, where he doth eate til one,
    Then sees a play till five, and suppers at seaven,
    And after supper straight to bed is gone,
And there till tenne next day he doth remaine,
And then he dines, then sees a Commedie,
And then he suppes, and goes to bed againe,
Thus rounde he runnes without varietie,
    Save that sometimes he comes not to the play,
    But falles into a whore house by the way.

                     –sig. Dr

Meditations of a Gull. 47

See yonder melancholy Gentleman,
Which hoodwinck'd with his hat, alone doth sit,
Thinke what he thinkes, and tel me if you can,
What great affaires troubles his little wit:
    He thinkes not of the warre twixt France & Spain,
    Whether it be for Europes good or ill,
    Nor whether the Empire can it selfe maintaine
    Against the Turkish powre encroching still.
Nor what great towne in all the nether lands,
The States determine to besiege this spring,
Nor how the Scottish pollicie now standes,
Nor what becomes of th' Irish mutining:
    But he doth seriouslie bethinke him whether
    Of the guld people he be more esteemde,
    For his long cloake, or for his great blacke feather,
    By which each gull is now a gallant deemde.
Or of a Journey he deliberates,
To Paris garden cock-pit, or the play,
Or how to steale a dogge he meditates,
Or what he shall unto his mistris say:
    Yet with these thoughts he thinks himselfe most fit
    To be of counsell with a King for wit.

                           —sigs. D3r–v

Weever's *Epigrammes in the oldest cut, and newest fashion*

When in Epigrammes in the oldest cut, and newest fashion *(1599) John Weever mocks an actor who has "lost his tongue," he is not referring to forgotten lines: he alludes to Thomas Kyd's* The Spanish Tragedy *(circa 1587), in which Hieronimo bites out his tongue to prevent his further interrogation, although without then announcing, as the subject of Weever's poem does, that he is tongueless. In the event some of his readers missed the joke, Weever explains it in the next epigram.*

Epig. 6. In Ruffinum.

Ruffinus lost his tongue on stage,
And wot ye how he made it knowne?
He spittes it out in bloudy rage,
And told the people he had none:
    The fond spectators said, he acted wrong,
    The dumbest man may say, he hath no tongue.

Epig 7. In eundem.

Ruffinus hath no tongue, why?
    For now he lost one:
Ruffinus hath a tongue, why?
    He says he hath none.

                           —sig. C1v

1600

Rowlands's *The Letting Of Humours Blood In The Head-Vaine*

In The Letting Of Humours Blood In The Head-Vaine *(1600) satirist Samuel Rowlands issues a plea to playwrights to stop providing words for actors to parrot and instead turn their skills to producing worthwhile poetry. In the margin beside lines 8–11 of "To Poets," there is a bracket and a note: "P. B. by / writing / won a / golden / Penne."*

TO POETS.

Good honest *Poets*, let me crave a boone,
That you would write, I do not care how soone,
Against the bastard humours howerly bred,
In every mad brain'd wit-worne giddie head:
At such grosse follies do not sit and wincke,
Belabour these same Gulles with pen and incke.
You see some strive for faire hand-writing fame,
As *Peeter Bales* his signe can prove the same,
Gracing his credite with a golden Pen:
I would have *Poets* prove more taller men:
In perfect Letters rested his contention,
But yours consist's in Wits choyce rare invention.
Will you stand spending your inventions treasure,
To teach Stage parrats speake for pennie pleasure,
While you your selves like musicke sounding Lutes
fretted and strunge, gaine them their silken sutes.
Leave *Cupids* cut, Womens face flatt'ring praise,
Loves subject growes too thredbare now adayes.
Change *Venus* Swannes, to write of *Vulcans* Greefe,
And you shall merite Golden Pennes a peece.

                           —sig. A3r

4. SATIRE.

Melfluvious, sweete Rose-watred elloquence,
Thou that hast hunted Barbarisme hence,
And taught the goodman *Cobbin* at his plow,
To be as elloquent as *Tullie* now:
Who nominicates his Bread and Cheese a name,
(That doth untrusse the nature of the same)
His stomacke stayer. How dee like the phrase?
Are Plowmen simple fellowes now a dayes?
Not so my Maisters: What meanes *Singer* then?
And *Pope* the Clowne, to speake so Boorish, when
They counterfaite the clownes upon the Stage?
Since Countrey fellowes grow in this same age,
To be so quaint in their new printed speech,
That cloth will now compare with Velvet breech. . . .

                           —sig. D8r

1605

A Translation of Dedekind's *Grobianus et Grobiana*

The Schoole of Slovenrie: Or, Cato turnd wrong side outward. Translated out of Latine into English verse, to the use of all English Christendome except Court and Cittie *(1605) is an anonymous English translation of Friedrich Dedekind's* Grobianus et Grobiana *(1549). A satiric guide to bad behavior, the book includes a stanza on going to see a theatrical performance.*

Meane time perchance unto the cittie Players there are come,
Which round about the towne proclaime their Play by sownd of drum.
Unto the vulgars store of feates and active trickes theile show,
That they upon them to maintaine them, something may bestow.
Many profane and base, both words and actions they will have,
Which are mislikte of such as are of life and manners grave.
And yet it is thy dutie unto every word to harke,
And all their gestures and their actions carefully to marke.
To all their wanton words, you your attentive care must give,
According unto that you heare, heereafter you must live,
Whether you naughty words do heare, or beastly sights do see,
To blush at either of them both is not beseeming thee.
For one which for some great offence hath suffred some disgrace,
You will be thought, if blushing colours are within your face.
Let nothing in your cheekes a red unseemely colour raise,
Keepe still this rule, there can be found no neerer way to praise.
All men will thinke that you the way to vice did never know,
If in your gestures you no signe of blushing use to show.
But if you use to laugh alowd as if that you were madde,
All men will thinke that of my Book the practice you have had.

                                        —sigs. R4v–S

1607

Merrie Conceited Jests of George Peele Gentleman

In Merrie Conceited Jests of George Peele Gentleman, sometimes a student in Oxford. Wherein is shewed the course of his life how he lived: a man very well knowne in the Citie of London and elsewhere *(1607) poet and playwright Peele is the subject of this short and perhaps apocryphal tale describing an impromptu— and criminal—stage performance. The anecdote includes details of the practices of touring companies of actors.*

The Jest of George Peele at
Bristow.

George was at Bristow, and there staying somwhat longer then his coyne would last him, his palfrey that should be his carier to London, his head was growne so big that he could not get him out of the stable, it so fortuned at that instant, certaine players came to the towne, and lay at that Inne where *George Peele* was: to whome *George* was well knowne, beeing in that time an excellent Poet, and had acquaintance of most of the best Players in England, from the triviall sort he was but so so: of which these were, only knew *George* by name no otherwise, there was not past three of the company come with the Cariage, the rest were behinde, by the reason of a long Jorney they had, so that night they could not inact, which *George* hearing had presently a stratagam in his head, to get his Horse free out of the stable: and money in his purse to beare his Charges up to Londone, and thus it was, hee goes directly to the Mayor tels him he was a scholler and a gentleman, and that he had a tertan historie of the knight of Rodes & withall how Bristow was first founded and by whome, & a briefe of all those that before him had succeeded in office in that worshipfull City desiring the Mayor that he with his presence, & the rest of his Brethren would grace his labours: The Mayor agreed to it, gave him leave and withall apointed him a place, but for himselfe he could not be there beeing in the evening, but bid him make his best benefit he could of the City: and very liberally gave him an Angell, which George thankfully receives, and about his businesse hee goes, got his stadge made, his history cryed, and hyred the players Apparell, to flourish out his show, promising to pay them liberally and withall desired them they favour him so much as to gather him his mony at the doore, for he thought it his best course to imploy them, least they should spy out his knavery, for they have parlous heads, they willingly yeeld to doe him any kindnesse that lies in them, in briefe caries their apparell to the Hall. placeth themselves at the doore, where *George* in the meane time with the ten shillings hee had of the Mayor, delivered his horse out of purgatory and caries him to the Townes end, and there placeth him, to be ready at his comming. By this time the Audience were come, and some forty shillings gathered, which mony *George* put in his purse, and putting on one of the Players silke Robes, after the trumpet had sounded thrise: out he comes, makes lowe obaysance goes forward with his prologue, which was thus,

A tryfling toy, a Jest of no account, pardie.
The Knight perhaps, you thinke for to be I.

Thinke on so still, for why you know that thought is free
Sit still a while, Ile send the Actors to ye.

Which beeing said after some fire workes that hee had made of purpose, threw out among them, & down staires goes he gets to his horse and so with his forty shillings to London leaves the Players to answere it, who when the Jest was knowne, their Inocence excused them, beeing as well gulled as the Mayor, and the Audience.

–pp. 16–17

1609

Dekker's *The Guls Horne-booke*

In The Gull's Horne-booke *(1609) playwright and pamphlet writer Thomas Dekker mocks the behavior of London's young gallants by providing them with an advice book to guide their bad behavior. In the following excerpt he describes how to make a fool of yourself at the theater.*

CHAP. VI.
How a Gallant should behave himselfe in a Play-house.

The Theater is your Poets Royal-Exchange, upon which their Muses (that are now turnd to Merchants) meeting, barter away that light commodity of words for a lighter ware then words. *Plaudities* and the *Breath* of the great *Beast*, which (like the threatnings of two Cowards) vanish all into aire. *Plaiers* and their *Factors*, who put away the stuffe, and make the best of it they possibly can (as indeed tis their parts so to doe) your Gallant, your Courtier and your Capten, had wont to be the soundest paymaisters, and I thinke are still the surest chapmen: and these by meanes that their heades are well stockt, deale upon this comical freight by the grosse: when your *Groundling*, and *Gallery Commoner* buyes his sport by the penny, and, like a *Hagler*, is glad to utter it againe by retailing.

Sithence then the place is so free in entertainement, allowing a stoole as well to the Farmers sonne as to your Templer: that your Stinkard has the selfe same libertie to be there in his Tabacco-Fumes, which your sweet Courtier hath: and that your Car-man and Tinker claime as strong a voice in their suffrage, and sit to give judgement on the plaies life and death, as well as the prowdest *Momus* among the tribe of *Critick*: It is fit that hee, whom the most tailors bils do make roome for, when he comes should not be basely (like a vyoll) casd up in a corner.

Whether therefore the gatherers of the publique or private Play-house stand to receive the afternoones

rent let our Gallant (having paid it) presently advance himselfe up to the Throne of the Stage. I meane not into the Lords roome, (which is now but the Stages Suburbs) No, those boxes by the iniquity of custome, conspiracy of waiting-women and Gentlemen-Ushers, that there sweat together, and the covetousnes of Sharers, are contemptibly thrust into the reare, and much new Satten is there dambd by being smothred to death in darknesse. But on the very Rushes where the Commedy is to daunce, yea and under the state of *Cambiles* himselfe must our fetherd *Estridge*, like a peece of Ordnance be planted valiantly (because impudently) beating downe the mewes & hisses of the opposed rascality.

For do but cast up a reckoning, what large cummings in are pursd up by sitting on the Stage, First a conspicuous *Eminence* is gotten, by which meanes the best and most essenciall parts of a Gallant (good cloathes, a proportionable legge, white hand, the Persian lock, and a tollerable beard) are perfectly revealed.

By sitting on the stage, you have a signd pattent to engrosse the whole commodity of Censure; may lawfully presume to be a Girder; & stand at the helme to steere the passage of Scænes yet no man shal once offer to hinder you from obtaining the title of an insolent over-weening Coxcombe.

By sitting on the stage, you may (without travelling for it) at the very next doore, aske whose play it is: and by that *Quest* of *Inquiry*, the law warrants you to avoid much mistaking: if you know not the author, you may raile against him: and peradventure so behave your selfe, that you may enforce the Author to know you.

By sitting on the stage, if you be a Knight, you may happily get you a Mistresse: if a meere *Fleet street* Gentleman, a wife; but assure your selfe by continuall residence, you are the first and principall man in election to begin the number of *We three*.

By spreading your body on the stage, and by being a Justice in examining of plaies, you shall put your selfe into such true *Scænicall* authority that some Poet shall not dare to present his Muse rudely upon your eyes, without having first unmaskt her, rifled her, and discovered all her bare and most mysticall parts before you at a Taverne, when you most knightly shal for his paines, pay for both their suppers.

By sitting on the stage, you may (with small cost) purchase the deere acquaintance of the boyes: have a good stoole for sixpence: at any time know what particular part any of the infants present: get your match lighted, examine the play-suits lace, and perhaps win wagers upon laying tis copper, &c. And to conclude whether you be a foole or a Justice of peace, a Cuckold or a Capten, a Lord Maiors sonne or a dawcocke, a knave or an under Shreife, of what stamp soever you be, currant or counterfet, the Stagelike time will bring you to most perfect light, and lay you open: neither are you to be hunted from thence though the Scar-crowes in the yard, hoot at you, hisse at you, spit at you, yea throw durt even in your teeth: tis most Gentlemanlike patience to endure all this, and to laugh at the silly Animals; but if the *Rabble* with a full throat, crie away with the foole, you were worse then a mad-man to tarry by it: for the Gentleman and the foole should never sit on the Stage together.

Mary let this observation go hand in hand with the rest: or rather like a country-servingman, some five yards before them. Present not your selfe on the Stage (especially at a new play) untill the quaking prologue hath (by rubbing) got cullor into his cheekes, and is ready to give the trumpets their Cue that hees upon point to enter: for then it is time, as though you were one of the *Properties*, or that you dropt out of the *Hangings* to creepe from behind the Arras with your *Tripos* or three-footed stoole in one hand, and a teston mounted betweene a fore-finger and a thumbe in the other: for if you should bestow your person upon the vulgar, when the belly of the house is but halfe full, your apparell is quite eaten up, the fashion lost, and the proportion of your body in more danger to be devoured, then if it were servd up in the Counter amongst the Powltry: avoid that as you would the Bastome. It shall crowne you with rich commendation to laugh alowd in the middest of the most serious and saddest scene of the terriblest Tragedy: and to let that clapper (your tongue) be tost so high that all the house may ring of it: your Lords use it; your Knights are Apes to the Lords, and do so too: your Inne-a-court-man is Zany to the Knights, and (many very scurvily) comes likewise limping after it: bee thou a beagle to them all, and never lin snuffing till you have sented them: for by talking and laughing (like a Plough-man in a Morris) you heap *Pelion* upon *Ossa*, glory upon glory: As first, all the eyes in the galleries will leave walking after the Players, and onely follow you: the simplest dolt in the house snatches up your name, and when he meetes you in the streetes, or that you fall into his hands in the middle of a Watch, his word shall be taken for you, heele cry, *Hees such a Gallant*, and you passe. Secondly, you publish your temperance to the world, in that you seeme not to resort thither to taste vaine pleasures with a hungrie appetite; but onely as a Gentleman, to spend a foolish houre or two, because you can doe nothing else. Thirdly you mightily disrelish the Audience, and disgrace the Author: mary you take up (though it be at the worst hand) a strong opinion of your owne judgement and inforce the Poet to take pitty of your weakenesse, and by some dedicated sonnet to bring you into a better paradice, onely to stop your mouth.

If you can (either for love or money) provide your selfe a lodging by the water side: for above the conveniencie it brings to shun Shoulder-clapping, and to ship away your Cockatrice betimes in the morning it adds a kind of state unto you, to be carried from thence to the staires of your Play-house: hate a Sculler (remember that) worse then to be acquainted with one ath Scullery. No, your Oares are your onely Sea-crabs, boord them, & take heed you never go twice together with one paire: often shifting is a great credit to Gentlemen: & that dividing of your Fare wil make the poore watersnaks be ready to pul you in peeces to enjoy your custome: No matter whether upon landing you have money or no, you may swim in twentie of their boates over the river, upon *Ticket*: mary when silver comes in, remember to pay trebble their fare, & it will make your Flounder catchers to send more thankes after you, when you doe not draw, then when you doe: for they know, It will be their owne another daie.

Before the Play begins, fall to cardes, you may win or loose (as Fencers doe in a prize) and beate one another by confederacie, yet share the money when you meete at supper: notwithstanding, to gul the *Ragga-muffins* that stand a loofe gaping at you, throw the cards (having first torne foure or five of them) round about the Stage, just upon the third sound, as though you had lost: it skils not if the foure knaves ly on their backs, and outface the Audience, theres none such fooles as dare take exceptions at them, because ere the play go off better knaves then they, will fall into the company.

Now sir, if the writer be a fellow that hath either epigramd you, or hath had a flirt at your mistris, or hath brought either your feather or your red beard, or your little legs &c. on the stage, you shall disgrace him worse then by tossing him in a blancket, or giving him the bastinado in a Taverne, if in the middle of his play, (bee it Pastorall or Comedy, Morall or Tragedie) you rise with a skreud and discontented face from your stoole to be gone: no matter whether the Scenes be good or no, the better they are, the worse doe you distast them: and beeing on your feete, sneake not away like a coward, but salute all your gentle acquaintance, that are spred either on the rushes or on stooles about you, and draw what troope you can from the stage after you: the *Mimicks* are beholden to you, for allowing them elbow roome: their Poet cries perhaps a pox go with you, but care not you for that, theres no musick without frets.

Mary if either the company, or indisposition of the weather binde you to sit it out, my counsell is then that you turne plaine Ape, take up a rush and tickle the earnest eares of your fellow gallants, to make other fooles fall a laughing: mewe at passionate speeches, blare at merrie, finde fault with the musicke, whew at the childrens Action, whistle at the songs: and above all, curse the sharers, that whereas the same day you had bestowed forty shillings on an embrodered Felt and Feather, (scotch-fashion) for your mistres in the Court, or your punck in the Cittie, within two houres after, you encounter with the very same block on the stage, when the haberdasher swore to you the impression was extant but that morning.

To conclude, hoord up the finest play-scraps you can get, uppon which your leane wit may most savourly feede for want of other stuffe, when the *Arcadian* and *Euphuird* gentlewomen have their tongues sharpened to set upon you: that qualitie (next to your shittlecocke) is the onely furniture to a Courtier thats but a new beginner, and is but in his *A B C* of complement. The next places that are fild, after the Playhouses bee emptied, are (or ought to be) Tavernes, into a Taverne then let us next march, where the braines of one Hogshead must be beaten out to make up another.

—pp. 27–30

1613

Parrot's *Laquei ridiculosi*

In Laquei ridiculosi: Or Springes for Woodcocks *(1613) Henry Parrot follows John Marston's advice, given in* The Scourge of Villany *(1599), about writing satire: the poet's duty is "under feigned, private names to note general vice." Parrot mocks actors and audience members for their social pretensions in these excerpts.*

55
Veniunt spectentur ut ipsi.

When yong *Rogero* goes to see a play,
His pleasure is you place him on the Stage,
The better to demonstrate his aray,
And how he sits attended by his Page,
 That onely serves to fill those pipes with smoke,
 For which he pawned hath his riding Cloke.

—sigs. C6v

117
Sic ars diluditur absens.

When *Ralph* returnes each evening from a play,
He tells his wife he was at shop that while,
Which simply she beleeves and goes her way,
Then laughes to see he could her so beguile
 And come upon her: but if all be true,
 Ther's many (*Ralph*) playes on her more then you.

—sig. E6r

131
Theatrum licentis.

Cotta's become a Player, most men know,
And will no longer take such toyling paines;
For heer's the spring (saith he) whence pleasures flow,
And brings them damnable excessive gaines,
 That now are Cedars growne from shrubs and sprigs
 Since *Greenes Tu-quoq*; and those Garlicke Jigs.

—sig. F1v

163
Cignus per plumas Anser.

Put off thy Buskins (*Sophocles* the great,)
And Morter tread with thy disdained shancks,
Thou think'st thy skill hath done a wondrous feat,
For which the world should give thee many thancks:
 Alas, it seemes thy feathers are but loose,
 Pluckt from a Swanne, and set upon a Goose.

—sig. G1v

125
Qui deierat peierat.

Dacus hath damn'd himselfe on due regard
From Tavernes, Plaies, Tobacco, and from Wine,
Swearing hee'l live like *John* of Paules-Church-yard
At least will often with *Duke Humphry* dine:
 T'were well done (*Dacus*) hadst thou power to do it
 But Dice and Drabs (I feare) will hold thee to it.

—sig. N3v

144
Incidit in Syllam cupiens vitare Charibdim.

Marcellus museth how to spend that day,
Wherein it likes him not to see a play;
But then he falles in some worse place (I doubt)
And staies so long till he be fired out.

—sig. N8r

1613

Wither's *Abuses Stript, And Whipt*

The precision of Shakespeare's vocabulary sometimes leads scholars to speculate that he worked as a soldier, sailor, schoolmaster, or grave digger. In the following excerpt from Abuses Stript, And Whipt. Or Satirical Essayes *(1613), poet and pamphlet writer George Wither offers another explanation: that poets have an excellent ear for "tearms and words," sharing Prince Hal's self-described ability to become "so good a proficient in one quarter of an hour, that I can drink with any tinker in his own language during my life" (*1 Henry IV, *2.4.17–20).*

For, of all sorts of men here's my beliefe,
The Poet is most worthy and the chiefe,
His *Science* is the absolut'st and best,
And deserves *honor* above all the rest;
For 'tis no humane knowledge gain'd by *art*,
But rather 'tis inspir'd into the heart
By *divine* meanes; and I do muse men dare,
Twixt it and their professions make compare,
For why should he that's but *Philosopher?*
Geometrician, or *Astrologer?*
Physician, Lawyer, Rethorician,
Historian, Arethmetician?
Or some such like, why should he having found
The meanes but by one *Art* to be renown'd,
Compare with time that claimes to have a part
And interest almost in every *Art?*
And if that men may ad unto their name,
By one of these an everlasting fame,
How much more should it unto them befall,
That have not only one of these, but all?
As Poets have; for do but search their works
And you shall find within their writing lurks
All *knowledge*; if they undertake
Of *divine* matters any speech to make,
You'l think them *Doctors*; if they need to tell
The course of *starres*, they seem for to excell
Great *Ptolemy*; entend they to perswade,
You'l think that they were *Retoritians* made:
What *Law?* what *Physick?* or what *History*
Can these not treat of? Nay, what *mistery*
Are they not learn'd in? If of *Trades* they write,
Have they not all their tearms and words as right
As if they had serv'd an *Apprenteship?*
Can they not name all *tooles* for workmanship?
We see tis true; if one entreat of *wars*,
Of cruell bloudy fraies, of wounds, of scars,
Why then he speaks so like a *souldier* there,
That he hath been begot in arms thou'lt sweare:
Againe, he writes so like a *Navigator*,
As if he had serv'd *Neptune* in the water,
And thou wouldst think he might of travaile make
As great a Volume, as our famous *Drake*;
Old *Proteus*, and *Vertumnus* are but *Apes*,
Compar'd to these, for shifting of their shapes;
There is no hum'rous *Passion* so strange,
To which they cannot in a moment change:
Note but their *Drammaticks*, and you shall see
They'l speak for every *sex*; for each degree,
And in all causes, as if they had been
In every thing, or (at least) all things seen.
If need be, they can like a *Lawyer* prate,
Or talke more gravely like a man of *state*,
They'l have a *Trades-mans* tongue to praise their ware,
And counterfeit him right, (but they'l not sweare):
The curioust *Physicians* (if they please)
Shall not coine words to give their patients ease
So well as they; And if occasion urge,
They'l *Choller*, yea and *Melancholly* purge
Only with charmes and words, and yet it shall,
Be honest meanes, and meerly naturall.
Are they dispos'd to gossip't like a *woman?*

They'l show their tricks so right, that almost no man,
But would so think them: *Virgins* that are purest,
And *Matrons*, that make shew to be demurest,
Speak not so like chast *Cynthia*, as they can,
Nor *Newbery* so like a *Curtezan*,
They'l give words either fitting for a *Clowne*,
Or such as shall not unbeseem a *Crowne*,
In show they will be *chollerick, ambitious,*
Desperate, jealous, mad, or *envious,*
In *sorrow*, or in any *passion* be;
But yet remaine still, from all *passions* free.
For, they have only to this end exprest them,
That men may see them plainer, and detest them.
But some will say that these have on the *stage*,
So painted out the *vices* of this age,
That it not only tells that they have bin,
Experienc't in every kind of *sin*:
But that it also doth corrupt and show,
How men should act those *sins* they did not know.
Oh hatefull saying, not pronounc't by *chance*,
But spewd out of malitious *ignorance*,
Weigh it, and you wil either thinke these weak,
Or say that they do out of envy speake:
Can none declare th'effects of *Drunkennes*,
Unless they used such-like beastlines?
Are all men ignorant what comes by *lust*,
Excepting those, that were themselves unjust?
Or think they no man can describe a *sin*
But that which *he himselfe* hath wallowed in?
If they suppose so, I no cause can tell:
But they may also boldly say as well
They were *apprentices* to every trade,
Of which they find they have descriptions made:
Or for because they see them write those things,
That do belong ro rule, best say th'are *Kings*:
As though that *sacred Poesy* inspir'd,
No other *knowledge* then might be acquir'd
By the dull outward *sense*; yes this is Shee
That showes us not alone all things that be,
But by her powers laies before our view,
Such wondrous things as *Nature* never knew:
And then, wheras they say that *men* are worse,
By reading what these write, 'tis their owne *curse*:
For is the *flower* faulty cause we see
The loathsom *spider* and the painfull *Bee*
Make divers use on't? No, it is the same
Unto the spider, though she cannot frame
Like sweetnes as the Bee thence; But indeed
I must confess that this bad age doth breed
Too many that without respect presume,
This worthy *title* on them to assume,
And undeserv'd; base fellowes, whom meere time
Hath made sufficient to bring forth a *Rime*,
A *Curtaine* Jigge, a libell, or a ballet
For fidlers, or some rogues with staffe and wallet
To sing at dores, men only wise enough
Out of some rotten old worm-eaten stuffe
To patch up a bald witles *Comedy*,
And trim it here and there with *Ribaldry*
Learn'd at a baudy house. I say there's such,
And they can never be disgrac't too much,

For though the name of *Poet* such abuses,
Yet they are enemies to all the *Muses*,
And dare not sort with them for feare they will
Tumble them headlong downe *Pernassus* hill:
Why then should their usurping of it wrong
That *title*, which doth not to them belong?
And wherfore should the shame of this lewd *crew*,
Betide them, unto whom true *honour's* due?
It shall not; for how e're they use the *name*,
Their works will shew how they do merit *fame*;
And though it be disgrace't through ignorance,
The *Generous* will *Poesie* advance,
As the most Antique *Science*, that is found:
And that which hath beene the first root, & ground
Of ev'ry Art; yea that which only brings
Content; And hath beene the delight of *Kings*.

—pp. 220–225

1614

Breton's *I would, And would not*

In I would, And would not *(1614) poet Nicholas Breton offers double perspectives on a variety of professions, including a life in the theater.*

74.

I would I were a Player, and could Act
    As many partes, as came upon a Stage:
And in my braine, could make a full Compact,
    Of all that passeth betwixt Youth and Age.
That I might have five-shares in every Play,
    And let them laugh, that beare the *Bell*-away.

75.

And yet I would not: For then doe I feare,
    If I should gall some *Goos-cappe* with my speech:
That he would freat & fume, and chase, and sweare,
    As if some Flea had bit him by the Breech.
And in some passion, or strange *Agonie*,
    Disturbe both mee, and all the Companie.

—sig. C4r

170.

Time hath a course, which nature cannot stay,
    For youth must die, or come to doting Age:
What is our life on Earth? but as a play,
    Where many a part doth come upon the Stage.
Rich, poore, wise, fond, faire, fowle, & great & smal
    And olde, and young, death makes an ende of al.

171.

Where he that makes his life a Comedy,
    To laugh and sing, and talke away the time:
May finde it in the ende a Tragedy,
    When mournefull Bells doe make no merry chime.
When sad despaire shall feare Infernall evill,
    While Sinne and death, are Agents for the divel.

172.

But doe not Rave, nor Raile, nor stampe, nor stare,
    As if thy care would goe to cuffes with sinne:
But shew how mercy doth Repentance spare,
    While working faith, doth heav'nly favour winne.
And loves obedience to the law doth prove,
    The chosen Soule, that God doth chiefly love.

—sig. Flv

1615

Overbury's *New And Choice Characters*

The following excerpts are from New And Choice Characters, *of severall Authors. Together with that exquisite and unmatcht Poeme,* The Wife, *Written by Syr Thomas Overburie (1615). The "character" is a short prose sketch describing and often mocking a recognizable human type; in this collection by Thomas Overbury, the characters expose Londoners to scrutiny, and the occasional references to the theater provide details about costuming and audience behavior.*

An Hypocrite.

Is a gilded *Pill*, compos'd of two vertuous ingredients, *Naturall dishonestie,* and *Artificiall dissimulation.*

. . . .

If he be a Cleargy Hypocrite, then all manner of vice is for the most part so proper to him, as hee will grudge any man the practise of it but himselfe; like that grave Burgesse, who being desired to lende his Cloathes to represent a part in a Comedy, answered; *No, by his leave, he would have no body play the foole in his cloathes but himselfe.*

. . . .

The author then shows how the Hypocrite demonstrates his "zealous Ignorance."

All this, and much more is in him, that abhorring *Degrees* and *Universities,* as reliques of *Superstition,* hath leapt from a Shop-bord, or a Cloke-bag, to a Deske, or Pulpit, and that like a Sea god in a *Pageant,* hath the rotten laths of his culpable life, and palpable ignorance, covered over with the painted-cloth of a pure gowne, and a night-cap; & with a false Trumpet of *Fained-zeale,* draweth after him some poore *Nymphes* and *Madmen,* that delight more to resort to dark Caves and secrete places, then to open and publike Assemblies.

. . . .

[Hypocrites] must not only be obeyed, fedde, & defended, but admired too: and that their Lay followers do as syncerely, as a shirtlesse fellow with a Cudgell under his arme, doeth a face-wringing *Ballet-singer*, a *Water-bearer* on the floore of a *Play-house*, a wide-mouth'de *Player*; or your Countrey gentleman, a fustian *Poet*, that speakes nothing but bladders and bombast.

—sigs. Ir–I3v

A Fantasticke Innes of Court man.

He is distinguished from a Scholler by a paire of silke stockings, and a Beaver Hatte, which makes him contemne a Scholler as much as a scholler doth a schoolmaister. By that he hath heard one mooting, and seene two playes, he thinks as basely of the *Universitie*, as a young *Sophister* doth of the *Grammar-schoole*.

—sig. I6r

A meere Fellow of an House.

Hee is one whose Hopes commonly exceede his Fortunes, and whose minde soares above his purse. If he hath read *Tacitus*, *Guicchardine*, or *Gallo-Belgicus*, he contemns the *late Lord-Treasurer*, for all the State-policie hee had; and laughes to thinke what a Foole he could make of *Salomon*, if he were now alive. He never weares new cloathes, but against an act or a good time, & is commonly a degree behind the fashion. He hath sworn to see *London* once a yeare, though all his businesse be, to see a Play, walke a turne in *Paules*, and observe the fashion.

—sigs. I6v–I7r

A Puny-clarke.

He is tane from *Grammar-schoole* halfe codled, and can hardly shake off his dreames of breeching in a twelve-month. Hee is a Farmers sonne, and his Fathers utmost ambition is to make him an *Atturney*. He doth itch towards a Poet, and greases his breches extreamely with feeding without a napkin. He studies false dice to cheate Costermongers, & is most chargeable to the butler of some *Inne of Chancery*, for pissing in their Greene-pots. Hee eates Ginger bread at a Play-house; and is so saucy, that he venters fairely for a broken pate, at the banketing house, and hath it.

—sig. K2r

An Improvident young Gallant,

There is a confederacy betweene him and his Cloathes, to be made a puppy: view him well, and you'll say his Gentry sits as ill upon him, as if hee had bought it with his penny. Hee hath more places to send money to, then the Divell hath to send his Spirits: and to furnish each Mistresse, would make him runne beside his wits, if he had any to lose. Hee accounts bashfulnes the wicked'st thing in the world; and therefore studies Impudence. If all men were of his minde, all honestie would bee out of fashion. He withers his Cloathes on the Stage, as a Sale-man is forc't to doe his Suits in Birchin-Lane; and when the Play is done, if you but mark his rising, 'tis a kind of walking Epilogue betweene the two Candles, to know if his Suite may passe for currant.

—sig. K8v

A Water-man

[. . .]His daily labour teaches him the Art of dissembling; for like a fellow that rides to the Pillory, hee goes not that way he lookes. [. . .] The Play-houses only keepe him sober; and as it doth many other Gallants, make him an afternoones man. London Bridge is the most terriblest eye-sore to him that can be. And to conclude, nothing but a *great Presse*, makes him flye from the River; nor any thing, but a *great Frost*, can teach him any good manners.

—sig. L7r

An excellent Actor.

Whatsoever is commendable in the grave Orator, is most exquisitly perfect in him; for by a full and significant action of body, he charmes our attention: sit in a full Theater, and you will thinke you see so many lines drawne from the circumference of so many eares, whiles the *Actor* is the *Center*. He doth not strive to make nature monstrous, she is often seene in the same Scæne with him, but neither on Stilts nor Crutches; and for his voice tis not lower then the prompter, nor lowder then the Foile and Target. By his action he fortifies morall precepts with example; for what we see him personate, we thinke truely done before us: a man of a deepe thought might apprehend, the Ghosts of our ancient *Heroes* walk't againe, and take him (at severall times) for many of them. Hee is much affected to painting, and tis a question whether that make him an excellent Plaier, or his playing an exquisite painter. Hee addes grace to the Poets labours: for what in the Poet is but ditty, in him is both ditty and musicke. He entertaines us in the best leasure of our life, that is betweene meales, the most unfit time, either for study or bodily exercise: the flight of Hawkes, and chase of wilde beastes, either of them are delights noble: but some think this sport of men the worthier, despight all *calumny*. All men have beene of his occupation: and indeed, what hee doth fainedly that doe others essentially: this day one plaies a Monarch, the next a private person. Heere one Acts a Tyrant, on the morrow an Exile: A Parasite this man to night, too morow a

Precisian, and so of divers others. I observe, of all men living, a worthy Actor in one kind is the strongest motive of affection that can be: for when he dies, we cannot be perswaded any man can doe his parts like him. Therefore the imitating Characterist was extreame idle in calling them Rogues. His Muse it seemes, with all his loud invocation, could not be wak't to light him a snuffe to read the Statute: for I would let his malicious ignorance understand, that Rogues are not to be imploide as maine ornaments to his Majesties Revels: but the itch of bestriding the Presse, or getting up on this wodden Pacolet, hath defil'd more innocent paper, then ever did Laxative Physicke: yet is their invention such tyred stuffe, that like Kentish Post-horse they can not go beyond their ordinary stage, should you flea them. But to conclude, I valew a worthy Actor by the corruption of some few of the quality, as I would doe gold in the oare; I should not minde the drosse, but the purity of the metall.

—sigs. M5v–M6v

Stephens's *Satyrical Essayes Characters And Others*

These two excerpts are from John Stephens's Satyrical Essayes Characters And Others. Or Accurate and quick Descriptions, fitted to the life of their Subjects *(1615) and from* Satyrical Essayes and Characters. Ironicall, and Instructive. The Second Impression . . . *(1615). Stephens includes a sketch of actors among his satirical characters, but in the later edition of his collection, he is careful to distinguish between common actors and those wearing the king's livery.*

CHARAC. IIII.

A common Player

Is a *slow Payer, seldome a Purchaser, never a Puritan.* The Statute hath done wisely to acknowledge him a Rogue; for his chiefe Essence is, *A dayly Counterfeite:* Hee hath been familiar so long with out-sides, that hee professes himselfe, (beeing unknowne) to bee an apparant Gentleman. But his thinne Felt, and his Silke Stockings, or his foule Linnen, and faire Doublet, doe (in him) bodily reveale the Broaker: So beeing not sutable, hee proves a *Motley:* his minde observing the same fashion of his body: both consist of parcells and remnants: but his minde hath commonly the newer fashion, and the newer stuffe: hee would not else hearken so passionately after new Tunes, new Trickes, new Devises: These together apparrell his braine and understanding, whilest hee takes the materialls upon trust, and is himselfe the Taylor to take measure of his soules liking. If hee cannot beleeve, hee doth conjecture strongly; but dares not resolve upon particulars, till he hath either spoken, or heard the *Epilogue;* unlesse he be prevented: neither dares hee entitle good things *Good,* unlesse hee bee heartned on by the Multitude: till then, hee saith faintly what hee thinkes, with a willing purpose to recant or persist: So howsoever he pretends to have a royall Master, or Mistresse, his wages and dependance prove him to bee the servant of the people. The cautions of his judging humour (if hee dares undertake it) bee a certaine number of lying jests against the common Lawyer; hansome conceits against the fine Courtiers; delicate quirkes against the rich Cuckold a Cittizen; shadowed glaunces for good innocent Ladies and Gentlewomen; with a nipping scoffe for some honest Justice, who hath once imprisoned him: or some thriftie Trades-man, who hath allowed him no credit: always remembred, his object is, *A new Play,* or *A Play newly revised.* Other Poems hee admits, as good fellowes take Tobacco, or ignorant Burgesses give a voyce, for company sake; as things that neither maintaine, nor bee against him. Hee can seeme no lesse then one in honour, or at least one mounted: for unto miseries which persecute such, hee is most incident. Hence it proceedes, that in the prosperous fortune of a Play frequented, hee proves immoderate, and falles into a Drunkards paradise, till it be *last* no longer. Otherwise when adversities come, they come together: for Lent and Shrove-tuesday bee not farre asunder: then hee is dejected daily and weekely: his blessings be neither lame nor monstrous; they goe upon foure legges; but move slowly; and make as great a distance betweene their steppes, as betweene the foure Tearmes. If he marries, hee mistakes the Woman for the Boy in Womans attire, by not respecting a difference in the mischiefe. But so long as hee lives unmarried, he mistakes the Boy, or a Whore for the Woman; by courting the first on the stage, or visiting the second at her devotions. Take him at the best, he is but a shifting companion; for he lives effectually by putting on, and putting off. If his profession were single, hee would thinke himselfe a simple fellow, as hee doth all professions besides his owne: His owne therefore is compounded of all Natures, all Humours, all professions. Hee is politick enough to perceive the Common-wealths doubts of his licence, and therefore in spight of Parliaments or Statutes he incorporates himselfe by the title of a Brother-hood. I need not multiply his character; for boyes and every one, will no sooner see men of this Faculty walke along, but they will (unasked) informe you what hee is by the vulgar denomination.

—pp. 244–249

In the second impression of Essayes and Characters, *in response to the criticism in* New and Choice Characters *of severall Authors (1615), Stephens provides a more diplomatic conclusion for "A Common Player." The final sentence is replaced with the following:*

Painting & fine cloths may not by the same reason be called abusive, that players may not be called rogues: *For they bee chiefe ornaments of his Majesties Revells.* I need not multiplie his character; for boyes and every one, wil no sooner see men of this Facultie walke along, but they wil unasked, informe you what he is by the vulgar title. Yet in the generall number of them, many may deserve a wise mans commendation: and therefore did I prefix an Epithite of *common,* to distinguish the base and artlesse appendants of our citty companies, which often time start away into rusticall wanderers and then (like Proteus) start backe again into the Citty number.

—p. 301

1616

Jonson's *Epigrammes*

In these passages, which were included in The Workes of Benjamin Jonson *(1616), the playwright and poet critiques his fellow dramatists.*

XLIX.

TO PLAY-WRIGHT.

Play-wright me reades, and still my verses damnes,
  He sayes, I want the tongue of *Epigrammes*;
I have no salt: no bawdrie he doth meane.
  For wittie, in his language, is obscene.
Play-wright, I loath to have thy manners knowne
  In my chast booke: professe them in thine owne.

—p. 781

LVI.

ON POET-APE.

Poore Poet-Ape, that would be thought our chiefe,
  Whose workes are eene the fripperie of wit,

From brocage is become so bold a thiefe,
  As we, the rob'd, leave rage, and pittie it.
At first he made low shifts, would picke and gleane,
  Buy the reversion of old playes; now growne
To a little wealth, and credit in the *scene,*
  He takes up all, makes each mans wit his owne.
And, told of this, he slights it. Tut, such crimes
  The sluggish gaping auditor devoures;
He markes not whose 'twas first: and after-times
  May judge it to be his, as well as ours.
Foole, as it halfe eyes will not know a fleece
  From locks of wooll, or shreds from the whole peece?

—p. 783

LXVIII.

ON PLAY-WRIGHT.

Play-wright convict of publike wrongs to men,
  Takes private beatings, and begins againe.
Two kinds of valour he doth shew at ones;
  Active in's braine, and passive in his bones.

—p. 787

LXXV.

ON LIPPE, THE TEACHER.

I cannot thinke there's that antipathy
  'Twixte *puritanes,* and *players,* as some cry;
Though Lippe, at Pauls, ranne from his text away,
  T'inveigh 'gainst playes: what did he then but play?

—p. 789

C.

ON PLAY-WRIGHT.

Play-wright, by chance, hearing some toyes I'had writ,
  Cry'd to my face, they were th'*elixir* of wit:
And I must now beleeve him: for, to day,
  Five of my jests, then stolne, past him a play.

—p. 799

Anti-Theatrical Tracts

The religious opposition to public theatrical performance has a long and vocal history. Sermons, pamphlets, and endless but often eloquent diatribes regularly warned good Christians to avoid the sin and contamination to be found at the theater. Occasionally these tracts provide details about performance practices, audience sizes, or theater architecture.

1583

Stubbes's "Of Stage-playes and Enterluds, with their wickednes"

These excerpts are from a section titled "Of Stage-playes and Enterluds, with their wickednes" in Phillip Stubbes's The Anatomie of Abuses . . . *(1583).*

All Stage-playes, Enterluds and Commedies, are either of divyne, or prophane matter: If they be of divine matter, than are they most intollerable, or rather Sacrilegious, for that the blessed word of GOD, is to be handled, reverently, gravely, and sagely, with veneration to the glorious Majestie of God, which shineth therin, and not scoffingly, flowtingly, & jybingly, as it is upon stages in Playes & Enterluds, without any reverence, worship, or veneration to the same: the word of our Salvation, the price of Christ his bloud, & the merits of his passion, were not given, to be derided, and jested at as they be in these filthie playes and enterluds on stages & scaffolds, or to be mixt and interlaced with bawdry, wanton shewes & uncomely gestures, as is used (every Man knoweth) in these playes and enterludes.

Stubbes then provides a long list of biblical and classical evidence against players abusing the word of God.

. . . .

Constantius, ordeined that no Player shold be admitted to the table of the Lord. Than seeing, that Playes were first invented by the Devil, practised by the heathen gentiles, and dedicat to their false ydols, Goddes and Goddesses: as the howse, stage and apparell, to *Venus:* the musicke, to *Appollo:* the penning, to *Minerva,*

and the Muses: the action and pronuntiation to *Mercurie* and the rest, it is more than manifest, that they are no fit exercyses for a Christen Man to follow. But if there were no evill in them, save this, namely, that the arguments of tragedies, is anger, wrath, immunitie, crueltie, injurie, incest, murther & such like: the Persons or Actors, are Goddes, Goddesses, Furies, Fyends, Hagges, Kings, Queenes, or Potentates. Of Commedies, the matter and ground is love, bawdrie, cosenage, flattery, whordome, adulterie: the Persons, or agents, whores, queanes, bawdes, scullions, Knaves, Curtezans, lecherous old men, amorous yong men, with such like of infinit varietie: If I say there were nothing els, but this, it were sufficient to withdraw a good christian from the using of them. For so often, as they goe to those howses where Players frequent, thei go to *Venus* pallace & sathans synagogue to worship devils, & betray Christ Jesus.

. . . .

The author treats "The fruits of theathers, & playes," the title given in the margin, at the beginning of this next excerpt.

Do they not maintaine bawdrie, insinuat folery, & renue the remembrance of hethen ydolatrie? Do they not induce whordome & unclennes? nay, are they not rather plaine devourers of maydenly virginitie and chastitie? For proofe wherof, but marke the flocking and running to Theaters & curtens, daylie and hourely, night and daye, tyme and tyde to see Playes and Enterludes, where such wanton gestures, such bawdie speaches: such laughing and fleering: such kissing and bussing: such clipping and culling: Suche winckinge and glancinge of wanton eyes, and the like is used, as is wonderfull to behold. Than these goodly pageants being done, every mate sorts to his mate, every one brings another homeward of their way verye friendly, and in their secret conclaves (covertly) they play the *Sodomits,* or worse. And these be the fruits of Playes and Enterluds, for the most part. And wheras, you say, there are good Examples to be learned in them:

Trulie, so there are: if you will learne falshood, if you will learn cosenage: if you will learn to deceive: if you will learn to play the Hipocrit: to cogge, lye and falsifie: if you will learn to jest, laugh and fleer, to grin, to nodd, and mow: if you will learn to playe the vice, to swear, teare, and blaspheme, both Heaven and Earth: If you will learn to become a bawde, uncleane, and to deverginat Mayds, to deflour honest Wyves: if you will learne to murther, slaie, kill, picke, steal, robbe and rove: If you will learn to rebel against Princes, to comit treasons, to consume treasurs, to practise ydlenes, to sing and talke of bawdie love and venery: if you will lerne to deride, scoffe, mock & flowt, to flatter & smooth: If you will learn to play the whore-maister, the glutton, Drunkard, or incestuous person: if you will learn to become proude, hawtie & arrogant: and finally, if you will learne to comtemne GOD and al his lawes, to care neither for heaven nor hel, and to commit al kinde of sinne and mischeef you need to goe to no other schoole, for all these good Examples, may you see painted before your eyes in enterludes and playes: wherfore, that man who giveth money for the maintenance of them, must needs incurre the damage of *premunire*, that is, eternall damnation except they repent.

. . . .

Therefore I beseech all players & Founder of plaies and enterludes, in the bowels of Jesus Christe, as they tender the salvation of their soules, and others, to leave of that cursed kind of life, and give them selves to such honest exercises, and godly misteries, as God hath commaunded them [. . . .]

—sigs. Lvr–Mr

1599

Rainolds's *Th'overthrow of Stage-Playes*

In Th'overthrow of Stage-Playes, By the way of controversie betwixt D. Gager and D. Rainoldes (1599) *John Rainolds refutes William Gager's defense of academic drama by using a wide array of classical and biblical authorities. The complexity of his argument is matched by the abundance of his footnotes; he is particularly disturbed by the spectacle of young men dressed in women's clothes. In this brief excerpt Rainolds shares the disdain many anti-theater writers express for male actors who play female characters. He is replying to Gager's argument that, as long as the mind is chaste, it does not matter how the body is dressed.*

Yet the third reason, wherein playes are charged, not for making young men come foorth in hoores attire, like[d] the lewde woman in the *Proverbs*; but for teaching them to counterfeit her[e] actions, her[f] wanton kisse, her impudent face, her [g] wicked

speeches and entisements; should have bene allowed even by your owne glosse and exposition of the text: sith[4] you say upon it, that *different behaviour becommeth different sexes, and, it beseemeth not men to folow wemens maners.* [h]*Thetis* taught *Achilles* howe to play the woman in gate, in speech, in gesture: *Sic ergo gradus; sic ora, manusque nate feres, comitesque modis imitabere fictis.* And because his mother had not taught him enough, or he was but a bad scholer: [i]*Deidamia* gave him farder advertisements, how *he must hold his naked brest, his hands,* & so foorth. These are wemens maners unseemelie for *Achilles* to imitate: he should not have done it. How much lesse seemely then is it for young men to danse like wemen, though like [k]those, who praised God with danses: and much lesse seemelie yet to danse like unhonest wemen, like [l]*Herodias?* whereby what a flame of lust may bee kindled in the hearts of men, as redie for the most part to conceve this fire, as flaxe is the other, [m]Christian writers shewe in parte by *Herodes* example: but a [n]Heathen *Poët* more fullie by his owne experience; affirming that hee was not ravished so much with his mistresses face, though marvellous faire and beautifull, nor with her *heare hanging downe loose after the facion about her smooth necke*; nor *with her radiant eyes, like starres*; nor *with her silkes,* & outlandish braverie; as hee was with *her galant dansing.* And greater reason is it you should condemne all stage-playes, wherein young men are trained to play such wemens partes . . .

[d] Prov. 7.10

[e] verse 11.

[f] verse 12.

[g] verse 18.

[4] Distincta sexum forma distinctum decet, Virile non est fœminæ more sequi.

[h] Stat. Achilleid. lib. 1.

[i] lib. 2.

[k] exod 15.20.

[l] Mar. 6.22.

[m] Chrysost. hom. 49. in Matth. Hyperius de feriis Bacchan. Vives de instit. fæminin. Christ lib. 1. cap. de saltationibus.

[n] Propertius lib. 2. eleg.

—pp. 17–18

1600

Vaughan's *The Golden grove*

In this excerpt from William Vaughan's The Golden grove, moralized in three Bookes: A worke very necessary for all such, as would know how to governe themselves, their houses, or their countrey *(1600), marginal notations are embedded in the text and enclosed in brackets.*

Stageplaies fraught altogether with scurrilities and knavish pastimes, are intolerable in a wel governed commonwealth. And chiefly for six reasons. First, *all Stageplayes were dedicated unto Bacchus* the drunken God of the Heathen, and therefore damnable [*Tertull. lib. de speculo.*]. Secondly, *they were forbidden by Christian parliaments* [*Concil. 30. Carthag. & Synod. Laodic. cap. 54.*]. Thirdly, men spend their flourishing time ingloriously and without credit, in contemplating of playes, All other things being spent may be recovered againe, but time is like unto the latter wheele of a coach, that followeth after the former, and yet can never attayne equally unto it. Fourthly, *no foolish and idle talking, nor jesting should be once named amongst us* [*Ephe. 5*]. Fiftly, stageplaies are nothing els, but pompes and showes, in which there is a declining from our beleefe. For what is the promise of Christians at their Baptisme? namely, to renounce the Divell and all his workes, pompes, and vanities. Sixtly, *Stageplayes are the very mockery of the word of God, and the toyes of our life* [*Salvian. lib. 6. de Gubern. Dei.*]. For while we be at the stage, wee are ravished with the love therof, according to the wise mans wordes: *It is a pastime for a foole to doe wickedly*; and so in laughing at filthy things, we sinne [*Prov. 10. 23.*].

—sig. Kr

A Defense of Actors

Playwright Thomas Heywood's Apology *is the only substantial surviving defense of actors and their trade. Compared to the large number of surviving anti-theatrical tracts, his argument may seem like a weak defense, but perhaps the players offered their skilled performances and large audiences as the best answer to the Puritans' complaints.*

1612

Heywood's *An Apology for Actors*

Thomas Heywood's An Apology for Actors. Containing three briefe Treatises. 1. Their Antiquity. 2. Their ancient Dignity. 3. The true use of their quality *(1612) is prefaced by several commendatory poems. Each supports Heywood's argument, and many offer details about theatrical practices: Arthur Hopton comments on the naturalistic acting practiced on the English stage and on the social "profit" that may be attained when "Brave men, brave acts, being bravely acted too, Makes, as men see things done, desire to do" (A1v–A2r); Richard Perkins describes an additional benefit of attending plays rather than reading them: "when I come to playes, I love to sit, / That all may see me in a publike place" (A3r); Christopher Beeston finds that plays, "Of all the modest pastimes [he] can finde," are the art form "most agreeing with a generous minde," making his time at the playhouse "Two houres well spent" (A3r).*

In the two poems that follow, John Taylor provides a lively definition of the purposes of playing, and Heywood reinterprets the conventional notion that all the world's a stage.

To my approved good friend
M. Thomas Heywood.

Of thee, and thy *Apology* for playes,
I will not much speake in contempt or praise:
Yet in these following lines Il'e shew my minde,
Of Playes, and such as have 'gainst Playes repin'd.
A Play's a briefe *Epitome* of time,
Where man m[a]y see his vertue or his crime
Layd open, either to their vices shame,
Or to their vertues memorable fame.
A Play's a true transparant Christall mirror,
To shew good minds their mirth, the bad their terror:
Where stabbing, drabbing, dicing, drinking, swearing
Are all proclaim'd unto the sight and hearing,
In ugly shapes of Heaven-abhorrid sinne,
Where men may see the mire they wallow in.
And well I know it makes the Divell rage,
To see his servants flouted on a stage.
A Whore, a Thiefe, a Pander, or a Bawd,
A Broker, or a slave that lives by fraud:
An Usurer, whose soule is in his chest,
Untill in hell it comes to restlesse rest.
A Fly-blowne gull, that faine would be a Gallant,
A Raggamuffin that hath spent his Tallant:
A selfe-wise foole, that sees his wits out-stript,

Or any vice that feeles it selfe but nipt,
Either in Tragedy, or Comedy,
In Morall, Pastorall, or History:
But straight the poyson of their envious tongues,
Breakes out in vollyes of Calumnious wronges.
And then a Tinker, or a Dray-man sweares,
I would the house were fir'd about their eares.
Thus when a play nips Sathan by the nose,
Streight all his vassails are the Actors foes.
But feare not man, let envy swell and burst,
Proceed, and bid the Divell do his worst.
For Playes are good or bad, as they are us'd,
And best inventions often are abus'd.

Yours ever
John Taylor.
—sigs. A3v–Av

There are two notes in the margin in Heywood's poem: at the beginning of the poem, "So compared by the Fathers"; and at the end, "No Theaters, no world".

The Author to his Booke.

The world's a Theater, the earth a Stage,
Which God, and nature doth with Actors fill,
Kings have their entrance in due equipage,
And some there parts play well and others ill.
The best no better are (in this Theater,)
Where every humor's fitted in his kinde,
This a true subjects acts, and that a Traytor,
The first applauded, and the last confin'd
This plaies an honest man, and that a knave
A gentle person this, and he a clowne
One man is ragged, and another brave.
All men have parts, and each man acts his owne.
She a chaste Lady acteth all her life,
A wanton Curtezan another playes.
This, covets marriage love, that nuptial strife,
Both in continuall action spend their dayes.
Some Citizens, some Soldiers, borne to adventer,
Sheepheards, and Sea-men; then our play's begun,
When we are borne, and to the world first enter,
And all finde *Exits* when their parts are done.
If then the worlds a Theater present,
As by the roundnesse it appeares most fit,
Built with starre-galleries of hye ascent,
In which *Jehove* doth as spectator sit.
And chiefe determiner to applaud the best,
And their indevours crowne with more then merit.
But by their evill actions doomes the rest,
To end disgrac't whilst others praise inherit.
    He that denyes then Theaters should be,
    He may as well deny a world to me.

Thomas Heywood.
—sigs. A3v–Av

In the first part of his argument Heywood musters an abundance of evidence, much of it from classical texts, to support his argument that plays and players are an essential part of a commonwealth. The following excerpts provide some practical details about the theater and show that Hamlet was not the only one who thought the play's the thing wherein to catch a conscience. After naming some of the most popular actors of the early seventeenth century, most of them dead by the time he was writing, Heywood describes the characteristics of good actors.

Actors should be men pick'd out personable, according to the parts they present, they should be rather schollers, that though they cannot speake well, know how to speake, or else to have that volubility, that they can speake well, though they understand not what, & so both imperfections may by instructions be helped & amended: but where a good tongue & a good conceit both faile, there can never be good actor. I also could wish, that such as are condemned for their licentiousnesse, might by a generall consent bee quite excluded our society: for as we are men that stand in the broad eye of the world, so should our manners, gestures, and behaviours, savour of such government and modesty, to deserve the good thoughts and reports of all men, and to abide the sharpest censures even of those that are the greatest opposites to the quality. Many amongst us, I know, to be of substance, of government, of sober lives, and temperate carriages, house-keepers, and contributary to all duties enjoyned them, equally with them that are rank't with the most bountifull; and if amongst so many of sort, there be any few degenerate from the rest in that good demeanor, which is both requisite & expected at their hands, let me entreat you not to censure hardly of all for the misdeeds of some . . .
—sig. E3r

Playes are writ with this ayme, and carryed with this methode, to teach the subjects obedience to their King, to shew the people the untimely ends of such as have moved tumults, commotions, and insurrections, to present them with the flourishing estate of such as live in obedience, exhorting them to allegeance, dehorting them from all trayterous and fellonious stratagems.

Omne genus scripti gravitate Tragedia vincit.

If we present a Tragedy, we include the fatall and abortive ends of such as commit notorious murders, which is aggravated and acted with all the Art that may be, to terrifie men from the like abhorred practises. If wee present a forreigne History, the subject is so intended, that in the lives of *Romans, Grecians,* or others, either the vertues of our Country-men are extolled, or their vices reproved, as thus, by the example of *Cæsar* to stir souldiers to valour, & magnanimity: by the fall of *Pompey*, that no man trust in his owne strength: we present *Alexander*, killing his friend in his rage, to reprove rashnesse: *Mydas*, choked with his gold, to taxe covetousnesse: *Nero* against tyranny: *Sardanapalus*, against luxury: *Nynus*, against ambition, with infinite others, by sundry instances, either animating men to noble attempts, or attaching the consciences of the spectators, finding themselves toucht in presenting the vices of others. If a morall, it is to perswade men to humanity and good life, to instruct them in civility and good manners, shewing them the fruits of honesty, and the end of villany.

–sig. F3v

If a Comedy, it is pleasantly contrived with merry accidents, and intermixt with apt and witty jests, to present before the Prince at certain times of solemnity, or else merily fitted to the stage. And what is then the subject of this harmlesse mirth? either in the shape of a Clowne, to shew others their slovenly and unhansome behaviour, that they may reforme that simplicity in themselves, which others make their sport, lest they happen to become the like subject of generall scorne to an auditory, else it intreates of love, deriding foolish inamorates, who spend their ages, their spirits, nay themselves, in the servile and ridiculous imployments of their Mistresses: and these are mingled with sportfull accidents, to recreate such as of themselves are wholly devoted to Melancholly, which corrupts the bloud: or to refresh such weary spirits as are tired with labour, or study, to moderate the cares and heavinesse of the minde, that they may returne to their trades and faculties with more zeale and earnestnesse; after some small soft and pleasant retirment. Sometimes they discourse of Pantaloones, Usurers that have unthrifty sonnes, which both the fathers and sonnes may behold to their instructions: sometimes of Curtesans, to divulge their subtelties and snares, in which yong men may be intangled, shewing them the meanes to avoyd them. If we present a Pastorall, we shew the harmelesse love of Sheepheards diversly moralized, distinguishing betwixt the craft of the Citty, and the innocency of the sheep-coat. Briefly, there is neither Tragedy, History, Comedy, Morrall or Pastorall, from which an infinite use cannot be gathered. I speake not in the defence of any lascivious shewes, scurrelous jeasts, or scandalous invectives: If there be any such, I banish them quite from my patronage . . .

–sigs. F3v–F4v

Art thou addicted to prodigallity? envy? cruelty? perjury? flattery? or rage? our Scenes affoord thee store of men to shape your lives by, who be frugall, loving, gentle, trusty, without soothing, and in all things temperate. Wouldst thou be honourable? just, friendly, moderate, devout, mercifull, and loving concord? thou mayest see many of their fates and ruines, who have beene dishonourable, unjust, false, gluttenous, sacrilegious, bloudy-minded, and brochers of dissention. Women likewise that are chaste, are by us extolled, and encouraged in their vertues, being instanced by *Diana, Belphebe, Matilda, Lucrece* and the Countesse of *Salisbury*. The unchaste are by us shewed their errors, in the persons of *Phrine, Lais, Thais, Flora*: and amongst us, *Rosamond*, and *Mistresse Shore*. What can sooner print modesty in the soules of the wanton, then by discovering unto them the monstrousnesse of their sin? It followes that we prove these exercises to have beene the discoverers of many notorious murders, long concealed from the eyes of the world. To omit all farre-fetcht instances, we wil prove it by a domestike, and home-borne truth, which within these few yeares happened. At *Lin* in *Norfolke*, the then Earle of *Sussex* players acting the old History of Fryer *Francis*, & presenting a woman, who insatiately doting on a yong gentleman, had (the more securely to enjoy his affection) mischievously and secretly murdered her husband, whose ghost haunted her, and at divers times in her most solitary and private contemplations, in most horrid and fearefull shapes, appeared, and stood before her. As this was acted, a townes-woman (till then of good estimation and report) finding her conscience (at this presen[t]ment) extremely troubled, suddenly skritched and cryd out O my husband, my husband! I see the ghost of my husband fiercely threatning and menacing me. At which shrill and u[n]expected out-cry, the people about her, moov'd to a strange amazement, inquired the reason of her clamour, when presently un-urged, she told them, that seven yeares ago, she, to be possest of such a Gentleman (meaning him) had poysoned her husband, whose fearefull image personated it selfe in the shape of that ghost: whereupon the murdresse was apprehended, before the Justices further examined, & by her voluntary confession after condemned. That this is true, as well by the report of the Actors as the records of the Towne, there are many eye-witnesses of this accident yet living, vocally to confirme it.

As strange an accident happened to a company of the same quality some 12 yeares ago, or not so much, who playing late in the night at a place called *Perin* in *Cornwall*, certaine *Spaniards* were landed the same night unsuspected, and undiscovered, with intent to take in the towne, spoyle and burne it, when suddenly, even upon their entrance, the players (ignorant as the townes-men of any such attempt) presenting a battle on the stage with their drum and trumpets strooke up a lowd alarme: which the enemy hearing, and fearing they were discovered, amazedly retired, made some few idle shot in a bravado, and so in a hurly-burly fled disorderly to their boats. At the report of this tumult, the townes-men were immediatly armed, and pursued them to the sea, praysing God for their happy deliverance from so great a danger, who by his providence made these strangers the instrument and secondary meanes of their escape from such imminent mischife, and the tyranny of so remorcelesse an enemy.

Another of the like wonder happened at *Amsterdam* in *Holland*, a company of our *English* Comedians (well knowne) travelling those Countryes, as they were before the Burgers and other the chiefe inhabitants, acting the last part of the 4 sons of *Aymon*, towards the last act of the history, where penitent *Renaldo*, like a common labourer, lived in disguise, vowing as his last pennance, to labour & carry burdens to the structure of a goodly Church there to be erected: whose diligence the labourers envying, since by reason of his stature and strength, hee did usually perfect more worke in a day, then a dozen of the best, (hee working for his conscience, they for their lucres.) Whereupon by reason his industry had so much disparaged their living, conspired amongst themselves to kill him, waiting some opportunity to finde him asleepe, which they might easily doe, since the forest labourers are the soundest sleepers, and industry is the best preparative to rest. Having spy'd their opportunity, they drave a naile into his temples, of which wound immediatly he dyed. As the Actors handled this, the audience might on a sodaine understand an out-cry, and loud shrike in a remote gallery, and pressing about the place, they might perceive a woman of great gravity, strangely amazed, who with a distracted & troubled braine oft sighed out these words: Oh my husband, my husband! The play, without further interruption, proceeded; the woman was to her owne house conducted, without any appa-

rant suspition, every one conjecturing as their fancies led them. In this agony she some few dayes languished, and on a time, as certaine of her well disposed neighbours came to comfort her, one amongst the rest being Church-warden, to him the Sexton posts, to tell him of a strange thing happening him in the ripping up of a grave: see here (quoth he) what I have found, and shewes them a faire skull, with a great nayle pierst quite through the braine-pan, but we cannot conjecture to whom it should belong, nor how long it hath laine in the earth, the grave being confused, and the flesh consumed. At the report of this accident, the woman, out of the trouble of her afflicted conscience, discovered a former murder. For 12 yeares ago, by driving that nayle into that skull, being the head of her husband, she had trecherously slaine him. This being publickly confest, she was arraigned, condemned, adjudged, and burned.

—sigs. G1r–G3r

In his conclusion Heywood returns to the antiquity of the acting profession and notes that in England actors are and have long been licensed by the monarch, but he ends on a more cautious note.

Now to speake of some abuse lately crept into the quality, as an inveighing against the State, the Court, the Law, the Citty, and their governements, with the particularizing of private mens humors (yet alive) Noble-men, & others. I know it distates many; neither do I any way approve it, nor dare I by any meanes excuse it. The liberty which some arrogate to themselves, committing their bitternesse, and liberall invectives against all estates, to the mouthes of Children, supposing their juniority to be a priviledge for any rayling, be it never so violent, I could advise all such, to curbe and limit this presumed liberty within the bands of discretion and government. But wise and juditial Censurers, before whom such complaints shall at any time hereafter come, wil not (I hope) impute these abuses to any transgression in us, who have ever been carefull and provident to shun the like.

—sig. G3v

Practical Matters

Those involved in producing theatrical effects are often reluctant to reveal how they have created them—particularly to describe them in print—because this would allow a competitor to copy them. A few examples survive, though, along with entrepreneur Philip Henslowe's costume and stage properties lists, to show that the ability to create magical effects on stage is not a recent invention.

1598

Inventories of Theatrical Costumes and Properties

These lists, first printed by Edmund Malone in his 1790 edition of The Plays and Poems of William Shakespeare, *are no longer extant. Probably compiled by Philip Henslowe, the lists show the elaborate costumes and props available to early modern theater companies. Some of the costume entries—"knaves sewtes," "Danes sewtes," "gostes sewt," or "anteckes cootes"—illustrate theatrical conventions whereby the apparel proclaims the man; others—"branhowlttes bodeys," "merlen gowne and cape," and "Will. Sommers sewtte"—refer to specific characters or actors. It is impossible to know whether or not Henslowe's inventories are typical; a list of props called for in Shakespeare's stage directions would be far shorter, but printed play texts from this period rarely provide production details. For further information see the analysis of these lists in Appendix 2 of* Henslowe's Diary: Edited with Supplementary Material, Introduction, and Notes *(1961), edited by R. A. Foakes and R. T. Rickert. The text here is from* The Plays and Poems of William Shakespeare, *volume 3 (1821), edited by Edmond Malone.*

"The booke of the Inventary of the goods of my Lord Admeralles men, tacken the 10 of Marche in the yeare 1598."

Gone and loste.

Item, i orenge taney satten dublet, layd thycke with gowld lace.

Item, i blew tafetie sewt.

Item, i payr of carnatyon satten Venesyons, layd with gold lace.

Item, i longe-shanckes sewte.

Item, i Sponnes dublet pyncket.

Item, i Spanerds gyrcken.

Item, Harey the fyftes dublet.

Item, Harey the fyftes vellet gowne.

Item, i fryers gowne.

Item, i lyttell dublet for boye.

"The Enventary of the Clownes Sewtes and Hermetes Sewtes, with dievers other sewtes, as followeth, 1598, the 10 of March."

Item, i senetores gowne, i hoode, and 5 senetores capes.

Item, i sewtte for Nepton; Fierdrackes sewtes for Dobe.

Item, iiii genesareyes gownes, and iiii torchberers sewtes.

Item, iii payer of red strasers, and iii fares gowne of buckrome.

Item, iiii Herwodes cottes, and iii sogers cottes, and i green gown for Maryan.

Item, vi grene cottes for Roben Hoode, and iiii knaves sewtes.

Item, ii payer of grene hosse, and Andersones sewte. i whitt shepen clocke.

Item, ii rosset cottes, and i black frese cotte, and iii prestes cottes.

Item, ii whitt sheperdes cottes, and ii Danes sewtes, and i payer of Danes hosse.

Item, The Mores lymes, and Hercolles lymes, and Will. Sommers sewtte.

Item, ii Orlates sewtes, hates and gorgetts, and vii anteckes cootes.

Item, Cathemer sewte, i payer of cloth whitte stockens, iiii Turckes hedes.

Item, iiii freyers gownes and iiii hooodes to them, and i fooles coate, cape, and babell, and branhowlttes bodeys, and merlen gowne and cape.

Item, ii black saye gownes, and ii cotton gownes, and i rede saye gowne.

Item, i mawe gowne of calleco for the quene, i carnowll hatte.

Item, i red sewt of cloth for pyge, layed with whitt lace.

Item, v payer of hosse for the clowne, and v gerkenes for them.

Item, iii payer of canvas hosse for asane, ii payer of black strocers.

Item, i yelow leather dublett for a clowne, i Whittcomes dublett poke.

Item, Eves bodeyes, i pedante trusser, and iii donnes hattes.

Item, i payer of yelow cotton sleves, i gostes sewt, and i gostes bodeyes.

Item, xviii copes and hattes, Verones sonnes hosse.

Item, iii trumpettes and a drum, and a trebel viall, a basse viall, a bandore, a sytteren, i anshente, i whitt hatte.

Item, i hatte for Robin Hoode, i hobihorse.

Item, v shertes, and i serpelowes, iiii ferdingalles.

Item, vi head-tiers, i fane, iiii rebatos, ii gyrketruses.

Item, i longe sorde.

. . . .

"The Enventary tacken of all the properties for my Lord Admeralles men, the 10 of Marche 1598."

Item, i rocke, i cage, i tombe, i Hell mought.

Item, i tome of Guido, i tome of Dido, i bedsteade.

Item, viii lances, i payer of stayers for Fayeton.

Item, ii stepells, & i chyme of belles, & i beacon.

Item, i hecfor for the playe of Faeton, the limes dead.

Item, i globe, & i golden scepter; iii clobes.

Item, ii marchepanes, & the sittie of Rome.

Item, i gowlden flece; ii rackets; i baye tree.

Item, i wooden hatchett; i lether hatchete.

Item, i wooden canepie; owld Mahemetes head.

Item, i lyone skin; i beares skyne; & Faetones lymes, & Faeton charete; & Argosse heade.

Item, Nepun forcke & garland.

Item, i crosers stafe; Kentes woden leage.

Item, Ierosses head, & raynbowe; i littell alter.

Item, viii viserdes; Tamberlyne brydell; i wooden matook.

Item, Cupedes bowe, and quiver; the clothe of the Sone & Mone.

Item, i bores heade & Serberosse iii heades.

Item, i Cadeseus; ii mose banckes, & i snake.

Item, ii fanes of feathers; Belendon stable; i tree of gowlden apelles; Tantelouse tre; ix eyorn targates.

Item, i copper targate, & xvii foyles.

Item, iiii wooden targates; i greve armer.

Item, i syne for Mother Readcap; i buckler.

Item, Mercures wings; Tasso picter; i helmet with a dragon; i shelde, with iii lyones; i elmee bowle.

Item, i chayne of dragons; i gylte speare.

Item, ii coffenes; i bulles head; and i vylter.

Item, iii tymbrells, i dragon in fostes.

Item, i lyone; ii lyon heades; i great horse with his leages; i sack-bute.

Item, i whell and frame in the Sege of London.

Item, i paire of rowghte gloves.

Item, i poopes miter.

Item, iii Imperial crownes; i playne crowne.

Item, i gostes crown; i crown with a sone.

Item, i frame for the heading in Black Jone.

Item, i black dogge.

Item, i cauderm for the Jewe.

—pp. 308–313

1611

Serlio's *The Second Booke of Architecture*

In The Second Booke of Architecture *(1611) Sebastiano Serlio's description of stage business focuses on "some things that are pleasing to the beholders," such as elaborate scenery and sophisticated lights. Such pleasures were confined to private theaters and court masques, although Serlio also describes some techniques that could be used in the public theater.*

Sometime you shall have occasion to shew thunder and lightning as the play requireth; then you must make thunder in this manner: commonly all Scenes are made at the end of a great Hall, wheras usually there is a Chamber above it, wherein you must roule a great Bullet of a Cannon or of some other great Ordinance, and then counterfeit Thunder. Lightning must be made in this maner, there must be a man placed behind the Scene or Scaffold in a high place with a bore in his hand, the cover whereof must be full with holes, and in the middle of that place there shall be a burning candle placed, the bore must be filled with powder of vernis or sulphire, and casting his hand with the bore upwards the powder flying in the candle, will shew as if it were lightning. But touching the beames of the lightning, you must draw a piece of wyre over the Scene, which must hang downewards, whereon you must put a squib covered over with pure gold or shining lattin which you will: and while the Bullet is rouling, you must shoote of some piece of Ordinance, and with the same giving fire to the squibs, it will worke the effect which is desired.

—sig. N3v

1612

Rid's *The Art of Jugling or Legerdemaine*

The following excerpt is from Samuel Rid's The Art of Jugling or Legerdemaine. Wherein is deciphered, all the conveyances of Legerdemaine and Jugling, how they are effected, & wherein they chiefly consist. Cautions to beware of cheating at Cardes and Dice. The detection of the beggerly Art of Alcumistry. &, The foppery of foolish cousoning Charmes. All tending to mirth and recreation, especially for those that desire to have the insight and private practise thereof *(1612)*.

To thrust a bodkin through your head,
without any hurt.

Take a Bodkin so made, as the haft being hollow, the blade thereof may slip thereinto: as soone as you holde the poynt downeward, and set the same to your forehead, and seeme to thrust it into your head: and so (with a little sponge in your hand) you may wringe out blood or wine, making the beholders thinke the blood or wine (whereof you may say you have drunke very much) runneth out of your forehead: Then after countenance of pains and greefe, pull away your hand suddenly, holding the poynt downeward, and it will fall so out, as it will seeme never to have bin thrusted into the hafte: But immediately thrust that bodkin into your lappe or pocket, and pull out another playne bodkin like the same, saving in that conceite.

—sig. E3v

Education

The early modern grammar school education, with its emphasis on Latin grammar and classical rhetoric, demanded that students work hard to train their memories. Many exercises also involved imitating Greek and Roman writers, a skill that translates easily to playwriting, where different voices are adopted in telling a story. Speaking aloud in the classroom was thought to help train students to be confident and eloquent public speakers.

1592

Letter of Gager

In his 31 July 1592 letter to John Rainolds (Christ Church College manuscript 352) William Gager defends the practice of university students performing in plays; he provides an apt summary of the reasons plays might be used in schools of all levels. The following excerpt is from W. G. Hiscock's A Christ Church Miscellany *(1946).*

we . . . doe it to recreate owre selves, owre House, and the better part of the *Universitye*, with some learned *Poeme* or other; to practyse owre owne style eyther in prose or verse; to be well acquainted with *Seneca* or *Plautus*; honestly to embolden owre pathe; to trye their voyces and confirme their memoryes; to frame their speeche; to conforme them to convenient action; to trye what mettell is in evrye one, and of what disposition they are of; whereby never any one amongst us, that I knowe was made the worse, many have byn muche the better; as I dare reporte to all the *Universitye*. Of whom some of them have lefte us such domesticall examples and preceptes of well speakinge, as if many that dislike such exercises, and others, and owre selves had followed; so many solecismes in utterance shoulde not be comitted so often as there are.

—p. 174

Checklist of Further Reading

Astington, John H. *English Court Theatre 1558–1642.* Cambridge: Cambridge University Press, 1999.

Baldwin, T. W. *William Shakespere's Small Latine and Lesse Greeke,* 2 volumes. Urbana: University of Illinois Press, 1944.

Bate, Jonathan. *The Genius of Shakespeare.* New York: Oxford University Press, 1997.

Bearman, Robert. *Shakespeare in the Stratford Records.* Stroud, U.K.: A. Sutton, 1994.

Bentley, Gerald Eades. *The Professions of Dramatist and Player in Shakespeare's Time, 1590–1642.* Princeton: Princeton University Press, 1986.

Berry, Herbert. *Shakespeare's Playhouses.* New York: AMS Press, 1987.

Bradbrook, M. C. *Shakespeare: The Poet in His World.* New York: Columbia University Press, 1978.

Brinkworth, E. R. C. *Shakespeare and the Bawdy Court of Stratford.* Chichester, U.K.: Phillimore, 1972.

Brooke, Tucker. *Shakespeare of Stratford: A Handbook for Students.* New Haven: Yale University Press, 1926.

Carson, Neil. *A Companion to Henslowe's Diary.* Cambridge: Cambridge University Press, 1988.

Chambers, E. K. *The Elizabethan Stage,* 4 volumes. Oxford: Clarendon Press, 1923.

Chambers. *Sources for a Biography of Shakespeare.* Oxford: Clarendon Press, 1946.

Chambers. *William Shakespeare: A Study of Facts and Problems,* 2 volumes. Oxford: Clarendon Press, 1930.

Cook, Ann Jennalie. *The Privileged Playgoer of Shakespeare's London, 1576–1642.* Princeton: Princeton University Press, 1981.

Cox, John D. and David Scott Kastan. *A New History of Early English Drama.* New York: Columbia University Press, 1997.

Cunningham, Peter, ed. *Extracts from the Accounts of the Revels at Court, in the Reigns of Queen Elizabeth and King James I, from the Original Office Books of the Masters and Yeomen.* London, 1842; reprinted, New York: AMS Press, 1971.

Davidson, Clifford and Jennifer Alexander. *The Early Art of Coventry, Stratford-upon-Avon, Warwick and Lesser Sites in Warwickshire: A Subject List of Extant and Lost Art Including Items Relevant to Early Drama.* Kalamazoo, Mich.: Medieval Institute Publications, Western Michigan University, 1985.

Davies, Marie-Helene. *Reflections of Renaissance England: Life, Thought and Religion Mirrored in Illustrated Pamphlets 1535–1640.* Allison Park, Pa.: Pickwick Publications, 1986.

Duncan-Jones, Katherine. *Ungentle Shakespeare: Scenes from His Life.* London: Arden Shakespeare, 2001.

Eccles, Mark. *Shakespeare in Warwickshire.* Madison: University of Wisconsin Press, 1961.

Evans, G. Blakemore, ed. *Elizabethan-Jacobean Drama: The Theatre in Its Time.* New York: New Amsterdam, 1988.

Fraser, Russell. *Shakespeare: The Later Years.* New York: Columbia University Press, 1992.

Fraser. *Young Shakespeare.* New York: Columbia University Press, 1988.

Fripp, Edgar I. *Shakespeare, Man and Artist,* 2 volumes. London: Oxford University Press, 1938.

Greg, W. W. *A Bibliography of the English Printed Drama to the Restoration,* volume 1: Stationers' Records: Plays to 1616: Nos. 1–349. London: Printed for the Bibliographical Society at the University Press, Oxford, 1939.

Greg. *Henslowe Papers: Being Documents Supplementary to Henslowe's Diary.* London: A. H. Bullen, 1907.

Gurr, Andrew. *Playgoing in Shakespeare's London,* second edition. Cambridge: Cambridge University Press, 1996.

Gurr. *The Shakespearian Playing Companies.* Oxford: Clarendon Press, 1996.

Gurr and Mariko Ichikawa. *Staging in Shakespeare's Theatres.* Oxford: Oxford University Press, 2000.

Halliwell-Phillips, J. O. *Outlines of the Life of Shakespeare,* 2 volumes. London: Longmans, Green, Reader & Dyer, 1887.

Harbage, Alfred, S. Schoenbaum, and Sylvia S. Wagonheim. *Annals of English drama, 975–1700,* revised edition. London: Routledge, 1989.

Henslowe, Philip. *Henslowe's Diary,* edited by R. A. Foakes and R. T. Rickert. Cambridge: Cambridge University Press, 1961.

Hinman, Charlton. *The Norton Facsimile: The First Folio of Shakespeare.* London: Hamlyn, 1968.

Hinman. *The Printing and Proofreading of the First Folio of Shakespeare,* 2 volumes. Oxford: Clarendon Press, 1963.

Honan, Park. *Shakespeare: A Life.* Oxford: Oxford University Press, 1998.

Honigman, E. A. J. and Susan Brock. *Playhouse Wills 1558–1642: An Edition of Wills by Shakespeare and His Contemporaries in the London Theatre.* Manchester: Manchester University Press, 1993.

Ingleby, C. M. and others. *The Shakespeare Allusion Book: A Collection of Allusions to Shakespeare from 1591 to 1700,* 2 volumes. London: Chatto & Windus, 1909.

Kay, Dennis. *Shakespeare: His Life, Work, and Era.* New York: Morrow, 1992.

Knutson, Roslyn Lander. *The Repertory of Shakespeare's Company 1594–1613.* Fayetteville, Ark.: University of Arkansas Press, 1991.

Levi, Peter. *The Life and Times of William Shakespeare.* London: Macmillan, 1988.

Lewis, B. Roland. *The Shakespeare Documents: Facsimiles, Transliterations, Translations & Commentary,* 2 volumes. London: Oxford University Press, 1940.

Matus, Irvin Leigh. *Shakespeare, In Fact.* New York: Continuum, 1994.

McDonald, Russ. *The Bedford Companion to Shakespeare: An Introduction with Documents,* second edition. Boston: Bedford/ St. Martin's Press, 2001.

McDonald. *Shakespeare and the Arts of Language.* Oxford: Oxford University Press, 2001.

Miola, Robert S. *Shakespeare's Reading.* Oxford: Oxford University Press, 2000.

Orrell, John. *The Quest for Shakespeare's Globe.* Cambridge: Cambridge University Press, 1983.

Rowe, Nicholas. "Some Account of the Life, &c. of Mr. William Shakespear," in volume 1, *The Works of Mr. William Shakespear,* 6 volumes. London: Printed for Jacob Tonson, 1709.

Rutter, Carol Chillington. *Documents of the Rose Playhouse.* Manchester: Manchester University Press, 1984.

Savage, Richard, and Fripp. *Minutes and Accounts of the Corporation of Stratford-upon-Avon and Other Records, 1553–1620,* 3 volumes. Oxford: Printed for the Dugdale Society by F. Hall, 1921–1930.

Schoenbaum, Samuel. *Shakespeare's Lives.* Oxford: Clarendon Press, 1970.

Schoenbaum. *William Shakespeare: A Documentary Life.* New York: Oxford University Press, 1975.

Schoenbaum. *William Shakespeare: Records and Images.* New York: Oxford University Press, 1981.

Sisson, C. J. *Lost Plays of Shakespeare's Age.* Cambridge: Cambridge University Press, 1936.

Thomas, David. *Shakespeare in the Public Records.* London: H.M.S.O., 1985.

Thomson, Peter. *Shakespeare's Professional Career.* Cambridge: Cambridge University Press, 1992.

Thomson. *Shakespeare's Theatre.* London: Routledge, 1983.

Wells, Gary Taylor and others. *William Shakespeare: A Textual Companion.* Oxford: Clarendon Press, 1987.

Wells, Stanley. *Shakespeare: A Dramatic Life.* London: Sinclair-Stevenson, 1994.

Wells, ed. *Shakespeare in the Theatre: An Anthology of Criticism.* Oxford: Clarendon Press, 1997.

Wiggins, Martin. *Shakespeare and the Drama of His Time.* Oxford: Oxford University Press, 2000.

Cumulative Index

Dictionary of Literary Biography, Volumes 1-263
Dictionary of Literary Biography Yearbook, 1980-2001
Dictionary of Literary Biography Documentary Series, Volumes 1-19
Concise Dictionary of American Literary Biography, Volumes 1-7
Concise Dictionary of British Literary Biography, Volumes 1-8
Concise Dictionary of World Literary Biography, Volumes 1-4

Cumulative Index

DLB before number: *Dictionary of Literary Biography,* Volumes 1-263
Y before number: *Dictionary of Literary Biography Yearbook,* 1980-2001
DS before number: *Dictionary of Literary Biography Documentary Series,* Volumes 1-19
CDALB before number: *Concise Dictionary of American Literary Biography,* Volumes 1-7
CDBLB before number: *Concise Dictionary of British Literary Biography,* Volumes 1-8
CDWLB before number: *Concise Dictionary of World Literary Biography,* Volumes 1-4

A

Aakjær, Jeppe 1866-1930 . . . . DLB-214

Abbey, Edward 1927-1989 . . . . DLB-256

Abbey, Edwin Austin 1852-1911 . . . . DLB-188

Abbey, Maj. J. R. 1894-1969 . . . . DLB-201

Abbey Press DLB-49

The Abbey Theatre and Irish Drama,
1900-1945 . . . . DLB-10

Abbot, Willis J. 1863-1934 . . . . DLB-29

Abbott, Jacob 1803-1879 . . . . DLB-1, 42, 243

Abbott, Lee K. 1947- DLB-130

Abbott, Lyman 1835-1922 . . . . DLB-79

Abbott, Robert S. 1868-1940 . . . . DLB-29, 91

Abe Kōbō 1924-1993 . . . . DLB-182

Abelard, Peter circa 1079-1142? DLB-115, 208

Abelard-Schuman DLB-46

Abell, Arunah S. 1806-1888 . . . . DLB-43

Abell, Kjeld 1901-1961 . . . . DLB-214

Abercrombie, Lascelles 1881-1938 . . . . DLB-19

Aberdeen University Press Limited DLB-106

Abish, Walter 1931- DLB-130, 227

Ablesimov, Aleksandr Onisimovich
1742-1783 . . . . DLB-150

Abraham à Sancta Clara 1644-1709 . . . . . DLB-168

Abrahams, Peter
1919- DLB-117, 225; CDWLB-3

Abrams, M. H. 1912- DLB-67

Abramson, Jesse 1904-1979 . . . . DLB-241

Abrogans circa 790-800 . . . . DLB-148

Abschatz, Hans Aßmann von
1646-1699 . . . . DLB-168

Abse, Dannie 1923- DLB-27, 245

Abutsu-ni 1221-1283 . . . . DLB-203

Academy Chicago Publishers DLB-46

Accius circa 170 B.C.-circa 80 B.C. DLB-211

Accrocca, Elio Filippo 1923- DLB-128

Ace Books DLB-46

Achebe, Chinua 1930- DLB-117; CDWLB-3

Achtenberg, Herbert 1938- DLB-124

Ackerman, Diane 1948- DLB-120

Ackroyd, Peter 1949- DLB-155, 231

Acorn, Milton 1923-1986 . . . . DLB-53

Acosta, Oscar Zeta 1935?- DLB-82

Acosta Torres, José 1925- DLB-209

Actors Theatre of Louisville DLB-7

Adair, Gilbert 1944- DLB-194

Adair, James 1709?-1783? DLB-30

Adam, Graeme Mercer 1839-1912 . . . . DLB-99

Adam, Robert Borthwick II 1863-1940 . . . DLB-187

Adame, Leonard 1947- DLB-82

Adameşteanu, Gabriel 1942- DLB-232

Adamic, Louis 1898-1951 . . . . DLB-9

Adams, Abigail 1744-1818 . . . . DLB-200

Adams, Alice 1926-1999 . . . . DLB-234; Y-86

Adams, Bertha Leith (Mrs. Leith Adams,
Mrs. R. S. de Courcy Laffan)
1837?-1912 . . . . DLB-240

Adams, Brooks 1848-1927 . . . . DLB-47

Adams, Charles Francis, Jr. 1835-1915 . . . . DLB-47

Adams, Douglas 1952- DLB-261; Y-83

Adams, Franklin P. 1881-1960 . . . . DLB-29

Adams, Hannah 1755-1832 . . . . DLB-200

Adams, Henry 1838-1918 . . . . DLB-12, 47, 189

Adams, Herbert Baxter 1850-1901 . . . . DLB-47

Adams, J. S. and C. [publishing house] DLB-49

Adams, James Truslow
1878-1949 . . . . DLB-17; DS-17

Adams, John 1735-1826 . . . . DLB-31, 183

Adams, John 1735-1826 and
Adams, Abigail 1744-1818 . . . . DLB-183

Adams, John Quincy 1767-1848 . . . . DLB-37

Adams, Léonie 1899-1988 . . . . DLB-48

Adams, Levi 1802-1832 . . . . DLB-99

Adams, Richard 1920- DLB-261

Adams, Samuel 1722-1803 . . . . DLB-31, 43

Adams, Sarah Fuller Flower
1805-1848 . . . . DLB-199

Adams, Thomas 1582 or 1583-1652 . . . . . . DLB-151

Adams, William Taylor 1822-1897 . . . . DLB-42

Adamson, Sir John 1867-1950 . . . . DLB-98

Adcock, Arthur St. John 1864-1930 . . . . . . DLB-135

Adcock, Betty 1938- DLB-105

"Certain Gifts" DLB-105

Adcock, Fleur 1934- DLB-40

Addison, Joseph 1672-1719 . . . DLB-101; CDBLB-2

Ade, George 1866-1944 . . . . DLB-11, 25

Adeler, Max (see Clark, Charles Heber)

Adlard, Mark 1932- DLB-261

Adonias Filho 1915-1990 . . . . DLB-145

Adorno, Theodor W. 1903-1969 . . . . DLB-242

Advance Publishing Company DLB-49

Ady, Endre 1877-1919 . . . . . . DLB-215; CDWLB-4

AE 1867-1935 . . . . DLB-19; CDBLB-5

Ælfric circa 955-circa 1010 . . . . DLB-146

Aeschines
circa 390 B.C.-circa 320 B.C. DLB-176

Aeschylus 525-524 B.C.-456-455 B.C.
. . . . DLB-176; CDWLB-1

Afro-American Literary Critics:
An Introduction DLB-33

After Dinner Opera Company Y-92

Agassiz, Elizabeth Cary 1822-1907 . . . . . . DLB-189

Agassiz, Louis 1807-1873 . . . . DLB-1, 235

Agee, James
1909-1955 . . . . DLB-2, 26, 152; CDALB-1

The Agee Legacy: A Conference at the University
of Tennessee at Knoxville Y-89

Aguilera Malta, Demetrio 1909-1981 . . . . DLB-145

Ahlin, Lars 1915-1997 . . . . DLB-257

Ai 1947- DLB-120

Aichinger, Ilse 1921- DLB-85

Aickman, Robert 1914-1981 . . . . DLB-261

Aidoo, Ama Ata 1942- DLB-117; CDWLB-3

Aiken, Conrad
1889-1973 . . . . DLB-9, 45, 102; CDALB-5

Aiken, Joan 1924- DLB-161

Aikin, Lucy 1781-1864 . . . . DLB-144, 163

Ainsworth, William Harrison 1805-1882 . . DLB-21

Aistis, Jonas 1904-1973 . . . . . DLB-220; CDWLB-4

Aitken, George A. 1860-1917 . . . . DLB-149

Aitken, Robert [publishing house] DLB-49

Akenside, Mark 1721-1770 . . . . DLB-109

Akins, Zoë 1886-1958 . . . . DLB-26

Aksahov, Sergei Timofeevich
1791-1859 . . . . DLB-198

Akutagawa, Ryūnsuke 1892-1927 . . . . DLB-180

Alabaster, William 1568-1640 . . . . DLB-132

Alain de Lille circa 1116-1202/1203 . . . . . DLB-208

Alain-Fournier 1886-1914 . . . . DLB-65

Alanus de Insulis (see Alain de Lille)

Alarcón, Francisco X. 1954- DLB-122

Alarcón, Justo S. 1930- DLB-209

Alba, Nanina 1915-1968 . . . . DLB-41

Albee, Edward 1928- DLB-7; CDALB-1

Albert the Great circa 1200-1280 . . . . DLB-115

Albert, Octavia 1853-ca. 1889 . . . . DLB-221

Alberti, Rafael 1902-1999 . . . . DLB-108

Albertinus, Aegidius circa 1560-1620 . . . . DLB-164

Alcaeus born circa 620 B.C. DLB-176

Alcott, Bronson 1799-1888 . . . . DLB-1, 223

Alcott, Louisa May 1832-1888
. . . DLB-1, 42, 79, 223, 239; DS-14; CDALB-3

Alcott, William Andrus 1798-1859 . . . . DLB-1, 243

Alcuin circa 732-804 . . . . DLB-148

Alden, Beardsley and Company DLB-49

Alden, Henry Mills 1836-1919 . . . . DLB-79

Alden, Isabella 1841-1930 . . . . DLB-42

Alden, John B. [publishing house] DLB-49

Aldington, Richard
1892-1962 . . . . .DLB-20, 36, 100, 149

Aldis, Dorothy 1896-1966 . . . . DLB-22

Aldis, H. G. 1863-1919 . . . . DLB-184

Aldiss, Brian W. 1925- DLB-14, 261

Aldrich, Thomas Bailey
1836-1907 . . . . .DLB-42, 71, 74, 79

Alegría, Ciro 1909-1967 . . . . DLB-113

Alegría, Claribel 1924- DLB-145

Aleixandre, Vicente 1898-1984 . . . . DLB-108

Aleksandravičius, Jonas (see Aistis, Jonas)

Aleksandrov, Aleksandr Andreevich
(see Durova, Nadezhda Andreevna)

Aleramo, Sibilla 1876-1960 . . . . DLB-114

Alexander, Cecil Frances 1818-1895 . . . . . DLB-199

Alexander, Charles 1868-1923 . . . . DLB-91

Alexander, Charles Wesley
[publishing house] DLB-49

Alexander, James 1691-1756 . . . . DLB-24

Alexander, Lloyd 1924- DLB-52

Alexander, Sir William, Earl of Stirling
1577?-1640 . . . . DLB-121

Alexie, Sherman 1966- DLB-175, 206

Alexis, Willibald 1798-1871 . . . . DLB-133

Alfred, King 849-899 . . . . DLB-146

Alger, Horatio, Jr. 1832-1899 . . . . DLB-42

Algonquin Books of Chapel Hill DLB-46

Algren, Nelson
1909-1981 . . . . .DLB-9; Y-81, Y-82; CDALB-1

Nelson Algren: An International
Symposium Y-00

"All the Faults of Youth and Inexperience":
A Reader's Report on
Thomas Wolfe's O Lost Y-01

Allan, Andrew 1907-1974 . . . . DLB-88

Allan, Ted 1916-1995 . . . . DLB-68

Allbeury, Ted 1917- DLB-87

Alldritt, Keith 1935- DLB-14

Allen, Ethan 1738-1789 . . . . DLB-31

Allen, Frederick Lewis 1890-1954 . . . . . . DLB-137

Allen, Gay Wilson 1903-1995 . . . . .DLB-103; Y-95

Allen, George 1808-1876 . . . . DLB-59

Allen, George [publishing house] DLB-106

Allen, George, and Unwin Limited DLB-112

Allen, Grant 1848-1899 . . . . .DLB-70, 92, 178

Allen, Henry W. 1912- Y-85

Allen, Hervey 1889-1949 . . . . DLB-9, 45

Allen, James 1739-1808 . . . . DLB-31

Allen, James Lane 1849-1925 . . . . DLB-71

Allen, Jay Presson 1922- DLB-26

Allen, John, and Company DLB-49

Allen, Paula Gunn 1939- DLB-175

Allen, Samuel W. 1917- DLB-41

Allen, Woody 1935- DLB-44

Allende, Isabel 1942- DLB-145; CDWLB-3

Alline, Henry 1748-1784 . . . . DLB-99

Allingham, Margery 1904-1966 . . . . DLB-77

Allingham, William 1824-1889 . . . . DLB-35

Allison, W. L. [publishing house] DLB-49

The Alliterative Morte Arthure and the Stanzaic
Morte Arthur circa 1350-1400 . . . . DLB-146

Allott, Kenneth 1912-1973 . . . . DLB-20

Allston, Washington 1779-1843 . . . . . . DLB-1, 235

Almon, John [publishing house] DLB-154

Alonzo, Dámaso 1898-1990 . . . . DLB-108

Alsop, George 1636-post 1673 . . . . DLB-24

Alsop, Richard 1761-1815 . . . . DLB-37

Altemus, Henry, and Company DLB-49

Altenberg, Peter 1885-1919 . . . . DLB-81

Althusser, Louis 1918-1990 . . . . DLB-242

Altolaguirre, Manuel 1905-1959 . . . . DLB-108

Aluko, T. M. 1918- DLB-117

Alurista 1947- DLB-82

Alvarez, A. 1929- DLB-14, 40

Alver, Betti 1906-1989 . . . . . DLB-220; CDWLB-4

Amadi, Elechi 1934- DLB-117

Amado, Jorge 1912- DLB-113

Ambler, Eric 1909-1998 . . . . DLB-77

American Conservatory Theatre DLB-7

American Fiction and the 1930s DLB-9

American Humor: A Historical Survey
East and Northeast
South and Southwest
Midwest
West DLB-11

The American Library in Paris Y-93

American News Company DLB-49

The American Poets' Corner: The First
Three Years (1983-1986) Y-86

American Publishing Company DLB-49

American Stationers' Company DLB-49

American Sunday-School Union DLB-49

American Temperance Union DLB-49

American Tract Society DLB-49

The American Trust for the
British Library Y-96

The American Writers Congress
(9-12 October 1981) Y-81

The American Writers Congress: A Report
on Continuing Business Y-81

Ames, Fisher 1758-1808 . . . . DLB-37

Ames, Mary Clemmer 1831-1884 . . . . . . DLB-23

Amiel, Henri-Frédéric 1821-1881 . . . . . . .DLB-217

Amini, Johari M. 1935- DLB-41

Amis, Kingsley 1922-1995
. . . . DLB-15, 27, 100, 139, Y-96; CDBLB-7

Amis, Martin 1949- DLB-194

Ammianus Marcellinus
circa A.D. 330-A.D. 395 . . . . DLB-211

Ammons, A. R. 1926- DLB-5, 165

Amory, Thomas 1691?-1788 . . . . DLB-39

Anania, Michael 1939- DLB-193

Anaya, Rudolfo A. 1937- DLB-82, 206

Ancrene Riwle circa 1200-1225 . . . . DLB-146

Andersch, Alfred 1914-1980 . . . . DLB-69

Andersen, Benny 1929- DLB-214

Anderson, Alexander 1775-1870 . . . . DLB-188

Anderson, David 1929- DLB-241

Anderson, Frederick Irving 1877-1947 . . . DLB-202

Anderson, Margaret 1886-1973 . . . . . . DLB-4, 91

Anderson, Maxwell 1888-1959 . . . . . . .DLB-7, 228

Anderson, Patrick 1915-1979 . . . . DLB-68

Anderson, Paul Y. 1893-1938 . . . . DLB-29

Anderson, Poul 1926- DLB-8

Anderson, Robert 1750-1830 . . . . DLB-142

Anderson, Robert 1917- DLB-7

Anderson, Sherwood
1876-1941 . . . . . DLB-4, 9, 86; DS-1; CDALB-4

Andreae, Johann Valentin 1586-1654 . . . . DLB-164

Andreas Capellanus
flourished circa 1185 . . . . DLB-208

Andreas-Salomé, Lou 1861-1937 . . . . DLB-66

Andres, Stefan 1906-1970 . . . . DLB-69

Andreu, Blanca 1959- DLB-134

Andrewes, Lancelot 1555-1626 . . . . .DLB-151, 172

Andrews, Charles M. 1863-1943 . . . . .DLB-17

Andrews, Miles Peter ?-1814 . . . . DLB-89

Andrews, Stephen Pearl 1812-1886 . . . . . DLB-250

Andrian, Leopold von 1875-1951 . . . . DLB-81

Andrić, Ivo 1892-1975 . . . . . .DLB-147; CDWLB-4

Andrieux, Louis (see Aragon, Louis)

Andrus, Silas, and Son DLB-49

Andrzejewski, Jerzy 1909-1983 . . . . DLB-215

Angell, James Burrill 1829-1916 . . . . DLB-64

Angell, Roger 1920- DLB-171, 185

Angelou, Maya 1928- DLB-38; CDALB-7

Anger, Jane flourished 1589 . . . . DLB-136

Angers, Félicité (see Conan, Laure)

Anglo-Norman Literature in the Development
  of Middle English Literature DLB-146

The Anglo-Saxon Chronicle circa 890-1154 . . .DLB-146

The "Angry Young Men" DLB-15

Angus and Robertson (UK) Limited DLB-112

Anhalt, Edward 1914-2000 . . . . .DLB-26

Anners, Henry F. [publishing house] DLB-49

Annolied between 1077 and 1081 . . . . .DLB-148

Annual Awards for *Dictionary of Literary
  Biography* Editors
  and Contributors Y-98, Y-99, Y-00, Y-01

Anscombe, G. E. M. 1919-2001 . . . . .DLB-262

Anselm of Canterbury 1033-1109 . . . . . . .DLB-115

Anstey, F. 1856-1934 . . . . DLB-141, 178

Anthony, Michael 1932- DLB-125

Anthony, Piers 1934- DLB-8

Anthony, Susanna 1726-1791 . . . . .DLB-200

Antin, David 1932- DLB-169

Antin, Mary 1881-1949 . . . . DLB-221; Y-84

Anton Ulrich, Duke of Brunswick-Lüneburg
  1633-1714 . . . . .DLB-168

Antschel, Paul (see Celan, Paul)

Anyidoho, Kofi 1947- DLB-157

Anzaldúa, Gloria 1942- DLB-122

Anzengruber, Ludwig 1839-1889 . . . . . . .DLB-129

Apess, William 1798-1839 . . . . DLB-175, 243

Apodaca, Rudy S. 1939- DLB-82

Apollinaire, Guillaume 1880-1918 . . . . . .DLB-258

Apollonius Rhodius third century B.C. . . .DLB-176

Apple, Max 1941- DLB-130

Appleton, D., and Company DLB-49

Appleton-Century-Crofts DLB-46

Applewhite, James 1935- DLB-105

Applewood Books DLB-46

April, Jean-Pierre 1948- DLB-251

Apuleius circa A.D. 125-post A.D. 164
  . . . . .DLB-211; CDWLB-1

Aquin, Hubert 1929-1977 . . . . .DLB-53

Aquinas, Thomas 1224 or 1225-1274 . . . .DLB-115

Aragon, Louis 1897-1982 . . . . .DLB-72, 258

Aralica, Ivan 1930- DLB-181

Aratus of Soli
  circa 315 B.C.-circa 239 B.C. DLB-176

Arbasino, Alberto 1930- DLB-196

Arbor House Publishing Company DLB-46

Arbuthnot, John 1667-1735 . . . . .DLB-101

Arcadia House DLB-46

Arce, Julio G. (see Ulica, Jorge)

Archer, William 1856-1924 . . . . .DLB-10

Archilochhus
  mid seventh century B.C.E. DLB-176

The Archpoet circa 1130?-? DLB-148

Archpriest Avvakum (Petrovich)
  1620?-1682 . . . . .DLB-150

Arden, John 1930- DLB-13, 245

Arden of Faversham DLB-62

Ardis Publishers Y-89

Ardizzone, Edward 1900-1979 . . . . .DLB-160

Arellano, Juan Estevan 1947- DLB-122

The Arena Publishing Company DLB-49

Arena Stage DLB-7

Arenas, Reinaldo 1943-1990 . . . . .DLB-145

Arendt, Hannah 1906-1975 . . . . .DLB-242

Arensberg, Ann 1937- Y-82

Arghezi, Tudor 1880-1967 . . .DLB-220; CDWLB-4

Arguedas, José María 1911-1969 . . . . . . .DLB-113

Argueta, Manlio 1936- DLB-145

Arias, Ron 1941- DLB-82

Arishima, Takeo 1878-1923 . . . . .DLB-180

Aristophanes circa 446 B.C.-circa 386 B.C.
  . . . . .DLB-176; CDWLB-1

Aristotle 384 B.C.-322 B.C.
  . . . . .DLB-176; CDWLB-1

Ariyoshi Sawako 1931-1984 . . . . .DLB-182

Arland, Marcel 1899-1986 . . . . .DLB-72

Arlen, Michael 1895-1956 . . . . . . DLB-36, 77, 162

Armah, Ayi Kwei 1939- . . .DLB-117; CDWLB-3

Armantrout, Rae 1947- DLB-193

Der arme Hartmann ?-after 1150 . . . . . . .DLB-148

Armed Services Editions DLB-46

Armstrong, Martin Donisthorpe
  1882-1974 . . . . .DLB-197

Armstrong, Richard 1903- DLB-160

Armstrong, Terence Ian Fytton (see Gawsworth, John)

Arndt, Ernst Moritz 1769-1860 . . . . .DLB-90

Arnim, Achim von 1781-1831 . . . . .DLB-90

Arnim, Bettina von 1785-1859 . . . . .DLB-90

Arnim, Elizabeth von (Countess Mary
  Annette Beauchamp Russell)
  1866-1941 . . . . .DLB-197

Arno Press .DLB-46

Arnold, Edward [publishing house] DLB-112

Arnold, Edwin 1832-1904 . . . . .DLB-35

Arnold, Edwin L. 1857-1935 . . . . .DLB-178

Arnold, Matthew
  1822-1888 . . . . .DLB-32, 57; CDBLB-4

Preface to *Poems* (1853) DLB-32

Arnold, Thomas 1795-1842 . . . . .DLB-55

Arnott, Peter 1962- DLB-233

Arnow, Harriette Simpson 1908-1986 . . . . .DLB-6

Arp, Bill (see Smith, Charles Henry)

Arpino, Giovanni 1927-1987 . . . . .DLB-177

Arreola, Juan José 1918- DLB-113

Arrian circa 89-circa 155 . . . . .DLB-176

Arrowsmith, J. W. [publishing house] DLB-106

The Art and Mystery of Publishing:
  Interviews Y-97

Artaud, Antonin 1896-1948 . . . . .DLB-258

Arthur, Timothy Shay
  1809-1885 . . . . DLB-3, 42, 79, 250; DS-13

The Arthurian Tradition and
  Its European Context DLB-138

Artmann, H. C. 1921-2000 . . . . .DLB-85

Arvin, Newton 1900-1963 . . . . .DLB-103

Asch, Nathan 1902-1964 . . . . .DLB-4, 28

Ascham, Roger 1515 or 1516-1568 . . . . .DLB-236

Ash, John 1948- DLB-40

Ashbery, John 1927- DLB-5, 165; Y-81

Ashbridge, Elizabeth 1713-1755 . . . . . . .DLB-200

Ashburnham, Bertram Lord
  1797-1878 . . . . .DLB-184

Ashendene Press DLB-112

Asher, Sandy 1942- Y-83

Ashton, Winifred (see Dane, Clemence)

Asimov, Isaac 1920-1992 . . . . .DLB-8; Y-92

Askew, Anne circa 1521-1546 . . . . .DLB-136

Aspazija 1865-1943 . . . . .DLB-220; CDWLB-4

Asselin, Olivar 1874-1937 . . . . .DLB-92

The Association of American Publishers Y-99

The Association for Documentary Editing . . . Y-00

Astell, Mary 1666-1731 . . . . .DLB-252

Astley, William (see Warung, Price)

Asturias, Miguel Angel
  1899-1974 . . . . .DLB-113; CDWLB-3

At Home with Albert Erskine Y-00

Atheneum Publishers DLB-46

Atherton, Gertrude 1857-1948 . . . . .DLB-9, 78, 186

Athlone Press DLB-112

Atkins, Josiah circa 1755-1781 . . . . .DLB-31

Atkins, Russell 1926- DLB-41

Atkinson, Louisa 1834-1872 . . . . .DLB-230

The Atlantic Monthly Press DLB-46

Attaway, William 1911-1986 . . . . .DLB-76

Atwood, Margaret 1939- DLB-53, 251

Aubert, Alvin 1930- DLB-41

Aubert de Gaspé, Phillipe-Ignace-François
  1814-1841 . . . . .DLB-99

Aubert de Gaspé, Phillipe-Joseph
  1786-1871 . . . . .DLB-99

Aubin, Napoléon 1812-1890 . . . . .DLB-99

Aubin, Penelope
  1685-circa 1731 . . . . .DLB-39

Preface to *The Life of Charlotta
  du Pont* (1723) DLB-39

Aubrey-Fletcher, Henry Lancelot (see Wade, Henry)

Auchincloss, Louis 1917- DLB-2, 244; Y-80

Auction of Jack Kerouac's *On the Road* Scroll . . Y-01

Auden, W. H. 1907-1973 . . .DLB-10, 20; CDBLB-6

Audio Art in America: A Personal Memoir . . . Y-85

Audubon, John James 1785-1851 . . . . .DLB-248

Audubon, John Woodhouse
  1812-1862 . . . . .DLB-183

Auerbach, Berthold 1812-1882 . . . . .DLB-133

Auernheimer, Raoul 1876-1948 . . . . .DLB-81

Augier, Emile 1820-1889 . . . . .DLB-192

Augustine 354-430 . . . . .DLB-115

Responses to Ken Auletta Y-97

Aulus Cellius
  circa A.D. 125-circa A.D. 180? DLB-211

Austen, Jane
1775-1817 . . . . DLB-116; CDBLB-3

Auster, Paul 1947- DLB-227

Austin, Alfred 1835-1913 . . . . DLB-35

Austin, J. L. 1911-1960 . . . . DLB-262

Austin, Jane Goodwin 1831-1894 . . . . . . DLB-202

Austin, John 1790-1859 . . . . DLB-262

Austin, Mary 1868-1934 . . . . . .DLB-9, 78, 206, 221

Austin, William 1778-1841 . . . . DLB-74

Australie (Emily Manning)
1845-1890 . . . . DLB-230

Author-Printers, 1476–1599 . . . . DLB-167

Author Websites Y-97

Authors and Newspapers Association DLB-46

Authors' Publishing Company DLB-49

Avallone, Michael 1924-1999 . . . . Y-99

Avalon Books DLB-46

Avancini, Nicolaus 1611-1686 . . . . DLB-164

Avendaño, Fausto 1941- DLB-82

Averroëö 1126-1198 . . . . DLB-115

Avery, Gillian 1926- DLB-161

Avicenna 980-1037 . . . . DLB-115

Avison, Margaret 1918- DLB-53

Avon Books DLB-46

Avyžius, Jonas 1922-1999 . . . . DLB-220

Awdry, Wilbert Vere 1911-1997 . . . . DLB-160

Awoonor, Kofi 1935- DLB-117

Ayckbourn, Alan 1939- DLB-13, 245

Ayer, A. J. 1910-1989 . . . . DLB-262

Aymé, Marcel 1902-1967 . . . . DLB-72

Aytoun, Sir Robert 1570-1638 . . . . DLB-121

Aytoun, William Edmondstoune
1813-1865 . . . . DLB-32, 159

B

B. V. (see Thomson, James)

Babbitt, Irving 1865-1933 . . . . DLB-63

Babbitt, Natalie 1932- DLB-52

Babcock, John [publishing house] DLB-49

Babits, Mihály 1883-1941 . . . DLB-215; CDWLB-4

Babrius circa 150-200 . . . . .DLB-176

Baca, Jimmy Santiago 1952- DLB-122

Bache, Benjamin Franklin 1769-1798 . . . . . DLB-43

Bacheller, Irving 1859-1950 . . . . DLB-202

Bachmann, Ingeborg 1926-1973 . . . . DLB-85

Bačinskaitė-Bučienė, Salomėja (see Nėris, Salomėja)

Bacon, Delia 1811-1859 . . . . DLB-1, 243

Bacon, Francis
1561-1626 . . . . DLB-151, 236, 252; CDBLB-1

Bacon, Sir Nicholas circa 1510-1579 . . . . . DLB-132

Bacon, Roger circa 1214/1220-1292 . . . . . DLB-115

Bacon, Thomas circa 1700-1768 . . . . DLB-31

Bacovia, George
1881-1957 . . . . DLB-220; CDWLB-4

Badger, Richard G., and Company DLB-49

Bagaduce Music Lending Library Y-00

Bage, Robert 1728-1801 . . . . DLB-39

Bagehot, Walter 1826-1877 . . . . DLB-55

Bagley, Desmond 1923-1983 . . . . DLB-87

Bagley, Sarah G. 1806-1848 . . . . DLB-239

Bagnold, Enid 1889-1981 . . .DLB-13, 160, 191, 245

Bagryana, Elisaveta
1893-1991 . . . . .DLB-147; CDWLB-4

Bahr, Hermann 1863-1934 . . . . DLB-81, 118

Bailey, Abigail Abbot 1746-1815 . . . . DLB-200

Bailey, Alfred Goldsworthy 1905- DLB-68

Bailey, Francis [publishing house] DLB-49

Bailey, H. C. 1878-1961 . . . . DLB-77

Bailey, Jacob 1731-1808 . . . . DLB-99

Bailey, Paul 1937- DLB-14

Bailey, Philip James 1816-1902 . . . . DLB-32

Baillargeon, Pierre 1916-1967 . . . . DLB-88

Baillie, Hugh 1890-1966 . . . . DLB-29

Baillie, Joanna 1762-1851 . . . . DLB-93

Bailyn, Bernard 1922- DLB-17

Bainbridge, Beryl 1933- DLB-14, 231

Baird, Irene 1901-1981 . . . . DLB-68

Baker, Augustine 1575-1641 . . . . DLB-151

Baker, Carlos 1909-1987 . . . . DLB-103

Baker, David 1954- DLB-120

Baker, Herschel C. 1914-1990 . . . . DLB-111

Baker, Houston A., Jr. 1943- DLB-67

Baker, Nicholson 1957- DLB-227

Baker, Samuel White 1821-1893 . . . . DLB-166

Baker, Thomas 1656-1740 . . . . DLB-213

Baker, Walter H., Company
("Baker's Plays") DLB-49

The Baker and Taylor Company DLB-49

Bakhtin, Mikhail Mikhailovich
1895-1975 . . . . DLB-242

Balaban, John 1943- DLB-120

Bald, Wambly 1902- DLB-4

Balde, Jacob 1604-1668 . . . . DLB-164

Balderston, John 1889-1954 . . . . DLB-26

Baldwin, James 1924-1987
. . . . DLB-2, 7, 33, 249; Y-87; CDALB-1

Baldwin, Joseph Glover
1815-1864 . . . . DLB-3, 11, 248

Baldwin, Louisa (Mrs. Alfred Baldwin)
1845-1925 . . . . DLB-240

Baldwin, Richard and Anne
[publishing house] DLB-170

Baldwin, William circa 1515-1563 . . . . . . DLB-132

Bale, John 1495-1563 . . . . DLB-132

Balestrini, Nanni 1935- DLB-128, 196

Balfour, Sir Andrew 1630-1694 . . . . DLB-213

Balfour, Arthur James 1848-1930 . . . . DLB-190

Balfour, Sir James 1600-1657 . . . . DLB-213

Ballantine Books DLB-46

Ballantyne, R. M. 1825-1894 . . . . DLB-163

Ballard, J. G. 1930- DLB-14, 207, 261

Ballard, Martha Moore 1735-1812 . . . . . . DLB-200

Ballerini, Luigi 1940- DLB-128

Ballou, Maturin Murray
1820-1895 . . . . .DLB-79, 189

Ballou, Robert O. [publishing house] DLB-46

Balzac, Honoré de 1799-1855 . . . . DLB-119

Bambara, Toni Cade
1939- DLB-38, 218; CDALB-7

Bamford, Samuel 1788-1872 . . . . DLB-190

Bancroft, A. L., and Company DLB-49

Bancroft, George 1800-1891 . . . DLB-1, 30, 59, 243

Bancroft, Hubert Howe 1832-1918 . . .DLB-47, 140

Bandelier, Adolph F. 1840-1914 . . . . DLB-186

Bangs, John Kendrick 1862-1922 . . . . . .DLB-11, 79

Banim, John 1798-1842 . . . . .DLB-116, 158, 159

Banim, Michael 1796-1874 . . . . DLB-158, 159

Banks, Iain 1954- DLB-194, 261

Banks, John circa 1653-1706 . . . . DLB-80

Banks, Russell 1940- DLB-130

Bannerman, Helen 1862-1946 . . . . DLB-141

Bantam Books DLB-46

Banti, Anna 1895-1985 . . . . .DLB-177

Banville, John 1945- DLB-14

Banville, Théodore de 1823-1891 . . . . . . .DLB-217

Baraka, Amiri
1934- DLB-5, 7, 16, 38; DS-8; CDALB-1

Barańczak, Stanisław 1946- DLB-232

Baratynsky, Evgenii Abramovich
1800-1844 . . . . DLB-205

Barbauld, Anna Laetitia
1743-1825 . . . . DLB-107, 109, 142, 158

Barbeau, Marius 1883-1969 . . . . DLB-92

Barber, John Warner 1798-1885 . . . . DLB-30

Bàrberi Squarotti, Giorgio 1929- DLB-128

Barbey d'Aurevilly, Jules-Amédée
1808-1889 . . . . DLB-119

Barbier, Auguste 1805-1882 . . . . .DLB-217

Barbilian, Dan (see Barbu, Ion)

Barbour, John circa 1316-1395 . . . . DLB-146

Barbour, Ralph Henry 1870-1944 . . . . . . DLB-22

Barbu, Ion 1895-1961 . . . . . . DLB-220; CDWLB-4

Barbusse, Henri 1873-1935 . . . . DLB-65

Barclay, Alexander circa 1475-1552 . . . . . DLB-132

Barclay, E. E., and Company DLB-49

Bardeen, C. W. [publishing house] DLB-49

Barham, Richard Harris 1788-1845 . . . . . DLB-159

Barich, Bill 1943- DLB-185

Baring, Maurice 1874-1945 . . . . DLB-34

Baring-Gould, Sabine
1834-1924 . . . . DLB-156, 190

Barker, A. L. 1918- DLB-14, 139

Barker, Arthur, Limited DLB-112

Barker, Clive 1952- DLB-261

Barker, George 1913-1991 . . . . DLB-20

Barker, Harley Granville 1877-1946 . . . . . . DLB-10

Barker, Howard 1946- DLB-13, 233

Barker, James Nelson 1784-1858 . . . . DLB-37

Barker, Jane 1652-1727 . . . . .DLB-39, 131

Barker, Lady Mary Anne 1831-1911. . . . .DLB-166

Barker, William circa 1520-after 1576 . . . .DLB-132

Barkov, Ivan Semenovich 1732-1768 . . . . .DLB-150

Barks, Coleman 1937- DLB-5

Barlach, Ernst 1870-1938 . . . . .DLB-56, 118

Barlow, Joel 1754-1812. . . . . .DLB-37

The Prospect of Peace (1778). DLB-37

Barnard, John 1681-1770 . . . . .DLB-24

Barnard, Marjorie 1879-1987 and Eldershaw, Flora
(M. Barnard Eldershaw) 1897-1956. . .DLB-260

Barne, Kitty (Mary Catherine Barne)
1883-1957 . . . . .DLB-160

Barnes, A. S., and Company DLB-49

Barnes, Barnabe 1571-1609 . . . . .DLB-132

Barnes, Djuna 1892-1982. . . . . .DLB-4, 9, 45

Barnes, Jim 1933- DLB-175

Barnes, Julian 1946- DLB-194; Y-93

Julian Barnes Checklist Y-01

Barnes, Margaret Ayer 1886-1967 . . . . .DLB-9

Barnes, Peter 1931- DLB-13, 233

Barnes, William 1801-1886 . . . . .DLB-32

Barnes and Noble Books DLB-46

Barnet, Miguel 1940- DLB-145

Barney, Natalie 1876-1972 . . . . .DLB-4

Barnfield, Richard 1574-1627. . . . . .DLB-172

Baron, Richard W.,
Publishing Company. DLB-46

Barr, Amelia Edith Huddleston
1831-1919 . . . . .DLB-202, 221

Barr, Robert 1850-1912 . . . . .DLB-70, 92

Barral, Carlos 1928-1989 . . . . .DLB-134

Barrax, Gerald William 1933- DLB-41, 120

Barrès, Maurice 1862-1923 . . . . .DLB-123

Barrett, Eaton Stannard 1786-1820 . . . . . .DLB-116

Barrie, J. M.
1860-1937 . . . . . .DLB-10, 141, 156; CDBLB-5

Barrie and Jenkins DLB-112

Barrio, Raymond 1921- DLB-82

Barrios, Gregg 1945- DLB-122

Barry, Philip 1896-1949 . . . . .DLB-7, 228

Barry, Robertine (see Françoise)

Barry, Sebastian 1955- DLB-245

Barse and Hopkins. DLB-46

Barstow, Stan 1928- DLB-14, 139

Barth, John 1930- DLB-2, 227

Barthelme, Donald
1931-1989 . . . . DLB-2, 234; Y-80, Y-89

Barthelme, Frederick 1943- DLB-244; Y-85

Bartholomew, Frank 1898-1985. . . . . . . .DLB-127

Bartlett, John 1820-1905 . . . . .DLB-1, 235

Bartol, Cyrus Augustus 1813-1900 . . . .DLB-1, 235

Barton, Bernard 1784-1849 . . . . .DLB-96

Barton, John ca. 1610-1675 . . . . .DLB-236

Barton, Thomas Pennant 1803-1869 . . . . .DLB-140

Bartram, John 1699-1777 . . . . .DLB-31

Bartram, William 1739-1823 . . . . .DLB-37

Basic Books DLB-46

Basille, Theodore (see Becon, Thomas)

Bass, Rick 1958- DLB-212

Bass, T. J. 1932- Y-81

Bassani, Giorgio 1916- DLB-128, 177

Basse, William circa 1583-1653 . . . . .DLB-121

Bassett, John Spencer 1867-1928 . . . . .DLB-17

Bassler, Thomas Joseph (see Bass, T. J.)

Bate, Walter Jackson 1918-1999 . . . . .DLB-67, 103

Bateman, Christopher
[publishing house] DLB-170

Bateman, Stephen circa 1510-1584 . . . . .DLB-136

Bates, H. E. 1905-1974. . . . . .DLB-162, 191

Bates, Katharine Lee 1859-1929 . . . . .DLB-71

Batiushkov, Konstantin Nikolaevich
1787-1855. .DLB-205

Batsford, B. T. [publishing house] DLB-106

Battiscombe, Georgina 1905- DLB-155

The Battle of Maldon circa 1000 . . . . .DLB-146

Baudelaire, Charles 1821-1867 . . . . .DLB-217

Bauer, Bruno 1809-1882 . . . . .DLB-133

Bauer, Wolfgang 1941- DLB-124

Baum, L. Frank 1856-1919 . . . . .DLB-22

Baum, Vicki 1888-1960 . . . . .DLB-85

Baumbach, Jonathan 1933- Y-80

Bausch, Richard 1945- DLB-130

Bausch, Robert 1945- DLB-218

Bawden, Nina 1925- DLB-14, 161, 207

Bax, Clifford 1886-1962 . . . . .DLB-10, 100

Baxter, Charles 1947- DLB-130

Bayer, Eleanor (see Perry, Eleanor)

Bayer, Konrad 1932-1964 . . . . .DLB-85

Bayley, Barrington J. 1937- DLB-261

Baynes, Pauline 1922- DLB-160

Baynton, Barbara 1857-1929 . . . . .DLB-230

Bazin, Hervé 1911-1996. . . . . .DLB-83

Beach, Sylvia 1887-1962. . . . . .DLB-4; DS-15

Beacon Press DLB-49

Beadle and Adams. DLB-49

Beagle, Peter S. 1939- Y-80

Beal, M. F. 1937- Y-81

Beale, Howard K. 1899-1959. . . . . .DLB-17

Beard, Charles A. 1874-1948 . . . . .DLB-17

A Beat Chronology: The First Twenty-five
Years, 1944-1969. . . . . .DLB-16

Periodicals of the Beat Generation. DLB-16

The Beats in New York City DLB-237

The Beats in the West DLB-237

Beattie, Ann 1947- DLB-218; Y-82

Beattie, James 1735-1803 . . . . .DLB-109

Beatty, Chester 1875-1968 . . . . .DLB-201

Beauchemin, Nérée 1850-1931 . . . . .DLB-92

Beauchemin, Yves 1941- DLB-60

Beaugrand, Honoré 1848-1906 . . . . .DLB-99

Beaulieu, Victor-Lévy 1945- DLB-53

Beaumont, Francis circa 1584-1616
and Fletcher, John 1579-1625
. . . . .DLB-58; CDBLB-1

Beaumont, Sir John 1583?-1627 . . . . .DLB-121

Beaumont, Joseph 1616-1699 . . . . .DLB-126

Beauvoir, Simone de 1908-1986 . . . . DLB-72; Y-86

Becher, Ulrich 1910- DLB-69

Becker, Carl 1873-1945 . . . . .DLB-17

Becker, Jurek 1937-1997. . . . . .DLB-75

Becker, Jurgen 1932- DLB-75

Beckett, Samuel 1906-1989
. . . . DLB-13, 15, 233; Y-90; CDBLB-7

Beckford, William 1760-1844 . . . . .DLB-39

Beckham, Barry 1944- DLB-33

Becon, Thomas circa 1512-1567 . . . . . . .DLB-136

Becque, Henry 1837-1899 . . . . .DLB-192

Beddoes, Thomas 1760-1808. . . . . .DLB-158

Beddoes, Thomas Lovell 1803-1849 . . . . .DLB-96

Bede circa 673-735. . . . . .DLB-146

Bedford-Jones, H. 1887-1949 . . . . .DLB-251

Beecher, Catharine Esther 1800-1878 . .DLB-1, 243

Beecher, Henry Ward 1813-1887 . .DLB-3, 43, 250

Beer, George L. 1872-1920 . . . . .DLB-47

Beer, Johann 1655-1700 . . . . .DLB-168

Beer, Patricia 1919-1999 . . . . .DLB-40

Beerbohm, Max 1872-1956 . . . . .DLB-34, 100

Beer-Hofmann, Richard 1866-1945 . . . . . .DLB-81

Beers, Henry A. 1847-1926 . . . . .DLB-71

Beeton, S. O. [publishing house] DLB-106

Bégon, Elisabeth 1696-1755 . . . . .DLB-99

Behan, Brendan
1923-1964 . . . . .DLB-13, 233; CDBLB-7

Behn, Aphra 1640?-1689 . . . . .DLB-39, 80, 131

Behn, Harry 1898-1973 . . . . .DLB-61

Behrman, S. N. 1893-1973 . . . . DLB-7, 44

Belaney, Archibald Stansfeld (see Grey Owl)

Belasco, David 1853-1931 . . . . .DLB-7

Belford, Clarke and Company DLB-49

Belinksy, Vissarion Grigor'evich
1811-1848 .DLB-198

Belitt, Ben 1911- DLB-5

Belknap, Jeremy 1744-1798 . . . . .DLB-30, 37

Bell, Adrian 1901-1980 . . . . .DLB-191

Bell, Clive 1881-1964. . . . . DS-10

Bell, Daniel 1919- DLB-246

Bell, George, and Sons. DLB-106

Bell, Gertrude Margaret Lowthian
1868-1926 . . . . .DLB-174

Bell, James Madison 1826-1902. . . . . .DLB-50

Bell, Madison Smartt 1957- DLB-218

Bell, Marvin 1937- DLB-5

Bell, Millicent 1919- DLB-111

Bell, Quentin 1910-1996 . . . . .DLB-155

Bell, Robert [publishing house] DLB-49

Bell, Vanessa 1879-1961 . . . . DS-10

Bellamy, Edward 1850-1898 . . . . DLB-12

Bellamy, John [publishing house] DLB-170

Bellamy, Joseph 1719-1790 . . . . DLB-31

La Belle Assemblée 1806-1837 . . . . DLB-110

Bellezza, Dario 1944-1996 . . . . DLB-128

Belloc, Hilaire 1870-1953 . . . . DLB-19, 100, 141, 174

Belloc, Madame (see Parkes, Bessie Rayner)

Bellonci, Maria 1902-1986 . . . . DLB-196

Bellow, Saul
1915- DLB-2, 28; Y-82; DS-3; CDALB-1

Belmont Productions DLB-46

Bels, Alberts 1938- DLB-232

Belševica, Vizma 1931- . . . DLB-232; CDWLB-4

Bemelmans, Ludwig 1898-1962 . . . . DLB-22

Bemis, Samuel Flagg 1891-1973 . . . . DLB-17

Bemrose, William [publishing house] DLB-106

Ben no Naishi 1228?-1271?. DLB-203

Benchley, Robert 1889-1945. . . . . DLB-11

Bencúr, Matej (see Kukučin, Martin)

Benedetti, Mario 1920- DLB-113

Benedict, Pinckney 1964- DLB-244

Benedict, Ruth 1887-1948. . . . . DLB-246

Benedictus, David 1938- DLB-14

Benedikt, Michael 1935- DLB-5

Benediktov, Vladimir Grigor'evich
1807-1873 . . . . DLB-205

Benét, Stephen Vincent
1898-1943 . . . . DLB-4, 48, 102, 249

Benét, William Rose 1886-1950 . . . . DLB-45

Benford, Gregory 1941- Y-82

Benjamin, Park 1809-1864 . . . . DLB-3, 59, 73, 250

Benjamin, S. G. W. 1837-1914 . . . . DLB-189

Benjamin, Walter 1892-1940 . . . . DLB-242

Benlowes, Edward 1602-1676. . . . . DLB-126

Benn Brothers Limited DLB-106

Benn, Gottfried 1886-1956 . . . . DLB-56

Bennett, Arnold
1867-1931. . . . DLB-10, 34, 98, 135; CDBLB-5

Bennett, Charles 1899-1995 . . . . DLB-44

Bennett, Emerson 1822-1905 . . . . DLB-202

Bennett, Gwendolyn 1902- DLB-51

Bennett, Hal 1930- DLB-33

Bennett, James Gordon 1795-1872 . . . . . DLB-43

Bennett, James Gordon, Jr. 1841-1918 . . . . DLB-23

Bennett, John 1865-1956 . . . . DLB-42

Bennett, Louise 1919- DLB-117; CDWLB-3

Benni, Stefano 1947- DLB-196

Benoit, Jacques 1941- DLB-60

Benson, A. C. 1862-1925 . . . . DLB-98

Benson, E. F. 1867-1940 . . . . DLB-135, 153

Benson, Jackson J. 1930- DLB-111

Benson, Robert Hugh 1871-1914 . . . . DLB-153

Benson, Stella 1892-1933 . . . . DLB-36, 162

Bent, James Theodore 1852-1897. . . . . . .DLB-174

Bent, Mabel Virginia Anna ?-? DLB-174

Bentham, Jeremy 1748-1832. . . . DLB-107, 158, 252

Bentley, E. C. 1875-1956 . . . . DLB-70

Bentley, Phyllis 1894-1977 . . . . DLB-191

Bentley, Richard 1662-1742 . . . . DLB-252

Bentley, Richard [publishing house] DLB-106

Benton, Robert 1932- and Newman,
David 1937- DLB-44

Benziger Brothers DLB-49

Beowulf circa 900-1000 or 790-825
. . . . DLB-146; CDBLB-1

Berent, Wacław 1873-1940. . . . . DLB-215

Beresford, Anne 1929- DLB-40

Beresford, John Davys
1873-1947 . . . . .DLB-162, 178, 197

"Experiment in the Novel" (1929) DLB-36

Beresford-Howe, Constance 1922- DLB-88

Berford, R. G., Company DLB-49

Berg, Stephen 1934- DLB-5

Bergengruen, Werner 1892-1964 . . . . DLB-56

Berger, John 1926- DLB-14, 207

Berger, Meyer 1898-1959. . . . . DLB-29

Berger, Thomas 1924- DLB-2; Y-80

Bergman, Hjalmar 1883-1931. . . . . DLB-259

Bergman, Ingmar 1918- DLB-257

Berkeley, Anthony 1893-1971 . . . . DLB-77

Berkeley, George 1685-1753 . . . . DLB-31, 101, 252

The Berkley Publishing Corporation DLB-46

Berlin, Lucia 1936- DLB-130

Berman, Marshall 1940- DLB-246

Bernal, Vicente J. 1888-1915 . . . . DLB-82

Bernanos, Georges 1888-1948 . . . . DLB-72

Bernard, Harry 1898-1979 . . . . DLB-92

Bernard, John 1756-1828 . . . . DLB-37

Bernard of Chartres circa 1060-1124? . . . DLB-115

Bernard of Clairvaux 1090-1153 . . . . DLB-208

The Bernard Malamud Archive at the
Harry Ransom Humanities
Research Center. Y-00

Bernard Silvestris
flourished circa 1130-1160 . . . . DLB-208

Bernari, Carlo 1909-1992 . . . . .DLB-177

Bernhard, Thomas
1931-1989 . . . . .DLB-85, 124; CDWLB-2

Bernstein, Charles 1950- DLB-169

Berriault, Gina 1926-1999 . . . . DLB-130

Berrigan, Daniel 1921- DLB-5

Berrigan, Ted 1934-1983 . . . . DLB-5, 169

Berry, Wendell 1934- DLB-5, 6, 234

Berryman, John 1914-1972 . . . . DLB-48; CDALB-1

Bersianik, Louky 1930- DLB-60

Berthelet, Thomas [publishing house] DLB-170

Berto, Giuseppe 1914-1978. . . . . .DLB-177

Bertolucci, Attilio 1911- DLB-128

Berton, Pierre 1920- DLB-68

Bertrand, Louis "Aloysius"
1807-1841. . . . . DLB-217

Besant, Sir Walter 1836-1901 . . . . . . DLB-135, 190

Bessette, Gerard 1920- DLB-53

Bessie, Alvah 1904-1985. . . . . DLB-26

Bester, Alfred 1913-1987 . . . . DLB-8

Besterman, Theodore 1904-1976 . . . . . . DLB-201

The Bestseller Lists: An Assessment. Y-84

Bestuzhev, Aleksandr Aleksandrovich
(Marlinsky) 1797-1837 . . . . DLB-198

Bestuzhev, Nikolai Aleksandrovich
1791-1855. . . . . DLB-198

Betham-Edwards, Matilda Barbara (see Edwards,
Matilda Barbara Betham-)

Betjeman, John
1906-1984 . . . . DLB-20; Y-84; CDBLB-7

Betocchi, Carlo 1899-1986 . . . . DLB-128

Bettarini, Mariella 1942- DLB-128

Betts, Doris 1932- DLB-218; Y-82

Beùkoviù, Matija 1939- DLB-181

Beveridge, Albert J. 1862-1927 . . . . .DLB-17

Beverley, Robert circa 1673-1722 . . . . . DLB-24, 30

Bevilacqua, Alberto 1934- DLB-196

Bevington, Louisa Sarah 1845-1895 . . . . . DLB-199

Beyle, Marie-Henri (see Stendhal)

Białoszewski, Miron 1922-1983 . . . . DLB-232

Bianco, Margery Williams 1881-1944 . . . DLB-160

Bibaud, Adèle 1854-1941 . . . . DLB-92

Bibaud, Michel 1782-1857 . . . . DLB-99

Bibliographical and Textual Scholarship
Since World War II. Y-89

Bichsel, Peter 1935- DLB-75

Bickerstaff, Isaac John 1733-circa 1808 . . . . DLB-89

Biddle, Drexel [publishing house]. DLB-49

Bidermann, Jacob
1577 or 1578-1639 . . . . DLB-164

Bidwell, Walter Hilliard 1798-1881 . . . . . . DLB-79

Bienek, Horst 1930- DLB-75

Bierbaum, Otto Julius 1865-1910 . . . . DLB-66

Bierce, Ambrose 1842-1914?
. . . . . . .DLB-11, 12, 23, 71, 74, 186; CDALB-3

Bigelow, William F. 1879-1966. . . . . DLB-91

Biggle, Lloyd, Jr. 1923- DLB-8

Bigiaretti, Libero 1905-1993 . . . . .DLB-177

Bigland, Eileen 1898-1970 . . . . DLB-195

Biglow, Hosea (see Lowell, James Russell)

Bigongiari, Piero 1914- DLB-128

Billinger, Richard 1890-1965 . . . . DLB-124

Billings, Hammatt 1818-1874 . . . . DLB-188

Billings, John Shaw 1898-1975 . . . . .DLB-137

Billings, Josh (see Shaw, Henry Wheeler)

Binding, Rudolf G. 1867-1938 . . . . DLB-66

Bingay, Malcolm 1884-1953. . . . . DLB-241

Bingham, Caleb 1757-1817 . . . . DLB-42

Bingham, George Barry 1906-1988 . . . . . . .DLB-127

Bingham, Sallie 1937- DLB-234

Bingley, William [publishing house]. DLB-154

Binyon, Laurence 1869-1943 . . . . DLB-19

Biographia Brittanica DLB-142

Biographical Documents I Y-84

Biographical Documents II Y-85

Bioren, John [publishing house] DLB-49

Bioy Casares, Adolfo 1914- DLB-113

Bird, Isabella Lucy 1831-1904 . . . . .DLB-166

Bird, Robert Montgomery 1806-1854 . . . .DLB-202

Bird, William 1888-1963 . . . . .DLB-4; DS-15

Birken, Sigmund von 1626-1681 . . . . .DLB-164

Birney, Earle 1904-1995 . . . . .DLB-88

Birrell, Augustine 1850-1933 . . . . .DLB-98

Bisher, Furman 1918- DLB-171

Bishop, Elizabeth
1911-1979 . . . . .DLB-5, 169; CDALB-6

Bishop, John Peale 1892-1944 . . . . . . .DLB-4, 9, 45

Bismarck, Otto von 1815-1898 . . . . .DLB-129

Bisset, Robert 1759-1805 . . . . .DLB-142

Bissett, Bill 1939- DLB-53

Bitzius, Albert (see Gotthelf, Jeremias)

Bjørnvig, Thorkild 1918- DLB-214

Black, David (D. M.) 1941- DLB-40

Black, Walter J. [publishing house] DLB-46

Black, Winifred 1863-1936 . . . . .DLB-25

The Black Aesthetic: Background DS-8

Black Theaters and Theater Organizations in
America, 1961-1982:
A Research List DLB-38

Black Theatre: A Forum [excerpts] DLB-38

Blackamore, Arthur 1679-? DLB-24, 39

Blackburn, Alexander L. 1929- Y-85

Blackburn, John 1923- DLB-261

Blackburn, Paul 1926-1971 . . . . .DLB-16; Y-81

Blackburn, Thomas 1916-1977 . . . . .DLB-27

Blackmore, R. D. 1825-1900 . . . . .DLB-18

Blackmore, Sir Richard 1654-1729 . . . . . . .DLB-131

Blackmur, R. P. 1904-1965 . . . . .DLB-63

Blackwell, Basil, Publisher DLB-106

Blackwood, Algernon Henry
1869-1951 . . . . DLB-153, 156, 178

Blackwood, Caroline 1931-1996 . . . . .DLB-14, 207

Blackwood, William, and Sons, Ltd. DLB-154

Blackwood's Edinburgh Magazine
1817-1980 . . . . .DLB-110

Blades, William 1824-1890 . . . . .DLB-184

Blaga, Lucian 1895-1961 . . . . .DLB-220

Blagden, Isabella 1817?-1873 . . . . .DLB-199

Blair, Eric Arthur (see Orwell, George)

Blair, Francis Preston 1791-1876 . . . . .DLB-43

Blair, James circa 1655-1743 . . . . .DLB-24

Blair, John Durburrow 1759-1823 . . . . . . .DLB-37

Blais, Marie-Claire 1939- DLB-53

Blaise, Clark 1940- DLB-53

Blake, George 1893-1961 . . . . .DLB-191

Blake, Lillie Devereux 1833-1913 . . .DLB-202, 221

Blake, Nicholas 1904-1972 . . . . .DLB-77
(see Day Lewis, C.)

Blake, William
1757-1827 . . . . . . .DLB-93, 154, 163; CDBLB-3

The Blakiston Company DLB-49

Blandiana, Ana 1942- DLB-232; CDWLB-4

Blanchot, Maurice 1907- DLB-72

Blanckenburg, Christian Friedrich von
1744-1796 . . . . .DLB-94

Blaser, Robin 1925- DLB-165

Blaumanis, Rudolfs 1863-1908 . . . . .DLB-220

Bleasdale, Alan 1946- DLB-245

Bledsoe, Albert Taylor 1809-1877 . . DLB-3, 79, 248

Bleecker, Ann Eliza 1752-1783 . . . . .DLB-200

Blelock and Company DLB-49

Blennerhassett, Margaret Agnew
1773-1842 . . . . .DLB-99

Bles, Geoffrey [publishing house] DLB-112

Blessington, Marguerite, Countess of
1789-1849 . . . . .DLB-166

Blew, Mary Clearman 1939- DLB-256

The Blickling Homilies circa 971 . . . . .DLB-146

Blind, Mathilde 1841-1896 . . . . .DLB-199

Blish, James 1921-1975 . . . . .DLB-8

Bliss, E., and E. White
[publishing house] DLB-49

Bliven, Bruce 1889-1977 . . . . .DLB-137

Blixen, Karen 1885-1962 . . . . .DLB-214

Bloch, Robert 1917-1994 . . . . .DLB-44

Block, Lawrence 1938- DLB-226

Block, Rudolph (see Lessing, Bruno)

Blondal, Patricia 1926-1959 . . . . .DLB-88

Bloom, Harold 1930- DLB-67

Bloomer, Amelia 1818-1894 . . . . .DLB-79

Bloomfield, Robert 1766-1823 . . . . .DLB-93

Bloomsbury Group DS-10

Blotner, Joseph 1923- DLB-111

Blount, Thomas 1618?-1679 . . . . .DLB-236

Bloy, Léon 1846-1917 . . . . .DLB-123

Blume, Judy 1938- DLB-52

Blunck, Hans Friedrich 1888-1961 . . . . . .DLB-66

Blunden, Edmund 1896-1974 . . .DLB-20, 100, 155

Blundeville, Thomas 1522?-1606 . . . . . . .DLB-236

Blunt, Lady Anne Isabella Noel
1837-1917 .DLB-174

Blunt, Wilfrid Scawen 1840-1922 . . . .DLB-19, 174

Bly, Nellie (see Cochrane, Elizabeth)

Bly, Robert 1926- DLB-5

Blyton, Enid 1897-1968 . . . . .DLB-160

Boaden, James 1762-1839 . . . . .DLB-89

Boas, Frederick S. 1862-1957 . . . . .DLB-149

The Bobbs-Merrill Archive at the
Lilly Library, Indiana University Y-90

Boborykin, Petr Dmitrievich 1836-1921 . .DLB-238

The Bobbs-Merrill Company DLB-46

Bobrov, Semen Sergeevich
1763?-1810 .DLB-150

Bobrowski, Johannes 1917-1965 . . . . .DLB-75

The Elmer Holmes Bobst Awards in Arts
and Letters Y-87

Bodenheim, Maxwell 1892-1954 . . . . . . .DLB-9, 45

Bodenstedt, Friedrich von 1819-1892 . . . .DLB-129

Bodini, Vittorio 1914-1970 . . . . .DLB-128

Bodkin, M. McDonnell 1850-1933 . . . . . . .DLB-70

Bodley, Sir Thomas 1545-1613 . . . . .DLB-213

Bodley Head .DLB-112

Bodmer, Johann Jakob 1698-1783 . . . . . . .DLB-97

Bodmershof, Imma von 1895-1982 . . . . . .DLB-85

Bodsworth, Fred 1918- DLB-68

Boehm, Sydney 1908- DLB-44

Boer, Charles 1939- DLB-5

Boethius circa 480-circa 524 . . . . .DLB-115

Boethius of Dacia circa 1240-? DLB-115

Bogan, Louise 1897-1970 . . . . .DLB-45, 169

Bogarde, Dirk 1921- DLB-14

Bogdanovich, Ippolit Fedorovich
circa 1743-1803 . . . . .DLB-150

Bogue, David [publishing house] DLB-106

Böhme, Jakob 1575-1624 . . . . .DLB-164

Bohn, H. G. [publishing house] DLB-106

Bohse, August 1661-1742 . . . . .DLB-168

Boie, Heinrich Christian 1744-1806 . . . . . .DLB-94

Bok, Edward W. 1863-1930 . . . . . .DLB-91; DS-16

Boland, Eavan 1944- DLB-40

Boldrewood, Rolf (Thomas Alexander Browne)
1826?-1915 .DLB-230

Bolingbroke, Henry St. John, Viscount
1678-1751 .DLB-101

Böll, Heinrich
1917-1985 . . . . . . .DLB-69; Y-85; CDWLB-2

Bolling, Robert 1738-1775 . . . . .DLB-31

Bolotov, Andrei Timofeevich
1738-1833 .DLB-150

Bolt, Carol 1941- DLB-60

Bolt, Robert 1924-1995 . . . . .DLB-13, 233

Bolton, Herbert E. 1870-1953 . . . . .DLB-17

Bonaventura DLB-90

Bonaventure circa 1217-1274 . . . . .DLB-115

Bonaviri, Giuseppe 1924- DLB-177

Bond, Edward 1934- DLB-13

Bond, Michael 1926- DLB-161

Boni, Albert and Charles
[publishing house] DLB-46

Boni and Liveright DLB-46

Bonnefoy, Yves 1923- DLB-258

Bonner, Marita 1899-1971 . . . . .DLB-228

Bonner, Paul Hyde 1893-1968 . . . . DS-17

Bonner, Sherwood (see McDowell, Katharine
Sherwood Bonner)

Robert Bonner's Sons DLB-49

Bonnin, Gertrude Simmons (see Zitkala-Ša)

Bonsanti, Alessandro 1904-1984 . . . . .DLB-177

Bontemps, Arna 1902-1973 . . . . .DLB-48, 51

The Book Arts Press at the University
of Virginia Y-96

The Book League of America DLB-46

Book Publishing Accounting: Some Basic
    Concepts Y-98

Book Reviewing in America: I Y-87

Book Reviewing in America: II Y-88

Book Reviewing in America: III Y-89

Book Reviewing in America: IV Y-90

Book Reviewing in America: V Y-91

Book Reviewing in America: VI Y-92

Book Reviewing in America: VII Y-93

Book Reviewing in America: VIII Y-94

Book Reviewing in America and the
    Literary Scene Y-95

Book Reviewing and the
    Literary Scene Y-96, Y-97

Book Supply Company DLB-49

The Book Trade History Group Y-93

The Book Trade and the Internet Y-00

The Booker Prize Y-96

Address by Anthony Thwaite,
    Chairman of the Booker Prize Judges
    Comments from Former Booker
    Prize Winners Y-86

The Books of George V. Higgins:
    A Checklist of Editions and Printings Y-00

Boorde, Andrew circa 1490-1549 . . . . DLB-136

Boorstin, Daniel J. 1914- DLB-17

Booth, Franklin 1874-1948 . . . . DLB-188

Booth, Mary L. 1831-1889 . . . . DLB-79

Booth, Philip 1925- Y-82

Booth, Wayne C. 1921- DLB-67

Booth, William 1829-1912 . . . . DLB-190

Borchardt, Rudolf 1877-1945 . . . . DLB-66

Borchert, Wolfgang 1921-1947 . . . . . . DLB-69, 124

Borel, Pétrus 1809-1859 . . . . DLB-119

Borges, Jorge Luis
    1899-1986 . . . . DLB-113; Y-86; CDWLB-3

Börne, Ludwig 1786-1837 . . . . DLB-90

Bornstein, Miriam 1950- DLB-209

Borowski, Tadeusz
    1922-1951 . . . . DLB-215; CDWLB-4

Borrow, George 1803-1881 . . . . . DLB-21, 55, 166

Bosanquet, Bernard 1848-1923 . . . . DLB-262

Bosch, Juan 1909- DLB-145

Bosco, Henri 1888-1976 . . . . DLB-72

Bosco, Monique 1927- DLB-53

Bosman, Herman Charles 1905-1951 . . . . DLB-225

Bostic, Joe 1908-1988 . . . . DLB-241

Boston, Lucy M. 1892-1990 . . . . DLB-161

Boswell, James
    1740-1795 . . . . DLB-104, 142; CDBLB-2

Boswell, Robert 1953- DLB-234

Bote, Hermann
    circa 1460-circa 1520 . . . . DLB-179

Botev, Khristo 1847-1876 . . . . DLB-147

Botta, Anne C. Lynch 1815-1891 . . . . . DLB-3, 250

Botto, Ján (see Krasko, Ivan)

Bottome, Phyllis 1882-1963 . . . . DLB-197

Bottomley, Gordon 1874-1948 . . . . DLB-10

Bottoms, David 1949- DLB-120; Y-83

Bottrall, Ronald 1906- DLB-20

Bouchardy, Joseph 1810-1870 . . . . DLB-192

Boucher, Anthony 1911-1968 . . . . DLB-8

Boucher, Jonathan 1738-1804 . . . . DLB-31

Boucher de Boucherville, George
    1814-1894 . . . . DLB-99

Boudreau, Daniel (see Coste, Donat)

Bourassa, Napoléon 1827-1916 . . . . DLB-99

Bourget, Paul 1852-1935 . . . . DLB-123

Bourinot, John George 1837-1902 . . . . DLB-99

Bourjaily, Vance 1922- DLB-2, 143

Bourne, Edward Gaylord
    1860-1908 . . . . DLB-47

Bourne, Randolph 1886-1918 . . . . DLB-63

Bousoño, Carlos 1923- DLB-108

Bousquet, Joë 1897-1950 . . . . DLB-72

Bova, Ben 1932- Y-81

Bovard, Oliver K. 1872-1945 . . . . DLB-25

Bove, Emmanuel 1898-1945 . . . . DLB-72

Bowen, Elizabeth
    1899-1973 . . . . DLB-15, 162; CDBLB-7

Bowen, Francis 1811-1890 . . . . . . DLB-1, 59, 235

Bowen, John 1924- DLB-13

Bowen, Marjorie 1886-1952 . . . . DLB-153

Bowen-Merrill Company DLB-49

Bowering, George 1935- DLB-53

Bowers, Bathsheba 1671-1718 . . . . DLB-200

Bowers, Claude G. 1878-1958 . . . . DLB-17

Bowers, Edgar 1924-2000 . . . . DLB-5

Bowers, Fredson Thayer
    1905-1991 . . . . DLB-140; Y-80, 91

Bowles, Paul 1910-1999 . . . . . . DLB-5, 6, 218; Y-99

Bowles, Samuel III 1826-1878 . . . . DLB-43

Bowles, William Lisles 1762-1850 . . . . DLB-93

Bowman, Louise Morey 1882-1944 . . . . . . DLB-68

Boyd, James 1888-1944 . . . . DLB-9; DS-16

Boyd, John 1919- DLB-8

Boyd, Martin 1893-1972 . . . . DLB-260

Boyd, Thomas 1898-1935 . . . . DLB-9; DS-16

Boyd, William 1952- DLB-231

Boye, Karin 1900-1941 . . . . DLB-259

Boyesen, Hjalmar Hjorth
    1848-1895 . . . . DLB-12, 71; DS-13

Boyle, Kay 1902-1992 . . . . . DLB-4, 9, 48, 86; Y-93

Boyle, Roger, Earl of Orrery 1621-1679 . . . DLB-80

Boyle, T. Coraghessan 1948- DLB-218; Y-86

Božić, Mirko 1919- DLB-181

Brackenbury, Alison 1953- DLB-40

Brackenridge, Hugh Henry
    1748-1816 . . . . DLB-11, 37

Brackett, Charles 1892-1969 . . . . DLB-26

Brackett, Leigh 1915-1978 . . . . DLB-8, 26

Bradburn, John [publishing house] DLB-49

Bradbury, Malcolm 1932-2000 . . . . . DLB-14, 207

Bradbury, Ray 1920- DLB-2, 8; CDALB-6

Bradbury and Evans DLB-106

Braddon, Mary Elizabeth
    1835-1915 . . . . DLB-18, 70, 156

Bradford, Andrew 1686-1742 . . . . . . DLB-43, 73

Bradford, Gamaliel 1863-1932 . . . . DLB-17

Bradford, John 1749-1830 . . . . DLB-43

Bradford, Roark 1896-1948 . . . . DLB-86

Bradford, William 1590-1657 . . . . . . DLB-24, 30

Bradford, William III 1719-1791 . . . . DLB-43, 73

Bradlaugh, Charles 1833-1891 . . . . DLB-57

Bradley, David 1950- DLB-33

Bradley, F. H. 1846-1924 . . . . DLB-262

Bradley, Ira, and Company DLB-49

Bradley, J. W., and Company DLB-49

Bradley, Katherine Harris (see Field, Michael)

Bradley, Marion Zimmer 1930-1999 . . . . . . DLB-8

Bradley, William Aspenwall 1878-1939 . . . . DLB-4

Bradshaw, Henry 1831-1886 . . . . DLB-184

Bradstreet, Anne
    1612 or 1613-1672 . . . . DLB-24; CDABL-2

Bradūnas, Kazys 1917- DLB-220

Bradwardine, Thomas circa
    1295-1349 . . . . DLB-115

Brady, Frank 1924-1986 . . . . DLB-111

Brady, Frederic A. [publishing house] DLB-49

Bragg, Melvyn 1939- DLB-14

Brainard, Charles H. [publishing house] . . DLB-49

Braine, John 1922-1986 . DLB-15; Y-86; CDBLB-7

Braithwait, Richard 1588-1673 . . . . DLB-151

Braithwaite, William Stanley
    1878-1962 . . . . DLB-50, 54

Braker, Ulrich 1735-1798 . . . . DLB-94

Bramah, Ernest 1868-1942 . . . . DLB-70

Branagan, Thomas 1774-1843 . . . . DLB-37

Branch, William Blackwell 1927- DLB-76

Brand, Max (see Faust, Frederick Schiller)

Branden Press DLB-46

Branner, H.C. 1903-1966 . . . . DLB-214

Brant, Sebastian 1457-1521 . . . . DLB-179

Brassey, Lady Annie (Allnutt)
    1839-1887 . . . . DLB-166

Brathwaite, Edward Kamau
    1930- DLB-125; CDWLB-3

Brault, Jacques 1933- DLB-53

Braun, Matt 1932- DLB-212

Braun, Volker 1939- DLB-75

Brautigan, Richard
    1935-1984 . . . . DLB-2, 5, 206; Y-80, Y-84

Braxton, Joanne M. 1950- DLB-41

Bray, Anne Eliza 1790-1883 . . . . DLB-116

Bray, Thomas 1656-1730 . . . . DLB-24

Brazdžionis, Bernardas 1907- DLB-220

Braziller, George [publishing house] DLB-46

The Bread Loaf Writers' Conference 1983 . . . Y-84

Breasted, James Henry 1865-1935 . . . . DLB-47

Brecht, Bertolt
  1898-1956 . . . . DLB-56, 124; CDWLB-2

Bredel, Willi 1901-1964 . . . . DLB-56

Bregendahl, Marie 1867-1940 . . . . DLB-214

Breitinger, Johann Jakob 1701-1776 . . . . DLB-97

Bremser, Bonnie 1939- DLB-16

Bremser, Ray 1934- DLB-16

Brennan, Christopher 1870-1932 . . . . DLB-230

Brentano, Bernard von 1901-1964 . . . . DLB-56

Brentano, Clemens 1778-1842 . . . . DLB-90

Brentano's DLB-49

Brenton, Howard 1942- DLB-13

Breslin, Jimmy 1929-1996 . . . . DLB-185

Breton, André 1896-1966 . . . . DLB-65, 258

Breton, Nicholas circa 1555-circa 1626 . . . DLB-136

The Breton Lays
  1300-early fifteenth century DLB-146

Brewer, Luther A. 1858-1933 . . . . DLB-187

Brewer, Warren and Putnam DLB-46

Brewster, Elizabeth 1922- DLB-60

Breytenbach, Breyten 1939- DLB-225

Bridge, Ann (Lady Mary Dolling Sanders
  O'Malley) 1889-1974 . . . . DLB-191

Bridge, Horatio 1806-1893 . . . . DLB-183

Bridgers, Sue Ellen 1942- DLB-52

Bridges, Robert
  1844-1930 . . . . DLB-19, 98; CDBLB-5

The Bridgewater Library DLB-213

Bridie, James 1888-1951 . . . . DLB-10

Brieux, Eugene 1858-1932 . . . . DLB-192

Brigadere, Anna 1861-1933 . . . . DLB-220

Briggs, Charles Frederick
  1804-1877 . . . . DLB-3, 250

Brighouse, Harold 1882-1958 . . . . DLB-10

Bright, Mary Chavelita Dunne (see Egerton, George)

Brimmer, B. J., Company DLB-46

Brines, Francisco 1932- DLB-134

Brink, André 1935- DLB-225

Brinley, George, Jr. 1817-1875 . . . . DLB-140

Brinnin, John Malcolm 1916-1998 . . . . DLB-48

Brisbane, Albert 1809-1890 . . . . DLB-3, 250

Brisbane, Arthur 1864-1936 . . . . DLB-25

British Academy DLB-112

The British Critic 1793-1843 . . . . DLB-110

The British Library and the Regular
  Readers' Group Y-91

British Literary Prizes Y-98

*The British Review and London Critical
  Journal* 1811-1825 . . . . DLB-110

British Travel Writing, 1940-1997 . . . . DLB-204

Brito, Aristeo 1942- DLB-122

Brittain, Vera 1893-1970 . . . . DLB-191

Brizeux, Auguste 1803-1858 . . . . DLB-217

Broadway Publishing Company DLB-46

Broch, Hermann
  1886-1951 . . . . DLB-85, 124; CDWLB-2

Brochu, André 1942- DLB-53

Brock, Edwin 1927- DLB-40

Brockes, Barthold Heinrich 1680-1747 . . . DLB-168

Brod, Max 1884-1968 . . . . DLB-81

Brodber, Erna 1940- DLB-157

Brodhead, John R. 1814-1873 . . . . DLB-30

Brodkey, Harold 1930-1996 . . . . DLB-130

Brodsky, Joseph 1940-1996 . . . . Y-87

Brodsky, Michael 1948- DLB-244

Broeg, Bob 1918- DLB-171

Brøgger, Suzanne 1944- DLB-214

Brome, Richard circa 1590-1652 . . . . DLB-58

Brome, Vincent 1910- DLB-155

Bromfield, Louis 1896-1956 . . . . DLB-4, 9, 86

Bromige, David 1933- DLB-193

Broner, E. M. 1930- DLB-28

Bronk, William 1918-1999 . . . . DLB-165

Bronnen, Arnolt 1895-1959 . . . . DLB-124

Brontë, Anne 1820-1849 . . . . DLB-21, 199

Brontë, Charlotte
  1816-1855 . . . . . . DLB-21, 159, 199; CDBLB-4

Brontë, Emily
  1818-1848 . . . . . . DLB-21, 32, 199; CDBLB-4

Brook, Stephen 1947- DLB-204

Brook Farm 1841-1847 . . . . DLB-223

Brooke, Frances 1724-1789 . . . . DLB-39, 99

Brooke, Henry 1703?-1783 . . . . DLB-39

Brooke, L. Leslie 1862-1940 . . . . DLB-141

Brooke, Margaret, Ranee of Sarawak
  1849-1936 . . . . DLB-174

Brooke, Rupert
  1887-1915 . . . . DLB-19, 216; CDBLB-6

Brooker, Bertram 1888-1955 . . . . DLB-88

Brooke-Rose, Christine 1923- DLB-14, 231

Brookner, Anita 1928- DLB-194; Y-87

Brooks, Charles Timothy 1813-1883 . . . DLB-1, 243

Brooks, Cleanth 1906-1994 . . . . DLB-63; Y-94

Brooks, Gwendolyn
  1917-2000 . . . . DLB-5, 76, 165; CDALB-1

Brooks, Jeremy 1926- DLB-14

Brooks, Mel 1926- DLB-26

Brooks, Noah 1830-1903 . . . . DLB-42; DS-13

Brooks, Richard 1912-1992 . . . . DLB-44

Brooks, Van Wyck
  1886-1963 . . . . DLB-45, 63, 103

Brophy, Brigid 1929-1995 . . . . DLB-14

Brophy, John 1899-1965 . . . . DLB-191

Brossard, Chandler 1922-1993 . . . . DLB-16

Brossard, Nicole 1943- DLB-53

Broster, Dorothy Kathleen 1877-1950 . . . . DLB-160

Brother Antoninus (see Everson, William)

Brotherton, Lord 1856-1930 . . . . DLB-184

Brougham and Vaux, Henry Peter Brougham,
  Baron 1778-1868 . . . . DLB-110, 158

Brougham, John 1810-1880 . . . . DLB-11

Broughton, James 1913-1999 . . . . DLB-5

Broughton, Rhoda 1840-1920 . . . . DLB-18

Broun, Heywood 1888-1939 . . . . DLB-29, 171

Brown, Alice 1856-1948 . . . . DLB-78

Brown, Bob 1886-1959 . . . . DLB-4, 45

Brown, Cecil 1943- DLB-33

Brown, Charles Brockden
  1771-1810 . . . . DLB-37, 59, 73; CDALB-2

Brown, Christy 1932-1981 . . . . DLB-14

Brown, Dee 1908- Y-80

Brown, Frank London 1927-1962 . . . . DLB-76

Brown, Fredric 1906-1972 . . . . DLB-8

Brown, George Mackay
  1921-1996 . . . . DLB-14, 27, 139

Brown, Harry 1917-1986 . . . . DLB-26

Brown, Larry 1951- DLB-234

Brown, Marcia 1918- DLB-61

Brown, Margaret Wise 1910-1952 . . . . DLB-22

Brown, Morna Doris (see Ferrars, Elizabeth)

Brown, Oliver Madox 1855-1874 . . . . DLB-21

Brown, Sterling 1901-1989 . . . . . . DLB-48, 51, 63

Brown, T. E. 1830-1897 . . . . DLB-35

Brown, Thomas Alexander (see Boldrewood, Rolf)

Brown, Warren 1894-1978 . . . . DLB-241

Brown, William Hill 1765-1793 . . . . DLB-37

Brown, William Wells
  1815-1884 . . . . DLB-3, 50, 183, 248

Browne, Charles Farrar 1834-1867 . . . . DLB-11

Browne, Frances 1816-1879 . . . . DLB-199

Browne, Francis Fisher 1843-1913 . . . . DLB-79

Browne, Howard 1908-1999 . . . . DLB-226

Browne, J. Ross 1821-1875 . . . . DLB-202

Browne, Michael Dennis 1940- DLB-40

Browne, Sir Thomas 1605-1682 . . . . DLB-151

Browne, William, of Tavistock
  1590-1645 . . . . DLB-121

Browne, Wynyard 1911-1964 . . . . DLB-13, 233

Browne and Nolan DLB-106

Brownell, W. C. 1851-1928 . . . . DLB-71

Browning, Elizabeth Barrett
  1806-1861 . . . . DLB-32, 199; CDBLB-4

Browning, Robert
  1812-1889 . . . . DLB-32, 163; CDBLB-4

Introductory Essay: *Letters of Percy
  Bysshe Shelley* (1852) DLB-32

Brownjohn, Allan 1931- DLB-40

Brownson, Orestes Augustus
  1803-1876 . . . . DLB-1, 59, 73, 243

Bruccoli, Matthew J. 1931- DLB-103

Bruce, Charles 1906-1971 . . . . DLB-68

John Edward Bruce: Three Documents DLB-50

Bruce, Leo 1903-1979 . . . . DLB-77

Bruce, Mary Grant 1878-1958 . . . . DLB-230

Bruce, Philip Alexander 1856-1933 . . . . DLB-47

Bruce Humphries [publishing house] DLB-46

Bruce-Novoa, Juan 1944- DLB-82

Bruckman, Clyde 1894-1955 . . . . DLB-26

Bruckner, Ferdinand 1891-1958 . . . . DLB-118

Brundage, John Herbert (see Herbert, John)

Brunner, John 1934-1995 . . . . DLB-261

Brutus, Dennis
1924- DLB-117, 225; CDWLB-3

Bryan, C. D. B. 1936- DLB-185

Bryant, Arthur 1899-1985 . . . . DLB-149

Bryant, William Cullen 1794-1878
. . . . DLB-3, 43, 59, 189, 250; CDALB-2

Bryce Echenique, Alfredo
1939- DLB-145; CDWLB-3

Bryce, James 1838-1922 . . . . DLB-166, 190

Bryden, Bill 1942- DLB-233

Brydges, Sir Samuel Egerton 1762-1837 . . DLB-107

Bryskett, Lodowick 1546?-1612 . . . . DLB-167

Buchan, John 1875-1940 . . . . DLB-34, 70, 156

Buchanan, George 1506-1582 . . . . DLB-132

Buchanan, Robert 1841-1901 . . . . DLB-18, 35

"The Fleshly School of Poetry and Other
Phenomena of the Day" (1872), by
Robert Buchanan DLB-35

"The Fleshly School of Poetry: Mr. D. G.
Rossetti" (1871), by Thomas Maitland
(Robert Buchanan) DLB-35

Buchman, Sidney 1902-1975 . . . . DLB-26

Buchner, Augustus 1591-1661 . . . . DLB-164

Büchner, Georg 1813-1837 . . DLB-133; CDWLB-2

Bucholtz, Andreas Heinrich 1607-1671 . . . DLB-168

Buck, Pearl S. 1892-1973 . . DLB-9, 102; CDALB-7

Bucke, Charles 1781-1846 . . . . DLB-110

Bucke, Richard Maurice 1837-1902 . . . . . . DLB-99

Buckingham, Joseph Tinker 1779-1861 and
Buckingham, Edwin 1810-1833 . . . . . . DLB-73

Buckler, Ernest 1908-1984 . . . . DLB-68

Buckley, William F., Jr. 1925- DLB-137; Y-80

Buckminster, Joseph Stevens
1784-1812 . . . . DLB-37

Buckner, Robert 1906- DLB-26

Budd, Thomas ?-1698 . . . . DLB-24

Budrys, A. J. 1931- DLB-8

Buechner, Frederick 1926- Y-80

Buell, John 1927- DLB-53

Bufalino, Gesualdo 1920-1996 . . . . DLB-196

Buffum, Job [publishing house] DLB-49

Bugnet, Georges 1879-1981 . . . . DLB-92

Buies, Arthur 1840-1901 . . . . DLB-99

Building the New British Library
at St Pancras Y-94

Bukowski, Charles 1920-1994 . . . DLB-5, 130, 169

Bulatović, Miodrag
1930-1991 . . . . DLB-181; CDWLB-4

Bulgarin, Faddei Venediktovich
1789-1859 . . . . DLB-198

Bulger, Bozeman 1877-1932 . . . . .DLB-171

Bullein, William
between 1520 and 1530-1576 . . . . DLB-167

Bullins, Ed 1935- DLB-7, 38, 249

Bulwer, John 1606-1656 . . . . DLB-236

Bulwer-Lytton, Edward (also Edward Bulwer)
1803-1873 . . . . DLB-21

"On Art in Fiction "(1838) DLB-21

Bumpus, Jerry 1937- Y-81

Bunce and Brother DLB-49

Bunner, H. C. 1855-1896 . . . . .DLB-78, 79

Bunting, Basil 1900-1985 . . . . DLB-20

Buntline, Ned (Edward Zane Carroll Judson)
1821-1886 . . . . DLB-186

Bunyan, John 1628-1688 . . . . . DLB-39; CDBLB-2

Burch, Robert 1925- DLB-52

Burciaga, José Antonio 1940- DLB-82

Burdekin, Katharine 1896-1963 . . . . DLB-255

Bürger, Gottfried August 1747-1794 . . . . . . DLB-94

Burgess, Anthony
1917-1993 . . . . . . DLB-14, 194, 261; CDBLB-8

The Anthony Burgess Archive at
the Harry Ransom Humanities
Research Center Y-98

Anthony Burgess's 99 Novels:
An Opinion Poll Y-84

Burgess, Gelett 1866-1951 . . . . DLB-11

Burgess, John W. 1844-1931 . . . . DLB-47

Burgess, Thornton W. 1874-1965 . . . . DLB-22

Burgess, Stringer and Company DLB-49

Burick, Si 1909-1986 . . . . .DLB-171

Burk, John Daly circa 1772-1808 . . . . DLB-37

Burk, Ronnie 1955- DLB-209

Burke, Edmund 1729?-1797 . . . . DLB-104, 252

Burke, James Lee 1936- DLB-226

Burke, Kenneth 1897-1993 . . . . DLB-45, 63

Burke, Thomas 1886-1945 . . . . DLB-197

Burley, Dan 1907-1962 . . . . DLB-241

Burlingame, Edward Livermore
1848-1922 . . . . DLB-79

Burman, Carina 1960- DLB-257

Burnet, Gilbert 1643-1715 . . . . DLB-101

Burnett, Frances Hodgson
1849-1924 . . . . .DLB-42, 141; DS-13, 14

Burnett, W. R. 1899-1982 . . . . DLB-9, 226

Burnett, Whit 1899-1973 and
Martha Foley 1897-1977 . . . . DLB-137

Burney, Fanny 1752-1840 . . . . DLB-39

Dedication, The Wanderer (1814) DLB-39

Preface to Evelina (1778) DLB-39

Burns, Alan 1929- DLB-14, 194

Burns, John Horne 1916-1953 . . . . Y-85

Burns, Robert 1759-1796 . . . . DLB-109; CDBLB-3

Burns and Oates DLB-106

Burnshaw, Stanley 1906- DLB-48

Burr, C. Chauncey 1815?-1883 . . . . DLB-79

Burr, Esther Edwards 1732-1758 . . . . . . DLB-200

Burroughs, Edgar Rice 1875-1950 . . . . DLB-8

Burroughs, John 1837-1921 . . . . DLB-64

Burroughs, Margaret T. G. 1917- DLB-41

Burroughs, William S., Jr. 1947-1981 . . . . DLB-16

Burroughs, William Seward 1914-1997
. . . . DLB-2, 8, 16, 152, 237; Y-81, Y-97

Burroway, Janet 1936- DLB-6

Burt, Maxwell Struthers
1882-1954 . . . . DLB-86; DS-16

Burt, A. L., and Company DLB-49

Burton, Hester 1913- DLB-161

Burton, Isabel Arundell 1831-1896 . . . . . DLB-166

Burton, Miles (see Rhode, John)

Burton, Richard Francis
1821-1890 . . . . .DLB-55, 166, 184

Burton, Robert 1577-1640 . . . . DLB-151

Burton, Virginia Lee 1909-1968 . . . . DLB-22

Burton, William Evans 1804-1860 . . . . . . DLB-73

Burwell, Adam Hood 1790-1849 . . . . DLB-99

Bury, Lady Charlotte 1775-1861 . . . . DLB-116

Busch, Frederick 1941- DLB-6, 218

Busch, Niven 1903-1991 . . . . DLB-44

Bushnell, Horace 1802-1876 . . . . .DS-13

Bussieres, Arthur de 1877-1913 . . . . DLB-92

Butler, Charles ca. 1560-1647 . . . . DLB-236

Butler, Guy 1918- DLB-225

Butler, E. H., and Company DLB-49

Butler, Joseph 1692-1752 . . . . DLB-252

Butler, Josephine Elizabeth 1828-1906 . . . DLB-190

Butler, Juan 1942-1981 . . . . DLB-53

Butler, Judith 1956- DLB-246

Butler, Octavia E. 1947- DLB-33

Butler, Pierce 1884-1953 . . . . .DLB-187

Butler, Robert Olen 1945- DLB-173

Butler, Samuel 1613-1680 . . . . .DLB-101, 126

Butler, Samuel 1835-1902 . . . . . DLB-18, 57, 174

Butler, William Francis 1838-1910 . . . . . . DLB-166

Butor, Michel 1926- DLB-83

Butter, Nathaniel [publishing house] DLB-170

Butterworth, Hezekiah 1839-1905 . . . . DLB-42

Buttitta, Ignazio 1899- DLB-114

Butts, Mary 1890-1937 . . . . DLB-240

Buzzati, Dino 1906-1972 . . . . .DLB-177

Byars, Betsy 1928- DLB-52

Byatt, A. S. 1936- DLB-14, 194

Byles, Mather 1707-1788 . . . . DLB-24

Bynneman, Henry
[publishing house] DLB-170

Bynner, Witter 1881-1968 . . . . DLB-54

Byrd, William circa 1543-1623 . . . . .DLB-172

Byrd, William II 1674-1744 . . . . DLB-24, 140

Byrne, John Keyes (see Leonard, Hugh)

Byron, George Gordon, Lord
1788-1824 . . . . DLB-96, 110; CDBLB-3

Byron, Robert 1905-1941 . . . . DLB-195

C

Caballero Bonald, José Manuel
1926- DLB-108

Cabañero, Eladio 1930- DLB-134

Cabell, James Branch 1879-1958 . . . . . . .DLB-9, 78

Cabeza de Baca, Manuel 1853-1915 . . . . . DLB-122

Cabeza de Baca Gilbert, Fabiola
1898- DLB-122

Cable, George Washington
1844-1925 .... DLB-12, 74; DS-13

Cable, Mildred 1878-1952 ....DLB-195

Cabrera, Lydia 1900-1991 ....DLB-145

Cabrera Infante, Guillermo
1929- DLB-113; CDWLB-3

Cadell [publishing house]..............DLB-154

Cady, Edwin H. 1917- DLB-103

Caedmon flourished 658-680...........DLB-146

Caedmon School circa 660-899 ....DLB-146

Cafés, Brasseries, and Bistros.......... DS-15

Cage, John 1912-1992 ....DLB-193

Cahan, Abraham 1860-1951 ....DLB-9, 25, 28

Cain, George 1943- DLB-33

Cain, James M. 1892-1977 ....DLB-226

Caird, Edward 1835-1908 ....DLB-262

Caird, Mona 1854-1932...............DLB-197

Čaks, Aleksandrs
1901-1950 ....DLB-220; CDWLB-4

Caldecott, Randolph 1846-1886 ....DLB-163

Calder, John (Publishers), Limited......DLB-112

Calderón de la Barca, Fanny
1804-1882 ....DLB-183

Caldwell, Ben 1937- DLB-38

Caldwell, Erskine 1903-1987 ....DLB-9, 86

Caldwell, H. M., Company DLB-49

Caldwell, Taylor 1900-1985 .... DS-17

Calhoun, John C. 1782-1850 ....DLB-3, 248

Călinescu, George 1899-1965 ....DLB-220

Calisher, Hortense 1911- DLB-2, 218

A Call to Letters and an Invitation
to the Electric Chair,
by Siegfried Mandel DLB-75

Callaghan, Mary Rose 1944- DLB-207

Callaghan, Morley 1903-1990 ....DLB-68

Callahan, S. Alice 1868-1894 .... DLB-175, 221

Callaloo Y-87

Callimachus circa 305 B.C.-240 B.C...... DLB-176

Calmer, Edgar 1907- DLB-4

Calverley, C. S. 1831-1884 ....DLB-35

Calvert, George Henry
1803-1889 ....DLB-1, 64, 248

Calvino, Italo 1923-1985 ....DLB-196

Cambridge, Ada 1844-1926...........DLB-230

Cambridge Press DLB-49

Cambridge Songs (Carmina Cantabrigensia)
circa 1050 ....DLB-148

Cambridge University Press DLB-170

Camden, William 1551-1623...........DLB-172

Camden House: An Interview with
James Hardin...................... Y-92

Cameron, Eleanor 1912- DLB-52

Cameron, George Frederick
1854-1885 ....DLB-99

Cameron, Lucy Lyttelton 1781-1858.....DLB-163

Cameron, Peter 1959- DLB-234

Cameron, William Bleasdell 1862-1951 ...DLB-99

Camm, John 1718-1778 ....DLB-31

Camon, Ferdinando 1935- DLB-196

Camp, Walter 1859-1925 ....DLB-241

Campana, Dino 1885-1932 ....DLB-114

Campbell, Bebe Moore 1950- DLB-227

Campbell, David 1915-1979...........DLB-260

Campbell, Gabrielle Margaret Vere
(see Shearing, Joseph, and Bowen, Marjorie)

Campbell, James Dykes 1838-1895 ......DLB-144

Campbell, James Edwin 1867-1896 ....DLB-50

Campbell, John 1653-1728.............DLB-43

Campbell, John W., Jr. 1910-1971 ....DLB-8

Campbell, Ramsey 1946- DLB-261

Campbell, Roy 1901-1957 ....DLB-20, 225

Campbell, Thomas 1777-1844 ....DLB-93, 144

Campbell, William Wilfred 1858-1918 ....DLB-92

Campion, Edmund 1539-1581 ....DLB-167

Campion, Thomas
1567-1620 ....DLB-58, 172; CDBLB-1

Campton, David 1924- DLB-245

Camus, Albert 1913-1960 ....DLB-72

The Canadian Publishers' Records
Database Y-96

Canby, Henry Seidel 1878-1961 ....DLB-91

Candelaria, Cordelia 1943- DLB-82

Candelaria, Nash 1928- DLB-82

Canetti, Elias
1905-1994 ....DLB-85, 124; CDWLB-2

Canham, Erwin Dain 1904-1982........DLB-127

Canitz, Friedrich Rudolph Ludwig von
1654-1699 ....DLB-168

Cankar, Ivan 1876-1918..... DLB-147; CDWLB-4

Cannan, Gilbert 1884-1955 .... DLB-10, 197

Cannan, Joanna 1896-1961 ....DLB-191

Cannell, Kathleen 1891-1974.............DLB-4

Cannell, Skipwith 1887-1957 ....DLB-45

Canning, George 1770-1827............DLB-158

Cannon, Jimmy 1910-1973 ....DLB-171

Cano, Daniel 1947- DLB-209

Cantú, Norma Elia 1947- DLB-209

Cantwell, Robert 1908-1978 ....DLB-9

Cape, Jonathan, and Harrison Smith
[publishing house] DLB-46

Cape, Jonathan, Limited DLB-112

Čapek, Karel 1890-1938 .... DLB-215; CDWLB-4

Capen, Joseph 1658-1725...............DLB-24

Capes, Bernard 1854-1918.............DLB-156

Capote, Truman 1924-1984
..... DLB-2, 185, 227; Y-80, Y-84; CDALB-1

Capps, Benjamin 1922- DLB-256

Caproni, Giorgio 1912-1990 ....DLB-128

Caragiale, Mateiu Ioan 1885-1936......DLB-220

Cardarelli, Vincenzo 1887-1959........DLB-114

Cárdenas, Reyes 1948- DLB-122

Cardinal, Marie 1929- DLB-83

Carew, Jan 1920- DLB-157

Carew, Thomas 1594 or 1595-1640.....DLB-126

Carey, Henry circa 1687-1689-1743......DLB-84

Carey, M., and Company DLB-49

Carey, Mathew 1760-1839.......... DLB-37, 73

Carey and Hart DLB-49

Carlell, Lodowick 1602-1675...........DLB-58

Carleton, William 1794-1869...........DLB-159

Carleton, G. W. [publishing house]......DLB-49

Carlile, Richard 1790-1843 .... DLB-110, 158

Carlson, Ron 1947- DLB-244

Carlyle, Jane Welsh 1801-1866 ....DLB-55

Carlyle, Thomas
1795-1881 ....DLB-55, 144; CDBLB-3

"The Hero as Man of Letters: Johnson,
Rousseau, Burns" (1841) [excerpt] DLB-57

The Hero as Poet. Dante;
Shakspeare (1841).................DLB-32

Carman, Bliss 1861-1929...............DLB-92

Carmina Burana circa 1230 ....DLB-138

Carnero, Guillermo 1947- DLB-108

Carossa, Hans 1878-1956 ....DLB-66

Carpenter, Humphrey
1946- DLB-155; Y-84, Y-99

The Practice of Biography III: An Interview
with Humphrey Carpenter Y-84

Carpenter, Stephen Cullen ?-1820?.......DLB-73

Carpentier, Alejo
1904-1980 ....DLB-113; CDWLB-3

Carr, Marina 1964- DLB-245

Carrier, Roch 1937- DLB-53

Carrillo, Adolfo 1855-1926 ....DLB-122

Carroll, Gladys Hasty 1904- DLB-9

Carroll, John 1735-1815..............DLB-37

Carroll, John 1809-1884 ....DLB-99

Carroll, Lewis
1832-1898 ...... DLB-18, 163, 178; CDBLB-4

The Lewis Carroll Centenary Y-98

Carroll, Paul 1927- DLB-16

Carroll, Paul Vincent 1900-1968.........DLB-10

Carroll and Graf Publishers DLB-46

Carruth, Hayden 1921- DLB-5, 165

Carryl, Charles E. 1841-1920 ....DLB-42

Carson, Anne 1950- DLB-193

Carswell, Catherine 1879-1946 ....DLB-36

Cărtărescu, Mirea 1956- DLB-232

Carter, Angela 1940-1992 ...... DLB-14, 207, 261

Carter, Elizabeth 1717-1806 ....DLB-109

Carter, Henry (see Leslie, Frank)

Carter, Hodding, Jr. 1907-1972 ....DLB-127

Carter, John 1905-1975 ....DLB-201

Carter, Landon 1710-1778 ....DLB-31

Carter, Lin 1930- Y-81

Carter, Martin 1927-1997.... DLB-117; CDWLB-3

Carter, Robert, and Brothers...........DLB-49

Carter and Hendee DLB-49

Cartwright, Jim 1958- DLB-245

Cartwright, John 1740-1824 . . . . DLB-158

Cartwright, William circa 1611-1643 . . . . DLB-126

Caruthers, William Alexander
1802-1846 . . . . DLB-3, 248

Carver, Jonathan 1710-1780 . . . . DLB-31

Carver, Raymond
1938-1988 . . . . DLB-130; Y-83, Y-88

First Strauss "Livings" Awarded to Cynthia
Ozick and Raymond Carver
An Interview with Raymond Carver Y-83

Cary, Alice 1820-1871 . . . . DLB-202

Cary, Joyce 1888-1957 . . . DLB-15, 100; CDBLB-6

Cary, Patrick 1623?-1657 . . . . DLB-131

Casey, Gavin 1907-1964 . . . . DLB-260

Casey, Juanita 1925- DLB-14

Casey, Michael 1947- DLB-5

Cassady, Carolyn 1923- DLB-16

Cassady, Neal 1926-1968 . . . . DLB-16, 237

Cassell and Company DLB-106

Cassell Publishing Company DLB-49

Cassill, R. V. 1919- DLB-6, 218

Cassity, Turner 1929- DLB-105

Cassius Dio circa 155/164-post 229 . . . . . DLB-176

Cassola, Carlo 1917-1987 . . . . DLB-177

The Castle of Perserverance circa 1400-1425 . DLB-146

Castellano, Olivia 1944- DLB-122

Castellanos, Rosario
1925-1974 . . . . DLB-113; CDWLB-3

Castillo, Ana 1953- DLB-122, 227

Castillo, Rafael C. 1950- DLB-209

Castlemon, Harry (see Fosdick, Charles Austin)

Čašule, Kole 1921- DLB-181

Caswall, Edward 1814-1878 . . . . DLB-32

Catacalos, Rosemary 1944- DLB-122

Cather, Willa 1873-1947
. . . . DLB-9, 54, 78, 256; DS-1; CDALB-3

Catherine II (Ekaterina Alekseevna), "The Great,"
Empress of Russia 1729-1796 . . . . DLB-150

Catherwood, Mary Hartwell 1847-1902 . . . DLB-78

Catledge, Turner 1901-1983 . . . . DLB-127

Catlin, George 1796-1872 . . . . DLB-186, 189

Cato the Elder 234 B.C.-149 B.C. DLB-211

Cattafi, Bartolo 1922-1979 . . . . DLB-128

Catton, Bruce 1899-1978 . . . . DLB-17

Catullus circa 84 B.C.-54 B.C.
. . . . DLB-211; CDWLB-1

Causley, Charles 1917- DLB-27

Caute, David 1936- DLB-14, 231

Cavendish, Duchess of Newcastle,
Margaret Lucas 1623-1673 . . . . DLB-131, 252

Cawein, Madison 1865-1914 . . . . DLB-54

Caxton, William [publishing house] DLB-170

The Caxton Printers, Limited DLB-46

Caylor, O. P. 1849-1897 . . . . DLB-241

Cayrol, Jean 1911- DLB-83

Cecil, Lord David 1902-1986 . . . . DLB-155

Cela, Camilo José 1916- Y-89

Celan, Paul 1920-1970 . . . . . . DLB-69; CDWLB-2

Celati, Gianni 1937- DLB-196

Celaya, Gabriel 1911-1991 . . . . DLB-108

A Celebration of Literary Biography Y-98

Céline, Louis-Ferdinand 1894-1961 . . . . . . DLB-72

The Celtic Background to Medieval English
Literature DLB-146

Celtis, Conrad 1459-1508 . . . . DLB-179

Cendrars, Blaise 1887-1961 . . . . DLB-258

Center for Bibliographical Studies and
Research at the University of
California, Riverside Y-91

The Center for the Book in the Library
of Congress Y-93

Center for the Book Research Y-84

Centlivre, Susanna 1669?-1723 . . . . DLB-84

The Centre for Writing, Publishing and
Printing History at the University
of Reading Y-00

The Century Company DLB-49

Cernuda, Luis 1902-1963 . . . . DLB-134

Cervantes, Lorna Dee 1954- DLB-82

Ch., T. (see Marchenko, Anastasiia Iakovlevna)

Chaadaev, Petr Iakovlevich
1794-1856 . . . . DLB-198

Chacel, Rosa 1898- DLB-134

Chacón, Eusebio 1869-1948 . . . . DLB-82

Chacón, Felipe Maximiliano 1873-? DLB-82

Chadwick, Henry 1824-1908 . . . . DLB-241

Chadwyck-Healey's Full-Text Literary Databases:
Editing Commercial Databases of
Primary Literary Texts Y-95

Challans, Eileen Mary (see Renault, Mary)

Chalmers, George 1742-1825 . . . . DLB-30

Chaloner, Sir Thomas 1520-1565 . . . . . . DLB-167

Chamberlain, Samuel S. 1851-1916 . . . . . DLB-25

Chamberland, Paul 1939- DLB-60

Chamberlin, William Henry 1897-1969 . . . DLB-29

Chambers, Charles Haddon 1860-1921 . . . DLB-10

Chambers, María Cristina (see Mena, María Cristina)

Chambers, Robert W. 1865-1933 . . . . DLB-202

Chambers, W. and R.
[publishing house] DLB-106

Chamisso, Albert von 1781-1838 . . . . DLB-90

Champfleury 1821-1889 . . . . DLB-119

Chandler, Harry 1864-1944 . . . . DLB-29

Chandler, Norman 1899-1973 . . . . DLB-127

Chandler, Otis 1927- DLB-127

Chandler, Raymond
1888-1959 . . . DLB-226, 253; DS-6; CDALB-5

Raymond Chandler Centenary Tributes
from Michael Avallone, James Ellroy,
Joe Gores, and William F. Nolan Y-88

Channing, Edward 1856-1931 . . . . DLB-17

Channing, Edward Tyrrell
1790-1856 . . . . DLB-1, 59, 235

Channing, William Ellery
1780-1842 . . . . DLB-1, 59, 235

Channing, William Ellery II
1817-1901 . . . . DLB-1, 223

Channing, William Henry
1810-1884 . . . . DLB-1, 59, 243

Chaplin, Charlie 1889-1977 . . . . DLB-44

Chapman, George
1559 or 1560-1634 . . . . DLB-62, 121

Chapman, John DLB-106

Chapman, Olive Murray 1892-1977 . . . . . DLB-195

Chapman, R. W. 1881-1960 . . . . DLB-201

Chapman, William 1850-1917 . . . . DLB-99

Chapman and Hall DLB-106

Chappell, Fred 1936- DLB-6, 105

"A Detail in a Poem" DLB-105

Chappell, William 1582-1649 . . . . DLB-236

Char, René 1907-1988 . . . . DLB-258

Charbonneau, Jean 1875-1960 . . . . DLB-92

Charbonneau, Robert 1911-1967 . . . . DLB-68

Charles, Gerda 1914- DLB-14

Charles, William [publishing house] DLB-49

Charles d'Orléans 1394-1465 . . . . DLB-208

Charley (see Mann, Charles)

Charteris, Leslie 1907-1993 . . . . DLB-77

Chartier, Alain circa 1385-1430 . . . . DLB-208

Charyn, Jerome 1937- Y-83

Chase, Borden 1900-1971 . . . . DLB-26

Chase, Edna Woolman 1877-1957 . . . . . . DLB-91

Chase, Mary Coyle 1907-1981 . . . . DLB-228

Chase-Riboud, Barbara 1936- DLB-33

Chateaubriand, François-René de
1768-1848 . . . . DLB-119

Chatterton, Thomas 1752-1770 . . . . DLB-109

Essay on Chatterton (1842), by
Robert Browning DLB-32

Chatto and Windus DLB-106

Chatwin, Bruce 1940-1989 . . . . DLB-194, 204

Chaucer, Geoffrey
1340?-1400 . . . . DLB-146; CDBLB-1

Chauncy, Charles 1705-1787 . . . . DLB-24

Chauveau, Pierre-Joseph-Olivier
1820-1890 . . . . DLB-99

Chávez, Denise 1948- DLB-122

Chávez, Fray Angélico 1910- DLB-82

Chayefsky, Paddy 1923-1981 . . . . . DLB-7, 44; Y-81

Cheesman, Evelyn 1881-1969 . . . . DLB-195

Cheever, Ezekiel 1615-1708 . . . . DLB-24

Cheever, George Barrell 1807-1890 . . . . . DLB-59

Cheever, John 1912-1982
. . . . . . DLB-2, 102, 227; Y-80, Y-82; CDALB-1

Cheever, Susan 1943- Y-82

Cheke, Sir John 1514-1557 . . . . DLB-132

Chelsea House DLB-46

Chênedollé, Charles de 1769-1833 . . . . . . DLB-217

Cheney, Ednah Dow 1824-1904 . . . . . DLB-1, 223

Cheney, Harriet Vaughn 1796-1889 . . . . . DLB-99

Chénier, Marie-Joseph 1764-1811 . . . . . . DLB-192

Chernyshevsky, Nikolai Gavrilovich
1828-1889 . . . . .DLB-238

Cherry, Kelly 1940 . . . . Y-83

Cherryh, C. J. 1942- Y-80

Chesebro', Caroline 1825-1873 . . . . .DLB-202

Chesney, Sir George Tomkyns
1830-1895 . . . . .DLB-190

Chesnut, Mary Boykin 1823-1886. . . . . . .DLB-239

Chesnutt, Charles Waddell
1858-1932 . . . . DLB-12, 50, 78

Chesson, Mrs. Nora (see Hopper, Nora)

Chester, Alfred 1928-1971 . . . . .DLB-130

Chester, George Randolph 1869-1924 . . . .DLB-78

The Chester Plays circa 1505-1532;
revisions until 1575 . . . . .DLB-146

Chesterfield, Philip Dormer Stanhope,
Fourth Earl of 1694-1773 . . . . .DLB-104

Chesterton, G. K. 1874-1936
. . DLB-10, 19, 34, 70, 98, 149, 178; CDBLB-6

Chettle, Henry circa 1560-circa 1607 . . . . .DLB-136

Cheuse, Alan 1940- DLB-244

Chew, Ada Nield 1870-1945 . . . . .DLB-135

Cheyney, Edward P. 1861-1947 . . . . .DLB-47

Chiara, Piero 1913-1986 . . . . .DLB-177

Chicano History .DLB-82

Chicano Language. DLB-82

Child, Francis James 1825-1896. . . .DLB-1, 64, 235

Child, Lydia Maria 1802-1880 . . . . DLB-1, 74, 243

Child, Philip 1898-1978 . . . . .DLB-68

Childers, Erskine 1870-1922 . . . . .DLB-70

Children's Book Awards and Prizes. DLB-61

Children's Illustrators, 1800-1880 . . . . . . .DLB-163

Childress, Alice 1916-1994 . . . . DLB-7, 38, 249

Childs, George W. 1829-1894. . . . . .DLB-23

Chilton Book Company DLB-46

Chin, Frank 1940- DLB-206

Chinweizu 1943- DLB-157

Chitham, Edward 1932- DLB-155

Chittenden, Hiram Martin 1858-1917 . . . . .DLB-47

Chivers, Thomas Holley 1809-1858 . . .DLB-3, 248

Cholmondeley, Mary 1859-1925. . . . . . . .DLB-197

Chomsky, Noam 1928- DLB-246

Chopin, Kate 1850-1904 . . .DLB-12, 78; CDALB-3

Chopin, Rene 1885-1953. . . . . .DLB-92

Choquette, Adrienne 1915-1973 . . . . .DLB-68

Choquette, Robert 1905- DLB-68

Choyce, Lesley 1951- DLB-251

Chrétien de Troyes
circa 1140-circa 1190. . . . . .DLB-208

Christensen, Inger 1935- DLB-214

The Christian Publishing Company DLB-49

Christie, Agatha
1890-1976 . . . . . . .DLB-13, 77, 245; CDBLB-6

Christine de Pizan
circa 1365-circa 1431. . . . . .DLB-208

Christopher, John 1922- DLB-255

Christus und die Samariterin circa 950 . . . . . .DLB-148

Christy, Howard Chandler 1873-1952 . . .DLB-188

Chulkov, Mikhail Dmitrievich
1743?-1792. .DLB-150

Church, Benjamin 1734-1778. . . . . .DLB-31

Church, Francis Pharcellus 1839-1906 . . . .DLB-79

Church, Peggy Pond 1903-1986 . . . . .DLB-212

Church, Richard 1893-1972. . . . . .DLB-191

Church, William Conant 1836-1917 . . . . . .DLB-79

Churchill, Caryl 1938- DLB-13

Churchill, Charles 1731-1764. . . . . .DLB-109

Churchill, Winston 1871-1947. . . . . .DLB-202

Churchill, Sir Winston
1874-1965 . . . . . . .DLB-100; DS-16; CDBLB-5

Churchyard, Thomas 1520?-1604. . . . . . . .DLB-132

Churton, E., and Company. DLB-106

Chute, Marchette 1909-1994 . . . . .DLB-103

Ciardi, John 1916-1986 . . . . .DLB-5; Y-86

Cibber, Colley 1671-1757. . . . . .DLB-84

Cicero
106 B.C.-43 B.C. DLB-211, CDWLB-1

Cima, Annalisa 1941- DLB-128

Čingo, Živko 1935-1987 . . . . .DLB-181

Cioran, E. M. 1911-1995. . . . . .DLB-220

Čipkus, Alfonsas (see Nyka-Niliūnas, Alfonsas)

Cirese, Eugenio 1884-1955 . . . . .DLB-114

Cīrulis, Jānis (see Bels, Alberts)

Cisneros, Sandra 1954- DLB-122, 152

City Lights Books DLB-46

Cixous, Hélène 1937- DLB-83, 242

The Claims of Business and Literature:
An Undergraduate Essay by
Maxwell Perkins Y-01

Clampitt, Amy 1920-1994 . . . . .DLB-105

Clancy, Tom 1947- DLB-227

Clapper, Raymond 1892-1944. . . . . .DLB-29

Clare, John 1793-1864 . . . . .DLB-55, 96

Clarendon, Edward Hyde, Earl of
1609-1674 . . . . .DLB-101

Clark, Alfred Alexander Gordon (see Hare, Cyril)

Clark, Ann Nolan 1896- DLB-52

Clark, C. E. Frazer, Jr. 1925- DLB-187; Y-01

Clark, C. M., Publishing Company. DLB-46

Clark, Catherine Anthony 1892-1977 . . . . .DLB-68

Clark, Charles Heber 1841-1915. . . . . .DLB-11

Clark, Davis Wasgatt 1812-1871 . . . . .DLB-79

Clark, Eleanor 1913- DLB-6

Clark, J. P. 1935- DLB-117; CDWLB-3

Clark, Lewis Gaylord
1808-1873 . . . . .DLB-3, 64, 73, 250

Clark, Walter Van Tilburg
1909-1971 . . . . .DLB-9, 206

Clark, William (see Lewis, Meriwether)

Clark, William Andrews Jr. 1877-1934 . . .DLB-187

Clarke, Sir Arthur C. 1917- DLB-261

Clarke, Austin 1896-1974. . . . . .DLB-10, 20

Clarke, Austin C. 1934- DLB-53, 125

Clarke, Gillian 1937- DLB-40

Clarke, James Freeman
1810-1888 . . . . .DLB-1, 59, 235

Clarke, Lindsay 1939- DLB-231

Clarke, Marcus 1846-1881 . . . . .DLB-230

Clarke, Pauline 1921- DLB-161

Clarke, Rebecca Sophia 1833-1906 . . . . . . .DLB-42

Clarke, Robert, and Company DLB-49

Clarke, Samuel 1675-1729 . . . . .DLB-252

Clarkson, Thomas 1760-1846 . . . . .DLB-158

Claudel, Paul 1868-1955 . . . . .DLB-192, 258

Claudius, Matthias 1740-1815 . . . . .DLB-97

Clausen, Andy 1943- DLB-16

Clawson, John L. 1865-1933 . . . . .DLB-187

Claxton, Remsen and Haffelfinger DLB-49

Clay, Cassius Marcellus 1810-1903 . . . . . . .DLB-43

Cleage, Pearl 1948- DLB-228

Cleary, Beverly 1916- DLB-52

Cleary, Kate McPhelim 1863-1905 . . . . . .DLB-221

Cleaver, Vera 1919- and
Cleaver, Bill 1920-1981. . . . . .DLB-52

Cleland, John 1710-1789 . . . . .DLB-39

Clemens, Samuel Langhorne (Mark Twain)
1835-1910 . . . . .DLB-11, 12, 23, 64, 74,
186, 189; CDALB-3

Mark Twain on Perpetual Copyright Y-92

Clement, Hal 1922- DLB-8

Clemo, Jack 1916- DLB-27

Clephane, Elizabeth Cecilia
1830-1869 . . . . .DLB-199

Cleveland, John 1613-1658 . . . . .DLB-126

Cliff, Michelle 1946- DLB-157; CDWLB-3

Clifford, Lady Anne 1590-1676. . . . . .DLB-151

Clifford, James L. 1901-1978 . . . . .DLB-103

Clifford, Lucy 1853?-1929. . . . . DLB-135, 141, 197

Clift, Charmian 1923-1969 . . . . .DLB-260

Clifton, Lucille 1936- DLB-5, 41

Clines, Francis X. 1938- DLB-185

Clive, Caroline (V) 1801-1873. . . . . .DLB-199

Clode, Edward J. [publishing house] DLB-46

Clough, Arthur Hugh 1819-1861 . . . . .DLB-32

Cloutier, Cécile 1930- DLB-60

Clouts, Sidney 1926-1982 . . . . .DLB-225

Clutton-Brock, Arthur 1868-1924 . . . . .DLB-98

Coates, Robert M. 1897-1973. . . . . . DLB-4, 9, 102

Coatsworth, Elizabeth 1893- DLB-22

Cobb, Charles E., Jr. 1943- DLB-41

Cobb, Frank I. 1869-1923 . . . . .DLB-25

Cobb, Irvin S. 1876-1944. . . . . . . .DLB-11, 25, 86

Cobbe, Frances Power 1822-1904 . . . . . . .DLB-190

Cobbett, William 1763-1835 . . . . .DLB-43, 107

Cobbledick, Gordon 1898-1969 . . . . .DLB-171

Cochran, Thomas C. 1902- DLB-17

Cochrane, Elizabeth 1867-1922 . . . . . .DLB-25, 189

Cockerell, Sir Sydney 1867-1962 . . . . . . .DLB-201

Cockerill, John A. 1845-1896 . . . . .DLB-23

Cocteau, Jean 1889-1963. . . . . .DLB-65, 258

Coderre, Emile (see Jean Narrache)

Coe, Jonathan 1961- DLB-231

Coetzee, J. M. 1940- DLB-225

Coffee, Lenore J. 1900?-1984 .... DLB-44

Coffin, Robert P. Tristram 1892-1955 .... DLB-45

Coghill, Mrs. Harry (see Walker, Anna Louisa)

Cogswell, Fred 1917- DLB-60

Cogswell, Mason Fitch 1761-1830 .... DLB-37

Cohan, George M. 1878-1942 .... DLB-249

Cohen, Arthur A. 1928-1986 .... DLB-28

Cohen, Leonard 1934- DLB-53

Cohen, Matt 1942- DLB-53

Colbeck, Norman 1903-1987 .... DLB-201

Colden, Cadwallader 1688-1776...... DLB-24, 30

Colden, Jane 1724-1766 .... DLB-200

Cole, Barry 1936- DLB-14

Cole, George Watson 1850-1939 .... DLB-140

Colegate, Isabel 1931- DLB-14, 231

Coleman, Emily Holmes 1899-1974 .... DLB-4

Coleman, Wanda 1946- DLB-130

Coleridge, Hartley 1796-1849 .... DLB-96

Coleridge, Mary 1861-1907 .... DLB-19, 98

Coleridge, Samuel Taylor
1772-1834.......... DLB-93, 107; CDBLB-3

Coleridge, Sara 1802-1852 .... DLB-199

Colet, John 1467-1519................ DLB-132

Colette 1873-1954................... DLB-65

Colette, Sidonie Gabrielle (see Colette)

Colinas, Antonio 1946- DLB-134

Coll, Joseph Clement 1881-1921 .... DLB-188

Collier, John 1901-1980 ....DLB-77, 255

Collier, John Payne 1789-1883 .... DLB-184

Collier, Mary 1690-1762............. DLB-95

Collier, P. F. [publishing house] DLB-49

Collier, Robert J. 1876-1918 .... DLB-91

Collin and Small.................... DLB-49

Collingwood, R. G. 1889-1943........ DLB-262

Collingwood, W. G. 1854-1932 .... DLB-149

Collins, An floruit circa 1653 .... DLB-131

Collins, Anthony 1676-1729 .... DLB-252

Collins, Isaac [publishing house]........ DLB-49

Collins, Merle 1950- DLB-157

Collins, Mortimer 1827-1876 ...... DLB-21, 35

Collins, Tom (see Furphy, Joseph)

Collins, Wilkie
1824-1889 ...... DLB-18, 70, 159; CDBLB-4

Collins, William 1721-1759........... DLB-109

Collins, William, Sons and Company ... DLB-154

Collis, Maurice 1889-1973 .... DLB-195

Collyer, Mary 1716?-1763?............ DLB-39

Colman, Benjamin 1673-1747 .... DLB-24

Colman, George, the Elder 1732-1794 .... DLB-89

Colman, George, the Younger
1762-1836.................... DLB-89

Colman, S. [publishing house] DLB-49

Colombo, John Robert 1936- DLB-53

Colquhoun, Patrick 1745-1820 .... DLB-158

Colter, Cyrus 1910- DLB-33

Colum, Padraic 1881-1972 .... DLB-19

Columella fl. first century A.D. DLB-211

Colvin, Sir Sidney 1845-1927 .... DLB-149

Colwin, Laurie 1944-1992 ....DLB-218; Y-80

Comden, Betty 1919- and
Green, Adolph 1918- DLB-44

Come to Papa.......................... Y-99

Comi, Girolamo 1890-1968 .... DLB-114

The Comic Tradition Continued
[in the British Novel] DLB-15

Commager, Henry Steele 1902-1998 ..... DLB-17

The Commercialization of the Image of
Revolt, by Kenneth Rexroth DLB-16

Community and Commentators: Black
Theatre and Its Critics DLB-38

Commynes, Philippe de
circa 1447-1511.................. DLB-208

Compton, D. G. 1930- DLB-261

Compton-Burnett, Ivy 1884?-1969....... DLB-36

Conan, Laure 1845-1924 .... DLB-99

Concord History and Life DLB-223

Concord Literary History of a Town.... DLB-223

Conde, Carmen 1901- DLB-108

Conference on Modern Biography......... Y-85

Congreve, William
1670-1729.......... DLB-39, 84; CDBLB-2

Preface to *Incognita* (1692) DLB-39

Conkey, W. B., Company DLB-49

Conn, Stewart 1936- DLB-233

Connell, Evan S., Jr. 1924- DLB-2; Y-81

Connelly, Marc 1890-1980.........DLB-7; Y-80

Connolly, Cyril 1903-1974 .... DLB-98

Connolly, James B. 1868-1957 .... DLB-78

Connor, Ralph 1860-1937 .... DLB-92

Connor, Tony 1930- DLB-40

Conquest, Robert 1917- DLB-27

Conrad, John, and Company DLB-49

Conrad, Joseph
1857-1924.... DLB-10, 34, 98, 156; CDBLB-5

Conroy, Jack 1899-1990................. Y-81

Conroy, Pat 1945- DLB-6

Considine, Bob 1906-1975 .... DLB-241

The Consolidation of Opinion: Critical
Responses to the Modernists DLB-36

Consolo, Vincenzo 1933- DLB-196

Constable, Archibald, and Company DLB-154

Constable, Henry 1562-1613 .... DLB-136

Constable and Company Limited DLB-112

Constant, Benjamin 1767-1830 .... DLB-119

Constant de Rebecque, Henri-Benjamin de
(see Constant, Benjamin)

Constantine, David 1944- DLB-40

Constantin-Weyer, Maurice 1881-1964 ... DLB-92

Contempo Caravan: Kites in a Windstorm ... Y-85

A Contemporary Flourescence of Chicano
Literature Y-84

Continental European Rhetoricians,
1400-1600 .... DLB-236

The Continental Publishing Company.... DLB-49

Conversations with Editors Y-95

Conversations with Publishers I: An Interview
with Patrick O'Connor Y-84

Conversations with Publishers II: An Interview
with Charles Scribner III Y-94

Conversations with Publishers III: An Interview
with Donald Lamm Y-95

Conversations with Publishers IV: An Interview
with James Laughlin................. Y-96

Conversations with Rare Book Dealers I: An
Interview with Glenn Horowitz......... Y-90

Conversations with Rare Book Dealers II: An
Interview with Ralph Sipper Y-94

Conversations with Rare Book Dealers
(Publishers) III: An Interview with
Otto Penzler.................... Y-96

The Conversion of an Unpolitical Man,
by W. H. Bruford DLB-66

Conway, Anne 1631-1679 .... DLB-252

Conway, Moncure Daniel
1832-1907 .... DLB-1, 223

Cook, David C., Publishing Company ... DLB-49

Cook, Ebenezer circa 1667-circa 1732..... DLB-24

Cook, Edward Tyas 1857-1919 .... DLB-149

Cook, Eliza 1818-1889 .... DLB-199

Cook, Michael 1933-1994 .... DLB-53

Cooke, George Willis 1848-1923 .... DLB-71

Cooke, Increase, and Company DLB-49

Cooke, John Esten 1830-1886 .... DLB-3, 248

Cooke, Philip Pendleton
1816-1850 .... DLB-3, 59, 248

Cooke, Rose Terry 1827-1892 ....DLB-12, 74

Cook-Lynn, Elizabeth 1930- DLB-175

Coolbrith, Ina 1841-1928 .... DLB-54, 186

Cooley, Peter 1940- DLB-105

"Into the Mirror" DLB-105

Coolidge, Clark 1939- DLB-193

Coolidge, George [publishing house] DLB-49

Coolidge, Susan (see Woolsey, Sarah Chauncy)

Cooper, Anna Julia 1858-1964........ DLB-221

Cooper, Edith Emma (see Field, Michael)

Cooper, Giles 1918-1966 .... DLB-13

Cooper, J. California 19??- DLB-212

Cooper, James Fenimore
1789-1851........ DLB-3, 183, 250; CDALB-2

Cooper, Kent 1880-1965 .... DLB-29

Cooper, Susan 1935- DLB-161, 261

Cooper, Susan Fenimore 1813-1894..... DLB-239

Cooper, William [publishing house]......DLB-170

Coote, J. [publishing house] DLB-154

Coover, Robert 1932- DLB-2, 227; Y-81

Copeland and Day DLB-49

Ćopić, Branko 1915-1984............. DLB-181

Copland, Robert 1470?-1548 .... DLB-136

Coppard, A. E. 1878-1957 . . . . .DLB-162

Coppée, François 1842-1908 . . . . .DLB-217

Coppel, Alfred 1921- Y-83

Coppola, Francis Ford 1939- DLB-44

Copway, George (Kah-ge-ga-gah-bowh)
 1818-1869 . . . . DLB-175, 183

Corazzini, Sergio 1886-1907 . . . . .DLB-114

Corbett, Richard 1582-1635 . . . . .DLB-121

Corbière, Tristan 1845-1875 . . . . .DLB-217

Corcoran, Barbara 1911- DLB-52

Cordelli, Franco 1943- DLB-196

Corelli, Marie 1855-1924. . . . . .DLB-34, 156

Corle, Edwin 1906-1956 . . . . Y-85

Corman, Cid 1924- DLB-5, 193

Cormier, Robert 1925-2000. . . .DLB-52; CDALB-6

Corn, Alfred 1943- DLB-120; Y-80

Cornford, Frances 1886-1960 . . . . .DLB-240

Cornish, Sam 1935- DLB-41

Cornish, William circa 1465-circa 1524. . .DLB-132

Cornwall, Barry (see Procter, Bryan Waller)

Cornwallis, Sir William, the Younger
 circa 1579-1614 . . . . .DLB-151

Cornwell, David John Moore (see le Carré, John)

Corpi, Lucha 1945- DLB-82

Corrington, John William
 1932-1988 . . . . .DLB-6, 244

Corriveau, Monique 1927-1976 . . . . .DLB-251

Corrothers, James D. 1869-1917 . . . . .DLB-50

Corso, Gregory 1930- DLB-5, 16, 237

Cortázar, Julio 1914-1984 . . .DLB-113; CDWLB-3

Cortéz, Carlos 1923- DLB-209

Cortez, Jayne 1936- DLB-41

Corvinus, Gottlieb Siegmund
 1677-1746. . . . . .DLB-168

Corvo, Baron (see Rolfe, Frederick William)

Cory, Annie Sophie (see Cross, Victoria)

Cory, William Johnson 1823-1892 . . . . . . .DLB-35

Coryate, Thomas 1577?-1617 . . . . . .DLB-151, 172

Ćosić, Dobrica 1921- DLB-181; CDWLB-4

Cosin, John 1595-1672. . . . . .DLB-151, 213

Cosmopolitan Book Corporation DLB-46

The Cost of *The Cantos:* William Bird
 to Ezra Pound Y-01

Costain, Thomas B. 1885-1965 . . . . .DLB-9

Coste, Donat 1912-1957 . . . . .DLB-88

Costello, Louisa Stuart 1799-1870 . . . . . . .DLB-166

Cota-Cárdenas, Margarita 1941- DLB-122

Côté, Denis 1954- DLB-251

Cotten, Bruce 1873-1954 . . . . .DLB-187

Cotter, Joseph Seamon, Sr. 1861-1949. . . . .DLB-50

Cotter, Joseph Seamon, Jr. 1895-1919 . . . . .DLB-50

Cottle, Joseph [publishing house]. DLB-154

Cotton, Charles 1630-1687 . . . . .DLB-131

Cotton, John 1584-1652. . . . . .DLB-24

Cotton, Sir Robert Bruce 1571-1631 . . . . .DLB-213

Coulter, John 1888-1980 . . . . .DLB-68

Cournos, John 1881-1966 . . . . .DLB-54

Courteline, Georges 1858-1929 . . . . .DLB-192

Cousins, Margaret 1905-1996 . . . . .DLB-137

Cousins, Norman 1915-1990. . . . . .DLB-137

Couvreur, Jessie (see Tasma)

Coventry, Francis 1725-1754 . . . . .DLB-39

Dedication, *The History of Pompey
 the Little* (1751) DLB-39

Coverdale, Miles 1487 or 1488-1569. . . . .DLB-167

Coverly, N. [publishing house] DLB-49

Covici-Friede DLB-46

Cowan, Peter 1914- DLB-260

Coward, Noel
 1899-1973 . . . . .DLB-10, 245; CDBLB-6

Coward, McCann and Geoghegan DLB-46

Cowles, Gardner 1861-1946 . . . . .DLB-29

Cowles, Gardner "Mike" Jr.
 1903-1985 . . . . DLB-127, 137

Cowley, Abraham 1618-1667 . . . . . .DLB-131, 151

Cowley, Hannah 1743-1809 . . . . .DLB-89

Cowley, Malcolm
 1898-1989 . . . . DLB-4, 48; Y-81, Y-89

Cowper, Richard 1926-2002 . . . . .DLB-261

Cowper, William 1731-1800 . . . . . . .DLB-104, 109

Cox, A. B. (see Berkeley, Anthony)

Cox, James McMahon 1903-1974 . . . . . . .DLB-127

Cox, James Middleton 1870-1957 . . . . . . .DLB-127

Cox, Leonard ca. 1495-ca. 1550 . . . . .DLB-236

Cox, Palmer 1840-1924. . . . . .DLB-42

Coxe, Louis 1918-1993 . . . . .DLB-5

Coxe, Tench 1755-1824. . . . . .DLB-37

Cozzens, Frederick S. 1818-1869 . . . . . . .DLB-202

Cozzens, James Gould
 1903-1978 . . . . .DLB-9; Y-84; DS-2; CDALB-1

James Gould Cozzens—A View from Afar. . . . Y-97

James Gould Cozzens Case Re-opened Y-97

James Gould Cozzens: How to Read Him. . . . Y-97

Cozzens's *Michael Scarlett* Y-97

James Gould Cozzens Symposium and
 Exhibition at the University of
 South Carolina, Columbia Y-00

Crabbe, George 1754-1832 . . . . .DLB-93

Crace, Jim 1946- DLB-231

Crackanthorpe, Hubert 1870-1896 . . . . . .DLB-135

Craddock, Charles Egbert (see Murfree, Mary N.)

Cradock, Thomas 1718-1770 . . . . .DLB-31

Craig, Daniel H. 1811-1895. . . . . .DLB-43

Craik, Dinah Maria 1826-1887 . . . . . .DLB-35, 136

Cramer, Richard Ben 1950- DLB-185

Cranch, Christopher Pearse
 1813-1892 . . . . .DLB-1, 42, 243

Crane, Hart 1899-1932 . . . . .DLB-4, 48; CDALB-4

Crane, R. S. 1886-1967 . . . . .DLB-63

Crane, Stephen
 1871-1900 . . . . .DLB-12, 54, 78; CDALB-3

Crane, Walter 1845-1915 . . . . .DLB-163

Cranmer, Thomas 1489-1556 . . . . . .DLB-132, 213

Crapsey, Adelaide 1878-1914. . . . . .DLB-54

Crashaw, Richard 1612 or 1613-1649. . . .DLB-126

Craven, Avery 1885-1980 . . . . .DLB-17

Crawford, Charles 1752-circa 1815 . . . . . .DLB-31

Crawford, F. Marion 1854-1909 . . . . .DLB-71

Crawford, Isabel Valancy 1850-1887 . . . . .DLB-92

Crawley, Alan 1887-1975 . . . . .DLB-68

Crayon, Geoffrey (see Irving, Washington)

Crayon, Porte (see Strother, David Hunter)

Creamer, Robert W. 1922- DLB-171

Creasey, John 1908-1973 . . . . .DLB-77

Creative Age Press. DLB-46

Creech, William [publishing house]. DLB-154

Creede, Thomas [publishing house] DLB-170

Creel, George 1876-1953 . . . . .DLB-25

Creeley, Robert 1926- . . . DLB-5, 16, 169; DS-17

Creelman, James 1859-1915 . . . . .DLB-23

Cregan, David 1931- DLB-13

Creighton, Donald Grant 1902-1979 . . . . . .DLB-88

Cremazie, Octave 1827-1879 . . . . .DLB-99

Crémer, Victoriano 1909?- DLB-108

Crescas, Hasdai circa 1340-1412? DLB-115

Crespo, Angel 1926- DLB-134

Cresset Press DLB-112

Cresswell, Helen 1934- DLB-161

Crèvecoeur, Michel Guillaume Jean de
 1735-1813 . . . . .DLB-37

Crewe, Candida 1964- DLB-207

Crews, Harry 1935- DLB-6, 143, 185

Crichton, Michael 1942- Y-81

A Crisis of Culture: The Changing Role
 of Religion in the New Republic DLB-37

Crispin, Edmund 1921-1978 . . . . .DLB-87

Cristofer, Michael 1946- DLB-7

Crnjanski, Miloš
 1893-1977 . . . . .DLB-147; CDWLB-4

Crocker, Hannah Mather 1752-1829 . . . . .DLB-200

Crockett, David (Davy)
 1786-1836 . . . . . . .DLB-3, 11, 183, 248

Croft-Cooke, Rupert (see Bruce, Leo)

Crofts, Freeman Wills 1879-1957. . . . . . . .DLB-77

Croker, John Wilson 1780-1857 . . . . . . .DLB-110

Croly, George 1780-1860. . . . . .DLB-159

Croly, Herbert 1869-1930 . . . . .DLB-91

Croly, Jane Cunningham 1829-1901 . . . . . .DLB-23

Crompton, Richmal 1890-1969 . . . . .DLB-160

Cronin, A. J. 1896-1981. . . . . .DLB-191

Cros, Charles 1842-1888. . . . . .DLB-217

Crosby, Caresse 1892-1970 . . . . .DLB-48

Crosby, Caresse 1892-1970
 and Crosby, Harry
 1898-1929 . . . . .DLB-4; DS-15

Crosby, Harry 1898-1929 . . . . .DLB-48

Crosland, Camilla Toulmin
 (Mrs. Newton Crosland)
 1812-1895 . . . . .DLB-240

Cross, Gillian 1945- DLB-161

Cross, Victoria 1868-1952 . . . . .DLB-135, 197

Crossley-Holland, Kevin 1941- . . . DLB-40, 161

Crothers, Rachel 1878-1958 . . . . DLB-7

Crowell, Thomas Y., Company DLB-49

Crowley, John 1942- Y-82

Crowley, Mart 1935- DLB-7

Crown Publishers DLB-46

Crowne, John 1641-1712 . . . . DLB-80

Crowninshield, Edward Augustus
1817-1859 . . . . DLB-140

Crowninshield, Frank 1872-1947 . . . . DLB-91

Croy, Homer 1883-1965 . . . . DLB-4

Crumley, James 1939- DLB-226; Y-84

Cruse, Mary Anne 1825?-1910. . . . . DLB-239

Cruz, Migdalia 1958- DLB-249

Cruz, Victor Hernández 1949- DLB-41

Csokor, Franz Theodor 1885-1969 . . . . . . DLB-81

Csoóri, Sándor 1930- DLB-232; CDWLB-4

Cuala Press DLB-112

Cudworth, Ralph 1617-1688. . . . . DLB-252

Cullen, Countee
1903-1946 . . . . DLB-4, 48, 51; CDALB-4

Culler, Jonathan D. 1944- DLB-67, 246

Cullinan, Elizabeth 1933- DLB-234

The Cult of Biography
Excerpts from the Second Folio Debate:
"Biographies are generally a disease of
English Literature" – Germaine Greer,
Victoria Glendinning, Auberon Waugh,
and Richard Holmes Y-86

Culverwel, Nathaniel 1619?-1651?. DLB-252

Cumberland, Richard 1732-1811 . . . . DLB-89

Cummings, Constance Gordon
1837-1924. . . . . .DLB-174

Cummings, E. E.
1894-1962 . . . . DLB-4, 48; CDALB-5

Cummings, Ray 1887-1957. . . . . DLB-8

Cummings and Hilliard DLB-49

Cummins, Maria Susanna
1827-1866. . . . . DLB-42

Cumpián, Carlos 1953- DLB-209

Cunard, Nancy 1896-1965 . . . . DLB-240

Cundall, Joseph [publishing house]. DLB-106

Cuney, Waring 1906-1976 . . . . DLB-51

Cuney-Hare, Maude 1874-1936 . . . . DLB-52

Cunningham, Allan 1784-1842. . . . . DLB-116, 144

Cunningham, J. V. 1911- DLB-5

Cunningham, Peter F.
[publishing house] DLB-49

Cunquiero, Alvaro 1911-1981 . . . . DLB-134

Cuomo, George 1929- Y-80

Cupples, Upham and Company. DLB-49

Cupples and Leon DLB-46

Cuppy, Will 1884-1949 . . . . DLB-11

Curiel, Barbara Brinson 1956- DLB-209

Curll, Edmund [publishing house] DLB-154

Currie, James 1756-1805. . . . . DLB-142

Currie, Mary Montgomerie Lamb Singleton,
Lady Currie
(see Fane, Violet)

Cursor Mundi circa 1300. . . . . DLB-146

Curti, Merle E. 1897- DLB-17

Curtis, Anthony 1926- DLB-155

Curtis, Cyrus H. K. 1850-1933 . . . . DLB-91

Curtis, George William
1824-1892 . . . . DLB-1, 43, 223

Curzon, Robert 1810-1873 . . . . DLB-166

Curzon, Sarah Anne 1833-1898 . . . . DLB-99

Cusack, Dymphna 1902-1981 . . . . DLB-260

Cushing, Harvey 1869-1939. . . . . DLB-187

Custance, Olive (Lady Alfred Douglas)
1874-1944. . . . . DLB-240

Cynewulf circa 770-840 . . . . DLB-146

Czepko, Daniel 1605-1660 . . . . DLB-164

Czerniawski, Adam 1934- DLB-232

D

Dabit, Eugène 1898-1936 . . . . DLB-65

Daborne, Robert circa 1580-1628. . . . . . . DLB-58

Dąbrowska, Maria
1889-1965 . . . . DLB-215; CDWLB-4

Dacey, Philip 1939- DLB-105

"Eyes Across Centuries: Contemporary
Poetry and 'That Vision Thing,'" . . . DLB-105

Dach, Simon 1605-1659 . . . . DLB-164

Dagerman, Stig 1923-1954 . . . . DLB-259

Daggett, Rollin M. 1831-1901 . . . . DLB-79

D'Aguiar, Fred 1960- DLB-157

Dahl, Roald 1916-1990. . . . . DLB-139, 255

Dahlberg, Edward 1900-1977 . . . . DLB-48

Dahn, Felix 1834-1912 . . . . DLB-129

Dal', Vladimir Ivanovich (Kazak Vladimir
Lugansky) 1801-1872. . . . . DLB-198

Dale, Peter 1938- DLB-40

Daley, Arthur 1904-1974 . . . . .DLB-171

Dall, Caroline Healey 1822-1912 . . . . . DLB-1, 235

Dallas, E. S. 1828-1879 . . . . DLB-55

From *The Gay Science* (1866) DLB-21

The Dallas Theater Center. DLB-7

D'Alton, Louis 1900-1951 . . . . DLB-10

Daly, Carroll John 1889-1958 . . . . DLB-226

Daly, T. A. 1871-1948 . . . . DLB-11

Damon, S. Foster 1893-1971 . . . . DLB-45

Damrell, William S. [publishing house] . . . DLB-49

Dana, Charles A. 1819-1897 . . . . . . DLB-3, 23, 250

Dana, Richard Henry, Jr.
1815-1882 . . . . DLB-1, 183, 235

Dandridge, Ray Garfield DLB-51

Dane, Clemence 1887-1965 . . . . .DLB-10, 197

Danforth, John 1660-1730 . . . . DLB-24

Danforth, Samuel, I 1626-1674. . . . . DLB-24

Danforth, Samuel, II 1666-1727 . . . . DLB-24

Dangerous Years: London Theater,
1939-1945 . . . . DLB-10

Daniel, John M. 1825-1865 . . . . DLB-43

Daniel, Samuel 1562 or 1563-1619. . . . . . DLB-62

Daniel Press DLB-106

Daniells, Roy 1902-1979. . . . . DLB-68

Daniels, Jim 1956- DLB-120

Daniels, Jonathan 1902-1981 . . . . .DLB-127

Daniels, Josephus 1862-1948 . . . . DLB-29

Daniels, Sarah 1957- DLB-245

Danilevsky, Grigorii Petrovich
1829-1890 . . . . DLB-238

Dannay, Frederic 1905-1982 and
Manfred B. Lee 1905-1971. . . . . .DLB-137

Danner, Margaret Esse 1915- DLB-41

Danter, John [publishing house] DLB-170

Dantin, Louis 1865-1945 . . . . DLB-92

Danzig, Allison 1898-1987 . . . . .DLB-171

D'Arcy, Ella circa 1857-1937. . . . . DLB-135

Dark, Eleanor 1901-1985 . . . . DLB-260

Darke, Nick 1948- DLB-233

Darley, Felix Octavious Carr 1822-1888 . DLB-188

Darley, George 1795-1846 . . . . DLB-96

Darmesteter, Madame James
(see Robinson, A. Mary F.)

Darwin, Charles 1809-1882 . . . . .DLB-57, 166

Darwin, Erasmus 1731-1802. . . . . DLB-93

Daryush, Elizabeth 1887-1977. . . . . DLB-20

Dashkova, Ekaterina Romanovna
(née Vorontsova) 1743-1810 . . . . DLB-150

Dashwood, Edmée Elizabeth Monica de la Pasture
(see Delafield, E. M.)

Daudet, Alphonse 1840-1897 . . . . DLB-123

d'Aulaire, Edgar Parin 1898- and
d'Aulaire, Ingri 1904- DLB-22

Davenant, Sir William 1606-1668 . . . DLB-58, 126

Davenport, Guy 1927- DLB-130

Davenport, Marcia 1903-1996 . . . . DS-17

Davenport, Robert ?-? DLB-58

Daves, Delmer 1904-1977. . . . . DLB-26

Davey, Frank 1940- DLB-53

Davidson, Avram 1923-1993 . . . . DLB-8

Davidson, Donald 1893-1968. . . . . DLB-45

Davidson, John 1857-1909 . . . . DLB-19

Davidson, Lionel 1922- DLB-14

Davidson, Robyn 1950- DLB-204

Davidson, Sara 1943- DLB-185

Davie, Donald 1922- DLB-27

Davie, Elspeth 1919- DLB-139

Davies, Sir John 1569-1626 . . . . .DLB-172

Davies, John, of Hereford 1565?-1618 . . . DLB-121

Davies, Peter, Limited DLB-112

Davies, Rhys 1901-1978. . . . . DLB-139, 191

Davies, Robertson 1913-1995. . . . . DLB-68

Davies, Samuel 1723-1761 . . . . DLB-31

Davies, Thomas 1712?-1785. . . . . DLB-142, 154

Davies, W. H. 1871-1940 . . . . .DLB-19, 174

Daviot, Gordon 1896?-1952 . . . . .DLB-10
(see also Tey, Josephine)

Davis, Arthur Hoey (see Rudd, Steele)

Davis, Charles A. 1795-1867 . . . . .DLB-11

Davis, Clyde Brion 1894-1962. . . . . .DLB-9

Davis, Dick 1945- DLB-40

Davis, Frank Marshall 1905-? DLB-51

Davis, H. L. 1894-1960 . . . . .DLB-9, 206

Davis, John 1774-1854 . . . . .DLB-37

Davis, Lydia 1947- DLB-130

Davis, Margaret Thomson 1926- DLB-14

Davis, Ossie 1917- DLB-7, 38, 249

Davis, Owen 1874-1956. . . . . .DLB-249

Davis, Paxton 1925-1994. . . . . Y-89

Davis, Rebecca Harding 1831-1910. . .DLB-74, 239

Davis, Richard Harding 1864-1916
. . . . DLB-12, 23, 78, 79, 189; DS-13

Davis, Samuel Cole 1764-1809 . . . . .DLB-37

Davis, Samuel Post 1850-1918. . . . . . . .DLB-202

Davison, Frank Dalby 1893-1970 . . . . . . .DLB-260

Davison, Peter 1928- DLB-5

Davydov, Denis Vasil'evich
1784-1839 . . . . .DLB-205

Davys, Mary 1674-1732 . . . . .DLB-39

Preface to *The Works of
Mrs. Davys* (1725) DLB-39

DAW Books. DLB-46

Dawson, Ernest 1882-1947 . . . . .DLB-140

Dawson, Fielding 1930- DLB-130

Dawson, Sarah Morgan 1842-1909 . . . . . .DLB-239

Dawson, William 1704-1752 . . . . .DLB-31

Day, Angel flourished 1583-1599 . . . DLB-167, 236

Day, Benjamin Henry 1810-1889 . . . . . . .DLB-43

Day, Clarence 1874-1935. . . . . .DLB-11

Day, Dorothy 1897-1980 . . . . .DLB-29

Day, Frank Parker 1881-1950 . . . . .DLB-92

Day, John circa 1574-circa 1640 . . . . .DLB-62

Day, John [publishing house] DLB-170

Day, The John, Company DLB-46

Day Lewis, C. 1904-1972. . . . . .DLB-15, 20
(see also Blake, Nicholas)

Day, Mahlon [publishing house] DLB-49

Day, Thomas 1748-1789 . . . . .DLB-39

Dazai Osamu 1909-1948 . . . . .DLB-182

Deacon, William Arthur 1890-1977. . . . . . .DLB-68

Deal, Borden 1922-1985 . . . . .DLB-6

de Angeli, Marguerite 1889-1987 . . . . .DLB-22

De Angelis, Milo 1951- DLB-128

De Bow, J. D. B.
1820-1867 . . . . .DLB-3, 79, 248

de Bruyn, Günter 1926- DLB-75

de Camp, L. Sprague 1907-2000 . . . . .DLB-8

De Carlo, Andrea 1952- DLB-196

De Casas, Celso A. 1944- DLB-209

Dechert, Robert 1895-1975 . . . . .DLB-187

Dedications, Inscriptions, and Annotations . . . Y-01

Dee, John 1527-1608 or 1609. . . . . . .DLB-136, 213

Deeping, George Warwick 1877-1950 . . . .DLB 153

Defoe, Daniel
1660-1731 . . . . . . .DLB-39, 95, 101; CDBLB-2

Preface to *Colonel Jack* (1722) DLB-39

Preface to *The Farther Adventures of
Robinson Crusoe* (1719) DLB-39

Preface to *Moll Flanders* (1722) DLB-39

Preface to *Robinson Crusoe* (1719). DLB-39

Preface to *Roxana* (1724). DLB-39

de Fontaine, Felix Gregory 1834-1896. . . . .DLB-43

De Forest, John William 1826-1906. . .DLB-12, 189

DeFrees, Madeline 1919- DLB-105

"The Poet's Kaleidoscope: The Element
of Surprise in the Making of
the Poem" DLB-105

DeGolyer, Everette Lee 1886-1956 . . . . . .DLB-187

de Graff, Robert 1895-1981. . . . . Y-81

de Graft, Joe 1924-1978 . . . . .DLB-117

De Heinrico circa 980? DLB-148

Deighton, Len 1929- DLB-87; CDBLB-8

DeJong, Meindert 1906-1991. . . . . .DLB-52

Dekker, Thomas
circa 1572-1632 . . . . . .DLB-62, 172; CDBLB-1

Delacorte, Jr., George T. 1894-1991 . . . . . .DLB-91

Delafield, E. M. 1890-1943 . . . . .DLB-34

Delahaye, Guy 1888-1969 . . . . .DLB-92

de la Mare, Walter 1873-1956
. . . . .DLB-19, 153, 162, 255; CDBLB-6

Deland, Margaret 1857-1945 . . . . .DLB-78

Delaney, Shelagh 1939- DLB-13; CDBLB-8

Delano, Amasa 1763-1823 . . . . .DLB-183

Delany, Martin Robinson 1812-1885 . . . . .DLB-50

Delany, Samuel R. 1942- DLB-8, 33

de la Roche, Mazo 1879-1961 . . . . .DLB-68

Delavigne, Jean François Casimir
1793-1843 .DLB-192

Delbanco, Nicholas 1942- DLB-6, 234

Delblanc, Sven 1931-1992 . . . . .DLB-257

Del Castillo, Ramón 1949- DLB-209

De León, Nephtalí 1945- DLB-82

Delgado, Abelardo Barrientos 1931- DLB-82

Del Giudice, Daniele 1949- DLB-196

De Libero, Libero 1906-1981 . . . . .DLB-114

DeLillo, Don 1936- DLB-6, 173

de Lint, Charles 1951- DLB-251

de Lisser H. G. 1878-1944 . . . . .DLB-117

Dell, Floyd 1887-1969 . . . . .DLB-9

Dell Publishing Company DLB-46

delle Grazie, Marie Eugene 1864-1931 . . . .DLB-81

Deloney, Thomas died 1600 . . . . .DLB-167

Deloria, Ella C. 1889-1971. . . . . .DLB-175

Deloria, Vine, Jr. 1933- DLB-175

del Rey, Lester 1915-1993 . . . . .DLB-8

Del Vecchio, John M. 1947- DS-9

Del'vig, Anton Antonovich 1798-1831. . . .DLB-205

de Man, Paul 1919-1983 . . . . .DLB-67

DeMarinis, Rick 1934- DLB-218

Demby, William 1922- DLB-33

De Mille, James 1833-1880 . . . . .DLB-251

Deming, Philander 1829-1915 . . . . .DLB-74

Deml, Jakub 1878-1961 . . . . .DLB-215

Demorest, William Jennings 1822-1895 . . .DLB-79

De Morgan, William 1839-1917 . . . . .DLB-153

Demosthenes 384 B.C.-322 B.C. DLB-176

Denham, Henry [publishing house]. DLB-170

Denham, Sir John 1615-1669. . . . . . .DLB-58, 126

Denison, Merrill 1893-1975. . . . . .DLB-92

Denison, T. S., and Company DLB-49

Dennery, Adolphe Philippe 1811-1899 . . .DLB-192

Dennie, Joseph 1768-1812 . . . . . DLB-37, 43, 59, 73

Dennis, C. J. 1876-1938 . . . . .DLB-260

Dennis, John 1658-1734. . . . . .DLB-101

Dennis, Nigel 1912-1989 . . . . .DLB-13, 15, 233

Denslow, W. W. 1856-1915 . . . . .DLB-188

Dent, J. M., and Sons. DLB-112

Dent, Tom 1932-1998 . . . . .DLB-38

Denton, Daniel circa 1626-1703. . . . . .DLB-24

DePaola, Tomie 1934- DLB-61

Department of Library, Archives, and Institutional
Research, American Bible Society. Y-97

De Quille, Dan 1829-1898. . . . . .DLB-186

De Quincey, Thomas
1785-1859 . . . . .DLB-110, 144; CDBLB-3

"Rhetoric" (1828; revised, 1859)
[excerpt] DLB-57

Derby, George Horatio 1823-1861 . . . . . . .DLB-11

Derby, J. C., and Company. DLB-49

Derby and Miller. DLB-49

De Ricci, Seymour 1881-1942 . . . . .DLB-201

Derleth, August 1909-1971 . . . . DLB-9; DS-17

Derrida, Jacques 1930- DLB-242

The Derrydale Press DLB-46

Derzhavin, Gavriil Romanovich
1743-1816 .DLB-150

Desaulniers, Gonsalve 1863-1934 . . . . . . .DLB-92

Desbordes-Valmore, Marceline
1786-1859 .DLB-217

Deschamps, Emile 1791-1871. . . . . .DLB-217

Deschamps, Eustache 1340?-1404 . . . . . .DLB-208

Desbiens, Jean-Paul 1927- DLB-53

des Forêts, Louis-Rene 1918- DLB-83

Desiato, Luca 1941- DLB-196

Desnica, Vladan 1905-1967 . . . . .DLB-181

Desnos, Robert 1900-1945. . . . . .DLB-258

DesRochers, Alfred 1901-1978. . . . . .DLB-68

Desrosiers, Léo-Paul 1896-1967. . . . . .DLB-68

Dessì, Giuseppe 1909-1977 . . . . .DLB-177

Destouches, Louis-Ferdinand
(see Céline, Louis-Ferdinand)

De Tabley, Lord 1835-1895 . . . . .DLB-35

Deutsch, André, Limited DLB-112

Deutsch, Babette 1895-1982 . . . . DLB-45

Deutsch, Niklaus Manuel (see Manuel, Niklaus)

Devanny, Jean 1894-1962. . . . . DLB-260

Deveaux, Alexis 1948- DLB-38

The Development of the Author's Copyright
    in Britain DLB-154

The Development of Lighting in the Staging
    of Drama, 1900-1945 . . . . DLB-10

"The Development of Meiji Japan" DLB-180

De Vere, Aubrey 1814-1902. . . . . DLB-35

Devereux, second Earl of Essex, Robert
    1565-1601 . . . . DLB-136

The Devin-Adair Company DLB-46

De Vinne, Theodore Low 1828-1914. . . . DLB-187

Devlin, Anne 1951- DLB-245

De Voto, Bernard 1897-1955 . . . . DLB-9, 256

De Vries, Peter 1910-1993 . . . . DLB-6; Y-82

Dewdney, Christopher 1951- DLB-60

Dewdney, Selwyn 1909-1979 . . . . DLB-68

Dewey, John 1859-1952 . . . . DLB-246

Dewey, Orville 1794-1882 . . . . DLB-243

Dewey, Thomas B. 1915-1981 . . . . DLB-226

DeWitt, Robert M., Publisher DLB-49

DeWolfe, Fiske and Company DLB-49

Dexter, Colin 1930- DLB-87

de Young, M. H. 1849-1925. . . . . DLB-25

Dhlomo, H. I. E. 1903-1956 . . . . DLB-157, 225

Dhuoda circa 803-after 843 . . . . DLB-148

The Dial 1840-1844 . . . . DLB-223

The Dial Press DLB-46

Diamond, I. A. L. 1920-1988 . . . . DLB-26

Dibble, L. Grace 1902-1998 . . . . DLB-204

Dibdin, Thomas Frognall 1776-1847. . . . . DLB-184

Di Cicco, Pier Giorgio 1949- DLB-60

Dick, Philip K. 1928-1982 . . . . DLB-8

Dick and Fitzgerald DLB-49

Dickens, Charles 1812-1870
    . . . . DLB-21, 55, 70, 159, 166; CDBLB-4

Dickey, James 1923-1997
    . . . . DLB-5, 193; Y-82, Y-93, Y-96;
                                    DS-7, DS-19; CDALB-6

James Dickey Tributes Y-97

The Life of James Dickey: A Lecture to
    the Friends of the Emory Libraries,
    by Henry Hart Y-98

Dickey, William 1928-1994 . . . . DLB-5

Dickinson, Emily
    1830-1886 . . . . DLB-1, 243; CDWLB-3

Dickinson, John 1732-1808. . . . . DLB-31

Dickinson, Jonathan 1688-1747. . . . . DLB-24

Dickinson, Patric 1914- DLB-27

Dickinson, Peter 1927- DLB-87, 161

Dicks, John [publishing house] DLB-106

Dickson, Gordon R. 1923- DLB-8

Dictionary of Literary Biography Yearbook Awards
    . . . . . . Y-92, Y-93, Y-97, Y-98, Y-99, Y-00, Y-01

The Dictionary of National Biography DLB-144

Didion, Joan 1934-
    . . . . . DLB-2, 173, 185; Y-81, Y-86; CDALB-6

Di Donato, Pietro 1911- DLB-9

Die Fürstliche Bibliothek Corvey Y-96

Diego, Gerardo 1896-1987 . . . . DLB-134

Digges, Thomas circa 1546-1595 . . . . DLB-136

The Digital Millennium Copyright Act:
    Expanding Copyright Protection in
    Cyberspace and Beyond Y-98

Diktonius, Elmer 1896-1961 . . . . DLB-259

Dillard, Annie 1945- Y-80

Dillard, R. H. W. 1937- DLB-5, 244

Dillingham, Charles T., Company DLB-49

The Dillingham, G. W., Company DLB-49

Dilly, Edward and Charles
    [publishing house] DLB-154

Dilthey, Wilhelm 1833-1911 . . . . DLB-129

Dimitrova, Blaga 1922- . . . DLB-181; CDWLB-4

Dimov, Dimitr 1909-1966 . . . . DLB-181

Dimsdale, Thomas J. 1831?-1866 . . . . DLB-186

Dinescu, Mircea 1950- DLB-232

Dinesen, Isak (see Blixen, Karen)

Dingelstedt, Franz von 1814-1881 . . . . . . DLB-133

Dintenfass, Mark 1941- Y-84

Diogenes, Jr. (see Brougham, John)

Diogenes Laertius circa 200 . . . . DLB-176

DiPrima, Diane 1934- DLB-5, 16

Disch, Thomas M. 1940- DLB-8

Disney, Walt 1901-1966. . . . . DLB-22

Disraeli, Benjamin 1804-1881 . . . . DLB-21, 55

D'Israeli, Isaac 1766-1848 . . . . DLB-107

Ditlevsen, Tove 1917-1976 . . . . DLB-214

Ditzen, Rudolf (see Fallada, Hans)

Dix, Dorothea Lynde 1802-1887 . . . . . DLB-1, 235

Dix, Dorothy (see Gilmer, Elizabeth Meriwether)

Dix, Edwards and Company DLB-49

Dix, Gertrude circa 1874-? DLB-197

Dixie, Florence Douglas 1857-1905 . . . . . DLB-174

Dixon, Ella Hepworth
    1855 or 1857-1932 . . . . DLB-197

Dixon, Paige (see Corcoran, Barbara)

Dixon, Richard Watson 1833-1900 . . . . . . DLB-19

Dixon, Stephen 1936- DLB-130

Dmitriev, Ivan Ivanovich 1760-1837 . . . . . DLB-150

Do They Or Don't They?
    Writers Reading Book Reviews Y-01

Dobell, Bertram 1842-1914 . . . . DLB-184

Dobell, Sydney 1824-1874 . . . . DLB-32

Dobie, J. Frank 1888-1964 . . . . DLB-212

Döblin, Alfred 1878-1957 . . . . DLB-66; CDWLB-2

Dobson, Austin 1840-1921 . . . . DLB-35, 144

Dobson, Rosemary 1920- DLB-260

Doctorow, E. L.
    1931- DLB-2, 28, 173; Y-80; CDALB-6

Documents on Sixteenth-Century
    Literature DLB-167, 172

Dodd, Anne [publishing house] DLB-154

Dodd, Mead and Company DLB-49

Dodd, Susan M. 1946- DLB-244

Dodd, William E. 1869-1940 . . . . DLB-17

Doderer, Heimito von 1896-1968 . . . . . . DLB-85

Dodge, B. W., and Company. DLB-46

Dodge, Mary Abigail 1833-1896 . . . . DLB-221

Dodge, Mary Mapes
    1831?-1905. . . . . DLB-42, 79; DS-13

Dodge Publishing Company DLB-49

Dodgson, Charles Lutwidge (see Carroll, Lewis)

Dodsley, R. [publishing house] DLB-154

Dodsley, Robert 1703-1764. . . . . DLB-95

Dodson, Owen 1914-1983 . . . . DLB-76

Dodwell, Christina 1951- DLB-204

Doesticks, Q. K. Philander, P. B.
    (see Thomson, Mortimer)

Doheny, Carrie Estelle 1875-1958 . . . . . . DLB-140

Doherty, John 1798?-1854 . . . . DLB-190

Doig, Ivan 1939- DLB-206

Doinaş, Ştefan Augustin 1922- DLB-232

Domínguez, Sylvia Maida 1935- DLB-122

Donahoe, Patrick [publishing house] DLB-49

Donald, David H. 1920- DLB-17

The Practice of Biography VI: An
    Interview with David Herbert Donald. . . . Y-87

Donaldson, Scott 1928- DLB-111

Doni, Rodolfo 1919- DLB-177

Donleavy, J. P. 1926- DLB-6, 173

Donnadieu, Marguerite (see Duras, Marguerite)

Donne, John
    1572-1631 . . . . DLB-121, 151; CDBLB-1

Donnelley, R. R., and Sons Company DLB-49

Donnelly, Ignatius 1831-1901. . . . . DLB-12

Donohue and Henneberry DLB-49

Donoso, José 1924-1996 . . . . . DLB-113; CDWLB-3

Doolady, M. [publishing house] DLB-49

Dooley, Ebon (see Ebon)

Doolittle, Hilda 1886-1961 . . . . DLB-4, 45

Doplicher, Fabio 1938- DLB-128

Dor, Milo 1923- DLB-85

Doran, George H., Company. DLB-46

Dorgelès, Roland 1886-1973. . . . . DLB-65

Dorn, Edward 1929-1999. . . . . DLB-5

Dorr, Rheta Childe 1866-1948. . . . . DLB-25

Dorris, Michael 1945-1997 . . . . DLB-175

Dorset and Middlesex, Charles Sackville,
    Lord Buckhurst, Earl of 1643-1706 . . . DLB-131

Dorsey, Candas Jane 1952- DLB-251

Dorst, Tankred 1925- DLB-75, 124

Dos Passos, John 1896-1970
    . . . . DLB-4, 9; DS-1, DS-15; CDALB-5

John Dos Passos: Artist Y-99

John Dos Passos: A Centennial
    Commemoration Y-96

Dostoevsky, Fyodor 1821-1881 . . . . DLB-238

Doubleday and Company DLB-49

Dougall, Lily 1858-1923 . . . . .DLB-92

Doughty, Charles M.
 1843-1926 . . . . DLB-19, 57, 174

Douglas, Lady Alfred (see Custance, Olive)

Douglas, Gavin 1476-1522 . . . . .DLB-132

Douglas, Keith 1920-1944 . . . . .DLB-27

Douglas, Norman 1868-1952 . . . . . . .DLB-34, 195

Douglass, Frederick 1818-1895
 . . . . .DLB-1, 43, 50, 79, 243; CDALB-2

Frederick Douglass Creative Arts Center Y-01

Douglass, William circa 1691-1752 . . . . . . .DLB-24

Dourado, Autran 1926- DLB-145

Dove, Arthur G. 1880-1946 . . . . .DLB-188

Dove, Rita 1952- DLB-120; CDALB-7

Dover Publications DLB-46

Doves Press DLB-112

Dowden, Edward 1843-1913 . . . . . . .DLB-35, 149

Dowell, Coleman 1925-1985 . . . . .DLB-130

Dowland, John 1563-1626 . . . . .DLB-172

Downes, Gwladys 1915- DLB-88

Downing, J., Major (see Davis, Charles A.)

Downing, Major Jack (see Smith, Seba)

Dowriche, Anne
 before 1560-after 1613 . . . . .DLB-172

Dowson, Ernest 1867-1900 . . . . .DLB-19, 135

Doxey, William [publishing house] DLB-49

Doyle, Sir Arthur Conan
 1859-1930 . . . DLB-18, 70, 156, 178; CDBLB-5

Doyle, Kirby 1932- DLB-16

Doyle, Roddy 1958- DLB-194

Drabble, Margaret
 1939- DLB-14, 155, 231; CDBLB-8

Drach, Albert 1902- DLB-85

Dragojević, Danijel 1934- DLB-181

Drake, Samuel Gardner 1798-1875 . . . . . .DLB-187

The Dramatic Publishing Company DLB-49

Dramatists Play Service DLB-46

Drant, Thomas early 1540s?-1578 . . . . . . .DLB-167

Draper, John W. 1811-1882 . . . . .DLB-30

Draper, Lyman C. 1815-1891 . . . . .DLB-30

Drayton, Michael 1563-1631 . . . . .DLB-121

Dreiser, Theodore 1871-1945
 . . . . . . .DLB-9, 12, 102, 137; DS-1; CDALB-3

Dresser, Davis 1904-1977 . . . . .DLB-226

Drewitz, Ingeborg 1923-1986 . . . . .DLB-75

Drieu La Rochelle, Pierre 1893-1945 . . . . . .DLB-72

Drinker, Elizabeth 1735-1807 . . . . .DLB-200

Drinkwater, John
 1882-1937 . . . . DLB-10, 19, 149

Droste-Hülshoff, Annette von
 1797-1848 . . . . .DLB-133; CDWLB-2

The Drue Heinz Literature Prize
 Excerpt from "Excerpts from a Report
 of the Commission," in David
 Bosworth's *The Death of Descartes*
 An Interview with David Bosworth Y-82

Drummond, William, of Hawthornden
 1585-1649 . . . . .DLB-121, 213

Drummond, William Henry
 1854-1907 . . . . .DLB-92

Druzhinin, Aleksandr Vasil'evich
 1824-1864 . . . . .DLB-238

Dryden, Charles 1860?-1931 . . . . .DLB-171

Dryden, John
 1631-1700 . . . . . .DLB-80, 101, 131; CDBLB-2

Držić, Marin
 circa 1508-1567 . . . . . . .DLB-147; CDWLB-4

Duane, William 1760-1835 . . . . .DLB-43

Dubé, Marcel 1930- DLB-53

Dubé, Rodolphe (see Hertel, François)

Dubie, Norman 1945- DLB-120

Dubois, Silvia
 1788 or 1789?-1889 . . . . .DLB-239

Du Bois, W. E. B.
 1868-1963 . . . . DLB-47, 50, 91, 246; CDALB-3

Du Bois, William Pène 1916-1993 . . . . .DLB-61

Dubrovina, Ekaterina Oskarovna
 1846-1913 . . . . .DLB-238

Dubus, Andre 1936-1999 . . . . .DLB-130

Ducange, Victor 1783-1833 . . . . .DLB-192

Du Chaillu, Paul Belloni 1831?-1903 . . . . .DLB-189

Ducharme, Réjean 1941- DLB-60

Dučić, Jovan
 1871-1943 . . . . .DLB-147; CDWLB-4

Duck, Stephen 1705?-1756 . . . . .DLB-95

Duckworth, Gerald, and Company
 Limited DLB-112

Duclaux, Madame Mary (see Robinson, A. Mary F.)

Dudek, Louis 1918- DLB-88

Duell, Sloan and Pearce DLB-46

Duerer, Albrecht 1471-1528 . . . . .DLB-179

Duff Gordon, Lucie 1821-1869 . . . . .DLB-166

Dufferin, Helen Lady, Countess of Gifford
 1807-1867 . . . . .DLB-199

Duffield and Green DLB-46

Duffy, Maureen 1933- DLB-14

Dufief, Nicholas Gouin 1776-1834 . . . . . . .DLB-187

Dugan, Alan 1923- DLB-5

Dugard, William [publishing house] DLB-170

Dugas, Marcel 1883-1947 . . . . .DLB-92

Dugdale, William [publishing house] DLB-106

Duhamel, Georges 1884-1966 . . . . .DLB-65

Dujardin, Edouard 1861-1949 . . . . .DLB-123

Dukes, Ashley 1885-1959 . . . . .DLB-10

Dumas, Alexandre *père* 1802-1870 . . . . .DLB-119, 192

Dumas, Alexandre *fils*
 1824-1895 . . . . .DLB-192

Dumas, Henry 1934-1968 . . . . .DLB-41

du Maurier, Daphne 1907-1989 . . . . .DLB-191

Du Maurier, George
 1834-1896 . . . . DLB-153, 178

Dummett, Michael 1925- DLB-262

Dunbar, Paul Laurence
 1872-1906 . . . . .DLB-50, 54, 78; CDALB-3

Dunbar, William
 circa 1460-circa 1522 . . . . .DLB-132, 146

Duncan, Dave 1933- DLB-251

Duncan, David James 1952- DLB-256

Duncan, Norman 1871-1916 . . . . .DLB-92

Duncan, Quince 1940- DLB-145

Duncan, Robert 1919-1988 . . . . . . .DLB-5, 16, 193

Duncan, Ronald 1914-1982 . . . . .DLB-13

Duncan, Sara Jeannette 1861-1922 . . . . . . .DLB-92

Dunigan, Edward, and Brother DLB-49

Dunlap, John 1747-1812 . . . . .DLB-43

Dunlap, William 1766-1839 . . . . . . .DLB-30, 37, 59

Dunn, Douglas 1942- DLB-40

Dunn, Harvey Thomas 1884-1952 . . . . . .DLB-188

Dunn, Stephen 1939- DLB-105

"The Good, The Not So Good" DLB-105

Dunne, Finley Peter 1867-1936 . . . . . . .DLB-11, 23

Dunne, John Gregory 1932- Y-80

Dunne, Philip 1908-1992 . . . . .DLB-26

Dunning, Ralph Cheever 1878-1930 . . . . . . .DLB-4

Dunning, William A. 1857-1922 . . . . .DLB-17

Dunsany, Lord (Edward John Moreton
 Drax Plunkett, Baron Dunsany)
 1878-1957 . . . . DLB-10, 77, 153, 156, 255

Duns Scotus, John
 circa 1266-1308 . . . . .DLB-115

Dunton, John [publishing house] DLB-170

Dunton, W. Herbert 1878-1936 . . . . .DLB-188

Dupin, Amantine-Aurore-Lucile (see Sand, George)

Dupuy, Eliza Ann 1814-1880 . . . . .DLB-248

Durack, Mary 1913-1994 . . . . .DLB-260

Durand, Lucile (see Bersianik, Louky)

Duranti, Francesca 1935- DLB-196

Duranty, Walter 1884-1957 . . . . .DLB-29

Duras, Marguerite 1914-1996 . . . . .DLB-83

Durfey, Thomas 1653-1723 . . . . .DLB-80

Durova, Nadezhda Andreevna
 (Aleksandr Andreevich Aleksandrov)
 1783-1866 . . . . .DLB-198

Durrell, Lawrence 1912-1990
 . . . . DLB-15, 27, 204; Y-90; CDBLB-7

Durrell, William [publishing house] DLB-49

Dürrenmatt, Friedrich
 1921-1990 . . . . DLB-69, 124; CDWLB-2

Duston, Hannah 1657-1737 . . . . .DLB-200

Dutt, Toru 1856-1877 . . . . .DLB-240

Dutton, E. P., and Company DLB-49

Duvoisin, Roger 1904-1980 . . . . .DLB-61

Duyckinck, Evert Augustus
 1816-1878 . . . . DLB-3, 64, 250

Duyckinck, George L.
 1823-1863 . . . . .DLB-3, 250

Duyckinck and Company DLB-49

Dwight, John Sullivan 1813-1893 . . . . .DLB-1, 235

Dwight, Timothy 1752-1817 . . . . .DLB-37

Dybek, Stuart 1942- DLB-130

Dyer, Charles 1928- DLB-13

Dyer, Sir Edward 1543-1607 . . . . .DLB-136

Dyer, George 1755-1841 . . . . .DLB-93

Dyer, John 1699-1757 . . . . .DLB-95

Dyk, Viktor 1877-1931 . . . . DLB-215

Dylan, Bob 1941- DLB-16

E

Eager, Edward 1911-1964 . . . . DLB-22

Eagleton, Terry 1943- DLB-242

Eames, Wilberforce 1855-1937. . . . . DLB-140

Earle, Alice Morse 1853-1911. . . . . DLB-221

Earle, James H., and Company DLB-49

Earle, John 1600 or 1601-1665 . . . . DLB-151

Early American Book Illustration,
    by Sinclair Hamilton DLB-49

Eastlake, William 1917-1997 . . . . DLB-6, 206

Eastman, Carol ?- DLB-44

Eastman, Charles A. (Ohiyesa)
    1858-1939 . . . . .DLB-175

Eastman, Max 1883-1969 . . . . DLB-91

Eaton, Daniel Isaac 1753-1814 . . . . DLB-158

Eaton, Edith Maude 1865-1914 . . . . DLB-221

Eaton, Winnifred 1875-1954. . . . . DLB-221

Eberhart, Richard 1904- DLB-48; CDALB-1

Ebner, Jeannie 1918- DLB-85

Ebner-Eschenbach, Marie von
    1830-1916. . . . . DLB-81

Ebon 1942- DLB-41

E-Books Turn the Corner. Y-98

Ecbasis Captivi circa 1045 . . . . DLB-148

Ecco Press. DLB-46

Eckhart, Meister circa 1260-circa 1328. . . DLB-115

The Eclectic Review 1805-1868. . . . . DLB-110

Eco, Umberto 1932- DLB-196, 242

Eddison, E. R. 1882-1945. . . . . DLB-255

Edel, Leon 1907-1997 . . . . DLB-103

Edelfeldt, Inger 1956- DLB-257

Edes, Benjamin 1732-1803 . . . . DLB-43

Edgar, David 1948- DLB-13, 233

Edgeworth, Maria
    1768-1849. . . . . .DLB-116, 159, 163

The Edinburgh Review 1802-1929 . . . . DLB-110

Edinburgh University Press DLB-112

The Editor Publishing Company DLB-49

Editorial Institute at Boston University Y-00

Editorial Statements DLB-137

Edmonds, Randolph 1900- DLB-51

Edmonds, Walter D. 1903-1998. . . . . DLB-9

Edschmid, Kasimir 1890-1966 . . . . DLB-56

Edson, Russell 1935- DLB-244

Edwards, Amelia Anne Blandford
    1831-1892 .DLB-174

Edwards, Dic 1953- DLB-245

Edwards, Edward 1812-1886 . . . . DLB-184

Edwards, James [publishing house]. DLB-154

Edwards, Jonathan 1703-1758. . . . . DLB-24

Edwards, Jonathan, Jr. 1745-1801 . . . . DLB-37

Edwards, Junius 1929- DLB-33

Edwards, Matilda Barbara Betham
    1836-1919 . . . . .DLB-174

Edwards, Richard 1524-1566 . . . . DLB-62

Edwards, Sarah Pierpont 1710-1758 . . . . . DLB-200

Effinger, George Alec 1947- DLB-8

Egerton, George 1859-1945 . . . . DLB-135

Eggleston, Edward 1837-1902. . . . . DLB-12

Eggleston, Wilfred 1901-1986 . . . . DLB-92

Eglītis, Anšlavs 1906-1993 . . . . DLB-220

Ehrenreich, Barbara 1941- DLB-246

Ehrenstein, Albert 1886-1950. . . . . DLB-81

Ehrhart, W. D. 1948- DS-9

Ehrlich, Gretel 1946- DLB-212

Eich, Günter 1907-1972. . . . . DLB-69, 124

Eichendorff, Joseph Freiherr von
    1788-1857 . . . . DLB-90

Eifukumon'in 1271-1342. . . . . DLB-203

1873 Publishers' Catalogues DLB-49

Eighteenth-Century Aesthetic
    Theories. DLB-31

Eighteenth-Century Philosophical
    Background DLB-31

Eigner, Larry 1926-1996 . . . . DLB-5, 193

Eikon Basilike 1649. . . . . DLB-151

Eilhart von Oberge
    circa 1140-circa 1195 . . . . DLB-148

Einhard circa 770-840 . . . . DLB-148

Eiseley, Loren 1907-1977 . . . . .DS-17

Eisenberg, Deborah 1945- DLB-244

Eisenreich, Herbert 1925-1986. . . . . DLB-85

Eisner, Kurt 1867-1919 . . . . DLB-66

Ekelöf, Gunnar 1907-1968 . . . . DLB-259

Eklund, Gordon 1945- Y-83

Ekman, Kerstin 1933- DLB-257

Ekwensi, Cyprian
    1921- DLB-117; CDWLB-3

Elaw, Zilpha circa 1790-? DLB-239

Eld, George [publishing house]. DLB-170

Elder, Lonne III 1931- DLB-7, 38, 44

Elder, Paul, and Company DLB-49

The Electronic Text Center and the Electronic
    Archive of Early American Fiction at the
    University of Virginia Library Y-98

Eliade, Mircea 1907-1986 . . . DLB-220; CDWLB-4

Elie, Robert 1915-1973 . . . . DLB-88

Elin Pelin 1877-1949 . . . . .DLB-147; CDWLB-4

Eliot, George
    1819-1880 . . . . DLB-21, 35, 55; CDBLB-4

Eliot, John 1604-1690 . . . . DLB-24

Eliot, T. S. 1888-1965
    . . . . .DLB-7, 10, 45, 63, 245; CDALB-5

T. S. Eliot Centennial Y-88

Eliot's Court Press DLB-170

Elizabeth I 1533-1603. . . . . DLB-136

Elizabeth of Nassau-Saarbrücken
    after 1393-1456 . . . . .DLB-179

Elizondo, Salvador 1932- DLB-145

Elizondo, Sergio 1930- DLB-82

Elkin, Stanley 1930-1995 . . . .DLB-2, 28, 218; Y-80

Elles, Dora Amy (see Wentworth, Patricia)

Ellet, Elizabeth F. 1818?-1877 . . . . DLB-30

Elliot, Ebenezer 1781-1849 . . . . DLB-96, 190

Elliot, Frances Minto (Dickinson)
    1820-1898 . . . . DLB-166

Elliott, Charlotte 1789-1871 . . . . DLB-199

Elliott, George 1923- DLB-68

Elliott, George P. 1918-1980. . . . . DLB-244

Elliott, Janice 1931- DLB-14

Elliott, Sarah Barnwell 1848-1928 . . . . . . DLB-221

Elliott, Thomes and Talbot DLB-49

Elliott, William III 1788-1863. . . . . . . DLB-3, 248

Ellis, Alice Thomas (Anna Margaret Haycraft)
    1932- DLB-194

Ellis, Edward S. 1840-1916. . . . . DLB-42

Ellis, Frederick Staridge
    [publishing house] DLB-106

The George H. Ellis Company. DLB-49

Ellis, Havelock 1859-1939 . . . . DLB-190

Ellison, Harlan 1934- DLB-8

Ellison, Ralph
    1914-1994 . . .DLB-2, 76, 227; Y-94; CDALB-1

Ellmann, Richard 1918-1987 . . . . . .DLB-103; Y-87

Ellroy, James 1948- DLB-226; Y-91

Eluard, Paul 1895-1952 . . . . DLB-258

Elyot, Thomas 1490?-1546 . . . . DLB-136

Emanuel, James Andrew 1921- DLB-41

Emecheta, Buchi 1944- DLB-117; CDWLB-3

Emendations for *Look Homeward, Angel* Y-00

The Emergence of Black Women Writers DS-8

Emerson, Ralph Waldo 1803-1882
    . . . . DLB-1, 59, 73, 183, 223; CDALB-2

Ralph Waldo Emerson in 1982 . . . . Y-82

Emerson, William 1769-1811 . . . . DLB-37

Emerson, William 1923-1997 . . . . .Y-97

Emin, Fedor Aleksandrovich
    circa 1735-1770 . . . . DLB-150

Emmanuel, Pierre 1916-1984 . . . . DLB-258

Empedocles fifth century B.C. DLB-176

Empson, William 1906-1984 . . . . DLB-20

Enchi Fumiko 1905-1986 . . . . DLB-182

"Encounter with the West" DLB-180

The End of English Stage Censorship,
    1945-1968 . . . . DLB-13

Ende, Michael 1929-1995 . . . . DLB-75

Endō Shūsaku 1923-1996 . . . . DLB-182

Engel, Marian 1933-1985 . . . . DLB-53

Engels, Friedrich 1820-1895 . . . . DLB-129

Engle, Paul 1908- DLB-48

English, Thomas Dunn 1819-1902 . . . . . . DLB-202

English Composition and Rhetoric (1866),
    by Alexander Bain [excerpt]. DLB-57

The English Language: 410 to 1500 . . . . . DLB-146

Ennius 239 B.C.-169 B.C. DLB-211

Enquist, Per Olov 1934- DLB-257

Enright, D. J. 1920- DLB-27

Enright, Elizabeth 1909-1968 . . . . .DLB-22

Epic and Beast Epic DLB-208

Epictetus circa 55-circa 125-130 . . . . .DLB-176

Epicurus 342/341 B.C.-271/270 B.C. DLB-176

Epps, Bernard 1936- DLB-53

Epstein, Julius 1909- and
  Epstein, Philip 1909-1952 . . . . .DLB-26

Equiano, Olaudah
  circa 1745-1797 . . . . . . .DLB-37, 50; DWLB-3

Olaudah Equiano and Unfinished Journeys:
  The Slave-Narrative Tradition and
  Twentieth-Century Continuities, by
  Paul Edwards and Pauline T.
  Wangman DLB-117

The E-Researcher: Possibilities and Pitfalls . . . Y-00

Eragny Press DLB-112

Erasmus, Desiderius 1467-1536 . . . . .DLB-136

Erba, Luciano 1922- DLB-128

Erdrich, Louise
  1954- DLB-152, 175, 206; CDALB-7

Erichsen-Brown, Gwethalyn Graham
  (see Graham, Gwethalyn)

Eriugena, John Scottus circa 810-877 . . . . .DLB-115

Ernst, Paul 1866-1933 . . . . .DLB-66, 118

Ershov, Petr Pavlovich 1815-1869 . . . . . .DLB-205

Erskine, Albert 1911-1993 . . . . Y-93

Erskine, John 1879-1951 . . . . .DLB-9, 102

Erskine, Mrs. Steuart ?-1948 . . . . .DLB-195

Ertel', Aleksandr Ivanovich
  1855-1908 .DLB-238

Ervine, St. John Greer 1883-1971 . . . . . . .DLB-10

Eschenburg, Johann Joachim 1743-1820 . . .DLB-97

Escoto, Julio 1944- DLB-145

Esdaile, Arundell 1880-1956 . . . . .DLB-201

Eshleman, Clayton 1935- DLB-5

Espriu, Salvador 1913-1985 . . . . .DLB-134

Ess Ess Publishing Company DLB-49

Essex House Press DLB-112

Esson, Louis 1878-1993 . . . . .DLB-260

Essop, Ahmed 1931- DLB-225

Esterházy, Péter 1950- DLB-232; CDWLB-4

Estes, Eleanor 1906-1988 . . . . .DLB-22

Estes and Lauriat DLB-49

Estleman, Loren D. 1952- DLB-226

Eszterhas, Joe 1944- DLB-185

Etherege, George 1636-circa 1692 . . . . . . .DLB-80

Ethridge, Mark, Sr. 1896-1981 . . . . .DLB-127

Ets, Marie Hall 1893- DLB-22

Etter, David 1928- DLB-105

Ettner, Johann Christoph 1654-1724 . . . . .DLB-168

Eugene Gant's Projected Works Y-01

Eupolemius flourished circa 1095 . . . . . . .DLB-148

Euripides circa 484 B.C.-407/406 B.C.
  .DLB-176; CDWLB-1

Evans, Augusta Jane 1835-1909 . . . . .DLB-239

Evans, Caradoc 1878-1945 . . . . .DLB-162

Evans, Charles 1850-1935 . . . . .DLB-187

Evans, Donald 1884-1921 . . . . .DLB-54

Evans, George Henry 1805-1856 . . . . .DLB-43

Evans, Hubert 1892-1986 . . . . .DLB-92

Evans, M., and Company DLB-46

Evans, Mari 1923- DLB-41

Evans, Mary Ann (see Eliot, George)

Evans, Nathaniel 1742-1767 . . . . .DLB-31

Evans, Sebastian 1830-1909 . . . . .DLB-35

Evaristi, Marcella 1953- DLB-233

Everett, Alexander Hill 1790-1847 . . . . . . .DLB-59

Everett, Edward 1794-1865 . . . . . . .DLB-1, 59, 235

Everson, R. G. 1903- DLB-88

Everson, William 1912-1994 . . . . .DLB-5, 16, 212

Ewart, Gavin 1916-1995 . . . . .DLB-40

Ewing, Juliana Horatia 1841-1885 . . . .DLB-21, 163

The Examiner 1808-1881 . . . . .DLB-110

Exley, Frederick 1929-1992 . . . . . . .DLB-143; Y-81

von Eyb, Albrecht 1420-1475 . . . . .DLB-179

Eyre and Spottiswoode DLB-106

Ezera, Regīna 1930- DLB-232

Ezzo ?-after 1065 . . . . .DLB-148

F

Faber, Frederick William 1814-1863 . . . . . .DLB-32

Faber and Faber Limited DLB-112

Faccio, Rena (see Aleramo, Sibilla)

Fagundo, Ana María 1938- DLB-134

Fair, Ronald L. 1932- DLB-33

Fairfax, Beatrice (see Manning, Marie)

Fairlie, Gerard 1899-1983 . . . . .DLB-77

Fallada, Hans 1893-1947 . . . . .DLB-56

Fancher, Betsy 1928- Y-83

Fane, Violet 1843-1905 . . . . .DLB-35

Fanfrolico Press DLB-112

Fanning, Katherine 1927 . . . . .DLB-127

Fanshawe, Sir Richard 1608-1666 . . . . . . .DLB-126

Fantasy Press Publishers DLB-46

Fante, John 1909-1983 . . . . .DLB-130; Y-83

Al-Farabi circa 870-950 . . . . .DLB-115

Farabough, Laura 1949- DLB-228

Farah, Nuruddin 1945- DLB-125; CDWLB-3

Farber, Norma 1909-1984 . . . . .DLB-61

Fargue, Léon-Paul 1876-1947 . . . . .DLB-258

Farigoule, Louis (see Romains, Jules)

Farjeon, Eleanor 1881-1965 . . . . .DLB-160

Farley, Harriet 1812-1907 . . . . .DLB-239

Farley, Walter 1920-1989 . . . . .DLB-22

Farmborough, Florence 1887-1978 . . . . . .DLB-204

Farmer, Penelope 1939- DLB-161

Farmer, Philip José 1918- DLB-8

Farnaby, Thomas 1575?-1647 . . . . .DLB-236

Farningham, Marianne (see Hearn, Mary Anne)

Farquhar, George circa 1677-1707 . . . . . . .DLB-84

Farquharson, Martha (see Finley, Martha)

Farrar, Frederic William 1831-1903 . . . . .DLB-163

Farrar and Rinehart DLB-46

Farrar, Straus and Giroux DLB-46

Farrell, J. G. 1935-1979 . . . . .DLB-14

Farrell, James T. 1904-1979 . . . .DLB-4, 9, 86; DS-2

Fast, Howard 1914- DLB-9

Faulkner, George [publishing house] DLB-154

Faulkner, William 1897-1962
  . . .DLB-9, 11, 44, 102; DS-2; Y-86; CDALB-5

William Faulkner Centenary Y-97

"Faulkner 100–Celebrating the Work,"
  University of South Carolina, Columbia . .Y-97

Impressions of William Faulkner Y-97

Faulkner and Yoknapatawpha Conference,
  Oxford, Mississippi Y-97

Faulks, Sebastian 1953- DLB-207

Fauset, Jessie Redmon 1882-1961 . . . . . . .DLB-51

Faust, Frederick Schiller (Max Brand)
  1892-1944 .DLB-256

Faust, Irvin 1924- DLB-2, 28, 218; Y-80

Fawcett, Edgar 1847-1904 . . . . .DLB-202

Fawcett, Millicent Garrett 1847-1929 . . . . .DLB-190

Fawcett Books .DLB-46

Fay, Theodore Sedgwick 1807-1898 . . . . .DLB-202

Fearing, Kenneth 1902-1961 . . . . .DLB-9

Federal Writers' Project DLB-46

Federman, Raymond 1928- Y-80

Fedorov, Innokentii Vasil'evich
  (see Omulevsky, Innokentii Vasil'evich)

Feiffer, Jules 1929- DLB-7, 44

Feinberg, Charles E. 1899-1988 . . . .DLB-187; Y-88

Feind, Barthold 1678-1721 . . . . .DLB-168

Feinstein, Elaine 1930- DLB-14, 40

Feiss, Paul Louis 1875-1952 . . . . .DLB-187

Feldman, Irving 1928- DLB-169

Felipe, Léon 1884-1968 . . . . .DLB-108

Fell, Frederick, Publishers DLB-46

Felltham, Owen 1602?-1668 . . . . . . .DLB-126, 151

Felman, Soshana 1942- DLB-246

Fels, Ludwig 1946- DLB-75

Felton, Cornelius Conway 1807-1862 . .DLB-1, 235

Fenn, Harry 1837-1911 . . . . .DLB-188

Fennario, David 1947- DLB-60

Fenner, Dudley 1558?-1587? DLB-236

Fenno, Jenny 1765?-1803 . . . . .DLB-200

Fenno, John 1751-1798 . . . . .DLB-43

Fenno, R. F., and Company DLB-49

Fenoglio, Beppe 1922-1963 . . . . .DLB-177

Fenton, Geoffrey 1539?-1608 . . . . .DLB-136

Fenton, James 1949- DLB-40

Ferber, Edna 1885-1968 . . . . .DLB-9, 28, 86

Ferdinand, Vallery III (see Salaam, Kalamu ya)

Ferguson, Sir Samuel 1810-1886 . . . . .DLB-32

Ferguson, William Scott 1875-1954 . . . . . . .DLB-47

Fergusson, Robert 1750-1774 . . . . .DLB-109

Ferland, Albert 1872-1943 . . . . .DLB-92

Ferlinghetti, Lawrence 1919- DLB-5, 16; CDALB-1

Fermor, Patrick Leigh 1915- DLB-204

Fern, Fanny (see Parton, Sara Payson Willis)

Ferrars, Elizabeth 1907- DLB-87

Ferré, Rosario 1942- DLB-145

Ferret, E., and Company DLB-49

Ferrier, Susan 1782-1854 . . . . DLB-116

Ferril, Thomas Hornsby 1896-1988 . . . . . DLB-206

Ferrini, Vincent 1913- DLB-48

Ferron, Jacques 1921-1985 . . . . DLB-60

Ferron, Madeleine 1922- DLB-53

Ferrucci, Franco 1936- DLB-196

Fetridge and Company DLB-49

Feuchtersleben, Ernst Freiherr von 1806-1849 . . . . DLB-133

Feuchtwanger, Lion 1884-1958 . . . . DLB-66

Feuerbach, Ludwig 1804-1872 . . . . DLB-133

Feuillet, Octave 1821-1890 . . . . DLB-192

Feydeau, Georges 1862-1921 . . . . DLB-192

Fichte, Johann Gottlieb 1762-1814 . . . . . . DLB-90

Ficke, Arthur Davison 1883-1945 . . . . DLB-54

Fiction Best-Sellers, 1910-1945 . . . . DLB-9

Fiction into Film, 1928-1975: A List of Movies Based on the Works of Authors in British Novelists, 1930-1959 . . . . DLB-15

Fiedler, Leslie A. 1917- DLB-28, 67

Field, Barron 1789-1846 . . . . DLB-230

Field, Edward 1924- DLB-105

Field, Joseph M. 1810-1856 . . . . DLB-248

Field, Michael (Katherine Harris Bradley [1846-1914] and Edith Emma Cooper [1862-1913]) DLB-240

"The Poetry File" DLB-105

Field, Eugene 1850-1895 . . . . DLB-23, 42, 140; DS-13

Field, John 1545?-1588 . . . . DLB-167

Field, Marshall, III 1893-1956 . . . . DLB-127

Field, Marshall, IV 1916-1965 . . . . DLB-127

Field, Marshall, V 1941- DLB-127

Field, Nathan 1587-1619 or 1620 . . . . DLB-58

Field, Rachel 1894-1942 . . . . DLB-9, 22

A Field Guide to Recent Schools of American Poetry Y-86

Fielding, Helen 1958- DLB-231

Fielding, Henry 1707-1754 . . . . . . DLB-39, 84, 101; CDBLB-2

"Defense of *Amelia*" (1752) DLB-39

From *The History of the Adventures of Joseph Andrews* (1742) DLB-39

Preface to *Joseph Andrews* (1742) DLB-39

Preface to Sarah Fielding's *The Adventures of David Simple* (1744) DLB-39

Preface to Sarah Fielding's *Familiar Letters* (1747) [excerpt] DLB-39

Fielding, Sarah 1710-1768 . . . . DLB-39

Preface to *The Cry* (1754) DLB-39

Fields, Annie Adams 1834-1915 . . . . DLB-221

Fields, James T. 1817-1881 . . . . DLB-1, 235

Fields, Julia 1938- DLB-41

Fields, Osgood and Company DLB-49

Fields, W. C. 1880-1946 . . . . DLB-44

Fifty Penguin Years Y-85

Figes, Eva 1932- DLB-14

Figuera, Angela 1902-1984 . . . . DLB-108

Filmer, Sir Robert 1586-1653 . . . . DLB-151

Filson, John circa 1753-1788 . . . . DLB-37

Finch, Anne, Countess of Winchilsea 1661-1720 . . . . DLB-95

Finch, Robert 1900- DLB-88

Findley, Timothy 1930- DLB-53

Finlay, Ian Hamilton 1925- DLB-40

Finley, Martha 1828-1909 . . . . DLB-42

Finn, Elizabeth Anne (McCaul) 1825-1921 . . . . DLB-166

Finnegan, Seamus 1949- DLB-245

Finney, Jack 1911-1995 . . . . DLB-8

Finney, Walter Braden (see Finney, Jack)

Firbank, Ronald 1886-1926 . . . . DLB-36

Firmin, Giles 1615-1697 . . . . DLB-24

First Edition Library/Collectors' Reprints, Inc. Y-91

Fischart, Johann 1546 or 1547-1590 or 1591 . . . . DLB-179

Fischer, Karoline Auguste Fernandine 1764-1842 . . . . DLB-94

Fischer, Tibor 1959- DLB-231

Fish, Stanley 1938- DLB-67

Fishacre, Richard 1205-1248 . . . . DLB-115

Fisher, Clay (see Allen, Henry W.)

Fisher, Dorothy Canfield 1879-1958 . . . DLB-9, 102

Fisher, Leonard Everett 1924- DLB-61

Fisher, Roy 1930- DLB-40

Fisher, Rudolph 1897-1934 . . . . DLB-51, 102

Fisher, Steve 1913-1980 . . . . DLB-226

Fisher, Sydney George 1856-1927 . . . . . . DLB-47

Fisher, Vardis 1895-1968 . . . . DLB-9, 206

Fiske, John 1608-1677 . . . . DLB-24

Fiske, John 1842-1901 . . . . DLB-47, 64

Fitch, Thomas circa 1700-1774 . . . . DLB-31

Fitch, William Clyde 1865-1909 . . . . DLB-7

FitzGerald, Edward 1809-1883 . . . . DLB-32

Fitzgerald, F. Scott 1896-1940 . . . . DLB-4, 9, 86, 219; Y-81, Y-92; DS-1, 15, 16; CDALB-4

F. Scott Fitzgerald Centenary Celebrations Y-96

F. Scott Fitzgerald: A Descriptive Bibliography, Supplement (2001) Y-01

F. Scott Fitzgerald Inducted into the American Poets' Corner at St. John the Divine; Ezra Pound Banned Y-99

"F. Scott Fitzgerald: St. Paul's Native Son and Distinguished American Writer": University of Minnesota Conference, 29-31 October 1982 . . . . Y-82

First International F. Scott Fitzgerald Conference Y-92

Fitzgerald, Penelope 1916- DLB-14, 194

Fitzgerald, Robert 1910-1985 . . . . Y-80

FitzGerald, Robert D. 1902-1987 . . . . . . DLB-260

Fitzgerald, Thomas 1819-1891 . . . . DLB-23

Fitzgerald, Zelda Sayre 1900-1948 . . . . Y-84

Fitzhugh, Louise 1928-1974 . . . . DLB-52

Fitzhugh, William circa 1651-1701 . . . . . . DLB-24

Flagg, James Montgomery 1877-1960 . . . . DLB-188

Flanagan, Thomas 1923- Y-80

Flanner, Hildegarde 1899-1987 . . . . DLB-48

Flanner, Janet 1892-1978 . . . . DLB-4

Flannery, Peter 1951- DLB-233

Flaubert, Gustave 1821-1880 . . . . DLB-119

Flavin, Martin 1883-1967 . . . . DLB-9

Fleck, Konrad (flourished circa 1220) DLB-138

Flecker, James Elroy 1884-1915 . . . . . . .DLB-10, 19

Fleeson, Doris 1901-1970 . . . . DLB-29

Fleißer, Marieluise 1901-1974 . . . . DLB-56, 124

Fleischer, Nat 1887-1972 . . . . DLB-241

Fleming, Abraham 1552?-1607 . . . . DLB-236

Fleming, Ian 1908-1964 . . .DLB-87, 201; CDBLB-7

Fleming, Paul 1609-1640 . . . . DLB-164

Fleming, Peter 1907-1971 . . . . DLB-195

Fletcher, Giles, the Elder 1546-1611 . . . . . DLB-136

Fletcher, Giles, the Younger 1585 or 1586-1623 . . . . DLB-121

Fletcher, J. S. 1863-1935 . . . . DLB-70

Fletcher, John (see Beaumont, Francis)

Fletcher, John Gould 1886-1950 . . . . DLB-4, 45

Fletcher, Phineas 1582-1650 . . . . DLB-121

Flieg, Helmut (see Heym, Stefan)

Flint, F. S. 1885-1960 . . . . DLB-19

Flint, Timothy 1780-1840 . . . . .DLB-73, 186

Flores-Williams, Jason 1969- DLB-209

Florio, John 1553?-1625 . . . . .DLB-172

Fo, Dario 1926- Y-97

Foix, J. V. 1893-1987 . . . . DLB-134

Foley, Martha (see Burnett, Whit, and Martha Foley)

Folger, Henry Clay 1857-1930 . . . . DLB-140

Folio Society DLB-112

Follain, Jean 1903-1971 . . . . DLB-258

Follen, Charles 1796-1840 . . . . DLB-235

Follen, Eliza Lee (Cabot) 1787-1860 . . . DLB-1, 235

Follett, Ken 1949- DLB-87; Y-81

Follett Publishing Company DLB-46

Folsom, John West [publishing house] DLB-49

Folz, Hans between 1435 and 1440-1513 . . . . . . .DLB-179

Fontane, Theodor 1819-1898 . . . . .DLB-129; CDWLB-2

Fontes, Montserrat 1940- DLB-209

Fonvisin, Denis Ivanovich 1744 or 1745-1792 . . . . DLB-150

Foote, Horton 1916- DLB-26

Foote, Mary Hallock
1847-1938 . . . . . . .DLB-186, 188, 202, 221

Foote, Samuel 1721-1777 . . . . .DLB-89

Foote, Shelby 1916- DLB-2, 17

Forbes, Calvin 1945- DLB-41

Forbes, Ester 1891-1967. . . . . .DLB-22

Forbes, Rosita 1893?-1967 . . . . .DLB-195

Forbes and Company. DLB-49

Force, Peter 1790-1868 . . . . .DLB-30

Forché, Carolyn 1950- DLB-5, 193

Ford, Charles Henri 1913- DLB-4, 48

Ford, Corey 1902-1969 . . . . .DLB-11

Ford, Ford Madox
1873-1939 . . . . . . .DLB-34, 98, 162; CDBLB-6

Ford, J. B., and Company DLB-49

Ford, Jesse Hill 1928-1996 . . . . .DLB-6

Ford, John 1586-?. DLB-58; CDBLB-1

Ford, R. A. D. 1915- DLB-88

Ford, Richard 1944- DLB-227

Ford, Worthington C. 1858-1941 . . . . . . .DLB-47

Fords, Howard, and Hulbert DLB-49

Foreman, Carl 1914-1984 . . . . .DLB-26

Forester, C. S. 1899-1966. . . . . .DLB-191

Forester, Frank (see Herbert, Henry William)

Forman, Harry Buxton 1842-1917. . . . . . .DLB-184

Fornés, María Irene 1930- DLB-7

Forrest, Leon 1937-1997. . . . . .DLB-33

Forster, E. M.
1879-1970 . . . . .DLB-34, 98, 162, 178, 195;
DS-10; CDBLB-6

Forster, Georg 1754-1794 . . . . .DLB-94

Forster, John 1812-1876 . . . . .DLB-144

Forster, Margaret 1938- DLB-155

Forsyth, Frederick 1938- DLB-87

Forten, Charlotte L. 1837-1914 . . . . . .DLB-50, 239

Charlotte Forten: Pages from
her Diary. DLB-50

Fortini, Franco 1917- DLB-128

Fortune, Mary ca. 1833-ca. 1910 . . . . . . .DLB-230

Fortune, T. Thomas 1856-1928. . . . . .DLB-23

Fosdick, Charles Austin 1842-1915 . . . . . .DLB-42

Foster, Genevieve 1893-1979 . . . . .DLB-61

Foster, Hannah Webster 1758-1840. . . DLB-37, 200

Foster, John 1648-1681 . . . . .DLB-24

Foster, Michael 1904-1956. . . . . .DLB-9

Foster, Myles Birket 1825-1899 . . . . .DLB-184

Foucault, Michel 1926-1984. . . . . .DLB-242

Foulis, Robert and Andrew / R. and A.
[publishing house] DLB-154

Fouqué, Caroline de la Motte
1774-1831 . . . . .DLB-90

Fouqué, Friedrich de la Motte
1777-1843. . . . . .DLB-90

Four Seas Company. DLB-46

Four Winds Press. DLB-46

Fournier, Henri Alban (see Alain-Fournier)

Fowler and Wells Company DLB-49

Fowles, John
1926- DLB-14, 139, 207; CDBLB-8

Fox, John 1939- DLB-245

Fox, John, Jr. 1862 or 1863-1919. . . .DLB-9; DS-13

Fox, Paula 1923- DLB-52

Fox, Richard K. [publishing house] DLB-49

Fox, Richard Kyle 1846-1922 . . . . .DLB-79

Fox, William Price 1926- DLB-2; Y-81

Foxe, John 1517-1587 . . . . .DLB-132

Fraenkel, Michael 1896-1957. . . . . .DLB-4

France, Anatole 1844-1924 . . . . .DLB-123

France, Richard 1938- DLB-7

Francis, C. S. [publishing house] DLB-49

Francis, Convers 1795-1863. . . . . .DLB-1, 235

Francis, Dick 1920- DLB-87

Francis, Sir Frank 1901-1988. . . . . .DLB-201

Francis, Jeffrey, Lord 1773-1850 . . . . . . .DLB-107

François 1863-1910 . . . . .DLB-92

François, Louise von 1817-1893. . . . . . . .DLB-129

Franck, Sebastian 1499-1542 . . . . .DLB-179

Francke, Kuno 1855-1930 . . . . .DLB-71

Frank, Bruno 1887-1945 . . . . .DLB-118

Frank, Leonhard 1882-1961 . . . . . . .DLB-56, 118

Frank, Melvin (see Panama, Norman)

Frank, Waldo 1889-1967. . . . . .DLB-9, 63

Franken, Rose 1895?-1988 . . . . .DLB-228, Y-84

Franklin, Benjamin
1706-1790 . . . .DLB-24, 43, 73, 183; CDALB-2

Franklin, James 1697-1735 . . . . .DLB-43

Franklin, Miles 1879-1954 . . . . .DLB-230

Franklin Library DLB-46

Frantz, Ralph Jules 1902-1979 . . . . .DLB-4

Franzos, Karl Emil 1848-1904 . . . . .DLB-129

Fraser, G. S. 1915-1980 . . . . .DLB-27

Fraser, Kathleen 1935- DLB-169

Frattini, Alberto 1922-. DLB-128

Frau Ava ?-1127 . . . . .DLB-148

Fraunce, Abraham 1558?-1592 or 1593. . .DLB-236

Frayn, Michael 1933- DLB-13, 14, 194, 245

Frederic, Harold
1856-1898 . . . . .DLB-12, 23; DS-13

Freeling, Nicolas 1927- DLB-87

Freeman, Douglas Southall
1886-1953 . . . . .DLB-17; DS-17

Freeman, Judith 1946- DLB-256

Freeman, Legh Richmond 1842-1915 . . . . .DLB-23

Freeman, Mary E. Wilkins
1852-1930 . . . . .DLB-12, 78, 221

Freeman, R. Austin 1862-1943 . . . . .DLB-70

Freidank circa 1170-circa 1233. . . . . .DLB-138

Freiligrath, Ferdinand 1810-1876 . . . . . . .DLB-133

Frémont, John Charles 1813-1890. . . . . . .DLB-186

Frémont, John Charles 1813-1890 and
Frémont, Jessie Benton 1834-1902 . . .DLB-183

French, Alice 1850-1934 . . . . .DLB-74; DS-13

French Arthurian Literature DLB-208

French, David 1939- DLB-53

French, Evangeline 1869-1960. . . . . .DLB-195

French, Francesca 1871-1960 . . . . .DLB-195

French, James [publishing house]. DLB-49

French, Samuel [publishing house] DLB-49

Samuel French, Limited. DLB-106

Freneau, Philip 1752-1832 . . . . DLB-37, 43

Freni, Melo 1934- DLB-128

Freshfield, Douglas W. 1845-1934 . . . . . .DLB-174

Freytag, Gustav 1816-1895 . . . . .DLB-129

Fridegård, Jan 1897-1968 . . . . .DLB-259

Fried, Erich 1921-1988 . . . . .DLB-85

Friedan, Betty 1921- DLB-246

Friedman, Bruce Jay 1930- DLB-2, 28, 244

Friedrich von Hausen circa 1171-1190. . . .DLB-138

Friel, Brian 1929- DLB-13

Friend, Krebs 1895?-1967? DLB-4

Fries, Fritz Rudolf 1935- DLB-75

Fringe and Alternative Theater in
Great Britain .DLB-13

Frisch, Max
1911-1991 . . . . .DLB-69, 124; CDWLB-2

Frischlin, Nicodemus 1547-1590 . . . . .DLB-179

Frischmuth, Barbara 1941- DLB-85

Fritz, Jean 1915- DLB-52

Froissart, Jean circa 1337-circa 1404. . . . . .DLB-208

From John Hall Wheelock's Oral Memoir . . . Y-01

Fromentin, Eugene 1820-1876. . . . . .DLB-123

Frontinus circa A.D. 35-A.D. 103/104 . . . .DLB-211

Frost, A. B. 1851-1928. . . . . .DLB-188; DS-13

Frost, Robert
1874-1963 . . . . .DLB-54; DS-7; CDALB-4

Frostenson, Katarina 1953- DLB-257

Frothingham, Octavius Brooks
1822-1895 . . . . .DLB-1, 243

Froude, James Anthony
1818-1894 . . . . DLB-18, 57, 144

Fruitlands 1843-1844 . . . . .DLB-223

Fry, Christopher 1907- DLB-13

Fry, Roger 1866-1934 . . . . DS-10

Fry, Stephen 1957- DLB-207

Frye, Northrop 1912-1991 . . . . . . .DLB-67, 68, 246

Fuchs, Daniel 1909-1993 . . . . .DLB-9, 26, 28; Y-93

Fuentes, Carlos 1928- DLB-113; CDWLB-3

Fuertes, Gloria 1918- DLB-108

Fugard, Athol 1932- DLB-225

The Fugitives and the Agrarians:
The First Exhibition Y-85

Fujiwara no Shunzei 1114-1204. . . . . . . .DLB-203

Fujiwara no Tameaki 1230s?-1290s?. DLB-203

Fujiwara no Tameie 1198-1275 . . . . .DLB-203

Fujiwara no Teika 1162-1241 . . . . .DLB-203

Fulbecke, William 1560-1603?. DLB-172

Fuller, Charles H., Jr. 1939- DLB-38

Fuller, Henry Blake 1857-1929 . . . . .DLB-12

Fuller, John 1937- DLB-40

Fuller, Margaret (see Fuller, Sarah)

Fuller, Roy 1912-1991 .... DLB-15, 20

Fuller, Samuel 1912- DLB-26

Fuller, Sarah 1810-1850
..... DLB-1, 59, 73, 183, 223, 239; CDALB-2

Fuller, Thomas 1608-1661 .... DLB-151

Fullerton, Hugh 1873-1945............ DLB-171

Fullwood, William flourished 1568 ..... DLB-236

Fulton, Alice 1952- DLB-193

Fulton, Len 1934- Y-86

Fulton, Robin 1937- DLB-40

Furbank, P. N. 1920- DLB-155

Furman, Laura 1945- Y-86

Furness, Horace Howard
1833-1912...................... DLB-64

Furness, William Henry
1802-1896 .... DLB-1, 235

Furnivall, Frederick James
1825-1910...................... DLB-184

Furphy, Joseph
(Tom Collins) 1843-1912.......... DLB-230

Furthman, Jules 1888-1966............ DLB-26

Furui Yoshikichi 1937- DLB-182

Fushimi, Emperor 1265-1317 .... DLB-203

Futabatei, Shimei
(Hasegawa Tatsunosuke)
1864-1909 .... DLB-180

The Future of the Novel (1899), by
Henry James.................... DLB-18

Fyleman, Rose 1877-1957 .... DLB-160

G

Gadallah, Leslie 1939- DLB-251

Gadda, Carlo Emilio 1893-1973 .... DLB-177

Gaddis, William 1922-1998 .... DLB-2, Y-99

Gág, Wanda 1893-1946 .... DLB-22

Gagarin, Ivan Sergeevich 1814-1882 .... DLB-198

Gagnon, Madeleine 1938- DLB-60

Gaiman, Neil 1960- DLB-261

Gaine, Hugh 1726-1807 .... DLB-43

Gaine, Hugh [publishing house] DLB-49

Gaines, Ernest J.
1933- DLB-2, 33, 152; Y-80; CDALB-6

Gaiser, Gerd 1908-1976 .... DLB-69

Gaitskill, Mary 1954- DLB-244

Galarza, Ernesto 1905-1984 .... DLB-122

Galaxy Science Fiction Novels DLB-46

Gale, Zona 1874-1938........... DLB-9, 228, 78

Galen of Pergamon 129-after 210........ DLB-176

Gales, Winifred Marshall 1761-1839 .... DLB-200

Gall, Louise von 1815-1855 .... DLB-133

Gallagher, Tess 1943- DLB-120, 212, 244

Gallagher, Wes 1911- DLB-127

Gallagher, William Davis 1808-1894 ..... DLB-73

Gallant, Mavis 1922- DLB-53

Gallegos, María Magdalena 1935- DLB-209

Gallico, Paul 1897-1976.............DLB-9, 171

Gallop, Jane 1952- DLB-246

Galloway, Grace Growden 1727-1782.... DLB-200

Gallup, Donald 1913- DLB-187

Galsworthy, John 1867-1933
..... DLB-10, 34, 98, 162; DS-16; CDBLB-5

Galt, John 1779-1839 .... DLB-99, 116

Galton, Sir Francis 1822-1911 .... DLB-166

Galvin, Brendan 1938- DLB-5

Gambit DLB-46

Gamboa, Reymundo 1948- DLB-122

Gammer Gurton's Needle................. DLB-62

Gan, Elena Andreevna (Zeneida R-va)
1814-1842 .... DLB-198

Gannett, Frank E. 1876-1957 .... DLB-29

Gao Xingjian 1940- Y-00

Gaos, Vicente 1919-1980 .... DLB-134

García, Andrew 1854?-1943 .... DLB-209

García, Lionel G. 1935- DLB-82

García, Richard 1941- DLB-209

García-Camarillo, Cecilio 1943- DLB-209

García Lorca, Federico 1898-1936 ...... DLB-108

García Márquez, Gabriel
1928- DLB-113; Y-82; CDWLB-3

Gardam, Jane 1928- DLB-14, 161, 231

Gardell, Jonas 1963- DLB-257

Garden, Alexander circa 1685-1756 ...... DLB-31

Gardiner, John Rolfe 1936- DLB-244

Gardiner, Margaret Power Farmer
(see Blessington, Marguerite, Countess of)

Gardner, John
1933-1982 .... DLB-2; Y-82; CDALB-7

Garfield, Leon 1921-1996............. DLB-161

Garis, Howard R. 1873-1962 .... DLB-22

Garland, Hamlin 1860-1940...DLB-12, 71, 78, 186

Garneau, Francis-Xavier 1809-1866...... DLB-99

Garneau, Hector de Saint-Denys
1912-1943 .... DLB-88

Garneau, Michel 1939- DLB-53

Garner, Alan 1934- DLB-161, 261

Garner, Hugh 1913-1979 .... DLB-68

Garnett, David 1892-1981 .... DLB-34

Garnett, Eve 1900-1991 .... DLB-160

Garnett, Richard 1835-1906.......... DLB-184

Garrard, Lewis H. 1829-1887 .... DLB-186

Garraty, John A. 1920- DLB-17

Garrett, George
1929- DLB-2, 5, 130, 152; Y-83

Fellowship of Southern Writers Y-98

Garrett, John Work 1872-1942........ DLB-187

Garrick, David 1717-1779 .... DLB-84, 213

Garrison, William Lloyd
1805-1879........ DLB-1, 43, 235; CDALB-2

Garro, Elena 1920-1998 .... DLB-145

Garth, Samuel 1661-1719 .... DLB-95

Garve, Andrew 1908- DLB-87

Gary, Romain 1914-1980............. DLB-83

Gascoigne, George 1539?-1577........ DLB-136

Gascoyne, David 1916- DLB-20

Gaskell, Elizabeth Cleghorn
1810-1865 ..... DLB-21, 144, 159; CDBLB-4

Gaskell, Jane 1941- DLB-261

Gaspey, Thomas 1788-1871 .... DLB-116

Gass, William H. 1924- DLB-2, 227

Gates, Doris 1901- DLB-22

Gates, Henry Louis, Jr. 1950- DLB-67

Gates, Lewis E. 1860-1924............ DLB-71

Gatto, Alfonso 1909-1976............ DLB-114

Gault, William Campbell 1910-1995 .... DLB-226

Gaunt, Mary 1861-1942..........DLB-174, 230

Gautier, Théophile 1811-1872 .... DLB-119

Gauvreau, Claude 1925-1971.......... DLB-88

The Gawain-Poet
flourished circa 1350-1400........ DLB-146

Gawsworth, John (Terence Ian Fytton Armstrong)
1912-1970...................... DLB-255

Gay, Ebenezer 1696-1787 .... DLB-24

Gay, John 1685-1732 .... DLB-84, 95

Gayarré, Charles E. A. 1805-1895 .... DLB-30

Gaylord, Charles [publishing house] DLB-49

Gaylord, Edward King 1873-1974 .... DLB-127

Gaylord, Edward Lewis 1919- DLB-127

Geda, Sigitas 1943- DLB-232

Geddes, Gary 1940- DLB-60

Geddes, Virgil 1897- DLB-4

Gedeon (Georgii Andreevich Krinovsky)
circa 1730-1763.................. DLB-150

Gee, Maggie 1948- DLB-207

Gee, Shirley 1932- DLB-245

Geßner, Salomon 1730-1788........... DLB-97

Geibel, Emanuel 1815-1884 .... DLB-129

Geiogamah, Hanay 1945- DLB-175

Geis, Bernard, Associates DLB-46

Geisel, Theodor Seuss 1904-1991 ...DLB-61; Y-91

Gelb, Arthur 1924- DLB-103

Gelb, Barbara 1926- DLB-103

Gelber, Jack 1932- DLB-7, 228

Gelinas, Gratien 1909- DLB-88

Gellert, Christian Fürchtegott
1715-1769...................... DLB-97

Gellhorn, Martha 1908-1998 .... Y-82, Y-98

Gems, Pam 1925- DLB-13

Genet, Jean 1910-1986 ....DLB-72; Y-86

Genette, Gérard 1930- DLB-242

Genevoix, Maurice 1890-1980 .... DLB-65

Genovese, Eugene D. 1930- DLB-17

Gent, Peter 1942- Y-82

Geoffrey of Monmouth
circa 1100-1155 .... DLB-146

George, Henry 1839-1897 .... DLB-23

George, Jean Craighead 1919- DLB-52

George, W. L. 1882-1926.............DLB-197

George III, King of Great Britain and Ireland 1738-1820 . . . . .DLB-213

George V. Higgins to Julian Symons Y-99

Georgslied 896? DLB-148

Gerber, Merrill Joan 1938- DLB-218

Gerhardie, William 1895-1977 . . . . .DLB-36

Gerhardt, Paul 1607-1676 . . . . .DLB-164

Gérin, Winifred 1901-1981 . . . . .DLB-155

Gérin-Lajoie, Antoine 1824-1882 . . . . .DLB-99

German Drama 800-1280 . . . . .DLB-138

German Drama from Naturalism to Fascism: 1889-1933 . . . . .DLB-118

German Literature and Culture from Charlemagne to the Early Courtly Period DLB-148; CDWLB-2

German Radio Play, The DLB-124

German Transformation from the Baroque to the Enlightenment, The DLB-97

The Germanic Epic and Old English Heroic Poetry: *Widsith, Waldere,* and *The Fight at Finnsburg* DLB-146

Germanophilism, by Hans Kohn DLB-66

Gernsback, Hugo 1884-1967 . . . . .DLB-8, 137

Gerould, Katharine Fullerton 1879-1944 . . . . .DLB-78

Gerrish, Samuel [publishing house] DLB-49

Gerrold, David 1944- DLB-8

The Ira Gershwin Centenary Y-96

Gerson, Jean 1363-1429 . . . . .DLB-208

Gersonides 1288-1344 . . . . .DLB-115

Gerstäcker, Friedrich 1816-1872 . . . . .DLB-129

Gerstenberg, Heinrich Wilhelm von 1737-1823 . . . . .DLB-97

Gervinus, Georg Gottfried 1805-1871 . . . . .DLB-133

Geston, Mark S. 1946- DLB-8

Al-Ghazali 1058-1111 . . . . .DLB-115

Gibbings, Robert 1889-1958 . . . . .DLB-195

Gibbon, Edward 1737-1794 . . . . .DLB-104

Gibbon, John Murray 1875-1952 . . . . .DLB-92

Gibbon, Lewis Grassic (see Mitchell, James Leslie)

Gibbons, Floyd 1887-1939 . . . . .DLB-25

Gibbons, Reginald 1947- DLB-120

Gibbons, William ?-? DLB-73

Gibson, Charles Dana 1867-1944 . . . . .DLB-188; DS-13

Gibson, Graeme 1934- DLB-53

Gibson, Margaret 1944- DLB-120

Gibson, Margaret Dunlop 1843-1920 . . . .DLB-174

Gibson, Wilfrid 1878-1962 . . . . .DLB-19

Gibson, William 1914- DLB-7

Gibson, William 1948- DLB-251

Gide, André 1869-1951 . . . . .DLB-65

Giguère, Diane 1937- DLB-53

Giguère, Roland 1929- DLB-60

Gil de Biedma, Jaime 1929-1990 . . . . .DLB-108

Gil-Albert, Juan 1906- DLB-134

Gilbert, Anthony 1899-1973 . . . . .DLB-77

Gilbert, Sir Humphrey 1537-1583 . . . . . . .DLB-136

Gilbert, Michael 1912- DLB-87

Gilbert, Sandra M. 1936- DLB-120, 246

Gilchrist, Alexander 1828-1861 . . . . .DLB-144

Gilchrist, Ellen 1935- DLB-130

Gilder, Jeannette L. 1849-1916 . . . . .DLB-79

Gilder, Richard Watson 1844-1909 . . . .DLB-64, 79

Gildersleeve, Basil 1831-1924 . . . . .DLB-71

Giles of Rome circa 1243-1316 . . . . .DLB-115

Giles, Henry 1809-1882 . . . . .DLB-64

Gilfillan, George 1813-1878 . . . . .DLB-144

Gill, Eric 1882-1940 . . . . .DLB-98

Gill, Sarah Prince 1728-1771 . . . . .DLB-200

Gill, William F., Company DLB-49

Gillespie, A. Lincoln, Jr. 1895-1950 . . . . . . .DLB-4

Gilliam, Florence ?-? DLB-4

Gilliatt, Penelope 1932-1993 . . . . .DLB-14

Gillott, Jacky 1939-1980 . . . . .DLB-14

Gilman, Caroline H. 1794-1888 . . . . . . .DLB-3, 73

Gilman, Charlotte Perkins 1860-1935 . . . .DLB-221

Gilman, W. and J. [publishing house] DLB-49

Gilmer, Elizabeth Meriwether 1861-1951 . .DLB-29

Gilmer, Francis Walker 1790-1826 . . . . . . .DLB-37

Gilmore, Mary 1865-1962 . . . . .DLB-260

Gilroy, Frank D. 1925- DLB-7

Gimferrer, Pere (Pedro) 1945- DLB-134

Gingrich, Arnold 1903-1976 . . . . .DLB-137

Ginsberg, Allen 1926-1997 . . . .DLB-5, 16, 169, 237; CDALB-1

Ginzburg, Natalia 1916-1991 . . . . .DLB-177

Ginzkey, Franz Karl 1871-1963 . . . . .DLB-81

Gioia, Dana 1950- DLB-120

Giono, Jean 1895-1970 . . . . .DLB-72

Giotti, Virgilio 1885-1957 . . . . .DLB-114

Giovanni, Nikki 1943- DLB-5, 41; CDALB-7

Gipson, Lawrence Henry 1880-1971 . . . . . .DLB-17

Girard, Rodolphe 1879-1956 . . . . .DLB-92

Giraudoux, Jean 1882-1944 . . . . .DLB-65

Gissing, George 1857-1903 . . . . .DLB-18, 135, 184

The Place of Realism in Fiction (1895) DLB-18

Giudici, Giovanni 1924- DLB-128

Giuliani, Alfredo 1924- DLB-128

Glackens, William J. 1870-1938 . . . . .DLB-188

Gladstone, William Ewart 1809-1898 . . . . .DLB-57, 184

Glaeser, Ernst 1902-1963 . . . . .DLB-69

Glancy, Diane 1941- DLB-175

Glanvill, Joseph 1636-1680 . . . . .DLB-252

Glanville, Brian 1931- DLB-15, 139

Glapthorne, Henry 1610-1643? DLB-58

Glasgow, Ellen 1873-1945 . . . . .DLB-9, 12

Glasier, Katharine Bruce 1867-1950 . . . . .DLB-190

Glaspell, Susan 1876-1948 . . . . .DLB-7, 9, 78, 228

Glass, Montague 1877-1934 . . . . .DLB-11

Glassco, John 1909-1981 . . . . .DLB-68

Glauser, Friedrich 1896-1938 . . . . .DLB-56

F. Gleason's Publishing Hall DLB-49

Gleim, Johann Wilhelm Ludwig 1719-1803 . . . . .DLB-97

Glendinning, Victoria 1937- DLB-155

The Cult of Biography Excerpts from the Second Folio Debate: "Biographies are generally a disease of English Literature" Y-86

Glidden, Frederick Dilley (Luke Short) 1908-1975 . . . . .DLB-256

Glinka, Fedor Nikolaevich 1786-1880 . . . .DLB-205

Glover, Keith 1966- DLB-249

Glover, Richard 1712-1785 . . . . .DLB-95

Glück, Louise 1943- DLB-5

Glyn, Elinor 1864-1943 . . . . .DLB-153

Gnedich, Nikolai Ivanovich 1784-1833 . . .DLB-205

Gobineau, Joseph-Arthur de 1816-1882 . . . . .DLB-123

Godber, John 1956- DLB-233

Godbout, Jacques 1933- DLB-53

Goddard, Morrill 1865-1937 . . . . .DLB-25

Goddard, William 1740-1817 . . . . .DLB-43

Godden, Rumer 1907-1998 . . . . .DLB-161

Godey, Louis A. 1804-1878 . . . . .DLB-73

Godey and McMichael DLB-49

Godfrey, Dave 1938- DLB-60

Godfrey, Thomas 1736-1763 . . . . .DLB-31

Godine, David R., Publisher DLB-46

Godkin, E. L. 1831-1902 . . . . .DLB-79

Godolphin, Sidney 1610-1643 . . . . .DLB-126

Godwin, Gail 1937- DLB-6, 234

Godwin, M. J., and Company DLB-154

Godwin, Mary Jane Clairmont 1766-1841 . . . . .DLB-163

Godwin, Parke 1816-1904 . . . . .DLB-3, 64, 250

Godwin, William 1756-1836 . . . . DLB-39, 104, ... 142, 158, 163, 262; CDBLB-3

Preface to *St. Leon* (1799) DLB-39

Goering, Reinhard 1887-1936 . . . . .DLB-118

Goes, Albrecht 1908- DLB-69

Goethe, Johann Wolfgang von 1749-1832 . . . . .DLB-94; CDWLB-2

Goetz, Curt 1888-1960 . . . . .DLB-124

Goffe, Thomas circa 1592-1629 . . . . .DLB-58

Goffstein, M. B. 1940- DLB-61

Gogarty, Oliver St. John 1878-1957 . . . .DLB-15, 19

Gogol, Nikolai Vasil'evich 1809-1852 . . . .DLB-198

Goines, Donald 1937-1974 . . . . .DLB-33

Gold, Herbert 1924- DLB-2; Y-81

Gold, Michael 1893-1967 . . . . .DLB-9, 28

Goldbarth, Albert 1948- DLB-120

Goldberg, Dick 1947- DLB-7

Golden Cockerel Press DLB-112

Golding, Arthur 1536-1606 . . . . .DLB-136

Golding, Louis 1895-1958 . . . . .DLB-195

Golding, William 1911-1993
.... DLB-15, 100, 255; Y-83; CDBLB-7

Goldman, Emma 1869-1940.......... DLB-221

Goldman, William 1931- DLB-44

Goldring, Douglas 1887-1960......... DLB-197

Goldsmith, Oliver 1730?-1774
.... DLB-39, 89, 104, 109, 142; CDBLB-2

Goldsmith, Oliver 1794-1861 .... DLB-99

Goldsmith Publishing Company DLB-46

Goldstein, Richard 1944- DLB-185

Gollancz, Sir Israel 1864-1930 .... DLB-201

Gollancz, Victor, Limited DLB-112

Gombrowicz, Witold
1904-1969 .... DLB-215; CDWLB-4

Gómez-Quiñones, Juan 1942- DLB-122

Gomme, Laurence James
[publishing house] DLB-46

Goncharov, Ivan Aleksandrovich
1812-1891............... DLB-238

Goncourt, Edmond de 1822-1896 ...... DLB-123

Goncourt, Jules de 1830-1870.......... DLB-123

Gonzales, Rodolfo "Corky" 1928- DLB-122

González, Angel 1925- DLB-108

Gonzalez, Genaro 1949- DLB-122

Gonzalez, Ray 1952- DLB-122

Gonzales-Berry, Erlinda 1942- DLB-209

"Chicano Language"................. DLB-82

González de Mireles, Jovita
1899-1983 .... DLB-122

González-T., César A. 1931- DLB-82

Goodbye, Gutenberg? A Lecture at the
New York Public Library,
18 April 1995, by Donald Lamm........ Y-95

Goodis, David 1917-1967 .... DLB-226

Goodison, Lorna 1947- DLB-157

Goodman, Allegra 1967- DLB-244

Goodman, Paul 1911-1972 .... DLB-130, 246

The Goodman Theatre DLB-7

Goodrich, Frances 1891-1984 and
Hackett, Albert 1900-1995 .... DLB-26

Goodrich, Samuel Griswold
1793-1860.............. DLB-1, 42, 73, 243

Goodrich, S. G. [publishing house]....... DLB-49

Goodspeed, C. E., and Company........ DLB-49

Goodwin, Stephen 1943- Y-82

Googe, Barnabe 1540-1594 .... DLB-132

Gookin, Daniel 1612-1687 .... DLB-24

Goran, Lester 1928- DLB-244

Gordimer, Nadine 1923- DLB-225; Y-91

Gordon, Adam Lindsay 1833-1870...... DLB-230

Gordon, Caroline
1895-1981 ....DLB-4, 9, 102; DS-17; Y-81

Gordon, Giles 1940- DLB-14, 139, 207

Gordon, Helen Cameron, Lady Russell
1867-1949..................... DLB-195

Gordon, Lyndall 1941- DLB-155

Gordon, Mary 1949- DLB-6; Y-81

Gordone, Charles 1925-1995 .... DLB-7

Gore, Catherine 1800-1861 .... DLB-116

Gore-Booth, Eva 1870-1926 .... DLB-240

Gores, Joe 1931- DLB-226

Gorey, Edward 1925-2000 .... DLB-61

Gorgias of Leontini
circa 485 B.C.-376 B.C. DLB-176

Görres, Joseph 1776-1848 .... DLB-90

Gosse, Edmund 1849-1928......DLB-57, 144, 184

Gosson, Stephen 1554-1624 ....DLB-172

The Schoole of Abuse (1579) DLB-172

Gotlieb, Phyllis 1926- DLB-88, 251

Go-Toba 1180-1239 .... DLB-203

Gottfried von Straßburg
died before 1230 ...... DLB-138; CDWLB-2

Gotthelf, Jeremias 1797-1854.......... DLB-133

Gottschalk circa 804/808-869 .... DLB-148

Gottsched, Johann Christoph
1700-1766...................... DLB-97

Götz, Johann Nikolaus 1721-1781....... DLB-97

Goudge, Elizabeth 1900-1984.......... DLB-191

Gough, John B. 1817-1886 .... DLB-243

Gould, Wallace 1882-1940............. DLB-54

Govoni, Corrado 1884-1965 .... DLB-114

Gower, John circa 1330-1408 .... DLB-146

Goyen, William 1915-1983 .....DLB-2, 218; Y-83

Goytisolo, José Augustín 1928- DLB-134

Gozzano, Guido 1883-1916 .... DLB-114

Grabbe, Christian Dietrich 1801-1836 ... DLB-133

Gracq, Julien 1910- DLB-83

Grady, Henry W. 1850-1889 .... DLB-23

Graf, Oskar Maria 1894-1967 .... DLB-56

Graf Rudolf
between circa 1170 and circa 1185 ... DLB-148

Graff, Gerald 1937- DLB-246

Grafton, Richard [publishing house]......DLB-170

Grafton, Sue 1940- DLB-226

Graham, Frank 1893-1965 .... DLB-241

Graham, George Rex 1813-1894 .... DLB-73

Graham, Gwethalyn 1913-1965 .... DLB-88

Graham, Jorie 1951- DLB-120

Graham, Katharine 1917- DLB-127

Graham, Lorenz 1902-1989 .... DLB-76

Graham, Philip 1915-1963 .... DLB-127

Graham, R. B. Cunninghame
1852-1936 ....DLB-98, 135, 174

Graham, Shirley 1896-1977 .... DLB-76

Graham, Stephen 1884-1975........... DLB-195

Graham, W. S. 1918- DLB-20

Graham, William H. [publishing house]... DLB-49

Graham, Winston 1910- DLB-77

Grahame, Kenneth
1859-1932 ....DLB-34, 141, 178

Grainger, Martin Allerdale 1874-1941 .... DLB-92

Gramatky, Hardie 1907-1979 .... DLB-22

Grand, Sarah 1854-1943..........DLB-135, 197

Grandbois, Alain 1900-1975 .... DLB-92

Grandson, Oton de circa 1345-1397..... DLB-208

Grange, John circa 1556-? DLB-136

Granich, Irwin (see Gold, Michael)

Granovsky, Timofei Nikolaevich
1813-1855 .... DLB-198

Grant, Anne MacVicar 1755-1838 ..... DLB-200

Grant, Duncan 1885-1978...............DS-10

Grant, George 1918-1988.............. DLB-88

Grant, George Monro 1835-1902........ DLB-99

Grant, Harry J. 1881-1963 .... DLB-29

Grant, James Edward 1905-1966 .... DLB-26

Grass, Günter 1927- ...DLB-75, 124; CDWLB-2

Grasty, Charles H. 1863-1924 .... DLB-25

Grau, Shirley Ann 1929- DLB-2, 218

Graves, John 1920- Y-83

Graves, Richard 1715-1804 .... DLB-39

Graves, Robert 1895-1985
....DLB-20, 100, 191; DS-18; Y-85; CDBLB-6

Gray, Alasdair 1934- DLB-194, 261

Gray, Asa 1810-1888 .... DLB-1, 235

Gray, David 1838-1861 .... DLB-32

Gray, Simon 1936- DLB-13

Gray, Thomas 1716-1771 .... DLB-109; CDBLB-2

Grayson, Richard 1951- DLB-234

Grayson, William J. 1788-1863.... DLB-3, 64, 248

The Great Bibliographers Series............ Y-93

The Great Modern Library Scam........... Y-98

The Great War and the Theater, 1914-1918
[Great Britain] DLB-10

The Great War Exhibition and Symposium at
the University of South Carolina........ Y-97

Grech, Nikolai Ivanovich 1787-1867..... DLB-198

Greeley, Horace 1811-1872 ...DLB-3, 43, 189, 250

Green, Adolph (see Comden, Betty)

Green, Anna Katharine
1846-1935 .... DLB-202, 221

Green, Duff 1791-1875 .... DLB-43

Green, Elizabeth Shippen 1871-1954 .... DLB-188

Green, Gerald 1922- DLB-28

Green, Henry 1905-1973 .... DLB-15

Green, Jonas 1712-1767............... DLB-31

Green, Joseph 1706-1780............... DLB-31

Green, Julien 1900-1998............. DLB-4, 72

Green, Paul 1894-1981.......DLB-7, 9, 249; Y-81

Green, T. and S. [publishing house]...... DLB-49

Green, T. H. 1836-1882.............. DLB-262

Green, Terence M. 1947- DLB-251

Green, Thomas Hill 1836-1882 .... DLB-190, 262

Green, Timothy [publishing house] DLB-49

Greenaway, Kate 1846-1901 .... DLB-141

Greenberg: Publisher DLB-46

Green Tiger Press..................... DLB-46

Greene, Asa 1789-1838................ DLB-11

Greene, Belle da Costa 1883-1950 ....DLB-187

Greene, Benjamin H.
[publishing house] DLB-49

Greene, Graham 1904-1991
............DLB-13, 15, 77, 100, 162, 201, 204;
Y-85, Y-91; CDBLB-7

Greene, Robert 1558-1592.........DLB-62, 167

Greene, Robert Bernard (Bob) Jr.
1947- DLB-185

Greenfield, George 1917-2000 .... Y-00

Greenhow, Robert 1800-1854 ....DLB-30

Greenlee, William B. 1872-1953 ....DLB-187

Greenough, Horatio 1805-1852......DLB-1, 235

Greenwell, Dora 1821-1882.........DLB-35, 199

Greenwillow Books DLB-46

Greenwood, Grace (see Lippincott, Sara Jane Clarke)

Greenwood, Walter 1903-1974 ......DLB-10, 191

Greer, Ben 1948- DLB-6

Greflinger, Georg 1620?-1677 ....DLB-164

Greg, W. R. 1809-1881 ....DLB-55

Greg, W. W. 1875-1959................DLB-201

Gregg, Josiah 1806-1850 ....DLB-183, 186

Gregg Press DLB-46

Gregory, Isabella Augusta Persse, Lady
1852-1932 ....DLB-10

Gregory, Horace 1898-1982 ....DLB-48

Gregory of Rimini circa 1300-1358 ......DLB-115

Gregynog Press DLB-112

Greiffenberg, Catharina Regina von
1633-1694 ....DLB-168

Greig, Noël 1944- DLB-245

Grenfell, Wilfred Thomason
1865-1940.......................DLB-92

Gress, Elsa 1919-1988 ....DLB-214

Greve, Felix Paul (see Grove, Frederick Philip)

Greville, Fulke, First Lord Brooke
1554-1628 ....DLB-62, 172

Grey, Sir George, K.C.B. 1812-1898.....DLB-184

Grey, Lady Jane 1537-1554 ....DLB-132

Grey Owl 1888-1938...........DLB-92; DS-17

Grey, Zane 1872-1939.............DLB-9, 212

Grey Walls Press DLB-112

Griboedov, Aleksandr Sergeevich
1795?-1829 ....DLB-205

Grier, Eldon 1917- DLB-88

Grieve, C. M. (see MacDiarmid, Hugh)

Griffin, Bartholomew flourished 1596....DLB-172

Griffin, Gerald 1803-1840 ....DLB-159

The Griffin Poetry Prize Y-00

Griffith, Elizabeth 1727?-1793 ....DLB-39, 89

Preface to *The Delicate Distress* (1769) DLB-39

Griffith, George 1857-1906 ....DLB-178

Griffiths, Ralph [publishing house] DLB-154

Griffiths, Trevor 1935- DLB-13, 245

Griggs, S. C., and Company DLB-49

Griggs, Sutton Elbert 1872-1930 ....DLB-50

Grignon, Claude-Henri 1894-1976.......DLB-68

Grigorovich, Dmitrii Vasil'evich
1822-1899 ....DLB-238

Grigson, Geoffrey 1905- DLB-27

Grillparzer, Franz
1791-1872 ....DLB-133; CDWLB-2

Grimald, Nicholas
circa 1519-circa 1562.............DLB-136

Grimké, Angelina Weld 1880-1958....DLB-50, 54

Grimké, Sarah Moore 1792-1873........DLB-239

Grimm, Hans 1875-1959 ....DLB-66

Grimm, Jacob 1785-1863 ....DLB-90

Grimm, Wilhelm
1786-1859 ....DLB-90; CDWLB-2

Grimmelshausen, Johann Jacob Christoffel von
1621 or 1622-1676......DLB-168; CDWLB-2

Grimshaw, Beatrice Ethel 1871-1953.....DLB-174

Grindal, Edmund 1519 or 1520-1583 ....DLB-132

Gripe, Maria (Kristina) 1923- DLB-257

Griswold, Rufus Wilmot
1815-1857...........DLB-3, 59, 250

Grosart, Alexander Balloch 1827-1899 ...DLB-184

Gross, Milt 1895-1953................DLB-11

Grosset and Dunlap....................DLB-49

Grossman, Allen 1932- DLB-193

Grossman Publishers...................DLB-46

Grosseteste, Robert circa 1160-1253 .....DLB-115

Grosvenor, Gilbert H. 1875-1966 ....DLB-91

Groth, Klaus 1819-1899...............DLB-129

Groulx, Lionel 1878-1967 ....DLB-68

Grove, Frederick Philip 1879-1949 ....DLB-92

Grove Press DLB-46

Grubb, Davis 1919-1980 ....DLB-6

Gruelle, Johnny 1880-1938 ....DLB-22

von Grumbach, Argula
1492-after 1563? DLB-179

Grymeston, Elizabeth
before 1563-before 1604 ....DLB-136

Gryphius, Andreas
1616-1664 ....DLB-164; CDWLB-2

Gryphius, Christian 1649-1706 ....DLB-168

Guare, John 1938- DLB-7, 249

Guerra, Tonino 1920-................DLB-128

Guest, Barbara 1920- DLB-5, 193

Guèvremont, Germaine 1893-1968 ....DLB-68

Guidacci, Margherita 1921-1992 ....DLB-128

Guide to the Archives of Publishers, Journals,
and Literary Agents in North American
Libraries Y-93

Guillén, Jorge 1893-1984 ....DLB-108

Guilloux, Louis 1899-1980 ....DLB-72

Guilpin, Everard
circa 1572-after 1608? DLB-136

Guiney, Louise Imogen 1861-1920 ....DLB-54

Guiterman, Arthur 1871-1943 ....DLB-11

Günderrode, Caroline von
1780-1806 ....DLB-90

Gundulić, Ivan
1589-1638 ....DLB-147; CDWLB-4

Gunn, Bill 1934-1989.................DLB-38

Gunn, James E. 1923- DLB-8

Gunn, Neil M. 1891-1973 ....DLB-15

Gunn, Thom 1929- DLB-27; CDBLB-8

Gunnars, Kristjana 1948- DLB-60

Günther, Johann Christian
1695-1723 ....DLB-168

Gurik, Robert 1932- DLB-60

Gustafson, Ralph 1909-1995 ....DLB-88

Gustafsson, Lars 1936- DLB-257

Gütersloh, Albert Paris 1887-1973 ....DLB-81

Guthrie, A. B., Jr. 1901-1991.........DLB-6, 212

Guthrie, Ramon 1896-1973 ....DLB-4

The Guthrie Theater DLB-7

Guthrie, Thomas Anstey (see Anstey, FC)

Gutzkow, Karl 1811-1878 ....DLB-133

Guy, Ray 1939- DLB-60

Guy, Rosa 1925- DLB-33

Guyot, Arnold 1807-1884 .... DS-13

Gwynne, Erskine 1898-1948 ....DLB-4

Gyles, John 1680-1755 ....DLB-99

Gyllensten, Lars 1921- DLB-257

Gysin, Brion 1916- DLB-16

H

H.D. (see Doolittle, Hilda)

Habermas, Jürgen 1929- DLB-242

Habington, William 1605-1654.........DLB-126

Hacker, Marilyn 1942- DLB-120

Hackett, Albert (see Goodrich, Frances)

Hacks, Peter 1928- DLB-124

Hadas, Rachel 1948- DLB-120

Hadden, Briton 1898-1929 ....DLB-91

Hagedorn, Friedrich von 1708-1754......DLB-168

Hagelstange, Rudolf 1912-1984.........DLB-69

Haggard, H. Rider
1856-1925 ....DLB-70, 156, 174, 178

Haggard, William 1907-1993.............. Y-93

Hagy, Alyson 1960-................DLB-244

Hahn-Hahn, Ida Gräfin von
1805-1880 ....DLB-133

Haig-Brown, Roderick 1908-1976 ....DLB-88

Haight, Gordon S. 1901-1985 ....DLB-103

Hailey, Arthur 1920- DLB-88; Y-82

Haines, John 1924- DLB-5, 212

Hake, Edward flourished 1566-1604.....DLB-136

Hake, Thomas Gordon 1809-1895 ....DLB-32

Hakluyt, Richard 1552?-1616 ....DLB-136

Halas, František 1901-1949 ....DLB-215

Halbe, Max 1865-1944 ....DLB-118

Halberstam, David 1934- DLB-241

Haldane, J. B. S. 1892-1964 ....DLB-160

Haldeman, Joe 1943- DLB-8

Haldeman-Julius Company DLB-46

Haldone, Charlotte 1894-1969 ....DLB-191

Hale, E. J., and Son DLB-49

Hale, Edward Everett
1822-1909 .... DLB-1, 42, 74, 235

Hale, Janet Campbell 1946- DLB-175

Hale, Kathleen 1898- DLB-160

Hale, Leo Thomas (see Ebon)

Hale, Lucretia Peabody 1820-1900....... DLB-42

Hale, Nancy
1908-1988 ....DLB-86; DS-17; Y-80, Y-88

Hale, Sarah Josepha (Buell)
1788-1879.............. DLB-1, 42, 73, 243

Hale, Susan 1833-1910............... DLB-221

Hales, John 1584-1656 .... DLB-151

Halévy, Ludovic 1834-1908 .... DLB-192

Haley, Alex 1921-1992....... DLB-38; CDALB-7

Haliburton, Thomas Chandler
1796-1865.................... DLB-11, 99

Hall, Anna Maria 1800-1881 .... DLB-159

Hall, Donald 1928- DLB-5

Hall, Edward 1497-1547 .... DLB-132

Hall, Halsey 1898-1977............... DLB-241

Hall, James 1793-1868 ....DLB-73, 74

Hall, Joseph 1574-1656 .... DLB-121, 151

Hall, Radclyffe 1880-1943 .... DLB-191

Hall, Samuel [publishing house] DLB-49

Hall, Sarah Ewing 1761-1830 .... DLB-200

Hall, Stuart 1932- DLB-242

Hallam, Arthur Henry 1811-1833 .... DLB-32

On Some of the Characteristics of Modern
Poetry and On the Lyrical Poems of
Alfred Tennyson (1831)............. DLB-32

Halleck, Fitz-Greene 1790-1867 ...... DLB-3, 250

Haller, Albrecht von 1708-1777......... DLB-168

Halliday, Brett (see Dresser, Davis)

Halliwell-Phillipps, James Orchard
1820-1889 .... DLB-184

Hallmann, Johann Christian
1640-1704 or 1716? DLB-168

Hallmark Editions DLB-46

Halper, Albert 1904-1984.............. DLB-9

Halperin, John William 1941- DLB-111

Halstead, Murat 1829-1908 .... DLB-23

Hamann, Johann Georg 1730-1788....... DLB-97

Hamburger, Michael 1924- DLB-27

Hamilton, Alexander 1712-1756 .... DLB-31

Hamilton, Alexander 1755?-1804 .... DLB-37

Hamilton, Cicely 1872-1952.........DLB-10, 197

Hamilton, Edmond 1904-1977 .... DLB-8

Hamilton, Elizabeth 1758-1816..... DLB-116, 158

Hamilton, Gail (see Corcoran, Barbara)

Hamilton, Gail (see Dodge, Mary Abigail)

Hamilton, Hamish, Limited DLB-112

Hamilton, Ian 1938- DLB-40, 155

Hamilton, Janet 1795-1873 .... DLB-199

Hamilton, Mary Agnes 1884-1962 ...... DLB-197

Hamilton, Patrick 1904-1962 .... DLB-10, 191

Hamilton, Virginia 1936- DLB-33, 52

Hamilton, Sir William 1788-1856 .... DLB-262

Hammett, Dashiell
1894-1961 .... DLB-226; DS-6; CDALB-5

The Glass Key and Other Dashiell Hammett
Mysteries.................... Y-96

Dashiell Hammett: An Appeal in *TAC*....... Y-91

Hammon, Jupiter 1711-died between
1790 and 1806 .... DLB-31, 50

Hammond, John ?-1663 .... DLB-24

Hamner, Earl 1923- DLB-6

Hampson, John 1901-1955............ DLB-191

Hampton, Christopher 1946- DLB-13

Handel-Mazzetti, Enrica von 1871-1955... DLB-81

Handke, Peter 1942- DLB-85, 124

Handlin, Oscar 1915- DLB-17

Hankin, St. John 1869-1909 .... DLB-10

Hanley, Clifford 1922- DLB-14

Hanley, James 1901-1985............. DLB-191

Hannah, Barry 1942- DLB-6, 234

Hannay, James 1827-1873 .... DLB-21

Hano, Arnold 1922- DLB-241

Hansberry, Lorraine
1930-1965 .... DLB-7, 38; CDALB-1

Hansen, Martin A. 1909-1955 .... DLB-214

Hansen, Thorkild 1927-1989 .... DLB-214

Hanson, Elizabeth 1684-1737 .... DLB-200

Hapgood, Norman 1868-1937 .... DLB-91

Happel, Eberhard Werner 1647-1690.... DLB-168

The Harbinger 1845-1849............. DLB-223

Harcourt Brace Jovanovich DLB-46

Hardenberg, Friedrich von (see Novalis)

Harding, Walter 1917- DLB-111

Hardwick, Elizabeth 1916- DLB-6

Hardy, Frank 1917-1994.............. DLB-260

Hardy, Thomas
1840-1928 ...... DLB-18, 19, 135; CDBLB-5

"Candour in English Fiction" (1890) DLB-18

Hare, Cyril 1900-1958 .... DLB-77

Hare, David 1947- DLB-13

Hare, R. M. 1919-2002............... DLB-262

Hargrove, Marion 1919- DLB-11

Häring, Georg Wilhelm Heinrich
(see Alexis, Willibald)

Harington, Donald 1935- DLB-152

Harington, Sir John 1560-1612......... DLB-136

Harjo, Joy 1951- DLB-120, 175

Harkness, Margaret (John Law)
1854-1923 .... DLB-197

Harley, Edward, second Earl of Oxford
1689-1741..................... DLB-213

Harley, Robert, first Earl of Oxford
1661-1724..................... DLB-213

Harlow, Robert 1923- DLB-60

Harman, Thomas flourished 1566-1573.. DLB-136

Harness, Charles L. 1915- DLB-8

Harnett, Cynthia 1893-1981........... DLB-161

Harper, Edith Alice Mary (see Wickham, Anna)

Harper, Fletcher 1806-1877 .... DLB-79

Harper, Frances Ellen Watkins
1825-1911 .... DLB-50, 221

Harper, Michael S. 1938- DLB-41

Harper and Brothers DLB-49

Harpur, Charles 1813-1868 .... DLB-230

Harraden, Beatrice 1864-1943 .... DLB-153

Harrap, George G., and Company
Limited...................... DLB-112

Harriot, Thomas 1560-1621........... DLB-136

Harris, Alexander 1805-1874 .... DLB-230

Harris, Benjamin ?-circa 1720....... DLB-42, 43

Harris, Christie 1907- DLB-88

Harris, Frank 1856-1931 ....DLB-156, 197

Harris, George Washington
1814-1869 .... DLB-3, 11, 248

Harris, Joel Chandler
1848-1908 ....DLB-11, 23, 42, 78, 91

Harris, Mark 1922- DLB-2; Y-80

Harris, Wilson 1921- DLB-117; CDWLB-3

Harrison, Mrs. Burton
(see Harrison, Constance Cary)

Harrison, Charles Yale 1898-1954....... DLB-68

Harrison, Constance Cary 1843-1920 ... DLB-221

Harrison, Frederic 1831-1923........DLB-57, 190

"On Style in English Prose" (1898) DLB-57

Harrison, Harry 1925- DLB-8

Harrison, James P., Company DLB-49

Harrison, Jim 1937- Y-82

Harrison, M. John 1945- DLB-261

Harrison, Mary St. Leger Kingsley
(see Malet, Lucas)

Harrison, Paul Carter 1936- DLB-38

Harrison, Susan Frances 1859-1935...... DLB-99

Harrison, Tony 1937- DLB-40, 245

Harrison, William 1535-1593.......... DLB-136

Harrison, William 1933- DLB-234

Harrisse, Henry 1829-1910 .... DLB-47

The Harry Ransom Humanities
Research Center at the University
of Texas at Austin Y-00

Harryman, Carla 1952- DLB-193

Harsdörffer, Georg Philipp 1607-1658 ... DLB-164

Harsent, David 1942- DLB-40

Hart, Albert Bushnell 1854-1943 ....DLB-17

Hart, Anne 1768-1834 .... DLB-200

Hart, Elizabeth 1771-1833............. DLB-200

Hart, Julia Catherine 1796-1867 .... DLB-99

The Lorenz Hart Centenary............... Y-95

Hart, Moss 1904-1961 .... DLB-7

Hart, Oliver 1723-1795............... DLB-31

Hart-Davis, Rupert, Limited.......... DLB-112

Harte, Bret 1836-1902
.........DLB-12, 64, 74, 79, 186; CDALB-3

Harte, Edward Holmead 1922- DLB-127

Harte, Houston Harriman 1927- DLB-127

Hartlaub, Felix 1913-1945 .... DLB-56

Hartlebon, Otto Erich 1864-1905....... DLB-118

Hartley, David 1705-1757 .... DLB-252

Hartley, L. P. 1895-1972.......... DLB-15, 139

Hartley, Marsden 1877-1943 . . . . .DLB-54

Hartling, Peter 1933- DLB-75

Hartman, Geoffrey H. 1929- DLB-67

Hartmann, Sadakichi 1867-1944 . . . . .DLB-54

Hartmann von Aue
circa 1160-circa 1205. . . .DLB-138; CDWLB-2

Harvey, Gabriel 1550?-1631 . . . DLB-167, 213, 236

Harvey, Jean-Charles 1891-1967 . . . . .DLB-88

Harvill Press Limited DLB-112

Harwood, Lee 1939- DLB-40

Harwood, Ronald 1934- DLB-13

Hašek, Jaroslav 1883-1923 . . .DLB-215; CDWLB-4

Haskins, Charles Homer 1870-1937 . . . . . .DLB-47

Haslam, Gerald 1937- DLB-212

Hass, Robert 1941- DLB-105, 206

Hasselstrom, Linda M. 1943- DLB-256

Hastings, Michael 1938- DLB-233

Hatar, Győző 1914- DLB-215

The Hatch-Billops Collection. DLB-76

Hathaway, William 1944- DLB-120

Hauff, Wilhelm 1802-1827 . . . . .DLB-90

A Haughty and Proud Generation (1922),
by Ford Madox Hueffer DLB-36

Haugwitz, August Adolph von
1647-1706. .DLB-168

Hauptmann, Carl 1858-1921 . . . . . . .DLB-66, 118

Hauptmann, Gerhart
1862-1946 . . . . .DLB-66, 118; CDWLB-2

Hauser, Marianne 1910- Y-83

Havel, Václav 1936- DLB-232; CDWLB-4

Haven, Alice B. Neal 1827-1863. . . . . . . .DLB-260

Havergal, Frances Ridley 1836-1879 . . . . .DLB-199

Hawes, Stephen 1475?-before 1529 . . . . . .DLB-132

Hawker, Robert Stephen 1803-1875 . . . . . .DLB-32

Hawkes, John
1925-1998 . . . . .DLB-2, 7, 227; Y-80, Y-98

John Hawkes: A Tribute Y-98

Hawkesworth, John 1720-1773. . . . . .DLB-142

Hawkins, Sir Anthony Hope (see Hope, Anthony)

Hawkins, Sir John 1719-1789 . . . . . . .DLB-104, 142

Hawkins, Walter Everette 1883-? DLB-50

Hawthorne, Nathaniel
1804-1864 . . . .DLB-1, 74, 183, 223; CDALB-2

Hawthorne, Nathaniel 1804-1864 and
Hawthorne, Sophia Peabody
1809-1871 .DLB-183

Hawthorne, Sophia Peabody
1809-1871 . . . . .DLB-183, 239

Hay, John 1835-1905. . . . . DLB-12, 47, 189

Hayashi, Fumiko 1903-1951 . . . . .DLB-180

Haycox, Ernest 1899-1950. . . . . .DLB-206

Haycraft, Anna Margaret (see Ellis, Alice Thomas)

Hayden, Robert
1913-1980 . . . . .DLB-5, 76; CDALB-1

Haydon, Benjamin Robert
1786-1846 .DLB-110

Hayes, John Michael 1919- DLB-26

Hayley, William 1745-1820 . . . . . . .DLB-93, 142

Haym, Rudolf 1821-1901 . . . . .DLB-129

Hayman, Robert 1575-1629. . . . . .DLB-99

Hayman, Ronald 1932- DLB-155

Hayne, Paul Hamilton
1830-1886 . . . . DLB-3, 64, 79, 248

Hays, Mary 1760-1843 . . . . .DLB-142, 158

Hayward, John 1905-1965. . . . . .DLB-201

Haywood, Eliza 1693?-1756. . . . . .DLB-39

From the Dedication, *Lasselia* (1723) DLB-39

From *The Tea-Table* *DLB-39*

From the Preface to *The Disguis'd
Prince* (1723) .DLB-39

Hazard, Willis P. [publishing house] DLB-49

Hazlitt, William 1778-1830 . . . . . . .DLB-110, 158

Hazzard, Shirley 1931- Y-82

Head, Bessie
1937-1986 . . . . DLB-117, 225; CDWLB-3

Headley, Joel T. 1813-1897 . . .DLB-30, 183; DS-13

Heaney, Seamus
1939- DLB-40; Y-95; CDBLB-8

Heard, Nathan C. 1936- DLB-33

Hearn, Lafcadio 1850-1904 . . . . . .DLB-12, 78, 189

Hearn, Mary Anne (Marianne Farningham,
Eva Hope) 1834-1909 . . . . .DLB-240

Hearne, John 1926- DLB-117

Hearne, Samuel 1745-1792. . . . . .DLB-99

Hearne, Thomas 1678?-1735 . . . . .DLB-213

Hearst, William Randolph 1863-1951 . . . . .DLB-25

Hearst, William Randolph, Jr.
1908-1993 .DLB-127

Heartman, Charles Frederick
1883-1953 .DLB-187

Heath, Catherine 1924- DLB-14

Heath, James Ewell 1792-1862. . . . . .DLB-248

Heath, Roy A. K. 1926- DLB-117

Heath-Stubbs, John 1918- DLB-27

Heavysege, Charles 1816-1876 . . . . .DLB-99

Hebbel, Friedrich
1813-1863 . . . . .DLB-129; CDWLB-2

Hebel, Johann Peter 1760-1826 . . . . .DLB-90

Heber, Richard 1774-1833 . . . . .DLB-184

Hébert, Anne 1916-2000 . . . . .DLB-68

Hébert, Jacques 1923- DLB-53

Hecht, Anthony 1923- DLB-5, 169

Hecht, Ben 1894-1964 . . . DLB-7, 9, 25, 26, 28, 86

Hecker, Isaac Thomas 1819-1888 . . . . .DLB-1, 243

Hedge, Frederic Henry
1805-1890 . . . . .DLB-1, 59, 243

Hefner, Hugh M. 1926- DLB-137

Hegel, Georg Wilhelm Friedrich
1770-1831 .DLB-90

Heide, Robert 1939- DLB-249

Heidish, Marcy 1947- Y-82

Heißenbüttel, Helmut 1921-1996 . . . . . . .DLB-75

Heike monogatari DLB-203

Hein, Christoph 1944- DLB-124; CDWLB-2

Hein, Piet 1905-1996 . . . . .DLB-214

Heine, Heinrich 1797-1856. . . . DLB-90; CDWLB-2

Heinemann, Larry 1944- DS-9

Heinemann, William, Limited DLB-112

Heinesen, William 1900-1991 . . . . .DLB-214

Heinlein, Robert A. 1907-1988 . . . . .DLB-8

Heinrich Julius of Brunswick
1564-1613 .DLB-164

Heinrich von dem Türlîn
flourished circa 1230. . . . . .DLB-138

Heinrich von Melk
flourished after 1160 . . . . .DLB-148

Heinrich von Veldeke
circa 1145-circa 1190. . . . . .DLB-138

Heinrich, Willi 1920- DLB-75

Heinse, Wilhelm 1746-1803. . . . . .DLB-94

Heinz, W. C. 1915- DLB-171

Heiskell, John 1872-1972 . . . . .DLB-127

Hejinian, Lyn 1941- DLB-165

Heliand circa 850 . . . . .DLB-148

Heller, Joseph
1923-1999 . . . . DLB-2, 28, 227; Y-80, Y-99

Heller, Michael 1937- DLB-165

Hellman, Lillian 1906-1984 . . . . . DLB-7, 228; Y-84

Hellwig, Johann 1609-1674 . . . . .DLB-164

Helprin, Mark 1947- Y-85; CDALB-7

Helwig, David 1938- DLB-60

Hemans, Felicia 1793-1835. . . . . .DLB-96

Hemenway, Abby Maria 1828-1890 . . . . .DLB-243

Hemingway, Ernest 1899-1961
. . . . .DLB-4, 9, 102, 210; Y-81, Y-87, Y-99;
DS-1, DS-15, DS-16; CDALB-4

The Hemingway Centenary Celebration at the
JFK Library. Y-99

Ernest Hemingway: A Centennial
Celebration Y-99

The Ernest Hemingway Collection at the
John F. Kennedy Library Y-99

Ernest Hemingway Declines to Introduce
War and Peace. Y-01

Ernest Hemingway's Reaction to James Gould
Cozzens. Y-98

Ernest Hemingway's Toronto Journalism
Revisited: With Three Previously
Unrecorded Stories Y-92

Falsifying Hemingway Y-96

Hemingway: Twenty-Five Years Later Y-85

Not Immediately Discernible . . . but Eventually
Quite Clear: The *First Light* and *Final Years*
of Hemingway's Centenary Y-99

Hemingway Salesmen's Dummies. Y-00

Second International Hemingway Colloquium:
Cuba. Y-98

Hémon, Louis 1880-1913 . . . . .DLB-92

Hempel, Amy 1951- DLB-218

Hemphill, Paul 1936- Y-87

Hénault, Gilles 1920- DLB-88

Henchman, Daniel 1689-1761 . . . . .DLB-24

Henderson, Alice Corbin 1881-1949 . . . . . .DLB-54

Henderson, Archibald 1877-1963. . . . . . . .DLB-103

Henderson, David 1942- DLB-41

Henderson, George Wylie 1904- DLB-51

Henderson, Zenna 1917-1983 .... DLB-8

Henighan, Tom 1934- DLB-251

Henisch, Peter 1943- DLB-85

Henley, Beth 1952- Y-86

Henley, William Ernest 1849-1903 ...... DLB-19

Henning, Rachel 1826-1914 .... DLB-230

Henningsen, Agnes 1868-1962 .... DLB-214

Henniker, Florence 1855-1923 .... DLB-135

Henry, Alexander 1739-1824 .... DLB-99

Henry, Buck 1930- DLB-26

Henry VIII of England 1491-1547 ...... DLB-132

Henry of Ghent
circa 1217-1229 - 1293 .... DLB-115

Henry, Marguerite 1902-1997 .... DLB-22

Henry, O. (see Porter, William Sydney)

Henry, Robert Selph 1889-1970 .... DLB-17

Henry, Will (see Allen, Henry W.)

Henryson, Robert
1420s or 1430s-circa 1505 .... DLB-146

Henschke, Alfred (see Klabund)

Hensley, Sophie Almon 1866-1946 ...... DLB-99

Henson, Lance 1944- DLB-175

Henty, G. A. 1832?-1902 .... DLB-18, 141

Hentz, Caroline Lee 1800-1856 ...... DLB-3, 248

Heraclitus
flourished circa 500 B.C. DLB-176

Herbert, Agnes circa 1880-1960 .... DLB-174

Herbert, Alan Patrick 1890-1971 .... DLB-10, 191

Herbert, Edward, Lord, of Cherbury
1582-1648 .... DLB-121, 151, 252

Herbert, Frank 1920-1986 ..... DLB-8; CDALB-7

Herbert, George 1593-1633 .. DLB-126; CDBLB-1

Herbert, Henry William 1807-1858 .... DLB-3, 73

Herbert, John 1926- DLB-53

Herbert, Mary Sidney, Countess of Pembroke
(see Sidney, Mary)

Herbert, Xavier 1901-1984 .... DLB-260

Herbert, Zbigniew
1924-1998 .... DLB-232; CDWLB-4

Herbst, Josephine 1892-1969 .... DLB-9

Herburger, Gunter 1932- DLB-75, 124

Hercules, Frank E. M. 1917-1996 .... DLB-33

Herder, Johann Gottfried 1744-1803 ..... DLB-97

Herder, B., Book Company DLB-49

Heredia, José-María de 1842-1905 ...... DLB-217

Herford, Charles Harold 1853-1931 .... DLB-149

Hergesheimer, Joseph 1880-1954 ..... DLB-9, 102

Heritage Press DLB-46

Hermann the Lame 1013-1054 .... DLB-148

Hermes, Johann Timotheus
1738-1821 .... DLB-97

Hermlin, Stephan 1915-1997 .... DLB-69

Hernández, Alfonso C. 1938- DLB-122

Hernández, Inés 1947- DLB-122

Hernández, Miguel 1910-1942 .... DLB-134

Hernton, Calvin C. 1932- DLB-38

Herodotus circa 484 B.C.-circa 420 B.C.
.... DLB-176; CDWLB-1

Heron, Robert 1764-1807 .... DLB-142

Herr, Michael 1940- DLB-185

Herrera, Juan Felipe 1948- DLB-122

Herrick, E. R., and Company DLB-49

Herrick, Robert 1591-1674 .... DLB-126

Herrick, Robert 1868-1938 .... DLB-9, 12, 78

Herrick, William 1915- Y-83

Herrmann, John 1900-1959 .... DLB-4

Hersey, John 1914-1993 ... DLB-6, 185; CDALB-7

Hertel, François 1905-1985 .... DLB-68

Hervé-Bazin, Jean Pierre Marie (see Bazin, Hervé)

Hervey, John, Lord 1696-1743 .... DLB-101

Herwig, Georg 1817-1875 .... DLB-133

Herzog, Emile Salomon Wilhelm
(see Maurois, André)

Hesiod eighth century B.C. DLB-176

Hesse, Hermann
1877-1962 .... DLB-66; CDWLB-2

Hessus, Helius Eobanus 1488-1540 ..... DLB-179

Hewat, Alexander circa 1743-circa 1824 ... DLB-30

Hewitt, John 1907- DLB-27

Hewlett, Maurice 1861-1923 .... DLB-34, 156

Heyen, William 1940- DLB-5

Heyer, Georgette 1902-1974 .... DLB-77, 191

Heym, Stefan 1913- DLB-69

Heyse, Paul 1830-1914 .... DLB-129

Heytesbury, William
circa 1310-1372 or 1373 .... DLB-115

Heyward, Dorothy 1890-1961 .... DLB-7, 249

Heyward, DuBose 1885-1940 ...DLB-7, 9, 45, 249

Heywood, John 1497?-1580? DLB-136

Heywood, Thomas
1573 or 1574-1641 .... DLB-62

Hibbs, Ben 1901-1975 .... DLB-137

Hichens, Robert S. 1864-1950 .... DLB-153

Hickey, Emily 1845-1924 .... DLB-199

Hickman, William Albert 1877-1957 ..... DLB-92

Hicks, Granville 1901-1982 .... DLB-246

Hidalgo, José Luis 1919-1947 .... DLB-108

Hiebert, Paul 1892-1987 .... DLB-68

Hieng, Andrej 1925- DLB-181

Hierro, José 1922- DLB-108

Higgins, Aidan 1927- DLB-14

Higgins, Colin 1941-1988 .... DLB-26

Higgins, George V.
1939-1999 .... DLB-2; Y-81, Y-98, Y-99

George V. Higgins to Julian Symons Y-99

Higginson, Thomas Wentworth
1823-1911 .... DLB-1, 64, 243

Highwater, Jamake 1942?- DLB-52; Y-85

Hijuelos, Oscar 1951- DLB-145

Hildegard von Bingen 1098-1179 .... DLB-148

Das Hildebrandslied
circa 820 .... DLB-148; CDWLB-2

Hildesheimer, Wolfgang
1916-1991 .... DLB-69, 124

Hildreth, Richard 1807-1865 .. DLB-1, 30, 59, 235

Hill, Aaron 1685-1750 .... DLB-84

Hill, Geoffrey 1932- DLB-40; CDBLB-8

Hill, George M., Company DLB-49

Hill, "Sir" John 1714?-1775 .... DLB-39

Hill, Lawrence, and Company,
Publishers DLB-46

Hill, Leslie 1880-1960 .... DLB-51

Hill, Susan 1942- DLB-14, 139

Hill, Walter 1942- DLB-44

Hill and Wang DLB-46

Hillberry, Conrad 1928- DLB-120

Hillerman, Tony 1925- DLB-206

Hilliard, Gray and Company DLB-49

Hills, Lee 1906- DLB-127

Hillyer, Robert 1895-1961 .... DLB-54

Hilton, James 1900-1954 .... DLB-34, 77

Hilton, Walter died 1396 .... DLB-146

Hilton and Company DLB-49

Himes, Chester 1909-1984 ....DLB-2, 76, 143, 226

Hindmarsh, Joseph [publishing house] DLB-170

Hine, Daryl 1936- DLB-60

Hingley, Ronald 1920- DLB-155

Hinojosa-Smith, Rolando 1929- DLB-82

Hinton, S. E. 1948- CDALB-7

Hippel, Theodor Gottlieb von
1741-1796 .... DLB-97

Hippocrates of Cos flourished circa 425 B.C.
.... DLB-176; CDWLB-1

Hirabayashi, Taiko 1905-1972 .... DLB-180

Hirsch, E. D., Jr. 1928- DLB-67

Hirsch, Edward 1950- DLB-120

Hoagland, Edward 1932- DLB-6

Hoagland, Everett H., III 1942- DLB-41

Hoban, Russell 1925- DLB-52; Y-90

Hobbes, Thomas 1588-1679 ...... DLB-151, 252

Hobby, Oveta 1905- DLB-127

Hobby, William 1878-1964 .... DLB-127

Hobsbaum, Philip 1932- DLB-40

Hobson, Laura Z. 1900- DLB-28

Hobson, Sarah 1947- DLB-204

Hoby, Thomas 1530-1566 .... DLB-132

Hoccleve, Thomas
circa 1368-circa 1437 .... DLB-146

Hochhuth, Rolf 1931- DLB-124

Hochman, Sandra 1936- DLB-5

Hocken, Thomas Morland
1836-1910 .... DLB-184

Hodder and Stoughton, Limited DLB-106

Hodgins, Jack 1938- DLB-60

Hodgman, Helen 1945- DLB-14

Hodgskin, Thomas 1787-1869 .... DLB-158

Hodgson, Ralph 1871-1962 .... DLB-19

Hodgson, William Hope
1877-1918. . . . . DLB-70, 153, 156, 178

Hoe, Robert III 1839-1909 . . . . DLB-187

Hoeg, Peter 1957- DLB-214

Højholt, Per 1928- DLB-214

Hoffenstein, Samuel 1890-1947 . . . . .DLB-11

Hoffman, Charles Fenno 1806-1884 . . .DLB-3, 250

Hoffman, Daniel 1923- DLB-5

Hoffmann, E. T. A.
1776-1822 . . . . DLB-90; CDWLB-2

Hoffman, Frank B. 1888-1958 . . . . .DLB-188

Hoffman, William 1925- DLB-234

Hoffmanswaldau, Christian Hoffman von
1616-1679 .DLB-168

Hofmann, Michael 1957- DLB-40

Hofmannsthal, Hugo von
1874-1929 . . . . DLB-81, 118; CDWLB-2

Hofstadter, Richard 1916-1970 . . . . . . DLB-17, 246

Hogan, Desmond 1950- DLB-14

Hogan, Linda 1947- DLB-175

Hogan and Thompson. DLB-49

Hogarth Press DLB-112

Hogg, James 1770-1835 . . . . .DLB-93, 116, 159

Hohberg, Wolfgang Helmhard Freiherr von
1612-1688 .DLB-168

von Hohenheim, Philippus Aureolus
Theophrastus Bombastus (see Paracelsus)

Hohl, Ludwig 1904-1980. . . . . .DLB-56

Holbrook, David 1923- DLB-14, 40

Holcroft, Thomas 1745-1809 . . . . .DLB-39, 89, 158

Preface to *Alwyn* (1780). DLB-39

Holden, Jonathan 1941- DLB-105

"Contemporary Verse Story-telling" DLB-105

Holden, Molly 1927-1981 . . . . .DLB-40

Hölderlin, Friedrich 1770-1843 DLB-90; CDWLB-2

Holdstock, Robert 1948- DLB-261

Holiday House. DLB-46

Holinshed, Raphael died 1580. . . . . .DLB-167

Holland, J. G. 1819-1881 . . . . DS-13

Holland, Norman N. 1927- DLB-67

Hollander, John 1929- DLB-5

Holley, Marietta 1836-1926 . . . . .DLB-11

Hollinghurst, Alan 1954- DLB-207

Hollingsworth, Margaret 1940- DLB-60

Hollo, Anselm 1934- DLB-40

Holloway, Emory 1885-1977 . . . . .DLB-103

Holloway, John 1920- DLB-27

Holloway House Publishing Company DLB-46

Holme, Constance 1880-1955 . . . . .DLB-34

Holmes, Abraham S. 1821?-1908 . . . . . . .DLB-99

Holmes, John Clellon 1926-1988 . . . . .DLB-16, 237

"Four Essays on the Beat Generation". DLB-16

Holmes, Mary Jane 1825-1907. . . . . .DLB-202, 221

Holmes, Oliver Wendell
1809-1894 . . . . . . .DLB-1, 189, 235; CDALB-2

Holmes, Richard 1945- DLB-155

The Cult of Biography
Excerpts from the Second Folio Debate:
"Biographies are generally a disease of
English Literature" Y-86

Holmes, Thomas James 1874-1959 . . . . . .DLB-187

Holroyd, Michael 1935- DLB-155; Y-99

Holst, Hermann E. von 1841-1904 . . . . . . .DLB-47

Holt, Henry, and Company DLB-49

Holt, John 1721-1784 . . . . .DLB-43

Holt, Rinehart and Winston DLB-46

Holtby, Winifred 1898-1935 . . . . .DLB-191

Holthusen, Hans Egon 1913- DLB-69

Hölty, Ludwig Christoph Heinrich
1748-1776. . . . . .DLB-94

Holub, Miroslav
1923-1998 . . . . .DLB-232; CDWLB-4

Holz, Arno 1863-1929 . . . . .DLB-118

Home, Henry, Lord Kames
(see Kames, Henry Home, Lord)

Home, John 1722-1808 . . . . .DLB-84

Home, William Douglas 1912- DLB-13

Home Publishing Company DLB-49

Homer circa eighth-seventh centuries B.C.
. . . . DLB-176; CDWLB-1

Homer, Winslow 1836-1910 . . . . .DLB-188

Homes, Geoffrey (see Mainwaring, Daniel)

Honan, Park 1928- DLB-111

Hone, William 1780-1842 . . . . DLB-110, 158

Hongo, Garrett Kaoru 1951- DLB-120

Honig, Edwin 1919- DLB-5

Hood, Hugh 1928- DLB-53

Hood, Mary 1946- DLB-234

Hood, Thomas 1799-1845 . . . . .DLB-96

Hook, Theodore 1788-1841 . . . . .DLB-116

Hooker, Jeremy 1941- DLB-40

Hooker, Richard 1554-1600 . . . . .DLB-132

Hooker, Thomas 1586-1647 . . . . .DLB-24

hooks, bell 1952- DLB-246

Hooper, Johnson Jones
1815-1862 . . . . .DLB-3, 11, 248

Hope, Anthony 1863-1933 . . . . .DLB-153, 156

Hope, Christopher 1944- DLB-225

Hope, Eva (see Hearn, Mary Anne)

Hope, Laurence (Adela Florence
Cory Nicolson) 1865-1904 . . . . .DLB-240

Hopkins, Ellice 1836-1904 . . . . .DLB-190

Hopkins, Gerard Manley
1844-1889 . . . . .DLB-35, 57; CDBLB-5

Hopkins, John (see Sternhold, Thomas)

Hopkins, John H., and Son DLB-46

Hopkins, Lemuel 1750-1801 . . . . .DLB-37

Hopkins, Pauline Elizabeth 1859-1930 . . . .DLB-50

Hopkins, Samuel 1721-1803 . . . . .DLB-31

Hopkinson, Francis 1737-1791 . . . . .DLB-31

Hopkinson, Nalo 1960- DLB-251

Hopper, Nora (Mrs. Nora Chesson)
1871-1906 .DLB-240

Hoppin, Augustus 1828-1896 . . . . .DLB-188

Hora, Josef 1891-1945 . . . . . .DLB-215; CDWLB-4

Horace 65 B.C.-8 B.C. DLB-211; CDWLB-1

Horgan, Paul 1903-1995 . . . . . DLB-102, 212; Y-85

Horizon Press .DLB-46

Hornby, C. H. St. John 1867-1946. . . . . . .DLB-201

Hornby, Nick 1957- DLB-207

Horne, Frank 1899-1974 . . . . .DLB-51

Horne, Richard Henry (Hengist)
1802 or 1803-1884 . . . . .DLB-32

Horney, Karen 1885-1952. . . . . .DLB-246

Hornung, E. W. 1866-1921. . . . . .DLB-70

Horovitz, Israel 1939- DLB-7

Horton, George Moses 1797?-1883? DLB-50

Horváth, Ödön von 1901-1938 . . . . . .DLB-85, 124

Horwood, Harold 1923- DLB-60

Hosford, E. and E. [publishing house] DLB-49

Hoskens, Jane Fenn 1693-1770?. DLB-200

Hoskyns, John 1566-1638 . . . . .DLB-121

Hosokawa Yūsai 1535-1610 . . . . .DLB-203

Hostovský, Egon 1908-1973 . . . . .DLB-215

Hotchkiss and Company. DLB-49

Hough, Emerson 1857-1923 . . . . .DLB-9, 212

Houghton, Stanley 1881-1913 . . . . .DLB-10

Houghton Mifflin Company DLB-49

Household, Geoffrey 1900-1988 . . . . .DLB-87

Housman, A. E. 1859-1936 . . . .DLB-19; CDBLB-5

Housman, Laurence 1865-1959. . . . . .DLB-10

Houston, Pam 1962- DLB-244

Houwald, Ernst von 1778-1845 . . . . .DLB-90

Hovey, Richard 1864-1900 . . . . .DLB-54

Howard, Donald R. 1927-1987 . . . . .DLB-111

Howard, Maureen 1930- Y-83

Howard, Richard 1929- DLB-5

Howard, Roy W. 1883-1964. . . . . .DLB-29

Howard, Sidney 1891-1939 . . . . DLB-7, 26, 249

Howard, Thomas, second Earl of Arundel
1585-1646 .DLB-213

Howe, E. W. 1853-1937 . . . . .DLB-12, 25

Howe, Henry 1816-1893 . . . . .DLB-30

Howe, Irving 1920-1993 . . . . .DLB-67

Howe, Joseph 1804-1873 . . . . .DLB-99

Howe, Julia Ward 1819-1910 . . . .DLB-1, 189, 235

Howe, Percival Presland 1886-1944 . . . . .DLB-149

Howe, Susan 1937- DLB-120

Howell, Clark, Sr. 1863-1936 . . . . .DLB-25

Howell, Evan P. 1839-1905. . . . . .DLB-23

Howell, James 1594?-1666. . . . . .DLB-151

Howell, Soskin and Company. DLB-46

Howell, Warren Richardson
1912-1984 .DLB-140

Howells, William Dean 1837-1920
. . . . DLB-12, 64, 74, 79, 189; CDALB-3

Introduction to Paul Laurence Dunbar,
Lyrics of Lowly Life (1896) DLB-50

Howitt, Mary 1799-1888 . . . . DLB-110, 199

Howitt, William 1792-1879 and
   Howitt, Mary 1799-1888 . . . . DLB-110

Hoyem, Andrew 1935- DLB-5

Hoyers, Anna Ovena 1584-1655 . . . . DLB-164

Hoyle, Fred 1915-2001 . . . . DLB-261

Hoyos, Angela de 1940- DLB-82

Hoyt, Henry [publishing house] DLB-49

Hoyt, Palmer 1897-1979 . . . . DLB-127

Hrabal, Bohumil 1914-1997 . . . . DLB-232

Hrabanus Maurus 776?-856 . . . . DLB-148

Hronský, Josef Cíger 1896-1960 . . . . DLB-215

Hrotsvit of Gandersheim
   circa 935-circa 1000 . . . . DLB-148

Hubbard, Elbert 1856-1915 . . . . DLB-91

Hubbard, Kin 1868-1930 . . . . DLB-11

Hubbard, William circa 1621-1704 . . . . . . DLB-24

Huber, Therese 1764-1829 . . . . DLB-90

Huch, Friedrich 1873-1913 . . . . DLB-66

Huch, Ricarda 1864-1947 . . . . DLB-66

Huck at 100: How Old Is
   Huckleberry Finn? Y-85

Huddle, David 1942- DLB-130

Hudgins, Andrew 1951- DLB-120

Hudson, Henry Norman 1814-1886 . . . . . . DLB-64

Hudson, Stephen 1868?-1944 . . . . DLB-197

Hudson, W. H. 1841-1922 . . . . . DLB-98, 153, 174

Hudson and Goodwin DLB-49

Huebsch, B. W. [publishing house] DLB-46

Oral History: B. W. Huebsch. Y-99

Hueffer, Oliver Madox 1876-1931 . . . . . . DLB-197

Hugh of St. Victor circa 1096-1141 . . . . . DLB-208

Hughes, David 1930- DLB-14

Hughes, Dusty 1947- DLB-233

Hughes, Hatcher 1881-1945 . . . . DLB-249

Hughes, John 1677-1720 . . . . DLB-84

Hughes, Langston 1902-1967
   . . . . DLB-4, 7, 48, 51, 86, 228; CDALB-5

Hughes, Richard 1900-1976 . . . . DLB-15, 161

Hughes, Ted 1930-1998 . . . . DLB-40, 161

Hughes, Thomas 1822-1896 . . . . DLB-18, 163

Hugo, Richard 1923-1982 . . . . DLB-5, 206

Hugo, Victor 1802-1885 . . . . DLB-119, 192, 217

Hugo Awards and Nebula Awards DLB-8

Hull, Richard 1896-1973 . . . . DLB-77

Hulme, T. E. 1883-1917 . . . . DLB-19

Hulton, Anne ?-1779? DLB-200

Humboldt, Alexander von 1769-1859 . . . . . DLB-90

Humboldt, Wilhelm von 1767-1835 . . . . . . DLB-90

Hume, David 1711-1776 . . . . DLB-104, 252

Hume, Fergus 1859-1932 . . . . DLB-70

Hume, Sophia 1702-1774 . . . . DLB-200

Hume-Rothery, Mary Catherine
   1824-1885 . . . . DLB-240

Humishuma (see Mourning Dove)

Hummer, T. R. 1950- DLB-120

Humorous Book Illustration DLB-11

Humphrey, Duke of Gloucester
   1391-1447 . . . . DLB-213

Humphrey, William 1924-1997 . . DLB-6, 212, 234

Humphreys, David 1752-1818 . . . . DLB-37

Humphreys, Emyr 1919- DLB-15

Huncke, Herbert 1915-1996 . . . . DLB-16

Huneker, James Gibbons 1857-1921 . . . . . DLB-71

Hunold, Christian Friedrich 1681-1721 . . DLB-168

Hunt, Irene 1907- DLB-52

Hunt, Leigh 1784-1859 . . . . DLB-96, 110, 144

Hunt, Violet 1862-1942 . . . . DLB-162, 197

Hunt, William Gibbes 1791-1833 . . . . DLB-73

Hunter, Evan 1926- Y-82

Hunter, Jim 1939- DLB-14

Hunter, Kristin 1931- DLB-33

Hunter, Mollie 1922- DLB-161

Hunter, N. C. 1908-1971 . . . . DLB-10

Hunter-Duvar, John 1821-1899 . . . . DLB-99

Huntington, Henry E. 1850-1927 . . . . DLB-140

Huntington, Susan Mansfield
   1791-1823 . . . . DLB-200

Hurd and Houghton DLB-49

Hurst, Fannie 1889-1968 . . . . DLB-86

Hurst and Blackett DLB-106

Hurst and Company DLB-49

Hurston, Zora Neale
   1901?-1960 . . . . DLB-51, 86; CDALB-7

Husson, Jules-François-Félix (see Champfleury)

Huston, John 1906-1987 . . . . DLB-26

Hutcheson, Francis 1694-1746 . . . . . . DLB-31, 252

Hutchinson, Ron 1947- DLB-245

Hutchinson, R. C. 1907-1975 . . . . DLB-191

Hutchinson, Thomas 1711-1780
   . . . . DLB-30, 31

Hutchinson and Company
   (Publishers) Limited DLB-112

Hutton, Richard Holt 1826-1897 . . . . DLB-57

von Hutton, Ulrich 1488-1523 . . . . DLB-179

Huxley, Aldous 1894-1963
   . . . . . DLB-36, 100, 162, 195, 255; CDBLB-6

Huxley, Elspeth Josceline
   1907-1997 . . . . DLB-77, 204

Huxley, T. H. 1825-1895 . . . . DLB-57

Huyghue, Douglas Smith 1816-1891 . . . . . DLB-99

Huysmans, Joris-Karl 1848-1907 . . . . DLB-123

Hwang, David Henry
   1957- DLB-212, 228

Hyde, Donald 1909-1966 and
   Hyde, Mary 1912- DLB-187

Hyman, Trina Schart 1939- DLB-61

I

Iavorsky, Stefan 1658-1722 . . . . DLB-150

Iazykov, Nikolai Mikhailovich
   1803-1846 . . . . DLB-205

Ibáñez, Armando P. 1949- DLB-209

Ibn Bajja circa 1077-1138 . . . . DLB-115

Ibn Gabirol, Solomon
   circa 1021-circa 1058 . . . . DLB-115

Ibuse, Masuji 1898-1993 . . . . DLB-180

Ichijō Kanera
   (see Ichijō Kaneyoshi)

Ichijō Kaneyoshi (Ichijō Kanera)
   1402-1481 . . . . DLB-203

The Iconography of Science-Fiction Art DLB-8

Iffland, August Wilhelm 1759-1814 . . . . . . DLB-94

Ignatow, David 1914-1997 . . . . DLB-5

Ike, Chukwuemeka 1931- DLB-157

Ikkyū Sōjun 1394-1481 . . . . DLB-203

Iles, Francis (see Berkeley, Anthony)

Illich, Ivan 1926- DLB-242

The Illustration of Early German Literar
   Manuscripts, circa 1150-circa 1300 . . DLB-148

Illyés, Gyula 1902-1983 . . . . . DLB-215; CDWLB-4

Imbs, Bravig 1904-1946 . . . . DLB-4

Imbuga, Francis D. 1947- DLB-157

Immermann, Karl 1796-1840 . . . . DLB-133

Inchbald, Elizabeth 1753-1821 . . . . DLB-39, 89

Ingamells, Rex 1913-1955 . . . . DLB-260

Inge, William 1913-1973 . . . . DLB-7, 249; CDALB-1

Ingelow, Jean 1820-1897 . . . . DLB-35, 163

Ingersoll, Ralph 1900-1985 . . . . DLB-127

The Ingersoll Prizes Y-84

Ingoldsby, Thomas (see Barham, Richard Harris)

Ingraham, Joseph Holt 1809-1860 . . . . DLB-3, 248

Inman, John 1805-1850 . . . . DLB-73

Innerhofer, Franz 1944- DLB-85

Innis, Harold Adams 1894-1952 . . . . DLB-88

Innis, Mary Quayle 1899-1972 . . . . DLB-88

Inō Sōgi 1421-1502 . . . . DLB-203

Inoue Yasushi 1907-1991 . . . . DLB-181

International Publishers Company DLB-46

Interviews:

Adoff, Arnold and Virginia Hamilton Y-01

Anastas, Benjamin Y-98

Baker, Nicholson Y-00

Bank, Melissa Y-98

Bernstein, Harriet Y-82

Betts, Doris Y-82

Bosworth, David Y-82

Bottoms, David Y-83

Bowers, Fredson Y-80

Burnshaw, Stanley Y-97

Carpenter, Humphrey Y-84, Y-99

Carr, Virginia Spencer Y-00

Carver, Raymond Y-83

Cherry, Kelly Y-83

Coppel, Alfred Y-83

Cowley, Malcolm Y-81

Davis, Paxton Y-89

De Vries, Peter Y-82

Dickey, James Y-82

Donald, David Herbert Y-87

Ellroy, James Y-91

Fancher, Betsy Y-83

Faust, Irvin Y-00

Fulton, Len Y-86

Furst, Alan Y-01

Garrett, George Y-83

Greenfield, George Y-91

Griffin, Bryan Y-81

Groom, Winston Y-01

Guilds, John Caldwell Y-92

Hardin, James Y-92

Harrison, Jim Y-82

Hazzard, Shirley Y-82

Herrick, William Y-01

Higgins, George V. Y-98

Hoban, Russell Y-90

Holroyd, Michael Y-99

Horowitz, Glen Y-90

Iggulden, John Y-01

Jakes, John Y-83

Jenkinson, Edward B. Y-82

Jenks, Tom Y-86

Kaplan, Justin Y-86

King, Florence Y-85

Klopfer, Donald S. Y-97

Krug, Judith Y-82

Lamm, Donald Y-95

Laughlin, James Y-96

Lindsay, Jack Y-84

Mailer, Norman Y-97

Manchester, William Y-85

McCormack, Thomas Y-98

McNamara, Katherine Y-97

McTaggart, J. M. E. 1866-1925 . . . . DLB-262

Mellen, Joan Y-94

Menaher, Daniel Y-97

Mooneyham, Lamarr Y-82

Murray, Les Y-01

Nosworth, David Y-82

O'Connor, Patrick Y-84, Y-99

Ozick, Cynthia Y-83

Penner, Jonathan Y-83

Pennington, Lee Y-82

Penzler, Otto Y-96

Plimpton, George Y-99

Potok, Chaim Y-84

Powell, Padgett Y-01

Prescott, Peter S. Y-86

Rabe, David Y-91

Rallyson, Carl Y-97

Rechy, John Y-82

Reid, B. L. Y-83

Reynolds, Michael Y-95, Y-99

Schlafly, Phyllis Y-82

Schroeder, Patricia Y-99

Schulberg, Budd Y-81, Y-01

Scribner, Charles III Y-94

Sipper, Ralph Y-94

Staley, Thomas F. Y-00

Styron, William Y-80

Toth, Susan Allen Y-86

Tyler, Anne Y-82

Vaughan, Samuel Y-97

Von Ogtrop, Kristin Y-92

Wallenstein, Barry Y-92

Weintraub, Stanley Y-82

Williams, J. Chamberlain Y-84

Editors, Conversations with Y-95

Interviews on E-Publishing Y-00

Into the Past: William Jovanovich's
Reflections in Publishing Y-01

Irving, John 1942- DLB-6; Y-82

Irving, Washington 1783-1859
. . . . DLB-3, 11, 30, 59, 73, 74,
183, 186, 250; CDALB-2

Irwin, Grace 1907- DLB-68

Irwin, Will 1873-1948 . . . . DLB-25

Isaksson, Ulla 1916-2000 . . . . DLB-257

Iser, Wolfgang 1926- DLB-242

Isherwood, Christopher
1904-1986 . . . . DLB-15, 195; Y-86

The Christopher Isherwood Archive,
The Huntington Library Y-99

Ishiguro, Kazuo
1954- DLB-194

Ishikawa Jun
1899-1987 . . . . DLB-182

The Island Trees Case: A Symposium on
School Library Censorship
An Interview with Judith Krug
An Interview with Phyllis Schlafly
An Interview with Edward B. Jenkinson
An Interview with Lamarr Mooneyham
An Interview with Harriet Bernstein Y-82

Islas, Arturo
1938-1991 . . . . DLB-122

Issit, Debbie 1966- DLB-233

Ivanišević, Drago
|1907-1981 . . . . DLB-181

Ivaska, Astrīde 1926- DLB-232

Ivers, M. J., and Company DLB-49

Iwaniuk, Wacław 1915- DLB-215

Iwano, Hōmei 1873-1920 . . . . DLB-180

Iwaszkiewicz, Jarosław 1894-1980 . . . . DLB-215

Iyayi, Festus 1947- DLB-157

Izumi, Kyōka 1873-1939 . . . . DLB-180

J

Jackmon, Marvin E. (see Marvin X)

Jacks, L. P. 1860-1955 . . . . DLB-135

Jackson, Angela 1951- DLB-41

Jackson, Charles 1903-1968 . . . . DLB-234

Jackson, Helen Hunt
1830-1885 . . . . DLB-42, 47, 186, 189

Jackson, Holbrook 1874-1948 . . . . DLB-98

Jackson, Laura Riding 1901-1991 . . . . DLB-48

Jackson, Shirley
1916-1965 . . . . DLB-6, 234; CDALB-1

Jacob, Max 1876-1944 . . . . DLB-258

Jacob, Naomi 1884?-1964 . . . . DLB-191

Jacob, Piers Anthony Dillingham
(see Anthony, Piers)

Jacob, Violet 1863-1946 . . . . DLB-240

Jacobi, Friedrich Heinrich 1743-1819 . . . . . DLB-94

Jacobi, Johann Georg 1740-1841 . . . . DLB-97

Jacobs, George W., and Company DLB-49

Jacobs, Harriet 1813-1897 . . . . DLB-239

Jacobs, Joseph 1854-1916 . . . . DLB-141

Jacobs, W. W. 1863-1943 . . . . DLB-135

Jacobsen, Jørgen-Frantz 1900-1938 . . . . . . DLB-214

Jacobsen, Josephine 1908- DLB-244

Jacobson, Dan 1929- DLB-14, 207, 225

Jacobson, Howard 1942- DLB-207

Jacques de Vitry circa 1160/1170-1240 . . . DLB-208

Jæger, Frank 1926-1977 . . . . DLB-214

Jaggard, William [publishing house] DLB-170

Jahier, Piero 1884-1966 . . . . DLB-114

Jahnn, Hans Henny 1894-1959 . . . . . . DLB-56, 124

Jakes, John 1932- Y-83

Jakobson, Roman 1896-1982 . . . . DLB-242

James, Alice 1848-1892 . . . . DLB-221

James, C. L. R. 1901-1989 . . . . DLB-125

James, George P. R. 1801-1860 . . . . DLB-116

James, Henry 1843-1916
. . . . . DLB-12, 71, 74, 189; DS-13; CDALB-3

James, John circa 1633-1729 . . . . DLB-24

James, M. R. 1862-1936 . . . . DLB-156, 201

James, Naomi 1949- DLB-204

James, P. D. 1920- . . . DLB-87; DS-17; CDBLB-8

James VI of Scotland, I of England
1566-1625 . . . . DLB-151, 172

*Ane Schort Treatise Conteining Some Revlis
and Cautelis to Be Obseruit and Eschewit
in Scottis Poesi* (1584) DLB-172

James, Thomas 1572?-1629 . . . . DLB-213

James, U. P. [publishing house] DLB-49

James, Will 1892-1942 . . . . DS-16

Jameson, Anna 1794-1860 . . . . DLB-99, 166

Jameson, Fredric 1934- DLB-67

Jameson, J. Franklin 1859-1937 . . . . DLB-17

Jameson, Storm 1891-1986 . . . . DLB-36

Jančar, Drago 1948- DLB-181

Janés, Clara 1940- DLB-134

Janevski, Slavko 1920- DLB-181; CDWLB-4

Jansson, Tove 1914-2001 . . . . DLB-257

Janvier, Thomas 1849-1913 . . . . DLB-202

Jaramillo, Cleofas M. 1878-1956 . . . . DLB-122

Jarman, Mark 1952- DLB-120

Jarrell, Randall 1914-1965 . DLB-48, 52; CDALB-1

Jarrold and Sons DLB-106

Jarry, Alfred 1873-1907 . . . . DLB-192, 258

Jarves, James Jackson 1818-1888 . . . . DLB-189

Jasmin, Claude 1930- DLB-60

Jaunsudrabiņš, Jānis 1877-1962 . . . . DLB-220

Jay, John 1745-1829 . . . . DLB-31

Jean de Garlande (see John of Garland)

Jefferies, Richard 1848-1887 . . . . DLB-98, 141

Jeffers, Lance 1919-1985 . . . . DLB-41

Jeffers, Robinson
1887-1962 . . . . DLB-45, 212; CDALB-4

Jefferson, Thomas
1743-1826 . . . . DLB-31, 183; CDALB-2

Jégé 1866-1940 . . . . DLB-215

Jelinek, Elfriede 1946- DLB-85

Jellicoe, Ann 1927- DLB-13, 233

Jemison, Mary circa 1742-1833 . . . . DLB-239

Jenkins, Dan 1929- DLB-241

Jenkins, Elizabeth 1905- DLB-155

Jenkins, Robin 1912- DLB-14

Jenkins, William Fitzgerald (see Leinster, Murray)

Jenkins, Herbert, Limited DLB-112

Jennings, Elizabeth 1926- DLB-27

Jens, Walter 1923- DLB-69

Jensen, Johannes V. 1873-1950 . . . . DLB-214

Jensen, Merrill 1905-1980 . . . . DLB-17

Jensen, Thit 1876-1957 . . . . DLB-214

Jephson, Robert 1736-1803 . . . . DLB-89

Jerome, Jerome K. 1859-1927 . . . . DLB-10, 34, 135

Jerome, Judson 1927-1991 . . . . DLB-105

Jerrold, Douglas 1803-1857 . . . . DLB-158, 159

Jersild, Per Christian 1935- DLB-257

Jesse, F. Tennyson 1888-1958 . . . . DLB-77

Jewel, John 1522-1571 . . . . DLB-236

Jewett, John P., and Company DLB-49

Jewett, Sarah Orne 1849-1909 . . . . DLB-12, 74, 221

The Jewish Publication Society DLB-49

Jewitt, John Rodgers 1783-1821 . . . . DLB-99

Jewsbury, Geraldine 1812-1880 . . . . DLB-21

Jewsbury, Maria Jane 1800-1833 . . . . DLB-199

Jhabvala, Ruth Prawer 1927- DLB-139, 194

Jiménez, Juan Ramón 1881-1958 . . . . DLB-134

Jimmy, Red, and Others: Harold Rosenthal
Remembers the Stars of the Press Box Y-01

Jin, Ha 1956- DLB-244

Joans, Ted 1928- DLB-16, 41

Jōha 1525-1602 . . . . DLB-203

Johannis de Garlandia (see John of Garland)

John, Errol 1924-1988 . . . . DLB-233

John, Eugenie (see Marlitt, E.)

John of Dumbleton
circa 1310-circa 1349 . . . . DLB-115

John of Garland (Jean de Garlande, Johannis de
Garlandia) circa 1195-circa 1272 . . . . DLB-208

Johns, Captain W. E. 1893-1968 . . . . DLB-160

Johnson, Mrs. A. E. ca. 1858-1922 . . . . . . DLB-221

Johnson, Amelia (see Johnson, Mrs. A. E.)

Johnson, B. S. 1933-1973 . . . . DLB-14, 40

Johnson, Benjamin [publishing house] DLB-49

Johnson, Benjamin, Jacob, and
Robert [publishing house] DLB-49

Johnson, Charles 1679-1748 . . . . DLB-84

Johnson, Charles R. 1948- DLB-33

Johnson, Charles S. 1893-1956 . . . . DLB-51, 91

Johnson, Denis 1949- DLB-120

Johnson, Diane 1934- Y-80

Johnson, Dorothy M. 1905–1984 . . . . DLB-206

Johnson, E. Pauline (Tekahionwake)
1861-1913 . . . . DLB-175

Johnson, Edgar 1901-1995 . . . . DLB-103

Johnson, Edward 1598-1672 . . . . DLB-24

Johnson, Eyvind 1900-1976 . . . . DLB-259

Johnson, Fenton 1888-1958 . . . . DLB-45, 50

Johnson, Georgia Douglas
1877?-1966 . . . . DLB-51, 249

Johnson, Gerald W. 1890-1980 . . . . DLB-29

Johnson, Greg 1953- DLB-234

Johnson, Helene 1907-1995 . . . . DLB-51

Johnson, Jacob, and Company DLB-49

Johnson, James Weldon
1871-1938 . . . . DLB-51; CDALB-4

Johnson, John H. 1918- DLB-137

Johnson, Joseph [publishing house] DLB-154

Johnson, Linton Kwesi 1952- DLB-157

Johnson, Lionel 1867-1902 . . . . DLB-19

Johnson, Nunnally 1897-1977 . . . . DLB-26

Johnson, Owen 1878-1952 . . . . Y-87

Johnson, Pamela Hansford 1912- DLB-15

Johnson, Pauline 1861-1913 . . . . DLB-92

Johnson, Ronald 1935-1998 . . . . DLB-169

Johnson, Samuel 1696-1772 . . . DLB-24; CDBLB-2

Johnson, Samuel
1709-1784 . . . . DLB-39, 95, 104, 142, 213

Johnson, Samuel 1822-1882 . . . . DLB-1, 243

Johnson, Susanna 1730-1810 . . . . DLB-200

Johnson, Terry 1955- DLB-233

Johnson, Uwe 1934-1984 . . . . . DLB-75; CDWLB-2

Johnston, Annie Fellows 1863-1931 . . . . . . DLB-42

Johnston, Basil H. 1929- DLB-60

Johnston, David Claypole 1798?-1865 . . . DLB-188

Johnston, Denis 1901-1984 . . . . DLB-10

Johnston, Ellen 1835-1873 . . . . DLB-199

Johnston, George 1912-1970 . . . . DLB-260

Johnston, George 1913- DLB-88

Johnston, Sir Harry 1858-1927 . . . . .DLB-174

Johnston, Jennifer 1930- DLB-14

Johnston, Mary 1870-1936 . . . . DLB-9

Johnston, Richard Malcolm 1822-1898 . . . DLB-74

Johnstone, Charles 1719?-1800? DLB-39

Johst, Hanns 1890-1978 . . . . DLB-124

Jolas, Eugene 1894-1952 . . . . DLB-4, 45

Jones, Alice C. 1853-1933 . . . . DLB-92

Jones, Charles C., Jr. 1831-1893 . . . . DLB-30

Jones, D. G. 1929- DLB-53

Jones, David 1895-1974 . . DLB-20, 100; CDBLB-7

Jones, Diana Wynne 1934- DLB-161

Jones, Ebenezer 1820-1860 . . . . DLB-32

Jones, Ernest 1819-1868 . . . . DLB-32

Jones, Gayl 1949- DLB-33

Jones, George 1800-1870 . . . . DLB-183

Jones, Glyn 1905- DLB-15

Jones, Gwyn 1907- DLB-15, 139

Jones, Henry Arthur 1851-1929 . . . . DLB-10

Jones, Hugh circa 1692-1760 . . . . DLB-24

Jones, James 1921-1977 . . . . .DLB-2, 143; DS-17

James Jones Papers in the Handy Writers'
Colony Collection at the University of
Illinois at Springfield Y-98

The James Jones Society Y-92

Jones, Jenkin Lloyd 1911- DLB-127

Jones, John Beauchamp 1810-1866 . . . . . . DLB-202

Jones, LeRoi (see Baraka, Amiri)

Jones, Lewis 1897-1939 . . . . DLB-15

Jones, Madison 1925- DLB-152

Jones, Major Joseph
(see Thompson, William Tappan)

Jones, Marie 1955- DLB-233

Jones, Preston 1936-1979 . . . . DLB-7

Jones, Rodney 1950- DLB-120

Jones, Thom 1945- DLB-244

Jones, Sir William 1746-1794 . . . . DLB-109

Jones, William Alfred
1817-1900 . . . . DLB-59

Jones's Publishing House DLB-49

Jong, Erica 1942- DLB-2, 5, 28, 152

Jonke, Gert F. 1946- DLB-85

Jonson, Ben
1572?-1637 . . . . DLB-62, 121; CDBLB-1

Jordan, June 1936- DLB-38

Joseph and George Y-99

Joseph, Jenny 1932- DLB-40

Joseph, Michael, Limited DLB-112

Josephson, Matthew 1899-1978 . . . . DLB-4

Josephus, Flavius 37-100 . . . . .DLB-176

Josiah Allen's Wife (see Holley, Marietta)

Josipovici, Gabriel 1940- DLB-14

Josselyn, John ?-1675 . . . . DLB-24

Joudry, Patricia 1921- DLB-88

Jouve, Pierre-Jean 1887-1976 . . . . DLB-258

Jovanovich, William
1920-2001 . . . . Y-01

Into the Past: William Jovanovich's
Reflections on Publishing Y-01

Jovine, Giuseppe 1922- DLB-128

Joyaux, Philippe (see Sollers, Philippe)

Joyce, Adrien (see Eastman, Carol)

Joyce, James 1882-1941
. . . . DLB-10, 19, 36, 162, 247; CDBLB-6

James Joyce Centenary: Dublin, 1982 . . . . Y-82

James Joyce Conference Y-85

A Joyce (Con)Text: Danis Rose and the
Remaking of *Ulysses* Y-97

The New *Ulysses* Y-84

Jozsef, Attila
1905-1937 . . . . DLB-215; CDWLB-4

Judd, Orange, Publishing Company DLB-49

Judd, Sylvester 1813-1853 . . . . DLB-1, 243

Judith circa 930 . . . . DLB-146

Julian Barnes Checklist Y-01

Julian of Norwich
1342-circa 1420 . . . . DLB-1146

Julius Caesar
100 B.C.-44 B.C. DLB-211; CDWLB-1

June, Jennie
(see Croly, Jane Cunningham)

Jung, Franz 1888-1963 . . . . DLB-118

Jünger, Ernst 1895- DLB-56; CDWLB-2

Der jüngere Titurel circa 1275 . . . . DLB-138

Jung-Stilling, Johann Heinrich
1740-1817 . . . . DLB-94

Justice, Donald 1925- Y-83

Juvenal circa A.D. 60-circa A.D. 130
. . . . DLB-211; CDWLB-1

The Juvenile Library
(see Godwin, M. J., and Company)

K

Kacew, Romain (see Gary, Romain)

Kafka, Franz 1883-1924 . . . . . . DLB-81; CDWLB-2

Kahn, Roger 1927- DLB-171

Kaikō Takeshi 1939-1989 . . . . DLB-182

Kaiser, Georg 1878-1945 . . . . DLB-124; CDWLB-2

Kaiserchronik circca 1147 . . . . DLB-148

Kaleb, Vjekoslav 1905- DLB-181

Kalechofsky, Roberta 1931- DLB-28

Kaler, James Otis 1848-1912 . . . . DLB-12

Kames, Henry Home, Lord
1696-1782 . . . . DLB-31, 104

Kamo no Chōmei (Kamo no Nagaakira)
1153 or 1155-1216 . . . . DLB-203

Kamo no Nagaakira (see Kamo no Chōmei)

Kampmann, Christian 1939-1988 . . . . DLB-214

Kandel, Lenore 1932- DLB-16

Kanin, Garson 1912-1999 . . . . DLB-7

Kant, Hermann 1926- DLB-75

Kant, Immanuel 1724-1804 . . . . DLB-94

Kantemir, Antiokh Dmitrievich
1708-1744 . . . . DLB-150

Kantor, MacKinlay 1904-1977 . . . . DLB-9, 102

Kanze Kōjirō Nobumitsu 1435-1516 . . . . DLB-203

Kanze Motokiyo (see Zeimi)

Kaplan, Fred 1937- DLB-111

Kaplan, Johanna 1942- DLB-28

Kaplan, Justin 1925- DLB-111; Y-86

The Practice of Biography V:
An Interview with Justin Kaplan Y-86

Kaplinski, Jaan 1941- DLB-232

Kapnist, Vasilii Vasilevich 1758?-1823 . . . DLB-150

Karadžić,Vuk Stefanović
1787-1864 . . . . DLB-147; CDWLB-4

Karamzin, Nikolai Mikhailovich
1766-1826 . . . . DLB-150

Karinthy, Frigyes 1887-1938 . . . . DLB-215

Karsch, Anna Louisa 1722-1791 . . . . DLB-97

Kasack, Hermann 1896-1966 . . . . DLB-69

Kasai, Zenzō 1887-1927 . . . . DLB-180

Kaschnitz, Marie Luise 1901-1974 . . . . DLB-69

Kassák, Lajos 1887-1967 . . . . DLB-215

Kaštelan, Jure 1919-1990 . . . . DLB-147

Kästner, Erich 1899-1974 . . . . DLB-56

Katenin, Pavel Aleksandrovich
1792-1853 . . . . DLB-205

Kattan, Naim 1928- DLB-53

Katz, Steve 1935- Y-83

Kauffman, Janet 1945- DLB-218; Y-86

Kauffmann, Samuel 1898-1971 . . . . DLB-127

Kaufman, Bob 1925- DLB-16, 41

Kaufman, George S. 1889-1961 . . . . DLB-7

Kavan, Anna 1901-1968 . . . . DLB-255

Kavanagh, P. J. 1931- DLB-40

Kavanagh, Patrick 1904-1967 . . . . DLB-15, 20

Kawabata, Yasunari 1899-1972 . . . . DLB-180

Kay, Guy Gavriel 1954- DLB-251

Kaye-Smith, Sheila 1887-1956 . . . . DLB-36

Kazin, Alfred 1915-1998 . . . . DLB-67

Keane, John B. 1928- DLB-13

Keary, Annie 1825-1879 . . . . DLB-163

Keary, Eliza 1827-1918 . . . . DLB-240

Keating, H. R. F. 1926- DLB-87

Keatley, Charlotte 1960- DLB-245

Keats, Ezra Jack 1916-1983 . . . . DLB-61

Keats, John 1795-1821 . . . . DLB-96, 110; CDBLB-3

Keble, John 1792-1866 . . . . DLB-32, 55

Keckley, Elizabeth 1818?-1907 . . . . DLB-239

Keeble, John 1944- Y-83

Keeffe, Barrie 1945- DLB-13, 245

Keeley, James 1867-1934 . . . . DLB-25

W. B. Keen, Cooke and Company DLB-49

Keillor, Garrison 1942- Y-87

Keith, Marian 1874?-1961 . . . . DLB-92

Keller, Gary D. 1943- DLB-82

Keller, Gottfried
1819-1890 . . . . DLB-129; CDWLB-2

Kelley, Edith Summers 1884-1956 . . . . DLB-9

Kelley, Emma Dunham ?-? DLB-221

Kelley, William Melvin 1937- DLB-33

Kellogg, Ansel Nash 1832-1886 . . . . DLB-23

Kellogg, Steven 1941- DLB-61

Kelly, George E. 1887-1974 . . . . DLB-7, 249

Kelly, Hugh 1739-1777 . . . . DLB-89

Kelly, Piet and Company DLB-49

Kelly, Robert 1935- DLB-5, 130, 165

Kelman, James 1946- DLB-194

Kelmscott Press DLB-112

Kelton, Elmer 1926- DLB-256

Kemble, E. W. 1861-1933 . . . . DLB-188

Kemble, Fanny 1809-1893 . . . . DLB-32

Kemelman, Harry 1908- DLB-28

Kempe, Margery circa 1373-1438 . . . . . . DLB-146

Kempner, Friederike 1836-1904 . . . . DLB-129

Kempowski, Walter 1929- DLB-75

Kendall, Claude [publishing company] DLB-46

Kendall, Henry 1839-1882 . . . . DLB-230

Kendall, May 1861-1943 . . . . DLB-240

Kendell, George 1809-1867 . . . . DLB-43

Kenedy, P. J., and Sons DLB-49

Kenkō circa 1283-circa 1352 . . . . DLB-203

Kennan, George 1845-1924 . . . . DLB-189

Kennedy, Adrienne 1931- DLB-38

Kennedy, John Pendleton 1795-1870 . . . DLB-3, 248

Kennedy, Leo 1907- DLB-88

Kennedy, Margaret 1896-1967 . . . . DLB-36

Kennedy, Patrick 1801-1873 . . . . DLB-159

Kennedy, Richard S. 1920- DLB-111

Kennedy, William 1928- DLB-143; Y-85

Kennedy, X. J. 1929- DLB-5

Kennelly, Brendan 1936- DLB-40

Kenner, Hugh 1923- DLB-67

Kennerley, Mitchell [publishing house] DLB-46

Kenny, Maurice 1929- DLB-175

Kent, Frank R. 1877-1958 . . . . DLB-29

Kenyon, Jane 1947-1995 . . . . DLB-120

Keough, Hugh Edmund 1864-1912 . . . . . . DLB-171

Keppler and Schwartzmann DLB-49

Ker, John, third Duke of Roxburghe
1740-1804 . . . . DLB-213

Ker, N. R. 1908-1982 . . . . DLB-201

Kerlan, Irvin 1912-1963 . . . . DLB-187

Kermode, Frank 1919- DLB-242

Kern, Jerome 1885-1945 . . . . DLB-187

Kernaghan, Eileen 1939- DLB-251

Kerner, Justinus 1776-1862 . . . . DLB-90

Kerouac, Jack
1922-1969 . . . DLB-2, 16, 237; DS-3; CDALB-1

The Jack Kerouac Revival Y-95

"Re-meeting of Old Friends":
The Jack Kerouac Conference Y-82

Auction of Jack Kerouac's *On the Road* Scroll . . Y-01

Kerouac, Jan 1952-1996 . . . . DLB-16

Kerr, Charles H., and Company DLB-49

Kerr, Orpheus C. (see Newell, Robert Henry)

Kersh, Gerald 1911-1968 . . . . DLB-255

Kesey, Ken
1935-2001 . . . . DLB-2, 16, 206; CDALB-6

Kessel, Joseph 1898-1979 . . . . DLB-72

Kessel, Martin 1901- DLB-56

Kesten, Hermann 1900- DLB-56

Keun, Irmgard 1905-1982 . . . . DLB-69

Key, Ellen 1849-1926 . . . . DLB-259

Key and Biddle DLB-49

Keynes, Sir Geoffrey 1887-1982 . . . . DLB-201

Keynes, John Maynard 1883-1946 . . . . DS-10

Keyserling, Eduard von 1855-1918 . . . . . DLB-66

Khan, Ismith 1925- DLB-125

Khaytov, Nikolay 1919- DLB-181

Khemnitser, Ivan Ivanovich
1745-1784 . . . . DLB-150

Kheraskov, Mikhail Matveevich
1733-1807 . . . . DLB-150

Khomiakov, Aleksei Stepanovich
1804-1860 . . . . DLB-205

Khristov, Boris 1945- DLB-181

Khvoshchinskaia, Nadezhda Dmitrievna
1824-1889 . . . . DLB-238

Khvostov, Dmitrii Ivanovich
1757-1835 . . . . DLB-150

Kidd, Adam 1802?-1831 . . . . DLB-99

Kidd, William [publishing house] DLB-106

Kidder, Tracy 1945- DLB-185

Kiely, Benedict 1919- DLB-15

Kieran, John 1892-1981 . . . . .DLB-171

Kiggins and Kellogg DLB-49

Kiley, Jed 1889-1962 . . . . DLB-4

Kilgore, Bernard 1908-1967 . . . . DLB-127

Kilian, Crawford 1941- DLB-251

Killens, John Oliver 1916- DLB-33

Killigrew, Anne 1660-1685 . . . . DLB-131

Killigrew, Thomas 1612-1683 . . . . DLB-58

Kilmer, Joyce 1886-1918 . . . . DLB-45

Kilroy, Thomas 1934- DLB-233

Kilwardby, Robert circa 1215-1279 . . . . . DLB-115

Kilworth, Garry 1941- DLB-261

Kimball, Richard Burleigh 1816-1892 . . . DLB-202

Kincaid, Jamaica 1949-
. . . . .DLB-157, 227; CDALB-7; CDWLB-3

King, Charles 1844-1933 . . . . DLB-186

King, Clarence 1842-1901 . . . . DLB-12

King, Florence 1936 . . . . Y-85

King, Francis 1923- DLB-15, 139

King, Grace 1852-1932 . . . . DLB-12, 78

King, Harriet Hamilton 1840-1920 . . . . . . DLB-199

King, Henry 1592-1669 . . . . DLB-126

King, Solomon [publishing house] DLB-49

King, Stephen 1947- DLB-143; Y-80

King, Susan Petigru 1824-1875 . . . . DLB-239

King, Thomas 1943- DLB-175

King, Woodie, Jr. 1937- DLB-38

Kinglake, Alexander William
1809-1891 . . . . DLB-55, 166

Kingsbury, Donald 1929- DLB-251

Kingsley, Charles
1819-1875 . . . . .DLB-21, 32, 163, 178, 190

Kingsley, Henry 1830-1876 . . . . DLB-21, 230

Kingsley, Mary Henrietta 1862-1900 . . . . .DLB-174

Kingsley, Sidney 1906- DLB-7

Kingsmill, Hugh 1889-1949 . . . . DLB-149

Kingsolver, Barbara
1955- DLB-206; CDALB-7

Kingston, Maxine Hong
1940- DLB-173, 212; Y-80; CDALB-7

Kingston, William Henry Giles
1814-1880 . . . . DLB-163

Kinnan, Mary Lewis 1763-1848 . . . . DLB-200

Kinnell, Galway 1927- DLB-5; Y-87

Kinsella, Thomas 1928- DLB-27

Kipling, Rudyard 1865-1936
. . . . DLB-19, 34, 141, 156; CDBLB-5

Kipphardt, Heinar 1922-1982 . . . . DLB-124

Kirby, William 1817-1906 . . . . DLB-99

Kircher, Athanasius 1602-1680 . . . . DLB-164

Kireevsky, Ivan Vasil'evich 1806-1856 . . . DLB-198

Kireevsky, Petr Vasil'evich 1808-1856 . . . DLB-205

Kirk, Hans 1898-1962 . . . . DLB-214

Kirk, John Foster 1824-1904 . . . . DLB-79

Kirkconnell, Watson 1895-1977 . . . . DLB-68

Kirkland, Caroline M.
1801-1864 . . . . . . .DLB-3, 73, 74, 250; DS-13

Kirkland, Joseph 1830-1893 . . . . DLB-12

Kirkman, Francis [publishing house] DLB-170

Kirkpatrick, Clayton 1915- DLB-127

Kirkup, James 1918- DLB-27

Kirouac, Conrad (see Marie-Victorin, Frère)

Kirsch, Sarah 1935- DLB-75

Kirst, Hans Hellmut 1914-1989 . . . . DLB-69

Kiš, Danilo 1935-1989 . . . . . DLB-181; CDWLB-4

Kita Morio 1927- DLB-182

Kitcat, Mabel Greenhow 1859-1922 . . . . . DLB-135

Kitchin, C. H. B. 1895-1967 . . . . DLB-77

Kittredge, William 1932- DLB-212, 244

Kiukhel'beker, Vil'gel'm Karlovich
1797-1846 . . . . DLB-205

Kizer, Carolyn 1925- DLB-5, 169

Klabund 1890-1928 . . . . DLB-66

Klaj, Johann 1616-1656 . . . . DLB-164

Klappert, Peter 1942- DLB-5

Klass, Philip (see Tenn, William)

Klein, A. M. 1909-1972 . . . . DLB-68

Kleist, Ewald von 1715-1759 . . . . DLB-97

Kleist, Heinrich von
1777-1811 . . . . DLB-90; CDWLB-2

Klinger, Friedrich Maximilian
1752-1831 . . . . DLB-94

Klíma, Ivan 1931- DLB-232; CDWLB-4

Kliushnikov, Viktor Petrovich
1841-1892 . . . . DLB-238

Oral History Interview with Donald S.
Klopfer Y-97

Klopstock, Friedrich Gottlieb
1724-1803 . . . . DLB-97

Klopstock, Meta 1728-1758 . . . . DLB-97

Kluge, Alexander 1932- DLB-75

Knapp, Joseph Palmer 1864-1951 . . . . DLB-91

Knapp, Samuel Lorenzo 1783-1838 . . . . . . DLB-59

Knapton, J. J. and P.
[publishing house] DLB-154

Kniazhnin, Iakov Borisovich
1740-1791 . . . . DLB-150

Knickerbocker, Diedrich (see Irving, Washington)

Knigge, Adolf Franz Friedrich Ludwig,
Freiherr von 1752-1796 . . . . DLB-94

Knight, Charles, and Company DLB-106

Knight, Damon 1922- DLB-8

Knight, Etheridge 1931-1992 . . . . DLB-41

Knight, John S. 1894-1981 . . . . DLB-29

Knight, Sarah Kemble 1666-1727 . . . . DLB-24, 200

Knight-Bruce, G. W. H. 1852-1896 . . . . . .DLB-174

Knister, Raymond 1899-1932 . . . . DLB-68

Knoblock, Edward 1874-1945 . . . . DLB-10

Knopf, Alfred A. 1892-1984 . . . . Y-84

Knopf, Alfred A. [publishing house] DLB-46

Knopf to Hammett: The Editoral
Correspondence Y-00

Knorr von Rosenroth, Christian
1636-1689 . . . . DLB-168

"Knots into Webs: Some Autobiographical
Sources," by Dabney Stuart DLB-105

Knowles, John 1926- DLB-6; CDALB-6

Knox, Frank 1874-1944 . . . . DLB-29

Knox, John circa 1514-1572 . . . . DLB-132

Knox, John Armoy 1850-1906 . . . . DLB-23

Knox, Lucy 1845-1884 . . . . DLB-240

Knox, Ronald Arbuthnott 1888-1957 . . . . . DLB-77

Knox, Thomas Wallace 1835-1896 . . . . . DLB-189

Kobayashi Takiji 1903-1933 . . . . DLB-180

Kober, Arthur 1900-1975 . . . . DLB-11

Kobiakova, Aleksandra Petrovna
1823-1892 . . . . DLB-238

Kocbek, Edvard 1904-1981 . . . DLB-147; CDWB-4

Koch, Howard 1902- DLB-26

Koch, Kenneth 1925- DLB-5

Kōda, Rohan 1867-1947 . . . . DLB-180

Koenigsberg, Moses 1879-1945 . . . . DLB-25

Koeppen, Wolfgang 1906-1996 . . . . DLB-69

Koertge, Ronald 1940- DLB-105

Koestler, Arthur 1905-1983 . . . . . .Y-83; CDBLB-7

Kohn, John S. Van E. 1906-1976 and
Papantonio, Michael 1907-1978 . . . . . .DLB-187

Kokoschka, Oskar 1886-1980 . . . . DLB-124

Kolb, Annette 1870-1967 . . . . DLB-66

Kolbenheyer, Erwin Guido
1878-1962 . . . . DLB-66, 124

Kolleritsch, Alfred 1931- DLB-85

Kolodny, Annette 1941- DLB-67

Kol'tsov, Aleksei Vasil'evich
1809-1842 . . . . DLB-205

Komarov, Matvei circa 1730-1812 . . . . . DLB-150

Komroff, Manuel 1890-1974 . . . . DLB-4

Komunyakaa, Yusef 1947- DLB-120

Koneski, Blaže 1921-1993 . . . DLB-181; CDWLB-4

Konigsburg, E. L. 1930- DLB-52

Konparu Zenchiku 1405-1468? DLB-203

Konrád, György 1933- DLB-232; CDWLB-4

Konrad von Würzburg
circa 1230-1287 . . . . .DLB-138

Konstantinov, Aleko 1863-1897 . . . . .DLB-147

Konwicki, Tadeusz 1926- DLB-232

Kooser, Ted 1939- DLB-105

Kopit, Arthur 1937- DLB-7

Kops, Bernard 1926?- DLB-13

Kornbluth, C. M. 1923-1958 . . . . .DLB-8

Körner, Theodor 1791-1813 . . . . .DLB-90

Kornfeld, Paul 1889-1942 . . . . .DLB-118

Kosinski, Jerzy 1933-1991 . . . . .DLB-2; Y-82

Kosmač, Ciril 1910-1980 . . . . .DLB-181

Kosovel, Srečko 1904-1926 . . . . .DLB-147

Kostrov, Ermil Ivanovich 1755-1796 . . . . .DLB-150

Kotzebue, August von 1761-1819 . . . . .DLB-94

Kotzwinkle, William 1938- DLB-173

Kovačić, Ante 1854-1889 . . . . .DLB-147

Kovič, Kajetan 1931- DLB-181

Kozlov, Ivan Ivanovich 1779-1840 . . . . . .DLB-205

Kraf, Elaine 1946- Y-81

Kramer, Jane 1938- DLB-185

Kramer, Larry 1935- DLB-249

Kramer, Mark 1944- DLB-185

Kranjčević, Silvije Strahimir
1865-1908 .DLB-147

Krasko, Ivan 1876-1958 . . . . .DLB-215

Krasna, Norman 1909-1984 . . . . .DLB-26

Kraus, Hans Peter 1907-1988 . . . . .DLB-187

Kraus, Karl 1874-1936 . . . . .DLB-118

Krause, Herbert 1905-1976 . . . . .DLB-256

Krauss, Ruth 1911-1993 . . . . .DLB-52

Kreisel, Henry 1922- DLB-88

Krestovsky V. (see Khvoshchinskaia,
Nadezhda Dmitrievna)

Krestovsky, Vsevolod Vladimirovich
1839-1895 .DLB-238

Kreuder, Ernst 1903-1972 . . . . .DLB-69

Krėvė-Mickevičius, Vincas 1882-1954 . . . .DLB-220

Kreymborg, Alfred 1883-1966 . . . . .DLB-4, 54

Krieger, Murray 1923- DLB-67

Krim, Seymour 1922-1989 . . . . .DLB-16

Kristensen, Tom 1893-1974 . . . . .DLB-214

Kristeva, Julia 1941- DLB-242

Krleža, Miroslav 1893-1981 . . DLB-147; CDWLB-4

Krock, Arthur 1886-1974 . . . . .DLB-29

Kroetsch, Robert 1927- DLB-53

Kross, Jaan 1920- DLB-232

Krúdy, Gyula 1878-1933 . . . . .DLB-215

Krutch, Joseph Wood
1893-1970 . . . . .DLB-63, 206

Krylov, Ivan Andreevich
1769-1844 .DLB-150

Kubin, Alfred 1877-1959 . . . . .DLB-81

Kubrick, Stanley 1928-1999 . . . . .DLB-26

Kudrun circa 1230-1240 . . . . .DLB-138

Kuffstein, Hans Ludwig von
1582-1656 .DLB-164

Kuhlmann, Quirinus 1651-1689 . . . . . . .DLB-168

Kuhnau, Johann 1660-1722 . . . . .DLB-168

Kukol'nik, Nestor Vasil'evich
1809-1868 .DLB-205

Kukučín, Martin
1860-1928 . . . . DLB-215; CDWLB-4

Kumin, Maxine 1925- DLB-5

Kuncewicz, Maria 1895-1989 . . . . .DLB-215

Kundera, Milan 1929- DLB-232; CDWLB-4

Kunene, Mazisi 1930- DLB-117

Kunikida, Doppo 1869-1908 . . . . .DLB-180

Kunitz, Stanley 1905- DLB-48

Kunjufu, Johari M. (see Amini, Johari M.)

Kunnert, Gunter 1929- DLB-75

Kunze, Reiner 1933- DLB-75

Kupferberg, Tuli 1923- DLB-16

Kurahashi Yumiko 1935- DLB-182

Kureishi, Hanif 1954- DLB-194, 245

Kürnberger, Ferdinand 1821-1879 . . . . . .DLB-129

Kurz, Isolde 1853-1944 . . . . .DLB-66

Kusenberg, Kurt 1904-1983 . . . . .DLB-69

Kushchevsky, Ivan Afanas'evich
1847-1876 .DLB-238

Kushner, Tony 1956- DLB-228

Kuttner, Henry 1915-1958 . . . . .DLB-8

Kyd, Thomas 1558-1594 . . . . .DLB-62

Kyffin, Maurice circa 1560?-1598 . . . . . .DLB-136

Kyger, Joanne 1934- DLB-16

Kyne, Peter B. 1880-1957 . . . . .DLB-78

Kyōgoku Tamekane 1254-1332 . . . . .DLB-203

Kyrklund, Willy 1921- DLB-257

L

L. E. L. (see Landon, Letitia Elizabeth)

Laberge, Albert 1871-1960 . . . . .DLB-68

Laberge, Marie 1950- DLB-60

Labiche, Eugène 1815-1888 . . . . .DLB-192

Labrunie, Gerard (see Nerval, Gerard de)

La Capria, Raffaele 1922- DLB-196

Lacombe, Patrice
(see Trullier-Lacombe, Joseph Patrice)

Lacretelle, Jacques de 1888-1985 . . . . . . .DLB-65

Lacy, Ed 1911-1968 . . . . .DLB-226

Lacy, Sam 1903- DLB-171

Ladd, Joseph Brown 1764-1786 . . . . .DLB-37

La Farge, Oliver 1901-1963 . . . . .DLB-9

Laffan, Mrs. R. S. de Courcy (see Adams,
Bertha Leith)

Lafferty, R. A. 1914- DLB-8

La Flesche, Francis 1857-1932 . . . . .DLB-175

Laforge, Jules 1860-1887 . . . . .DLB-217

Lagerkvist, Pär 1891-1974 . . . . .DLB-259

Lagerlöf, Selma 1858-1940 . . . . .DLB-259

Lagorio, Gina 1922- DLB-196

La Guma, Alex
1925-1985 . . . . DLB-117, 225; CDWLB-3

Lahaise, Guillaume (see Delahaye, Guy)

Lahontan, Louis-Armand de Lom d'Arce,
Baron de 1666-1715? DLB-99

Laing, Kojo 1946- DLB-157

Laird, Carobeth 1895- Y-82

Laird and Lee .DLB-49

Lalić, Ivan V. 1931-1996 . . . . .DLB-181

Lalić, Mihailo 1914-1992 . . . . .DLB-181

Lalonde, Michèle 1937- DLB-60

Lamantia, Philip 1927- DLB-16

Lamartine, Alphonse de 1790-1869 . . . . . .DLB-217

Lamb, Lady Caroline 1785-1828 . . . . .DLB-116

Lamb, Charles
1775-1834 . . . . . . DLB-93, 107, 163; CDBLB-3

Lamb, Mary 1764-1874 . . . . .DLB-163

Lambert, Betty 1933-1983 . . . . .DLB-60

Lamming, George 1927- . . . DLB-125; CDWLB-3

L'Amour, Louis 1908-1988 . . . . DLB-206; Y-80

Lampman, Archibald 1861-1899 . . . . .DLB-92

Lamson, Wolffe and Company DLB-49

Lancer Books .DLB-46

Landesman, Jay 1919-   and
Landesman, Fran 1927- DLB-16

Landolfi, Tommaso 1908-1979 . . . . .DLB-177

Landon, Letitia Elizabeth 1802-1838 . . . . .DLB-96

Landor, Walter Savage 1775-1864 . . . . DLB-93, 107

Landry, Napoléon-P. 1884-1956 . . . . .DLB-92

Lane, Charles 1800-1870 . . . . .DLB-1, 223

Lane, F. C. 1885-1984 . . . . .DLB-241

Lane, John, Company DLB-49

Lane, Laurence W. 1890-1967 . . . . .DLB-91

Lane, M. Travis 1934- DLB-60

Lane, Patrick 1939- DLB-53

Lane, Pinkie Gordon 1923- DLB-41

Laney, Al 1896-1988 . . . . DLB-4, 171

Lang, Andrew 1844-1912 . . . . . . DLB-98, 141, 184

Langevin, André 1927- DLB-60

Langford, David 1953- DLB-261

Langgässer, Elisabeth 1899-1950 . . . . .DLB-69

Langhorne, John 1735-1779 . . . . .DLB-109

Langland, William
circa 1330-circa 1400 . . . . .DLB-146

Langton, Anna 1804-1893 . . . . .DLB-99

Lanham, Edwin 1904-1979 . . . . .DLB-4

Lanier, Sidney 1842-1881 . . . . DLB-64; DS-13

Lanyer, Aemilia 1569-1645 . . . . .DLB-121

Lapointe, Gatien 1931-1983 . . . . .DLB-88

Lapointe, Paul-Marie 1929- DLB-88

Larcom, Lucy 1824-1893 . . . . .DLB-221, 243

Lardner, John 1912-1960 . . . . .DLB-171

Lardner, Ring 1885-1933
......DLB-11, 25, 86, 171; DS-16; CDALB-4

Lardner 100: Ring Lardner
Centennial Symposium Y-85

Lardner, Ring, Jr. 1915-2000 ......DLB-26, Y-00

Larkin, Philip 1922-1985 .....DLB-27; CDBLB-8

La Roche, Sophie von 1730-1807 ....DLB-94

La Rocque, Gilbert 1943-1984 ....DLB-60

Laroque de Roquebrune, Robert
(see Roquebrune, Robert de)

Larrick, Nancy 1910- DLB-61

Larsen, Nella 1893-1964..............DLB-51

Larson, Clinton F. 1919-1994.........DLB-256

La Sale, Antoine de
circa 1386-1460/1467............DLB-208

Lasch, Christopher 1932-1994 ......DLB-246

Lasker-Schüler, Else 1869-1945 .....DLB-66, 124

Lasnier, Rina 1915- DLB-88

Lassalle, Ferdinand 1825-1864 ......DLB-129

Latham, Robert 1912-1995..........DLB-201

Lathrop, Dorothy P. 1891-1980 ....DLB-22

Lathrop, George Parsons 1851-1898 .....DLB-71

Lathrop, John, Jr. 1772-1820............DLB-37

Latimer, Hugh 1492?-1555...........DLB-136

Latimore, Jewel Christine McLawler
(see Amini, Johari M.)

La Tour du Pin, Patrice de 1911-1975 ...DLB-258

Latymer, William 1498-1583 ....DLB-132

Laube, Heinrich 1806-1884 ....DLB-133

Laud, William 1573-1645............DLB-213

Laughlin, James 1914-1997.......DLB-48; Y-96

James Laughlin Tributes.................Y-97

Conversations with Publishers IV:
An Interview with James Laughlin.......Y-96

Laumer, Keith 1925- DLB-8

Lauremberg, Johann 1590-1658 ....DLB-164

Laurence, Margaret 1926-1987.........DLB-53

Laurentius von Schnüffis 1633-1702.....DLB-168

Laurents, Arthur 1918- DLB-26

Laurie, Annie (see Black, Winifred)

Laut, Agnes Christiana 1871-1936 ....DLB-92

Lauterbach, Ann 1942- DLB-193

Lautreamont, Isidore Lucien Ducasse, Comte de
1846-1870....................DLB-217

Lavater, Johann Kaspar 1741-1801.......DLB-97

Lavin, Mary 1912-1996 ....DLB-15

Law, John (see Harkness, Margaret)

Lawes, Henry 1596-1662 ....DLB-126

Lawless, Anthony (see MacDonald, Philip)

Lawless, Emily (The Hon. Emily Lawless) 1845-1913
DLB-240

Lawrence, D. H. 1885-1930
..... DLB-10, 19, 36, 98, 162, 195; CDBLB-6

Lawrence, David 1888-1973...........DLB-29

Lawrence, Jerome 1915-   and
Lee, Robert E. 1918-1994........DLB-228

Lawrence, Seymour 1926-1994 ....Y-94

Lawrence, T. E. 1888-1935 ....DLB-195

Lawson, George 1598-1678 ....DLB-213

Lawson, Henry 1867-1922 ....DLB-230

Lawson, John ?-1711................DLB-24

Lawson, John Howard 1894-1977 ......DLB-228

Lawson, Louisa Albury 1848-1920......DLB-230

Lawson, Robert 1892-1957............DLB-22

Lawson, Victor F. 1850-1925 ....DLB-25

Layard, Sir Austen Henry
1817-1894....................DLB-166

Layton, Irving 1912- DLB-88

LaZamon flourished circa 1200 ....DLB-146

Lazarević, Laza K. 1851-1890......DLB-147

Lazarus, George 1904-1997 ....DLB-201

Lazhechnikov, Ivan Ivanovich
1792-1869....................DLB-198

Lea, Henry Charles 1825-1909 ....DLB-47

Lea, Sydney 1942- DLB-120

Lea, Tom 1907- DLB-6

Leacock, John 1729-1802 ....DLB-31

Leacock, Stephen 1869-1944 ....DLB-92

Lead, Jane Ward 1623-1704 ....DLB-131

Leadenhall Press...................DLB-106

Leakey, Caroline Woolmer 1827-1881...DLB-230

Leapor, Mary 1722-1746.............DLB-109

Lear, Edward 1812-1888 ......DLB-32, 163, 166

Leary, Timothy 1920-1996..............DLB-16

Leary, W. A., and Company DLB-49

Léautaud, Paul 1872-1956 ....DLB-65

Leavis, F. R. 1895-1978..............DLB-242

Leavitt, David 1961- DLB-130

Leavitt and Allen DLB-49

Le Blond, Mrs. Aubrey 1861-1934......DLB-174

le Carré, John 1931- DLB-87; CDBLB-8

Lécavelé, Roland (see Dorgeles, Roland)

Lechlitner, Ruth 1901- DLB-48

Leclerc, Félix 1914- DLB-60

Le Clézio, J. M. G. 1940- DLB-83

Lectures on Rhetoric and Belles Lettres (1783),
by Hugh Blair [excerpts] DLB-31

Leder, Rudolf (see Hermlin, Stephan)

Lederer, Charles 1910-1976 ....DLB-26

Ledwidge, Francis 1887-1917 ....DLB-20

Lee, Dennis 1939- DLB-53

Lee, Don L. (see Madhubuti, Haki R.)

Lee, George W. 1894-1976.............DLB-51

Lee, Harper 1926- DLB-6; CDALB-1

Lee, Harriet (1757-1851) and
Lee, Sophia (1750-1824)............DLB-39

Lee, Laurie 1914-1997 ....DLB-27

Lee, Li-Young 1957- DLB-165

Lee, Manfred B. (see Dannay, Frederic, and
Manfred B. Lee)

Lee, Nathaniel circa 1645-1692 ....DLB-80

Lee, Sir Sidney 1859-1926 ....DLB-149, 184

Lee, Sir Sidney, "Principles of Biography," in
Elizabethan and Other Essays DLB-149

Lee, Tanith 1947- DLB-261

Lee, Vernon
1856-1935 ....DLB-57, 153, 156, 174, 178

Lee and Shepard.....................DLB-49

Le Fanu, Joseph Sheridan
1814-1873.............DLB-21, 70, 159, 178

Leffland, Ella 1931- Y-84

le Fort, Gertrud von 1876-1971.........DLB-66

Le Gallienne, Richard 1866-1947 ....DLB-4

Legaré, Hugh Swinton
1797-1843 ....DLB-3, 59, 73, 248

Legaré, James Mathewes 1823-1859... DLB-3, 248

The Legends of the Saints and a Medieval
Christian Worldview.............DLB-148

Léger, Antoine-J. 1880-1950 ....DLB-88

Leggett, William 1801-1839 ....DLB-250

Le Guin, Ursula K.
1929- DLB-8, 52, 256; CDALB-6

Lehman, Ernest 1920- DLB-44

Lehmann, John 1907- DLB-27, 100

Lehmann, John, Limited............DLB-112

Lehmann, Rosamond 1901-1990 ....DLB-15

Lehmann, Wilhelm 1882-1968..........DLB-56

Leiber, Fritz 1910-1992................DLB-8

Leibniz, Gottfried Wilhelm 1646-1716 ... DLB-168

Leicester University Press DLB-112

Leigh, W. R. 1866-1955............DLB-188

Leinster, Murray 1896-1975............DLB-8

Leiser, Bill 1898-1965............DLB-241

Leisewitz, Johann Anton 1752-1806 ......DLB-94

Leitch, Maurice 1933- DLB-14

Leithauser, Brad 1943- DLB-120

Leland, Charles G. 1824-1903 ....DLB-11

Leland, John 1503?-1552 ....DLB-136

Lemay, Pamphile 1837-1918............DLB-99

Lemelin, Roger 1919-1992 ....DLB-88

Lemercier, Louis-Jean-Népomucène
1771-1840.....................DLB-192

Le Moine, James MacPherson
1825-1912 ....DLB-99

Lemon, Mark 1809-1870 ....DLB-163

Le Moyne, Jean 1913-1996.............DLB-88

Lemperly, Paul 1858-1939 ....DLB-187

L'Engle, Madeleine 1918- DLB-52

Lennart, Isobel 1915-1971 ....DLB-44

Lennox, Charlotte
1729 or 1730-1804 ....DLB-39

Lenox, James 1800-1880..............DLB-140

Lenski, Lois 1893-1974...............DLB-22

Lentricchia, Frank 1940- DLB-246

Lenz, Hermann 1913-1998............DLB-69

Lenz, J. M. R. 1751-1792..............DLB-94

Lenz, Siegfried 1926- DLB-75

Leonard, Elmore 1925- DLB-173, 226

Leonard, Hugh 1926- DLB-13

Leonard, William Ellery 1876-1944 . . . . . . .DLB-54

Leonowens, Anna 1834-1914 . . . . . . .DLB-99, 166

LePan, Douglas 1914- DLB-88

Lepik, Kalju 1920-1999 . . . . .DLB-232

Leprohon, Rosanna Eleanor 1829-1879 . . . .DLB-99

Le Queux, William 1864-1927. . . . . .DLB-70

Lermontov, Mikhail Iur'evich
1814-1841 . . . . .DLB-205

Lerner, Max 1902-1992 . . . . .DLB-29

Lernet-Holenia, Alexander 1897-1976 . . . . .DLB-85

Le Rossignol, James 1866-1969 . . . . .DLB-92

Lescarbot, Marc circa 1570-1642 . . . . .DLB-99

LeSeur, William Dawson 1840-1917 . . . . . .DLB-92

LeSieg, Theo. (see Geisel, Theodor Seuss)

Leskov, Nikolai Semenovich 1831-1895 . .DLB-238

Leslie, Doris before 1902-1982 . . . . .DLB-191

Leslie, Eliza 1787-1858 . . . . .DLB-202

Leslie, Frank 1821-1880 . . . . .DLB-43, 79

Leslie, Frank, Publishing House DLB-49

Leśmian, Bolesław 1878-1937 . . . . .DLB-215

Lesperance, John 1835?-1891 . . . . .DLB-99

Lessing, Bruno 1870-1940 . . . . .DLB-28

Lessing, Doris
1919- DLB-15, 139; Y-85; CDBLB-8

Lessing, Gotthold Ephraim
1729-1781 . . . . .DLB-97; CDWLB-2

Lettau, Reinhard 1929- DLB-75

Letter from Japan. Y-94, Y-98

Letter from London. Y-96

Letter to [Samuel] Richardson on *Clarissa*
(1748), by Henry Fielding DLB-39

A Letter to the Editor of *The Irish Times* Y-97

Lever, Charles 1806-1872 . . . . .DLB-21

Lever, Ralph ca. 1527-1585 . . . . .DLB-236

Leverson, Ada 1862-1933 . . . . .DLB-153

Levertov, Denise
1923-1997 . . . . .DLB-5, 165; CDALB-7

Levi, Peter 1931- DLB-40

Levi, Primo 1919-1987 . . . . .DLB-177

Lévi-Strauss, Claude 1908- DLB-242

Levien, Sonya 1888-1960. . . . . .DLB-44

Levin, Meyer 1905-1981 . . . . .DLB-9, 28; Y-81

Levine, Norman 1923- DLB-88

Levine, Philip 1928- DLB-5

Levis, Larry 1946- DLB-120

Levy, Amy 1861-1889 . . . . .DLB-156, 240

Levy, Benn Wolfe 1900-1973 . . . . . .DLB-13; Y-81

Lewald, Fanny 1811-1889 . . . . .DLB-129

Lewes, George Henry 1817-1878 . . . . .DLB-55, 144

"Criticism In Relation To
Novels" (1863) DLB-21

The Principles of Success in Literature
(1865) [excerpt]. DLB-57

Lewis, Agnes Smith 1843-1926 . . . . .DLB-174

Lewis, Alfred H. 1857-1914 . . . . .DLB-25, 186

Lewis, Alun 1915-1944 . . . . .DLB-20, 162

Lewis, C. Day (see Day Lewis, C.)

Lewis, C. S. 1898-1963
. . . . .DLB-15, 100, 160, 255; CDBLB-7

Lewis, Charles B. 1842-1924 . . . . .DLB-11

Lewis, Henry Clay 1825-1850 . . . . . . .DLB-3, 248

Lewis, Janet 1899-1999 . . . . Y-87

Lewis, Matthew Gregory
1775-1818 . . . . .DLB-39, 158, 178

Lewis, Meriwether 1774-1809 and
Clark, William 1770-1838 . . . . . .DLB-183, 186

Lewis, Norman 1908- DLB-204

Lewis, R. W. B. 1917- DLB-111

Lewis, Richard circa 1700-1734 . . . . .DLB-24

Lewis, Sinclair
1885-1951 . . . . . .DLB-9, 102; DS-1; CDALB-4

Sinclair Lewis Centennial Conference Y-85

Lewis, Wilmarth Sheldon 1895-1979. . . . .DLB-140

Lewis, Wyndham 1882-1957 . . . . .DLB-15

Lewisohn, Ludwig 1882-1955 . . .DLB-4, 9, 28, 102

Leyendecker, J. C. 1874-1951 . . . . .DLB-188

Lezama Lima, José 1910-1976 . . . . .DLB-113

L'Heureux, John 1934- DLB-244

Libbey, Laura Jean 1862-1924. . . . . .DLB-221

The Library of America. DLB-46

Library History Group Y-01

The Licensing Act of 1737 . . . . .DLB-84

Lichfield, Leonard I [publishing house] . . .DLB-170

Lichtenberg, Georg Christoph 1742-1799 . .DLB-94

The Liddle Collection Y-97

Lidman, Sara 1923- DLB-257

Lieb, Fred 1888-1980. . . . . .DLB-171

Liebling, A. J. 1904-1963 . . . . .DLB-4, 171

Lieutenant Murray (see Ballou, Maturin Murray)

Lighthall, William Douw 1857-1954 . . . . .DLB-92

Lilar, Françoise (see Mallet-Joris, Françoise)

Lili'uokalani, Queen 1838-1917. . . . . . . .DLB-221

Lillo, George 1691-1739. . . . . .DLB-84

Lilly, J. K., Jr. 1893-1966 . . . . .DLB-140

Lilly, Wait and Company DLB-49

Lily, William circa 1468-1522 . . . . .DLB-132

Limited Editions Club DLB-46

Limón, Graciela 1938- DLB-209

Lincoln and Edmands DLB-49

Lindesay, Ethel Forence
(see Richardson, Henry Handel)

Lindgren, Astrid 1907-2002 . . . . .DLB-257

Lindgren, Torgny 1938- DLB-257

Lindsay, Alexander William, Twenty-fifth Earl
of Crawford 1812-1880. . . . . .DLB-184

Lindsay, Sir David circa 1485-1555. . . . . .DLB-132

Lindsay, David 1878-1945 . . . . .DLB-255

Lindsay, Jack 1900- Y-84

Lindsay, Lady (Caroline Blanche Elizabeth Fitzroy
Lindsay) 1844-1912. . . . . .DLB-199

Lindsay, Norman 1879-1969 . . . . .DLB-260

Lindsay, Vachel 1879-1931 . . . .DLB-54; CDALB-3

Linebarger, Paul Myron Anthony
(see Smith, Cordwainer)

Link, Arthur S. 1920-1998. . . . . .DLB-17

Linn, Ed 1922-2000 . . . . .DLB-241

Linn, John Blair 1777-1804. . . . . .DLB-37

Lins, Osman 1924-1978. . . . . .DLB-145

Linton, Eliza Lynn 1822-1898 . . . . .DLB-18

Linton, William James 1812-1897 . . . . . . .DLB-32

Lintot, Barnaby Bernard
[publishing house] DLB-170

Lion Books DLB-46

Lionni, Leo 1910-1999. . . . . .DLB-61

Lippard, George 1822-1854. . . . . .DLB-202

Lippincott, J. B., Company DLB-49

Lippincott, Sara Jane Clarke 1823-1904 . . .DLB-43

Lippmann, Walter 1889-1974 . . . . .DLB-29

Lipton, Lawrence 1898-1975 . . . . .DLB-16

Liscow, Christian Ludwig 1701-1760. . . . .DLB-97

Lish, Gordon 1934- DLB-130

Lisle, Charles-Marie-René Leconte de
1818-1894 .DLB-217

Lispector, Clarice
1925-1977 . . . . .DLB-113; CDWLB-3

LitCheck Website Y-01

A Literary Archaeologist Digs On: A Brief
Interview with Michael Reynolds by
Michael Rogers Y-99

The Literary Chronicle and Weekly Review
1819-1828. .DLB-110

Literary Documents: William Faulkner
and the People-to-People Program Y-86

Literary Documents II: *Library Journal*
Statements and Questionnaires from
First Novelists Y-87

Literary Effects of World War II
[British novel] DLB-15

Literary Prizes Y-00

Literary Prizes [British] DLB-15

Literary Research Archives: The Humanities
Research Center, University of Texas . . . Y-82

Literary Research Archives II: Berg Collection
of English and American Literature of
the New York Public Library Y-83

Literary Research Archives III:
The Lilly Library Y-84

Literary Research Archives IV:
The John Carter Brown Library. Y-85

Literary Research Archives V:
Kent State Special Collections. Y-86

Literary Research Archives VI: The Modern
Literary Manuscripts Collection in the
Special Collections of the Washington
University Libraries Y-87

Literary Research Archives VII:
The University of Virginia Libraries Y-91

Literary Research Archives VIII:
The Henry E. Huntington Library Y-92

Literary Research Archives IX:
Special Collections at Boston University. . Y-99

The Literary Scene and Situation and . . . Who
(Besides Oprah) Really Runs American
Literature?. Y-99

Literary Societies Y-98, Y-99, Y-00, Y-01

"Literary Style" (1857), by William
    Forsyth [excerpt]. DLB-57

Literatura Chicanesca: The View From
    Without DLB-82

Literature at Nurse, or Circulating Morals (1885),
    by George Moore. DLB-18

The Literature of Boxing in England
    through Arthur Conan Doyle Y-01

The Literature of the
    Modern Breakthrough DLB-259

Littell, Eliakim 1797-1870 .... DLB-79

Littell, Robert S. 1831-1896 .... DLB-79

Little, Brown and Company DLB-49

Little Magazines and Newspapers. DS-15

The Little Review 1914-1929 .... DS-15

Littlewood, Joan 1914- DLB-13

Lively, Penelope 1933- DLB-14, 161, 207

Liverpool University Press DLB-112

The Lives of the Poets DLB-142

Livesay, Dorothy 1909- DLB-68

Livesay, Florence Randal 1874-1953 ..... DLB-92

"Living in Ruin," by Gerald Stern DLB-105

Livings, Henry 1929-1998 .... DLB-13

Livingston, Anne Howe 1763-1841 ...DLB-37, 200

Livingston, Myra Cohn 1926-1996 ...... DLB-61

Livingston, William 1723-1790 .... DLB-31

Livingstone, David 1813-1873 .... DLB-166

Livingstone, Douglas 1932-1996 .... DLB-225

Livy 59 B.C.-A.D. 17 ...... DLB-211; CDWLB-1

Liyong, Taban lo (see Taban lo Liyong)

Lizárraga, Sylvia S. 1925- DLB-82

Llewellyn, Richard 1906-1983 .... DLB-15

Lloyd, Edward [publishing house] DLB-106

Lobel, Arnold 1933- DLB-61

Lochridge, Betsy Hopkins (see Fancher, Betsy)

Locke, David Ross 1833-1888 .... DLB-11, 23

Locke, John 1632-1704 ..... DLB-31, 101, 213, 252

Locke, Richard Adams 1800-1871 .... DLB-43

Locker-Lampson, Frederick
    1821-1895 .... DLB-35, 184

Lockhart, John Gibson
    1794-1854 .... DLB-110, 116 144

Lockridge, Ross, Jr. 1914-1948 ..... DLB-143; Y-80

Locrine and Selimus DLB-62

Lodge, David 1935- DLB-14, 194

Lodge, George Cabot 1873-1909 .... DLB-54

Lodge, Henry Cabot 1850-1924 .... DLB-47

Lodge, Thomas 1558-1625. .... DLB-172

From *Defence of Poetry* (1579) DLB-172

Loeb, Harold 1891-1974 .... DLB-4

Loeb, William 1905-1981 .... DLB-127

Lofting, Hugh 1886-1947 .... DLB-160

Logan, Deborah Norris 1761-1839 ...... DLB-200

Logan, James 1674-1751 .... DLB-24, 140

Logan, John 1923- DLB-5

Logan, Martha Daniell 1704?-1779 ..... DLB-200

Logan, William 1950- DLB-120

Logau, Friedrich von 1605-1655 .... DLB-164

Logue, Christopher 1926- DLB-27

Lohenstein, Daniel Casper von
    1635-1683 .... DLB-168

Lo-Johansson, Ivar 1901-1990 .... DLB-259

Lomonosov, Mikhail Vasil'evich
    1711-1765 .... DLB-150

London, Jack
    1876-1916..... DLB-8, 12, 78, 212; CDALB-3

The London Magazine 1820-1829........ DLB-110

Long, David 1948- DLB-244

Long, H., and Brother DLB-49

Long, Haniel 1888-1956............... DLB-45

Long, Ray 1878-1935................. DLB-137

Longfellow, Henry Wadsworth
    1807-1882........ DLB-1, 59, 235; CDALB-2

Longfellow, Samuel 1819-1892. .... DLB-1

Longford, Elizabeth 1906- DLB-155

Longinus circa first century DLB-176

Longley, Michael 1939- DLB-40

Longman, T. [publishing house]........ DLB-154

Longmans, Green and Company........ DLB-49

Longmore, George 1793?-1867.......... DLB-99

Longstreet, Augustus Baldwin
    1790-1870 ....DLB-3, 11, 74, 248

Longworth, D. [publishing house] DLB-49

Lonsdale, Frederick 1881-1954....... DLB-10

A Look at the Contemporary Black Theatre
    Movement DLB-38

Loos, Anita 1893-1981 ..... DLB-11, 26, 228; Y-81

Lopate, Phillip 1943- Y-80

Lopez, Barry 1945- DLB-256

López, Diana
    (see Isabella, Ríos)

López, Josefina 1969- DLB-209

Loranger, Jean-Aubert 1896-1942........ DLB-92

Lorca, Federico García 1898-1936 ...... DLB-108

Lord, John Keast 1818-1872............ DLB-99

The Lord Chamberlain's Office and Stage
    Censorship in England............. DLB-10

Lorde, Audre 1934-1992 .... DLB-41

Lorimer, George Horace 1867-1939...... DLB-91

Loring, A. K. [publishing house]........ DLB-49

Loring and Mussey.................. DLB-46

Lorris, Guillaume de (see *Roman de la Rose*)

Lossing, Benson J. 1813-1891.......... DLB-30

Lothar, Ernst 1890-1974............... DLB-81

Lothrop, D., and Company DLB-49

Lothrop, Harriet M. 1844-1924 .... DLB-42

Loti, Pierre 1850-1923 .... DLB-123

Lotichius Secundus, Petrus 1528-1560....DLB-179

Lott, Emeline ?-? DLB-166

Louisiana State University Press Y-97

The Lounger, no. 20 (1785), by Henry
    Mackenzie DLB-39

Lounsbury, Thomas R. 1838-1915 ...... DLB-71

Louÿs, Pierre 1870-1925.............. DLB-123

Lovelace, Earl 1935- DLB-125; CDWLB-3

Lovelace, Richard 1618-1657 .... DLB-131

Lovell, Coryell and Company DLB-49

Lovell, John W., Company DLB-49

Lover, Samuel 1797-1868 .... DLB-159, 190

Lovesey, Peter 1936- DLB-87

Lovinescu, Eugen
    1881-1943 .... DLB-220; CDWLB-4

Lovingood, Sut
    (see Harris, George Washington)

Low, Samuel 1765-? DLB-37

Lowell, Amy 1874-1925 .... DLB-54, 140

Lowell, James Russell 1819-1891
    ......DLB-1, 11, 64, 79, 189, 235; CDALB-2

Lowell, Robert 1917-1977 .. DLB-5, 169; CDALB-7

Lowenfels, Walter 1897-1976 .... DLB-4

Lowndes, Marie Belloc 1868-1947 .... DLB-70

Lowndes, William Thomas 1798-1843... DLB-184

Lownes, Humphrey [publishing house] ...DLB-170

Lowry, Lois 1937- DLB-52

Lowry, Malcolm 1909-1957 ... DLB-15; CDBLB-7

Lowther, Pat 1935-1975 .... DLB-53

Loy, Mina 1882-1966............... DLB-4, 54

Lozeau, Albert 1878-1924.............. DLB-92

Lubbock, Percy 1879-1965............ DLB-149

Lucan A.D. 39-A.D. 65 .... DLB-211

Lucas, E. V. 1868-1938 ....DLB-98, 149, 153

Lucas, Fielding, Jr. [publishing house] DLB-49

Luce, Clare Booth 1903-1987 .... DLB-228

Luce, Henry R. 1898-1967 .... DLB-91

Luce, John W., and Company DLB-46

Lucian circa 120-180. ....DLB-176

Lucie-Smith, Edward 1933- DLB-40

Lucilius circa 180 B.C.-102/101 B.C..... DLB-211

Lucini, Gian Pietro 1867-1914 .... DLB-114

Lucretius circa 94 B.C.-circa 49 B.C.
    .... DLB-211; CDWLB-1

Luder, Peter circa 1415-1472 ....DLB-179

Ludlum, Robert 1927- Y-82

Ludus de Antichristo circa 1160 .... DLB-148

Ludvigson, Susan 1942- DLB-120

Ludwig, Jack 1922- DLB-60

Ludwig, Otto 1813-1865 .... DLB-129

Ludwigslied 881 or 882 .... DLB-148

Luera, Yolanda 1953- DLB-122

Luft, Lya 1938- DLB-145

Lugansky, Kazak Vladimir
    (see Dal', Vladimir Ivanovich)

Lugn, Kristina 1948- DLB-257

Lukács, Georg (see Lukács, György)

Lukács, György
    1885-1971........DLB-215, 242; CDWLB-4

Luke, Peter 1919- DLB-13

Lummis, Charles F. 1859-1928........ DLB-186

Lundkvist, Artur 1906-1991 . . . . .DLB-259

Lupton, F. M., Company. DLB-49

Lupus of Ferrières
circa 805-circa 862. . . . . .DLB-148

Lurie, Alison 1926- DLB-2

Lustig, Arnošt 1926- DLB-232

Luther, Martin 1483-1546 . . . DLB-179; CDWLB-2

Luzi, Mario 1914- DLB-128

L'vov, Nikolai Aleksandrovich 1751-1803 . .DLB-150

Lyall, Gavin 1932- DLB-87

Lydgate, John circa 1370-1450 . . . . .DLB-146

Lyly, John circa 1554-1606 . . . . .DLB-62, 167

Lynch, Patricia 1898-1972 . . . . .DLB-160

Lynch, Richard flourished 1596-1601 . . . .DLB-172

Lynd, Robert 1879-1949 . . . . .DLB-98

Lyon, Matthew 1749-1822. . . . . .DLB-43

Lyotard, Jean-François 1924-1998 . . . . . . .DLB-242

Lysias circa 459 B.C.-circa 380 B.C. DLB-176

Lytle, Andrew 1902-1995 . . . . .DLB-6; Y-95

Lytton, Edward
(see Bulwer-Lytton, Edward)

Lytton, Edward Robert Bulwer
1831-1891 . . . . .DLB-32

M

Maass, Joachim 1901-1972. . . . . .DLB-69

Mabie, Hamilton Wright 1845-1916 . . . . . .DLB-71

Mac A'Ghobhainn, Iain (see Smith, Iain Crichton)

MacArthur, Charles 1895-1956. . . . . DLB-7, 25, 44

Macaulay, Catherine 1731-1791. . . . . . . .DLB-104

Macaulay, David 1945- DLB-61

Macaulay, Rose 1881-1958 . . . . .DLB-36

Macaulay, Thomas Babington
1800-1859 . . . . DLB-32, 55; CDBLB-4

Macaulay Company DLB-46

MacBeth, George 1932- DLB-40

Macbeth, Madge 1880-1965 . . . . .DLB-92

MacCaig, Norman 1910-1996 . . . . .DLB-27

MacDiarmid, Hugh
1892-1978 . . . . DLB-20; CDBLB-7

MacDonald, Cynthia 1928- DLB-105

MacDonald, George 1824-1905 . . . DLB-18, 163, 178

MacDonald, John D. 1916-1986 . . . . . DLB-8; Y-86

MacDonald, Philip 1899?-1980 . . . . .DLB-77

Macdonald, Ross (see Millar, Kenneth)

Macdonald, Sharman 1951- DLB-245

MacDonald, Wilson 1880-1967. . . . . .DLB-92

Macdonald and Company (Publishers) . . .DLB-112

MacEwen, Gwendolyn 1941-1987. . . .DLB-53, 251

Macfadden, Bernarr 1868-1955. . . . . .DLB-25, 91

MacGregor, John 1825-1892 . . . . .DLB-166

MacGregor, Mary Esther (see Keith, Marian)

Machado, Antonio 1875-1939 . . . . .DLB-108

Machado, Manuel 1874-1947. . . . . .DLB-108

Machar, Agnes Maule 1837-1927. . . . . . . .DLB-92

Machaut, Guillaume de
circa 1300-1377 . . . . .DLB-208

Machen, Arthur Llewelyn Jones
1863-1947 . . . . DLB-36, 156, 178

MacInnes, Colin 1914-1976. . . . . .DLB-14

MacInnes, Helen 1907-1985. . . . . .DLB-87

Mac Intyre, Tom 1931- DLB-245

Mačiulis, Jonas (see Maironis, Jonas)

Mack, Maynard 1909- DLB-111

Mackall, Leonard L. 1879-1937. . . . . . . .DLB-140

MacKaye, Percy 1875-1956. . . . . .DLB-54

Macken, Walter 1915-1967 . . . . .DLB-13

Mackenzie, Alexander 1763-1820 . . . . . . .DLB-99

Mackenzie, Alexander Slidell
1803-1848 . . . . .DLB-183

Mackenzie, Compton 1883-1972 . . . . .DLB-34, 100

Mackenzie, Henry 1745-1831 . . . . .DLB-39

Mackenzie, Kenneth (Seaforth)
1913-1955 . . . . .DLB-260

Mackenzie, William 1758-1828 . . . . .DLB-187

Mackey, Nathaniel 1947- DLB-169

Mackey, Shena 1944- DLB-231

Mackey, William Wellington
1937- DLB-38

Mackintosh, Elizabeth (see Tey, Josephine)

Mackintosh, Sir James 1765-1832 . . . . . . .DLB-158

Maclaren, Ian (see Watson, John)

Macklin, Charles 1699-1797. . . . . .DLB-89

MacLean, Katherine Anne 1925- DLB-8

Maclean, Norman 1902-1990 . . . . .DLB-206

MacLeish, Archibald 1892-1982
. . . . DLB-4, 7, 45, 228; Y-82; CDALB-7

MacLennan, Hugh 1907-1990 . . . . .DLB-68

MacLeod, Alistair 1936- DLB-60

Macleod, Fiona (see Sharp, William)

Macleod, Norman 1906-1985 . . . . .DLB-4

Mac Low, Jackson 1922- DLB-193

Macmillan and Company DLB-106

The Macmillan Company DLB-49

Macmillan's English Men of Letters,
First Series (1878-1892) DLB-144

MacNamara, Brinsley 1890-1963 . . . . . . .DLB-10

MacNeice, Louis 1907-1963. . . . . .DLB-10, 20

MacPhail, Andrew 1864-1938. . . . . .DLB-92

Macpherson, James 1736-1796. . . . . .DLB-109

Macpherson, Jay 1931- DLB-53

Macpherson, Jeanie 1884-1946 . . . . .DLB-44

Macrae Smith Company DLB-46

MacRaye, Lucy Betty (see Webling, Lucy)

Macrone, John [publishing house] DLB-106

MacShane, Frank 1927-1999 . . . . .DLB-111

Macy-Masius DLB-46

Madden, David 1933- DLB-6

Madden, Sir Frederic 1801-1873 . . . . .DLB-184

Maddow, Ben 1909-1992. . . . . .DLB-44

Maddux, Rachel 1912-1983. . . . . . . .DLB-234; Y-93

Madgett, Naomi Long 1923- DLB-76

Madhubuti, Haki R. 1942- DLB-5, 41; DS-8

Madison, James 1751-1836 . . . . .DLB-37

Madsen, Svend Åge 1939- DLB-214

Maeterlinck, Maurice 1862-1949 . . . . . . .DLB-192

Mafūz, Najīb 1911- Y-88

Magee, David 1905-1977. . . . . .DLB-187

Maginn, William 1794-1842 . . . . . . .DLB-110, 159

Magoffin, Susan Shelby 1827-1855 . . . . . .DLB-239

Mahan, Alfred Thayer 1840-1914. . . . . . . .DLB-47

Maheux-Forcier, Louise 1929- DLB-60

Mahin, John Lee 1902-1984 . . . . .DLB-44

Mahon, Derek 1941- DLB-40

Maikov, Vasilii Ivanovich 1728-1778. . . . .DLB-150

Mailer, Norman 1923-
. . . . DLB-2, 16, 28, 185; Y-80, Y-83, Y-97;
DS-3; CDALB-6

Maillart, Ella 1903-1997. . . . . .DLB-195

Maillet, Adrienne 1885-1963 . . . . .DLB-68

Maillet, Antonine 1929- DLB-60

Maillu, David G. 1939- DLB-157

Maimonides, Moses 1138-1204 . . . . .DLB-115

Main Selections of the Book-of-the-Month
Club, 1926-1945 . . . . .DLB-9

Main Trends in Twentieth-Century Book
Clubs. DLB-46

Mainwaring, Daniel 1902-1977 . . . . .DLB-44

Mair, Charles 1838-1927 . . . . .DLB-99

Maironis, Jonas
1862-1932 . . . . DLB-220; CDWLB-4

Mais, Roger 1905-1955 . . . . . DLB-125; CDWLB-3

Major, Andre 1942- DLB-60

Major, Charles 1856-1913 . . . . .DLB-202

Major, Clarence 1936- DLB-33

Major, Kevin 1949- DLB-60

Major Books DLB-46

Makemie, Francis circa 1658-1708. . . . . . .DLB-24

The Making of Americans Contract Y-98

The Making of a People, by
J. M. Ritchie .DLB-66

Maksimović, Desanka
1898-1993 . . . . DLB-147; CDWLB-4

Malamud, Bernard 1914-1986
. . . . . . DLB-2, 28, 152; Y-80, Y-86; CDALB-1

Mălăncioiu, Ileana 1940- DLB-232

Malerba, Luigi 1927- DLB-196

Malet, Lucas 1852-1931. . . . . .DLB-153

Mallarmé, Stéphane 1842-1898 . . . . .DLB-217

Malleson, Lucy Beatrice (see Gilbert, Anthony)

Mallet-Joris, Françoise 1930- DLB-83

Mallock, W. H. 1849-1923 . . . . .DLB-18, 57

"Every Man His Own Poet; or,
The Inspired Singer's Recipe
Book" (1877). DLB-35

Malone, Dumas 1892-1986 . . . . .DLB-17

Malone, Edmond 1741-1812 . . . . .DLB-142

Malory, Sir Thomas
circa 1400-1410 - 1471. . . .DLB-146; CDBLB-1

Malpede, Karen 1945- DLB-249

Malraux, André 1901-1976. . . . . DLB-72

Malthus, Thomas Robert
1766-1834. . . . . DLB-107, 158

Maltz, Albert 1908-1985 . . . . DLB-102

Malzberg, Barry N. 1939- DLB-8

Mamet, David 1947- DLB-7

Mamin, Dmitrii Narkisovich 1852-1912. . DLB-238

Manaka, Matsemela 1956- DLB-157

Manchester University Press DLB-112

Mandel, Eli 1922-1992 . . . . DLB-53

Mandeville, Bernard 1670-1733 . . . . DLB-101

Mandeville, Sir John
mid fourteenth century DLB-146

Mandiargues, André Pieyre de 1909- . . . DLB-83

Manea, Norman 1936- DLB-232

Manfred, Frederick 1912-1994 . . . .DLB-6, 212, 227

Manfredi, Gianfranco 1948- DLB-196

Mangan, Sherry 1904-1961 . . . . DLB-4

Manganelli, Giorgio 1922-1990 . . . . DLB-196

Manilius fl. first century A.D. DLB-211

Mankiewicz, Herman 1897-1953 . . . . DLB-26

Mankiewicz, Joseph L. 1909-1993 . . . . . . DLB-44

Mankowitz, Wolf 1924-1998 . . . . DLB-15

Manley, Delarivière 1672?-1724 . . . . . . DLB-39, 80

Preface to The Secret History, of Queen Zarah,
and the Zarazians (1705) DLB-39

Mann, Abby 1927- DLB-44

Mann, Charles 1929-1998 . . . . Y-98

Mann, Heinrich 1871-1950 . . . . DLB-66, 118

Mann, Horace 1796-1859 . . . . DLB-1, 235

Mann, Klaus 1906-1949 . . . . DLB-56

Mann, Mary Peabody 1806-1887 . . . . DLB-239

Mann, Thomas 1875-1955 . . . DLB-66; CDWLB-2

Mann, William D'Alton 1839-1920 . . . . . DLB-137

Mannin, Ethel 1900-1984 . . . . DLB-191, 195

Manning, Emily (see Australie)

Manning, Frederic 1882-1935. . . . . DLB-260

Manning, Laurence 1899-1972 . . . . DLB-251

Manning, Marie 1873?-1945 . . . . DLB-29

Manning and Loring. DLB-49

Mannyng, Robert
flourished 1303-1338 . . . . DLB-146

Mano, D. Keith 1942- DLB-6

Manor Books DLB-46

Mansfield, Katherine 1888-1923. . . . . . . DLB-162

Manuel, Niklaus circa 1484-1530 . . . . . . .DLB-179

Manzini, Gianna 1896-1974 . . . . .DLB-177

Mapanje, Jack 1944- DLB-157

Maraini, Dacia 1936- DLB-196

Marcel Proust at 129 and the Proust Society
of America Y-00

Marcel Proust's Remembrance of Things Past:
The Rediscovered Galley Proofs Y-00

March, William 1893-1954. . . . . DLB-9, 86

Marchand, Leslie A. 1900-1999 . . . . DLB-103

Marchant, Bessie 1862-1941. . . . . DLB-160

Marchant, Tony 1959- DLB-245

Marchenko, Anastasiia Iakovlevna
1830-1880 . . . . DLB-238

Marchessault, Jovette 1938- DLB-60

Marcinkevičius, Justinas 1930- DLB-232

Marcus, Frank 1928- DLB-13

Marcuse, Herbert 1898-1979 . . . . DLB-242

Marden, Orison Swett 1850-1924. . . . . . . DLB-137

Marechera, Dambudzo 1952-1987 . . . . . . DLB-157

Marek, Richard, Books. DLB-46

Mares, E. A. 1938- DLB-122

Margulies, Donald 1954- DLB-228

Mariani, Paul 1940- DLB-111

Marie de France flourished 1160-1178 . . . DLB-208

Marie-Victorin, Frère 1885-1944 . . . . DLB-92

Marin, Biagio 1891-1985 . . . . DLB-128

Marincović, Ranko
1913- DLB-147; CDWLB-4

Marinetti, Filippo Tommaso
1876-1944. . . . . DLB-114

Marion, Frances 1886-1973 . . . . DLB-44

Marius, Richard C. 1933-1999 . . . . Y-85

Markevich, Boleslav Mikhailovich
1822-1884 . . . . DLB-238

Markfield, Wallace 1926- DLB-2, 28

Markham, Edwin 1852-1940 . . . . DLB-54, 186

Markle, Fletcher 1921-1991 . . . . .DLB-68; Y-91

Marlatt, Daphne 1942- DLB-60

Marlitt, E. 1825-1887 . . . . DLB-129

Marlowe, Christopher
1564-1593 . . . . DLB-62; CDBLB-1

Marlyn, John 1912- DLB-88

Marmion, Shakerley 1603-1639 . . . . DLB-58

Der Marner before 1230-circa 1287 . . . . . DLB-138

Marnham, Patrick 1943- DLB-204

The Marprelate Tracts 1588-1589 . . . . DLB-132

Marquand, John P. 1893-1960 . . . . . . DLB-9, 102

Marqués, René 1919-1979 . . . . DLB-113

Marquis, Don 1878-1937 . . . . DLB-11, 25

Marriott, Anne 1913- DLB-68

Marryat, Frederick 1792-1848 . . . . . . DLB-21, 163

Marsh, Capen, Lyon and Webb. DLB-49

Marsh, George Perkins
1801-1882 . . . . DLB-1, 64, 243

Marsh, James 1794-1842. . . . . DLB-1, 59

Marsh, Narcissus 1638-1713 . . . . DLB-213

Marsh, Ngaio 1899-1982 . . . . DLB-77

Marshall, Alan 1902-1984 . . . . DLB-260

Marshall, Edison 1894-1967 . . . . DLB-102

Marshall, Edward 1932- DLB-16

Marshall, Emma 1828-1899 . . . . DLB-163

Marshall, James 1942-1992. . . . . DLB-61

Marshall, Joyce 1913- DLB-88

Marshall, Paule 1929- DLB-33, 157, 227

Marshall, Tom 1938-1993 . . . . DLB-60

Marsilius of Padua
circa 1275-circa 1342 . . . . DLB-115

Mars-Jones, Adam 1954- DLB-207

Marson, Una 1905-1965. . . . . .DLB-157

Marston, John 1576-1634 . . . . .DLB-58, 172

Marston, Philip Bourke 1850-1887. . . . . . DLB-35

Martens, Kurt 1870-1945 . . . . DLB-66

Martial circa A.D. 40-circa A.D. 103
. . . . .DLB-211; CDWLB-1

Martien, William S. [publishing house] . . . DLB-49

Martin, Abe (see Hubbard, Kin)

Martin, Catherine ca. 1847-1937. . . . . . . DLB-230

Martin, Charles 1942- DLB-120

Martin, Claire 1914- DLB-60

Martin, David 1915-1997 . . . . DLB-260

Martin, Jay 1935- DLB-111

Martin, Johann (see Laurentius von Schnüffis)

Martin, Thomas 1696-1771 . . . . DLB-213

Martin, Violet Florence (see Ross, Martin)

Martin du Gard, Roger 1881-1958. . . . . . DLB-65

Martineau, Harriet
1802-1876. . . . . .DLB-21, 55, 159, 163, 166, 190

Martínez, Demetria 1960- DLB-209

Martínez, Eliud 1935- DLB-122

Martínez, Max 1943- DLB-82

Martínez, Rubén 1962- DLB-209

Martinson, Harry 1904-1978 . . . . DLB-259

Martinson, Moa 1890-1964 . . . . DLB-259

Martone, Michael 1955- DLB-218

Martyn, Edward 1859-1923 . . . . DLB-10

Marvell, Andrew
1621-1678. . . . . DLB-131; CDBLB-2

Marvin X 1944- DLB-38

Marx, Karl 1818-1883 . . . . DLB-129

Marzials, Theo 1850-1920 . . . . DLB-35

Masefield, John
1878-1967. . . DLB-10, 19, 153, 160; CDBLB-5

Masham, Damaris Cudworth Lady
1659-1708. . . . . DLB-252

Mason, A. E. W. 1865-1948. . . . . DLB-70

Mason, Bobbie Ann
1940- DLB-173; Y-87; CDALB-7

Mason, William 1725-1797 . . . . DLB-142

Mason Brothers DLB-49

Massey, Gerald 1828-1907 . . . . DLB-32

Massey, Linton R. 1900-1974. . . . . .DLB-187

Massinger, Philip 1583-1640 . . . . DLB-58

Masson, David 1822-1907 . . . . DLB-144

Masters, Edgar Lee
1868-1950 . . . . DLB-54; CDALB-3

Masters, Hilary 1928- DLB-244

Mastronardi, Lucio 1930-1979 . . . . .DLB-177

Matevski, Mateja 1929- . . .DLB-181; CDWLB-4

Mather, Cotton
1663-1728. . . . . . . DLB-24, 30, 140; CDALB-2

Mather, Increase 1639-1723 . . . . DLB-24

Mather, Richard 1596-1669 . . . . DLB-24

Matheson, Annie 1853-1924 . . . . .DLB-240

Matheson, Richard 1926- DLB-8, 44

Matheus, John F. 1887- DLB-51

Mathews, Cornelius 1817?-1889 . . .DLB-3, 64, 250

Mathews, Elkin [publishing house] DLB-112

Mathews, John Joseph 1894-1979 . . . . . . .DLB-175

Mathias, Roland 1915- DLB-27

Mathis, June 1892-1927 . . . . .DLB-44

Mathis, Sharon Bell 1937- DLB-33

Matković, Marijan 1915-1985 . . . . .DLB-181

Matoš, Antun Gustav 1873-1914 . . . . . . .DLB-147

Matsumoto Seichō 1909-1992 . . . . .DLB-182

The Matter of England 1240-1400. . . . . . .DLB-146

The Matter of Rome early twelfth to late
    fifteenth century DLB-146

Matthew of Vendôme
    circa 1130-circa 1200. . . . . .DLB-208

Matthews, Brander
    1852-1929 . . . . DLB-71, 78; DS-13

Matthews, Jack 1925- DLB-6

Matthews, Victoria Earle 1861-1907 . . . . .DLB-221

Matthews, William 1942-1997 . . . . .DLB-5

Matthiessen, F. O. 1902-1950 . . . . .DLB-63

Matthiessen, Peter 1927- DLB-6, 173

Maturin, Charles Robert 1780-1824 . . . . .DLB-178

Maugham, W. Somerset 1874-1965
    . . . . DLB-10, 36, 77, 100, 162, 195; CDBLB-6

Maupassant, Guy de 1850-1893 . . . . .DLB-123

Mauriac, Claude 1914-1996. . . . . .DLB-83

Mauriac, François 1885-1970 . . . . .DLB-65

Maurice, Frederick Denison
    1805-1872 . . . . .DLB-55

Maurois, André 1885-1967 . . . . .DLB-65

Maury, James 1718-1769 . . . . .DLB-31

Mavor, Elizabeth 1927- DLB-14

Mavor, Osborne Henry (see Bridie, James)

Maxwell, Gavin 1914-1969 . . . . .DLB-204

Maxwell, H. [publishing house] DLB-49

Maxwell, John [publishing house] DLB-106

Maxwell, William 1908- DLB-218; Y-80

May, Elaine 1932- DLB-44

May, Karl 1842-1912 . . . . .DLB-129

May, Thomas 1595 or 1596-1650 . . . . .DLB-58

Mayer, Bernadette 1945- DLB-165

Mayer, Mercer 1943- DLB-61

Mayer, O. B. 1818-1891 . . . . .DLB-3, 248

Mayes, Herbert R. 1900-1987 . . . . .DLB-137

Mayes, Wendell 1919-1992 . . . . .DLB-26

Mayfield, Julian 1928-1984 . . . . .DLB-33; Y-84

Mayhew, Henry 1812-1887 . . . . . .DLB-18, 55, 190

Mayhew, Jonathan 1720-1766 . . . . .DLB-31

Mayne, Ethel Colburn 1865-1941 . . . . . . .DLB-197

Mayne, Jasper 1604-1672 . . . . .DLB-126

Mayne, Seymour 1944- DLB-60

Mayor, Flora Macdonald 1872-1932 . . . . . .DLB-36

Mayröcker, Friederike 1924- DLB-85

Mazrui, Ali A. 1933- DLB-125

Mažuranić, Ivan 1814-1890 . . . . .DLB-147

Mazursky, Paul 1930- DLB-44

McAlmon, Robert 1896-1956 . . .DLB-4, 45; DS-15

Robert McAlmon's "A Night at Bricktop's" . . Y-01

McArthur, Peter 1866-1924. . . . . .DLB-92

McAuley, James 1917-1976. . . . . .DLB-260

McBride, Robert M., and Company DLB-46

McCabe, Patrick 1955- DLB-194

McCaffrey, Anne 1926- DLB-8

McCarthy, Cormac 1933- DLB-6, 143, 256

McCarthy, Mary 1912-1989 . . . . . . .DLB-2; Y-81

McCay, Winsor 1871-1934 . . . . .DLB-22

McClane, Albert Jules 1922-1991 . . . . . . .DLB-171

McClatchy, C. K. 1858-1936. . . . . .DLB-25

McClellan, George Marion 1860-1934 . . .DLB-50

McCloskey, Robert 1914- DLB-22

McClung, Nellie Letitia 1873-1951 . . . . . .DLB-92

McClure, Joanna 1930- DLB-16

McClure, Michael 1932- DLB-16

McClure, Phillips and Company DLB-46

McClure, S. S. 1857-1949. . . . . .DLB-91

McClurg, A. C., and Company DLB-49

McCluskey, John A., Jr. 1944- DLB-33

McCollum, Michael A. 1946 . . . . Y-87

McConnell, William C. 1917- DLB-88

McCord, David 1897-1997. . . . . .DLB-61

McCord, Louisa S. 1810-1879 . . . . .DLB-248

McCorkle, Jill 1958- DLB-234; Y-87

McCorkle, Samuel Eusebius
    1746-1811 . . . . .DLB-37

McCormick, Anne O'Hare 1880-1954 . . . .DLB-29

Kenneth Dale McCormick Tributes Y-97

McCormick, Robert R. 1880-1955 . . . . . . .DLB-29

McCourt, Edward 1907-1972. . . . . .DLB-88

McCoy, Horace 1897-1955 . . . . .DLB-9

McCrae, Hugh 1876-1958 . . . . .DLB-260

McCrae, John 1872-1918 . . . . .DLB-92

McCullagh, Joseph B. 1842-1896. . . . . . . .DLB-23

McCullers, Carson
    1917-1967 . . . . . DLB-2, 7, 173, 228; CDALB-1

McCulloch, Thomas 1776-1843. . . . . .DLB-99

McDonald, Forrest 1927- DLB-17

McDonald, Walter 1934- DLB-105, DS-9

"Getting Started: Accepting the Regions
    You Own—or Which Own You," DLB-105

McDougall, Colin 1917-1984 . . . . .DLB-68

McDowell, Katharine Sherwood Bonner
    1849-1883 . . . . .DLB-202, 239

McDowell, Obolensky. DLB-46

McEwan, Ian 1948- DLB-14, 194

McFadden, David 1940- DLB-60

McFall, Frances Elizabeth Clarke
    (see Grand, Sarah)

McFarlane, Leslie 1902-1977 . . . . .DLB-88

McFarland, Ronald 1942- DLB-256

McFee, William 1881-1966 . . . . .DLB-153

McGahern, John 1934- DLB-14, 231

McGee, Thomas D'Arcy 1825-1868 . . . . . .DLB-99

McGeehan, W. O. 1879-1933 . . . . . . .DLB-25, 171

McGill, Ralph 1898-1969 . . . . .DLB-29

McGinley, Phyllis 1905-1978 . . . . .DLB-11, 48

McGinniss, Joe 1942- DLB-185

McGirt, James E. 1874-1930 . . . . .DLB-50

McGlashan and Gill. DLB-106

McGough, Roger 1937- DLB-40

McGrath, John 1935- DLB-233

McGrath, Patrick 1950- DLB-231

McGraw-Hill DLB-46

McGuane, Thomas 1939- DLB-2, 212; Y-80

McGuckian, Medbh 1950- DLB-40

McGuffey, William Holmes 1800-1873 . . . .DLB-42

McGuinness, Frank 1953- DLB-245

McHenry, James 1785-1845. . . . . .DLB-202

McIlvanney, William 1936- DLB-14, 207

McIlwraith, Jean Newton 1859-1938. . . . . .DLB-92

McIntosh, Maria Jane 1803-1878. . . .DLB-239, 248

McIntyre, James 1827-1906 . . . . .DLB-99

McIntyre, O. O. 1884-1938. . . . . .DLB-25

McKay, Claude 1889-1948 . . . .DLB-4, 45, 51, 117

The David McKay Company DLB-49

McKean, William V. 1820-1903 . . . . .DLB-23

McKenna, Stephen 1888-1967 . . . . .DLB-197

The McKenzie Trust Y-96

McKerrow, R. B. 1872-1940 . . . . .DLB-201

McKinley, Robin 1952- DLB-52

McKnight, Reginald 1956- DLB-234

McLachlan, Alexander 1818-1896. . . . . . . .DLB-99

McLaren, Floris Clark 1904-1978 . . . . . . .DLB-68

McLaverty, Michael 1907- DLB-15

McLean, John R. 1848-1916 . . . . .DLB-23

McLean, William L. 1852-1931. . . . . .DLB-25

McLennan, William 1856-1904 . . . . .DLB-92

McLoughlin Brothers DLB-49

McLuhan, Marshall 1911-1980 . . . . .DLB-88

McMaster, John Bach 1852-1932. . . . . . . .DLB-47

McMurtry, Larry 1936-
    . . . . . DLB-2, 143, 256; Y-80, Y-87; CDALB-6

McNally, Terrence 1939- DLB-7, 249

McNeil, Florence 1937- DLB-60

McNeile, Herman Cyril 1888-1937 . . . . . . .DLB-77

McNickle, D'Arcy 1904-1977 . . . . . .DLB-175, 212

McPhee, John 1931- DLB-185

McPherson, James Alan 1943- DLB-38, 244

McPherson, Sandra 1943- Y-86

McTaggart, J. M. E. 1866-1925. . . . . . . .DLB-262

McWhirter, George 1939- DLB-60

McWilliams, Carey 1905-1980 . . . . .DLB-137

Mda, Zakes 1948- DLB-225

Mead, L. T. 1844-1914 . . . . .DLB-141

Mead, Matthew 1924- DLB-40

Mead, Taylor ?- DLB-16

Meany, Tom 1903-1964.............DLB-171

Mechthild von Magdeburg
circa 1207-circa 1282 .... DLB-138

Medieval French Drama.............. DLB-208

Medieval Travel Diaries.............. DLB-203

Medill, Joseph 1823-1899 .... DLB-43

Medoff, Mark 1940- DLB-7

Meek, Alexander Beaufort
1814-1865. .... DLB-3, 248

Meeke, Mary ?-1816?................ DLB-116

Meinke, Peter 1932- DLB-5

Mejia Vallejo, Manuel 1923- DLB-113

Melanchthon, Philipp 1497-1560 ....DLB-179

Melançon, Robert 1947- DLB-60

Mell, Max 1882-1971 .... DLB-81, 124

Mellow, James R. 1926-1997 .... DLB-111

Mel'nikov, Pavel Ivanovich 1818-1883... DLB-238

Meltzer, David 1937- DLB-16

Meltzer, Milton 1915- DLB-61

Melville, Elizabeth, Lady Culross
circa 1585-1640 .... DLB-172

Melville, Herman
1819-1891........ DLB-3, 74, 250; CDALB-2

Memoirs of Life and Literature (1920),
by W. H. Mallock [excerpt] DLB-57

Mena, María Cristina 1893-1965 ... DLB-209, 221

Menander 342-341 B.C.-circa 292-291 B.C.
.................DLB-176; CDWLB-1

Menantes (see Hunold, Christian Friedrich)

Mencke, Johann Burckhard
1674-1732.................... DLB-168

Mencken, H. L. 1880-1956
........DLB-11, 29, 63, 137, 222; CDALB-4

H. L. Mencken's "Berlin, February, 1917" Y-00

Mencken and Nietzsche: An Unpublished
Excerpt from H. L. Mencken's *My Life
as Author and Editor* Y-93

Mendelssohn, Moses 1729-1786 .... DLB-97

Mendes, Catulle 1841-1909 .... DLB-217

Méndez M., Miguel 1930- DLB-82

Mens Rea (or Something)................Y-97

The Mercantile Library of New York Y-96

Mercer, Cecil William (see Yates, Dornford)

Mercer, David 1928-1980.............. DLB-13

Mercer, John 1704-1768 .... DLB-31

Meredith, George
1828-1909 ....DLB-18, 35, 57, 159; CDBLB-4

Meredith, Louisa Anne 1812-1895.. DLB-166, 230

Meredith, Owen
(see Lytton, Edward Robert Bulwer)

Meredith, William 1919- DLB-5

Mergerle, Johann Ulrich
(see Abraham ä Sancta Clara)

Mérimée, Prosper 1803-1870 ...... DLB-119, 192

Merivale, John Herman 1779-1844...... DLB-96

Meriwether, Louise 1923- DLB-33

Merlin Press..................... DLB-112

Merriam, Eve 1916-1992 .... DLB-61

The Merriam Company............... DLB-49

Merril, Judith 1923-1997............. DLB-251

Merrill, James 1926-1995 ....DLB-5, 165; Y-85

Merrill and Baker................... DLB-49

The Mershon Company.............. DLB-49

Merton, Thomas 1915-1968........DLB-48; Y-81

Merwin, W. S. 1927- DLB-5, 169

Messner, Julian [publishing house] DLB-46

Mészöly, Miklós 1921- DLB-232

Metcalf, J. [publishing house] DLB-49

Metcalf, John 1938- DLB-60

The Methodist Book Concern DLB-49

Methuen and Company DLB-112

Meun, Jean de (see *Roman de la Rose*)

Mew, Charlotte 1869-1928........ DLB-19, 135

Mewshaw, Michael 1943- Y-80

Meyer, Conrad Ferdinand 1825-1898 ... DLB-129

Meyer, E. Y. 1946- DLB-75

Meyer, Eugene 1875-1959 .... DLB-29

Meyer, Michael 1921-2000........... DLB-155

Meyers, Jeffrey 1939- DLB-111

Meynell, Alice 1847-1922 .... DLB-19, 98

Meynell, Viola 1885-1956 .... DLB-153

Meyrink, Gustav 1868-1932........... DLB-81

Mézières, Philipe de circa 1327-1405 .... DLB-208

Michael, Ib 1945- DLB-214

Michaëlis, Karen 1872-1950 .... DLB-214

Michaels, Leonard 1933- DLB-130

Michaux, Henri 1899-1984........... DLB-258

Micheaux, Oscar 1884-1951........... DLB-50

Michel of Northgate, Dan
circa 1265-circa 1340 .... DLB-146

Micheline, Jack 1929-1998 .... DLB-16

Michener, James A. 1907?-1997 .... DLB-6

Micklejohn, George
circa 1717-1818.................. DLB-31

Middle English Literature:
An Introduction DLB-146

The Middle English Lyric DLB-146

Middle Hill Press DLB-106

Middleton, Christopher 1926- DLB-40

Middleton, Richard 1882-1911........ DLB-156

Middleton, Stanley 1919- DLB-14

Middleton, Thomas 1580-1627 .... DLB-58

Miegel, Agnes 1879-1964 .... DLB-56

Mieželaitis, Eduardas 1919-1997 .... DLB-220

Mihailović, Dragoslav 1930- DLB-181

Mihalić, Slavko 1928- DLB-181

Mikhailov, A. (see Sheller, Aleksandr
Konstantinovich)

Mikhailov, Mikhail Larionovich
1829-1865 .... DLB-238

Miles, Josephine 1911-1985 .... DLB-48

Miles, Susan (Ursula Wyllie Roberts)
1888-1975..................... DLB-240

Miliković, Branko 1934-1961......... DLB-181

Milius, John 1944- DLB-44

Mill, James 1773-1836........ DLB-107, 158, 262

Mill, John Stuart
1806-1873...... DLB-55, 190, 262; CDBLB-4

Millar, Andrew [publishing house] DLB-154

Millar, Kenneth
1915-1983 ....DLB-2, 226; Y-83; DS-6

Millay, Edna St. Vincent
1892-1950 .... DLB-45, 249; CDALB-4

Millen, Sarah Gertrude 1888-1968...... DLB-225

Miller, Arthur 1915- DLB-7; CDALB-1

Miller, Caroline 1903-1992 .... DLB-9

Miller, Eugene Ethelbert 1950- DLB-41

Miller, Heather Ross 1939- DLB-120

Miller, Henry
1891-1980 .... DLB-4, 9; Y-80; CDALB-5

Miller, Hugh 1802-1856 .... DLB-190

Miller, J. Hillis 1928- DLB-67

Miller, James [publishing house]........ DLB-49

Miller, Jason 1939- DLB-7

Miller, Joaquin 1839-1913 .... DLB-186

Miller, May 1899- DLB-41

Miller, Paul 1906-1991...............DLB-127

Miller, Perry 1905-1963 ....DLB-17, 63

Miller, Sue 1943- DLB-143

Miller, Vassar 1924-1998 .... DLB-105

Miller, Walter M., Jr. 1923- DLB-8

Miller, Webb 1892-1940 .... DLB-29

Millett, Kate 1934- DLB-246

Millhauser, Steven 1943- DLB-2

Millican, Arthenia J. Bates 1920- DLB-38

Milligan, Alice 1866-1953............. DLB-240

Mills and Boon.................... DLB-112

Milman, Henry Hart 1796-1868........ DLB-96

Milne, A. A. 1882-1956 ..... DLB-10, 77, 100, 160

Milner, Ron 1938- DLB-38

Milner, William [publishing house] DLB-106

Milnes, Richard Monckton (Lord Houghton)
1809-1885 .... DLB-32, 184

Milton, John
1608-1674........ DLB-131, 151; CDBLB-2

Miłosz, Czesław 1911- DLB-215; CDWLB-4

Minakami Tsutomu 1919- DLB-182

Minamoto no Sanetomo 1192-1219 ..... DLB-203

The Minerva Press.................. DLB-154

Minnesang circa 1150-1280............. DLB-138

Minns, Susan 1839-1938 .... DLB-140

Minor Illustrators, 1880-1914.......... DLB-141

Minor Poets of the Earlier Seventeenth
Century DLB-121

Minton, Balch and Company.......... DLB-46

Mirbeau, Octave 1848-1917....... DLB-123, 192

Mirk, John died after 1414?........... DLB-146

Miron, Gaston 1928- DLB-60

A Mirror for Magistrates DLB-167

Mishima Yukio 1925-1970 . . . . DLB-182

Mitchel, Jonathan 1624-1668 . . . . DLB-24

Mitchell, Adrian 1932- DLB-40

Mitchell, Donald Grant
1822-1908 . . . . DLB-1, 243; DS-13

Mitchell, Gladys 1901-1983 . . . . DLB-77

Mitchell, James Leslie 1901-1935 . . . . DLB-15

Mitchell, John (see Slater, Patrick)

Mitchell, John Ames 1845-1918 . . . . DLB-79

Mitchell, Joseph 1908-1996 . . . . DLB-185; Y-96

Mitchell, Julian 1935- DLB-14

Mitchell, Ken 1940- DLB-60

Mitchell, Langdon 1862-1935 . . . . DLB-7

Mitchell, Loften 1919- DLB-38

Mitchell, Margaret 1900-1949 . . . DLB-9; CDALB-7

Mitchell, S. Weir 1829-1914 . . . . DLB-202

Mitchell, W. J. T. 1942- DLB-246

Mitchell, W. O. 1914- DLB-88

Mitchison, Naomi Margaret (Haldane)
1897-1999 . . . . DLB-160, 191, 255

Mitford, Mary Russell 1787-1855 . . . . DLB-110, 116

Mitford, Nancy 1904-1973 . . . . DLB-191

Mittelholzer, Edgar
1909-1965 . . . . DLB-117; CDWLB-3

Mitterer, Erika 1906- DLB-85

Mitterer, Felix 1948- DLB-124

Mitternacht, Johann Sebastian
1613-1679 . . . . DLB-168

Miyamoto, Yuriko 1899-1951 . . . . DLB-180

Mizener, Arthur 1907-1988 . . . . DLB-103

Mo, Timothy 1950- DLB-194

Moberg, Vilhelm 1898-1973 . . . . DLB-259

Modern Age Books DLB-46

"Modern English Prose" (1876),
by George Saintsbury DLB-57

The Modern Language Association of America
Celebrates Its Centennial Y-84

The Modern Library DLB-46

"Modern Novelists – Great and Small" (1855),
by Margaret Oliphant DLB-21

"Modern Style" (1857), by Cockburn
Thomson [excerpt] DLB-57

The Modernists (1932),
by Joseph Warren Beach DLB-36

Modiano, Patrick 1945- DLB-83

Moffat, Yard and Company DLB-46

Moffet, Thomas 1553-1604 . . . . DLB-136

Mohr, Nicholasa 1938- DLB-145

Moix, Ana María 1947- DLB-134

Molesworth, Louisa 1839-1921 . . . . DLB-135

Möllhausen, Balduin 1825-1905 . . . . DLB-129

Molnár, Ferenc
1878-1952 . . . . DLB-215; CDWLB-4

Molnár, Miklós (see Mészöly, Miklós)

Momaday, N. Scott
1934- DLB-143, 175, 256; CDALB-7

Monkhouse, Allan 1858-1936 . . . . DLB-10

Monro, Harold 1879-1932 . . . . DLB-19

Monroe, Harriet 1860-1936 . . . . DLB-54, 91

Monsarrat, Nicholas 1910-1979 . . . . DLB-15

Montagu, Lady Mary Wortley
1689-1762 . . . . DLB-95, 101

Montague, C. E. 1867-1928 . . . . DLB-197

Montague, John 1929- DLB-40

Montale, Eugenio 1896-1981 . . . . DLB-114

Montalvo, José 1946-1994 . . . . DLB-209

Monterroso, Augusto 1921- DLB-145

Montesquiou, Robert de 1855-1921 . . . . . DLB-217

Montgomerie, Alexander
circa 1550?-1598 . . . . DLB-167

Montgomery, James 1771-1854 . . . . . . DLB-93, 158

Montgomery, John 1919- DLB-16

Montgomery, Lucy Maud
1874-1942 . . . . DLB-92; DS-14

Montgomery, Marion 1925- DLB-6

Montgomery, Robert Bruce (see Crispin, Edmund)

Montherlant, Henry de 1896-1972 . . . . DLB-72

The Monthly Review 1749-1844 . . . . DLB-110

Montigny, Louvigny de 1876-1955 . . . . DLB-92

Montoya, José 1932- DLB-122

Moodie, John Wedderburn Dunbar
1797-1869 . . . . DLB-99

Moodie, Susanna 1803-1885 . . . . DLB-99

Moody, Joshua circa 1633-1697 . . . . DLB-24

Moody, William Vaughn 1869-1910 . . . . DLB-7, 54

Moorcock, Michael 1939- DLB-14, 231, 261

Moore, Alan 1953- DLB-261

Moore, Brian 1921-1999 . . . . DLB-251

Moore, Catherine L. 1911- DLB-8

Moore, Clement Clarke 1779-1863 . . . . DLB-42

Moore, Dora Mavor 1888-1979 . . . . DLB-92

Moore, G. E. 1873-1958 . . . . DLB-262

Moore, George 1852-1933 . . . DLB-10, 18, 57, 135

Moore, Lorrie 1957- DLB-234

Moore, Marianne
1887-1972 . . . . DLB-45; DS-7; CDALB-5

Moore, Mavor 1919- DLB-88

Moore, Richard 1927- DLB-105

Moore, T. Sturge 1870-1944 . . . . DLB-19

Moore, Thomas 1779-1852 . . . . DLB-96, 144

Moore, Ward 1903-1978 . . . . DLB-8

Moore, Wilstach, Keys and Company DLB-49

Moorehead, Alan 1901-1983 . . . . DLB-204

Moorhouse, Geoffrey 1931- DLB-204

The Moorland-Spingarn Research
Center DLB-76

Moorman, Mary C. 1905-1994 . . . . DLB-155

Mora, Pat 1942- DLB-209

Moraga, Cherríe 1952- DLB-82, 249

Morales, Alejandro 1944- DLB-82

Morales, Mario Roberto 1947- DLB-145

Morales, Rafael 1919- DLB-108

Morality Plays: *Mankind* circa 1450-1500 and
Everyman circa 1500 . . . . DLB-146

Morante, Elsa 1912-1985 . . . . DLB-177

Morata, Olympia Fulvia 1526-1555 . . . . . . DLB-179

Moravia, Alberto 1907-1990 . . . . DLB-177

Mordaunt, Elinor 1872-1942 . . . . DLB-174

Mordovtsev, Daniil Lukich 1830-1905 . . . DLB-238

More, Hannah
1745-1833 . . . . DLB-107, 109, 116, 158

More, Henry 1614-1687 . . . . DLB-126, 252

More, Sir Thomas
1477 or 1478-1535 . . . . DLB-136

Moreno, Dorinda 1939- DLB-122

Morency, Pierre 1942- DLB-60

Moretti, Marino 1885-1979 . . . . DLB-114

Morgan, Berry 1919- DLB-6

Morgan, Charles 1894-1958 . . . . DLB-34, 100

Morgan, Edmund S. 1916- DLB-17

Morgan, Edwin 1920- DLB-27

Morgan, John Pierpont 1837-1913 . . . . DLB-140

Morgan, John Pierpont, Jr. 1867-1943 . . . . DLB-140

Morgan, Robert 1944- DLB-120

Morgan, Sydney Owenson, Lady
1776?-1859 . . . . DLB-116, 158

Morgner, Irmtraud 1933- DLB-75

Morhof, Daniel Georg 1639-1691 . . . . DLB-164

Mori, Ōgai 1862-1922 . . . . DLB-180

Móricz, Zsigmond 1879-1942 . . . . DLB-215

Morier, James Justinian
1782 or 1783?-1849 . . . . DLB-116

Mörike, Eduard 1804-1875 . . . . DLB-133

Morin, Paul 1889-1963 . . . . DLB-92

Morison, Richard 1514?-1556 . . . . DLB-136

Morison, Samuel Eliot 1887-1976 . . . . DLB-17

Morison, Stanley 1889-1967 . . . . DLB-201

Moritz, Karl Philipp 1756-1793 . . . . DLB-94

Moriz von Craûn circa 1220-1230 . . . . DLB-138

Morley, Christopher 1890-1957 . . . . DLB-9

Morley, John 1838-1923 . . . . . . DLB-57, 144, 190

Morris, George Pope 1802-1864 . . . . DLB-73

Morris, James Humphrey (see Morris, Jan)

Morris, Jan 1926- DLB-204

Morris, Lewis 1833-1907 . . . . DLB-35

Morris, Margaret 1737-1816 . . . . DLB-200

Morris, Richard B. 1904-1989 . . . . DLB-17

Morris, William 1834-1896
. . . . DLB-18, 35, 57, 156, 178, 184; CDBLB-4

Morris, Willie 1934-1999 . . . . Y-80

Morris, Wright
1910-1998 . . . . DLB-2, 206, 218; Y-81

Morrison, Arthur 1863-1945 . . . . DLB-70, 135, 197

Morrison, Charles Clayton 1874-1966 . . . . DLB-91

Morrison, John 1904-1988 . . . . DLB-260

Morrison, Toni 1931-
. . . . . . DLB-6, 33, 143; Y-81, Y-93; CDALB-6

Morrow, William, and Company DLB-46

Morse, James Herbert 1841-1923 . . . . DLB-71

Cumulative Index

Morse, Jedidiah 1761-1826 . . . . DLB-37

Morse, John T., Jr. 1840-1937 . . . . DLB-47

Morselli, Guido 1912-1973 . . . . .DLB-177

Mortimer, Favell Lee 1802-1878 . . . . DLB-163

Mortimer, John
1923- DLB-13, 245; CDBLB-8

Morton, Carlos 1942- DLB-122

Morton, H. V. 1892-1979 . . . . DLB-195

Morton, John P., and Company DLB-49

Morton, Nathaniel 1613-1685 . . . . DLB-24

Morton, Sarah Wentworth 1759-1846 . . . . DLB-37

Morton, Thomas circa 1579-circa 1647 . . . DLB-24

Moscherosch, Johann Michael
1601-1669 . . . . DLB-164

Moseley, Humphrey
[publishing house] DLB-170

Möser, Justus 1720-1794 . . . . DLB-97

Mosley, Nicholas 1923- DLB-14, 207

Moss, Arthur 1889-1969. . . . . DLB-4

Moss, Howard 1922-1987. . . . . DLB-5

Moss, Thylias 1954- DLB-120

The Most Powerful Book Review
in America
[New York Times Book Review] Y-82

Motion, Andrew 1952- DLB-40

Motley, John Lothrop
1814-1877. . . . . DLB-1, 30, 59, 235

Motley, Willard 1909-1965 . . . . DLB-76, 143

Mott, Lucretia 1793-1880 . . . . DLB-239

Motte, Benjamin Jr. [publishing house]. . . DLB-154

Motteux, Peter Anthony 1663-1718 . . . . . DLB-80

Mottram, R. H. 1883-1971 . . . . DLB-36

Mount, Ferdinand 1939- DLB-231

Mouré, Erin 1955- DLB-60

Mourning Dove (Humishuma) between
1882 and 1888?-1936. . . . . .DLB-175, 221

Movies from Books, 1920-1974 . . . . DLB-9

Mowat, Farley 1921- DLB-68

Mowbray, A. R., and Company,
Limited. DLB-106

Mowrer, Edgar Ansel 1892-1977 . . . . DLB-29

Mowrer, Paul Scott 1887-1971 . . . . DLB-29

Moxon, Edward [publishing house] DLB-106

Moxon, Joseph [publishing house] DLB-170

Mphahlele, Es'kia (Ezekiel)
1919- DLB-125; CDWLB-3

Mrożek, Sławomir 1930- . . DLB-232; CDWLB-4

Mtshali, Oswald Mbuyiseni 1940- DLB-125

Mucedorus DLB-62

Mudford, William 1782-1848 . . . . DLB-159

Mueller, Lisel 1924- DLB-105

Muhajir, El (see Marvin X)

Muhajir, Nazzam Al Fitnah (see Marvin X)

Mühlbach, Luise 1814-1873 . . . . DLB-133

Muir, Edwin 1887-1959 . . . . .DLB-20, 100, 191

Muir, Helen 1937- DLB-14

Muir, John 1838-1914. . . . . DLB-186

Muir, Percy 1894-1979 . . . . DLB-201

Mujū Ichien 1226-1312. . . . . DLB-203

Mukherjee, Bharati 1940- DLB-60, 218

Mulcaster, Richard
1531 or 1532-1611 . . . . DLB-167

Muldoon, Paul 1951- DLB-40

Müller, Friedrich (see Müller, Maler)

Müller, Heiner 1929-1995 . . . . DLB-124

Müller, Maler 1749-1825 . . . . DLB-94

Muller, Marcia 1944- DLB-226

Müller, Wilhelm 1794-1827 . . . . DLB-90

Mumford, Lewis 1895-1990 . . . . DLB-63

Munby, A. N. L. 1913-1974 . . . . DLB-201

Munby, Arthur Joseph 1828-1910 . . . . . . DLB-35

Munday, Anthony 1560-1633 . . . . . . .DLB-62, 172

Mundt, Clara (see Mühlbach, Luise)

Mundt, Theodore 1808-1861 . . . . DLB-133

Munford, Robert circa 1737-1783 . . . . DLB-31

Mungoshi, Charles 1947- DLB-157

Munk, Kaj 1898-1944. . . . . DLB-214

Munonye, John 1929- DLB-117

Munro, Alice 1931- DLB-53

Munro, George [publishing house] DLB-49

Munro, H. H.
1870-1916. . . . . DLB-34, 162; CDBLB-5

Munro, Neil 1864-1930 . . . . DLB-156

Munro, Norman L.
[publishing house] DLB-49

Munroe, James, and Company. DLB-49

Munroe, Kirk 1850-1930 . . . . DLB-42

Munroe and Francis DLB-49

Munsell, Joel [publishing house] DLB-49

Munsey, Frank A. 1854-1925 . . . . DLB-25, 91

Munsey, Frank A., and Company DLB-49

Murakami Haruki 1949- DLB-182

Murav'ev, Mikhail Nikitich
1757-1807 . . . . DLB-150

Murdoch, Iris 1919-1999
. . . . . . DLB-14, 194, 233, 262; CDBLB-8

Murdoch, Rupert 1931- DLB-127

Murfree, Mary N. 1850-1922 . . . . .DLB-12, 74

Murger, Henry 1822-1861 . . . . DLB-119

Murger, Louis-Henri (see Murger, Henry)

Murner, Thomas 1475-1537 . . . . .DLB-179

Muro, Amado 1915-1971 . . . . DLB-82

Murphy, Arthur 1727-1805 . . . . DLB-89, 142

Murphy, Beatrice M. 1908- DLB-76

Murphy, Dervla 1931- DLB-204

Murphy, Emily 1868-1933 . . . . DLB-99

Murphy, Jack 1923-1980 . . . . DLB-241

Murphy, John, and Company DLB-49

Murphy, John H., III 1916- DLB-127

Murphy, Richard 1927-1993 . . . . DLB-40

Murray, Albert L. 1916- DLB-38

Murray, Gilbert 1866-1957 . . . . DLB-10

Murray, Jim 1919-1998 . . . . DLB-241

Murray, John [publishing house] DLB-154

Murry, John Middleton 1889-1957. . . . . DLB-149

"The Break-Up of the Novel" (1922) DLB-36

Murray, Judith Sargent
1751-1820. . . . . .DLB-37, 200

Murray, Pauli 1910-1985 . . . . DLB-41

Musäus, Johann Karl August 1735-1787 . . . DLB-97

Muschg, Adolf 1934- DLB-75

The Music of Minnesang DLB-138

Musil, Robert
1880-1942 . . . . .DLB-81, 124; CDWLB-2

Muspilli circa 790-circa 850 . . . . DLB-148

Musset, Alfred de 1810-1857 . . . . . . .DLB-192, 217

Mussey, Benjamin B., and Company DLB-49

Mutafchieva, Vera 1929- DLB-181

Mwangi, Meja 1948- DLB-125

My Summer Reading Orgy: Reading for Fun
and Games: One Reader's Report
on the Summer of 2001 . . . . .Y-01

Myers, Frederic W. H. 1843-1901 . . . . . . DLB-190

Myers, Gustavus 1872-1942 . . . . DLB-47

Myers, L. H. 1881-1944 . . . . DLB-15

Myers, Walter Dean 1937- DLB-33

Mykolaitis-Putinas, Vincas 1893-1967 . . . DLB-220

Myles, Eileen 1949- DLB-193

Myrdal, Jan 1927- DLB-257

N

Na Prous Boneta circa 1296-1328 . . . . . . DLB-208

Nabl, Franz 1883-1974 . . . . DLB-81

Nabokov, Vladimir 1899-1977
. . . . .DLB-2, 244; Y-80, Y-91; DS-3; CDALB-1

The Vladimir Nabokov Archive
in the Berg Collection Y-91

Nabokov Festival at Cornell. Y-83

Nádaši, Ladislav (see Jégé)

Naden, Constance 1858-1889. . . . . DLB-199

Nadezhdin, Nikolai Ivanovich
1804-1856 . . . . DLB-198

Naevius circa 265 B.C.-201 B.C. DLB-211

Nafis and Cornish DLB-49

Nagai, Kafū 1879-1959 . . . . DLB-180

Naipaul, Shiva 1945-1985. . . . . .DLB-157; Y-85

Naipaul, V. S. 1932-
. . . . .DLB-125, 204, 207; Y-85, Y-01;
CDBLB-8; CDWLB-3

Nakagami Kenji 1946-1992 . . . . DLB-182

Nakano-in Masatada no Musume (see Nijō, Lady)

Nałkowska, Zofia 1884-1954 . . . . DLB-215

Nancrede, Joseph [publishing house] DLB-49

Naranjo, Carmen 1930- DLB-145

Narezhny, Vasilii Trofimovich
1780-1825 . . . . DLB-198

Narrache, Jean 1893-1970. . . . . DLB-92

Nasby, Petroleum Vesuvius (see Locke, David Ross)

Nash, Eveleigh [publishing house] DLB-112

Nash, Ogden 1902-1971 . . . . DLB-11

Nashe, Thomas 1567-1601? DLB-167

Nason, Jerry 1910-1986 . . . . .DLB-241

Nast, Conde 1873-1942 . . . . .DLB-91

Nast, Thomas 1840-1902 . . . . .DLB-188

Nastasijević, Momčilo 1894-1938 . . . . . . .DLB-147

Nathan, George Jean 1882-1958 . . . . .DLB-137

Nathan, Robert 1894-1985 . . . . .DLB-9

National Book Critics Circle Awards Y-00; Y-01

The National Jewish Book Awards Y-85

The National Theatre and the Royal
　　Shakespeare Company: The
　　National Companies DLB-13

Natsume, Sōseki 1867-1916 . . . . .DLB-180

Naughton, Bill 1910- DLB-13

Navarro, Joe 1953- DLB-209

Naylor, Gloria 1950- DLB-173

Nazor, Vladimir 1876-1949 . . . . .DLB-147

Ndebele, Njabulo 1948- DLB-157

Neagoe, Peter 1881-1960 . . . . .DLB-4

Neal, John 1793-1876 . . . . .DLB-1, 59, 243

Neal, Joseph C. 1807-1847 . . . . .DLB-11

Neal, Larry 1937-1981 . . . . .DLB-38

The Neale Publishing Company DLB-49

Nebel, Frederick 1903-1967 . . . . .DLB-226

Neely, F. Tennyson [publishing house] DLB-49

Negoiţescu, Ion 1921-1993 . . . . .DLB-220

Negri, Ada 1870-1945 . . . . .DLB-114

"The Negro as a Writer," by
　　G. M. McClellan DLB-50

"Negro Poets and Their Poetry," by
　　Wallace Thurman DLB-50

Neidhart von Reuental
　　circa 1185-circa 1240 . . . . .DLB-138

Neihardt, John G. 1881-1973 . . . . . .DLB-9, 54, 256

Neilson, John Shaw 1872-1942 . . . . .DLB-230

Neledinsky-Meletsky, Iurii Aleksandrovich
　　1752-1828 . . . . .DLB-150

Nelligan, Emile 1879-1941 . . . . .DLB-92

Nelson, Alice Moore Dunbar 1875-1935 . . .DLB-50

Nelson, Antonya 1961- DLB-244

Nelson, Kent 1943- DLB-234

Nelson, Thomas, and Sons [U.K.] DLB-106

Nelson, Thomas, and Sons [U.S.] DLB-49

Nelson, William 1908-1978 . . . . .DLB-103

Nelson, William Rockhill 1841-1915 . . . . .DLB-23

Nemerov, Howard 1920-1991 . . . . .DLB-5, 6; Y-83

Németh, László 1901-1975 . . . . .DLB-215

Nepos circa 100 B.C.-post 27 B.C. DLB-211

Nėris, Salomėja
　　1904-1945 . . . . .DLB-220; CDWLB-4

Nerval, Gerard de 1808-1855 . . . . .DLB-217

Nesbit, E. 1858-1924 . . . . .DLB-141, 153, 178

Ness, Evaline 1911-1986 . . . . .DLB-61

Nestroy, Johann 1801-1862 . . . . .DLB-133

Nettleship, R. L. 1846-1892 . . . . .DLB-262

Neugeboren, Jay 1938- DLB-28

Neukirch, Benjamin 1655-1729 . . . . .DLB-168

Neumann, Alfred 1895-1952 . . . . .DLB-56

Neumann, Ferenc (see Molnár, Ferenc)

Neumark, Georg 1621-1681 . . . . .DLB-164

Neumeister, Erdmann 1671-1756 . . . . . . .DLB-168

Nevins, Allan 1890-1971 . . . . DLB-17; DS-17

Nevinson, Henry Woodd 1856-1941 . . . .DLB-135

The New American Library DLB-46

New Approaches to Biography: Challenges
　　from Critical Theory, USC Conference
　　on Literary Studies, 1990 . . . . Y-90

New Directions Publishing Corporation . . .DLB-46

A New Edition of *Huck Finn* Y-85

New Forces at Work in the American Theatre:
　　1915-1925 . . . . .DLB-7

New Literary Periodicals:
　　A Report for 1987 . . . . Y-87

New Literary Periodicals:
　　A Report for 1988 . . . . Y-88

New Literary Periodicals:
　　A Report for 1989 . . . . Y-89

New Literary Periodicals:
　　A Report for 1990 . . . . Y-90

New Literary Periodicals:
　　A Report for 1991 . . . . Y-91

New Literary Periodicals:
　　A Report for 1992 . . . . Y-92

New Literary Periodicals:
　　A Report for 1993 . . . . Y-93

The New Monthly Magazine
　　1814-1884 . . . . .DLB-110

The New Variorum Shakespeare Y-85

A New Voice: The Center for the Book's First
　　Five Years Y-83

The New Wave [Science Fiction] DLB-8

New York City Bookshops in the 1930s and 1940s:
　　The Recollections of Walter Goldwater . . Y-93

Newbery, John [publishing house] DLB-154

Newbolt, Henry 1862-1938 . . . . .DLB-19

Newbound, Bernard Slade (see Slade, Bernard)

Newby, Eric 1919- DLB-204

Newby, P. H. 1918- DLB-15

Newby, Thomas Cautley
　　[publishing house] DLB-106

Newcomb, Charles King 1820-1894 . . .DLB-1, 223

Newell, Peter 1862-1924 . . . . .DLB-42

Newell, Robert Henry 1836-1901 . . . . .DLB-11

Newhouse, Samuel I. 1895-1979 . . . . .DLB-127

Newman, Cecil Earl 1903-1976 . . . . .DLB-127

Newman, David (see Benton, Robert)

Newman, Frances 1883-1928 . . . . Y-80

Newman, Francis William 1805-1897 . . . .DLB-190

Newman, John Henry
　　1801-1890 . . . . .DLB-18, 32, 55

Newman, Mark [publishing house] DLB-49

Newmarch, Rosa Harriet 1857-1940 . . . . .DLB-240

Newnes, George, Limited DLB-112

Newsome, Effie Lee 1885-1979 . . . . .DLB-76

Newspaper Syndication of American
　　Humor DLB-11

Newton, A. Edward 1864-1940 . . . . .DLB-140

Newton, Sir Isaac 1642-1727 . . . . .DLB-252

Nexø, Martin Andersen 1869-1954 . . . . . .DLB-214

Nezval, Vítěslav
　　1900-1958 . . . . .DLB-215; CDWLB-4

Ngugi wa Thiong'o
　　1938- DLB-125; CDWLB-3

Niatum, Duane 1938- DLB-175

The *Nibelungenlied* and the *Klage*
　　circa 1200 . . . . .DLB-138

Nichol, B. P. 1944-1988 . . . . .DLB-53

Nicholas of Cusa 1401-1464 . . . . .DLB-115

Nichols, Ann 1891?-1966 . . . . .DLB-249

Nichols, Beverly 1898-1983 . . . . .DLB-191

Nichols, Dudley 1895-1960 . . . . .DLB-26

Nichols, Grace 1950- DLB-157

Nichols, John 1940- Y-82

Nichols, Mary Sargeant (Neal) Gove
　　1810-1884 . . . . .DLB-1, 243

Nichols, Peter 1927- DLB-13, 245

Nichols, Roy F. 1896-1973 . . . . .DLB-17

Nichols, Ruth 1948- DLB-60

Nicholson, Edward Williams Byron
　　1849-1912 . . . . .DLB-184

Nicholson, Norman 1914- DLB-27

Nicholson, William 1872-1949 . . . . .DLB-141

Ní Chuilleanáin, Eiléan 1942- DLB-40

Nicol, Eric 1919- DLB-68

Nicolai, Friedrich 1733-1811 . . . . .DLB-97

Nicolas de Clamanges circa 1363-1437 . . .DLB-208

Nicolay, John G. 1832-1901 and
　　Hay, John 1838-1905 . . . . .DLB-47

Nicolson, Adela Florence Cory (see Hope, Laurence)

Nicolson, Harold 1886-1968 . . . . . . .DLB-100, 149

Nicolson, Harold, "The Practice of Biography," in
　　The English Sense of Humour and
　　Other Essays DLB-149

Nicolson, Nigel 1917- DLB-155

Niebuhr, Reinhold 1892-1971 . . . . . DLB-17; DS-17

Niedecker, Lorine 1903-1970 . . . . .DLB-48

Nieman, Lucius W. 1857-1935 . . . . .DLB-25

Nietzsche, Friedrich
　　1844-1900 . . . . .DLB-129; CDWLB-2

Nievo, Stanislao 1928- DLB-196

Niggli, Josefina 1910- Y-80

Nightingale, Florence 1820-1910 . . . . . . .DLB-166

Nijō, Lady (Nakano-in Masatada no Musume)
　　1258-after 1306 . . . . .DLB-203

Nijō Yoshimoto 1320-1388 . . . . .DLB-203

Nikolev, Nikolai Petrovich
　　1758-1815 . . . . .DLB-150

Niles, Hezekiah 1777-1839 . . . . .DLB-43

Nims, John Frederick 1913-1999 . . . . .DLB-5

Nin, Anaïs 1903-1977 . . . . .DLB-2, 4, 152

1985: The Year of the Mystery:
　　A Symposium Y-85

The 1997 Booker Prize Y-97

The 1998 Booker Prize Y-98

Niño, Raúl 1961- DLB-209

Nissenson, Hugh 1933- DLB-28

Niven, Frederick John 1878-1944 . . . . DLB-92

Niven, Larry 1938- DLB-8

Nixon, Howard M. 1909-1983 . . . . DLB-201

Nizan, Paul 1905-1940 . . . . DLB-72

Njegoš, Petar II Petrović
1813-1851 . . . . .DLB-147; CDWLB-4

Nkosi, Lewis 1936- DLB-157

"The No Self, the Little Self, and the Poets,"
by Richard Moore DLB-105

Noah, Mordecai M. 1785-1851 . . . . DLB-250

Noailles, Anna de 1876-1933 . . . . DLB-258

Nobel Peace Prize

The 1986 Nobel Peace Prize: Elie Wiesel Y-86

The Nobel Prize and Literary Politics Y-86

Nobel Prize in Literature

The 1982 Nobel Prize in Literature:
Gabriel García Márquez. Y-82

The 1983 Nobel Prize in Literature:
William Golding Y-83

The 1984 Nobel Prize in Literature:
Jaroslav Seifert Y-84

The 1985 Nobel Prize in Literature:
Claude Simon. Y-85

The 1986 Nobel Prize in Literature:
Wole Soyinka. Y-86

The 1987 Nobel Prize in Literature:
Joseph Brodsky Y-87

The 1988 Nobel Prize in Literature:
Najīb Mahfūz. Y-88

The 1989 Nobel Prize in Literature:
Camilo José Cela Y-89

The 1990 Nobel Prize in Literature:
Octavio Paz Y-90

The 1991 Nobel Prize in Literature:
Nadine Gordimer. Y-91

The 1992 Nobel Prize in Literature:
Derek Walcott Y-92

The 1993 Nobel Prize in Literature:
Toni Morrison Y-93

The 1994 Nobel Prize in Literature:
Kenzaburō Ōe Y-94

The 1995 Nobel Prize in Literature:
Seamus Heaney Y-95

The 1996 Nobel Prize in Literature:
Wisława Szymborsha Y-96

The 1997 Nobel Prize in Literature:
Dario Fo. Y-97

The 1998 Nobel Prize in Literature:
José Saramago Y-98

The 1999 Nobel Prize in Literature:
Günter Grass Y-99

The 2000 Nobel Prize in Literature:
Gao Xingjian Y-00

The 2001 Nobel Prize in Literature:
V. S. Naipaul Y-01

Nodier, Charles 1780-1844 . . . . DLB-119

Noël, Marie 1883-1967 . . . . DLB-258

Noel, Roden 1834-1894 . . . . DLB-35

Nogami, Yaeko 1885-1985 . . . . DLB-180

Nogo, Rajko Petrov 1945- DLB-181

Nolan, William F. 1928- DLB-8

Noland, C. F. M. 1810?-1858 . . . . DLB-11

Noma Hiroshi 1915-1991 . . . . DLB-182

Nonesuch Press DLB-112

Noonan, Robert Phillipe (see Tressell, Robert)

Noonday Press DLB-46

Noone, John 1936- DLB-14

Nora, Eugenio de 1923- DLB-134

Nordan, Lewis 1939- DLB-234

Nordbrandt, Henrik 1945- DLB-214

Nordhoff, Charles 1887-1947 . . . . DLB-9

Norén, Lars 1944- DLB-257

Norman, Charles 1904-1996 . . . . DLB-111

Norman, Marsha 1947- Y-84

Norris, Charles G. 1881-1945 . . . . DLB-9

Norris, Frank
1870-1902 . . . . . . DLB-12, 71, 186; CDALB-3

Norris, John 1657-1712 . . . . DLB-252

Norris, Leslie 1921- DLB-27, 256

Norse, Harold 1916- DLB-16

Norte, Marisela 1955- DLB-209

North, Marianne 1830-1890 . . . . .DLB-174

North Point Press DLB-46

Nortje, Arthur 1942-1970 . . . . DLB-125

Norton, Alice Mary (see Norton, Andre)

Norton, Andre 1912- DLB-8, 52

Norton, Andrews 1786-1853. . . . . DLB-1, 235

Norton, Caroline 1808-1877 . . . DLB-21, 159, 199

Norton, Charles Eliot 1827-1908 . . DLB-1, 64, 235

Norton, John 1606-1663. . . . . DLB-24

Norton, Mary 1903-1992 . . . . DLB-160

Norton, Thomas (see Sackville, Thomas)

Norton, W. W., and Company DLB-46

Norwood, Robert 1874-1932 . . . . DLB-92

Nosaka Akiyuki 1930- DLB-182

Nossack, Hans Erich 1901-1977 . . . . DLB-69

Not Immediately Discernible . . . but Eventually
Quite Clear: The *First Light* and *Final Years*
of Hemingway's Centenary Y-99

A Note on Technique (1926), by
Elizabeth A. Drew [excerpts] DLB-36

Notes from the Underground
of *Sister Carrie* Y-01

Notker Balbulus circa 840-912 . . . . DLB-148

Notker III of Saint Gall
circa 950-1022 . . . . DLB-148

Notker von Zweifalten ?-1095 . . . . DLB-148

Nourse, Alan E. 1928- DLB-8

Novak, Slobodan 1924- DLB-181

Novak, Vjenceslav
1859-1905 . . . . DLB-147

Novakovich, Josip 1956- DLB-244

Novalis 1772-1801 . . . . DLB-90; CDWLB-2

Novaro, Mario 1868-1944 . . . . DLB-114

Novás Calvo, Lino
1903-1983 . . . . DLB-145

"The Novel in [Robert Browning's]
'The Ring and the Book'" (1912),
by Henry James DLB-32

The Novel of Impressionism,
by Jethro Bithell DLB-66

Novel-Reading: *The Works of
Charles Dickens, The Works of
W. Makepeace Thackeray*
(1879), by Anthony Trollope DLB-21

Novels for Grown-Ups Y-97

The Novels of Dorothy Richardson (1918),
by May Sinclair. DLB-36

Novels with a Purpose (1864), by
Justin M'Carthy DLB-21

Noventa, Giacomo 1898-1960 . . . . DLB-114

Novikov, Nikolai
Ivanovich 1744-1818 . . . . DLB-150

Novomeský, Laco
1904-1976. . . . . DLB-215

Nowlan, Alden 1933-1983 . . . . DLB-53

Noyes, Alfred 1880-1958 . . . . DLB-20

Noyes, Crosby S. 1825-1908 . . . . DLB-23

Noyes, Nicholas 1647-1717 . . . . DLB-24

Noyes, Theodore W. 1858-1946 . . . . DLB-29

N-Town Plays circa 1468 to early
sixteenth century. DLB-146

Nugent, Frank 1908-1965. . . . . DLB-44

Nugent, Richard Bruce 1906- DLB-151

Nušić, Branislav
1864-1938 . . . . .DLB-147; CDWLB-4

Nutt, David [publishing house]. DLB-106

Nwapa, Flora
1931-1993 . . . . .DLB-125; CDWLB-3

Nye, Bill 1850-1896 . . . . DLB-186

Nye, Edgar Wilson (Bill)
1850-1896 . . . . DLB-11, 23

Nye, Naomi Shihab 1952- DLB-120

Nye, Robert 1939- DLB-14

Nyka-Niliūnas, Alfonsas
1919- DLB-220

O

Oakes Smith, Elizabeth
1806-1893 . . . . DLB-1, 239, 243

Oakes, Urian circa 1631-1681 . . . . DLB-24

Oakley, Violet 1874-1961 . . . . DLB-188

Oates, Joyce Carol 1938- . . .DLB-2, 5, 130; Y-81

Ōba Minako 1930- DLB-182

Ober, Frederick Albion 1849-1913 . . . . . . DLB-189

Ober, William 1920-1993. . . . . Y-93

Oberholtzer, Ellis Paxson 1868-1936 . . . . . DLB-47

Obradović, Dositej 1740?-1811. . . . . .DLB-147

O'Brien, Charlotte Grace 1845-1909 . . . . DLB-240

O'Brien, Edna 1932- . . . DLB-14, 231; CDBLB-8

O'Brien, Fitz-James 1828-1862 . . . . DLB-74

O'Brien, Flann (see O'Nolan, Brian)

O'Brien, Kate 1897-1974 . . . . DLB-15

O'Brien, Tim
    1946- DLB-152; Y-80; DS-9; CDALB-7

O'Casey, Sean 1880-1964 .....DLB-10; CDBLB-6

Occom, Samson 1723-1792 ....DLB-175

Ochs, Adolph S. 1858-1935 ....DLB-25

Ochs-Oakes, George Washington
    1861-1931 ....DLB-137

O'Connor, Flannery 1925-1964
    ....DLB-2, 152; Y-80; DS-12; CDALB-1

O'Connor, Frank 1903-1966 ....DLB-162

Octopus Publishing Group DLB-112

Oda Sakunosuke 1913-1947 ....DLB-182

Odell, Jonathan 1737-1818 ....DLB-31, 99

O'Dell, Scott 1903-1989 ....DLB-52

Odets, Clifford 1906-1963 ....DLB-7, 26

Odhams Press Limited DLB-112

Odoevsky, Aleksandr Ivanovich
    1802-1839 ....DLB-205

Odoevsky, Vladimir Fedorovich
    1804 or 1803-1869 ....DLB-198

O'Donnell, Peter 1920- DLB-87

O'Donovan, Michael (see O'Connor, Frank)

O'Dowd, Bernard 1866-1953 ....DLB-230

Ōe Kenzaburō 1935- DLB-182; Y-94

O'Faolain, Julia 1932- DLB-14, 231

O'Faolain, Sean 1900- DLB-15, 162

Off Broadway and Off-Off Broadway DLB-7

Off-Loop Theatres DLB-7

Offord, Carl Ruthven 1910- DLB-76

O'Flaherty, Liam 1896-1984 ... DLB-36, 162; Y-84

Ogilvie, J. S., and Company DLB-49

Ogilvy, Eliza 1822-1912 ....DLB-199

Ogot, Grace 1930- DLB-125

O'Grady, Desmond 1935- DLB-40

Ogunyemi, Wale 1939- DLB-157

O'Hagan, Howard 1902-1982 ....DLB-68

O'Hara, Frank 1926-1966 ....DLB-5, 16, 193

O'Hara, John
    1905-1970 ....DLB-9, 86; DS-2; CDALB-5

John O'Hara's Pottsville Journalism Y-88

O'Hegarty, P. S. 1879-1955 ....DLB-201

Okara, Gabriel 1921- DLB-125; CDWLB-3

O'Keeffe, John 1747-1833 ....DLB-89

Okes, Nicholas [publishing house] DLB-170

Okigbo, Christopher
    1930-1967 ....DLB-125; CDWLB-3

Okot p'Bitek 1931-1982 .....DLB-125; CDWLB-3

Okpewho, Isidore 1941- DLB-157

Okri, Ben 1959- DLB-157, 231

Olaudah Equiano and Unfinished Journeys:
    The Slave-Narrative Tradition and
    Twentieth-Century Continuities, by
    Paul Edwards and Pauline T.
    Wangman DLB-117

Old English Literature:
    An Introduction DLB-146

Old English Riddles
    eighth to tenth centuries DLB-146

Old Franklin Publishing House DLB-49

Old German Genesis and *Old German Exodus*
    circa 1050-circa 1130 ....DLB-148

Old High German Charms and
    Blessings DLB-148; CDWLB-2

The *Old High German Isidor*
    circa 790-800 ....DLB-148

The Old Manse DLB-223

Older, Fremont 1856-1935 ....DLB-25

Oldham, John 1653-1683 ....DLB-131

Oldman, C. B. 1894-1969 ....DLB-201

Olds, Sharon 1942- DLB-120

Olearius, Adam 1599-1671 ....DLB-164

O'Leary, Ellen 1831-1889 ....DLB-240

Oliphant, Laurence 1829?-1888......DLB-18, 166

Oliphant, Margaret 1828-1897...DLB-18, 159, 190

Oliver, Chad 1928- DLB-8

Oliver, Mary 1935- DLB-5, 193

Ollier, Claude 1922- DLB-83

Olsen, Tillie 1912 or 1913-
    ....DLB-28, 206; Y-80; CDALB-7

Olson, Charles 1910-1970 ....DLB-5, 16, 193

Olson, Elder 1909- DLB-48, 63

Omotoso, Kole 1943- DLB-125

Omulevsky, Innokentii Vasil'evich
    1836 [or 1837]-1883 ....DLB-238

On Learning to Write Y-88

Ondaatje, Michael 1943- DLB-60

O'Neill, Eugene 1888-1953 .....DLB-7; CDALB-5

Eugene O'Neill Memorial Theater
    Center DLB-7

Eugene O'Neill's Letters: A Review Y-88

Onetti, Juan Carlos
    1909-1994 ....DLB-113; CDWLB-3

Onions, George Oliver 1872-1961.......DLB-153

Onofri, Arturo 1885-1928 ....DLB-114

O'Nolan, Brian 1911-1966 ....DLB-231

Opie, Amelia 1769-1853 ....DLB-116, 159

Opitz, Martin 1597-1639 ....DLB-164

Oppen, George 1908-1984 ....DLB-5, 165

Oppenheim, E. Phillips 1866-1946 ......DLB-70

Oppenheim, James 1882-1932 ....DLB-28

Oppenheimer, Joel 1930-1988 ....DLB-5, 193

Optic, Oliver (see Adams, William Taylor)

Oral History: B. W. Huebsch Y-99

Oral History Interview with Donald S.
    Klopfer Y-97

Orczy, Emma, Baroness 1865-1947.......DLB-70

Oregon Shakespeare Festival Y-00

Origo, Iris 1902-1988 ....DLB-155

Orlovitz, Gil 1918-1973 ....DLB-2, 5

Orlovsky, Peter 1933- DLB-16

Ormond, John 1923- DLB-27

Ornitz, Samuel 1890-1957 ....DLB-28, 44

O'Rourke, P. J. 1947- DLB-185

Orten, Jiří 1919-1941 ....DLB-215

Ortese, Anna Maria 1914- DLB-177

Ortiz, Simon J. 1941- DLB-120, 175, 256

Ortnit and *Wolfdietrich* circa 1225-1250 ....DLB-138

Orton, Joe 1933-1967 ....DLB-13; CDBLB-8

Orwell, George (Eric Arthur Blair)
    1903-1950 ...DLB-15, 98, 195, 255; CDBLB-7

The Orwell Year Y-84

(Re-)Publishing Orwell Y-86

Ory, Carlos Edmundo de 1923- DLB-134

Osbey, Brenda Marie 1957- DLB-120

Osbon, B. S. 1827-1912 ....DLB-43

Osborn, Sarah 1714-1796 ....DLB-200

Osborne, John 1929-1994 .....DLB-13; CDBLB-7

Osgood, Frances Sargent 1811-1850 .....DLB-250

Osgood, Herbert L. 1855-1918 ....DLB-47

Osgood, James R., and Company DLB-49

Osgood, McIlvaine and Company DLB-112

O'Shaughnessy, Arthur 1844-1881 ....DLB-35

O'Shea, Patrick [publishing house]
    ....DLB-49

Osipov, Nikolai Petrovich
    1751-1799 ....DLB-150

Oskison, John Milton 1879-1947 ....DLB-175

Osler, Sir William 1849-1919 ....DLB-184

Osofisan, Femi
    1946- DLB-125; CDWLB-3

Ostenso, Martha 1900-1963 ....DLB-92

Ostrauskas, Kostas 1926- DLB-232

Ostriker, Alicia 1937- DLB-120

Osundare, Niyi 1947- DLB-157; CDWLB-3

Oswald, Eleazer 1755-1795 ....DLB-43

Oswald von Wolkenstein
    1376 or 1377-1445 ....DLB-179

Otero, Blas de 1916-1979 ....DLB-134

Otero, Miguel Antonio 1859-1944 ....DLB-82

Otero, Nina 1881-1965 ....DLB-209

Otero Silva, Miguel 1908-1985 ....DLB-145

Otfried von Weißenburg
    circa 800-circa 875? DLB-148

Otis, Broaders and Company DLB-49

Otis, James (see Kaler, James Otis)

Otis, James, Jr. 1725-1783 ....DLB-31

Ottaway, James 1911- DLB-127

Ottendorfer, Oswald 1826-1900 ....DLB-23

Ottieri, Ottiero 1924- DLB-177

Otto-Peters, Louise 1819-1895 ....DLB-129

Otway, Thomas 1652-1685 ....DLB-80

Ouellette, Fernand 1930- DLB-60

Ouida 1839-1908 ....DLB-18, 156

Outing Publishing Company DLB-46

Outlaw Days, by Joyce Johnson DLB-16

Overbury, Sir Thomas
    circa 1581-1613 ....DLB-151

The Overlook Press DLB-46

Overview of U.S. Book Publishing,
    1910-1945 ....DLB-9

Ovid 43 B.C.-A.D. 17 ......DLB-211; CDWLB-1

Owen, Guy 1925- DLB-5

Owen, John 1564-1622 . . . . DLB-121

Owen, John [publishing house] DLB-49

Owen, Peter, Limited DLB-112

Owen, Robert 1771-1858 . . . . DLB-107, 158

Owen, Wilfred
1893-1918 . . . . DLB-20; DS-18; CDBLB-6

The Owl and the Nightingale
circa 1189-1199 . . . . DLB-146

Owsley, Frank L. 1890-1956 . . . . DLB-17

Oxford, Seventeenth Earl of, Edward
de Vere 1550-1604 . . . . .DLB-172

Ozerov, Vladislav Aleksandrovich
1769-1816 . . . . DLB-150

Ozick, Cynthia 1928- DLB-28, 152; Y-83

First Strauss "Livings" Awarded to Cynthia
Ozick and Raymond Carver
An Interview with Cynthia Ozick Y-83

P

Pace, Richard 1482?-1536 . . . . DLB-167

Pacey, Desmond 1917-1975 . . . . DLB-88

Pack, Robert 1929- DLB-5

Packaging Papa: *The Garden of Eden* Y-86

Padell Publishing Company DLB-46

Padgett, Ron 1942- DLB-5

Padilla, Ernesto Chávez 1944- DLB-122

Page, L. C., and Company DLB-49

Page, Louise 1955- DLB-233

Page, P. K. 1916- DLB-68

Page, Thomas Nelson
1853-1922 . . . . .DLB-12, 78; DS-13

Page, Walter Hines 1855-1918 . . . . . . DLB-71, 91

Paget, Francis Edward 1806-1882 . . . . . . DLB-163

Paget, Violet (see Lee, Vernon)

Pagliarani, Elio 1927- DLB-128

Pain, Barry 1864-1928 . . . . .DLB-135, 197

Pain, Philip ?-circa 1666 . . . . DLB-24

Paine, Robert Treat, Jr. 1773-1811 . . . . DLB-37

Paine, Thomas
1737-1809 . . . . DLB-31, 43, 73, 158; CDALB-2

Painter, George D. 1914- DLB-155

Painter, William 1540?-1594 . . . . DLB-136

Palazzeschi, Aldo 1885-1974 . . . . DLB-114

Paley, Grace 1922- DLB-28, 218

Paley, William 1743-1805 . . . . DLB-251

Palfrey, John Gorham 1796-1881 . . DLB-1, 30, 235

Palgrave, Francis Turner 1824-1897 . . . . . . DLB-35

Palmer, Joe H. 1904-1952 . . . . .DLB-171

Palmer, Michael 1943- DLB-169

Palmer, Nettie 1885-1964 . . . . DLB-260

Palmer, Vance 1885-1959 . . . . DLB-260

Paltock, Robert 1697-1767 . . . . DLB-39

Paludan, Jacob 1896-1975 . . . . DLB-214

Pan Books Limited DLB-112

Panama, Norman 1914- and
Frank, Melvin 1913-1988 . . . . DLB-26

Panaev, Ivan Ivanovich 1812-1862 . . . . . . DLB-198

Panaeva, Avdot'ia Iakovlevna
1820-1893 . . . . DLB-238

Pancake, Breece D'J 1952-1979 . . . . DLB-130

Panduro, Leif 1923-1977 . . . . DLB-214

Panero, Leopoldo 1909-1962 . . . . DLB-108

Pangborn, Edgar 1909-1976 . . . . DLB-8

"Panic Among the Philistines": A Postscript,
An Interview with Bryan Griffin Y-81

Panizzi, Sir Anthony 1797-1879 . . . . DLB-184

Panneton, Philippe (see Ringuet)

Panshin, Alexei 1940- DLB-8

Pansy (see Alden, Isabella)

Pantheon Books DLB-46

Papadat-Bengescu, Hortensia
1876-1955 . . . . DLB-220

Papantonio, Michael (see Kohn, John S. Van E.)

Paperback Library DLB-46

Paperback Science Fiction DLB-8

Paquet, Alfons 1881-1944 . . . . DLB-66

Paracelsus 1493-1541 . . . . .DLB-179

Paradis, Suzanne 1936- DLB-53

Páral, Vladimír, 1932- DLB-232

Pardoe, Julia 1804-1862 . . . . DLB-166

Paredes, Américo 1915-1999 . . . . DLB-209

Pareja Diezcanseco, Alfredo 1908-1993 . . DLB-145

Parents' Magazine Press DLB-46

Parfit, Derek 1942- DLB-262

Parise, Goffredo 1929-1986 . . . . .DLB-177

Parisian Theater, Fall 1984: Toward
A New Baroque Y-85

Parizeau, Alice 1930- DLB-60

Park, Ruth 1923- DLB-260

Parke, John 1754-1789 . . . . DLB-31

Parker, Dan 1893-1967 . . . . DLB-241

Parker, Dorothy 1893-1967 . . . . . . DLB-11, 45, 86

Parker, Gilbert 1860-1932 . . . . DLB-99

Parker, J. H. [publishing house] DLB-106

Parker, James 1714-1770 . . . . DLB-43

Parker, John [publishing house] DLB-106

Parker, Matthew 1504-1575 . . . . DLB-213

Parker, Stewart 1941-1988 . . . . DLB-245

Parker, Theodore 1810-1860 . . . . DLB-1, 235

Parker, William Riley 1906-1968 . . . . DLB-103

Parkes, Bessie Rayner (Madame Belloc)
1829-1925 . . . . DLB-240

Parkman, Francis
1823-1893 . . . . .DLB-1, 30, 183, 186, 235

Parks, Gordon 1912- DLB-33

Parks, Tim 1954- DLB-231

Parks, William 1698-1750 . . . . DLB-43

Parks, William [publishing house] DLB-49

Parley, Peter (see Goodrich, Samuel Griswold)

Parmenides
late sixth-fifth century B.C. DLB-176

Parnell, Thomas 1679-1718 . . . . DLB-95

Parnicki, Teodor 1908-1988 . . . . DLB-215

Parr, Catherine 1513?-1548 . . . . DLB-136

Parrington, Vernon L. 1871-1929 . . . . . DLB-17, 63

Parrish, Maxfield 1870-1966 . . . . DLB-188

Parronchi, Alessandro 1914- DLB-128

Parton, James 1822-1891 . . . . DLB-30

Parton, Sara Payson Willis
1811-1872 . . . . .DLB-43, 74, 239

Partridge, S. W., and Company DLB-106

Parun, Vesna 1922- DLB-181; CDWLB-4

Pasinetti, Pier Maria 1913- DLB-177

Pasolini, Pier Paolo 1922- DLB-128, 177

Pastan, Linda 1932- DLB-5

Paston, George (Emily Morse Symonds)
1860-1936 . . . . .DLB-149, 197

The Paston Letters 1422-1509 . . . . DLB-146

Pastorius, Francis Daniel
1651-circa 1720 . . . . DLB-24

Patchen, Kenneth 1911-1972 . . . . DLB-16, 48

Pater, Walter
1839-1894 . . . . .DLB-57, 156; CDBLB-4

Aesthetic Poetry (1873) DLB-35

Paterson, A. B. "Banjo" 1864-1941 . . . . . DLB-230

Paterson, Katherine 1932- DLB-52

Patmore, Coventry 1823-1896 . . . . DLB-35, 98

Paton, Alan 1903-1988 . . . . .DS-17

Paton, Joseph Noel 1821-1901 . . . . DLB-35

Paton Walsh, Jill 1937- DLB-161

Patrick, Edwin Hill ("Ted") 1901-1964 . . .DLB-137

Patrick, John 1906-1995 . . . . DLB-7

Pattee, Fred Lewis 1863-1950 . . . . DLB-71

Pattern and Paradigm: History as
Design, by Judith Ryan DLB-75

Patterson, Alicia 1906-1963 . . . . .DLB-127

Patterson, Eleanor Medill 1881-1948 . . . . . DLB-29

Patterson, Eugene 1923- DLB-127

Patterson, Joseph Medill 1879-1946 . . . . . . DLB-29

Pattillo, Henry 1726-1801 . . . . DLB-37

Paul, Elliot 1891-1958 . . . . DLB-4

Paul, Jean (see Richter, Johann Paul Friedrich)

Paul, Kegan, Trench, Trubner and
Company Limited DLB-106

Paul, Peter, Book Company DLB-49

Paul, Stanley, and Company Limited DLB-112

Paulding, James Kirke
1778-1860 . . . . .DLB-3, 59, 74, 250

Paulin, Tom 1949- DLB-40

Pauper, Peter, Press DLB-46

Pavese, Cesare 1908-1950 . . . . .DLB-128, 177

Pavić, Milorad 1929- DLB-181; CDWLB-4

Pavlov, Konstantin 1933- DLB-181

Pavlov, Nikolai Filippovich 1803-1864 . . . . DLB-198

Pavlova, Karolina Karlovna 1807-1893 . . . . DLB-205

Pavlović, Miodrag
1928- DLB-181; CDWLB-4

Paxton, John 1911-1985 . . . . DLB-44

Payn, James 1830-1898 . . . . DLB-18

Payne, John 1842-1916 . . . . DLB-35

Payne, John Howard 1791-1852 . . . . .DLB-37

Payson and Clarke. DLB-46

Paz, Octavio 1914-1998 . . . . .Y-90, Y-98

Pazzi, Roberto 1946- DLB-196

Peabody, Elizabeth Palmer 1804-1894. .DLB-1, 223

Peabody, Elizabeth Palmer
   [publishing house] DLB-49

Peabody, Josephine Preston 1874-1922 . . .DLB-249

Peabody, Oliver William Bourn
   1799-1848 . . . . .DLB-59

Peace, Roger 1899-1968. . . . . .DLB-127

Peacham, Henry 1578-1644? DLB-151

Peacham, Henry, the Elder
   1547-1634 . . . . DLB-172, 236

Peachtree Publishers, Limited DLB-46

Peacock, Molly 1947- DLB-120

Peacock, Thomas Love 1785-1866 . . .DLB-96, 116

Pead, Deuel ?-1727. . . . . .DLB-24

Peake, Mervyn 1911-1968 . . . . . .DLB-15, 160, 255

Peale, Rembrandt 1778-1860 . . . . .DLB-183

Pear Tree Press .DLB-112

Pearce, Philippa 1920- DLB-161

Pearson, H. B. [publishing house] DLB-49

Pearson, Hesketh 1887-1964 . . . . .DLB-149

Pechersky, Andrei (see Mel'nikov, Pavel Ivanovich)

Peck, George W. 1840-1916 . . . . .DLB-23, 42

Peck, H. C., and Theo. Bliss
   [publishing house] DLB-49

Peck, Harry Thurston 1856-1914 . . . . .DLB-71, 91

Peden, William 1913-1999. . . . . .DLB-234

Peele, George 1556-1596 . . . . .DLB-62, 167

Pegler, Westbrook 1894-1969 . . . . .DLB-171

Péguy, Charles Pierre 1873-1914 . . . . . . .DLB-258

Pekić, Borislav 1930-1992 . . .DLB-181; CDWLB-4

Pellegrini and Cudahy DLB-46

Pelletier, Aimé (see Vac, Bertrand)

Pelletier, Francine 1959- DLB-251

Pemberton, Sir Max 1863-1950 . . . . .DLB-70

de la Peña, Terri 1947- DLB-209

Penfield, Edward 1866-1925 . . . . .DLB-188

Penguin Books [U.K.] DLB-112

Penguin Books [U.S.] DLB-46

Penn Publishing Company DLB-49

Penn, William 1644-1718. . . . . .DLB-24

Penna, Sandro 1906-1977. . . . . .DLB-114

Pennell, Joseph 1857-1926 . . . . .DLB-188

Penner, Jonathan 1940- Y-83

Pennington, Lee 1939- Y-82

Penton, Brian 1904-1951 . . . . .DLB-260

Pepys, Samuel
   1633-1703 . . . . .DLB-101, 213; CDBLB-2

Percy, Thomas 1729-1811 . . . . .DLB-104

Percy, Walker 1916-1990 . . . . . DLB-2; Y-80, Y-90

Percy, William 1575-1648 . . . . .DLB-172

Perec, Georges 1936-1982 . . . . .DLB-83

Perelman, Bob 1947- DLB-193

Perelman, S. J. 1904-1979. . . . . .DLB-11, 44

Perez, Raymundo "Tigre" 1946- DLB-122

Peri Rossi, Cristina 1941- DLB-145

Perkins, Eugene 1932- DLB-41

Perkoff, Stuart Z. 1930-1974 . . . . .DLB-16

Perley, Moses Henry 1804-1862 . . . . .DLB-99

Permabooks. DLB-46

Perovsky, Aleksei Alekseevich
   (Antonii Pogorel'sky) 1787-1836 . . . . .DLB-198

Perri, Henry 1561-1617 . . . . .DLB-236

Perrin, Alice 1867-1934 . . . . .DLB-156

Perry, Bliss 1860-1954. . . . . .DLB-71

Perry, Eleanor 1915-1981 . . . . .DLB-44

Perry, Henry (see Perri, Henry)

Perry, Matthew 1794-1858. . . . . .DLB-183

Perry, Sampson 1747-1823 . . . . .DLB-158

Perse, Saint-John 1887-1975 . . . . .DLB-258

Persius A.D. 34-A.D. 62 . . . . .DLB-211

Perutz, Leo 1882-1957 . . . . .DLB-81

Pesetsky, Bette 1932- DLB-130

Pestalozzi, Johann Heinrich 1746-1827 . . .DLB-94

Peter, Laurence J. 1919-1990 . . . . .DLB-53

Peter of Spain circa 1205-1277 . . . . .DLB-115

Peterkin, Julia 1880-1961 . . . . .DLB-9

Peters, Lenrie 1932- DLB-117

Peters, Robert 1924- DLB-105

"Foreword to *Ludwig of Bavaria*" DLB-105

Petersham, Maud 1889-1971 and
   Petersham, Miska 1888-1960 . . . . . . .DLB-22

Peterson, Charles Jacobs 1819-1887 . . . .DLB-79

Peterson, Len 1917- DLB-88

Peterson, Levi S. 1933- DLB-206

Peterson, Louis 1922-1998. . . . . .DLB-76

Peterson, T. B., and Brothers DLB-49

Petitclair, Pierre 1813-1860 . . . . .DLB-99

Petrescu, Camil 1894-1957 . . . . .DLB-220

Petronius circa A.D. 20-A.D. 66
   . . . . .DLB-211; CDWLB-1

Petrov, Aleksandar 1938- DLB-181

Petrov, Gavriil 1730-1801 . . . . .DLB-150

Petrov, Valeri 1920- DLB-181

Petrov, Vasilii Petrovich 1736-1799 . . . . .DLB-150

Petrović, Rastko
   1898-1949 . . . . .DLB-147; CDWLB-4

Petruslied circa 854? DLB-148

Petry, Ann 1908-1997 . . . . .DLB-76

Pettie, George circa 1548-1589 . . . . .DLB-136

Peyton, K. M. 1929- DLB-161

Pfaffe Konrad flourished circa 1172 . . . . . .DLB-148

Pfaffe Lamprecht flourished circa 1150 . . .DLB-148

Pfeiffer, Emily 1827-1890 . . . . .DLB-199

Pforzheimer, Carl H. 1879-1957 . . . . . . .DLB-140

Phaedrus circa 18 B.C.-circa A.D. 50. . . . .DLB-211

Phaer, Thomas 1510?-1560 . . . . .DLB-167

Phaidon Press Limited. DLB-112

Pharr, Robert Deane 1916-1992 . . . . .DLB-33

Phelps, Elizabeth Stuart 1815-1852 . . . . .DLB-202

Phelps, Elizabeth Stuart 1844-1911 . . .DLB-74, 221

Philander von der Linde
   (see Mencke, Johann Burckhard)

Philby, H. St. John B. 1885-1960 . . . . . . .DLB-195

Philip, Marlene Nourbese 1947- DLB-157

Philippe, Charles-Louis 1874-1909. . . . . . .DLB-65

Philips, John 1676-1708 . . . . .DLB-95

Philips, Katherine 1632-1664 . . . . .DLB-131

Phillipps, Sir Thomas 1792-1872 . . . . . . .DLB-184

Phillips, Caryl 1958- DLB-157

Phillips, David Graham 1867-1911 . . . . .DLB-9, 12

Phillips, Jayne Anne 1952- Y-80

Phillips, Robert 1938- DLB-105

"Finding, Losing, Reclaiming: A Note
   on My Poems" DLB-105

Phillips, Sampson and Company DLB-49

Phillips, Stephen 1864-1915. . . . . .DLB-10

Phillips, Ulrich B. 1877-1934 . . . . .DLB-17

Phillips, Wendell 1811-1884 . . . . .DLB-235

Phillips, Willard 1784-1873 . . . . .DLB-59

Phillips, William 1907- DLB-137

Phillpotts, Adelaide Eden (Adelaide Ross)
   1896-1993 . . . . .DLB-191

Phillpotts, Eden 1862-1960 . . DLB-10, 70, 135, 153

Philo circa 20-15 B.C.-circa A.D. 50 . . . . .DLB-176

Philosophical Library. DLB-46

Phinney, Elihu [publishing house] DLB-49

Phoenix, John (see Derby, George Horatio)

PHYLON (Fourth Quarter, 1950),
   The Negro in Literature:
   The Current Scene DLB-76

Physiologus circa 1070-circa 1150 . . . . . . .DLB-148

Piccolo, Lucio 1903-1969. . . . . .DLB-114

Pickard, Tom 1946- DLB-40

Pickering, William [publishing house] DLB-106

Pickthall, Marjorie 1883-1922 . . . . .DLB-92

Pictorial Printing Company DLB-49

Piercy, Marge 1936- DLB-120, 227

Pierro, Albino 1916- DLB-128

Pignotti, Lamberto 1926- DLB-128

Pike, Albert 1809-1891 . . . . .DLB-74

Pike, Zebulon Montgomery
   1779-1813 . . . . .DLB-183

Pillat, Ion 1891-1945 . . . . .DLB-220

Pilon, Jean-Guy 1930- DLB-60

Pinckney, Eliza Lucas 1722-1793 . . . . . . .DLB-200

Pinckney, Josephine 1895-1957 . . . . .DLB-6

Pindar circa 518 B.C.-circa 438 B.C.
   . . . . .DLB-176; CDWLB-1

Pindar, Peter (see Wolcot, John)

Pineda, Cecile 1942- DLB-209

Pinero, Arthur Wing 1855-1934 . . . . .DLB-10

Pinget, Robert 1919-1997 . . . . .DLB-83

Pinkney, Edward Coote 1802-1828. . . . . .DLB-248

Pinnacle Books DLB-46

Piñon, Nélida 1935- DLB-145

Pinsky, Robert 1940- Y-82

Robert Pinsky Reappointed Poet Laureate Y-98

Pinter, Harold 1930- DLB-13; CDBLB-8

Piontek, Heinz 1925- DLB-75

Piozzi, Hester Lynch [Thrale]
1741-1821 . . . . DLB-104, 142

Piper, H. Beam 1904-1964 . . . . DLB-8

Piper, Watty DLB-22

Pirckheimer, Caritas 1467-1532 . . . . DLB-179

Pirckheimer, Willibald 1470-1530 . . . . DLB-179

Pisar, Samuel 1929- Y-83

Pisemsky, Aleksai Feofilaktovich
1821-1881 . . . . DLB-238

Pitkin, Timothy 1766-1847 . . . . DLB-30

The Pitt Poetry Series: Poetry Publishing
Today Y-85

Pitter, Ruth 1897- DLB-20

Pix, Mary 1666-1709 . . . . DLB-80

Pixerécourt, René Charles Guilbert de
1773-1844 . . . . DLB-192

Plaatje, Sol T. 1876-1932 . . . . DLB-125, 225

Plante, David 1940- Y-83

Platen, August von 1796-1835 . . . . DLB-90

Plath, Sylvia
1932-1963 . . . . DLB-5, 6, 152; CDALB-1

Plato circa 428 B.C.-348-347 B.C.
. . . . DLB-176; CDWLB-1

Plato, Ann 1824?-? DLB-239

Platon 1737-1812 . . . . DLB-150

Platt, Charles 1945- DLB-261

Platt and Munk Company DLB-46

Plautus circa 254 B.C.-184 B.C.
. . . . DLB-211; CDWLB-1

Playboy Press DLB-46

Playford, John [publishing house] DLB-170

Plays, Playwrights, and Playgoers DLB-84

Playwrights on the Theater DLB-80

Der Pleier flourished circa 1250 . . . . DLB-138

Pleijel, Agneta 1940- DLB-257

Plenzdorf, Ulrich 1934- DLB-75

Plessen, Elizabeth 1944- DLB-75

Pletnev, Petr Aleksandrovich
1792-1865 . . . . DLB-205

Pliekšāne, Elza Rozenberga (see Aspazija)

Pliekšāns, Jānis (see Rainis, Jānis)

Plievier, Theodor 1892-1955 . . . . DLB-69

Plimpton, George 1927- DLB-185, 241; Y-99

Pliny the Elder A.D. 23/24-A.D. 79 . . . . . DLB-211

Pliny the Younger
circa A.D. 61-A.D. 112 . . . . DLB-211

Plomer, William
1903-1973 . . . . DLB-20, 162, 191, 225

Plotinus 204-270 . . . . DLB-176; CDWLB-1

Plowright, Teresa 1952- DLB-251

Plume, Thomas 1630-1704 . . . . DLB-213

Plumly, Stanley 1939- DLB-5, 193

Plumpp, Sterling D. 1940- DLB-41

Plunkett, James 1920- DLB-14

Plutarch
circa 46-circa 120 . . . . . . DLB-176; CDWLB-1

Plymell, Charles 1935- DLB-16

Pocket Books DLB-46

Poe, Edgar Allan 1809-1849
. . . . DLB-3, 59, 73, 74, 248; CDALB-2

Poe, James 1921-1980 . . . . DLB-44

The Poet Laureate of the United States
Statements from Former Consultants
in Poetry Y-86

Pogodin, Mikhail Petrovich
1800-1875 . . . . DLB-198

Pogorel'sky, Antonii
(see Perovsky, Aleksei Alekseevich)

Pohl, Frederik 1919- DLB-8

Poirier, Louis (see Gracq, Julien)

Poláček, Karel 1892-1945 . . . DLB-215; CDWLB-4

Polanyi, Michael 1891-1976 . . . . DLB-100

Pole, Reginald 1500-1558 . . . . DLB-132

Polevoi, Nikolai Alekseevich
1796-1846 . . . . DLB-198

Polezhaev, Aleksandr Ivanovich
1804-1838 . . . . DLB-205

Poliakoff, Stephen 1952- DLB-13

Polidori, John William 1795-1821 . . . . DLB-116

Polite, Carlene Hatcher 1932- DLB-33

Pollard, Alfred W. 1859-1944 . . . . DLB-201

Pollard, Edward A. 1832-1872 . . . . DLB-30

Pollard, Graham 1903-1976 . . . . DLB-201

Pollard, Percival 1869-1911 . . . . DLB-71

Pollard and Moss DLB-49

Pollock, Sharon 1936- DLB-60

Polonsky, Abraham 1910-1999 . . . . DLB-26

Polotsky, Simeon 1629-1680 . . . . DLB-150

Polybius circa 200 B.C.-118 B.C. DLB-176

Pomialovsky, Nikolai Gerasimovich
1835-1863 . . . . DLB-238

Pomilio, Mario 1921-1990 . . . . DLB-177

Ponce, Mary Helen 1938- DLB-122

Ponce-Montoya, Juanita 1949- DLB-122

Ponet, John 1516?-1556 . . . . DLB-132

Ponge, Francis 1899-1988 . . . . DLB-258

Poniatowski, Elena
1933- DLB-113; CDWLB-3

Ponsard, François 1814-1867 . . . . DLB-192

Ponsonby, William [publishing house] DLB-170

Pontiggia, Giuseppe 1934- DLB-196

Pony Stories DLB-160

Poole, Ernest 1880-1950 . . . . DLB-9

Poole, Sophia 1804-1891 . . . . DLB-166

Poore, Benjamin Perley 1820-1887 . . . . . . DLB-23

Popa, Vasko 1922-1991 . . . . DLB-181; CDWLB-4

Pope, Abbie Hanscom 1858-1894 . . . . DLB-140

Pope, Alexander
1688-1744 . . . . . . DLB-95, 101, 213; CDBLB-2

Popov, Mikhail Ivanovich
1742-circa 1790 . . . . DLB-150

Popović, Aleksandar 1929-1996 . . . . DLB-181

Popper, Sir Karl R. 1902-1994 . . . . DLB-262

Popular Library DLB-46

Porete, Marguerite ?-1310 . . . . DLB-208

Porlock, Martin (see MacDonald, Philip)

Porpoise Press DLB-112

Porta, Antonio 1935-1989 . . . . DLB-128

Porter, Anna Maria 1780-1832 . . . . . DLB-116, 159

Porter, David 1780-1843 . . . . DLB-183

Porter, Eleanor H. 1868-1920 . . . . DLB-9

Porter, Gene Stratton (see Stratton-Porter, Gene)

Porter, Hal 1911-1984 . . . . DLB-260

Porter, Henry ?-? DLB-62

Porter, Jane 1776-1850 . . . . DLB-116, 159

Porter, Katherine Anne 1890-1980
. . . . . . DLB-4, 9, 102; Y-80; DS-12; CDALB-7

Porter, Peter 1929- DLB-40

Porter, William Sydney
1862-1910 . . . . DLB-12, 78, 79; CDALB-3

Porter, William T. 1809-1858 . . . . DLB-3, 43, 250

Porter and Coates DLB-49

Portillo Trambley, Estela 1927-1998 . . . . . DLB-209

Portis, Charles 1933- DLB-6

Posey, Alexander 1873-1908 . . . . DLB-175

Postans, Marianne circa 1810-1865 . . . . . DLB-166

Postl, Carl (see Sealsfield, Carl)

Poston, Ted 1906-1974 . . . . DLB-51

Potekhin, Aleksei Antipovich 1829-1908 . DLB-238

Potok, Chaim 1929- DLB-28, 152

A Conversation with Chaim Potok Y-84

Potter, Beatrix 1866-1943 . . . . DLB-141

Potter, David M. 1910-1971 . . . . DLB-17

Potter, Dennis 1935-1994 . . . . DLB-233

The Harry Potter Phenomenon Y-99

Potter, John E., and Company DLB-49

Pottle, Frederick A. 1897-1987 . . . . DLB-103; Y-87

Poulin, Jacques 1937- DLB-60

Pound, Ezra 1885-1972
. . . . DLB-4, 45, 63; DS-15; CDALB-4

Poverman, C. E. 1944- DLB-234

Povich, Shirley 1905-1998 . . . . DLB-171

Powell, Anthony 1905-2000 . . . DLB-15; CDBLB-7

The Anthony Powell Society: Powell and
the First Biennial Conference Y-01

Dawn Powell, Where Have You Been All
Our Lives? Y-97

Powell, John Wesley 1834-1902 . . . . DLB-186

Powell, Padgett 1952- DLB-234

Powers, J. F. 1917-1999 . . . . DLB-130

Powers, Jimmy 1903-1995 . . . . DLB-241

Pownall, David 1938- DLB-14

Powys, John Cowper 1872-1963 . . . . . DLB-15, 255

Powys, Llewelyn 1884-1939 . . . . DLB-98

Powys, T. F. 1875-1953 . . . . DLB-36, 162

Poynter, Nelson 1903-1978 . . . . DLB-127

The Practice of Biography: An Interview
with Stanley Weintraub Y-82

The Practice of Biography II: An Interview
with B. L. Reid Y-83

The Practice of Biography III: An Interview
with Humphrey Carpenter Y-84

The Practice of Biography IV: An Interview with
William Manchester Y-85

The Practice of Biography VI: An Interview with
David Herbert Donald Y-87

The Practice of Biography VII: An Interview with
John Caldwell Guilds Y-92

The Practice of Biography VIII: An Interview
with Joan Mellen Y-94

The Practice of Biography IX: An Interview
with Michael Reynolds Y-95

Prados, Emilio 1899-1962 . . . . DLB-134

Praed, Mrs. Caroline (see Praed, Rosa)

Praed, Rosa (Mrs. Caroline Praed)
1851-1935 . . . . DLB-230

Praed, Winthrop Mackworth 1802-1839. . . DLB-96

Praeger Publishers DLB-46

Praetorius, Johannes 1630-1680. . . . . DLB-168

Pratolini, Vasco 1913-1991 . . . . DLB-177

Pratt, E. J. 1882-1964. . . . . DLB-92

Pratt, Samuel Jackson 1749-1814 . . . . DLB-39

Preciado Martin, Patricia 1939- DLB-209

Preface to *The History of Romances* (1715), by
Pierre Daniel Huet [excerpts] DLB-39

Préfontaine, Yves 1937- DLB-53

Prelutsky, Jack 1940- DLB-61

Premisses, by Michael Hamburger DLB-66

Prentice, George D. 1802-1870 . . . . DLB-43

Prentice-Hall DLB-46

Prescott, Orville 1906-1996 . . . . Y-96

Prescott, William Hickling
1796-1859 . . . . DLB-1, 30, 59, 235

The Present State of the English Novel (1892),
by George Saintsbury DLB-18

Prešeren, Francè
1800-1849 . . . . DLB-147; CDWLB-4

Preston, Margaret Junkin
1820-1897 . . . . DLB-239, 248

Preston, May Wilson 1873-1949 . . . . DLB-188

Preston, Thomas 1537-1598. . . . . DLB-62

Prévert, Jacques 1900-1977 . . . . DLB-258

Prichard, Katharine Susannah
1883-1969 . . . . DLB-260

Price, Reynolds 1933- DLB-2, 218

Price, Richard 1723-1791 . . . . DLB-158

Price, Richard 1949- Y-81

Prideaux, John 1578-1650 . . . . DLB-236

Priest, Christopher 1943- DLB-14, 207, 261

Priestley, J. B. 1894-1984
. . . DLB-10, 34, 77, 100, 139; Y-84; CDBLB-6

Priestley, Joseph 1733-1804 . . . . DLB-252

Primary Bibliography: A Retrospective Y-95

Prime, Benjamin Young 1733-1791 . . . . DLB-31

Primrose, Diana floruit circa 1630. . . . . . . DLB-126

Prince, F. T. 1912- DLB-20

Prince, Nancy Gardner 1799-?. DLB-239

Prince, Thomas 1687-1758. . . . . DLB-24, 140

Pringle, Thomas 1789-1834 . . . . DLB-225

Printz, Wolfgang Casper 1641-1717. . . . . . DLB-168

Prior, Matthew 1664-1721 . . . . DLB-95

Prisco, Michele 1920- DLB-177

Pritchard, William H. 1932- DLB-111

Pritchett, V. S. 1900-1997 . . . . DLB-15, 139

Probyn, May 1856 or 1857-1909 . . . . DLB-199

Procter, Adelaide Anne 1825-1864 . . . DLB-32, 199

Procter, Bryan Waller 1787-1874 . . . . . DLB-96, 144

Proctor, Robert 1868-1903 . . . . DLB-184

*Producing Dear Bunny, Dear Volodya: The Friendship
and the Feud* Y-97

The Profession of Authorship:
Scribblers for Bread. Y-89

Prokopovich, Feofan 1681?-1736. . . . . DLB-150

Prokosch, Frederic 1906-1989 . . . . DLB-48

The Proletarian Novel DLB-9

Pronzini, Bill 1943- DLB-226

Propertius circa 50 B.C.-post 16 B.C.
. . . . DLB-211; CDWLB-1

Propper, Dan 1937- DLB-16

Prose, Francine 1947- DLB-234

Protagoras circa 490 B.C.-420 B.C. DLB-176

Proud, Robert 1728-1813. . . . . DLB-30

Proust, Marcel 1871-1922 . . . . DLB-65

Prynne, J. H. 1936- DLB-40

Przybyszewski, Stanislaw 1868-1927 . . . . . . DLB-66

Pseudo-Dionysius the Areopagite floruit
circa 500 . . . . DLB-115

Public Domain and the Violation of Texts . . . Y-97

The Public Lending Right in America Statement by
Sen. Charles McC. Mathias, Jr. PLR and the
Meaning of Literary Property Statements on
PLR by American Writers Y-83

The Public Lending Right in the United Kingdom
Public Lending Right: The First Year in the
United Kingdom. Y-83

The Publication of English
Renaissance Plays DLB-62

Publications and Social Movements
[Transcendentalism] DLB-1

Publishers and Agents: The Columbia
Connection Y-87

Publishing Fiction at LSU Press. Y-87

The Publishing Industry in 1998:
Sturm-und-drang.com Y-98

The Publishing Industry in 1999. . . . . Y-99

Pückler-Muskau, Hermann von
1785-1871. . . . . DLB-133

Pufendorf, Samuel von 1632-1694. . . . . . . DLB-168

Pugh, Edwin William 1874-1930 . . . . DLB-135

Pugin, A. Welby 1812-1852. . . . . DLB-55

Puig, Manuel 1932-1990 . . . . DLB-113; CDWLB-3

Pulitzer, Joseph 1847-1911 . . . . DLB-23

Pulitzer, Joseph, Jr. 1885-1955 . . . . DLB-29

Pulitzer Prizes for the Novel,
1917-1945 . . . . DLB-9

Pulliam, Eugene 1889-1975 . . . . DLB-127

Purchas, Samuel 1577?-1626 . . . . DLB-151

Purdy, Al 1918-2000 . . . . DLB-88

Purdy, James 1923- DLB-2, 218

Purdy, Ken W. 1913-1972 . . . . DLB-137

Pusey, Edward Bouverie 1800-1882 . . . . . . DLB-55

Pushkin, Aleksandr Sergeevich
1799-1837 . . . . DLB-205

Pushkin, Vasilii L'vovich
1766-1830 . . . . DLB-205

Putnam, George Palmer
1814-1872 . . . . DLB-3, 79, 250, 254

G. P. Putnam [publishing house] DLB-254

G. P. Putnam's Sons [U.K.] DLB-106

G. P. Putnam's Sons [U.S.] DLB-49

A Publisher's Archives: G. P. Putnam Y-92

Putnam, Samuel 1892-1950 . . . . DLB-4

Puzo, Mario 1920-1999 . . . . DLB-6

Pyle, Ernie 1900-1945 . . . . DLB-29

Pyle, Howard
1853-1911 . . . . DLB-42, 188; DS-13

Pym, Barbara 1913-1980 . . . . . . DLB-14, 207; Y-87

Pynchon, Thomas 1937- DLB-2, 173

Pyramid Books DLB-46

Pyrnelle, Louise-Clarke 1850-1907 . . . . DLB-42

Pythagoras circa 570 B.C.-? DLB-176

Q

Quad, M. (see Lewis, Charles B.)

Quaritch, Bernard 1819-1899 . . . . DLB-184

Quarles, Francis 1592-1644 . . . . DLB-126

The Quarterly Review 1809-1967 . . . . DLB-110

Quasimodo, Salvatore 1901-1968 . . . . DLB-114

Queen, Ellery (see Dannay, Frederic, and
Manfred B. Lee)

Queen, Frank 1822-1882 . . . . DLB-241

The Queen City Publishing House DLB-49

Queneau, Raymond 1903-1976 . . . . . . DLB-72, 258

Quennell, Sir Peter 1905-1993 . . . . . . DLB-155, 195

Quesnel, Joseph 1746-1809 . . . . DLB-99

The Question of American Copyright
in the Nineteenth Century
Preface, by George Haven Putnam
The Evolution of Copyright, by
Brander Matthews
Summary of Copyright Legislation in
the United States, by R. R. Bowker
Analysis of the Provisions of the
Copyright Law of 1891, by
George Haven Putnam
The Contest for International Copyright,
by George Haven Putnam
Cheap Books and Good Books,
by Brander Matthews DLB-49

Quiller-Couch, Sir Arthur Thomas
1863-1944 . . . . DLB-135, 153, 190

Quin, Ann 1936-1973 . . . . DLB-14, 231

Quincy, Samuel, of Georgia ?-? DLB-31

Quincy, Samuel, of Massachusetts
1734-1789 . . . . DLB-31

Quinn, Anthony 1915- DLB-122

The Quinn Draft of James Joyce's
Circe Manuscript Y-00

Quinn, John 1870-1924 . . . . DLB-187

Quiñónez, Naomi 1951- DLB-209

Quintana, Leroy V. 1944- DLB-82

Quintana, Miguel de 1671-1748
A Forerunner of Chicano Literature . DLB-122

Quintillian
circa A.D. 40-circa A.D. 96 . . . . DLB-211

Quintus Curtius Rufus fl. A.D. 35 . . . . . . DLB-211

Quist, Harlin, Books DLB-46

Quoirez, Françoise (see Sagan, Françoise)

R

R-va, Zeneida (see Gan, Elena Andreevna)

Raabe, Wilhelm 1831-1910 . . . . DLB-129

Raban, Jonathan 1942- DLB-204

Rabe, David 1940- DLB-7, 228

Raboni, Giovanni 1932- DLB-128

Rachilde 1860-1953 . . . . DLB-123, 192

Racin, Kočo 1908-1943 . . . . DLB-147

Rackham, Arthur 1867-1939 . . . . DLB-141

Radauskas, Henrikas
1910-1970 . . . . DLB-220; CDWLB-4

Radcliffe, Ann 1764-1823 . . . . DLB-39, 178

Raddall, Thomas 1903-1994 . . . . DLB-68

Radford, Dollie 1858-1920 . . . . DLB-240

Radichkov, Yordan 1929- DLB-181

Radiguet, Raymond 1903-1923 . . . . DLB-65

Radishchev, Aleksandr Nikolaevich
1749-1802 . . . . DLB-150

Radnóti, Miklós
1909-1944 . . . . DLB-215; CDWLB-4

Radványi, Netty Reiling (see Seghers, Anna)

Rahv, Philip 1908-1973 . . . . DLB-137

Raich, Semen Egorovich 1792-1855 . . . . . DLB-205

Raičković, Stevan 1928- DLB-181

Raimund, Ferdinand Jakob 1790-1836 . . . . DLB-90

Raine, Craig 1944- DLB-40

Raine, Kathleen 1908- DLB-20

Rainis, Jānis 1865-1929 . . . . . DLB-220; CDWLB-4

Rainolde, Richard
circa 1530-1606 . . . . DLB-136, 236

Rakić, Milan 1876-1938 . . . . . DLB-147; CDWLB-4

Rakosi, Carl 1903- DLB-193

Ralegh, Sir Walter
1554?-1618 . . . . DLB-172; CDBLB-1

Ralin, Radoy 1923- DLB-181

Ralph, Julian 1853-1903 . . . . DLB-23

Ramat, Silvio 1939- DLB-128

Rambler, no. 4 (1750), by Samuel Johnson
[excerpt] DLB-39

Ramée, Marie Louise de la (see Ouida)

Ramírez, Sergío 1942- DLB-145

Ramke, Bin 1947- DLB-120

Ramler, Karl Wilhelm 1725-1798 . . . . DLB-97

Ramon Ribeyro, Julio 1929- DLB-145

Ramos, Manuel 1948- DLB-209

Ramous, Mario 1924- DLB-128

Rampersad, Arnold 1941- DLB-111

Ramsay, Allan 1684 or 1685-1758 . . . . . . DLB-95

Ramsay, David 1749-1815 . . . . DLB-30

Ramsay, Martha Laurens 1759-1811 . . . . DLB-200

Ramsey, Frank P. 1903-1930 . . . . DLB-262

Ranck, Katherine Quintana 1942- DLB-122

Rand, Avery and Company DLB-49

Rand, Ayn 1905-1982 . . . . . . DLB-227; CDALB-7

Rand McNally and Company DLB-49

Randall, David Anton 1905-1975 . . . . DLB-140

Randall, Dudley 1914- DLB-41

Randall, Henry S. 1811-1876 . . . . DLB-30

Randall, James G. 1881-1953 . . . . DLB-17

The Randall Jarrell Symposium:
A Small Collection of Randall Jarrells
Excerpts From Papers Delivered at the
Randall Jarrel Symposium Y-86

Randolph, A. Philip 1889-1979 . . . . DLB-91

Randolph, Anson D. F.
[publishing house] DLB-49

Randolph, Thomas 1605-1635 . . . . . . DLB-58, 126

Random House DLB-46

Ranlet, Henry [publishing house] DLB-49

Ransom, Harry 1908-1976 . . . . DLB-187

Ransom, John Crowe
1888-1974 . . . . DLB-45, 63; CDALB-7

Ransome, Arthur 1884-1967 . . . . DLB-160

Raphael, Frederic 1931- DLB-14

Raphaelson, Samson 1896-1983 . . . . DLB-44

Rashi circa 1040-1105 . . . . DLB-208

Raskin, Ellen 1928-1984 . . . . DLB-52

Rastell, John 1475?-1536 . . . . DLB-136, 170

Rattigan, Terence
1911-1977 . . . . DLB-13; CDBLB-7

Rawlings, Marjorie Kinnan 1896-1953
. . . . DLB-9, 22, 102; DS-17; CDALB-7

Rawlinson, Richard 1690-1755 . . . . DLB-213

Rawlinson, Thomas 1681-1725 . . . . DLB-213

Raworth, Tom 1938- DLB-40

Ray, David 1932- DLB-5

Ray, Gordon Norton 1915-1986 . . . DLB-103, 140

Ray, Henrietta Cordelia 1849-1916 . . . . DLB-50

Raymond, Ernest 1888-1974 . . . . DLB-191

Raymond, Henry J. 1820-1869 . . . . . . DLB-43, 79

Michael M. Rea and the Rea Award for the
Short Story Y-97

Reach, Angus 1821-1856 . . . . DLB-70

Read, Herbert 1893-1968 . . . . DLB-20, 149

Read, Martha Meredith DLB-200

Read, Opie 1852-1939 . . . . DLB-23

Read, Piers Paul 1941- DLB-14

Reade, Charles 1814-1884 . . . . DLB-21

Reader's Digest Condensed Books DLB-46

Readers Ulysses Symposium Y-97

Reading, Peter 1946- DLB-40

Reading Series in New York City Y-96

The Reality of One Woman's Dream:
The de Grummond Children's
Literature Collection Y-99

Reaney, James 1926- DLB-68

Rebhun, Paul 1500?-1546 . . . . DLB-179

Rèbora, Clemente 1885-1957 . . . . DLB-114

Rebreanu, Liviu 1885-1944 . . . . DLB-220

Rechy, John 1934- DLB-122; Y-82

The Recovery of Literature:
Criticism in the 1990s: A Symposium Y-91

Redding, J. Saunders 1906-1988 . . . . . . DLB-63, 76

Redfield, J. S. [publishing house] DLB-49

Redgrove, Peter 1932- DLB-40

Redmon, Anne 1943- Y-86

Redmond, Eugene B. 1937- DLB-41

Redpath, James [publishing house] DLB-49

Reed, Henry 1808-1854 . . . . DLB-59

Reed, Henry 1914- DLB-27

Reed, Ishmael
1938- DLB-2, 5, 33, 169, 227; DS-8

Reed, Rex 1938- DLB-185

Reed, Sampson 1800-1880 . . . . DLB-1, 235

Reed, Talbot Baines 1852-1893 . . . . DLB-141

Reedy, William Marion 1862-1920 . . . . . . DLB-91

Reese, Lizette Woodworth 1856-1935 . . . . DLB-54

Reese, Thomas 1742-1796 . . . . DLB-37

Reeve, Clara 1729-1807 . . . . DLB-39

Preface to *The Old English Baron* (1778) DLB-39

The Progress of Romance (1785) [excerpt] DLB-39

Reeves, James 1909-1978 . . . . DLB-161

Reeves, John 1926- DLB-88

Reeves-Stevens, Garfield 1953- DLB-251

"Reflections: After a Tornado,"
by Judson Jerome DLB-105

Regnery, Henry, Company DLB-46

Rehberg, Hans 1901-1963 . . . . DLB-124

Rehfisch, Hans José 1891-1960 . . . . DLB-124

Reich, Ebbe Kløvedal 1940- DLB-214

Reid, Alastair 1926- DLB-27

Reid, B. L. 1918-1990 . . . . DLB-111; Y-83

The Practice of Biography II:
An Interview with B. L. Reid Y-83

Reid, Christopher 1949- DLB-40

Reid, Forrest 1875-1947 . . . . DLB-153

Reid, Helen Rogers 1882-1970 . . . . DLB-29

Reid, James ?-? DLB-31

Reid, Mayne 1818-1883 . . . . DLB-21, 163

Reid, Thomas 1710-1796 . . . . DLB-31, 252

Reid, V. S. (Vic) 1913-1987 . . . . DLB-125

Reid, Whitelaw 1837-1912 . . . . DLB-23

Reilly and Lee Publishing Company DLB-46

Reimann, Brigitte 1933-1973 . . . . DLB-75

Reinmar der Alte
  circa 1165-circa 1205 . . . . DLB-138

Reinmar von Zweter
  circa 1200-circa 1250 . . . . DLB-138

Reisch, Walter 1903-1983 . . . . DLB-44

Reizei Family DLB-203

Remarks at the Opening of "The Biographical
  Part of Literature" Exhibition, by
  William R. Cagle. Y-98

Remarque, Erich Maria
  1898-1970 . . . . DLB-56; CDWLB-2

Remington, Frederic
  1861-1909 . . . . DLB-12, 186, 188

Reminiscences, by Charles Scribner Jr. DS-17

Renaud, Jacques 1943- DLB-60

Renault, Mary 1905-1983 . . . . Y-83

Rendell, Ruth 1930- DLB-87

Rensselaer, Maria van Cortlandt van
  1645-1689 . . . . DLB-200

Repplier, Agnes 1855-1950 . . . . DLB-221

Representative Men and Women: A Historical
  Perspective on the British Novel,
  1930-1960 . . . . DLB-15

Research in the American Antiquarian Book
  Trade Y-97

Reshetnikov, Fedor Mikhailovich
  1841-1871 . . . . DLB-238

Rettenbacher, Simon 1634-1706. . . . . DLB-168

Reuchlin, Johannes 1455-1522. . . . . DLB-179

Reuter, Christian 1665-after 1712 . . . . . . DLB-168

Revell, Fleming H., Company DLB-49

Reverdy, Pierre 1889-1960 . . . . DLB-258

Reuter, Fritz 1810-1874 . . . . DLB-129

Reuter, Gabriele 1859-1941 . . . . DLB-66

Reventlow, Franziska Gräfin zu
  1871-1918 . . . . DLB-66

Review of Nicholson Baker's *Double Fold:
  Libraries and the Assault on Paper*. Y-00

Review of Reviews Office DLB-112

Review of [Samuel Richardson's] *Clarissa* (1748),
  by Henry Fielding DLB-39

The Revolt (1937), by Mary Colum
  [excerpts] DLB-36

Rexroth, Kenneth 1905-1982
  . . . . . . DLB-16, 48, 165, 212; Y-82; CDALB-1

Rey, H. A. 1898-1977 . . . . DLB-22

Reynal and Hitchcock DLB-46

Reynolds, G. W. M. 1814-1879 . . . . DLB-21

Reynolds, John Hamilton 1794-1852 . . . . . DLB-96

Reynolds, Sir Joshua 1723-1792 . . . . DLB-104

Reynolds, Mack 1917- DLB-8

A Literary Archaelogist Digs On: A Brief
  Interview with Michael Reynolds by
  Michael Rogers Y-99

Reznikoff, Charles 1894-1976 . . . . . . DLB-28, 45

Rhett, Robert Barnwell 1800-1876. . . . . . . DLB-43

Rhode, John 1884-1964 . . . . DLB-77

Rhodes, Eugene Manlove 1869-1934 . . . . DLB-256

Rhodes, James Ford 1848-1927 . . . . DLB-47

Rhodes, Richard 1937- DLB-185

Rhys, Jean 1890-1979
  . . . . DLB-36, 117, 162; CDBLB-7; CDWLB-3

Ricardo, David 1772-1823 . . . . DLB-107, 158

Ricardou, Jean 1932- DLB-83

Rice, Elmer 1892-1967 . . . . DLB-4, 7

Rice, Grantland 1880-1954 . . . . DLB-29, 171

Rich, Adrienne 1929- DLB-5, 67; CDALB-7

Richard de Fournival
  1201-1259 or 1260 . . . . DLB-208

Richard, Mark 1955- DLB-234

Richards, David Adams 1950- DLB-53

Richards, George circa 1760-1814 . . . . DLB-37

Richards, Grant [publishing house] DLB-112

Richards, I. A. 1893-1979. . . . . DLB-27

Richards, Laura E. 1850-1943 . . . . DLB-42

Richards, William Carey 1818-1892 . . . . . DLB-73

Richardson, Charles F. 1851-1913 . . . . DLB-71

Richardson, Dorothy M. 1873-1957 . . . . . DLB-36

Richardson, Henry Handel
  (Ethel Florence Lindesay
  Robertson) 1870-1946 . . . . DLB-197, 230

Richardson, Jack 1935- DLB-7

Richardson, John 1796-1852 . . . . DLB-99

Richardson, Samuel
  1689-1761 . . . . DLB-39, 154; CDBLB-2

Introductory Letters from the Second
  Edition of *Pamela* (1741). DLB-39

Postscript to [the Third Edition of]
  Clarissa (1751) DLB-39

Preface to the First Edition of
  Pamela (1740) DLB-39

Preface to the Third Edition of
  Clarissa (1751) [excerpt] DLB-39

Preface to Volume 1 of *Clarissa* (1747) DLB-39

Preface to Volume 3 of *Clarissa* (1748) DLB-39

Richardson, Willis 1889-1977 . . . . DLB-51

Riche, Barnabe 1542-1617 . . . . DLB-136

Richepin, Jean 1849-1926 . . . . DLB-192

Richler, Mordecai 1931- DLB-53

Richter, Conrad 1890-1968 . . . . DLB-9, 212

Richter, Hans Werner 1908- DLB-69

Richter, Johann Paul Friedrich
  1763-1825 . . . . DLB-94; CDWLB-2

Rickerby, Joseph [publishing house] DLB-106

Rickword, Edgell 1898-1982 . . . . DLB-20

Riddell, Charlotte 1832-1906. . . . . DLB-156

Riddell, John (see Ford, Corey)

Ridge, John Rollin 1827-1867 . . . . DLB-175

Ridge, Lola 1873-1941 . . . . DLB-54

Ridge, William Pett 1859-1930 . . . . DLB-135

Riding, Laura (see Jackson, Laura Riding)

Ridler, Anne 1912- DLB-27

Ridruego, Dionisio 1912-1975 . . . . DLB-108

Riel, Louis 1844-1885 . . . . DLB-99

Riemer, Johannes 1648-1714 . . . . DLB-168

Rifbjerg, Klaus 1931- DLB-214

Riffaterre, Michael 1924- DLB-67

Riggs, Lynn 1899-1954 . . . . DLB-175

Riis, Jacob 1849-1914 . . . . DLB-23

Riker, John C. [publishing house] DLB-49

Riley, James 1777-1840. . . . . DLB-183

Riley, John 1938-1978 . . . . DLB-40

Rilke, Rainer Maria
  1875-1926 . . . . DLB-81; CDWLB-2

Rimanelli, Giose 1926- DLB-177

Rimbaud, Jean-Nicolas-Arthur
  1854-1891 . . . . DLB-217

Rinehart and Company DLB-46

Ringuet 1895-1960. . . . . DLB-68

Ringwood, Gwen Pharis 1910-1984 . . . . . . DLB-88

Rinser, Luise 1911- DLB-69

Ríos, Alberto 1952- DLB-122

Ríos, Isabella 1948- DLB-82

Ripley, Arthur 1895-1961 . . . . DLB-44

Ripley, George 1802-1880 . . . . . DLB-1, 64, 73, 235

The Rising Glory of America:
  Three Poems DLB-37

The Rising Glory of America:
  Written in 1771 (1786),
  by Hugh Henry Brackenridge and
  Philip Freneau DLB-37

Riskin, Robert 1897-1955. . . . . DLB-26

Risse, Heinz 1898- DLB-69

Rist, Johann 1607-1667 . . . . DLB-164

Ristikivi, Karl 1912-1977 . . . . DLB-220

Ritchie, Anna Mowatt 1819-1870 . . . . . DLB-3, 250

Ritchie, Anne Thackeray 1837-1919 . . . . . . DLB-18

Ritchie, Thomas 1778-1854 . . . . DLB-43

Rites of Passage [on William Saroyan] Y-83

The Ritz Paris Hemingway Award Y-85

Rivard, Adjutor 1868-1945 . . . . DLB-92

Rive, Richard 1931-1989 . . . . DLB-125, 225

Rivera, José 1955- DLB-249

Rivera, Marina 1942- DLB-122

Rivera, Tomás 1935-1984 . . . . DLB-82

Rivers, Conrad Kent 1933-1968 . . . . DLB-41

Riverside Press DLB-49

Rivington, Charles [publishing house] DLB-154

Rivington, James circa 1724-1802 . . . . DLB-43

Rivkin, Allen 1903-1990 . . . . DLB-26

Roa Bastos, Augusto 1917- DLB-113

Robbe-Grillet, Alain 1922- DLB-83

Robbins, Tom 1936- Y-80

Roberts, Charles G. D. 1860-1943 . . . . DLB-92

Roberts, Dorothy 1906-1993 . . . . DLB-88

Roberts, Elizabeth Madox
  1881-1941 . . . . DLB-9, 54, 102

Roberts, James [publishing house] DLB-154

Roberts, Keith 1935-2000 . . . . DLB-261

Roberts, Kenneth 1885-1957 . . . . DLB-9

Roberts, Michèle 1949- DLB-231

Roberts, Ursula Wyllie (see Miles, Susan)

Roberts, William 1767-1849 . . . . DLB-142

Roberts Brothers. DLB-49

Robertson, A. M., and Company DLB-49

Robertson, Ethel Florence Lindesay
(see Richardson, Henry Handel)

Robertson, William 1721-1793 . . . . DLB-104

Robins, Elizabeth 1862-1952 . . . . DLB-197

Robinson, A. Mary F. (Madame James
Darmesteter, Madame Mary
Duclaux) 1857-1944 . . . . DLB-240

Robinson, Casey 1903-1979 . . . . DLB-44

Robinson, Edwin Arlington
1869-1935 . . . . DLB-54; CDALB-3

Robinson, Henry Crabb 1775-1867 . . . . . DLB-107

Robinson, James Harvey 1863-1936 . . . . . DLB-47

Robinson, Lennox 1886-1958 . . . . DLB-10

Robinson, Mabel Louise 1874-1962 . . . . . . DLB-22

Robinson, Marilynne 1943- DLB-206

Robinson, Mary 1758-1800 . . . . DLB-158

Robinson, Richard circa 1545-1607 . . . . . DLB-167

Robinson, Therese 1797-1870 . . . . DLB-59, 133

Robison, Mary 1949- DLB-130

Roblès, Emmanuel 1914-1995 . . . . DLB-83

Roccatagliata Ceccardi, Ceccardo
1871-1919 . . . . DLB-114

Roche, Billy 1949- DLB-233

Rochester, John Wilmot, Earl of
1647-1680 . . . . DLB-131

Rochon, Esther 1948- DLB-251

Rock, Howard 1911-1976 . . . . DLB-127

Rockwell, Norman Perceval 1894-1978 . . DLB-188

Rodgers, Carolyn M. 1945- DLB-41

Rodgers, W. R. 1909-1969 . . . . DLB-20

Rodney, Lester 1911- DLB-241

Rodríguez, Claudio 1934-1999 . . . . DLB-134

Rodríguez, Joe D. 1943- DLB-209

Rodríguez, Luis J. 1954- DLB-209

Rodriguez, Richard 1944- DLB-82, 256

Rodríguez Julia, Edgardo 1946- DLB-145

Roe, E. P. 1838-1888 . . . . DLB-202

Roethke, Theodore
1908-1963 . . . . DLB-5, 206; CDALB-1

Rogers, Jane 1952- DLB-194

Rogers, Pattiann 1940- DLB-105

Rogers, Samuel 1763-1855 . . . . DLB-93

Rogers, Will 1879-1935 . . . . DLB-11

Rohmer, Sax 1883-1959 . . . . DLB-70

Roiphe, Anne 1935- Y-80

Rojas, Arnold R. 1896-1988 . . . . DLB-82

Rolfe, Frederick William
1860-1913. . . . . DLB-34, 156

Rolland, Romain 1866-1944. . . . . DLB-65

Rolle, Richard circa 1290-1300 - 1340 . . . DLB-146

Rölvaag, O. E. 1876-1931 . . . . DLB-9, 212

Romains, Jules 1885-1972 . . . . DLB-65

Roman, A., and Company DLB-49

Roman de la Rose: Guillaume de Lorris
1200 to 1205-circa 1230, Jean de Meun
1235-1240-circa 1305 . . . . DLB-208

Romano, Lalla 1906- DLB-177

Romano, Octavio 1923- DLB-122

Romero, Leo 1950- DLB-122

Romero, Lin 1947- DLB-122

Romero, Orlando 1945- DLB-82

Rook, Clarence 1863-1915 . . . . DLB-135

Roosevelt, Theodore 1858-1919 . . . . .DLB-47, 186

Root, Waverley 1903-1982 . . . . DLB-4

Root, William Pitt 1941- DLB-120

Roquebrune, Robert de 1889-1978 . . . . . . DLB-68

Rorty, Richard 1931- DLB-246

Rosa, João Guimarães 1908-1967 . . . . . . DLB-113

Rosales, Luis 1910-1992 . . . . DLB-134

Roscoe, William 1753-1831 . . . . DLB-163

Danis Rose and the Rendering of *Ulysses* Y-97

Rose, Reginald 1920- DLB-26

Rose, Wendy 1948- DLB-175

Rosegger, Peter 1843-1918 . . . . DLB-129

Rosei, Peter 1946- DLB-85

Rosen, Norma 1925- DLB-28

Rosenbach, A. S. W. 1876-1952 . . . . DLB-140

Rosenbaum, Ron 1946- DLB-185

Rosenberg, Isaac 1890-1918 . . . . DLB-20, 216

Rosenfeld, Isaac 1918-1956 . . . . DLB-28

Rosenthal, Harold 1914-1999 . . . . DLB-241

Jimmy, Red, and Others: Harold Rosenthal
Remembers the Stars of the Press Box . . . Y-01

Rosenthal, M. L. 1917-1996 . . . . DLB-5

Rosenwald, Lessing J. 1891-1979 . . . . DLB-187

Ross, Alexander 1591-1654 . . . . DLB-151

Ross, Harold 1892-1951 . . . . DLB-137

Ross, Leonard Q. (see Rosten, Leo)

Ross, Lillian 1927- DLB-185

Ross, Martin 1862-1915 . . . . DLB-135

Ross, Sinclair 1908-1996. . . . . DLB-88

Ross, W. W. E. 1894-1966. . . . . DLB-88

Rosselli, Amelia 1930-1996. . . . . DLB-128

Rossen, Robert 1908-1966 . . . . .DLB-26

Rossetti, Christina 1830-1894 . . . DLB-35, 163, 240

Rossetti, Dante Gabriel
1828-1882 . . . . DLB-35; CDBLB-4

Rossner, Judith 1935- DLB-6

Rostand, Edmond 1868-1918 . . . . DLB-192

Rosten, Leo 1908-1997 . . . . DLB-11

Rostenberg, Leona 1908- DLB-140

Rostopchina, Evdokiia Petrovna
1811-1858 . . . . DLB-205

Rostovsky, Dimitrii 1651-1709 . . . . DLB-150

Rota, Bertram 1903-1966 . . . . DLB-201

Bertram Rota and His Bookshop Y-91

Roth, Gerhard 1942- DLB-85, 124

Roth, Henry 1906?-1995 . . . . DLB-28

Roth, Joseph 1894-1939 . . . . DLB-85

Roth, Philip 1933-
. . . . .DLB-2, 28, 173; Y-82; CDALB-6

Rothenberg, Jerome 1931- DLB-5, 193

Rothschild Family. DLB-184

Rotimi, Ola 1938- DLB-125

Routhier, Adolphe-Basile 1839-1920 . . . . . DLB-99

Routier, Simone 1901-1987 . . . . DLB-88

Routledge, George, and Sons DLB-106

Roversi, Roberto 1923- DLB-128

Rowe, Elizabeth Singer 1674-1737 . . . . DLB-39, 95

Rowe, Nicholas 1674-1718 . . . . DLB-84

Rowlands, Samuel circa 1570-1630. . . . . . DLB-121

Rowlandson, Mary
circa 1637-circa 1711 . . . . DLB-24, 200

Rowley, William circa 1585-1626 . . . . DLB-58

Rowse, A. L. 1903-1997 . . . . DLB-155

Rowson, Susanna Haswell
circa 1762-1824 . . . . .DLB-37, 200

Roy, Camille 1870-1943 . . . . DLB-92

Roy, Gabrielle 1909-1983. . . . . DLB-68

Roy, Jules 1907- DLB-83

The G. Ross Roy Scottish Poetry Collection
at the University of South Carolina Y-89

The Royal Court Theatre and the English
Stage Company DLB-13

The Royal Court Theatre and the New
Drama DLB-10

The Royal Shakespeare Company
at the Swan Y-88

Royall, Anne Newport 1769-1854 . . . DLB-43, 248

The Roycroft Printing Shop DLB-49

Royde-Smith, Naomi 1875-1964 . . . . DLB-191

Royster, Vermont 1914- DLB-127

Royston, Richard [publishing house] DLB-170

Różewicz, Tadeusz 1921- DLB-232

Ruark, Gibbons 1941- DLB-120

Ruban, Vasilii Grigorevich 1742-1795 . . . DLB-150

Rubens, Bernice 1928- DLB-14, 207

Rudd and Carleton. DLB-49

Rudd, Steele (Arthur Hoey Davis) DLB-230

Rudkin, David 1936- DLB-13

Rudolf von Ems circa 1200-circa 1254 . . . DLB-138

Ruffin, Josephine St. Pierre
1842-1924 . . . . DLB-79

Ruganda, John 1941- DLB-157

Ruggles, Henry Joseph 1813-1906 . . . . DLB-64

Ruiz de Burton, María Amparo
1832-1895 . . . . DLB-209, 221

Rukeyser, Muriel 1913-1980 . . . . DLB-48

Rule, Jane 1931- DLB-60

Rulfo, Juan 1918-1986 . . . . . .DLB-113; CDWLB-3

Rumaker, Michael 1932- DLB-16

Rumens, Carol 1944- DLB-40

Rummo, Paul-Eerik 1942- DLB-232

Runyon, Damon 1880-1946 . . . . . .DLB-11, 86, 171

Ruodlieb circa 1050-1075 . . . . DLB-148

Rush, Benjamin 1746-1813 . . . . DLB-37

Rush, Rebecca 1779-?. DLB-200

Rushdie, Salman 1947- DLB-194

Rusk, Ralph L. 1888-1962. . . . . .DLB-103

Ruskin, John
  1819-1900 . . . . . .DLB-55, 163, 190; CDBLB-4

Russ, Joanna 1937- DLB-8

Russell, B. B., and Company. DLB-49

Russell, Benjamin 1761-1845 . . . . .DLB-43

Russell, Bertrand 1872-1970. . . . . . . .DLB-100, 262

Russell, Charles Edward 1860-1941 . . . . .DLB-25

Russell, Charles M. 1864-1926 . . . . .DLB-188

Russell, Eric Frank 1905-1978 . . . . .DLB-255

Russell, Fred 1906- DLB-241

Russell, George William (see AE)

Russell, Countess Mary Annette Beauchamp
  (see Arnim, Elizabeth von)

Russell, R. H., and Son DLB-49

Russell, Willy 1947- DLB-233

Rutebeuf flourished 1249-1277 . . . . .DLB-208

Rutherford, Mark 1831-1913. . . . . .DLB-18

Ruxton, George Frederick
  1821-1848 . . . . .DLB-186

Ryan, Michael 1946- Y-82

Ryan, Oscar 1904- DLB-68

Ryder, Jack 1871-1936. . . . . .DLB-241

Ryga, George 1932- DLB-60

Rylands, Enriqueta Augustina Tennant
  1843-1908 . . . . .DLB-184

Rylands, John 1801-1888. . . . . .DLB-184

Ryle, Gilbert 1900-1976 . . . . .DLB-262

Ryleev, Kondratii Fedorovich
  1795-1826 . . . . .DLB-205

Rymer, Thomas 1643?-1713 . . . . .DLB-101

Ryskind, Morrie 1895-1985. . . . . .DLB-26

Rzhevsky, Aleksei Andreevich
  1737-1804. . . . . .DLB-150

S

The Saalfield Publishing Company DLB-46

Saba, Umberto 1883-1957 . . . . .DLB-114

Sábato, Ernesto 1911- DLB-145; CDWLB-3

Saberhagen, Fred 1930- DLB-8

Sabin, Joseph 1821-1881 . . . . .DLB-187

Sacer, Gottfried Wilhelm 1635-1699 . . . . .DLB-168

Sachs, Hans 1494-1576 . . . . . DLB-179; CDWLB-2

Sack, John 1930- DLB-185

Sackler, Howard 1929-1982. . . . . .DLB-7

Sackville, Lady Margaret 1881-1963 . . . . .DLB-240

Sackville, Thomas 1536-1608 . . . . .DLB-132

Sackville, Thomas 1536-1608
  and Norton, Thomas 1532-1584. . . . . .DLB-62

Sackville-West, Edward 1901-1965 . . . . . .DLB-191

Sackville-West, V. 1892-1962 . . . . . . .DLB-34, 195

Sadlier, D. and J., and Company. DLB-49

Sadlier, Mary Anne 1820-1903 . . . . .DLB-99

Sadoff, Ira 1945- DLB-120

Sadoveanu, Mihail 1880-1961 . . . . .DLB-220

Sáenz, Benjamin Alire 1954- DLB-209

Saenz, Jaime 1921-1986 . . . . .DLB-145

Saffin, John circa 1626-1710. . . . . .DLB-24

Sagan, Françoise 1935- DLB-83

Sage, Robert 1899-1962. . . . . .DLB-4

Sagel, Jim 1947- DLB-82

Sagendorph, Robb Hansell 1900-1970. . . .DLB-137

Sahagún, Carlos 1938- DLB-108

Sahkomaapii, Piitai (see Highwater, Jamake)

Sahl, Hans 1902- DLB-69

Said, Edward W. 1935- DLB-67

Saigyō 1118-1190. . . . . .DLB-203

Saiko, George 1892-1962. . . . . .DLB-85

St. Dominic's Press DLB-112

Saint-Exupéry, Antoine de 1900-1944 . . . . .DLB-72

St. John, J. Allen 1872-1957 . . . . .DLB-188

St. Johns, Adela Rogers 1894-1988 . . . . . . .DLB-29

The St. John's College Robert Graves Trust. . Y-96

St. Martin's Press. DLB-46

St. Omer, Garth 1931- DLB-117

Saint Pierre, Michel de 1916-1987 . . . . . . .DLB-83

Sainte-Beuve, Charles-Augustin
  1804-1869 . . . . .DLB-217

Saints' Lives. .DLB-208

Saintsbury, George 1845-1933. . . . . . DLB-57, 149

Saiokuken Sōchō 1448-1532 . . . . .DLB-203

Saki (see Munro, H. H.)

Salaam, Kalamu ya 1947- DLB-38

Šalamun, Tomaž 1941- . . .DLB-181; CDWLB-4

Salas, Floyd 1931- DLB-82

Sálaz-Marquez, Rubén 1935- DLB-122

Salemson, Harold J. 1910-1988 . . . . .DLB-4

Salinas, Luis Omar 1937- DLB-82

Salinas, Pedro 1891-1951. . . . . .DLB-134

Salinger, J. D.
  1919- DLB-2, 102, 173; CDALB-1

Salkey, Andrew 1928- DLB-125

Sallust circa 86 B.C.-35 B.C.
  . . . . .DLB-211; CDWLB-1

Salt, Waldo 1914- DLB-44

Salter, James 1925- DLB-130

Salter, Mary Jo 1954- DLB-120

Saltus, Edgar 1855-1921 . . . . .DLB-202

Saltykov, Mikhail Evgrafovich
  1826-1889 . . . . .DLB-238

Salustri, Carlo Alberto (see Trilussa)

Salverson, Laura Goodman 1890-1970 . . . .DLB-92

Samain, Albert 1858-1900 . . . . .DLB-217

Sampson, Richard Henry (see Hull, Richard)

Samuels, Ernest 1903-1996 . . . . .DLB-111

Sanborn, Franklin Benjamin
  1831-1917 . . . . .DLB-1, 223

Sánchez, Luis Rafael 1936- DLB-145

Sánchez, Philomeno "Phil" 1917- DLB-122

Sánchez, Ricardo 1941-1995 . . . . .DLB-82

Sánchez, Saúl 1943- DLB-209

Sanchez, Sonia 1934- DLB-41; DS-8

Sand, George 1804-1876 . . . . .DLB-119, 192

Sandburg, Carl
  1878-1967 . . . . DLB-17, 54; CDALB-3

Sanders, Edward 1939- DLB-16, 244

Sandoz, Mari 1896-1966 . . . . .DLB-9, 212

Sandwell, B. K. 1876-1954. . . . . .DLB-92

Sandy, Stephen 1934- DLB-165

Sandys, George 1578-1644. . . . . .DLB-24, 121

Sangster, Charles 1822-1893 . . . . .DLB-99

Sanguineti, Edoardo 1930- DLB-128

Sanjōnishi Sanetaka 1455-1537 . . . . .DLB-203

Sansay, Leonora ?-after 1823. . . . . .DLB-200

Sansom, William 1912-1976 . . . . .DLB-139

Santayana, George
  1863-1952. . . . . .DLB-54, 71, 246; DS-13

Santiago, Danny 1911-1988. . . . . .DLB-122

Santmyer, Helen Hooven 1895-1986 . . . . Y-84

Sanvitale, Francesca 1928- DLB-196

Sapidus, Joannes 1490-1561. . . . . .DLB-179

Sapir, Edward 1884-1939 . . . . .DLB-92

Sapper (see McNeile, Herman Cyril)

Sappho circa 620 B.C.-circa 550 B.C.
  . . . . .DLB-176; CDWLB-1

Saramago, José 1922- Y-98

Sarban (John F. Wall) 1910-1989 . . . . . . .DLB-255

Sardou, Victorien 1831-1908. . . . . .DLB-192

Sarduy, Severo 1937- DLB-113

Sargent, Pamela 1948- DLB-8

Saro-Wiwa, Ken 1941- DLB-157

Saroyan, William
  1908-1981 . . . . . DLB-7, 9, 86; Y-81; CDALB-7

Sarraute, Nathalie 1900-1999. . . . . .DLB-83

Sarrazin, Albertine 1937-1967 . . . . .DLB-83

Sarris, Greg 1952- DLB-175

Sarton, May 1912-1995 . . . . .DLB-48; Y-81

Sartre, Jean-Paul 1905-1980. . . . . .DLB-72

Sassoon, Siegfried
  1886-1967 . . . . .DLB-20, 191; DS-18

Siegfried Loraine Sassoon:
  A Centenary Essay
  Tributes from Vivien F. Clarke and
  Michael Thorpe Y-86

Sata, Ineko 1904- DLB-180

Saturday Review Press DLB-46

Saunders, James 1925- DLB-13

Saunders, John Monk 1897-1940. . . . . . . .DLB-26

Saunders, Margaret Marshall
  1861-1947 . . . . .DLB-92

Saunders and Otley DLB-106

Saussure, Ferdinand de 1857-1913 . . . . . . .DLB-242

Savage, James 1784-1873 . . . . .DLB-30

Savage, Marmion W. 1803?-1872 . . . . . . .DLB-21

Savage, Richard 1697?-1743 . . . . .DLB-95

Savard, Félix-Antoine 1896-1982. . . . . . . .DLB-68

Savery, Henry 1791-1842 . . . . .DLB-230

Saville, (Leonard) Malcolm 1901-1982 . . . DLB-160

Sawyer, Robert J. 1960- DLB-251

Sawyer, Ruth 1880-1970 . . . . DLB-22

Sayers, Dorothy L.
1893-1957 . . . . . DLB-10, 36, 77, 100; CDBLB-6

Sayle, Charles Edward 1864-1924 . . . . . . DLB-184

Sayles, John Thomas 1950- DLB-44

Sbarbaro, Camillo 1888-1967 . . . . DLB-114

Scalapino, Leslie 1947- DLB-193

Scannell, Vernon 1922- DLB-27

Scarry, Richard 1919-1994 . . . . DLB-61

Schaefer, Jack 1907-1991 . . . . DLB-212

Schaeffer, Albrecht 1885-1950 . . . . DLB-66

Schaeffer, Susan Fromberg 1941- DLB-28

Schaff, Philip 1819-1893 . . . . DS-13

Schaper, Edzard 1908-1984 . . . . DLB-69

Scharf, J. Thomas 1843-1898 . . . . DLB-47

Schede, Paul Melissus 1539-1602 . . . . .DLB-179

Scheffel, Joseph Viktor von 1826-1886 . . . DLB-129

Scheffler, Johann 1624-1677 . . . . DLB-164

Schelling, Friedrich Wilhelm Joseph von
1775-1854 . . . . DLB-90

Scherer, Wilhelm 1841-1886 . . . . DLB-129

Scherfig, Hans 1905-1979 . . . . DLB-214

Schickele, René 1883-1940 . . . . DLB-66

Schiff, Dorothy 1903-1989 . . . . DLB-127

Schiller, Friedrich
1759-1805 . . . . DLB-94; CDWLB-2

Schirmer, David 1623-1687 . . . . DLB-164

Schlaf, Johannes 1862-1941 . . . . DLB-118

Schlegel, August Wilhelm 1767-1845 . . . . . DLB-94

Schlegel, Dorothea 1763-1839 . . . . DLB-90

Schlegel, Friedrich 1772-1829 . . . . DLB-90

Schleiermacher, Friedrich 1768-1834 . . . . DLB-90

Schlesinger, Arthur M., Jr. 1917- DLB-17

Schlumberger, Jean 1877-1968 . . . . DLB-65

Schmid, Eduard Hermann Wilhelm
(see Edschmid, Kasimir)

Schmidt, Arno 1914-1979 . . . . DLB-69

Schmidt, Johann Kaspar (see Stirner, Max)

Schmidt, Michael 1947- DLB-40

Schmidtbonn, Wilhelm August
1876-1952 . . . . DLB-118

Schmitz, James H. 1911- DLB-8

Schnabel, Johann Gottfried
1692-1760 . . . . DLB-168

Schnackenberg, Gjertrud 1953- DLB-120

Schnitzler, Arthur
1862-1931 . . . . DLB-81, 118; CDWLB-2

Schnurre, Wolfdietrich 1920-1989 . . . . . . DLB-69

Schocken Books DLB-46

Scholartis Press DLB-112

Scholderer, Victor 1880-1971 . . . . DLB-201

The Schomburg Center for Research
in Black Culture DLB-76

Schönbeck, Virgilio (see Giotti, Virgilio)

Schönherr, Karl 1867-1943 . . . . DLB-118

Schoolcraft, Jane Johnston 1800-1841 . . . . .DLB-175

School Stories, 1914-1960 . . . . DLB-160

Schopenhauer, Arthur 1788-1860 . . . . DLB-90

Schopenhauer, Johanna 1766-1838 . . . . . . DLB-90

Schorer, Mark 1908-1977 . . . . DLB-103

Schottelius, Justus Georg 1612-1676 . . . . . DLB-164

Schouler, James 1839-1920 . . . . DLB-47

Schoultz, Solveig von 1907-1996 . . . . DLB-259

Schrader, Paul 1946- DLB-44

Schreiner, Olive
1855-1920 . . . . .DLB-18, 156, 190, 225

Schroeder, Andreas 1946- DLB-53

Schubart, Christian Friedrich Daniel
1739-1791 . . . . DLB-97

Schubert, Gotthilf Heinrich 1780-1860 . . . . DLB-90

Schücking, Levin 1814-1883 . . . . DLB-133

Schulberg, Budd 1914- DLB-6, 26, 28; Y-81

Schulte, F. J., and Company DLB-49

Schulz, Bruno 1892-1942 . . . DLB-215; CDWLB-4

Schulze, Hans (see Praetorius, Johannes)

Schupp, Johann Balthasar 1610-1661 . . . . DLB-164

Schurz, Carl 1829-1906 . . . . DLB-23

Schuyler, George S. 1895-1977 . . . . DLB-29, 51

Schuyler, James 1923-1991 . . . . DLB-5, 169

Schwartz, Delmore 1913-1966 . . . . DLB-28, 48

Schwartz, Jonathan 1938- Y-82

Schwartz, Lynne Sharon 1939- DLB-218

Schwarz, Sibylle 1621-1638 . . . . DLB-164

Schwerner, Armand 1927-1999 . . . . DLB-165

Schwob, Marcel 1867-1905 . . . . DLB-123

Sciascia, Leonardo 1921-1989 . . . . .DLB-177

Science Fantasy DLB-8

Science-Fiction Fandom and Conventions . . DLB-8

Science-Fiction Fanzines: The Time
Binders DLB-8

Science-Fiction Films DLB-8

Science Fiction Writers of America and the
Nebula Awards DLB-8

Scot, Reginald circa 1538-1599 . . . . DLB-136

Scotellaro, Rocco 1923-1953 . . . . DLB-128

Scott, Alicia Anne (Lady John Scott)
1810-1900 . . . . DLB-240

Scott, Catharine Amy Dawson
1865-1934 . . . . DLB-240

Scott, Dennis 1939-1991 . . . . DLB-125

Scott, Dixon 1881-1915 . . . . DLB-98

Scott, Duncan Campbell 1862-1947 . . . . . . DLB-92

Scott, Evelyn 1893-1963 . . . . DLB-9, 48

Scott, F. R. 1899-1985 . . . . DLB-88

Scott, Frederick George 1861-1944 . . . . DLB-92

Scott, Geoffrey 1884-1929 . . . . DLB-149

Scott, Harvey W. 1838-1910 . . . . DLB-23

Scott, Lady Jane (see Scott, Alicia Anne)

Scott, Paul 1920-1978 . . . . .DLB-14, 207

Scott, Sarah 1723-1795 . . . . DLB-39

Scott, Tom 1918- DLB-27

Scott, Sir Walter 1771-1832
. . . . . . .DLB-93, 107, 116, 144, 159; CDBLB-3

Scott, Walter, Publishing
Company Limited DLB-112

Scott, William Bell 1811-1890 . . . . DLB-32

Scott, William R. [publishing house] DLB-46

Scott-Heron, Gil 1949- DLB-41

Scribe, Eugene 1791-1861 . . . . DLB-192

Scribner, Arthur Hawley 1859-1932 . . . . DS-13, 16

Scribner, Charles 1854-1930 . . . . DS-13, 16

Scribner, Charles, Jr. 1921-1995 . . . . Y-95

Reminiscences DS-17

Charles Scribner's Sons DLB-49; DS-13, 16, 17

Scripps, E. W. 1854-1926 . . . . DLB-25

Scudder, Horace Elisha 1838-1902 . . . . .DLB-42, 71

Scudder, Vida Dutton 1861-1954 . . . . DLB-71

Scupham, Peter 1933- DLB-40

Seabrook, William 1886-1945 . . . . DLB-4

Seabury, Samuel 1729-1796 . . . . DLB-31

Seacole, Mary Jane Grant 1805-1881 . . . . DLB-166

The Seafarer circa 970 . . . . DLB-146

Sealsfield, Charles (Carl Postl)
1793-1864 . . . . DLB-133, 186

Sears, Edward I. 1819?-1876 . . . . DLB-79

Sears Publishing Company DLB-46

Seaton, George 1911-1979 . . . . DLB-44

Seaton, William Winston 1785-1866 . . . . . DLB-43

Secker, Martin [publishing house] DLB-112

Secker, Martin, and Warburg Limited . . . DLB-112

The Second Annual New York Festival
of Mystery Y-00

Second-Generation Minor Poets of the
Seventeenth Century DLB-126

Sedgwick, Arthur George 1844-1915 . . . . . DLB-64

Sedgwick, Catharine Maria
1789-1867 . . . . .DLB-1, 74, 183, 239, 243

Sedgwick, Ellery 1872-1930 . . . . DLB-91

Sedgwick, Eve Kosofsky 1950- DLB-246

Sedley, Sir Charles 1639-1701 . . . . DLB-131

Seeberg, Peter 1925-1999 . . . . DLB-214

Seeger, Alan 1888-1916 . . . . DLB-45

Seers, Eugene (see Dantin, Louis)

Segal, Erich 1937- Y-86

Šegedin, Petar 1909- DLB-181

Seghers, Anna 1900-1983 . . . . DLB-69; CDWLB-2

Seid, Ruth (see Sinclair, Jo)

Seidel, Frederick Lewis 1936- Y-84

Seidel, Ina 1885-1974 . . . . DLB-56

Seifert, Jaroslav
1901-1986 . . . . . . .DLB-215; Y-84; CDWLB-4

Seigenthaler, John 1927- DLB-127

Seizin Press DLB-112

Séjour, Victor 1817-1874 . . . . DLB-50

Séjour Marcou et Ferrand, Juan Victor
(see Séjour, Victor)

Sekowski, Jósef-Julian, Baron Brambeus
(see Senkovsky, Osip Ivanovich)

Selby, Bettina 1934- DLB-204

Selby, Hubert, Jr. 1928- DLB-2, 227

Selden, George 1929-1989 . . . . .DLB-52

Selden, John 1584-1654 . . . . .DLB-213

Selected English-Language Little Magazines
 and Newspapers [France, 1920-1939] . . .DLB-4

Selected Humorous Magazines
 (1820-1950) DLB-11

Selected Science-Fiction Magazines and
 Anthologies DLB-8

Selenić, Slobodan 1933-1995 . . . . .DLB-181

Self, Edwin F. 1920- DLB-137

Self, Will 1961- DLB-207

Seligman, Edwin R. A. 1861-1939 . . . . . . .DLB-47

Selimović, Meša
 1910-1982 . . . . .DLB-181; CDWLB-4

Sellings, Arthur 1911-1968 . . . . .DLB-261

Selous, Frederick Courteney
 1851-1917 . . . . .DLB-174

Seltzer, Chester E. (see Muro, Amado)

Seltzer, Thomas [publishing house] DLB-46

Selvon, Sam 1923-1994 . . . . .DLB-125; CDWLB-3

Semmes, Raphael 1809-1877 . . . . .DLB-189

Senancour, Etienne de 1770-1846 . . . . . . .DLB-119

Sendak, Maurice 1928- DLB-61

Seneca the Elder
 circa 54 B.C.-circa A.D. 40 . . . . .DLB-211

Seneca the Younger
 circa 1 B.C.-A.D. 65 . . . .DLB-211; CDWLB-1

Senécal, Eva 1905- DLB-92

Sengstacke, John 1912- DLB-127

Senior, Olive 1941- DLB-157

Senkovsky, Osip Ivanovich
 (Józef-Julian Sekowski, Baron Brambeus)
 1800-1858 . . . . .DLB-198

Šenoa, August 1838-1881 . . . .DLB-147; CDWLB-4

"Sensation Novels" (1863), by
 H. L. Manse DLB-21

Sepamla, Sipho 1932- DLB-157, 225

Seredy, Kate 1899-1975 . . . . .DLB-22

Sereni, Vittorio 1913-1983 . . . . .DLB-128

Seres, William [publishing house] DLB-170

Serling, Rod 1924-1975 . . . . .DLB-26

Sernine, Daniel 1955- DLB-251

Serote, Mongane Wally 1944- DLB-125, 225

Serraillier, Ian 1912-1994 . . . . .DLB-161

Serrano, Nina 1934- DLB-122

Service, Robert 1874-1958 . . . . .DLB-92

Sessler, Charles 1854-1935 . . . . .DLB-187

Seth, Vikram 1952- DLB-120

Seton, Elizabeth Ann 1774-1821 . . . . .DLB-200

Seton, Ernest Thompson
 1860-1942 . . . . .DLB-92; DS-13

Setouchi Harumi 1922- DLB-182

Settle, Mary Lee 1918- DLB-6

Seume, Johann Gottfried 1763-1810 . . . . . .DLB-94

Seuse, Heinrich 1295?-1366 . . . . .DLB-179

Seuss, Dr. (see Geisel, Theodor Seuss)

The Seventy-fifth Anniversary of the Armistice:
 The Wilfred Owen Centenary and
 the Great War Exhibit
 at the University of Virginia Y-93

Severin, Timothy 1940- DLB-204

Sewall, Joseph 1688-1769 . . . . .DLB-24

Sewell, Richard B. 1908- DLB-111

Sewell, Anna 1820-1878 . . . . .DLB-163

Sewell, Samuel 1652-1730 . . . . .DLB-24

Sex, Class, Politics, and Religion [in the
 British Novel, 1930-1959] DLB-15

Sexton, Anne 1928-1974 . . .DLB-5, 169; CDALB-1

Seymour-Smith, Martin 1928-1998 . . . . . .DLB-155

Sgorlon, Carlo 1930- DLB-196

Shaara, Michael 1929-1988 . . . . Y-83

Shabel'skaia, Aleksandra Stanislavovna
 1845-1921 . . . . .DLB-238

Shadwell, Thomas 1641?-1692 . . . . .DLB-80

Shaffer, Anthony 1926- DLB-13

Shaffer, Peter 1926- DLB-13, 233; CDBLB-8

Shaftesbury, Anthony Ashley Cooper,
 Third Earl of 1671-1713 . . . . .DLB-101

Shairp, Mordaunt 1887-1939 . . . . .DLB-10

Shakespeare, Nicholas 1957- DLB-231

Shakespeare, William
 1564-1616 . . . . . .DLB-62, 172, 263; CDBLB-1

$6,166,000 for a *Book!* Observations on
 *The Shakespeare First Folio: The History
 of the Book* Y-01

The Shakespeare Globe Trust Y-93

Shakespeare Head Press DLB-112

Shakhovskoi, Aleksandr Aleksandrovich
 1777-1846 . . . . .DLB-150

Shange, Ntozake 1948- DLB-38, 249

Shapiro, Karl 1913-2000 . . . . .DLB-48

Sharon Publications DLB-46

Sharp, Margery 1905-1991 . . . . .DLB-161

Sharp, William 1855-1905 . . . . .DLB-156

Sharpe, Tom 1928- DLB-14, 231

Shaw, Albert 1857-1947 . . . . .DLB-91

Shaw, George Bernard
 1856-1950 . . . . . . .DLB-10, 57, 190, CDBLB-6

Shaw, Henry Wheeler 1818-1885 . . . . .DLB-11

Shaw, Joseph T. 1874-1952 . . . . .DLB-137

Shaw, Irwin
 1913-1984 . . . . . .DLB-6, 102; Y-84; CDALB-1

Shaw, Mary 1854-1929 . . . . .DLB-228

Shaw, Robert 1927-1978 . . . . .DLB-13, 14

Shaw, Robert B. 1947- DLB-120

Shawn, William 1907-1992 . . . . .DLB-137

Shay, Frank [publishing house] DLB-46

Shchedrin, N. (see Saltykov, Mikhail Evgrafovich)

Shea, John Gilmary 1824-1892 . . . . .DLB-30

Sheaffer, Louis 1912-1993 . . . . .DLB-103

Shearing, Joseph 1886-1952 . . . . .DLB-70

Shebbeare, John 1709-1788 . . . . .DLB-39

Sheckley, Robert 1928- DLB-8

Shedd, William G. T. 1820-1894 . . . . .DLB-64

Sheed, Wilfred 1930- DLB-6

Sheed and Ward [U.S.] DLB-46

Sheed and Ward Limited [U.K.] DLB-112

Sheldon, Alice B. (see Tiptree, James, Jr.)

Sheldon, Edward 1886-1946 . . . . .DLB-7

Sheldon and Company DLB-49

Sheller, Aleksandr Konstantinovich
 1838-1900 . . . . .DLB-238

Shelley, Mary Wollstonecraft 1797-1851
 . . . . .DLB-110, 116, 159, 178; CDBLB-3

Shelley, Percy Bysshe
 1792-1822 . . . . . .DLB-96, 110, 158; CDBLB-3

Shelnutt, Eve 1941- DLB-130

Shenstone, William 1714-1763 . . . . .DLB-95

Shepard, Clark and Brown DLB-49

Shepard, Ernest Howard 1879-1976 . . . . . .DLB-160

Shepard, Sam 1943- DLB-7, 212

Shepard, Thomas I, 1604 or 1605-1649 . . .DLB-24

Shepard, Thomas II, 1635-1677 . . . . .DLB-24

Shepherd, Luke
 flourished 1547-1554 . . . . .DLB-136

Sherburne, Edward 1616-1702 . . . . .DLB-131

Sheridan, Frances 1724-1766 . . . . .DLB-39, 84

Sheridan, Richard Brinsley
 1751-1816 . . . . .DLB-89; CDBLB-2

Sherman, Francis 1871-1926 . . . . .DLB-92

Sherman, Martin 1938- DLB-228

Sherriff, R. C. 1896-1975 . . . . . . .DLB-10, 191, 233

Sherrod, Blackie 1919- DLB-241

Sherry, Norman 1935- DLB-155

Sherry, Richard 1506-1551 or 1555 . . . . . .DLB-236

Sherwood, Mary Martha 1775-1851 . . . . .DLB-163

Sherwood, Robert E. 1896-1955 . . .DLB-7, 26, 249

Shevyrev, Stepan Petrovich
 1806-1864 . . . . .DLB-205

Shiel, M. P. 1865-1947 . . . . .DLB-153

Shiels, George 1886-1949 . . . . .DLB-10

Shiga, Naoya 1883-1971 . . . . .DLB-180

Shiina Rinzō 1911-1973 . . . . .DLB-182

Shikishi Naishinnō 1153?-1201 . . . . .DLB-203

Shillaber, Benjamin Penhallow
 1814-1890 . . . . .DLB-1, 11, 235

Shimao Toshio 1917-1986 . . . . .DLB-182

Shimazaki, Tōson 1872-1943 . . . . .DLB-180

Shine, Ted 1931- DLB-38

Shinkei 1406-1475 . . . . .DLB-203

Ship, Reuben 1915-1975 . . . . .DLB-88

Shirer, William L. 1904-1993 . . . . .DLB-4

Shirinsky-Shikhmatov, Sergii Aleksandrovich
 1783-1837 . . . . .DLB-150

Shirley, James 1596-1666 . . . . .DLB-58

Shishkov, Aleksandr Semenovich
 1753-1841 . . . . .DLB-150

Shockley, Ann Allen 1927- DLB-33

Shōno Junzō 1921- DLB-182

Shore, Arabella 1820?-1901 and
 Shore, Louisa 1824-1895 . . . . .DLB-199

Short, Luke (see Glidden, Frederick Dilley)

Short, Peter [publishing house] DLB-170

Shorter, Dora Sigerson 1866-1918 . . . . . . DLB-240

Shorthouse, Joseph Henry 1834-1903 . . . . DLB-18

Shōtetsu 1381-1459. . . . . DLB-203

Showalter, Elaine 1941- DLB-67

Shulevitz, Uri 1935- DLB-61

Shulman, Max 1919-1988. . . . . DLB-11

Shute, Henry A. 1856-1943 . . . . DLB-9

Shute, Nevil 1899-1960. . . . . DLB-255

Shuttle, Penelope 1947- DLB-14, 40

Sibbes, Richard 1577-1635 . . . . DLB-151

Sibiriak, D. (see Mamin, Dmitrii Narkisovich)

Siddal, Elizabeth Eleanor 1829-1862 . . . . DLB-199

Sidgwick, Ethel 1877-1970. . . . . DLB-197

Sidgwick, Henry 1838-1900 . . . . DLB-262

Sidgwick and Jackson Limited DLB-112

Sidney, Margaret (see Lothrop, Harriet M.)

Sidney, Mary 1561-1621 . . . . DLB-167

Sidney, Sir Philip
1554-1586 . . . . DLB-167; CDBLB-1

An Apologie for Poetrie (the Olney
edition, 1595, of *Defence of Poesie*) DLB-167

Sidney's Press. DLB-49

Sierra, Rubén 1946- DLB-122

Sierra Club Books. DLB-49

Siger of Brabant circa 1240-circa 1284 . . . DLB-115

Sigourney, Lydia Huntley
1791-1865. . . . . . .DLB-1, 42, 73, 183, 239, 243

Silkin, Jon 1930- DLB-27

Silko, Leslie Marmon 1948- . . DLB-143, 175,256

Silliman, Benjamin 1779-1864. . . . . DLB-183

Silliman, Ron 1946- DLB-169

Silliphant, Stirling 1918- DLB-26

Sillitoe, Alan 1928- DLB-14, 139; CDBLB-8

Silman, Roberta 1934- DLB-28

Silva, Beverly 1930- DLB-122

Silverberg, Robert 1935- DLB-8

Silverman, Kaja 1947- DLB-246

Silverman, Kenneth 1936- DLB-111

Simak, Clifford D. 1904-1988. . . . . DLB-8

Simcoe, Elizabeth 1762-1850. . . . . DLB-99

Simcox, Edith Jemima 1844-1901. . . . . . . DLB-190

Simcox, George Augustus 1841-1905. . . . . DLB-35

Sime, Jessie Georgina 1868-1958 . . . . DLB-92

Simenon, Georges 1903-1989 . . . . . .DLB-72; Y-89

Simic, Charles 1938- DLB-105

"Images and 'Images,'" DLB-105

Simionescu, Mircea Horia 1928- DLB-232

Simmel, Johannes Mario 1924- DLB-69

Simmes, Valentine [publishing house] DLB-170

Simmons, Ernest J. 1903-1972 . . . . DLB-103

Simmons, Herbert Alfred 1930- DLB-33

Simmons, James 1933- DLB-40

Simms, William Gilmore
1806-1870. . . . . .DLB-3, 30, 59, 73, 248

Simms and M'Intyre. DLB-106

Simon, Claude 1913- DLB-83; Y-85

Simon, Neil 1927- DLB-7

Simon and Schuster DLB-46

Simons, Katherine Drayton Mayrant
1890-1969 . . . . Y-83

Simović, Ljubomir 1935- DLB-181

Simpkin and Marshall
[publishing house] DLB-154

Simpson, Helen 1897-1940 . . . . DLB-77

Simpson, Louis 1923- DLB-5

Simpson, N. F. 1919- DLB-13

Sims, George 1923- DLB-87; Y-99

Sims, George Robert 1847-1922 . . .DLB-35, 70, 135

Sinán, Rogelio 1904- DLB-145

Sinclair, Andrew 1935- DLB-14

Sinclair, Bertrand William 1881-1972. . . . . DLB-92

Sinclair, Catherine 1800-1864. . . . . DLB-163

Sinclair, Jo 1913-1995 . . . . DLB-28

Sinclair, Lister 1921- DLB-88

Sinclair, May 1863-1946. . . . . DLB-36, 135

Sinclair, Upton 1878-1968 . . . . . DLB-9; CDALB-5

Sinclair, Upton [publishing house] DLB-46

Singer, Isaac Bashevis
1904-1991 . . . DLB-6, 28, 52; Y-91; CDALB-1

Singer, Mark 1950- DLB-185

Singmaster, Elsie 1879-1958 . . . . DLB-9

Sinisgalli, Leonardo 1908-1981. . . . . DLB-114

Siodmak, Curt 1902-2000. . . . . DLB-44

Sîrbu, Ion D. 1919-1989 . . . . DLB-232

Siringo, Charles A. 1855-1928 . . . . DLB-186

Sissman, L. E. 1928-1976 . . . . DLB-5

Sisson, C. H. 1914- DLB-27

Sitwell, Edith 1887-1964 . . . . . . DLB-20; CDBLB-7

Sitwell, Osbert 1892-1969. . . . . .DLB-100, 195

Skácel, Jan 1922-1989. . . . . DLB-232

Skalbe, Kārlis 1879-1945. . . . . DLB-220

Skármeta, Antonio
1940- DLB-145; CDWLB-3

Skavronsky, A. (see Danilevsky, Grigorii Petrovich)

Skeat, Walter W. 1835-1912 . . . . DLB-184

Skeffington, William
[publishing house] DLB-106

Skelton, John 1463-1529. . . . . DLB-136

Skelton, Robin 1925- DLB-27, 53

Škéma, Antanas 1910-1961. . . . . DLB-220

Skinner, Constance Lindsay
1877-1939 . . . . DLB-92

Skinner, John Stuart 1788-1851 . . . . DLB-73

Skipsey, Joseph 1832-1903 . . . . DLB-35

Skou-Hansen, Tage 1925- DLB-214

Škvorecký, Josef 1924- DLB-232; CDWLB-4

Slade, Bernard 1930- DLB-53

Slamnig, Ivan 1930- DLB-181

Slančeková, Božena (see Timrava)

Slater, Patrick 1880-1951 . . . . DLB-68

Slaveykov, Pencho 1866-1912 . . . . .DLB-147

Slaviček, Milivoj 1929- DLB-181

Slavitt, David 1935- DLB-5, 6

Sleigh, Burrows Willcocks Arthur
1821-1869 . . . . DLB-99

A Slender Thread of Hope:
The Kennedy Center Black
Theatre Project DLB-38

Slesinger, Tess 1905-1945 . . . . DLB-102

Slessor, Kenneth 1901-1971 . . . . DLB-260

Slick, Sam (see Haliburton, Thomas Chandler)

Sloan, John 1871-1951 . . . . DLB-188

Sloane, William, Associates DLB-46

Small, Maynard and Company DLB-49

Small Presses in Great Britain and Ireland,
1960-1985 . . . . DLB-40

Small Presses I: Jargon Society. Y-84

Small Presses II: The Spirit That Moves
Us Press. Y-85

Small Presses III: Pushcart Press Y-87

Smart, Christopher 1722-1771 . . . . DLB-109

Smart, David A. 1892-1957 . . . . .DLB-137

Smart, Elizabeth 1913-1986 . . . . DLB-88

Smart, J. J. C. 1920- DLB-262

Smedley, Menella Bute 1820?-1877 . . . . . DLB-199

Smellie, William [publishing house] DLB-154

Smiles, Samuel 1812-1904 . . . . DLB-55

Smiley, Jane 1949- DLB-227, 234

Smith, A. J. M. 1902-1980 . . . . DLB-88

Smith, Adam 1723-1790 . . . . DLB-104, 252

Smith, Adam (George Jerome Waldo Goodman)
1930- DLB-185

Smith, Alexander 1829-1867 . . . . DLB-32, 55

"On the Writing of Essays" (1862) DLB-57

Smith, Amanda 1837-1915 . . . . DLB-221

Smith, Betty 1896-1972. . . . . .Y-82

Smith, Carol Sturm 1938- Y-81

Smith, Charles Henry 1826-1903. . . . . DLB-11

Smith, Charlotte 1749-1806 . . . . DLB-39, 109

Smith, Chet 1899-1973 . . . . .DLB-171

Smith, Cordwainer 1913-1966 . . . . DLB-8

Smith, Dave 1942- DLB-5

Smith, Dodie 1896- DLB-10

Smith, Doris Buchanan 1934- DLB-52

Smith, E. E. 1890-1965. . . . . DLB-8

Smith, Elder and Company DLB-154

Smith, Elihu Hubbard 1771-1798 . . . . DLB-37

Smith, Elizabeth Oakes (Prince)
(see Oakes Smith, Elizabeth)

Smith, Eunice 1757-1823. . . . . DLB-200

Smith, F. Hopkinson 1838-1915 . . . . .DS-13

Smith, George D. 1870-1920. . . . . DLB-140

Smith, George O. 1911-1981 . . . . DLB-8

Smith, Goldwin 1823-1910. . . . . DLB-99

Smith, H. Allen 1907-1976 . . . . .DLB-11, 29

Smith, Harrison, and Robert Haas
[publishing house] DLB-46

Smith, Harry B. 1860-1936 . . . . .DLB-187

Smith, Hazel Brannon 1914- DLB-127

Smith, Henry circa 1560-circa 1591 . . . . . .DLB-136

Smith, Horatio (Horace) 1779-1849 . . . . . .DLB-116

Smith, Horatio (Horace) 1779-1849 and
James Smith 1775-1839 . . . . .DLB-96

Smith, Iain Crichton 1928- DLB-40, 139

Smith, J. Allen 1860-1924 . . . . .DLB-47

Smith, J. Stilman, and Company DLB-49

Smith, Jessie Willcox 1863-1935 . . . . .DLB-188

Smith, John 1580-1631 . . . . .DLB-24, 30

Smith, John 1618-1652 . . . . .DLB-252

Smith, Josiah 1704-1781 . . . . .DLB-24

Smith, Ken 1938- DLB-40

Smith, Lee 1944- DLB-143; Y-83

Smith, Logan Pearsall 1865-1946 . . . . .DLB-98

Smith, Margaret Bayard 1778-1844 . . . . .DLB-248

Smith, Mark 1935- Y-82

Smith, Michael 1698-circa 1771 . . . . .DLB-31

Smith, Pauline 1882-1959 . . . . .DLB-225

Smith, Red 1905-1982 . . . . DLB-29, 171

Smith, Roswell 1829-1892 . . . . .DLB-79

Smith, Samuel Harrison 1772-1845 . . . . . . .DLB-43

Smith, Samuel Stanhope 1751-1819 . . . . . . .DLB-37

Smith, Sarah (see Stretton, Hesba)

Smith, Sarah Pogson 1774-1870 . . . . .DLB-200

Smith, Seba 1792-1868 . . . . .DLB-1, 11, 243

Smith, Stevie 1902-1971 . . . . .DLB-20

Smith, Sydney 1771-1845 . . . . .DLB-107

Smith, Sydney Goodsir 1915-1975 . . . . . . .DLB-27

Smith, Sir Thomas 1513-1577 . . . . .DLB-132

Smith, W. B., and Company DLB-49

Smith, W. H., and Son DLB-106

Smith, Wendell 1914-1972 . . . . .DLB-171

Smith, William flourished 1595-1597 . . . . .DLB-136

Smith, William 1727-1803 . . . . .DLB-31

A General Idea of the College of Mirania
(1753) [excerpts] DLB-31

Smith, William 1728-1793 . . . . .DLB-30

Smith, William Gardner 1927-1974 . . . . . . .DLB-76

Smith, William Henry 1808-1872 . . . . .DLB-159

Smith, William Jay 1918- DLB-5

Smithers, Leonard [publishing house] DLB-112

Smollett, Tobias
1721-1771 . . . . .DLB-39, 104; CDBLB-2

Dedication, *Ferdinand Count
Fathom* (1753) DLB-39

Preface to *Ferdinand Count Fathom* (1753) DLB-39

Preface to *Roderick Random* (1748) DLB-39

Smythe, Francis Sydney 1900-1949 . . . . .DLB-195

Snelling, William Joseph 1804-1848 . . . . .DLB-202

Snellings, Rolland (see Touré, Askia Muhammad)

Snodgrass, W. D. 1926- DLB-5

Snow, C. P.
1905-1980 . . . . .DLB-15, 77; DS-17; CDBLB-7

Snyder, Gary 1930- . . . DLB-5, 16, 165, 212, 237

Sobiloff, Hy 1912-1970 . . . . .DLB-48

The Society for Textual Scholarship and
TEXT Y-87

The Society for the History of Authorship,
Reading and Publishing Y-92

Söderberg, Hjalmar 1869-1941 . . . . .DLB-259

Södergran, Edith 1892-1923 . . . . .DLB-259

Soffici, Ardengo 1879-1964 . . . . .DLB-114

Sofola, 'Zulu 1938- DLB-157

Solano, Solita 1888-1975 . . . . .DLB-4

Soldati, Mario 1906-1999 . . . . .DLB-177

Šoljan, Antun 1932-1993 . . . . .DLB-181

Sollers, Philippe 1936- DLB-83

Sollogub, Vladimir Aleksandrovich
1813-1882 . . . . .DLB-198

Sollors, Werner 1943- DBL-246

Solmi, Sergio 1899-1981 . . . . .DLB-114

Solomon, Carl 1928- DLB-16

Solway, David 1941- DLB-53

Solzhenitsyn and America Y-85

Somerville, Edith Œnone 1858-1949 . . . . .DLB-135

Somov, Orest Mikhailovich
1793-1833 . . . . .DLB-198

Sønderby, Knud 1909-1966 . . . . .DLB-214

Song, Cathy 1955- DLB-169

Sonnevi, Göran 1939- DLB-257

Sono Ayako 1931- DLB-182

Sontag, Susan 1933- DLB-2, 67

Sophocles 497/496 B.C.-406/405 B.C.
. . . . DLB-176; CDWLB-1

Šopov, Aco 1923-1982 . . . . .DLB-181

Sørensen, Villy 1929- DLB-214

Sorensen, Virginia 1912-1991 . . . . .DLB-206

Sorge, Reinhard Johannes 1892-1916 . . . .DLB-118

Sorrentino, Gilbert 1929- DLB-5, 173; Y-80

Sotheby, James 1682-1742 . . . . .DLB-213

Sotheby, John 1740-1807 . . . . .DLB-213

Sotheby, Samuel 1771-1842 . . . . .DLB-213

Sotheby, Samuel Leigh 1805-1861 . . . . . . .DLB-213

Sotheby, William 1757-1833 . . . . .DLB-93, 213

Soto, Gary 1952- DLB-82

Sources for the Study of Tudor and Stuart
Drama DLB-62

Souster, Raymond 1921- DLB-88

The *South English Legendary* circa thirteenth-fifteenth
centuries DLB-146

Southerland, Ellease 1943- DLB-33

Southern, Terry 1924-1995 . . . . .DLB-2

Southern Illinois University Press Y-95

Southern Writers Between the Wars DLB-9

Southerne, Thomas 1659-1746 . . . . .DLB-80

Southey, Caroline Anne Bowles
1786-1854 . . . . .DLB-116

Southey, Robert 1774-1843 . . . . . DLB-93, 107, 142

Southwell, Robert 1561?-1595 . . . . .DLB-167

Southworth, E. D. E. N. 1819-1899 . . . . . .DLB-239

Sowande, Bode 1948- DLB-157

Sowle, Tace [publishing house] DLB-170

Soyfer, Jura 1912-1939 . . . . .DLB-124

Soyinka, Wole
1934- DLB-125; Y-86, Y-87; CDWLB-3

Spacks, Barry 1931- DLB-105

Spalding, Frances 1950- DLB-155

Spark, Muriel 1918- DLB-15, 139; CDBLB-7

Sparke, Michael [publishing house] DLB-170

Sparks, Jared 1789-1866 . . . . .DLB-1, 30, 235

Sparshott, Francis 1926- DLB-60

Späth, Gerold 1939- DLB-75

Spatola, Adriano 1941-1988 . . . . .DLB-128

Spaziani, Maria Luisa 1924- DLB-128

Special Collections at the University of Colorado
at Boulder Y-98

The Spectator 1828- DLB-110

Spedding, James 1808-1881 . . . . .DLB-144

Spee von Langenfeld, Friedrich
1591-1635 . . . . .DLB-164

Speght, Rachel 1597-after 1630 . . . . .DLB-126

Speke, John Hanning 1827-1864 . . . . .DLB-166

Spellman, A. B. 1935- DLB-41

Spence, Catherine Helen 1825-1910 . . . . .DLB-230

Spence, Thomas 1750-1814 . . . . .DLB-158

Spencer, Anne 1882-1975 . . . . .DLB-51, 54

Spencer, Charles, third Earl of Sunderland
1674-1722 . . . . .DLB-213

Spencer, Elizabeth 1921- DLB-6, 218

Spencer, George John, Second Earl Spencer
1758-1834 . . . . .DLB-184

Spencer, Herbert 1820-1903 . . . . DLB-57, 262

"The Philosophy of Style" (1852) DLB-57

Spencer, Scott 1945- Y-86

Spender, J. A. 1862-1942 . . . . .DLB-98

Spender, Stephen 1909-1995 . . .DLB-20; CDBLB-7

Spener, Philipp Jakob 1635-1705 . . . . .DLB-164

Spenser, Edmund
circa 1552-1599 . . . . .DLB-167; CDBLB-1

Envoy from *The Shepheardes Calender* DLB-167

"The Generall Argument of the
Whole Booke," from
The Shepheardes Calender DLB-167

"A Letter of the Authors Expounding
His Whole Intention in the Course
of this Worke: Which for that It Giueth
Great Light to the Reader, for the Better
Vnderstanding Is Hereunto Annexed,"
from *The Faerie Queene* (1590) DLB-167

"To His Booke," from
The Shepheardes Calender (1579) DLB-167

"To the Most Excellent and Learned Both
Orator and Poete, Mayster Gabriell Haruey,
His Verie Special and Singular Good Frend
E. K. Commendeth the Good Lyking of
This His Labour, and the Patronage of
the New Poete," from
The Shepheardes Calender DLB-167

Sperr, Martin 1944- DLB-124

Spicer, Jack 1925-1965 . . . . DLB-5, 16, 193

Spielberg, Peter 1929- Y-81

Spielhagen, Friedrich 1829-1911. . . . . . . DLB-129

"Spielmannsepen" (circa 1152-circa 1500) . . DLB-148

Spier, Peter 1927- DLB-61

Spillane, Mickey 1918- DLB-226

Spink, J. G. Taylor 1888-1962 . . . . DLB-241

Spinrad, Norman 1940- DLB-8

Spires, Elizabeth 1952- DLB-120

Spitteler, Carl 1845-1924 . . . . DLB-129

Spivak, Lawrence E. 1900- DLB-137

Spofford, Harriet Prescott
1835-1921 . . . . DLB-74, 221

Sprigge, T. L. S. 1932- DLB-262

Spring, Howard 1889-1965. . . . . DLB-191

Squibob (see Derby, George Horatio)

Squier, E. G. 1821-1888 . . . . DLB-189

Stableford, Brian 1948- DLB-261

Stacpoole, H. de Vere 1863-1951 . . . . DLB-153

Staël, Germaine de 1766-1817 . . . . . . DLB-119, 192

Staël-Holstein, Anne-Louise Germaine de
(see Staël, Germaine de)

Stafford, Jean 1915-1979 . . . . .DLB-2, 173

Stafford, William 1914-1993 . . . . DLB-5, 206

Stage Censorship: "The Rejected Statement"
(1911), by Bernard Shaw [excerpts] . . . DLB-10

Stallings, Laurence 1894-1968 . . . . .DLB-7, 44

Stallworthy, Jon 1935- DLB-40

Stampp, Kenneth M. 1912- DLB-17

Stănescu, Nichita 1933-1983. . . . . DLB-232

Stanev, Emiliyan 1907-1979 . . . . DLB-181

Stanford, Ann 1916- DLB-5

Stangerup, Henrik 1937-1998 . . . . DLB-214

Stanitsky, N. (see Panaeva, Avdot'ia Iakovlevna)

Stankevich, Nikolai Vladimirovich
1813-1840. . . . . DLB-198

Stanković, Borisav ("Bora")
1876-1927. . . . . .DLB-147; CDWLB-4

Stanley, Henry M. 1841-1904. . . . DLB-189; DS-13

Stanley, Thomas 1625-1678 . . . . DLB-131

Stannard, Martin 1947- DLB-155

Stansby, William [publishing house]. DLB-170

Stanton, Elizabeth Cady 1815-1902 . . . . . . DLB-79

Stanton, Frank L. 1857-1927 . . . . DLB-25

Stanton, Maura 1946- DLB-120

Stapledon, Olaf 1886-1950 . . . . DLB-15, 255

Star Spangled Banner Office. DLB-49

Stark, Freya 1893-1993. . . . . DLB-195

Starkey, Thomas circa 1499-1538 . . . . . DLB-132

Starkie, Walter 1894-1976. . . . . DLB-195

Starkweather, David 1935- DLB-7

Starrett, Vincent 1886-1974 . . . . DLB-187

The State of Publishing. Y-97

Statements on the Art of Poetry DLB-54

Stationers' Company of London, The DLB-170

Statius circa A.D. 45-A.D. 96 . . . . DLB-211

Stead, Christina 1902-1983. . . . . DLB-260

Stead, Robert J. C. 1880-1959 . . . . DLB-92

Steadman, Mark 1930- DLB-6

The Stealthy School of Criticism (1871), by
Dante Gabriel Rossetti. DLB-35

Stearns, Harold E. 1891-1943. . . . . DLB-4

Stebnitsky, M. (see Leskov, Nikolai Semenovich)

Stedman, Edmund Clarence 1833-1908 . . . DLB-64

Steegmuller, Francis 1906-1994 . . . . DLB-111

Steel, Flora Annie 1847-1929 . . . . . . DLB-153, 156

Steele, Max 1922- Y-80

Steele, Richard
1672-1729. . . . . DLB-84, 101; CDBLB-2

Steele, Timothy 1948- DLB-120

Steele, Wilbur Daniel 1886-1970 . . . . DLB-86

Steere, Richard circa 1643-1721 . . . . DLB-24

Stefanovski, Goran 1952- DLB-181

Stegner, Wallace 1909-1993 . . . . .DLB-9, 206; Y-93

Stehr, Hermann 1864-1940 . . . . DLB-66

Steig, William 1907- DLB-61

Stein, Gertrude 1874-1946
. . . . DLB-4, 54, 86, 228; DS-15; CDALB-4

Stein, Leo 1872-1947. . . . . DLB-4

Stein and Day Publishers DLB-46

Steinbeck, John
1902-1968 . . . .DLB-7, 9, 212; DS-2; CDALB-5

John Steinbeck Research Center. Y-85

Steinem, Gloria 1934- DLB-246

Steiner, George 1929- DLB-67

Steinhoewel, Heinrich 1411/1412-1479. . . .DLB-179

Steloff, Ida Frances 1887-1989 . . . . DLB-187

Stendhal 1783-1842. . . . . DLB-119

Stephen Crane: A Revaluation Virginia
Tech Conference, 1989 . . . . .Y-89

Stephen, Leslie 1832-1904 . . . . . .DLB-57, 144, 190

Stephen Vincent Benét Centenary Y-97

Stephens, A. G. 1865-1933 . . . . DLB-230

Stephens, Alexander H. 1812-1883. . . . . . DLB-47

Stephens, Alice Barber 1858-1932 . . . . . . DLB-188

Stephens, Ann 1810-1886 . . . . DLB-3, 73, 250

Stephens, Charles Asbury 1844?-1931 . . . . DLB-42

Stephens, James 1882?-1950. . . . .DLB-19, 153, 162

Stephens, John Lloyd 1805-1852 . . . DLB-183, 250

Stephens, Michael 1946- DLB-234

Stephenson, P. R. 1901-1965 . . . . DLB-260

Sterling, George 1869-1926 . . . . DLB-54

Sterling, James 1701-1763 . . . . DLB-24

Sterling, John 1806-1844. . . . . DLB-116

Stern, Gerald 1925- DLB-105

Stern, Gladys B. 1890-1973 . . . . DLB-197

Stern, Madeleine B. 1912- DLB-111, 140

Stern, Richard 1928- DLB-218; Y-87

Stern, Stewart 1922- DLB-26

Sterne, Laurence
1713-1768 . . . . DLB-39; CDBLB-2

Sternheim, Carl 1878-1942 . . . . DLB-56, 118

Sternhold, Thomas ?-1549 and
John Hopkins ?-1570 . . . . DLB-132

Steuart, David 1747-1824 . . . . DLB-213

Stevens, Henry 1819-1886 . . . . DLB-140

Stevens, Wallace 1879-1955 . . . DLB-54; CDALB-5

Stevenson, Anne 1933- DLB-40

Stevenson, D. E. 1892-1973 . . . . DLB-191

Stevenson, Lionel 1902-1973 . . . . DLB-155

Stevenson, Robert Louis
1850-1894 . . . . . . .DLB-18, 57, 141, 156, 174;
DS-13; CDBLB-5

"On Style in Literature:
Its Technical Elements" (1885) DLB-57

Stewart, Donald Ogden
1894-1980 . . . . DLB-4, 11, 26

Stewart, Douglas 1913-1985. . . . . DLB-260

Stewart, Dugald 1753-1828. . . . . DLB-31

Stewart, George, Jr. 1848-1906. . . . . DLB-99

Stewart, George R. 1895-1980 . . . . DLB-8

Stewart, Harold 1916-1995. . . . . DLB-260

Stewart, Maria W. 1803?-1879 . . . . DLB-239

Stewart, Randall 1896-1964 . . . . DLB-103

Stewart, Sean 1965- DLB-251

Stewart and Kidd Company. DLB-46

Stickney, Trumbull 1874-1904 . . . . DLB-54

Stieler, Caspar 1632-1707 . . . . DLB-164

Stifter, Adalbert
1805-1868 . . . . .DLB-133; CDWLB-2

Stiles, Ezra 1727-1795 . . . . DLB-31

Still, James 1906- DLB-9; Y01

Stirling, S. M. 1954- DLB-251

Stirner, Max 1806-1856 . . . . DLB-129

Stith, William 1707-1755 . . . . DLB-31

Stock, Elliot [publishing house]. DLB-106

Stockton, Frank R.
1834-1902 . . . . .DLB-42, 74; DS-13

Stockton, J. Roy 1892-1972 . . . . DLB-241

Stoddard, Ashbel [publishing house] DLB-49

Stoddard, Charles Warren
1843-1909 . . . . DLB-186

Stoddard, Elizabeth 1823-1902. . . . . DLB-202

Stoddard, Richard Henry
1825-1903 . . . . DLB-3, 64, 250; DS-13

Stoddard, Solomon 1643-1729 . . . . DLB-24

Stoker, Bram
1847-1912. . . . . . .DLB-36, 70, 178; CDBLB-5

Stokes, Frederick A., Company DLB-49

Stokes, Thomas L. 1898-1958 . . . . DLB-29

Stokesbury, Leon 1945- DLB-120

Stolberg, Christian Graf zu 1748-1821 . . . . DLB-94

Stolberg, Friedrich Leopold Graf zu
1750-1819 . . . . DLB-94

Stone, Herbert S., and Company DLB-49

Stone, Lucy 1818-1893. . . . . .DLB-79, 239

Stone, Melville 1848-1929 . . . . DLB-25

Stone, Robert 1937- DLB-152

Stone, Ruth 1915- DLB-105

Stone, Samuel 1602-1663 . . . . DLB-24

Stone, William Leete 1792-1844 . . . . .DLB-202

Stone and Kimball .DLB-49

Stoppard, Tom
    1937- DLB-13, 233; Y-85; CDBLB-8

Playwrights and Professors DLB-13

Storey, Anthony 1928- DLB-14

Storey, David 1933- DLB-13, 14, 207, 245

Storm, Theodor 1817-1888 . .DLB-129; CDWLB-2

Story, Thomas circa 1670-1742 . . . . .DLB-31

Story, William Wetmore 1819-1895 . . .DLB-1, 235

Storytelling: A Contemporary Renaissance . . . Y-84

Stoughton, William 1631-1701. . . . . .DLB-24

Stow, John 1525-1605 . . . . .DLB-132

Stow, Randolph 1935- DLB-260

Stowe, Harriet Beecher 1811-1896
    . . DLB-1, 12, 42, 74, 189, 239, 243; CDALB-3

Stowe, Leland 1899- DLB-29

Stoyanov, Dimitr Ivanov (see Elin Pelin)

Strabo 64 or 63 B.C.-circa A.D. 25 . . . . . .DLB-176

Strachey, Lytton 1880-1932. . . . .DLB-149; DS-10

Strachey, Lytton, Preface to Eminent
    Victorians DLB-149

Strahan, William [publishing house] DLB-154

Strahan and Company. DLB-106

Strand, Mark 1934- DLB-5

The Strasbourg Oaths 842. . . . . .DLB-148

Stratemeyer, Edward 1862-1930 . . . . .DLB-42

Strati, Saverio 1924- DLB-177

Stratton and Barnard DLB-49

Stratton-Porter, Gene
    1863-1924 . . . . .DLB-221; DS-14

Straub, Peter 1943- Y-84

Strauß, Botho 1944- DLB-124

Strauß, David Friedrich 1808-1874 . . . . . .DLB-133

The Strawberry Hill Press DLB-154

Strawson, P. F. 1919- DLB-262

Streatfeild, Noel 1895-1986 . . . . .DLB-160

Street, Cecil John Charles (see Rhode, John)

Street, G. S. 1867-1936. . . . . .DLB-135

Street and Smith. DLB-49

Streeter, Edward 1891-1976. . . . . .DLB-11

Streeter, Thomas Winthrop 1883-1965 . . .DLB-140

Stretton, Hesba 1832-1911. . . . . . . .DLB-163, 190

Stribling, T. S. 1881-1965 . . . . .DLB-9

Der Stricker circa 1190-circa 1250 . . . . . .DLB-138

Strickland, Samuel 1804-1867 . . . . .DLB-99

Strindberg, August 1849-1912 . . . . .DLB-259

Stringer, Arthur 1874-1950 . . . . .DLB-92

Stringer and Townsend DLB-49

Strittmatter, Erwin 1912- DLB-69

Strniša, Gregor 1930-1987 . . . . .DLB-181

Strode, William 1630-1645 . . . . .DLB-126

Strong, L. A. G. 1896-1958 . . . . .DLB-191

Strother, David Hunter (Porte Crayon)
    1816-1888 .DLB-3, 248

Strouse, Jean 1945- DLB-111

Stuart, Dabney 1937- DLB-105

Stuart, Jesse 1906-1984 . . . . . DLB-9, 48, 102; Y-84

Stuart, Lyle [publishing house] DLB-46

Stuart, Ruth McEnery 1849?-1917 . . . . .DLB-202

Stubbs, Harry Clement (see Clement, Hal)

Stubenberg, Johann Wilhelm von
    1619-1663 . . . . .DLB-164

Studebaker, William V. 1947- DLB-256

Studio. DLB-112

The Study of Poetry (1880), by
    Matthew Arnold DLB-35

Stump, Al 1916-1995 . . . . .DLB-241

Sturgeon, Theodore 1918-1985 . . . . . .DLB-8; Y-85

Sturges, Preston 1898-1959 . . . . .DLB-26

"Style" (1840; revised, 1859), by
    Thomas de Quincey [excerpt]. DLB-57

"Style" (1888), by Walter Pater. DLB-57

Style (1897), by Walter Raleigh
    [excerpt]. DLB-57

"Style" (1877), by T. H. Wright
    [excerpt]. DLB-57

"Le Style c'est l'homme" (1892), by
    W. H. Mallock DLB-57

Styron, William
    1925- DLB-2, 143; Y-80; CDALB-6

Suárez, Mario 1925- DLB-82

Such, Peter 1939- DLB-60

Suckling, Sir John 1609-1641?. DLB-58, 126

Suckow, Ruth 1892-1960. . . . . .DLB-9, 102

Sudermann, Hermann 1857-1928 . . . . . . .DLB-118

Sue, Eugène 1804-1857 . . . . .DLB-119

Sue, Marie-Joseph (see Sue, Eugène)

Suetonius circa A.D. 69-post A.D. 122 . . .DLB-211

Suggs, Simon (see Hooper, Johnson Jones)

Sui Sin Far (see Eaton, Edith Maude)

Suits, Gustav 1883-1956 . . . . DLB-220; CDWLB-4

Sukenick, Ronald 1932- DLB-173; Y-81

Suknaski, Andrew 1942- DLB-53

Sullivan, Alan 1868-1947 . . . . .DLB-92

Sullivan, C. Gardner 1886-1965 . . . . .DLB-26

Sullivan, Frank 1892-1976 . . . . .DLB-11

Sulte, Benjamin 1841-1923 . . . . .DLB-99

Sulzberger, Arthur Hays 1891-1968 . . . . .DLB-127

Sulzberger, Arthur Ochs 1926- DLB-127

Sulzer, Johann Georg 1720-1779 . . . . .DLB-97

Sumarokov, Aleksandr Petrovich
    1717-1777 . . . . .DLB-150

Summers, Hollis 1916- DLB-6

A Summing Up at Century's End Y-99

Sumner, Charles 1811-1874. . . . . .DLB-235

Sumner, Henry A. [publishing house] DLB-49

Sundman, Per Olof 1922-1992 . . . . .DLB-257

Supervielle, Jules 1884-1960 . . . . .DLB-258

Surtees, Robert Smith 1803-1864. . . . . . . .DLB-21

Survey of Literary Biographies Y-00

A Survey of Poetry Anthologies,
    1879-1960 . . . . .DLB-54

Surveys: Japanese Literature,
    1987-1995 . . . . .DLB-182

Sutherland, Efua Theodora
    1924-1996 . . . . .DLB-117

Sutherland, John 1919-1956. . . . . .DLB-68

Sutro, Alfred 1863-1933. . . . . .DLB-10

Svendsen, Hanne Marie 1933- DLB-214

Swados, Harvey 1920-1972 . . . . .DLB-2

Swain, Charles 1801-1874 . . . . .DLB-32

Swallow Press DLB-46

Swan Sonnenschein Limited DLB-106

Swanberg, W. A. 1907- DLB-103

Swenson, May 1919-1989 . . . . .DLB-5

Swerling, Jo 1897- DLB-44

Swift, Graham 1949- DLB-194

Swift, Jonathan
    1667-1745 . . . . . . .DLB-39, 95, 101; CDBLB-2

Swinburne, A. C.
    1837-1909 . . . . .DLB-35, 57; CDBLB-4

Swineshead, Richard
    floruit circa 1350 . . . . .DLB-115

Swinnerton, Frank 1884-1982 . . . . .DLB-34

Swisshelm, Jane Grey 1815-1884. . . . . . . .DLB-43

Swope, Herbert Bayard 1882-1958 . . . . . . .DLB-25

Swords, T. and J., and Company DLB-49

Swords, Thomas 1763-1843 and
    Swords, James ?-1844 . . . . .DLB-73

Sykes, Ella C. ?-1939 . . . . .DLB-174

Sylvester, Josuah
    1562 or 1563-1618 . . . . .DLB-121

Symonds, Emily Morse (see Paston, George)

Symonds, John Addington
    1840-1893 . . . . DLB-57, 144

"Personal Style" (1890) DLB-57

Symons, A. J. A. 1900-1941. . . . . .DLB-149

Symons, Arthur 1865-1945 . . . . . . DLB-19, 57, 149

Symons, Julian
    1912-1994 . . . . DLB-87, 155; Y-92

Julian Symons at Eighty. Y-92

Symons, Scott 1933- DLB-53

A Symposium on *The Columbia History of
    the Novel*. Y-92

Synge, John Millington
    1871-1909 . . . . .DLB-10, 19; CDBLB-5

Synge Summer School: J. M. Synge and the
    Irish Theater, Rathdrum, County Wiclow,
    Ireland. Y-93

Syrett, Netta 1865-1943 . . . . DLB-135, 197

Szabó, Lőrinc 1900-1957 . . . . .DLB-215

Szabó, Magda 1917- DLB-215

Szymborska, Wisława
    1923- DLB-232, Y-96; CDWLB-4

T

Taban lo Liyong 1939?- DLB-125

Tabori, George 1914- DLB-245

Tabucchi, Antonio 1943- DLB-196

Taché, Joseph-Charles 1820-1894 . . . . . . .DLB-99

Tachihara Masaaki 1926-1980 . . . . .DLB-182

Tacitus circa A.D. 55-circa A.D. 117 . . . . DLB-211; CDWLB-1

Tadijanović, Dragutin 1905- DLB-181

Tafdrup, Pia 1952- DLB-214

Tafolla, Carmen 1951- DLB-82

Taggard, Genevieve 1894-1948 . . . . DLB-45

Taggart, John 1942- DLB-193

Tagger, Theodor (see Bruckner, Ferdinand)

Taiheiki late fourteenth century DLB-203

Tait, J. Selwin, and Sons DLB-49

Tait's Edinburgh Magazine 1832-1861 . . . . . DLB-110

The Takarazaka Revue Company Y-91

Talander (see Bohse, August)

Talese, Gay 1932- DLB-185

Talev, Dimitr 1898-1966 . . . . DLB-181

Taliaferro, H. E. 1811-1875 . . . . DLB-202

Tallent, Elizabeth 1954- DLB-130

TallMountain, Mary 1918-1994 . . . . DLB-193

Talvj 1797-1870 . . . . DLB-59, 133

Tamási, Áron 1897-1966 . . . . DLB-215

Tammsaare, A. H. 1878-1940 . . . . DLB-220; CDWLB-4

Tan, Amy 1952- DLB-173; CDALB-7

Tandori, Dezső 1938- DLB-232

Tanner, Thomas 1673/1674-1735 . . . . . DLB-213

Tanizaki Jun'ichirō 1886-1965 . . . . DLB-180

Tapahonso, Luci 1953- DLB-175

The Mark Taper Forum DLB-7

Taradash, Daniel 1913- DLB-44

Tarbell, Ida M. 1857-1944 . . . . DLB-47

Tardivel, Jules-Paul 1851-1905 . . . . DLB-99

Targan, Barry 1932- DLB-130

Tarkington, Booth 1869-1946 . . . . DLB-9, 102

Tashlin, Frank 1913-1972 . . . . DLB-44

Tasma (Jessie Couvreur) 1848-1897 . . . . DLB-230

Tate, Allen 1899-1979 . . . . . . .DLB-4, 45, 63; DS-17

Tate, James 1943- DLB-5, 169

Tate, Nahum circa 1652-1715 . . . . DLB-80

Tatian circa 830 . . . . DLB-148

Taufer, Veno 1933- DLB-181

Tauler, Johannes circa 1300-1361 . . . . . . .DLB-179

Tavčar, Ivan 1851-1923 . . . . DLB-147

Taverner, Richard ca. 1505-1575 . . . . DLB-236

Taylor, Ann 1782-1866 . . . . DLB-163

Taylor, Bayard 1825-1878 . . . . . . DLB-3, 189, 250

Taylor, Bert Leston 1866-1921 . . . . DLB-25

Taylor, Charles H. 1846-1921 . . . . DLB-25

Taylor, Edward circa 1642-1729 . . . . DLB-24

Taylor, Elizabeth 1912-1975 . . . . DLB-139

Taylor, Henry 1942- DLB-5

Taylor, Sir Henry 1800-1886 . . . . DLB-32

Taylor, Jane 1783-1824 . . . . DLB-163

Taylor, Jeremy circa 1613-1667 . . . . DLB-151

Taylor, John 1577 or 1578 - 1653 . . . . DLB-121

Taylor, Mildred D. ?- DLB-52

Taylor, Peter 1917-1994 . . . . . DLB-218; Y-81, Y-94

Taylor, Susie King 1848-1912 . . . . DLB-221

Taylor, William Howland 1901-1966 . . . DLB-241

Taylor, William, and Company DLB-49

Taylor-Made Shakespeare? Or Is "Shall I Die?" the Long-Lost Text of Bottom's Dream? Y-85

Teasdale, Sara 1884-1933 . . . . DLB-45

Telles, Lygia Fagundes 1924- DLB-113

Temple, Sir William 1628-1699 . . . . DLB-101

Temple, William F. 1914-1989 . . . . DLB-255

Temrizov, A. (see Marchenko, Anastasia Iakovlevna)

Tench, Watkin ca. 1758-1833 . . . . DLB-230

Tenn, William 1919- DLB-8

Tennant, Emma 1937- DLB-14

Tenney, Tabitha Gilman 1762-1837 .DLB-37, 200

Tennyson, Alfred 1809-1892 . . . . DLB-32; CDBLB-4

Tennyson, Frederick 1807-1898 . . . . DLB-32

Tenorio, Arthur 1924- DLB-209

Tepliakov, Viktor Grigor'evich 1804-1842 . . . . DLB-205

Terence circa 184 B.C.-159 B.C. or after DLB-211; CDWLB-1

Terhune, Albert Payson 1872-1942 . . . . DLB-9

Terhune, Mary Virginia 1830-1922 . . . . .DS-13, DS-16

Terry, Megan 1932- DLB-7, 249

Terson, Peter 1932- DLB-13

Tesich, Steve 1943-1996 . . . . Y-83

Tessa, Delio 1886-1939 . . . . DLB-114

Testori, Giovanni 1923-1993 . . . . . . .DLB-128, 177

Tey, Josephine 1896?-1952 . . . . DLB-77

Thacher, James 1754-1844 . . . . DLB-37

Thackeray, William Makepeace 1811-1863 . . DLB-21, 55, 159, 163; CDBLB-4

Thames and Hudson Limited DLB-112

Thanet, Octave (see French, Alice)

Thatcher, John Boyd 1847-1909 . . . . DLB-187

Thaxter, Celia Laighton 1835-1894 . . . . . DLB-239

Thayer, Caroline Matilda Warren 1785-1844 . . . . DLB-200

Thayer, Douglas 1929- DLB-256

The Theatre Guild DLB-7

The Theater in Shakespeare's Time DLB-62

Thegan and the Astronomer flourished circa 850 . . . . DLB-148

Thelwall, John 1764-1834 . . . . DLB-93, 158

Theocritus circa 300 B.C.-260 B.C. DLB-176

Theodorescu, Ion N. (see Arghezi, Tudor)

Theodulf circa 760-circa 821 . . . . DLB-148

Theophrastus circa 371 B.C.-287 B.C. DLB-176

Theriault, Yves 1915-1983 . . . . DLB-88

Thério, Adrien 1925- DLB-53

Theroux, Paul 1941- DLB-2, 218; CDALB-7

Thesiger, Wilfred 1910- DLB-204

They All Came to Paris DS-16

Thibaudeau, Colleen 1925- DLB-88

Thielen, Benedict 1903-1965 . . . . DLB-102

Thiong'o Ngugi wa (see Ngugi wa Thiong'o)

Third-Generation Minor Poets of the Seventeenth Century DLB-131

This Quarter 1925-1927, 1929-1932 . . . . .DS-15

Thoma, Ludwig 1867-1921 . . . . DLB-66

Thoma, Richard 1902- DLB-4

Thomas, Audrey 1935- DLB-60

Thomas, D. M. 1935- . . DLB-40, 207; CDBLB-8

D. M. Thomas: The Plagiarism Controversy Y-82

Thomas, Dylan 1914-1953 . . . . . . DLB-13, 20, 139; CDBLB-7

The Dylan Thomas Celebration Y-99

Thomas, Edward 1878-1917 . . . . .DLB-19, 98, 156, 216

Thomas, Frederick William 1806-1866 . . DLB-202

Thomas, Gwyn 1913-1981 . . . . DLB-15, 245

Thomas, Isaiah 1750-1831 . . . . . . .DLB-43, 73, 187

Thomas, Isaiah [publishing house] DLB-49

Thomas, Johann 1624-1679 . . . . DLB-168

Thomas, John 1900-1932 . . . . DLB-4

Thomas, Joyce Carol 1938- DLB-33

Thomas, Lorenzo 1944- DLB-41

Thomas, R. S. 1915-2000 . . . . . DLB-27; CDBLB-8

Thomasîn von Zerclære circa 1186-circa 1259 . . . . DLB-138

Thomasius, Christian 1655-1728 . . . . DLB-168

Thompson, Daniel Pierce 1795-1868 . . . . DLB-202

Thompson, David 1770-1857 . . . . DLB-99

Thompson, Dorothy 1893-1961 . . . . DLB-29

Thompson, E. P. 1924-1993 . . . . DLB-242

Thompson, Flora 1876-1947 . . . . DLB-240

Thompson, Francis 1859-1907 . . . . DLB-19; CDBLB-5

Thompson, George Selden (see Selden, George)

Thompson, Henry Yates 1838-1928 . . . . DLB-184

Thompson, Hunter S. 1939- DLB-185

Thompson, Jim 1906-1977 . . . . DLB-226

Thompson, John 1938-1976 . . . . DLB-60

Thompson, John R. 1823-1873 . . . . .DLB-3, 73, 248

Thompson, Lawrance 1906-1973 . . . . DLB-103

Thompson, Maurice 1844-1901 . . . . . . .DLB-71, 74

Thompson, Ruth Plumly 1891-1976 . . . . . DLB-22

Thompson, Thomas Phillips 1843-1933 . . DLB-99

Thompson, William 1775-1833 . . . . DLB-158

Thompson, William Tappan 1812-1882 . . . . DLB-3, 11, 248

Thomson, Edward William 1849-1924 . . . DLB-92

Thomson, James 1700-1748 . . . . DLB-95

Thomson, James 1834-1882 . . . . DLB-35

Thomson, Joseph 1858-1895 . . . . .DLB-174

Thomson, Mortimer 1831-1875 . . . . DLB-11

Thon, Melanie Rae 1957- DLB-244

Thoreau, Henry David 1817-1862 . . . . DLB-1, 183, 223; CDALB-2

The Thoreauvian Pilgrimage: The Structure of an
American Cult. DLB-223

Thorpe, Adam 1956- DLB-231

Thorpe, Thomas Bangs
1815-1878 . . . . .DLB-3, 11, 248

Thorup, Kirsten 1942- DLB-214

Thoughts on Poetry and Its Varieties (1833),
by John Stuart Mill DLB-32

Thrale, Hester Lynch
(see Piozzi, Hester Lynch [Thrale])

Thubron, Colin 1939- DLB-204, 231

Thucydides
circa 455 B.C.-circa 395 B.C. DLB-176

Thulstrup, Thure de 1848-1930 . . . . . . .DLB-188

Thümmel, Moritz August von
1738-1817 . . . . .DLB-97

Thurber, James
1894-1961 . . . . .DLB-4, 11, 22, 102; CDALB-5

Thurman, Wallace 1902-1934. . . . . .DLB-51

Thwaite, Anthony 1930- DLB-40

The Booker Prize
Address by Anthony Thwaite,
Chairman of the Booker Prize Judges
Comments from Former Booker
Prize Winners Y-86

Thwaites, Reuben Gold 1853-1913 . . . . . . .DLB-47

Tibullus circa 54 B.C.-circa 19 B.C.. . . . . .DLB-211

Ticknor, George 1791-1871 . . .DLB-1, 59, 140, 235

Ticknor and Fields. DLB-49

Ticknor and Fields (revived) DLB-46

Tieck, Ludwig 1773-1853. . . . .DLB-90; CDWLB-2

Tietjens, Eunice 1884-1944 . . . . .DLB-54

Tikkanen, Märta 1935- DLB-257

Tilghman, Christopher circa 1948. . . . . . .DLB-244

Tilney, Edmund circa 1536-1610. . . . . . . .DLB-136

Tilt, Charles [publishing house]. DLB-106

Tilton, J. E., and Company DLB-49

Time and Western Man (1927), by Wyndham
Lewis [excerpts]. DLB-36

Time-Life Books DLB-46

Times Books .DLB-46

Timothy, Peter circa 1725-1782 . . . . .DLB-43

Timrava 1867-1951 . . . . .DLB-215

Timrod, Henry 1828-1867. . . . . .DLB-3, 248

Tindal, Henrietta 1818?-1879 . . . . .DLB-199

Tinker, Chauncey Brewster 1876-1963 . . .DLB-140

Tinsley Brothers DLB-106

Tiptree, James, Jr. 1915-1987. . . . . .DLB-8

Tišma, Aleksandar 1924- DLB-181

Titus, Edward William
1870-1952 . . . . .DLB-4; DS-15

Tiutchev, Fedor Ivanovich 1803-1873 . . . .DLB-205

Tlali, Miriam 1933- DLB-157, 225

Todd, Barbara Euphan 1890-1976. . . . . . .DLB-160

Todorov, Tzvetan 1939- DLB-242

Tofte, Robert
1561 or 1562-1619 or 1620. . . . . . . .DLB-172

Toklas, Alice B. 1877-1967. . . . . .DLB-4

Tokuda, Shūsei 1872-1943. . . . . .DLB-180

Toland, John 1670-1722. . . . . .DLB-252

Tolkien, J. R. R.
1892-1973 . . . . . .DLB-15, 160, 255; CDBLB-6

Toller, Ernst 1893-1939. . . . . .DLB-124

Tollet, Elizabeth 1694-1754 . . . . .DLB-95

Tolson, Melvin B. 1898-1966 . . . . . . .DLB-48, 76

Tolstoy, Aleksei Konstantinovich
1817-1875. . . . . .DLB-238

Tolstoy, Leo 1828-1910. . . . . .DLB-238

Tom Jones (1749), by Henry Fielding
[excerpt]. DLB-39

Tomalin, Claire 1933- DLB-155

Tomasi di Lampedusa, Giuseppe
1896-1957 .DLB-177

Tomlinson, Charles 1927- DLB-40

Tomlinson, H. M. 1873-1958 . . .DLB-36, 100, 195

Tompkins, Abel [publishing house]. DLB-49

Tompson, Benjamin 1642-1714 . . . . .DLB-24

Tomson, Graham R.
(see Watson, Rosamund Marriott)

Ton'a 1289-1372 . . . . .DLB-203

Tondelli, Pier Vittorio 1955-1991 . . . . . . .DLB-196

Tonks, Rosemary 1932- DLB-14, 207

Tonna, Charlotte Elizabeth 1790-1846 . . .DLB-163

Tonson, Jacob the Elder
[publishing house] DLB-170

Toole, John Kennedy 1937-1969 . . . . Y-81

Toomer, Jean 1894-1967 . . .DLB-45, 51; CDALB-4

Tor Books DLB-46

Torberg, Friedrich 1908-1979 . . . . .DLB-85

Torrence, Ridgely 1874-1950. . . . . . .DLB-54, 249

Torres-Metzger, Joseph V. 1933- DLB-122

Toth, Susan Allen 1940- Y-86

Tottell, Richard [publishing house] DLB-170

"The Printer to the Reader," (1557)
by Richard Tottell. DLB-167

Tough-Guy Literature DLB-9

Touré, Askia Muhammad 1938- DLB-41

Tourgée, Albion W. 1838-1905. . . . . .DLB-79

Tournemir, Elizaveta Sailhas de (see Tur, Evgeniia)

Tourneur, Cyril circa 1580-1626. . . . . . . .DLB-58

Tournier, Michel 1924- DLB-83

Tousey, Frank [publishing house] DLB-49

Tower Publications DLB-46

Towne, Benjamin circa 1740-1793 . . . . . . .DLB-43

Towne, Robert 1936- DLB-44

The Townely Plays fifteenth and sixteenth
centuries DLB-146

Townshend, Aurelian
by 1583-circa 1651 . . . . .DLB-121

Toy, Barbara 1908- DLB-204

Tracy, Honor 1913- DLB-15

Traherne, Thomas 1637?-1674 . . . . .DLB-131

Traill, Catharine Parr 1802-1899. . . . . . . .DLB-99

Train, Arthur 1875-1945 . . . . .DLB-86; DS-16

The Transatlantic Publishing Company . . .DLB-49

The Transatlantic Review 1924-1925 . . . . DS-15

The Transcendental Club 1836-1840 . . . .DLB-223

Transcendentalism. DLB-223

Transcendentalists, American DS-5

A Transit of Poets and Others: American
Biography in 1982. . . . . Y-82

transition 1927-1938. . . . . DS-15

Translators of the Twelfth Century: Literary Issues
Raised and Impact Created. DLB-115

Tranströmer, Tomas 1931- DLB-257

Travel Writing, 1837-1875. . . . . .DLB-166

Travel Writing, 1876-1909 . . . . .DLB-174

Travel Writing, 1910-1939 . . . . .DLB-195

Traven, B. 1882? or 1890?-1969? DLB-9, 56

Travers, Ben 1886-1980 . . . . .DLB-10, 233

Travers, P. L. (Pamela Lyndon)
1899-1996 .DLB-160

Trediakovsky, Vasilii Kirillovich
1703-1769 .DLB-150

Treece, Henry 1911-1966 . . . . .DLB-160

Trejo, Ernesto 1950- DLB-122

Trelawny, Edward John
1792-1881 . . . . .DLB-110, 116, 144

Tremain, Rose 1943- DLB-14

Tremblay, Michel 1942- DLB-60

Trends in Twentieth-Century
Mass Market Publishing DLB-46

Trent, William P. 1862-1939. . . . . .DLB-47

Trescot, William Henry 1822-1898. . . . . . .DLB-30

Tressell, Robert (Robert Phillipe Noonan)
1870-1911 .DLB-197

Trevelyan, Sir George Otto
1838-1928 .DLB-144

Trevisa, John circa 1342-circa 1402. . . . . .DLB-146

Trevor, William 1928- DLB-14, 139

Trierer Floyris circa 1170-1180 . . . . .DLB-138

Trillin, Calvin 1935- DLB-185

Trilling, Lionel 1905-1975 . . . . .DLB-28, 63

Trilussa 1871-1950. . . . . .DLB-114

Trimmer, Sarah 1741-1810 . . . . .DLB-158

Triolet, Elsa 1896-1970 . . . . .DLB-72

Tripp, John 1927- DLB-40

Trocchi, Alexander 1925- DLB-15

Troisi, Dante 1920-1989 . . . . .DLB-196

Trollope, Anthony
1815-1882 . . . . . . .DLB-21, 57, 159; CDBLB-4

Trollope, Frances 1779-1863 . . . . .DLB-21, 166

Trollope, Joanna 1943- DLB-207

Troop, Elizabeth 1931- DLB-14

Trotter, Catharine 1679-1749. . . . . . .DLB-84, 252

Trotti, Lamar 1898-1952. . . . . .DLB-44

Trottier, Pierre 1925- DLB-60

Trotzig, Birgitta 1929- DLB-257

Troubadours, *Trobairitz,* and Trouvères . .DLB-208

Troupe, Quincy Thomas, Jr. 1943- DLB-41

Trow, John F., and Company DLB-49

Trowbridge, John Townsend 1827-1916 . .DLB-202

Trudel, Jean-Louis 1967- DLB-251

Truillier-Lacombe, Joseph-Patrice
  1807-1863. . . . . DLB-99

Trumbo, Dalton 1905-1976 . . . . DLB-26

Trumbull, Benjamin 1735-1820 . . . . DLB-30

Trumbull, John 1750-1831 . . . . DLB-31

Trumbull, John 1756-1843 . . . . DLB-183

Truth, Sojourner 1797?-1883 . . . . DLB-239

Tscherning, Andreas 1611-1659. . . . . DLB-164

Tsubouchi, Shōyō 1859-1935. . . . . DLB-180

Tucholsky, Kurt 1890-1935 . . . . DLB-56

Tucker, Charlotte Maria
  1821-1893 . . . . DLB-163, 190

Tucker, George 1775-1861 . . . . DLB-3, 30, 248

Tucker, James 1808?-1866? DLB-230

Tucker, Nathaniel Beverley
  1784-1851. . . . . DLB-3, 248

Tucker, St. George 1752-1827 . . . . DLB-37

Tuckerman, Frederick Goddard
  1821-1873. . . . . DLB-243

Tuckerman, Henry Theodore 1813-1871. . DLB-64

Tumas, Juozas (see Vaizgantas)

Tunis, John R. 1889-1975. . . . . .DLB-22, 171

Tunstall, Cuthbert 1474-1559. . . . . DLB-132

Tunström, Göran 1937-2000 . . . . DLB-257

Tuohy, Frank 1925- DLB-14, 139

Tupper, Martin F. 1810-1889 . . . . DLB-32

Tur, Evgeniia 1815-1892 . . . . DLB-238

Turbyfill, Mark 1896- DLB-45

Turco, Lewis 1934- Y-84

Turgenev, Aleksandr Ivanovich
  1784-1845. . . . . DLB-198

Turgenev, Ivan Sergeevich 1818-1883 . . . DLB-238

Turnball, Alexander H. 1868-1918. . . . . . DLB-184

Turnbull, Andrew 1921-1970. . . . . DLB-103

Turnbull, Gael 1928- DLB-40

Turner, Arlin 1909-1980 . . . . DLB-103

Turner, Charles (Tennyson)
  1808-1879. . . . . DLB-32

Turner, Ethel 1872-1958. . . . . DLB-230

Turner, Frederick 1943- DLB-40

Turner, Frederick Jackson
  1861-1932 . . . . .DLB-17, 186

Turner, Joseph Addison 1826-1868 . . . . . . DLB-79

Turpin, Waters Edward 1910-1968 . . . . . . DLB-51

Turrini, Peter 1944- DLB-124

Tutuola, Amos 1920-1997 . . DLB-125; CDWLB-3

Twain, Mark (see Clemens, Samuel Langhorne)

Tweedie, Ethel Brilliana circa 1860-1940 . .DLB-174

The 'Twenties and Berlin, by Alex Natan . DLB-66

Two Hundred Years of Rare Books and
  Literary Collections at the
  University of South Carolina. Y-00

Twombly, Wells 1935-1977 . . . . DLB-241

Twysden, Sir Roger 1597-1672 . . . . DLB-213

Tyler, Anne
  1941- DLB-6, 143; Y-82; CDALB-7

Tyler, Mary Palmer 1775-1866. . . . . DLB-200

Tyler, Moses Coit 1835-1900. . . . . . . .DLB-47, 64

Tyler, Royall 1757-1826 . . . . DLB-37

Tylor, Edward Burnett 1832-1917 . . . . . . DLB-57

Tynan, Katharine 1861-1931 . . . . . DLB-153, 240

Tyndale, William circa 1494-1536 . . . . . . DLB-132

U

Uchida, Yoshika 1921-1992 . . . . .CDALB-7

Udall, Nicholas 1504-1556. . . . . DLB-62

Ugrêsić, Dubravka 1949- DLB-181

Uhland, Ludwig 1787-1862. . . . . DLB-90

Uhse, Bodo 1904-1963 . . . . DLB-69

Ujević, Augustin ("Tin") 1891-1955. . . . . DLB-147

Ulenhart, Niclas flourished circa 1600 . . . DLB-164

Ulibarrí, Sabine R. 1919- DLB-82

Ulica, Jorge 1870-1926 . . . . DLB-82

Ulivi, Ferruccio 1912- DLB-196

Ulizio, B. George 1889-1969 . . . . DLB-140

Ulrich von Liechtenstein
  circa 1200-circa 1275 . . . . DLB-138

Ulrich von Zatzikhoven
  before 1194-after 1214 . . . . DLB-138

Ulysses, Reader's Edition. Y-97

Unaipon, David 1872-1967. . . . . DLB-230

Unamuno, Miguel de 1864-1936 . . . . DLB-108

Under, Marie 1883-1980
  . . . . DLB-220; CDWLB-4

Under the Microscope (1872), by
  A. C. Swinburne DLB-35

Underhill, Evelyn
  1875-1941. . . . . DLB-240

Ungaretti, Giuseppe 1888-1970 . . . . DLB-114

Unger, Friederike Helene 1741-1813 . . . . DLB-94

United States Book Company DLB-49

Universal Publishing and Distributing
  Corporation DLB-46

The University of Iowa
  Writers' Workshop
  Golden Jubilee Y-86

University of Missouri Press Y-01

The University of South Carolina Press. Y-94

University of Wales Press DLB-112

University Press of Florida. Y-00

University Press of Kansas. Y-98

University Press of Mississippi. Y-99

"The Unknown Public" (1858), by
  Wilkie Collins [excerpt] DLB-57

Uno, Chiyo 1897-1996 . . . . DLB-180

Unruh, Fritz von 1885-1970 . . . . DLB-56, 118

Unspeakable Practices II:
  The Festival of Vanguard
  Narrative at Brown University Y-93

Unsworth, Barry 1930- DLB-194

Unt, Mati 1944- DLB-232

The Unterberg Poetry Center of the
  92nd Street Y Y-98

Unwin, T. Fisher [publishing house] DLB-106

Upchurch, Boyd B. (see Boyd, John)

Updike, John 1932-
  . . . . .DLB-2, 5, 143, 218, 227; Y-80, Y-82;
                                        DS-3; CDALB-6

John Updike on the Internet. Y-97

Upīts, Andrejs 1877-1970 . . . . DLB-220

Upton, Bertha 1849-1912. . . . . DLB-141

Upton, Charles 1948- DLB-16

Upton, Florence K. 1873-1922 . . . . DLB-141

Upward, Allen 1863-1926 . . . . DLB-36

Urban, Milo 1904-1982 . . . . DLB-215

Urista, Alberto Baltazar (see Alurista)

Urquhart, Fred 1912- DLB-139

Urrea, Luis Alberto 1955- DLB-209

Urzidil, Johannes 1896-1976. . . . . DLB-85

The Uses of Facsimile. Y-90

Usk, Thomas died 1388. . . . . DLB-146

Uslar Pietri, Arturo 1906- DLB-113

Ussher, James 1581-1656 . . . . DLB-213

Ustinov, Peter 1921- DLB-13

Uttley, Alison 1884-1976 . . . . DLB-160

Uz, Johann Peter 1720-1796 . . . . DLB-97

V

Vac, Bertrand 1914- DLB-88

Vācietis, Ojārs 1933-1983. . . . . DLB-232

Vaičiulaitis, Antanas 1906-1992. . . . . . . DLB-220

Vaculík, Ludvík 1926- DLB-232

Vaičiūnaite, Judita 1937- DLB-232

Vail, Laurence 1891-1968 . . . . DLB-4

Vailland, Roger 1907-1965 . . . . DLB-83

Vaižgantas 1869-1933 . . . . DLB-220

Vajda, Ernest 1887-1954. . . . . DLB-44

Valdés, Gina 1943- DLB-122

Valdez, Luis Miguel 1940- DLB-122

Valduga, Patrizia 1953- DLB-128

Valente, José Angel 1929-2000. . . . . DLB-108

Valenzuela, Luisa 1938-   . . .DLB-113; CDWLB-3

Valeri, Diego 1887-1976 . . . . DLB-128

Valerius Flaccus fl. circa A.D. 92 . . . . . . DLB-211

Valerius Maximus fl. circa A.D. 31 . . . . . DLB-211

Valéry, Paul 1871-1945 . . . . DLB-258

Valesio, Paolo 1939- DLB-196

Valgardson, W. D. 1939- DLB-60

Valle, Víctor Manuel 1950- DLB-122

Valle-Inclán, Ramón del 1866-1936 . . . . DLB-134

Vallejo, Armando 1949- DLB-122

Vallès, Jules 1832-1885. . . . . DLB-123

Vallette, Marguerite Eymery (see Rachilde)

Valverde, José María 1926-1996 . . . . DLB-108

Van Allsburg, Chris 1949- DLB-61

Van Anda, Carr 1864-1945 . . . . DLB-25

van der Post, Laurens 1906-1996. . . . . . . DLB-204

Van Dine, S. S. (see Wright, Williard Huntington)

Van Doren, Mark 1894-1972 . . . . DLB-45

van Druten, John 1901-1957 . . . . DLB-10

Van Duyn, Mona 1921- DLB-5

Van Dyke, Henry 1852-1933 . . . . .DLB-71; DS-13

Van Dyke, Henry 1928- DLB-33

Van Dyke, John C. 1856-1932 . . . . .DLB-186

van Gulik, Robert Hans 1910-1967 . . . . DS-17

van Itallie, Jean-Claude 1936- DLB-7

Van Loan, Charles E. 1876-1919 . . . . .DLB-171

Van Rensselaer, Mariana Griswold
    1851-1934 .DLB-47

Van Rensselaer, Mrs. Schuyler
    (see Van Rensselaer, Mariana Griswold)

Van Vechten, Carl 1880-1964 . . . . .DLB-4, 9

van Vogt, A. E. 1912-2000 . . . . .DLB-8, 251

Vanbrugh, Sir John 1664-1726 . . . . .DLB-80

Vance, Jack 1916?- DLB-8

Vančura, Vladislav
    1891-1942 . . . . .DLB-215; CDWLB-4

Vane, Sutton 1888-1963 . . . . .DLB-10

Vanguard Press DLB-46

Vann, Robert L. 1879-1940 . . . . .DLB-29

Vargas Llosa, Mario
    1936- DLB-145; CDWLB-3

Varley, John 1947- Y-81

Varnhagen von Ense, Karl August
    1785-1858 . . . . .DLB-90

Varnhagen von Ense, Rahel
    1771-1833 . . . . .DLB-90

Varro 116 B.C.-27 B.C. DLB-211

Vasiliu, George (see Bacovia, George)

Vásquez, Richard 1928- DLB-209

Vásquez Montalbán, Manuel 1939- DLB-134

Vassa, Gustavus (see Equiano, Olaudah)

Vassalli, Sebastiano 1941- DLB-128, 196

Vaughan, Henry 1621-1695 . . . . .DLB-131

Vaughan, Thomas 1621-1666 . . . . .DLB-131

Vaughn, Robert 1592?-1667 . . . . .DLB-213

Vaux, Thomas, Lord 1509-1556 . . . . .DLB-132

Vazov, Ivan 1850-1921 . . . . . DLB-147; CDWLB-4

Véa Jr., Alfredo 1950- DLB-209

Veblen, Thorstein 1857-1929 . . . . .DLB-246

Vega, Janine Pommy 1942- DLB-16

Veiller, Anthony 1903-1965 . . . . .DLB-44

Velásquez-Trevino, Gloria 1949- DLB-122

Veley, Margaret 1843-1887 . . . . .DLB-199

Velleius Paterculus
    circa 20 B.C.-circa A.D. 30 . . . . .DLB-211

Veloz Maggiolo, Marcio 1936- DLB-145

Vel'tman Aleksandr Fomich
    1800-1870 . . . . .DLB-198

Venegas, Daniel ?-? DLB-82

Venevitinov, Dmitrii Vladimirovich
    1805-1827 . . . . .DLB-205

Vergil, Polydore circa 1470-1555 . . . . .DLB-132

Veríssimo, Erico 1905-1975 . . . . .DLB-145

Verlaine, Paul 1844-1896 . . . . .DLB-217

Verne, Jules 1828-1905 . . . . .DLB-123

Verplanck, Gulian C. 1786-1870 . . . . .DLB-59

Very, Jones 1813-1880 . . . . .DLB-1, 243

Vian, Boris 1920-1959 . . . . .DLB-72

Viazemsky, Petr Andreevich
    1792-1878 . . . . .DLB-205

Vicars, Thomas 1591-1638 . . . . .DLB-236

Vickers, Roy 1888?-1965 . . . . .DLB-77

Vickery, Sukey 1779-1821 . . . . .DLB-200

Victoria 1819-1901 . . . . .DLB-55

Victoria Press .DLB-106

Vidal, Gore 1925- DLB-6, 152; CDALB-7

Vidal, Mary Theresa 1815-1873 . . . . .DLB-230

Vidmer, Richards 1898-1978 . . . . .DLB-241

Viebig, Clara 1860-1952 . . . . .DLB-66

Viereck, George Sylvester
    1884-1962 . . . . .DLB-54

Viereck, Peter 1916- DLB-5

Viets, Roger 1738-1811 . . . . .DLB-99

Viewpoint: Politics and Performance, by
    David Edgar DLB-13

Vigil-Piñon, Evangelina 1949- DLB-122

Vigneault, Gilles 1928- DLB-60

Vigny, Alfred de
    1797-1863 . . . . DLB-119, 192, 217

Vigolo, Giorgio 1894-1983 . . . . .DLB-114

The Viking Press DLB-46

Vilde, Eduard 1865-1933 . . . . .DLB-220

Vilinskaia, Mariia Aleksandrovna
    (see Vovchok, Marko)

Villanueva, Alma Luz 1944- DLB-122

Villanueva, Tino 1941- DLB-82

Villard, Henry 1835-1900 . . . . .DLB-23

Villard, Oswald Garrison
    1872-1949 . . . . .DLB-25, 91

Villarreal, Edit 1944- DLB-209

Villarreal, José Antonio 1924- DLB-82

Villaseñor, Victor 1940- DLB-209

Villegas de Magnón, Leonor
    1876-1955 . . . . .DLB-122

Villehardouin, Geoffroi de
    circa 1150-1215 . . . . .DLB-208

Villemaire, Yolande 1949- DLB-60

Villena, Luis Antonio de 1951- DLB-134

Villiers, George, Second Duke
    of Buckingham 1628-1687 . . . . .DLB-80

Villiers de l'Isle-Adam, Jean-Marie Mathias
    Philippe-Auguste, Comte de
    1838-1889 . . . . DLB-123, 192

Villon, François 1431-circa 1463? DLB-208

Vine Press DLB-112

Viorst, Judith ?- DLB-52

Vipont, Elfrida (Elfrida Vipont Foulds,
    Charles Vipont) 1902-1992 . . . . .DLB-160

Viramontes, Helena María 1954- DLB-122

Virgil 70 B.C.-19 B.C. DLB-211; CDWLB-1

Virtual Books and Enemies of Books Y-00

Vischer, Friedrich Theodor 1807-1887 . . .DLB-133

Vitruvius circa 85 B.C.-circa 15 B.C. DLB-211

Vitry, Philippe de 1291-1361 . . . . .DLB-208

Vivanco, Luis Felipe 1907-1975 . . . . .DLB-108

Vivian, E. Charles 1882-1947 . . . . .DLB-255

Viviani, Cesare 1947- DLB-128

Vivien, Renée 1877-1909 . . . . .DLB-217

Vizenor, Gerald 1934- DLB-175, 227

Vizetelly and Company DLB-106

Voaden, Herman 1903- DLB-88

Voß, Johann Heinrich 1751-1826 . . . . .DLB-90

Voigt, Ellen Bryant 1943- DLB-120

Vojnović, Ivo 1857-1929 . . . . DLB-147; CDWLB-4

Volkoff, Vladimir 1932- DLB-83

Volland, P. F., Company DLB-46

Vollbehr, Otto H. F.
    1872?-1945 or 1946 . . . . .DLB-187

Vologdin (see Zasodimsky, Pavel Vladimirovich)

Volponi, Paolo 1924- DLB-177

Vonarburg, Élisabeth 1947- DLB-251

von der Grün, Max 1926- DLB-75

Vonnegut, Kurt 1922-
    . . . . . . .DLB-2, 8, 152; Y-80; DS-3; CDALB-6

Voranc, Prežihov 1893-1950 . . . . .DLB-147

Vovchok, Marko 1833-1907 . . . . .DLB-238

Voynich, E. L. 1864-1960 . . . . .DLB-197

Vroman, Mary Elizabeth
    circa 1924-1967 . . . . .DLB-33

W

Wace, Robert ("Maistre")
    circa 1100-circa 1175 . . . . .DLB-146

Wackenroder, Wilhelm Heinrich
    1773-1798 . . . . .DLB-90

Wackernagel, Wilhelm 1806-1869 . . . . . .DLB-133

Waddell, Helen 1889-1965 . . . . .DLB-240

Waddington, Miriam 1917- DLB-68

Wade, Henry 1887-1969 . . . . .DLB-77

Wagenknecht, Edward 1900- DLB-103

Wägner, Elin 1882-1949 . . . . .DLB-259

Wagner, Heinrich Leopold 1747-1779 . . . .DLB-94

Wagner, Henry R. 1862-1957 . . . . .DLB-140

Wagner, Richard 1813-1883 . . . . .DLB-129

Wagoner, David 1926- DLB-5, 256

Wah, Fred 1939- DLB-60

Waiblinger, Wilhelm 1804-1830 . . . . .DLB-90

Wain, John
    1925-1994 . . . DLB-15, 27, 139, 155; CDBLB-8

Wainwright, Jeffrey 1944- DLB-40

Waite, Peirce and Company DLB-49

Wakeman, Stephen H. 1859-1924 . . . . . .DLB-187

Wakoski, Diane 1937- DLB-5

Walahfrid Strabo circa 808-849 . . . . .DLB-148

Walck, Henry Z. DLB-46

Walcott, Derek
    1930- DLB-117; Y-81, Y-92; CDWLB-3

Waldegrave, Robert [publishing house] . . .DLB-170

Waldman, Anne 1945- DLB-16

Waldrop, Rosmarie 1935- DLB-169

Walker, Alice 1900-1982 . . . . DLB-201

Walker, Alice
1944- DLB-6, 33, 143; CDALB-6

Walker, Annie Louisa (Mrs. Harry Coghill)
circa 1836-1907 . . . . DLB-240

Walker, George F. 1947- DLB-60

Walker, John Brisben 1847-1931 . . . . DLB-79

Walker, Joseph A. 1935- DLB-38

Walker, Margaret 1915- DLB-76, 152

Walker, Ted 1934- DLB-40

Walker and Company DLB-49

Walker, Evans and Cogswell Company . . . DLB-49

Wall, John F. (see Sarban)

Wallace, Alfred Russel 1823-1913 . . . . . . DLB-190

Wallace, Dewitt 1889-1981 and
Lila Acheson Wallace 1889-1984 . . . . DLB-137

Wallace, Edgar 1875-1932 . . . . DLB-70

Wallace, Lew 1827-1905 . . . . DLB-202

Wallace, Lila Acheson
(see Wallace, Dewitt, and Lila Acheson Wallace)

Wallace, Naomi 1960- DLB-249

Wallant, Edward Lewis
1926-1962 . . . . DLB-2, 28, 143

Waller, Edmund 1606-1687 . . . . DLB-126

Walpole, Horace 1717-1797 . . . . . DLB-39, 104, 213

Preface to the First Edition of
The Castle of Otranto (1764) DLB-39

Preface to the Second Edition of
The Castle of Otranto (1765) DLB-39

Walpole, Hugh 1884-1941 . . . . DLB-34

Walrond, Eric 1898-1966 . . . . DLB-51

Walser, Martin 1927- DLB-75, 124

Walser, Robert 1878-1956 . . . . DLB-66

Walsh, Ernest 1895-1926 . . . . DLB-4, 45

Walsh, Robert 1784-1859 . . . . DLB-59

Walters, Henry 1848-1931 . . . . DLB-140

Waltharius circa 825 . . . . DLB-148

Walther von der Vogelweide
circa 1170-circa 1230 . . . . DLB-138

Walton, Izaak
1593-1683 . . . . DLB-151, 213; CDBLB-1

Wambaugh, Joseph 1937- DLB-6; Y-83

Wand, Alfred Rudolph 1828-1891 . . . . . . DLB-188

Waniek, Marilyn Nelson 1946- DLB-120

Wanley, Humphrey 1672-1726 . . . . DLB-213

Warburton, William 1698-1779 . . . . DLB-104

Ward, Aileen 1919- DLB-111

Ward, Artemus (see Browne, Charles Farrar)

Ward, Arthur Henry Sarsfield (see Rohmer, Sax)

Ward, Douglas Turner 1930- DLB-7, 38

Ward, Mrs. Humphry 1851-1920 . . . . DLB-18

Ward, James 1843-1925 . . . . DLB-262

Ward, Lynd 1905-1985 . . . . DLB-22

Ward, Lock and Company DLB-106

Ward, Nathaniel circa 1578-1652 . . . . DLB-24

Ward, Theodore 1902-1983 . . . . DLB-76

Wardle, Ralph 1909-1988 . . . . DLB-103

Ware, Henry, Jr. 1794-1843 . . . . DLB-235

Ware, William 1797-1852 . . . . DLB-1, 235

Warfield, Catherine Ann 1816-1877 . . . . . DLB-248

Waring, Anna Letitia 1823-1910 . . . . DLB-240

Warne, Frederick, and Company [U.K.] . . . DLB-106

Warne, Frederick, and Company [U.S.] . . . DLB-49

Warner, Anne 1869-1913 . . . . DLB-202

Warner, Charles Dudley 1829-1900 . . . . . DLB-64

Warner, Marina 1946- DLB-194

Warner, Rex 1905- DLB-15

Warner, Susan 1819-1885 . . . DLB-3, 42, 239, 250

Warner, Sylvia Townsend
1893-1978 . . . . DLB-34, 139

Warner, William 1558-1609 . . . . DLB-172

Warner Books DLB-46

Warr, Bertram 1917-1943 . . . . DLB-88

Warren, John Byrne Leicester (see De Tabley, Lord)

Warren, Lella 1899-1982 . . . . Y-83

Warren, Mercy Otis 1728-1814 . . . . . DLB-31, 200

Warren, Robert Penn 1905-1989
. . . . DLB-2, 48, 152; Y-80, Y-89; CDALB-6

Warren, Samuel 1807-1877 . . . . DLB-190

Die Wartburgkrieg circa 1230-circa 1280 . . . DLB-138

Warton, Joseph 1722-1800 . . . . DLB-104, 109

Warton, Thomas 1728-1790 . . . . DLB-104, 109

Warung, Price (William Astley)
1855-1911 . . . . DLB-230

Washington, George 1732-1799 . . . . DLB-31

Wassermann, Jakob 1873-1934 . . . . DLB-66

Wasserstein, Wendy 1950- DLB-228

Wasson, David Atwood 1823-1887 . . . DLB-1, 223

Watanna, Onoto (see Eaton, Winnifred)

Waterhouse, Keith 1929- DLB-13, 15

Waterman, Andrew 1940- DLB-40

Waters, Frank 1902-1995 . . . . DLB-212; Y-86

Waters, Michael 1949- DLB-120

Watkins, Tobias 1780-1855 . . . . DLB-73

Watkins, Vernon 1906-1967 . . . . DLB-20

Watmough, David 1926- DLB-53

Watson, Ian 1943- DLB-261

Watson, James Wreford (see Wreford, James)

Watson, John 1850-1907 . . . . DLB-156

Watson, Rosamund Marriott
(Graham R. Tomson) 1860-1911 . . . . DLB-240

Watson, Sheila 1909- DLB-60

Watson, Thomas 1545?-1592 . . . . DLB-132

Watson, Wilfred 1911- DLB-60

Watt, W. J., and Company DLB-46

Watten, Barrett 1948- DLB-193

Watterson, Henry 1840-1921 . . . . DLB-25

Watts, Alan 1915-1973 . . . . DLB-16

Watts, Franklin [publishing house] DLB-46

Watts, Isaac 1674-1748 . . . . DLB-95

Waugh, Alec 1898-1981 . . . . DLB-191

Waugh, Auberon 1939-2000 . . . DLB-14, 194; Y-00

The Cult of Biography
Excerpts from the Second Folio Debate:
"Biographies are generally a disease of
English Literature" Y-86

Waugh, Evelyn
1903-1966 . . . . . DLB-15, 162, 195; CDBLB-6

Way and Williams DLB-49

Wayman, Tom 1945- DLB-53

We See the Editor at Work Y-97

Weatherly, Tom 1942- DLB-41

Weaver, Gordon 1937- DLB-130

Weaver, Robert 1921- DLB-88

Webb, Beatrice 1858-1943 and
Webb, Sidney 1859-1947 . . . . DLB-190

Webb, Francis 1925-1973 . . . . DLB-260

Webb, Frank J. ?-? DLB-50

Webb, James Watson 1802-1884 . . . . DLB-43

Webb, Mary 1881-1927 . . . . DLB-34

Webb, Phyllis 1927- DLB-53

Webb, Walter Prescott 1888-1963 . . . . . . DLB-17

Webbe, William ?-1591 . . . . DLB-132

Webber, Charles Wilkins 1819-1856? . . . DLB-202

Webling, Lucy (Lucy Betty MacRaye)
1877-1952 . . . . DLB-240

Webling, Peggy (Arthur Weston)
1871-1949 . . . . DLB-240

Webster, Augusta 1837-1894 . . . . . . DLB-35, 240

Webster, Charles L., and Company DLB-49

Webster, John
1579 or 1580-1634? DLB-58; CDBLB-1

John Webster: The Melbourne
Manuscript Y-86

Webster, Noah
1758-1843 . . . . DLB-1, 37, 42, 43, 73, 243

Weckherlin, Georg Rodolf 1584-1653 . . . DLB-164

Wedekind, Frank
1864-1918 . . . . DLB-118; CDBLB-2

Weeks, Edward Augustus, Jr.
1898-1989 . . . . DLB-137

Weeks, Stephen B. 1865-1918 . . . . DLB-187

Weems, Mason Locke 1759-1825 . . . DLB-30, 37, 42

Weerth, Georg 1822-1856 . . . . DLB-129

Weidenfeld and Nicolson DLB-112

Weidman, Jerome 1913-1998 . . . . DLB-28

Weiß, Ernst 1882-1940 . . . . DLB-81

Weigl, Bruce 1949- DLB-120

Weinbaum, Stanley Grauman 1902-1935 . . DLB-8

Weiner, Andrew 1949- DLB-251

Weintraub, Stanley 1929- DLB-111; Y82

The Practice of Biography: An Interview
with Stanley Weintraub Y-82

Weise, Christian 1642-1708 . . . . DLB-168

Weisenborn, Gunther 1902-1969 . . . . DLB-69, 124

Weiss, John 1818-1879 . . . . DLB-1, 243

Weiss, Peter 1916-1982 . . . . DLB-69, 124

Weiss, Theodore 1916- DLB-5

Weisse, Christian Felix 1726-1804 . . . . . . DLB-97

Weitling, Wilhelm 1808-1871 . . . . DLB-129

Welch, James 1940- DLB-175, 256

Welch, Lew 1926-1971? DLB-16

Weldon, Fay 1931- DLB-14, 194; CDBLB-8

Wellek, René 1903-1995 . . . . DLB-63

Wells, Carolyn 1862-1942 . . . . DLB-11

Wells, Charles Jeremiah circa 1800-1879 . . . DLB-32

Wells, Gabriel 1862-1946 . . . . DLB-140

Wells, H. G.
1866-1946 . . . DLB-34, 70, 156, 178; CDBLB-6

Wells, Helena 1758?-1824 . . . . DLB-200

Wells, Robert 1947- DLB-40

Wells-Barnett, Ida B. 1862-1931 . . . . . DLB-23, 221

Welty, Eudora 1909- DLB-2, 102, 143;
. . . . Y-87, Y-01; DS-12; CDALB-1

Eudora Welty: Eye of the Storyteller Y-87

Eudora Welty Newsletter Y-99

Eudora Welty's Funeral Y-01

Eudora Welty's Ninetieth Birthday Y-99

Wendell, Barrett 1855-1921 . . . . DLB-71

Wentworth, Patricia 1878-1961 . . . . DLB-77

Wentworth, William Charles
1790-1872 . . . . DLB-230

Werder, Diederich von dem 1584-1657 . . . DLB-164

Werfel, Franz 1890-1945 . . . . DLB-81, 124

Werner, Zacharias 1768-1823 . . . . DLB-94

The Werner Company DLB-49

Wersba, Barbara 1932- DLB-52

Wescott, Glenway 1901- DLB-4, 9, 102

Wesker, Arnold 1932- DLB-13; CDBLB-8

Wesley, Charles 1707-1788 . . . . DLB-95

Wesley, John 1703-1791 . . . . DLB-104

Wesley, Mary 1912- DLB-231

Wesley, Richard 1945- DLB-38

Wessels, A., and Company DLB-46

Wessobrunner Gebet circa 787-815 . . . . DLB-148

West, Anthony 1914-1988 . . . . DLB-15

West, Cornel 1953- DLB-246

West, Dorothy 1907-1998 . . . . DLB-76

West, Jessamyn 1902-1984 . . . . DLB-6; Y-84

West, Mae 1892-1980 . . . . DLB-44

West, Michelle Sagara 1963- DLB-251

West, Nathanael
1903-1940 . . . . DLB-4, 9, 28; CDALB-5

West, Paul 1930- DLB-14

West, Rebecca 1892-1983 . . . . DLB-36; Y-83

West, Richard 1941- DLB-185

West and Johnson DLB-49

Westcott, Edward Noyes 1846-1898 . . . . DLB-202

The Western Messenger 1835-1841 . . . . DLB-223

Western Publishing Company DLB-46

Western Writers of America Y-99

The Westminster Review 1824-1914 . . . . DLB-110

Weston, Arthur (see Webling, Peggy)

Weston, Elizabeth Jane circa 1582-1612 . . DLB-172

Wetherald, Agnes Ethelwyn 1857-1940 . . . . DLB-99

Wetherell, Elizabeth (see Warner, Susan)

Wetherell, W. D. 1948- DLB-234

Wetzel, Friedrich Gottlob 1779-1819 . . . . . DLB-90

Weyman, Stanley J. 1855-1928 . . . . . DLB-141, 156

Wezel, Johann Karl 1747-1819 . . . . DLB-94

Whalen, Philip 1923- DLB-16

Whalley, George 1915-1983 . . . . DLB-88

Wharton, Edith 1862-1937
. . . . . DLB-4, 9, 12, 78, 189; DS-13; CDALB-3

Wharton, William 1920s?- Y-80

"What You Lose on the Swings You Make Up
on the Merry-Go-Round" Y-99

Whately, Mary Louisa 1824-1889 . . . . . . DLB-166

Whately, Richard 1787-1863 . . . . DLB-190

From *Elements of Rhetoric* (1828;
revised, 1846) DLB-57

What's Really Wrong With Bestseller Lists . . Y-84

Wheatley, Dennis 1897-1977 . . . . DLB-77, 255

Wheatley, Phillis
circa 1754-1784 . . . . DLB-31, 50; CDALB-2

Wheeler, Anna Doyle 1785-1848? DLB-158

Wheeler, Charles Stearns 1816-1843 . . . DLB-1, 223

Wheeler, Monroe 1900-1988 . . . . DLB-4

Wheelock, John Hall 1886-1978 . . . . DLB-45

From John Hall Wheelock's Oral Memoir . . . Y-01

Wheelwright, J. B. 1897-1940 . . . . DLB-45

Wheelwright, John circa 1592-1679 . . . . . . DLB-24

Whetstone, George 1550-1587 . . . . DLB-136

Whetstone, Colonel Pete (see Noland, C. F. M.)

Whewell, William 1794-1866 . . . . DLB-262

Whichcote, Benjamin 1609?-1683 . . . . DLB-252

Whicher, Stephen E. 1915-1961 . . . . DLB-111

Whipple, Edwin Percy 1819-1886 . . . . . . DLB-1, 64

Whitaker, Alexander 1585-1617 . . . . DLB-24

Whitaker, Daniel K. 1801-1881 . . . . DLB-73

Whitcher, Frances Miriam
1812-1852 . . . . DLB-11, 202

White, Andrew 1579-1656 . . . . DLB-24

White, Andrew Dickson 1832-1918 . . . . . DLB-47

White, E. B. 1899-1985 . . . . DLB-11, 22; CDALB-7

White, Edgar B. 1947- DLB-38

White, Edmund 1940- DLB-227

White, Ethel Lina 1887-1944 . . . . DLB-77

White, Hayden V. 1928- DLB-246

White, Henry Kirke 1785-1806 . . . . DLB-96

White, Horace 1834-1916 . . . . DLB-23

White, James 1928-1999 . . . . DLB-261

White, Patrick 1912-1990 . . . . DLB-260

White, Phyllis Dorothy James (see James, P. D.)

White, Richard Grant 1821-1885 . . . . DLB-64

White, T. H. 1906-1964 . . . . DLB-160, 255

White, Walter 1893-1955 . . . . DLB-51

White, William, and Company DLB-49

White, William Allen 1868-1944 . . . . DLB-9, 25

White, William Anthony Parker
(see Boucher, Anthony)

White, William Hale (see Rutherford, Mark)

Whitechurch, Victor L. 1868-1933 . . . . DLB-70

Whitehead, Alfred North 1861-1947 . . . . . DLB-100

Whitehead, James 1936- Y-81

Whitehead, William 1715-1785 . . . . . . DLB-84, 109

Whitfield, James Monroe 1822-1871 . . . . . DLB-50

Whitfield, Raoul 1898-1945 . . . . DLB-226

Whitgift, John circa 1533-1604 . . . . DLB-132

Whiting, John 1917-1963 . . . . DLB-13

Whiting, Samuel 1597-1679 . . . . DLB-24

Whitlock, Brand 1869-1934 . . . . DLB-12

Whitman, Albert, and Company DLB-46

Whitman, Albery Allson 1851-1901 . . . . . . DLB-50

Whitman, Alden 1913-1990 . . . . Y-91

Whitman, Sarah Helen (Power)
1803-1878 . . . . DLB-1, 243

Whitman, Walt
1819-1892 . . . . DLB-3, 64, 224, 250; CDALB-2

Whitman Publishing Company DLB-46

Whitney, Geoffrey 1548 or 1552?-1601 . . DLB-136

Whitney, Isabella flourished 1566-1573 . . . DLB-136

Whitney, John Hay 1904-1982 . . . . DLB-127

Whittemore, Reed 1919-1995 . . . . DLB-5

Whittier, John Greenleaf
1807-1892 . . . . DLB-1, 243; CDALB-2

Whittlesey House DLB-46

Who Runs American Literature? Y-94

Whose *Ulysses?* The Function of Editing Y-97

Wickham, Anna (Edith Alice Mary Harper)
1884-1947 . . . . DLB-240

Wicomb, Zoë 1948- DLB-225

Wideman, John Edgar 1941- DLB-33, 143

Widener, Harry Elkins 1885-1912 . . . . . . DLB-140

Wiebe, Rudy 1934- DLB-60

Wiechert, Ernst 1887-1950 . . . . DLB-56

Wied, Martina 1882-1957 . . . . DLB-85

Wiehe, Evelyn May Clowes (see Mordaunt, Elinor)

Wieland, Christoph Martin 1733-1813 . . . . DLB-97

Wienbarg, Ludolf 1802-1872 . . . . DLB-133

Wieners, John 1934- DLB-16

Wier, Ester 1910- DLB-52

Wiesel, Elie
1928- DLB-83; Y-86, 87; CDALB-7

Wiggin, Kate Douglas 1856-1923 . . . . DLB-42

Wigglesworth, Michael 1631-1705 . . . . DLB-24

Wilberforce, William 1759-1833 . . . . DLB-158

Wilbrandt, Adolf 1837-1911 . . . . DLB-129

Wilbur, Richard
1921- DLB-5, 169; CDALB-7

Wild, Peter 1940- DLB-5

Wilde, Lady Jane Francesca Elgee
1821?-1896 . . . . DLB-199

Wilde, Oscar 1854-1900
. . . . DLB-10, 19, 34, 57, 141, 156, 190;
CDBLB-5

"The Critic as Artist" (1891) DLB-57

Oscar Wilde Conference at Hofstra
University Y-00

From "The Decay of Lying" (1889) DLB-18

"The English Renaissance of
Art" (1908)..................... DLB-35

"L'Envoi" (1882) DLB-35

Wilde, Richard Henry 1789-1847...... DLB-3, 59

Wilde, W. A., Company DLB-49

Wilder, Billy 1906- DLB-26

Wilder, Laura Ingalls 1867-1957..... DLB-22, 256

Wilder, Thornton
1897-1975 ....DLB-4, 7, 9, 228; CDALB-7

Thornton Wilder Centenary at Yale Y-97

Wildgans, Anton 1881-1932........... DLB-118

Wiley, Bell Irvin 1906-1980 .... DLB-17

Wiley, John, and Sons DLB-49

Wilhelm, Kate 1928- DLB-8

Wilkes, Charles 1798-1877 .... DLB-183

Wilkes, George 1817-1885 .... DLB-79

Wilkins, John 1614-1672............. DLB-236

Wilkinson, Anne 1910-1961 .... DLB-88

Wilkinson, Eliza Yonge
1757-circa 1813................. DLB-200

Wilkinson, Sylvia 1940- Y-86

Wilkinson, William Cleaver 1833-1920 ... DLB-71

Willard, Barbara 1909-1994 .... DLB-161

Willard, Emma 1787-1870 .... DLB-239

Willard, Frances E. 1839-1898 .... DLB-221

Willard, L. [publishing house] DLB-49

Willard, Nancy 1936- DLB-5, 52

Willard, Samuel 1640-1707............ DLB-24

Willeford, Charles 1919-1988.......... DLB-226

William of Auvergne 1190-1249........ DLB-115

William of Conches
circa 1090-circa 1154 .... DLB-115

William of Ockham circa 1285-1347 .... DLB-115

William of Sherwood
1200/1205-1266/1271.............. DLB-115

The William Chavrat American Fiction Collection
at the Ohio State University Libraries Y-92

Williams, A., and Company............ DLB-49

Williams, Ben Ames 1889-1953 .... DLB-102

Williams, C. K. 1936- DLB-5

Williams, Chancellor 1905- DLB-76

Williams, Charles 1886-1945 ...DLB-100, 153, 255

Williams, Denis 1923-1998............ DLB-117

Williams, Emlyn 1905-1987 ....DLB-10, 77

Williams, Garth 1912-1996 .... DLB-22

Williams, George Washington
1849-1891 .... DLB-47

Williams, Heathcote 1941- DLB-13

Williams, Helen Maria 1761-1827 ...... DLB-158

Williams, Hugo 1942- DLB-40

Williams, Isaac 1802-1865 .... DLB-32

Williams, Joan 1928- DLB-6

Williams, Joe 1889-1972 .... DLB-241

Williams, John A. 1925- DLB-2, 33

Williams, John E. 1922-1994 .... DLB-6

Williams, Jonathan 1929- DLB-5

Williams, Miller 1930- DLB-105

Williams, Nigel 1948- DLB-231

Williams, Raymond 1921- ... DLB-14, 231, 242

Williams, Roger circa 1603-1683 .... DLB-24

Williams, Rowland 1817-1870 .... DLB-184

Williams, Samm-Art 1946- DLB-38

Williams, Sherley Anne 1944-1999 ...... DLB-41

Williams, T. Harry 1909-1979 .... DLB-17

Williams, Tennessee
1911-1983 .... DLB-7; Y-83; DS-4; CDALB-1

Williams, Terry Tempest 1955- DLB-206

Williams, Ursula Moray 1911- DLB-160

Williams, Valentine 1883-1946 .... DLB-77

Williams, William Appleman 1921- DLB-17

Williams, William Carlos
1883-1963 ..... DLB-4, 16, 54, 86; CDALB-4

Williams, Wirt 1921- DLB-6

Williams Brothers.................... DLB-49

Williamson, Henry 1895-1977 .... DLB-191

Williamson, Jack 1908- DLB-8

Willingham, Calder Baynard, Jr.
1922-1995 .... DLB-2, 44

Williram of Ebersberg circa 1020-1085 .. DLB-148

Willis, Nathaniel Parker 1806-1867
................DLB-3, 59, 73, 74, 183, 250; DS-13

Willkomm, Ernst 1810-1886 .... DLB-133

Willumsen, Dorrit 1940- DLB-214

Wills, Garry 1934- DLB-246

Wilmer, Clive 1945- DLB-40

Wilson, A. N. 1950- DLB-14, 155, 194

Wilson, Angus 1913-1991 ......DLB-15, 139, 155

Wilson, Arthur 1595-1652 .... DLB-58

Wilson, August 1945- DLB-228

Wilson, Augusta Jane Evans 1835-1909 ... DLB-42

Wilson, Colin 1931- DLB-14, 194

Wilson, Edmund 1895-1972............ DLB-63

Wilson, Effingham [publishing house] ... DLB-154

Wilson, Ethel 1888-1980 .... DLB-68

Wilson, F. P. 1889-1963 .... DLB-201

Wilson, Harriet E.
1827/1828?-1863? DLB-50, 239, 243

Wilson, Harry Leon 1867-1939 .... DLB-9

Wilson, John 1588-1667.............. DLB-24

Wilson, John 1785-1854 .... DLB-110

Wilson, John Dover 1881-1969 .... DLB-201

Wilson, Lanford 1937- DLB-7

Wilson, Margaret 1882-1973 .... DLB-9

Wilson, Michael 1914-1978 .... DLB-44

Wilson, Mona 1872-1954............. DLB-149

Wilson, Robert Charles 1953- DLB-251

Wilson, Robley 1930- DLB-218

Wilson, Romer 1891-1930 .... DLB-191

Wilson, Thomas 1524-1581....... DLB-132, 236

Wilson, Woodrow 1856-1924 .... DLB-47

Wimsatt, William K., Jr. 1907-1975 ...... DLB-63

Winchell, Walter 1897-1972........... DLB-29

Winchester, J. [publishing house] DLB-49

Winckelmann, Johann Joachim
1717-1768 .... DLB-97

Winckler, Paul 1630-1686 .... DLB-164

Wind, Herbert Warren 1916- DLB-171

Windet, John [publishing house] DLB-170

Windham, Donald 1920- DLB-6

Wing, Donald Goddard 1904-1972 ......DLB-187

Wing, John M. 1844-1917 ....DLB-187

Wingate, Allan [publishing house] DLB-112

Winnemucca, Sarah 1844-1921 ....DLB-175

Winnifrith, Tom 1938- DLB-155

Winning an Edgar Y-98

Winsloe, Christa 1888-1944........... DLB-124

Winslow, Anna Green 1759-1780...... DLB-200

Winsor, Justin 1831-1897 .... DLB-47

John C. Winston Company DLB-49

Winters, Yvor 1900-1968.............. DLB-48

Winterson, Jeanette 1959- DLB-207, 261

Winthrop, John 1588-1649.......... DLB-24, 30

Winthrop, John, Jr. 1606-1676 .... DLB-24

Winthrop, Margaret Tyndal 1591-1647.. DLB-200

Winthrop, Theodore 1828-1861 .... DLB-202

Wirt, William 1772-1834 .... DLB-37

Wise, John 1652-1725.................. DLB-24

Wise, Thomas James 1859-1937 .... DLB-184

Wiseman, Adele 1928-1992 .... DLB-88

Wishart and Company................ DLB-112

Wisner, George 1812-1849............ DLB-43

Wister, Owen 1860-1938 ....DLB-9, 78, 186

Wister, Sarah 1761-1804.............. DLB-200

Wither, George 1588-1667 .... DLB-121

Witherspoon, John 1723-1794 .... DLB-31

Withrow, William Henry 1839-1908..... DLB-99

Witkacy (see Witkiewicz, Stanisław Ignacy)

Witkiewicz, Stanisław Ignacy
1885-1939 ....DLB-215; CDWLB-4

Wittgenstein, Ludwig 1889-1951 .... DLB-262

Wittig, Monique 1935- DLB-83

Wodehouse, P. G.
1881-1975.......... DLB-34, 162; CDBLB-6

Wohmann, Gabriele 1932- DLB-75

Woiwode, Larry 1941- DLB-6

Wolcot, John 1738-1819............. DLB-109

Wolcott, Roger 1679-1767 .... DLB-24

Wolf, Christa 1929- DLB-75; CDWLB-2

Wolf, Friedrich 1888-1953 .... DLB-124

Wolfe, Gene 1931- DLB-8

Wolfe, John [publishing house] DLB-170

Wolfe, Reyner (Reginald)
[publishing house] DLB-170

Wolfe, Thomas
1900-1938 .... DLB-9, 102, 229; Y-85;
DS-2, DS-16; CDALB-5

"All the Faults of Youth and Inexperience":
A Reader's Report on
Thomas Wolfe's *O Lost* Y-01

Eugene Gant's Projected Works Y-01

The Thomas Wolfe Collection at the University
of North Carolina at Chapel Hill Y-97

Thomas Wolfe Centennial
Celebration in Asheville Y-00

Fire at Thomas Wolfe Memorial Y-98

The Thomas Wolfe Society Y-97

Wolfe, Tom 1931- DLB-152, 185

Wolfenstein, Martha 1869-1906 . . . . DLB-221

Wolff, Helen 1906-1994 . . . . Y-94

Wolff, Tobias 1945- DLB-130

Wolfram von Eschenbach
circa 1170-after 1220 . . . . DLB-138; CDWLB-2

Wolfram von Eschenbach's *Parzival:*
Prologue and Book 3 . . . . DLB-138

Wolker, Jiří 1900-1924 . . . . DLB-215

Wollstonecraft, Mary 1759-1797
. . . . DLB-39, 104, 158, 252; CDBLB-3

Wondratschek, Wolf 1943- DLB-75

Wood, Anthony à 1632-1695 . . . . DLB-213

Wood, Benjamin 1820-1900 . . . . DLB-23

Wood, Charles 1932- DLB-13

Wood, Mrs. Henry 1814-1887 . . . . DLB-18

Wood, Joanna E. 1867-1927 . . . . DLB-92

Wood, Sally Sayward Barrell Keating
1759-1855 . . . . DLB-200

Wood, Samuel [publishing house] DLB-49

Wood, William ?-? DLB-24

The Charles Wood Affair:
A Playwright Revived Y-83

Woodberry, George Edward
1855-1930 . . . . DLB-71, 103

Woodbridge, Benjamin 1622-1684 . . . . . . DLB-24

Woodcock, George 1912-1995 . . . . DLB-88

Woodhull, Victoria C. 1838-1927 . . . . DLB-79

Woodmason, Charles circa 1720-? DLB-31

Woodress, Jr., James Leslie 1916- DLB-111

Woods, Margaret L. 1855-1945 . . . . DLB-240

Woodson, Carter G. 1875-1950 . . . . DLB-17

Woodward, C. Vann 1908-1999 . . . . DLB-17

Woodward, Stanley 1895-1965 . . . . DLB-171

Woodworth, Samuel 1785-1842 . . . . DLB-260

Wooler, Thomas 1785 or 1786-1853 . . . . . DLB-158

Woolf, David (see Maddow, Ben)

Woolf, Douglas 1922-1992 . . . . DLB-244

Woolf, Leonard 1880-1969 . . . . . . DLB-100; DS-10

Woolf, Virginia 1882-1941
. . . . DLB-36, 100, 162; DS-10; CDBLB-6

Woolf, Virginia, "The New Biography," *New York
Herald Tribune,* 30 October 1927 . . . . . DLB-149

Woollcott, Alexander 1887-1943 . . . . DLB-29

Woolman, John 1720-1772 . . . . DLB-31

Woolner, Thomas 1825-1892 . . . . DLB-35

Woolrich, Cornell 1903-1968 . . . . DLB-226

Woolsey, Sarah Chauncy 1835-1905 . . . . . DLB-42

Woolson, Constance Fenimore
1840-1894 . . . . DLB-12, 74, 189, 221

Worcester, Joseph Emerson
1784-1865 . . . . DLB-1, 235

Worde, Wynkyn de [publishing house] . . . DLB-170

Wordsworth, Christopher 1807-1885 . . . . DLB-166

Wordsworth, Dorothy 1771-1855 . . . . DLB-107

Wordsworth, Elizabeth 1840-1932 . . . . DLB-98

Wordsworth, William
1770-1850 . . . . DLB-93, 107; CDBLB-3

Workman, Fanny Bullock 1859-1925 . . . . DLB-189

The Works of the Rev. John Witherspoon
(1800-1801) [excerpts] DLB-31

A World Chronology of Important Science
Fiction Works (1818-1979) DLB-8

World Literature Today: A Journal for the
New Millennium Y-01

World Publishing Company DLB-46

World War II Writers Symposium
at the University of South Carolina,
12–14 April 1995 . . . . Y-95

Worthington, R., and Company DLB-49

Wotton, Sir Henry 1568-1639 . . . . DLB-121

Wouk, Herman 1915- Y-82; CDALB-7

Wreford, James 1915- DLB-88

Wren, Sir Christopher 1632-1723 . . . . DLB-213

Wren, Percival Christopher
1885-1941 . . . . DLB-153

Wrenn, John Henry 1841-1911 . . . . DLB-140

Wright, C. D. 1949- DLB-120

Wright, Charles 1935- DLB-165; Y-82

Wright, Charles Stevenson 1932- DLB-33

Wright, Frances 1795-1852 . . . . DLB-73

Wright, Harold Bell 1872-1944 . . . . DLB-9

Wright, James
1927-1980 . . . . DLB-5, 169; CDALB-7

Wright, Jay 1935- DLB-41

Wright, Judith 1915-2000 . . . . DLB-260

Wright, Louis B. 1899-1984 . . . . DLB-17

Wright, Richard
1908-1960 . . . . . DLB-76, 102; DS-2; CDALB-5

Wright, Richard B. 1937- DLB-53

Wright, S. Fowler 1874-1965 . . . . DLB-255

Wright, Sarah Elizabeth 1928- DLB-33

Wright, Willard Huntington ("S. S. Van Dine")
1888-1939 . . . . DS-16

Wrigley, Robert 1951- DLB-256

A Writer Talking: A Collage Y-00

Writers and Politics: 1871-1918,
by Ronald Gray DLB-66

Writers and their Copyright Holders:
the WATCH Project Y-94

Writers' Forum Y-85

Writing for the Theatre,
by Harold Pinter DLB-13

Wroth, Lawrence C. 1884-1970 . . . . DLB-187

Wroth, Lady Mary 1587-1653 . . . . DLB-121

Wurlitzer, Rudolph 1937- DLB-173

Wyatt, Sir Thomas circa 1503-1542 . . . . . DLB-132

Wycherley, William
1641-1715 . . . . DLB-80; CDBLB-2

Wyclif, John
circa 1335-31 December 1384 . . . . . . DLB-146

Wyeth, N. C. 1882-1945 . . . . DLB-188; DS-16

Wylie, Elinor 1885-1928 . . . . DLB-9, 45

Wylie, Philip 1902-1971 . . . . DLB-9

Wyllie, John Cook 1908-1968 . . . . DLB-140

Wyman, Lillie Buffum Chace
1847-1929 . . . . DLB-202

Wymark, Olwen 1934- DLB-233

Wyndham, John 1903-1969 . . . . DLB-255

Wynne-Tyson, Esmé 1898-1972 . . . . DLB-191

X

Xenophon circa 430 B.C.-circa 356 B.C. DLB-176

Y

Yasuoka Shōtarō 1920- DLB-182

Yates, Dornford 1885-1960 . . . . DLB-77, 153

Yates, J. Michael 1938- DLB-60

Yates, Richard
1926-1992 . . . . DLB-2, 234; Y-81, Y-92

Yau, John 1950- DLB-234

Yavorov, Peyo 1878-1914 . . . . DLB-147

The Year in Book Publishing Y-86

The Year in Book Reviewing and the Literary
Situation Y-98

The Year in British Drama Y-99, Y-00, Y-01

The Year in British Fiction Y-99, Y-00, Y-01

The Year in Children's
Books Y-92–Y-96, Y-98, Y-99, Y-00, Y-01

The Year in Children's Literature Y-97

The Year in Drama Y-82-Y-85, Y-87–Y-96

The Year in Fiction . . . Y-84–Y-86, Y-89, Y-94–Y-99

The Year in Fiction: A Biased View Y-83

The Year in Literary
Biography Y-83–Y-98, Y-00, Y-01

The Year in Literary Theory Y-92–Y-93

The Year in London Theatre Y-92

The Year in the Novel Y-87, Y-88, Y-90–Y-93

The Year in Poetry . . Y-83–Y-92, Y-94, Y-95, Y-96,
. . . . Y-97, Y-98, Y-99, Y-00, Y-01

The Year in Science Fiction
and Fantasy Y-00, Y-01

The Year in Short Stories Y-87

The Year in the Short Story Y-88, Y-90–Y-93

The Year in Texas Literature Y-98

The Year in U.S. Drama Y-00

The Year in U.S. Fiction Y-00, Y-01

The Year's Work in American Poetry Y-82

The Year's Work in Fiction: A Survey Y-82

Yearsley, Ann 1753-1806 . . . . DLB-109

Yeats, William Butler
1865-1939 . . . . DLB-10, 19, 98, 156; CDBLB-5

Yep, Laurence 1948- DLB-52

Yerby, Frank 1916-1991 . . . . DLB-76

Yezierska, Anzia
1880-1970 . . . . DLB-28, 221

Yolen, Jane 1939- DLB-52

Yonge, Charlotte Mary
1823-1901 . . . . DLB-18, 163

The York Cycle circa 1376-circa 1569 . . . . DLB-146

A Yorkshire Tragedy DLB-58

Yoseloff, Thomas [publishing house] DLB-46

Young, A. S. "Doc" 1919-1996 . . . . DLB-241

Young, Al 1939- DLB-33

Young, Arthur 1741-1820 . . . . DLB-158

Young, Dick 1917 or 1918 - 1987 . . . . . . .DLB-171

Young, Edward 1683-1765 . . . . DLB-95

Young, Frank A. "Fay" 1884-1957 . . . . . . DLB-241

Young, Francis Brett 1884-1954 . . . . DLB-191

Young, Gavin 1928- DLB-204

Young, Stark 1881-1963 . . . . . . DLB-9, 102; DS-16

Young, Waldeman 1880-1938 . . . . DLB-26

Young, William
publishing house] DLB-49

Young Bear, Ray A. 1950- DLB-175

Yourcenar, Marguerite
1903-1987 . . . . .DLB-72; Y-88

"You've Never Had It So Good," Gusted by
"Winds of Change": British Fiction in the
1950s, 1960s, and After DLB-14

Yovkov, Yordan 1880-1937 . .DLB-147; CDWLB-4

Z

Zachariä, Friedrich Wilhelm 1726-1777 . . . DLB-97

Zagajewski, Adam 1945- DLB-232

Zagoskin, Mikhail Nikolaevich
1789-1852 . . . . DLB-198

Zajc, Dane 1929- DLB-181

Zālīte, Māra 1952- DLB-232

Zamora, Bernice 1938- DLB-82

Zand, Herbert 1923-1970 . . . . DLB-85

Zangwill, Israel 1864-1926 . . . . . .DLB-10, 135, 197

Zanzotto, Andrea 1921- DLB-128

Zapata Olivella, Manuel 1920- DLB-113

Zasodimsky, Pavel Vladimirovich
1843-1912 . . . . DLB-238

Zebra Books DLB-46

Zebrowski, George 1945- DLB-8

Zech, Paul 1881-1946 . . . . DLB-56

Zeidner, Lisa 1955- DLB-120

Zeidonis, Imants 1933- DLB-232

Zeimi (Kanze Motokiyo) 1363-1443 . . . . . DLB-203

Zelazny, Roger 1937-1995 . . . . DLB-8

Zenger, John Peter 1697-1746 . . . . DLB-24, 43

Zepheria DLB-172

Zesen, Philipp von 1619-1689 . . . . DLB-164

Zhukovsky, Vasilii Andreevich
1783-1852 . . . . DLB-205

Zieber, G. B., and Company DLB-49

Ziedonis, Imants 1933- CDWLB-4

Zieroth, Dale 1946- DLB-60

Zigler und Kliphausen, Heinrich
Anshelm von 1663-1697 . . . . DLB-168

Zimmer, Paul 1934- DLB-5

Zinberg, Len (see Lacy, Ed)

Zindel, Paul 1936- DLB-7, 52; CDALB-7

Zingref, Julius Wilhelm 1591-1635 . . . . . . DLB-164

Zinnes, Harriet 1919- DLB-193

Zinzendorf, Nikolaus Ludwig von
1700-1760 . . . . DLB-168

Zitkala-Ša 1876-1938 . . . . .DLB-175

Zīverts, Mārtiņš 1903-1990 . . . . DLB-220

Zlatovratsky, Nikolai Nikolaevich
1845-1911 . . . . DLB-238

Zola, Emile 1840-1902 . . . . DLB-123

Zolla, Elémire 1926- DLB-196

Zolotow, Charlotte 1915- DLB-52

Zschokke, Heinrich 1771-1848 . . . . DLB-94

Zubly, John Joachim 1724-1781 . . . . DLB-31

Zu-Bolton II, Ahmos 1936- DLB-41

Zuckmayer, Carl 1896-1977 . . . . DLB-56, 124

Zukofsky, Louis 1904-1978 . . . . DLB-5, 165

Zupan, Vitomil 1914-1987 . . . . DLB-181

Župančič, Oton 1878-1949 . . .DLB-147; CDWLB-4

zur Mühlen, Hermynia 1883-1951 . . . . DLB-56

Zweig, Arnold 1887-1968 . . . . DLB-66

Zweig, Stefan 1881-1942 . . . . DLB-81, 118

ISBN 0-7876-6007-8

90000